Inside Judaism

ALSO BY ALFRED J. KOLATCH

Best Baby Names for Jewish Children

A Child's First Book of Jewish Holidays

Classic Bible Stories for Jewish Children

The Complete Dictionary of English and Hebrew First Names

The Comprehensive Dictionary of English and Hebrew First Names

The Concise Family Seder

El Libro Judio del Por Que

The Family Seder

A Handbook for the Jewish Home

Great Jewish Quotations

The Jewish Book of Why

The Jewish Book of Why: The Torah

The Jewish Child's First Book of Why

The Jewish Heritage Quiz Book

The Jewish Mourner's Book of Why

The Jonathan David Dictionary of First Names

Let's Celebrate Our Jewish Holidays!

Masters of the Talmud

The New Name Dictionary

Our Religion: The Torah

The Second Jewish Book of Why

These Are the Names

Today's Best Baby Names

What Jews Say About God

Inside Judaism

The Concepts, Customs, and Celebrations of the Jewish People

Alfred J. Kolatch

JONATHAN DAVID PUBLISHERS, INC.
Middle Village, New York 11379

INSIDE JUDAISM

Jonathan David Publishers, Inc.
68-22 Eliot Avenue
Middle Village, New York 11379

www.jdbooks.com

2 4 6 8 10 9 7 5 3 1

Library of Congress Cataloging-in-Publication Data

Library of Congress Cataloging-in-Publication Data

Kolatch, Alfred J.
    Inside Judaism : the concepts, customs, and celebrations of the Jewish people / Alfred J. Kolatch.
        p. cm.
    Includes biographical references and index.
    ISBN 0-8246-0466-0
    1. Judaism—Encyclopedias.   I. Title.
    BM50.K65 2006
    296.03'dc22
                                                                2005054315

Book design and composition by John Reinhardt Book Design

Printed in the United States of America

Contents

In Appreciation

ix

Introduction

xi

A Note on Style

xiii

Alphabetical Entries

1

Index

615

About the Author

704

In Appreciation

Inside Judaism is the result of the efforts of many individuals over a period of years. I am deeply indebted to all those who nurtured this project in ways large and small from the moment of inception to the moment of publication.

To the entire staff of Jonathan David Publishers, my appreciation for their overall help in researching, organizing, and preparing the manuscript. Particular thanks are due Kathy Gluszak, Allison Gordon Mastropieri, and Debbie Seiden for their word-processing wizardry; Rachel Taller for checking each of the biblical references, reading the entries for factual accuracy, and helping to establish a consistent style of transliteration; Taneya Sheffey for reading the page proofs; and Barbara Burke for her proofreading skills and general assistance in moving the project along.

Marvin Sekler, Jonathan David's vice-president and director of marketing, has been helpful in countless ways. His long experience in guiding books through the publication process has proven invaluable here as well.

My brother, Rabbi Arthur J. Kolatch, graciously read the entire manuscript and noted areas needing further research and points requiring clarification. I thank him particularly for sharing his knowledge of the practices of the Reform movement.

My friend and colleague, Rabbi Emanuel S. Goldsmith, professor of Jewish Studies at Queens College of the City University of New York, was always available for consultation on a wide range of issues.

Judy Gitenstein edited the manuscript with great care and dedication, putting herself in the position of those new to the subject matter. Her astute queries and suggestions for cross-references contributed greatly toward making this a more readable and useful book.

Crucial to the success of a work such as this is the ability of the reader to access information with ease. The superbly detailed index prepared by Rachel Dadusc will make that possible. My gratitude to her for providing such an invaluable resource.

Needless to say, the "look" of any book is also crucial to its success. I am deeply indebted to Mike Stromberg for his elegant jacket design and to John Reinhardt for his sophisticated yet reader-friendly book design.

My sons, Jonathan and David, gave unselfishly of their time and energy, seeking to ensure that this work would be appreciated by as wide an audience as possible. Jonathan read the manuscript with a sharply critical eye, noting lapses in logical development and adding focus to the text. David skillfully coordinated the many details involved in bringing a project such as this to fruition. My gratitude to both of them.

And to my wife, Thelma, I extend heartfelt thanks for her continued devotion and encouragement.

Introduction

Judaism is more than a religion of ideas; it is also a religion of action. The timeless principles that are the very heart of Judaism are brought to life through the observance of specific customs, rites, and celebrations that have been embellished and modified over time. The two—core beliefs and everyday practice—have a strong interrelationship, and together they serve to unite the Jewish people and keep Judaism strong and relevant.

Most of the basic concepts and values of Judaism derive from the Torah, the first five books of the Bible. One need only leaf through chapter 20 of the Book of Exodus or chapters 18 and 19 of the Book of Leviticus to discover such universally cherished values as "Love thy neighbor as thyself," "Honor thy father and mother," "Thou shalt not covet," "Thou shalt not take vengeance or bear a grudge against thy countrymen," and "Thou shalt not place a stumbling-block before the blind."

Basic Judaic principles are elaborated upon in the Talmud, which is essentially a commentary on the Torah. The talmudic masters interpreted the Torah in order to uncover that which is not explicitly revealed in Scripture or that which may be obscure or not applicable to the times. Scholars of the tenth, eleventh, and twelfth centuries including Sa'adya Gaon of Egypt, Rabbi Gershom Me'or Ha-Golah of Germany, the famous commentator Rashi of France, and the great philosopher Moses Maimonides of Spain not only continued the tradition of interpreting biblical text, but also assumed the difficult undertaking of clarifying talmudic rulings. In subsequent centuries, down to the present day, the work of these brilliant thinkers has been carried on by such latter-day equals as Joseph Caro, Moses Isserles, Jacob Emden, Ezekiel Landau, Isaac Elchanan Spektor, Moshe Feinstein, and Solomon B. Freehof.

Although commentary on biblical and rabbinic law comprises a large part of Jewish literature, it is important to remember that Jewish law, or *halakhah*, does not operate in a vacuum. It is inextricably bound to custom, or *minhag*, the actual manner in which Jews carry out religious mandates.

While law is imposed from without, custom develops from within. That Jews are required to bless the *lulav* bouquet on the holiday of Sukkot is mandated biblically, but precisely how the *lulav* is to be waved and when the blessing is to be recited is a matter of custom. Local practice is not to be regarded lightly, warns the Talmud (Yerushalmi *Pesachim* 4:1): "Do not change [abandon] the custom of your ancestors." This is developed further in Joseph Caro's *Code of Jewish Law* (*Shulchan Arukh*, Yoreh Dei'ah 376:4), where custom is actually equated with law.

Many Jews are surprised to learn that some practices that are widely considered absolute religious requirements are in fact firmly entrenched customs. Such
is the case with the wearing of a headcovering, particularly a *yarmulke*. Except
for Priests, the Bible does not require men entering the sanctuary or participating in a religious rite or service to cover their heads. We learn from the tractate
Nedarim (30b) that in talmudic times practices varied: "Men sometimes cover
their heads and sometimes do not. But women's hair is always covered, and children are always bareheaded." That the Talmud goes out of its way to report that
the third/fourth-century scholar Assi would cover his head with a kerchief when
reciting *Grace After Meals* would indicate that, routinely, he went bareheaded.

It was not until the Middle Ages that it became a practice for observant Jewish men to cover their heads when praying, studying, eating, and, for some,
even when going about their daily secular tasks. Yet today, a Jew insisting upon
praying in a traditional synagogue bareheaded, without a *yarmulke*, would be
considered at a minimum disrespectful and, more likely, heretical. What began
as mere custom, in time, assumed the power of law.

For many Jews, distinguishing between what is mandatory and what is traditional is difficult. Eating potato *latkes* on Chanukkah is not mandated anywhere.
But for some, this custom, which draws a connection between the oil in which
the pancakes are fried and the oil used to light the *menorah*, is the essence of the
holiday. Similarly with eating *hamantaschen* on Purim or dipping apples in honey
on Rosh Hashanah.

Inside Judaism explores the connection between Jewish ideology and common
practice, between thought and observance, between principle and action. By offering readers deeper insight into the concepts, customs, and celebrations that
have united the Jewish people for millennia, it is hoped that this volume will
enhance their appreciation of the Jewish heritage.

Readers of this book can satisfy their curiosity in various ways. For the brows-
er, random reading of the alphabetical entries and consulting the cross-references at the end of the entries might provide the richest harvest. For those seeking
specific information, the comprehensive index will provide easy access to the
material. Whatever path you take, I wish you an enriching experience.

ALFRED J. KOLATCH

A Note on Style

The task of transliterating Hebrew, Yiddish, and Aramaic names into English is more complex than it might appear. This is because there are two styles of pronunciation: Ashkenazic and Sephardic. The Ashkenazic system was commonly used in Central and Eastern Europe and is still widely used, particularly by older Jews and by some Orthodox groups when engaged in study. The Sephardic style of pronunciation, which today is the official style of speech in Israel and in many communities around the world, has largely replaced Ashkenazic pronunciation.

In this volume, transliterated terms are rendered following the Sephardic dialect, although frequently used Askenazic pronunciations of some terms are occasionally given as variant forms. It should be noted, however, that because of the range of accents found among speakers, it is impossible to achieve absolute consistency.

Key to Transliteration

- The gutteral *khaf* (כ) sound found in words such as *barukh* is represented by the letters *kh*.
- The gutteral *chet* (ח) sound found in words such as *chutzpah* is represented by the letters *ch*.
- The vowel sound in the English word *pique* and the Hebrew word *bimah* is represented by the letter *i*.
- The vowel sound in the English word *pin* and the Hebrew word *minchah* is also represented by the letter *i*.
- The diphthong sound in the English word *pie* and the Hebrew word *chai* is represented by the letters *ai*.
- The diphthong sound in the English word *eight* and the Hebrew word *eish* is represented by the letters *ei*.
- The vowel sound in the English word *hot* and the Hebrew word *chag* is represented by the letter *a*.
- The vowel sound in the English word *met* and the Hebrew word *get* is represented by the letter *e*.
- The vowel sound in the English word *to* and the Hebrew word *zu* is represented by the letter *u*.
- Except for the letters *shin* and *tzadi*, consonants with a *dagesh* forte are represented by a double letter, as in *tefillin*.
- The final letter *hei* in such Hebrew words as *mishnah* or *chuppah* is represented by the letter *h*.

Alphabetical
Entries

Abortion

The Greek philosopher Aristotle believed that the soul becomes part of the unborn male child on the fortieth day after conception and of the female child on the eightieth. Perhaps influenced by these teachings, the Rabbis of the Talmud and later centuries regarded the fertilized ovum as mere fluid until the fortieth day after conception, when the embryo, or fetus, is said to be formed. From this point until birth, the fetus is considered part of the mother. In many references in the Talmud and later rabbinic sources, the fetus is not characterized as a person (*nefesh* in Hebrew), for it is not yet considered an autonomous, viable entity (*ben* or *bar ka'yamah*). Appropriately, then, in Hebrew the fetus is called *ubar yerekh imo*, "an appendage of its mother" (*Yevamot* 69b and *Niddah* 15b). This view was reinforced by the eleventh-century French commentator Rashi, who said, "So long as the fetus does not enter the 'atmosphere of the world,' it is not to be considered a person" (*Sanhedrin* 17b. See also Choshen Mishpat 423, 425).

Essentially, the Sages based their point of view on the statement in the Book of Exodus (21:22) that if a pregnant woman is struck by someone and her unborn child is destroyed, the person causing the mishap must pay damages. The individual is not, however, characterized as a murderer, because the unborn child is not yet considered a person.

Talmudic View on Abortion

The Talmud is quite specific in presenting the guidelines for abortion: "If a woman is having difficulty giving birth and her life is in danger, the fetus may be removed surgically, limb by limb, because the woman's life takes precedence over the fetus. However, if delivery has already begun, and the child's head or the greater part of its body has al-ready emerged, the child may not be harmed to save the mother, because one person's life may not be taken to save another" (Mishnah *Oholot* 7:6).

Nevertheless, despite the fact that in Jewish law the unborn child is not considered a person, the law does not approve of abortion unless there is sufficient justification (*Tosafot* on *Chullin* 33a).

The Contemporary View

Both the Orthodox and the non-Orthodox rabbinate oppose indiscriminate abortion, but they do favor abortion when the mother's life or well-being is at stake. Disagreements do arise, however, over the definition of "well-being." Conservative and Reform rabbis tend to be more liberal in their interpretation of what constitutes valid medical intervention, although many Orthodox authorities have, in recent centuries, expressed progressive views as well.

Rabbi Jacob Emden (1697–1776) permitted abortion if the procedure would relieve the pregnant woman of great pain or discomfort, even if her life were not in danger (*She'eilot Yavetz* 1:43). Rabbi Emden also permitted an abortion in the case of a woman who was impregnated as a result of an adulterous union. The stigma of bastardy that the child would bear was considered sufficient justification (*Lechem Ha-Panim*, section 19).

Ben Zion Uziel, who served as Sephardic Chief Rabbi of Israel from 1939 to 1953, permitted an abortion that was in the best interests of the mother, even if not crucial to her health (*Mishpetei Uzi'el* II, No. 47).

Contemporary rabbis of all denominations generally agree that it is proper to end a pregnancy if its continuation would cause the mother severe physical or psychological harm. Many rabbis also approve of abortions if there is considerable likelihood that the child would be born deformed (for example, if the mother has contracted a disease such as rubella, known to cause severe fetus malformation). To some authorities, unfavorable indications from an amniocentesis analysis are sufficient grounds for abortion. However, Orthodox authorities such as Rabbi David Bleich, professor of Jewish law and ethics at the Benjamin N. Cardozo School of Law, in New York City, take the position that even an abnormal fetus should not be aborted unless it is a threat to the mother's life. In 1971, this position was subscribed to by the Union of Orthodox Jewish Scientists.

Acharon

This Hebrew term, meaning "last," is used by Ashkenazim to refer to the last Torah honor (*aliyah*) before the *maftir*. Traditionally, this *aliyah* is considered highly desirable because of its association with the expression *acharon acharon chaviv*, "the last [one] is most beloved."

The expression was first used in the Midrash (*Genesis Rabbah* 78:8) in a comment on the verse in Genesis (33:2) that describes the order in which Jacob arranged his family when he anticipated a confrontation with his brother, Esau. Jacob placed Rachel and her son Joseph at the very end of the formation, says the Midrash, because he loved them most, thus securing for them the safest position.

Among Ashkenazim the last *aliyah* is generally offered to pious people, particularly when each of the Five Books of Moses is concluded and especially on Simchat Torah, when the concluding portion of the entire Pentateuch is read.

Sephardim refer to the last *aliyah* by the name *mashlim*, meaning "concluder." The honor is usually reserved for a bridegroom, for it symbolizes the hope that the man's life will now be complete and fulfilled. Among Moroccan Jews, by whom sons are particularly coveted, the *mashlim aliyah* is reserved for the father of a newborn girl; it is an expression of the father's hope that with the birth of the child he will have "completed" his fathering of daughters and that in the future he will father only sons.

See Maftir.

Acronyms

Known in Hebrew as *roshei teivot*, meaning "heads of words," acronyms are words formed from the first (or first few) letters of a series of words or names. *Roshei teivot* often serve as mnemonic devices. A famous example is found in the Passover *Haggadah*: *detzakh*, *adash*, *b'achav*, an acronym formed from the first letter of each of the ten plagues.

The names of famous Jewish scholars are often mentioned only in their acronymic form. Thus, the famous eleventh-century French scholar Rabbi Shlomo Yitzchaki is best known as Rashi, and the twelfth-century philosopher/scholar Rabbi Moses ben Maimon is most often referred to as Rambam. The eighteenth-century Israel ben Eliezer, founder of chasidism, became known as the Ba'al Shem Tov, from which the acronym Besht was created.

The Talmud uses the term *notarikon*, derived from the Latin *notarium* ("writing quickly") to refer to the concept of acronym. *Shabbat* 105a states: "Rabbi Yochanan quoted Rabbi Yosei ben Zimra as saying, 'How do we know that *notarikon* ["abbreviated forms"] are recognized by the Torah?'" This is followed by examples of abbreviated names and words created to help one remember the details.

Many acronyms are in popular use in Israel

today. These include *Tzahal* for *Tzava Haga-nah Le-Yisra'el*, referring to Israel Defense Forces; *Ramatkal* for *Rosh Ha-Mateh Ha-Kela-li*, referring to the Chief-of-Staff of the Israeli army; and *duach* for *din ve-cheshbon*, referring to an oral or written report. Other widely used acronyms are *zal*, standing for *zikhrono li-ve-rakhah*, meaning "may his memory serve as a blessing," and perhaps one of the earliest and most famous, *Tanakh*, which represents the words *Torah*, *Nevi'im* (Prophets), and *Ketuvim* (Holy Writings, Hagiographa).

See Amen; Mnemonic Devices; Tanakh; Yavneh and Yaknehaz.

Acrostic

A literary device whereby the first (or middle or last) letter of a verse or of a series of words, when taken in order, spell out a name, slogan, or simply the letters of the alphabet. The device has been employed by Jewish poets, particularly liturgists, to serve as a mnemonic device, an aid to memory.

Many Psalms and medieval hymns contain acrostics. For example, the first letter of each line of the *Ashrei* prayer (Psalm 84:5 and 145:15–21) begins with a different letter of the Hebrew alphabet, running from *alef* to *tav* (except for the missing *nun*). The first letter of each stanza in the *Ein Keloheinu* hymn form the two Hebrew words *amen ba*, meaning "the end [of the service] has come."

Each successive word of the first twenty-two words of the prayer *Tikanta Shabbat* ("Thou hast established the Sabbath"), which is recited as part of the Sabbath *Musaf* service, begins with a different letter of the *alef bet* in reverse order, from *tav* to *alef*. Kabbalists believe that this will remind Jews that once they have learned everything from *alef* to *tav*, they must reverse gears and deepen their knowl-edge and spirituality by learning everything anew, from the end to the beginning.

Each stanza of the *Lekhah Dodi* prayer, which is recited at the Friday evening service, begins with a different Hebrew letter. When combined, they spell out the name of the author: Shlomo Halevi.

See Al Cheit; Geshem; Maccabee; Tal.

Adloyada

The name of the Purim carnival held annu-ally in Tel Aviv. The word is a composite of the three Hebrew words *ad*, *de-lo*, and *yada*, meaning "until he no longer knows [how to distinguish]," referring to a state of inebria-tion.

Excessive drinking is discouraged in Jewish tradition, except on one occasion: the joyous holiday of Purim. In fact, Rabba (Rava), the renowned fourth-century Babylonian scholar, said that a man is obliged to drink so much wine on Purim that he is no longer capable of distinguishing between the words "blessed is Mordekhai" and "cursed is Haman" (*Megillah* 7b).

This tradition is said to have its roots in a song that was sung on Purim in talmudic times. The stanzas of the song ended with the alternate refrains "blessed is Mordekhai" and "cursed is Haman." Often, celebrants were so inebriated that they would mix up the refrains. (They would also mix up other refrains, such as "blessed is Esther" and "cursed is Zeresh [wife of Haman].")

See Megillah; Purim; Wine.

Adonai

A Hebrew term literally meaning "My Lord, My Master." One of the names used for God.

See God, Names of.

Adon Olam

A Hebrew phrase meaning "Master of the Universe." The name of a popular hymn composed by the illustrious eleventh-century liturgical poet and philosopher Solomon ibn Gabirol. *Adon Olam* extols God for His creative power, His uniqueness, and the protective wing with which He shields those who trust in Him. In the fifteenth century, it was added to the liturgy of the morning (*Shacharit*) service, and ever since has been used as the concluding hymn of the Sabbath and holiday morning service in Ashkenazic congregations.

Adoption

By definition, adoption is the taking of a child into one's family through a legal process and raising the child as one's own. There is no actual evidence that such a procedure existed in biblical times, nor is there evidence that legal adoption was known in talmudic times. The closest that Judaism comes to the modern concept of adoption is found in such statements as: "If anyone brings up an orphan boy or girl in his house, Scripture considers it as if he had begotten him" (*Megillah* 13a and *Sanhedrin* 19b).

The Talmud (Mishnah *Gittin* 5:4 and *Pesachim* 49b) also speaks of a category of individuals known as "legal guardians," designated by the term *epitropos* (sometimes written as *apotropos*). These people, the Talmud says, are appointed by the courts to administer the estate of orphans. However, because the guardians are not considered adoptive parents, the orphans are not their legal heirs.

While the guardian of the child assumes full responsibility for the upbringing and nurturing of the child, he or she does not have the same relationship toward the child as do the natural parents. The child inherits the natural father's estate and continues to be called the offspring of the natural father. If the father is a Priest (*Kohen*) or Levite (*Levi*), the child is a Priest or Levite. When Torah honors are distributed at the coming-of-age ceremonies of bar mitzvah and bat mitzvah, the natural parents are the first to receive the honors; and when a natural parent dies, the child recites the *Kaddish* and observes all mourning rites.

Adoption was introduced into Jewish life in a legal sense for the first time in 1960, when the Knesset enacted the Adoption of Children Law. This statute allows any child under eighteen years of age to be adopted by a person who is at least eighteen years older than the person being adopted. Under this law, there can be no legal adoption of persons over age eighteen, and the blood relationship between the adoptee and his or her natural parents continues undisturbed. The law also provides that a registry of adoptions with complete information about the natural parents be kept.

Adultery

Civil law, unlike Jewish law (*halakhah*), generally defines adultery as voluntary sexual intercourse between a married person and a person of the opposite sex, whether single or married.

In Jewish law, however, adultery refers only to sexual relations between a married woman and a man who is not her husband, regardless of the man's marital status. It does not apply to sexual relations between a married man and a single woman. The reason is rooted in the fact that under biblical law a man can be married to more than one woman, but a woman can be married to only one man.

The basic law prohibiting adultery is stated in the seventh of the Ten Commandments (Exodus 20:13 and Deuteronomy 5:17) and is elaborated upon in the Book of Leviticus

(20:10), where a man is also considered an adulterer. The punishment for both a man and a woman is death.

In biblical times, a woman suspected of being willingly adulterous (called a *sotah* in Hebrew) was required to undergo a complicated ritual procedure to determine the veracity of the allegation. The details are outlined in the Book of Numbers (5:12—31). A tractate of the Talmud entitled *Sotah* is devoted to the subject of a wife accused of being unfaithful.

A child born of an adulterous union is a *mamzer* ("bastard") in Jewish law. A *mamzer* is permitted to marry only another *mamzer* or a convert to Judaism.

See Capital Punishment; Sotah; Mamzer.

Afikomon

See Seder.

Afterlife

The Bible reports that all who died were buried in the ground, with the exception of Enokh, "for God took him" (Genesis 5:24), and Elijah, who the Bible (II Kings 2:11) says "was swept up into heaven in a whirlwind." The ultimate fate of each of these figures is not recorded.

Not until postbiblical times did Jewish literature begin to address the question of one's fate after life on earth. Centuries later, when religious leaders felt a need to assure those who live virtuously in this world that a reward awaits them in a future life, the branch of theology dealing with death, resurrection, and immortality—known as eschatology—became of interest to philosophers and scholars. The future came to be referred to in Hebrew as *olam ha-ba*, the world to come.

Nature of the Afterlife

There is no universally accepted view among Jewish thinkers about the nature of the hereaf-

ter. Professor George Foot Moore of Harvard commented on the multiplicity of viewpoints as follows: "Any attempt to systematize the Jewish notions of the hereafter imposes upon them an order and consistency which does not exist in them" (*Judaism*, vol. II, p. 380).

The wide variety of conceptions of the world to come led to the creation of numerous designations, including *olam ha-emet*, "world of truth"; *olam ha-menuchah*, "world of rest"; *olam ha-nefashot*, "world of souls"; and *olam she-kulo tov*, "world of complete goodness."

Early Thinkers

The idea that one's earthly experience does not terminate with one's physical demise took on special importance for Jews during the period following the Babylonian Exile in the sixth century B.C.E. and especially after the Second Temple was destroyed in 70 C.E. In order to endure the degrading and sometimes oppressive conditions of the Babylonian captivity and to cope with prolonged suffering during the Roman occupation of Palestine, culminating in the destruction of the Second Temple, the Jewish people were eager to accept the concept of an afterlife.

Substantially differing views of the hereafter emerged toward the end of the Second Temple period. The Sadducees, consisting of prominent aristocrats, Priests, and other influential members of society, believed solely in the here and now and refused to accept interpretations linking biblical texts to the concept of a hereafter. Reward and punishment, they maintained, will be administered in this life, the only life man knows.

By contrast, the Pharisees, the less affluent members of society, hoped that a better life awaited them after earthly existence. The Bible is subject to interpretation, they said, but even vague biblical allusions to a hereafter should be taken seriously. The Pharisees embraced the concepts of resurrection of the dead, judgment day, and the coming of the Messiah, views expressed throughout the Talmud by the many Rabbis who were of the Pharisaic persuasion.

Talmudic Views

Later Rabbis expanded upon Pharisaic beliefs, exploring the meaning of immortality, the nature of reward and punishment, and the advent of the Messiah and the Messianic Age. No general consensus was reached, however, and the debate on the nature of the hereafter continued. Of the views expressed in the Talmud, that of Rabbi Jacob captured the imagination of many Jews: "This world is like a vestibule [*prozdor*] before the world to come [*olam ha-ba*].... Prepare yourself in the vestibule so that you may enter into the grand salon" (Ethics of the Fathers 4:21).

To encourage a hopeful outlook among Jews, other Rabbis of the Talmud presented various descriptions of the beautiful and easy life that lay ahead for those who conduct themselves properly in this world. The world to come will be "not like this world. In this world, man [often] has trouble harvesting and crushing [grapes], but in the world to come a man will place one grape [which, as all other grapes, will be huge] on a wagon or a ship, transfer it to a corner of his house, and use its contents to make enough wine to fill a large keg..." (*Ketubbot* 111b).

Rava, the third-century Babylonian talmudic scholar, construed the world to come as a place where man will be closely questioned before he is allowed to enter (*Shabbat* 31a). The following questions, he said, will first have to be answered about the person's behavior in this world: Did you act honorably and honestly in your business dealings? Did you set aside time each day to engage in study? Did you marry and have children? Did you have faith in your salvation? Did you engage in examining opinions and ideas logically? Did you use your knowledge to arrive at proper conclusions?

Post-Talmudic Attitudes

As far back as the eleventh century, scholars of the caliber of the Spanish religious philosopher Bachya ibn Pakuda (*c.* 1050–*c.* 1120) visualized the afterlife as a world of souls, not bodies. Moses Maimonides, the most respected rabbi, scholar, and philosopher of the twelfth century, likewise did not believe in a literal world to come; that is, they did not see a locale to which actual physical bodies would be transported after death.

To Maimonides, the hereafter was an imaginary place where the souls of the righteous would repose, where they would be rewarded for their virtuous lives by a new type of purely intellectual experience. Maimonides' belief, based on a statement of Rav in the tractate *Berakhot* (17a), is expressed in the *Mishneh Torah* (Hilkhot Teshuvah 8:2):

> In the world to come, there is nothing corporeal, no material substance; there exist only souls of righteous people without bodies—like the ministering angels. And since in that world there are no bodies, there is neither eating there, nor drinking, nor any of the activities human beings engage in in this world, such as sitting, standing, sleeping, dying, grieving, and making merriment...

Maimonides concludes: "The righteous will sit with crowns on their heads, enjoying the radiance of the *Shekhinah* [God's presence]."

In explaining his father's belief, Abraham Maimuni, the son of Maimonides, noted that when philosophers speak of matter never being completely destroyed, they mean that it assumes new form. In like manner, he says, man's nature or spirit or soul is not propelled into oblivion after death. It merely assumes new form, and that new form is pure intelligence. Since man on earth has no experience in such matters, he adds, it is difficult for him to grasp the concept of spirit or soul that is totally independent of bodily form.

Rabbi Moses ben Nachman (Nachmanides), the thirteenth-century authority, was of the opinion that the world to come refers to an interim period, which begins after the dead are resurrected, when the fate of each soul will be weighed to determine whether it is worthy of entering Paradise (*Gan Eden*).

The Italian scholar and philosopher Leon de Modena (1571–1648) regarded as unlikely that at death a human life ends completely. How man, a creature of such great intellect that he can build cities, move mountains, and change the course of rivers should suddenly altogether cease being and "perish entirely like a horse or a dog or a fly" is unfathomable.

Baruch Spinoza (1632–1677) shared de Modena's view. "The human mind cannot be absolutely destroyed with the human body. . . . There is some part of it that remains eternal," he wrote in his *Spinoza's Ethics*.

The prominent Orthodox Israeli scientist, philosopher, and historian Yeshayahu Leibowitz (1903–1994) expressed his concept of life after death very forthrightly, even though it does not square with the traditional Orthodox view. In an interview with Israeli students in "*Sof Shavua*," weekend supplement of the newspaper *Maariv* (February 8, 1991), the renowned Hebrew University professor was asked about his personal view of the afterlife.

"Death has no significance," he said. "Only life matters."

"What is Judaism's attitude toward death?" a student asked.

Leibowitz replied, "In the entire Torah there is not the slightest suggestion that anything happens after death. All the ideas and theories articulated on the subject of a world to come and the resurrection of the dead have no relationship to religious faith. It is sheer folklore. After you die, you simply do not exist."

See Gilgul; Heaven and Hell; Reincarnation; Resurrection.

Aggadah

An Aramaic talmudic word meaning "narrative," used interchangeably with the Hebrew word *haggadah*. The term specifically refers to the sections of the Talmud that contain stories, parables, and words of wisdom through which the Rabbis sought to make a point, teach a lesson, or interpret the biblical narrative. It includes discussions of ethics, philosophy, and theology as well as popular tales, legends, and folklore. It also includes such topics as astronomy, astrology, medicine, magic, and mysticism.

Leopold Zunz, an outstanding nineteenth-century German Jewish scholar, summarized the contents of the *aggadah* when he wrote, "Everything the imagination can conceive is found in the *aggadah* with one great exception: it contains no frivolity. It is there to teach love of God and fear of God."

Aggadah, interspersed throughout the Talmud, is distinct from the Talmud's major component, *halakhah*, which addresses legal matters only. The interconnection between the two was once described by the poet laureate of Israel, Chaim Nachman Bialik (1873–

1934): "The *halakhah* is the exemplification and crystallization of the *aggadah*, while the *aggadah* is the crucible of *halakhah*."

An example of *aggadah* is the famous parable of the fox and the fishes in which Rabbi Akiba cautions Israel not to succumb to enticements offered by its natural enemies (*Berakhot* 61b):

Once the wicked Roman government that controlled Palestine decreed that it is forbidden for Jews to study Torah or practice it—and certainly to teach it. One day, Pappus ben Judah found his colleague, Rabbi Akiba, assembling groups of Jews to whom he would teach Torah.

Pappus said to Akiba: "Aren't you afraid of the government?"

Akiba replied: "Let me answer you with a parable. Once a fox was walking alongside a river and he saw the fishes rushing by in schools, from one place to another. Said the fox to them: 'From what are you fleeing?'

"The fish replied: 'We are fleeing the fishermen's nets that are cast to entrap us.'

"'Why don't you come up here on the dry land,' said the fox, 'so you and I can live together, just the way our ancestors once lived together?'

"To which the fish replied: 'Are you the foolish one? You are called the most clever of animals, but you are the most foolish. If we are afraid here in the water which is our own element, how much more so would we be on dry land, which is a strange environment?'"

"So it is with us," said Akiba. "If we are not safe when we study Torah, how much less safe would we be when we neglect the Torah?"

Palestinian scholars use the term *aggadah* whereas Babylonian scholars use the term *haggadah*.

See Haggadah.

Aging

The Bible (Numbers 8:25–26) states that the Levites, who served in a variety of capacities in the Tabernacle in the desert, were compelled to retire upon reaching the age of fifty because their work was physically demanding. Jewish tradition, however, regards seventy as the time when old age begins to set in. The Psalmist (90:10) says: "The span of our life is seventy years; or, given by reason of strength, eighty years..." Several thousand years later, the *Code of Jewish Law* (*Shulchan Arukh*, Yoreh Dei'ah 244:1) reiterated the view that old age begins at seventy.

In the Holiness Code, the Bible (Leviticus 19:32) spells out how the elderly are to be treated: "You shall rise before the aged and show deference to the old; you shall fear the Lord: I am the Lord."

The Talmud (*Kiddushin* 33a) says of Rabbi Yochanan, the third-century Palestinian scholar, that he would rise before the elderly, even when aged heathens passed by. Yochanan said that he was showing the heathens deference because of the many experiences they have had in their long lives.

Rabbi Judah said (*Berakhot* 8b), "Be careful to respect an old man who has forgotten his learning through no fault of his own [because he is ill or distressed from the burden of making a livelihood], for it was said, 'Both the whole Tablets of the Law [Ten Commandments] and the fragments of the Tablets [which were broken by Moses] were placed in the ark [for safekeeping] (*Bava Batra* 14b).'"

The great twentieth-century Jewish philosopher Abraham Joshua Heschel summarized the Jewish attitude toward the elderly (*Judaism* magazine, spring 1977) when he wrote: "The years of old age…are indeed formative years, rich in possibilities to unlearn the follies of a lifetime, to see through inbred self-deceptions, to deepen understanding and compassion, to widen the horizon of honesty, to refine the sense of fairness."

See Hekdeish; Moshav Zekeinim.

Agunah

Plural, *agunot*. A Hebrew term meaning "chained woman," referring to a married woman who has not been granted a Jewish divorce document (*get*) and is therefore "chained" to her present condition. Unable to remarry, an *agunah* is a woman in limbo.

Two types of women are in this category:

1. A woman whose husband has disappeared and whose whereabouts cannot be definitely established. A popular talmudic example of such a case involves a man who has disappeared in a body of water. If the disappearance took place in a small body of water whose perimeters are clearly visible (*ma'yim she-yeish la-hem sof*), and the husband was not seen to surface at any point, it is assumed that he drowned. In this case, the wife is free to remarry.

However, if the disappearance took place in a large body of water, such as a sea or ocean, whose perimeters are not totally visible to the naked eye (*ma'yim she-ein la-hem sof*), it is assumed that the husband might have been rescued or might have made his way to dry land without having been seen by anyone. In such a case, the wife is considered an *agunah*—that is, she is chained to her husband and may not remarry (*Bava Kama* 121a).

2. A woman who has been divorced in the eyes of a civil court but whose husband has refused to grant her a Jewish divorce.

The Disappearance Dilemma

The status of the *agunah* has been seriously debated for over two thousand years, since the days of the great first-century talmudic scholars Hillel and Shammai. In the view of Hillel and most of his colleagues, an *agunah* may remarry even if the husband's death is probable but cannot be absolutely proved. Shammai, on the other hand, required that witnesses come forth and offer positive testimony.

At the end of the nineteenth century, the leading rabbinic authority of Kovno, Lithuania, Rabbi Isaac Elchanan Spektor (1817–1896), set his mind to alleviate the plight of the *agunah*. He ruled that in cases where a husband is lost at sea, regardless of how large the body of water, such water is to be presumed to be *ma'yim she-yeish la-hem sof*. As such, the missing husband can be presumed to have drowned, and the widow is allowed to remarry.

Spektor also adopted an unconventional method of avoiding the problem from the outset. He made it a practice of visiting recently drafted married soldiers and trying to persuade them to write an actual divorce document. The *get* would be held in safekeeping by the *Beit Din* (court), which was authorized by the soldier to serve the divorce on his wife only in the event that he is missing in action and presumed dead.

The Obstinate Husband

Over the years, various rabbis have suggested ways of dealing with the plight of the *agunah* whose husband refuses to execute a *get*. Despite these efforts, largely because of the antipathy of rabbinic authorities toward changing established law, the issue remains unresolved.

The Conservative movement has attempted to deal with the *agunah* dilemma by adding a clause to the marriage contract (*ketubbah*), stipulating that in the event that the marriage is to be dissolved, the husband and wife agree to abide by the decisions of the *Beit Din* of the Rabbinical Assembly. In effect, if the husband persists in his refusal to grant a *get*, the marriage will be annulled and the woman will be free to remarry.

The text of this clause was prepared in 1953 by Professor Saul Lieberman, an outstanding authority on Jewish law, but the Orthodox rabbinate considered it not in full compliance with Jewish law. However, in the late twentieth century, a number of modern Orthodox rabbis, led by Rabbi Emanuel Rackman, president of Bar-Ilan University, and his daughter-in-law, Honey Rackman, began to press their fundamentalist colleagues to find a solution to the plight of Orthodox *agunot*.

See Heter Mei'ah Rabbanim.

Ahavat Yisra'el

A Hebrew phrase meaning "love of Israel; love of fellow Jews." A concept inherent in the expression "All Jews are responsible one for the other" (*Shevuot* 39a), which implies a sense of personal identification with the plight of Jews regardless of where they live. All Jews are considered part of one extended family.

See Mitnagdim.

Akdamut

A Hebrew word meaning "introduction" or "beginning," *Akdamut* is the name of a mystical Aramaic poem recited on the first day of Shavuot before the first Torah portion is read. Composed in the eleventh century by Meir ben Isaac of Worms, this ninety-seven verse poem celebrating God's gift of the Torah to the Jewish people opens with the words *akdamut milin*, meaning "an introduction to the words [of the Ten Commandments]." It goes on to say that it is practically impossible to express in words the gratitude of the Jewish people for having been blessed with the Torah.

In its introductory verses, *Akdamut* expresses the Jewish love of God and His Torah:

> Could we with ink the ocean fill,
> Were every blade of grass a quill,
> Were the world of parchment made,
> And every man a scribe by trade,
> To write the love of God above
> Would drain the ocean dry;
> Nor would the scroll contain the whole,
> Though stretch from sky to sky.
> …[last] Then let us rejoice that He blessed
>   us and gave us the Law.

Azharot

On the second day of Shavuot, Sephardic congregations recite a different poem prior to the Torah reading. Called *Azharot* ("warnings"), it amplifies upon the contents of the 365 negative commandments (*mitzvot lo ta'aseh*) found in the Torah.

See Mitzvah.

Akeidah

A Hebrew term meaning "the binding." In the Book of Genesis (22), God puts Abraham to the test, saying, "Take your son, your favored one, Isaac, whom you love, and go to the Land of Moriah, and offer him there as a burnt offering on one of the hills that I will point out to you." Abraham did all that God commanded him in preparation for the sacrifice, even to the point of binding Isaac on the altar. In the end, at God's command, Abraham did not harm the child.

The Hebrew word for binding is *akeidah*, and so in Jewish literature the proposed sacrifice of Isaac became known as the *Akeidah* or *Akeidat Yitzchak*, "The Binding of Isaac." Based on the parallel drawn by Paul (Romans 8:32) between the *Akeidah* and the sacrifice (crucifixion) of Jesus, the Christian Church introduced the misleading term "Sacrifice of Isaac" to refer to what is known in Jewish literature simply as the "Binding of Isaac."

In Jewish tradition, Rosh Hashanah became a time of testing and proving one's loyalty to God. Therefore, in the synagogue on the second day of the holiday, the story of the Binding of Isaac is read aloud from the Torah. The ram's horn (*shofar*) is blown during the Rosh Hashanah service as a reminder of the ram that Abraham used as a substitute for the sacrifice of his son.

In the Middle Ages, Isaac was exalted as a symbol of Jewish martyrdom.

Akum

An acronym formed by combining the first letter of the first two words and the first two letters of the third word in the expression *oveid kokhavim u-mazalot*, "worshipper of stars and constellations." The term is used frequently in the Talmud and later Jewish literature to describe a heathen or a non-Jew. In the Middle Ages, the term was used euphemistically to mislead Christian censors who examined Jewish writings for use of any term that might be an affront to Christians or Christianity. *Akum*, being unfamiliar, was not censored.

Many medieval rabbis went out of their way to indicate that the term did not apply to Christians or Moslems, who share the belief in one God.

Al Cheit

This Hebrew term meaning "for the sin" is the name given to a confession of sins that is included in each of the five Yom Kippur services. Composed in the post-talmudic period (sixth to tenth centuries), the *Al Cheit* enumerates forty-four transgressions for which the individual seeks forgiveness. Particular emphasis is placed on sins of speech.

These confessions, arranged in a double alphabetical acrostic (the first two sins begin with *alef*, the next two with *bet*, and so on) are framed in the plural: "For the sin *we* have committed...," rather than "for the sin *I* have committed." This formulation reminds us that we are all responsible for each other.

In reciting the *Al Cheit* prayer, which focuses on personal moral failures—such as callousness, pride, insolence, hatred, envy, slander, deception, and corrupt business practices—the individual expresses contrition and asks for God's forgiveness. As each of the transgressions is recited aloud, it is traditional for the worshipper to beat one's breast.

See Ashamnu; Breast-beating; Confession of Sins.

Aleinu

A Hebrew word meaning "it is our duty." This, the final prayer recited at all religious services, begins with the sentence "It is our duty to praise the Master of the Universe, to ascribe greatness to the Creator." Using verses from various books of the Bible—including Isaiah, Habakkuk, and Psalms—the *Aleinu* articulates the struggle of Jews to eradicate idolatry and polytheism from the face of the earth and to encourage the acceptance of a belief in one God. It expresses the hope that the day will come when God will be worshipped by all humankind.

Scholars believe that the *Aleinu* was composed by Rav, also known as Abba Arikha, a leading Babylonian talmudic teacher of the third century C.E. In its original form, it contained a phrase taken from the Book of Isaiah

(30:7) which reads, "For the help of Egypt shall be vanity and emptiness [*hevel va-rik* in Hebrew]." In Europe, around the year 1400, an apostate Jew complained to Church authorities that this was a slanderous phrase referring to Jesus and his teachings, when in fact it was referring to Egypt. To prove his point, the apostate used the method known as *gematriah*, through which he equated the numerical value of the word *va-rik* ("emptiness") with the numerical value of Yeshu, the Hebrew name for Jesus. The numerical value of each is 316. The Church accepted the apostate's false charge that each day Jews were casting aspersions on the Savior, and they successfully pressured the Jews to drop the phrase from their prayerbooks. Only the Sephardim, who did not live in Christian countries at that time and were therefore not subject to Church influence, retained the phrase in their prayerbooks.

See Gematriah; Spitting.

Al Ha-Nisim

This Hebrew phrase meaning "for the miracles" are the first two words of a special prayer of thanksgiving that is added to the *Amidah* (*Shemoneh Esrei*) during Chanukkah and Purim. The prayer is also added to the *Grace After Meals* on these holidays.

Al Ha-Nisim, which was introduced in the post-talmudic era sometime before the eighth century, thanks God for delivering "the strong into the hands of the weak, the many into the hands of the few, the impure into the hands of the pure, the wicked into the hands of the righteous, and the arrogant into the hands of those who occupy themselves with Thy Torah."

On Chanukkah, the paragraph that follows *Al Ha-Nisim* describes the miracle of Chanukkah. On Purim, the paragraph that follows relates to the story of Esther.

See Eighteen Benedictions.

Aliyah to Israel

Aliyah is a Hebrew word literally meaning "going up." When one immigrates to Israel, he or she is said to be making *aliyah* ("going up") to Israel. Jews have always felt a strong affinity with and devotion to the Land of Israel (*Eretz Yisra'el*). This is traceable to the covenant made between God and Abraham in which the Land of Israel was promised to Abraham and his descendants (Genesis 12). To live on the land became a requirement of Jewish law. "A person who dwells in the Diaspora," says the Talmud (*Ketubbot* 110b), "is like one who has no God." And in the same talmudic tractate there is a complementary statement: "Whoever lives outside of Israel may be regarded as one who worships idols."

The great thirteenth-century Spanish scholar Moses ben Nachman (Nachmanides) affirmed that settling in Israel is a positive Torah commandment, and he set an example by moving there from Spain. Nachmanides lived out the last three years of his life, from 1267 to 1270, in Acre. Maimonides, on the other hand, does not include *aliyah* among his list of 613 commandments.

Throughout the centuries, other individuals and small groups have taken the talmudic caveat seriously and have settled in the Holy Land. This activity intensified after World War II, peaking after 1948, when the State of Israel was established. A large percentage of Jews who have immigrated to Israel in the latter half of the twentieth century have done so to seek refuge from persecution, while many others have done so for religious or nationalistic reasons.

Opposition to Aliyah

As far back as talmudic times, some Jews have been opposed to the concept of *aliyah* on grounds that it interferes with the fulfillment of biblical prophecy. Jeremiah said, "They [Israel, the defeated nation] shall be carried to Babylon and shall remain there [in the Diaspora] until the day I [God] remember them" (Jeremiah 27:22). To Rabbi Judah this meant, "Whoever goes up [returns] from Babylonia [the Diaspora] to Israel transgresses a positive commandment of the Torah" (*Ketubbot* 110b). God must be the instrument through which Jews return to Israel.

Today, a considerable number of ultra-Orthodox Jews continue to accept the view of Rabbi Judah, believing, as Jeremiah implied, that only through divine intervention can the Children of Israel be returned to the Holy Land. Typical of those who support this position are members of the Satmar chasidic sect, which originated in Hungary.

Since the establishment of the State of Israel in 1948, millions of Jews from all over the world have made *aliyah*. The largest mass immigration to Israel in recent years has been that of the Jews of Russia and Ethiopia in the late 1980s and early 1990s.

The influx from the Soviet Union reached a crisis stage when, from 1989 through 1994, roughly 500,000 immigrants arrived in Israel at a time when the population of Israel was about four million. Additionally, Israeli officials estimated that one-third of the new arrivals were distant descendants of Jews, had non-Jewish spouses, and did not consider themselves Jews. But they were allowed into Israel because of an amendment to the 1950 Law of Return. The law, which specifies who could immigrate, was altered in 1970 to include the right of immigration to any person with a single Jewish grandparent.

See Jewish Identity; Law of Return.

Aliyah to the Torah

An *aliyah* (plural, *aliyot*) to the Torah is an invitation to ascend the pulpit (*bimah*) and approach the Torah. The honoree recites an initial blessing before the Torah portion is read aloud and then a concluding blessing after the reading is finished. An *aliyah* may be assigned only to an adult—that is, a male who is past bar mitzvah age or, in most non-Orthodox congregations, a female who is past bat mitzvah age.

In the Sephardic tradition, an *aliyah* to the Torah is often referred to as a *mitzvah*, meaning "commandment," because the reading and study of the Torah is considered a primary religious obligation.

When Ezra the Scribe assumed leadership of the Jewish people in the middle of the fifth century B.C.E., he introduced a new concept: individual Jews were to be called upon to read a portion of the Torah to the assembly at prescribed times, principally on the Sabbath. Initially, the honor of reading from the Torah was reserved for the "seven illustrious members of the community," and for that reason seven Torah honors are awarded each Sabbath.

Allocation of Aliyot

Initially, the first person called to read from the Torah was a Priest (*Kohen*); the second a Levite (*Levi*), a member of the family of priestly assistants; and all the others were Israelites (*Yisra'elim*, plural form of *Yisra'el*), the balance of the community (Orach Cha'yim 135:3–4). This procedure is still followed in traditional synagogues. If a *Kohen* is not present, a *Yisra'el* is to receive the first *aliyah*, even if a *Levi* is present. If a *Kohen* receives the first *aliyah* and there is no *Levi* present to receive the second *aliyah*, the same *Kohen* is awarded the second *aliyah* as well, and he repeats all the blessings, (*Mishneh Torah*, Hilkhot Tefillah 12:19 and Orach Cha'yim 135:6).

Reform Judaism does not give preference to a *Kohen* or *Levi* over a *Yisra'el*. In Conservative Judaism, the *Kohen/Levi* system is followed by most congregations, but sometimes a *Yisra'el* is called to the Torah for the first *aliyah* even if a *Kohen* is present.

The first three *aliyot* are considered "*aliyot* of distinction," and those who receive them are referred to in Jewish literature by the Aramaic term *telata gavrei* ("three gentlemen"), a phrase based on Daniel 3:24, where the three courageous friends of Daniel—Shadrach, Meshach, and Abed-Nego—are mentioned. Some scholars say that these first three *aliyot* represent the patriarchs, and some say that they represent the three divisions of the Bible: Torah, Prophets, and Holy Writings.

When the Palestinian *amora* Isaac Nappacha was asked (*Gittin* 60a) who is to be called up to the Torah after *Kohen* and *Levi*, he replied: First *parnassim* (lay leaders), followed by the scholars who are qualified to be *parnassim*, then sons of scholars whose fathers had been *parnassim*, and finally heads of synagogues and members of the general public.

Number of Aliyot

The total number of *aliyot* awarded at a Torah reading service varies with the occasion; the general rule is that the more important the holiday, the more honors are assigned. As follows:

- *three aliyot:*
  Sabbath afternoon
  Monday and Thursday mornings
  weekdays during Chanukkah
  Purim
  Tishah B'Av and other minor fast day mornings
  Yom Kippur afternoon

- *four aliyot:*
  Rosh Chodesh (New Moon) unless it falls on the Sabbath
  Chol Ha-Moed (Intermediate Days of Passover and Sukkot) unless it falls on the Sabbath

- *five aliyot:*
  Rosh Hashanah, Passover, Shavuot, Sukkot, Shemini Atzeret, Simchat Torah

- *six aliyot:*
  Yom Kippur morning

- *seven aliyot:*
  Sabbath morning

It is improper to award fewer than the number of *aliyot* prescribed for a given occasion. Additional *aliyot*, known as *hosafot*, may be awarded only on occasions when five, six, or seven *aliyot* are prescribed. However, when fewer than five *aliyot* are mandated, the sixteenth-century Ashkenazic authority Moses Isserles makes an exception in the awarding of additional *aliyot*. When two bridegrooms who are *Yisra'elim* are present at a service, he rules, an additional *aliyah* may be awarded so that both celebrants can be honored. The same applies when two fathers of newborn sons are present.

The Maftir

Aside from the prescribed number of *aliyot* assigned on holidays and the Sabbath, an additional *aliyah* called *maftir* is mandated. The Talmud (*Megillah* 23a) says that the person who reads the *haftarah* (selection from the Prophets) should first read the *maftir* portion from the Torah. The scholar Ulla explains that this is done in order to show respect for the Torah: by reading from the Torah first, the person designated to read the *haftarah* is showing deference to the Pentateuch, which is higher in sanctity than the Prophets.

In Ashkenazic congregations today, *maftir* is generally reserved for the bar or bat mitzvah. In Sephardic congregations, the bar mitzvah generally receives the fifth *aliyah*; he does not chant the *haftarah*. (Sephardic congregations do not celebrate a bat mitzvah at a religious service.)

Reform congregations, which in past years reduced the number of *aliyot*, offering as few as one honor, have in more recent years been adding to that number, some even awarding the prescribed minimum of seven on a Sabbath morning.

Special Occasions

According to tradition, there are special occasions when an individual is entitled to receive an *aliyah* on demand. Not all authorities agree as to which milestones take precedence over others, but the following is the generally accepted sequence:

1. a groom on the Sabbath before his wedding (*Aufruf*)

2. a groom on the Sabbath following his wedding

3. a bar mitzvah (and today, in Conservative and Reform congregations, a bat mitzvah)

4. the father of a newborn child who has come to the synagogue to name the baby

5. one who will observe a *yahrzeit* in the week

6. one who is obligated to recite the *Birkat Ha-Gomel* prayer after emerging unscathed from a life-threatening experience

7. visiting dignitaries

In strictly traditional synagogues, only one person at a time is called to the Torah to recite the blessings. This is based on the talmudic observation that it is difficult to understand what is being said when two people speak simultaneously. If honorees were to recite the blessings together, the congregation may not hear them clearly and know when to respond by saying "Amen."

Most non-Orthodox congregations reject this prohibition and in fact quite often will honor two people with the same *aliyah*. Sometimes one person will recite the first Torah blessing and the second person will recite the concluding blessing; at other times, both blessings are recited in unison.

Blood Relatives

When pronouncing the Torah blessings, one is in effect giving testimony to God and to the Jewish people. In Jewish law, the testimony of two witnesses is required to convict an individual of wrongdoing, but the witnesses may not be blood relatives. Using this law as a basis, the Rabbis ruled that blood relatives should not be awarded consecutive *aliyot*.

Some authorities believe that the ruling is based on the superstitious belief that if two members of a family receive *aliyot* one after the other, the evil eye will cast a spell on the family. Non-Orthodox congregations consider this ban nonbinding.

In Sephardic congregations, members of the immediate family (male and female) stand when a member of the family is honored with an *aliyah*, and they remain standing until the honoree returns to his seat.

Aliyot for Women

In early talmudic times (from approximately 100 B.C.E. to 200 C.E.) women as well as men were called to the Torah, and all read their own Torah portions (*Megillah* 23a and the Tosefta, *Megillah* 4:11). On occasions when a congregation consisted of very few males who were knowledgeable enough to read the unvocalized Torah script, most of the *aliyot* were given to women. This proved embarrassing to the male population and was probably one of the factors that led to the appointment of the *ba'al korei*, "master of the reading," who read all Torah portions.

At this same time, in what has been interpreted as a move to insure male dominance in Jewish life, another change was put into effect by the Rabbis. Women, who originally had *read* from the Torah, were now denied the right even to ascend the pulpit and recite the Torah blessings. The reason for this was given as *mipnei kevod tzibur*, because of the "honor [dignity] of the public [congregation]." The Rabbis felt that since the presence of women on the pulpit would be distracting to men, females should be banned from all participation in the synagogue service.

It is quite evident that as far back as the thirteenth century authorities did not unanimously subscribe to the ban on women receiving *aliyot*. The eminent German scholar Rabbi Meir of Rothenberg (1215–1293) ruled that if on the Sabbath a congregation consists only of *Kohanim* (Priests), women, and children, the women and children may be called to the Torah. And if there are no women and children present, the Torah may not be read because a *Kohen* may not be given the third, fourth, fifth, sixth, or seventh *aliyot* on Sabbath. If one of those *aliyot* were given to a *Kohen*, an observer might be misled into thinking that the honoree was not really a *Kohen*.

A younger contemporary of Rabbi Meir, Rabbi Yerucham, author of *Toldot Adam ve-Chavah*, is quoted by Joseph Caro in his *Beit*

Yosef (Orach Cha'yim 135) as having ruled that in a city where all residents are *Kohanim*, a *Kohen* is called to the Torah for the first *aliyah* and he repeats the blessings for the second *aliyah* (since a *Levi* is not present) and then women are called for subsequent *aliyot*, since "all may be counted to the number seven" as stated in the Talmud (*Megillah* 23a).

Today, most Conservative and all Reform and Reconstructionist congregations award *aliyot* to women because they no longer regard as valid the prohibition based on *kevod tzibur*. Since the individual who is called to the Torah no longer reads the Torah portion, they consider the original reason of causing embarrassment to oneself or the congregation no longer applicable.

Torah Blessings and Non-Jews

Only a Jew may be called to recite the Torah blessings. If a Gentile were called to the Torah for an *aliyah*, even if he knew the Torah blessings and pronounced them properly, each of the blessings would be a *berakhah le-vatalah*, a wasted blessing. The blessings are considered wasted because a non-Jew is not eligible to recite a blessing containing the words "*asher kideshanu be-mitzvotav ve-tzivanu...*," meaning "Who has sanctified us with His commandments and commanded us to..." Non-Jews, not being members of the Covenant People, were not commanded to observe the *mitzvot* of the Torah.

Auctioning Aliyot

In the Middle Ages it was not uncommon for minors to read the Torah and to conduct the entire service. The leading fourteenth-century rabbi of North Africa, Rabbi Simon Duran, observes in one of his responsa that the *maftir* was auctioned off each week at the Sabbath service, and he who made the largest offer would bestow the *haftarah* honor upon a minor so that he might gain experience.

There are authorities, however, who limit this practice and prohibit the calling up of a minor for *maftir* on Shabbat Chazon, Shabbat Shuvah, the seventh day of Passover, Shabbat Zakhor, Shabbat Parah, and on the first day of Shavuot. The *haftarot* selected for these occasions contain subject matter more appropriately read by adults.

Until comparatively recent times, it was commonplace in Orthodox synagogues for *aliyot* to be auctioned, particularly on holidays. Joseph Caro's *Code of Jewish Law* (*Shulchan Arukh*, Orach Cha'yim 147:1) notes that it was common practice to auction the *hagbahah* (raising of the Torah) and *gelilah* (rolling and dressing of the Torah) honors. Sephardic synagogues, particularly Iranian, consider these to be distinguished honors. However, strictly speaking, they are not *aliyot* since a blessing is not pronounced by the honoree.

See Aliyah to Israel.

Alphabet, Hebrew

There are a total of twenty-two letters in the Hebrew alphabet, five of which are scripted differently when used as the final letter of a word. Thus, including the final letters, there are actually twenty-seven different characters in the Hebrew alphabet.

The Letters of the Alphabet

The following are the twenty-two letters of the alphabet: *alef, bet/vet, gimmel, dalet, hei, vav, za'yin, chet, tet, yud, kaf/khaf, lamed, mem, nun, samekh, a'yin, pei/fei, tzadi, kuf, reish, shin/sin, tav.* The meaning of most of these letters is uncertain, although there has been reasonable speculation about the origin of some.

Alef – א

Also spelled *aleph*. The first letter in the Hebrew alphabet, paralleling the Greek *alpha*, is mentioned in the Mishnah of tractate *Shekalim* (3:2). *Alef* has a numerical value of one. In the form *aluf*, the term is often used to refer to a prince or ruler. When an *alef* with a stroke over it precedes other numbers, it has a value of 1,000.

Bet/Vet – ב/ב

Also spelled *beth*. The second letter of the Hebrew alphabet, paralleling the Greek letter *beta*. When the *bet* has no *dagesh* (dot) in it, it is pronounced *vet*. It is speculated that the *bet*, which means "house" (*ba'yit*) in Hebrew, is so called because it looked like a house in ancient Hebrew-Canaanitish script. The letter is shaped like a box, with its left side open, indicating an entrance or a vestibule of a house. The numerical value of *bet* is two. When a *bet* with a stroke over it precedes other numbers, it has a value of 2,000.

Gimmel – ג

The third letter in the Hebrew alphabet, paralleling the Greek *gamma*, as noted in the Mishnah of tractate *Shekalim* (3:2). Some philologists claim that the name *gimmel* is related to *gamal*, meaning "camel." In ancient Hebrew-Canaanitish script the *gimmel* resembles the shape of a camel. The numerical value of *gimmel* is three. When a *gimmel* with a stroke over it precedes other numbers, it has a value of 3,000.

Dalet – ד

Also spelled *daleth*. This letter, meaning "door," is the fourth letter of the Hebrew alphabet. Scholars believe that it is so named because in its original Hebrew-Canaanitish script it was shaped like a door. The numerical value of *dalet* is four. When a *dalet* with a stroke over it precedes other numbers, it has a value of 4,000.

Hei – ה

The fifth letter in the Hebrew alphabet, when used at the beginning of some words, *hei* means "this" or "this one." When a *hei* with a stroke over it precedes other numbers, it has a value of 5,000. *Hei* with a stroke over it is also used as an abbreviation for the name of God.

Vav – ו

The sixth letter in the Hebrew alphabet, *vav*, meaning "a screw [that which joins parts]," has a numerical value of six. When a *vav* with a stroke over it precedes other numbers, it has a value of 6,000.

Za'yin – ז

The seventh letter in the Hebrew alphabet, *za'yin* is sometimes said to be so named because it resembles the shape of the letter used in the ancient Hebrew-Canaanitish script. *Za'yin* means "armament" or "sword" in Hebrew and has a numerical value of seven. When a *za'yin* with a stroke over it precedes other numbers, it has a value of 7,000.

Chet – ח

Also spelled *het*. It is speculated that the *chet* originated by placing two of the letter *za'yin* next to each other. It is the eighth letter in the Hebrew alphabet and has a numerical value of eight. When a *chet* with a stroke over it precedes other numbers, it has a value of 8,000.

Tet – ט

The ninth letter in the Hebrew alphabet, *tet* has a numerical value of nine. When a *tet*

with a stroke over it precedes other numbers, it has a value of 9,000.

Yud – י

Also spelled and pronounced *yod*. The tenth letter in the Hebrew alphabet, *yud* has a numerical value of ten. *Yud* with a stroke after it is often used as an abbreviation for the name of God. When a *yud* with a stroke over it precedes other numbers, it has a value of 10,000.

Kaf/Khaf – כ/כ

Two forms of the eleventh letter of the Hebrew alphabet. Both the *kaf* and *khaf* are shaped the same, except when they appear at the end of a word. The *khaf* has no *dagesh* (dot) in it, except when it appears at the beginning of a word or a syllable within the word. In those instances a dot is placed in the *khaf* and it is pronounced *kaf*. When the *khaf* appears at the end of a word, it is elongated by extending the vertical line. In the ancient Hebrew-Canaanitish script the *khaf* was portrayed as resembling the hollow of a hand with fingers bent.

The numerical value of this letter is twenty. Occasionally, it appears in its elongated form at the beginning of a series of numbers, and in such cases it has a value of 500.

Lamed – ל

The twelfth letter in the Hebrew alphabet, the *lamed* is so named because in the ancient Hebrew-Canaanitish script it had the shape of an oxgoad, a plow. Reference to such an instrument is made in the Book of Judges (3:31). *Lamed* has a numerical value of thirty.

Mem – מ

The thirteenth letter in the Hebrew alphabet, the *mem* has a numerical value of forty.

When it appears as the final letter of a word, it takes a different shape and is called *mem sofit* ("final *mem*") or *mem setumah* ("enclosed *mem*") because it is enclosed on all sides.

When the *mem* appears in the middle or beginning of a word, it is called *mem petuchah* ("open *mem*") because there is an open space between the horizontal bar at the base of the letter and the vertical stroke on the left side. When the *mem* appears in its final form at the beginning of a calendar date, its numerical value is 600.

In ancient Hebrew-Canaanitish script, the *mem* was shaped like waves. Hence, the definition "water" has been ascribed to it.

Nun – נ

The fourteenth letter of the Hebrew alphabet, *nun* has a numerical value of fifty. It is one of five letters that is shaped differently when it appears as the final letter of a word, and in those cases it is called *nun sofit* ("final *nun*") or *nun peshutah* ("simple *nun*"). When it appears at the beginning or middle of a word, it is called *nun kefufah* ("bent *nun*"). When the final form of the letter is placed at the beginning of a word, as is sometimes done when giving a date, its numerical value is 700.

The *nun* is generally defined as "fish," and in the ancient Hebrew-Canaanitish script it is indeed shaped like a fish. The Hebrew word for fish is *dag*, and the Aramaic word for fish is *nuna* (see Jonah 2:1).

Samekh – ס

Also spelled *samech*. The fifteenth letter in the Hebrew alphabet, the *samekh* has a numerical value of sixty. In the ancient Hebrew-Canaanitish script, the *samekh* appears in the shape of a fish skeleton, which is why it is sometimes defined as "prop" or "support," as the spine is for the body.

A'yin – ע

The sixteenth letter in the Hebrew alphabet, the *a'yin*, meaning "eye," has a numerical value of seventy. In the ancient Hebrew-Canaanitish script the *a'yin* has the shape of an eye.

Pei/fei – פ/פ

The seventeenth letter in the Hebrew alphabet, the *pei* has a dot (*dagesh* in Hebrew) in it and is therefore also known as *pei degushah*. Without the *degesh*, the letter is pronounced *fei*. The *pei* and *fei,* which have a numerical value of eighty, have been defined as "mouth" because in the ancient Hebrew-Canaanitish script the letter took the shape of an open mouth. *Pei* is one of the five final Hebrew letters that are shaped differently when they appear at the end of a word. When it appears at the beginning or in the middle of a word, it is called *pei kefufah* ("bent *pei*"). When it appears at the end of a word, it is called *pei sofit* ("final *pei*") or *pei peshutah* ("simple *pei*"). The final *pei* has a numerical value of 800.

Tzadi – צ

Also pronounced *tzadik*. The eighteenth letter in the Hebrew alphabet, the *tzadi* has the numerical value of ninety. It is speculated that the *tzadi* is so named because in the ancient Hebrew-Canaanitish script it is shaped like a net for catching fish, and *tzadi* means "fishing" or "hunting." The *tzadi* is one of the five Hebrew letters that are shaped differently when they appear at the end of a word. When a *tzadi* appears at the beginning or middle of a word, it is called *tzadi kefufah* ("bent *tzadi*"); and when it appears at the end of a word, it is called *tzadi sofit* ("final *tzadi*") or *tzadi peshutah* ("simple *tzadi*"). The final *tzadi* has a numerical value of 900.

Kuf – ק

The nineteenth letter in the Hebrew alphabet, it is speculated that the *kuf* is so named because in the ancient Hebrew-Canaanitish script it was shaped like the eye of a needle, which is *kuf* in Hebrew. The numerical value of *kuf* is 100.

Reish – ר

The twentieth letter in the Hebrew alphabet, the *reish* carries a numerical value of 200. It is thought to be so named because in the ancient Hebrew-Canaanitish script the letter was shaped like a head, which is *rosh* in Hebrew.

Shin/Sin – שׁ / שׂ

The twenty-first letter in the Hebrew alphabet, the *shin/sin* has a numerical value of 300. The *shin* is shaped like a three-branched candelabrum and has a dot above its right branch; it is pronounced "sh." When the dot appears above the left branch, it is pronounced "s" and is called *sin*.

Tav – ת

The twenty-second (and final) letter in the Hebrew alphabet has a numerical value of 400.

The Final Letters

The earliest manuscripts of the Torah (and the rest of the Bible) had no chapter or verse delineations. One verse ran into another, and even words themselves had no spacing between them. To solve the problem faced by the Torah reader (*ba'al korei*) and by students who had difficulty determining where words begin or end, the early scribes introduced final letters for the following five consonants: *kaf, mem, nun, pei, tzadi*. Whenever a word ended with one of these letters, the shape of the letter was changed—usually it was elongated. The need for a device to indicate where a word ended was particularly acute with two-letter words, such as *akh, im, min, af,* and *ben*. Two-letter words, it was found, were often mistakenly combined with the short words that preceded them.

The Rabbis of the Talmud wondered about the origin of the final letters. Some concluded that they were instituted by the prophets (*Shabbat* 104a), while others believed that when Moses received the Torah on Mount Sinai, he was instructed to use them.

Mystics have theorized that the final letters originated at the time of Creation but were stored away until the Children of Israel entered the Promised Land. They were then revealed and were added to the other twenty-two letters of the alphabet. (See *Shabbat* 104a. See also Palestinian Talmud, *Megillah* 1:9).

Alef vs. Bet

A great deal of discussion in the Talmud and Midrash relates to various Hebrew letters, particularly to the *alef* and *bet* (see *Shabbat* 104a). Early Bible commentators questioned why the first letter of the first word of the first book of the Bible is a *bet* rather than an *alef*, the first letter of the alphabet. Speculation continued for centuries, and a variety of explanations are offered in talmudic texts and later midrashic commentaries (see *Genesis Rabbah* 1:10 and Palestinian Talmud, *Chagigah* 10a):

- The Torah begins with a *bet* to serve as a reminder not to probe too deeply into the origin of the world, which might lead to heresy. Rabbi Levi, the third-century Babylonian scholar (*Genesis*

Rabbah 1:10), said, "Just as the letter *bet* is closed on three sides but open in the front [on the left side], so are you *not* permitted to investigate matters that are above and below, what is before and what is behind." Sensing that this explanation could be misleading (since Rabbi Levi lists *four* forbidden areas of investigation, although the *bet* is sealed on only *three* sides), his colleague Bar Kapparah comments, "You may speculate about things that happened after Creation, but you may not speculate about that which transpired before Creation."

- A more reasonable explanation for the discrepancy in the interpretation of Rabbi Levi and Bar Kapparah is that each may have owned Torah manuscripts with different texts. It is known that in the early Hebrew-Phoenician script used by Jews before the Assyrian script (*ketav Ashuri*) was adopted, the *bet* did not have an open panel on its left side as it does today.

- *Bet* was selected because it has a numerical value of two and therefore represents the two worlds: this world and the world to come (the Messianic Age).

- *Bet* pleaded before God that it deserved the honor of being the first letter of the Torah because it is the first letter of the word *barukh*, meaning "blessed."

- *Bet* was preferred over *alef* because *alef* is the first letter of the Hebrew word *arur*, meaning "cursed."

- *Alef* is a weak letter. It stands on two spindly legs, while *bet* has a flat, strong base.

- *Bet* has two points that protrude from it: the first extends from the base of the letter and points behind it; the second extends from the top of the letter and faces upward. To anyone who questions the origin of the Torah by asking, "Who created you?" the *bet* can answer by pointing upward, toward God. And to anyone who asks, "What is the name of the One who created you?" *bet* can answer by pointing behind it to the letter *alef*, which is the first letter of the name of God.

- In one *midrash*, the alert *alef* is portrayed as very modest. It did not push its claim to be the first letter of the Torah and was rewarded instead by becoming the first letter of the Decalogue (Exodus 20:2). (The *alef* is the first letter of *anokhi*, meaning "I," and *anokhi* is the first word of the Ten Commandments.)

- In a different *midrash*, Rabbi Eleazar portrays the *alef* as being rather pushy: For twenty-six generations from the time of Adam the *alef* complained to God, "Sovereign of the universe, I am the first of the letters of the alphabet, yet you did not create the world with me!" "When I reveal My Torah at Sinai," God answered, "I will place you at the head of the commandments, as the first letter of *anokhi*."

See Numbers.

Amen

In the Book of Numbers (5:22), the word *Amen* is used to indicate assent. Often defined as "true" or "faithful," the term is uttered in response to all prayers that begin with the words *Barukh atah Adonai*, "Blessed art Thou O God."

In Temple times, the response to the blessings conferred upon the public by Priests was "Blessed be His glorious Name forever and ever." After the Temples were destroyed, "Amen" was used in its stead (*Ta'anit* 16).

The Talmud (*Shabbat* 119b) quotes Resh Lakish as saying, "He who responds 'Amen' to a prayer with all his strength will have the gates of Paradise opened for him."

Rabbi Chaninah was of the opinion that the Hebrew word *Amen*—spelled *alef, mem, nun*—is an acronym formed from the first letter of the Hebrew phrase *El Melekh Ne'eman*, meaning "God is a faithful King." The phrase is used as a prelude to the *Shema* ("Hear, O Israel") when one is engaged in private prayer.

Kabbalists believe that in the days of the Messiah the gates of the Garden of Eden (Paradise) will be open to all who have responded "Amen" to the words of the *Kaddish*.

Am Ha-Aretz

This Hebrew term meaning "person of the land" was initially used to refer to farmers, who were largely unlearned and therefore presumed not to be pious. This belief was first expressed in the Ethics of the Fathers (2:6): "*lo am ha-aretz chasid*—An ignorant man cannot be pious."

Generally, in talmudic literature an *am ha-aretz* is not invited to be a witness, and if he is called to testify, his testimony is not accepted. Maimonides, however, disagreed, stating that if it is known that an *am ha-aretz* has been leading a righteous life, his testimony is accepted (*Mishneh Torah*, Book of Judges 11:2).

See Talmid Chakham.

Amidah

This Hebrew word literally meaning "standing" is the name of a prayer known in English as *Eighteen Benedictions*.

See Eighteen Benedictions.

Amora

Plural, *amora'im*. Derived from the Hebrew and Aramaic verb *amar*, meaning "to say" or "to speak," an *amora* is literally a speaker or interpreter.

In the Talmud, the term is used to refer to (1) a person who stood alongside the presiding teacher or lecturer and interpreted or explained the lesson in an oratorical manner. Since the lesson was sometimes difficult to follow, the *amora* simplified it and expressed it in Aramaic, the vernacular of the period, and (2) all teachers in Palestine and Babylonia who flourished during a period of about three hundred years, from the death of Judah the Prince (220 C.E.) to the redaction of the Babylonian Talmud (about 500 C.E.).

The primary function of *amora'im* was to elaborate upon the teachings of the Mishnah, although they did sometimes offer legal opinions and did attempt to reconcile differences in the views expressed by their predecessors, the *tanna'im* ("teachers").

As a general rule, *amora'im* in Palestine were ordained by the Palestinian *nasi* (Prince) and carried the title "Rabbi." Babylonian *amora'im* carried the title "Rav" or "Mar," and although they were generally ordained, their ordination was not usually recognized by Palestinian authorities.

The activity of the Palestinian *amora'im* took place primarily in the academies of Tiberias, Sepphoris, and Caesarea. At the same time, the task of interpreting the rulings of the Mishnah was underway in Babylonia, principally in the academies of Nehardea, Sura, and Pumbedita. Since the teachings of the Mishnah are quite concise, the task of elaborating upon them, explaining their full implications, and reconciling contradictions involved much discussion and debate. The written record of their discourses is called the *Gemara*, an Aramaic word that means "learning."

A major difference between Babylonian and Palestinian *amora'im* was their method of teaching and studying the texts of the Mishnah. Palestinians used a more simple and direct method, while Babylonian *amora'im* were noted for their dialectical discussions and hair-splitting analyses of the text. This characteristic of the Babylonians is noted in the talmudic tractate *Bava Metzia* (38b): "In [the Babylonian academy of] Pumbedita, the students know how to pass an elephant through the eye of a needle," meaning that they can force acceptance of statements or positions that are absolutely illogical or untenable.

The prominent Palestinian *amora'im* included Yannai the Elder, Jonathan the Elder, Jonathan bar Nappacha (Ha-Nappach), Shimon ben Lakish, and Joshua ben Levi. The last of the Palestinian *amora'im*—including Jeremiah, Jonah, and Yossi bar Zavda—were active in Tiberias until the year 359.

The outstanding Babylonian *amora'im* included Mar Samuel and Shila, who headed academies in Nehardea, and Rav (also known as Abba Arikha), who was master of the prestigious academy in Sura. The analysis of the Babylonian *amora'im* concluded in the year 500.

Am Segulah

See Chosen People.

Amulet

A charm that is said to have magical or mystical powers to protect against demons or evil spirits. The Hebrew word for amulet is *ka'mei'a*, which literally means "tie, bind." The use of such antidemonic charms was commonplace throughout Jewish history. The Talmud (Mishnah *Shabbat* 8:3) refers to an amulet consisting of animal skin on which magical writing was inscribed; it also refers

to the *even tekumah*, or "preservation stone" (*Shabbat* 66b), which was worn by pregnant women to prevent miscarriages. Women in labor as well as women who had just given birth were protected by a variety of amulets. (Herbs and aromatic roots were also used to ward off evil spirits. A sprig of fennel over which an incantation had been pronounced was hung in the home or carried around on one's person.)

Amulets were generally hung on the wall of the home or tied around the neck as a charm to ward off demons and evil spirits intent upon causing harm. In the Middle Ages, it was not uncommon for people to save a piece of the *matzah* that had been served as *afikomon* at the Passover *Seder* for use as an amulet. The *matzah* was hung in the house or carried in a pouch as a protection against evil people and evil spirits.

Amulet Inscriptions

Verses from Psalm 126, which became known as the Antidemonic Psalm because it was believed to protect infants, were frequently inscribed on amulets that were hung on a child's crib. Psalm 127 was believed to guard children and many "wore its words" as a pendant-charm throughout life.

Sometimes a metal plate inscribed with the Hebrew letter *hei*, which stands for God's name, was appended to a neckchain.

In the Middle Ages, when kabbalistic influence was at its height, the use of amulets containing the name of God in a variety of letter combinations was widespread. As a result, three nonwords appeared on the obverse side of *mezuzah* parchments in the form of the phrase *kozu be-muchsaz kozu*, which in reality is the Hebrew phrase *Adonai Eloheinu Adonai*. The letters of each word were substituted by ones that followed in alphabetical order. Thus

Adonai, which is spelled *yud, hei, vav, hei,* is spelled *kaf, vav, za'yin, vav.*

God's names always played an important role in the efficacy of amulets. The twelfth-century scholar Abraham ibn Ezra described an unusual amulet known as the *Zahlenquadrat,* or "magic square." The square was divided into nine boxes in which the numbers one to nine were inserted. The sum of the three numbers that appear in each direction (vertical, horizontal, or diagonal) is fifteen. The number fifteen is the numerical value of *yah,* another name for God, spelled *yud* plus *hei,* which is ten plus five. The number five—which is the numerical value of the Hebrew letter *hei,* a short form of God's name—is always placed in the center box.

4	9	2
3	5	7
8	1	6

In addition to the name of God, the names of angels also appear on amulets. *Sefer Razi'el,* a book of secrets supposedly revealed to Adam, stressed the importance of writing on the amulet the name of the angel who had the power to control the particular evil force.

Prominent rabbis such as the twelfth-century Moses Maimonides and eighteenth-century Jacob Emden condemned the use of amulets, characterizing them as pure superstition. On the other hand, authorities such as David Hoffman (1843–1921), director of the Berlin Rabbinical Seminary, permitted their use because of their beneficial psychological effects.

Angel of Death

Although only mentioned once in the Bible, the Angel of Death, known in Hebrew as *ma-lakh ha-mavet*, plays an important role in the Jewish heritage. The Book of Proverbs (16:14) states, "The king's wrath is a messenger of death, but a wise man can appease it."

The Talmud (*Avodah Zarah* 5a) discusses the place of the Angel of Death in the scheme of things: how he acts "full of eyes," sometimes standing above the head of a sick person with sword drawn and ready to act (ibid. 20b). To many of the Rabbis the existence of a *malakh ha-mavet* is more than sheer fantasy, and they therefore required that upon death in a household all water in the house be poured out in case poison from the angel's sword fell into it. Traditional commentators explain that the water poured out when a death occurs was the water that families stored up and kept in jugs at the entrances to homes.

This water is called *ma'yim she'uvim* ("drawn waters" in Hebrew), as opposed to *ma'yim cha'yim* ("living, natural waters"), such as well water or rain water gathered in pits. The *ma'yim she'uvim,* which has been drawn through pipes (tap water, for example), must be poured out because the water is considered tainted by virtue of its proximity to the deceased (*Bava Batra* 60b).

In kabbalistic literature the Angel of Death is known by the Aramaic term *sitra achara,* meaning "[the] Other Side"—the side of defilement, the side of Satan—and is often identified with Samael, the Prince of Dark Forces. Kabbalists believe that in the world to come (*olam ha-ba*) the Angel of Death will be slain by God. This view is expressed in the popular *Chad Gadya* folk song with which the Passover *Seder* is concluded.

See Angels; Demonology.

Angels

Although there are references in the Bible to God and a heavenly court where celestial beings minister to Him (I Kings 22:19; Isaiah 61ff.), angelology did not originate with Judaism. It was quite common for peoples of the Near East to describe a heavenly world inhabited by beings belonging to a species distinct and separate from humans.

In the Bible, these heavenly creatures are known generally as *malakhim* (singular, *malakh*) of which many species exist, such as those that go by the name *seraphim* (Isaiah 6:2) and *keruvim*, or cherubim in English (Genesis 3:24). In general, the angels of the Bible are assigned two tasks: (1) to serve as man's advocate and to assist him in meeting life's difficulties and (2) to minister to God, to serve in His heavenly court, and to sing His praises. However, in contrast to the way angels are characterized in other religious disciplines, in biblical and postbiblical Judaism angels never functioned as intermediaries between man and God.

Among the instances in biblical literature of angels helping man are:

- When Jacob is having difficulty with his father-in-law, Laban, he is visited by an "angel of God," who helps extricate him from his predicament (Genesis 31:11).

- When Abraham sends his faithful servant on a mission to find a wife for Isaac, an angel is sent to help make the mission successful (Genesis 24:40).

- When Hagar, Abraham's second wife, runs away because Sarah is treating her badly, an angel urges Hagar to return to Abraham, assuring her that she will be blessed with many offspring (Genesis 16:7–11).

- When Lot, Abraham's nephew, is having difficulty with the wicked people of Sodom, two angels appear on the scene to rescue him (Genesis 19:1ff.).

- When Jacob sets out for Haran to find a wife among his kinfolk, he has a dream in which he sees angels of God ascending and descending a ladder that reaches from earth to heaven. In the dream, God appears to Jacob and assures him of divine guidance and protection and the promise of success (Genesis 28:12).

Evidence that angels serve as members of the heavenly court and are occasionally consulted by God exists in the Bible as well. In Genesis (1:26), God says: "Let us create man in our image." To whom was God speaking? To the angels of His heavenly court is the widely accepted explanation.

In the Midrash (*Genesis Rabbah* 1:3), the Rabbis debated when angels were created. Rabbi Yochanan said, "They were created on the second day of the week." Rabbi Chaninah said, "They were created on the fifth day." A third view was that they were created even before the world was created.

The Language of Angels

The Rabbis, curious about the language used by the angels, concluded (*Chagigah* 16a) that "Angels, like human beings, speak the holy tongue [Hebrew]." Rabbi Yochanan said (*Sotah* 33a) that if anyone prays for his needs in Aramaic, the ministering angels do not pay attention to him because they do not understand that language [and therefore cannot transmit Aramaic prayers to the throne of glory].

The Hierarchy of Angels

While there were legions of angels doing God's work and serving man, the Bible refers to only two by name, both in the Book of Daniel. Gabriel is mentioned in 8:16 and 9:21 and Mikhael in 10:13 and 10:21. They

were assigned the most important roles and were closest to God, and hence they became known as *archangels* or *superangels*. In the Midrash (*Genesis Rabbah* 8:13), Rabbi Judah ben Simon goes so far as to say, "Mikhael and Gabriel were Adam's best men."

Two other angels, Raphael and Uriel, also emerge in Jewish literature as archangels. They were called upon to perform many unimaginable missions, usually with the assistance of angels of lesser status.

The Rabbis of the Midrash (*Numbers Rabbah* 2:10) describe the status and function of the four archangels. God, they said, established four cardinal directions in the world: east, west, north, and south, each with a specific purpose relating to the physical environment. Likewise did He station four angels in four directions to surround His throne. Mikhael was stationed to the south, on the right side of God; Uriel was on the north side; Gabriel was stationed to the east, in front of the throne; and Raphael behind the throne, to the west. Mikhael and Gabriel are often mentioned together as participants in a particular task, but never as duplicating each others' mission. The Rabbis believed that one angel never carries out dual tasks, nor do two angels perform the same task. Of the two archangels, Mikhael was superior in rank (*Berakhot* 4b), for whenever he appears, God's presence (the *Shekhinah*) is nearby (*Exodus Rabbah* 2:5).

The Rabbis of the Talmud (*Yoma* 37a) established the angel hierarchy based on the way the three angels who came to visit Abraham while he was recuperating from his circumcision conducted themselves: Mikhael walked in the middle, Gabriel to his right, and Raphael to his (Mikhael's) left.

Although Mikhael is considered the guardian angel of Israel and was therefore assigned the most important roles, Gabriel was chosen to resolve many crucial situations in the lives of biblical heroes: he was assigned the task of overthrowing Sodom (*Bava Metzia* 86b) so as to extricate Lot and his family from a perilous situation; he played an important role in rescuing the infant Moses (*Sotah* 12b and *Exodus Rabbah* 1:24, 1:26); and later he rescued Hananiah, Mishael, and Azariah from the fiery furnace in which they had been cast (*Pesachim* 118 a, b).

In Christian theology, it was the archangel Gabriel who announced to the Virgin of Nazareth that she would mother a son (Luke 1:33).

Among the lesser angels who were often called upon to assist the archangels, the most important of these have names ending with *el*, meaning "God," for it is from God that they derived their power. The first part of their names was related to their specific role and function. Thus Shamriel (from the Hebrew root *shamor*) was a guardian angel, Chasdiel (from *chesed*) and Rachmiel (from *rachmanut*) were angels of compassion and mercy, and Zakhriel (from *zakhor*) was an angel who ruled over memory. Other angel names that appear frequently in magical incantations and prayers are Aniel or Anael, Samael, Sachiel, Cassiel, Kaftziel, Tzadkiel, Barkiel, Nuriel, and Yeshamiel.

Evil Angels

While it seems clear that the Rabbis of the Talmud believed in the presence and influence of angels, not all angels were considered good. Satan is the generic name for the wicked ones; and Samael was the chief of all Satans. The Talmud (*Bava Batra* 16a) says: "Satan, the *yeitzer ha-ra* [evil inclination], and the Angel of Death are all one." As is evident from the Book of Job, God permits Satan to be active and influential, and it is man's task to combat him. Much advice has been given by the Rabbis as to the best way to offset the demonic, seductive forces let loose by Satan.

Maimonides' View

In his twelfth-century *Guide of the Perplexed* (I:49; II:6), Moses Maimonides downgrades the belief in the existence of angels as corporeal beings. He asserts that angels are natural forces placed in the world by God, and that these forces shape and control all that happens in the universe.

While some Jews with mystic leanings still believe in angels as celestial beings with special access to God, most Jews today subscribe to the view of Maimonides.

Animals, Treatment of

The concept of treating animals compassionately, maintaining an awareness of actions that are painful to them, is known by the Hebrew term *tza'ar ba'alei cha'yim* (literally, "the pain caused to living creatures").

See Tza'ar Ba'alei Cha'yim.

Ani Ma'amin

Meaning "I Believe [with perfect faith]," these are the opening Hebrew words to each of the Thirteen Principles of Faith enunciated by Moses Maimonides in the twelfth century. These principles, detailed in many editions of the prayerbook, were first presented by Maimonides in his commentary on the Mishnah (*Sanhedrin*, chapter 10).

Maimonides' twelfth Principle of Faith, which expresses hope for salvation through the coming of the Messiah, became the theme song of Jews incarcerated in Nazi concentration camps. It reads: "I believe with perfect faith in the coming of the Messiah, and though he may tarry, yet do I hope in him and look for his coming every day."

See Thirteen Principles of Faith.

Anim Zemirot

Literally meaning "I shall recite songs," these are the first words and popular designation of a Hebrew hymn entitled *Shir Ha-Kavod* ("Song of Glory"). Attributed to the twelfth-century German scholar and mystic Rabbi Yehudah He-Chasid, the hymn acclaims God's greatness and has been serving, primarily in Orthodox synagogues, as the concluding hymn of the Sabbath and holiday morning service. *Shir Ha-Kavod* is often led responsively by a pre-bar mitzvah youngster.

Aninut

This Hebrew word meaning "period of distress" refers to the first stage of mourning following the death of an immediate family member. It begins with the moment of death and ends when the burial is completed. During this time, the mourner (*onein* in Hebrew) is exempt from the obligation of carrying out the positive commandments (*mitzvot*), including prayer, and is forbidden from shaving, cutting the hair, and conducting usual business affairs.

See Onein; Shivah.

Anthropomorphism

A term, derived from the Greek, that refers to assigning human form or attributes to a god, animal, or inanimate object. God is anthropomorphized repeatedly in the Bible: He *expels* man from the Garden of Eden, *orders* Noah to build an ark, *smells* the pleasant odor of the offering brought by Noah, *confuses* the language of men when they decide to build the Tower of Babel, and so on.

Jewish philosophers and theologians generally agree that God is not to be conceived of as having human form, pointing to the biblical description of the Revelation on Mount Sinai

(Deuteronomy 4:12): "You heard the sound of words, but you saw no form…" Portraying God as having physical form was a heathen practice, which the Bible condemns.

Moses Maimonides (1135–1204) was probably the first Jewish philosopher to state categorically that "whoever conceives of God as a corporeal being is an apostate" (*Mishneh Torah*, Hilkhot Teshuvah 3:7). One of his contemporaries, the French talmudist Abraham ben David of Posquières (1120–1190), also known by the acronym Ravad, argued that many good Jews believe that God has human form, and they are not to be considered heretics; they are simply in error for failing to understand that the anthropomorphic passages in Scripture and rabbinic literature were not meant to be taken literally.

Nonetheless, Jews continue to speak of God in human terms. However, when doing so, some people add the Hebrew expression *kiv'yakhol*, meaning "as if it were possible [to think of God in such mortal terms]." An example of early usage of the term *kiv'yakhol* can be found in the Midrash (*Mekhilta* 44): "When God created this world, He used only one hand; but when it came to building the Holy Temple in Jerusalem, He, used both hands, as if it were possible [*kiv' yakhol*]."

See God; Monotheism.

Anti-Semitism

The first major manifestation of anti-Semitism can be traced to the Book of Exodus (1:8ff.), where it is said that "a new king arose in Egypt who did not know Joseph [and all the good he had done for the Egyptian people]." The Egyptian ruler refused to acknowledge the contribution of the Hebrew Joseph, who had saved the country during seven years of famine. When the new Pharaoh saw how numerous and successful Joseph's family, the Israelite people, had become, he grew fearful that in time of crisis they would turn against him. To prevent this, Pharaoh decided to enslave the Jews, and they remained in bondage for four centuries.

The second major manifestation of hate toward Jews as a people is described in the Book of Esther. In 486 B.C.E., Xerxes (Ahasueros) succeeded his father, Darius, to the throne of Persia. The king's prime minister, Haman, who harbored an abiding hatred of the Jews of the kingdom, complained to the king about "a certain people, scattered and dispersed among the other peoples in all the provinces of your realm, whose laws are different from those of any other people, and who do not obey the king's laws." Haman gained the king's approval to exterminate the Jews, but his plot was foiled by Esther, a Jewish woman who had become queen.

Attitude of the New Testament

Pontius Pilate, the Roman governor of Palestine in the time of Jesus, is portrayed in the New Testament as a leader without control over events. Although the Book of Matthew describes him as accusing Jesus of being the King of the Jews and hence a threat to Roman authority, Pontius is presented as unwilling to condemn Jesus and sentence him to execution. The blame for the Crucifixion is placed on the "chief Priests and the elders," who cry out, "Let him be crucified" (Matthew 27:11–25). Pontius Pilate then literally washes his hands in public and says, "This blood is not shed by my hands," while the Jews respond, "His [Jesus'] blood be upon us and our children." Here, Matthew shifts the guilt for the Crucifixion from the Romans to the Jews.

This account is the basis for the twenty-century-old libel that labels Jews as "Christ-killers." Some Christian New Testament scholars have explained away Matthew's representation of Pilate as a victim of circumstance rather than as a ruthless ruler responsible for the execution of Jesus. They point out that when the Gospels were written, relations between the emerging Church and the Jewish community were extremely strained, and new Christians were eager to portray Jews unfavorably.

It has been pointed out that the charge that Jews crucified Jesus is without historical foundation. In fact, crucifixion was a practice begun in Persia and later used by the Romans. The Roman ritual of crucifixion began with a severe beating. Following the beating, the person was hanged on two crossed wood beams by driving nails through the hands and feet. The body of the victim was not permitted to touch—and thereby defile—the ground. The Jewish historian Flavius Josephus, who lived around the time of Jesus, tells of thousands of Jews who were crucified by the Romans. It is an established fact that crucifixion was the Roman way of executing criminals.

The Christian charge that the Jews crucified Jesus can be refuted on a number of counts:

1. By the time Jesus appeared on the scene, the *Sanhedrin* (the superior judicial body in Jewish life) had lost all authority to pass sentence in capital cases. The authority was held completely by the Romans. The order to execute Jesus could only have come from the supreme Roman authority—namely, Pontius Pilate, governor of Palestine.

2. According to New Testament accounts in Mark (14:54) and Matthew (26:57), the *Sanhedrin* convened a session on the same night that Jesus was arrested; this was Passover eve, which in that year fell on the Sabbath. According to the Talmud (Mishnah *Sanhedrin* 6:11), this could not have occurred because (a) capital cases could legally be tried only during the day, and (b) the *Sanhedrin* would not have heard a case on a holiday and certainly not on a Sabbath. The Gospel of Luke (22:54, 66) does not agree with the other two Synoptic Gospels (Mark and Matthew) on this point. Luke says that the *Sanhedrin* met in the morning of that day.

3. While crucifixion was a method of capital punishment widely used by the Romans, there is no evidence of it ever having been used by Jews. The Jewish methods of execution were stoning, burning, strangling, and slaying by the sword. The first three methods are mentioned in the Bible, and the fourth is mentioned in the Talmud.

During the first two centuries of the Common Era, the Romans exhibited tolerance toward Jews. However, in the year 313 Emperor Constantine legalized the practice of Christianity and gave it favored status over Judaism. Two years later, Constantine declared it illegal for Jews to seek out converts; the crime was made punishable by death. Constantine characterized the Jews as a "despicable sect," and thus began long centuries of persecution.

Early Role of the Papacy

Among the earliest dispensers of theological hatred was Pope Gregory VII, who in 1080 addressed a letter to Castilian king Alonso VI:

As we feel impelled to congratulate you on the progress of your fame, so at the same time must we deprecate the harm you do. We admonish your Highness that you must cease to suffer the Jews to rule over the Christians and exercise authority over them. For to allow the Christians to be subordinate to the Jews, and to subject them to their judgment, is the same as oppressing God's Church and exalting Satan's synagogue. To wish to please Christ's enemies means to treat Christ himself with contumely.

The Crusaders were inspired by this communication, and beginning in the year 1096 embarked on a two-century adventure through Europe, despoiling Jewish property and senselessly murdering Jews as they made their way to the Holy Land to retrieve control of the Holy Sepulchre in Jerusalem from the hands of Muslim "infidels."

Following Gregory's example, Pope Innocent III, who occupied the papacy from 1198 to 1216, urged Christian rulers to so treat Jews that they "will not dare to raise their neck, bowed under the yoke of perpetual slavery, against the reverence of the Christian faith." He insisted that because the Jews were guilty of the crucifixion of Jesus, they are assigned to perpetual servitude. In 1208 Pope Innocent III wrote in a letter to Count Nevers:

> Jews, like the fratricide Cain, are doomed to wander about the earth as fugitives and vagabonds, and their faces must be covered with shame. They are under no circumstances to be protected by princes, but on the contrary, they are to be condemned to serfdom.

After the Crusades and throughout the Middle Ages, Jews were forbidden to own land, engage in agriculture, or take up a trade. One of the few occupations left open to them was moneylending, and this only because the Church had prohibited Christians from lending money at interest to fellow Christians. This was based on Exodus 22:24–26, which declares that one is not permitted to lend money at interest to one's *own* people. As Jews became increasingly involved in moneylending, they became criticized and condemned as usurers. The penalty for violating the law was excommunication.

Later Role of the Papacy

In 1442, Pope Eugenius IV fed fuel to the fires of anti-Semitism when he issued a decree urging total social ostracism of Jews:

> We decree and order that from now on, and for all time, Christians shall not eat or drink with Jews, nor admit them to feasts, nor cohabit with them, nor bathe with them. Christians shall not allow Jews to hold civil honors over Christians, or to exercise public offices in the state.

The Spanish Inquisition

The year 1480 marked the beginning of the Spanish Inquisition, a tribunal established by the Catholic Church to investigate and suppress all acts of heresy. Many of the Jews who chose conversion to avoid expulsion from Spain but who continued to practice Judaism secretly (the *marranos* or *conversos*) were a target of the Inquisition. Those found guilty were punished in what was called an *auto de fe* ("act of faith"). The Spanish Inquisition, which was later extended to Portugal and even into Spanish territories in the Americas, continued until the 1800s.

Decades after the beginning of the Inquisition, Pope Pius IV wrote a decree, issued posthumously in 1565, stating that the Jews of Rome be confined to a ghetto:

We order that each and every Jew of both sexes in our temporal domain, and in all the cities, lands, places and baronies subject to them, shall depart completely out of the confines thereof within the space of three months....

This and other papal pronouncements influenced the general population of Europe to despise Jews. In 1543, following a visit to Greece, Benjamin of Tudela, the twelfth-century Spanish-born Jewish world-traveler, wrote, "The Greeks hate the Jews, good and bad alike, and beat them in the street.... No Jew is allowed to ride on horseback. The one exception is Solomon Ha-Mitzri, who is the king's physician, and through whom the Jews enjoy considerable alleviation of their oppression."

The Protestant Reformation

In the sixteenth century, with the Reformation came a renewed interest in the Old Testament and Hebrew studies. Anti-Semitism eased for a time as the disgruntled priest Martin Luther turned to Jews for approbation of his new Bible translation and his rejection of papal claims. But when Luther saw that Jews were reluctant to join his cause and were averse to his expectation that they convert to Christianity en masse, he turned against them, just as he had turned against the Catholic Church. Luther's German publication, *On the Jews and Their Lies* (1543), published in Wittenberg, has been called the first work of anti-Semitism. In it, he urged, "Their synagogues should be set on fire, and whatever is left should be buried in dirt so that no one may ever be able to see a stone or cinder of it."

The vicious attacks upon Jews and their way of life by this leader of the Protestant Ref-

ormation inspired others to follow his lead. Most prominent among them was the French philosopher François Voltaire (1694–1778), who predicted that "these [Jewish] people would some day become deadly to the human race."

The Spread of Anti-Jewish Sentiment

Between 1894 and 1906, strong anti-Semitic feelings were aroused in France, especially as a result of the Dreyfus case. A French-Jewish officer, Alfred Dreyfus, was falsely accused of selling military secrets to Germany.

About the same time, the term "anti-Semite" was introduced by William Marr (1818–1904). An unemployed journalist who blamed Jews for the loss of his job, Marr founded the League of Anti-Semites, a popular German political movement. His contemporary, historian Heinrich von Treitschke (1834–1896), justified German anti-Semitism and attacks upon Jews based on their refusal to assimilate. He characterized Jews as Germans who had established a "mongrel" German-Jewish culture. Said von Treitschke, "Jews are our misfortune," and because of his scholarly standing, anti-Semitism became encased in a cloak of acceptability and respectability.

The Protocols of the Elders of Zion, which claimed that a Jewish conspiracy to dominate the world was in place, first appeared in 1903. The veracity of this document, which later was proved to be a forgery, was accepted by many prominent public personalities, including automobile magnate Henry Ford, as late as 1920. In that year, having had some unpleasant financial encounters with Jewish bankers, Ford acquired the Dearborn *Independent* and used the pages of that newspaper to run a series of articles about "the international Jew" as the source of the world's problems. Years later, having been convinced that the *Protocols* was a fraud, Ford apologized for his gullibility. Nonetheless, Ford's articles had contributed to the spread of anti-Semitism worldwide.

As a result of the Dreyfus case, assimilated Viennese Jewish journalist Theodor Herzl became involved in Jewish causes and became convinced that the only solution to the disease of anti-Semitism was the establishment of a Jewish state. In 1904, when Herzl approached Pope Pius X for the pontiff's support of the Zionist cause, the Pope responded:

> We cannot encourage this movement. We cannot prevent the Jews from going to Jerusalem, but we can never encourage them. . . . The Jews have not recognized our Lord; therefore we cannot recognize the Jewish people. . . . If you come to Palestine and settle your people there, we shall have churches and priests ready to baptize all of you.

In 1905, two million Jews fled from Russia, most to the United States, as a result of organized anti-Semitic violence. And in 1911 anti-Jewish riots broke out in Great Britain when Welsh miners ransacked Jewish shops.

Modern Anti-Semitism

As a result of its defeat in World War I, Germany became ripe for the acceptance of anti-Semitism, which was exploited by Adolph Hitler, who blamed Germany's woes on the Jews. In 1922, Adolph Hitler declared that if he were to win power, "the annihilation of the Jews will be my first and foremost task. . . . They cannot protect themselves and no one will come forward as their protectors." Within four months after being appointed chancellor of the Reich in January 1933, Hitler's Nazi party staged a one-day boycott

of all Jewish stores, doctors, and lawyers. Nazi leaders began urging the expulsion of Jews from schools and universities. In March 1933, Dachau, the first concentration camp for political opponents, was erected outside Munich. Thus began the Holocaust and the extermination of six million Jews.

Changes in Church Thinking

By the end of the third decade of the twentieth century, a slight change in attitude was evident in the leadership of the Catholic Church. In 1929 Pope Pius XI declared: "Christians cannot possibly have a hand in anti-Semitism. Anti-Semitism is not admissible. Spiritually, we are Semites." Again, in a September 1938 address to Belgian pilgrims, this Pope said: "Through Christ and in Christ we are the spiritual descendants of Abraham. No, it is not possible for Christians to participate in anti-Semitism."

With the ascendancy to the papacy of John XXIII in 1958, and the appointment in 1962 of Augustin Cardinal Bea as president of the Secretariat for Promoting Christian Unity, a profound change in Jewish-Christian relations began. Immediately after his appointment, the Cardinal stated: "[It must be acknowledged] honestly and clearly what God has accomplished in the Jewish people and through them, the whole human race."

This attitude was soon reflected in a document known as *Nostra Aetate* ("In Our Time"), issued by the Vatican. The pronouncement, stating that "the Jewish covenant had never been revoked" and that "Jews remain people of God," repudiated the old Christian charge that Christians have displaced Jews as the Chosen People.

Hoping to make amends with the Jews, Pope John XXIII composed this prayer shortly before his death in 1963:

We realize now that many, many centuries of blindness have dimmed our eyes, so that we no longer see the beauty of Thy Chosen People and no longer recognize in their faces the features of our first-born brother. We realize that our brows are branded with the mark of Cain. Centuries long has Abel lain in blood and tears, because we have forgotten Thy love. Forgive us the curse which we unjustly laid on the name of the Jews. Forgive us, that with our curse, we crucified Thee a second time.

When John Paul II ascended to the papacy in 1978, he continued the policy of reconciliation begun by John XXIII. In April 1986, he visited the main synagogue in Rome and joined with the Chief Rabbi in reading from the Book of Psalms. In an address to the congregation at that momentous occasion, he said:

The Jewish religion is not "extrinsic" to us, but in a certain way is "intrinsic" to our own religion. With Judaism, therefore, we have a relationship which we do not have with any other religion. You are our dearly beloved brothers, and in a certain way, it could be said that you are our elder brother.

By the 1990s, impressive changes aimed at reducing tensions and improving relations between Jews and non-Jews were already in place. Catholic and Protestant textbooks were being revised to accommodate reconciliation. A 1992 doctoral thesis that studied eight Sunday School textbooks, used by about sixty percent of American Protestant Churches, found that Jews are no longer depicted as eternally cursed or blamed for the crucifixion of Jesus.

Nonetheless, despite the progress made and the continued efforts of organizations such as the World Jewish Congress and the Anti-Defamation League of B'nai Brith, with entry into the third millennium anti-Semitism remained visible in America, Europe, and the rest of the civilized world.

The issue of anti-Semitism was heightened on February 25, 2004, with the Ash Wednesday release of filmmaker Mel Gibson's *The Passion of the Christ*. Grossing a phenomenal $250 million in the first three weeks of its showing, the controversial film was criticized by Jews not only for its extreme brutality but also for inaccurately exonerating Pontius Pilate in the death of Jesus and instead implicating the Jews. Compared in offensiveness to the *Passion Play* presented every ten years in Oberammergau, Germany, Jewish leaders expressed the fear that the film would lead to a rise in anti-Jewish feeling worldwide.

See Blood Libels; Holocaust.

Apikores

Plural, *apikorsim*. From the Greek, meaning "disbeliever, skeptic," the term is related to the name of the fourth-century B.C.E. Greek philosopher Epicurus, who inspired the school of thought which maintained that the goal of life is to attain fulfillment through sensuous pleasure. Epicureans followed the hedonistic "eat, drink, and be merry, for tomorrow we die" philosophy, yet Epicurus himself also believed that the search for pleasure must be guided by a sense of morality and moderation.

While Jews believed that the pleasures of this world are to be enjoyed, they distanced themselves from Epicurus, who disputed the Jewish view that God is the source of moral law, that man learns to be moral by imitating God. Since the Epicurean attitude was tantamount to a denial of God, the Rabbis branded any Jew who subscribed to it an *apikores*, a heretic.

See Apostate and Apostasy; Excommunication.

Apocrypha

This Latin term derived from the Greek, meaning "hidden," applies specifically to a group of books by unknown authors written at the time the Bible itself was being compiled and edited—sometime after 200 B.C.E.—but not considered sufficiently authentic and sacred to warrant inclusion in the canon, the official Hebrew Bible. The Talmud refers to these books as *Sefarim Chitzonim*, "Outside Books."

The following are the fourteen books of the Apocrypha:

1. *Book of Tobit*. The story of a Jew who was among those exiled to Assyria and had buried King Sennacherib's victims. He was rewarded by being cured of his blindness. The Book of Tobit is the earliest of the books of the Apocrypha.

2. *First Book of Esdras* (Ezra). An account of Jewish history from King Josiah's celebration of Passover (II Kings 23:1–9) to the reading of the Law in the time of Ezra.

3. *Second Book of Esdras*. A narrative of Ezra urging Jews to undergo a spiritual rejuvenation.

4. *Book of Judith*. The dramatic story of a woman of Samaria who decapitated the commander of the army that was besieging her city.

5. *Book of Esther*. An expanded version of the biblical story which elaborates on some of the actions described in the biblical book.

6. *Wisdom of Solomon*. A discussion of the fate of the righteous people and wicked people as well as the folly of idolatry.

7. *Wisdom of Ben Sira*. A book of hymns and proverbs on the model of the biblical Book of Proverbs. Also called the Wisdom of Jesus, Son of Sirach (Ecclesiasticus).

8. *Book of Barukh*. An elaboration on the Book of Jeremiah, written by Jeremiah's scribe, Barukh ben Neriah.

9. *Song of the Three Holy Children*. The story of Daniel's three friends who were cast into a fiery furnace and survived.

10. *Susanna and the Elders*. A short story about a woman who was saved from death by Daniel.

11. *Bel and the Dragon*. An expansion of the Book of Daniel in which Daniel succeeds in convincing monarchs of the futility of idol worship.

12. *Prayer of Manasseh*. A penitential prayer recited by Manasseh, king of Judah.

13. *First Book of Maccabees*. The story of the Maccabees and their successful revolt against the Syrian-Greeks.

14. *Second Book of Maccabees*. A detailed description of the leadership of Judah the Maccabee.

Some of the early Rabbis of the Talmud considered the books of the Apocrypha to be tainted by Christian attitudes. Scholars such as Rabbi Akiba believed that any Jew who reads from the Apocrypha will have no share in the world to come (*Sanhedrin* 10:1). Unlike Jews, most Christian denominations, especially Catholics, consider the books of the

Apocrypha to be divinely inspired and reckon them as part of the Septuagint.

Apostate and Apostasy

The word "apostate" is the accepted English translation of both the Hebrew word *mumar*, meaning "one who changes," and the word *meshumad*, meaning "one who destroys." The Tosefta (Mishnah *Chullin* 1:1), a supplement to the Mishnah that was composed in Palestine, uses the word *meshumad*, while the Babylonian Talmud (ibid. 4b) uses the word *mumar* in the same quotation.

Although the Talmud in general defines an "Israelite apostate" as a Jew who has turned to idol worship and because of this is to be equated with one who has abandoned the whole Torah, the word in later times took on the meaning of a Jew who abandons Judaism for another religion.

The Babylonian Talmud on occasion uses the word *min* (plural, *minim*) to describe an apostate. In response to the question Who is a *min*? the Talmud says: "Anyone who worships idols" (*Avodah Zarah* 26b). In the same tractate, *min* and *apikores* are placed in the same category, while in the tractate *Rosh Hashanah* (17a) the *min* is also described as one who has rejected the Torah and does not believe in the resurrection of the dead. The tractate *Chullin* (4b), in using the word *mumar* for apostate, concurs, adding that one is an apostate if he denies the *authenticity* of the Torah.

In actual practice, the Rabbis believe an apostate to be a Jew who abandons the practice of ritual law. The Midrash (introduction to *Lamentations Rabbah* 2) speaks of God saying about Israel, "I would have been satisfied if they [the Jews] abandoned Me but did not forsake my Torah." The idea is that even if a Jew is an atheist, by observing the commandments (*mitzvot*) of the Torah he will return to a belief in God.

As evidence of the fact that the ritual forms are essential in the Jewish tradition, the *Code of Jewish Law* (*Shulchan Arukh*, Yoreh Dei'ah 158:2) classifies an apostate as a Jew who deliberately and spitefully (*le-hakhis*) eats non-kosher food or wears articles made of *shaatnez* (forbidden mixtures of fabrics, such as wool and linen) or the like.

Types of Apostate

Rabbinic authorities (*Avodah Zarah* 26b) distinguish between the *mumar le-hakhis*, the spiteful apostate, who wishes to get even with his community, whom he feels has wronged him in one fashion or another; and the apostate *mumar le-tei'avon*, who forsakes his religion for personal advantage.

A classic example of the *mumar le-tei'avon* is Judah Monis, who was born in 1683 either in Algiers or Italy, received his Jewish education in Leghorn and Amsterdam, and served as a rabbi in New York. Monis had a deep interest in the Hebrew language and its grammar. He yearned to teach Hebrew at Harvard College and receive its aid in publishing a Hebrew grammar that he had written. He was advised by the highly respected Dr. Increase Mather and his colleagues at Harvard that the price of becoming an instructor was conversion to Christianity.

Monis eagerly accepted the opportunity, and on March 27, 1722, at a public ceremony in College Hall, embraced Christianity. In his baptismal sermon, he declared that the reason behind his conversion was that he found Christianity to be the only religion through which he could be saved. This was, of course, a blatant lie. Monis was clearly a *mumar le-tei'avon*.

The Apostate Who Lost Faith

The classic apostate in talmudic literature is Elishah ben Avuyah, who was given the appellation Acher, meaning "the other" (*Berakhot* 57b). The Talmud advances several theories as to why Elishah lost his faith in God and was labelled Acher.

According to one theory, this brilliant scholar, the teacher of the respected Rabbi Meir, was witness to a faith-shaking mishap. Elishah saw a man climb a rickety ladder to fetch some young birds. A religious person, the man was careful to follow the law as specified in the Bible (Deuteronomy 22:–7): "Do not take the mother with her young. Let the mother go and take only the young, in order that you may fare well and have a long life." But as the man was descending the ladder, it collapsed and the man fell to his death.

Elishah wondered, Is this the reward for obeying the Torah? Why would God do such a thing to a man following His Law? Where is this man's long life, which was promised to those who observe the Law? Whatever happened to Rabbi Eleazar's teaching that "those engaged in the performance of a *mitzvah* never come to harm"? (*Pesachim* 8a). These questions consumed Elishah ben Avuyah's thoughts and led to his loss of faith.

Another theory put forth to explain Elishah's apostasy involves the humiliation suffered by the great scholar Chutzpit the Meturgeman, the translator and expositor of the Law in the *Sanhedrin* led by Rabbi Gamaliel. Chutzpit was one of the ten martyrs put to death by Hadrian of Rome in the second century C.E.; his tongue was cut out and dragged through the village by a pig. Upon observing this, Elishah exclaimed, "The mouth that delivered pearls [of wisdom] licks the dust." And his faith was markedly weakened (*Kiddushin* 39b).

A final theory as to what caused the pub-lic to demean the famous scholar Elishah ben Avuya by referring to him as Acher revolves around an apocryphal tale described in several tractates of the Talmud. It is said (Bavli, *Chagigah* 14b and Jerusalem Talmud 2:1, 77a) that Elishah shared a mystical experience along with his colleagues Shimon ben Zomah, Rabbi Akiba, and Shimon ben Azzai. In this happening, the four rabbinic scholars entered the King's Orchard (*pardeis* in Hebrew; Paradise in English) "while still alive." There, they beheld the *Shekhinah* (God), a sight so mind-boggling that when Ben Zomah gazed upon it, he was stricken and died. Rabbi Akiba, the most mature of all the scholars, was not affected; he left the orchard in peace. But, the tale goes, Elishah ben Avuyah was so overwhelmed that he lost all faith and became a heretic. The Jewish community turned against him, and from that time on called him not Elishah, but Acher.

Concerning the three scholars, the Talmud comments, "If one sees Ben Azzai in a dream, he may hope to become pious. If one sees Ben Zomah, he may hope to become wise. But if he sees Acher, let him fear that he will be punished."

The Worst Apostate

The worst of all apostates in the eyes of Jewish law is the Jew who violates the Sabbath publicly (*Eruvin* 69a and Orach Cha'yim 385:3).

The Talmud (*Eruvin* 69a and 69b) draws a sharp distinction between one who violates the Sabbath in public and one who does so privately. While the appellation *mumar*, "apostate," is applied to both, the public violator is equated with a Gentile, a heathen, an idolator (because by his actions he has seemingly denied the faith completely) while the private violator is not so stigmatized.

This point was reasserted by Moses Maimonides in the *Mishneh Torah*, where he equates a person who desecrates the Sabbath publicly with an atheist and an idolator. (This equation is also made in Orach Cha'yim 385:3).

In discussing the blatant violation of the Sabbath, the Talmud emphasizes *public* violation (the Greek word *be-farhesya*, meaning "open, frankly," is used). The Rabbis focused their discussion on public violation because they were aware that the person who violates the Sabbath publicly is a much greater threat to Judaism than one who violates it in the privacy of his own home. While the private violator's actions go unnoticed, the actions of the public violator might encourage sinning by others.

Apparently, exclusion of Jews from the Jewish fold for violating the Sabbath in public was a serious problem, and an attempt to mitigate the situation was made from the very beginning. The first indication of this effort is found in the Talmud (*Sanhedrin* 74b), where the question is asked, "How many persons must be present for an action to be called a *public* action?" And the answer is, "Rabbi Jacob said in the name of Rabbi Yochanan: 'The minimum is ten.'" The comment is added that all ten must be Jews.

Clearly, since ten Jews had to witness a violation of the Sabbath for it to be labeled a public violation, it is evident that the Rabbis were not anxious, nor did they make it easy, to characterize Jews as apostates for violating the Sabbath.

Rabbis who adhere to the letter of Jewish law will not permit a Jew who violates the Sabbath publicly to sign a Jewish marriage contract (*ketubbah*) as a witness.

Ultra-Orthodox rabbis such as Moshe Feinstein (1895–1986) have ruled as invalid marriages performed by Reform rabbis because the Reform *ketubbot* must be presumed to have been witnessed by Sabbath violators. In one responsum (*Igrot Moshe*, Even Ha-Ezer 76) he allowed an *agunah* to remarry after ascertaining that her first marriage had been performed by a Reform rabbi. (An *agunah* is a "chained woman." She is unable to remarry because it is not known whether her missing husband is dead or alive.) The presumption was that the witnesses to the Reform marriage contract were not Sabbath observers, and hence the marriage was invalid, freeing the woman to remarry.

Rights of the Apostate

Regardless of all the conjecture about exactly who belongs in the category of apostate, a basic principle was laid down in the Talmud (*Sanhedrin* 44a) and is encapsulated in the following dictum: af al pi she-chata, Yisra'el hu, "[A Jew,] even though he has sinned, continues to be counted as a Jew."

While an apostate loses much credibility as a Jew, the privileges denied depend upon the degree of apostasy.

- The apostate is denied the privilege of writing *tefillin* parchments, because the Bible (Deuteronomy 6:8–9) says, "...and *you* shall bind them. . . and *you* shall write them..." This means that only such people who bind them [the *tefillin*] can write them. This applies to the writing of a Torah scroll and *mezuzot* as well, since the apostate does not subscribe to their use or importance.

- The apostate is denied the right, if he is a Priest (*Kohen*) to bless the people. However, if he renounces his apostasy, the right is restored to him.

- The apostate is denied an *aliyah* and is no longer counted to a *minyan*.
- The apostate may be denied the privileges received by Jews under the Law of Return.

However, an apostate continues to retain many of the obligations, rights, and privileges accorded every other Jew:

- The apostate inherits his parent's property, and if he is a firstborn (*bekhor*), he has not forfeited his firstborn rights (*Choshen Mishpat* 283:2).
- If the apostate is a ritual slaughterer (*shochet*), he may continue at his occupation, but his slaughtering (*shechitah*) is carefully monitored (*Chullin* 4b and Yoreh Dei'ah 2:2, 4).
- The obligation of an apostate to marry the widow of his deceased childless brother—known as levirate marriage (*yibum* in Hebrew)–still applies. If the apostate refuses to marry his childless sister-in-law, he must perform the *chalitzah* ("removal of the sandal") ceremony.

The Penitent Apostate

There is general agreement among authorities that if an apostate decides to return to Judaism, he or she is not required to undergo any ritual, although some require immersion in a mikveh. Moses Isserles, in his Notes to the Code of Jewish Law (Shulchan Arukh, Yoreh Dei'ah 268:12), reiterates the point that even when a Jew abandons Judaism, he is still a Jew. In fact, Jewish law insists that those who return to Judaism are to be treated with kindness and consideration; they are not to be embarrassed by being reminded of their defection.

Mourning When Apostasy Occurs

The issue of whether one is required to sit *shivah* for a family member who has abandoned Judaism has been the subject of debate. Actually, the practice dates back to the publication of the twelfth-century work *Or Zaru'a*, by Rabbi Isaac of Vienna. In this book, Rabbi Isaac reported that the great eleventh-century scholar Rabbenu Gershom ben Yehudah, known as the Luminary of the Diaspora (*Me'or Ha-Golah*), sat *shivah* for his son who had converted to Christianity. Upon publication of the book, it became widespread practice to sit *shivah* for a child who converts, despite the fact that outstanding scholars, including Joseph Caro, author of the *Code of Jewish Law*, insisted that doing so is not demanded by the law and is not appropriate conduct.

Caro states (*Shulchan Arukh*, Yoreh Dei'ah 345:5) that "[one] does not mourn for an apostate." (See also *Chokhmat Adam* 156:6.) Why, then, did Rabbenu Gershom sit *shivah* for his son? Further delving by scholars revealed that Rabbenu Gershom did not sit *shivah* for his son at the time of the young man's conversion. He sat *shivah* for him at a later date, at the time of the son's death. And the misunderstanding grew out of the misreading of one word in Isaac of Vienna's work. Isaac wrote that Rabbenu Gershom sat *shivah* for his son—and he used the Hebrew word *she-nishtamed*, meaning "who had converted." Some of the texts erroneously added one letter to the word and spelled it *ke-she-nishtamed*, meaning "when he converted." Because of the error, it was believed that Rabbenu Gershom sat *shivah* at the time of his son's conversion, when in fact he sat *shivah* after his son died.

Sitting *shivah* for a child who joins another faith has never been a legal requirement for Jews, and authorities do not favor the practice.

Mourning a member of the family who has abandoned Judaism runs counter to the basic talmudic principle that one never loses his Jewish identity; he may return to the fold unceremoniously whenever he so decides. To sit *shivah* for a family member who converts is, in a sense, damning that person forever, thus precluding the possibility of his ever returning to the faith of his ancestors.

Upon the Death of an Apostate

The Talmud (*Semachot* 2:8) says that mourning is not to be observed for any Jew who has become an apostate. In the Talmud a Jewish defector is placed in the same category as an intentional suicide and an executed criminal.

Scholars have pointed out that when Maimonides, in his *Mishneh Torah*, lists those for whom Jews do not mourn "because they have separated themselves from the community," he includes "apostates to idolatry" (Hilkhot Aveilut 1:10). Since today (and for the past eight or more centuries) a Christian is no longer considered to be an idolater in the eyes of Jewish law, the question of whether a family is to sit *shivah* upon the death of one of its members who had earlier joined the Church is moot.

A point to be considered, however, is whether the apostate abandoned Judaism as an act of rebellion toward his family or teachers or whether he truly loved his newly adopted faith. When the motivation of the apostate is spite, some authorities argue, there is always a degree of hope that he may reconsider at a future date and return to the fold. Such an apostate is to be considered a full Jew, and when he dies, *shivah* may be observed for him under the talmudic principle of *al pi shechata, Yisra'el hu* (see above). However, when the motivation of the apostate is genuine love for another faith, the individual is not to be

mourned (Yoreh Dei'ah 345:5).

Some authorities are of the opinion that one who denounces Judaism publicly should not be mourned. His action, they believe, will encourage others to defect, and it is therefore inexcusable.

Moses Sofer (Schreiber), distinguished rabbi of Slovakia from 1803 onward, widely known for his popular legal work *Chatam Sofer*, disagreed, maintaining (Yoreh Dei'ah 341) that not only do we engage in burying apostates, but we even provide shrouds for them. (See also *Shulchan Arukh*, Yoreh Dei'ah 333:3.)

There is a difference of opinion among authorities as to whether a child may recite *Kaddish* for an apostate parent—that is, one who has forsaken his faith and severed all ties with the Jewish community. Rabbi Moses Isserles (1525–1572) wrote that a son may recite *Kaddish* for an apostate father who was murdered by idolators, because it is presumed that through his death the father has made atonement for his sin, and that in all probability the man repented just before life left his body (Yoreh Dei'ah 340:5).

Other authorities follow the lead of the famous Rabbi Akiba Eger (1761–1837), of Posen, Poland, who ruled that a son is permitted to mourn and say *Kaddish* for an apostate parent even if the death was natural. This is in keeping with the talmudic view that the biblical commandment (Exodus 20:12) to honor one's father and mother is to be obeyed under all circumstances. It is also in keeping with the talmudic view that a Jew who has abandoned the faith is still considered to be a Jew.

Appearance Principle

The concept known as *marit a'yin* (literally, "how things appear to the eye") plays a vital role in Jewish law. Since people often tend to judge others by how they perceive them, Jewish law cautions that care must be taken to avoid situations that would lead the observer to arrive at faulty conclusions.

What has come to be called the "appearance principle" evolved from an interpretation of the biblical commandment that one must not "boil a kid in its mother's milk," which is repeated twice in the Book of Exodus (23:19 and 34:26) and once in the Book of Deuteronomy (14:21). Both eating and profiteering from a mixture of meat and milk are forbidden.

The question arose: if the Bible prohibits cooking meat (a kid) in its mother's milk, why then should it be forbidden to cook fowl in milk? The answer of the Rabbis is *mipnei marit a'yin*, because of how the act appears to the public. If chicken were to be cooked or mixed with milk in any fashion, it might appear to an outsider that the person is actually cooking meat (specifically veal, since veal and chicken have similar coloring) with milk. To avoid the possibility of the observer arriving at this erroneous conclusion, the Rabbis forbade the mixing of all meat products with all dairy products.

By extension, some contemporary authorities, applying the principle of *marit a'yin*, have forbidden the serving of margarine (a *pareve* product) at a meat meal. Doing so, they fear, might leave the false impression that butter is being served. For the same reason, those who are especially meticulous in their observance will not serve nondairy creamer with coffee at a meat meal.

The *marit a'yin* principle can be applied to countless situations in Jewish law. For example, in the case of building a house Jewish law states that work may be done for a Jew by a Gentile on the Sabbath if it is not done at the express order of the Jew. Thus, a Jew may make a specific type of contract with a Gentile to build him a house. The contract, called *kablanut*, establishes no time limit for completion of the work. The Gentile labors at his own pace and on whatever days he chooses.

Such an arrangement is acceptable in Jewish law for the building of a home but not for the building of a synagogue. The reasoning is that people seeing work being done on the synagogue on the Sabbath might conclude that the leaders of the congregation ordered that the work be performed on the Sabbath, which would be a violation of Jewish law.

A classic example of the appearance principle at work is seen in a responsum of Rabbi Solomon Luria (1510–1573) of Poland. Luria was asked whether a man who was subject to headaches might, in the privacy of his home, eat his meals without wearing a hat. He replied that doing so is permissible, explaining that there is no prohibition against even praying without a hat. Luria added that he personally would not conduct himself in that manner because of the appearance factor. He felt that eating bareheaded might disturb people who believe that the wearing of a hat is essential.

Similarly, the outspoken German rabbinic authority Jacob (Yaakov) Israel Emden (1697–1776), who was critical of women who wore wigs, wrote in one of his responsa that a married woman should not cover her hair with a beautiful wig because one might be misled into believing that the wig is her own hair, which according to Jewish law should not be exposed. Instead, he suggested, a married women must wear a *tikhl* (cloth covering).

The appearance factor is also the basis for the rabbinic ruling that if it is necessary for a mourner to leave the house of mourning in order to sleep elsewhere, he or she should do so late at night when there is less likelihood of being seen. If the person were to be seen, the observer might conclude that the mourner is not sitting *shivah* at all.

The appearance principle would also apply to a case in which a Jew is in need of making an urgent telephone call while walking down the street. The person should not walk into a nonkosher meat market in order to use its pay telephone, for observers might be left with the false impression that the Jew was in the store to purchase nonkosher meat. Likewise, a Jew may not enter a bookstore on the Sabbath just to browse. Being sighted in the bookstore could lead someone to think the Jew intends to make a purchase, in clear violation of Sabbath law.

Another potentially misleading situation occurs when a non-Jew attending a synagogue service is provided with a prayershawl (*tallit*) by the usher. Congregants might be misled into thinking that the individual is a Jew.

See Stumbling-Block Principle.

Aravah

See Four Species.

Arba Imma'hot

Literally meaning "the four matriarchs," this term refers specifically to Sarah, Rebecca, Rachel, and Leah. Sarah was the wife of Abraham; Rebecca the wife of Isaac; and Rachel and Leah the wives of Jacob. *Imma'hot* is the plural form of *imma*, meaning "mother."

See Patriarchs.

Arba Kanfot

Originally, fringes (*tzitziot;* singular, *tzitzit*) were attached to the four corners of the overgarment, as prescribed in the Book of Deuteronomy (22:12): "You shall place twisted

cords [*gedilim* or *tzitziot*] on the four corners of your garment." In talmudic times a full-length prayershawl (*tallit*) was worn all day long, but when it became too cumbersome, and especially when styles changed and overgarments no longer always had four distinct corners, a lightweight undergarment that could be draped over the neck was used in its place. This undergarment became known as *arba kanfot*, meaning "four corners," or *tallit katan*, meaning "small *tallit*." In the vernacular, this undergarment is referred to simply as *tzitzit*.

Another explanation for the introduction of the *arba kanfot* is that in the Middle Ages, when anti-Semitism was rampant, Jews who wore the large *tallit* with its fringes fully exposed were in danger of being attacked. The smaller undergarment was therefore created.

See Tallit; Tzitzit.

Arba Kosot

Literally meaning "four cups," this term refers to the number of cups of wine that one is required to drink during the Passover *Seder*.

See Seder; Wine on Passover.

Arba Minim

Literally meaning "four species," this term refers to the primary symbols of the Sukkot holiday: palm branch (*lulav*), citron (*etrog*), willow (*aravah*), and myrtle (*hadas*).

These are taken in hand and waved during the Sukkot holiday in order to express appreciation for having enjoyed a year of agricultural abundance.

See Four Species.

Arbitration

Resolving conflicts by means of arbitration is favored in Jewish law. The reasoning, presented in the talmudic tractate *Sanhedrin* (6b) by the second-century Palestinian scholar Rabbi Joshua ben Korcha, is that absolute reconciliation can be effected only when judges temper justice with mercy. Solely through such arbitration can peace exist.

The procedure—known in modern Hebrew as *borerut*, meaning "choosing," or by the acronym *zabla*, which stands for the Hebrew words [*ve-*]*zeh borer lo echad*, "this one chooses one [arbitration]"; that is, one litigant chooses an arbitrator and the other does likewise. If the two agree on a settlement, the case is closed. If the two cannot agree, they choose a third arbitrator, and his decision must be accepted by both parties to the dispute.

Arbor Day

A midwinter holiday that falls on the fifteenth day of the Hebrew month Shevat.

See Chamishah Asar Bi-Shevat.

Ark

The cabinet that houses the Torot (singular, Torah) in the synagogue was originally known as the Ark of the Covenant (Exodus 31:7). Most commonly it is simply called *Aron*, meaning "box," a short form of *Aron Ha-Kodesh*, meaning "the holy box," a term first used in II Chronicles (35:3). The tractate *Ta'anit* refers to the *Aron Ha-Kodesh* as *Teivah*, also meaning "box."

In the Mishnah *Ta'anit* (2:2), the expression *yoreid lifnei ha-teivah* is used to mean "to go down and stand before the cabinet [and lead the prayers]." The *teivah* in which the Torot were kept was generally placed on a platform above floor level. The cantor led the congregation in prayer from a lectern on floor level; hence, one would "go down" from the ark area to floor level and stand before the lectern to conduct the service. In many Or-thodox congregations today, a portion of the prayer service is still conducted from a lectern at floor level.

Whereas Ashkenazim generally use the term *Aron Ha-Kodesh* for ark, Sephardim favor the biblical word *Heikhal*, meaning "sanctuary." This word is found in I Kings 6:3 and Isaiah 6:1, among other places in the Bible; it is also used as a synonym for the Temple built by Solomon.

The First Ark

The first holy ark was constructed by the gifted craftsman Bezalel, son of Uri of the tribe of Judah, a wise, talented man appointed by Moses upon instructions from God. Bezalel's assignment was to construct a portable Tabernacle that would be carried by the Israelites during their forty-year trek through the wilderness to the Promised Land. The centerpiece of the Tabernacle was to be the ark, for it was to house the Ten Commandments brought down from Mount Sinai by Moses (Exodus 31:1ff.). (See *Berakhot* 55a for the rabbinic view relating to Bezalel's appointment.)

Since the Israelites were in transit as they made their way to the Promised Land, the Tabernacle and its appurtenances were designed to be assembled quickly and transported without difficulty. The sacred assignment of carrying the Ark fell to the Levites, who, according to biblical tradition, were so honored because they alone did not participate in the building of the Golden Calf (Exodus 32:26; Numbers 3:27ff.; I Chronicles 15:2).

The tractate *Yoma* (53b) notes that most Rabbis believe with Rabbi Yochanan ben Zakkai that when Nebukhadnezzar, king of Babylonia, exiled the Jews of Palestine, the Ark went with them into exile.

Second Ark Theory

When Moses returned from Mount Sinai carrying the Ten Commandments, he found that the Israelites had convinced Aaron to build a Golden Calf so that they might worship it. In his anger, Moses threw the tablets to the ground, shattering them. He then ascended the mountain a second time (Deuteronomy 10:2) and received from God another set of the Ten Commandments.

Some Rabbis of the talmudic period theorized that one ark was built to house the second set of whole tablets and another to house the shattered pieces of the first Ten Commandments. Rabbi Judah ben Lakish held (Tosefta *Sotah* 7:18) that it was the second ark, the one for the shattered tablets—that accompanied the Children of Israel whenever they went out to battle an enemy. Other Rabbis believed that only one ark was in existence and that it contained both the broken and whole tablets (*Menachot* 99a and *Bava Batra* 14b).

An Object of Holiness

The Ark was to be treated with utmost care, for it represented God's holiness and presence. Disrespecting the Ark was tantamount to disrespecting God.

During their years of wandering through the wilderness and later, after they had entered the Promised Land, there were times when the Israelites had to hide the Ark lest it be captured by the enemy. While David, king of Israel, was battling the Philistines, the Ark was stored for many years in the home of Avinadav, who lived in the safer, hilly countryside of the Land of Canaan. When victory over the Philistines was achieved, David ordered that the Ark be brought to Jerusalem, where he would establish his capital.

To emphasize the holiness of the Ark and its centrality in the Jewish religion, the Bible (II Samuel 6:1–8) relates an incident involving a man named Uzzah. The Ark had been placed on an ox-cart as a means of transport, and, as it was being moved, Uzzah reached up to steady it and keep it from falling when the oxen faltered. Touching the Holy Ark was forbidden. The Bible (II Samuel 6:7) says: "And the anger of the Lord was kindled against Uzzah, and God smote him for his misdeed; and he died there next to the Ark of God."

The Temple Period

When Solomon, son of David, finally built the Holy Temple in Jerusalem, the Ark was given a permanent home in a room known as the Holy of Holies (I Kings 8:6. *See Ta'anit* 16b).

Scholars believe that at the time of the destruction of the First Temple the Ark was removed and never found again. When the Second Temple was built, the Holy of Holies was left empty. Only the High Priest could enter this area, and only once each year, on Yom Kippur. God's presence (*Shekhinah*) was said to reside in the Holy of Holies.

What happened to the Ark after the Temple was destroyed is unknown. Graham Hancock, a correspondent for *The* [London] *Economist*, speculates that before the Temple was razed in 586 B.C.E., the Ark was sent to Ethiopia via the Elephantine Island near Aswan, Egypt, and that it rests there to this day in the Church of St. Mary of Zion at Axam.

The Synagogue Ark

Next to the Torah itself, the synagogue ark is considered the most sacred object in Jewish life. It is the focal point of the interior of the synagogue, and the most important rites and rituals of Judaism center around it.

In countries east of Jerusalem, the ark is placed on the western wall of the synagogue, in the direction of Jerusalem. In Western countries—Europe and the Americas—the ark is placed on the synagogue's eastern wall. Synagogues in Israel itself place the ark on the wall that faces the Temple Mount, where the Temples stood in ancient times.

Jewish tradition demands that an ark never be left without a Torah in it, for that would be an act of disrespect to the sacred ark (Orach Cha'yim 1:54:3). In some communities, when all Torot are removed from the ark in order to parade them through the synagogue on Hoshanah Rabbah and Simchat Torah, a lighted candle is placed in the ark. The light of the candle symbolizes the "light" of the Torah, which is referred to in the *Code of Jewish Law (Shulchan Arukh)*. This sixteenth-century work as well as the Talmud many years before caution against turning one's back on the Torah, and this admonition has led to the practice of taking three steps backward when retreating from the ark area.

Why precisely three steps are taken is not certain, but the custom is possibly related to the fact that many important events in Jewish history are associated with the number three.

Storing Torah Scrolls

How Torot are stored has changed over the centuries. From artistic renderings on the walls of the Jewish catacombs in Rome it is evident that in early times Torah scrolls were stored horizontally in wall niches. In fact, the Talmud (*Megillah* 27a) permits one Torah scroll to be placed on top of another. (See also *Mishneh Torah*, Hilkhot Sefer Torah 10:5.)

Beginning in the Middle Ages, Torah scrolls were placed vertically in tall niches and cabinets. This eventually became the common practice, even though vertical storage was apparently not particularly desirable, as evidenced from the statement of the emi-

nent thirteenth-century scholar Rabbi Meir of Rothenburg, who wrote the following to a correspondent:

> You ask, "Why do we not lay the Torah horizontally in the ark, just as the Ten Commandments were kept in the Temple?" This is a good question [said Rabbi Meir]. Rabbenu Tam [the grandson of Rashi] once wrote in a responsum that it would be a good idea to lay the Torah flat in the ark . . . and had he [Rabbenu Tam] thought of it when he built his own ark, he would have made it wider [so as to be able to place his Torah horizontally rather than vertically].

It would appear that the universally accepted practice of storing Torah scrolls vertically is primarily based on space considerations and ease of access.

The Open Ark

As a sign of respect, the Rabbis of the Talmud (*Makkot* 22b and *Kiddushin* 33b) ruled that members of a congregation should rise and remain standing when the ark is opened and the Torah is exposed. The ruling is based on the verse in Leviticus (19:32), "You shall rise before the aged and show deference to the old." In the Talmud, "aged" means "old in wisdom," people who are "wise and learned." The Rabbis reasoned: If, when a learned person is in our presence, we must rise in deference to his wisdom and knowledge, how much more so it should be required that we rise in the presence of the Torah, which is the source of all wisdom.

However, when it became more common to place the ark on an elevated platform (*bimah*), the question arose anew, since now the sacred area in which the ark was located was considered to be a separate domain. In the *Code of Jewish Law*, Joseph Caro rules that one must stand when a Torah passes in procession before him, and one must stand until the Torah is placed on the reading table or until it is no longer within one's field of vision (*Shulchan Arukh*, Yoreh Dei'ah 282:2). In a note on this subject, Isserles wrote that when the Torah is placed on the reading table (which is normally on a platform at least ten handbreadths—approximately three feet—above the floor level of the congregation) the Torah is then considered to be in a different domain or area (the Hebrew word used is *reshut*), and it is therefore not necessary for the congregation to remain standing, despite the fact that the Torah is visible (ibid. 242:18).

These views were supported by Rabbi David ben Samuel Halevi, the seventeenth-century author of *Turei Zahav* (also known by the acronym Taz), the authoritative commentary on the *Code of Jewish Law*, who pointed out that when the Torah is in the ark it is considered to be in a different domain, and even if the ark is open and the Torot are visible, the congregation is not obligated to stand. It is for this reason that members of a congregation may be seated during the actual Torah reading service without manifesting disrespect toward the Torah. The "separate domain" concept also applies to being seated throughout *Ne'ilah*, the concluding service of Yom Kippur, during which the doors of the ark are kept open and the Torot are in full view of the congregants.

Many later authorities have been less permissive in this matter. The eighteenth-century Dutch scholar Meir Eisenstadt is of the opinion that congregants should remain standing when the ark is open and the Torot visible (*Panim Me-irot* 1:74). Moses Sofer, the famous Hungarian authority, agrees. "If the ark is open," he says, "it is forbidden to remain seated" (*Chatam Sofer*, Choshen Mishpat 73).

Yechiel Mikhael Epstein (1829–1908), the rabbi and halakhic authority, says in his *Arukh Ha-Shulchan* (Yoreh Dei'ah 282:13) that since *most* people rise for the open ark, *all* people should rise; although the law does not require one to do so (since the Torah is in another domain), members of the congregation may think that the person who remains seated is acting disrespectfully toward the Torah. Only if a person is known to be weak or ill, adds Epstein, may he or she remain seated.

Rabbi Epstein also discusses the propriety of rabbis preaching to their congregations with their backs to the ark (Yoreh Dei'ah 282:2). He justifies this practice by stating that the ark is generally raised above the pulpit floor and consequently is in a separate, self-contained area. The preacher cannot therefore be charged with showing disrespect toward the Torah if he stands with his back to the Ark. Rabbi Epstein also argues that by his very activities a preacher is actually showing great respect for the Torah, because in his preachments he is urging acceptance of the Torah's laws.

While almost all Orthodox congregations forbid the Torah reader (*ba'al korei*) from having his back to the ark when reading from the Torah, non-Orthodox congregations, in keeping with the reasoning of the *Arukh Ha-Shulchan*, permit it. Most synagogues today are constructed so that the reading table is to the side of the ark rather than directly in front of it, which solves the problem completely.

So important is the ark in Jewish life that the Babylonian Talmud quotes Rav Huna as saying that if a congregation was shy one person to make up a *minyan* (ritual quorum of ten), the ark may be counted as the tenth person, and a full service may be held. (*Berakhot* 47b.)

Since, as stated earlier, the ark itself achieves a status of holiness second only to the Torah, just as a Torah scroll is stored away in a *genizah* or buried when no longer usable or needed, so, too, is an ark. In fact, the same treatment is accorded a Torah mantle or any religious article that has been in direct contact with a Torah scroll (*Shulchan Arukh*, Orach Cha'yim 154:3–8).

Rabbi Ephraim Oshry, once a leading rabbi of the Kovno (Lithuania) Jewish community, ruled that a fragment of wood from a destroyed ark that is found in a pile of rubble must be buried or stored away; it is to be treated with the same sanctity as a whole ark.

The Ark Curtain

In traditional synagogues, an often elaborately embroidered curtain (*parokhet* in Hebrew) hangs in front of the ark. The Ashkenazic tradition is to hang the *parokhet* in front of the ark doors, while Sephardic practice is to place the curtain behind the doors. In synagogues where ark coverings are not used, the ark doors themselves are usually elaborately decorated. The origin of the practice of not using an ark curtain is uncertain, but it may be part of an old tradition that bans the duplication of the precise form of the appurtenances used in the two Temples in Jerusalem. Use of an ark curtain did not become widespread until after the sixteenth century.

The Book of Exodus (26:31–33) explains that the ark curtain is to be made of "blue, purple, and crimson yarns, and fine twisted linen..." and that it should serve as a partition between the Holy of Holies, in which the ark was housed, and the rest of the Tabernacle. Reference is again made to the *parokhet* in Exodus (40:21), when Moses "brought the Ark into the Tabernacle and set up the curtain and screened the Ark."

Ark curtains used throughout the year are usually blue, purple, or maroon. On holidays, particularly the High Holidays, practically all synagogues change the ark covering as well as the Torah mantles and lectern covers to white. The choice of the color white, a symbol of purity and hope, is linked to one of the popular prophecies of Isaiah (1:18): "If your sins be like crimson, they can turn snow white." The message is that man can change and be redeemed.

On Tishah B'Av, the *parokhet* is removed from the ark to accentuate the mournful mood of the day. On that day, the ninth day of the month of Av, both the First and Second Temples were burned to the ground—the First Temple by the Babylonians in the year 586 B.C.E. and the Second Temple by the Romans in 70 C.E.

The Ark Valance

The short valance that hangs across the top of the ark curtain, first mentioned in Exodus 26:34, is called the *kapporet*. This horizontal piece of fabric was created to match the ark curtain and round out the design.

In Eastern Europe of the sixteenth through the eighteenth centuries, it was not uncommon for ladies of a community to create a *kapporet* from the swaddling clothes worn by children at their circumcision ceremonies. This custom is being revived in some American communities.

Armageddon

A Greek word from the Hebrew words Har Megiddo, "mountain of Megiddo," a location in central Israel where decisive battles were fought in biblical times (Judges 5:19 and II Kings 23:29).

Based upon a prophecy in the Book of Ezekiel (38, 39), it is at Megiddo where a final, mammoth war will take place. The enemy will be Gog, ruler over the Land of Magog. His forces will be defeated, and Israel's primacy will be established. The world stage will be set for the arrival of the Messiah, who will prepare the world for an age of peace.

See Gog and Magog.

Art and Sculpture

In the Book of Exodus, the second of the Ten Commandments states (20:4): "Thou shalt not make unto thee a graven image, nor any manner of likeness of anything that is in the heaven above or on the earth beneath..."

Deuteronomy (4:16–18) repeats this proscription and elaborates upon it, specifying that it is forbidden to make "the form of any figure, the likeness of male or female, the likeness of any beast that is on earth." Subsequently (Deuteronomy 4:19), it explains the reason for the prohibition: nothing must stand in the way of Israel worshipping the one and only God.

The Rabbis of talmudic and post-talmudic times interpreted the Bible to mean that all art forms are permissible if there is no danger that they will be worshipped (*Avodah Zarah* 43b). Despite this liberal ruling of the Rabbis, in building their synagogues in ancient times Jews largely refrained from using decorations that depicted the human form in any way—high relief, bas relief, or flat surface. They believed that all such decorations would interfere with a congregant's complete concentration on the spirituality of God.

Early on, however, there were many exceptions to this view. The Talmud makes a distinction between images made for the purpose of worship and those made for other reasons. It tells of a synagogue in Nehardea, Babylonia,

in which a statue of the king had been erected, where the great second/third-century C.E. talmudic scholars Rav and Samuel, as well as the father of Samuel, used to go to pray (*Rosh Hashanah* 24b).

In his *Mishneh Torah*, Moses Maimonides (1135–1204) summarizes the opinions expressed in the Talmud. The prohibition against making graven images, he says, applies only to representations of the human form (*Avodat Kokhavim* 3:10,11). Possibly reacting to the ever-increasing appearance of statues of Jesus and the saints, Maimonides emphasizes that a human figure may not be made in high relief (three-dimensional), but it may be rendered in bas relief or may be painted on a flat surface or woven into a tapestry. These views are also codified in Joseph Caro's *Code of Jewish Law*, which states that it is permissible to paint, draw, or weave into a tapestry parts of the human form, but not the complete human being (*Shulchan Arukh*, Yoreh Dei'ah 141:4–7). Shaping an entire body is prohibited because it imitates heathen practices.

Beautifying Religious Objects

Some authorities, such as the thirteenth-century Meir of Rothenburg, took their lead from the Rabbis of the Talmud (*Shabbat* 133b), who interpreted the words of the Bible (Exodus 5:2), "This is my God and I will glorify Him," to mean that God is glorified when He is worshipped with love in the most beautiful manner possible. It therefore became customary, beginning primarily in the thirteenth century, to adorn to the maximum extent all ritual objects used in the performance of a *mitzvah*—the fulfillment of a commandment. This concept, known as *hiddur mitzvah*, led to the creation of illuminated prayerbooks, Bibles, and religious documents such as marriage contracts (*ketubbot*) with colorful borders and drawings of birds, animals, and even figures of humans.

In one of his responsa, Rabbi Meir of Rothenburg addressed a question posed by his outstanding disciple, Rabbi Asher ben Yechiel (1250–1327), who asked why Rabbi Meir did not object to the illumination of holiday prayerbooks (machzorim) with decorative representations of animals and birds. Was this not a violation of the law prohibiting the painting of any living form or figure? Such decorations, Rabbi Meir answered, should be discouraged because they interfere with one's concentration on prayer. However, he said, painting figures that are not three-dimensional is permissible. He adds: "Moreover, the Talmud (Avodah Zarah 43 a–b) seems to imply that a Jew is permitted even to make three-dimensional figures of animals and birds, since only the fashioning of figures of the human body or the figure of man, lion, ox, and eagle is forbidden."

Ovadiah Yosef (1920–), former Sephardic Chief Rabbi of Israel, disagrees with this position. In one of his responsa (Yechaveh Daat III:62) he clearly disapproves of the use of an ark curtain (parokhet) on which the figure of lions are embroidered and of the placement of bronze lions atop an ark on either side of the Ten Commandments. But on the question of having one's picture taken (III:63), he is permissive, since a photograph is only two-dimensional and its purpose is "for beauty and not for worship."

In 1926, Rabbi Abraham Kook, Chief Rabbi of Palestine, responded to a question posed by the painter Abraham Neumann by saying that while some pious Jews object to being painted or photographed, the majority follow Caro's Code of Jewish Law, which permits it.

Archaeological Discoveries

Twentieth-century excavations of ancient Palestinian synagogues have revealed that the structures were beautified with a considerable amount of art. The most famous of these synagogues is the Dura Europos, which was erected in 245 C.E. along the Euphrates River in Babylonia. Its ruins were discovered in 1932 in a remarkable state of preservation. The synagogue contained a surprising number of exquisite frescoes, mosaics, symbols of the zodiac, and even large panels of biblical scenes showing the full human form. Later, however, when using the human form in art was banned as being a violation of the second of the Ten Commandments, synagogues were no longer so decorated. Additionally, so as not to seem to imitate the Church, Jewish communities were careful to refrain from adorning the interior or exterior of their synagogues with sculptured forms.

Artificial Insemination

Because there is more than one type of artificial insemination procedure, and because there are many different circumstances under which they can be used, there is no clear-cut attitude toward artificial insemination that is shared by Jewish scholars.

One type of artificial insemination involves injecting the semen of the donor directly into the women's uterus. The egg (ovum) of the woman is fertilized by the sperm of the donor, an embryo develops, and the woman carries the child to term.

A second type of artificial insemination is implemented in situations where the fallopian tubes of the woman are blocked and the egg cannot reach the uterus to be fertilized by the sperm of the male. In these cases the ovum is removed from the woman by means of a minor operation. The egg is placed in a dish or test tube and the male's sperm—freshly obtained or frozen—is introduced. If the fertilization is successful, the resulting embryo is implanted in the uterus of the mother. Babies born as a result of this *in vitro* (in glass) procedure were characterized as test-tube babies.

In 1979, Professor Shlomo Mashiah, heading a team of Sheba Hospital doctors, performed a Caesarian section on a thirty-three-year-old woman and delivered the first test-tube baby ever "made in Israel." This came just one year (July 25, 1978) after the world's first test-tube baby, a healthy girl, had been born in England to a Mr. and Mrs. Brown.

In both artificial insemination procedures, the husband of the woman who provides the egg for fertilization may or may not be the donor of the sperm. If he is, the procedure is referred to as AIH (Artificial Insemination Husband). If, for one reason or another, the husband is unable to provide the sperm and the semen of a stranger must be used, the procedure is known as AID (Artificial Insemination Donor).

Many Jewish (as well as Christian) theologians have criticized these procedures on moral grounds. They argue that whatever good may be accomplished by helping infertile couples to have a family is by far outweighed by the danger of allowing humans to "play God." However, the consensus among Jewish scholars is that AIH is a permissible procedure while AID is questionable.

AIH—The Rabbinic View

Great scholars such as Rabbi Shalom Mordechai Schwadron, the nineteenth-century Galician authority; Aaron Walkin, the celebrated rabbi of Pinsk after World War I; and Rabbi Eliezer Waldenberg of Israel in the 1950s all believed that it is quite proper for a woman who cannot otherwise conceive—because the male has difficulty depositing sperm—to be impregnated artificially with the seed of her husband. They did not regard this as "wasting seed" or "destroying seed" (*hashchatat zera*) because the purpose of the procedure is the propagation of life. Most contemporary rabbinic authorities subscribe to the same view.

In his *Judaism and Healing*, Rabbi J. David Bleich (p. 80–84) points out that the AIH method, preferred by (Orthodox) rabbinic authorities, is to retrieve and use the semen from the vagina after intercourse. This eliminates any question of "wasting seed." He also points out that some authorities are opposed to AIH because to achieve pregnancy some physicians have been tempted, in order to assure more potency, to add the semen of a foreign donor to the husband's without disclosing that fact.

In cases where artificial insemination with the husband as donor is performed outside the wife's body (*in vitro*), there is strong rabbinic opposition. While in August 1978, in an address to the annual Torah Shebe'al Peh convocation in Israel, Rabbi Ovadiah Yosef gave his qualified approval to the procedure, Rabbi Shlomo Goren, the Ashkenazic Chief Rabbi at the time, disapproved of *in vitro* fertilization as morally repugnant. He and those who shared his view argued that children who are the product of fertilization outside the female body may be born with physical abnormalities because of the extra handling of the ovum when it is extracted from the womb to be fertilized and then reimplanted.

AID—The Rabbinic View

As a matter of practical law, rabbinic authorities are opposed to artificial insemination by a donor other than the husband (AID). While some equate AID with adultery, most oppose it because it could conceivably lead to a situation where sperm from the same donor might be used to impregnate other women, and the children born as a result of these procedures (who would actually all be half-brothers and half-sisters) might one day meet and marry. Such marriages, say the opponents of AID, would be incestuous and strictly forbidden by biblical law (Leviticus 18).

Opponents of AID also argue that the donor, the stranger, is "wasting seed" since the semen he emits is not used to establish a family for himself. "Wasting seed" (onanism) is a direct violation of traditional Jewish law.

Under certain circumstances, however, rabbinic authorities have permitted artificial insemination in which the semen of a stranger is used. One such case is referred to in a responsum of Rabbi Moshe Feinstein. He ruled (*Igrot Moshe*, Even Ha-Ezer 1:10) that in a case where a married woman has been unable to conceive for ten years and doctors concur that the husband is sterile, the woman may be impregnated with the semen of a stranger. This conclusion is based on an incident related in the Talmud (*Chagigah* 14b–15a). While immersing herself in a ritual bath (*mikveh*) that had earlier been used by a man, a virgin was unknowingly impregnated by semen that remained floating in the water. The Talmud explains that a High Priest, who by biblical law (Leviticus 21:13–14) can marry only a virgin, was permitted to marry this woman.

Citing this as a legal precedent, rabbinic authorities have said that impregnating a woman with the semen of a donor (AID) is permissible so long as there is no direct physical contact between the man and the woman. A child born from such a pregnancy is considered legitimate in every respect. Yet, while

Jewish law theoretically permits AID, it does not encourage it in actual practice.

The liberal view is expressed by Rabbi Solomon B. Freehof (*Central Conference of American Rabbis Yearbook,* LXII [1952], pp. 123–25), who sees no reason not to allow AID. He considers the primary objection to AID—namely, that a child born as a result of the procedure may unknowingly marry a close blood relative and thus violate biblical law—so farfetched that it should not be considered a factor in determining the law.

AID and Parentage

When a child is born from seed provided by a donor other than the husband, Jewish law considers the child legitimate in every respect. But unlike secular law, Jewish law does not consider the husband of the woman to be the legal father of the child. The donor of the seed is the legitimate father, and the woman's husband has no legal connection with the child because he did not provide the seed. And although the man's wife has had a child while married to him, this child does not satisfy the biblical commandment incumbent upon the husband to beget children.

In emphasizing the fact that the child is the son of the donor of the semen, Samuel ben Uri Phoebus, the seventeenth-century commentator on the *Shulchan Arukh* (Bet Shmuel on Even Ha-Ezer 1, Note 10), says that if this were not the case, Jewish law would not be concerned that the child might marry his own blood sister. Concern arises because the donor is, indeed, the father.

See Host Mothers; Mamzer.

Asarah B'Tevet

Literally meaning "the tenth of Tevet," this is the name of a minor fast day observed from dawn to nightfall on the tenth day of the Hebrew month Tevet, the month before Chanukkah. It commemorates the sad day in the year 588 B.C.E. when the siege of Jerusalem began, culminating two years later in the razing of the First Temple, which had been built by King Solomon.

The Chief Rabbinate of Israel has set aside this fast day as one on which *Kaddish* is to be said in Israeli synagogues to commemorate the lives of the victims of the Holocaust who died without leaving a family to say *Kaddish* for them.

Asceticism

The religious doctrine that one can be elevated to a higher spiritual plane through self-discipline and self-denial was embraced by early Christianity. It encouraged the renunciation of the pleasures of the flesh. Abstinence from sex, food, wine, as well as the submission to flagellation were opted for by those who followed the ascetic lifestyle. In Galatians (5:16), Paul says, "Walk in the Spirit and ye shall not fulfill the lust of the flesh." Physical cravings and spiritual cravings are antithetical, he goes on to say.

In biblical times, Hebrew sects such as the Nazirites (Numbers 6:1–21) took vows to refrain from cutting their hair or drinking wine or other intoxicants for a specified period of time. The Bible does not applaud such conduct, for when the period of abstinence ended, the *nazir* was required to bring a sacrifice to atone for the sin he had committed against his own person. The Book of Jeremiah (35) describes a similar sect, called the Rechabites, who lived in tents and drank no wine.

In later years, particularly between the first century B.C.E. and the first century C.E., sects of this kind continued to exist. One such sect was the Essenes, who lived on the western shore of the Dead Sea area of Palestine. Punctilious about religious observance, they devoted themselves to study and prayer, fasted frequently, did not marry and abstained from sex. The historian Josephus, in his *The Jewish War* (II:160), mentions one group of Essenes who were the exception: they *did* marry for the sole purpose of having children.

Jewish tradition is generally opposed to the ascetic way of life, which it considers aberrant—in fact, sinful—for it reflects a rejection of the bounty and goodness that God intended for man's enjoyment. Maimonides, in his *Mishneh Torah*, forbids a Jew from leading a celibate life, eating no meat, drinking no wine, and generally living a life of self-deprivation (Dei'ot 3:1). This position of Maimonides is representative of the beliefs of the Rabbis of the Talmud. The Jerusalem Talmud (Mishnah *Kiddushin* 4:12) expresses the popular rabbinic attitude when it says that man will have to account before God on the Day of Judgment for every legitimate pleasure he denied himself in life. Another reference (Jerusalem Talmud, Mishnah *Nedarim* 9:1) is even more direct when it asks of those who aspire to asceticism: "Were not enough things forbidden to you by the Torah that you should want to add to them?"

Aseret Yemei Teshuvah

The ten days between Rosh Hashanah and Yom Kippur.

See Ten Days of Repentance.

Ashamnu

Like the *Al Cheit*, the *Ashamnu* ("We Have Sinned") is a Confession of Sins recited on Yom Kippur. Consisting of only twenty-eight words, it lists alphabetically, in general terms, the sins we as members of the community may have committed and for which we seek forgiveness. Traditionally, as each sin is mentioned, worshippers beat their left breast (over the heart) as a symbolic expression of remorse.

In Orthodox congregations, at most morning services the *Ashamnu* prayer is recited after the *Amidah*, but it is particularly associated with Yom Kippur, when all Jews repeat it several times in the course of the day.

See Yom Kippur.

Ashkenazim

Literally, "Germans." Over the centuries many Jews living in the Middle East moved north and settled in the Germanic countries, in France, and in the neighboring countries of Eastern Europe. Since Germany received most of the migrants, these Jews became known as *Ashkenazim*. *Ashkenaz* (singular) appears as a personal name in the Book of Genesis (10:3) and as a kingdom in the Book of Jeremiah (51:27).

The largest influx of Jews to the United States after the middle of the nineteenth century consisted of Ashkenazim. They were in flight from the revolutionary activity that was engulfing the European continent. Customs and practices of the Ashkenazim, as well as the institutions they established, have shaped and dominated American Jewish life.

See Sephardim.

Ashrei

This song of praise to God expressing complete confidence in His concern for all creatures is recited during every morning service and every afternoon service. *Ashrei*, which in the Talmud is called *Tehillah*, consists of the twenty-one verses of Psalm 145. It is introduced by two additional verses, one from Psalm 84:5 and one from Psalm 144:15, both of which begin with the word *Ashrei*, meaning "happy, fortunate," hence, the name of the prayer. The concluding verse of the *Ashrei* is taken from Psalm 115: "And we will bless the Lord from this time forth and forever. Halleluyah!"

The Rabbis of the Talmud said that anyone who recites the *Ashrei* faithfully three times a day is assured of a share in the world to come.

Astrology

Astrology is generally defined as a pseudoscience that forecasts human events and destinies by means of observing and interpreting the relative positions of the stars, sun, and moon. The Bible is clearly opposed to astrology and all forms of divination. (See Deuteronomy 18:9–14.)

In the Talmud (*Nedarim* 32a) and the Midrash (*Genesis Rabbah* 44:12), reference is made to the patriarch Abraham as a believer in astrology. One Rabbi of the Talmud even claimed that Abraham wore an astrological chart over his heart and that many kings came to visit him to consult it. In the talmudic tractate *Shabbat* (156a), Abraham says, "Lord of the universe! I have consulted my horoscope and it is not fated that I should beget a son." And God answers, "Away with your astrology! The planets [stars] have no influence over Israel." The Hebrew original of this phrase, *ein mazal le-Yisra'el*, is often mistranslated as "Israel [Jews] has no luck," *mazal* being the Hebrew word for both star and luck. (In the vernacular, *mazal tov*, which is literally "good star," has taken on the popular meaning of "good luck.")

A strong denunciation of the claims of astrology and divination is found in the talmudic tractate *Nedarim* (32a), where the following teaching is set forth: "A person who refrains from practicing divination is assigned a place in heaven, which even [God's] ministering angels are unable to attain." (See also *Pesachim* 113b.) However, many Rabbis of the Talmud believed in the efficacy of astrology and even searched for biblical passages to support their views.

The tractate *Shabbat* (129a–b; 156b) has a great deal to say about astrology and the influence of the planets (*mazalim*) on man's condition. In one instance, Nachman bar Isaac's mother was told by astrologers, "Your son will be a thief." So she did not let him go bareheaded and said to him, "Cover your head so that the fear of heaven may be upon you." And this has been one of the reasons advanced for observant Jews not to go about bareheaded.

The outstanding twelfth-century Spanish scholar Moses Maimonides maintained that using astrological calculations to determine dates on which it is advisable to perform certain tasks is sheer nonsense. Nonetheless, many prominent rabbis and scholars—as well as the masses in general—looked with favor upon the "art" of astrology: Sa'adya Gaon (tenth century), Abraham ibn Ezra (twelfth century), and Nachmanides (thirteenth century). In the seventeenth century, the prominent Dutch rabbi Manasseh ben Israel (1604–1675) claimed: "In all periods there have been great astrologers among our people, and most notably in the Land of Spain." (See Joshua Trachtenberg's *Jewish Magic and Superstition*, 1939.)

Many of the beliefs and practices of Jewish mystics are rooted in astrology. These include avoidance of starting a new project on a Monday or a Wednesday, or preferring Tuesday as the best day for a wedding. Some believe that people born on Sunday will be distinguished; on Monday, angry; on Tuesday, wealthy; on Wednesday, intelligent; on Thursday, kind and generous; on Friday, pious; and those born on Saturday will die on Saturday. An eclipse of the moon was considered a bad omen for Jews and an eclipse of the sun bad luck for Gentiles.

Many contemporary Jewish figures believe in the efficacy of astrology or, at the very least, that it is neither harmful nor contrary to Jewish law.

See Kabbalah; Mysticism; Zodiac.

Atonement, Day of

See Yom Kippur.

Attributes of Mercy

See Thirteen Attributes of Mercy.

Atzeret

In the Book of Numbers (29:35) and the Book of Deuteronomy (16:8), the term *atzeret* ("assembly") is used to designate the festival observed on the eighth day after the seven days of Sukkot, which became popularly known as Shemini Atzeret, or "eighth day of assembly."

In the Talmud, Atzeret is the only name by which the Shavuot holiday is called. The Rabbis regarded Shavuot as the concluding day of the Passover holiday, which was to be celebrated as a day of "solemn assembly" and "holy convocation." They considered the relationship of Shavuot to Passover to be the same as that of Shemini Atzeret to Sukkot. Shemini Atzeret was considered the conclusion of Sukkot; Shavuot was considered the conclusion of Passover. [See *Pesikta* 193, where Shavuot is referred to as Atzeret Shel Pesach. See also *Megillah* 32a and Mishnah *Rosh Hashanah* 1:2.]

Aufruf

This German word meaning "calling up" is the name given to the honor bestowed upon a bridegroom in the synagogue on the Sabbath before his wedding. At the *Aufruf,* the bridegroom is called up to the Torah, thus affording the community an opportunity to publicly congratulate him. After reciting the second Torah blessing, the groom is sometimes showered with nuts and is often serenaded with song.

The practice of showering a groom with nuts at his *Aufruf* is of European origin. The custom evolved because of the Hebrew word *egoz,* meaning "nut," and the Hebrew word, *tov,* meaning "good," both have a numerical value of seventeen. The *Aufruf* ceremony symbolizes entry into a new phase of life which, it is hoped, will be good and fruitful. In some communities, raisins and other sweets are thrown at the bridegroom, expressing the same hope.

Today, in many non-Orthodox congregations, the bride accompanies her husband-to-be to the pulpit during the *Aufruf* and both recite the Torah blessings jointly.

Among some Russian Jews, it is customary to pass out candy during the synagogue service and to spray the wrist of each worshipper with perfume. The groom (*chatan*) wears a long, elaborately embroidered robe and skullcap.

See Marriage.

Autopsy

Since talmudic times, the post-mortem dissection of a body has been strictly forbidden. Because man is made in the image of God, the Rabbis of the Talmud and those of later centuries considered any form of mutilation of the body an affront to God, a denial of the belief that "in the end of days" God will resurrect the dead. Disfigurement of the body in any fashion would impinge upon the process of resurrection.

A more liberal view of autopsy was introduced in the eighteenth century when Rabbi Ezekiel Landau (1713–1793), the respected rabbi of Prague, responded to a person from London who asked whether it is permissible to perform an autopsy on a Jew in order to ascertain the cause of death, in the hope that what would be learned might help save the lives of future patients.

Rabbi Landau ruled that an autopsy may be performed only if there is reason to believe that as a result of the procedure doctors will gain knowledge and be able to cure a *particular* patient who is nearby and in *immediate* need of help. In all other cases, autopsy is to be considered *nivul ha-met,* "dishonoring the dead," a violation of the biblical commandment (Deuteronomy 21:22–23) that the dead be buried immediately, "on the same day" (*Noda Bi-Yehudah* II, Yoreh Dei'ah 210). Rabbi Moses Sofer (1763–1839), the esteemed authority from Pressburg, Ukraine, concurred (see *Chatam Sofer,* Yoreh Dei'ah 336).

After almost two hundred years of status quo, an even more liberal attitude toward autopsy emerged. The former Chief Rabbi of the British Commonwealth, Immanuel Jakobovits (1921–1999), author of *Jewish Medical Ethics,* permitted autopsy, citing the talmudic passage (*Berakhot* 45a) wherein it is noted that Rabbi Ishmael's disciples boiled the body of a condemned prostitute to determine the number of bones it contained—and without protest.

In Israel, when the need for cadavers for teaching purposes in medical schools had become acute, outstanding scholars including former Chief Rabbis of Israel Abraham Kook and Ben Zion Uziel approved the dissection of Jewish corpses so long as proper respect and care were taken. They were of the opinion that performing an autopsy may, in certain cases, be aptly called reverence for the dead (*kevod ha-met*)—that life is thus being sanctified, rather than desecrated, since the result of the procedure may eventually lead to the saving of another life. In Jewish law, nothing is of greater importance than preserving life, known in Hebrew as *pikuach nefesh*.

The Law of Anatomy and Pathology, passed by the Israeli Knesset in 1953, permits autopsy when the cause of death is doubtful, and especially if the procedure may lead to the saving of future lives. Doctors are required to respect the wishes of the family of the deceased wherever possible, and must turn over for proper burial all dissected organs after the necessary examinations have been performed.

While most contemporary Orthodox authorities agree with these more recent liberal views, especially when civil law demands that an autopsy be performed in order to investigate a homicide (*Chullin* 11b), a declaration made by 356 of their colleagues in 1966 stated that "autopsies in any form are prohibited by Torah Law."

Aveilut

A Hebrew word literally meaning "[condition of] mourning." One who has lost a close family member (mother, father, sister, brother, son, daughter, or spouse) is called an *aveil* (feminine, *aveilah*) for the duration of the mourning period, which extends up to one year depending on the relationship to the deceased.

There are three mourning periods: *shivah*, the first seven days after burial; *sheloshim*, the first thirty days after burial; and *yud bet chodesh*, the first twelve months after burial.

See Mourners and Mourning; Sheloshim; Shivah; Yud Bet Chodesh.

Avinu Malkeinu

Consisting of forty-four verses, each beginning with the words *Avinu Malkeinu* ("Our Father, our King"), this prayer is recited each morning except the Sabbath during the Ten Days of Repentance, the period between Rosh Hashanah and Yom Kippur. The *Avinu Malkeinu*, which is usually recited by the cantor and repeated by the congregation, is an expression of remorse for sins that have been committed and a plea for forgiveness.

Scholars attribute the authorship of about half of the *Avinu Malkeinu* supplications to Rabbi Akiba of the second century and the balance to liturgical poets who lived as late as the fourteenth century. Although the forty-four verses are all couched in the plural ("*Our* Father, *our* King, *we* have sinned before Thee"), they apply to each member of the community.

Why the *Avinu Malkeinu* prayer is not recited on the Sabbath can be traced to an incident described in the Talmud (*Ta'anit* 25b). It is reported that, in the second century C.E., when Rabbi Eliezer pronounced twenty-four benedictions for rain before the Holy Ark, his petitions were not answered. Then, Rabbi Akiba approached the ark and prayed: "Our Father, Our King, we have no King but Thee. Our Father, our King, for Thy sake have mercy upon us." And the rains fell. Since it was considered improper to pray for personal gain on the Sabbath, the *Avinu Malkeinu* was not recited on that day.

Avodah

In its original meaning, *Avodah* (literally, "work") referred to the Temple ritual of offering sacrifices on the altar. The importance of the ritual is reflected in a statement of Shimon the Just: "The world rests on three foundations: Torah, divine service (*Avodah*), and practices of lovingkindness" (Ethics of the Fathers 1:2).

When the Temple was destroyed in the

year 70 C.E. and the sacrificial system was abandoned, the prayer service continued. The Rabbis of the Talmud (*Ta'anit* 2a), led by Yochanan ben Zakkai, refused to concede that the Temple would not be rebuilt and its ritual reconstituted. They therefore kept its memory alive by reciting on Yom Kippur afternoon the elaborate sacrificial procedures conducted by the High Priest on that sacred day in the Jewish calendar. An account of how the ceremony was carried out is detailed in the Mishnah (*Yoma* 1).

A'yin Ha-Ra

A Hebrew term literally meaning "evil eye." Superstition has it that demons and evil spirits must be guarded against. So for example, to ward off forces bent on harming someone who is being praised verbally, the expression *b'li a'yin ha-ra* ("without incurring the evil eye") is added immediately after the complimentary words are spoken. This same sentiment is expressed in the Hebrew-Yiddish expression *kein a'yin hara,* or in popular folk-talk, *kenahora.*

In the talmudic tractate *Berakhot* (20a), when the Rabbis asked the famous Yochanan bar Nappacha whether he was fearful of the evil eye, he replied, "I come from the seed of Joseph over whom the evil eye had no power, for it is written (Genesis 49:22), 'Joseph is a fruitful vine above the a'yin' [which in Hebrew means 'fountain' or 'eye']."

Nevertheless, in ancient times and even today, the average Jew, whether educated or not, was fearful of the influence of demons and evil spirits that might attack if provoked. Thus, special precautions were taken to protect a newborn child and its mother as well as those on their deathbed, for it was believed that evil spirits considered humans to be most vulnerable at birth and death.

Among the devices and measures created to mislead, scare, or waylay the "otherworldly" opponents of man are the recitation of psalms, particularly Psalm 91 (the Antidemonic Psalm, sometimes called the Psalm of Afflictions); surrounding the bed of a mother and newborn baby; marching a bride around a groom three times or seven times; breaking a glass at the conclusion of a wedding ceremony; and washing hands after leaving a cemetery, where it was believed evil spirits congregate.

The fifteenth-century rabbi Jacob Weil let it be known that "when I prepare for my afternoon nap, I recite the Antidemonic Psalm, for all sleep is dangerous because of demons."

During Operation Desert Storm, in 1991, when Iraq began launching SCUD ballistic missiles against Saudi Arabia and Israel, Major Kathleen Murray, a registered nurse from Madeira, Florida, who ran an Air Force medical facility, reported that soldiers read Psalm 91, with special emphasis on verses 5 and 6:

> You need not fear the terror by night
> Nor the arrow that flies by day,
> Nor the pestilence that stalks in the darkness,
> Nor the destruction that ravages at noon.

A'yin Tachat A'yin

Literally, "an eye for an eye." A concept more popularly known as *lex talionis.*
See Lex Talionis.

Azazel

The Book of Leviticus (16:6ff.) notes that before Aaron the High Priest could make atonement for all the people of Israel on Yom Kippur day, he first had to purge himself of sin. After offering sacrifices on his own behalf and on behalf of his family, he would take two he-goats and place lots upon them: one marked "for the Lord" and the other "for Azazel." The goat designated "for the Lord" was offered as a sin-offering, while the other was led into the wilderness, carrying with it all the sins of Israel. There, in an inaccessible region, it was set free.

In Temple times, a different procedure was followed. The goat, bearing the sins of the High Priest, was pushed off a steep cliff, and thus it met its death. The entire episode is dramatically reenacted in a moving narrative recited on Yom Kippur as part of the *Musaf* (afternoon) service.

The exact meaning of the term "Azazel" has not been firmly established. In modern parlance it has come to mean "hell," which has led to the pejorative Hebrew expression *leikh la-azazel*, "go to hell." Scholars, however, differ as to the word's origin and meaning. Some believe that it is a combination of the two words *eiz azal*, meaning "the goat has left [gone]." Others define it as "steep mountain." Still others believe that the term derives from the Akkadian *azlu* and refers to a type of goat.

In John Milton's *Paradise Lost*, Azazel is one of the angels who rebelled against Satan.

See Heaven and Hell.

Ba'al Korei

A Hebrew term meaning "master of the reading."

See Torah Reading.

Ba'al Tefillah

A Hebrew term meaning "master of prayer."
See Cantor.

Ba'al Teki'ah

A Hebrew term meaning "master of the *teki'ah*," referring to the expert who blows the *shofar*. Also referred to as *ba'al tokei'ah*.
See Shofar.

Ba'al Teshuvah

A Hebrew term meaning "master of repentance."

See Repentance.

Badekn Di Kallah

A Yiddish-Hebrew term meaning "veiling the bride."

See Veiling the Bride.

Bal Tashchit

This basic biblical concept, which literally means "do not waste," condemns wanton waste or destruction. The term is first used in the Book of Genesis (38:9), when the Israelites are cautioned not to destroy (*lo tashchit*) the sidegrowth (*pei'ot*) of their beards.

The "preservation principle," as it is sometimes called, is emphasized once again in the Book of Deuteronomy (20:19): "When you wage war against a city, and you have to besiege it for a long time in order to capture it, you must not destroy [*lo tashchit*] its trees by wielding an ax against them." This biblical proscription applied only to fruit-bearing trees. Destroying other trees, those required to build siegeworks against the city, did not fall into the category of wanton destruction.

In time, the Rabbis extended the *bal tashchit* principle to include wanton destruction of any kind. In one reference, the Talmud (*Semachot* 9:23) describes as wasteful the ancient practice of placing valuables in the coffin of the deceased. In another, the Talmud (*Bava Kamma* 91b) uses the term *bal tashchit* in connection with a mourner who extends the tear in his garment (*keri'ah*), more than necessary, thus making its repair very costly.

The Rabbis of the Talmud applied the concept of preserving natural resources to the spilling of human seed, as detailed in the Book of Genesis (38), where the story of Judah and his sons Er and Onan is told. The conclusion drawn from this episode is that masturbation is a biblically forbidden act.

Chaim Vital (1542–1620), the chief disciple of the mystic Rabbi Isaac Luria (the Ari) wrote: "My master, of blessed memory, used to be careful never to destroy any insect, even the smallest, most insignificant among them, such as a flea or a gnat or a bee—even if they were annoying him."

Modern Attitudes

Today, religiously-oriented scientists and environmentalists stress that polluting the air, wasting energy, destroying forests, neglecting to recycle goods, and similar actions are violations of the Preservation Principle. However, they do not consider masturbation sinful or in any way harmful to the well-being of the individual.

See Ecology.

Bal Tosif

By adhering to this biblical proscription (Deuteronomy 4:2 and 13:1), which literally means "refrain from adding [to the laws specified in the Torah]," an individual is manifesting the

belief that the Torah is complete and need not be improved upon in any way. Thus, a person is frowned upon if he performs a *mitzvah* that he is not obligated to perform, such as sitting in a *sukkah* on Shemini Atzeret, which is not part of the Sukkot holiday but a totally separate one observed on the day following Sukkot.

Rashi, quoting the Midrash (Sifri on *R'ei* 82), offers as examples that one may not add a fifth passage to the four that are inscribed on the *tefillin* parchment, or add a fifth variety to the four species that are part of the *lulav* bouquet, or add a fifth to the four *tzitziot* on a *tallit*; or add a fourth verse to the three that form the *Priestly Benediction*.

See Chasid Shoteh.

Baraita

Plural, *baraitot*. An Aramaic term meaning "outside," referring specifically to rabbinic teachings that were not included in the Mishnah of Judah the Prince (219 C.E.).

Although these studies expressed the view of respected talmudic teachers, (*tanna'im*), they were not included in the Mishnah proper, possibly because Rabbi Judah was unaware of them. They were, however, well known to talmudic scholars of a later period (*amora'im*), who alluded to these teachings in their explication of the Mishnah.

Baraitot are found scattered throughout both the Babylonian Talmud and the Jerusalem Talmud. When the Babylonian Talmud introduces a *baraita*, it uses the Aramaic words *tanya*, meaning "we have learned," or *tannu rabbanan*, "our Rabbis have taught." The Jerusalem Talmud uses the word *matnito*, which has a similar meaning.

During the geonic period (500–1000 C.E.) the *baraitot* were assembled to form a body of work known as the Tosefta, meaning "additions, supplements [to the Mishnah]."

Bar Mitzvah

Plural, *b'nei mitzvah*. An Aramaic/Hebrew term meaning "son of the commandment." The expression *bar mitzvah* is first found in the talmudic tractate *Bava Metzia* (96a), where it refers to every adult Jew who is subject to biblical law. Not until the fourteenth century was the term applied specifically to a boy who has reached the age of thirteen plus one day, at which point Jewish law considers him a mature adult. As such, he is counted as part of a *minyan* (a religious quorum of ten adults) and is thus obligated to live up to biblical and talmudic commandments, such as donning *tefillin* (phylacteries) and fasting on Yom Kippur.

The bar mitzvah boy is trained in the donning of *tefillin* several months before his actual bar mitzvah so that he will become adept at performing the ritual (Be'er Hetev commentary on Orach Cha'yim 37:1). The phrase "entering the *minyan*" is the way Sephardim refer to a bar mitzvah boy. Once he begins donning his *tefillin*, he is counted as part of the quorum of ten who make up a *minyan*. In some North African (Sephardic) communities, a bar mitzvah is called *Tefillin*.

The bar mitzvah is generally marked at a synagogue service on the Sabbath immediately following the young man's date of birth, although a formal synagogue commemoration is not required by law.

The Synagogue Commemoration

At the synagogue service, the bar mitzvah is awarded an *aliyah*—he is called to the Torah. The young man recites the Torah blessings before and after a portion of the Torah is read. Sometimes he chants his own Torah portion, which is usually the *maftir*, the last portion of the day. After the Torah is returned to the ark, the bar mitzvah also usually chants the *haftarah*, a selection from one of the books of the Prophets. Special blessings are read by him prior to and following the prophetic portion.

The custom of assigning to the bar mitzvah the *maftir aliyah* and the reading of the *haftarah* began in the fourteenth century, when many rabbis feared that an *aliyah* might be given to a boy who had not yet reached his thirteenth birthday. The rabbis ruled that only the *maftir aliyah*, which is not one of the prescribed seven *aliyot*, may be given to the bar mitzvah. In most Sephardic congregations, the bar mitzvah is awarded the fifth or sixth *aliyah* and he does not chant the *haftarah*.

Since a bar mitzvah may be celebrated during any synagogue service at which the Torah is read, in addition to the Sabbath and holidays, the event may be held on Mondays, Thursdays, and Rosh Chodesh (the beginning of the Hebrew month). Observant Jews often schedule a bar mitzvah on weekdays so that family members and friends can attend without violating the law prohibiting travel on the Sabbath. In instances when a child is unable to learn the *haftarah*, or when an observant family wishes to hold the party after the conclusion of the Sabbath, a bar mitzvah is sometimes celebrated at the Sabbath afternoon (*Minchah*) service.

Some communities still follow an old tradition of filling small bags with candy, nuts, raisins, or other sweets and throwing them at a bar mitzvah following the recitation of the closing Torah blessing as an expression of hope that a sweet life will be the lot of the celebrant.

Parental Rights

A natural parent of a son who had been given out for adoption at a young age retains all religious paternal rights and obligations pertaining to the child. If the natural father is present at the bar mitzvah of his son, it is he rather than the adoptive father who recites the *Barukh She-petarani* prayer, and it is he who must be honored with an *aliyah* if a choice must be made between the two.

Opposition to the Bar Mitzvah

For many years, Reform rabbis were opposed to the bar mitzvah ceremony, instead favoring confirmation, which was held when children were between fifteen and seventeen years of age and hence more mature. Rabbi Kaufmann Kohler, who was appointed president of Hebrew Union College in 1903 and held that post for eighteen years, adamantly opposed the bar mitzvah. In an article in the Central Conference of American Rabbis *Yearbook* (No. 23, 1913), he maintained that "the bar mitzvah rite ought not to be encouraged by any Reform rabbi as it is a survival of Orientalism, like the covering of the head during services...." However, his colleague David Neumark (1866–1924) favored allowing the ceremony to be held in Reform congregations where such was already the practice. Currently, Reform congregations do hold the bar mitzvah ceremony.

Bar Mitzvah Parties

As far back as the sixteenth century, rabbinic authorities condemned unbridled celebrating at bar mitzvah parties, which were often held just for the purpose of enabling guests to gorge themselves with food and to carry on in an uninhibited fashion. Lavish, expensive parties are discouraged by present-day rabbis as well, and families are encouraged to donate the financial savings to organizations that feed the poor. One such organization is Mazon, which has offices in many large cities in the United States.

See Bat Mitzvah.

Barukh She-petarani

Literally meaning "Blessed Is He Who Has Freed Me," this blessing of thanksgiving is recited by a father at the bar mitzvah of his son immediately after the boy has pronounced the second Torah blessing. The practice, now observed primarily by Orthodox Jews, was introduced in talmudic times by Rabbi Eleazar ben Rabbi Shimon, who said: "A man is responsible for [educating] his son until the age of thirteen, thereafter he must say: 'Blessed is He who has freed me from the responsibility of this boy'" (*Genesis Rabbah* 63:10). Thenceforth, the boy is considered an adult and is obligated to carry out the religious rites incumbent upon adult Jews.

Many Conservative and Reform congregations have substituted the *She-heche'yanu* blessing for the *Barukh She-petarani*, which some say carries a negative connotation. After the bar mitzvah has recited the second Torah blessing, the immediate family often stands and joins in expressing thanks for having reached this joyous day.

Bastardy

The Hebrew term for bastard is *mamzer*, which in the Jewish legal tradition does not mean a child born out of wedlock, but rather one who is born of an adulterous or incestuous marriage.

See Adultery; Mamzer.

Batel B'Shishim

Literally meaning "nullified in one-sixtieth," this Jewish legal concept refers to forbidden food that has been mixed with permitted food. If the permitted substances are sixty times greater in quantity or volume than the prohibited item, the permitted substances are considered to have neutralized the forbidden one. This neutralization would apply when a particle of cooked meat falls into a pot with a milk product and settles there. It would not apply, however, if the meat is from a nonkosher animal, and it would only apply if the mixing is the result of an accident (*Chullin* 97a).

In cases of *chametz* (leaven) becoming admixed with a Passover dish, regardless of how small the quantity of *chametz*, the mixture is prohibited.

The rules that apply to special situations in this regard are detailed in Joseph Caro's *Code of Jewish Law* (*Shulchan Arukh*, Yoreh Dei'ah 91, 92).

See Dietary Laws.

Bat Mitzvah

Plural, *b'not mitzvah*. A Hebrew term meaning "daughter of the commandment." Because girls usually reach physical maturity earlier than boys, in Jewish tradition the female is considered an adult either at the age of twelve plus one day, at which time the Talmud (*Ta'anit* 13b) refers to her as a *na'arah*, or at the age of twelve and one-half plus one day, at which time she is called a *bogeret*. Authorities have established twelve plus one day as the official age of maturity (see *Arukh Ha-Shulchan* 225:4), and today it is on or about that time that a girl becomes a bat mitzvah.

The bat mitzvah ceremony was not introduced until 1922, when Rabbi Mordecai Kaplan, founder of the Reconstructionist movement, introduced it to correspond to the bar mitzvah celebration enjoyed by boys. His belief was that just as boys are called to the Torah for the *maftir aliyah* and to recite the prophetic portion, so should girls be honored. The ceremony, he maintained, would encourage young girls to pursue Jewish studies and would also restore some of the equality denied Jewish women under Jewish law.

Rabbi Kaplan's daughter, Judith, was the first girl to become a bat mitzvah. The ceremony was held in New York City at the Society for the Advancement of Judaism, the mother synagogue of the Reconstructionist movement.

Variant Practices

In non-Orthodox synagogues, the bat mitzvah celebration closely parallels that of the bar mitzvah, although in some instances the girl is not awarded an *aliyah*. In these cases, the young woman is generally permitted to recite the *haftarah*, including the blessings that accompany it.

Congregations that do not honor a woman with an *aliyah* often hold the bat mitzvah celebration at the Friday evening service, when the Torah is not normally read. Generally, at a Friday night bat mitzvah service the young lady chants from the prophetic portion scheduled to be read the next morning. Some Conservative rabbis who conduct a Friday night bat mitzvah do not permit the *haftarah* blessings to be recited, arguing that these would be wasted blessings (*berakhot le-vatalah*) since the reading of the prophetic portion is not required by law.

In Reform congregations, where the Torah itself is often read on Friday night, the bat mitzvah reads from the Torah and from the Prophets.

Mainstream Orthodoxy does not generally recognize the bat mitzvah as a religious celebration. While not conceding that the onset of a girl's maturity is of religious significance and in any way comparable to a boy's having reached the age of bar mitzvah, in recent years the Orthodox have given recognition to the bat mitzvah concept by allowing a party for the girl to be held outside the precincts of the synagogue. At these festivities, the girl some-times gives a talk on a religious theme. Some Orthodox object to this practice, favoring instead that a male adult make a speech praising the girl for her attendance at synagogue or Hebrew school, and offering congratulations to her parents.

Among the ultra-Orthodox, there is a wide range of attitudes on the subject. Rabbi Moshe Feinstein (1895–1986) opposed attendance at either the bat mitzvah service (which he referred to as *hevel*, meaning "nonsense") or the party that follows (*Igrot Moshe*, Orach Cha'yim 104). Other ultra-Orthodox authorities—such as René-Samuel Sirat (1930–), the Chief Rabbi of France, a Sephardic Jew—oppose the ritual as well, but with less vituperation.

The former Sephardic Chief Rabbi of Israel, Ovadiah Yosef (1920–), is much more liberal in his approach. While he does not advocate calling a girl to the Torah, he does believe that inasmuch as she has passed her twelfth birthday and is obligated to assume religious responsibilities like other adult women, the day should be marked by a festive meal that may legitimately be called a *se'udat mitzvah*, a religious meal of celebration (Yechaveh Daat 2:29).

The late Lubavitcher Rebbe, Menachem Mendel Schneerson (1902–1994), favored giving recognition to a young woman as she enters maturity, maintaining that the traditional ban against teaching girls Torah can no longer be seen as applicable in this age when women receive advanced education and have achieved distinction as scholars and scientists.

See Se'udat Mitzvah.

Battered Women

Although neither the Bible nor the Talmud have much to say about the physical abuse of women by their spouses, scholars of the Middle Ages and thereafter have commented on the phenomenon. Rabbenu Jacob Tam (1100–1171), the grandson of Rashi, said that "wifebeating is not done in Israel," and Moses Isserles, in his notes to the sixteenth-century *Code of Jewish Law* (*Shulchan Arukh*, Even Ha-Ezer 154:3), states that "a man who beats his wife commits a sin; it is as though he has beaten a neighbor." He then adds that if a man persists in such behavior, the court may compel him to divorce his wife. Isserles follows this with the observation that wifebeating is not customary among Jews, obviously echoing the view of earlier scholars such as Rabbenu Tam and later ones such as Mordechai ben Hillel (died 1298), author of the influential code *Sefer Mordechai*, who wrote: "It is not the custom of our people [to beat wives], only of the Gentiles."

The contention that Jewish men did not engage in physical abuse of women is not supported by fact. Domestic violence was prevalent among Jews in medieval times, and prominent legal authorities such as the twelfth-century Moses Maimonides and the thirteenth/fourteenth-century Asher ben Yechiel (the Rosh) condoned wifebeating as wholly acceptable.

While Maimonides subscribed to the teachings of the Rabbis of the Talmud that one must care for his wife and treat her gently and with compassion, he also ruled that if a wife refuses to carry out such domestic duties as washing her husband's hands or feet, or serving him at the table, "she should be beaten with rods" (*Mishneh Torah*, Hilkhot Ishut 21:3 and 10). However, Maimonides' outspoken critic, the French talmudist Abraham ben David of Posquières (1120–1198), wrote: "I never heard that it is permitted to raise a rod to strike a woman."

The prominent thirteenth-century German scholar Rabbi Meir ben Baruch of Rothenburg (the Maharam), in answer to a question on the subject of wifebeating, wrote:

> A Jew must honor his wife more than he honors himself. If one strikes one's wife, one should be punished more severely than for striking another person. For one is enjoined to honor one's wife but is not enjoined to honor the other person.... If he persists in striking her, he should be excommunicated, lashed, and suffer the severest punishments, even to the extent of amputating his arm. If his wife is willing to accept a divorce, he must divorce her and pay her [the money stipulated in] the *ketubbah* [Jewish marriage contract].
> (Quoted in Irving A. Agus's *Rabbi Meir of Rothenberg*, 1970)

A Contemporary Problem

According to reports issued by the Histadrut Parliament's Welfare Committee, as reported in *The Jerusalem Post* (December 3, 1994), 200,000 Israeli women were beaten or mistreated by their husbands in 1994. Seventeen were murdered by their husbands in 1994, and in both 1992 and 1993 twenty-one were murdered by their husbands, boyfriends, former husbands, or sons.

In 1996, Naamat, a women's organization that provides legal advice and shelter to battered women, estimated that there were 250,000 battered women in Israel, 20,000 of them in Tel Aviv.

A comprehensive scholarly report on this subject entitled "Family Violence," by Rabbi Elliot N. Dorff, was issued in September 1995 by the Committee on Jewish Law and Standards of the Rabbinical Assembly.

Beauty and Beautification

The importance of appreciating the beauty around us is an essential aspect of Jewish tradition. The Rabbis of ancient times introduced special blessings expressing man's gratitude for the beauty and awesome power of nature. These appear in the opening pages of most prayerbooks.

An appreciation of beauty was associated with the carrying out of religious commandments (*mitzvot*), and thus evolved the concept of *hiddur mitzvah* ("beautification of the commandment"). Tradition urges Jews to select beautiful ceremonial objects to be used in carrying out the commandments. The *etrog* (citron) used on Sukkot is to be nicely shaped, free of all blemishes, and of good color. Artisans created many handsome containers in a variety of styles, metals, and woods to house the *etrog* during the week of Sukkot. Spice boxes used during the *havdalah* ceremony at the close of the Sabbath and holidays were designed in a variety of decorative shapes, often fashioned of wood, silver, and other materials. *Kiddush* cups, candlesticks, and other religious objects, including eternal lights, synagogue candelabra, and Torah appurtenances were likewise beautifully designed and crafted by skilled artisans.

The concept of *hiddur mitzvah* has been applied to the manufacture of *tallitot* (prayershawls). Whereas in the past the *tallit* was made of white fabric (wool, rayon, or silk) with black and sometimes blue stripes, in recent years colorful designs have been created using a variety of materials. Purple, scarlet, and blue—the hues used in the Tabernacle and in the garments of the High Priest—are becoming preferred colors.

Bedikat Chametz

Literally meaning "the search for leaven," this procedure takes place in the Jewish home on the night of the fourteenth of Nissan—the night before the Passover *Seder*.

After the house has been thoroughly cleaned and scoured in preparation for the Passover holiday, the head of the household conducts a symbolic search for the last vestige of leaven in the house. The procedure begins with a member of the household placing small pieces of bread (*chametz*) in key places, usually on a windowsill in each room of the house. In some families it is customary to distribute ten pieces of bread, representing the kabbalistic notion of ten *sefirot*—ten manifestations of God.

Before beginning the search for the *chametz*, the head of the house recites the blessing ending with the words *al bi'ur chametz*, "for the removal and burning of *chametz*." Followed by children present, the leader then proceeds from room to room by candlelight. Using a feather, the bread pieces are brushed into a wooden spoon. All of this (spoon, collected pieces of bread, and feather) is wrapped together, and on the following morning it is burned. Prior to the burning, appropriate prayers are recited. Once this task has been completed, the house is considered officially kosher for Passover.

Beit Din

A Hebrew term literally meaning "house of judgment," referring to a court of law.

In Temple times (prior to 70 C.E.) there existed two major courts, its members appointed by leaders of the Jewish community. Each court had a different jurisdiction:

1. Great Sanhedrin (*Sanhedrin Ha-Gedolah*). This tribunal, consisting of seventy-one

judges, concerned itself with some capital cases, but primarily with matters affecting the priesthood and the sacrificial system. It was vested with the authority of deciding all matters of profound national concern, such as going to war, and was responsible for ruling on all cases that were left undecided by lower courts. Its rulings were final and binding.

Sessions of the Great Sanhedrin were held each workday until 3:00 P.M. in the Chamber of Hewn Stone (*Lishkat Ha-Gazit*). While the titular head of the body was the *nasi* ("Prince"), an outstanding scholar and community leader, the day-to-day operations of the court were under the supervision of the *Av Beit Din* ("Father of the Court"), who was second in command (Mishnah *Chagigah* 2:2).

2. Court of Twenty-three (*Beit Din Shel Esrim ve-Shalosh*), also known as *Sanhedrin Ketanah* (the Lesser Sanhedrin). Next in importance to the Great Sanhedrin, this court had the authority to hear cases in which the death penalty could be imposed. Such courts sat in session in all regions of the country and when necessary were convened as district courts in settlements consisting of at least 120 men.

After Jewish autonomy in Palestine came to an end as a result of the Roman occupation of Palestine in 70 C.E., the large and small Sanhedrins were no longer operative, and so it remained over the centuries of exile. This was so because it was believed that only the rabbinic authorities in the Holy Land had the power to ordain rabbis. And since it was rabbis who sat on these tribunals as judges, the tribunals could no longer be reestablished.

But smaller, local courts were operative over the centuries. These were established and existed within local communities to adjudicate civil cases, thus making it possible for Jews to avoid airing their personal disputes before the general non-Jewish population.

In Israel today, aside from local courts, a Supreme Court consisting of fourteen judges is in place. Three or more may listen to a case and rule upon it at any one time. The Supreme Court has the power to overrule decisions of the District Courts.

Possibly the best organized *Beit Din* in the world functions in England. It consists of five judges called *da'yanim* (singular, *da'yan*) who, because of their scholarship, rank higher than the congregational rabbi. They are members of an independent body not accountable to the Chief Rabbi, although technically he is the *ex-officio* head of the Court. The judges meet five times a week to discuss issues such as divorce, conversion, and the supervision of dietary laws.

Beit Knesset

Literally meaning "house of assembly," this popular Hebrew term for synagogue was first used in the talmudic tractate *Megillah* (21a and 26a).

See Synagogue.

Beit Midrash

Literally meaning "house of study," this term refers to the school in which adults study Talmud, Midrash, and other advanced subjects. It was first used in the talmudic tractates *Megillah* (26a) and *Chagigah* (3a).

See Synagogue.

Beit Sefer

Literally meaning "house of the book," this is the generic name for a school in which Jewish children receive their primary education. It was first used in the talmudic tractate *Ketubbot* (2:10). Another popular term for school is *cheder* ("room").

See Cheder.

Benevolence

See Zeh Ne'heneh Ve-Zeh Lo Chaser.

Berakhah Le-Vatalah

The third of the Ten Commandments (Exodus 20:7) prohibits taking the name of God in vain, and from this proscription the concept of *berakhah le-vatalah*, "wasted blessing," evolved. A blessing is considered to be wasted or superfluous, said the Rabbis of the Talmud, when it employs God's name for no legitimate purpose. There are two categories of wasted blessing.

Action Not Taken

A blessing becomes superfluous when it calls for an action that is then not taken. For example, if one recites the blessing over bread (*Hamotzi*) but then does not taste the bread, the blessing is considered wasted. Similarly, if on a Sabbath or holiday one recites the blessing over wine (*Kiddush*) after reciting the *Hamotzi* blessing, the *Kiddush* would be considered a *berakhah le-vatalah*, since according to Jewish law the blessing over bread, which is recited at the beginning of the meal, covers all foods consumed at the meal, including wine (*Pesachim* 105a and *Berakhot* 33a).

The *berakhah le-vatalah* concept explains why blessings were not assigned to a number of important positive Torah commandments (*mitzvot*) that would seem to require them. The first commandment in the Torah is, "Be fruitful and multiply" (Genesis 1:28). To have children is of the highest priority in Jewish law, yet before engaging in sexual intercourse no blessing is recited. The reason can probably be explained by the Wasted Blessing Principle. Should the intercourse not result in pregnancy, the blessing would have been uttered for naught.

The same is true with regard to fulfill-ing the primary commandment (*mitzvah*) of giving charity (*tzedakah*) (Deuteronomy 15:7–8). Surprisingly, no blessing was assigned to this Torah-based commandment. The thirteenth-century Spanish scholar Rabbi Solomon ben Adret of Barcelona (the Rashba) explained that fulfilling the commandment is not wholly dependent upon the giver; the receiver must acquiesce in the action. There is always the possibility that the person in need will reject the charitable gift of the donor. Thus, a blessing recited before giving charity might be wasted.

Persons Not Obligated

The second type of wasted blessing is uttered by a person who is not required or obligated to pronounce the blessing. If a Gentile were called to the Torah for an *aliyah*, and if he knew the Torah blessings and pronounced them properly, each of the blessings would be a *berakhah le-vatalah*. The blessings are considered wasted because a non-Jew is not eligible to recite a blessing containing the words *asher kideshanu be-mitzvotav ve-tzivanu*, meaning "Who has sanctified us with Your commandments and commanded us to…" Non-Jews, not being part of the Covenant People, were not commanded to observe the *mitzvot* of the Torah.

Bible

The Bible—referred to in Hebrew as the *Mikra*, *Kitvei Ha-Kodesh*, or *Tanakh*—consists of three parts: the Torah, the Prophets, and the Holy Writings. In all, it is comprised of thirty-nine books.

The Torah: This term applies to the Five Books of Moses, the first five books of the Bible. The word *Pentateuch*, a Latin work derived from the Greek, meaning "five books," is commonly used to refer to these five books. Pentateuch corresponds to the Hebrew word

Chumash, meaning "five." The Torah consists of the books of Genesis, Exodus, Leviticus, Numbers, and Deuteronomy.

The Prophets: This second of the three parts of the Bible is referred to in Hebrew as *Nevi'im*. The Prophets consists of the books of Joshua, Judges, I Samuel, II Samuel, I Kings, II Kings, Isaiah, Jeremiah, Ezekiel, Hosea, Joel, Amos, Ovadiah, Jonah, Micah, Nahum, Habakkuk, Zephaniah, Haggai, Zekhariah, and Malakhi.

The Holy Writings: Also known as the Hagiographa and referred to in Hebrew as *Ketuvim*, this part of the Bible is comprised of the books of Psalms, Proverbs, Job, Song of Songs, Ruth, Lamentations, Ecclesiastes, Esther, Daniel, Ezra, Nechemiah, I Chronicles, and II Chronicles.

The biblical triad of Torah, Prophets, and Holy Writings is most commonly referred to as the *Tanakh*, a Hebrew acronym fashioned after the first letters of the Hebrew words *Torah* (Pentateuch), *Nevi'im* (Prophets), and *Ketuvim* (Holy Writings).

According to an early talmudic method of counting, the total number of books in the Bible was said to be twenty-four. This figure was arrived at by counting the twelve Minor Prophets as one book (in Aramaic the group is called *Trei Asar*, "twelve") and also by counting each of the following as one book: I Samuel and II Samuel, I Kings and II Kings; I Chronicles and II Chronicles; and Ezra and Nechemiah. In classical literature, the term used to designate these twenty-four books is *Esrim Ve-Arba'ah*, or *Esrim Ve-Arba*.

Christians do not recognize the Holy Writings as a separate part of the Bible. Instead, they intersperse the various books in this division among the books of the Prophets.

Christians refer to the Jewish Bible as "Old Testament," which implies that there is a "New Testament" that supersedes it. The term "Old Testament" is, therefore, anathema to Jews.

See Torah.

Bikur Cholim

The Rabbis considered the act of *bikur cholim* ("visiting the sick") to be a religious commandment (*mitzvah*) of such magnitude that all who do so will have a share in the world to come (*Shabbat* 127a; Yoreh Dei'ah 335:1; *Chokhmat Adam* 151:1). They went so far as to rule that if a close relative (father, mother, brother, sister, son, daughter, spouse) is seriously ill and it seems likely that a visit will cheer up the individual and improve his or her chances for recovery, even violating the Sabbath is permitted. Saving a life by any means is a cardinal principle of Judaism. Rabbi Abba said (*Nedarim* 39b): "He who visits the sick reduces his pain by one-sixtieth."

The Rabbis (Yoreh Dei'ah 337:1) were careful to advise that one must be extremely cautious about the words one uses when visiting a seriously ill person. For example, if it is suspected that by notifying the ill person that a relative has died, it will cause great mental anguish and possibly lead to a worsening of the patient's condition, that news should not be transmitted.

See Mitzvah.

Bimah

Literally, "platform, elevated stage." In early biblical times, the hills and high places on which sacrifices were brought were called *bamot* (singular, *bamah*), akin to the word *bimah* (I Samuel 9:12). After the destruction of the Second Temple, the synagogue became the spiritual center of Jewish life, and the reading of the Torah replaced sacrifices as the highlight of the religious service. The altar on which sacrifices were brought in Temple times was replaced by a large table set on a slightly elevated stage from which the synagogue *chazzan* (cantor) or *ba'al tefillah* (prayer leader) would chant the prayers. In many smaller synagogues the table was placed at, or near, floor level.

The *bimah*, also called by the Hebrew term *amud* (II Kings 11:14), always faced the ark. Under normal circumstances, it was located on a platform a step or two above floor level, but always much lower than the platform on which the ark itself was located. It was for this reason that it was said—many references to this can be found in the Talmud—that the leader of the service "*goes down* before the ark" (*yoreid lifnei ha-teivah*) when he conducts a service. This was in keeping with the verse in Psalms (130:1), "Out of the depths have I called upon You, O Lord."

There are also many talmudic references to the *bimah* being located in the center of the synagogue, close to floor level. One of the early significant comments relating to this custom was uttered by Rabbi Jose ben Chaninah (*Berakhot* 10b). Quoting Rabbi Eliezer ben Jacob, he said: "A man should not stand in a high place when he prays, but should pray in a lowly place."

An early reference to the *bimah* being situated in the center of a synagogue is found in the talmudic tractate *Sukkah* (51b), where Rabbi Judah the Prince states that anyone who has not seen the beautiful synagogue in third-century B.C.E. Alexandria, Egypt, has not seen a magnificent building in his life. The synagogue was so large that it was able to accommodate many thousands of worshippers at one time. The *bimah* was situated in the center of the sanctuary, and the *gabbai* (sexton) held a scarf in his hand. When the time came for the congregation to respond *Amen*, he would wave the scarf, since his voice could not carry to every corner of the huge room.

In most Orthodox synagogues today, the service is conducted from a *bimah* in the center (or near the center) of the sanctuary. All non-Orthodox congregations conduct the entire service from the pulpit, the area immediately in front of the ark, which is also known as the *bimah*, since it is a raised platform.

See Synagogue.

Birkat Ha-Chamah

A Hebrew term literally meaning "the blessing of the sun." The popular Hebrew word for sun, *shemesh*, appears over one hundred times in the Bible; its synonym *chamah* appears but six times. Yet, the prayer relating to the blessing of the sun is called *Birkat Ha-Chamah*. In the Book of Genesis (1:14–19), where the creation of the sun and moon are described as occurring on the fourth day, the sun is referred to by neither designation. It is called simply "the great light."

In biblical times there were sun-worshipping cults, as is attested to by the fact that a number of locations in the Holy Land carry a "sun" name, such as Beit Shemesh (Jeremiah 43:13), where cult members lived. In the Book of Deuteronomy (4:19), Israel is warned not to bow down or serve the sun, the moon, or stars.

Although the sun and the other heavenly bodies are no longer looked upon as deities but as servants of God, the ancient adoration of the sun has left its mark on Jewish life. Based upon calculations by the third/fourth-century talmudic scholar Abbayei (*Berakhot* 59b), who concluded that the vernal equinox (when the sun crosses the equator, making night and day of equal length) always begins its cycle in the month of Nissan (roughly, April), when the sun is ninety degrees above the eastern horizon. This is presumed to be what the alignment of the heavenly bodies was on Wednesday, the fourth day of Creation.

It takes twenty-eight years for the full equinox cycle to be completed. Hence, every twenty-eight years, on the fourth day of the week, special prayers of thanksgiving are recited in the synagogue after the morning service to commemorate the occasion. The Rabbis taught (ibid.): "He who sees the sun at its turning point, the moon in its power, the planets in their orbits, and the signs of the zodiac in their orderly progress, should say: 'Blessed be He who has wrought the work of Creation.'" In addition, verses 84:12, 72:5, 75:2, and 97:6 from the Book of Psalms as well as the entire Psalm 19, 121, and 148 are recited.

The first occasion to bless the sun in the twenty-first century occurs in the year 2009.

Birkat Ha-Chodesh

Literally, "blessing of the month [new moon]." Originally a private prayer recited daily by Rav, founder of the Babylonian academy of Sura in the third century (Berakhot 16b), the Birkat Ha-Chodesh was adopted by synagogues as a prayer to announce the coming of a hoped for, blessed new month. In this prayer, which is recited in the synagogue on the Sabbath preceding the beginning of the new Hebrew month, the name of the new month is announced as well as the day or days on which it will fall.

The one month of the year for which this special blessing is not recited is Tishrei. Three reasons have been given:

1. Tishrei needs no announcement because everyone is aware that the High Holidays are approaching.
2. Tishrei is already a blessed month since it contains so many holidays (Rosh Hashanah, Yom Kippur, and Sukkot).

3. Satan is always eager to voice ill feelings about the Children of Israel. What better time to do this than in a month with so many important holidays. By omitting the blessing for the new month of Tishrei, thus not announcing its coming, Satan will be misled and will not testify against Israel while the Jews are petitioning God for forgiveness in their synagogues.

Birkat Ha-Gomel

Literally, "Blessing of Him who bestows [blessings upon man]."

According to the Talmud (Berakhot 54b), four types of persons who have escaped harm should recite a prayer of thanksgiving: one who has safely completed a sea trip; one who has crossed the desert successfully; one who has recovered from a serious illness; and one who has been released from prison.

Although the benediction may be recited at any time, it is traditionally recited after one has received an aliyah and completed the recitation of the second Torah blessing.

In the Birkat Ha-Gomel, the individual gives thanks to God for "granting favors to people as unworthy as he." The congregation responds by saying, "May He who was good to you continue to bestow His goodness upon you." In Yiddish, the ceremony is referred to as benshn goimel.

The practice of giving thanks to God for having been delivered from danger has been traced to Temple times, when a person who survived a life-threatening experience would express thanksgiving by bringing a sacrificial offering. When the Temple was destroyed in the year 70 C.E. and individuals could no longer offer sacrifices, thanksgiving was expressed through prayer. Synagogue officials became obliged to call to the Torah (within three days of the event if possible) anyone who had emerged safely from a perilous predicament and wished to express thankfulness. (See *Shulchan Arukh*, Orach Cha'yim 219:9, and the comment of the Magen Avraham, note 10.)

Birkat Ha-Levanah

Literally, "blessing of the moon." Also referred to as *Kiddush Levanah*, "sanctification of the moon." This blessing, instituted in mishnaic times (100–200 C.E.), thanks God for the renewal of the moon each month, once its appearance has been confirmed by members of the court (*Beit Din*).

Observant Jews recite the blessing while standing outside the synagogue on a Saturday night after *havdalah*, sometime between the fourth and sixteenth of the month, when the new moon is visible.

Various versions of *Birkat Ha-Levanah* are mentioned in the Talmud and Tosefta, the briefest being, "Blessed is God, Creator of the world" and "Blessed is He who sanctifies the months." The minor talmudic tractate *Soferim* (2:1–2) discusses the subject in detail and suggests the way in which the individual is to conduct himself when blessing the new moon.

Birkat Ha-Mazon

Literally, "blessing of the food." This prayer of thanksgiving is recited after consuming a full meal, that is, one in which bread is consumed.

See Grace After Meals.

Birkat Kohanim

Literally, "blessing of the Priests." Popularly referred to as *dukhening*, this blessing is conferred upon the congregation by members of priestly families.

See Priestly Benediction.

Birth Control

The biblical precept to "be fruitful and multiply" (Genesis 1:28) has been interpreted by the Rabbis of the Talmud as applying to men only. It is they, not their wives, who are obligated to carry out this commandment. Despite the fact that the Talmud says that a man has complied with the law once he has fathered two children (*Yevamot* 61b), he may not employ birth control devices even after he has done so. Jewish law, as interpreted by all leading authorities, considered the prohibition against "destroying" or "wasting" seed (in Hebrew, *hashchatat zera*) to be an inviolable law in its own right, and the use of a condom by a male is prohibited, except in special cases where pregnancy may cause injury or death to the woman.

Opposition to Vasectomy

In Jewish law, it is the duty of the male to propagate the race. Since vasectomy prevents the man from fulfilling this duty, submitting to the procedure is considered a direct violation of biblical law.

Opposition to male sterilization is also based on Deuteronomy 23:2, which states: "He whose testes are crushed or whose male organ is cut off may not be admitted to the congregation of the Lord." Intentional castration was inflicted by heathens who were selected to high positions in families of the aristocracy. Jewish tradition considers castration—and by extension any action that permanently damages the male's power of propagation—an affront to human dignity and damaging to the status of Israel as a holy nation. Accordingly, the *Code of Jewish Law* (Shulchan Arukh, Even Ha-Ezer 5:1–2) condemns it.

In recent years, since the medical profession has learned to reverse vasectomies, some rabbinic authorities have permitted men to undergo the operation, especially when the health of the wife is a factor.

Female Birth Control

Although the primary obligation of building a family belongs to the male, the wife may nevertheless not use contraceptive devices even if she and her husband have already established a basic family, which according to the School of Hillel means having a boy and a girl, and according to the School of Shammai means having two boys (*Yevamot* 61b). The sole exception to this rule is the use of the birth control pill, which is discussed below.

The main argument advanced in support of this attitude is the talmudic reference to three kinds of woman who according to Rashi "may" use and, according to Rabbenu Tam, "should" use a contraceptive device called a *mokh*—a soft tuft of wool or cotton that is inserted into the vagina. The three categories are the minor, the pregnant woman, and the nursing mother. In each case, the reason for permitting (or requiring) the use of the *mokh* is to prevent a pregnancy that might be harmful to the health of the mother or the child. (The *mokh* is mentioned five times in the Talmud: *Yevamot* 12b and 100b, *Ketubbot* 39a, *Niddah* 45a, and *Nedarim* 35b.)

The Talmud (*Yevamot* 12b) offers reasons why these three categories of woman may use the *mokh*. A minor may otherwise become pregnant and, being so young, may die as a result. A pregnant woman may use the device because, it was believed, sperm may cause damage to the fetus. And, in the case of nursing women it was felt that should a woman become pregnant while still breastfeeding her first child, the child may have to be weaned prematurely, thus causing harm or even death to the infant.

Based on the fact that in the above cases the well-being of the mother and/or the child is the basis for permitting the use of a contraceptive device, rabbis in post-talmudic times permitted the use of contraceptives only by women in similar circumstances.

Changing View on Birth Control

In post-talmudic times, more and more rabbinic authorities began to regard sex as having a purpose beyond procreation, namely the sexual gratification of both male and female. Authorities such as the thirteenth-century Nachmanides of Spain and Isaiah da Trani of Italy, the sixteenth-century Solomon Luria of Poland, and the nineteenth-century Moses Sofer of Hungary were among those who propounded the idea that mutual pleasure and gratification from intercourse is a legitimate activity and that the *mokh* (and similar devices employed by a woman) may be used. They believed, however, that contraceptives must not interfere with sexual gratification and should allow for unrestricted penetration by the male. Although not all rabbinic authorities agree with these views, it is the dominant opinion.

The Birth Control Pill

The birth control pill for women that was introduced in the United States in the late 1950s is akin to an oral contraceptive mentioned in the Talmud (*Shabbat* 10a and *Yevamot* 65b) and later rabbinic literature. The Talmud refers to it as a "potion of sterility," "cup of sterility," and "potion of roots" (*kos ikrin* in Hebrew). Depending on the dosage of the concoction (its exact contents are not known), sterility could be prevented or induced. This potion was believed to be effective for both men and women, but the Talmud and the *Code of Jewish Law* (*Shulchan Arukh*, Even Ha-Ezer 5:12) permit its use only by the

woman so that she might make herself sterile—temporarily or permanently—depending upon her health requirements and physical condition.

Practically all rabbinic authorities permit women to use the birth control pill after the birth of a boy and a girl (or two boys) because, unlike other contraceptives, it does not in any way interfere with the sexual act. Being a nonuterine device, the pill satisfies critics who argue that Jewish law forbids use by the woman of any device that interferes with the passage of semen or that prevents the husband and wife from achieving direct and full physical contact during cohabitation.

Contemporary Views on Birth Control

Today, almost all rabbinic authorities permit the use of contraceptive devices by women—even if a family has not already been established—in cases where pregnancy may imperil the life of the mother or where it is certain that the newborn might be afflicted with a serious congenital disease or abnormality. More liberal authorities also generally take into account the mental attitude of the woman and the stress to which she might be subject if she were to become pregnant.

However, Rabbi I. Jakobovits (1921–1999), former Chief Rabbi of Great Britain, interpreted Jewish law as not sanctioning any form of contraception by the male.

See Bal Tashchit; Sex and Sexuality.

Birthdays

Based upon the verse in the Book of Ecclesiastes (7:1), "A good name is better than fragrant oil, and the day of death is better than the day of birth," Jewish tradition assigned little importance to birthdays. The time for celebration is after one has successfully completed his or her mission on earth.

The only biblical reference to a birthday is found in the Book of Genesis (40:20): "On the third day—his birthday—Pharaoh made a banquet for all the officials..." Not until talmudic times do we find another reference to individual birthdays of Jews. The talmudic tractate *Kiddushin* (72b) notes: "When Rabbi Akiba died, Rabbi Judah [the Prince] was born; when Rabbi Judah died, Rabba was born; when Rabba died, Rabbi Ashi was born." The inference is that since the death and birth occurred on the same day, "a righteous man does not depart this earth before another righteous man like him is created."

Contemporary Practice

In recent years, Reform and Conservative congregations have introduced the practice of awarding *aliyot* and reciting a special prayer for individuals who are celebrating special birthdays, such as the fiftieth, seventieth, or eightieth. It has been noted that some *chasidim* do celebrate birthdays, and that the birthday of the Lubavitcher *rebbe* is celebrated annually by his followers.

Yom huledet, the current Hebrew term for birthday, is the same expression as that used in the Book of Genesis, in reference to Pharaoh.

Birthright

In Jewish tradition, the concept of the firstborn son having special rights dates back to the relationship between Jacob and Esau. The Book of Genesis recounts that Esau, the elder son of Isaac and Rebecca, sold his birthright to his younger twin brother, Jacob, for a dish of lentil stew (Genesis 25:32–34).

In many cultures the firstborn son was given special privileges in connection with inheritance and general family status. In Judaism, he also had a special relationship to

God. Like the first fruits of the land and the firstlings of the herd and flock, the firstborn son of man was considered sacred, for he was the guarantor of the continuation of the family line.

The people of Israel as a group were called "God's firstborn" (Exodus 4:22), meaning that they occupied a special place in the divine scheme of things.

See Siyyum Bekhorim.

Bi'ur Chametz

Literally, "the removal and burning of the leaven [on the morning of the Passover *Seder*]."

See Bedikat Chametz.

Black Jews

See Falashas.

Blech

A Yiddish word meaning "tin." Although a fire may not be kindled on the Sabbath, tradition demands that to be true to the designation "Sabbath, a day of delight" some hot or warm food should be served. Because actual cooking on the Sabbath is forbidden, in observant homes one or more of the stove burners is kept at a moderate temperature—enough to keep food warm but not cook it—and the burner(s) is covered by a *blech*, a sheet of tin or aluminum. The heat is thus retained and distributed over a larger area than is covered by the burner itself, and pots of precooked food and preboiled water are set on it to be kept warm.

Blessings and Praises

In one sense, the English word "blessing" means an act or prayer of one who praises, glorifies, or offers thanks to God. The Middle English term "benediction" derives from the Latin *benedicto*, meaning "to speak well

[of God]." The Hebrew term for blessing, *berakhah*, comes from a root meaning "to bend the knee." The Book of Psalms (95:6–7) says: "Come, let us bow down and kneel, bend the knee before the Lord our Maker, for He is our God and we are His people...."

The Obligation to Give Thanks

A Jewish tradition established by the Rabbis as far back as talmudic times demands that "one not enjoy the pleasures of this world without first reciting a blessing" (*Berakhot* 35a). To this admonition, a caveat is added: "Any blessing that does not mention God's name is not a blessing" (ibid. 40b).

The Rabbis of the Talmud debated the number of blessings an individual should recite each day. The view of the second-century scholar, Rabbi Meir, a pupil of Rabbi Akiba, prevailed: "A person is obligated to recite one hundred blessings each day" (*Menachot* 43b).

This number was arrived at based on the biblical verse (Deuteronomy 10:12), "What does the Lord demand of you?" The Hebrew word for "what," pronounced *ma*, is spelled *mem, hei*. The word for one hundred, *mei'ah* is spelled *mem, alef, hei*. Rabbi Meir interpreted the word *mah* (what) as if it were spelled *mei'ah* (one hundred), assuming that the middle letter, *alef*, was there originally but had been purposely dropped to make the point that the Lord requires that we pronounce one hundred blessings each day.

The Nature of the Blessings

The largest percentage of the one hundred required blessings are included in the three daily *Shacharit* (morning), *Minchah* (afternoon), and *Ma'ariv* (evening) prayer services: The *Eighteen Benedictions* (*Shemoneh Esrei*), which are recited at each service comprise fifty-four of the daily requirement. The remaining forty-six blessings are expressions of gratitude for the foods people eat, and for the various religious obligations that they fulfill during the course of their lives—such as donning a *tallit* (prayershawl) and *tefillin* (phylacteries), lighting candles to welcome the Sabbath and holidays, building a *sukkah* and "dwelling" in it, and taking up the *etrog* (citron) and *lulav* (palm branch).

In addition to the blessings that are recited on a regular basis, the Rabbis prescribed blessings for special moments and experiences in life. These include returning safely from a perilous journey, seeing trees blossoming in springtime, meeting a friend after a long absence, viewing the majestic ocean, experiencing lightning and thunder, seeing a rainbow in the sky or strange creatures on earth. Hardly any dramatic event that one might experience in life has been overlooked, extending even to life's tragedies, when one is expected to express continued belief in God and His administration of justice.

Activities Without Blessings

Activities or procedures that are pure custom and are not mandated by the Bible, the Scribes, or the Rabbis of the talmudic and post-talmudic period do not require that a blessing be recited when they are carried out. This, for example, is the reason why one does not recite a blessing when putting on a *kippah* or any other headcovering. In his *Mishneh Torah*, Hilkhot Chanukkah 3:7, Maimonides says: *ein mevarkhin al ha-minhag*, "one does not say a blessing when carrying out a custom."

One of the questions that some authorities wrestled with in post-talmudic times was why the Rabbis of the Talmud ordered blessings for some Torah *mitzvot* ("commandments") but not others. No benedictions were ordered, for example, for such important commandments as visiting the sick, comforting mourners, and attending a funeral. Addressing this question in one of his responsa, the twelfth-century Spanish authority Rabbi Joseph ibn Plat said that one rule cannot explain every such case, but generally no benediction is recited when the performance of the *mitzvah* depends upon a second person. When one gives charity to an individual, the charity must be accepted by another person. Likewise, no blessing is recited if the *mitzvah* comes about because a second person has sinned. Thus, if one recovers stolen goods and restores it to its owner (a commendable act), a blessing is not recited.

The Sanctification Phrase

As a general rule, only such blessings that are recited before an activity that is biblically mandated must include the phrase *asher kideshanu be-mitzvotav*, "Who has sanctified us by His commandments." Thus, for example, when one affixes a *mezuzah* to a doorpost, as commanded in the Bible (Deuteronomy 6:9), the prayer recited is "Blessed art thou, O Lord our God, Who has sanctified us by His commandments and commanded us to affix a *mezuzah*." When one eats *matzah*, he likewise is observing a biblical commandment (Deuteronomy 16:3), and thus the blessing recited over the *matzah* includes the sanctification phrase.

On the other hand, one who recites the *Hamotzi* blessing before eating a piece of bread ("Blessed art thou, O Lord our God, Who brings forth bread from the earth") omits *asher kideshanu be-mitzvotav* because there is no biblical commandment to eat bread. The blessing over bread was introduced by the Rabbis of the Talmud; it does not derive from the Bible.

Notable exceptions to the rule are the

blessings recited when kindling the Sabbath and Chanukkah candles. In both instances the sanctification phrase is part of the prayer despite the fact that the kindling of candles on these occasions is not biblically mandated. The Bible requires that the Sabbath be observed but not that candles be lighted. There is no reference at all to Chanukkah in the Bible because it is of postbiblical origin. However, to the early Scribes of the pre-talmudic period and to the Rabbis of the Talmud, the Sabbath represented the essence of Judaism, and Chanukkah represented a victory that saved Judaism from extinction. The candle-lighting prayer for each occasion was therefore deemed worthy of containing the words *asher kideshanu be-mitzvotav.*

Blessing Precedes Activity

Generally speaking, when a blessing is required, it is to be pronounced before the activity is performed. There are exceptions, however, such as when one lights the Sabbath candles. The blessing is recited after the candles are lighted because once the candlelighting blessing has been recited, the Sabbath has officially begun. To light the candles after the blessing has been pronounced would be in violation of the Sabbath law that prohibits the lighting of a fire on the Sabbath.

Jewish law also demands that after a blessing is recited, the activity take place immediately. Thus, for example, when a person says the prayer before donning a *tallit,* he may not pause to carry on a conversation before actually putting on the *tallit.* Or, when a person recites a prayer over food, he or she must taste the food immediately thereafter, without interruption. The act of interruption is known as *hafsakah* in Hebrew (*Shulchan Arukh, Orach Cha'yim* 162).

Blessings and Nonkosher Food

Recognizing that there are emergency situations—times of war, when stranded in a strange city, and the like—when one has no choice but to eat forbidden food, authorities have addressed the question of whether it is proper to recite a blessing before eating a meal that is not strictly kosher. Maimonides (1135–1204) wrote that one should not recite a blessing before or after he has eaten forbidden food. However, his critic, the French talmudist Abraham ben David of Posquières (1120–1198), also known as the Ravad, disagreed. In the Ravad's view a blessing should be recited before eating all food, kosher or nonkosher. He does, however, register his disapproval of eating forbidden food by stating that when two other persons are partaking of the same nonkosher meal, the introductory verses of the *Grace After Meals* should not be recited.

Most contemporary authorities are of the opinion that when one recites the blessing over bread at the beginning of a nonkosher meal, he is in essence condoning the eating of nonkosher food. The blessing, it is believed, should therefore not be said.

See Barukh She-petarani; Berakhah Le-Vatalah; Birkat Ha-Gomel; Prayer; She-heche'yanu.

Blood

Throughout the Bible, blood is spoken of as the essence of life. Therefore, the consumption of blood is strictly forbidden. The Book of Deuteronomy says (12:23ff.), "But make sure that you do not partake of the blood, for the blood is the life, and you must not consume the life with the flesh. You must not partake of it; you must pour it out on the ground like water."

The Book of Leviticus (17:11–12) states the

penalty for violating the ban on the consumption of blood: "If anyone of the House of Israel, or of the strangers who live among them, partakes of blood, I will set My face against the person . . . I will cut him off from his kin. For the life of the flesh is in the blood..."

The prohibition against the consumption of blood was taken very seriously in Jewish tradition, as reflected in the laws of *kashrut*, which require that the maximum amount of blood be removed from food before cooking it. A distinction was made, however, between the oral consumption of blood and the intravenous consumption of blood.

Based upon the text in Leviticus (19:16), "Do not stand aside while the blood of your neighbor is being shed," rabbinic authorities have ruled that one should not let a neighbor die if one's own blood can save him. Thus, the taking in of blood orally is prohibited, but the administering of blood intravenously is not.

Rabbi Moshe Feinstein (*Igrot Moshe*, Choshen Mishpat 103) went even further, ruling in one of his responsa that it is permissible to sell blood to be used for transfusion, especially if one is in dire financial need. The pleasure of earning the money, he argues, far outweighs the pain of a pinprick to the skin.

Viewing blood as the essence of life is reflected in the Jewish ban on embalming. Jewish law regards the blood as part of the body, and as such it may not be separated from the deceased prior to burial, unless government requirement demands it.

Blood Libels

The charge that Jews murder Christian children in order to use their blood for the baking of *matzah* for Passover is centuries old. The first such blood libel dates back to the first century C.E., when the Alexandrian writer and orator Apion traveled and lectured widely throughout Egypt, making malicious charges against Jews. The Jewish historian Flavius Josephus answered Apion's baseless claims in a treatise entitled *Contra Apionem* (*Against Apion*).

Through the centuries, charges of the ritual use of Christian blood by Jews surfaced mainly at Eastertime, which falls close to Passover, when Jews eat *matzah*. In fact, the charge that Christian blood—or any blood, for that matter—is used in the preparation of *matzah* is without foundation, since *matzah* must be made of flour and water only.

In the Middle Ages, blood libels were hurled at Jews with regularity. In 1144, in Norwich, England, a charge was made in connection with the disappearance of a Christian child named William. In 1171, a similar charge was leveled in Bloise, France. Accusations became increasingly frequent. Two of the more noteworthy are the cases of Hugh of Lincoln (1255) and Simon of Trent (1475).

So widespread was the charge that Jews used Christian blood on Passover that Rabbi David Halevi (1586–1667) noted in his commentary on the *Code of Jewish Law* (*Shulchan Arukh*, Orach Cha'yim 472:11) that although it is preferable to use red wine for the Passover *Seder*, "nowadays we do not use red wine because of false accusations [that it contains Christian blood]."

Over the centuries, Christian clergy at the highest level condemned blood libels: in 1272, Pope Gregory X; in 1758, Cardinal Lorenzo Ganganelli, who later became Pope Clement XIV; and, in 1935, Pope Pius XI. These condemnations notwithstanding, the blood libels continued, among the most notorious being the Damascus Affair (1840) and Beilis Trial in Kiev (1913).

In Karel Capek's *President Masaryk Tells His Story*, Thomas Masaryk (1850–1937), the liberal first president of Czechoslovakia, is quoted as saying:

> Mother would forbid us to go near the Lechners because, as she said, Jews were using the blood of Christian children.... The superstition of Christian blood being used for Passover cakes has become so much a part and parcel of my existence that whenever I chanced to come near a Jew—I wouldn't do it on purpose—I would look at his fingers to see if blood was there.

Ahad Ha-Am (18561927), one of the greatest of all modern Jewish writers, placed the blood libel accusations in the following perspective:

> This [blood libel] accusation is the solitary case in which the general acceptance of an idea about ourselves does not make us doubt whether all the world can be wrong, and we right, because it is based on an absolute lie. Every Jew who has been brought up among Jews knows as an indisputable fact that throughout the length and breadth of Jewry there is not a single individual who drinks human blood for religious purposes.... "But," you ask, "is it possible that everybody can be wrong and the Jews right?" Yes, it is possible: the blood accusation proves it possible.

Blood libel accusations have persisted well into the twentieth century. In 1928, in Messina, New York, a Christian girl disappeared on the eve of Yom Kippur. Ancient blood ritual rumors began to surface, and the local rabbi was accused of kidnapping the child. Soon thereafter, the girl turned up unharmed and the embarrassed local officials apologized publicly.

As late as 1995, front-page news was made when Scotland Yard was called upon to investigate the publication and distribution to twenty London nursery schools of a leaflet headlined "Avoid Orthodox Jews; Child Ritual Murder Outbreak Is Feared." The leaflet featured an illustration showing an anti-Semitic caricature of an Orthodox Jew and of a group of bearded Jews sucking blood from a child—all in the form of a "warning" to non-Jewish parents.

See Anti-Semitism.

Brazen Serpents

When the trek of the Israelites through the wilderness became difficult and burdensome, they began to cry out against God and Moses. "Why did you make us leave Egypt to die in the wilderness? There is no bread and no water, and we are tired of this miserable food."

When God heard these complaints, he sent fiery serpents among the people. "And they bit the people and many of the Israelites died." The people then turned to Moses, apologized for speaking against him and God, and pleaded that he intercede with God to get rid of the serpents. Moses complied, and God ordered that Moses mount a serpent figure on a pole. Moses then fashioned one out of copper, mounted it on a standard, and anyone who was bitten by a serpent could look at the copper (brazen) figure and be healed (Numbers 21:4–9).

In later centuries, brazen serpents mounted on poles were idolized by Jews. In the eighth century B.C.E., Hezekiah, the thirteenth king of Judah, destroyed these idols (II Kings 18:4).

It is interesting to note that the symbol worn by medical healers is the caduceus, a winged staff with a snake coiled around it.

Bread

In Jewish tradition, the two most important foods are bread and wine, for no Sabbath, holiday, or special party meal (*se'udah*) is considered complete without them. Their distinction has been linked to Scripture, which speaks of bread as the food that sustains life and wine as the food that adds joy to life (Psalms 104:14–15).

Special Significance

The importance of bread is first indicated in the Book of Deuteronomy (8:8), where this food—or, more specifically, wheat from which most bread is made—is mentioned before all other foods. Because of this primary status, when the blessing over bread (*Hamotzi*) is recited at the beginning of a meal, it is said to cover all foods to be eaten during the course of the meal. Individual blessings need not be recited over each specific food eaten, unless a particular food is not considered an integral part of the meal—fruit, for example.

So highly regarded is bread in the Jewish tradition that the Talmud makes this statement: "Four things have been said in connection with bread: (1) Raw meat should not be placed on it [the meat might spoil the bread]; (2) a full cup [of wine] should not be passed over it [some wine might spill on the bread]; (3) it should not be thrown around; and (4) it should not be used as a prop for a dish (*Berakhot* 50b).

Jewish law requires that hands be ritually washed (with a vessel) before eating a regular meal, that is, a meal at which bread is served. One is not required to wash before eating a meal at which no bread is served.

One reason for the washing of the hands is purely mundane: to cleanse them before eating. The second and more important reason is to render the hands ritually clean before touching bread, which is a holy object.

Breaking Bread

In post-Temple times (after 70 C.E.), it became customary for the head of the household to break off pieces of bread after the *Hamotzi* blessing was recited and to pass the bread to those at the table. The custom is described in the Talmud: Rabbi Abbahu, a third-century Palestinian scholar, made a dinner for Rabbi Ze'eira, the most distinguished rabbinic authority in Palestine. Abbahu said to Ze'eira when they sat down to eat, "Will your honor please commence [meaning 'break bread'] for us?" Ze'eira replied, "Doesn't your honor accept the ruling of Rabbi Yochanan that the host should break bread?" So Rabbi Abbahu broke the bread for those assembled at the dinner (*Berakhot* 46a).

The *Code of Jewish Law* (*Shulchan Arukh*, Orach Cha'yim 167:1) suggests that the piece of bread (*challah*) that is first tasted after the *Hamotzi* benediction is pronounced should include part of the crust. This, the most baked part of the bread, is a reminder of the meal-offering that was burned on the Temple altar. Salt is sprinkled on the bread as an additional reminder that in Temple times all sacrifices were treated with salt: *Al kol korbankha takriv melach*, "On all your [meal] offerings shall you sprinkle salt" (Leviticus 2:13).

Rabbi Meir Ha-Kohen, in his commentary *Hagahot Maimuniyyot* (chapter 7 in Maimonides' *Hilkhot Berakhot*), records the view of his teacher, Rabbi Meir of Rothenburg (thirteenth century). Noting that the French custom was to cut the bread on the bottom and break it upward, while the German practice was to cut the bread on top and break it downward, Meir of Rothenburg avoided slighting either group by cutting the loaf part way through, top and bottom, and then breaking off pieces.

In many homes today, particularly on the

Sabbath, after cutting the loaf of bread part way through, the head of the household breaks off pieces of bread with the hard crust intact and passes a piece to each family member. Ashkenazim often score the loaf top and bottom before breaking off pieces for distribution to family members (Orach Cha'yim 158:1, Be'er Hetev commentary).

Before reciting *Grace After Meals*, in some traditional homes today it is customary to leave bread on the table. Although the reasoning is uncertain, the practice is said to be based on the comment of Rabbi Elazar (*Sanhedrin* 92a), "He who does not leave bread on the table at the end of a meal will never be blessed."

See Challah; Hamotzi; Salt.

Breastbeating

The ancient practice of beating one's breast when reciting certain prayers of penitence has become common among Jews.

Particularly during the High Holidays, but throughout the year as well, when the words "we have sinned" or "we have transgressed" are uttered during prayer, the words are accompanied by beating the left breast (over the heart) with the right hand. The breastbeating is not intended to induce pain but to remind one of the words being uttered and to encourage sincere penitence.

The two prayers most commonly associated with breastbeating are the *Al Cheit* ("For the Sin") and the *Ashamnu* ("We Have Sinned").

See Prayer.

Brit

This Hebrew word meaning "covenant" is an abbreviated form of the term *brit milah*, "Covenant of Circumcision."

See Circumcision.

Burial

Jewish law demands that the deceased be buried promptly, within twenty-four hours, unless there are extenuating circumstances, such as the need to await the arrival of close relatives from distant places (*Shulchan Arukh*, Yoreh Dei'ah 357:1). The basis for the prompt burial practice is a passage from the Book of Deuteronomy (21:23):

> You must not permit his corpse to remain impaled on the stake overnight; you must bury him the same day. For an impaled body is an affront to God; you shall not defile the land that the Lord your God is giving you to possess.

It was considered an affront to God to allow a human being, created in His image, to remain exposed to the mercy of the elements and not be accorded a dignified, speedy burial. Although the passage refers to burial of a criminal who had been executed by order of the court, prompt burial was extended to include all deceased.

Some scholars have pointed out that it was once widely believed that for as long as the dead is unburied the ghost (spirit) of the deceased can be exceedingly harmful to mourners, especially to those who were disrespectful to the deceased. It therefore became common practice to bury the dead promptly.

Permissible Delay

When it is important to await the arrival of very close relatives, when a government regulation so dictates, or when a strike occurs and burials cannot take place, funerals may be delayed—but never for more than three days. Leaving the body unburied for a longer time dishonors the dead, referred to in Hebrew as *nivul ha-met* (*Shulchan Arukh*, Yoreh Dei'ah 357:1).

If extenuating circumstances demand a delay longer than three days, the procedure is to hold the chapel service and then to take the body to the cemetery, where it is stored in a vault until burial can take place. In such an instance, the body is embalmed to prevent early decay and malodor.

Time of Day

Although nighttime burials are not in any way prohibited by Jewish law, they never became the norm. This is based on the Deuteronomic law (21:23) that states, "You must bury him [on] the same *day*." The Rabbis took the word "day" literally and encouraged daytime funerals.

In medieval times burials were held after dark, but the practice was later rejected, mainly owing to a belief in demonology shared by many Rabbis of the Talmud. According to the talmudic scholar Rabbi Yochanan, "One may not greet anyone at night [when he cannot be certain that he is a fellow human being] for fear he may be a demon" (*Sanhedrin* 44a). The tractate *Chagigah* (3b) says, "Our Rabbis taught: 'He who goes out alone at night or spends the night in a cemetery is a fool [because demons are active at night].'"

That burials were occasionally held at night is also evident from the comment of Rabbi Moses Isserles in his Notes to the sixteenth-century *Code of Jewish Law*: "There are some who say that if you bury the dead at night, you may not recite the *Kaddish* or *Tziduk Ha-Din* prayers" (*Shulchan Arukh*, Yoreh Dei'ah 401:6). Other authorities, such as Yekutiel Greenwald, in his *Akh le-Tzara*, have added that one may also not deliver a eulogy at night.

Modern biblical scholars, such as Dr. Julian Morgenstern, clearly connect the avoidance of nighttime funerals to demonology. In his *Rites of Birth, Marriage, and Death Among the Semites*, Morgenstern writes: "Evil spirits are generally thought by the Semites, ancient and modern, to be dangerous at night. With the rising of the sun, their power wanes or departs completely."

While nighttime funerals are generally avoided today, there are exceptions. In the Mea She'arim section of Jerusalem, funerals are sometimes held after dark.

Burial in the Earth

In the Book of Genesis (3:19) God addresses Adam, saying, "For dust thou art and unto dust shalt thou return." Based on this statement, Jewish law demands that the dead be buried in the ground, covered by earth. Cremation is not sanctioned under Jewish law because the body must be returned to the earth in the form in which it existed in life.

Above-ground burial is also prohibited in Jewish law.

Although the Rabbis of the Talmud were aware that Abraham was buried in Me'arat Ha-Makhpelah (Genesis 23:9), a cave located in Hebron, they nonetheless ruled that it is a violation of Jewish law (*Shulchan Arukh*, Yoreh Dei'ah 362:1 and *Eruvin* 53a) for a corpse to be buried in hewn rock, which prevents it from making direct contact with the earth. It is known that the prominent rabbinic authority Isaac Elchanan Spektor (1817–1896) permitted burial in a mausoleum, but only as a temporary measure, until arrangements could be made for permanent burial in the ground.

The stone structures that are built over graves in Jewish cemeteries are not usually mausoleums in the accepted sense of the word. Most often these are erected after the deceased has already been buried in the earth. In Jewish law, burial in mausoleums is permitted only when a coffin placed in it is covered by earth.

Burial of Holy Objects

As an expression of respect and adoration, religious articles such as worn-out Torah scrolls and sacred printed books are to be discarded ceremoniously. They are brought to the cemetery for burial in a grave alongside a pious individual (*Shulchan Arukh*, Yoreh Dei'ah 282:10 and *Megillah* 26b).

After the Burial

As mourners leave the gravesite after a burial, it has been customary for some to pick up a clod of grass and throw it backward over their shoulder. Justification for this custom is associated with the verse in the Book of Psalms (72:16) which ends with the words, "And let men sprout up in towns like country grass," an illusion to the hoped-for resurrection of the dead.

See Death; Funeral Practices.

Burial Society

First established in the Middle Ages, the Burial Society is possibly the most prestigious organization in Jewish life. It is also perhaps the least known, the least publicized, and surely the least glamorous. The Society consists of Jewish volunteers—members of a particular synagogue or members of the community at large—who prepare the dead for burial and sometimes even manage the administration of the local cemetery. Those who volunteer for this service are regarded as among the most selfless, most dedicated people in the Jewish fold.

Whereas Ashkenazim call the Burial Society by the Hebrew name *chevrah kaddishah*, meaning "Holy Society," Sephardim use a variety of terms that are indicative of the noble nature of the work to which the men and women of the group have dedicated themselves. Syrian Jews call the *chevrah kaddishah* by the name *chevrah rodfei tzedek*, "Society of Pursuers of Justice." The Spanish-Portuguese community calls the group *hebrah chased va-emet* [sic], "Society of Lovingkindness and Truth." Moroccans call it by a variety of names, including *chevrat gomlei chasadim*, "Society of Providers of Lovingkindness," *chevrat chesed ve-emet*, and *chevrat Rabbi Shimon bar Yocha'i*, "Society of Rabbi Shimon bar Yocha'i." Rabbi Shimon, the legendary charismatic mystic, is buried atop Mount Meron in northern Israel. Each year on Lag Ba-Omer, which is the anniversary of Rabbi Shimon's death, thousands of his followers make a pilgrimage to Mount Meron.

The Chevrah Kaddishah Today

When Jewish communities were close-knit, each town or village and often each individual synagogue had its own Burial Society. Although the Jewish community is no longer as cohesive as it once was, the *chevrah kaddishah* still functions, either under the aegis of one or more of the synagogues in a community or under the auspices of a funeral parlor. After the funeral director has arranged for the attending physician to certify a death, and after the body has been transported to the chapel, the Burial Society is called in by the rabbi or the funeral director to attend to the corpse and prepare it for burial.

Guarding the Deceased

As a way of showing respect for the deceased, Jewish tradition demands that between the time of death and burial the body be guarded at all times. This is a function of the *chevrah kaddishah*. One of its members, called a *shomer*, meaning "watchman" (feminine, *shomeret*), remains on duty and recites Psalm 23, Psalm 91, or selected verses from Psalm 119. The verses from Psalm 119 are selected so that when the first letter of each verse is put side by side, they spell out the name of the deceased. (See *Moed Katan* 25a and Yoreh Dei'ah 373:5.)

Holy Land Earth

Because earth from the Land of Israel is considered to have atoning powers (*Ketubbot* 111a), burial societies in many communities adopted the custom of placing a bag of earth from Israel under the head of the deceased, or of sprinkling some of the earth over the body. Both procedures are intended to symbolize that regardless of where one lives or dies, the individual remains connected to the Land of Israel.

Two Guiding Principles

The two guiding principles that govern the activities of the Burial Societies are the same as those that govern all Jewish death and mourning rites. First, that proper respect and reverence be shown the dead, referred to in the Talmud as *yekarah de-shichvah*. And, second, that due respect be accorded the bereaved, referred to in the Talmud as *yekarah de-chayei* (*Sanhedrin* 46b and 47a). These terms are Aramaic, which was the vernacular of the Jews in the talmudic and post-talmudic periods. The Hebrew term for the Aramaic *yekarah de-shichvah* is *kevod ha-met* ("honor of the dead"); and for *yekarah de-chayei*, *kevod he-chai* ("honor of the living").

The primary function of the *chevrah kaddishah* is to perform the ritual purification known as *tohorah*, which involves cleansing the body and dressing it in shrouds.

See Purity and Impurity; Shrouds.

Calendar

The noted philosopher and rabbi Samson Raphael Hirsch (1808–1888) wrote (*Judaism Eternal*, 1959): "The catechism of the Jew consists of his calendar. On the pinions of time which bear us through life, God has inscribed the eternal words of His soul-inspiring doctrine, making days and weeks, months and years the heralds to proclaim His truths."

Story of the Calendar

Until the year 359 C.E., the arrival of the New Moon (Rosh Chodesh, the beginning of the Hebrew month) was announced each month by the *Sanhedrin* (Supreme Court). The proclamation was based on the testimony of two eyewitnesses who appeared before the *Sanhedrin* and were questioned about the crescent shape of the moon that they reported having observed. If the *Sanhedrin* was satisfied with the integrity of the witnesses and their testimony, it then checked that testimony against its own secret calculations, which had been worked out in advance using mathematical and astrological methodology. The secret was under the control of a special Calendar Council called *Sod Ha-Ibur* (literally, "secret of the calendar intercalation [inserting a day or month into the calendar]"). This group decided when a leap year would occur and whether the months Cheshvan and Kislev should have twenty-nine or thirty days.

If everything harmonized, the *Sanhedrin* would transmit a torch signal from one mountaintop to the next, thereby advising each community that the new moon had officially been sighted. At a later date, the *Sanhedrin* decided to relay the information by messenger rather than by torch signal. This new system was instituted because dissidents such as the Samaritans, who did not accept the authority of the *Sanhedrin*, were known to send up false flares in order to obscure the message being transmitted.

When the Romans, who ruled Palestine, curtailed some of the privileges that the *Sanhedrin*, its president, Patriarch Hillel II, and his court had enjoyed for many years, and the situation became generally grave for the Jewish community, Hillel II decided to publish a calendar. The official day or days marking the beginning of the new month (Rosh Chodesh) and the date of each of the Jewish holidays were thereby fixed, and the testimony of witnesses was no longer required.

The establishment of a process of intercalating, or adjusting the calendar by adding extra days or months, was necessary in order to harmonize the Jewish calendar with the Civil (Gregorian) calendar. The Jewish calendar is a lunar calendar with 354 days in one year, whereas the Civil calendar is a solar calendar with roughly 365 days in one year—an eleven-day discrepancy.

Synchronizing the Calendar

The Calendar Council of the *Sanhedrin* was concerned with synchronizing the Jewish calendar with the Civil calendar for the simple reason that the Jewish holidays were based on the seasons of the year and had to be observed at their "appointed times," as specified in the Bible. Passover, for example, had to be celebrated in the spring. If adjustments to the calendar were not made, the biblical command to observe the holiday at that time of year would be violated, for if allowed to fall behind by eleven days each year, Passover would eventually be observed in the winter months.

The annual eleven-day discrepancy between the Jewish and Civil calendars was reconciled by adding an extra month (Adar II) every two or three years (seven times in nineteen years). In addition, each year one day was added or subtracted from the months Cheshvan and Kislev, as needed. These were the "swing" months: in some years they would have twenty-nine days, in some years thirty days.

The following months in the Jewish calendar always have twenty-nine days: Iyyar, Tammuz, Elul, Tevet, and Adar. The following months always have thirty days: Nissan, Sivan, Av, Tishrei, and Shevat.

In a common (nonleap) year, Adar has twenty-nine days; in a leap year, Adar I has thirty days and Adar II has twenty-nine days.

Delineating the Days

In the Civil calendar, a new day begins at midnight and extends for twenty-four hours. In the Jewish calendar, the day begins and ends at sunset. Therefore, according to the Jewish calendar a person born at nine P.M. on Thursday night, January 1, 1981, is considered to have been born on Friday, January 2. His Jewish birthday is Friday, 26 Tevet 5741, which corresponds to January 2, 1981. By the same token, according to the Jewish calendar, one who died on Thursday night, January 1, 1981, is considered to have died on Friday, 26 Tevet 5741. In future years the *yahrzeit* (anniversary of death) of that person must always be observed on the Jewish date: 26 Tevet.

Months of the Jewish Year

Tishrei—*Also spelled* Tishri. The seventh month of the Jewish year counting from Nissan. Coming at the end of summer, almost always in September and occasionally in October, it was a time in ancient Palestine when the crops were being harvested. Farmers now had more leisure and this was an ideal moment to celebrate the High Holidays—Rosh Hashanah and Yom Kippur.

Although this was ample reason for Tishrei to be considered the most important—and therefore the first—month of the year, the Bible considers Nissan to be first, because it is the month in which the Israelites were freed from bondage in Egypt.

The zodiacal sign of Tishrei is Libra.

Cheshvan—The eighth month of the Jewish year counting from Nissan, or the second month counting from Tishrei, the original form of which is Mar-Cheshvan, is called Bul in I Kings (6:38). Cheshvan is a short form of Mar-Cheshvan.

Mar-Cheshvan, meaning "bitter [*mar*] Cheshvan," has been interpreted as being so named because in stark contrast to the preceding month, Tishrei, this month contains no holidays and is therefore sad (bitter).

Cheshvan usually begins at the end of October. Its zodiacal sign is Scorpio.

Kislev—The ninth month of the Jewish year counting from Nissan, or the third month counting from Tishrei. The festival of Chanukkah is celebrated during Kislev, beginning with the twenty-fifth day of the month. Kislev generally falls in the month of December (and usually begins in mid-November). Its zodiacal sign is Sagittarius.

Tevet—The tenth month of the Jewish year counting from Nissan, or the fourth month counting from Tishrei. According to tradition, it was on the tenth day of Tevet that the siege of Jerusalem by the Babylonians was begun, culminating in the destruction of the First Temple in 586 B.C.E.

Tevet usually begins in the second half of December or the beginning of January. Its zodiacal sign is Capricorn.

Shevat—The eleventh month of the Jewish year counting from Nissan, and the fifth month counting from Tishrei. Falling in January/February, Shevat always has thirty days. Its zodiacal sign is Aquarius. The minor holiday called Chamishah Asar Bi-Shevat (Tu Bi-Shevat) is celebrated on the fifteenth day of the month, particularly in Israel, when school children plant trees.

Adar—The last (twelfth) month of the year counting from Nissan, and the sixth counting from Tishrei. In order to harmonize the solar-centered secular calendar with the lunar-based Jewish calendar (the former having 365 days and the latter 354 days), there will be seven leap years in every cycle of nineteen years. The added month is called Adar Sheini (Adar II), which means "second Adar."

Adar is the month in which Purim falls, and because Purim is such a joyous occasion, the Rabbis said (*Ta'anit* 29a–b), "When Adar enters, joy should be increased." Thus, Adar came to be considered a good-luck month.

Adar usually falls in the month of March. Its zodiacal sign is Pisces.

Adar Sheini—*See* Adar.

Nissan—Despite the fact that Rosh Hashanah is referred to as New Year's Day and occurs at the beginning of the month of Tishrei, the Bible (Exodus 12:2) speaks of Nissan as the first month of the year because it is during this month that the Exodus from Egypt took place. Nissan is the time of year when the earth reawakens and begins a new cycle of growth.

Nissan usually begins in late March or early April. Its zodiacal sign is Aries (ram). Aries is a reminder of the *Akeidah* and represents the sacrificial animal Abraham found to be sacrificed in place of Isaac. The lamb is a reminder of the paschal lamb, which the Rabbis associated with the month of Nissan.

Iyyar—The second month of the Jewish year counting from Nissan, or the eighth month counting from Tishrei. Iyyar begins in April or May. Its zodiacal sign is Taurus, meaning "ox" in Latin. Lag Ba-Omer is celebrated during the month of Iyyar.

Sivan—The third month of the Jewish year counting from Nissan, or the ninth month counting from Tishrei. Sivan, the month in which the holiday of Shavuot is celebrated, always has thirty days. Sivan usually begins in the month of June. Its zodiacal sign is Gemini.

Tammuz—The fourth month of the Jewish year counting from Nissan, or the tenth month counting from Tishrei. It is the month in which the "Three Weeks" mourning period for the destruction of the Jerusalem Temples is observed. Weddings are traditionally not held from the seventeenth of Tammuz until Tishah B'Av. Tammuz begins in late June or early July. Its zodiacal sign is Cancer.

Av—The fifth month of the Jewish year counting from Nissan, or the eleventh month counting from Tishrei. Av falls in late July or early August. Its zodiacal sign is Leo.

Av is the saddest month in the year, for it was on the ninth day of this month that both the First and Second Temples were destroyed. The ninth of Av (Tishah B'Av) is a fast day, second in importance only to Yom Kippur.

In ancient times, the fifteenth day of Av was celebrated as a minor festival. It was on that date when marriages between persons of different tribes was permitted, and it became customary for marriageable girls to parade themselves before prospective husbands. The Mishnah (*Ta'anit* 4:1; 26b) records Rabbi Shimon ben Gamaliel's description of that day:

> Never were there festive days in Israel greater than the fifteenth of Av and the Day of Atonement. On these days the daughters of Jerusalemites used to go out in borrowed white garments so as to avoid putting to shame those who had no garments of their own.... They danced in the vineyards, exclaiming at the same time, "Young man, lift up your eyes and see what you are choosing for yourself. Do not look for beauty, but set your eyes on good family..."

One of the prophetic portions (*haftarot*) read in the synagogue during the month of Av begins with the words *nachamu, nachamu ami*, "Comfort, O comfort My people" (Isaiah 40). The Hebrew name Menachem is a form of the word *nachamu*; hence, boys born on or about the Sabbath on which this prophetic portion is read are sometimes called Menachem, as was Menachem Begin.

Elul—The sixth month of the Jewish year counting from Nissan, or the twelfth month counting from Tishrei. Elul, the month before Rosh Hashanah, begins in late August. Its zodiacal sign is Virgo.

During the month of Elul, it is customary for individuals to visit family graves (*kever avot*). *Chasidim* in particular also visit the graves of illustrious leaders.

Calculating the Hebrew Year

Sometime during the second century C.E., the principal of the academy in Sepphoris (Tzipori in Hebrew), Yosei ben Chalafta, wrote a book entitled *Seder Olam* ("The Chro-

nology of the World"). In it he traces the generations of mankind from Adam to Hadrian, the Roman ruler of Palestine from 117 to 138. About fifty years earlier, in the year 69 or 70—the exact year is in dispute—the Romans destroyed the Temple.

Considering all the information provided in the Bible, Yosei arrived at the following chronology from Creation onward:

- Adam was created in the year 1 and lived 930 years.
- Noah was born 126 years later, in the year 1056.
- Abraham was born 892 years after Noah, corresponding to the year 1949 after Creation.
- Isaac was born when Abraham was 100 years old.
- 190 years elapsed from the birth of Isaac to the time Jacob and his sons moved to Egypt, which is the year 2239.
- 210 years elapsed from the time Joseph was enslaved in Egypt to the Exodus of the Israelites from Egypt, which is the year 2449.
- 480 years later, in 2929, Solomon dedicated the First Temple.
- Solomon's Temple existed for 410 years before it was destroyed, in 3339, by the Babylonian conqueror Nebukhadnezzar, who sent the Jews into exile.
- Jews remained in Babylonian exile for seventy years. They were allowed to return to Palestine in 3409, at which time they erected the Second Temple.
- 420 years later, the Second Temple was destroyed by the Romans. This was the year 69 C.E. according to Yosei—3,829 years after Creation.

Subtracting 69 from 3,829 leaves 3,760, which corresponded to the year 1 in the civil calendar. To determine the current Hebrew calendar year, one must add the total number of years that have passed since the year 1. For example, the year 2000 in the civil calendar added to 3,760 will yield the equivalent Hebrew calendar year (5760).

Some of Yosei ben Chalafta's calculations defy confirmation. They have, however, been validated by tradition, and Jews the world over accept them.

See Zodiac.

Candles and Candlelighting

In ancient times, Jews, like their neighbors, believed in the existence of evil spirits that were intent on harming humans. Many antidotes were used to neutralize those destructive forces, foremost among them being light and fire, for the evil spirits thrived only in the dark.

As far back as the first century, lighting torches and candles was a popular way of fending off demons. Carrying lighted torches at Jewish weddings was a common practice in the early centuries because, as the Talmud suggests (*Berakhot* 54b), a bride and groom are prone to attack by demons anxious to disturb happy occasions.

Similarly, candlelight was used to keep evil spirits at bay following a death. Even today, immediately upon a death, it is customary to place a lighted candle near the head of a deceased. Kabbalists are known to surround the body with twenty-six lighted tapers, twenty-six being the numerical value of the Hebrew word *Yehovah*, meaning "God."

In the Middle Ages it was common for people to avoid walking in the dark without a candle or lantern for fear that evil spirits would pounce upon them. The famous scholar Rabbi Jacob Levi Mollin, better known as the Maharil (died 1427), warned: "One should not walk through his yard without a light. God forbid!"

In his classic seventeenth-century work *Maavar Yabok*, Rabbi Aaron Berekhiah ben Moses of Modena writes that the placing of a lighted candle near a deceased is also explained as a way of showing respect for the soul of the departed. Mystics believe that the flame of the candle eases the soul's ascent to heaven.

Sabbath and Holiday Candlelighting

Some scholars are of the opinion that Sabbath candles are lighted to keep harmful spirits away so that the Sabbath peace might be enjoyed without disturbance. The practice of lighting candles on holidays is said to be based on the verse in the Book of Esther (8:16) that describes the victory of Esther and Mordekhai over Haman as having been celebrated with "light and joy." It is also for this reason that candles are often lit at weddings and other joyous occasions.

The earliest Sabbath and holiday "candlesticks" were star-shaped oil lamps that were hung from the ceiling. Created by Jews in fourteenth-century Germany, each lamp had four to eight small containers that were filled with oil sufficient to burn throughout the night on Friday. Candlesticks and candelabra with two to five arms, designed for use with wax candles, were introduced in Eastern Europe at a much later date.

It is traditional on both the Sabbath and holidays to use at least two candles. This custom is traceable to the fact that in early talmudic times oil lamps were kindled in every household every night of the week for the practical purpose of illuminating a room. An average dwelling consisted of two rooms, and usually one lighted candle would be carried from room to room to provide light as needed. But on Friday night two candles were used for illumination, one for each room, since the carrying of lighted candles was prohibited.

The lighting of two candles is also said to represent the two important references to the Sabbath in the Bible: "*Remember* the Sabbath" (Exodus 20:8) and "*Observe* the Sabbath" (Deuteronomy 5:12).

A variety of customs has emerged over the centuries, differing from community to community and family to family. Some people light seven candles, or a seven-branched candelabrum, to correspond to the seven days of the week or the seven-branch *menorah* that was a centerpiece of the Temple in Jerusalem. In some homes the woman will light a candle for each member of the family, including grandchildren. The Talmud (*Shabbat* 23b) encouraged this custom when it said, "The multiplication of candles [light] is a Sabbath blessing."

Blessing the Candles

Until the eighth century, a blessing over the candles was not recited. But afterward, in order to negate the hostility of the Jewish Karaite community, which forbade the use of all light on the Sabbath, it became obligatory to recite a blessing.

Sadducees and Karaites took literally the prohibition against making a fire on the Sabbath (Exodus 35:3) and extends it to making use of all artificial light on the Sabbath. They therefore observed the Sabbath in darkness.

After lighting the candles and before pronouncing the blessing, it is traditional to wave one's hands three times over the flames, then rotate the hands in a circular motion over the eyes, and then to cover the eyes with the hands. Rotating the hands and then gathering them toward oneself is a gesture of embracing

the entire household of Israel—*Kohen*, *Levi*, and *Yisra'el*.

Several explanations have been offered for the covering of the eyes *before* reciting the blessing, the most popular being that by so doing the person is blocking out extraneous thoughts and concentrating fully upon the intent of the words being expressed. Another is that one thus avoids seeing the embarrassment caused the *challah*, which has to wait for its blessing while the candles are blessed.

The more legalistic explanation is that one may not enjoy the fruits of a blessing until *after* the blessing has been recited. Normally, when a blessing is to be pronounced, the recitation precedes the activity. However, in the case of Sabbath candlelighting, the activity—the candlelighting itself—is performed before the blessing is recited. If a person were to recite the blessing first, she would in effect have ushered in the Sabbath before actually having kindled the candles. This would constitute a violation of Jewish law, which forbids making a fire on the Sabbath.

Although the Rabbis considered the lighting of a candle to be a spiritual act, they did not mandate that a blessing be recited over it when it is associated with death and mourning. The Mishnah (*Berakhot* 8:6) notes that a blessing may be pronounced over a candle only when its light will be enjoyed, which is not the case when a candle is to commemorate a death.

The Candlelighting Obligation

The primary obligation of lighting Sabbath and holiday candles has been assigned by tradition to the woman of the house. The explanation for this is found in the Talmud (*Shabbat* 31b), where Rashi comments that since it was a woman who was the cause of man's downfall, which resulted in the light of the world being dimmed, it is woman's obligation to light the candles and bring back light.

If for some reason the woman of the house cannot carry out the candlelighting duty (if she is ill, giving birth, or the like), the obligation rests with the man. The twelfth-century philosopher and scholar Moses Maimonides (*Shabbat* 5:2) says that where women assume the chief responsibility of caring for the home, they should light candles, but where the man assumes or shares the responsibility, he may light the candles. Single men and women who run their own households are also obligated to light Sabbath candles.

Candlelighting Time

In the Jewish calendar, all days begin at nightfall (of the evening before the actual day in question) and extend for twenty-four hours. So as not to desecrate the Sabbath by miscalculating the time night actually falls, it has become customary to usher in the Sabbath early. Candles are lighted at sundown, usually eighteen minutes before sunset and approximately forty minutes before nightfall.

Special Circumstances

In some households, especially those of senior citizens, electric candles are used for safety reasons. This has been permitted by rabbinic authorities because the prayer for Sabbath candlelighting does not specifically indicate that there must be a flame on the candle. The prayer reads, "Blessed art Thou, O Lord our God, King of the universe, who has commanded us to kindle the Sabbath lights [*ner shel Shabbat*]." The word *ner* mentioned in the blessing means "light" or "candle," not "fire" or "flame." In the *havdalah* ceremony, where a candle with an actual flame is required, the Hebrew word *eish* ("fire") is used in the blessing.

When it was announced that Jewish astronaut Judith Resnick would be a member of the space shuttle *Challenger* team (which met a tragic fate on January 29, 1986), the question was put to the Chief Rabbi of Israel Shlomo Goren: Are Jews in space required to light Sabbath and holiday candles? Goren responded that time is calculated on earth according to the sun and moon, which does not apply to travel in space. Hence, a Jew cannot celebrate the Sabbath and holidays in space.

See Chanukkah *and* Yahrzeit *for details concerning candlelighting on these occasions.*

Cantillation

The cantillation notations found in printed copies of the Hebrew Bible indicate the melody a Torah reader is to use when chanting Scripture at public readings in the synagogue. The Hebrew word for the musical notation is *te'amim* (singular, *ta'am*), literally meaning "tastes" or "flavors," but the term *trop* is more popularly used. Although assumed to be of Yiddish origin *trop* actually derives from the Greek *tropus* and the Latin *tropos*, both meaning "turning, to turn," referring to the melodic ups and downs that occur as the Torah selection is chanted.

Historical Background

The cantillation system now in use was introduced as far back as talmudic times (*Megillah* 32a) but was not perfected until the ninth century as an outgrowth of the work initiated by Aaron ben Asher of Tiberias. Because the project was carved out primarily in Tiberias by Aaron's family, the system of cantillation became known as the Tiberian system.

The Ben Asher style of notation was accepted in most Jewish communities throughout the world, primarily among *Ashkenazim*. However, different melodies developed among

the Jews of the Sephardic communities, particularly those of the Eastern world (including Iraq [formerly Babylonia], Syria, Yemen, Iran [formerly Persia], Egypt, and India). These tunes showed Arab influence.

Both Ashkenazim and Sephardim have remained loyal to their traditional styles of cantillation. To deviate from them, said the Rabbis, would be a serious breach of the scriptural injunction (Deuteronomy 19:14), "You shall not move your neighbor's landmarks [traditions] established by previous generations."

Special Melodies

The Maharil (Rabbi Jacob Halevi Mollin), leading fifteenth-century Ashkenazic authority on matters of custom and liturgy, suggested that the melody for the Torah reading on the High Holidays (except for the afternoon *Minchah* reading on Yom Kippur) be different from the melody employed throughout the year so as to remind the public that these are special days in the Jewish calendar, days calling for introspection. Distinctive melodies were also introduced for the special readings on the various holidays and fast days. The Song of Songs, which is read on Passover, has its own style, as does the Book of Lamentations, which is read on Tishah B'Av, and the Book of Ruth, which is read on Shavuot.

Cantillation Prompter

As an aid to the Torah reader (*ba'al ko-rei*) in some Sephardic congregations an official stands next to the reader and indicates through hand movements when the reader's voice should rise or be lowered and when a note should be extended or curtailed. Rashi, (eleventh century) mentions this practice in his commentary on the Talmud. He recalls seeing Jews from Palestine who had settled in France motioning with the right hand to

indicate the melody to be used by the Torah reader (*Berakhot* 62a).

The custom of using hand movements is not widespread today, but it is still practiced in the synagogues of Rome, and at times can also be observed in synagogues that follow the Moroccan and Yemenite rituals.

See Hand Gestures; Nusach; Torah Reading.

Cantor

Synagogue prayer services may be conducted by any adult. The leader is generally referred to as the *shli'ach tzibur*, meaning "messenger [representative] of the public" or *ba'al tefillah*, meaning "master of prayer."

A professional who is hired by a congregation to lead its prayer services, particularly on the Sabbath and holidays, is called a cantor, a term derived from the Latin *cantus*, meaning "one who chants." The Hebrew word for cantor is *chazzan* (also spelled *hazzan*).

In response to a question as to whether it is better for a congregation to have a professional cantor or a nonpaid volunteer, the thirteenth-century authority Rabbi Solomon ben Abraham Adret (also known as the Rashba) responded that a paid professional is preferred "so that amateurs who are not capable will not have an opportunity to display their flimsy efforts and annoy the public at large" (*Teshuvot She-elot Ha-Rashba*, responsum no. 265).

Women are not accepted as cantors in Orthodox and many Conservative synagogues. Reform and Reconstructionist congregations freely accept women as cantors.

See Eighteen Benedictions.

Capital Punishment

The Bible is quite clear in demanding the death penalty for those who commit murder. The Book of Genesis (9:6) states: "Whoever

sheds human blood, the blood of that person shall be shed, for in His image did God make man." The Book of Job (1:21) says: "God gave life and only God has the right to take it away." Shedding man's blood is on par with deicide.

The Bible explicitly calls for the death penalty, not only for homicide, but for crimes such as cursing one's parents (Exodus 21:15, 17), blasphemy (Leviticus 24:14), adultery by a man or woman (Leviticus 20:10), incest (Leviticus 20:11–12), homosexual activity, bestiality (Leviticus 20:13), kidnapping (Exodus 21:16), and Sabbath violation (Exodus 35:2–3).

The Mishnah (*Sanhedrin* 7:1) states that the court has the power to use four methods of execution: stoning, burning, decapitation, and strangling. Despite the right granted the court to implement such penalties, many Rabbis of the Talmud were not in favor of capital punishment. Cognizant of man's fallibility, they said (*Makkot* 7a): "A *Sanhedrin* [judicial court] that effects an execution once in seven years is deemed to be a wicked tribunal." Rabbi Eliezer ben Azariah went even further in saying that a court that puts a person to death deserves to be called "wicked" even if it executes a criminal only once in seventy years.

First/second-century scholars Akiba and Tarphon opposed capital punishment under all circumstances. They said: "Had we been in the *Sanhedrin*, no one would ever have been executed" (Mishnah *Makkot* 1:10). However, Rabbi Shimon ben Gamaliel, president of the *Sanhedrin* in the second century, disagreed, saying that *not* to execute a criminal guilty of a capital offense is terribly wrong, for it would encourage criminal activity. Criminals would be quick to appreciate the fact that carrying out the death penalty is not being taken seriously by the courts.

The gravity with which members of the *Sanhedrin* viewed the imposition of the death penalty upon a criminal is evidenced by the fact that individual members took it upon themselves to fast on the day on which they sentenced a person to death (*Sanhedrin* 63a).

Actually, the Bible itself (Deuteronomy 17:6) makes it very difficult for an accused killer to be put to death, for it requires the testimony of at least two eyewitnesses to the crime. Circumstantial evidence is not sufficient.

Since those Rabbis of the Talmud who were averse to executing a person could not summarily disregard laws of the Torah that demanded the death penalty, they searched for verses in Scripture that would justify their opposition to capital punishment. Careful study of the Bible led them to the verse in Exodus (21:15) that concludes with the words *mot yumat*, meaning "that man [the criminal] shall surely be put to death." Since the word for death is repeated in this Hebrew phrase (both *mot* and *yumat* are forms of the Hebrew word for death), the Rabbis concluded that the Torah intended to teach that the death penalty is to be imposed only by God, not by man. For, when the Bible wishes to indicate death at the hands of a human tribunal (as in Exodus 35:2), the word *mot* alone is used.

Although the Rabbis of the Talmud continued to discuss and debate the issue of capital punishment, the fact is that once the Temple was destroyed in the year 70 C.E. and the *Sanhedrin* lost its power, imposition of the death penalty lapsed entirely. Rabbi Shila said: "Since we have been exiled from our land, we have no authority to put [anyone] to death" (*Berakhot* 58a).

The modern State of Israel, like all Western industrialized nations except the United States, has disallowed the death penalty for all criminals except Holocaust murderers. The only person executed since Israel was established was Adolph Eichmann, in 1962.

At the 1996 convention of the Rabbinical Assembly (Conservative), noting that in the twentieth century as many as 300 people have been wrongly convicted of capital crimes, passed a resolution opposing the death penalty and urged its abolition throughout the United States.

See Sanhedrin.

Cave of Makhpelah

Also spelled Cave of Machpelah. When Sarah died at age 127 in Kiryat Arba, also known as Hebron, Abraham needed a burial place for her. As a nonresident, Abraham could not own property there, so he approached a wealthy landowner, Ephron the Hittite, and asked that he sell him the land containing the Cave of Makhpelah, which was at the very edge of his property.

Magnanimously, Ephron offered the land and the cave as a gift. But Abraham insisted on paying and tendered Ephron four hundred *shekels* of silver. By paying in full for the burial site in Hebron, Abraham established a claim that no one could ever deny was legally his (Midrash *Genesis Rabbah* 79:7).

Abraham wanted this site to be burial grounds not only for Sarah but also for their descendants. And, indeed, the Cave of Makhpelah is where Isaac and Rebecca (49:31), as well as Jacob (50:13) and Leah (49:31), were later buried.

In the tractate *Eruvin* (53a), Rabbi Isaac explains that Kiryat Arba, meaning "the city of four [couples]" is so called because in addition to the three Patriarchs and Matriarchs, Adam and Eve are also buried there.

After the Roman Empire was divided at the end of the fourth century, the Orthodox Eastern Church of the Byzantine Empire controlled Palestine, and they built a church over the Cave of Makhpelah. Later, when the Moslems conquered the area, they converted the church into a mosque, and only Moslems were permitted to pray there. In 1967, after the Six-Day War, the Israelis took control of the area, and all faiths were welcome to visit and pray at the cave once purchased by Abraham.

Celibacy

Until modern times, the Western world, under the influence of Christianity, considered sex and sin to be virtually synonymous. Based on New Testament teachings (I Corinthians 7:19), throughout the centuries Christian scholars have viewed sex as a concession to human weakness and marriage as an "evil" necessary for the propagation of the human race. Celibacy, it was believed, is the ideal state. Galatians (5:24) considers the body a repository of "passions and desires," and Paul supports this view when he says in Romans (7:24–25), "Wretched man that I am! Who will deliver me from this body of death? ... With the mind I serve the law of God, but with the flesh the law of sin."

In Jewish tradition, sex is not considered sinful. Genesis (1:28) stresses man's duty "to be fruitful and multiply" as a *positive* commandment. Man is *obligated* to propagate the race. Isaiah later taught that God did not create the earth to keep it as a wasteland. "He formed it for habitation" (Isaiah 45:18).

See Sex and Sexuality.

Cemetery

The basic Hebrew term for cemetery is *beit kevarot*, meaning "House of Graves," (Mishnah *Sanhedrin* 6:5) but in keeping with an ancient Jewish tradition, abrasive terminology and harsh appellations such as this one are often softened and even eliminated. Instead of *beit kevarot*, a cemetery is sometimes referred to euphemistically as *beit olam* ("Eternal House"), *beit cha'yim* ("House of the Living"), or *beit avot* ("House of the Fathers [Ancestors]"). In the Book of Job (30:23) a cemetery is called "The House Assigned for All the Living," and in the Midrash (*Ecclesiastes Rabbah* 10:9) the Aramaic form, *bet almin*, is used.

The poet Henry Wadsworth Longfellow reminded us of a very unusual and appealing term for cemetery: "I like that ancient Saxon phrase that called the burial ground 'God's Acre,'" he wrote. This designation has had much appeal for Jews as well, for in Jewish tradition the burial ground is accorded the highest degree of respect. This was once reflected in the advice given to Nebukhadnezzar of Babylonia by his lieutenants. He was looking for a place to set up camp in anticipation of his conquest of Palestine. "There are no better or neater places than Jewish cemeteries," the lieutenants advised. "Their graveyards are better than your palaces" (*Sanhedrin* 96b).

Cemetery Origins

In early times, there were no Jewish cemeteries. The first known Jewish burial site was purchased by Abraham from a man named Ephron, a member of the pagan Hittite nation (Genesis 23). Abraham bought from him a plot of land in a place called Makhpelah, near Hebron, and there he buried his wife Sarah. The fact that Sarah's burial site was not a Jewish "cemetery" but a private parcel of land led the Rabbis of the Talmud to declare that a person should be buried *be-tokh shelo*, meaning "in his own property" (*Bava Batra* 112a). They give no indication that the site must be totally separate from the burial place of non-Jews.

In talmudic times, while ancestral tombs continued to be used, public burial plots were already established. In one reference, the Talmud suggests that a righteous man not be buried next to a sinner (*Sanhedrin* 47a), whether Jewish or not, which would indicate that burial in communal cemeteries did take place. The sinner the Talmud speaks of is one guilty of a capital offense, which includes those convicted of idol worship (Mishnah *Sanhedrin* 5:1).

At a later point in history the custom of burying Jews in their own cemeteries was introduced. However, since this was pure custom, and not law, Jewish burial practices varied in different communities.

Today, Jewish cemeteries are owned and operated either by individual synagogues, by the community at large, or by private parties.

Cemetery Etiquette

The cemetery is considered a holy place and proper respect is demanded when one enters the premises. Although a cemetery is not considered to have the same sanctity as a synagogue, it has become a strong Jewish custom to show respect for the deceased by keeping one's head covered within its confines (Yoreh Dei'ah 368:1).

Joseph Caro's sixteenth-century *Code of Jewish Law* (*Shulchan Arukh*) cautions that all activities smacking of disrespect (called *kalut rosh* in Hebrew) be avoided in a cemetery. In general, Jews have heeded this caution with one exception: the serving of food.

When cemeteries were far from cities and a trip to a cemetery might occupy as much as one full day, it was considered proper to feed those who made the long trek. Serving food in the cemetery became a necessity and was not done in a spirit of celebration. Today, with travel time reduced considerably, rabbinic authorities consider it inappropriate for food to be served at graveside after a funeral or unveiling.

Jewish law prohibits one from bringing a Torah scroll into a cemetery as well as from wearing *tefillin* or engaging in formal prayer there (Yoreh Dei'ah 367). (In talmudic times *tefillin* were worn all day long.) These prohibitions are based on the interpretation of a verse in Proverbs (17:5), "He who mocks the poor [*lo'eg la-rash* in Hebrew, literally meaning 'teasing the dead'] blasphemes God." In Jewish literature a poor man is equated with a dead man. Hence, those lying in their graves are sometimes referred to as "the poor ones." Tradition considers it a mockery of the dead to come into a cemetery with religious articles that the deceased may have once used and enjoyed but no longer can.

Restricted Access

Members of the priestly family (*Kohanim*) are forbidden to come in contact with or be in close proximity to the dead. The *Kohen* may walk the cemetery paths so long as he is not within six feet of a grave. He may, however, approach the grave of an immediate family member.

Leaving the Cemetery

It is customary to wash one's hands as one leaves the cemetery. If water is not available, the washing of hands is done before entering the home.

This custom stems from the ancient practice of purification through washing after being near the dead. It is also connected with the ancient belief that demons follow the dead and hover around graves, so that those who have followed the cortege must purify themselves because of having been in close proximity to the unclean demons.

See Burial; Funeral Practices; Grave Visitations; Tombstones.

Chad Gadya

This popular Passover melody, which is sung at the conclusion of the *Seder*, carries a profound message. Composed in Aramaic in nursery-rhyme style, *Chad Gadya* (literally, "One [Only] Kid") was adapted from a popular German ballad and was introduced into the Haggadah by German Jews. In fanciful form and with great simplicity, it tells the story of the Jewish people: a father bought a little goat for two *zuzim*, two small coins. And then along came a cat and devoured the goat; a dog came along and bit the cat; a stick came along and beat the dog; and so on.

So it was with the Jewish people. One nation after another tried to conquer it, but unsuccessfully. The message: evil designs may be planned and even carried out, but in the end God conquers all, and justice will prevail.

Chad gadya is used in Israel as a slang term for jail. A prisoner is said to languish in a *chad gadya*—that is, all alone.

See Seder.

Chai

Spelled *chet yud* in Hebrew, *chai* (literally, "life") has the numerical equivalent of eighteen. The letter *chet* equals 8, and the letter *yud* equals 10.

In Jewish tradition the number eighteen is considered lucky because of its association with *chai*. Eighteen dollars or multiples thereof has become a sum to donate to charity. *Chai* charms or other jewelry with the traditional Hebrew word applied to it are worn by many Jews as a symbol of Jewish identity. Even non-Jews, such as the singer Pat Boone, sometimes wear a *chai* charm to show their closeness to the Jewish people and their Zionist ideals.

Chai also figures in the procedure followed in the waving of the palm branch (*lulav*) on

Sukkot. The Spanish scholar Rabbi David ibn Abi Zimra (1479–1573) was the first person to note that when the *lulav* is used during the recitation of the *Hallel* prayer, it should be waved three times in each of six directions: north, south, east, west, up, and down, for a total of eighteen (*chai*) waves. This, he says, reflects the gift of life that God has given to all creatures everywhere.

See Gematriah.

Chalitzah

According to biblical law (Deuteronomy 25:5ff.), a man is required to marry the childless widow of his deceased brother in order to perpetuate the name of the deceased. If the man refuses to comply with this law of levirate marriage, he must subject himself to the Ceremony of the Removed Sandal, known in Hebrew as *chalitzah*. The widow loosens or removes the brother-in-law's shoe (sandal), spits in his face, and says, "So shall be done to a man who refuses to build up his brother's house." (The words *yarkah be-fanav*, usually translated as "spit in front of him," would seem to be more accurately translated as "spit in his face." This would be more in keeping with the purpose of the act, which is to humiliate this man who is violating the law. This is the sense in which Hosea (5:5) uses the word *be-fanav* and is the way the *Targum* translates it [Deuteronomy 25:9 and Numbers 12:14]). Only after this symbolic act has been performed is the widow free to marry a stranger.

See Levirate Marriage.

Challah

Plural, *challot*. This egg-rich bread with a crusty exterior and soft interior is traditionally prepared for Sabbaths and holidays.

Origin of the Word

The Hebrew word *challah*, usually translated as "cake" or "loaf," is mentioned in the Book of Numbers (15:20). The Children of Israel were commanded to set aside, from the bread they bake, a small portion of dough for the sustenance of the Priests. This ritual, referred to as "taking *challah*" (*Challah* 1:4), applied only to dough prepared for the baking of bread, not pastry. Hence, the word *challah* became associated with bread only.

The word *challah* was first used in the Bible (Leviticus 24:5) to describe the twelve showbreads (*lechem ha-panim*) that were arranged on the altar in the Tabernacle. According to most authorities, this is the origin of the use of *challah* on the Sabbath and holidays.

From Temple to Post-Temple Times

In 70 C.E., with the destruction of the Second Temple and the discontinuance of the sacrificial system, the Rabbis of the Talmud began to think of the table in the home as representing the altar in the Temple: "As long as the Temple existed, the altar atoned for Israel, but now a man's table atones for him," says the Talmud (*Berakhot* 50b).

It was then that the bread served at mealtime began to take on new meaning as a symbol of and a replacement for the cereal sacrifice that was brought in Temple times—one consisting of a mixture of fine flour, oil, and frankincense, often baked into loaves (*challot*). In the Temple, the Priest burned up some of these loaves on the altar to serve as a memorial to God, and the remainder were for his personal use.

After the destruction of the Second Temple in 70 C.E., *challah* continued to be "taken" by those who baked bread. Since Priests no longer carried on their former Temple activities, however, bakers would remove a portion of dough before baking and throw it into the oven, to be burned as a symbolic reminder of past practice. This procedure is referred to even today as "[the] taking [of] *challah.*"

The Two-Challah Tradition

According to traditional explanation, the origin of the custom of placing two *challot* on the Sabbath and holiday table can be traced to the time of the Children of Israel's forty-year trek through the desert, after escaping enslavement in Egypt. When there was no food, God miraculously sent down manna from heaven, which settled on the earth like dew. Enough manna fell each day to meet the needs of only one day.

So that the Israelites would not have to collect the manna on the Sabbath (which would have constituted work), on the sixth day a double portion of manna was sent down, and each person gathered *twice* as much manna as usual (Exodus 16:22). The Hebrew words *lechem mishneh* are used here, meaning "double allotment." Hence, as a remembrance of that event two *challot* are served on the Sabbath.

A second explanation is that two *challot* serve as a reminder of the loaves of bread (*lechem ha-panim*) permanently displayed first on the Tabernacle table (Exodus 25:30) and later in the Temple in Jerusalem. In each case twelve loaves were laid out in *two* rows; they were displayed all week long. These showbreads were required to be continually displayed in the presence of God. Each Sabbath fresh breads were prepared to replace the old ones, which became the property of the Priests. The Priests were required to eat them in a holy place, since the bread was holy. The two *challot* used today represent the two rows of showbreads displayed in the Tabernacle and Temple.

The custom of placing two loaves of bread on the Sabbath table has also been explained as an extension of the old practice of serving a loaf of bread with each cooked dish. In ancient times it was customary on weekdays to eat only one cooked dish, and therefore only one loaf of bread was placed on the table. But the Sabbath was special, and two cooked dishes were served in order to add to the joyous nature of the day—each with its own loaf of bread. Thus, it became traditional to serve two loaves of bread with each Sabbath meal.

Special Challah Designs

In order to glorify and celebrate the Sabbath and holidays, over the years, in different communities, Sabbath and holiday *challot* have been fashioned in a variety of shapes and styles: rectangular, oblong, flat, braided, round, filled with raisins, and often sprinkled with seeds to represent the manna of the desert.

On Rosh Hashanah round *challot* are commonly used. The shape is symbolic of the cyclical and eternal nature of life, expressing the hope that the coming year will be complete, unbroken by tragedy. This custom was begun in Eastern Europe in the late nineteenth century.

In various European communities, *challot* in the form of a ladder were made for Rosh Hashanah and Yom Kippur to symbolize the theme of the popular *Netaneh Tokef* prayer, in which the destiny of man is decreed: "Who will live and who will die; who will be rich and who poor. . ." Man will either ascend the ladder of life and find success in the year to follow or he will descend and suffer an unfortunate fate.

On Rosh Hashanah, in Volhynia (in the Russian Ukraine), *challot* were sometimes made in

the form of a bird. This was based on a verse in Isaiah (31:5): "As hovering birds, so will the Lord protect Jerusalem." A bird-shaped or bird-trimmed *challah* reflects the hope that man's prayers be carried to heaven. This *challah* shape was also prepared for Yom Kippur for the same reason.

In some parts of the Russian Ukraine it was customary to decorate the top of *challot* served on the first Sabbath after Passover with an extra piece of dough shaped in the form of a key. This represented the key to the "gate of release" from the bondage of Egypt. According to tradition, the "gate of release" can be opened for one month after the festival.

Shavuot *challot* are often shaped round in some communities and elongated in others. A ladder design is placed on top of the bread to commemorate the giving of the Torah on Mount Sinai. The ladder design was chosen because the numerical value of the Hebrew word for Sinai is the same (130) as that of the Hebrew word for ladder (*sulam*). The ladder symbolizes the ascent of Moses to heaven to receive the Ten Commandments.

Challot prepared for Hoshanah Rabbah (the seventh and last day of Sukkot) often have a hand fashioned out of dough mounted on them. The hand represents the hand of God, which sealed in writing the judgment that was passed on the previous Yom Kippur, and our acceptance of the verdict.

The Purim *challah*, called *keylitsh* in Russian, is giant-sized and braided. It is designed to represent the long ropes used to hang Haman.

Covering the Challot

The *challot* on the Sabbath and holiday table are customarily covered. This tradition stems from the comparison of the Sabbath to a bride. Just as the veil of a bride under the canopy is removed after the blessings have been recited, so should the *challot* be uncovered once the blessing over bread (*Hamotzi*) has been recited.

A second explanation for covering the *challot* is that since the *Kiddush* is recited over the wine before the *challah* blessing is recited, the *challah* is kept covered so that it should not be slighted. When one does not have wine for *Kiddush*, the *Kiddush* is recited over the *challot*. In such cases, the *challot* are not covered.

Before tasting the *challah*, it is customary, among some Jews, to dip a small piece in salt or to sprinkle salt on the bread. This stems from an old Jewish tradition based on the talmudic statement that "A man's table is like an altar that brings atonement" (*Berakhot* 55a). Salt was used with all sacrifices brought on the altar in Temple times, and the custom of dipping bread in salt evolved as a reminder of this aspect of the sacrificial system.

After the *Hamotzi* blessing is recited, the *challot* are usually sliced and the bread distributed to each person at the table. However, in some families, pieces of *challah* are torn rather than sliced and the pieces actually thrown to those at the table.

After the Sabbath meal, before *Grace* is recited, it is customary to leave a small piece of *challah* (the size of an olive [*k'zayit*]) on the table. This is based on a statement of Rabbi Eleazar (*Sanhedrin* 92a), who said: "Anyone who does not leave a bit of bread on the table [at the end of the meal, before reciting *Grace*] will not enjoy blessings in his lifetime."

See Bread.

Chametz

In ancient times, anything leavened (*chametz*) was considered impure because it had fermented or soured. The Talmud (*Berakhot* 17a) says: "Leaven represents the evil impulse of the heart." *Matzah*, unleavened bread, was a symbol of purity.

The Meal Offerings brought as sacrifices during Temple times had to be absolutely pure, and *matzah* was used for this purpose.

What Constitutes Chametz?

From biblical times onward, Jewish law has required that every bit of *chametz* be removed from the house during Passover.

The following five grains, and food items made from their flour, are considered *chametz*: wheat, barley, spelt (a primitive species of wheat), rye, and oats. Use of these grains is prohibited on Passover, except for the making of *matzah*. The exception was made because the eating of *matzah* is mandated in the Bible (Exodus 13:7), and to make *matzah*, grain has to be used. And, since *matzah* is made only from two ingredients—flour and water—it can be prepared for baking quickly and will not ferment. Traditionally, *matzah* is made from wheat flour.

Because flour is subject to fermentation (*chametz*), pastries and cakes for Passover may be made only from *matzah*-flour, that is, *matzah* that has been ground fine. This flour is made from *matzah* that has been previously baked and is therefore no longer subject to fermentation.

Originally, in the Ashkenazic community only the five grains mentioned above were considered *chametz*. Post-talmudic authorities (the *ge'onim*) added rice and legumes (*kitni'ot*) to this group. Legumes include beans, peas, and the fruit of any plant of the pea family.

The Sephardic community did not accept this geonic prohibition, because the main articles of food in their geographic locations were rice and legumes. Consequently, today Sephardic Jews eat both legumes and rice on Passover, while Ashkenazic Jews do not.

"Selling" Chametz

Jewish law requires that one not possess or own any *chametz* during Passover. Because of the hardship often involved in accomplishing this, a procedure known as *mekhirat* [selling of] *chametz* was created, whereby a Jew "sells" his *chametz* to a rabbi, who in turn "sells" it to a non-Jewish person with the understanding that the sale is only symbolic. The non-Jew is considered the owner of the *chametz* throughout Passover, but once the holiday is over, it is understood that for some monetary consideration the transaction is to be reversed and that the *chametz* once again becomes the property of the Jew.

See Bedikat Chametz; Legal Fiction.

Chamishah Asar Bi-Shevat

Literally, "the fifteenth day of Shevat." Hillel and his disciples declared this day a semiholiday. They called it "Rosh Hashanah Le-Ilanot" (New Year for Trees) because at about this time in Israel (January-February) the annual rains have ended and a new annual cycle of tree growth has begun.

Tu Bi-Shevat (*tu* is an acronym consisting of the Hebrew letters *tet* [nine] and *vav* [six] with the combined numerical value of fifteen) is another name for Chamishah Asar Bi-Shevat. The holiday, also known as Arbor (Tree) Day, is celebrated on the fifteenth day of Shevat by the eating of various fruits, especially those grown in Israel. In Europe, some Ashkenazic Jews were said to eat fifteen different kinds of fruit on this day. *bokser*—carob—has long been a popular holiday treat.

In Israel today, the holiday is celebrated by schoolchildren going on camping trips and planting trees. In many communities throughout the world a new focus has been given to the holiday by those who want to call attention to environmental issues.

Chanukkah

A Hebrew word meaning "dedication." This postbiblical minor holiday is celebrated for eight days, beginning on the twenty-fifth day of the Hebrew month Kislev, which falls during the month of December.

Origin and Nature of the Holiday

Chanukkah marks the deliverance of the Jews of Palestine from the oppression of the Syrian-Greeks, who in the second century B.C.E. attempted to impose heathen practices upon the Jewish population. Judah the Maccabee (meaning "Judah the hammer") and his four brothers, all sons of Mattathias the High Priest of the Hasmonean family, led a successful rebellion against them.

The Maccabean revolt reached its climax when King Antiochus IV of Syria prohibited Sabbath observance, the study of Torah, and sacred Jewish practices such as circumcision. The decisive insult was the conversion of the Temple into a pagan shrine, an act through which Antiochus demonstrated his intention to impose upon Jews the paganism of the Hellenistic world.

In 165 B.C.E., the Hasmoneans recaptured the Temple from the Syrian-Greek army and rebuilt the desecrated altar. According to the Mishnah, this military operation took eight days, and that is why Chanukkah became an eight-day observance (*Ta'anit* 2:10).

Other Theories

There are a number of other theories as to why Chanukkah is celebrated for eight days. The Talmud (*Shabbat* 21b) notes that when the Syrian-Greeks captured the Temple, they desecrated all the jugs of oil that the High Priest had prepared for lighting the Temple *menorah* (candelabrum). After much searching, only one small undefiled jug, still bearing the unbroken seal of the High Priest, could be found. This cruse contained only enough oil to burn in the *menorah* for one day. Nevertheless, the High Priest kindled the *menorah*—and a miracle happened: the *menorah* flame continued to burn for eight days. In commemoration, it was decided that thenceforth the holiday would be observed annually by kindling lights for eight days. Thus, Chanukkah came to be called the Feast (or Festival) of Lights (Chag Ha-Urim in Hebrew).

Another explanation is noted in the Apocrypha, Second Book of Maccabees (1, 10). There, the eight days are associated with the eight days of the Sukkot holiday. When the wars with the Syrian-Greeks were being fought, Jews were unable to celebrate the eight days of the Sukkot festival, and so when victory was finally achieved on the twenty-fifth day of Kislev in the year 165 B.C.E., it was ordained that Chanukkah, celebrating the rededication of the Temple, be an eight-day holiday as a reminder of the Sukkot celebration that had not been held.

A further explanation is found in the Midrash. After the sons of Mattathias defeated the Syrian-Greeks, it was said, they entered the Temple, where they found eight iron spears. The spears were pushed into the earth and a lighted oil lamp was placed on each one.

The Chanukkah Menorah

Whereas the candelabrum used in the Temple was seven-branched, the *menorah* designated to celebrate the Chanukkah holiday has nine branches, each of which holds a cup into which oil or a candle is placed. Just as one of the lights on the seven-branched *menorah* in the Jerusalem Temple was used to kindle the other six, so the ninth light of the Chanukkah *menorah*—or *chanukkiyah*, as it is now often called—is used to kindle the other eight.

The ninth light, which is usually elevated above the others, is known as the *shamash*, the "servant." Since its only function is to serve the others, it is not reckoned as one of the official *menorah* lights. It is improper to use any of the candles except the *shamash* to light another candle, for as Rav explained (*Shabbat* 22a), to do so cheapens the commandment because it would appear that one candle is being diminished by giving some of its light to another.

Menorot (plural of *menorah*) are made of all types of materials, including brass, copper, wood, ceramic, and sterling silver. Some are made to accommodate candles, some oil, and some both. *Menorot* with oil cups have removable pierced lids through which wicks are inserted. Olive oil is generally preferred because that was the oil used in Temple times. However, candles are acceptable because they contain an oil base.

Electric *menorot* are popularly used as decorative pieces. Traditionally, a candle or oil *menorah* is used for the recitation of the candlelighting blessings, but where it is unsafe to do so, such as in hospitals or homes for the elderly, blessings may be recited over an electric *menorah*.

Candlelighting Procedure

During the Festival of Lights, candles are lit as soon after nightfall as possible. On Friday nights, the regular Sabbath candles are lit after the Chanukkah lighting ceremony has been completed. When the Sabbath is over on Saturday night, *Havdalah* is recited before lighting the Chanukkah candles.

The Chanukkah candlelighting procedure is as follows: Each night the *shamash* candle is lighted first, without reciting a blessing over it. On the first night, the flame of the *shamash* is used to light a candle that has been placed in the extreme right holder of the *menorah*.

As it is lit, the appropriate blessings are recited. (These are found in most prayerbooks.) On the second night, two candles are lit, until the eighth day, when the *menorah* is ablaze with eight burning candles plus the *shamash*. On the first night, a third blessing, the *Sheheche'yanu*, is recited as well.

The system of adding one candle each night was proposed by the great scholar Hillel in the first century B.C.E. (*Shabbat* 21b). Shammai, a contemporary of Hillel, was of the opinion that eight candles should be lighted on the first night of Chanukkah and that one less candle should be lighted each subsequent night.

Hillel's view prevailed because Jewish tradition follows the principle that "in matters of holiness one should increase rather than decrease." Shammai held that one should follow the system used in offering the sacrificial animals throughout the eight days of Sukkot (Numbers 29:12): thirteen were sacrificed on the first day, and one less on each succeeding day.

Over the centuries various customs have been adopted relative to the positioning and lighting of the candles. The practice generally accepted today follows the tradition of giving equal importance to the right and left side of the *menorah*, indicating that God's presence is everywhere. The candles are therefore inserted from right to left as one faces the *menorah* (the newest addition to be on the left), but they are kindled from left to right (the newest addition to be kindled first).

Unlike the Sabbath and holiday candles, which were originally also used for general house illumination, the light of the Chanukkah *menorah* was intended exclusively to celebrate the holiday. For this reason the *menorah* has traditionally been placed in a front window of the house so that its light is visible to passerby, thus publicizing the miracle of Chanukkah.

In early times, the *menorah* was placed outside the house entrance, on the left side, so that as one entered he or she would walk between the door *mezuzah*, which hung on the right doorpost, and the lighted *menorah*, which stood on the left—that is, between two *mitzvot* (commandments).

Ma'oz Tzur

Literally meaning "rock of refuge," but popularly known as "Rock of Ages," this hymn is sung by members of the Ashkenazic community each night of Chanukkah after the lighting of the candles. Composed by a poet between the eleventh and thirteenth centuries, the poem extols God as Israel's deliverer. Undoubtedly, the author's first name was Mordekhai, since the first letter of each of the five stanzas when taken together spells out that name. The "Rock of Ages" melody was adopted from a German folk song that dates back to the fifteenth century.

Holiday Foods

Although cheese dishes are generally associated with Shavuot, longstanding tradition dictates that cheese delicacies be eaten on Chanukkah as well. The origin of the practice can be traced to the story of Judith, one of the heroines in the Book of Judith of the Apocrypha (about the sixth century B.C.E.).

Judith, according to legend, was a daughter of one of the Hasmoneans who fed salty cheese to Holofernes, the general of Nebukhadnezzar's army, an archenemy of the Jewish people. As a result, the general became very thirsty, consumed large amounts of wine, became drunk, and was beheaded by Judith, leading to a Jewish victory. To commemorate this event, it is said, Jews eat cheese and

cheese products on Chanukkah. This custom achieved popularity in the Middle Ages.

Potato *latkes*, or pancakes, are a popular Chanukkah dish because they are fried in oil, and oil symbolizes the miracle of the cruse of oil that lasted for eight days instead of one. *Latkes* are called *fasputshes* or *pontshkes* by some Ashkenazim. In Israel these Chanukkah pancakes are called *levivot*.

On Chanukkah, Israelis also eat doughnuts (*sufganiyot*) which, like *latkes*, are fried in oil. The 1995 edition of the *Guinness Book of World Records* honored the culinary students of the Hadassah College of Technology for having created the world's largest *sufganiyah*. Weighing thirty-five pounds, it consisted of thirteen pounds of flour, five pounds of jelly, six pints of oil, ten eggs, and one pound of yeast. It was fried in nine gallons of oil.

In earlier centuries, the rendered fat of chicken and other fowl was needed to prepare holiday delicacies. Because goose is so fatty a bird, it became traditional to serve goose on Chanukkah and to render its fat, some of which was then set aside and saved until Passover. Some of the crisp pieces of poultry, called *grivn* or *gribenes*, that are a byproduct of the rendering process are served with *latkes* on Chanukkah by some families.

Giftgiving and Other Traditions

Giftgiving was part of the early Purim tradition but was not associated with Chanukkah. In Eastern Europe, on the fifth night of Chanukkah families gathered for a special celebration during which children were given Chanukkah *gelt* (money). Later, when Christians and Jews mingled more freely, Jews were influenced by the Christian tradition of giving gifts to children at Christmastime. Soon, Jewish parents began the practice of giving gifts other than Chanukkah *gelt* to their children, and before long the custom evolved of giving children a gift on each night of the holiday.

Although gambling was looked upon with disfavor in the Jewish tradition, on Chanukkah cardplaying has long been permitted and enjoyed. The practice began five or six hundred years ago, in the Middle Ages, when *yeshivah* students temporarily abandoned their studies on Chanukkah to involve themselves in a game of chance. Contemporary Rabbis have condemned this practice, but it continues nonetheless.

Rabbi Levi Yitzhak, the famous chasidic rabbi of Berditchev, defended cardplaying on Chanukkah by explaining that it trains Jews to stay up late, which would enable them to study Torah for longer hours throughout the year. This is not to say that Rabbi Levi Yitzhak condoned gambling throughout the year.

Dreidel

The most popular Chanukkah game is *dreidel*. This Yiddish word, derived from the German *drehen*, meaning "to turn," refers to the four-sided top that is used in a Chanukkah game as well as to the name of the game itself. The Hebrew name for *dreidel* is *sevivon*, from the root *savov*, meaning "to turn."

On each side of the *dreidel* there is a different Hebrew letter. *Dreidels* used throughout the world before the State of Israel was established in 1948 have the Hebrew letters *nun*, *gimmel*, *hei*, *shin*, which stand for the Hebrew words *nes gadol ha'yah sham*, "a great miracle happened there [in Israel]." After the State was established, the letter *pei* for *po*, meaning "here," replaced the *shin* for *sham*, meaning "there." The four letters found on *dreidels* used in Israel today are *nun*, *gimmel*, *hei*, and *pei*, standing for "a great miracle happened *here* [in Israel]."

There are a variety of ways to play the *dreidel* game, which was introduced by German Jews. Generally, each participant places a coin or piece of candy (or some other item) in the "pot" to start the game. Each player spins in turn. If the *dreidel* comes up with a *nun*, which stands for *Nichts* ("nothing" in German), the spinner takes nothing out of the pot; according to another version, everyone puts an equal amount in the pot. If the *dreidel* lands with the *gimmel*, which stands for the German word *Ganze* ("whole, total amount"), facing up, then the spinner takes all. If the top lands with the letter *hei*, representing the German word *Halb* ("half"), facing up, then the spinner takes half of the pot. If the *dreidel* comes up with a *shin*, which stands for the German *Stellen* ("to put or place"), the spinner has to put a coin or candy in the pot.

On December 7, 2000, the *Guinness Book of World Records* announced a new record of 530 for the most *dreidels* spinning simultaneously, set by Jewish students at the University of Maryland. The earlier record was 528.

Chanukkat Ha-Ba'yit

Literally, "dedication of the [new] house." The term was originally used in reference to the dedication of the Temple built by King Solomon (I Kings 8), but was later adopted by Jews as the name of a ceremony conducted when moving into a new home and affixing a *mezuzah* to the doorpost of the entrance.

See Mezuzah.

Charity

The Hebrew term for charity, *tzedakah*, literally means "justice, righteousness," but in a popular sense it refers particularly to the performance of acts of charity and compassion.

To be charitable is a basic Jewish concept that derives from the Torah. In the Book of Deuteronomy (15:4), we are told "there shall be no needy among you." And in Deuteronomy (14:22–29), the Bible says that the produce of one's field must be tithed (taxed) before it can be enjoyed by the owner. The Rabbis established three types of tithe to be set aside from the farmer's produce after it had ripened and had been brought into his premises. These are *ma'aseir rishon*, "first tithe," *ma'aseir sheini*, "second tithe," and *ma'aseir ani*, "poor man's tithe."

First tithing consisted of giving one-tenth of the produce of the field to the Levites, after a portion of the crop (called *terumah*) had been given for the sustenance of the Priests (*Kohanim*).

Second tithing consisted of a portion of the produce remaining after the Priests and Levites had received their portion. This was brought to the Temple in Jerusalem, where it was consumed by the owner.

Poor man's tithe was a special tithe set aside for the poor from the produce of the field, on the third and sixth years of the seven-year Sabbath cycle, after the tithing for the Priest and Levites had been taken.

The needs of the poor, however, were met in other ways.

The Bible (Leviticus 19:9) makes it mandatory for the owner of a field, after it had been harvested, to refrain from returning to the field to collect stalks that had fallen off the wagon. These sheaves were to be left for the poor to glean, as is clearly described in the Book of Ruth (2:2ff.), where she follows the reapers and gleans stalks from the field of Boaz. The produce left behind for the poor is called *leket*, meaning "gleanings." The same ruling applies to the fallen fruit of the vineyard.

Aside from the gleanings that the Torah prescribed to be left behind for the poor, it also mandates (ibid.) that the farmer leave each corner (*pei'ah*) of his field uncut, so the poor can come and reap this section for themselves.

The Torah (Leviticus 19:10) concludes the section on gifts to the poor with the simple explanation: "For I am the Lord your God," implying that by caring for the less fortunate members of society we are emulating God's holiness. The rich are not to patronize the poor, and when they are providing for their needs, it is not to be considered a gift, but an obligation, as that which is rightfully theirs. It is a matter of justice (*tzedakah*).

This attitude was best illustrated by the folktale concerning a poor man who came to a rich man seeking alms. The rich man said that he could not spare any money because his son had lost a great deal of money gambling and he had to pay off his debts. The poor man responded: "If your son wants to gamble, let him do it with his own money, not mine."

Eight Levels of Charitable Giving

In his *Mishneh Torah* (Matnat Aniyim 10:7–14), Moses Maimonides delineates the parameters of *tzedakah*:

> Whoever sees a poor person asking [for aid] and ignores him and does not give him *tzedakah* has transgressed a negative commandment, as it is written: "Do not harden your heart nor close your hand against your needy brother" (Deuteronomy 15:7).

He amplifies by listing eight degrees of charitable giving from the most to the least desirable:

1. Assisting a poor Jew by offering him a gift or loan, by accepting the person into a business partnership, or by helping the person find employment, so as

to support himself until such time as the person can be self-sufficient.

2. Performing the meritorious act for its own sake: Giving alms to the poor in such a manner that neither giver nor receiver knows each other's identity.

3. Depositing money in a charity box if one is certain that the person in charge is honorable and will handle the funds honestly.

4. Giving in such a manner that the recipient knows the identity of the giver but the giver does not know the identity of the recipient.

5. Personally presenting a gift to a poor person before being asked.

6. Presenting a gift to a poor person after being asked.

7. Giving less than one can afford to but doing so graciously.

8. Giving without enthusiasm.

These eight degrees are repeated in the *Shulchan Arukh* (Yoreh Dei'ah 249:6–13), which also lays down specific guidelines for the treatment of the poor and even emphasizes that he who receives charity must also give charity.

Acts of Kindness

In Jewish tradition the concept of *tzedakah* is not limited to helping those in financial or material needs. It extends to the fair and compassionate treatment of one's fellow man. This aspect of the concept is based on the verse in Deuteronomy (16:20), *tzedek, tzedek, tirdof,* "Justice, justice, shall you pursue." A second biblical verse often quoted in relationship to this concept is found in Leviticus (19:15): *b'tzedek tishpot amitekha,* "You shall judge your neighbor justly."

The importance of treating one's fellow man justly and with lovingkindness is embodied in the parallel concept known as *gemilut chasadim*.

Synagogue Contributions

When a monetary contribution is made to a synagogue, it is customary among Ashkenazic Jews to offer the sum of eighteen dollars, or a multiple thereof, the number eighteen being the numerical value of the Hebrew word *chai*, meaning "life" (*chet* equals 8, *yud* equals 10).

Many Sephardim and mystics contribute the sum of twenty-six dollars, this number representing the total value of the Hebrew letters *yud* (10), *hei* (5), *vav* (6), *hei* (5), which spell out Yehovah, one of God's names. Occasionally a contribution of 101 dollars is made, this sum being the numerical value of the letters in the name of the archangel Mikhael: *mem* (40), *yud* (10), *khaf* (20), *alef* (1), *lamed* (30).

Many Jewish schools and organizations often send traveling messengers known as *meshulachim* to collect charitable funds and donations from the public.

Charity Box

During weekday religious services in Orthodox synagogues, it was once common practice to pass a metal container among the congregants, who would deposit coins to be distributed to charitable causes. Often the box, called a *pushke* in Yiddish, was left in the rear of the room, and those present would deposit a coin as they left the service.

This practice has all but ceased, but in many homes one still sees the readily identifiable blue-and-white Jewish National Fund (Keren Ka-yemet Le-Yisra'el) box on display. The JNF was established in 1901 at the Fifth Zionist Congress on a proposal by Theodor

Herzl that the Land of Israel be redeemed and rebuilt through voluntary contributions by Jews from all parts of the world. Monies donated to the JNF are used for the reforestation of Israel.

At the conclusion of a cemetery burial service, it has become customary, particularly among Sephardim, for the rabbi to pronounce the words *tzedakah tatzil mi-mavet*, "Charity saves from death." A charity box is then passed around and all deposit coins. This practice is associated with a verse in the Book of Proverbs (11:4), "Wealth is of no help on the day of tragedy, but righteousness [*tzedakah*] saves from death."

See Shnudder.

Chasidei Umot Ha-Olam

A Hebrew term literally meaning "the righteous of all nations." This basic concept considers righteous non-Jews to be equal with all Jews in the sight of God and in the reward that awaits them in the world to come. The concept was first enunciated by Moses Maimonides in his *Mishneh* Torah (Melakhim 8:11): "Anyone who willingly accepts the Seven Noahide Laws and adheres to them is considered to be one of the *chasidei umot ha-olam* and is assured a portion in the world to come."

The State of Israel officially recognizes all *chasidei umot ha-olam* at its Yad Vashem memorial, established in 1953 to memorialize those who perished in the Holocaust. Over six hundred such righteous gentiles have been so recognized. To honor these individuals, the Yad Vashem struck a coin bearing the talmudic maxim, "He who save one life is considered to have saved the whole world."

See Yad Vashem.

Chasidism

Also spelled *hasidism* and *hassidism*. Although the term applies to a movement that emerged in the second half of the eighteenth century, the word from which it derives—*chasid*, "pious one"—applied originally to Jews who lived during the time of the Maccabees. The staunch community of pietists, or *chasidim* (plural of *chasid*) who lived at that time, formed the backbone of the revolt against Antiochus Epiphanes, culminating in the Jewish victory over the Syrian-Greek armies, which led to the celebration of Chanukkah.

Birth of a Movement

Chasidism (*chasidut* in Hebrew) did not play an important role in Jewish life until the middle of the eighteenth century, when Israel ben Eliezer (1700–1760), better known as the Ba'al Shem Tov ("Master of the Good Name"), or simply as the Besht, an acronym of Ba'al Shem Tov, appeared on the scene and attempted to restore faith and piety as the main ingredients of a wholesome Jewish life. His emphasis was on redirecting energy toward deeper and purer religious worship and devotion to God. This appealed to large numbers of unlettered and untutored Jews of Poland and Lithuania, but it was opposed by the leading rabbinic figure of that period, Elijah ben Solomon, better known as the Vilna Gaon, who emphasized intensive Bible and Talmud study.

The Ba'al Shem Tov's unassuming lifestyle was attractive to the simple, hardworking average Jew, for he was one of them. As a young man, he made his living from a variety of occupations, including teacher (*melamed*) of young children, lime burner, and ritual slaughterer (*shochet*). At the same time, he devoted himself to the study of *kabbalah*, the world of mysticism, and became proficient at effecting miraculous cures by pronouncing magical words and formulas, particularly by invoking God's name in various mystical formations.

Over a twenty-year period prior to his death in 1760, the Besht attracted some ten thousand followers. His doctrines were based primarily on the teachings of the master kabbalist of Safed, Rabbi Isaac Luria (1542–1572), better known as the Ari. These teachings, in essence, contend that man must learn to appreciate the fact that the entire physical world and nature are nothing more than God's outer garment and are therefore infused with spirituality. Man's mission in life is to appreciate the physical world and master it. By achieving such mastery, he will be in a position to reach God and cling to Him.

This basic concept of chasidism is called *deveikut*, meaning "clinging [to God]" or "communion [with God]," a goal that is accomplished through fervent prayer and study and joyful expression through song and dance. Equally attractive to the common man was the Ba'al Shem Tov's belief that every Jew must love every other Jew, a concept known in Hebrew as *ahavat Yisra'el*, "love of Israel."

The Besht, like his predecessor the Ari, never committed his teachings to writing. However, twenty years after the Besht's death, a disciple by the name of Jacob Joseph of Polonnoye, recorded them, just as Chayim Vital had done with the teachings of his master, the Ari.

From the eighteenth century on, the basic concepts of chasidism were propagated by chasidic leaders called *rebbes*, meaning "teachers." Because they were believed to serve as mediators between man and God, these charismatic individuals were also called *tzadikim* (singular, *tzadik*), "righteous ones."

Outstanding Chasidic Personalities

Outstanding among the chasidic leaders of the eighteenth century was Dov Ber of Mezerich (*c.* 1710–1772), the disciple and successor of the Ba'al Shem Tov, who enlarged the movement by attracting to it many learned Jews. Dov Ber's pupil, Levi Yitzchak of Berdichev (1740–1809), succeeded him. He preached the doctrine of *ahavat Yisra'el* and prayed fervently for the welfare of fellow Jews everywhere. Levi Yitzchak was held in such high regard that when he died, his followers did not elect a successor.

Nachman of Brazlav (1772–1811), the grandson of Odel, the daughter of the Ba'al Shem Tov, was another charismatic leader. He emphasized in particular the importance of prayer enlivened by song and dance, and became beloved and famous for his many parables.

The Chabad Movement

The most popular of the many modern chasidic sects was founded by Shneur Zalman of Lyady (1747–1813), a small town in White Russia, where he settled in 1804 and became a disciple of Dov Ber of Mezerich. There, Shneur Zalman composed his popular *Likutei Amarim* ("Collection of Sayings"), better known as the *Tanya*, containing his interpretation of kabbalistic teachings. This work became the bible of the chasidic sect founded by Shneur Zalman.

In time, Shneur Zalman's devotees (*chasidim*) concentrated in the town of Lubavitch or Lubavici, and it became the center of their activities, which led to their designation as Lubavitch *chasidim*. The Lubavitchers were considered more intellectual than other emerging sects, emphasizing study over emotionalism. They adhered to the teaching of their master, Shneur Zalman, that three attributes emanate from God: *chokhmah* ("wisdom"), *binah* ("understanding" or "reason"), and *dei'ah* ("knowledge"). Hence the Lubavitch movement acquired the name Chabad, an acronym formed from the first letter of the words *chokhmah*, *binah*, and *dei'ah*.

In the course of the nineteenth and twentieth centuries, a number of rebbes emerged as leaders of the Chabad movement. After the outbreak of World War II, Yosef Yitzchak Schneerson, then leader of the movement, moved the Chabad headquarters to Crown Heights, in Brooklyn, New York. Upon his death in 1950, he was succeeded by his son-in-law, Menachem Mendel Schneerson. Menachem Mendel (1902–1994), seventh leader of the Chabad movement, was a well-educated and charismatic leader who turned the movement into an organization with 3,000 emissaries and worldwide influence. Many of these emissaries are known as *shlichim*, or *shluchim* (messengers). They are dedicated to the task of *keiruv*, or outreach, to those Jews who are not observant. The late Rabbi Schneerson is still being promoted as the Messiah by many of his followers, although he himself never made the claim overtly.

Other Sects

There are many active chasidic sects throughout the world today. Among the best known and most influential are the Belz, Ger, and Satmar. The last group, founded by Moses ben Tzevi (1759–1854) and named after the town of Satmar, where its dynamic leader Rabbi Joel Teitelbaum lived when he assumed leadership in 1928, is notorious for its anti-Zionist stand. The Satmar *chasidim* maintain that the Holy Land will be returned to the Jews not through the efforts of human beings but with the advent of the Messiah.

Distinctive Dress Codes

Different chasidic sects are distinguishable by the type of headgear they wear and by the style of their outer garments. Most wear black coats. Bratzlav *chasidim* wear gold-striped coats. Gerer *chasidim* wear knickers; Lithuanian *chasidim* wear double-breasted frocks; the number of buttons on their coats range from two to four. Members of particular sects are also distinguished by the shape of their beards; the length of their earlocks; the color of their socks; the length of their trousers, the type of neckties worn (although many *chasidim* go tieless, considering the use of a tie to be a non-Jewish custom), and the type of skullcap worn, usually under a black hat.

Spiritual Use of the Gartl

There are two types of *gartl* (Yiddish for "girdle") associated with Jewish religious life. One is used to secure the rolled-up Torah scroll; the other is a ropelike belt worn by *chasidim*. The latter is worn around the midsection in order to establish a separation between the upper region of the body where the heart and mind reside and the lower region, where the sexual impulse resides. Use of this type of *gartl* dates back to talmudic times (*Shabbat* 9b–10a).

Some *chasidim*, such as those in Jerusalem who are members of the Toldos Aharon group, wear a white sash four inches wide (as opposed to the standard *gartl*, which is less than one-half inch wide) because they believe the wider the separation between the two halves of the body, the greater the expression of piety.

Opponents of Chasidism

From its very inception, the most vigorous opponent of the chasidic movement was Elijah ben Solomon (1720–1797), of Vilna,

Lithuania. Better known as the Vilna Gaon, he contended that *chasidim* were not Jews and that one could not eat food prepared by them. He and his followers were known as *mitnagdim*, meaning "opponents [of the chasidic movement]."

See Headcovering; Intermediaries; Keiruv, Mitnagdim.

Chasid Shoteh

A Hebrew term literally meaning "pious fool," referring to a person who suffers from an arrogance of piety. Such a person so misconstrues the purpose of the commandments of the Torah that he goes to an extreme in observing them.

The tractate *Sotah* (21b), of the Babylonian Talmud, gives the following example of a pious fool: A woman is drowning in a river. A pious man sees her and says, "It is against the law for me to look at a woman, so I cannot rescue her."

In a second example, a man wearing *tefillin* notices a child drowning. He says to himself: "*After* I remove my *tefillin* [so as not to desecrate them], I will jump into the water to save the child." In the interim the child drowns (*Yerushalmi Sotah* 3:4).

The characterization of *chasid shoteh* has been used for one who prays more than is necessary. The Talmud refers to one who recites the *Hallel* prayers every day as a "blasphemer of God." These prayers were to be reserved for holidays only, and as Rashi put it, by reciting them every day, one reduces them to mere songs. Thus the *chasid shoteh* is defaming God (*Shabbat* 118b).

Chatan Bereishit

This Hebrew term literally meaning "bridegroom of Genesis" is the designation bestowed upon the person who is honored with the Torah honor (*aliyah*) at which time the

first section of the Book of Genesis is read on Simchat Torah.

See Aliyah to the Torah; Simchat Torah.

Chatan Torah

This Hebrew term literally meaning "bridegroom of the Torah" is the designation bestowed upon the person being awarded the Torah honor (*aliyah*) at which time the last portion of the Book of Deuteronomy is read on Simchat Torah. This Torah honor is generally reserved for a scholar who is forever "wedded" to the Torah.

See Aliyah to the Torah; Simchat Torah.

Chavrutah

An Aramaic word, the equivalent of the Hebrew *chaverut*, meaning "friendship." Akin to the word *chevrah*, also meaning "association." *Chavrutah* refers to the idea that one can learn best when associating himself with a partner rather than studying alone. This approach is followed in Jewish academies of higher learning today.

In *Shabbat* 63a, Rabbi Jeremiah said in the name of Rabbi Elazar, "When two scholars sharpen each other in studying the law [halakhah], the Holy One, blessed be He gives them success." And *Ta'anit* 23a sums up the importance of study with a friend by reporting the proclamation of Rava: "Either companionship [*chavrutah*] or death."

See Yeshivah.

Chavurah

A term derived from the Hebrew *chevrah*, meaning "association," and referring to a group of persons that meets for the purpose of study and social activity.

See Chavrutah; Chevrah.

Chazakah

A Hebrew term literally meaning "claim to possession," indicating that one has an ironclad right that supersedes the claims of others.

According to the Talmud, a person who has been using a property for three or more years, depending on the local code, has the right of access to or ownership of the property if no one has ever objected to his presence (*Bava Batra* 28a). A storekeeper conducting business at a particular site over a period of time may object to a competitor opening the same type of business nearby, the former asserting that he has a *chazakah* that may not be infringed upon.

The *chazakah* claim is often used by an individual who, for example, has for many years been given the third *aliyah* on Yom Kippur afternoon and has chanted the *haftarah* (Yonah). Should anyone wish to deny him this honor, he can claim that he has a *chazakah*, a proprietary right, to the *maftir* because he has been receiving the honor for many years.

Cheder

A Hebrew word literally meaning "room." In Eastern Europe prior to World War II, a teacher (*melamed*) would conduct religious studies in one of the rooms of his home. Thus, the term *cheder* later took on the meaning of school.

See Education.

Cheirem

A Hebrew term literally meaning "ban," which may be applied to an object or an individual.

See Excommunication.

Chesed Shel Emet

A Hebrew term literally meaning "a true [totally selfless] act of kindness," that is, an act of kindness done without any expectation of reward. Attending a funeral and joining a funeral cortege is a favored example of an action that Jewish law views as totally altruistic, for one can expect no thanks from the dead, who are being accorded this honor.

See Met Mitzvah.

Cheshbon Ha-Nefesh

A Hebrew term literally meaning "accounting of the soul" or "self-reckoning." This concept, which dates back to early talmudic times, requires the individual to submit to moral self-examination. In the Ethics of the Fathers (3:1), the first-century B.C.E. scholar Akavya ben Mehalalel said: "Know from where you came, and where you are heading, and before whom you are to give an accounting (*din ve-cheshbon*) of your life." Akavya's contemporaries said of him: "There was not a person who was his equal in wisdom and the avoidance of sin."

This concept, known as *cheshbon ha-nefesh*, became an integral part of Jewish religious life and eventually evolved into a central theme of the High Holiday liturgy. During this period, from Rosh Hashanah through Yom Kippur, the individual is encouraged to engage in soul-searching and to acknowledge and make amends for any wrongdoing.

The eleventh/twelfth-century Spanish religious philosopher Bachya ibn Pakuda popularized the concept when he wrote his famous book *Chovot Ha-Levavot* (*Duties of the Heart*), in which he examines subjects such as trust in God, love of God, humility, and asceticism.

Some scholars have theorized that the celebrated twelfth-century scholar Moses Maimonides wrote his *Guide of the Perplexed* (*Moreh Nevukhim*) because he felt the need to engage in *cheshbon ha-nefesh* by articulating where he stands on important aspects of Jewish law and theology.

See High Holidays; Rosh Hashanah; Yamim Nora'im; Yom Kippur

Chevrah

A Hebrew word literally meaning "association."

See Chavrutah; Chavurah.

Chevrah Kaddishah

An Aramaic term for the Burial Society, an organization of Jewish volunteers whose primary responsibility is preparing the deceased for burial.

See Burial Society; Purity and Impurity.

Chillul Ha-Shem

A Hebrew term literally meaning "desecration of the Name [of God]." Judaism characterizes actions that are dishonest or deceitful to Jew or non-Jew as an affront to God as well as man. *Kiddush Ha-Shem* ("sanctification of the Name") is the opposite of *chillul Ha-Shem*.

See Deceit; Profanation of God's Name.

Chol Ha-Moed

A Hebrew term literally meaning "secular days of the holiday." The designation applies specifically to the intermediate days between the first two days and the last two days of Passover, and between the first two days of Sukkot and Hoshanah Rabbah, the last day of the holiday.

The days of Chol Ha-Moed are considered secular in the sense that they are half-holidays. Most traditional Jews conduct business affairs on Chol Ha-Moed. However, many ultra-Orthodox Jews and *chasidim* abstain from all or most business activities. They also do not don *tefillin* on these days, which they consider closer to a full holiday than a half-holiday.

See Passover; Sukkot.

Chosen People

The Book of Exodus (19:5) and the Book of Deuteronomy (7:6, 14:2) both refer to the Children of Israel as *Am Segulah*, "a treasured people," chosen by God. The first reference makes it clear that the relationship is conditional, dependent upon Israel's behavior: "*If you will obey me faithfully and keep My covenant, you shall be My treasured possession among all the peoples. Indeed, all the earth is Mine, but you shall be to Me a kingdom of Priests and a holy nation.*"

According to scholars such as Martin Buber, the word *segulah* ("treasure") is derived from the Akkadian word for cattle or property. Just as in nomadic times cattle was man's treasured property, so is Israel considered by God to be His treasured possession.

The Concept Interpreted

The Rabbis of the Talmud (*Bava Kama* 84a) offer a variety of approaches to the concept of the chosenness of Israel. Rabbi Yochanan (Johanan) says that Israel was not actually chosen by God, but that Israel did the choosing. He bases this view on verses in Deuteronomy (33:2) and Habakkuk (3:3) which he interprets to mean that God offered the Torah to every nation and they refused it. He then offered the Torah to Israel and they accepted it. Thus, Israel chose God (*Avodah Zarah* 2b).

Rabbi Dimi (also called Avdimi) ben Chama, a fourth-century Palestinian scholar who lived during the time when Constantine ruled Rome (327–330) and controlled the Church, introduced another explanation of how the Jews became the Chosen People (ibid.). Unlike Rabbi Yochanan, who believed that Israel chose God, Rabbi Dimi believed that God chose Israel, which in fact made them God's Chosen People. Israel, he said, was not willing at first to accept the Torah and its many commandments, but God imposed His will upon them. Rabbi Dimi based this conclusion on his interpretation of the verse in Exodus (19:17), "And Moses brought forth the people out of the camp to meet God, and they [Israel] stood *at the foot* of the mountain." The fact that the Torah mentions that Israel was brought to meet God at the foot of the mountain teaches us, says Rabbi Dimi, that God wanted Israel to come close to the mountain so that he might suspend the mountain over them like a huge dome and warn them, "If you accept the Torah, it will be good with you; if not, this [place] will be your grave" (*Shabbat* 88a).

Few Jews have expressed the opinion that the notion of chosenness implies that Jews are a superior people or that special privileges have been conferred upon them. On the contrary, chosenness has meant that the people of Israel bear special responsibility to lead exemplary lives. The prophet Amos (3:2) said, "I have known you [Israel] of all peoples on the earth; therefore, I will visit your iniquities upon you..."

Opposition to the Concept

Over the centuries many Jewish as well as non-Jewish authorities have scoffed at the claim of Jews that they are the Chosen People, while others have applauded the idea. Martin Luther (1483–1546), the breakaway Catholic priest who found serious fault with the Church and nailed Ninety-five Theses to church doors to protest some of the Church's scandalous behavior, initially thought well of the Jews. But when he discovered that they would not convert to Christianity, he changed his attitude radically. In a vicious 1543 book, *Jews and Their Lies*, he wrote: "The sun never shone on a more bloodthirsty and vengeful people who imagine they are God's people."

In 1980, the Reverend Bailey Smith, president of the Southern Baptist Conference, echoed these sentiments: "With all due respect to those dear [Jewish] people, God Almighty does not hear the prayer of a Jew." He then went on to explain: "I believe Jews are God's special people, but without Jesus Christ Jews are lost."

Pope John XXIII (1881–1963) did not agree, and just before his death he composed a prayer beginning with the words: "We realize now that many, many centuries of blindness have dimmed our eyes so that we no longer see the beauty of Thy Chosen People."

Despite centuries-old charges by the non-Jewish community that the concept of a Chosen People reflects an attitude of superiority, traditional, and even nontraditional, Jews have clung to the idea. The enlightened Jewish philosopher Moses Mendelssohn (1729–1786) was in close contact with the Christian community but never abandoned the belief in Jewish chosenness. Because of the Revelation at Mount Sinai, Mendelssohn explained, Jews were singled out as the Chosen People, and as such they have the obligation to be bearers of that revelation to the rest of the world. Chosenness carries with it responsibility; it does not imply superiority.

Rabbi Mordecai Kaplan, who founded the Jewish Reconstructionist Society in the 1930s rejected the concept of Israel's chosenness, and substituted for the words *asher bachar banu* ("Who has chosen us"), which are the essence of the first Torah blessing, the words *asher kervanu la-avodato* ("Who has drawn us close to His service"). Nonetheless, in the 1980s and 1990s many of Kaplan's disciples rejected his rejection and have reverted to the traditional words.

See Covenant People; Reconstructionism.

Chozer Bi-Teshuvah

A Hebrew term literally meaning "one who returns in repentance."

See Repentance.

Chug Ivri

A Hebrew term literally meaning "Hebrew-speaking circle," referring to a group of Jews who meet regularly to speak in Hebrew and thus improve their language skills.

Chukat Ha-Goy

A Hebrew term literally meaning "the law of the non-Jew." This concept is based upon the biblical statement (Leviticus 20:23), "You shall not follow the customs of the nation that I am driving out before you," a reference to the heathen practices mentioned earlier in Leviticus (18:3).

Viewing the customs and practices of non-Jews as something to be avoided was embraced by Jews in order to strengthen the biblical notion that Israel was to be "a holy nation and a kingdom of Priests." To maintain this status, Israel was to avoid emulating the heathen practices of idolatrous nations (*Tosafot* on *Avodah Zarah* 11).

This was later extended to encompass all non-Jewish religious practices. Thus, for example, what prompted Jews to require the wearing of a headcovering at religious services was the fact that Christians kept their heads uncovered during worship. Rashi, the eleventh-century French scholar, points out that there existed a custom "to place myrtle branches on a coffin to honor the dead" (*Beitzah* 6a). However, this practice did not endure because adorning a coffin in this manner was considered a non-Jewish custom and, as such, one to be avoided by Jews.

The tractate *Ta'anit* (22a) suggests that Jews in mourning refrain from wearing black shoes because this was a distinctly Gentile custom.

In the twelfth century, Moses Maimonides explained the reasoning behind the rabbinic prohibition against serving meat and dairy at the same meal—that doing so was a pagan practice. Maimonides also noted that Jews are not to wear the type of clothing worn by non-Jews, not to shave their beards as non-Jews do, and not to build houses as they do (*Mishneh Torah*, Hilkhot Akum 11). In his notes to Joseph Caro's *Code of Jewish Law* (*Shulchan Arukh*, Yoreh Dei'ah 178), Moses Isserles says that this does not mean that Jews cannot adopt any non-Jewish practices.

Rabbi Abraham Menachem Steinberg (1847–1928) of Brody forbade the holding of a wedding in the synagogue, claiming that to hold a wedding in a place of worship is a Gentile custom and to do so would be copying a Gentile form of worship. (Quoted in Louis Jacob's *Theology in the Responsa* [1975].)

Celebrating the New Year

In its original form, the Sylvester (meaning "from the forest") new year celebration was a Roman heathen practice in which products of the forest were given as gifts. Later, more expensive gifts were exchanged. When the Romans invaded England (43 B.C.E.), their priests brought with them the New Year gift-giving custom. The priests cut off branches of mistletoe that grew on their sacred oaks, and these were handed out to the people as good luck charms.

Not until 487 did New Year's Day become associated with Christianity. In that year it was incorporated into the Church calendar as a holy day to celebrate the circumcision of Jesus. The association of New Year's Day with pagan customs and Christian doctrine was ample reason for many Jews to refrain from celebrating New Year's Day as a holiday.

Despite the fact that the New Year's celebration has lost its religious significance, and despite the fact that practically all Jews celebrate the holiday today, some authorities still oppose holding New Year's parties. In 1981, Bezalel Zolti, Chief Rabbi of Jerusalem, warned hotels not to hold New Year's parties "because Sylvester celebrations may offend the sensibilities of Jewish religious people." Almost all hotels complied so that their certificates of *kashrut* would not be withdrawn.

Celebrating Halloween

Many Jews consider Halloween to be in the same category as New Year's, and as such they object to having their children participate in its celebration. Halloween originated in early Roman times (before the advent of Christianity) as a holiday celebrated by Druids (priests of a religious order in ancient Gaul and Britain). The celebration marked the end of summer, and pumpkins, cornstalks, and similar products of the earth were used in the feasting and merrymaking.

In the eighth century, when the Church saw that it would not succeed in weaning its people away from observing this pagan holiday, it incorporated Halloween into the Christian calendar. The holiday would be celebrated on the first of November as a day honoring all saints, hence the name All Saints' Day. The night before (October 31) was called "holy [hallowed] evening," and many of the old pagan Druid practices were retained in its celebration, including the dressing up as ghosts, goblins, witches, fairies, and elves.

Notable Exceptions

Even though Caro's *Code of Jewish Law* (*Shulchan Arukh*, Yoreh Dei'ah 178:1) warns against mimicking "the ways of the heathen," it does contain many laws that perpetuate ancient heathen and Gentile practice. For example, the Roman superstition of putting on the right shoe first when dressing became the basis for the prescription that a Jew put on his right shoe first in the morning, although a new Torah-based reason was found to justify this action.

The Rabbis of talmudic and later times (see Tosafot on *Avodah Zarah* 11a) and the Notes of Isserles on *Shulchan Arukh*, Yoreh Dei'ah 178:1) condemned all practices that were once part of heathen worship. However, for the sake of retaining an amicable relationship with Gentiles, they did not forbid joining with Christians in some of the celebrations. Moses Isserles (1525–1572), in his Notes (*Shulchan Arukh*, Yoreh Dei'ah 184:12), writes that for the sake of retaining goodwill and avoiding enmity, Jews who find themselves in the midst of a Gentile holiday celebration should join in the festivities. He suggests that Jews not seek out such celebrations, but he considers it proper for Jews to send gifts to non-Jews on non-Jewish holidays.

The liberal attitudes expressed by some of the foremost Orthodox rabbis were criticized by many segments of the Orthodox community, and this minority applied a more strict definition of the *chukat ha-goy* concept. Thus, many chasidic groups refuse to wear a tie or cut their hair simply "because *goyim* do these things." When the Satmar Rebbe, Moshe Teitelbaum, arrived in Israel for a visit in the 1990s, a supporter who planned the two-week trip was asked if a red carpet would be rolled out. "We'll have everything except a red carpet. The red carpet idea is a *goyish* custom," he declared.

See Goodwill Principle; Superstition and Magic.

Chukim

Singular, *chok*. A Hebrew word literally meaning "laws." From talmudic times onward, the traditional Jewish view has been that all the commandments of the Torah, with four often-cited exceptions, are subject to rational explanation. The four exceptions, commonly referred to as *chukim*, are:

- the law of *yibum*, which obligates a man to marry his widowed childless sister-in-law (Deuteronomy 25:5);

- the law of *shaatnez*, which forbids the mingling of wool and linen—animal and vegetable—in a single garment (Deuteronomy 22:11);

- the law of the scapegoat (*sa'ir la-azazel*), which requires that on Yom Kippur a scapegoat be sent off to die in the desert carrying the sins of the Children of Israel (Leviticus 16:26, 34);

- the law of the red heifer (*parah adumah*), which requires that a red cow that had never carried a load and is without blemish be sacrificed and that water of purification be created from the cow's ashes to be used to purify those who have come in contact with the dead. Strangely, in the process of preparing the concoction, the preparer becomes impure (Numbers 19).

Rabbi Yochanan ben Zakkai, a leading first-century talmudic scholar, characterized the irrationality of this fourth example by saying (*Numbers Rabbah* 19:8): "It is not the dead that defile, nor the water [with the ashes mixed in] that purifies. The Holy One, blessed be He, merely said: 'I have laid down a statute. I have issued a decree. You are not allowed to disobey my commandment.'"

Laws of this kind (*chukim*), which defy logical explanation, continue to confound scholars to this day.

See Law, Jewish.

Chuppah

A Hebrew term literally meaning "canopy," used most often in reference to the wedding canopy. The original meaning of the word *chuppah* is "a cover of garlands," which explains why very often a *chuppah* consists of a bower of leaves and flowers.

Some scholars believe the *chuppah* to be a reminder of the tents in which the early Israelites lived, whereas others say that it recalls the laurel wreath worn by the bride and groom during a marriage ceremony in talmudic times. Still other authorities believe that the *chuppah* represents the room in the groom's house to which the bride was brought after the ceremony and where the couple cohabited. The consummation of the marriage, known as *yichud*, was once an essential part of the marriage ceremony.

During the Middle Ages, when marriages were performed in the synagogue, it became customary to erect the type of *chuppah* that has become most familiar today. The modern structure—approximately six feet square—is supported by wooden or metal poles and is covered with satin, silk, or velvet material on which is embroidered Hebrew words or phrases connoting good luck.

The Tallit as Chuppah

The use of a *tallit* (prayershawl) as a *chuppah* dates back to seventeenth-century Germany and France, where the groom spread his *tallit* over the bride's head to symbolize his intention to always protect her. German Jews based this custom on an interpretation of a verse in Ezekiel (16:8): "Your time was the time of love, and I spread my mantle over you…" French Jews based it on the words of Ruth to Boaz (Ruth 2:9): "Spread…thy cloak over thy handmaid, for thou art a near kinsman."

In Israel today, at the weddings of soldiers the *chuppah* is often a *tallit* held up by four rifles.

Among Sephardim, the *tallit* that is given to a groom as a gift is often used as the wedding canopy. In some communities both sets of parents hold the prayershawl over the heads of the bride and groom.

In Reform practice, the use of a *chuppah* is optional.

See Circles and Circling; Weddings.

Chutz La-Aretz

Literally "outside the Land [of Israel]," referring to the Diaspora. Because Israel is the focus of Jewish thought and emotion, it is known simply as "the Land." Even in everyday Hebrew conversation, Israelis refer to their country simply as "the Land." Every place outside of Israel is considered *chutz la-aretz* or, in abbreviated form, *chul*.

See Diaspora.

Circles and Circling

In Judaism, as in other religions and cultures, forming a circle around a person was a way of safeguarding the individual from harmful spirits. There are numerous examples:

- Traditionally, under the wedding canopy a bride circles the groom three or seven times, depending on local custom. He is thus protected from evil spirits intent upon marring the joyous occasion.
- After lighting the Sabbath candles, the homemaker circles the hands over the flames and then recites the blessing.
- In Jewish folklore, Choni Ha-Me'agel, a popular legendary character, drew a circle around himself as a protection from demons.
- While reciting certain prayers during the Sukkot holiday, the congregants encircle the synagogue while holding the *etrog*

and *lulav*. This encirclement is known in Hebrew as *hakafot*.

- It was once widely believed that demons follow the dead to the grave and that they can be warded off by forming a protective circle around the body of the deceased. Demons are able to operate only in the public domain, and the circle creates a private area within which they are neutralized.
- It is a violation of Jewish law for a Priest (*Kohen*) to enter a cemetery, because the impurity of graves will render him ritually unclean. Therefore, friends who are not Priests surround the Priest and accompany him as he enters the cemetery and makes his way to the grave he is visiting. The encircled Priest is thus considered to be in a separate domain, and the impurity (*tumah* in Hebrew) that pervades the burial place cannot reach him.
- It was customary in many European communities to conduct a vigil, called *Wachnacht*, a German word meaning "night of watching." Schoolchildren would be invited to encircle the crib of a newborn child and recite the *Shema* prayer, followed by adults, who would then spend the night in study. This circle of protection, an innovation of kabbalists, was considered an effective safeguard against evil spirits.
- Among some Sephardim, it is customary to take the coffin into the cemetery chapel before burial and for mourners to then march around the coffin seven times while reciting special prayers known in Spanish as *Rodeamentos* (*hakafot ha-met* in Hebrew; "Processions Around the Dead" in English). Other Sephardim perform the ritual of encirclement when the

coffin is placed on top of the grave, just before it is lowered into the ground.

See Hakafot; Kapparot; Weddings.

Circumcision

Circumcision represents the external sign of the covenant that was concluded between Abraham and God as specified in the Book of Genesis (17:10): "This is My covenant which you shall keep between Me and you and your seed after you: Every male among you shall be circumcised..."

The popular Hebrew word for circumcision is *brit*. In the Talmud (*Menachot* 53b), this rite is referred to as *brit milah*, meaning "covenant of the circumcision." In later times, the procedure was referred to simply as *milah*. During the second-century Hadrianic persecution of the Jews, when circumcision was banned, the rite was referred to as *shavu'a ha-ben*, "the week of the son" (*Bava Batra* 60b). The term was used by the talmudic scholar Ishmael ben Elishah.

Circumcision was widely performed in the ancient Near East during the time of Abraham. Although the removal of the foreskin of the penis was unheard of in Mesopotamia, where Abraham came from, the rite was practiced extensively in Egypt, where Abraham had visited. The fifth-century Greek historian Herodotus noted that the Egyptians performed circumcision "for the sake of cleanliness, considering it better to be clean than comely." In the Bible itself (Joshua 5:9), we are reminded that the Egyptians regarded an uncircumcised male as a "disgrace." In the Book of Jeremiah (9:24), reference is also made to the practice of circumcision by Egyptians.

Terms of the Covenant

In the Book of Genesis (17:4), God said to Abraham: "This is my covenant with you. You shall be the father of a multitude of nations."

The terms of the Covenant are further spelled out in verse 12: "And he that is eight days old shall be circumcised, every male throughout your generations." This section in Genesis (concluding with verse 14) ends with the words: "And the uncircumcised male, that soul shall be cut off from his people; he has broken My commandment."

So important is the circumcision requirement that Jewish law demands that it be carried out even if the eighth day falls on the holiest days in the Jewish calendar, namely the Sabbath and Yom Kippur, when all types of work are prohibited. Circumcision may be postponed beyond the eighth day only if the health of the child is at stake. In such cases, after the child has returned to good health, seven days are allowed to elapse before the rite is performed; the day of the boy's recovery is considered to be his day of birth.

Based on the verse, "On the eighth *day* the flesh of his foreskin shall be circumcised" (Leviticus 12:3), the Rabbis of the Talmud (*Yevamot* 72b and Palestinian Talmud, *Shabbat* 15a) ruled that the circumcision rite should take place in daylight.

The Circumcision Ceremony

The circumcision ceremony is conducted as follows:

- `A religious quorum is assembled if possible. Included in the *minyan* are those who will be main participants in the circumcision ceremony: the circumciser (*mohel*), the father, the godfather (*sandek*).

- The mother and baby remain in a separate room together with the godmother (*kvaterin*).

- The father designates a man (the *kvater*, usually the husband of the *kvaterin*) to enter the mother's room and bring the baby in for the *brit*. The *kvaterin* takes the baby from the mother and hands it to the *kvater*.

- When the *kvater* arrives with the baby, everyone except the *sandek* rises and remains standing throughout the brief ceremony.

- The *mohel* takes the baby from the *kvater* and sings out *Barukh ha-ba*, meaning "Blessed is he who has arrived."

- The *mohel* places the child for a moment on the Chair of Elijah and recites the appropriate blessings. If a doctor who is unfamiliar with the blessings is to perform the circumcision, a knowledgeable layman should recite them.

- The *mohel* then hands the child to the father, who in turn hands it to the *sandek*. The *sandek* holds the child firmly in his lap while the circumcision is performed. Occasionally, especially when a doctor performs the circumcision, the child is placed on a table, with the *sandek* holding him securely.

- Immediately before the foreskin is removed, the father recites the *brit* blessing: *Barukh atah Adonai, Eloheinu melekh ha-olam, asher kideshanu be-mitzvotav ve-tzivanu lehakhniso bi-verito shel Avraham avinu* ("Blessed art Thou, O Lord our God, King of the universe, who has sanctified us with His commandments and commanded us to bring him into the Covenant of Abraham, our father"). If the father of the child is not present at the *brit*, the blessing is recited by the *sandek*.

- After the operation is complete, the *mohel* recites a blessing over a cup of wine, at which time the Hebrew name selected for the baby is pronounced for the first time.

- After the naming of the child, the *mohel* dips a piece of cotton or gauze into the wine and lets the baby suck on it while the *mohel* pronounces the concluding blessings of the ceremony.

- Refreshments or a festive meal (*se'udat mitzvah*) are now served and the assembly joins in singing.

Metzitzah B'feh

The Mishnah (*Shabbat* 133a) requires what is called *metzitzah b'feh*, "sucking the blood [of circumcision] by mouth [of the *mohel*]." After the foreskin has been removed, the membrane is split, called *peri'ah* in Hebrew, and pulled down. The *mohel* then sucks the blood by mouth so as to draw it out from all crevices to avoid later complications. He then spits it out (*Shulchan Arukh*, Yoreh Dei'ah 264:3).

This practice was followed precisely as mandated in the Talmud and codes especially by *chasidim*. Most Orthodox rabbis, however, have abandoned this procedure and use a syringe or glass suction tube to draw out the blood. Rabbi J. David Bleich, a professor of Talmud at Yeshiva University and a professor of Law and Ethics at Benjamin N. Cardozo School of Law, insists that the procedure is perfectly safe if the *mohel* rinses out his mouth with 151 proof rum. Rabbi Moshe Tendler, also a professor at Yeshiva University and a medical doctor, insists that the practice of sucking the blood directly by mouth may lead to the transmission of the AIDS virus to the *mohel* if the mother had transmitted it to her child.

Special Cases

If a boy is born with the foreskin of his penis absent, the *mohel* who performs the procedure simply draws a drop of blood from the glans, and that blood droplet represents the sign of the *brit*. This procedure, known as *hatafat dam brit*, is followed by the recital of the regular *Brit* blessing.

Jews not circumcised as children are obligated to be circumcised at a later date. Persons wanting to convert to Judaism also must be circumcised.

The *Code of Jewish Law* (*Shulchan Arukh*, Yoreh Dei'ah 263:5) specifies that if a child lives for less than eight days, he is to be circumcised (omitting the blessing) and named at the grave site before burial. But the outstanding eleventh-century scholar Rashi indicated his disapproval of such a practice, and the twelfth-century authority Moses Maimonides makes no mention of it in his code. Conservative and Reform Jews oppose this practice, but Orthodox Jews honor it.

The Christian Attitude

The Gospel of Luke (2:21) reports that Jesus was taken by his parents to the Temple in Jerusalem to be circumcised, like all other Jewish boys. On that occasion he was given the name Yeshu, a form of Yehoshua, meaning "God has saved."

In the Early Church the question was hotly debated as to whether the rite of circumcision should be observed. Saint Peter argued that to become a Christian one must be circumcised, as was Jesus. Saint Paul argued that physical circumcision should not be a requisite to becoming a member of the Church, and that "conversion of the heart" is sufficient (Romans 2:29).

Muslim Practice

Abraham is looked upon as a patriarch of the Arabic people, even as he is for Jews. But they also see Abraham's son, Ishmael, as their spiritual ancestor. And just as both Abraham and Ishmael were circumcised, so should their descendants be circumcised.

Muslims the world over, like Jews, practice circumcision (*khitan*) of their male children. The Koran refers to the rite but does not provide details as to its execution except to say that the act is to be performed before puberty. According to one tradition, circumcision is to take place on the seventh day after birth, but more commonly it is postponed until a later date. Converts to Islam are expected to undergo circumcision.

Modern Technology

In 1992, at Soroka Hospital in Beersheba, Israel, a teenage émigré from the Soviet Union underwent the first *brit* in which a surgical laser rather than a scalpel was employed. The laser causes minimal bleeding and is an extra safeguard in circumcising newborns or adults suffering from hemophilia. Since many in the Orthodox rabbinate consider the small amount of blood drawn by this procedure not sufficient to satisfy the legal requirement, they are opposed to its use, fearing that the use of lasers for circumcision may be adopted for use on healthy babies. In cases where the life of a child may be endangered by a normal circumcision, the laser procedure is endorsed by all authorities.

Opposition to Circumcision

In the nineteenth century, a group of Reform Jewish leaders in Frankfurt, Germany, advocated the abolition of circumcision on the grounds that it was antiquated and barbaric, but the prospect of abolition was vigorously opposed by the Reform movement as a whole. Oddly enough, it was the excommunicated semi-apostate Dutch philosopher Baruch (Benedict) Spinoza (1632–1677) who made the strongest case for the rite of circumcision: "Such great importance do I attach to the sign of the Covenant, that I am persuaded that it is sufficient by itself to maintain the separate existence of the nation forever."

Today, like all Jewish religious denominations, Reform Jews accept circumcision as an important religious rite, although some individuals still oppose it on the grounds that it is traumatic for the child and that it deprives the man of full sexual pleasure. Few medical authorities agree with this contention, citing the tens of millions of Jews and non-Jews who have been circumcised without ill effect. However, in his *Guide of the Perplexed* (3:49), Moses Maimonides does express the opinion that circumcision weakens (lessens) man's sexual desire and was ordained by the Torah to help man achieve self-mastery.

See Mohel.

Cities of Refuge

The Bible (Numbers 35:6; Deuteronomy 19:1) states that once the Israelites had captured and settled in the Promised Land, they were to set aside six cities of refuge, or *arei miklat*. It was in these prescribed areas—three in the Land of Canaan proper, three in Transjordan—where an individual who had unintentionally killed another human being could find refuge from the avenging relative of the deceased.

A blood-avenging relative, known in Hebrew as a *go'el ha-dam*, acted in accordance with the principle of *nefesh tachat nefesh*, prescribed in Leviticus (24:17–18): "If anyone kills any human being, he shall be put to death . . . a life for a life."

The Talmud (*Makkot* 11a) states that the murderer was safe in a city of refuge so long as the High Priest was alive. Upon his death, the unintentional murderer was open to attack, for it was believed that only through the prayers of the High Priest was the *go'el ha-dam* granted safe haven.

Code of Jewish Law

See Law, Jewish.

Coffins

Although the Book of Genesis (50:26) refers to Joseph as being "put in a coffin in Egypt," this Egyptian custom was not practiced by the early Israelites. In fact, when Jacob, Joseph's father, dies and is buried in Canaan (Genesis 50:13), no mention is made of placing him in a coffin.

The Talmud (*Moed Katan* 27a–b; *Ketubbot* 8b) calls attention to the fact that in the early centuries of the Common Era coffins were not used by Jews. It was customary to place a wealthy deceased person on a *dargesh*, a tall, richly ornamented, stately bed. The poor, wrapped only in shrouds, were brought out for burial on a simple bier or wooden platform. When it became apparent that the poor felt humiliated by the simple burials accorded their family members, it was ruled that all deceased persons should be brought out on a simple bier.

This ruling was not strictly followed, and by the Middle Ages, a variety of customs had developed. In France, coffins were used; in Spain, they were not. In the sixteenth century, kabbalists considered it important that the dead body make direct contact with the earth, and coffins were therefore banned. The corpse was placed in a body bag and carried to the grave on a wooden platform. A bed of interwoven reeds, prepared in advance, was first placed on the floor of the grave, and the corpse was laid on this mat.

Burial without a coffin is still practiced by many Orthodox Jews in Israel and by many Sephardim outside of Israel, particularly in Greece, Turkey, and other Balkan states. In Western countries, local law generally demands that the dead be buried in coffins.

Wood as the Material of Choice

In the Talmud, Rabbi Levi traces to the Garden of Eden the origin of the custom of using coffins made of wood. He says that the fact that Adam and Eve were hiding among the *trees* when God called to them (Genesis 3:8) "was a sign for his descendants that they would be placed in wooden coffins" (*Genesis Rabbah* 19:8).

The kind of wood used for coffins is of little consequence, but over the years inexpensive soft woods (especially pine) have been preferred, primarily because they were thought to decompose more rapidly than hardwoods such as oak. A metal casket, which is slow to decompose, is not used because it counters the biblical commandment, "Unto dust shalt thou return" (Genesis 3:19). This is also the reason why many people follow the custom of having holes drilled in the bottom of the casket, accelerating decomposition. Wood is also preferred over metal because the latter is considered a symbol of war. Burying a loved one in a metal coffin would not be in keeping with the idea of "resting in peace."

Finally, the use of wood—preferably un-polished wood—for coffins is seen by the Talmud (*Moed Katan* 27a and *Ketubbot* 8b) a sign that ostentatious funerals are to be frowned upon. Jewish tradition advocates humility and simplicity in its treatment of the dead.

The practice of draping a black cloth over a coffin probably began as local custom and then grew in popularity. The cloth covering may have been introduced to soften the harsh appearance of an unadorned pine coffin. A Star of David is usually embroidered on the covering for decorative purposes only.

Adorning the Coffin

Although there is no objection in Jewish law to covering a coffin with flowers (or adorning graves with shrubs and plants), Jewish custom has never favored the practice. Rashi, the eleventh-century French scholar, points out that there existed a custom "to place myrtle branch-es on a coffin to honor the dead" (*Beitzah* 6a). However, this practice did not endure because adorning a coffin in this manner was considered a non-Jewish custom and, as such, one not to be copied by Jews. Not adorning coffins and graves was more in keeping with the Jewish value that all people—rich and poor—are equal in death (*Moed Katan* 27b). Just as the burial garment of both the rich and the poor is to be simple white shrouds, so is the coffin and grave of both the rich and the poor to remain plain and unadorned.

See Burial; Death; Funeral Practices.

Colors

While many colors carry significance in Jewish tradition, white and blue are most often used.

Blue

The color blue is identified with the *tzitziot* ("fringes," plural of *tzitzit*) that were originally attached to the four corners of the overgarment, as prescribed in Deuteronomy 22:12. In ancient times it was required that one of the eight threads that make up each fringe be dyed blue. The Bible (Numbers 15:38) refers to this thread as *petil tekheilet*, "blue thread."

The Talmud (*Menachot* 42b) describes how the blue dye was made: The blood of a species of mollusk known as *chilazon*, even though not kosher, was mixed with other specified ingredients to obtain a precise shade of blue. In time, the identity of the particular species of mollusk could no longer be ascertained, and the practice of dyeing one thread blue was discontinued. However, in 1994 Israeli researchers claimed to have discovered the secret of the ancient dye mentioned in talmudic literature.

Rabbi Meir asked rhetorically (*Menachot* 43b and *Sotah* 17a): "Why is blue designated as the color for one of the *tzitziot*?" He answers:

"Because blue resembles the color of the sea, and the sea resembles the color of the sky, and the sky resembles the color of a sapphire, and a sapphire resembles the color of [God's] throne of glory [as it is written in the Book of Exodus 24:10]."

In Jewish tradition, blue, along with purple, is a symbol of royalty. The Ark curtain and Torah mantle are often made of blue or purple fabric.

Red

The color red, which is represented as possessing magical powers, figures prominently in Jewish ritual. In the Bible (Leviticus 4:4–7), the red blood of a sacrificed animal is not discarded, but is sprinkled on the altar, presumably to appease the powers of evil.

In the Middle Ages, red was regarded by peoples of all religious persuasions as having anti-demonic power capable of thwarting the plans of the evil eye. Jewish children, like Christian children, often were dressed in red clothing or wore coral necklaces as protection against the devil and other evil forces. In some communities, it was customary to place a red cloth wristband on a newborn baby for protection.

The prophet Isaiah was among the first to emphasize the negative aspect of the color red when he preached: "Though your sins be like crimson, they can turn [white] as snow [if you repent]; if they are as red as dyed wool, they can become [white] as fleece" (Isaiah 1:18). In the Middle Ages, some Jews of Eastern Europe refrained from eating tomatoes, which they considered *treif* ("ritually unclean") because of their red color and its association with blood.

White

In Jewish tradition, white is the bridal color. At a first marriage a bride is expected to wear a white gown, and at some Orthodox weddings a groom will also wear a white gown (*kittl*) as a symbol of purity. Likewise, many Jews wear a white *kittl* during High Holiday services, and some dress in white garments to honor the Sabbath. At the Passover *Seder*, the leader of the service also dons a white *kittl*. White is also the color of the shrouds in which the deceased is wrapped after being bathed and purified.

Black

Expressive of sadness and mourning, black is the color of the cloth used to drape a coffin and the color of the ribbon upon which *keri'ah* (tearing of the garment) is performed. Although the Bible makes no reference to the wearing of black mourning garments, the Talmud (*Shabbat* 114a) quotes Rabbi Yannai as having instructed, "Do not bury me in black garments [lest I appear to be without merit]," hence the association of black with death and mourning.

In the Talmud (*Bava Kama* 59b), Eleazar Ze'era is asked, "Why do you always wear black shoes?" He replies, "I am in mourning for Jerusalem."

In another talmudic reference (*Ta'anit* 22a), Rabbi Beroka asks a Jew why he is wearing black shoes when he is not in mourning. His answer is so that the Gentiles among whom he travels may not know that he is a Jew, so that he may learn in advance if any harsh decrees are being planned against Jews. On the other hand, another talmudic reference (*Sanhedrin* 74b) advises Jews not to abandon their most insignificant customs, such as wearing black shoelaces, so as to demonstrate their continued loyalty to Judaism.

Israel Abrahams, in his *Jewish Life in the Middle Ages* writes: "The Jews of all countries wore black; in Spain, Germany, and Italy the phenomenon was equally marked. Black being the color of grief of the Jews [who were in a constant state of mourning for the loss of Zion]."

Black vs. White

In his *Mishneh Torah* (Beit Ha-Mikdash 6:11), Maimonides writes that one of the primary functions of the *Sanhedrin* in Temple times was to investigate persons claiming to be of priestly heritage, desirous of officiating at Temple rituals. If a claimant turned out to be unqualified because of his genealogy, he was required to don black clothes and leave the Temple premises. Those whose claim was valid donned white and served with all the other *Kohanim* (Priests).

A talmudic legend tells of how, immediately following Yom Kippur, the High Priest Simon the Just announced that he would die within the year. When asked how he knew, the High Priest responded that every year, when he entered the Holy of Holies on the Day of Atonement to perform the special Yom Kippur service, he would see an old man dressed in white, and the old man would accompany him out of the holy chamber. This year, he said, the man was dressed in black and did not accompany the High Priest. Just as predicted, Simon died a short time later (around 310 B.C.E.), after the festival of Sukkot. This legend contributed to the association of black with sadness and hence with death, while white became a symbol of joy.

See Shrouds; Tallit; Torah Ornaments.

Commandments

See Law, Jewish; Mitzvah; Taryag Mitzvot; Ten Commandments.

Community

See Kehillah.

Compassion

The Jewish concept of showing compassion or mercy is expressed in the Jewish term *rachmanut*. In Jewish liturgy God is referred to as *El Malei Rachamim*, "God Full of Mercy," and as *El Rachum Ve-Chanun*, "Compassionate and Merciful God." He is also referred to as *Ba'al Ha-Rachamim*, "Master of Mercy," or simply by the Aramaic name *Rachmana*, "the Merciful One," as in the popular expression *Rachmana liba ba'i*, "God wants [a person's] heart" (*Sanhedrin* 106b).

In Jewish literature, Jews are characterized as "merciful people, children of the Merciful One," because they have accepted the "Yoke of the Law," which demands that they be merciful just as God is merciful. Their mission in life is to imitate God. This means that Jews must be kind to the proselyte, a commandment mentioned no less than thirty-six times in the Bible (*Bava Metzia* 59b), and to the stranger, a caution always coupled with the words (Exodus 22:20, Deuteronomy 10:19), "Because you were a stranger in the land of Egypt"; that Jews visit the sick, for as the Sages taught (*Nedarim* 39b), "whoever visits the sick reduces their illness by one-sixtieth"; that they be kind to the orphan and widow; and that they comfort the bereaved.

All Jews, regardless of socioeconomic status, are expected to help those less fortunate. The Rabbis taught that even a poor man who depends upon the dole must give a portion of that which he or she receives as charity.

So important is the concept of *rachmanut* that the Rabbis of the Talmud even instructed Jews to be compassionate even toward one's enemy. Commenting on the drowning of the Egyptians at the Red Sea (Exodus 14:20), Rabbi Yochanan said: "The ministering angels wanted to sing hymns of joy for the victory, but God exclaimed: "The work of My hands are drowned in the sea and you want to rejoice!" (*Megillah* 10b). To a compassionate God, such conduct was unthinkable.

See Lifnim Mi-Shurat Ha-Din; Truth; Tzedakah.

Compromise

Jewish law recognizes that there are times when the truth cannot prevail and one must be willing to accept less than one believes he or she is entitled to. A classic example is noted in the Tosefta (*Bava Metzia* 3:5), where a man is described as admitting to having stolen two hundred *maneh* (units of currency). Two people claim to be his victim and each demands the return of the full amount. The ruling is that the thief pay each claimant one *maneh*, the balance not to be paid out until the two arrive at a compromise (*pesharah* in Hebrew).

Regarding the concept of compromise, the second-century *tanna* Rabbi Shimon ben Gamaliel comments (*Sanhedrin* 5b): "The power of compromise [through arbitration] is more powerful than any legal judgment [because the parties have agreed in advance not to appeal the decision]." His Palestinian colleague Joshua ben Korcha concurred, but went even further by saying that compromise through arbitration is not merely a wise course but a morally correct one. He said (*Sanhedrin* 6b): "Surely where there is strict justice there is no peace, and where there is peace, there is no strict justice. But what is the kind of justice with which peace can coexist? We must say: Arbitration." To which Joshua ben Korcha adds: "Settling conflicts by arbitration is a meritorious course."

Despite Rabbi Shimon's strong advocacy of compromise as a means of settling disputes, the approach was not universally accepted. The Talmud (*Sanhedrin* 6b) illustrated the two positions in describing the views of Moses and his brother, Aaron, with regard to the importance of adherence to the strict demands of Jewish law. Moses differed from his more peace-loving brother by subscribing to the motto, "Let the law pierce the mountain,"

that is, nothing must give way to strict adherence to law. The law, Moses asserted (Deuteronomy 1:8), comes from God and must not be tampered with even if it causes hardship to one party. Arbitration and compromise, he believed, are not the way to resolve conflict peacefully.

While Jewish law recognizes that compromise is necessary for the sake of maintaining peace among individual members of society, especially in monetary matters, it is opposed to compromise in matters of morality. This is evident by the inclusion in the Yom Kippur martyrology of the story of the ten Sages who in Roman times accepted death rather than abandon the teaching of Torah to their students or compromise their convictions by being disloyal to their tradition.

See Arbitration.

Condolences

The Rabbis of the Talmud consider the act of condoling, of offering sympathy to mourners, to be a primary *mitzvah*, a godly act, the kind of activity in which God himself is involved (*Sotah* 14a). The first such instance is found in the Bible, after the death of Abraham, when God revealed Himself, paid Isaac (Abraham's son) a condolence call, and blessed him (Genesis 25:11).

Visiting the mourner during *shivah*, the seven-day mourning period following the burial of a loved one, is a deed of compassion that is intended to help the bereaved through the initial period of grieving. Theologically, the act is connected with God's message to the Jewish people as expressed by the prophet Isaiah: "Comfort ye, comfort ye, my people" (40:1). From this verse, which is intended to allay the fears of the threatened people of Jerusalem, the message was drawn that in times of tragedy every individual needs comforting. The Hebrew expression for comforting mourners is *nichum aveilim*. When one comforts a mourner, he is said to be *menachem aveil*, "comforting a mourner."

When to Visit

The proper time for casual acquaintances to visit the mourner is after the first two days of *shivah*. The Rabbis of the Talmud advised, "Do not comfort a mourner while his deceased relative is still before him [in the mind's eye]." Because memories are vivid and grief is most intense during the first two days of *shivah*, visitors should wait until the third day before paying a condolence call. An exception is made for the very closest of friends and for those who would have no other opportunity to pay their respects to the bereaved.

In any case, offering condolences to a mourner is best done in person. To resort to the telephone to offer sympathies can be considered only second best and is acceptable only if traveling to the *shivah* home would be exceedingly difficult or prohibitively costly. Otherwise, authorities feel, there should be no excuse for anyone's neglecting the duty to comfort a mourner personally.

Appropriate Conversation

The mere presence of a visitor in a *shivah* house is what offers the most comfort to the mourner. Words are unnecessary. The Bible, in describing the classic mourner, Job, says that when Job was mourning the loss of his family, he was visited by three friends, who sat with him for seven days without uttering a word, "for they saw how very great was his suffering" (2:13). And the Bible (Job 3:1) later says: "After this, Job opened his mouth and said...." Only when Job was finished talking did his friend Eliphaz the Temanite begin to speak (4:1).

In talmudic times it was customary in Babylonia for mourners, when being visited, to cover their heads and faces with a hood, a practice common among the general population. The Rabbis of the Talmud (*Moed Katan 24a*) encouraged this behavior and urged mourners to be sure to cover their mouths, leaving only the nose and eyes exposed. This reminded the mourners to be silent. For a mourner to be engaged in much conversation might leave the impression that he has forgotten his sorrow.

Rabbi Yochanan points out (*Moed Katan 27b*) that "as soon as the mourner nods his head [indicating that he would like the visitors to take leave of him], the comforters are no longer allowed to remain seated by him."

In the Midrash (*Ecclesiastes Rabbah 3:9*), the Rabbis suggest that a visitor can bestow no greater favor upon a mourner than to be silent in his presence, unless invited to speak. This message was driven home by an incident that occurred when the wife of Rabbi Mana of Sepphoris (fourth century C.E.) died. His colleague Rabbi Abun came to pay a condolence call. Rabbi Mana said: "Are there any words of Torah you would like to offer us in our time of grief?" Rabbi Abun replied: "At times such as this, the Torah takes refuge in silence."

This does not mean that one need remain absolutely silent when in the company of a mourner, but idle chatter should be avoided. The visitor is best advised to be prepared to respond to the mourner rather than to initiate conversation.

To pretend to be casual about the mourner's situation is considered an affront. Accordingly, authorities such as Rashi, citing God's words to Ezekiel (24:17), "Sigh in silence," state that those visiting the mourner during *shivah* should refrain from extending customary greetings such as "hello," "good morning," "how are you?" and "*shalom*." The mourner is obviously experiencing a great sorrow at this time, and an honest, positive response to these greetings can surely not be expected.

Some authorities are more lenient in this matter, maintaining that expressions such as "good morning" or "how are you?" are not intended to be taken as questions that call for a response.

When a mourner does not respond to words of greeting, it should be recognized that the individual has been traumatized by recent events and cannot be expected to respond normally. A visitor should not be insulted if a mourner does not respond to a greeting.

The Talmud (*Semachot* 6:2) advises that a mourner react in the following manner to those who greet him: "On the first and second day of mourning he should say to them: 'I am a mourner.' On the third day, he may return their greeting in hushed tones, but in no case should he greet anyone first." (*See* Yoreh Dei'ah 385:1.)

Upon leaving the presence of a mourner, it is traditional for Ashkenazim to say, *Ha-Makom ye-nacheim etkhem betokh she'ar avelei Tziyon vi-Yerushala'yim*, "May the Lord comfort you along with all the mourners of Zion and Jerusalem."

The traditional expression of condolence among Sephardim is: *min ha-shama'yim te-nuchamu*, "May heaven comfort you."

The loss of the Second Temple in 70 C.E. was a serious blow to Jews everywhere, a catastrophe for which Jews were to be in perpetual mourning. Reference to it is made whenever Jews take leave of mourners at the cemetery or when paying a visit to a *shivah* house. By associating the mourner's personal loss with the national catastrophe that befell all Jews when the Temple was destroyed, we are expressing how deeply we empathize with the bereaved.

See Nichum Aveilim; Shivah.

Confession of Sins

The Book of Ecclesiastes (7:20) says, "For there is not a righteous man upon earth who does good and does not sin." The Bible thus acknowledges that every individual, in the course of his life, knowingly or unknowingly, commits a sinful act. Accordingly, Jewish tradition established a mechanism for atonement.

Atonement Through Sacrifice and Prayer

The Bible requires that an offering be brought on the Temple altar. The Book of Leviticus (4:1–35) describes two types of such offerings: the sin offering (*korban chatat*) and the guilt offering (*korban asham*). However, with the destruction of the Second Temple in 70 C.E. the sacrificial system was abandoned, and from that time on Jews were deprived of the opportunity to atone for sins through animal sacrifices. To compensate, the Rabbis introduced the concept of confession of sin through prayer. These *Viddui* ("confession") prayers as they are called, are found in the daily, Sabbath, and holiday liturgies.

During Yom Kippur services, *Viddui* prayers are recited ten times. Through these confessions, which begin with the words *ashamnu* ("we have trespassed") or *al cheit* ("for the sin [we have committed before Thee]"), the individual as a member of the community expresses his imperfections.

Deathbed Atonement

The term *Viddui* has become associated with the approach of death. The Talmud says (*Shabbat* 32a), "When a man is sick and near death, they say to him, 'confess'." Based on this statement, the making of a formal deathbed confession has become part of Jewish custom.

The accepted deathbed prayer, which was composed by Moses Nachmanides (1194–1270),

begins with the words, "I acknowledge unto Thee, O Lord my God and God of my fathers, that both my cure and my death are in Thy hands...."

See Repentance; Sin; Viddui; Yom Kippur.

Confirmation

Probably inspired by the practice of the Christian Church, in the nineteenth century Reform rabbis in Germany substituted confirmation for bar mitzvah. Their contention was that the age of thirteen, when bar mitzvah is regularly celebrated, is too young for a Jewish boy to be ushered into the Jewish fold. Age sixteen or seventeen, when children are better equipped to understand and appreciate Jewish values, would be more appropriate, they maintained.

In 1849, while serving as rabbi of Temple Beth El, in Albany, New York, Bohemian-born Rabbi Isaac Mayer Wise introduced this concept to the United States. Wise called for the abandonment of the bar mitzvah rite, a demand that greatly upset many members of his congregation.

At first, only Reform congregations embraced the confirmation ceremony, but in time most Conservative congregations adopted it as well. However, unlike Reform congregations, Conservative congregations did not abandon the bar mitzvah ceremony. Today, most Reform and Conservative congregations celebrate both a bar mitzvah and a confirmation ceremony. Orthodox congregations deplore the confirmation concept.

The day designated for confirmation is Shavuot, the holiday commemorating the giving of the Torah on Mount Sinai. It is celebrated as a group affair by girls and boys who have completed a prescribed course of religious study.

See Reform Judaism; Shavuot.

Conservative Judaism

The Conservative movement within Judaism, which began to emerge in the early twentieth century, initially was referred to as Conservative-Orthodox Judaism or Traditional Judaism. Only after World War II, when Louis Finkelstein's (1895–1991) years of service as chancellor of the Jewish Theological Seminary—the mother institution of Conservative Judaism—came to an end and historian Gerson D. Cohen (1924–1991) succeeded him, did the term Conservative Judaism begin to gain acceptance.

In the eyes of the general public, the Conservative movement was considered a meeting ground for Jews who could not abide by the strict, unyielding demands of Orthodoxy or by the total disregard of traditional rituals and ceremonies as advocated by the early leaders of the Reform movement.

Origins

The ideological father of Conservative Judaism is said to be Zacharias Frankel (1801–1875), a Reform rabbi who led a traditional congregation in Dresden, Germany, in the mid-nineteenth century. When German-born Abraham Geiger (1810–1874), the protagonist of the Reform movement in Germany, began advocating prayer in the vernacular and the deletion of prayers relating to the restoration of the sacrificial system and a return to Zion, Frankel, who had subscribed to the views of Leopold Zunz (1810–1874), took issue with Geiger.

Zunz, a brilliant scholar in Judaic as well as general studies, believed that Judaism is never static, that it constantly evolves in keeping with the demands of each time and locale. Zunz advocated reacquainting Jews with their glorious past and instilling in them renewed pride in Jewish achievement, and he made these views amply clear to Reform leader Geiger, whom he admired at one point but whom he later accused of cavalierly discarding many traditional practices.

In a letter to Geiger dated May 4, 1845, Leopold Zunz wrote:

> I despise a rabbinical hierarchy, but I also have a contempt for Reform Judaism.... We must reform ourselves, not our religion. We should attack only evil practices that crept in our religious life, whether from within or without, but not the holy heritage.

One of the scholars who came to America from Germany (in 1824) was Isaac Leeser (1806–1868). In 1829, he was appointed *chazzan*/rabbi of the Sephardic Mikveh Israel Congregation, in Philadelphia, where he founded the Maimonides Rabbi's Training College. Profoundly influenced by Zunz's advocacy of loyalty to tradition, yet allowing for respectful and measured change, Leeser was the first to introduce sermons in English and render the Hebrew Bible into English.

While Zacharias Frankel was considered the spiritual father of Conservative Judaism in Europe, Isaac Leeser was so considered in America. Italian-born Sabato Morais (1823–1897), after officiating in London from 1846 to 1851, came to America and succeeded Leeser as rabbi of Mikveh Israel Congregation.

Morais, a strictly traditional rabbi, was friendly with his Reform colleagues and even served on the Board of Examiners of Hebrew Union College (HUC), the institution founded by Isaac Mayer Wise in 1875. However, when he attended HUC's first commencement supper in 1883 and noticed nonkosher food on the menu, Morais disassociated himself from the Reform movement.

The Jewish Theological Seminary

At a formal meeting of rabbis and laymen held at New York's Shearith Israel Congregation on January 31, 1886, a proposal to establish the Jewish Theological Seminary of America (JTSA) was ratified. Sabato Morais was selected to be president of the Advisory Board of Ministers.

The philosophy of the institution was based on ideas that had been enunciated by Zecharias Frankel. This approach, known as Positive Historical Judaism, acknowledges the reality of historical change and evolution in Jewish belief and practice, but without diminishing the validity of Jewish law (*halakhah*), which is the kernel that provides for Jewish continuity.

In 1902, the Romanian-born scholar Solomon Schechter (1850–1915), who had studied in Vienna and Berlin, was called from London's Cambridge College, where he was serving as a Reader in Rabbinics, to assume the presidency of the Jewish Theological Seminary of America (JTS). In time, JTS became so identified with its president's charismatic personality that for decades it was referred to as Schechter's Seminary.

During the years of Schechter's leadership, the seminary grew in stature, adding a distinguished faculty that included men the caliber of talmudist Louis Ginzberg, historian Alexander Marx, and medieval Hebrew poetry expert Israel Davidson. In 1913, Schechter organized the United Synagogue of America, an association of Conservative congregations, which was begun with twenty-two member congregations. Following his death in 1915, Schechter's wife, Mathilda, founded the Women's League (1918), later called the Women's League of Conservative Judaism. This was followed by the establishment of the Young People's League (1920) and of the National Federation of Men's Clubs (1928).

Cyrus Adler (1863–1940), who had earned a Ph.D. in Semitics at Johns Hopkins University and was assistant secretary of the Smithsonian Institution, succeeded Schechter as president of the Jewish Theological Seminary. Earlier, in 1906, he was one of the founders of the American Jewish Committee, and in 1908 he founded Dropsie College.

When Adler died in 1940, leadership of JTS was placed in the hands of Louis Finkelstein (1895–1991), who had been serving as provost since 1937. In 1951, his title was changed from president to chancellor.

In 1972, Gerson D. Cohen (1924–1991) succeeded Finkelstein as chancellor. He retired in 1986 and was succeeded by historian Ismar Schorsch (1925–   ).

Attitude Toward Jewish Law

In 1900, graduates of the Jewish Theological Seminary were organized into an Alumni Association. In 1940, the association was reorganized to form the Rabbinical Assembly of America, the vast majority of whose members were ordained at the seminary, although graduates of Orthodox and Reform seminaries were also eligible for admission. The Rabbinical Assembly's Committee on Jewish Law and Standards issues opinions (responsa) in matters of synagogue and personal practice.

While the Rabbinical Assembly membership considers the Written and Oral Law sacred, it does allow room for change to meet the exigencies of the modern age. Thus, after its Committee on Jewish Law and Standards has explored a problem, it will often issue a majority and a minority report. For a minority report to be issued, at least two members of the committee must support it. On the question of permitting travel to a synagogue on the Sabbath, for example, a majority report expressed approval, whereas a minority report

forbade it. In another instance, a minority report was issued allowing congregations that are so inclined to observe Jewish holidays for the same number of days as they are observed in Israel (one day less for Passover, Shavuot, and Sukkot). When both a majority and a minority report are issued, members of the assembly have the option of adopting either position.

On some matters of fundamental importance, the Committee on Jewish Law and Standards does not allow its members freedom of choice. Thus, members are not permitted to officiate at a marriage between a Jew and a non-Jew. Anyone who does so is subject to expulsion from the Rabbinical Assembly.

Conversion: Historical Background

In the Jewish past, non-Jews desirous of embracing Judaism have at times been readily accepted and at other times rejected. In the Bible, Ruth the Moabite was warmly welcomed into the Jewish fold. Although Ruth did not undergo formal conversion, she is revered in Jewish history as the ancestor of King David, from whom the Messiah would be descended. In the pre-exile portions of the Bible the idea of conversion was unknown, as evidenced by the fact that there is no Hebrew word for convert. One could only be a Jew by birth. The idea of conversion developed after the destruction of the Temple in 586 B.C.E.

Early Attitudes Toward Conversion

From the time of the Bar Kokhba rebellion against Rome (135 C.E.) onward, Jews began to regard proselytes with suspicion, realizing that much of the hatred toward, and persecution of, Jews was initiated by converts who spied on them and reported them to the authorities. This led many Rabbis of the talmudic period to condemn all efforts to welcome proselytes. Rabbi Chelbo, a fourth-century scholar, is the author of the oft-repeated diatribe, "Proselytes are as troublesome to Israel as a sore [scab]" (*Yevamot* 109b and *Kiddushin* 70b).

Chelbo's view was shared by other talmudic authorities who were concerned that foreigners might infiltrate the Jewish community. This is evident from the anonymous comment (*Niddah* 13b), "Our Rabbis taught: 'Proselytes and those who play with [molest] children delay the advent of the Messiah.'" Here proselytism is equated with pederasty (sodomy between males, especially as practiced by a man with a boy, which was common among heathens), because, the Rabbis feared, a proselyte might introduce these practices into the Jewish community. Elsewhere in the Talmud (the minor tractate *Kallah Rabbati* 2), proselytes are compared with those who masturbate, both condemned as causing a delay in the coming of the Messiah.

Conversion to Judaism was also discouraged by religious authorities because they knew how demanding in time and energy living a full Jewish life can be. Observing the 613 commandments and following the numerous customs, ceremonies, and traditions is difficult to all but the most dedicated. Thus, the Rabbis refused conversion to all with less than pure motives. Specifically, they refused to accept converts whose sole purpose was to be able to marry a Jew. Those who had already converted with only this goal in mind were regarded as inferior.

Geirei Ara'yot

Converts who did not exhibit a sincere desire to join the Jewish community were called *geirei ara'yot*, "leonine proselytes," indicating that they had converted under duress. The origin of the name can be traced to the Bible (II Kings 17:24ff.). After the Assyrians captured Israel in the eighth century B.C.E., the king of Assyria expelled all the inhabitants of Samaria (northern Israel) and replaced them with idolators from strange lands. Disapproving of idolatrous practices, God sent ferocious lions upon the strangers, who took this as a sign of God's disapproval and converted to Judaism. However, while professing a belief in one God, the strangers continued to practice idolatry. Based on this incident, the Rabbis of the Talmud condemned all conversions that were not purely motivated.

The Talmud suggests that when a Gentile expresses a desire to convert, he should be asked, Why do you want to convert to Judaism? Do you know that at present Jews are oppressed, despised, and harassed? If the Gentile answers that he is aware of these problems but nevertheless wants to join the Jewish community, he is accepted as a candidate for conversion (*Yevamot* 47a and Yoreh Dei'ah 262:2).

The above attitudes notwithstanding, the Rabbis of the Talmud were generally accepting of converts. The first-century talmudic sage Shimon ben Gamaliel said, "When a prospective proselyte shows an interest in Judaism, extend to him a hand of welcome" (*Leviticus Rabbah* 2:9). The Midrash (*Genesis Rabbah* 39:14) goes so far as to say, "Anyone who draws a Gentile closer to Judaism and converts him is comparable to being his creator." Rabbi Elazar, in the talmudic tractate *Pesachim* (87b), says: "The Holy One, blessed be He, sent Israel into exile for no reason other than that they should attract proselytes to join the Jewish fold."

Post-Talmudic Views

In post-talmudic times, rabbinic opposition to conversion intensified in response to legislation enacted by Romans and later by Christians that forced Jews to curb their growth. To satisfy those in power, proselytism was discouraged and standards for admission to the Jewish fold were raised.

Despite the strictures placed on conversion, an unusual event took place during the first half of the eighth century in the kingdom of the Khazars. This uncivilized half-Mongolian people who had earlier conquered what is now southern Russia began to cast off pagan practices. As a result of their conquests, the Khazar king and his noblemen mingled with the Slavic population of the conquered territories, and there they came into contact with Jewish merchants. Slowly, they were influenced by Jewish religious beliefs and practices and converted to Judaism.

Maimonides' View

Early in the twelfth century (about 1102), a Catholic priest named Obadiah followed the example of the archbishop of Bari (Italy) and converted to Judaism. Obadiah wrote religious poems and prayers and a book on Torah cantillation. He also kept a diary, fragments of which were found in the Cairo Genizah early in the twentieth century.

After Obadiah's conversion, he was still not accepted as a full-fledged Jew, even by his teacher. He therefore wrote a now-famous letter to Moses Maimonides in which he asked whether his teacher was correct in suggesting that in his prayers Obadiah not use the words, "Our God and God of our fathers," since Obadiah's father was not Jewish.

Maimonides strongly criticized the attitude of Obadiah's teacher and said to the convert, "Go tell your teacher that he owes you an apology. And tell him that he should fast and pray and ask God to forgive him for what he said to you. He must have been intoxicated and forgot that in thirty-six places the Torah reminds us to respect the convert and in thirty-six places it admonishes us to love the convert. Whoever maligns him commits a great sin."

Maimonides added that when Obadiah recites his prayers, he may say, "Our God and God of our fathers," because although he has no Jewish father from the generation that preceded him, the patriarch Abraham is now his father, as he is for all Jews.

Letter to Yemen

Known in Hebrew as *Iggeret Teiman*, this is a famous letter written by Moses Maimonides to the Jews of Yemen in 1172, when they were being forced to convert to Islam. Maimonides wrote the panic-stricken community a lengthy letter, comforting them and assuring them that the descendants of Jacob would survive those who degraded them. "Do not be dismayed," he wrote, "at the persecutions of your people, for these are trials, designed to test and purify us. You should take it upon yourselves to hearten one another. Let your elders guide the youth and let your leaders direct the masses." The letter of encouragement was read publicly in all the congregations of Yemen.

Modern Attitudes

Although in the past Jewish authorities have objected to conversion motivated solely by the desire to marry a Jew, and while to this day all rabbinic bodies urge their members to discourage conversion for an ulterior motive, the current practice, even by some Orthodox rabbis, is to allow such candidates to enter the conversion process. If, during the period of preparation, the rabbi discerns that the candidate is developing a sincere affinity for Judaism, and if it becomes evident that the individual will embrace Judaism unconditionally, acceptance into the Jewish community is granted.

According to a 1990 National Jewish Population Survey, approximately four thousand people were converting to Judaism each year. It is estimated that as many as one in thirty American Jews was not born to a Jewish mother.

In March 2000, the Israeli Supreme Court issued a ruling which ordered the Interior Ministry's Population Registrar to accept conversions conducted by non-Orthodox rabbis in Israel, and to recognize such converts as full Jews. Chief Rabbi Yisroel Meir Lau criticized the ruling.

See Dietary Laws; Euthanasia; Get; Intermarriage; Law, Jewish; Ordination; Orthodox Judaism; Reform Judaism.

Conversion: Rites and Procedures

Moses Maimonides emphasized that a proselyte must be taught the major principles governing the Jewish religion, such as the belief in the unity of God. Accordingly, all Jewish denominations today require that after demonstrating one's sincerity about wanting to convert, the candidate engage in a period of study to become acquainted with the history, laws, and customs of Judaism.

Interestingly, while today rabbis in practically all Jewish communities will accept converts as Jews once they have met prescribed standards, the Syrian Jewish community will not admit converts into their ranks under any circumstances because they want to maintain a close-knit, unadulterated community. This policy was established in 1937 by the Syrian Sephardic Rabbinical Council. A Syrian Jew who marries a convert is totally rebuffed by the community and excluded from its religious and social life.

To underscore the seriousness of the commitment being made, the Rabbis of the Talmud (*Keritot* 8b–9a) introduced a series of well-defined rites that the convert must undergo in order to become a Jew. These are based on the three rites that the Children of Israel (Hebrews) agreed to in entering a covenant with God: circumcision (*brit milah*), immersion (*tevilah*), and the offering of a sacrifice (*korban*) on the altar (Exodus 24:5ff.).

When the Temple was destroyed in the year 70 C.E. and sacrifices were no longer offered, only circumcision and immersion remained as conversion requirements.

In Jewish tradition, the process of conversion, culminating in the admission of a proselyte into the Jewish fold, is a legal matter. As such, it requires witnesses to attest to the fact that the ceremony is properly conducted. Three qualified men are to be present at the circumcision (*brit milah*) and immersion (*tevilah*) of a male convert. The three men (of whom usually at least one is a rabbi) constitute a legal entity known as a *Beit Din*, a court. There is no indication in the Talmud (*Yevamot* 46 a, b) or in the code of Maimonides that all members of the *Beit Din* must be rabbis or learned men, as is sometimes believed. Average, intelligent, knowledgeable Jews may be members of the court.

At the immersion of a female convert, a woman representing the *Beit Din* accompanies the convert into the ritual bath chamber (*mikveh*). She then reports to the three men, who wait in an outer room.

Circumcision

Abraham (Genesis 17:1–14) was the first person to accept God, and this acceptance was demonstrated by Abraham's willingness to submit himself to circumcision. This act was referred to as a "sign" of the Covenant.

When the Bible describes how the Jews prepared themselves for the Exodus from Egypt in anticipation of the Revelation at Mount Sinai, it notes that Moses circumcised all the males so they could be counted as members of the Covenant People and thus be permitted to eat of the paschal lamb (Exodus 12:48). The law was thus firmly established that all males who wish to be part of the Jewish people be circumcised. Circumcision became a sign of identification with the Covenant People.

Jewish law requires that all adult male converts be circumcised in the same manner as a Jewish male infant on the eighth day after his birth as God requires in the Bible (Genesis 17:12): "Throughout the generations, every male among you shall be circumcised at the age of eight days." In 1892, the Central Conference of American Rabbis (Reform) abolished this requirement. In recent years, however, most of its members have reinstituted it, but many will accept an existing circumcision even if it was not performed for the purpose of conversion. Orthodox and Conservative Judaism will not accept, for the purposes of conversion, a routine circumcision, that is, one that is performed for health reasons rather than for the purpose of fulfilling the conversion requirement.

A circumcised non-Jew must submit to a token circumcision if he plans to become a Jew. The *mohel* (a person trained as a specialist in circumcision) merely draws a drop of blood from the penis and then pronounces all the blessings normally recited at a *brit*. The drawing of the blood is known as *hatafat dam brit*, meaning "drawing the blood of the Covenant."

Immersion

The second rite through which Israel entered the Covenant was immersion. According to the Rabbis of the Talmud, the first instance of immersion occurred in the Sinai Desert before the Revelation (*Yevamot* 46b). When the Israelites arrived at the foot of Mount Sinai, Moses instructed them to prepare for a great religious experience. Before they could "meet" God, Moses told them to "sanctify" themselves and to wash their garments (Exodus 19:10). The Rabbis equated the word "sanctification" and the "washing of garments" with immersion in a ritual bath (*mikveh*). Hence, they said, immersion in a ritual bath is required before one may be admitted as a member of the Covenant People.

Orthodox and Conservative practice requires that all male and female candidates for conversion submit to immersion in a *mikveh*. While the 1892 Conference of Reform Rabbis eliminated this practice as it did the circumcision requirement, in recent years Reform rabbis have encouraged converts to submit to immersion. In fact, the Reform movement in Israel has required converts to submit to immersion as well as circumcision.

Strict compliance with Jewish law demands that the convert be naked when the immersion rite takes place. However, when a regular *mikveh* is not available and the immersion is done in a river, lake, or in the ocean, the convert may wear a loose-fitting garment. Such clothing is not considered a barrier (*chatzitzah* in Hebrew) because it does not prevent the water from making full contact with all parts of the body.

When neither a regular *mikveh* nor a natural body of water (lake, river, or ocean) is available, the Committee on Law and Standards of the Rabbinical Assembly (Conservative) permits the use of a swimming pool, particularly an in-ground pool. The Orthodox rabbinate is not as lenient in this regard.

Naming of Converts

Converted males are named during the circumcision ceremony, while converted females are named in the synagogue on a Sabbath after all the rites have been completed.

Although there is no legal requirement mandating that male converts to Judaism adopt the Hebrew name of Abraham or that female converts use Sarah or Ruth as a first name, there is a longstanding tradition to this effect. In most cases, at the time of conversion a male convert is named Avraham ben Avraham Avinu (Abraham the son of Abraham our father) and a female convert is named Sarah bat Avraham Avinu (Sarah the daughter of Abraham our father) or Rut bat Avraham Avinu (Ruth the daughter of Abraham our father). The use of "ben Avraham" and "bat Avraham" is generally insisted upon for purposes of identifying the individual as a proselyte (*Shulchan Arukh*, Even Ha-Ezer 129:20).

Several reasons are offered for naming converts Avraham. First, the Bible (Genesis 17:5) speaks of Abraham as being "the father of a multitude of nations," and since proselytes come from diverse peoples and backgrounds, it is appropriate that they be called the sons and daughters of Abraham. Second, Abraham became known as "the father of proselytes" because once non-Jews have converted to Judaism, their connection with their former non-Jewish families is in many ways severed, and the family of Abraham is now considered their family. It is for this reason that the Talmud calls proselytes "newborn babes" (*Yevamot* 22a).

Offering the convert the name of Abraham is also explained as an expression of deep love. The Midrash says, "God loves proselytes dearly. And we, too, should show our love for them because they left their father's house, and their people, and the Gentile community, and have joined us" (*Numbers Rabbah* 8:2).

It is, of course, a matter of history that not all proselytes have taken the name Abraham. The scholar Onkelos was a proselyte. Flavius Clemens, nephew of the Roman Vespasian, was a proselyte. The Talmud also refers to a proselyte named Judah the Ammonite (*Berakhot* 28a).

Bava Metzia (73b) mentions a contemporary of Rava named Mari bar Rachel. He was named after his mother, Rachel, who was a Jew married to a convert. He was conceived before the conversion but born afterward.

In more recent years, male converts have been named Ben Ami, meaning "son of my people."

Female converts take the name of Sarah because she was the wife of Abraham, the first Hebrew, and also because, as tradition has it, she and Abraham were active in "winning souls" (Genesis 12:5) to the worship of God, Abraham converting idol-worshipping men and Sarah converting the women (*Genesis Rabbah* 39:14).

Some female converts to Judaism take the name of Ruth because the Ruth of the Bible is regarded as the epitome of loyalty to Judaism, although she was not a convert in the formal sense, not having undergone immersion in a ritual bath. Ruth is famous for swearing eternal allegiance to her mother-in-law, Naomi, as expressed in the following immortal words from the Book of Ruth (1:16):

> Whither thou goest, I will go,
> Whither thou lodgest, I will lodge,
> Thy people shall be my people,
> And thy God my God.

Conversion of Children

If a baby born to a non-Jewish mother is adopted by a Jewish couple and is converted by them to Judaism, the child is considered to be a full Jew even though he or she is not old enough to consent to the conversion.

The conversion of a child by a parent without his or her consent is permitted based on the talmudic principle *zakhin le-adam shelo be-fanav*, "one can do another a favor without his knowledge" (*Ketubbot* 11a and Yoreh Dei'ah 268:7). Jews consider it a privilege to be a Jew and to bring someone into the Jewish fold. However, acknowledging the possibility that persons so converted might wish to renounce Judaism when they grow up, the Talmud (ibid.) reserves for them the right to do so when they reach the age of maturity (twelve years of age for a girl and thirteen for a boy). No formal announcement is required of the young man or young woman who wishes to continue to be a Jew after reaching maturity. Once that point has passed, Jewish law considers the person to be like all proselytes who were converted to Judaism as adults, none of whom has the right to annul the conversion. A proselyte remains a Jew in the eyes of Jewish law even if the person abandons the Jewish way of life (Yoreh Dei'ah 268:7, 12) as long as he does not adopt another faith formally.

The child of a Jewish man and Gentile woman must be converted in order to be Jewish. A child whose natural mother is not Jewish but who is adopted by Jewish parents must likewise undergo conversion to be considered Jewish. As is the case with all conversion, its execution must be done in the presence of a *Beit Din*. This tribunal will convene when expressly requested to do so by the adoptive parents.

Reform Judaism, which has adopted the concept of patrilineal descent in addition to the concept of matrilineal descent, considers the offspring of a Jewish father and non-Jewish mother to be Jewish if it is the expressed desire of the parents to bring up the child as a Jew. Formal conversion of the offspring is not required.

The Parents of a Proselyte

Although the Talmud speaks of a convert as being a "newborn babe" with little connection to his or her former family (*Yevamot* 22a), this view was not taken literally by many talmudic and post-talmudic authorities. Not only would it be unnatural for a convert to completely forsake his or her natural parents, they believed it would be impractical as well. The Talmud rules that a proselyte has not forfeited the right to an inheritance due upon the death of his or her non-Jewish parent (Mishnah *Demai* 6:10). Thus, the Rabbis did not consider a child's association with non-Jewish parents to be completely ended. They recognized that there is no law in Judaism more important than the fifth commandment, which demands that one accord respect to one's parents ("Honor thy father and thy mother" [Exodus 20:12]). Rabbis throughout the centuries have insisted that this commandment be followed in letter and in spirit, and they considered it fully applicable to a born Jew and to a proselyte alike. This attitude was emphasized in the twelfth century by Moses Maimonides, who wrote that a convert to Judaism must not cease respecting his or her Gentile father. Although the proselyte begins a whole new life, the individual's blood ties have not been totally severed.

Joseph Caro's sixteenth-century *Code of Jewish Law* (*Shulchan Arukh*, Yoreh Dei'ah 241:9) reminds one of the obligation of a proselyte to treat his or her parents respectfully. In a later section (Yoreh Dei'ah 374:5), Caro adds that when authorities say that a proselyte does not have to mourn parents, it means that the person is not *obligated* to do so, but *may* do so.

Generally, authorities are of the opinion that while not all mourning rites should be observed by a proselyte for non-Jewish parents, some should be observed as a sign of respect. They suggest, for example, that during the week of *shivah* the proselyte continue to wear shoes instead of changing to slippers as Jews by birth do. These authorities feel that those who visit the proselyte mourner and see that not *all* the mourning rites are being observed will understand that a *Jewish* parent is not being mourned.

The Priestly Family

Despite the acceptance of proselytes as the equals of all born-Jews, in Jewish law certain limitations are placed upon the convert, the most oppressive being that a Priest (*Kohen*) may not marry a convert, although the daughter of a *Kohen* may marry a convert. The reason offered is that since early proselytes came from heathen stock, they were considered tainted. Therefore, a Priest, who was expected to be as unblemished as the sacrifice he offered on the altar, was not permitted to marry a woman whose past life might reflect negatively upon his character or stigmatize his offspring.

Today, only the Orthodox community abides by these restrictions. The position taken by the Rabbinical Assembly (Conservative) is that since today's Priests in general are of uncertain genealogy and there is no way to prove that they are descendants of the family of Aaron of the tribe of Levi, the ruling has lost its validity. They also argue that it is unfair and even embarrassing to admit a female proselyte to the Jewish fold, but to then deny her the right to marry a *Kohen* based on a regulation that might have had validity when the Temple existed but is no longer a factor in Jewish life. The reestablishment of the Temple, they argue, is not anticipated. The Reform and Reconstructionist rabbinate share the Conservative view.

The non-Orthodox offer one additional argument: Since Jewish law (Even Ha-Ezer 6:1) considers a marriage between a Priest and a proselyte or a divorcee binding once it has taken place (called *be-di-avad* in Hebrew), there is no valid reason for denying the *Kohen* and his offspring all priestly privileges. Such privileges include officiation at a redemption ceremony for the firstborn (*pidyon ha-ben*) and being called to the Torah for the first honor (*aliyah*).

See Matrilineal Descent; Parents, Honoring; Patrilineal Descent; Sephardim.

Courtesy

See Derekh Eretz; Tircha De-Tzibura.

Court Jews

Better known by the German appellation *Hofjuden* (singular, *Hofjude*), these were men of wealth who in the seventeenth and eighteenth centuries were pressed into government service to assist Christian kings and princes in Central and Eastern Europe to organize their finances. Among their responsibilities were collecting taxes and providing supplies for the armies. Because of their association with those in power, the court Jews were given many privileges not enjoyed by other Jews. Since most of them rarely exercised their influence to alleviate the plight of their fellow Jews, they were generally held in low esteem by the Jewish community. Some, however, such as Samuel Oppenheimer and Samson Wertheimer of Vienna, who was known as the *Judenkaiser*, or Jewish Emperor, did obtain rights and privileges for their coreligionists. Amschel Rothschild, founder of the Rothschild family dynasty, was a *Hofjude* in Frankfurt on Main.

Covenant People

One of the cardinal beliefs of Judaism is that God made a covenant with Abraham and through him with the Jewish people. In this agreement, described in Genesis 12:1–3, God in effect says: Go forth and spread My name throughout the world, and as a reward I will bring blessings to you and your descendants forever.

In the last address of Moses to the Children of Israel, the Covenant is confirmed (Deuteronomy 29:9ff.):

> You stand this day before the Lord . . . to enter into the Covenant which the Lord your God is concluding this day . . . to the end that He may establish you this day as His people and be your God as He promised you and swore to your fathers, Abraham, Isaac, and Jacob. . . . I make this Covenant not with you alone . . . but with those who are not here this day. . . .

In Jewish tradition, the Covenant is regarded as a permanent link between the past and the present. It can never be dissolved. All Jews come under its umbrella by virtue of the fact that they are "of the seed of Abraham." The Jewish people thus became the "holy seed" (*zera kodesh* in Hebrew), and the members of this fellowship became known as the Covenant People. It matters not whether an individual Jew remains fully observant of Jewish law. Membership in the fellowship cannot be denied one who is of the seed of Abraham unless the person has totally abandoned Judaism and has openly adopted another faith.

A member of the Covenant People is called a *ben brit*, literally "Son of the Covenant" (plural, *b'nei brit*). This expression was first used in the Mishnah of the tractate *Bava Kama* (1:2).

See Chosen People.

Creation

That God created the world is an indisputable basic principle of traditional Judaism, but how and when this was accomplished has been the subject of debate throughout the ages.

Two frequently raised questions are: Did God create the world before any physical matter existed (*ex nihilo*), or did He use existent matter? Did God complete Creation in six days, or was Creation incomplete at that point?

The first question revolves about the first two words of the Hebrew Bible, *be-reishit bara*, and how they are translated and interpreted. Is "in the beginning God created [the heaven and the earth] . . ." the correct translation, or is "when God began to create . . ." more correct? The first translation could be interpreted to mean that in the beginning, when nothing yet existed, God created the world. The second translation could be interpreted to mean that matter already existed, and with that matter God began to create.

In Jewish literature, the first allusion to *creatio ex nihilo*, creation out of nothing, is found in the second verse of Genesis, where the term *tohu va-vohu*, "unformed and void," is used. In the Apocrypha (Second Maccabees 7:28), which was written in Second Temple times (fifth to first century B.C.E.), the text reads, "Look up to heaven and earth and all that is therein, and know that God made them out of things that did not exist."

Scholars such as Abraham ibn Ezra (1089–1164) dispute the contention that *be-reishit bara* means creation out of nothing. Some point to creation stories embraced by other cultures—such as the Assyro-Babylonian myth in which heaven and earth are described as having been fashioned out of the carcass of *ti'amat*, a sea-dragon. (The Hebrew word *tehom*, meaning "the deep," in Genesis 1:2 is equated with *ti'amat*.) However, the consensus among Jewish scholars, including Moses Maimonides (1135–1204), is that the doctrine of *creatio ex nihilo* should be accepted by traditional Jews even though the idea of creating something out of nothing runs counter to rational thinking. The explanation is offered that when it comes to the power of God, nothing is impossible.

The Question of Time

While there is agreement in traditional Judaism that God is the Creator of the universe, attitudes vary as to the process by which the world came into existence and the span of time over which this was accomplished. The Torah text itself gives rise to many questions:

- Is the biblical description of Creation lasting six days to be taken literally, or can "days" be interpreted as "years" or "millennia" or "eons"? To Philo of Alexandria, Creation was beyond time.

- How could light (which God called Daylight) have been created on the *first* day when the sun was created on the *fourth* day?

- Why are there two renditions of how Eve was created? Was she created at the same time as Adam (Genesis 1:27), or was she created later, out of Adam's rib (Genesis 2:22)?

The Bible vs. Evolution

In his notes to the Book of Genesis, Joseph H. Hertz (1872–1946), former Chief Rabbi of England, addresses what some consider to be a conflict between the biblical account of Creation and the Darwinian theory of evolution: "In the face of this great diversity of views as to the manner of Creation," he writes, "there is nothing inherently un-Jewish in the evolutionary conception of the origin and growth of exis-

tence from the simple to the complex, and from the lowest to the highest…from amorphous chaos to order, from inorganic to organic, from lifeless matter to vegetable, animal, and man."

Rabbi Hertz adds: "Rashi, the greatest Jewish commentator of all time, taught that the purpose of Scripture was not to give a strict chronology of Creation; while no less an authority than Maimonides declared: 'The account given in Scripture of the Creation is not, as is generally believed, intended to be in all its parts literal.'"

The popular view that the biblical account of Creation is not compatible with the concept of evolution has been discounted by many other Jewish scholars as well. Rabbi Simchah Bunam of Przysucha (1765–1827), a Polish chasidic leader, wrote:

> God created the world in a state of beginning. The universe is always in an uncompleted state, in the form of its beginning. It is not like a vessel at which the master works to finish it; it requires continuous labor and renewal by creative forces. Should these cease for only a second, the universe would return to primeval chaos (quoted in Louis Newman's *The Hasidic Anthology*, 1944).

Rabbi Abraham Isaac Kook, the first Ashkenazic Chief Rabbi of Palestine, wrote in his *Orot Ha-Kodesh* (1938):

> The idea that there is an evolutionary path upwards provides the world with a basis for optimism.…It is easy enough to see how the two [theory of evolution and Bible] can be reconciled. Everyone knows that these topics, which belong to life's mystery, are always dominated by metaphor, riddle, and hint. (Quoted in Louis Jacobs' *Jewish Ethics, Philosophy, and Mysticism*, 1978)

Finally, Morris Adler (1906–1966), a prominent Conservative American rabbi, summed up this attitude in his *May I Have a Word With You?* (1967):

> Creation is not a complete event, permitting God to withdraw into a cosmic vastness outside of it. Creation is a dynamic, ongoing process.

Cremation

Although there are instances in the Bible in which cremation is considered an acceptable practice, as when the bodies of King Saul and his sons who fell in the battle of Gilboa were cremated, most early rabbinic authorities considered cremation a violation of biblical law. Their view is based on two statements in the Book of Genesis. Genesis 2:7 says, "The Lord God formed man from the dust of the earth. He blew into his nostrils the breath of life, and man became a living being." In Genesis 3:19, God says to Adam, "For dust thou art, and unto dust shalt thou return." This, say the Rabbis, means that the body of a deceased must be returned to the earth from which it was formed.

The requirement that the body of a deceased be buried in the earth is a basic principle of Jewish law. The fact that the ashes of cremation are most often scattered or placed in an urn and stored in the home or in a crematorium led the authorities to ban cremation as a legitimate Jewish form of burial. A further reason for Jewish opposition to cremation is that burning the body of a deceased will make physical resurrection impossible.

The extent to which cremation is condemned in Jewish law and tradition is evident in the rabbinic ruling pertaining to a Jew who lived among non-Jews and who feared that when he died he would be buried in their Christian cemetery. The Jew therefore left word that upon his death his body was to be burned. When the man's wish became known, it was ruled that the wish was not to be satisfied because it is far better for a Jew to be buried among non-Jews than to be cremated, the latter being a clear violation of Jewish law.

Burying the Ashes of Cremation

There is a difference of opinion as to whether the ashes of a cremated body may be buried in a Jewish cemetery.

In a responsum, Rabbi Ben Zion Uziel (1880–1953), known as the Rishon Le-Tziyon, also prohibits the burial of ashes of cremation in a Jewish cemetery because a cemetery is a sacred place and cremation is an act done in violation of Jewish law. In a 1935 responsum, Rabbi Abraham Isaac Kook (1865–1935) arrives at the same conclusion.

While many authorities agree with this position, others do not accept it as an inviolable rule. In his *Guide to Life*, Rabbi H. Rabinowicz of London writes that when the wife of Dr. Maurice Davis was cremated (September 27, 1891), Chief Rabbi Hermann Adler was asked whether her ashes could be buried in the Jewish cemetery. He wrote, quoting from *The Jewish Chronicle*, October 2, 1891:

> I have given this request my full consideration in concert with the members of the *Beit Din*. We subscribe to the opinion stated by my venerated predecessor that there does not exist any precept prohibiting the interment in a Jewish cemetery of the ashes of a person who has already been cremated, an opinion supported by other eminent rabbis including the Chief Rabbi of Kovno [Rabbi Isaac Elchanan Spektor, 1817–1896]. We accordingly permit such a burial. At the same time we earnestly

beg you and the members of the community not to construe this permission into a sanction of the practice of cremation. We ardently hope that no brother or sister in faith will make a similar testamentary disposition, involving, as it does, a grave breach of Jewish law.

Some rabbinic organizations, such as London's Burial Society of the United Synagogue (Orthodox) and the Law Committee of the Rabbinical Assembly of America (Conservative), permit the ashes of cremation to be buried in a Jewish cemetery. In this way, these organizations maintain, at least part of the deceased is being returned to the earth, as demanded in Genesis 3:19.

Crucifixion

The practice of putting to death by nailing or binding to a cross and leaving to die of exposure was begun in Persia and later adopted by the Romans. The Roman crucifixion ritual began with a severe beating. Following the beating, the person was hanged on two crossed wooden beams by driving nails through the hands and feet. The body of the victim was not permitted to touch—and thereby defile—the ground. The Jewish historian Flavius Josephus, who lived in the time of Jesus, tells of thousands of Jews who were crucified by the Romans. It is established fact that crucifixion was the Roman way of executing criminals.

Pontius Pilate, the Roman governor of Palestine in the time of Jesus, is portrayed in the New Testament as a leader without control over events. Although the Book of Matthew describes him as accusing Jesus of being the "King of the Jews" and hence a threat to Roman authority, Pontius is presented as unwilling to condemn Jesus and sentence him to execution. The blame for the Crucifixion is placed on the "chief Priests and the elders," who cry out, "Let him be crucified" (Matthew 27:11–25). Pontius Pilate then literally washes his hands in public and says, "This blood is not shed by my hands," while the Jews respond boastfully, "his [Jesus'] blood be upon us and our children." Here, Matthew shifts the guilt for the Crucifixion from the Romans to the Jews.

This account, the basis for the twenty-century-old libel that labels Jews as Christ-killers, is refuted by these following facts:

1. By the time Jesus appeared on the scene, the *Sanhedrin* (the superior judicial body in Jewish life) had lost all authority to pass sentence in capital cases. This authority was held completely by the Romans. A statement (*Berakhot* 58a) by the third-century Babylonian scholar Rabbi Shila testifies to how well established was their control. While the Jews conducted their own courts, they were not empowered to execute criminals. When asked why a person found guilty of adultery had been subjected to thirty-nine lashes rather than to the death penalty, as was prescribed in Leviticus 20:10, Rabbi Shila replied: "Since we have been exiled from our land, we have no authority to execute people." The order to execute Jesus could only have come from the supreme Roman authority, namely Pontius Pilate.

2. According to New Testament accounts in Mark (14:54) and Matthew (26:57), the *Sanhedrin* convened a session on the same night that Jesus was arrested. But this was Passover eve, which in that year fell on the Sabbath. According to the Talmud (Mishnah *Sanhedrin* 6:11)

(a) capital cases could legally be tried only during the day and (b) the *Sanhedrin* would not have heard a case on a holiday and certainly not on a Sabbath. The Gospel of Luke (22:54, 66) does not agree with the other two Synoptic Gospels (Mark and Matthew) on this point. Luke says that the *Sanhedrin* met in the morning of that day.

3. While crucifixion was a method of capital punishment widely used by the Romans, there is no evidence of its ever having been used by Jews. The Jewish methods of execution were stoning, burning, strangling, and slaying by the sword. The first three methods are mentioned in the Bible, and the fourth is mentioned in the Talmud (*Sanhedrin* 52b).

Daf Yomi

Literally, "daily page [of Talmud study]." In 1922, the Lubliner Rav of Poland, Rabbi Meir Shapiro, concerned that Jews were not devoting enough time to study of the Talmud, introduced a concept whereby everyone would study one page (*daf*) of Talmud each day. By doing so, Rabbi Meir calculated, every Jew would complete a review of each of the 2,711 double-sided folios of the sixty-three tractates of the Babylonian Talmud in seven and one-half years. At that point, all who had completed the task would assemble to celebrate a *siyyum ha-Shas*, "the completion of the review of the Talmud." (*Siyyum* means completion; *Shas* is an acronym of *Shishah Sedarim*, the six divisions of the Mishnah.)

On September 28, 1997, under the sponsorship of the Agudas Ha-Rabbonim, 70,000 Jews gathered in New York's Madison Square Garden to celebrate the completion of the tenth cycle of daily study.

Daven (Davenen)

Yiddish words meaning "to pray." One who is praying is said to be davening (an Anglicized form).

The Latin word *divinum*, meaning "to do the divine thing" or "to pray," also means "to offer a sacrifice." Since bringing a sacrifice was the original form of Jewish prayer, the connection between *daven* and *divinum* is palpable. Today, the word *daven* is used in English to mean "to recite prayers of the daily or holiday liturgy."

It is historical fact that the Jews who lived on the Italian peninsula in the early years of the Common Era spoke Latin and developed a dialect called Judeo-Italian, which contained many Latin words. In post-talmudic times, many Roman Jews moved to East European countries, where Yiddish became the common language of Jews. In time, some Judeo-Italian was absorbed into the Yiddish language.

Among the many other theories about the origin of the word *daven* or *davenen*, a most probable one is that it stems from the Hebrew root *davav*, meaning "to speak." In the Song of Songs (7:10) it appears in the form of *doveiv*, and as *dovevot* (referring to the lips moving) in the talmudic tractate (*Yevamot* 97a).

Da'yeinu

A Hebrew word literally meaning "it would have been enough," the name of a popular hymn sung during the Passover *Seder*. The hymn consists of a series of statements, each ending with the word *da'yeinu*, in which God is thanked and praised by Jews for the miraculous release of their ancestors from Egyptian bondage and for His many other gifts to Israel.

It is customary among the Jews of Afghanistan to distribute to each of those at the *Seder* table an onion with its leafy stems attached. Every time the word *da'yeinu* is uttered, each participant strikes his neighbor lightly with the onion stems. The origin of this unique custom is associated with the statement in the Book of Numbers (11:5–6) describing how the freed slaves began to complain about the *manna* that was sent down from heaven for their daily diet. They began yearning for the "good old days of slavery in Egypt," where they were fed fish, cucumbers, watermelon, green leeks, onion, and garlic.

The word *da'yeinu* is used colloquially to indicate "Enough, already!"

Day of Atonement

The English name for Yom Kippur.
See Yom Kippur.

Death

The exact moment that a person ceases to be alive and may be declared officially dead has been the subject of debate among Jewish scholars for almost two thousand years. The Talmud (*Yoma* 85a) says that one can determine a death by checking the nostrils. If after a feather has been placed in front of the nostrils no movement is detected, the person is considered to be dead. (See also Maimonides' *Mishneh Torah*, Hilkhot Shabbat 2:19.)

Later authorities have insisted that in addition to making sure that breathing has ceased, one must ascertain that the heart has stopped functioning. This view was summarized by Immanuel Jakobovits, former Chief Rabbi of England, in his *Compendium on Medical Ethics*: "Cessation of spontaneous respiration and absence of heartbeat for a given time period represents the classical Jewish legal interpretation of death."

Rabbi Yechiel Tucatzinsky notes in his book *Gesher Ha-Cha'yim* that in Jerusalem today the custom is to wait twenty minutes after an individual is declared dead before removing the body from the deathbed.

In recent years, states such as New York have ruled that a person is considered clinically dead once all brain activity has ceased and all cognitive function is absent. Some Jewish scholars nevertheless insist that since there have been a significant number of cases where people declared brain dead have recovered, respiration and cardiac activity must also be carefully checked.

Decalogue

From the Greek *deka* and *logos*, meaning "ten" and "words," the term refers to the Ten Commandments (in Hebrew, *Aseret Ha-Dibrot*), which Moses received on Mount Sinai (Exodus 20, Deuteronomy 5).

See Ten Commandments.

Deceit

In Jewish law, deceit is known as *geneivat da'at*, "stealing the mind." Equating deceit with theft, the Talmud (*Chullin* 94a) explicitly condemns anyone who deceives his fellow man, Jew or non-Jew.

Elaborating on this talmudic teaching, Moses Maimonides (1135–1204) says that when one sells an article, the whole truth must be revealed, even to the extent of informing the buyer of a defect that is not apparent (*Mishneh Torah*, Sefer Kinyan 18).

A century later, the French rabbi-preacher Moses ben Jacob of Coucy expended much effort, traveling as far as Spain in an attempt to encourage Jews to live in accordance with the highest ethical standard. In his popular code *Semag* (an acronym for *Sefer Mitzvot Gadol*), he writes that Jews must not deceive anyone, whether Christian, Muslim, or Jew: "God has scattered Israel among the nations so that proselytes shall be gathered unto them. If Jews behave deceitfully toward non-Jews, who will want to join them? Jews should not lie either to Jew or to Gentile, nor mislead them in any matter."

Judaism characterizes behavior that is deceitful, dishonest, or misleading as a *chillul Ha-Shem*, "desecration of God's name," an affront to God as well as to man (Tosefta on *Bava Kama* 10:15).

Demonology

Although belief in the prevalence of evil spirits (*sheidim* in Hebrew) intent upon harming human beings was once strong in Jewish tradition, Scripture offers only two oblique references to demons. The Book of Deuteronomy (32:17) notes, "They sacrificed to demons, no-gods," and the Book of Psalms (106:37) refers to "their own sons they sacrificed to demons." However, later Jewish texts, particularly those

that emerged in midrashic and mystic literature, have had much more to say on the subject.

According to one school of thought, the
origin of evil spirits can be explained as follows: When God created man on the sixth day,
He created all the souls first and then clothed
them with flesh. Sabbath was fast approaching,
and God had on hand many souls still without
a physical body. But it was too late to complete
the task, for the Sabbath was to be a day of rest.
These "unfinished" souls, these spirits, were
then left to fend for themselves, and they continuously searched for human bodies in which
they might settle. Man, on the other hand, was
wary of the unwelcome, disturbing creatures,
and was constantly on guard, seeking ways to
keep the demons at bay.

While some Jewish authorities, such as Moses Maimonides (1135–1204) and Abraham
Ibn Ezra (1089–1164), took a strong stand
against the belief in demons, most scholars, including Rashi (1040–1105) (Numbers
22:23 and *Berakhot* 6a), believed in their efficacy.

Potential Victims

The Talmud (*Berakhot* 54b) specifies that
"three persons [in particular] require protection from demons: an invalid [a terminally ill
patient], a bride, and a groom." Some add, "a
mourner." This has led to the emergence of a
variety of customs and ceremonies designed
to offset the power of demons, who are constantly on the lookout for victims. The Rabbis
of the Talmud warned that evil spirits lurk in
the dark and attack unescorted people (*Berakhot* 6a and 43b). Therefore, if a person must
be out alone at night, he should carry a torch,
for fire and light are anathema to demons.

Demons were also thought to attack pregnant women and newborn babies. To ward

off such attacks, amulets were hung over the
bed of women who were about to give birth
or who had just given birth. Newborns were
sometimes protected by men who encircled
their cribs and recited psalms and prayers.
Demons, it was believed, were unable to penetrate circles.

Circumcision

On the night before a circumcision (*brit*),
it is customary among Sephardim to hold
the *shalom zakhar* ("Welcome to the Male
Child") ceremony. Sephardim believe that the
presence of a group of people will deter Satan,
who is eager to prevent Jews from observing
the rite of circumcision.

In the Middle Ages and for several centuries afterward, it was common practice for a
mohel who was to perform a *brit* on the Sabbath to leave a scalpel under the baby's pillow
on Friday for the Saturday morning circumcision. Aside from the fact that it is forbidden to
carry an object on the Sabbath, it was believed
that demons who are prone to attack newborn
infants would be scared off by knives and
similar sharp objects. This practice has largely
been abandoned.

Demons and Names

An old Jewish tradition, which still persists
in some quarters, involves the changing of a
baby's—or an adult's—name if the person has
been beset by a serious illness. The change of
name is intended to confuse the Angel of Death
and raise doubts as to the ill person's identity.
A male's name is usually changed to Cha'yim
and a female's name to Cha'ya, both meaning
"life." In cases of a seriously ill young person,
the name is changed to the Yiddish Alter for a
male and Alterke for a female, both meaning
"old one." Sometimes, an entirely new name
is added to the old one.

Demons and Weddings

Demons, lacking a physical body, are intent upon disturbing an individual's joyous celebrations, something they themselves cannot experience. Many features of the wedding ceremony were therefore introduced to safeguard the well-being of the bride and groom. Among Jews of the first century (as well as among Romans of that period), lighted torches were carried during the wedding ceremony as protection against evil spirits. Today, at some weddings, lighted candles are held aloft.

The old practice of creating a circle in order to keep demons at bay was transferred to the wedding ceremony. It became traditional for a bride and sometimes her parents to walk around the groom three or seven times at the beginning of the ceremony to prevent demons from reaching the groom.

Noise is thought to be unbearable to demons. In the Middle Ages, it was customary for the groom to taste of the wine after the seven wedding benedictions had been recited. He would then let his bride taste of it as well, after which he would turn to the north wall and throw the wine glass against it. In the world of Jewish magic and superstition, it was believed that evil spirits came from the north. (The prophets often spoke of the enemy as descending upon Israel from the north.) The most effective way to ward off evil spirits and demons, it was thought, was through noise, including that made by breaking a glass. The kabbalistic explanation for the breaking of the glass follows a similar rationale.

The custom of throwing a glass against a silver plate, rather than against a wall, later developed in some communities. A dented silver plate used for this purpose can be seen in the Jewish Cultural Museum in the Caribbean island of Curaçao's Mikvé Israel–Emanuel Synagogue.

The practice of throwing a glass against a wall following the wedding ceremony has long been abandoned, and today, instead of using the glass from which the wine was drunk, the groom crushes a separate glass with his heel at the conclusion of the ceremony. Since the main purpose of breaking a glass is to create noise, some rabbis prefer that a light bulb be used instead: it is easier to break and usually makes a louder noise.

Using noise as an antidote to offset the powers of evil spirits has been widespread in various cultures. Church bells were originally rung to ward off evil spirits, and the same is true of the noise created by smashing a bottle against the hull of a ship before it is launched. In many cultures a frontal attack was made upon evil spirits by cracking a whip, or throwing things to create noise, or by shooting into the air.

In talmudic times, Jews created noise to scare off demons by rattling nuts in a jar before visiting a privy, where demons were thought to make a home. They would also strike a vessel from which they were about to drink water so as to chase away evil spirits, lest they swallow any that may have settled in the vessel.

Demons and Death

The human fear of demons was heightened when man was most vulnerable, that is, during the last stages of human life and immediately following a death. Believing that fire and light would deter evil spirits, it became customary to place lighted candles at the bedside of the terminally ill. During a burial ceremony, while carrying the coffin to the grave, it became traditional for the procession to pause three or seven times until reaching the burial site. Gaon Sar Shalom, the ninth-century head of the great academy in Sura, pointed out that in his day the procession paused seven times after the burial in order to shake off evil spirits that clung to those returning from a funeral. With each stop, one of the spirits would disappear. Scholars in subsequent centuries (Rashi and Isserles, for example) repeated this explanation for halting the procession when approaching and leaving the grave. Other scholars believe that the custom of halting seven times stems from the seven references to the vanity of human life mentioned in the Book of Ecclesiastes (1:1). The word *hevel,* meaning "vanity," is used three times, and the plural form *havallim* is used twice. Each time the plural is used, it is counted as two references, for a total of four. Thus, the total number of references to the vanity of life (three plus four) is seven.

The custom of washing one's hands before entering a home after a funeral relates to the belief that demons follow the dead and hover around graves, and that those who have followed the cortege and have been in the presence of a corpse, which can impart ritual impurity, must wash to rid themselves of the unclean demons. To this end, a pitcher of water is left at the front door by friends or neighbors. Washing may also be performed before leaving the cemetery, but since water is not always available there, the washing is usually done upon returning home.

The Antidemonic Psalm

Psalm 91, which often appears in the prayerbook with the last verse of Psalm 90 as its opening sentence, beginning with the words *vi-yehi no'am* ["may the pleasantness of the Lord"], lists a series of plagues (punishments) that will befall all who are disloyal to God and promises protection for all who are faithful. Because the plagues are explicitly mentioned in verses 1–9, the Talmud refers to this psalm (*Shevuot* 15b) as *Shir Shel Pega'im,* meaning "Psalm of Affliction." It has also become known as the Antidemonic Psalm, because it was (and in some quarters still is) recited by Jews whenever they believe demons will or can attack. Saturday night is one such time. After a day of having been kept at bay by the holiness of the Sabbath, demons were expected to attack. Psalm 91 is recited to ward them off. Funerals are another occasion when demons were believed to be active, and Psalm 91 is therefore sometimes recited then as well.

In Frankfurt, Germany, it was once reported that on one Rosh Hashanah the *shofar* blower (*ba'al tokei'ah*) could not get the sounds to come out. He blamed it on evil spirits who had lodged themselves in the ram's horn. To remedy the situation, Psalm 91 was recited three times into the wide end of the *shofar.* The demons were dislodged, and the *shofar* was able to emit its beautiful sounds.

See Dybbuk; Exorcism; Superstition and Magic.

Derekh Eretz

A Hebrew term literally meaning "the way [of the people] of the land," this basic concept of Judaism demands that one act with courtesy, civility, and dignity. *Derekh eretz* includes everything from mode of dress to the manner of interacting with others. The tractate *Kiddushin* (40b) goes so far as to say that a person who eats in the street is to be compared to a dog. Some Rabbis view a person with poor manners as ill-suited to testify in court. One who is not concerned with one's public behavior, they maintain, will likely not be concerned with the absolute accuracy of his testimony.

Two minor talmudic tractates, *Derekh Eretz Rabbah* and *Derekh Eretz Zuta,* are devoted to the subject of proper behavior. The following reflects the kind of advice offered:

- A person should not break bread over a dish, wipe the plate with a piece of bread, or gather crumbs and leave them on the table.
- A scholar should not eat standing, lick his fingers, or belch in public.
- A wise man does not speak before one who is greater than he in wisdom.
- A scholar must control his eating and drinking habits.
- A person should not rejoice when among people who are grieving.

In his *Mishneh Torah*, Moses Maimonides devotes the entire section called Hilkhot Dei'ot to the subject of personal conduct. This includes extending love to neighbors and strangers, avoiding criticizing people publicly, refraining from gossip, resisting the temptation to take revenge, and imitating the ways of God by being compassionate and caring.

Deveikut

This basic kabbalistic concept, a name derived from a Hebrew root meaning "to cleave," is based on the words of Deuteronomy 4:4: "You who cleave to the Lord your God are all alive today." Life becomes meaningful and salvation is achieved, according to the teachings of the Jewish mystics, only by attaching oneself to God and following His commandments diligently.

See Kelippah.

Diaspora

Throughout history, Jews who lived outside of Palestine (today, outside of Israel) were said to be living in the Diaspora, a word derived from the Greek meaning "a scattering." The Hebrew word for Diaspora is *golah* or *galut*, although the term *chutz la-aretz*, meaning

"outside the land," is also commonly used, as is the abbreviated form *chul*. The word *kahal*, meaning "congregation," is used to refer to an organized local community in the Diaspora.

The Three Exiles

The first major exile of Jews from their homeland happened between the years 732 and 721 B.C.E., when two kings of Assyria invaded the northern part of Palestine and forced ten of the twelve tribes of Israel to flee. The tribes settled primarily in Assyria, but also in other lands, and although numerous theories have been offered as to the eventual fate of these "Ten Lost Tribes of Israel," all are speculation.

The second major exile of Jews occurred in the year 586 B.C.E., when Nebukhadnezzar of Babylonia, who had conquered many of the nations of the region, overran Palestine, occupied Jerusalem, and laid waste to the Temple built by King Solomon about five centuries earlier. Most of the Jews of the remaining two tribes were exiled to Babylonia.

Jewish enslavement in Babylonia ended when Cyrus the Great of Persia defeated the Babylonians some fifty years later, and in 538 B.C.E. permitted the Jews to return to their homeland. However, many Jews remained behind, establishing strong Jewish communities and important academies of learning in Babylonia. It was in these great institutions, which endured until the tenth century, that the monumental Babylonian Talmud was created.

The third major exile was suffered by Jews in the year 70 C.E., when the Romans captured Jerusalem and destroyed the Second Temple. Many Jews were taken to Rome, while others fled to all parts of Europe, where they established new communities.

Around the first century C.E., many Jews settled in Alexandria, Egypt, making up about forty percent of the city's population. Two of the city's five districts were inhabited exclusively by Jews, and it was reported that Alexandria's main synagogue was so large that not all worshippers could hear the cantor and that hand signals were used so that those seated far from the *bimah* (pulpit) would know when to say "Amen." By 115 C.E., the Jews of Alexandria began to suffer persecution, and the magnificent synagogue was set afire.

Expulsion: A Recurring Theme

Over the centuries, Jews were repeatedly expelled from many countries and principalities where they had established themselves. Among the most devastating expulsions in Jewish history was that from England on July 18, 1290. Sixteen thousand Jews left England, with about sixteen hundred settling in Flanders and the remainder in France.

On July 22, 1306, after living there for almost a thousand years, 100,000 Jews were expelled from France. They settled in neighboring countries, including Germany and Austria, but the acceptance of Jews in Austria was not long-lived, and for an extended period after March 12, 1421, no Jew was to be found in that country.

The relatively pleasant conditions that the Jews of Spain and Portugal enjoyed for many centuries ended in 1492 in Spain and 1497 in Portugal, when the cruel laws of the Inquisition forced many Jews to convert to Christianity; those who resisted were burned at the stake. Tens of thousands were forcibly expelled, fleeing as far north as Holland, as far east as Turkey, and as far south as North Africa.

The Modern Diaspora

The Jewish Diaspora following World War II—after the loss of six million Jews in the Holocaust—encompasses more than one hundred countries around the globe. According to *Jewish Communities of the World*, a 1996 publication of the World Jewish Congress, cities with the largest Jewish populations in the post-Nazi era aside from Israel were: New York City, 1,750,000; Miami, 535,000; Los Angeles, 490,000; Paris, France, 350,000; Philadelphia, 254,000; Chicago, 248,000; San Francisco, 210,000; Boston, 208,000; London, 200,000; Moscow, 200,000; Buenos Aires, 180,000; Toronto, 175,000; Washington, D.C., 165,000; Kiev, 110,000; Montreal, 100,000; and St. Petersburg, Russia, 100,000.

Among the countries with the fewest Jews are South Korea, El Salvador, Iraq, and Tahiti, which have less than 150 Jews each, and Afghanistan, Albania, Algeria, China, Cypress, Egypt, Indonesia, Taiwan, and Zambia, which have less than 100 Jews each.

While Jews of the various Diaspora communities follow different customs in their worship services and differ greatly in the degree of their adherence to Jewish law, what they share is a love of Israel and concern for its welfare.

Dietary Laws

The all-embracing Hebrew term for the Jewish dietary laws is *kashrut*, derived from *kasher* ("kosher" in English), meaning "ritually fit." While the word *kasher* is used mainly in connection with food and the way it is prepared and served, it is also associated with the legitimacy of religious articles such as a Torah scroll, *mezuzah*, *tefillin*, and *etrog*. A religious article is considered *kasher*, or kosher, if it is unflawed—that is, if it is in ritually fit condition for use in the execution of a religious commandment. The term *kasher* is also used to describe a witness who is fit—that is, competent—to testify or sign a marriage contract (*ketubbah*).

Sources of the Regulations

The basic laws of *kashrut* as they pertain to food are listed in chapter 11 of the Book of Leviticus and chapter 14 of the Book of Deuteronomy. These sources enumerate the types of animals, birds, and fish that fall into the kosher category. The Rabbis of the Talmud and later rabbinic authorities added regulations that specify the manner in which these kosher animals are to be slaughtered and prepared for the table. Local rabbinic authorities of later centuries often reinterpreted the rabbinic rulings, resulting in the establishment of different customs in different communities.

The Rationale

The reasons offered for the creation of the Jewish dietary laws are diverse. The Bible itself gives no explanation except to say (Leviticus 11:44–45) that by adhering to these laws, the Children of Israel shall be a holy people, just as God is holy. The Rabbis elaborated on this explanation (Midrash *Sifra* on Leviticus 20:26), saying: "A person should never say, 'I cannot eat the flesh of swine because I loathe it.' What he should be saying is, 'It appeals to me and I would like to eat it, but I can't because my Father in Heaven has decreed that I should not eat it.'"

Nonkosher food, in general, is prohibited to Jews not because it is abhorrent, distasteful, or unhealthy, but rather because eating it violates a biblical commandment. However, Bible scholar Jacob Milgrom pointed out that long before the Torah was written, the people of the Near East were known to have found swine abhorrent, not fit for human consumption, to be used only as a sacrifice to the gods of the netherworld or for other cultic purposes. Since Jews were warned not to imitate heathen practices, this may be the reason why the pig came to be forbidden to Jews.

In his *Guide of the Perplexed*, the twelfth-century philosopher and doctor Moses Maimonides states that the dietary laws are good for the individual Jew because they encourage self-control and teach people to temper their feelings and curb their appetite.

The reason most commonly set forth for the observance of the dietary laws is that they serve as a unifying factor for the Jewish people. The early Rabbis believed that the secret of Jewish survival is separatism; to be a holy people means to be a people apart. Observance of the dietary laws makes mingling with Gentiles more difficult, because socializing often involves dining together. By extension, the Rabbis concluded, if Jews are unable to eat with non-Jews, there will be less intermarriage.

Contemporary Observance

Orthodox and Conservative Jews subscribe to the basic dietary laws, although the degree of observance varies among individual members within each group. Reform Jews, by and large, are not strict about *kashrut* observance, although many willingly refrain from eating pork, shellfish, and other foods explicitly prohibited in the Bible.

It should be noted that during the festival of Passover special dietary laws are imposed in addition to those observed throughout the year. Passover laws are derived from the prohibition against eating *chametz* (leaven) during the Passover holiday. Traditionally, dishes and flatware that have come in contact with *chametz* during the year are replaced for Passover.

A 1993 survey by the Israeli Guttman Institute for Applied Research found that some 90 percent of Israelis observe or try to observe at least some of the dietary laws. Two-thirds said they eat only kosher food at home, although only about half keep separate sets of dishes for milk and meat.

Kosher Animals

For an animal to be kosher, it must meet the criteria in the Book of Leviticus, chapter 11, and in the Book of Deuteronomy, chapter 14. A mammal must have hooves that are fully split and it must chew its cud. If only one of these characteristics is present, the animal is not kosher. Thus, camels, horses, badgers, and hares—which chew the cud but do not have genuine split hooves—are not kosher. The same is true for animals that have split hooves but do not chew the cud, such as the pig. Oxen, sheep, deer, and goats are among the animals that fulfill both requirements and are therefore kosher.

The Stigma of the Pig

Although the pig (*chazir* in Hebrew) should be no more objectionable to Jews than any of the other prohibited animals that have split hooves but do not chew their cud, Jews in fact do find the pig particularly abhorrent. To this day, many Jews who do not observe the dietary laws as a whole still avoid eating the meat of swine.

The Talmud says, "It is not proper to raise pigs," noting that, "cursed is he who raises pigs" (*Bava Kamma* 79b and 82b). The reason is not given, but scholars have associated the deep Jewish aversion to the pig with the Hasmonean period in Jewish history (second century B.C.E.), when the Syrian-Greeks, led by Antiochus Epiphanes, dominated the Palestine scene and tried to force Jews to sacrifice pigs in the Temple and to eat of their flesh (I Maccabees 1:47).

Moses Maimonides, in his *Guide of the Perplexed* (III:48), expresses the opinion that health considerations are the reason for banning the consumption of pig meat:

To eat any of the various kinds of food that the Law has forbidden us is blameworthy. Among all those forbidden to us, only pork and fat may be imagined not to be harmful. But this is not so, for pork is more humid than is proper and contains much superfluous matter. The major reason why the Law abhors it is its being very dirty and feeding on dirty things. You know to what extent the Law insists upon the need to remove filth out of sight, even in the field and in a military camp, and all the more within cities.... You know the dictum of [the Sages], may their memory be blessed: The mouth of a swine is like walking excrement [*Berakhot* 25a].

In Israel pork is called *basar lavan*, "white meat." Supermarket chains do not carry pork, nor is it served in hotels.

Kosher Fowl

The Bible does not specifically name which birds may be eaten. It simply states that any "clean" bird is fit for consumption. Birds traditionally accepted as kosher include the chicken, turkey, duck, goose, and pigeon. In many localities rabbis classify the pheasant as kosher.

The Bible indicates the type of birds that are not kosher, and these include the ostrich, hawk, raven, eagle, owl, pelican, and stork.

Kosher Fish

To be considered kosher, a fish must have fins and scales, as indicated in the Bible (Leviticus 11:9–10; Deuteronomy 14:9–10). The reason is not given, although the thirteenth-century Bible commentator Moses ben Nachman (Nachmanides) believed the reason might be that fish with fins and scales generally swim near the surface of the water, where they are less likely to be contaminated by bacteria. All fish have fins, so to determine whether a fish is kosher, one must ascertain whether the fish has, or ever had, scales. While some fish, such as lumpfish and catfish, don't have scales, swordfish and sturgeon lose their scales at some point in development. According to the *Code of Jewish Law* (Yoreh Dei'ah 83:1), any fish that has scales at any point in its lifetime is considered kosher. Many in the Orthodox rabbinate are not convinced that the juvenile scales that swordfish and sturgeon have can truly be called scales, and they therefore do not consider these fish kosher.

Conservationist magazine (August 1994) describes the bodily covering of sturgeon as follows: "Instead of scales, five rows of large bony plates or shields (called scutes) cover the sturgeon's leatherlike skin. The scutes provide protection against predators and add to the fish's primitive appearance." The Conservative rabbinate, following a responsum issued by Rabbi Isaac Klein, classifies both swordfish and sturgeon as kosher. As far back as the twelfth century, German talmudist Ephraim ben Isaac of Regensburg permitted the consumption of sturgeon, but then reversed himself when he heard voices in a dream telling him it was not kosher.

Fish roe is kosher only if it comes from a kosher fish.

All shellfish—including shrimp, lobster, oysters, clams, and crabs—are not kosher, for they have neither fins nor scales.

Kosher Slaughtering

For the meat of a kosher animal to be considered kosher for consumption, it must be slaughtered by a ritual slaughterer (*shochet*). The purpose of such slaughtering is to drain off as much blood as possible, for the Bible considers blood to be the very essence of life (Leviticus 3:17).

According to the rules of kosher slaughtering, the throat of the animal must be cut with a sharp knife, a knife free of the slightest blemish. With one swift stroke, to inflict a minimum amount of pain upon the animal, its windpipe, esophagus, and jugular vein are severed so that the blood will quickly drain from the carcass.

The mandatory removal of blood applies to all animals except fish. The popular reason for not requiring that fish be slaughtered and koshered like other animals is that fish have only a small amount of blood in them, yet the Rabbis went to great lengths to offer another explanation. They noted in the tractate *Chullin* (27b) that after the Israelites in the desert complained that they were tired of a menu limited to manna, God promised he would provide them with meat and fish as they demanded. Moses says to God: "The people who are with me number 600,000 men.... Could enough flocks be slaughtered to satisfy them? Or could enough fish of the sea be *gathered* to suffice." From the use of the word "gather" when speaking of fish, rather than "slaughter" as used for animals, the Rabbis concluded that fish do not have to be slaughtered like animals.

Koshering Procedure

Before cooking the meat of an animal that has been ritually slaughtered, it is necessary to drain the flesh of as much blood as possible; according to biblical law (Leviticus 7:26–27), blood may not be consumed. If meat (such as liver) is to be broiled, it does not have to be koshered because the broiling process removes most of the blood.

Koshering—or kashering, as the procedure is often called—involves first washing the meat with water, then placing it in a large receptacle filled with water and soaking it for a half-hour to soften the flesh. The water must cover all surfaces of the meat. After this has been done, the meat is placed on a flat, grooved board, which has been set on an incline so liquids can drain off. The meat is then salted thoroughly on all sides with coarse ("kosher") salt; it remains on the board for one hour. Coarse salt is used because of its effectiveness in absorbing a large percentage of the blood from the meat. After the meat is rinsed twice, it is considered kashered—that is, fit for cooking. In the past this process was carried out by the homemaker. Nowadays, most butchers do the kashering for their customers.

The Hindquarter

The hindquarter of an otherwise kosher animal is unfit for use unless all of the blood vessels have been removed, since this is the only way to purge the flesh of enough blood to make it kosher. The prohibition against eating certain parts of the hindquarter is found in Genesis 32:33 and expanded upon in the Talmud (*Chullin* 90a) and *Shulchan Arukh* (Yoreh Dei'ah 65).

The purging process, called *treibening* in Anglo-Yiddish, is a tedious operation, and most butchers are neither capable nor desirous of executing it. For this reason, kosher butchers generally sell only the forequarter of an animal. In some communities outside the United States, specially trained butchers take the trouble to remove all veins, arteries, and forbidden fat from the hindquarter of an animal, thus making it kosher.

Meat, including fowl, that has been left unwashed and unsalted for more than three days after slaughtering cannot be koshered, since the blood has congealed. The only way of salvaging such meat is to broil it.

Kosher Certification

The Orthodox rabbinate generally supervises the *kashrut* of manufactured foods, although in some communities Conservative rabbis and organizations have assumed that role. There are more than fifty *kashrut*-certifying entities in the United States, ranging from the largest, the Union of Orthodox Jewish Congregations, which certifies thousands of products manufactured by eleven hundred firms, to one individual rabbi in Pittsburgh who certifies a single product: a brand of soft drinks.

Each of the rabbinic agencies, communal organizations, and individual rabbis called upon by food manufacturers to certify their products as kosher has its own identifying symbol. The symbol is printed on the box or label of the product receiving certification.

Some kosher food products carry the letter K on their packaging to indicate that they are under rabbinic supervision, but the name of the certifying agent cannot be known unless one writes directly to the manufacturer. The manufacturer will provide a copy of the certification upon request. Commonly used symbols include KD (kosher dairy), KP (kosher for Passover), and Pareve ("neutral"). The most commonly seen symbol is the Ⓤ of the Union of Orthodox Jewish Congregations.

Kosher Style

This misleading term is sometimes used by food stores or caterers who wish to appeal to the Jewish market. "Kosher style" connotes foods Jews enjoy (pastrami, bagels, lox—for example) without affirming the *kashrut* of the items.

Kosher Cooking

A household that observes the dietary laws does not mix meat and dairy products when preparing food, nor does it serve them at one meal. This is based on the biblical prohibition set forth in the Book of Exodus (23:19) and repeated in the Book of Deuteronomy (14:21): "Thou shalt not seethe [cook] a kid in its mother's milk." From this commandment, scholars whose opinions are recorded in the Talmud and other religious literature drew the conclusion that any mixing of meat and milk, whether in cooking or in serving, is prohibited. The kosher home, therefore, has separate dishes, cookware, and flatware for the preparation and serving of dairy and meat products.

Theoretically, nonabsorbent glass dishes can be used for meat and dairy foods, but the practice is not encouraged because, as scholars maintain, "it conflicts with the spirit of the dietary laws." However, the same water glasses are used at dairy and meat meals.

Flatware, pots, pans, and dishes used in conjunction with meat products are said to be *fleishik* or *fleishedik*, and those associated with dairy products are said to be *milchik* or *milchedik*.

Waiting Period

As an extension of the rule that prohibits the cooking of a kid in its mother's milk, the dietary laws forbid eating milk and meat products at the same meal.

The waiting period required between eating meat and dairy has varied from one to six hours, depending on the community and the views of rabbinic authorities on how long it takes to digest specific foods. Among German and most other West European Jews the custom has been to wait three hours between a meat meal and a dairy meal. East European Jews were in the habit of waiting six hours. Among Dutch Jews the prevailing custom has been to wait seventy-two minutes—one hour and twelve minutes.

Normally, a waiting period is not required if one wishes to eat meat after dairy foods. But since hard cheeses adhere to the teeth and take longer to digest, a number of authorities have ruled that a period of time should elapse between eating hard cheeses and meat or meat products. Depending on the rabbinic authority, the waiting requirement is one hour or longer. In all cases, authorities suggest that after eating dairy foods a person rinse his mouth with water before eating meat or meat products.

See Gidin; Passover.

Dignity

See Kevod Ha-Beriot; Kevod Ha-Met; Kevod He-Chai; Kevod Tzibur.

Dina De-Malchuta Dina

See Law-of-the-Land Principle.

Divorce

Judaism regards divorce as a tragedy. The prophet Hosea (2:21–22) considered the covenant of marriage, entered into by husband and wife, to be as sacred and eternal as the covenant established between God and Israel.

To the prophet Malakhi (2:14), dissolution of a marriage represented an act of faithlessness. He lamented: "The Lord has been witness between you and the wife of your youth against whom you have dealt treacherously, though she is your companion, the wife of your covenant."

The Rabbis of the Talmud (*Gittin* 90b; *Sanhedrin* 22a), in deploring the breakup of a marriage, expressed their feelings this way:

"Even the altar [of the Temple, symbolizing God's presence] sheds tears when anyone divorces his wife."

These sentiments aside, Jewish law from earliest times acknowledged the reality that some marriages do fail and that it is in the best interest of all parties to dissolve such unsuccessful unions.

Initiating a Divorce

The first biblical reference to divorce appears in the Book of Deuteronomy (24:1):

"When a man marries a woman in whom, after a time, he is displeased because he has discovered something unseemly about her, *he may write a document of divorce and give it to her....*" Use of the word "he" in this statement implies that only the husband has the right to initiate divorce proceedings and actually issue the divorce. The wife has no such right. According to some talmudic scholars, the man need not have convincing reasons for taking such action. Members of the School of Hillel believed that if a wife is a bad cook, even that would be sufficient grounds for divorce. Rabbi Akiba went even further and said that it is sufficient cause if the husband finds another woman more beautiful than his wife (*Gittin* 90a).

Acknowledging the basic unfairness of denying women the right to initiate a divorce, in post-talmudic times Jewish courts ruled that under certain conditions a man could be *compelled* to divorce his wife. Such reasons include the man's refusal to have marital relations or his inability to support the woman adequately. The courts also justified taking action in a woman's behalf if the husband was unfaithful, physically abusive, or had contracted a loathsome disease such as leprosy.

Until the tenth century, Jewish law permitted a man to have as many wives at one time as he wished, whereas a woman could have but one husband. Around the year 1000, the esteemed Rabbi Gershom ben Judah (Yehudah) of Mainz, Germany [965–1028], convened a synod of rabbis and leaders of nearby communities. This group issued a series of regulations (*takanot*), among them one that withdrew a man's right to obtain a divorce without first obtaining his wife's consent and another that related to a prohibition against polygamy, despite the fact that the Bible permits it. The bans issued by this synod was known as the *Cheirem* [excommunication] *de-Rabbenu Gershom*, meaning that anyone who violated the rules set down by the synod would be isolated from the Jewish community.

Rabbis of subsequent centuries recognized that the ban against divorce without mutual consent could become a hardship to a man who wished to be free of an insane wife. How could she agree to accept the *get*, the Jewish divorce document, if she is totally incompetent? Since the man would have no remedy, the authorities introduced a procedure known in Hebrew as *heter mei'ah rabbanim*, "permission by one hundred rabbis," whereby one hundred rabbis or knowledgeable laymen would sign a document granting the husband the right to issue a divorce to a wife not competent to receive it.

The "One Hundred Rabbis" principle did not apply to a woman seeking a divorce from an incompetent husband, since biblical law requires the man to write the divorce and to deliver it to his wife. A court could not be empowered to act in the woman's behalf, since it would contravene the legislation of the Torah. As a result, if a man either refuses or is unable to issue a divorce decree, the undivorced woman becomes an *agunah* ("chained woman"), and as such is unable to marry while her husband is still alive.

Civil vs. Religious Divorce

In a responsum (*Ma'arkhei Lev*, responsum 87) published in 1922, the great Romanian scholar Rabbi Yehudah Lev Zirelson (1859–1941) ruled that a civil marriage between two Jews is sufficiently valid to require that should the two divorce civilly, a Jewish divorce document (*get*) must be issued if either partner is to remarry in a Jewish ceremony. Zirelsohn's reasoning was that if a *get* were not issued, more harm than good would result. In the eyes of the Jewish community, the couple was assumed to be husband and wife. If they were suddenly divorced civilly but a *get* were not issued, the public might think the husband derelict in his duty. Furthermore, should either one be remarried by a rabbi in the future, the public might think that the rabbi was conducting a ceremony in which one of the partners was still married.

Divorce and Intermarriage

Jewish law does not recognize the validity of a civil marriage between a Jew and non-Jew. If a couple were so married and subsequently obtained a civil divorce, rabbis of all denominations would marry the Jewish partner to another eligible Jew. A *get* is not required since the marriage was not entered into "according to the laws of Moses and Israel."

Cohabitation Without Marriage

Jewish tradition does not look favorably upon couples living together without having been formally married. However, there is a mistaken notion that if it is public knowledge that a Jewish man and a Jewish woman have lived together for more than thirty days and then decide to separate, they must obtain a Jewish divorce before either can remarry. The fifteenth-century German talmudic scholar Rabbi Israel Isserlein and, in more recent times, Chief Rabbi Herzog of Israel have ruled that living together without having been formally married does not constitute a marriage and therefore a *get* is not required to end the relationship.

Dogma

Derived from the Greek meaning "opinion," the term dogma is used in theology to refer to a body of beliefs that have been authoritatively and formally approved by the leaders of a religious movement. Thus, for example, the Apostles' Creed and the catechism represent Catholic dogma. One is not a faithful Catholic if one does not accept the beliefs expressed therein.

Jewish authorities never formulated a firm and formal body of doctrine that Jews must embrace if they are to be counted among the faithful. In Judaism, it is practice rather than belief—deed, not creed—that determines the loyalty of a Jew. How a Jew behaves is more important than what he believes. This is not to say that over the ages Jewish authorities have not tried to formulate doctrinaire beliefs.

From Philo to Albo

The first-century C.E. Alexandrian Jewish philosopher Philo borrowed elements from Greek and Jewish teachings and fused them into one system of eight essential principles of faith. These principles, as A. Wolfson of Harvard University pointed out (*Philo, Foundations of Religious Philosophy*, 1947) are (1) God's existence, (2) God's unity, (3) divine providence, (4) creation of the world, (5) unity of the world, (6) existence of incorporeal ideas, (7) revelation of the Law, and (8) the eternity of the Law.

Philo's belief that Jewish Law is the purest revelation of God's presence greatly influenced Jewish thinkers for the next twenty centuries. Most prominent of these was Spanish-born Moses Maimonides (1135–1204), who spelled out Thirteen Principles of Faith that Jews are obliged to accept if they are to be counted as faithful members of the flock of Israel. Foremost among these are: a belief in the existence of God, God's unity, the advent of the Messiah, and resurrection of the dead. To Maimonides the Principles of Faith were dogma, which is evidenced from his statement that a person who disregards any of these fundamentals "has departed from the general body of Israel," for "he denies the root truth of Judaism."

Succeeding generations have accepted Maimonides' Articles of Faith, which is evidenced by the fact that it became the basis of the *Yigdal* prayer, said to have been composed around 1300 in Italy by Daniel ben Judah, a judge (*da'yan*) in Rome. The *Yigdal* became part of the Ashkenazic and Sephardic liturgies.

In the fifteenth century, the Spanish religious philosopher Joseph Albo (*c.* 1380–*c.* 1435) composed his book *Sefer Ha-Ikarim* (*Book of Root-Principles*) in which he reduced to three the number of primary beliefs that are to govern Jewish thinking: divine existence, divine revelation, and reward and punishment. From these root-principles all other beliefs flow, including belief in the coming of the Messiah, *creatio ex nihilo*, and resurrection of the dead.

The Shema and Monotheism

Of all Jewish beliefs, perhaps the most basic is embodied in the popular *Shema* prayer, which appears in the Book of Deuteronomy (6:4): "Hear, O Israel, the Lord is our God, the Lord is One." This, the first prayer that a young child is taught and the final prayer uttered by a dying person on his deathbed, has been the keynote of Judaism for 3,500 years.

What the *Shema* proclaims—the fundamental truth about the unity and uniqueness of God—is the source from which the concept of monotheism springs.

From this concept of the oneness—the unity—of God, the Rabbis of the Talmud and later scholars have extrapolated a profound lesson, namely, that just as God is One, so is all of humanity one; all mankind are brothers and are obligated to observe the commandment "Thou shalt love thy neighbor as thyself" (Leviticus 19:18).

Even Baruch (Benedict) Spinoza (1632–1677), the Dutch philosopher who was labelled an atheist for his unorthodox views, concluded that the *Shema* was a basic dogma of Judaism. In his *Tractatus Theologico-Politicus* (1670), he wrote: "He is One. Nobody will dispute that this doctrine is absolutely necessary for complete devotion, admiration, and love toward God. For devotion, admiration, and love spring from the superiority of one over all else."

Spinoza was considered a heretic and was excommunicated in 1656, not so much for his pantheistic views—which claimed that nothing is supernatural and that God is not transcendent, that each finite thing is part of God and God is immanent in all things—but because he flouted the authority of the rabbinical courts of Amsterdam.

Mendelssohn's Approach

The German-Jewish philosopher-scholar Moses Mendelssohn (1729–1786) was the chief proponent of the idea that Jews must distance themselves from the Christian belief that salvation is dependent upon acceptance of religious dogma. Mendelssohn believed that Judaism is a revealed *law*, not a revealed *religion*. The Jewish belief in God or in resurrection or in immortality, he contends, is mandated by reason, not blind faith.

Mendelssohn's view that Judaism is not governed by dogma is shared by few scholars—modern or ancient. The Romanian-born Solomon Schechter (1847–1915), who served as president of the Jewish Theological Seminary of America until his death, took strong issue with such views. In *Studies in Judaism* (1945), he wrote: "It is true [that] religion is a concentration of many ideas and ideals which make this religion able to adapt itself to various modes of thinking and living. But there must always be a point round which all these ideas concentrate themselves. This centre is *dogma*."

Dreams

The early Hebrews attached great significance to dreams, which were generally considered to be divinely inspired. The act of dreaming, they believed, was a method by which God communicated with individuals, particularly with His favored subjects, although sometimes with those of lesser status.

Early Biblical Dreams

The earliest dream recorded in the Bible (Genesis 28) is that experienced by Jacob after he left Beersheba en route to Haran. Stopping to rest for the night, he gathered some stones strewn on the ground to serve as a pillow. He soon fell asleep and dreamed that "a ladder was standing on earth and its top reached heaven. And, behold, angels of God were ascending and descending the ladder...." At this point God appeared to Jacob and promised that his descendants will be many and "all the families of the earth shall bless themselves through you and your descendants." The nineteenth-century English poet and essayist William Hazlitt (1778–1830) considered this description of Jacob's dream to be "the most beautiful in literature."

Shortly after this episode, the Bible (Genesis 31:24) describes a dream of Laban, Jacob's father-in-law, who was not one of God's favored sons. When Jacob was fleeing from Laban after having been accused of stealing his father-in-law's property, God appears to Laban in a dream and warns him not to "attempt anything with Jacob good or bad."

For the most part, the dreams in the Bible serve as an instrument through which God's favored sons can show their wisdom. The prime examples are the dreams of Pharaoh's baker and butler, as well as Pharaoh himself, which Joseph interpreted (Genesis 40, 41), and the dream of Nebukhadnezzar of Babylonia, which Daniel interpreted (Daniel 2).

Talmudic Views

The Rabbis of the Talmud could not agree on whether dreams represented good omens, bad omens, or had no particular meaning. They felt, generally, that dreams have "no effect one way or the other" (*Gittin* 52a).

When the third-century talmudic scholar Samuel had a bad dream, he would say, quoting Zekhariah 10:2, "The dream speaks falsely." When he had a good dream, he would question, "Do dreams ever speak falsely?" and would then quote the Book of Numbers (12:6): "I [God] speak with him [a prophet] in a dream." Samuel thereby implied, as did some of his colleagues, that there was an element of the prophetic in all dreams and dreams should therefore not be ignored. As one of Samuel's colleagues put it, "a dream is one-sixtieth prophecy" (*Berakhot* 57b).

This view was shared by the twelfth-century scholar and philosopher Moses Maimonides, who theorized that in a dream the imaginative faculty is inspired, which is the first step in authentic prophecy (*Guide of the Perplexed* III 36–38).

There is no coherent traditional view on the significance or efficacy of dreams in talmudic or later literature. In the tractate *Berakhot* (55a), Rabbi Chisda says that "a bad dream is better than a good dream," which Rabbi Huna explains (55b) as meaning that "a good man is not shown a good dream and a bad man is not shown a bad dream," that is, good people have bad dreams and bad people have good dreams. Rashi explains this incongruity by saying that a bad dream will cause a good person to think about his conduct and use the opportunity to improve himself. On the other hand, bad people will conclude from their good dreams that they have no need to improve their behavior and will thus be denied a reward in the world to come.

Notwithstanding their explanation of how bad dreams can be viewed in a positive light, the Rabbis of the Talmud recognized the validity of fasting after having had a bad dream in the hope of nullifying any ill-effects of the dream. The talmudic tractate *Ta'anit* (12b) refers to this personal fast as *ta'anit chalom*, a "dream fast." However, many of the rabbinic scholars in the Middle Ages, such as the Spanish authority Solomon ibn Adret (1235–1310), believed in the efficacy of dreams but had strong reservations about the need to fast following a bad dream.

The legal rulings of Jewish authorities were influenced by their dreams. Rabbi Ephraim ben Isaac of Regensburg, Germany (died 1175), who earlier had ruled that sturgeon is a kosher fish, reversed himself after a dream revealed to him the error in his thinking. Today, the consensus is that sturgeon is kosher.

Dress Code

Aside from the legislation in the Torah that (1) fringes (*tzitziot*) be attached to the four corners of an outer garment (Numbers 15:37–41); (2) that a garment not be made of two incompatible materials, such as a mixture of animal (wool or silk) and vegetable (linen/cotton) products, called *shaatnez* in Hebrew (Deuteronomy 22:11); and (3) that a man not dress in women's garments (Deuteronomy 22:5), there is no mandatory dress code in Jewish law.

Garment Colors

The only Jews required to wear special garments were members of the priestly family: Aaron and his descendants. The Bible says (Leviticus 16:4) that when Aaron, the High Priest, enters the Holy of Holies on Yom Kippur (the only time in the year when he is permitted to do so), he is to replace his usual garments made of gold with vestments of plain white linen, which represents purity and forgiveness.

The Rabbis of the Talmud compare the white garments to the black garb of an accused individual who appears before an earthly king and awaits judgment. He dresses like a mourner because he fears that he might be found guilty and be punished. Israelites, on the other hand, when appearing before God on Yom Kippur, dress in white because they are confident that He will excuse their sins and pardon them.

Black clothing was considered by the Rabbis of the Talmud to be suitable not only as a sign of mourning but also of distress (*Chagigah* 16a). The Talmud (*Bava Metzia* 59b) relates that when Rabbi Akiba was assigned the sad duty of notifying Rabbi Eliezer ben Hyrcanus that he was being excommunicated, "he dressed himself in black clothing."

Jewish women who lived in Babylonia wore colored garments, while those who lived in Palestine wore starched white linen garments (*Pesachim* 109a). No reason for the distinction is given.

Personal Appearance

The importance of personal appearance in the Jewish tradition was summed up in the talmudic tractate *Bava Metzia* (52a), where the fourth-century scholar Abbayei said: "Overpay for your back, but pay only the exact amount for your stomach," meaning that one should spend as much as necessary on one's clothing to appear well-groomed, but no more than is necessary for food to sustain oneself.

The Rabbis of the Talmud encouraged the wearing of fine garments. The tractate *Berakhot* (57b) says that fine garments are among the things that "enlarge a man's heart," that fill him with pride. The Midrash (*Exodus Rabbah* 18:5) notes that "a man's dignity is shown through his dress."

Scholars, especially, were expected to be meticulously dressed; their appearance was always expected to be elegant. The Talmud noted that the scholar must be careful not to wear patched shoes (*Berakhot* 43b). If he goes out of doors with a stained garment, he is "worthy of death" (*Shabbat* 114a).

Women, like men, were expected to maintain an attractive appearance and to abide by the principle of modesty (*tzeniut*). Their bodies were always to be fully covered, including their hair, which was to be hidden by a wig or a piece of cloth (*tikhl*). Depending on the customs of the country in which they lived, women would enhance their appearance with colorful garments.

Dressing up on the Sabbath and holidays was a tradition followed by men as well as women. A man was obligated to buy his wife new clothing and jewelry for the major holidays, and men were supposed to honor the Sabbath by wearing special clothes. This tradition has come to be known as *noi mitzvah*, "the beauty of the *mitzvah*," a concept comparable to *hiddur mitzvah*.

Biblical law (Deuteronomy 22:5), which prohibits men from wearing the garb of women, was extended by the Rabbis to include all practices that are specifically associated with women. Maimonides points out that the commandment in Deuteronomy implies that a man should not wear brightly colored clothing or shiny jewelry if such is the practice among women in his locality. He also points out that man should not pluck white hairs from his head or face or dye his graying hair, which are also the habits of women. Joseph Caro's *Code of Jewish Law* (*Shulchan Arukh*, Yoreh Dei'ah, 182:6) prohibits a man from looking in a mirror, calling it "a woman's way."

See Hiddur Mitzvah.

Dukhening

An Anglicized term derived from the Hebrew word *dukhan*. During morning prayer services on various occasions, Priests (*Kohanim*) mount the raised platform (*dukhan*) in front of the ark, then, arms extended, they confer upon the congregation the *Priestly Benediction*, which consists of the three verses from the Book of Numbers (6:24–26). The ceremony is popularly known by the Anglicized term *dukhening*. The Hebrew term is *Birkat Kohanim*.

See Priestly Benediction.

D'var Torah

A Hebrew term literally meaning "word of the Torah," generally referring to an explication of the Torah portion. This short discourse is delivered by a rabbi or a knowledgeable layman before or after the Torah reading on Sabbaths and holidays. Some rabbis suggest that a *D'var Torah* should be delivered at every meal, especially on the Sabbath and at joyous celebrations.

The French expression *explication de texte*,

meaning an intensive scrutiny and interpretation of the interrelated details of a written text, best sums up the precise meaning of the *d'var Torah* concept. In many congregations, the *d'var Torah* has replaced the traditional Sabbath sermon.

Dybbuk

From a Hebrew root meaning "to cleave," this term is used in reference to a demon that clings to the soul of a living person who has sinned. There, it finds a temporary safe haven. Although stories about dybbuks were common in ancient Middle Eastern and Roman literature, the first such story in Jewish literature appeared in the *Maaseh Book*, published in 1602. In this tale, the demon, which had resided in the body of a cow and was forced to leave when the cow was about to be slaughtered, infiltrated a young man.

Famous kabbalists, such as the sixteenth-century Ashkenazi rabbi Isaac ben Solomon Luria of Safed (better known by the acronym Ari), were known to have used their supernatural powers to exorcise a *dybbuk* from the body of a "possessed" person. In later centuries, wonder-working rabbis called *tzadikim* were known to invoke God's name in its various mystic configurations and thus rid sufferers from their tormentors. One such miracle worker was the Ba'al Shem Tov (1700–1760), the founder of the chasidic movement, who began his career by exorcising demons.

In some procedures, to force the demon to leave the body, a ram's horn is blown and the exorcist shouts, "Get out! Get out!"

Today, cases of exorcism take place in Israel, although rarely.

The Yiddish-Russian author Solomon Anski (1863–1920) popularized the subject through his play *The Dybbuk*.

See Demonology; Exorcism.

Ecology

Although Jewish sources do not address ecological issues to a great extent, some scholars cite a statement in the Book of Genesis (1:28) as proof that Jewish tradition is not environmentally friendly: "God blessed them [Adam and Eve] and said to them, 'Bear fruit and multiply and fill the earth and master it! Have dominion over the fish of the sea, the fowl of heavens, and all crawling things upon the earth.'" This verse has been construed by some as a mandate for man to exploit the environment, to poison the atmosphere, to despoil natural resources for the benefit of man.

Others claim that Judaism is concerned with preservation of the environment. They point to the Book of Deuteronomy (20:19–20), which legislates: "When you wage war against a city, and you have to besiege it for a long time in order to capture it, you must not destroy its trees by wielding an ax against them. You may eat of them but you must not cut them down....Only those trees of which you know are not trees for eating, those you may cut down to build siege works against the enemy." Most of the Rabbis of the Talmud shared the view of the scholar Rabina, who said: "If the trees' value for other purposes exceeds its value as a producer of fruit, it may be cut down" (*Bava Kama* 91b). This view, which was governed by the principle of *bal tashchit*, applied not only to trees but to the environment in general.

One of the reasons for the establishment of the sabbatical year (Exodus 23:10–11; Leviticus 25:1–7), which requires that farmers allow their land to lie fallow every seventh year, is that the land will be able to revitalize itself. This, it is noted, is proof of Judaism's desire to preserve the world's natural resources.

See Bal Tashchit.

Education

One of the early commandments in the Torah pertains to the education of all Israelites, young and old. In the Book of Deuteronomy (6:1ff.), the Children of Israel are instructed to observe the commandments of God embodied in the Torah and to teach them to their offspring: "...to speak of them when you are sitting in your house and when you are walking in the way..." From earliest times to the present, learning and study have been mainstays of Jewish life and have insured Jewish survival and continuity.

The initial effort at educating Jews was made from the third century B.C.E. through the fifth century C.E. Great energy was expended by the Rabbis of the Talmud as well as their forerunners, the 120-member Great Assembly (*Anshei Knesset Ha-Gedolah*) to establish a high standard of education and piety that they hoped would become the norm in Jewish life. The importance of education was summarized by the first-century scholar and leader of Jewry, Hillel the Elder: "An uncultured person cannot fear sin, and an ignorant person cannot be truly pious" (Ethics of the Fathers 2:6).

A reverence for learning has prevailed throughout Jewish history, and the Talmud (Mishnah *Hora'yot* 3:8), in a revealing passage, demonstrates this quite dramatically. It says that a Priest takes precedence over a Levite, a Levite takes precedence over an Israelite, and an Israelite over a *mamzer* (bastard), provided that all are equal in learning. However, if a *mamzer* is a scholar and the High Priest is an ignoramus, the learned *mamzer* takes precedence over the ignorant High Priest. The ideal man, to the Sages of the Talmud, is the one who studies Bible and Mishnah, attends to the needs of scholars, is honest in business, and speaks gently to his fellow man (*Yoma* 86a).

The emphasis placed on learning in Jewish tradition propelled Shimon ben Shetach, a first-century B.C.E. leader of Palestinian Jewry (and a brother-in-law of King Alexander Yannai), to establish community-sponsored public schools. A century later it motivated Joshua ben Gamala, the wealthy High Priest (about 64 B.C.E.) who was not learned himself, to establish in every town at least one school for children over five years of age (*Bava Batra* 21a). This was the beginning of a long tradition demanding excellence in education among Jews, young and old alike. Only through education, it was believed, will God-fearing citizens be produced.

The Age to Start

Later Rabbis of the Talmud, such as the second-century Judah ben Tema, amplified the importance of early and continued study when he said (Ethics of the Fathers 5:25): "Five years of age is the proper time for the study of Bible; ten years, for the study of Mishnah; fifteen, for the study of Talmud...." Actually, it was recommended that the study of Torah begin at an age earlier than five, and that no age was too young. In the Midrash, one Sage is quoted as saying: "At age three a child is ready to learn the letters of the Hebrew alphabet" (*Tanchuma* on Kedoshim 14).

Joshua ben Levi, the third-century Palestinian scholar, was once told how very young children were taught to remember the alphabet by associating the letters with valuable concepts. For example, they were taught to remember the first two letters, the *alef* and *bet* by repeating the words *alef binah*, meaning, as Rashi puts it, "The study of Torah is the beginning of wisdom." The *gimmel* is then combined with the *dalet* to form the words *gemul dalim*, which means, "Be compassionate to the poor." Similar associations were

established for the remaining letters of the alphabet (*Shabbat* 104a).

Resh Lakish, another third-century Palestinian scholar, commented on the importance of teaching little children: "The world continues to exist only for the sake of the breath of school children [engaged in sounding out the words of the Torah]" (*Shabbat* 119b).

This did not mean that children who did not have the capacity to study and learn were expected to achieve a high degree of knowledge. The Rabbis also encouraged fathers to teach their sons a trade. The second-century scholar Judah ben Ila'i warned that "anyone who does not teach his son a trade is as though he had taught him to be a thief" (*Kiddushin* 29a). In fact, some of the greatest Rabbis of the Talmud were also known to have a trade, including Yochanan bar Nappacha (the blacksmith) and Yochanan Ha-Sandler (the shoemaker).

The general theory of education that governed the thinking of the Rabbis was expressed by Abbayei, a third/fourth-century Babylonian scholar: "That which one learns in his youth is not forgotten" (*Shabbat* 21b). Two centuries earlier, the Palestinian scholar Elishah ben Avuyah suggested the same truth more poetically: "If one studies in his youth, to what can this be compared? To writing with ink on clean paper" (Ethics of the Fathers 4:25).

Education of Women

In talmudic times an occasional scholar, such as the second-century Ben Azzai, favored extending education to girls. The Mishnah (*Nedarim* 35b) says that daughters as well as sons may be taught Torah. However, most talmudic authorities agreed with Rabbi Eliezer, also of the second century, who put it rather crudely when he said: "Anyone who teaches his daughter Torah [which includes Talmud] teaches her lewdness" (Mishnah in *Sotah* 20a). Eliezer was concerned that if the girl learned the many laws in the Talmud that relate to sexuality, she might become unduly excited sexually.

The Rabbis of the Talmud (*Berakhot* 17a) tried to put a positive spin on the practice of denying women equal access to Torah studies by saying that women are amply rewarded by being successful in encouraging their husbands and sons to devote themselves to study. Women who fulfilled this role well were highly praised. For the guidance they gave the family and the support they lent their husbands, they were called "righteous women." For the sake of righteous women, say the Rabbis, the Israelites merited redemption from Egyptian bondage (*Sotah* 11b).

The more likely explanation for denying women an education equal to that of men is that women, unlike men, were not obligated to perform all of the positive commandments of the Torah, so their need for a formal education was not thought to be pressing. For girls, the primary place of learning was the home. They learned unsystematically by observing and helping their mothers and by listening in on lessons taught to the boys of the family by their father or a private tutor.

Over the centuries, various authorities have urged that girls be given a thorough Jewish education. However, aside from the legendary Beruriah, wife of the second-century Palestinian talmudic scholar Rabbi Meir (and the daughter of the illustrious scholar Chaninah ben Teradyon), few women achieved stature as learned persons or scholars. The Talmud was so enchanted by Beruriah that it exaggerated her accomplishments, claiming that "she learned three hundred laws from three hundred teachers in one day" (*Pesachim* 62b). In

fact, many of the scholars in talmudic times did not think highly of women, describing them as lightheaded, gossipy, and incapable of learning.

Throughout most of Jewish history, the role of the woman has been to foster education, not to become educated herself. Her responsibility was to ensure that her sons attended classes and that her husband was cared for upon returning home from work or from studying in the academy. Not until after World War I did the Orthodox establishment recognize the need for formally educating women. In 1917, the first school for girls was organized in Cracow, Poland, by Sarah Schenirer with the aid of the ultra-Orthodox Agudat Israel. This was the beginning of the Beth Jacob School educational system, which now boasts an international network of schools, including teacher training institutes.

Communal Responsibility

The concept of Jewish communal responsibility for the education of its youth, which was introduced by Shimon ben Shetach and Joshua ben Gamala, was accepted by all sizable Jewish communities over the centuries. The third-century Palestinian scholar Samuel ben Nachman observed: "When a man teaches Torah to his neighbor's son, Scripture regards it as though he had begotten him" (*Sanhedrin* 19b).

In the Jewish community everyone was considered a neighbor, and it was the duty of communal leaders to ensure that all children, rich and poor, including the fatherless, were properly educated. Education was compulsory for all boys beginning at age six; girls were not given a formal education. Class size was limited to twenty-five students.

Discipline was rigid, for teachers took literally the words of Solomon, "Spare the rod and spoil the child." (Proverbs 23:13). However, the famous talmudic scholar Rav tempered this admonition by saying, "When you wish to punish a pupil, hit him with nothing harder than a shoelace."

To ensure a morally pure school atmosphere, male teachers were expected to be married, so that mothers who brought their children to school would not be in a position of having contact with an unmarried man.

In the Middle Ages, the larger Jewish communities carried on their traditional role of providing education to all children. Tuition was free and teachers were paid from the communal treasury. In smaller communities that did not have resources to provide free educational services, a teacher (known as a *melamed* in Hebrew) would educate children in his home and parents would pay a fee to the teacher. Since the lessons were carried out in one room of the teacher's house, such informal schools were called *cheder* ("room" in Hebrew).

In some of the larger European communities, day schools called *yeshivot* (singular, *yeshivah*) were established for children and teenagers. In these schools—which subsisted on communal funds, but mostly on modest tuition fees and donations from the general public—intensive Jewish studies were carried on, often from early morning into the evening. In subsequent centuries *yeshivot* flourished in all parts of Eastern and Western Europe.

The Musar Movement

In European *yeshivot* the educational focus was on Talmud and its commentaries and also on Joseph Caro's *Code of Jewish Law* (*Shulchan Arukh*). In the nineteenth century, Rabbi Israel Lipkin (1810–1883), also known as Israel Salanter, introduced the idea of incorporating the teaching of morals and ethical living (*musar* in Hebrew) to *yeshivah* students in order to strengthen their inner piety and religious sensitivity. He traveled throughout Europe from his base in Lithuania to spread his belief, and as a result many schools began to devote one-half hour or more each day to lecture students about inculcating ethical values. Lipkin's own teachings were collected by one of his pupils, Isaac Belzer, in a volume titled *Or Yisra'el* ("*The Light of Israel*").

Religious Education in the U.S.

In the United States, the first Hebrew school was established in 1729 when New York's Shearith Israel Congregation erected a building that was designed to be a synagogue, but also incorporated a study hall for pupils. This was the first of the synagogue "Hebrew schools" that in time dotted the country. As the Jewish population grew and a number of synagogues existed side by side in one city, the communal Hebrew school, generally known as the Talmud Torah, was established.

In 1838, in Philadelphia, Rebecca Gratz (1781–1869) founded the first "Sunday school," which offered students from non-Orthodox families free instruction in Jewish history and related subjects. Children from Orthodox families received a more intensive education in congregational or communal Hebrew schools or in *yeshivot*. Torah Umesorah, the National Society for Hebrew Day Schools, was established, and by 1938 it was said to represent 377 Orthodox day schools in the United States and Canada.

In subsequent years, modern Orthodox institutions of higher learning became more amenable to the idea of women pursuing the same studies as men. Consequently, many women became expert talmudists and joined university faculties. Since the 1980s Conservative, Reform, and Reconstructionist seminaries have ordained hundreds of women as rabbis, some of whom occupy positions as professors in higher academies of learning. By the year 2000, isolated instances of Orthodox women ordained privately by Orthodox rabbis were being publicized, although the practice was rejected by Orthodox rabbinical seminaries.

See Cheder; Yeshivah.

Eighteen Benedictions

One of the oldest and most important prayers in Jewish liturgy, the *Eighteen Benedictions* (*Shemoneh Esrei*, in Hebrew), was originally called the *Tefillah*, meaning "Prayer." It was also called the *Amidah*, meaning "standing," because it was recited while standing.

According to tradition, the *Eighteen Benedictions* were formulated by the Men of the Great Assembly and were recited by Levites as part of a prayer service in Second Temple times. The Midrash (*Numbers Rabbah* 2:1) explains that the prayer consists of eighteen benedictions because the Torah mentions eighteen occasions on which God spoke to Moses and Aaron.

The Talmud (*Berakhot* 26b) informs us that the *Shemoneh Esrei* is to be recited three times each day, once at each of the three daily prayer services (*Shacharit*, *Minchah*, and *Ma'ariv*).

The Nineteenth Benediction

The requirement that the *Tefillah* be made up of eighteen blessings is emphasized in the Talmud (*Megillah* 17b). However, in 70 C.E., after his academy was reestablished at Yavneh following the razing of the Second Temple by the Romans, Rabbi Gamaliel II added a nineteenth. This blessing, called *Birkat Ha-Minim* ("Blessing Against the Heretics") but more commonly known as *Ve-la-malshinim*, was instituted as an antidote to such "heretical" Jewish sects as the Sadducees, Boethusians, Essenes, and Early Christians, who did not accept the authority of the Rabbis of the Tal-

mud. To different degrees, these groups were engaged in slandering the mainstream Jewish community and in reporting any untoward activity to the Roman conquerors of Palestine. The slanderers were called *malshinim* and that became the opening word of the blessing, which condemned their activity and expressed the hope that God would soon humble and punish these malicious sinners.

Notwithstanding the fact that the *Birkat Ha-Minim* was added as a nineteenth blessing, the name "Eighteen Benedictions" continued to be used. To add further confusion to the name, on the Sabbath an abbreviated version of the prayer, consisting of only seven blessings, is recited.

At morning and afternoon services, the leader repeats all nineteen benedictions aloud after they are recited silently by worshippers. At the evening (*Ma'ariv*) service, the leader does not repeat the benedictions.

In the tractate *Rosh Hashanah* (34b), Rabban Gamliel explains why the congregation recites the *Amidah* prayer before the reader (*chazzan*) repeats it. He says, "[The congregation recites the prayer] so as to give the *chazzan* time to prepare himself to be in the proper mood for his performance before the public." It must be remembered that in talmudic times prayers were recited from memory.

Silent Prayer

The *Shemoneh Esrei* is recited silently. In the Talmud (*Sotah* 13b), Rabbi Yochanan, quoting Rabbi Shimon bar Yocha'i, explains that the practice was adopted so that a worshipper should not be embarrassed if he is overheard confessing transgressions.

In a responsum of Rabbi Eleazar Fleckeles (1754–1826), the Prague authority, it is pointed out that the *Zohar* seems to hold that the *Amidah* should be recited so softly that even the worshipper himself does not hear it, while Joseph Caro's *Code of Jewish Law (Shulchan Arukh)* rules that only the worshipper should hear it. Fleckeles argues that the *Code* should be followed.

Maimonides summarized the content of the *Amidah* when he wrote, "The first three benedictions deal with praise of God, the last three with thanksgiving, and those in the middle with petitions for personal and communal needs."

It became traditional practice for the leaders of the service to recite the *Shemoneh Esrei* aloud after the congregation had recited it silently. Maimonides defied tradition when, during his leadership of the congregation in Cairo, Egypt, after congregants finished reciting the prayer they became engaged in loud conversation with their neighbors. Maimonides was embarrassed by such conduct, especially when Muslims who attended the Jewish services commented on the undignified conduct of the Jews in their synagogue. Maimonides reacted by ordering that the congregation no longer recite the *Amidah* before the cantor recited it aloud. The practice remained in effect for some three hundred years before it was discontinued.

See Kedushah; Prayer.

Ein Keloheinu

Literally meaning "There is no one like our God," these are the opening Hebrew words of a hymn, based on the theme of Psalm 145, that is chanted at the end of the Sabbath and holiday afternoon (*Musaf*) service. The first of its five stanzas reads:

There is none like our God,
There is none like our Master,
There is none like our King,
There is none like our Deliverer.

The remaining four stanzas are identical except for the first word.

When the first Hebrew letter of each of the first five stanzas (*alef, mem, nun, bet, alef*) are set side by side, they form the phrase *amen ba*, meaning "Amen [signifying the end of the service] is coming."

The *Ein Keloheinu* consists of twenty statements of faith. It is sometimes said that the prayer was introduced because the Sages taught that it is meritorious to recite one hundred blessings each day, and since on the Sabbath and holidays a short form of the *Eighteen Benedictions* is recited, these statements of faith help fill the gap.

See Faith.

Eirusin

In earlier centuries Jewish marriages were conducted in two stages. The first stage, referred to as *eirusin*, is often translated as "betrothal" or "engagement." The second stage, the marriage proper, which took place as much as one year later, is known as *nisuin* or *kiddushin*.

In the first stage, the wine was blessed, the bride received a ring, and the *ketubbah* (marriage contract) was read. In the second stage, a cup of wine was filled and seven blessings, called the *Sheva Berakhot*, were recited. With the completion of this second step, the bride and groom were officially married and were permitted to live together as man and wife.

In Germany and France during the twelfth century, the two ceremonies of *eirusin* and *nisuin* were combined, and that is how the marriage ceremony is conducted to this day. According to Maimonides, the terms *eirusin* and *kiddushin* are synonymous, although today we often refer to the combined portions of the marriage ceremony as *kiddushin*.

See Marriage.

Elijah

The courageous prophet Elijah, who was the conscience of Israel in the days when idol-worshipping King Ahab and Queen Jezebel ruled over Israel in the ninth century B.C.E. (I Kings 18:17ff.), left an indelible mark on Jewish life. He preached that Israel must not forsake God, so that the Covenant established between God and Abraham might endure.

In time, the name and person of Elijah became identified with the Messianic Age, and he came to be thought of as the guardian angel of the Jewish people and the forerunner of the Messiah. According to tradition, Elijah did not die: he ascended to heaven in a chariot and vanished. His eventual return has been anticipated by generations of Jews ever since.

Elijah's Cup

To concretize Elijah's importance in Jewish tradition, a cup of wine is reserved for him at the Passover *Seder* table in the hope that he will appear as an honored guest. At the beginning of the second half of the *Seder*, following the meal, the front door of the home is opened to welcome him. Through these symbolic actions, *Seder* participants express their willingness to bring the Messianic Age into their lives. Elijah's Cup reflects the belief that an age of peace and justice will become a reality at some unexpected time.

Elijah's Chair

During the circumcision (*brit*) ceremony, a chair is placed next to the seat reserved for the *sandek*, the person who holds the baby during the procedure. This chair, known as the Chair of Elijah, is reserved for the prophet, who according to tradition is an unseen guest who attends every *brit* to protect the newborn from danger.

In some synagogues, especially in Sephardic communities, a special chair is set aside for the prophet. To make sure that nobody occupies this Chair of Elijah, it is sometimes affixed to the wall of the synagogue and is removed only as needed.

El Malei Rachamim

A Hebrew term literally meaning "God full of mercy." This prayer for the peaceful repose of the soul under God's protective wings is chanted by a rabbi or cantor at all memorial (*Yizkor*) services and at funerals and unveilings. Ashkenazim refer to this prayer as the *Hazkarah* ("Remembrance") or *Hazkarat Neshamot* ("Remembrance of the Souls"). Sephardim use a similar prayer, known as *Hashkabah*, meaning "Rest in Peace."

Embalming

Preserving the remains of a deceased by draining the blood from the body was practiced by early Jews. Embalming was also common among Egyptians and, in fact, the Bible (Genesis 50:2–3 and 50:26) states that both Jacob and his son Joseph were embalmed when they died in Egypt.

Embalming was practiced in Second Temple times, as indicated in the writings of the first-century historian Josephus. In describing the death of Aristobulus II, King of Judea (67–63 B.C.E.), Josephus writes (*Antiquities*, Book Fourteen 7:4), "His dead body also lay for a good while embalmed in honey till Anthony afterward sent it to Judea and caused him to be buried in the royal sepulchre."

However, the Rabbis of the Talmud considered embalming disrespectful of the dead. They also objected to it because the procedure retards the hasty decomposition of the body, delaying its return to the earth from whence it came. Thus, the Rabbis banned enbalming.

Modern Attitudes

Contemporary Jewish authorities permit embalming when government regulations require it and in cases where the body cannot be buried within three days of death as prescribed by Jewish law. Until that time, refrigeration of the body is adequate to retard deterioration, but when burial is delayed because the body must be transported to another city, injection of embalming fluids is necessary to slow deterioration and eliminate foul odors.

Authorities (*Gesher Ha-Cha'yim* I, p. 73) are careful to warn that the blood or any organs removed during the embalming process must be saved in a container and ultimately buried in the coffin together with the corpse.

See Burial.

Emet

See Truth.

Encroachment

See Hasagat Gevul.

Eruv

Also spelled *eiruv*. The Hebrew word *eruv* (plural, *eruvin*) in its literal sense means "mixture, merging, amalgamation, or blending." In its legal sense the term refers to an instrument that permits a normally forbidden legal activity to be conducted.

The concept of *eruv* concerns the types of "work" that one may be engaged in on a Sabbath or holiday. Work, in Jewish law, need not involve intense physical exertion. Activities such as walking beyond certain set boundaries or carrying even the lightest of objects from private to public or from public to private domains are considered work.

Origin of the Concept

The word *eruv*, derived from *erev* ("mixture"), first appears in Scripture in connection with the Exodus. There, the Bible (Exodus 12:38) speaks of the *erev rav*, the "large mixture" of foreign people who joined the Israelites and left Egypt with them. But neither the word *eruv* nor the concept of *eruv* is mentioned in Scripture. Maimonides does not include the concept in his listing of the 613 commandments (*taryag mitzvot*) mandated by the Bible and, instead, considers it to be an institution introduced by the scribes in postbiblical times.

According to Maimonides, the laws of *eruv* established by the Rabbis of the Talmud are based on their interpretation of the verse in Exodus (16:29), "Let no man leave his place [domain] on the seventh day." This warning that the Israelites not leave their homes to gather manna on the Sabbath was taken to mean that on that day of the week it is forbidden to carry an object from the private domain into the public domain or the reverse. The verse is cited by Moses Maimonides as the basis for limiting the distance that one may walk on the Sabbath.

The origin of the concept of *eruv* is said to be more directly traceable to a statement in Jeremiah (17:27): "If you will not hearken to Me to keep the Sabbath holy, and do not refrain from bearing a burden when you enter the gates of Jerusalem on the Sabbath Day, then will I kindle a fire in the gates thereof and it shall devour the palaces of Jerusalem..."

The Laws and Types of Eruv

In the *Mishneh Torah* (Hilkhot Shabbat 14), Maimonides summarizes the many laws of *eruv* and the extensive discussions that appear in the talmudic tractates *Shabbat* and *Eruvin*.

Three types of *eruv* were introduced in order to alleviate Sabbath hardships:

- the *eruv* of cooked foods (*eruv tavshilin*), which permits one to cook food on a holiday falling on a Friday for the Sabbath that follows it;
- the *eruv* of boundaries (*eruv techumim*), which enables one to walk more than is normally permitted on the Sabbath;
- the *eruv* of yards (*eruv chatzeirot*), which permits one to carry objects in and out of a public courtyard and in the public domain on the Sabbath.

Eruv Tavshilin

The most widely used of the three types of *eruv* is the *eruv tavshilin* ("mixture of cooked foods"). Normally, on a holiday one is permitted to cook only food that will be eaten on the holiday itself. One is not permitted to cook food that will be eaten after the holiday.

When a holiday precedes the Sabbath, it is often a hardship for the homemaker to prepare Sabbath meals days in advance. Jewish law therefore permits the cooking of Sabbath food on the holiday by taking advantage of the *eruv tavshilin* procedure.

To implement the *eruv*, the homemaker prepares a dish of cooked food before the holiday begins. The dish may simply be an egg or a piece of roasted chicken along with bread (*matzah* is substituted on Passover). The food is set aside and a special *eruv* prayer is recited. By performing this ceremony, one is allowed to cook on the holiday for the Sabbath that follows it because the cooking process is considered to have been started before the holiday began. Thus, the food prepared on the holiday is "mixed" with the food prepared before the holiday.

The talmudic tractate *Yoma* (28b) states the Aramaic prayer to be recited when the *eruv tavshilin* is initiated.

Eruv Techumim

Jewish law considers it work if on a Sabbath or a festival one walks more than 2,000 cubits (about three-fifths of a mile) beyond the city limits or beyond the inhabited area of one's town. To overcome such a limitation for those who might want to visit a neighboring town to listen to a preacher (*magid*) or to socialize with friends, the *Eruv Techumim* ("mixture or fusion of boundaries") was introduced.

A person intending to walk more than 2,000 cubits on a Sabbath or festival selects a spot (perhaps a tree or similar landmark) and places some food there before the onset of the holy day. This new location, for purpose of law, becomes the person's new "residence," entitling him or her to walk an additional 2,000 cubits without being in violation of Jewish law. The reasoning is that the place where one eats a meal may be considered a residence. (See *Eruvin* 50b–51a. The earliest mention of 2,000 cubits as a noteworthy distance is to be found in Joshua 3:4. See also *Mishneh Torah* Hilkhot Shabbat 27:1–2.)

In Orthodox neighborhoods today an *eruv* is created by extending a wire or nylon cord from utility pole to utility pole until it encompasses the entire area, symbolically making the location common rather than public property. Besides allowing observant Jews to carry objects within the perimeter of the community, it permits them to push baby carriages, an activity hitherto forbidden because Jewish law views pushing an object as equivalent to carrying it.

According to most authorities, a public area in which more than 600,000 people live or work is too large to have an *eruv*. This conclusion was reached because Exodus 12:37 mentions 600,000 Israelites as the number of "men on foot" who fled Egypt during the Exodus. The verse that follows uses the words *erev rav* to explain that a "mixed multitude" of non-Israelites left Egypt with them. Use of a form of the word *eruv* immediately following reference to the 600,000 fixes the maximum population of an area that may have an *eruv*.

Eruv Chatzeirot

The third type of *eruv*, known as *Eruv Chatzeirot* ("mixture [pooling] of yards"), involves persons who live in an enclosed area consisting of a group of homes with entrances that open on a common courtyard. Since the courtyard is public property, none of the residents of the homes bordering the yard are permitted to carry objects into the yard on the Sabbath. In order to overcome this hardship, before the Sabbath each family brings a dish of food (or some flour for the baking of a large loaf of bread) to a designated home in the compound. Since all families bordering the courtyard contribute food, all have equal rights to the food, and they have joint "ownership" of the courtyard. Thus, the yard that was once considered public property becomes "mixed" or "pooled" (that is, an *eruv* is established), and the yard is considered private property in which all residents may carry objects without being in violation of Sabbath law.

Essenes

Three sects flourished in Second Temple times: Pharisees, Sadducees, and Essenes (*Isi'im* in Hebrew, meaning "Pietists"). While the first two were quite large and are mentioned frequently in talmudic literature, the Essenes are not. We know about them primarily from the writings of the second-century B.C.E. Philo and Josephus. It is believed that the Essenes, who took the words of the biblical texts literally and lived accordingly, were a sect that lived an isolated life in the caves of Qumran and produced the Dead Sea Scrolls.

See Asceticism.

Eternal Light

The eternal light (*ner tamid* in Hebrew), which in most synagogues hangs in front of the ark, was originally part of the seven-branched candelabrum (*menorah*) that was the centerpiece of the Temples in Jerusalem. Because it was the westernmost light of the candelabrum, it was called (Mishnah *Tamid* 6:1) *ner ma'aravi* ("western lamp").

Fed continuously with oil, the eternal light burned uninterrupted. Its chief function was to serve as a source from which the other six branches would be lighted. The other six lights were extinguished daily for cleaning purposes. The source branch was known in Hebrew as the *shamash*, meaning "that which serves," and the eternal light found in the modern synagogue represents that *shamash* of the Temple *menorah*. Hanging an eternal light in a synagogue, a practice first introduced in eighteenth-century Germany, is a matter of custom rather than law.

Ethics

Although the Hebrew term *musar*, meaning "discipline" (as in Proverbs 1:8), comes closest, there is no other Hebrew word that corresponds precisely to the English term ethics. The essential components of an ethical system—namely, justice, honesty, kindness, fair treatment of others—are nevertheless very much part of the fabric of Jewish law and Jewish thought. These elements comprise the code of morals that have governed Jewish life from biblical times to the present. The talmudic tractate *Avot*, known in English as Ethics of the Fathers, is the repository of most of the ethic principles that are integral to the Jewish way of life.

The Jewish attitude toward ethical living is based on the second and third discourses of Moses, which he delivered to the Children of Israel immediately before his death. In the Book of Deuteronomy (11:1ff. and 28:9ff.), he exhorts the people that if they are to be blessed by God with good fortune, they must subscribe to His commandments and discipline themselves to subdue pride and shun waywardness. Moses tells the Israelites that they are a holy people whom God will protect, but only if they imitate His ways.

The Rabbis of the Talmud expanded upon this theme when they answered the question, What are the ways of God that man should emulate? Abba Saul, the second-century Palestinian scholar, interpreted the words in the Book of Exodus (15:2), "This is my God and I will glorify Him," to mean "This is my God and I will be like Him." (He translates the Hebrew word *ve-anveihu*, "I will glorify Him," as though it should read *ani ve-hu*, "I and He [must act alike].") Consequently, says Abba Saul (*Shabbat* 133b), "Be like Him. Just as He is gracious, so be you gracious; just as He is compassionate, so be you compassionate."

Imitatio Dei

This Latin term meaning "imitating God" is the foundation of specific laws of the Torah and the cornerstone of the Jewish ethical system. It involves a relationship between man and God in which man expresses in human terms what God demands in moral terms. Professor Yechezkel Kaufmann, the eminent theologian, summed up the Jewish ethical system in his *The Religion of Israel*:

> Morality is an absolute value, for it is divine in essence. The God who demands righteousness, justice, kindness, and compassion is Himself just, gracious, kind, and compassionate. Moral goodness makes man share, as it were, in the divine nature.

In time, Jewish tradition extended the concept of ethical living to mean that being godlike by imitating God carries with it great responsibility. The individual must not only believe in God's qualities on a theoretical level, but must prove acceptance of these beliefs by assuming responsibility for his neighbor's welfare, as he does for his own. The teaching "Love thy neighbor as thyself" (Leviticus 19:18) implies that while God controls the universe, man controls his own life and bears the responsibility to make sure that the world is kind and fair to all of its inhabitants.

The fourth-century Babylonian talmudic scholar Chama (*Sotah* 14b) characterized this responsibility by interpreting the verse in Deuteronomy (13:5), "You shall walk after the Lord your God," to mean, "Just as God clothes the naked, so must you clothe the naked. Just as He visits the sick, so must you visit the sick. Just as He comforts mourners, so must you comfort mourners. Just as He buries the dead, so must you bury the dead."

Man's responsibility toward his fellow man is an essential part of the Jewish system of ethics. Couched in theological terms, it means, as is often stated, that man subject himself to the will of God and accept His code of living as man's goal and purpose in life.

See Musar Movement.

Eulogy

From the Greek meaning "good word, fine language," this term refers generally to a speech given in praise of a deceased person.

The first eulogy (*hespeid* in Hebrew) of record in Jewish sources was delivered by David when King Saul and Saul's son Jonathan died. Among the memorable words spoken by David are these (II Samuel 1:19):

Your glory, O Israel,
Lies slain on your heights:
How have the mighty fallen!

Who Is Eulogized

Many Rabbis of the Talmud (*Shulchan Arukh, Yoreh Dei'ah* 344) were of the opinion that if a person leaves instructions not to be eulogized, those wishes should be honored. Some authorities, however, believed that a great injustice is done the memory of the deceased when a eulogy is not delivered. Thus, based upon the principle that one may not give away that which is not his, rabbinic authorities are in general agreement that such a request may be ignored (*Shabbat* 105b).

The Rabbis of the Talmud and those who later codified the law believed that the delivery of a eulogy is important, not only to honor the dead by lavishing praise upon them, but secondarily to bring tears to the eyes of the mourners, thus helping them to express their grief. In a eulogy for the Talne Rebbetzin, Rebecca Twersky, the noted Orthodox authority Rabbi Joseph B. Soloveitchik said: "The *halakhah* [Jewish law] did not like to see the dead interred in silent indifference. It wanted to hear the shriek of despair and to see the hot tear washing away human cruelty and toughness."

Notwithstanding these formidable arguments emphasizing the importance of the eulogy, Jewish law generally favors honoring the expressed wishes of the deceased.

When Eulogies Are Delivered

In addition to the tradition of delivering eulogies at funerals, it has been the custom for many centuries to eulogize scholars and other important people on the last day of *shivah*, on the thirtieth day after death (the conclusion of *sheloshim*), and at the end of the year (when *yahrzeit* is observed). In rare instances, very prominent scholars are eulogized on each and every day during *shivah*.

When Eulogies Are Not Delivered

Traditionally, eulogies are not delivered when a burial takes place on a Friday afternoon or on the eve of a Jewish holiday, for this is when one must return home promptly in order to prepare for the joyous day that is to follow. Eulogies are also often omitted at funerals held on the day following one of the Pilgrim Festivals (Sukkot, Passover, Shavuot), a practice traceable to the times when the pilgrims were returning home from their journey to Jerusalem and were still in a joyous frame of mind (Orach Cha'yim 670:13 and 697:1).

These prohibitions are not always observed, especially when the funeral is held early in the day and the mourners and others in attendance will have ample time to reach their homes and prepare for the Sabbath or festival. Exceptions are often made for distinguished leaders and scholars (*Moed Katan* 27b) and even for laymen whose families insist that a eulogy be delivered.

The Rabbis of the Talmud (*Shabbat* 21b) ruled that for the eight days of Chanukkah, beginning with the twenty-fifth day of Kislev, one may not eulogize the dead or fast, presumably because these are joyous times. This ruling, by and large, is not followed today.

Since honest words of praise cannot be spoken for those who have taken their own lives, the Talmud (*Semachot* 2:1) and *Code of Jewish Law* (*Shulchan Arukh*, Yoreh Dei'ah 345:1) forbid eulogizing suicides. Exceptions are sometimes made for a suicide whose irrational action may have been the result of undue stress.

The Content of Eulogies

The Talmud (*Semachot* 3:5 and *Shabbat* 153a) and *Code of Jewish Law* (*Shulchan Arukh*, Yoreh Dei'ah 344:1) condemn the delivery of eulogies that are untruthful or that exaggerate the virtues and achievements of the deceased. The Rabbis did not condemn eulogies that embellish the truth just slightly. They did, however, object vigorously to outright distortion. The tractate *Berakhot* (62a) says: "Just as the dead are held responsible for their sins, so are funeral orators held accountable for delivering dishonest eulogies."

The Rabbis were more lenient with regard to exaggerated eulogies for the sons of the wealthy and of scholars. Out of deference to their parents, exaggerated eulogies were permitted, but a warning was issued against delivering speeches that are "woven out of nothing" (Yoreh Dei'ah 344:5).

See Funeral Practices.

Euphemism

To convey coarse or unpleasant realities in gentler tones, Judaism often substitutes less offensive language, or *euphemism* (from the Greek, literally meaning "good omen" or "good speech"). Thus, for example, Jews sometimes use the Hebrew word *niftar* ("freed [from the burden of the commandments]") for *met* ("died").

Euphemism has been used since biblical times, yet there is no precise Hebrew word for it. In the Talmud (*Berakhot* 58a), the Aramaic term *sagi-nehor*, meaning "one who sees much light," is used in referring to the blind Rav Sheshet.

This system of using a softer expression to describe a negative condition is rooted in the Bible. The Rabbis declare (*Megillah* 25b and *Sanhedrin* 68b): "Wherever an indelicate expression is written in the text, we must substitute for it a more polite and delicate reading."

Ishmael ben Elishah, the outstanding first-century scholar, a colleague of Rabbi Akiva and founder of a talmudic academy, emphasized to his students that "one must always carry on a discussion using clean language [*leshon nekiyah*]" (*Pesachim* 3a).

The Rabbis generally regarded the use of foul language and the recitation of unsavory biblical tales as out of keeping with the goal of establishing Israel as a holy people. Pointing to Leviticus 11, where kosher and nonkosher animals are listed, the Rabbis note that the text studiously avoids the word *tamei*, meaning "defiled, ritually unclean," using in its stead two words, *lo tehorah*, "not clean." The Bible, which is usually very sparing in its verbiage, here uses two words when one would have been quite adequate (*Leviticus Rabbah* 26:1–2).

The Rabbis (*Shabbat* 103b) adopted this same approach in their own writings. Thus, when they speak of a Torah scroll that is beyond repair and must be disposed of, the word *nignaz*, "hidden away," is used instead of the harsher term *nikbar*, "buried."

This desire to avoid using words with negative or unpleasant connotations led to unusual and unexpected situations. When printed books began to appear in the sixteenth century, some Jewish printers went so far as to alter the numbering of pages and chapters in order to avoid the use of letters that would spell out words with unsavory meanings. For example, in editions of Joseph Caro's *Code of Jewish Law*, the number 270, normally written in Hebrew as *reish a'yin* (*reish* being numerically equivalent to 200 and *a'yin* to 70) is reversed (*a'yin reish*), to avoid spelling out the word *ra*, meaning "bad" or "evil." The same procedure was followed for the number 275, which in Hebrew is *ra'ah*, the feminine form of *ra*. The spelling *reish a'yin hei* was changed to *a'yin reish hei*. For the number 344, Joseph Caro uses *shin dalet mem* instead of *shin mem dalet*, which spells *shmad*, the Hebrew word for destruction.

The names of entire books were sometimes changed in order to avoid the use of unpleasant words. Thus, the talmudic tractate on mourning, which should have properly been named *Aveilut* ("mourning"), is called *Semachot*, meaning "joys." And the tractate *Beitzah* is sometimes called by its Aramaic name *Bei'ah*, because *Beitzah* in its plural form, *Beitzim* ("eggs"), also refers to testicles. Likewise, the sixth section of the Talmud, which contains twelve tractates and deals with purities and impurities, is called by the Hebrew name *Tohorot*, meaning "cleanness."

Indelicate expressions occasionally appear in the Torah. To avoid reading these aloud in the synagogue, the Masoretes substituted euphemistic expressions. In the Book of Deuteronomy 28:27, the word *afolim*, "hemorrhoids," appears. However, the scribes considered this Hebrew word too coarse to be pronounced aloud in the synagogue, and so in a marginal note they inform us that the word *techorim* is to be substituted for it when the Torah is read in public. Both words have the same meaning, but the word *afolim* apparently carried a negative connotation with which we are no longer familiar. The written form in such instances are known as *ketiv* and the oral form as *keri*. Other places in the Bible where *afolim* is the *ketiv* and *techorim* is the *keri* are to be found in I Samuel 5:6, 9, 12; and 6:4, 5, 11, 17.

Another example of a word that was changed to a euphemistic form is found in Deuteronomy 28:30. Here, among the long list of curses that will befall one who does not observe the commandments, appears the word *yishgalenah*, meaning "violate her, have intercourse with her." The verse reads, "You

will betroth a woman, but another man will have intercourse with her." As indicated in the marginal note, when the Torah is read, the reader substitutes the word *yishkavenah*, meaning "he will lie with her," for *yishgalenah*. The Masoretes considered this a more delicate way of referring to sexual intercourse, so they established *yishgalenah* as the written form (*ketiv*) and the euphemistic *yishkavenah* as the spoken form (*keri*).

A striking example of the use of a euphemism is found in the Book of Job (2:9) where Job's wife tells him to curse God so God will put him to death. Here, instead of *kaleil*, the Hebrew word for "curse," *bareikh*, meaning "bless," is used instead.

See the *Mishneh Torah*, Hilkhot Sefer Torah 7:11, and the *Shulchan Arukh*, Yoreh Dei'ah 275:6, for more on euphemistic expressions.

Euthanasia

Derived from the Greek meaning "beautiful death," euthanasia is referred to in the vernacular as "mercy killing." The concept is alien to Jewish life and law, which emphasizes the positive biblical commandment to "choose life."

The Rabbis of the Talmud were quite emphatic in denouncing the practice of euthanasia, citing an action taken by King David as the basis of their opposition. The incident (II Samuel 1:1–16) occurred during the fierce battle near Mount Gilboa, where King Saul faced powerful Philistine troops. A young man appeared before David (who was not involved in the battle) and reported that he had seen the badly wounded King Saul leaning against a spear. In intense physical pain, Saul asked the young man to be merciful and end his (the king's) life. The young man acceded to Saul's wishes. When David learned of this, he ordered the young man executed, saying, "You have taken the life of God's anointed!"

Based upon this incident, the Rabbis ruled that since all life is anointed by God, no person has the right to hasten the death of another person, regardless of the motivation. In the talmudic tractate *Sanhedrin* (78a) they insist that he who kills a terminally ill person be punished with death.

This attitude is emphasized by Rabbi Judah of Regensburg, Bavaria (died 1217) in his *Book of the Pious*: "If one who suffers excruciating pain says to his fellow man, 'You see yourself I shall not live—not much longer, and as I cannot bear my pain any longer, I beg of you to kill me,' he must not so much as touch him."

Liberal Attitudes

More liberal attitudes toward euthanasia are to be found in the Talmud and later Jewish literature.

When the death of Rabbi Judah the Prince (135–219), editor of the Mishnah and the most outstanding scholar of the third century, was imminent, his disciples gathered around his bed and prayed continuously for his recovery. However, one of Rabbi Judah's maidservants (who was reputed to be a learned woman), realizing how intense was her master's suffering and how useless it would be to prolong his life, hurled an earthenware jug to the ground. The noise had its expected effect: it attracted the attention of everyone in the room and the praying ceased, whereupon Judah expired. By her action, Judah's maid hastened his death (*Ketubbot* 104a).

Rabbi Nissim ben Reuven Girondi, an outstanding fourteenth-century Spanish scholar and physician, known by the acronym Ran, used this incident in his commentary as the basis for his decision that one may refrain from praying for a sick person whose pain is intense and for whom there is no hope for recovery (*Nedarim* 40a).

Traditional Practices

A minority of authorities today cite the Rabbi Judah the Prince incident as grounds for adopting the passive euthanasia approach. They argue that when a terminally ill patient is living in great pain, doctors are not obligated to keep the patient alive by introducing artificial life-support systems, thus leaving therapeutic intervention in the hands of God.

The consensus of Orthodox thinking continues to be in line with the ruling set forth by Joseph Caro in his sixteenth century *Code of Jewish Law* (*Shulchan Arukh*, Yoreh Dei'ah 339:1). Caro reasserts the ruling of the Talmud and emphasizes that regardless of the seriousness of the ailment or how negative the prognosis, no effort may be made to shorten the life of the patient. Jewish tradition places the decision of who shall live and who shall die in God's hands alone and insists that one is not permitted to remove a pillow from under a dying person's head or create any kind of disturbance that is likely to hasten a death. He does, however, indicate that one is permitted to silence any *external* noise that prevents the departure of the soul, but the person himself may not be touched.

There is a practice among the Jews of Yemen to remove the *mezuzah* and sacred books from the room of a dying man who is in great pain. The Yemenites believe that the presence of holy objects lessens the power of the Angel of Death, and when they are removed, the power of the angel increases. Thus, the Angel of Death is able to take the life of the patient sooner.

In recent years, two noted Orthodox authorities have expressed definitive opinions on the subject of euthanasia. Rabbi Eliezer Yehuda Waldenberg (born 1917), chief justice of the Jerusalem District Rabbinical Court, writes in his book *Tzitz Eliezer; A Compendium of Jewish Halakhic Principles*: "Even if the patient himself cries out, 'Leave me be and do not give me any aid because for me death is preferable,' everything possible must be done to sustain the life of the patient."

In addition, he argues, that it is not permissible to pray for the death of an incurable patient, especially a relative, who is suffering greatly because the individual might be unconsciously motivated by self-interest, such as the desire to relieve himself of the heavy burden of caring for the sick person.

In his *Judaism and Healing, Halakhic Perspectives* (1981), Rabbi J. David Bleich, a dean at Yeshiva University and associate professor of law at the Benjamin Cardozo School of Law, writes that "passive euthanasia involving the omission of a therapeutic procedure or the withholding of medication which could sustain life is prohibited by Jewish law. The terminal nature of an illness in no way mitigates the physician's responsibilities. The physician is charged with prolonging life no less than with effecting a cure."

Some modern authorities, however, are of the view that there is no moral obligation to keep terminally ill patients alive by means of artificial support systems. In their view, the physician is free to follow a procedure that will accomplish the wishes of individuals writing a Living Will in which they instruct their families and their doctors that no heroic measures should be used to keep them alive if death is clearly imminent.

In 1994, Israel, following Holland, became the second country in the world to permit mercy killing by law. The Euthanasia Law, passed by the Knesset as an amendment to the penal law, states that "a person will not bear liability for a medical action or treatment performed with lawful permission on an individual for that person's benefit." Leading rabbis of the ultra-Orthodox community vigor-

ously demurred, stating: "One is obligated by Torah law to treat the ill, as is needed, with all the standard medicine and procedures, even if in the doctor's opinion the patient is terminally ill and will likely die."

Recent Attitudes

In the 1990s, with the much publicized activities of Dr. Jack Kevorkian, who helped many hopelessly ill patients terminate their lives, the issue of assisted suicide came to the fore. In July 1995, George Delury (a convert to Judaism) assisted his Jewish wife, Myrna Lebov, a longtime victim of multiple sclerosis, take her own life. After she took a lethal dose of antidepressants, Delury placed a pair of plastic bags over her head, hastening her death. He was sentenced to four months in prison.

Rabbis of all denominations deplored Delury's actions. Orthodox Rabbi J. David Bleich called it "homicide," and Fred Rosner, a medical doctor, denounced any form of suicide as "wrong on the part of the patient and on [the] part of the person assisting." Rabbi Kassel Abelson, chairman of the Rabbinical Assembly (Conservative) law committee, announced that "the Conservative movement does not allow assisted suicide, no matter what the intentions of the people involved." And, finally, Rabbi Richard Address, Reform Judaism's authority on issues of bioethics, said: "I would be hard pressed to condone putting a bag over another person's head. It goes against the conscience of Jewish tradition."

Evil Eye

See A'yin Ha-ra.

Evolution

The theory of evolution proposed by the nineteenth-century English naturalist Charles Darwin stands in stark contrast to the account of Creation as presented in the first chapter of the Book of Genesis. The Bible maintains that man, the world, and everything in it were created in six days, while Darwin's contention is that what exists today in the animal and plant world is the result of an ongoing evolutionary process that began three billion years ago. Each species, the Darwinian theory suggests, evolved from a common ancestor, and its members developed and changed over time as they adapted to environmental conditions in their battle for survival (natural selection).

Fundamentalists of all faiths have condemned Darwin's theory as heresy, and this is generally true of Jewish Orthodoxy. However, Menachem Mendel Schneerson (1902–1994), the Lubavitcher Rebbe, tried to harmonize the theory of evolution with the biblical account of Creation by saying that the fossils that have been presented as proof of the antiquity of the world were actually placed there by God at the time of Creation. His point was that while evidence of evolution may be discovered from time to time, this in no way negates the view that Creation was a spontaneous act.

The attempt to reconcile the biblical story of Creation with physical evidence of the antiquity of the world can be traced to talmudic times. The third century C.E. scholar Abbahu (*Genesis Rabbah* 3:7) proposed the idea that this world as we know it may not have been the only world that God created. "The Holy One," he said, "created many worlds and then destroyed them before He created this one. And when this one was created, He said, 'This one pleases Me. The others did not please Me.'"

Abbahu based this conclusion on an interpretation of the statement in Genesis (1:31) that after the six days of Creation "God saw all that He had made and found it very good. And there was evening and there was morning, the sixth day." Because the Bible uses the words "*very* good" rather than merely "good," says Abbahu, it can be inferred that the worlds that God had created previously and then destroyed were good but not good enough.

The fourth-century Palestinian scholar Judah ben Simon made a similar observation based on the concluding words of the above-mentioned verse. The fact that the words "and there *was* evening" rather than "let there be evening" are used led Judah to believe that evening already existed and did not have to be created.

Rabbi Israel Lipschutz (1782–1860), a modern Orthodox rabbi who published a commentary on the Mishnah entitled *Tiferet Yisra'el* (1892), was inclined to interpret the story of Creation in a nonliteral fashion. He agreed with the kabbalistic theory that Creation was cyclical and that the story in Genesis describes the beginning of a new cycle. The remains of dinosaurs and of primitive human forms that are discovered periodically are those of creatures from earlier cycles.

In his work *Orot Ha-kodesh*, the late Chief Rabbi of Palestine, Abraham I. Kook (1865–1935), asserts that the theory of evolution is in full accord with the *kabbalah*, to which he subscribed. The Creation narrative, he says, belongs to the "mysteries [secrets] that abound in the Torah," which are not to be taken literally.

Rabbi J. H. Hertz (1872–1946), the former British Chief Rabbi, argues in his *Pentateuch and Haftorahs* (1960) that in the face of the great diversity of views among earlier Jewish teachers there is nothing basically un-Jewish in accepting the evolutionary view about the origin and development of all forms of life.

Excommunication

Two Hebrew terms are used to express the concept of excommunication: *niddui* and *cheirem*. *Niddui* applies to the banning of individuals while *cheirem* applies to animate as well as inanimate objects. The Jerusalem Talmud (*Ta'anit* 3:10; 16b) says: "Anyone who causes people to desecrate God's name is to be subject to *niddui*. Such excommunication is to be not less than thirty days (*Moed Katan* 16a)."

The Hebrew term *cheirem* is first used in the Book of Leviticus (27:28) for an object that has been consecrated to God and therefore may not be used by man. In the Book of Joshua (6:17) the term is used in reference to the city of Jericho and its contents. After the walls of Jericho fell, Joshua warned his people that "the city and everything in it are to be proscribed [*cheirem*] for the Lord.... All the silver, gold, and objects of copper and iron are consecrated to the Lord; they must go into the treasury of the Lord [under the guardianship of the Priests]." So important is the concept of *cheirem*, says the Bible, that anyone who appropriates articles that have been declared *cheirem* is subject to the penalty of death. (Deuteronomy 7:25ff. and Joshua 7:1ff.)

Cheirem and the Individual

The concept of *cheirem* as it applies to an individual is first noted in the Mishnah. The tractate *Eruvin* (5:6–7) describes the excommunication of the scholar Akavya ben Mahalalel, a member of the *Sanhedrin* in the first century C.E. Akavya was offered the post of president of the Court on condition that he would renounce four of his minority opinions. He refused, declaring: "I would rather be called a fool all my days than that I should become even for one hour a wicked man in the sight of God; and that men should say,

'He withdrew his opinions for the sake of getting power.'" As a consequence, Akavyah was placed in *cheirem*—that is, excommunicated—by the Rabbis.

Elishah ben Avuyah, the second-century C.E. talmudic scholar, a teacher and friend of the celebrated Rabbi Meir, was likewise ostracized by his colleagues after expressing heretical views and doubts concerning the unity of God, reward and punishment, and the resurrection of the dead. Following his excommunication, he was no longer referred to as Elishah ben Avuyah, but as Acher, "the Other One."

In talmudic and later times, excommunication was used to enforce the rule of Jewish law and the enactments of the local community.

The Talmud (*Berakhot* 19a) cites twenty-four offenses punishable by excommunication. Among them are:

- insulting a learned man, even after the scholar's death

- insulting a messenger of the court

- refusing to appear before the court at the appointed time

- violating the second day of a holiday

- testifying against a fellow Jew in a Gentile court, which causes the person to lose money he would not have lost if the case were brought before a Jewish court

- taking the name of God in vain

- causing others to profane the name of God

- tempting another person to sin

- selling nonkosher meat as kosher meat

The ban on the above was usually issued by a rabbinic court after the offender had been duly warned about his offensive conduct. Sometimes the *cheirem* was pronounced by an individual rabbi or even a layman who felt wronged by another member of the community. The ban, which might last anywhere from a day to several years, often prohibited members of the community from having not only social dealings but also business dealings with the individual charged.

Rabbenu Gershom's Enactment

Throughout the ages, communal leaders employed the ban to keep delinquent Jews on the straight and narrow path. In the early Middle Ages, one of the luminaries of the Jewish community resorted to the *cheirem* in order to correct many abuses by Jews of Western Europe. About the year 1000, a series of enactments was introduced by Rabbi Gershom ben Judah. These ordinances became known in Hebrew as *Takanot d'Rabbenu Gershom* ("Ordinances of Our Rabbi Gershom"), and resulted in violators being placed in *cheirem*.

Rabbenu Gershom (965–1040), a brilliant scholar, founded a number of academies on both sides of the Rhine while serving as the rabbi of Mainz, Germany. His reputation as an outstanding teacher, in combination with his personal magnetism, earned him the respect of Jewish communities throughout Europe, particularly in Germany, France, and Italy. Questions were addressed to him from all parts of the Diaspora, and he soon became known as Rabbenu Gershom Me'or Ha-Golah, "Our Rabbi Gershom, the Light of the Diaspora."

At a meeting of the leading rabbis of Western Europe convened by Rabbenu Gershom, the following ordinances were enacted:

- An unequivocal ban was placed on polygamy. Although the practice had been condemned much earlier, not all European Jews had remained monogamous. This was due largely to the influence of Islamic communities in which polygamy was commonplace.

- Unilateral divorces were banned. A man could no longer divorce his wife without her consent. This talmudic law had often been violated.

- A ban was placed on all members of the community who mocked or mistreated a person who had converted to Christianity under duress and was now returning to the Jewish fold. Rabbenu Gershom also threatened to excommunicate anyone who refused to grant the returnees full participation in the social life of the community.

- A ban was placed on all who cut pages out of books not belonging to them.

- A ban was placed on persons who read letters not addressed to them.

Rabbenu Gershom died in 1040, the year of Rashi's birth, although some historians record the year of his death as 1028.

The Maimonides Controversy

The *cheirem* has also been used in the course of Jewish history to ban the writings of an individual. Rabbi Moses ben Maimon, better known as Maimonides or Rambam, is a case in point.

The great literary achievements of Maimonides were his encyclopedic code of Jewish law, the *Mishneh Torah*, and his philosophical work, *Moreh Nevukhim* (*Guide of the Perplexed*). While these two works earned Maimonides worldwide acclaim, they also incurred great disdain on the part of many rabbis in Spain, France, Germany, as well as in Akko, where kabbalists condemned the *Guide*, ordered that it be burned, and threatened excommunication to anyone who would study it. Kabbalists went so far as to desecrate the tomb of Maimonides in Tiberias, and instead of the laudatory inscription substituted "Moses Maimuni" [as he was called], the excommunicated heretic."

What most displeased the anti-Maimonists was Maimonides' claim in the introduction to his *Mishneh Torah* that this new code would replace the Talmud, and especially his hubris in naming it *Mishneh Torah*, meaning "Repetition of the Torah." Disdainfully, they referred to his code as *Yad Ha-Chazakah*, "The Mighty Hand," an allusion to the fact that the code consisted of fourteen chapters and the numerical equivalent of *yad* is fourteen (*yud* [10] plus *dalet* [4]). Considered objectionable were Maimonides' efforts at reconciling Revelation with science, his attempt to rationalize and explain away miracles, his belief that not everything in the Bible should be taken literally, and his condemnation of those who believe in an anthropomorphic God.

Almost two centuries were to pass before the feud fully subsided. Even the Church had become involved: in 1232, convinced that Maimonides was a heretic, the Dominicans burned his books.

Spinoza's Excommunication

Like Moses Maimonides, Baruch Spinoza was looked upon with distrust by certain elements within his community. Born in Amsterdam, by age fifteen Spinoza had become thoroughly acquainted with the teachings of all the great Jewish philosophers and the foremost natural scientists. Reason became his god, and he would not countenance beliefs founded on superstition or faulty thinking.

Spinoza rejected the Mosaic authorship of the Pentateuch and was critical of the Bible's internal contradictions. He argued that God and Nature are one, and that God acts only in accordance with the laws of His own nature, which are totally logical. This ruled out belief in miracles, belief in the supernatural, and belief in God's transcendence. It also ruled out an interplay between God and man.

Gradually, Spinoza stopped attending synagogue and began influencing young people. The leaders of the Jewish community in Amsterdam became alarmed upon learning that Spinoza was spreading radical ideas about God and particularly about immortality. Not very secure politically, the leaders feared that his teachings, which were contrary to those of the Church, would offend the Christian community. Such blasphemy, they felt, might be used to justify the expulsion of the Jews from Amsterdam, for their presence there at this time was merely tolerated.

The community elders pleaded with Spinoza to recant his heresies, but the rebel refused. Consequently, for defying the authority of the leadership, in 1656 Spinoza was excommunicated by the Sephardic community. All contact with him ceased, and even members of his own family no longer associated with him.

Spinoza was not terribly upset at having been placed in *cheirem*. Able to earn a living by giving private lessons and later by grinding lenses, he continued his studies and his philosophical writings until his death in 1677. Although Spinoza never recanted and was never formally returned to the Jewish fold, the Jewish community of later centuries harbored no ill-will toward him and his thinking.

Mordecai Kaplan's Excommunication

One of the most famous contemporary examples of a person being placed in *cheirem* involves Rabbi Mordecai M. Kaplan, founder of the Reconstructionist movement, who was excommunicated by the Orthodox rabbinate for his unorthodox views.

One year after publishing *Judaism as a Civilization* in 1934, Kaplan founded a biweekly magazine, *The Reconstructionist*, and organized the Jewish Reconstructionist Foundation. He created a new body of religious literature, including a Passover Haggadah and a Sabbath prayerbook (1945). In the latter, Kaplan eliminated references to the Jews as the Chosen People and offered a folkloristic rather than a literal interpretation of God's miracles. Allusions to a personal Messiah, priestly castes, and corporeal resurrection were also excised.

The ultra-Orthodox Union of Orthodox Rabbis was so incensed by Rabbi Kaplan's so-called heresy that in 1945 they excommunicated him in a dramatic ceremony described by *The New York Times* (January 1945) in these words:

> A tribunal of the rabbis gathered in a midtown hotel.... Wearing full beards and earlocks, caftans, even broad-rimmed velvet hats, seated on a dais which they had draped in funeral black, the assembled elders proceeded in effect to revive the heresy trial of Baruch Spinoza. They denounced the [prayer] book as "blasphemous," set the volume on fire (it was lying on the dais), lit candles for Kaplan as for a dead person, then, wrapped in prayer shawls, pronounced the ban of excommunication on Kaplan... demanding that "hereafter no soul in Israel shall traffic or communicate with him, and his name and presence shall be exorcised from the congregation of Israel." The decree was formalized by the blowing of a *shofar*.

The prayerbook issued by Mordecai Kaplan was also denounced by Louis Ginzberg and Saul Lieberman, fellow professors at the Jewish Theological Seminary.

Exilarchs

Around 600 B.C.E., after the Babylonians under Nebukhadnezzar had overthrown the powerful Assyrian and Egyptian empires and took control of Palestine, he allowed the Jews to form a self-governing community under the leadership of an exilarch, known as the *Reish Galuta* ("Head of the Exiles"). The man chosen to be exilarch, with the approval of Nebukhadnezzar, was to be a descendant of the ancient ruling dynasty of Judea, the House of David. Even after the Babylonians lost power in the region and were succeeded by Persians and Romans, the office of exilarch continued to govern the Jewish community.

The Jews of Babylonia regarded the exilarch with great respect even though he was not always a scholar. The exilarch was the middleman between the ruling power and the Jews. He appointed a marketing commissioner who regulated the economic life of the Jewish community, imposing strict controls and collecting taxes, a portion of which was sent to the ruling power's treasury. The erudite third-century Babylonian scholar Rav (Abba Arikha) was once appointed to this highly coveted position.

The exilarch was also responsible for the administration of justice in both civil and criminal matters. The judges whom he appointed enjoyed immunity: they could not be sued for making an error in judgment (*Sanhedrin* 4b). Many learned members of the exilarch's family were selected to serve as judges, and they were given the honorable title *Rabbana*, meaning "master" (*Pesachim* 115b and *Chullin* 92a).

Because of the great responsibility that the exilarch had to bear, he came to be highly regarded by the governing powers over the centuries. At the investiture, a new exilarch was introduced with great pomp and ceremony.

The monarch "laid hands" on the new appointee, trumpets were sounded, and governmental lay and spiritual leaders would participate in the ceremony.

The Jews looked upon the installation of a new exilarch with great pride. It was reported that when an ordinary Jew was given an *aliyah*, he would ascend the pulpit to pronounce the Torah blessings, but when the exilarch was given an *aliyah*, the Torah was carried to him. On the Sabbath following his investiture a special Sabbath service was held in his honor. At Sabbath services today, the *Yekum Purkan* prayer is recited for the welfare of the *Reish Galuta*.

The first exilarch of note is Huna, a second/third-century Babylonian scholar of whom Yehudah Ha-Nasi said that were he to come to Palestine he would be subservient to him, for Huna was a descendant of the male line of the House of David (Yerushalmi, *Kila'yim* 9:3). He was succeeded by fourteen exilarchs who held the office during the talmudic period.

Among the most prominent exilarchs was the third-century Ukba, also called Mar Ukba bar Nechemiah (*Kiddushin* 44b and *Bava Batra* 55a). He studied under Samuel, principal of the academy in Nehardea. Later he established his court (*Beit Din*) in Katri, a town near Sura in southern Babylonia.

The fourth-century Huna bar Nathan was another exilarch for which some details are provided in the Babylonian Talmud. *Gittin* 59a says that he deferred to the more learned scholar Ashi, and *Berakhot* 46b reveals that he engaged in a dispute with the blind *amora* Sheshet as to the proper etiquette to be followed at mealtime.

As time wore on, the power and influence of the exilarchate weakened and by the thirteenth century the office ceased to exist.

Exorcism

Unlike the Catholic Church, which established a procedure called Ordination of Exorcists, Jews never developed an official method of ridding humans of demons. Nonetheless, kabbalistic literature devotes much attention to the subject of exorcism. The twelfth-century publication *Sefer Chasidim* (*Book of the Pious*) presents a variety of prayers and incantations, many of them verses from the Bible that were especially recommended as an effective way of exorcising evil spirits. Foremost among these are three verses from the Book of Numbers (6:24–26) that constitute the *Birkat Kohanim* (*Priestly Benediction*):

> [May] the Lord bless thee and keep thee;
> [May] the Lord make His face to shine
> upon thee and be gracious unto thee;
> [May] the Lord lift up His countenance
> upon thee and give thee peace.

Also used is the blessing that Jacob, on his deathbed, conferred upon his beloved son Joseph (Genesis 49:22): "Joseph is a fruitful vine, a fruitful vine by the fountain; its branches extend over the wall."

Psalm 91 was widely employed not only in exorcism rites, but also as a preventative measure.

See Demonology.

Eye-for-an-Eye Principle

See Lex Talionis.

Ezrat Nashim

A Hebrew term literally meaning "Court (Quarters) of Women," referring to a specific section in the First and Second Temples.

See Women's Gallery.

Faith

In his well-known declaration, "The righteous person shall live by his faith," the prophet Habakkuk (2:4) says that the essence of a religious life is man's faith (*emunah* in Hebrew); that God's laws are just and that by observing the commandments enunciated in the Torah one attains spiritual perfection.

In the Jewish tradition, faith in God is demonstrated by action rather than simple verbal acknowledgment. Jeremiah stated this truism clearly when he equated faith with justice (5:1), and Hosea (2:21–22) likewise linked faithfulness and devotion to God with righteousness, justice, goodness, and mercy.

The Rabbis of the Talmud (*Shabbat* 31a) use the word *emunah* to exemplify the highest moral value to which one can aspire. When one dies and hopes to be admitted to Heaven, the scholar Rava said, the first question asked of the person is, "Have you carried out all your business dealings in good faith [*be-emunah*]?"

See Thirteen Principles of Faith.

Falashas

The only community of blacks that is believed to have an authentic claim on the Jewish heritage is that of the Falasha Jews, who have lived in Ethiopia (Abyssinia) for centuries. The Falashas believe that after the Queen of Sheba, ruler over the southern Arabian kingdom, visited King Solomon in Jerusalem (described in I Kings 10), she returned to her land full of admiration for the wisdom of the king. Accompanying her was a contingent of Jews who subsequently settled in Abyssinia. This contingent was the first of the Falasha community.

There is a belief among Falashas that they are descendants of a marriage between the Queen of Sheba and Solomon. But more likely, the Falashas are descended from a tribe that lived in Abyssinia in early biblical times and which adopted Judaism after being exposed to it by Jews who visited and/or settled there.

By the early centuries C.E., it is clear, the Falashas had become aware of the Bible and had accepted its teachings and commandments. However, the rabbinic interpretations and explanations of the biblical laws, as enunciated in the Talmud, did not reach them in their entirety. The Falashas were exposed only to teachings communicated to them by occasional visitors. Consequently, it became customary among Falashas to circumcise their sons on the eighth day after birth, observe the Sabbath and most holidays, and follow the biblical dietary laws. Yet the sounding of the *shofar* on Rosh Hashanah is not customary, the *lulav* and *etrog* are not used on Sukkot, and Purim is not observed at all.

The Falashas call themselves *Beta Israel*, meaning "House of Israel." Their Ethiopian neighbors look upon them as outsiders, however, calling them Falashas, meaning "exiles" in Amharic, the Semitic language used officially in Ethiopia.

The status of Falashas as Jews has been debated for centuries. As far back as the sixteenth century Rabbi David ben Zimri, who for many years was a rabbinical judge and Chief Rabbi in Cairo, accepted as fact the contention that Falashas were descendants of the tribe of Dan. Nevertheless, in one of his responsa he ruled that Falashas were like Karaites: we accept their marriages as valid marriages, but we do not accept their divorces as valid divorces.

With few exceptions, this view is generally subscribed to by rabbinic Judaism. It is based on the fact that the marriage ceremony of the Falashas incorporates all the elements necessary for a valid Jewish marriage, but their divorce document (*get*) does not comply with the demands of rabbinic law.

Saving the Jews of Ethiopia

The first man in modern times to devote himself to learning about the beliefs and customs of the Falashas was Jacques Faitlovitch (1881–1955). He studied Oriental languages in Paris, and in 1904 embarked on a trip to Ethiopia, where he spent eighteen months. Faitlovitch concluded that the Falashas were indeed Jews and that world Jewry was obligated to save them from extinction. As a result, pro-Falasha support groups were established in the United States, Europe, and Palestine.

Beginning late in 1984, until January 1985, in an Israeli government undertaking known as Operation Moses, over 7,000 Ethiopian Jews were airlifted to Israel after a waiting period in the Sudan. In March 1985, an additional 800 were secretly airlifted to Israel aboard a U.S. aircraft. In 1990, 3,000 more Ethiopian Jews arrived in Israel; and in May 1991, an additional 14,000 Falashas were airlifted from Addis Ababa to Israel in one day in what is known as Operation Solomon. This dramatic airlift of Ethiopian Jews was noted twice in the *Guinness Book of World Records*: for the most immigrants to arrive in any country in a single day and the most people to fly in a Boeing 747 on a single flight.

Acceptance of Falashas

The current practice in Israel is to accept Falashas as Jews, but nevertheless to require that they go through the conversion process before they can marry Jews. The first Chief Rabbi of Palestine, Rabbi Abraham Isaac Kook (died 1935), referred to the Falashas as "part of the Jewish people who because of trials and tribulations of the Exile have been far removed from us . . ." His successor, Yitzchak Halevi Herzog (died 1959), ruled that the origin and descent of the Falashas is too doubtful for them to be regarded as Jews, and he insisted that they undergo conversion. On February 9, 1973, the Sephardic Chief Rabbi of Israel, Ovadiah Yosef, ruled that Falashas are Jews according to Jewish law (*halakhah*). The Ashkenazic Chief Rabbi, Shlomo Goren, concurred. Nevertheless, despite their rulings, these two Chief Rabbis still required Falashas to undergo conversion before they could marry Jews.

Other Black Jews

A number of Jewish congregations in the United States consist of blacks who profess to be Jews and follow the precepts of the religion to some degree. One of the earliest such congregations was organized in 1930 in Harlem, New York, by Wentworth A. Matthew, a self-proclaimed rabbi.

Decades later, in 1966, Ben Ammi Carter, spiritual leader of B'nai Zakin Sar Shalom, a small Chicago congregation of black Hebrews, said to his followers, "Brothers and sisters: the American government does not wish to free the black people. The American people do not wish to free the blacks. Even our black leaders are faithless. . . . Brothers and sisters: *Elohim*, the Lord High God, has commanded me to lead you out of the American wilderness." To which the excited congregation responded, "Hallelujah!"

Thus began an odyssey that took the members of this group from Chicago to Liberia, where they settled for a period of two years, attempting to establish a viable Jewish community. When this experiment failed, they moved to Israel, where they were permitted to settle in the town of Dimona, in the Negev Desert. Even though the group considers itself Jewish, from the point of view of Jewish law that is questionable since their lineage is unproven.

Family and Family Life

In the books of Genesis (10:18) and Numbers (1:2), the family or clan is called *mishpachah*, a term widely used today. Judaism, like other ancient civilizations and religions, regards the father as head of the family; genealogy is therefore traced through him. A person's religion, on the other hand, is traced through the mother's side. Only the child of a Jewish mother or a convert to Judaism is regarded as a member of the Jewish family structure (*Bava Batra* 109b).

Since early biblical times, the family has been a central component of Jewish life. Abraham sought a mate for his son Isaac from among his family members, as did Isaac for his son Jacob. When the Children of Israel were about to be freed from bondage in Egypt, they celebrated their redemption by gathering as families to celebrate Passover, the holiday of freedom. And so it was when the Israelites settled in the Promised Land that each tribe received a portion of land, territory which would be owned by the tribal families in perpetuity.

In the ensuing centuries, after the two Jerusalem Temples were destroyed, first by the Babylonians and later by the Romans, the synagogue, supported by the family, became the focus of Jewish life. Observance of the Sabbath and holidays was marked by family gatherings, particularly at mealtime, which further strengthened the bond of its members; and the fathers' intense interest in the education of their children, primarily the boys, resulted in a closeness developing between the generations.

The Importance of Family

The Torah and Prophets, the Talmud and Midrash repeatedly emphasize the importance of family. In the Book of Malakhi (3:23), the main function of Elijah, who in Jewish tradition is to be the forerunner of the Messiah, is to "reconcile parents with children and children with parents."

Throughout the centuries of oppression in Europe and elsewhere, the home was refuge for the Jewish family and the place where Jewish values were taught. The religion of the Jew and his family life formed a network that enabled Jews to face an often hostile outside world. It also was a bulwark against assimilation. Religious celebrations and ceremonies that were observed in the bosom of the family served to keep Judaism alive and families close-knit. Observance of dietary laws was an accepted feature, as was the weekly celebration of the Sabbath. The lighting of candles on Friday night, the Sabbath meals, the annual *Seder* gathering, the building of a *sukkah*, and the joyful Purim and Chanukkah observances all added to the unity of family life.

The Obligation to Reproduce

Jewish tradition holds that through the institution of marriage man fulfills the divine plan to propagate the human race. The obligation to "be fruitful and multiply and populate the earth" (Genesis 1:28) is so important that the Rabbis (*Ketubbot* 17b) ruled that even the study of Torah may be suspended in order to rejoice with, and bring joy to, a bride and groom.

How many children one must have in order to comply with the biblical commandment to be fruitful and multiply was discussed in the Talmud (*Yevamot* 61b) by Hillel and Shammai, two prominent first-century scholars. Hillel and his followers believed that a married couple must have one boy and one girl in order to satisfy the commandment, whereas the School of Shammai contended that it was necessary to have two boys.

The Hillelites based their view on the verse in Genesis (1:27), "And God created man in his own image...male and female created He them." This statement, they said, emphasizes the equality of the sexes as perceived by God. The Shammaites, on the other hand, reasoned that since Moses, the great Lawgiver, had two sons and no daughters, two sons should be seen as the requirement for satisfying the biblical commandment.

Generally, the opinion of Hillel is followed, and rabbinic authorities are in agreement that one has fulfilled his religious obligation if his family consists of at least one son and one daughter.

Family Purity

See Niddah; Tohorat Ha-Mishpachah.

Fasting and Fast Days

In Jewish tradition, the fasting ritual serves more than one purpose. On a personal level, it is believed to cleanse the soul of one who has sinned, expressed remorse, and vowed to improve future conduct. For the Jewish people as a whole, abstaining from food and drink is a way of expressing grief over a tragedy that has befallen the community or a segment of it. The fasting ritual is also sometimes observed in the hope that an impending catastrophe might be averted through God's intercession. In almost all instances fasting is accompanied by prayer in which atonement for sins is hoped for.

In the tractate *Berakhot* (17a), the personal prayer recited by the fourth-century Babylonian scholar Sheshet is an indication of how the ancients regarded the true purpose of fasting. At the conclusion of a formal prayer session, Sheshet would add these words:

Sovereign of the Universe, Thou knowest full well that in the time when the Temple was standing, if a man sinned he used to bring a sacrifice, and although all that was offered of it was its fat and blood, atonement was made for him therewith.

Now, I have kept a fast and my fat and blood have diminished. May it be Thy will to account my fat and blood which have been diminished as if I had offered them before Thee on the altar, and do Thou favor me.

Of all fast days, only Yom Kippur is mentioned in the Torah (Leviticus 23:27–32). The Book of Zekhariah (8:19), named for the prophet who lived after the Babylonian Exile and the return of the Jews to Palestine in the sixth century B.C.E., speaks of four fasts:

1. The Fast of the Fourth Month, which occurs on the seventeenth of Tammuz and is popularly known as Shivah Asar B'Tammuz.

2. The Fast of the Fifth Month, which occurs on the ninth of Av and is popularly known as Tishah B'Av.

3. The Fast of the Seventh Month, which occurs on the tenth day of Tishrei and is popularly known as Yom Kippur.

4. The Fast of the Tenth Month, which occurs on the tenth day of Tevet and is popularly known as Asarah B'Tevet.

The three fasts other than Yom Kippur are associated with events leading up to the capture of Jerusalem and the sacking of the First Temple. The Fast of Esther and the Fast of Gedaliah, not mentioned by Zekhariah, are of an even later date.

The Fast of the Firstborn, known as *ta'anit bekhorim* in Hebrew, has biblical roots but was not introduced until the eighth or ninth century, during the geonic period. It is associated with the tenth plague inflicted upon the

Egyptians when Pharaoh refused to liberate the enslaved Israelites and all firstborn Egyptian males were struck dead (Exodus 12:29).

Fasting Regulations

Other than Yom Kippur, which must be observed on the day indicated in the Bible, the tenth of Tishrei, even if that day happens to be the Sabbath, fast days are postponed to Sunday if the actual date of observance falls on a Sabbath. The sole exception is the Fast of Esther. If the thirteenth of Adar, the actual fast day, falls on the Sabbath, the fast is observed two days earlier, on Thursday, since fasting is not permitted on the Sabbath, a day of joy, nor on Friday, a day needed to prepare for the Sabbath.

Fasting on Yom Kippur and Tishah B'Av lasts for a full twenty-four hours. All other fasts begin at dawn and end in the evening of the same day.

The obligation to fast falls upon those who have reached religious maturity. Boys below age thirteen and girls below age twelve are not subject to any of the commandments. However, the Talmud (*Yoma* 82a) advises that children should be trained to fast for part of Yom Kippur a year or two before they reach maturity.

Nonholiday Fasts

In earlier centuries, some pious Jews would fast on the Monday, Thursday, and again on the following Monday after the festivals of Passover and Sukkot. These fasts were a bid for forgiveness for any religious indiscretion the person might have committed during those lengthy holidays. Some Jews went so far as to fast every Monday and Thursday (days on which the Torah is read) throughout the year.

A number of traditions have evolved in which fasting is a central element. Among Orthodox Jews in particular, a bride and groom will fast on their wedding day until after the ceremony. This represents an expression of penance for past misdeeds and symbolizes entry into a new phase of life with a clean slate. In Jewish tradition, marriage is a watershed event in an individual's life when sins are forgiven and a new page in the life of the couple begins. The couple does not fast if the wedding is held on Rosh Chodesh, which is a half-holiday.

Strict adherence to Jewish law (*Shulchan Arukh*, Orach Cha'yim 44:1) demands fasting if one drops *tefillin* (phylacteries). Scholars infer from this that if one drops a Torah scroll, a fast is also required. Authorities differ as to whether it is appropriate only for the person who dropped the scroll to fast or whether all present at the time should do likewise. The prevailing view is that only the person who actually drops the scroll should fast on the next three weekdays on which the Torah is read. For example, if the Torah is dropped at a Sabbath service, the fast is held on the following Monday and Thursday and the subsequent Monday. According to the minority view, all present when the Torah is dropped are expected to fast, but only for one day. In all cases, the fasting period is from dawn to sundown, as on minor fast days. (See the Magen Avraham commentary on Orach Cha'yim 573:1.)

Fasting on the day of *yahrzeit* for a parent has been a popular practice, and some individuals even fast to commemorate the anniversary of death of a revered teacher. (See Isserles on Orach Cha'yim 376:6.)

Communal Fasts

There are occasions on which a community as a whole engages in fasting. Each such occasion has become known as a Purim Katan (Minor Purim) because it is reminiscent of the Fast of Esther (Ta'anit Esther), which precedes the Purim holiday. These communal fasts include:

- The Purim of Algiers, first observed on the fourth day of Cheshvan in the year 1540 to commemorate the community's having been saved from destruction during the Spanish-Algerian Wars of 1516–1517.
- The Purim of Baghdad, established on the eleventh of Av in the year 1773 on the occasion of the community having been freed from Persian oppression.
- The Purim of Fossano (Italy), established on the eighteenth of Nissan in the year 1796 on the occasion of the city having been saved from destruction by a bomb explosion.
- The Purim of Rhodes, established in 1840 on the fourteenth of Adar on the occasion of the community having been spared annihilation.
- The Purim of Casablanca (called Purim Hitler), established in 1943 on the second of Kislev on the occasion of Jews having been saved from Nazi occupation.

Fast of Silence

Of all the observances that are characterized as fast days, one does not involve the abstention from food and drink. The Jews of Morocco observe what is called Ta'anit Ha-Dibur, "The Fast Day of Speech." On a particular day of the year, all Moroccan Jews refrain from speaking and devote themselves exclusively to prayer and soul-searching. They pledge to guard their tongues from speaking evil and promise to use their gift of speech for expressing kindly thoughts. Kabbalists introduced this concept in the Middle Ages and called it Tzom Shetikah, "Fast of Silence."

Personal Fasts

According to a manuscript left behind by Moses Maimonides (1135–1204) and discovered by Samuel ben Abraham Shkeil of Acco, Palestine (where Maimonides settled temporarily after his escape from persecution in Spain), Maimonides set aside for himself and members of his family a special day of fasting. He wrote:

On Sunday evening, the fourth of Iyyar, I went to sea; on Sabbath, the tenth of Iyyar, in the year 4925 (1165) a heavy gale arose, and our lives were endangered. I vowed to observe these two days as strict fast days for myself, my family and all my household, and to order my descendants to keep these fasts also in future generations and to give charity in accordance with their means. I further vowed to observe the tenth of Iyyar in seclusion and to devote the day to prayer and study. On that day, God alone was with me on the sea; so upon the yearly return of this day, I do not wish to be in human society, unless I am compelled to.

In talmudic times it was believed bad dreams could have a devastating effect, and fasting could be a mitigating factor (*Shabbat* 11a).

Natan Sharansky, the outspoken dissident who was released from Soviet prison after nine years of incarceration (1976–86) for allegedly spying for Israel, eventually made his way to Israel. He became a member of the Knesset and came to revere Yitzhak Rabin, the prime minister. To demonstrate his intense feeling over the great loss, Sharansky established 11 Cheshvan 5756 (November 4, 1995), the day Rabin was murdered by Yigal Amir, a third-year law student at Bar-Ilan University, as a fast day. Sharansky said: "The day a Jew killed a Jew is a day of mourning for me."

See Fast of Esther; Fast of the Firstborn; Fast of Gedaliah; Fast of the Ninth of Av; Fast of the Seventeenth of Tammuz.

Fast of Esther

The day before Purim, the thirteenth day of the Hebrew month Adar, is known in Hebrew as Ta'anit Esther, the Fast of Esther. It was on this date that the Jews of Persia fasted to lend support to Queen Esther, who courageously entered the presence of King Ahasueros without prior permission, an act punishable by death. She dared do this only because the fate of her people was at stake.

Haman, second in command to the king, had proclaimed, with the king's consent, that the Jews of the kingdom were disloyal and were to be massacred on the thirteenth day of the month of Adar. Queen Esther managed successfully to be received by the king and to convince him of the inadvisability of allowing Haman to carry out his plan.

When the day of the Fast of Esther falls on a Sabbath, the day of fasting is moved back to Thursday since fasting is not permitted on the Sabbath, a day of joy. Fasting is also not permitted on Friday since that day is needed to prepare for the Sabbath.

See Fasting and Fast Days; Purim.

Fast of the Firstborn

Traditionally, the firstborn in a family is required to fast on the fourteenth of Nissan, the day before Passover. This custom, of biblical origin, is based on the account presented in Exodus (12:21–28) in which all Egyptian firstborn were slain and the firstborn of Israel were spared. The word "Passover" (*Pesach* in Hebrew) is derived from the verb *pasach*, meaning "to spare, to pass over [the houses of the Israelites]."

The Fast of the Firstborn, known in Hebrew as *ta'anit bekhorim*, commemorates and expresses gratitude for the sparing of the firstborn males of Israel. In time the requirement changed, and the fast was excused if the firstborn of the family undertook to study a talmudic tractate and to complete his studies on the day before Passover. In practice, and with exceptions, the studying is assumed by the local rabbi, who on the morning before the day of Passover assembles all the firstborn of the community. After morning prayers, the group joins the rabbi in studying the last section of the tractate that he has been studying in anticipation of the occasion. This *siyyum* or *siyyum massechta*, meaning "completing a tractate [of the Talmud]" is followed by the serving of light refreshments. The repast is known as a *se'udat mitzvah*, "*mitzvah* meal."

See Fasting and Fast Days.

Fast of Gedaliah

The minor fast day known in Hebrew as Tzom Gedaliah, the Fast of Gedaliah, falls on the third day of Tishrei, the day following Rosh Hashanah.

Gedaliah was a Jewish official appointed by King Nebukhadnezzar of Babylonia to govern the Jews who remained in Palestine after the destruction of the First Temple in 586 B.C.E. Considered a traitor by some Jews, Gedaliah was assassinated on the third day of Tishrei. In retaliation, Nebukhadnezzar inflicted reprisals on the Jewish people.

Gedaliah's efforts to rebuild Jewish life were not fully appreciated in his lifetime, but in death he is mourned as a hero, and the day of his assassination is observed as a fast day in the Jewish calendar. The fasting begins at sunrise on the third of Tishrei and ends when the stars appear the same evening.

See Fasting and Fast Days.

Fast of the Ninth of Av

Tishah B'Av, the ninth of Av, is a fast day second in importance only to Yom Kippur. As on Yom Kippur, the Tishah B'Av fast extends for a full twenty-four hours.

Tishah B'Av, which falls in summertime, is a day of mourning for the loss of the First Temple, destroyed in the year 586 B.C.E. by the Babylonians, and for the Second Temple, destroyed on the same day in the year 70 C.E. by the Romans. It marks the final day of a three-week period of intense national mourning for the loss of Jewish independence and the destruction of Judaism's holiest shrines.

Aside from these catastrophic events, other happenings in Jewish history are said to have occurred or reached a climax on the ninth of Av. These include the fall of Betar (the last Jewish stronghold during the Bar Kokhbah rebellion against Rome) in 135 C.E. and the beginning of the expulsion of the Jews from Spain in 1492.

The importance of Tishah B'Av as a fast day is emphasized in the Talmud (*Ta'anit* 30b), where the comment is made: "He who eats or drinks on the ninth day of Av must be considered as guilty as one who has eaten on Yom Kippur." The fast of Tishah B'Av, like Yom Kippur, begins at sunset and ends the next evening with the appearance of the first three stars.

In some communities, it is customary on Tishah B'av for Jews to observe some of the laws of mourning. During the synagogue service, worshippers remove their shoes and sit on low benches while the biblical Book of Lamentations (*Eikhah*) is being read. At the last meal prior to the fast, round-shaped foods (such as rolls, bagels, and eggs—the kind of food eaten by mourners after a funeral) are served. Some sprinkle ashes on the egg as an additional sign of mourning.

See Fasting and Fast Days.

Fast of the Seventeenth of Tammuz

Shivah Asar B'Tammuz, the seventeenth day of Tammuz, is observed as a fast day three weeks before Tishah B'Av. It commemorates the period when Jewish independence ended in the sixth century B.C.E. On that day in 586 B.C.E., during the reign of Nebukhadnezzar of Babylonia, the walls protecting Jerusalem were breached, and three weeks later the holy Temple itself was destroyed. Jews were then exiled to Babylonia.

Shivah Asar B'Tammuz is a minor fast day in the Jewish calendar. The fast lasts from dawn until stars appear in the evening sky.

See Fasting and Fast Days.

First Fruits

In the Bible, first fruits, whether of the vegetable or the animal world, belong to God and are to be consecrated to Him as an expression of thanksgiving. In the Book of Exodus (13:1), God says to Moses: "Consecrate unto Me every firstborn: man and beast, the first issue of every womb among the Israelites is Mine." This commandment is repeated several times. Similarly, the first fruits of the soil are to be consecrated to God each year as they are harvested. The Book of Exodus (23:19) is quite explicit: "The choice fruits of your soil shall you bring to the house of the Lord your God." The exact statement is repeated in Exodus 34:26.

The first fruits of the annual harvest became known as *bikkurim*, the Hebrew plural form of *bekhor*, meaning "first" or "oldest." Seven species of agricultural products grown by Jewish farmers in ancient Palestine were subject to the requirement that they be brought as an offering to God in the Sanctuary in Jerusalem. These highly-prized species of the Land of Israel, listed in the Book of

Deuteronomy (8:8), are wheat, barley, grapes, pomegranates, olives, and dates from which sweet honey was extracted. Other offerings were brought by pilgrims as well, but these were purely voluntary.

In the Book of Numbers (28:26), the offering of first fruits is associated with the holiday of Shavuot: "On the day of first fruits, your Feast of Weeks [Shavuot], when you bring an offering of new grain to the Lord...." Hence, the Shavuot holiday became known as Chag Ha-Bikkurim, the holiday of *bikkurim*.

Offerings of produce in season were also brought to the Temple in Jerusalem on the major holidays of Passover and Sukkot. Pilgrim-farmers and their families from all parts of Palestine would make the trek to Jerusalem to deliver their offerings. Since the pilgrimage ended with the pilgrims ascending on foot up the steep hills leading to the Jerusalem Temple, these pilgrims became known as *olei regel*, "ascenders on foot."

Bringing *bikkurim* to the Temple on the three pilgrimage festivals is first mentioned in the first chapter of the apocryphal Book of Tobit. While the appearance of all males in Jerusalem on the three festivals is mandated in the Book of Exodus (23:17), it is not specifically associated with the bringing of first fruits.

As commanded in the Book of Deuteronomy (26:1–11), the fruit-filled baskets carried by the pilgrims were set down in front of the altar as they recited prayers of thanksgiving to God for having given them rich, productive soil.

In the absence of the ancient Temple, in modern Israel the *bikkurim* festival is reenacted in an altered form. The courtyard of the Jewish agency building in the heart of Jerusalem serves as the termination point of a procession by children from various parts of the country carrying baskets laden with fruits that are left there for distribution to the poor.

The Mishnah *Bikkurim*, the last tractate of the mishnaic order Zera'im, discusses the subject in detail.

Flags and Emblems

The first mention of flags and emblems being used by Jews is found in the Book of Numbers (1:52): "The Israelites shall encamp, troop by troop, each man with his division and each under his own flag." The Hebrew word for flag is *degel*. Ot (plural, *otot*), meaning "sign" or "symbol," is a synonym.

The display of flags and emblems by the Israelites was in keeping with the practice of all the tribes and nations of antiquity who expressed their identity by displaying distinctive banners bearing emblems taken from nature. The Romans, for example, chose the eagle as the centerpiece of their flag.

The Bible itself does not indicate in what manner the flag of each of the Twelve Tribes of Israel was decorated, but the Midrash (*Numbers Rabbah* 2:7) suggests that each was decorated in a color of one of the twelve precious stones that were embedded in the breastplate worn by the High Priest. It has also been suggested that the emblem on each flag may have corresponded with the message implicit in Jacob's blessing to his sons (Genesis 49) or the blessing conferred by Moses upon the Israelites (Deuteronomy 33). Thus, Judah's flag may have borne the picture of the lion (Genesis 49:9).

According to one tradition the flag of the Maccabees, who battled the Syrian-Greeks in the second century B.C.E., bore the Hebrew inscription *Mi kamokhah ba-eilim Adonai*, "Who is like Thee among the gods, O Lord."

Long before the State of Israel was established in 1948, Theodor Herzl, in his book *Judenstadt* (Jewish State), published in 1896, suggested that Jews create a flag consisting of seven golden stars, symbolizing a seven-hour workday. However, when the state came into being, the flag that was adopted consisted of a blue Star of David in the center of a white banner, flanked by two horizontal blue stripes. It is assumed that the stripes and white background were inspired by the design of the traditional prayershawl (*tallit*).

The only other flag among all the nations on earth that bears a Star of David is the African nation Burundi. Its flag has three stars in its center, in the form of a triangle.

The insignias of many universities—Yale, Columbia, and Dartmouth among them—feature Hebraic themes and words. The Hebrew words *urim ve-tumim*, which appeared on the breastplate of the High Priest, are embossed on the Yale University seal (Exodus 28:30). Dartmouth uses the Hebrew words *El Shaddai*, "Almighty God," near the top of its seal, and Columbia uses the Tetragrammaton, *Yehovah*, on its emblem.

Flogging

As detailed in the Book of Deuteronomy (25:1–3), floggings (*malkot* in Hebrew) were used to punish a guilty person:

> When there is a dispute between two men and they go to court, and a decision is rendered declaring the one in the right and the other in the wrong—if the guilty one is to be flogged, the magistrate shall have him lie down and be given lashes...as his guilt warrants. He may be given up to forty lashes, but not more, for by excessive flogging, your brother may be degraded before your eyes.

Because the verse says "*up to* forty lashes," the Rabbis (*Makkot* 22b) set the limit at thirty-nine so that if a mistake were made the number would not exceed forty. If the guilty party was in ill-health, no more than three lashes were administered.

In talmudic times, the courts imposed flagellation upon persons whose actions, though not in violation of Torah law, were in opposition to accepted moral standards. The Talmud (*Sanhedrin* 46a) records a case of a man who had intercourse with his wife under a fig tree (that is, publicly—*befarhesya*). He was brought before the court and was flogged "not because it merited it [since the law did not prescribe this punishment for such conduct], but because the times warranted it [since those were times of loose morals]." *Malkot*, in such instances, were intended to serve as a deterrent.

In later times, the concept of *malkot* was introduced to "cleanse" a person who, although not guilty of a crime, voluntarily wished to rid himself of guilt feelings. On the day before Yom Kippur, he would appear before the synagogue sexton and submit himself to flogging as he confessed his sins. This purely symbolic act, particularly common in the Middle Ages, was carried out with a light strap.

On the Hoshanah Rabbah festival, the *malkot* symbolism is still carried out through the beating of willows, in the course of the morning service.

Flowers

While any number of flowers were known to dot the Holy Land in Bible times, only the rose and lily are prominently mentioned in Scripture, particularly in the Song of Songs. In the Talmud, the saffron, jasmine, and narcissus are singled out for their pleasant scent and medicinal value. Reference is also made to the fact that bridegrooms wore wreaths of rose and myrtle (Mishnah *Sotah* 9:14). This tradition was discontinued when Jews became aware that it was *chukat ha-goy*, "non-Jewish practice." *Avodah Zarah* (4:2) notes that idol worshippers followed the custom of placing flower wreaths on their idols during festival celebrations.

In time, the association of flowers with pagan practice lost its cogency and flowers began to be used at Jewish weddings and to adorn the synagogue pulpit, particularly on the Shavuot holiday. In some congregations, on Simchat Torah a canopy (*chuppah*) made of plants and flowers was erected on the pulpit to welcome the *chatan Torah* ("bridegroom of the Torah") and the *chatan Bereishit* ("bridegroom of Genesis"), members who were awarded special Torah honors (*aliyot*).

Funerals

Although there is no objection in Jewish law to covering a coffin with flowers or greenery, it has not been traditional to do so. According to the Talmud (*Berakhot* 53a and *Bava Kama* 16b), flowers, like spices, were used to offset the malodor of a decaying body. The presence of flowers at funerals was common among non-Jews, who sometimes kept their dead for extended periods before burial. The Jewish requirement that the dead be buried within three days made the use of flowers unnecessary.

Rashi, the eleventh-century French scholar, points out that there existed a custom "to place myrtle branches on a coffin to honor the dead" (*Beitzah* 6a). However, because adorning a coffin in this manner was considered a non-Jewish practice, Jews were discouraged from adopting it.

In Israel, a more lenient attitude has developed, even among the Orthodox. There, a distinction is made between potted flowers and cut flowers. Cut flowers are generally permitted because they are more intimately associated with the earth in which they grew.

Potted flowers are grown in soil that has been "separated" from the earth.

Food

The Bible, the Talmud, and later writings devote considerable attention to food and the important role it plays in life. Abba Arikha (also known as Rav), the outstanding third-century Babylonian scholar, said that the time will come when one will have to render an account for all the food he has seen but not tasted (Yerushalmi *Kiddushin* 4:12). Eating in moderation is considered a wholesome and pleasurable activity. Food is meant to be enjoyed, and it occupies a central position in the celebration of the Sabbath and holidays.

Nutrition

From the Talmud and other early sources, it is evident that the Rabbis were aware of the health values of certain foods. In *Berakhot* 44b, for example, Rabbi Yannai quotes his teacher Judah the Prince as saying that "an egg is superior in food value to the same quantity of any other kind of food." And Rabbi Dimi adds that "a [boiled] egg is better than the same quantity of every other kind of boiled food except meat." Some Rabbis considered cabbage, beets, and asparagus to be highly curative while others named roasted egg, roasted meat, fat meat, and poultry to be harmful. Others added nuts and cucumbers (ibid. 57b) to the list of harmful foods.

Rabbi Jose the son of Bun said (Yerushalmi *Kiddushin* 4:12), "One should not live in a city that does not have a vegetable garden." Two reasons have been offered in explanation of this statement. First, if there are no vegetables available in the city, a person's cost of living will be much higher because more of his or her diet will have to consist of meat and dairy products, which are more expensive. Second, vegetables provide nourishment for the body, and it is wise to live in a location where such food is plentiful.

In talmudic times, the weekday diet of the majority of people was vegetarian, with meat eaten only on Sabbaths, holidays, and special occasions. There is a difference of opinion among the Rabbis as to whether it is better to eat vegetables raw or cooked (*Berakhot* 44b; *Eruvin* 55b), and the Talmud recommends some vegetables over others. Lentils, if eaten once in thirty days, protect one from respiratory problems (*Berakhot* 40a). Of garlic, it is said, "It satisfies, it warms the body, it makes the face shine, it increases seminal fluid, and it cures tapeworm" (*Bava Kama* 82a). Radishes are considered good for one's the health (*Eruvin* 56a), and onions should be avoided because of the pungent fluid they contain (ibid. 29b).

Olives were extremely popular in talmudic times. White olives, it is said, cause one to forget what he has learned (*Hora'yot* 13b), but olive oil is said to be good for old men. A talmudic aphorism counsels, "Bread for young men, oil for old men, and honey for children" (*Yoma* 75b).

Many talmudic references are to be found relating to the influence of foods on sexual activity. The view is expressed that foods such as eggs, fish, garlic, wine, milk, cheese, and fatty meats increase sexual potency. On the other hand, salt and egg barley are said to diminish it.

The View of Maimonides

In the twelfth century, scholar-physician Moses Maimonides wrote a health book called *Sefer Refuot* (*Book of Remedies*), and his idea of what is good and bad for one's well-being is not always in agreement with the ideas expressed in the Talmud. Maimonides recommends bread baked from flour that is neither too old nor too fine. He considers cheese and butter, white-meated fish with firm flesh, and the meat of the goat, sheep, and chicken to be healthful. Wine and dried fruits are also wholesome foods, he maintains, but fresh fruits are considered unwholesome. Maimonides does not recommend garlic or onions.

Sabbath Food

The wide variety of dishes created to celebrate the special days in the calendar has been a positive element in keeping the family together and in making religion an exciting adventure. Jewish housewives seem to have taken seriously the answer to a question posed in the Talmud (*Shabbat* 118b), "How does one prove that he delights in the Sabbath?" To which Rabbi Judah, a disciple of Rav, replied, "He proves it by preparing a dish of beets, a large fish, and cloves of garlic."

The serving of fish on the Sabbath has been tied to the story of Creation. The Midrash suggests that since fish were created on the fifth day, man on the sixth, followed by Sabbath on the seventh day, this progression should be kept intact by man eating fish to celebrate the Sabbath.

Since it was expected that all homes serve fish at least once during the Sabbath, and since the cost was often beyond the reach of many families, a preparation called *gefilte* fish was created by the housewives of Eastern European communities. This recipe reduced the cost considerably. (The Talmud [ibid.] refers to an inexpensive pie made of fish-hash.)

Gefilte fish means "filled" or "stuffed" fish. The dish was so called because originally, after two or three types of boned fish used in its preparation (usually carp, pike, and whitefish) were ground up and seasoned with onions, salt, pepper, etc., the mixture was stuffed into the skin of the fish. It was then cooked for an hour or more.

Another preparation similar in some ways to *gefilte* fish is *gehakte* ("chopped") herring. Because of its lower cost, this was also often served as the Sabbath dinner fish dish. It was prepared by skinning a few herrings and chopping them together with hard-boiled eggs, onions, apples, sugar, pepper, and a bit of vinegar.

Meat is also traditionally enjoyed on the Sabbath.

Since food may not be cooked on the Sabbath, but can be kept warm until served, *cholent* proved to be a good dish to prepare for the Sabbath: it could be kept warm overnight in a closed oven.

The *cholent* dish itself is prepared differently in different communities, but it traditionally consists of meat, beans, potatoes, and various other local vegetables that are cooked for two to six hours. Late Friday afternoon, after it has been fully cooked, the *cholent* is placed in a closed oven and kept there until it is used at the Sabbath midday meal.

In ghettos of Eastern Europe, the *cholent* dish prepared by many housewives was often taken to the home of a neighbor who had a good stove. It was left in (or on top of) that stove until it was needed for lunch on the Sabbath.

Among Sephardim, the Sabbath food that is prepared before sundown on Friday and is left to stay warm all night is known as *chamin* (*dafina* in Morocco). *Chamin,* Ladino (Spanish-Hebrew) for oven, derives from the Hebrew word for hot (*cham*). Chickpeas or other legumes and meat or poultry are integral to the preparation, which also contains eggs that are cooked in their shells until they become light brown inside. Some recipes include cracked wheat; others are spiced with cinnamon or cloves.

A particularly popular Sabbath dish is *kugel,* a pudding made of noodles, potatoes, or other ingredients. *Kugel* in German means "ball," and the dish is so named because traditionally it is cooked in a round (ball-shaped) casserole.

The tradition of celebrating Sabbaths, holidays, and other happy occasions with specially prepared foods has added joy to Jewish life. See the holiday entries for references to foods associated with specific occasions.

See Dietary Laws.

Four Questions

See Seder.

Four Species

Four plant species (*arba minim* in Hebrew) prescribed in the Book of Leviticus (23:40) are taken in hand and blessed on each day of the Sukkot holiday. The Bible states the requirement as follows: "And you shall take on the first day [of the holiday] the fruit of goodly trees, branches of palm trees, boughs of thick trees, and willows of the brook; and you shall rejoice before your God seven days."

Although the Bible does not state specifically which fruit or which trees are to be "taken" on Sukkot, Jewish authorities have interpreted the "fruit of goodly trees" to mean the citron (*etrog*; plural, *etrogim*) and the "branches of palm trees" to mean the date palm (*lulav*; plural, *lulavim*). The "boughs of thick trees" are ascribed to the myrtle (*hadas*; plural, *hadasim*), and "willows of the brook" to the familiar willow tree (*aravot*).

The Etrog

The *etrog* is said to be the most distinguished of the four symbols because, in addition to its visual attractiveness, it has both fragrance and taste. The *lulav* tree bears delicious fruit with no fragrance. The myrtle branch has an aroma but does not bear edible fruit. The willow has no fragrance, and it does not bear fruit. When the blessing over the four species is recited, the *etrog*, because of its distinction, is held separately in the left hand while the *lulav* is tied together with the myrtles and willows and held in the right hand.

HOW THE ETROG GROWS

A question arose as to which way the *etrog* is to be held as the blessing is recited. Not being farmers, the Rabbis of the Talmud were not sure how the *etrog* grows. At one end of this lemon-shaped fruit is a round nipplelike protuberance called a *pittam* (plural, *pittamim*), and at the opposite end is a thick stem called an *ikutz*. The Rabbis (*Shulchan Arukh*, Orach Cha'yim 651:1) were under the mistaken impression that the *pittam* is the point of connection of the fruit to the tree, when in fact the *ikutz* is the connector.

THE PITTAM

Derived from the Aramaic *pittma*, and sometimes spelled *pittom*, the *pittam* is the knobby bulge at the tip of an *etrog* (citron). The Aramaic term *shoshanta* is also used to describe the protuberance. The *etrog* grows with the *pittam* facing downward.

For an *etrog* to be kosher—that is, fit for use—the *pittam* must not be broken or missing. However, a variety of *etrogim* grown in North Africa and other Mediterranean countries are naturally *pittam*-less, and these are considered kosher.

In Frankfurt, Germany, in the twelfth and thirteenth centuries, it was common practice for a pregnant woman to bite the *pittam* off the *etrog* after its last use on Hoshanah Rabbah, but not eat the fruit itself. In this manner she was demonstrating that unlike Eve she obeyed God's commandment not to eat the forbidden fruit. As a reward, it was thought, she would enjoy a painless and successful childbirth. Some believed she would be rewarded by giving birth to a male child.

RECITING THE BLESSING

In Jewish law, a blessing must be recited prior to performing a religious act. This legal concept is known by the Hebrew term *oveir la'asiyato* (plural *oveir la'asiyatam*), meaning "incumbent upon the performer [of the action]." Rabbi Judah summed up this ruling when he said (*Pesachim* 7b), "All the commandments over which a blessing is to be recited, the blessing must be recited before the action takes place." Hence, in a desire not to violate this precept, when holding the *etrog* prior to reciting the blessing, it was ruled that the *pittam* should be held facing downward, the opposite of the way the Rabbis thought the fruit actually grows on the tree. Only after the blessing has been recited is the *etrog* turned around and held with the *pittam* facing upward, again because this is the way the *etrog* was thought by the Rabbis to grow on the tree.

Two great nineteenth-century rabbinic authorities were aware of the mistaken traditional notion pertaining to the attachment of the *etrog* to the tree. However, Rabbi Yechiel Epstein (1835–1905), author of the *Arukh Ha-Shulchan* (651:12–13), and Rabbi Israel ben Meir Ha-Kohen (1838–1933), author of the *Mishnah Berurah* (651:2), were not about to make a break with established tradition. They opposed making a change in a custom that had been in effect for about five hundred years, and by doing so were abiding by one of the strictures of the Palestinian Talmud (*Pesachim* 4:1): *Al te-shanu minhag avoteikhem*, "Do not alter the customs of your ancestors."

SELECTING THE ETROG

In observing the Sukkot holiday, it is considered particularly meritorious to acquire a beautiful, choice *etrog*, but not all Jews agree on what constitutes "choice" (*muvchar* in Hebrew). Sephardic Jews prefer round, fat *etrogim*. Hungarians like oval ones with smooth surfaces; Jews of Galician extraction find an *etrog* with a furrowed surface to be most desirable. Some Jews consider an *etrog* to be *muvchar* only if its protuberance falls in a straight line with its stem.

POST-HOLIDAY USAGE

Since citrons grow on trees, and since in Jewish tradition Tu Bi-Shevat, the fifteenth day of the Hebrew month Shevat, is celebrated as the festival of trees, a custom developed to make jam from the *etrogim* used on Sukkot for consumption on Tu Bi-Shevat.

The Lulav

Modern linguists explain that since the *lulav* is the central branch of the palm (*tamar*) tree from which other branches would later stem, it is considered the heart (*lev*) of the tree, hence the name *lulav*.

After the *lulav/etrog* blessing is recited, the *lulav* is waved and/or shaken. It is also waved during the morning service when selections of the *Hallel* prayers are recited. The act of waving, common in Temple times when sacrifices were brought on the altar, was generally considered helpful in bringing the offerer closer to God. Talmudic authorities of a more mystical bent believed that the act of waving wards off evil spirits. The *lulav* is waved in six directions (north, east, south, west, up, and down) to indicate that God is everywhere.

The second-century talmudic scholar Eleazar ben Zadok, who was a *Kohen*, used to hold the *etrog* and *lulav* aloft during the entire prayer service except when he was blessing the congregation (*Birkat Kohanim*), reciting the *Shema*, or reading a portion from the Torah scroll. And the tractate *Sukkah* (41b) reports that the fourth-century Babylonian *amora* Mar bar Ameimar said to Rav Ashi, "My father used to recite all his Sukkot prayers while holding the *lulav* in his hand, and not merely when *Hallel* was recited. So dear was the *mitzvah* of *lulav* to him."

The third-century Babylonian *amora* Acha bar Yaakov (*Sukkah* 38a) used to wave the *lulav* to and fro in a stabbing fashion, as if to say to Satan, "I am thrusting an arrow in your eye." Many rabbis in Palestine adopted a similar procedure to ward off evil spirits and harmful winds.

There is a custom among some Jews to save the *lulav* until the Passover holiday, and to use it as fuel with which to bake *matzah*. Others use the *lulav* to sweep up the breadcrumbs during the search for leaven ceremony and to start the fire when burning the leaven the following morning.

The Hadasim

When the Torah speaks of the myrtle, it describes it in three words: *anaf eitz avot* ("the thick bough of a tree"). Because three words are used, it has become traditional to use three myrtle branches in the *lulav* bouquet.

Although myrtle is referred to in the Torah as "the boughs of thick trees," it is actually a bush. The Rabbis of the Talmud describe it as a "leafy tree" because its base is encased in leaves. Unlike most plants, the myrtle requires little water and little care, and after it is cut, its branches remain unwilted for an extended period. For this reason, the myrtle is associated with eternal life, happiness, and success. In fact, in ancient times brides carried a bouquet containing myrtle branches when they appeared under the marriage canopy.

The Aravot

Two willows are used in the *lulav* bouquet because the Bible speaks of willows in the plural (*aravot*), taken to mean two. The sixteenth-century *Code of Jewish Law* (*Shulchan Arukh*) recommends that the leaves of the willow be of the type with smooth rather than serrated edges. In Yiddish, the term *un zaiglach* ("without teeth") is used for the preferred type.

In addition to the two *aravot* that are used in the *lulav* bouquet, on Hoshanah Rabbah, the last day of Sukkot, five or six *aravot* are tied together into a bunch and beaten against the back of a synagogue pew as special prayers for salvation are recited.

Free Will

The issue of free will is presented in the Book of Deuteronomy (30:15–19), in which God says to the Children of Israel: "Behold, I have set before you this day life and prosperity, death and adversity.... I call heaven and earth to witness against you this day: I have put before you life and death, blessing and curse. Choose life if you and your offspring would live."

The message of the Torah is clear: humankind has the power to choose and is therefore accountable for its actions. However, the question of whether people are free to choose an unpredetermined course of action has been addressed by theologians and philosophers for millennia. If our fate has been preordained by God, then we in essence lack freedom of choice. If, on the other hand, we have the power to shape our own lives, how can God be characterized as omniscient or omnipotent?

The Rabbis of the Talmud tried to unravel the mystery in a variety of ways. Rabbi Akiba said (Ethics of the Fathers 3:19): "All things are foreseen [by God], yet freedom of choice has been given [to people]." Rabbi Chaninah declared (*Berakhot* 33b): "Everything is in the hand of Heaven except the fear of Heaven," meaning that people's physical characteristics are predetermined, but their moral character is molded by the choices they make.

Philosophers of subsequent centuries continued to address the problem. Sa'adya Gaon (882–942), the Egyptian-born Babylonian scholar, and Judah Ha-Levi (*c.* 1075–1141), the Spanish poet-philosopher who wrote the classic *Kuzari*, shared the same view: only after a person has determined how he will behave does God make up His mind about the individual's pattern of behavior. The twelfth-century Spanish thinker Moses Maimonides, author of the *Guide of the Perplexed*, confessed that just as it is impossible for people to understand the true essence of God, so is it impossible to understand the nature of His knowledge. Nevertheless, said Maimonides, humans do have freedom of choice. In his *Mishneh Torah* (Hilkhot Teshuvah 5:1–2), he wrote: "Free will is granted to every man. If he desires to incline toward the good way, and be righteous, he has the power to do so; and if he desires to incline toward the unrighteous way and be a wicked man, he has also the power to do so ... Do not believe, as stupid people do, that God decides at birth who will be righteous and who will be wicked. No, every human being can be either as righteous as Moses or as wicked as [the wicked king] Jeroboam..." In expressing this view, Maimonides takes vehement exception to the statement of the third/fourth-century Palestinian scholar Chaninah ben Papa, who said in *Niddah* (16b): "The name of the angel in charge of conception is Night. He takes a drop [of the semen] and places it before God and asks: 'What shall be of this drop? Shall it produce a strong man or a weak man, a wise man or a fool, a rich man or a poor man?'"

The fourteenth-century Chasdai Crescas (died 1410), the Chief Rabbi of Aragon, Spain, and author of the work *Or Adonai* ("*The Light of God*"), states that people are subject to the influences of cause and effect that are beyond their control, thus limiting their powers of free will. Even so, they are responsible for their actions.

Modern-day philosophers and theologians continue to struggle with the question of free will. Many take the position of Rabbi Mordecai Kaplan (1881–1983), who said: "The ethical choice of man operates within the framework of a morally determined world."

Educator Henry Slonimsky (1884–1970) wrote (*Essays*, 1967): "Man has freedom, he can choose God or reject God, he can lead the world to perdition and to redemption. The creation of this being Man with such power of freedom means that God has made room for a co-determining power alongside of Himself. Man is the crossroad of the world."

Funeral Practices

In the days when Jews lived in small towns, the entire funeral service was conducted in the cemetery. The deceased was carried in a coffin from the home to the cemetery, which was on the outskirts of the town, not far from the homes of the populace.

When cities grew and cemeteries were located increasingly far away from population centers, not all who wished to be present at each funeral could manage to reach the cemetery. It therefore became customary—although not required by Jewish law—to hold an additional service in the home of the deceased.

The eleventh-century scholar Rashi said (*Megillah* 28b) that an exception could be made in the case of a great scholar or community leader. For him, the home funeral service may be replaced by a synagogue service so that large numbers of people can attend.

The sixteenth-century *Code of Jewish Law* (*Shulchan Arukh*, Yoreh Dei'ah 344:20), in speaking of synagogue funerals, comments that if the deceased was a worthy community leader—rabbi or layman—it was the practice in some communities to bring the body into the synagogue for the funeral service and eulogy. But the distinction between the deserving and undeserving could not be clearly drawn, and the practice led to much confusion, as wealthy families sometimes demanded a synagogue service for a less than deserving relative. Consequently, synagogue funeral services were reserved for respected, pious persons and esteemed scholars.

Over the centuries, many scholars have opposed the idea of bringing a coffin into the synagogue. This attitude is based on the verse in the Book of Psalms (115:17), "The dead cannot praise the Lord." To bring a deceased, who obviously can no longer pray, into the synagogue would constitute an affront to the dead (*nivul ha-met*).

Today, almost all funerals are held in funeral parlors, largely for the convenience of having a funeral director take care of the many necessary details. However, funerals are sometimes conducted in the home of the deceased or in the synagogue if it suits the family and the congregation.

Some congregations in the United States have adopted a policy of holding the funerals of all their members in the synagogue so as to accord everyone the same degree of respect. Additionally, some Jewish communities are too small to support a Jewish funeral chapel, so funerals are often conducted in the synagogue. Where that is not feasible, it is permissible to hold funerals in non-Jewish chapels if all Christological symbols are removed.

During World War II, the Law Committee of the Jewish Welfare Board's Division of Religious Activities, consisting of Orthodox, Conservative, and Reform rabbis, ruled that Jewish chaplains may officiate at military funerals in national cemeteries such as Arlington, where Jewish and Christian soldiers are buried side by side.

After the formal service held in the funeral parlor or synagogue has concluded, the coffin is placed in a hearse. Among some Orthodox Jews, it is customary to walk behind the hearse for a block or two before mourners proceed by car to the cemetery, so as to fulfill the commandment (*mitzvah*) of "escorting the deceased" (*halva'yat ha-met*).

Upon arrival of the cortege at the cemetery, the funeral director presents to cemetery officials the legal documents required before the burial can take place. The hearse, followed by the mourners in their cars, then proceeds to the burial plot. The coffin is removed from the hearse, and the pallbearers, followed by the rabbi and the mourners, proceed slowly to the open grave.

Pallbearers

In Jewish tradition, carrying the deceased to his or her final resting place is considered a primary obligation incumbent upon all Jews. While it is customary for members of the family or close Jewish friends to carry the deceased to his or her burial plot, Jewish law does not prohibit non-Jews from acting as pallbearers. In fact, when non-Jews participate in Jewish funerals, they are according honor and respect to the dead (*kevod ha-met*). Since interfaith cooperation is encouraged by Jewish law, most rabbis have no objection to accepting the goodwill of non-Jews who agree to serve as pallbearers at Jewish funerals.

The Seven Stops

Traditionally, Psalm 91 is read by the rabbi as he leads the procession that follows the coffin as it is carried to the grave. As verse 11, consisting of seven Hebrew words (the English translation of which is "For He will order His angels to guard you wherever you go"), is recited, the procession usually stops after each word. (In some traditions only three stops are made.) Each pause is sometimes explained as an opportunity for the bereaved to express hesitation and reluctance to take leave of the departed.

A second explanation offered by the Rabbis of the Talmud (*Bava Batra* 100b) is that the seven stops reflect the seven times the Hebrew word *hevel*, "vanity [of life]," is mentioned in the Book of Ecclesiastes (1:2). "Vanity of Vanities," said Ecclesiastes, "vanity of vanities, all is vanity." (Actually the word "vanity," *hevel*, is mentioned only five times: three times in the singular and twice in the plural. But each plural is counted for two singular forms, making a total of seven.)

A third explanation for making seven stops during the procession from hearse to grave is to reflect the seven stages of man as described in Ecclesiastes, and expanded upon in the Midrash (*Kohelet Rabbah* 1:2), where Rabbi Samuel ben Isaac taught that the seven vanities mentioned by Ecclesiastes correspond to the seven worlds a man passes through in life:

- At age one he is fondled and kissed by all.
- At ages two and three he is like a pig, sticking his hands in filth.
- At ten he skips like a kid.
- At twenty he is like a neighing horse, preening his person and longing for a wife.

- Having married, he is like an ass (struggling for a living).
- When he has children, he battles like a dog to provide food for their needs.
- When he grows old, he is bent like an ape (and begins to lose the characteristics of a human).

Modern scholars generally believe that the origin of the custom of pausing during a procession has roots in the belief that the stopping and starting will cause the evil spirits that follow the dead to the grave to become confused and disoriented, uncertain over the whereabouts of the deceased. This is in keeping with the attitude of many early authorities. One such scholar, the Gaon Sar Shalom, a ninth-century head of the great academy in Sura, Babylonia, explained that in his day processions paused seven times in order to shake off evil spirits that clung to those who had attended the funeral. With each stop, one of the spirits would disappear.

Scholars in subsequent centuries (Rashi in the eleventh and Moses Isserles in the sixteenth) repeated this explanation of the practice of halting to and from the grave, noting that with each pause the evil spirits lose their effectiveness. Rashi adds that halting the procession allows a final opportunity to eulogize the dead.

Joshua Trachtenberg, in his *Jewish Magic and Superstition* (p. 178), recalls the instructions of Shabbetai, son of the mystic Isaiah Horowitz (died 1630), to his son. He wrote in his testament: "While my body is being lowered into the grave, have seven pious and learned men repeat Psalm 91 seven times."

The Burial

After the coffin is lowered into the grave, it is customary for some present to follow the tradition of transferring some earth onto the coffin with the back of a shovel. This is a symbolic way of relatives and friends fulfilling the obligation to bury their dead.

When one individual has done so, instead of the shovel being handed directly to the next person, it is pushed into the mound of earth alongside the grave. The next mourner then picks up the shovel and repeats the procedure. In some Sephardic communities, such as those in Turkey and Greece, the custom is for individuals to simply throw the shovel on the ground after using it.

The practice of not passing the shovel directly from hand to hand also has been explained as a way of saying that we do not wish to pass sorrow from one person to another.

The tradition of using the back side of the shovel probably originated as local custom and eventually became common practice. Its purpose was to indicate a difference (*shinui* in talmudic parlance) between ordinary shoveling and the shoveling of earth to bury a loved one. Using the backside of the shovel is a practice particularly common among the Sephardim of Greece, Turkey, and other parts of the Ottoman Empire, as well as in many parts of the Western world.

Depending on local practice, the grave is completely filled with earth at this time, or it is partially filled and then draped with a blanket of simulated grass. The Orthodox tradition is to fill the grave completely. The rabbi then recites one or two Psalms, after which the memorial prayer *El Malei Rachamim* is recited or chanted by the rabbi or cantor. Following this, the mourners recite the *Mourner's Kaddish* for the first time. The ceremony may end at this point, or the rabbi may conclude with a benediction.

The assembly now forms two lines on either side of the walkway. As the immediate family passes through, the appropriate expression of condolence is pronounced by those in attendance.

At one time, after the burial service, mourners would stand still while the people attending would pass between them. But, the Talmud tells us (*Sanhedrin* 19a), two families in Jerusalem attending a funeral together contended with one another, each maintaining that they deserve to pass between the mourners first. To solve this problem, the Rabbis established a rule that the public would form a double line and remain standing while the mourners passed through.

As all leave the cemetery, they wash their hands at the spigot provided near the exit of the cemetery. The cup that is used is not passed directly from person to person. As with the passing of the shovel, this is explained as a symbolic way of not transferring trouble from one individual to another. If handwashing is not done before leaving the cemetery, the hands are washed before entering the house of mourning.

See Burial; Cemetery; Flowers; Halva'yat Ha-Met; Nivul Ha-Met.

Gabbai

Plural, *gabba'im*. A Hebrew word literally meaning "elevated one," referring to an official who conducts synagogue and community affairs. Most often, the term is applied to ushers who distribute Torah honors (*aliyot*) and oversee synagogue decorum. In some congregations, one of the *gabba'im* is also assigned the task of calling out the *aliyot* and/or making the *Mi Shebeirakh* prayer, although these tasks are usually performed by the rabbi, the sexton, or the *ba'al korei* himself.

In earlier centuries, it was common for Jewish communities in Europe to appoint members to collect taxes and to distribute funds to the needy. These appointees were called *gabba'ei tzedakah*, "charity collectors." The first mention of such officials is found in the Mishnah of the tractate *Demai* (3:1).

See Torah Reading.

Gambling

The Bible does not make specific reference to gambling, but the Rabbis of the Talmud (*Sanhedrin* 24b–25b and *Shabbat* 149b) criticized the practice, describing anyone who gambles with dice (*mesachek be-kuvya*) as ineligible to serve as a judge or even appear as a witness. They went so far as to characterize all winnings from gambling as theft (*gezel*), because money is taken from a loser who derives nothing in return.

In his *Mishneh Torah* (*Gezeilah Va-Aveidah* 1:3, 6:7–16), Moses Maimonides sums up the rabbinic attitude:

Who are gamblers? Those who play with wooden blocks or stones or bones or similar objects and agree that whoever wins over his fellow in the game will take a certain sum of money from him—this is theft by rabbinic law. Even though the loss was by consent of the loser, yet inasmuch as the winner takes money by means of game or sport without giving anything in return, it is thievery. Similarly, those who play with a domestic or wild animal or with birds and agree that the owner of the animal that wins or runs faster will take from his fellow a certain amount of money, and all similar cases—this is all forbidden and is theft by rabbinic law.

Despite the rabbinic condemnation, gambling continued to be engaged in by Jews throughout the Middle Ages. During the Renaissance period, apparently influenced by the passion for games of chance among Christians, gambling among Italian Jews reached epidemic proportions. As early as 1416, Jewish communities in Bologna and Forli prohibited the playing of card games and the rolling of dice. In 1576, the rabbis of Cremona issued a ban on all those who engaged in gambling, but it had to be rescinded because of strong objection. Learned Jews who became addicted to gambling were able to muster ingenious arguments in favor of the practice, even contending, as did the prominent Italian physician and philosopher Abraham ben Chananiah Yagel (1553–c. 1624), author of *Gei Chizayon* (*Valley of Vision*), that "all of human perfection is in cards and dice."

There is one activity involving gambling which the Rabbis found acceptable—namely, the playing of the *dreidel* game on Chanukkah.

Gambling on Christmas

In addition to Chanukkah, the Rabbis permitted gambling on one other occasion during the year: the eve of Christmas, known as *Nitl Nacht*. On that night, much revelry took place in the streets, and it was dangerous for Jews of the European *shtetl* to leave their homes. So those who would customarily go out each evening to the study hall would stay indoors surrounded by family and friends. Many would sit around a table and play a card game known as *kvitl*, much like blackjack.

See Chanukkah.

Gaon

Plural, *ge'onim*. A Hebrew term literally meaning "illustrious one," used as a title for an outstanding scholar or leader, particularly in the Sephardic communities of Babylonia between the sixth and eleventh centuries. During this period, the two main academies of learning were in Sura and Pumbedita. Sherira Gaon, who died in 1006 at the age of 100, headed the Pumbedita *yeshivah*. He was succeeded by his son, Hai Gaon, who died in 1038 at age 99. Rabbi Sa'adya ben Joseph (882–942), who was born in Egypt and migrated to Babylonia in 921, was appointed *ga'on* of the academy of Sura in 928. Popularly known as Sa'adya Gaon, he was one of the most famous of all personalities to whom the title of *ga'on* was assigned. His main contribution was *Emunot Ve-Dei'ot (Beliefs and Opinions)*, originally written in Arabic, in which he denies any conflict between reason and revealed religion.

Despite the finalizing of the Babylonian Talmud by the scholars Ravina and Ashi toward the end of the fifth century, the *ge'onim* and later scholars introduced *takanot* (rulings) on matters not specifically treated in the Talmud itself.

In the sixth century and later, as groups of Jews settled farther away from the centers of Jewish learning in Babylonia and Palestine, old customs changed and new ones came into being. Local customs varied and had the power of law. Even the *ge'onim*, who were highly regarded by the Jews of the Diaspora between the seventh and eleventh centuries, did not dare tamper with local customs. They went so far as to support the retention of local practices even when they personally did not approve of them.

Garden of Eden

Called *Gan Eden* in Hebrew, this is the place where Adam and Eve enjoyed a happy, carefree existence before eating from the fruit of the Tree of Knowledge (Genesis 3:1ff.).

See Paradise.

Gebruchts

Gebruchts (also pronounced *gebrachts*) is Yiddish for "dipping [*matzah*] in [liquid]." During Passover, some observant Jews, concerned that they might violate the regulations prohibiting the use of *chametz*, are careful not to allow even baked *matzah* to come into contact with a liquid. They fear that if part of the *matzah* was not thoroughly baked, the liquid might cause the raw flour to ferment or leaven. Consequently, Jews who follow the custom of "no *gebruchts*" refrain from preparing *matzah brei*, *matzah* balls, and other dishes that require the mixing of water with *matzah* products. Since the Bible demands that *matzah* be eaten for seven days, "no *gebruchts*" is not practiced on the eighth day of Passover.

See Chametz; Passover.

Gehinnom

A Hebrew term literally meaning "Valley of Hinnom." The Greek name is Gehenna. The Books of Joshua (15:8), II Kings (23:10), and Jeremiah (7:31) refer to the "Valley [*gei* in Hebrew] of the son of Hinnom," a place located south of Jerusalem where children were sacrificed to the god Molokh. The valley was deemed accursed and later became the burning place for all the city's refuse. As a consequence, the word *Gehinnom* became associated with all that is evil and sinful. Hel (Hell), the Old Norse goddess of the underworld, was later associated with *Gehenna* and the two words became synonymous.

In Jewish tradition, those who did not lead exemplary lives on earth would be doomed to spend eternity in *Gehinnom*.

Disparate Visions of Gehinnom

The distinguished first-century talmudic scholar Rabbi Yochanan ben Zakkai fell ill and his disciples went to visit him. When he saw them, he began to weep, since he was unsure whether he was destined to go to Paradise or *Gehinnom*. In the course of their discussion, Rabbi Yochanan let it be known that he believed in a physical heaven and hell.

His disciple Rabbi Shimon ben Lakish did not agree: "There is no *Gehinnom* in the world to come," he said. "The Holy One, blessed be He, will draw forth the sun from its sheath and the righteous shall be healed while the wicked will be judged and punished."

Rabbi Judah ben Ila'i, another of Yochanan's disciples, likewise did not agree with the master. He said: "There will be neither a consuming sun nor a *Gehinnom*, but a fire will issue forth from the wicked and burn them up" (*Berakhot* 28b; *Nedarim* 8b; *Genesis Rabbah* 6:6).

Gelilah

See Hagbahah and Gelilah.

Gemara

This Aramaic term literally meaning "study, learn, infer, or conclude" is the name given to one of the two parts of the Talmud, the other being the Mishnah. In popular parlance, the term *Gemara* is often used to mean the entire Talmud.

The Mishnah sets forth the basic law, and the *Gemara* interprets, discusses, and expands upon it. The Rabbis whose views are mentioned in the *Gemara* are called *tanna'im*, while the opinions of Rabbis whose opinions are set forth in the Mishnah are called *amora'im*. The final editing of the *Gemara* of the Babylonian Talmud was accomplished by two Rabbis: Ravina and Ashi, around the year 500 C.E. The Mishnah itself was finalized two and one-half centuries earlier by Rabbi Judah the Prince.

See Talmud.

Gematriah

Of uncertain etymology but generally said to be of Greek origin, the term *gematriah* has become part of the Hebrew lexicon and refers to a system that converts the letters of the Hebrew alphabet into numbers. Hence, *alef*, the first letter of the alphabet, has the numerical value of one, *bet* equals two, and so on. *Tav*, the last letter, equals 400.

Gematriah was employed as far back as talmudic times to underscore or uncover teachings and values secreted in the text of the Torah and the rest of the Bible and was also used widely to expound creative interpretations of Scripture. The second-century Galilean scholar Eleazar ben Yosi introduced thirty-two hermeneutic systems that are used to interpret biblical text. One of these is *gematriah*.

When Rabbi Chiya bar Abba, a third-century Palestinian scholar, wished to point out that under the influence of too much wine one loses lucidity, he employed a *gematriah*. Rabbi Chiya pointed out that the numerical value of wine—*ya'yin* in Hebrew (spelled *yud* [10] *yud* [10] *nun* [50])—is seventy, and the Hebrew word for secret—*sod* in Hebrew (spelled *samekh* [60] *vav* [6] *dalet* [4])—is also seventy. From this he concluded that "when wine goes in[to one's body], secrets come out [of one's mouth]" (*Eruvin* 65a).

When the Rabbis wanted to elevate the status of the patriarch Abraham to that of angel, they found corroboration in the fact that the numerical value of both Avraham (Hebrew for Abraham) and of the angel Razi'el is 248. When they wanted to equate the ladder that Jacob saw in his dream, upon which angels were ascending to heaven and descending to earth (Genesis 28:12), with Moses' ascent to Mount Sinai to receive the Ten Commandments, they calculated that the Hebrew word for ladder (*sulam*) and the word for Sinai both have the numerical value of 130.

Kabbalists, in particular, have discovered many lessons through *gematriah*. The Italian mystic Leon de Modena (1571–1648) contended that it was quite proper to address a woman as "honey" because the Hebrew word for woman—*ishah*—and the Hebrew word for honey—*devash*—both have a numerical value of 306.

In modern times it is common for people to make a contribution of eighteen dollars, or a multiple thereof, to charity. Eighteen is the numerical value of *chai*, meaning "life" in Hebrew. Sephardim often make a contribution of twenty-six dollars, because twenty-six is the numerical value of Yehovah, one of God's names. Occasionally, Sephardim will contribute $101, representing the numerical value of the name of the archangel Mikhael.

See Alphabet, Hebrew *for the numerical value of each letter.*

Gemilut Chasadim

Singular, *gemilut chesed.* Rabbi Shimon the Just, one of the last members of the Great Assembly (*Anshei Knesset Ha-Gedolah*), the supreme religious body in Temple times, is reported to have said (Ethics of the Fathers 1:2): "The world rests on three foundations: Torah, divine service [*Avodah*], and acts of lovingkindness [*gemilut chasadim*] between man and his fellow man."

In the Jewish tradition, the concept of *gemilut chasadim* encompasses the giving of charity, visiting the sick, burying the dead, comforting mourners, and performing selfless acts without expecting a reward. The Talmud (*Shabbat* 120a) characterizes the performance of such virtuous deeds as *midat chasidut*, "a [high] degree of piety."

Early Charitable Institutions

At the height of talmudic times, between 100 and 500 C.E., two charitable public institutions had already achieved a high degree of sophistication in the performance of acts of lovingkindness. These are described in various talmudic tractates, principally Mishnah *Pei'ah* (8:7a), Mishnah *Nedarim* (4:4), *Bava Batra* (8b), and *Shabbat* (117b–118a).

The first institution was called *tamchui*, which is the name of a large dish in which food was placed to provide at least one day's supply for the poor, whether they were local residents or strangers. Two individuals were appointed in each community to collect funds for the purchase of food.

The second institution was called *kuppah*, or Communal Fund. The monies in this fund, collected on a weekly basis, were used to take care of those in greater need. It also provided food and lodging for transients who had to stay in town over the Sabbath. They were supplied with enough food to take care of the three obligatory Sabbath meals.

Three distinguished community leaders constituted the *kuppah* committee. They were called *gabba'ei tzedakah*, "charity administrators." The famous first/second-century Rabbi Akiva was a member of such a panel. Distributing the collected funds was considered an awesome responsibility and a great honor.

Over the centuries, *gemilut chasadim* societies flourished throughout Europe, continuing to be active even until the present time in America and elsewhere.

The tractate *Sukkah* (49b) compares the virtues of giving charity and performing acts of lovingkindness. The Rabbis point out that charity can be done only with money, but *gemilut chasadim* can be done with one's person as well as one's money. Charity can be given only to the poor, but *gemilut chasadim* can be extended to the rich and the poor.

In the centuries following talmudic times, European Jewish communities, as well as others throughout the world, established Hebrew Loan Societies to offer interest-free loans to those who were financially distressed.

According to S. D. Goitein, in his *A Mediterranean Society* (1971), records found among the *genizah* documents reveal how widespread the dispensation of charity was in Jewish communities throughout history. In the days when Maimonides lived in Fostat, Egypt, there was an average of one relief recipient for every four donors; twenty-five percent of the population was needy.

Today, acts of lovingkindness are sometimes referred to as *gemachs*, an acronym of *gemilut chasadim*.

Genizah

A Hebrew word literally meaning "hiding place," referring specifically to a storage space in a synagogue where worn or unusable Torah scrolls, prayerbooks, sacred writings, and other holy objects were deposited for safekeeping until such time as they could be accorded proper burial in a Jewish cemetery.

The most famous *genizah* was situated in the attic of the Ben Ezra Synagogue, built in 882 in Fostat, Egypt, near Cairo. (Maimonides was the leader of the Jewish community of Fostat in the twelfth century.) For centuries, until 1763, the Jewish world was unaware of the rich collection of manuscripts stored there.

Some of the manuscripts in the Cairo Genizah, as the Ben Ezra storage space came to be known, were brought to Cambridge University, where the renowned Romanian-born Solomon Schechter was teaching. Recognizing the importance of the documents, Schechter traveled to Fostat in 1896 and retrieved some 100,000 manuscript leaves of works that had been unknown or lost. Among the significant finds were hundreds of unknown poems by the great sixth-century Palestinian poet Yannai. Until this discovery, only one of Yannai's poems—which somehow found its way to Europe and into the Ashkenazic liturgy—had survived.

The Cairo Genizah was of extreme importance; since its restoration in 1025, following the devastation of the Ben Ezra Synagogue by fire, its contents had remained untouched. Furthermore, not only were religious artifacts found there, but also copies of deeds, wills, business contracts, private letters, and rabbinic responsa, a virtual treasure-trove of information that has engaged students and historians for the past century.

Gentile

The word *gentile*, derived from the Latin *gentilis*, referred originally to a member of the same race or clan. In later times it took on the meaning of "foreigner." Anyone who was not a Roman was a Gentile, and the term was later used by Jews to refer to anyone who was a pagan or heathen, not specifically to a Christian. Christians objected to being described as Gentiles because they considered the word pejorative, despite the fact that the New Testament often uses the word when referring to non-Jews.

The twelfth-century philosopher Moses Maimonides summed up the traditional Jewish attitude toward Gentiles as follows (*Teshuvot Ha-Rambam*, Friedman edition, Jerusalem, 1934):

> You asked about the Gentiles. Keep in mind, that "God requires the heart, and that everything depends on the intention of the heart." Therefore, our teachers said: "The pious among the Gentiles have a portion in the Future World—that is to say, [the pious are] those who have attained the required status of knowledge of the Creator and have endeavored to achieve ethical qualities. There is no doubt that he who achieves ethical qualities in the right ways of life and correct wisdom of belief in God merits the Future World."

See Goy; Noahide Laws.

Geshem

Literally, "rain." The name given to the prayer for rain that is recited during the *Musaf* service on Shemini Atzeret. Like the prayer for dew (*Tal*), which is recited on the first day of Passover, *Geshem* was composed by the eighth-century Palestinian poet Eleazar Ha-Kalir.

Geshem is constructed in the form of an alphabetical acrostic in which the meritorious deeds of Abraham, Isaac, Jacob, Moses, Aaron, and the Twelve Tribes of Israel are recalled. The prayer expresses the hope that because of their praiseworthy lives, God will bless the Land of Israel with much needed rain during the forthcoming winter months (*Ta'anit* 2b; *Rosh Hashanah* 33a).

Since in the *Geshem* prayer God is portrayed as a dispenser of justice, as he is in the Rosh Hashanah and Yom Kippur prayers, it is customary for the cantor and rabbi to don a white cap and robe when leading these prayers, as is done on the High Holidays.

See Tal.

Get

Before the bonds of matrimony can be officially severed, Jewish law requires that the husband issue a bill of divorcement to his wife, and that she willingly accept it.

The biblical term for the divorce document is *sefer keritut* (Deuteronomy 24:1), meaning "book of dissolution." However, the Talmud introduced the word *get*, which some authorities say derives from the Akkadian, meaning "court writ." When a *get* is issued, it serves to nullify the original marriage contract (*ketubbah*).

Orthodox and Conservative rabbis require that a *get* be obtained before a remarriage can take place; Reform rabbis generally accept a civil divorce as sufficient.

The Writing of the Get

Based on the verse in Deuteronomy (24:1), "...he *writes* her a bill of divorcement," the Rabbis concluded that the document must be handwritten by a scribe who is well versed in Jewish law. The *get* is written in Aramaic, which was the everyday language of the masses, particularly in Babylonia, where large numbers of Jews lived.

It is required that the divorce document be written by a Jewish scribe (*sofer*) in the presence of a *Beit Din*, a rabbinic court consisting of three rabbis. (Some authorities are of the opinion that even one rabbi can constitute a *Beit Din*.) Also present are the husband, sometimes the wife, and two male witnesses who are unrelated to the parties in the proceedings.

Using a sharp wooden stylus, the scribe rules twelve strong lines on the reverse side of a sheet of parchment or heavy white paper. The text itself must consist of twelve lines so as to comport with the numerical value of the letters that spell out the Hebrew word *get* (*gimmel* [3] plus *tet* [9]).

After a last-minute attempt at reconciliation is made by the *Beit Din*, the scribe uses a quill to write the *get* with black ink on the parchment or heavy white paper.

While the early codes of Jewish law forbid the use of a metal pen from ever being used to write a *get*, later authorities permit its use when it is impossible to find a scribe adept at the use of a quill. (See Isaac Klein's *A Guide to Jewish Religious Practice*, 1979, p. 478.)

Cutting the Get

After the document is written and witnessed, a tear is made in it with a knife or scissors. This assures that the script on the document will not be erased and the parchment reused for other divorce proceedings.

A second reason for cutting the *get* is historical. During Hadrian's rule over Palestine (117–138 C.E.), when all legal authority was denied the Jewish community, Jewish courts continued to function secretly. When a *get* was issued, the document was cut so that if it were discovered by Roman authorities, Jews could always deny that the document was a legal one.

After the *get* has been cut, the husband hands it to his wife if she is present. If she is not present, the husband appoints an agent to deliver the document to her. A member of the court or one of the two witnesses sometimes act as the husband's messenger.

Ghetto

Since early times, Jews, like other ethnic groups, have tended to live apart from other groups, establishing homes in a particular section of the towns or villages in which they resided. However, beginning in the sixteenth century, freedom of choice in deciding where to live was often denied Jews.

For a thousand years, the Catholic Church had tried unsuccessfully to convince Jews to abandon their beliefs and embrace Christianity. In 1516, realizing that their attempts were futile, Church officials influenced local authorities in Venice, Italy, to confine Jews to an isolated area so that they would not be able to spread their "sinful" teaching among the masses. This area was originally the location of an iron foundry—*geto* in the Venetian dialect, hence the English word "ghetto."

Ironically, in the very year that the Venetians enforced this oppressive ruling, a wealthy Christian named Daniel Bomberg, of Antwerp (born 1455), was granted permission by the Council of Venice to establish a Hebrew printing and publishing house in which he used Jewish editors, typesetters, printers, and proofreaders. The first printed Talmud was from Bomberg's presses, and the format established in that first edition is followed to this day.

Following the example of Venice, ghettos were established in many other cities throughout Europe, especially after the mid-sixteenth century when Protestantism came into existence. Over the centuries, the confinement of Jews to restricted areas became common in other European countries.

Nazi Ghettos

The International School for Holocaust Studies at Israel's Yad Vashem Holocaust Memorial Museum has published a map of the ghettos established by the Nazis between 1943 and 1944. The map shows approximately four hundred ghettos to which Jews were officially confined throughout Europe during the Nazi era. The last and perhaps most famous was the Warsaw Ghetto, which was decimated by the Nazis in 1943.

Ghosts

In the Bible, the most well-known reference to necromancy—the practice of claiming to be able to foretell the future by communication with the dead–concerned the prophet Samuel and King Saul. After Samuel died, King Saul was facing his last battle against the Philistines on Mount Gilboa. Eager to know beforehand how things would turn out, he persuaded an old witch who lived in the town of Endor to summon up the ghost of Samuel. When the apparition appeared in the form of an old man, Saul threw himself on the ground in supplication. The ghost demanded: "Why have you disturbed me...?" Saul replied: "I have summoned you *to tell me what I shall do*" (I Samuel 28:15).

With the dawn of the Middle Ages, belief in the power of ghosts became popular among Jews, although rabbis tried to stem the tide. Its influence was so widespread that it left an indelible mark on Jewish practices relating to death and burial, such as the customs of throwing clumps of grass over one's shoulder following a burial and of rapidly filling a grave once the casket has been lowered into the ground. These are considered ways of preventing the return of the ghost of the deceased, which may want to attack those still alive and which they believe may have caused pain to the deceased.

See Demonology.

Gidin

From an Akkadian and Aramaic root meaning "sinews," found in the hindquarter of a kosher animal. After the scribe has finished writing all the sheets of a Torah scroll, he sews one parchment to another with *gidin*, which are made from the dried veins of a kosher animal. These veins are stretched until they are as fine as thread.

The kosher animal from which the veins are taken need not be one that has been ritually slaughtered, but it must be one of those animals listed as kosher in the Book of Leviticus. Thus, if a deer (a wild animal that is kosher) is found dead in the field and had not been slaughtered in accordance with Jewish law, the carcass may not be used as food unless all its veins have been removed, but its veins may be used to make thread for sewing sheets of parchment. The prohibition against eating certain parts of the hindquarter is found in Genesis 32:33 and expanded upon in the Talmud [*Chullin* 90a] and *Shulchan Arukh* [Yoreh Dei'ah 65]).

Gidin are also sometimes made from tendons taken from the foot muscles of kosher animals.

See Dietary Laws.

Gilgul

A Hebrew word literally meaning "rolling," used in connection with two concepts: *gilgul mechilot*, meaning "rolling through underground passages," and *gilgul neshamot*, or *gilgul nefashot*, meaning "rolling [transmigration] of souls."

Gilgul Mechilot

This term meaning "rolling through underground passages" is used to express the ancient belief, still held by many, that when the Messiah comes, all Jewish dead who have lived righteous lives in the Diaspora will roll underground to the Holy Land, where they will be resurrected.

Abba Sala the Great, a third/fourth-century

Palestinian scholar, asked (*Ketubbot* 111a): "Will not the rolling be a painful experience for the righteous?" Abbayei answered: "Cavities [tunnels] will be made for them underground [to ease their trip]."

Gilgul Neshamot

There is a belief among many Jews, especially adherents of the philosophy of the sixteenth-century mystic Rabbi Isaac Luria of Safed, that after death the soul reappears in another body, human or animal. This concept is referred to by the Hebrew term *gilgul neshamot* (or *gilgul nefashot*), meaning "rolling [transmigration] of souls."

In his *Sefer Ha-Gilgulim* (*Book of Transmigration of Souls*), the famous disciple of Rabbi Luria, Chayim Vital, wrote: "The soul of a conceited community leader passed into the body of a bee; that of one who had been cruel to the poor into the body of a crow; the soul of a denunciator passed into the body of a barking dog; that of one who neglected to wash his hands before meals into a river." The rebirth of the soul in this new body is called reincarnation.

The *Sefer Ha-Bahir*, a small thirteenth-century book of unknown authorship, is the earliest source for teaching the concept of *gilgul*.

See Reincarnation.

Glassbreaking

The breaking of a glass at a wedding is generally explained as an expression of regret and sorrow over the destruction of the Temple in Jerusalem. The loud noise of the breaking glass is a stark reminder of the trauma caused by the loss of Jewish national independence suffered at the hands of the Romans in 70 C.E.

The piercing noise is also said to serve as a warning that man must temper life's joyous moments (such as the occasion of a wedding) with sober thoughts: that life is not all joy; that the happiness of the wedding day will not continue indefinitely; and that the young couple must prepare for life's eventualities. This reasoning became popular as a result of the talmudic story (*Berakhot* 30b–31a) in which the great scholar Mar, the son of Ravina, surprised the guests at his son's wedding during a moment of hilarity by smashing a valuable white porcelain vase before their eyes. His action reflected the ancient belief that it is wise to dampen enthusiasm so as to forestall misfortune.

A more plausible explanation of the origin of the glassbreaking custom lies in the realm of superstition. In the Middle Ages it was customary for the groom to taste of the wine after the seven wedding benedictions (*Sheva Berakhot*) had been recited. He would then let his bride taste of the wine as well, after which he would turn to the north wall and throw the glass against it. In the world of Jewish magic and superstition it was believed that evil spirits came from the North. (The biblical prophets often spoke of the evil enemy as descending upon Israel from the North.) The most effective way to repel evil spirits and demons, they believed, is by creating noise, including that made by breaking a glass. Kabbalists maintained that demons are intent upon disturbing the happiness of the new couple and that by shattering glass the evil spirits will be appeased.

It should be noted that in many cultures and civilizations noise was considered an antidote to the powers of evil spirits. Church bells were originally rung to ward off spirits. The same is true of the noise caused by the smashing of a bottle against the hull of a ship before it is launched.

The practice of throwing a glass against a wall has been abandoned. Today, a glass object other than the wine goblet is securely wrapped, and at the conclusion of the wedding ceremony the object is placed on the floor and crushed under the heel of the groom.

Early Reform Judaism considered the tradition of breaking a glass to be of little value and significance; its observance was deemed optional. A number of outstanding modern Orthodox authorities—including Hillel Posek of Tel Aviv and the former Sephardic Chief Rabbi of Israel, Ben-Zion Uziel—have criticized the practice, claiming that it causes many in the audience to shout, clap, and cheer, which is inappropriate, since they consider breaking a glass symbolic of the destruction of the Temple.

Since the main purpose of breaking a glass is to create noise, as explained earlier, some rabbis prefer that a light bulb or flashbulb be used: it is easier to break and usually makes a louder noise.

Mistaken Notion

Many people are under the false impression that the breaking of a glass by the groom is an essential part of the wedding custom, but the fact is that in the *Code of Jewish Law* (*Shulchan Arukh*, Even Ha-Ezer 65:3) Joseph Caro does not even mention the practice. His coauthor, Moses Isserles (an Ashkenazi), does mention it in his notes, saying that glassbreaking is practiced in some localities.

See Marriage; Weddings.

Glatt Kosher

The word *glatt*, Yiddish for smooth, refers to the condition of the lung of a kosher animal, particularly a mammal. Lungs that have incurred some sort of damage carry scar tissue, rendering the lung no longer smooth. Many persons who are fastidious about religious observance believe that an animal whose lungs are not perfectly smooth should not be used as food. Such strictness goes beyond the requirement of the law, which considers an animal kosher as long as there is no puncture in its lungs.

The term "glatt kosher" does not apply to fowl, the lungs of which are very small.

Dairy or vegetable products—such as cheese, butter, bread, candy, and cookies—are sometimes incorrectly labeled "*glatt* kosher." The term is applied only to the flesh of an animal with lungs.

God

The nature of God has long been debated by Jewish theologians. The Bible itself characterizes God as a "man of war" (Exodus 15:3; Psalms 24:8); as one who visits the sick (Genesis 18:1); as kind and merciful (Numbers 14:18; Psalms 145:8); as a source of healing (Numbers 12:13–15); as a source of peace (Psalm 29:11); as a fountainhead of understanding (Proverbs 28:5); and as One who rewards the righteous (Job 42:10). These anthropomorphic descriptions, however, do not represent mainstream Jewish thought.

Defining God

In the Bible, God appears to Moses in the midst of the bush that burned but would not be consumed and instructs Moses to tell the Children of Israel that He will free them from the bondage of Egypt. Moses then asks (Exodus 3:13): "When I come to the Israelites and say to them, 'The God of your fathers has sent me to you,' and they ask me, 'What is His name?' What shall I say to them?'"

God answers: "*Eh-heh-yeh asher Eh-heh-yeh.*" Say to the Israelites, "I will be who I shall be."

God identifies Himself not as a Being of the moment but as a Being of becoming. God is reaching out toward the future. Thus, man can state what God stands for, what God represents, but not what He is because He is not of the present. Thus, God is thought of as an ideal, an aspiration.

The Search for God

The Bible, the Talmud, and all subsequent traditional Jewish literature posit the existence of God as axiomatic, as indisputable fact. When pressed for proof, traditionalists point to the existence of the world and say, "This is God's handiwork, for only God could have the intelligence and power to put such a beautiful and complex world into motion."

As for God's continuing relationship to the world, the Psalmist says (115:16): "The heaven belongs to God, and the earth He has given to man."

God's Relationship to Man

Rabbi Chama ben Chaninah, in his interpretation of the text in Deuteronomy (13:5), sees God as man's role model: "You shall walk after the Lord your God." How does a human being walk after God? By emulating Him, said Rabbi Chama: Just as He clothes the naked, so must you clothe the naked. Just as He visits the sick, so must you visit the sick. Just as He comforts mourners, so must you comfort mourners. Just as He buries the dead, so must you bury the dead (*Sotah* 14a).

In attempting to explain the relationship of God to man, some Rabbis of the Talmud expressed the idea that man and God are partners. Just as man is dependent on God, so is God dependent on man. Although God, they say, created the world, and although He alone is sovereign, God needs man to help perfect it, a concept known in Hebrew as *tikkun olam*.

Other Rabbis of the Talmud (*Sanhedrin* 38a) reject the idea of a partnership existing between man and God. They present this view in answer to the question, "Why was Adam the last of all God's creations?" If, as Judaism believes, all of the world was created for man, why was Adam not the first of God's creations? The answer of the Rabbis is, "Man was created on the eve of the Sabbath [making him the last of all creations] so that the Sadducees should not say, 'Man was God's partner in creating the world.'"

Despite the initial aversion of the Rabbis to the idea of linking God to man as partners, this view was, and still is, subscribed to by most traditional theologians. This partnership, they say, is an expression of God's imminence, of God's concern for man, the crown of all His creations. Man, by his faith and actions, contributes to the perfection of the world. The Jew, in particular, makes his contribution toward creating an improved world through prayer and study and the observance of the commandments (*mitzvot*) (*Ta'anit* 2a).

See God, Names of.

God, Names of

Jewish tradition has assigned many names to God. The talmudic tractate *Soferim* (4:1–2) lists the following as divine names: *El* (a short form of *Elohim*), *Adonai*, *Yehovah* (also written *Yahweh*), *Shaddai*, *Tzeva'ot*, *E-he-yeh Asher E-he-yeh*, *Eloha* (a form of *Elohim*), and *Yah* (the first two letters of *Yahweh*). All of these names are considered holy and must be treated respectfully.

In the Midrash (*Exodus Rabbah* 3:6), the third-century Palestinian talmudic scholar Abba bar Mammel sums up the various usages of the names of God: "God said to Moses: 'Do you wish to know My name? I am called according to My work: sometimes I am called Almighty God, sometimes Lord of Hosts, sometimes God, and sometimes Lord. When I am judging mankind, I am called God; when I am waging war against the wicked, I am called Lord of Hosts; when I pardon a man for his sins, I am called Almighty God [*El Shaddai*]; and when I show mercy to the world, I am called *Adonai*, because this name denotes the quality of mercy in God.'"

The Tetragrammaton

From the Greek meaning "four letters," Tetragrammaton refers to the four Hebrew letters (*yud*, *hei*, *vav*, *hei*) that spell out God's name, Yehovah, which in Jewish law is too sacred to be pronounced. Yehovah is Anglicized as Jehova, and the Tetragrammaton is sometimes presented as YHWH.

Yehovah appears in Scripture 6,639 times. The talmudic tractates *Sanhedrin* (60a) and *Yoma* (66a) use the replacement expression *Shem Ha-Meforash*, meaning the "Explicit Name," when referring to the Tetragrammaton. Rabbi Nachman ben Isaac, in the talmudic tractate *Pesachim* (50a), said that all this will change in the world to come when "as God's name is written so will it be pronounced."

Traditionally, *Yehovah* may never be written out in Hebrew, and when the name is spoken during the Torah reading or prayer service, it is to be pronounced *Adonai* (*Kiddushin* 71a), meaning "Master" or "Lord." This form is used in the Bible 412 times. When spoken in a secular setting, however, replacement names such as *Adoshem* or *Ha-Shem* are used. The only time and the only person who was once permitted to pronounce the Tetragrammaton was the High Priest—and that was once a year, on Yom Kippur, when he offered the holy day sacrifices (Leviticus 16).

Yah (*yud* plus *hei*), which has the numerical value of 15, is a short form of *Yehovah* and is considered as sacred as the full name. Therefore, great care is taken not to place these two letters side by side. When it is necessary to do so, such as when the numerical value of 15 is being expressed, the letters *tet* (9) plus *vav* (6) are substituted. This will be noticed in the pagination of the Talmud, the *Code of Jewish Law* (*Shulchan Arukh*), and other religious books.

Elohim

The first verse of the Bible reads, "In the beginning, when *Elohim* began to create heaven and earth…" Many scholars find the use of the word *Elohim* problematic because it appears to be plural in form. How can God be spoken of in a plural sense when the foundation of Judaism is a belief in one God?

While it is true that the suffix *im* is generally used as a plural ending, in words such as *shama'yim* ("heaven") and *panim* ("face"), this is not the case; these words are not a plural form, just as *Elohim* is not a plural form.

The terms *El* and *Elo(h)a* are abbreviated forms of *Elohim*. The Book of Job uses *Eloha* as the name of God forty-one times.

Scholars such as J. H. Hertz (*Pentateuch and Haftorahs*, page 2) maintain that the word *Elohim* is not to be thought of as a plural form but as a term denoting great power. It is therefore proper, when speaking of God as Creator, to use this term rather than *Adonai* or one of the other names of God. Use of the word *Elohim* to denote power is evident from Exodus 22:27, which says: "Do not curse *Elohim*," referring to the judges, who are supreme in power and govern the nation. In Exodus 21:6, *elohim* likewise means "judges."

Other scholars, such as Nahum M. Sarna (*JPS Commentary on Genesis*, page 5), point out that *elohim* is a generic word for deity.

Pronouncing and Writing the Names of God

The third of the Ten Commandments (Exodus 20:7) forbids man from taking the name of God in vain. However, so as not to ban the expression of God's name totally from secular use, it became acceptable and commonplace to use God's name but not spell it out precisely. Thus, in writing and in speech, *Elokim* was used instead of *Elohim*, and *Eloheinu* became *Elokeinu*. *Ha-Shem* ("The Name") became a popular substitute for God when used in a secular setting. The first three Hebrew letters of *Adonai* and last two Hebrew letters of *Ha-Shem* were combined to make the word *Adoshem*, which is popularly used in a secular setting.

Ovadiah Yosef (1920–), former Chief Rabbi of Israel, stated that when one is studying Talmud or Midrash, it is quite proper for the student to pronounce God's name, and he need not use a substitute such as *Ha-Shem* (*Yechaveh Daat* III: 13). However, he limits such usage to the recitation of verses from the Bible and insists that at other times replacements such as *Ha-Shem*, *Elokim*, and *Elokenu* should be employed.

The Rabbis laid down strict rules concerning the treatment of the names of God in written form, emphasizing that their sanctity depends on how they are written and who writes them. The *Code of Jewish Law* (*Shulchan Arukh*, Yoreh Dei'ah 276:9) states categorically that the name of God written in a language other than Hebrew is not holy, because it is no longer the *actual* name of God, and its letters may be erased. Some later authorities do not agree, maintaining that the proper reverence must be accorded the name of God regardless of the language in which it is written. Therefore, in modern times one often sees the spelling of Lord as L-rd and God as G-d.

Fear that God's name may be dishonored if it is used indiscriminately is the reason why His name, in any of its forms, is not used on documents or letters that might eventually be discarded, destroyed, or even mishandled (see *Shavuot* 35a; *Rosh Hashanah* 18b). Rabbi Moses Isserles ruled (Yoreh Dei'ah 276:13) that one may write God's name in full in a book, since a book is not likely to be mistreated. All of this blends neatly into the reason why one book of the Bible does not mention the name of God, and that is the Book of Esther, called the *Megillah*. This book was written as a letter in scroll form sent out by Mordekhai to all the Jews throughout the kingdom of Ahasueros, informing them of the events that had transpired and that the fourteenth and fifteenth days of Adar each year are to be celebrated as days of joy and thanksgiving. Since this letter was intended for mass distribution, the name of God does not appear so that there is no chance that it will be desecrated.

Other Names for God

God has been referred to by many cognomens. The names King of Kings, Holy One Blessed Be He, and Our Father, Our King are often used in the liturgy. Shalom has also been considered a name of God based upon an incident described in the Book of Judges (6:24), where after seeing an angel of the Lord face-to-face, Gideon builds an altar and calls it *Adonai Shalom*, "The Lord is Peace." For this reason some people, when writing *shalom* in Hebrew, do not write out the final letter (*Shabbat* 10b).

When God is referred to in relation to Israel, the following names are used: Abir Yisra'el ("Strong One of Israel"), Kedosh Yisra'el ("Holy One of Israel"), Tzur Yisra'el ("Rock of Israel"), and Even Yisra'el ("Rock of Israel").

Invocation of the Name

While a number of God's names have been invoked to constrain demons and evil spirits, the name *Shaddai* ("Almighty") was most

commonly used. It was inscribed on the obverse side of the door *mezuzah* parchment and was exposed through the small aperture in the *mezuzah* casing. This, it was believed, protected the home. *Tefillin* straps were wrapped around the palm and fingers of the hand so as to form the three Hebrew letters *shin, dalet, yud,* which spells *Shaddai.* Likewise, when facing the congregation to bless it, *Kohanim* (Priests) raise both hands and spread out the fingers to form the letter *shin,* standing for *Shaddai.* In some Jewish communities, it was once the practice to spread the fingers of a corpse to form the letter *shin* as a protection against demons.

See Dybbuk; Exorcism; Profanation of God's Name.

Gog and Magog

The prophet Ezekiel, who lived in exile in Babylonia after the destruction of the First Temple in 586 B.C.E., prophesied (Ezekiel 38) that in the days leading up to the Messianic Age Israel will be restored to its former glory and will be resettled in its own land. However, this will not happen without fierce opposition, for powerful armies from the north under the leadership of Gog, ruler of the land of Magog, will invade Israel. The invasion will be repulsed and the enemy will be utterly destroyed.

While in the Book of Ezekiel Magog is portrayed as the land over which Gog ruled, in rabbinic literature Magog is pictured as a personality, a partner of Gog, hence the term Gog and Magog, which became a metaphor for heathen nations who are unsuccessful in destroying God's kingdom. In Christian literature, both Gog and Magog are hostile forces dominated by Satan (Revelations 16:16 and 20:7–10).

See Armageddon.

Golden Rule

The oft-quoted commandment "Love thy neighbor as thyself," mentioned in the Book of Leviticus (19:18), has spawned many offshoots and has been expressed in a variety of forms over the ages. According to the Talmud (*Shabbat* 31a), in the first century B.C.E. Hillel the Great responded to a stranger who asked to be taught the entire Torah while standing on one foot: "Do not do unto others what you would not have others do unto you," he said.

Rabbi Akiba, the leading scholar of the generation following the destruction of the Temple in 70 C.E. declared that the commandment in Leviticus 19:18 is a "fundamental rule of the Torah" (Jerusalem Talmud, *Nedarim* 9:4). His colleague Ben Azzai disagreed, maintaining that the phrase "This is the story of man" (Genesis 5:1) expresses an even greater Torah rule, especially in view of the fact that the verse ends by stating that man was made "in the likeness of God."

Over the centuries many scholars have interpreted and reinterpreted the meaning of Leviticus 19:18, because as simple as it may seem, the verse evokes many questions: What is meant by "neighbor"? A fellow Jew? One's countryman? A fellow human being?

Second, what is meant by the imperative "love"? How can one be commanded to love?

Third, what is meant by the words "as yourself"? Is it possible to love another as one loves oneself?

The Spanish scholar Abraham ibn Ezra (1089–1164) said that the Golden Rule should be understood as meaning that one must wish for his neighbor all the good fortune he wishes for himself.

In the thirteenth century, Nachmanides (1194–1270) described Leviticus 19:18 as an overstatement. The concept of loving one's neighbor as oneself is an ideal, he says, and not to be taken literally. Commenting on "as yourself," Nachmanides expresses doubt that Jewish law would obligate an individual to endanger his life for another person. He points to the statement of Rabbi Akiba, who said that when it comes to a choice between saving one's own life and that of another, one's own life comes first (Talmud Yerushalmi, *Nedarim* 9:4). However, the commentator adds, man should rejoice for the good fortune of his neighbor. He must never feel jealousy or envy.

In his commentary *Mikra Ki-Pheshuto*, Polish-born Arnold Ehrlich (1848–1919) observes that it is a serious error to assume that the word "neighbor" refers to anyone but an Israelite. He argues that when the Torah says, "Love your neighbor as yourself," it means love only your neighbor who is like yourself—namely, "one who is an Israelite, just as you are an Israelite" (*Mikra Ki-pheshuto*, Leviticus 19:19)

Golel

The Hebrew word *golel*, which means both "to roll" and "to cover" (see *Yoma* 68b, 70a; *Sotah* 39b), was originally used in connection with the burial procedure. In ancient times, when persons were buried in caves, the final act was to roll a stone over the cave opening, thus covering the grave. Therefore the term *golel*, which in the Talmud (*Shabbat* 142b and *Oholot* 2:4) is used to mean "rock," took on the meaning of "covering."

The eleventh-century French scholar Rashi (*Shabbat* 152b) was of the opinion that the word *golel*—in connection with the later burial procedure in which persons were laid to rest in coffins that were placed in the ground and covered with earth—referred to the top or covering of the coffin itself. This view was accepted by later authorities, such

as Nachmanides, who ruled that the seven-day mourning period (*shivah*) actually begins when the coffin is closed with its cover.

The second meaning of *golel* relates to the procedure carried out in the synagogue in connection with the reading from the Torah.

See Gilgul; Hagbahah and Gelilah.

Golem

Jewish literature contains many legendary accounts revolving about the creation of an artificial human being, a *golem*. It is said that those who are sufficiently pious and who know the secret names of God can breathe life into a lump of clay. However, because only God has the power to give a being the ability to speak, the *golem* remains mute.

The Hebrew word *golem* appears once in the Bible (Psalms 139:16) in reference to an unformed and imperfect mass. It is also used in the Talmud (*Sanhedrin* 38b) in a legend about the first hours of Adam's existence.

The story of the *golem*, which stresses the limitations of human power, has been told in many forms. The most famous is connected with the miracle-working Rabbi Judah Loew ben Bezalel of Prague (1512–1609, also known by the acronym Maharal), who made a *golem* to protect the Jews of Prague. It is said that on the twentieth day of the month of Adar in the year 5340 (1580 in the Civil calendar), assisted by his son-in-law and a favorite pupil probably named Sosson, the rabbi took a pile of clay and from it kneaded a human likeness about 60 inches in height. Then, the first of the rabbi's helpers marched around the awesome form seven times in a counterclockwise direction, and the mass turned red hot. The second assistant then walked around the robot in the same direction and the form became moist, the skin began to glow, and nails appeared on the fingers.

Rabbi Loew then programmed the figure by inserting in it a secret formula designed to provide the *golem* with intelligence and supernatural strength. The figure then came to life, was then dressed, given the name Yossele, and allowed to live in the rabbi's residence as a member of the family. During the week, the *golem* worked in the synagogue, serving as the sexton (*shammes*). On the Sabbath, when work is forbidden, Rabbi Loew removed the secret formula from the body of the *golem*, and it became immobile for an entire day.

One Sabbath, the rabbi forgot to remove the formula and the *golem* went berserk, destroying everything that got in its way. Rabbi Loew was called in and he removed the formula. Once again, the *golem* became a lifeless mass of clay.

Goodwill Principle

Although many laws in the Bible, Talmud, and later rabbinic writings were designed to limit contact between Jews and Gentiles, other laws were introduced to create a climate of friendship and peaceful coexistence. Especially after the Roman occupation of Palestine in the first century C.E., the need for the establishment of amity between Jews and non-Jews became pronounced, and many laws and practices were introduced to help achieve it. In talmudic literature, these laws and practices were explained as *mipnei darkei shalom*, "for the sake of the paths of peace," for the sake of maintaining goodwill between the Jewish and non-Jewish communities.

Rabbi Judah the Prince, the most outstanding Jewish scholar and leader of the second/third century C.E., was the first talmudic authority to espouse this policy of harmony between groups. He set the tone for future leaders by carrying on a dialogue with the Roman occupiers of Palestine, and owing to his political astuteness, succeeded in maintaining amicable relations between the Romans and the Jews. Many succeeding Jewish leaders followed Rabbi Judah's example in advocating peaceful coexistence with the non-Jewish world. The Talmud (*Gittin* 61a) states without equivocation: "We support the poor of the heathen along with the poor of Israel, and visit the sick of the heathen along with the sick of Israel, and bury their dead with the Jewish dead [if there is no other place for them to be buried] all for the sake of peace."

The desire to maintain a positive relationship with the non-Jewish community compelled the Rabbis to demand of Jews that they be more circumspect in their dealings with non-Jews than with Jews. They ruled, for example, that it is a greater breach of law to steal from or deceive a Gentile than a Jew. Stealing from a Jew, they said (Tosefta *Bava Kama* 10:15), "violates only the law that prohibits stealing. But when one steals from a Gentile, he violates a second law, namely the commandment not to profane God's name [Exodus 20:7]."

Even in medieval times, when oppressive measures against Jews were instituted by the Church, Jews continued to espouse the peaceful coexistence doctrine. Rabbi Isaac ben Moses Arama, the fifteenth-century Spanish philosopher who was forced to flee to Naples, Italy, because of the Spanish Inquisition, still found himself able to write in his famous homiletical work *Akeidat Yitzchak*: "Every pious Gentile is equal to a son of Israel." The same attitude was echoed by Joseph Caro in his sixteenth-century *Code of Jewish Law* (*Shulchan Arukh*, Yoreh Dei'ah 367:1).

The goodwill principle plays itself out in the internal religious life of Jews as well. The *Code of Jewish Law* (*Shulchan Arukh*, Orach Cha'yim 135:12) makes this point in a ruling with regard to a congregation consisting almost wholly of Priests (*Kohanim*) except for one Israelite (*Yisra'el*) who is present. The question arises: when the Torah is to be read, who shall be given the first *aliyah*? Normally the first Torah honor is assigned to a *Kohen* if one is present. But in this case, the ruling was made that *mipnei darkei shalom*—for the sake of the paths of peace—the first *aliyah* must be given to the *Yisra'el* so as to avoid conflict among the *Kohanim*. For, if one particular *Kohen* was selected over the others for the first honor, the others may resent not having been selected (*Gittin* 59a).

See Peace.

Goy

Plural, *goyim*. This Hebrew term literally meaning "nation" is used repeatedly in the Bible when referring to the Jewish people. In Exodus 19:6 the term *goy kadosh* is used, describing the Jewish people as a "holy nation." Isaiah 2:4 presents the prophet's often-quoted view of the Messianic Age as being a time when "nation [*goy*] will not lift up sword against nation [*goy*], nor will they learn to make war anymore."

In Jewish literature, the term *goy* does not refer to Gentiles or Christians, although many Church leaders have been under that impression. Over the centuries, they censored various editions of the Talmud, substituting other words for *goy* wherever it appeared so as to avoid any suggestion that the references might apply to Christians. Amazingly, the offensive acronym *oveid kokhavim u-mazalot*, "a worshipper of stars and constellations" (*Sanhedrin* 64a), the term used for an idolator, was substituted.

In the course of time, when non-Jews persecuted Jews or exhibited intense hatred toward them, Jews began using *goy* as a pejorative. When conditions improved, the word continued to be used, but without vindictiveness or malice. An example of its innocent usage is reflected in the following anecdote:

A well-to-do businessman wants to join a country club that does not admit Jews. So he changes his name from Hyman Cohen to Jeffrey Monroe Coleman, and poses as a Harvard alumnus. When applying for membership, he is asked, "Religion, please?" And his immediate response is "*goy* of course."

See Shabbes Goy.

Grace After Meals

The prayer recited at the conclusion of a meal, called *Birkat Ha-Mazon* (literally, "Blessing Over Food") in Hebrew, is popularly known by the Yiddish term *benshn*, which derives from the Latin *benedicere*, meaning "to bless."

The requirement to say *Grace After Meals* is biblical (Deuteronomy 8:10): "And you shall eat and be satisfied and bless the Lord for the good land that He gave you." This verse is preceded by a description of the good land: "A land wherein you shall eat bread without scarceness and not lack anything." The fact that these two verses appear side by side led the Rabbis to conclude that if one eats bread, considered to be the staff of life, he is then obligated to bless the Lord.

When bread is consumed, all four blessings of *Birkat Ha-Mazon* are recited, for only then is the repast considered to be a "true" meal. For meals or snacks at which bread has not been consumed, condensed versions of *Grace* are recited depending on what is eaten. The *Berakhah Acharonah* (literally, "Last Blessing") is recited when cakes, pastries, fruit, and the like are the essential part of the meal. An even shorter form of *Grace After Meals*, known as *Borei Nefashot*, is an expression of thanks to God for having created all living things. It is recited on occasions when neither the full *Grace* nor the *Berakhah Acharonah* is in order.

Presence of a Quorum

When three or more people are present at a meal, one of the participants issues an invitation to the others to join in the recitation of the *Grace After Meals* (Mishnah *Berakhot* 7:1). This call to prayer is known as *Birkat Zimun*, "Prayer of Invitation." The quorum of three is known as a *mezuman*, a name derived from the Hebrew word meaning "to invite."

Why *three* people are needed to recite the introductory prayer is linked to the fact that the dinner table represents the altar of sacrifice in Temple times. Three main varieties of sacrifice were brought in the Temple: animal sacrifices (*zevach* in Hebrew), grain offerings (*minchah*), and libations (*nesekh*).

Mystics have explained that the number three was favored because it was the first odd number after the unit (one). Early peoples found luck in odd numbers. The Talmud expresses the belief that even numbers are not merely unlucky, but dangerous.

Because the table in the home came to represent the altar in the Temple, and because it was prohibited to place iron implements on the altar (because of their association with war), it became customary among some families to remove knives from the table before the recitation of *Grace After Meals*. In some households, metal spoons and forks are also removed. In others, all metal utensils are covered with a cloth until the recitation of *Grace* is concluded.

There is a tradition for ten or more men (a *minyan*) to assemble at the head table at the end of the wedding meal. The *Grace After Meals*, concluding with the *sheva berakhot* (*Seven Benedictions*), is then recited. Orthodox Jews do not invite women to the table so as to insure that the ban against praying in mixed company is being honored.

Grass-tossing

After the burial service, it is customary among some Jews to toss a clump of grass behind them. This practice was first noted by the twelfth-century scholar Rabbi Eliezer ben Nathan, who believed the custom to be based on three biblical verses (Psalms 103:14, Psalms 72:16, and Job 2:12) that speak of grass and earth as symbols of sorrow. Other scholars, including the sixteenth-century Greek authority Rabbi Binyamin Ze'ev of Arta, have associated the custom with a reference in the Book of Isaiah (26:19) that speaks of the resurrection of the dead and the renewal of life.

Rabbi Ze'ev notes that uprooting a clump of grass is a reminder that the dead will one day rise up again as the grass, but also suggests that man came from the earth and must return to the earth. (The Hebrew name for the first man, Adam, means "earth," for he came from the earth" [Genesis 2:7].)

Scholars point out that the custom of throwing grass was borrowed by Jews from their Christian neighbors, primarily in Germany and France. Gentiles considered the practice particularly effective in driving off evil spirits, which follow mourners leaving the cemetery.

When Christians began claiming that Jews were employing this custom as an act of sorcery aimed at harming them, the practice was discontinued. Rabbi Moses ben Yechiel was able to persuade Church authorities that the throwing of a clod of grass was a harmless activity. Nonetheless, the custom was never completely abandoned. When practiced today, it is often accompanied by a recitation of the verse, "He [God] is mindful that we are but dust" (Psalms 103:14).

A clump of grass is also often left on a tombstone (just as stones are) by persons who have visited a grave. This serves as a calling card, notifying other visitors that the deceased has not been forgotten.

See Burial.

Grave Visitations

It has become a Jewish tradition to visit graves of loved ones periodically and to pray that through the merit of the deceased the living will gain favor and forgiveness in the eyes of God. Such visitations may take place at any time, but the month preceding Rosh Hashanah (Elul) up until Yom Kippur is considered especially appropriate.

It is customary for brides and grooms who have lost parents to visit the cemetery prior to the wedding and to recite the memorial prayer, *El Malei Rachamim*.

While there is no basis for it in Jewish law, it is generally considered improper to visit other graves when one is at the cemetery to attend a funeral. Nevertheless, the belief persists, with the following reasons offered:

- To visit other graves is an affront to the deceased and to the mourners, detracting attention and respect due the deceased.
- Those who wander off to visit other graves may become distraught and may accidentally step on graves that block their way.
- Evil spirits lurk in cemeteries at times of burial, and it is therefore wise for all to leave the cemetery as quickly as possible.

Since a Priest (*Kohen*) may not visit a cemetery because he would be in close proximity to the dead, some Orthodox Jews follow the practice of holding hands and forming a circle around a *Kohen* who wishes to visit a grave. By being enclosed in a circle, the *Kohen* is considered to be in a private domain, thus eliminating the possibility of his becoming ritually impure.

Greetings and Salutations

In the Jewish tradition, there are many forms of greeting expressed at different times of the day, month, and year. Some, such as *Shalom*, are casual daily greetings, but most revolve about holidays and synagogue activity.

Among the more popular greetings and salutations are:

Ad mei'ah ve-esrim shanah

A Hebrew phrase meaning "[May you live] until 120 years [of age]." The Yiddish equivalent of this Hebrew expression is *Biz hundert und tzvansig*. When introduced in the course of conversation, the phrase expresses the hope that one will live a full, rich life, as did Moses, who reached the age of 120.

The first mention of 120 years as the allotted lifespan for man on earth is found in the Book of Genesis (6:3), where God says, "My breath shall not abide in man forever, since he, too, is flesh; let the days allowed him be 120."

A Hebrew acronym formed from *Ad mei'ah ve-esrim shanah* is *Amush*. Some Jews, when addressing a person in a communication, will often add the word *Amush* after the salutation, as in "My dear Joseph, *Amush*." For women the salutation used is *Tichyi*, "May you live."

Alav ha-shalom

A Hebrew phrase meaning "May he rest in peace." For a woman the proper grammatical form is *Aleha ha-shalom*. The expression is uttered after mentioning the name of a deceased. When used in writing, it is often abbreviated by placing the first letter of each Hebrew word (the *a'yin* and the *hei*) side by side separated by two short vertical strokes similar to a quotation mark.

Throughout geonic literature (approximately 500 to 1000 C.E.) one encounters the Hebrew letter *nun* and *a'yin* after the name of a deceased person. These letters are the first letters of the Hebrew words *Nucho Eden*, meaning "May his resting place be in [the Garden of] Eden."

See Zikhrono li-verakhah.

Barukh ha-ba

A Hebrew expression meaning "Blessed is he who comes." The feminine form is *Berukhah ha-ba'ah*. These words are always uttered by the officiating clergyman as the bride and groom appear before him at their wedding. The plural form is *Berukhim ha-baim*.

Barukh Ha-Shem

This Hebrew term meaning "Blessed is the Name [of God]" is used as an expression of gratitude in a variety of situations. The abbreviation *B"H* is sometimes placed at the top of a written communication.

B'ezrat Ha-Shem

These Hebrew words meaning "With the help of the Name [of God]," are used to express the hope that things will turn out well.

Chag samei'ach

A Hebrew greeting meaning "[Have a] happy holiday."

Chazak, chazak, ve-nitchazek

This Hebrew salutation meaning "Be strong, be strong, and let us be strengthened" is pronounced by the congregation after one of the five books of the Torah has been completed by the Torah reader.

Chazak u-varuch

This expression meaning "Be strong and be blessed" is used in Sephardic congregations to congratulate one who has just received an *aliyah* or has just led the congregation in prayer.

Gemar chatimah tovah

This Hebrew term meaning "A final good sealing [of your fate]" is expressed on Yom Kippur, the last of the Ten Days of Awe when, according to Jewish tradition, one's fate for the coming year is "sealed."

See also *Ketivah va-chatimah tovah*.

Gezuntheit

This Yiddish formulation of the German word *Gesundheit*, meaning "To your health," is an expression of hoped-for well-being uttered when a person sneezes. The term stems from Genesis (2:7), which says, "And He [God] blew into his [man's] nostrils the soul of life." It was believed that the nostrils are the apertures through which life enters and leaves man's body.

Jewish legend relates that, until the time of the patriarch Jacob, people did not become ill before dying. They simply sneezed, then died immediately. Sneezing was believed to signal approaching death.

In early times, Jews as well as other peoples believed that sneezing was the work of evil spirits who were determined to take a man's life, and that their plan could be frustrated by uttering biblical quotations or other expressions. Jews have been known to respond to a sneeze with the verse uttered by Jacob on his deathbed, "For Thy salvation have I hoped, O Lord" (Genesis 49:18), or by exclamations such as "God bless you" or *Gezuntheit*."

In the talmudic tractate *Berakhot* (24a, b), there are two notions about the significance of the sneeze. One is that it is a bad omen; the other, that if one sneezes while praying, he will be blessed. In the same tractate (53a), the importance of the sneeze is downplayed. It states that while studying in the academy, the members of the household of Rabbi Gamaliel did not say "Good health" when someone sneezed, so as not to interrupt their studies. Rashi explains that when one person blesses another, all must stop what they are doing so that they can listen to the blessing and respond "Amen." However, so as not to waste time, says Rashi, one does not interrupt his studies to say "Good health" or "God bless you" upon hearing a sneeze.

In Hebrew, the expression *La-beriut*, "To [good] health," is the counterpart of the Yiddish *Gezuntheit*.

Gut Shabbes

A Yiddish greeting meaning "[Have a] good Sabbath." *Shabbat shalom* is the Hebrew equivalent. Very often, the popular Yiddish expression *A gutn Shabbes* is used.

Gut yontiff

A Yiddish greeting meaning "[Have a] good holiday." *Chag samei'ach* is the Hebrew equivalent.

Ketivah va-chatimah tovah

A Yom Kippur greeting very similar to *Gemar chatimah tovah* and meaning "May you be inscribed and [may your fate] be sealed for good."

La-beri'ut

See *Gezuntheit*.

Le-cha'yim

This Hebrew expression meaning "to life" is used as a toast before drinking wine or liquor. According to an incident described in the Talmud, it would appear that the Jewish custom of toasting someone with the term *Le-cha'yim* has its origin with the great scholar Akiba who, at a banquet he gave in honor of his son Shimon, is said to have offered each guest a glass of wine and to have saluted him with the words, "Wine and health to the mouth of our teachers; health and wine to the mouths of our teachers and their disciples" (*Shabbat* 67b).

Le-cha'yim tovim u-le-shalom

A Hebrew greeting meaning "For a good and peaceful life."

L'shanah tovah

A Hebrew Rosh Hashanah greeting meaning "Have a good New Year."

Le-shanah tovah tikateivu

This Hebrew greeting meaning "May you be inscribed [in the Book of Life] for a good life" is popularly used on Rosh Hashanah. The singular form, rarely used, is *Le-shanah tovah tikatev*. On Yom Kippur, the greeting is changed to *Le-shanah tovah tikateivu ve-tei-chateimu*.

Mazal tov

This Hebrew term literally meaning "Good [lucky] star" is a congratulatory expression used on happy occasions by Ashkenazic Jews. Sephardim use the expression *Siman tov*, meaning "[Let it be] a good sign."

To commemorate Queen Elizabeth's fiftieth anniversary on the British throne, the term *Mazal tov* appeared in Hebrew and English on a first-day cover stamp. The envelope, issued in a limited edition of 500, contains the opening words of the prayer for the queen and royal family that is recited in British synagogues on the Sabbath and festivals.

Mazal u-verakhah

This Hebrew expression meaning "Good luck and blessing," is used particularly by chasidic Jews of Antwerp, Belgium, who dominated the diamond trade. A business deal was sealed with a handshake and the words *Mazal u-verakhah*. No written contract was needed.

Mei-cha'yil le-cha'yil

A Hebrew greeting meaning "[May you go] from strength to strength."

Neiro ya'ir

This Hebrew phrase meaning "May his light shine [forever]" usually appears in abbreviated form, placing the letters *nun* and *yud* after a person's name.

Shabbat shalom

This Hebrew greeting meaning "[May you have] a Sabbath of peace" is comparable to the Yiddish greeting *Gut Shabbes* or *A gutn Shabbes*.

Shalom

Literally meaning "Peace [unto you]," this popular Hebrew greeting is used to say hello and goodbye. The Rabbis of the Talmud (*Berakhot* 64a) made a fine distinction when *Shalom* is used to say goodbye. They say that when taking leave of a friend, one should not say *Leikh be-shalom*, "Go in peace," but rather *Leikh le-shalom*, "Go to peace." However, when bidding farewell to the deceased, one should not say, *Leikh le-shalom*, "Go to peace," but *Leikh be-shalom*, "Go in peace."

The term *Leikh le-shalom*, "Go to peace," implies that one is expected to return, as is evident from the expression used by Jethro in Exodus 4:18 and by Jonathan in I Samuel 20:42.

Shalom aleikhem

This popular Hebrew greeting meaning "Peace unto you" is equivalent to "Hello" or "How are you?" The response is *Aleikhem shalom*. From earliest times it was believed that angels accompanied worshippers to and from the synagogue (*Shabbat* 119b) and that it is proper to welcome these visiting angels every Friday night. Based upon this legend, the kabbalists of the sixteenth century introduced a hymn entitled *Shalom Aleikhem*, which welcomes the coming of the Sabbath.

Shalom u-verakhah

A Hebrew greeting meaning "Peace and blessing [to you]." Commonly used by Sephardim as a congratulatory expression.

Shanah tovah

This popular Hebrew greeting meaning "A good year [to you]" is popularly used during the period between Rosh Hashanah and Yom Kippur. Some people use the full phrasing, *Le-shanah tovah tikateivu ve-tei-chateimu le-alter le-cha'yim*, meaning "May you be inscribed [in the Book of Life] immediately for a good year." The Talmud (*Rosh Hashanah* 16b) states that the fulfillment of this wish is experienced by those who are completely righteous.

Shanah tovah u-mevorakh

A Hebrew expression meaning "[Have a] good and blessed New Year."

Shlita

An acronym formed from the first letters of the Hebrew phrase *She-yichyeh le-orekh yamim tovim arukhim, Amen*, meaning "May he live a long and good life, Amen." The expression is used after mentioning the name of a living Torah scholar or a righteous person.

Siman tov

A Hebrew term meaning "Good sign" or "Good omen," used as an expression of congratulations primarily by Sephardim. Akin to the term *Mazal tov*, commonly used by Ashkenazim.

Yasher ko'ach

A popular Yiddish contraction of the Hebrew congratulatory expression *Yi-yasher kochakha*, meaning "May your strength continue from strength to strength." The expression is first used in the Talmud (*Shabbat* 87a) where Reish Lakish comments on the word *shibarta* in the verse (Deuteronomy 10:2) about the breaking of the Ten Commandments by Moses. Reish Lakish says *Yi-yasher kochakha she-shibarta*, "Congratulations on your having broken [the tablets]." The greeting is offered when one has successfully completed a synagogue honor, such as having recited the Torah blessings, raised the Torah (*hagbahah*) following the Torah reading, or opened the ark.

Zai gezunt

A Yiddish expression meaning "Be healthy!" Usually spoken when taking leave of someone after a conversation.

Zeikher tzadik li-verakhah

Literally meaning "May the memory of this righteous person serve as a blessing [in our lives]," this Hebrew expression, originally found in the Book of Proverbs (10: 7), is used after saying the name of a deceased pious person. In printed form, it is abbreviated as *z"t"l*, representing the first letter of each of the three Hebrew letters of the expression.

See Alav ha-shalom; Zikhrono li-verakhah.

Zikhrono li-verakhah

Literally, "May his memory be a blessing," an expression used after writing a deceased male's name. *Zikhronah li-verakhah* is the feminine equivalent. Akin to the term *Alav [aleha] ha-shalom* and *Aleha ha-shalom*, meaning "May he (she) rest in peace." First used in the tractate *Kiddushin* (31b), the expression is often abbreviated as *z"l* (*za'yin lamed*), formed from the first letter of the two Hebrew words.

See Alav ha-shalom; Zeikher tzadik li-verakhah.

Greeting a Non-Jew

One of the conflicts Jews had to face in the Middle Ages was how to greet and pay proper respect to noblemen and the clergy who wear a cross. Rabbi Israel Isserlein (1390–1460), the most prominent German rabbi of his day, was among those authorities who were asked this question. He answered that such meetings should be avoided if at all possible. He then described how, when he was a boy living in Vienna, a high Church official, out of respect to Jews, would cover his cross when the Jews were obliged to bow to him. Isserlein concludes that when a Jew is placed in a position that he must raise a hat or bow to a person wearing a cross, it should be understood that the Jew is paying respect to the person and not to the cross.

In the recent past, a similar situation arose in predominantly Catholic Peru, where it is a time-honored tradition for Cabinet members, when they are inducted, to kneel before the president, who wears a large crucifix. In February 1994, Efraim Goldenberg became the first Peruvian Jew to be named foreign minister. At the beginning of the induction ceremony, the president removed his cross and replaced it after Goldenberg was sworn in.

Guilt

See Confession of Sins; Kapparot; Original Sin; Sin; Tokheichah.

Haftarah

Plural, *haftarot*. This Hebrew term meaning "conclusion" refers to the reading from the Prophets that supplements and follows the Torah portion read in the synagogue on Sabbaths and holidays. It derives from the root *patar*, meaning "to be rid of, to be free of, to end or complete [a situation]."

After the *maftir* (concluding) portion has been read, the Torah scroll is removed from the reading table and the *maftir* honoree recites the *haftarah*.

Origins

The earliest reference to the actual reading of a *haftarah* is found in the New Testament in the Book of Acts (13:15), where Paul was invited to deliver a sermon "after the reading of the Law and the Prophets." There is also a reference in Luke (4:17) to Jesus reading from the Book of Isaiah during a Sabbath service in Nazareth.

According to the most widely accepted theory, the introduction of the *haftarah* reading dates back to the second century B.C.E., when Palestine and many of the countries bordering it had been conquered by Antiochus, ruler of Syria and Greece. Antiochus wished to impose idolatrous practices on the people of Judea, hoping to win them over to a pagan lifestyle. To achieve this during his reign in the years prior to 165 B.C.E., Antiochus tried to weaken Judaism by banning many basic Jewish practices, one of which was the public reading of the Torah.

Being without military might, Jews had no choice but to obey this ban. However, since a prohibition had not been placed on other types of public reading, synagogues replaced the Torah reading with selected readings from the Prophets. Because the Rabbis did not want the Torah lesson of each week to be forgotten, they took great pains to select as the prophetic reading of the week a portion directly or tangentially related to the theme of the Torah reading that would normally have been read on that particular Sabbath or holiday.

It had been customary to read a minimum of three verses from the Torah for each of the seven honorees at a Sabbath Torah reading service. When the Torah reading ban was instituted, the Rabbis established that a minimum of twenty-one verses be divided among the seven honorees called to read from the Prophets. The minor talmudic tractate *Soferim* (14:1) points out that actually twenty-two verses were read. The extra verse, read by one of the seven, was done out of respect to the synagogue sexton.

Exclusions

A *haftarah* reading does not follow the Torah reading at the Monday and Thursday synagogue service, for to read a prophetic portion on these workdays would prolong the service and inconvenience the congregation unduly. (The Aramaic term for such inconvenience is *tircha d'tzibura*, "public inconvenience," a principle of Jewish law that is often invoked when establishing religious and social communal practices.)

A *haftarah* selection is also not recited following the Torah reading at the Sabbath afternoon *Minchah* service—in part because a selection from the Prophets has already been read that morning. But perhaps the primary reason can be traced to earlier times, in Europe in particular, when it was customary for a preacher (*magid* in Hebrew) to deliver a sermon on Sabbath afternoon. To extend the Torah reading section of the service by reciting a *haftarah* as well would have used up time needed by the preacher.

Reinstitution of the Torah Reading

After the Maccabean (Hasmonean) victory over Antiochus in 165 B.C.E., the reading from the Torah was resumed. Nevertheless, the practice of reading from the Prophets continued, with only one person rather than seven called to do the entire prophetic reading. For a while thereafter, the *maftir* honor was no longer considered important or prestigious, so the Rabbis raised its status by declaring that the person honored with *maftir* should also chant the *haftarah* and be accorded the privilege of leading the congregation in the recital of the *Shema* or *Shemoneh Esrei* (*Amida*) prayers. To further enhance the importance of the *maftir*, the Rabbis ruled that before the *haftarah* is read on Sabbaths, the last verses of the Torah reading of the day should be repeated.

The fourth-century Palestinian scholar Ulla explained (*Megillah* 23a) that these verses are repeated so that the person who will be reciting the prophetic portion will first have an opportunity to accord the Torah ample respect, by reciting blessings over it. By following this procedure, he is reaffirming the fact that the Torah is greater in sanctity than the writings of the Prophets.

Maimonides, in his *Mishneh Torah* (Hilkhot Tefillah 12:13), says that he who reads the *haftarah* must first read at least three verses from the Torah.

Hagbahah and Gelilah

The honors known in Hebrew as *hagbahah*, literally meaning "raising (lifting)," and *gelilah*, literally meaning "rolling up," are both awarded as part of the Torah reading ritual.

Ashkenazic Practice

In Ashkenazic congregations, after the Torah reading has been completed, two persons are called to the pulpit: one to lift the Torah scroll and display its words to the congregation, the other to roll the scroll together, tie it with its sash (*gartl*), and cover it with its mantle and ornaments. The person who holds the Torah aloft is called the *magbi'ah*, "the lifter"; the second person is called the *golel*, "the roller." When the Torah is raised, the congregation rises and recites aloud: "This is the Torah that Moses set before the Children of Israel" (Deuteronomy 4:44) "at the command of the Lord through Moses" (Numbers 9:23).

The prayerbook composed by the Vilna Gaon (1720–1797) indicates that all of Numbers 9:23 was once recited, not merely part of it as we do today. Apparently *hagbahah* and *gelilah* were originally performed by the reader himself.

Sephardic Practice

In Sephardic congregations, those performing these honors are not called by the names *magbi'ah* and *golel*. Before the reading of the Torah begins, an unannounced person raises the scroll, revealing a minimum of three columns of the written Torah text. He turns from side to side, enabling congregants in every part of the synagogue to see the words on the parchment while the Torah reader (*ba'al korei*), using the Torah pointer (*yad*), indicates precisely where the reading will begin. The congregation then recites the above verse from Deuteronomy, after which the Torah scroll is placed on the reading table. When the reading has been completed, it is dressed unceremoniously.

The Hebrew term used by Sephardim for the Torah-raising ceremony is *hakamah*, meaning "elevating [the Torah]." In Spanish-Portuguese synagogues the ceremony is referred to by the Spanish term *levantador*.

The Golel in the Talmud

Why the Sephardic procedure differs from the Ashkenazic one is not readily explained, but it is quite clear that the Sephardic practice is the older. In the Talmud itself no mention is made of *magbi'ah*, and exactly when it became customary to call up a special person to raise the Torah is unknown. However, in medieval times the honor of elevating the scroll and carrying it in a procession was highly coveted.

The Talmud (*Megillah* 32a) does make reference to the *golel*, but not as a person specifically designated for this honor. The Talmud says that the "senior" person among all who have received an *aliyah* at a service is the *golel*, which is considered an honor "equal in importance to all the Torah honors combined."

Haggadah

The Hebrew word *haggadah* ("the telling") is used as a variant form of *aggadah* and also as the name of the prayerbook used at the Passover *Seder*. The Haggadah retells the story of the Exodus of the Israelites from Egypt—as recorded in the Book of Exodus—some three thousand years ago. It also includes psalms and songs that are recited and sung as part of the evening celebration.

The Haggadah was introduced by the Men of the Great Assembly (*Anshei Knesset Ha-Gedolah*), the supreme authority in matters of religion and law during the Second Temple period, in order to comply with the biblical verse, "And you shall instruct your offspring on that day..." (Exodus 13:8). Among other things, the Haggadah is a book of instruction.

Since the publication of the first Haggadah in the thirteenth century, more than 3,500 different Haggadot (plural) have been published world wide. Usually, the Hebrew text is accompanied by a translation into the vernacular of the country, along with notes, comments, and illustrations. Among the most famous Haggadot are the Copenhagen and Sarajevo editions, noted for their calligraphy, illustrations, and overall beauty. Haggadot vary in content as well as design.

See Aggadah.

Hagiographa

The Greek name for the third and last part of the Bible, known in Hebrew as *Ketuvim*, meaning "[Holy] Writings." The thirteen books that comprise this section appear in the Jewish Bible in this order: Psalms, Proverbs, Job, Song of Songs, Ruth, Lamentations, Ecclesiastes, Esther, Daniel, Ezra, Nehemiah, I Chronicles, and II Chronicles.

Of this group, five of the books are read as part of the synagogue service held on specific occasions. The Song of Songs is read on the intermediate Sabbath of Passover; the Book of Ruth, on Shavuot; Lamentations, on Tisha B'Av; Ecclesiastes, on Shemini Atzeret; the Scroll of Esther, on Purim.

Hair and Haircutting

Hair and the way it is cared for play an important role in Jewish tradition.

The Nazirites, the ancient Hebrew ascetic sect to which Samson (Judges 13–16) belonged, refrained from cutting their hair as a sign of their dedication to the service of God. In the Book of Jeremiah (7:29), cutting the hair is a sign of mourning. Speaking in the name of God, the prophet says, "Cut off your hair and cast it away, and take up a lament on the heights."

The highest officials in Jewish life in ancient times—the king and the High Priest—were expected to keep their hair in perfect condition. The Talmud (*Sanhedrin* 22 a–b) says that no one may watch the king when his hair is being cut and that it must be trimmed every day. As for the High Priest, his hair must be trimmed on the eve of every Sabbath, while an ordinary Priest must have his hair trimmed once every thirty days.

Ben Eleazar, the son-in-law of Rabbi Judah the Prince, was so enamored of the fashion in which the High Priest's hair was cut that he spent huge sums of money to have the style copied (see also *Shabbat* 9b).

Facial Hair

The Talmud considers hair, particularly the beard, to be a symbol of maturity, piety, and distinction. The tractate *Bava Metzia* (84a) describes the beard as "an adornment to a man's face," while the tractate *Yevamot* (80b) says, "A man without a beard is like a eunuch." In Temple times young Priests who had not yet grown beards were not permitted to pronounce the *Birkat Kohanim*, "Blessing of the Priests" (*Shabbat* 152a; *Bava Metzia* 84a).

The Torah (Leviticus 19:27) forbids the Israelites from "rounding off" or "destroying the sidegrowth [in Hebrew, *pei'ot*] of one's head" because those who ministered to idols were known to shave certain areas of the face with a sharp blade. Aside from the association with idolatry, the Rabbis objected to the use of an open blade (in Hebrew, *taar*, meaning "sword") because it is a lethal weapon, a symbol of war.

The twelfth-century philosopher Moses Maimonides was probably the first authority to note five specific areas of the male face that should not be shaved with an open blade: both upper sides of the jaw (next to the ears), both sides of the chin, and the peak of the chin. The penalty for removing hair from these areas with a blade is whipping (in Hebrew, *makkot*), said Maimonides, but there is no

punishment if the hair is removed with scissors. According to Maimonides, a blade may be used to remove hair from the soft areas of the face, including the upper lip and the area below the chin to the neck (*Mishneh Torah*, Avodat Kokhavim 12:7–8. See also *Shulchan Arukh*, Yoreh Dei'ah 181:11 and the notes of Isserles on this section).

There has never been unanimity among rabbinic authorities as to which areas of the face are actually meant by Leviticus 19:27, and in the sixteenth century a stricter attitude toward shaving was adopted. Joseph Caro and Moses Isserles ruled (Yoreh Dei'ah 181:10–11) that Jews may not remove *any* hair from the face. Later scholars, such as Ezekiel Landau (1713–1793) of Prague, noted (*Noda Bi-Yehudah*, Yoreh Dei'ah II:80) that trimming the beard is a violation of sacred Jewish tradition.

After the seventeenth century, however, as Jews were increasingly drawn into the mainstream of Western society, they found it necessary to make their appearance more acceptable to the general population. This was true particularly among the Sephardim of Western Europe. Since Jewish law permitted the removal of facial hair by means other than with a single swordlike blade, Jews began to remove hair from their faces by using scissors, clippers, or chemical depilatories. Today, most Orthodox Jews who shave use electric razors.

It is interesting to note that Jews from Bukhara, Uzbekistan, still follow the painful ritual of shaving a bride on the night before her wedding by pulling a fine, taut string across her cheek.

Chasidic Practice

While *chasidim* allow their sidelocks to grow long, they do not permit the hair on the top of the head to grow long. The Talmud (*Bava Kama* 83a) warns that to grow hair long is one of "the ways of the Amorites," and as is the rule with all pagan practices, it is avoided.

Chasidim also take seriously the admonition of the *Zohar* on Be-ha-alotekhah that "growing hair long increases the stern decree directed against the world." This is linked to a central concept of mysticism known as *kelippot* (plural of *kelippah*, meaning "shell, husk"). *Kelippot* are barriers and distractions that take a man's mind away from spiritual matters. To achieve spiritual purity and maturity, mystics believes that they must rid themselves of these barriers, which include allowing a man's hair to grow long.

In Eastern Europe, before a boy reached his thirteenth birthday, his hair was cropped on the top of his head so as to leave almost bare the spot where his *tefillin* are to be placed—in the area "between the eyes" above the bridge of the nose. The sidelocks, however, were left untouched, in compliance with the biblical commandment not to destroy the sidegrowth of one's head (Leviticus 19:27).

Chasidim add an interpretation to the admonition in the Book of Leviticus (19:23) that forbids eating the fruit of a tree during the first three years of its growth to mean that a boy's hair should not be cut until he is three years old. On his third birthday an elaborate haircutting ceremony, called *upsherenish* in Yiddish, is held, but the sidelocks are left intact. In Israel, the ceremony is called *chalakah*, derived from the Hebrew word *chalak*, meaning "smooth."

See Sheitl.

Hakafot

A Hebrew term literally meaning "encirclements," referring to the elaborate synagogue Torah processions held twice during the year.

Hoshanah Rabbah, the last day of Sukkot, is the first occasion in the Jewish calendar when all Torah scrolls are removed from the ark and carried around the synagogue. During this procession, congregants holding Torot (plural of Torah) circle the synagogue seven times, followed by others carrying the *lulav* and *etrog*. The Mishnah *Sukkah* (4:5) describes the ritual of Hoshanah Rabbah in Temple times: "Every day [of the first six days of the festival] they went round the altar once, saying, 'We beseech Thee, O Lord, save now; we beseech Thee, O Lord, make us now prosper [Psalms 118:25].' But on that [seventh] day they went round the altar seven times." (See also *Shulchan Arukh*, Orach Cha'yim 660:1.)

The most widely observed procession takes place on Simchat Torah. All Torot are removed from the ark and the congregation sings and dances as the scrolls are carried around the synagogue seven times, or as many times as required to give all persons present an opportunity to carry a scroll. This ceremony is mentioned for the first time in a book entitled *Minhagim*, composed at the beginning of the fifteenth century by Rabbi Isaac Tyrnau, an Austrian scholar.

In his *Toledot Chag Simchat Torah*, Avraham Yaari asserts that conducting *hakafot* on Simchat Torah was a practice totally unknown before the last third of the sixteenth century.

See Circles and Circling.

Halakhah

A Hebrew word literally meaning "the way, the path," referring specifically to Jewish law as first stated in the Bible and then interpreted and expanded upon by the Rabbis of the Talmud as well as later scholars.

See Law and Custom; Law, Jewish.

Halakhah Le-Moshe Mi-Sinai

A Hebrew term literally meaning "the Law transmitted to Moses from Mount Sinai." To

Orthodox Jews, the immutability of the Law is a basic tenet of Judaism.

The Mishnah *Pei'ah* (2:6) uses the term as a means of conveying the idea that the ancient laws of the Torah are to be eternally revered.

See Written Law.

Hallel

This Hebrew word literally meaning "praise" is the name given to a special selection of Psalms (113–118) that are recited on various occasions in the Jewish calendar. All six psalms (*Full Hallel*) are recited on the three Pilgrim Festivals (Sukkot, Passover, Shavuot), on New Moons (Rosh Chodesh), and on Chanukkah. *Hallel* is not recited on Rosh Hashanah, Yom Kippur, or Purim.

The reason why *Hallel* is not recited on Rosh Hashanah and Yom Kippur is found in the Talmud (*Rosh Hashanah* 32b). Rabbi Abbahu of Caesarea (third century) was once asked why *Hallel* is not recited on those days, and he replied that the angels ministering to God once asked this very question of God. God replied: "Is it possible that the King should be sitting on the throne of justice with the book of life and death open before Him, and Israel should chant hymns of praise? When people's fate is in the balance, one should not be expressing joy." For a similar reason *Hallel* is never recited during a service held in a house of mourning.

Rabbi Nachman explained (*Megillah* 14a and *Mishneh Torah*, Hilkhot Chanukkah 3:6) why *Hallel* is not recited on Purim: "The reading of the *Megillah* [with its joyful conclusion] is the equivalent of reciting *Hallel*."

In Temple times, the *Full Hallel* was recited only at the first Passover *Seder*, on the eight days of Sukkot, and on the eight days of Chanukkah. After the Temple was destroyed and the psalms of praise that traditionally accompanied the Shavuot offerings of first-fruits were no longer recited, the *Full Hallel* was added to the Shavuot synagogue liturgy.

Some time around the beginning of the third century C.E., the Jews of Babylonia added the practice of reciting *Hallel* on the last six days of Passover and on Rosh Chodesh. To mark a distinction between this new practice and the older one, the first eleven verses of both Psalm 115 and Psalm 116 were omitted on the last six days of Passover and on Rosh Chodesh. This shorter version of the *Hallel* became known as *Half Hallel*, although actually only a very small portion of the *Full Hallel* is omitted.

The *Full Hallel* is also known as the *Egyptian Hallel* because Psalm 114 deals with the Exodus from Egypt. This name was created by the Rabbis of the Talmud to distinguish the *Egyptian Hallel* from the *Great Hallel*, which consists of Psalm 136 and is recited daily during the *Shacharit* service. (*Pesachim* 118a. See also *Megillah* 10b and *Ta'anit* 28b for another explanation of the *Half Hallel* tradition.)

In Israel today, many Orthodox synagogues recite *Hallel* on Yom Ha-Atzma'ut (Israel Independence Day), although the right-wing among the Orthodox object to this innovation on the grounds that new religious observances may not be added to those traditionally in place.

Conservative synagogues add *Hallel* to the prayer service on Yom Ha-Atzma'ut. However, when the holiday falls on the Sabbath, *Hallel* is recited at the previous Wednesday night and Thursday morning services.

Halva'yat Ha-Met

A Hebrew term literally meaning "escorting the deceased." The Talmud (*Shabbat* 127a) considers escorting the dead (especially outstanding scholars) to their final resting place to be a cardinal principle of Judaism, an act worthy of great praise, one of the best acts a person can perform. Escorting the dead is characterized in Hebrew as *chesed shel emet*, "the ultimate kindness," for it is done without motive, without the expectation of reward from the recipient of the kindness.

The Talmud (*Berakhot* 18a) counsels that one should not allow a funeral cortege to pass by without joining it. To neglect doing so would be a violation of the law that cautions against "mocking the poor [the dead]," which is an affront to God (Proverbs 17:5). Caring for the poor and accompanying the dead to their final resting place are both godly activities of the highest priority in Jewish tradition. This was emphasized by the Rabbis (who considered studying Torah of such supreme importance that one should not waste time on any other activity) when they declared that students may suspend their studies in order to accompany the dead to their final resting place.

Today, the custom of escorting the dead is fulfilled, especially among some Orthodox Jews, by walking behind the hearse for a block or two after the funeral service has concluded and before the procession continues on to the cemetery.

In this connection, it should be noted that there are a variety of local customs in Sephardic communities. Among Jewish Kurds, for example, sons of the deceased do not follow the coffin but remain in the courtyard of their house. Among the Jews of Libya, sons do not stand close to the coffin. After it is taken into the cemetery, they wait on the outside, and that is where they recite the *Kaddish* after the burial service.

See Funeral Practices.

Hamotzi

This Hebrew term literally meaning "He who draws forth" is the name of the blessing recited at the beginning of every meal at which bread is served.

When Abraham (Genesis 18:5) was visited by three angels in the guise of men, he rushed to offer them a meal of which the first element was bread (*pat lechem*). Thus, the Rabbis concluded, a meal without bread cannot be considered a true meal. The Rabbis reasoned that just as one must thank God following a meal, so must one express thanks before beginning a meal. *Hamotzi lechem min ha-aretz*, "He [God] who draws forth bread from the earth," became the concluding phrase of the blessing recited.

The *Hamotzi* covers all foods eaten during a meal with the exception of wine, which requires its own blessing because it is considered a special gift of God. "Wine cheers the hearts of men," wrote the Psalmist (104:15) alongside the words "to draw forth bread from the earth."

See Bread.

Hamsa

Also spelled *chamsa*. An Arabic word literally meaning "five," referring to the five-fingered talismans commonly used by Jews of North Africa as protection against evil spirits. These hand-shaped good-luck amulets are used as pieces of jewelry on necklaces and earrings, as ornaments on the walls of a home, and even as part of the chain of the eternal light (*ner* tamid) that hangs in front of the synagogue ark.

On Chanukkah, Syrian parents traditionally gave their children a candle in the shape of a hand to protect them from the evil eye.

Hand Gestures

In Jewish tradition, dating back to biblical times, hand movements and gestures were used to express a spiritual message. The first such instance is found in the Book of Genesis (48:17–19), where Jacob extends his hands to bless his grandchildren Ephraim and Manasseh. In I Kings (8:54–55), when Solomon dedicated the Temple that he had built in Jerusalem and had offered to the Lord all his prayers and supplications, "he rose from where he had been kneeling in front of the altar of the Lord, his hands spread out toward heaven. He stood, and in a loud voice blessed the whole congregation of Israel."

In talmudic times, it became customary for the Priests in the Temple to bestow a blessing upon those who came to worship. When pronouncing the three verses in the Book of Numbers (6:24), the Priests raised their hands and spread out their fingers to form the Hebrew letter *shin*, the first letter of the word *Shaddai*, one of the names for God.

Aid to Torah Readers

Since it is essential that a Torah reader (*ba'al korei*) chant the text of a Torah scroll in accordance with the established cantillation, in some Sephardic congregations, particularly among Yemenites, an official who stands next to the *ba'al korei* indicates, through hand movements, when the reader's voice should rise or be lowered, when a note should be extended, and when it should be shortened.

Rashi (eleventh century) mentions this practice in his commentary on the Talmud (*Berakhot* 62a). He recalls seeing Jews from Palestine who had settled in France motion with the right hand to indicate the pattern of the melody when the Torah was being read.

The custom of using hand movements during the Torah reading, while not widespread today, is still practiced in the synagogues of Rome and at times can also be observed in synagogues that follow the Moroccan and Yemenite rituals.

See Handwashing; Priestly Benediction.

Handkerchief Ceremony

In its earliest form the concept of marriage was one in which a man "acquired" a woman with a fee paid by the father or the guardian of the girl. In Jewish law, one way to confirm a purchase or transaction was by *kinyan sudar*, meaning "acquisition by kerchief."

In the original form of this act of acquisition, as described in the Book of Ruth (4:1–8), the medium employed was a sandal. The transfer of property was done by one party removing a shoe and giving it to the other. In the story of Ruth, Boaz was the buyer and he removed his shoe to symbolize his purchase of the land that once belonged to Elimelekh (Naomi's husband) and their two sons. With this purchase, Boaz became free to marry Ruth.

During the nineteenth century, and to a limited extent today, after a marriage had been agreed to, a date was set for stipulations (*tena'im*) to be executed in writing. (In German and Yiddish the writing ceremony is known as *knas mahl*, "penalty meal.") When the agreement was finally set down, it was symbolically affirmed by the marriage performer (or some other person) holding up a handkerchief, with a representative of the bride holding one end and a representative of the groom holding the other. Since the *tena'im* ceremony is no longer very common, the handkerchief ceremony is held today at a private ceremony before the wedding proper, at which time the two witnesses to the *ketubbah* are present in addition to invited guests. The bridegroom indicates his agreement to fulfill the obligations of the *ketubbah* by taking hold of a handkerchief or piece of cloth held up by the officiating rabbi. Witnesses sign the *ketubbah*, and the groom is then escorted to the bride's chamber, where the bride-veiling ceremony takes place.

See Knas Mahl.

Handwashing

In Jewish tradition, the ritual washing of the hands is done for two reasons: as a health measure and in preparation for the execution of a religious commandment.

As a Religious Act

The first mention of handwashing as an expression of spirituality is found in the Book of Exodus (30:17–21), where Moses is commanded to make a copper laver and place it at the entrance to the altar area so that Aaron and his sons (the priestly family) could wash their hands before approaching the altar to offer sacrifices. Verses 20–21 conclude: "…and it shall be for them a statute forever."

Priests had to be in a constant state of readiness to accept the animal and cereal (grain) offerings that were brought to the Temple by the public as sacrifices to God. In his normal state, a *Kohen* (Priest), like all other individuals, was considered impure (*tamei*), ritually unclean. Before performing a ritual act, he was therefore required to wash his hands.

In the fifth century B.C.E., Ezra the Scribe, who was a member of a priestly family, insisted that Priests wash their hands before accepting the first-fruits of grain brought to the Temple as an offering.

When the Temple was destroyed in 70 C.E., the table in the home came to represent the Temple altar. The bread placed on it symbolized the offerings that had once been brought to the Priests. The Sages, who believed that the Temple and the functions of the priesthood would one day be restored, did not want the practice of washing the hands before handling an offering to be forgotten, so the washing of hands before eating a meal was strictly enforced. After the handwashing, the *Netilat Yada'yim* blessing was pronounced: "Blessed art Thou…Who commanded us to raise up hands and to pour water over them."

The vessel used for the washing of hands for religious purposes was a metal or glass pitcher called *natla*, hence the term *netilat yada'yim*, literally "the raising of hands" (*Chullin* 105a and 117a). In ancient times, the *Kohen*, before officiating, would raise his hands, and a Levite, using a pitcher filled with water, would pour water over them.

A semblance of this ritual is still followed today by observant Jews. Before sitting down to a meal at which bread is served, the hands are washed, after which the *Hamotzi*—the blessing over bread—is recited.

So widespread was ritual handwashing in talmudic times that the Midrash (*Be-midbar Rabbah* 20:21) reports that an innkeeper once said to a Jew, "When I saw that you ate without washing your hands and without a blessing, I thought you were a heathen."

Rabbi Zerika (*Sotah* 4b) was even more emphatic about the importance of carrying out this ritual. He said, in the name of Rabbi Eleazar, "Whoever makes light of washing the hands [before and after meals] will be uprooted from the world."

Handwashing Procedure

The most common handwashing procedure is to fill a cup with water and then to pour water from the cup onto each hand three times, starting with the right hand and alternating thereafter. In Jewish tradition, the right hand is always favored. "The right hand of the Lord doeth valiantly," says the Psalmist (118:15, 16).

The *Code of Jewish Law* explains that in ritual handwashing the first pouring cleanses the hand; the second removes the ritual impurity (*tumah* in Hebrew); and since the water of the second pouring becomes impure when it comes into contact with the (impure) hand, a third pouring is required to restore the hand to a condition of ritual purity (*tohorah* in Hebrew).

The *Code of Jewish Law* (*Shulchan Arukh*, Orach Cha'yim 162:2) explains that in order to ensure that the hands are removed of all ritual impurity, the water must reach all parts of the hand, including the area between the fingers, and the palm up to the wrist. In order to distribute the water, the hands are raised.

Ma'yim Achronim

It is also customary to wash the hands, particularly the fingers, after the meal has been eaten, before *Grace After Meals* is recited. The water that is poured on the fingers is known as *ma'yim achronim*, "final waters."

Moses Maimonides, in his *Mishneh Torah* (Book of Cleanness 11), explains that unlike the washing of hands at the beginning of a meal, which is a religious obligation, the washing of hands at the end of the meal is done for health reasons only. In early times, it was customary to use salt freely. Salt was taken in hand and sprinkled over the food. A residue of salt always remained on the diner's fingers when the meal was over, and if the diner rubbed his eyes, serious damage might result. It therefore became customary among Jews to wash the fingers at the end of the meal. Since this was a precautionary health measure rather than a religious obligation, no prayer was assigned the act.

Passover Handwashing

According to ancient practice recorded in the Talmud, hands are to be washed before food is dipped into a liquid or sauce. Although this practice has fallen into general disuse, it remains part of the Passover *Seder* ritual. A pitcher of water is carried around the table by the mistress of the house, and water is poured onto the hands of each participant. In some households, the participants leave the table to wash their hands. Before the actual *Seder* meal is served, the hands are once again washed.

Death-related Handwashing

Many Jews follow the tradition demanding that before entering a cemetery to recite prayers at the grave of a loved one, the hands should be washed so that the person will be in a state of purity. Based on the old folk belief that evil spirits follow those who have visited a grave, and that water will wash away the demons, it is also common for people to wash the hands immediately upon leaving a cemetery.

The esteemed Babylonian authority Hai Gaon (939–1039), head of the academy in Pumbedita, believed that it is not necessary to wash hands following a cemetery visit, but conceded that where it is a local custom to do so, there is no objection. However, most later authorities considered it an important rite.

Rabbi Jacob Levi Mollin, the fourteenth-century authority on Jewish customs and ceremonies, explains (*Teshuvot Maharil*, no. 23) that the reason for washing the hands after visiting a cemetery is to remove "the spirit of uncleanness that dwells in the cemetery" because of the demons that were believed to congregate there.

The sixteenth-century Greek authority Rabbi Binyamin Ze'ev of Arta considers the act of handwashing to be an expression of atonement. Just as in Deuteronomy (21:7) the elders washed their hands as an expression of innocence, so is the washing of hands upon leaving a cemetery a way of saying, "We are not responsible for this death."

Today, most traditional Jews wash the hands immediately upon leaving the cemetery after the burial or before entering the *shivah* home if they had just attended the funeral. A jug of water is generally placed at the entrance of the home for that purpose.

After washing the hands, some Jews recite a verse from the Book of Isaiah (25:8):

> He will destroy death forever.
> My Lord God will wipe the tears away
>   from all faces,
> And will put an end to the reproach of His
>   people over all the earth.
> For it is the Lord who has spoken.

Just as one does not pass a shovel from hand to hand when shoveling earth into a grave for fear that he may be passing trouble to his neighbor, so does one not pass the washing cup from person to person. After washing the hands, each individual places the cup down on the ground for the next person to use.

Hasagat Gevul

A Hebrew term literally meaning "encroachment upon a neighbor's property." Originally, the concept was merely a restatement of the biblical injunction (Deuteronomy 19:14), "You shall not move your neighbor's landmark that had been established by previous generations." The Rabbis of the Talmud (*Megillah* 32a), however, expanded the concept to include all types of infringement upon the rights of individuals and the spurning of communal regulations and traditions, such as changing the traditional Torah reading chants.

The most serious examples of *hasagat gevul* generally involve infringement upon a person's livelihood. If a person opens a store to sell the same products currently on sale in a nearby establishment, the established store owner may challenge the newcomer, on the grounds of *hasagat gevul*, of threatening his livelihood. The same would be true if a doctor opens a practice in a vicinity already being serviced by another practitioner, or if a teacher moves into a small town and tries to lure students from a teacher who has been making his living there for a long time.

Hashchatat Zera

A Hebrew term literally meaning "destroying the seed" or "wasting seed."

See Bal Tashchit; Birth Control.

Ha-Shem

A Hebrew word literally meaning "the Name [of God]," used in place of the more formal *Adonai*.

See God, Names of.

Haskalah

A Hebrew term literally meaning "enlightenment," referring specifically to a movement that took root in the eighteenth century, the aim of which was to spread modern European culture among Jews. Advocates of *Haskalah* were called *maskilim* (singular, *maskil*), meaning "enlightened ones." These intellectuals believed that in order for Jews to become fully emancipated and accepted by the elite of the non-Jewish community they would have to acquire a Western university education which would equip them to become comfortable intellectually and socially in their non-Jewish environment. To this end among other things, *maskilim* advocated the use of Hebrew, rather than Yiddish, as the language of discourse and cultural expression. Most *maskilim*, while learned in talmudic studies, believed that much more emphasis should be placed on biblical studies.

One of the outstanding pioneers of the *Haskalah* movement, and possibly its prime mover, was the brilliant German-born Moses Mendelssohn (1729–1786) who, in addition to his proficiency in Jewish subjects, spent years in Berlin studying philosophy, mathematics, Latin, French, and English. Believing that the study of Talmud had overtaken the study of Bible to an unhealthy degree, in 1783 he published the *Bi'ur*, meaning "explanation," which was a German translation of the Torah (Pentateuch) using Hebrew characters accompanied by a commentary.

Another force behind the *Haskalah* was David Friedlander (1750–1834), a leader of the Reform movement in Germany and an intimate friend of Mendelssohn. He advocated less concentration on talmudic studies and, in fact, proposed giving up the study of Talmud altogether and abolishing Jewish observances. His aim was to achieve complete Jewish assimilation into European society. In 1778, Friedlander was among the founders of the Jewish Free School in Berlin, which called for the banning of Yiddish as the language of instruction.

Other *maskilim* who sympathized with the views of Friedlander were the Galician Joshua Heschel Schorr (1814–1895) and the Russian Hebrew writer Moses Leib Lilienblum (1843–1910). While they did not denigrate the value of the Talmud completely, they did believe that its laws were obsolete and unworthy of support. They pressed for reform of Jewish law (*halakhah*).

Another pioneer of the *Haskalah* movement was Naphtali Herz Wessely (1725–1805). Like Moses Mendelssohn, he did not subscribe to the authority of talmudic law and both worked to diminish its position by stressing the importance of studying Bible more intensely and encouraging the masses to do so. "We were not all created to be talmudists," said Wessely.

Wessely also encouraged the implementation of an educational program for Jewish youth that would include secular studies. His views aroused great controversy and were strenuously opposed by the mainstream Orthodox community, which advocated concentrated study of Talmud and its commentaries.

Three other *maskilim* are worthy of note:

1. Solomon J. Rapoport (1760–1867), an ordained Galician rabbi, studied secular subjects and published a number of critical studies on Jewish history and culture. *Chasidim* and other ultra-Orthodox Jews did not appreciate his scholarship and attacked him for his enlightened views.

2. Nachman Krochmal (1785–1840), a Galician historian and philosopher, was deeply concerned with the survival of the Jewish people. He was a personal friend of Solomon Rapoport and shared many of his views. Krochmal's most famous book, *Moreh Nevuchei Ha-Zeman* ("Guide for the Perplexed of the Time"), was a takeoff on the title of the famous work of Moses Maimonides, *Moreh Nevukhim* ("Guide for the Perplexed"). Krochmal's work explains Jewish history in terms of its spirituality and states that it can only be understood if approached in religious terms.

3. Leopold Zunz (1794–1886), a German-born scholar of great renown, founded the Verein für Kultur und Wissenschaft

in Berlin in 1819. He was a pioneer in critical studies on such subjects as *Midrash Aggadah*, Jewish liturgy, Jewish biography, and Jewish folklore.

Havdalah

A Hebrew word literally meaning "separation, division." Thought to have been introduced between the fifth and fourth centuries B.C.E. by the Men of the Great Assembly (*Berakhot* 33a), the *havdalah* ceremony is conducted at the end of the Sabbath and holidays to mark the separation of the holy from the mundane. During the ceremony a blessing is made over wine, a candle, and spices. The *havdalah* service can be found in any Sabbath prayerbook.

The Wine Blessing

The *havdalah* ceremony begins with the chanting of the blessing over a cup of wine filled to overflowing, which some explain is an expression of hope that the workdays to follow will bring blessings in abundance. The origin of the custom, however, is rooted in the belief, common in early societies, that the spilling of wine is a safeguard against evil spirits. These spirits, it was believed, could be bribed with a bit of wine (*Eruvin* 65a). Although wine is usually sipped immediately after reciting the blessing, in the *havdalah* ceremony the wine is not drunk until all of the *Havdalah* blessings have been recited.

The Candle Blessing

Originally, two lighted candles were held during the *havdalah* ceremony because the prayer recited uses the plural form for light: "Blessed art Thou…who created the *lights* of fire [...*borei me-orei ha-eish*]." Today, as a substitute, a single braided candle with a double wick is usually used. It provides a torchlike flame to satisfy the verse in Psalms

(19:9), "The commandment of the Lord is pure, enlightening the eyes." Blue-and-white and red-and-white are the most popular color combinations of the strand.

A child is usually called upon to hold the *havdalah* candle. When a boy holds it, people sometimes say, "Hold it high so you will get a tall bride." When a girl holds it, she is told, "Hold the candle high so you will get a tall groom." This bit of fantasy notwithstanding, the custom was probably adopted so that people witnessing the ceremony would be able to see the dancing flame more easily.

When pronouncing the candle blessing, the leader as well as those present fold in and then sometimes extend the fingers of their hands to allow the light of the candle to reflect off their fingernails. This symbolic action shows that pleasure is being derived from the light emanating from the candle, and that the blessing is not being recited for naught. (*See* Berakhah Le-Vatalah.)

The Spices

A third part of the *havdalah* service is the recitation of a blessing over spices. Originally, spices were spread throughout the home after a meal in order to dissipate food odors. This was not done following Sabbath meals, however, because that would be a desecration of the holy day. When spices were used once again on Saturday night, for the first time in twenty-four or twenty-five hours, their use was given religious significance by associating the spices with the *havdalah* ceremony and by the recitation of a special prayer. In modern times, instead of spreading spices around the house, they are placed in a spice box, which is passed around for all to sniff after the blessing has been recited. The spices most commonly used are cinnamon, cloves, and allspice. Many Sephardic Jews favor lemon, myrtle, or mint.

It is sometimes said that the use of spices as part of the *havdalah* ceremony is intended to raise spirits and offset the sadness that may overcome us at the end of the joyous Sabbath Day, when the problems of everyday life have to be faced once again.

Dousing the Flame

After all the *Havdalah* blessings have been recited, the flame of the candle is doused in the wine that overflowed from the goblet into the wine tray beneath it. An ancient superstition states that if the eyes are touched with the overflow liquid, weak eyes will be cured. The origin is obscure but is probably associated with verse 9 of Psalm 19, mentioned earlier. There is also a custom whereby one dips his fingers into the wine and then puts his hand in his pocket as if to pray for a week of prosperity, or strokes his fingers across his forehead or temples for wisdom.

Drinking the Wine

The *havdalah* ceremony concludes with the individual who conducts the ceremony drinking some of the wine and saving some for children present to sip. Women traditionally do not taste the *havdalah* wine, probably based on an old, obscure belief that if a woman drinks from the *havdalah* cup she will grow a beard.

Another reason offered for women not partaking of the wine is that Adam's wife caused his downfall when she ate of the Tree of Knowledge. One legend has it that the fruit of the Tree of Knowledge was the grape, and Eve squeezed grapes to make wine. Because of her sin, the story goes, women do not drink the *havdalah* wine.

See Melaveh Malkah; Soul.

Havlagah

A Hebrew term literally meaning "self-restraint." A policy adopted in Palestine by the Haganah in response to Arab attacks against Jews from 1936 to 1939. The meager Israeli armed forces acted in self-defense, but avoided retaliation when it was deemed unwise or unnecessary.

Hazkarah

This Hebrew word literally meaning "remembrance" is the name by which Sephardim refer to the *El Malei Rachamim* memorial prayer. The *Hazkarah* is recited principally at funerals and on occasions when *Yizkor* is recited.

Hazkarat Neshamot

This Hebrew term literally meaning "remembering of the souls" is another name for the *Yizkor* service.

Headcovering

There are no regulations in the Bible that require Israelites to keep their heads covered. The Bible does not even require headcoverings for men entering the sanctuary or participating in a religious rite or service. Only Priests were expected to wear headgear (Exodus 28:4), and this only when officiating at the Temple altar or performing other priestly functions. Scholars explain that the priestly requirement was introduced in order to distinguish Jewish Priests from heathen priests, who offered sacrifices to their deities with heads uncovered. In other biblical references, the covering of the head and face is regarded as a sign of mourning. This is how King David expressed grief when his son Absalom rebelled against him (II Samuel 15:30), and again when he mourned Absalom's death (II Samuel 19:5).

Babylonian Practices in Talmudic Times

In talmudic times (*Berakhot* 60b) there was no established practice or binding law with regard to the covering of the head. It seems clear that the custom in Babylonia, where most Jews lived, was for a man, upon rising in the morning, to place a kerchief (called a *sudara* in Aramaic) over his head and to recite the blessing, "Blessed is He who crowns Israel with glory." This would indicate that men did keep their heads covered, yet the Talmud (*Nedarim* 30b) also states that the average man did not always keep his head covered: "Men sometimes cover their heads and sometimes do not. But women's hair is always covered, and children are always bareheaded."

We also know from the Talmud (*Kiddushin* 8a) that Babylonian scholars wore a *special* headcovering that indicated their status. The learned Rabbi Chiya bar Abba, a third-century Babylonian-born Palestinian, once reprimanded (*Kiddushin* 30a) his fellow Palestinian scholar Joshua ben Levi for wearing a plain kerchief rather than a scholar's cap on his head. In time, the habit of scholars covering their heads spread to the masses, and it became increasingly common for the average man to wear a headcovering, especially when reciting prayers and studying.

That the wearing of a headcovering was neither mandatory nor commonplace in talmudic times is revealed in a story relating to the fourth-century C.E. Babylonian scholar Rabbi Nachman ben Isaac. Nachman's mother had been told by astrologers that her son would be a thief. Thinking that wearing a headcovering might divert him from such a course, she cautioned (*Shabbat* 156b): "Cover your head so that the fear of heaven may be upon you, and pray [for mercy]." This comment may have led Joseph Caro to rule (Orach Cha'yim 2:6) that one may not walk more than four cubits (six feet) with uncovered head.

Several other talmudic references associate "fear of heaven [God]" with keeping one's head covered. In the first reference, the Talmud (*Kiddushin* 31a) says, "Rav Huna, son of Joshua [a great third-century Babylonian scholar], would not walk four cubits [six feet] without [wearing] a headcovering, for, he said, 'The *Shekhinah* [God's glory] is above my head.'" In a second reference (*Kiddushin* 29b), the same Rav Huna replied to a question by saying that the observance for which he hoped to be rewarded the most was "for never walking four cubits with uncovered head." However, the fact the Talmud (*Berakhot* 51a) goes out of its way to report that the third/fourth-century scholar Assi would cover his head with a kerchief when reciting *Grace After Meals* would indicate that normally he was bareheaded.

From the statement in *Kiddushin* 29b, it would appear that unmarried men did not wear headcoverings. When Rabbi Hamnuna appeared before Rabbi Chisda, he was not wearing a hat. "Why are you not wearing a headdress?" asked Rabbi Chisda. "Because I am not married," responded Hamnuna.

Palestinian Practices

All the above statements found in the Talmud represent the thinking, attitudes, and practices of the communities in Babylonia and those influenced by Babylonian scholars, including the Spanish communities under Arab rule. This is evident from such statements as the one noted in the Jerusalem Talmud (*Kila'yim* 9:4, and also noted in *Genesis Rabbah* 100:7) that when the third-century scholar Bar Kapparah mourned the passing of his teacher Rabbi Judah the Prince, he covered his head.

Apparently, the custom of wearing a head-covering at all times was not yet commonplace among Palestinian Jewry, although those in mourning sometimes did choose to cover the head (*Moed Katan* 15a and 24a). The minor tractate *Soferim*, which was composed in Palestine, clearly states (14:15) that a man with uncovered head may serve as the Torah reader (*ba'al korei*) and may lead the congregation in reciting the *Shema*.

The Palestinian practice of not wearing a headcovering spread to the Sephardic Jewish communities in the distant countries of Spain and Portugal, and in time the Ashkenazic communities in France and Germany also began to follow the Palestinian practice. Historian Israel Abrahams states that in the thirteenth century "boys in Germany and adults in France were called to the Torah bareheaded."

Rabbi Isaac ben Moses of Vienna (1200–1270), author of *Or Zaru'a*, tells us that rabbis in France prayed with uncovered heads. This would appear to have been normal conduct, because nowhere in his commentaries or responsa does the eleventh-century French authority Rashi (1040–1105) make reference to headcoverings worn by men, although he does mention the fact that women may not appear in public with heads uncovered.

In the Midrash (*Genesis Rabbah* 17:8), the Palestinian scholar, Rabbi Joshua, was asked why a man walks about with head uncovered while a woman walks about with head covered. He replied: "She is like one who committed a transgression and is ashamed of people. [Eve ate the forbidden fruit and then prevailed upon Adam to eat it]. It is that reason that a woman keeps her head covered."

This liberal attitude was echoed by the thirteenth-century rabbi Samson ben Zadok, a disciple of Rabbi Meir ben Baruch of Rothenburg (*c.* 1220–1293). In his *Tashbetz* (#549), he quotes the words of his master: "It is not forbidden to walk bareheaded."

Sixteenth-Century Practices

Polish scholar Solomon Luria (1510–1574), the esteemed rabbi of Lublin, popularly known as the Maharshal, was often attacked for his liberal attitudes. In one of his responsa (#72), he ruled that covering the head does not reflect a sign of piety and that one may study sacred books with uncovered head if he finds that the wearing of a headcovering is inconvenient. He wrote: "I do not know of any prohibition against praying with uncovered head."

In another inquiry, Luria was asked whether a person who suffers from headaches is permitted to eat bareheaded (and hence recite the blessings bareheaded). In his reply he states that he is aware that Rabbi Israel Isserlein (1390–1460), the leading German authority (whom Luria respected greatly), says that it is wrong to pronounce God's name without a headcovering. But he adds that he doesn't understand why Isserlein ruled in that manner, and that he himself would not hesitate to utter benedictions with an uncovered head. Luria bases his argument on the talmudic statement (*Soferim* 14:15) that says that one may recite the *Shema* with uncovered head. The Maharshal concludes that "since other teachers have said that it is not proper to pray without a headcovering, he will not contradict them and will support their view."

Solomon Luria goes on to explain the probable reason why most Rabbis insisted that the head be covered despite the leniency of Jewish law in this regard. It is a matter of public perception, he says. Since many Jews had become accustomed to thinking of anyone who walks around bareheaded as being frivolous and disrespectful of Jewish law, it is best that Jews should not go bareheaded.

The Spanish scholar Joseph Caro (1488–1575), compiler of the *Code of Jewish Law*, acknowledges (*Shulchan Arukh*, Orach Cha'yim 91:3) that some Jews go about bareheaded and even enter the synagogue and pray with uncovered heads. He does not condemn those who follow this practice, but he does suggest that to keep one's head covered is a more pious way of living (*midat chasidut*).

It is clear that according to Jewish law there is no compelling reason for Jews to wear a headcovering. Nonetheless, for the reasons indicated above, the Babylonian custom of keeping one's head covered not only during prayer but at all times became accepted by traditional Jews.

The Skullcap

The Yiddish word for the headcovering commonly seen today is *yarmulke*. Although of uncertain origin, one view is that the term is derived from *armucella*, a headcovering worn by medieval clergy. A second explanation is that *yarmulke* is related to the French *arme* (akin to the Latin *arma*), a type of round medieval helmut with a movable visor.

The popular view is that the word *yarmulke* is a distorted form of the Hebrew words *yarei mei-Elohim* "in fear [awe] of God." This idea is based, for the most part on a statement made by a fifth-century Babylonian talmudic scholar, Huna ben Joshua, who said, "I never walked four cubits with uncovered head because God dwells over my head." (*Kiddushin* 31a) Another Yiddish word for *yarmulke* is *koppel* (*kappel*) a form of the Latin *capitalis*, meaning "of the head." The Hebrew word for *yarmulke* is *kippah*.

The Covered Skullcap

The practice of wearing a skullcap under one's hat began in the Middle Ages (seventeenth century), when it was customary in German lands for one to doff his hat to a government official as a gesture of respect. In order to avoid being without a headcovering for even a moment, Orthodox Jews wore a skullcap under their hats. This practice is still observed by ultra-Orthodox Jews today.

Modern Attitudes

Despite the preponderance of opinion that keeping one's head covered is not required by biblical or talmudic law, and despite the fact that the practice was never unanimously espoused by rabbinic authorities, many observant Jews in recent centuries have shown a preference for keeping their heads covered at all times.

Probably the most plausible explanation for this development is that over the centuries Jews were accustomed to seeing Christians going about with head uncovered—particularly in church—and the uncovered head became associated with Christianity. To maintain their integrity as a community, Jews often avoided practices that were current among Christians.

Today, Orthodox Jews generally wear a skullcap at all times, although some do not while at work or in certain social situations. Conservative Jews are of various minds. Some keep their heads covered at all times; others only when reciting prayers, studying Bible or Talmud, and at mealtime; and still others only when reciting prayers. Reform Jews do not generally wear skullcaps, but the matter is optional. Many Reform Jews do wear headcoverings during prayer.

Black Hats

Among *chasidim* of nineteenth-century Eastern Europe, it was customary for men to keep their heads covered with black hats. Black was always considered the proper color for garments worn by Jews as a means of expressing a sense of mourning for the loss of the Jerusalem Temples, the First Temple in 587 B.C.E. and the Second Temple in 70 C.E. Even shoelaces were to be black rather than white (*Sanhedrin* 74b).

Today, when returning home from synagogue on the Sabbath or holidays, those who follow chasidic practice continue to wear their street hats at least until after reciting the *Kiddush* (prayer over wine). Some continue to wear their hats throughout the meal, while others wear only black *yarmulkes* after the *Kiddush* has been recited. The term "Black Hats" is sometimes used somewhat pejoratively by Jews when referring to those who are extremely observant.

Chasidic Practice

Chasidim assign considerable importance to the wearing of hats, and each sect established an identity by their individual style of headcovering, depending on their country of origin.

Belzer chasidim who are married wear a round fur *shtreiml* (headpiece) made of twelve fur tails, one for each of the twelve tribes of Israel.

Gerer chasidim, originally from Poland, who are disciples of the Kotzker Rebbe, wear a high hat with a rounded crown, and on the Sabbath and holidays don a special black fur hat called a *spodik*.

Romanian Vishnitzer *chasidim*, who today live mostly in Bnei Brak, Israel, wear low, rounded black velvet hats, as do the Belzer *chasidim*. The Belzer hats, however, have a bow on the band on the left side while the Vishnitzer do not. On the Sabbath, both the Vishnitzers and the Belzers wear low brown fur *shtreimels* (made of thirteen or twenty pelts).

Satmar *chasidim* are identifiable by their low, broad round headgear made of beaver fur. The Satmar hat is referred to as a *biber*, a Yiddish term adopted from the German *Biber*, meaning "beaver."

Before Menachem Mendel Schneerson became the Lubavitcher Rebbe after World War II, the Lubavitcher *chasidim* used to wear fur *shtreimels* on the Sabbath, but the new *rebbe* wore only fedoras, even on the Sabbath. So, since 1951 Lubavitchers have followed the style of their leader.

Headcovering and Mourning

Covering the head by drawing a cloth over the face and lips was a popular mourning ritual among Ishmaelites. When adopted by Israelites, it became known as *atifat Yishm'eilim*, "the wrapping of Ishmaelites."

In time, a great many authorities began to disparage this practice of covering the head and face to the lips because it led to ridicule by non-Jews, particularly non-Jewish servants and maids. Gradually, it was abandoned in its original form and it became customary for mourners to keep their heads, but not their faces, covered. (See the comments of Isserles and the Shach on Yoreh Dei'ah 386:1).

Many later legal authorities commented on the practice of mourners covering the head: the eleventh-century French authority Rashi was asked whether mourners (*aveilim*) must keep their heads covered throughout the *shivah* period. He replied: "Although non-Jews make fun of this custom, Jews should nevertheless follow the practice" (*Sefer Teshuvot Rashi*, by Israel Elfenbein, Bnei Brak, Israel, 1980).

The thirteenth-century Spanish scholar Moses ben Nachman (Nachmanides) (*Shulchan Arukh*, Yoreh Dei'ah 386:1) took the position that "the head is uncovered out of respect for the public." Thus when a mourner is alone, he is to keep his head covered; and when visitors come to offer comfort, the mourner is to uncover his head as a sign of respect.

Rabbi Jacob ben Moses Ha-Levi Mollin (1360–1427), popularly known as the Maharil, indicates in his famous book on customs and ceremonies, *Sefer Ha-Minhagim*, that it is proper for mourners to keep their heads covered at all times during *shivah*. This is the practice generally followed today by traditional Jews, and, out of respect for the mourner, visitors to a house of mourning usually wear a headcovering as well.

See Sheitl.

Heaven and Hell

The Bible makes no direct reference to a heaven or hell as a place to which people go after death. Chapters 2 and 3 of Genesis, as well as chapter 28 of Ezekiel, refer to an earthly Garden of Eden (*Gan Eden* in Hebrew), but this is not the celestial Paradise referred to in later Jewish literature. Only after the destruction of the First Temple in 586 B.C.E. and the subsequent exile of Jews to Babylonia (later conquered by Persia), at which time Jews came under the strong influence of Persian Zoroastrian teachings, did the concept of heaven and hell become the subject of serious discussion among Jews.

Talmudic Views

In talmudic times, especially during the periods of persecution by the Romans in the early centuries C.E., the concept of heaven and hell began to take root. Heaven was equated with *Gan Eden* (Paradise), a place where the righteous would go after death to enjoy the fruits of the good life they had led while on earth. Those who did not live exemplary lives on earth, talmudists felt, would be consigned to hell (*Gehinnom* or *Gehenna*).

To many Rabbis of the Talmud, heaven and hell were real places created by God. The Talmud (*Berakhot* 28b) notes that the illustrious Rabbi Yochanan ben Zakkai wept before his death because he was not sure whether he would go to heaven or to hell. Many talmudic references (*Ta'anit* 10a, *Bava Kama* 84a, *Eruvin* 19a) indicate that *Gan Eden* and *Gehinnom* are actual terrestrial places.

To other scholars, such as the third-century Babylonian Abba Arikha (better known as Rav), Paradise, or the world to come, is a spiritual place where there will be "no eating, or drinking, or procreation, or business dealings, or jealousy, or hatred, or competition. The righteous will sit there with crowns on their heads, enjoying the brightness of God's radiance" (*Berakhot* 17a).

Post-Talmudic Views of Heaven and Hell

Scholars of post-talmudic centuries were less and less inclined to view the hereafter as a physical place. *Gan Eden* to Rabbi Moses ben Nachman (Nachmanides) of the thirteenth century was a world of souls (*olam ha-neshamot* in Hebrew), a place where only the souls, not the bodies, of the departed would enter immediately after death. A century earlier, Maimonides wrote (*Mishneh Torah*, Hilkhot Teshuvah 8): "There are neither bodies nor bodily forms in the world to come, only the souls of the righteous..."

Rabbi Ben Zion Bokser, in his *Judaism: Profile of a Faith*, after surveying the classic Jewish writers on the concept of heaven and hell, sums up their thinking by noting that this doctrine is subject to two interpretations: "The exponents of conventional Jewish piety who remained untouched by philosophical thought tended to interpret this doctrine literally." They understood the rewards and punishments associated with heaven and hell to be real and physical. On the other hand, the idea of a physical heaven and a physical hell where rewards and punishments were assigned and carried out "has seemed repugnant to many people in modern no less than in ancient times."

Most Jews today—Orthodox and non-Orthodox—believe in the immortality of the soul, but not all believe in heaven and hell and in the physical resurrection of the dead. Reform Judaism and Reconstructionism accept only the idea of the immortality of the soul, and this is reflected in their respective liturgies.

Heavenly Voice

A concept better known by the Hebrew term *bat kol*, literally meaning "daughter of the voice," connoting an echo. In Jewish legend, the term *bat kol* refers to a voice from heaven that reveals the will of God. The Talmud (*Yoma* 9b) says that when the last of the prophets died, the Holy Spirit disappeared from Israel, and the people depended upon the *bat kol* for their guidance.

Hekdeish

Also spelled *hekdesh*. From the Hebrew word *kadosh*, meaning "holy," the *hekdeish* was a hospicelike institution that provided for the care and needs of the indigent members of a Jewish community as well as the sick and elderly. Wandering peddlers were also housed there for a night or two.

Even non-Jews were cared for in these institutions. It had been noted that in Krakow,

in 1599, a rule was established by the Jewish community that whenever a maid serving a Jewish family took sick, she could stay in the *hekdeish* and her employer would pay for her upkeep.

Hell

See Heaven and Hell.

Hermeneutics

A Greek word meaning "to interpret," especially as it applies to methods of interpreting the Bible. Rabbis of the Talmud used the system widely to uncover the underlying meaning of the Torah text. While the Rabbis insisted that the literal meaning of the text must be accepted as true and inviolable, they also validated allegorical (*aggadic*) and exegetical interpretations. (*See* Aggadah.)

According to an old tradition, Shemaiah and Avtalyon, teachers of first-century Hillel the Great, were the first exegetes, and it was Hillel himself who formulated seven hermeneutical rules that can be used in explaining the Bible text. Hillel's famous pupil Yochanan ben Zakkai followed in Hillel's footsteps.

Rabbi Ishmael ben Elishah, who died a martyr's death during the Roman persecutions of 135 C.E., expanded on Hillel's rules and established thirteen principles for interpreting texts. Still later, Rabbi Eliezer son of Yosei the Galilean expanded upon these thirteen and formulated thirty-two exegetical principles.

Two of the better-known rules that are standard in all systems of biblical interpretations are *kal va-chomer* and *gezeirah shavah*.

The *kal va-chomer* principle—which logicians refer to as *a fortiori*, "for a stronger reason"—involves arriving at a conclusion that follows with even greater logical necessity than another already accepted in the argument. The Tosefta (*Pesachim* 9:2) gives an example: since silence is a good course for wise people to follow, how much more so should this apply to stupid people. Another example: if eating is prohibited on Tishah B'Av, which is not a biblical holiday, how much more so is eating forbidden on Yom Kippur, which is biblically mandated.

The principle of *gezeirah shavah*—which is commonly referred to as "verbal analogy"—involves comparing verses or words to arrive at a conclusion. This method of interpretation can be seen in the tractate *Kiddushin* (2a), where the point is made that the "taking of a bride"—that is, marriage—becomes official with the transfer of money. (At a later time, the giving of money was replaced by the giving of a ring by the bridegroom to the bride). To prove that the transfer of money is what validates a marriage, the Rabbis used the word *kichah*, meaning "taking." They note that the word appears (in different forms) in two passages in the Torah. In Genesis 23:13, where Abraham wishes to acquire property from Ephron the Hittite as a burial plot for his wife Sarah, Abraham says: "I will give you money for the field, *take* it from me." And in Deuteronomy 22:13, the Bible says, "If a man *takes* a wife." The Rabbis ruled that the word *take* in both instances constitutes a *gezeirah shavah*. Thus, they concluded, just as property is acquired by the payment of money, so is a wife.

Hespeid

Also spelled *hesped*. A Hebrew word derived from the Akkadian meaning "to raise one's voice in lamentation over the dead."

See Eulogy.

Heter Mei'ah Rabbanim

Gershom ben Yehuda (*c.* 965–1028), better known as Rabbi Gershom Me'or Ha-Golah ("Light of the Diaspora") and usually referred to as Rabbenu Gershom, was the most famous West European scholar of his generation. His decisions on ritual and legal matters were accepted as binding by European Jewry, but not by Jews of Sephardic extraction. Rabbenu Gershom's rulings included a ban on polygamy; a reaffirmation of the law that a man may not divorce his wife without her consent; a prohibition against reading letters addressed to others even when not sealed; cutting pages out of books; and criticizing converts who had returned to Judaism after having accepted Christianity. Anyone failing to observe these rulings was subject to excommunication.

Scholars believe that it was Rabbenu Gershom's ban on polygamy and his insistence on the acceptance of the talmudic ruling that a man may not divorce his wife without her consent that resulted in the formulation of the concept known as *heter mei'ah rabbanim* ("permission of one hundred rabbis").

Under Jewish law, when a man wishes to divorce his wife, a divorce document known as a *get*, handwritten by a scribe (*sofer*), is given directly to the wife by the husband or his agent. She must accept it if the divorce is to be legal, but if she refuses, neither party is permitted to remarry.

The wife may have had legitimate reasons for not accepting the *get*, such as not agreeing to the custody arrangement being proposed, or to the property settlement, or to a demand of the husband that she pay a certain amount of money. Nonetheless, the Rabbis always favored the man over the woman, and in order to make it possible for the man to remarry, they conceived of the idea *of heter mei'ah rabbanim*.

According to this concept, if one hundred rabbis living in three different countries sign a document stating that in their opinion there is no reasonable justification for the wife's refusal to accept the *get*, the husband is free to remarry. Undoubtedly, the original intent was to give a man the freedom to remarry if his wife was mentally incompetent, in a coma, or simply obstinate and unreasonable, but its actual implementation was not limited to these extreme conditions. The result was that in many cases a woman who had refused to accept a *get* from her husband for legitimate reasons was forced to remain an *agunah*, a woman "chained" to her husband and thus unable to remarry.

Sephardim never felt bound by this *heter,* since they lived primarily in Muslim countries where polygamy was an accepted way of life.

See Agunah.

Hiddur Mitzvah

A Hebrew term literally meaning "beautification or enhancement of a commandment." This concept was first referred to in the talmudic tractate *Bava Kama* (9b), where Rabbi Ze'eira said that in the performance of a Torah commandment one should act in an exemplary manner and purchase articles that are beautiful in shape and form regardless of expense.

See Beauty and Beautification.

High Holidays

Of all the holidays in the Jewish year, aside from the Sabbath, Rosh Hashanah and Yom Kippur are the most holy, and thus they are referred to as High Holidays or High Holy Days. Unlike other major Jewish holidays, the High Holidays, which emphasize morality, self-examination, spirituality, and holiness, are not related to historical events. Because of their serious nature, they are referred to as Days of Awe (*Yamim Nora'im* in Hebrew).

Actually, the Days of Awe encompass more than the ten-day period from Rosh Hashanah through Yom Kippur. They commence a full month before Rosh Hashanah, on the first day of Elul. From that day on, at every weekday morning service, the blasts of the *shofar* (ram's horn) reverberate in the synagogue, reminding Jews that the most awesome and holy days in the Jewish calendar are approaching.

See Rosh Hashanah; Yamim Nora'im; Yom Kippur.

High Priesthood

The institution of the high priesthood was introduced in biblical times when the tribe of Levi was set apart from the other eleven tribes of Israel and its members were consecrated to the service of God. Aaron, the brother of Moses, was elevated above all other Levites and anointed as chief Priest (Leviticus 21:10). In the Book of Numbers (35:25), he is referred to as *Kohen Gadol* ("High Priest"), and the Book of Leviticus (21:10–15) details the following prescriptions and proscriptions that are to govern his life:

The Priest who is exalted above his fellows, on whose head the anointing oil has been poured, and who has been ordained to wear the vestments, shall not bare his head or rend his vestments. He shall not go in where there is any dead body; he shall not defile himself even for his father or mother....He may marry only a woman who is a virgin. A widow, or a divorced woman, or one who is degraded by harlotry—such he may not marry. Only a virgin of his own kin may he take to wife—that he may not profane his offspring among his kin, for I the Lord have sanctified him.

One of the main functions of the High Priest was to officiate at the annual Yom Kippur ceremony of purification, on the tenth day of Tishrei. The details of his attire, the offerings he was to bring, and the sins to which he was to confess, as set forth in Leviticus 16, are recapitulated each year at the afternoon Yom Kippur synagogue service. Among the important ceremonies enacted at this service was the entry of the High Priest into the Holy of Holies, a room in the Temple that was to be entered at no other time. According to tradition, the Holy of Holies contained the tablets of the Ten Commandments that Moses had brought down from Sinai. In addition, it is believed to have contained the broken pieces of the first tablets, which Moses had smashed upon the ground when he saw that a Golden Calf had been erected in his absence.

The Talmud (*Gittin* 7a) expresses the importance of the high priesthood when it declaims: "When the hat of the High Priest adorned his head, it reflected glory on all the people of Israel."

Traditionally, the High Priest was to be a descendant of King David through Zadok, a descendant of Aaron (I Chronicles 5:38). After the Babylonian Exile in 586 B.C.E., when the monarchy came to an end with the destruction of the First Temple and there was no longer a Davidic king, the High Priest became the chief spokesman of the Jews in dealing with other nations that ruled Palestine. With the destruction of the Second Temple in 70 C.E., the office ceased to exist.

Holidays and Holy Days

In an essay published in his *Judaism Eternal* (English translation 1959), Samson Raphael Hirsch (1808–1888), the astute leader of nineteenth-century Orthodox German Jewry, wrote: "The catechism of the Jew consists of his calendar. On the pinions of time, which bear us through life, God has inscribed the eternal words of his soul-inspired doctrine, making days and weeks, months and years the heralds to proclaim his truths."

Berl Katznelson (1887–1944), the Palestinian labor leader, amplified upon this observation: "The Jewish year is thickly sown with days of far deeper significance than anything found in the calendars of other peoples."

The days of special meaning in the Jewish calendar—its days of celebration—are generally divided as follows: fall holidays and spring holidays, major holidays and minor holidays.

Rosh Hashanah and Yom Kippur

The fall holiday season usually begins during the month of September, or in some years early October, on the first day of the Hebrew month Tishrei. The first ten days of this holiday period—from Rosh Hashanah through Yom Kippur—are called the Days of Awe. In the special prayers recited during these days, God is revered and celebrated as Creator and Master of the universe, and Jews are called upon to examine themselves and consider the state of their spiritual lives.

Although the Ten Days of Awe officially commence on the first day of Tishrei, the period of introspection in fact begins one month earlier, on the first of Elul. During Elul, special prayers are added to the liturgy, and the *shofar* (ram's horn) is sounded in the synagogue each day as part of the morning service to remind worshippers that the most awesome holidays in the Jewish calendar are approaching.

The focus of Rosh Hashanah is the synagogue service, which features the sounding of the *shofar*, as prescribed in the Bible. Rosh Hashanah is also a holiday of distinctive foods: the pomegranate, the many seeds of which represent the hope for a productive year; honey-laden treats that symbolize the hope for sweet days ahead; and bread loaves (*challot*) in various symbolic shapes and designs.

Yom Kippur is a solemn day of prayer and fasting, beginning with the *Kol Nidrei* service and ending with the sounding of the *shofar* twenty-five hours later. In traditional synagogues, many congregants wear white gowns (*kittls*) as a symbol of purity and avoid wearing leather shoes, which are a sign of luxurious living. During the recitation of the Yom Kippur prayers, the attention of Jews is on their relationship with God and their fellow man.

Sukkot, Shemini Atzeret, and Simchat Torah

A second group of fall holidays, which begins five days after Yom Kippur, includes Sukkot (Tabernacles), Shemini Atzeret, and Simchat Torah.

During the Sukkot holiday, the Bible (Leviticus 23:42–43) says, "You shall live in booths [*sukkot*] seven days in order that future generations may know that I made the Israelite people live in booths when I brought them out of the Land of Egypt." Today, this festival commemorating the forty-year trek of the Israelites through the desert to the Promised Land is celebrated as a seven-day holiday in both Israel and the Diaspora.

Shemini Atzeret and Simchat Torah are often erroneously assumed to be part of the Sukkot holiday, whereas they are actually individual holidays. In Israel today, Shemini Atzeret is observed as a one-day holiday that follows Sukkot; in the Diaspora, Shemini Atzeret is celebrated for two days. In Israel, Simchat Torah is observed as part of Shemini Atzeret. In the Diaspora, Simchat Torah is the second day of the two-day Shemini Atzeret celebration.

Passover and Shavuot

Two major holidays fall during the spring months: Passover (Pesach) and Shavuot (Pentecost). Passover, the most widely observed of all Jewish holidays, celebrates the escape of the Children of Israel from bondage in Egypt. Shavuot, which falls on the sixth of Sivan, seven weeks and one day after the second day of Passover, is both an agricultural festival and a celebration of the giving of the Torah on Mount Sinai.

Chanukkah, Purim, and Other Minor Holidays

Rosh Hashanah, Yom Kippur, Sukkot, Shemini Atzeret, Simchat Torah, Passover, and Shavuot are considered *major* holidays in the Jewish tradition. What makes them so is that they are all mandated in the Torah. All of the major holidays are observed as rest days, much like the Sabbath, with the same prohibitions against work applying to them.

In addition to the major holidays, the Jewish calendar includes a number of *minor* ones. Aside from the more popular Chanukkah and Purim, the minor holidays include Tishah B'Av, a day of mourning for the destruction of the two Temples; Tu Bi-Shevat, celebrated as the New Year for trees; and the more recently introduced Yom Ha-Atzma'ut (Israel Independence Day) and Yom Ha-Sho'ah (Holocaust Remembrance Day).

Other than Purim, the story of which is recounted in the Book of Esther, none of the minor holidays is biblically mandated. Each is celebrated by the observance of distinctive rituals and ceremonies and by the inclusion of special readings in the prayer service.

Also included in the category of minor holidays are the Intermediate Days (Chol Ha-Moed) of Sukkot and Passover. These days, which separate the first days from the last days of each holiday, are marked by the recitation of a special liturgy and special readings from the Torah but are not subject to the prohibitions associated with the Sabbath or the main days of the holiday.

See Fasting and Fast Days *and entries for individual holidays.*

Holiness

The Hebrew word for holiness, *kedushah*, derives from the word *kadosh*, meaning "holy." In the Book of Leviticus (19:1–2), Moses is commanded to speak to the whole community of Israel and say to them, "You shall be holy, for I the Lord your God am holy." Holiness was established as an ideal of moral purity that applied to all members of the community, not merely to the priestly family whose lives were dedicated exclusively to the service of God.

The concept is reiterated in Leviticus (22:31–32): "You shall observe My commandments diligently; I am the Lord. You shall not profane My holy name that I may be sanctified in the midst of the people of Israel. I am the Lord Who sanctifies you."

The third-century Babylonian scholar Rabbi Chama interpreted these verses to mean that one must imitate God, a concept that later came to be known by the Latin term *imitatio Dei*. Rabbi Chama said (*Sotah* 14a) that to believe in God means to behave like God: "Just as He is righteous, so must you be righteous; just as He is compassionate, so must you be compassionate...." The German-Austrian Bible scholar Adolf Jellinek (1821–1893) categorized the verses in Leviticus as "Israel's Bible in miniature."

The concept of holiness runs through the whole of Jewish life. The two Temples that serviced the Jewish people for over a thousand years, from the days of Solomon, builder of the First Temple, through the Roman oc-cupation of Jerusalem and the sacking of the Second Temple in 70 C.E., were both known as *Batei Mikdash* (singular, *Beit Mikdash*), "Holy Temples." (*Mikdash* is derived from *kadosh*.) The holiest room in these Temples was called *Kodesh Kodoshim*, "Holy of Holies."

The name of the prayer recited over wine on Sabbaths and holidays became known as the *Kiddush*, meaning "sanctification," also a form of *kadosh*. The marriage ceremony, known as *Kiddushin*, is likewise derived from *kadosh*. Rabbis, cantors, and sexton—all of whom minister to the Jewish people—are referred to as *klei kodesh*, meaning "holy vessels."

Hierarchy of Holiness

To impress the concept of holiness upon Jews for all time, the Rabbis created a ladder of holiness, and on the very top rung they placed the Torah itself. The Torah scroll that is written specifically for reading at public services is the most sanctified object in Jewish life, and any article that is associated with it, even remotely, is likewise invested with a degree of sanctity.

Not all religious articles are of equal rank. Thus, the Talmud (*Megillah* 26a) tells us, one may not sell a Torah scroll to purchase secondary books of the Bible (those in the Prophets or Holy Writings); nor may one sell these secondary books of Scripture to buy Torah wrappings (mantle, *gartl*, and so on); nor may one sell these wrappings to buy an ark to house the Torah; nor may one sell an ark and use its proceeds to buy a synagogue building.

The hierarchy of sanctity as established by the Rabbis is governed by the following rules: one may raise a religious article from one level of sanctity to another, but one may not lower the status of an article. This principle governs not only the buying and selling of holy articles, but also their use and disposition. Thus, one may not salvage any part of the parchment of a Torah scroll by erasing the previous script and writing on it the text used in *tefillin* or *mezuzot*. *Tefillin* are of lower sanctity than a Torah; *mezuzot* of lower sanctity than *tefillin*.

Tefillin are considered higher in sanctity than *mezuzot* because they contain four passages from the Torah, while *mezuzot* contain only two. Furthermore, *tefillin* make direct contact with a person's body, while *mezuzot* do not. (See *Shulchan Arukh*, Orach Cha'yim 38:12, and the comment of Magen Avraham.)

Regarding the principle that religious articles may only be elevated in status, not lowered—known in Hebrew as *ma'alin ba-kodesh ve-lo moridin* (see *Berakhot* 28a). It is quite likely that the idea stems from the manner in which the shewbreads were treated in Temple times (*see* Mishnah *Shekalim* 6:4).

See Holy Articles; Piety.

Holiness Code

Known as the Holiness Code, chapter 19 of the Book of Leviticus begins with the words, "Speak to the Children of Israel and say to them: you shall be holy, for I the Lord your God am holy." Israel was to separate itself from other idolatrous nations and thus become a holy nation, dedicated to God.

The Holiness Code repeats many of the laws found in the Ten Commandments and goes into greater detail, emphasizing that the highest degree of moral conduct is expected of Jews, who, in the words of Isaiah, are to be *nes la-goyim*, "a guiding symbol to the nations of the world" (Isaiah 5:26; 11:12).

Hollekreisch

During the course of this ceremony, once popular primarily in South Germany, a Jewish male child who had been given a Hebrew name at the time of circumcision (*brit*), or a female child who had been named in the synagogue on the first Sabbath after her birth, is given a *secular* name. The origin of the custom, first mentioned by the fifteenth-century writer Moses Mintz, is obscure. Mintz considered the name of the ceremony to derive from a combination of the Hebrew word *chol*, meaning "secular, mundane," and the German *kreischen*, meaning "to shout, to call out." Some scholars consider the word *Hollekreisch* to be a corruption of the French *haut au crèche*, meaning "raise the crib."

The *Hollekreisch* ceremony consisted of lifting the baby (or the cradle with the baby in it) three times; each time the name of the baby was shouted out in unison by all present. The format of the ceremony varied from community to community. In some locales, children performed the honors.

In some communities, several men raise the four legs of the crib and shout out, "Holeh [the name of the witch], Holeh, Holeh, what shall the name of the child be?" Then, someone responds by announcing the name of the child. As the announcement is made, the participants shouted, "Holeh," making it impossible for the witch to hear the name of the baby, and thus unable to put a curse on the child.

In another version of the *Hollekreisch* ceremony, the father of the baby would read to the assembled children verses from each of the first five books of the Bible: Genesis 1:1 and 2:1, Exodus 1:1, Leviticus 1:1, Numbers 1:1, Deuteronomy 1:1 and 34:12 (the last verse of the Torah). The children would repeat each verse word for word, then the cradle with the child in it is raised three times, with the father asking each time, "What shall we name the baby?" In unison, the children would call out the secular name of the baby.

Holocaust

The term "Holocaust," literally "a whole burnt offering," refers to the systematic annihilation of European civilians—including more than 6,000,000 Jews—by the Nazis before and during World War II. It had its inception on January 20, 1933, when the aging president of the German Republic, Paul von Hindenburg, appointed the leader of the National Socialist (Nazi) German Workers Party, Adolf Hitler, to be chancellor of the Reich. And it ended twelve years later, on May 8, 1945, with the surrender of the Nazis to the Allied Powers and the release of thousands of Jews incarcerated in Auschwitz and other concentration camps in Poland, Germany, and adjacent countries which had been overrun by Hitler's forces.

In 1925, Hitler published his notorious *Mein Kampf*, in which he spelled out his philosophy and his determination to cleanse Germany of Jews and establish racial purity as the criterion for German citizenship. This excluded all Jews who were considered non-Aryans and hence members of an inferior race. He characterized Jews as a subhuman, parasitical people—the source of all the ills that had befallen the German people.

To further demean the Jews of Germany, in 1933, when Hitler became chancellor, a law was enacted which declared that any person with one Jewish parent or grandparent was to be considered a Jew. Two years later, in 1935, after the passage of the Nuremberg Laws, the definition of who is a Jew was amplified to distinguish between full Jews and *Mischlings*. A person who had at least three Jewish grandparents was considered a Jew. Anyone with one full Jewish parent and one Aryan (non-Jewish) parent was a *Mischling* and was treated as a full Jew. Hitler's goal was to make Germany free of all Jews (*Judenrein*).

Little by little Jews were denied all civil rights. They were forced to sell their businesses at prices dictated by the government, public schools were closed to Jewish children and, in accordance with a decree dated October 5, 1938, the letter J (for Jude) was stamped on their passports. Earlier that year, on June 15, one-thousand five-hundred Jews were deported off to concentration camps.

Night of Broken Glass

A major event that accelerated drastic action against Jews occurred on November 7, 1938, when a defiant seventeen-year-old Polish Jew, Herschel Grynszpan, entered the German embassy in Paris and shot and killed the German Third Secretary. This gave Hitler the perfect pretext to encourage the populace of Germany to turn on the Jews with greater force than ever. Party members were encouraged to smash the windows of Jewish shops and loot them. And teams of police were sent out to burn down all synagogues. All this happened on the night of November 9–10, 1938. Five hundred synagogues were burned down, ninety-one Jews were killed. And because the streets of Germany were strewn with glass, that night became known as the Night of Broken Glass, or *Kristallnacht* in German. Thirty thousand Jews were taken captive that night and sent to concentration camps, and by the time the Nazi scourge ended in May 1945 millions of Jews had been deported to dozens of concentration and death camps primarily in Poland, where six million were murdered either by gassing, shooting, overwork, or starvation.

The first gas chamber was set up in Brandenburg toward the end of 1939, where Zyklon-B was experimented with as were other various gasses including carbon monoxide. Other mass gas chambers were established and Jews were sent into sealed "showers," where they were gassed. Six of the better-known well-equipped extermination camps that were deliberately designed to carry out mass slaughter by gassing were situated at Chelmo and Auschwitz, Polish areas that had been incorporated into the Reich, and at Treblinka, Sobibor, Majdanek, and Belzec in Poland proper.

At these camps Jews were divided into two groups. The elderly, the infirm, and those judged to be unable to do physical labor were sent to the gas chambers. The others were sent to the labor section of the camp where their heads were shaved and identification numbers tattooed on their arms.

Hitler, well on his way to accomplishing his dream of a Final Solution to the Jewish problem, finally miscalculated by invading Russia in June 1941 where he suffered a miserable defeat. And when the Allies landed on Normandy on June 6, 1944, in France and began to take back land that had been in Hitler's hands, his fate was doomed. On April 30, 1945, in his bunker in the Reich Chancellery, he committed suicide and the war in Europe was over.

In total, there were 1,634 concentration camps plus 900 labor camps in which Jews and other prisoners languished, were tortured, and perished. But Hitler's dream of a Final Solution to the Jewish problem never materialized.

The Hebrew term for Holocaust is *Shoah*, meaning "catastrophe." It is the title used by Claude Lanzmann for his sweeping 1985 documentary portraying the history of the incarceration and murder of the Jews during World War II.

Fearing that the Holocaust might be forgotten by future generations, especially since a number of university-connected scholars were denying that it ever took place in the manner being publicized, museums and memorials sprung up in all parts of the world to remind mankind that the Holocaust actually occurred. Today, almost every major city has at least one memorial commemorating some facet of the tragedy, and the largest such memorial in the United States is the Holocaust Memorial Museum in Washington, D.C., which opened in 1993. The largest such memorial in the world is Israel's Yad Vashem.

Jews throughout the world observe the twenty-seventh day of the Hebrew month Nissan as Holocaust Remembrance Day (*Yom Ha-Sho'ah* in Hebrew). On this day, which falls in April or May, special ceremonies are held at the Yad Vashem memorial in Jerusalem, as well as in many synagogues and places of memorial throughout the world.

In Israel, on the morning of Holocaust Remembrance Day, sirens are sounded and all pedestrian and vehicular traffic comes to a halt. People exit their cars and stand in silence. Radio and television broadcasts are suspended. No human sound is heard throughout the country for two full minutes. All places of entertainment are closed for the day.

Other Holocaust Victims

In addition to the 6,000,000 Jews murdered during the Holocaust, it is estimated that about 1,000,000 gypsies suffered the same fate. Gypsies are so-called because they originated in Egypt in the thirteenth-century and made their way via India to southeastern Europe. They were non-Aryan craftsmen always in search of work.

A second group that suffered—although comparatively less—were the pacifist Jehovah's Witnesses. About 25,000 lived in Germany during the Nazi era. They refused to take up arms or make the Nazi salute and proclaim *Sieg Heil*. They claimed allegiance only to the Kingdom of God. About 6,000 of them were incarcerated in concentration camps, of whom approximately 2,000 were murdered. The handicapped were also among those targeted for annihilation by the Nazis.

Deniers of the Holocaust

Authors like Austin J. App wrote a book in 1974 entitled *A Straight Look at the Third Reich* accused the Jews of directing allied policy and of resorting to a path "open to hypocrites and liars, namely to fabricate a mass atrocity. This they did with the legend of the six million Jews gassed.... This is a fabrication and swindle."

This attitude caused Elie Wiesel to remark: "I have an occasional nightmare. I wake up shivering thinking that when we die, no one will be able to persuade people that the Holocaust occurred." That such a situation is within the realm of possibility was confirmed in 1997 when a survey of 8,000 twelve- to eighteen-year-old students found that some 30 percent of Swedish secondary students stated that they had substantial doubts as to whether the Holocaust occurred (reported in *Dateline: World Jewry*, July 1987).

Holocaust Denier David Irving

In the year 2000, British Holocaust revisionist author David Irving brought a libel suit against American professor Deborah Lipstadt. He accused her of falsely accusing him in her writings of being an anti-Semite and a Holocaust denier. According to English law, the burden of proof lay upon Lipstadt, and she successfully defended herself. It was later revealed that FBI director J. Edgar Hoover had been warned as far back as 1969 that Irving had plans to tamper with U.S. archive transcripts of the Nuremberg war crimes trial held in Germany at the end of World War II.

Confirmers of the Holocaust

As far back as 1952, Menachem Begin was so moved by the tragic events of the Nazi era that he asked his followers in Israel to take an oath which he modeled after the famous verse in Psalm 137 which began, "If I forget thee, O Jerusalem, let my right hand wither, may my tongue stick to my palate if I cease to think of you, if I do not keep the extermination of the Jews in memory even at my happiest hour."

After laying a wreath at Auschwitz, where he said "that was one of the few times I cried," and after viewing Steven Spielberg's *Schindler's List*, the award-winning film that brought attention to the enormity of the Holocaust tragedy, Christian evangelist Billy Graham said: "I think *Schindler's List* has helped remind people [about the Holocaust] and that it could happen again. I think to keep it alive is wonderful, and television is the main medium to do that."

The New York Times (November 15, 1986) summed up the attitude of confirmers of the Holocaust when it commented: "The Holocaust has become a metaphor for our century. There cannot be an end to speaking and writing about it."

In 1994, Steven Spielberg established the Survivors of the Shoah Visual History Foundation, the purpose of which is to focus "on teaching my children and your children and their children's children, hopefully, how to conduct themselves in this world that is becoming increasingly less tolerant." Spielberg set out to videotape and share the testimonies of some 50,000 survivors. By the year 2000, he had recorded 51,182 testimonies in thirty languages and fifty-seven countries.

Holocaust Remembrance Day

In an enactment of the Israeli Knesset on April 25, 1951, the twenty-seventh day of the Hebrew month Nissan was designated as "Holocaust and Ghetto Uprising Remembrance Day," *Yom Ha-Sho'ah* in Hebrew. In countries of the Diaspora, Holocaust Remembrance Day is usually celebrated on April 19, the day when the Warsaw Ghetto uprising commenced in 1943.

In Israel, Yom Ha-Sho'ah is marked by wreath-laying ceremonies at Jerusalem's Yad Vashem memorial to the victims of the Nazis. All places of entertainment are closed, and at one point during the day two minutes of silence are observed, during which all traffic stops and people stand at attention. In the Diaspora, commemorative services are held in synagogues. At Reform services a special reading is done from II Samuel 1:17–22, in which King David laments the death of King Saul and of David's friend and brother-in-law, Jonathan. The eulogy includes the stirring words, "Your glory, O Israel, lies slain on your heights," a reflection of the sense of grief felt by all of Jewry over the loss of six million Holocaust victims.

Feeling that it is inappropriate to add holidays or fast days to the Jewish calendar, the Chief Rabbinate in Israel ruled that *Kaddish* should not be recited on Yom Ha-Sho'ah. Instead, they set aside the regular fast day of the tenth of Tevet (December/January), when all Jews mourn the loss of the First Temple in 586 B.C.E. at the hands of Nebukhadnezzar of Babylonia, as the day on which all Jews should say *Kaddish* for victims of the Holocaust who left behind no family member to memorialize them.

In Great Britain, Prime Minister Tony Blair personally endorsed a plan to make January 27—the anniversary of the liberation of the Auschwitz concentration camp—a national Holocaust Remembrance Day. The first observance of the day was held on January 27, 2001.

Holy Articles

The Talmud (*Megillah* 26b) makes a distinction between two types of holy article: *tashmishei kedushah*, meaning "accessories of holiness," and *tashmishei mitzvah*, "accessories of religious observance."

The first type includes articles that have some tactical association with a Torah scroll. Among these are the containers in which scrolls are kept or transported; the arks in which they are housed; the ark curtain (which was sometimes used to cover the table upon which the Torah is read), and the Torah mantle. Also included in this category are *mezuzot* and *tefillin* (which contain parchment upon which are inscribed selections from the Torah), *tefillin* straps, and the bags in which *tefillin* are kept. These accessories of holiness may not be discarded indiscriminately when no longer usable; they must be buried in a cemetery.

The second category of holy articles, the accessories of religious observance, include a *sukkah*, *lulav*, *shofar*, and fringes (*tzitziot*) of a garment. These may be discarded when their usefulness has been exhausted.

See Holiness.

Holy of Holies

In the Temple built in Jerusalem by King Solomon, a room was designated as the Holy of Holies (*Kodesh Ha-Kodoshim* in Hebrew), which the Talmud (*Ketubbot* 106a) refers to as *Devir*. This room housed the Holy Ark, in which was stored the Ten Commandments that Moses had brought down from Mount Sinai and, according to some authorities (*Berakhot* 8b; *Bava*

Batra 14b), also the broken pieces of the first set of Ten Commandments, which Moses smashed when he saw the Golden Calf.

Only the High Priest was permitted to enter the Holy of Holies, and even he only once a year, on Yom Kippur. God's presence (*Shekhinah*) was said to reside in this room, and it was dangerous for anyone to be there, for as the Bible says (Exodus 33:20), "No person can look upon Me and live." And so when the High Priest emerged unscathed from the Holy of Holies on Yom Kippur afternoon, safe, great merriment ensued. The revelry is recounted in the *Musaf* (afternoon) service of Yom Kippur.

See Ark; High Priesthood.

Holy Writings

Known in Hebrew as *Ketuvim* or *Kitvei Ha-Kodesh*, the Holy Writings is the third section of the Bible (*Tanakh*), the first two being the Torah and the Prophets.

See Bible.

Homosexuality

The Bible (Leviticus 18:22) considers male homosexuality to be an unnatural and depraved activity. Its condemnation is explicit: "Thou shalt not lie [cohabit] with a male as one lies with a woman; it is an abomination." Leviticus 20:13 repeats this characterization, adding, "The two of them shall be put to death." Female homosexuality, or lesbianism, is not specifically mentioned in the Bible.

The consequences of homosexuality are vividly portrayed throughout the Bible. In Genesis (19:5), a group of the inhabitants of Sodom demanded that Lot, Abraham's nephew, send out of his house male visitors so that they, the Sodomites, could cohabit with them. Lot refused to comply. Because of the apparent prevalence of homosexuality among the Sodomites, Jewish tradition says, Sodom was eventually destroyed. The word "sodomy" specifically refers to anal intercourse between two males, but it is commonly used in reference to any sexual act that is considered abnormal.

In the Book of Judges (19:22), members of the tribe of Benjamin from Gibeah demanded that a visitor who was being housed for the night be sent out of the house "that we may know [cohabit with] him." Gibeah, like Sodom, was destroyed for its homosexual practices.

Historical Perspective

Homosexuality was common among the Canaanites and among the early Egyptians. It was part of heathen worship in biblical times and was widely accepted as the norm among the Greeks. In the Athens of Pericles and Plato, love affairs between boys and men were common. In fact, the classical Greek system of education was built on an erotic association between teacher and pupil: the student was to "inspire" the teacher with his good looks, and the teacher in turn was to prove himself a worthy role model.

Even in the first three centuries B.C.E., when Greek influence was strongest, Jews never accepted homosexuality as a way of life. The Talmud (*Kiddushin* 82a) notes that Jews did not engage in such activity, but it was prevalent among non-Jews even those who were considered upstanding citizens, observers of the Seven Noahide Laws. This is evident from the comment of the third/fourth century C.E. Palestinian scholar Ulla, who noted (*Chullin* 92 a, b) that the Noahide Laws consist of thirty individual commandments, one of which mandates that a marriage contract (*ketubbah*) not be issued to males if they are suspected of indecent practices and sodomy.

Although not all the Rabbis of the Talmud agreed with the ruling, Rabbi Judah the Prince, editor of the Mishnah, went so far as to say, "An unmarried man may not herd cattle, nor may two unmarried men sleep together." Such were the lengths to which some of the Sages would go in order to keep temptation at a distance.

Centuries later, Moses Maimonides (1135–1204) and other codifiers of Jewish law observed (*Mishneh Torah*, Issurei Biah 22:2) that "Jews are not suspected of practicing homosexuality." Throughout the Middle Ages, until recent times, Jewish sources have focused little attention on the issue of homosexuality, although such activity was commonplace among the general population. Christian courts, throughout the Middle Ages, were known to execute some persons for sodomy.

Modern Attitudes

The twentieth century saw a gradual change in attitudes toward homosexuality. In a 1935 letter to the worried mother of a homosexual, Sigmund Freud wrote, "Homosexuality is assuredly no advantage, but it is nothing to be ashamed of, no vice, no degradation." By 1974 the American Psychiatric Association no longer considered homosexuality a mental illness.

As homosexuals began to be treated more equally by society at large, Jewish homosexuals began to demand that the Jewish community no longer regard them as sinners. Synagogues were established by and for homosexuals; some rabbis began to conduct marriages for homosexuals; and some rabbis openly announced their own homosexuality. The argument offered in defense of full recognition of the homosexual lifestyle is that although procreation is the primary purpose of Jewish marriage, it is not the sole purpose. Surely, it

is argued, homosexuals are made in God's image as everyone else, and they should therefore not be denied the right to a full free life.

Halakhists (masters of Jewish law) have not had sufficient time to assess the demands of the Jewish homosexual. However, Rabbi Norman Lamm, former president of Yeshiva University (Orthodox), advanced a response to the demands of the homosexual community in which he maintained that homosexuality is an abominable act, exactly as the Bible asserts. He argued that if Jews were to condone the practice of homosexuality, they would also have to condone other acts heretofore held immoral by Jewish tradition.

Most Conservative and Reform rabbis concur. Yet, while homosexuals are considered to be in violation of Jewish law, no group has argued in favor of banning them or expelling them from the Jewish community. There has been strong opposition to the establishment of special gay synagogues, but there has been little, if any, opposition to homosexuals freely joining established synagogues.

In 1973, Reform Judaism's leading authority on Jewish law, Rabbi Solomon Freehof, wrote a responsum in which he said that "homosexuality is deemed in Jewish law to be a sin . . . [but] it would be in direct contravention of Jewish law to keep sinners out of the congregation." In 1977, the Union of American Hebrew Congregations (Reform) voted to admit homosexuals to congregational membership.

A 1992 ruling of the Committee on Jewish Law and Standards of the Rabbinical Assembly (Conservative) states: "The [local] rabbi, in consultation with the congregation's leaders, will be entrusted to formulate policies regarding the eligibility of homosexuals for honors within worship and for lay leadership positions."

The Reconstructionist Rabbinical Association, at its 1992 convention approved commitment ceremonies for homosexual couples, its guidelines affirming "a full place for gay and lesbian members in the leadership of our movement organizations." In 1996 the Reconstructionist movement issued a daily prayerbook entitled *Kol Ha-Neshamah* in which it introduced a special reading on the loss of a gay or lesbian lover.

See Lesbianism; Noahide Laws; Sex and Sexuality.

Honesty

In the Hebrew language, there is no precise word for honesty, the closest being *emet*, meaning "truth." The Book of Proverbs (12:19) characterizes truthfulness as follows: "Truthful speech abides forever, a lying tongue endures but for a moment."

In the Jewish tradition, honesty implies not only telling the truth, but also acting upon it. This principle condemns the employer who fails to pay the wages due an employee as well as the employee who fails to give the employer a full day's work.

The Midrash (*Exodus Rabbah* 13:1) tells about the second-century talmudic scholar Abba Joseph, who was employed as a housebuilder. While standing upon a scaffold, someone asked him to come down to answer a question of Jewish law. "I cannot come down," he replied, "because I am hired by the day, to do a day's work."

The Rabbis of the Talmud (*Bava Metzia* 58b) elaborated further on this theme. They said that a person should not go into a store and pretend to be interested in purchasing an article, when he knows that he lacks the funds to pay for it. The Rabbis believed that this constitutes not only deceit but also theft of the proprietor's time.

The Rabbis also considered it dishonest to work one's own field at night and hire oneself out to work on someone else's field during the day. Under these circumstances, the worker would not be rested enough to give a full, honest day's work.

White Lies

The question of whether one must always tell the absolute truth, or whether telling a "white lie" is permissible under certain circumstances, was considered by the Rabbis of the Talmud. The tractate *Yevamot* (65b) states that it is quite proper to tell a lie so long as it causes no harm to another individual and serves to promote peace and harmony. As an example, the Rabbis bring the case of Joseph's brothers, who said to him (Genesis 50:16): "Your father gave orders before his death, saying, 'Forgive the dreadful deed of your brothers [who sold you into slavery] and their sin, for they have done you evil.'" The fact is that Jacob never made such a statement, but the Rabbis forgave the brothers and considered the statement of the brothers to be no more that a white lie, which served the good purpose of maintaining harmony in the family.

The Rabbis offer a second example of a white lie being told in which God Himself is the perpetrator. In the Book of Genesis (18:12), after Sarah is told by an angel that she and Abraham would have a child, she laughs and says, "How can we have a child when my husband is so old?"

Later, God says to Abraham: "Why did Sarah laugh and say 'Shall I really bear a child, though *I* am aged?'" The Rabbis point out the discrepancy. Sarah never said *she* was old. She said *Abraham* was old. But God preferred to alter the truth and tell a white lie so as not to offend Abraham and thus create disharmony between the couple.

The classic example of a white lie is found in the tractate *Yevamot* (65b) where the students of Hillel and Shammai were discussing which language should be used in singing the praises of a bride. Beth Shammai said: "The bride as she is," meaning that her qualities should be spelled out truthfully, even if they are not admirable. Beth Hillel said: "The bride, beautiful and graceful," meaning that one should tell a white lie and say nice things so as not to hurt the feelings of a bride who may, in fact, be ugly and ungraceful.

Hosafot

Singular, *hosafah*. A Hebrew term literally meaning "additions." On the Sabbath and holidays, before the *maftir* (the final honoree) is called to the Torah, the last verses of the final *aliyah* (*shevi'i* on Sabbath, *chamishi* on holidays) may be repeated one or more times in order to accommodate additional congregants who are deserving of being honored on that day. At least three verses are read for each of these extra *aliyot*.

Hoshanah Rabbah

A Hebrew term literally meaning "the great hosanna." Hoshanah Rabbah is the seventh and last day of the Sukkot holiday and is observed as a half-holiday in the same manner as the Intermediate Days of Sukkot.

Hoshanah Rabbah was endowed with special sanctity by the last of the Prophets: Chaggai, Zekhariah, and Malakhi. Occurring at the beginning of the rainy season, it became known as a Day of Judgment for Rain. (A special service for rain became part of the liturgy on Shemini Atzeret, the day following Hoshanah Rabbah.)

In Temple times, in addition to the two willows that were part of the *lulav* bouquet, it was customary to add to the bouquet an extra willow that was held high as it was carried in the procession that made its way around the altar seven times. Verses beginning with *hosha na*, "Please save us," were chanted, and the ceremony thus became known as *hoshanot*. In post-Temple days, the ceremony became part of the synagogue ritual, and at a later date it was enhanced: instead of using a single willow branch, a bunch of willows (five or six) were tied together.

On Hoshanah Rabbah, it became customary to beat the bunch of willows on the floor or against the synagogue seats. This custom grew out of the association of the final day of Sukkot with the final day of the High Holidays. Yom Kippur was regarded as the day that concluded the Season of Divine Judgment, and Hoshanah Rabbah was considered the day that brought to a close the long holiday period that began with Rosh Hashanah. Yom Kippur was the day on which the Heavenly Court decided the fate of man, and Hoshanah Rabbah represented one final opportunity for the evil decree to be reversed. Because Hoshanah Rabbah was also considered the Day of Judgment for Rain, the practice of self-flagellation conducted on Yom Kippur was transferred to Hoshanah Rabbah and was marked by the beating of willows. (*See* Malkot.)

On Hoshanah Rabbah, it is traditional to eat *kreplach*, dumplings filled with "beaten" (chopped) ingredients, usually onion and meat. Another food custom associated with Hoshanah Rabbah involves the preparation of a special *challah*. Since it was believed that the judgment of God that was passed on Yom Kippur must be sealed by a handwritten verdict, and since the verdict was sealed on Hoshanah Rabbah, a hand made of dough is placed on the *challah* before it is baked. The hand represents the acceptance of the *kvitl* (the receipt or document) on which the verdict is recorded. The tradition of preparing this type of *challah* was probably developed in Volhynia, Ukraine.

See Hakafot; Sukkot.

Hoshanot

The Hebrew term for the bunch of willows beaten on the floor or on the seats of the synagogue on Hoshanah Rabbah, the last day of Sukkot. A prayer beginning with the refrain *Hosha na* ("Please save us") is recited.

See Hoshanah Rabbah.

Hospitality

In the Talmud (*Shabbat* 127a), Rabbi Judah says in the name of Rav, "Giving a kindly reception to strangers is even more meritorious than receiving God's presence." The first record of such meritorious conduct is described in the Book of Genesis (18:1ff.), where Abraham welcomes three strangers (angels in the guise of men) who came to visit as he was recovering from his circumcision.

Showing hospitality toward strangers, known in Hebrew by the term *hakhnasat orchim* ("welcoming strangers"), took on great importance during the Middle Ages, when many Jews traveled about to earn a living and found themselves far from home on a Sabbath or holiday. Jewish communities considered it their responsibility to care for these "guests" during their stay in town. Thus they provided food as well as lodging for the out-of-towners.

The *Kiddush* recited in the synagogue on Friday nights at the conclusion of the *Ma'ariv* (evening) service was instituted for the sake of those who were away from home and were being lodged in the synagogue.

Host-Mothers

When a woman is known to be unable to carry a fetus to term (as when she has a tendency to abort), arrangements are sometimes made to have the fertilized egg of the woman implanted in the uterus of a second woman, called the host-mother. Sometimes the fertilized egg is extracted from the womb of the first woman and implanted in the second; sometimes the egg is fertilized in a test tube or dish outside of the womb. For a fee, the host-mother carries the fetus to term. Upon giving birth, the child is "returned" to the natural mother, the supplier of the ovum.

Rabbinic authorities, including the late Chief Rabbi Immanuel Jakobovits (1921–1999) of England, have condemned this practice of using a host-mother as an incubator as being morally reprehensible. However, since this is sometimes the only way in which a married couple can have a child, the practice is generally approved of as long as the sperm that fertilizes the egg is that of the husband and not a stranger.

Religion of Offspring

According to Jewish law, a child is Jewish if his or her mother is Jewish. However, the religion of a child carried to term by a host-mother is in question when a fertilized ovum of a Jewish woman is implanted in the womb of a host-mother who is not Jewish. Who is the real mother of the child? Is it the Jewish woman who supplied the fertilized egg, or is it the non-Jewish host-mother who nurtured the child in her womb and carried it to term?

Most authorities are of the opinion that it is the supplier of the ovum who is the real mother. However, the question is so new and so complex that very few rabbinic authorities have ventured definitive opinions.

See Artificial Insemination.

Humility

Jewish history prides itself on the fact that its first great leader, Moses, was a very humble man. The Hebrew term used in the Bible (Numbers 12:3) is *anav*, meaning "modest."

Micah, one of the great prophets of Israel, who lived in the eighth century B.C.E., was one of the first to hold up humility as an ideal. He asked rhetorically (Micah 6:7–8): "What does the Lord require of thee?" And his answer was: "Only to do justice, to love kindness, and to walk humbly with thy God."

The Rabbis of the Talmud (*Sotah* 5a) emphasized the value of leading a humble life: "Any person who is haughty and arrogant, God says of him, 'he and I cannot live together in this world.'" And the fourth-century scholar Rava, recognizing how easily wise people of great learning often tend to become arrogant, said (*Kallah Rabbati* 3:6): "Humility is a hedge to wisdom." With a small amount of humility, one can guard against having wisdom go to one's head.

The Rabbis (*Sotah* 5a) urged us to derive a lesson from the conduct of God, who ignored all the tall and mighty mountains and caused His presence to rest on Mount Sinai, and who ignored all the tall trees and settled His presence on a lowly, humble bush.

See Modesty.

Hunting

Jewish law concedes that while most people find it necessary to include meat in their diet, there is no justification for taking the life of an animal for any other purpose. To kill an animal solely for sport or to use its fur or skin is not condoned in Jewish law.

So distasteful is the maltreatment of animals that while the *She-heche'yanu* blessing is recited when wearing new apparel for the first time, it need not be said when wearing apparel made from animal hide. Clearly, the taking of animal life is not to be celebrated.

Hunting for Sport

Rabbi Ezekiel Landau of Prague (1713–1793) was once asked whether it is permissible to hunt animals for sport. Is hunting a violation of the law against causing pain to animals (*tza'ar ba'alei cha'yim*)? Landau replied (*Noda Bi-Yehudah* II, Yoreh Dei'ah 10) that technically there is no violation of Jewish law when one hunts, since man is permitted to slay animals for his own essential needs. However, he does condemn hunting for sport on moral and ethical grounds, emphasizing that killing an animal not only runs counter to the whole of Jewish tradition, but that when one enters the woods to hunt, he places his own life in jeopardy.

Heinrich Heine (1799–1856), the German-Jewish poet who was baptized in 1825 but remained close to the Jewish community, wrote the following about the Jewish attitude toward hunting: "My ancestors did not belong to the hunters so much as to the hunted, and the idea of attacking the descendants of those [animals] who were our comrades in suffering goes against my grain."

See She-heche'yanu.

Hygiene

The popular aphorism "Cleanliness is next to godliness" is an outgrowth of a thought expressed by Francis Bacon (1561–1626) in his *Advancement of Learning* (1605): "Cleanliness of body was ever deemed to proceed from a due reverence to God."

Many centuries earlier, the talmudic scholar Pinchas (Phineas) ben Yair commented on the verse in Deuteronomy (23:10), "You shall keep from you every evil thing," as meaning that one should be fastidious about studying and practicing the laws of the Torah, because "fastidiousness leads to cleanliness, and cleanliness leads to abstinence, and abstinence leads to purity, and purity leads to holiness, and holiness leads to humility, and humility leads to fear of sin, and fear of sin leads to piety, and piety leads to godliness . . ." (*Avodah Zarah* 20b).

In the tractate *Shabbat* (50b), the Rabbis taught that one honored God by the daily washing of hands, feet, and face, and that if a scholar (who represents the model of perfection and a high standard of cleanliness) dresses with a soiled garment, he is worthy of death (ibid. 114a). The Mishnah (*Megillah* 4:6–7) forbids anyone with soiled garments from reading the Torah before a congregation, and a *Kohen* from raising his hands to pronounce the *Priestly Benediction*.

Joseph Caro's sixteenth-century *Code of Jewish Law* (*Shulchan Arukh*, Orach Cha'yim 4:18 and 158–165) notes those occasions when hands should be washed. Included are the following: after one urinates or defecates; upon arising each morning; before eating a meal; after touching any part of the body that is usually covered; after removing one's shoes, after visiting a cemetery; after marital relations. Maimonides considered these regulations to serve as reminders to Jews that cleanliness is next to godliness and that displaying a clean outer appearance reflects inner purity. Many scholars, however, relegate such practices as washing hands after visiting a cemetery as having roots in superstitious belief.

Ritual cleanliness is a concept closely related to personal cleanliness, but is actually in a category of its own.

See Mikveh; Purity and Impurity; Tohorat Ha-Mishpachah.

Ibbur

A concept introduced by the disciples of the thirteenth-century kabbalist Isaac the Blind (c. 1160–1235), son of the illustrious French authority Abraham ben David of Posquières. He and other kabbalists spoke of "the secret *ibbur*," meaning "impregnation." This referred to a special gift possessed by "holy men," or *rebbes*, who were able to transfer a portion of their noble character and pure souls to another worthy individual who was in need of support to overcome and correct a moral deficiency that might lead him to sin.

See Gilgul.

Idolatry

In the ancient world, Judaism was the only religion to forbid idolatry, known in Hebrew as *avodah zarah* ["the worship of strange gods"]. The second and third commandments of the Decalogue (Exodus 20:4-5) warn unequivocally: "You shall not make for yourself a sculpture image or any likeness of what is in the heavens above and the earth below...You shall not bow down to them or serve them..." Paramount in Judaism is the worship of the One God whose identity is proclaimed each day in recitation of the *Shema*: "Hear O Israel, the Lord is our God, the Lord is One."

Judaism categorizes idolatry, along with adultery and murder, as one of the three cardinal sins of Judaism. In fact, the Talmud (*Pesachim* 25a) states that Jews are obligated to sacrifice their lives rather than engage in the worship of false gods. So anathema is the practice of idolatry to the Jewish way of life that the entire seventy-five pages of the talmudic tractate *Avodah Zarah* are devoted to the subject, with special emphasis on the measures to be taken to limit social interaction between Jews and the members of poly-theistic nations, in the hope of reducing the likelihood of intermarriage.

See Intermarriage; Moneylending; Wine.

Immersion

See Mikveh; Tevilah.

Incest

Incest is generally defined as sexual intercourse between persons so closely related that they are legally forbidden to marry. The Hebrew term for incest is *gilui ara'yot*, meaning "uncovering nakedness." *Ara'yot* is akin to the Hebrew *ervah*, meaning "nakedness" (Exodus 28:42).

Biblical Prohibition

The laws pertaining to incest are set forth in Leviticus 18 and repeated in Leviticus 20. The seventeen sexual liaisons condemned as incest in the Bible reflect the activity of a male only. A male person is forbidden to marry or have sex with his

1. mother
2. father's wife (stepmother)
3. sister
4. half-sister, on father or mother's side
5. daughter
6. son's daughter
7. daughter's daughter
8. father's sister
9. mother's sister
10. father's brother's wife
11. son's wife
12. brother's wife, except in the case of levirate marriage
13. wife's mother
14. wife's daughter
15. wife's son's daughter

16. wife's daughter's daughter

17. wife's sister

The only rationale offered for these prohibitions is that they were practiced by idolatrous cultures and are therefore forbidden to the Children of Israel. Leviticus (18:3) explains: "You shall not follow the practices of the land of Egypt, where you lived, nor of the land of Canaan, to which I am taking you."

Talmudic View

The Rabbis of the Talmud extended the biblical prohibitions to include "secondary" (*shniyot*) offenders. These include marriage or sex with a

1. paternal or maternal grandmother

2. father's or mother's stepmother

3. daughter of a son's daughter and daughter of a son's son

4. daughter of a daughter's daughter and daughter of a daughter's son

5. grandfather's maternal or paternal sister

6. sister of a mother's mother

7. wife of a father's brother from one mother, the wife of a mother's brother whether paternal of maternal, and the wife of a grandfather's brother from one father

8. son's daughter-in-law and a daughter's daughter-in-law

9. wife's paternal or maternal grandmother

10. daughter of a wife's grandson (son's son)

11. daughter of a wife's daughter's daughter

While unaware of the fact that chromosomes carry genes that determine and transmit hereditary characteristics, the Rabbis of the Talmud observed that the offspring of close relatives were more likely to be born with deformities. This is evident from the talmudic law prohibiting a woman from marrying into a family of lepers or epileptics. Rabbi J. David Bleich, a specialist in bioethics and a Talmud professor at Yeshiva University, believes that this ruling "is one of the oldest recorded pieces of genetic legislation."

The Rabbis of the Talmud and later rabbinic authorities did not agree as to which marriages should be avoided. While the Bible does not prohibit the marriage of an uncle to his niece, and while, on the other hand, the Talmud (*Sanhedrin* 76b) actually encourages it, the medieval Ukrainian scholar and kabbalist Judah the Pious (Yehudah Hechasid [1638–1700]) firmly opposed it, maintaining that the offspring of such marriages may suffer blindness. This ruling was accepted by later legal scholars.

See Mamzer; Levirate Marriage; Marriages, Prohibited.

Ingathering of Exiles

See Aliyah to Israel; Kibbutz Galu'yot.

Interest

See Moneylending.

Intermarriage

The prohibition of marriages between Jews and non-Jews is biblical in origin. Deuteronomy (7:3) sets forth the law explicitly: "You shall not intermarry with them; do not give your daughters to their sons or take their daughters for your sons." The reason: so that the Israelites would not be influenced to worship the gods of the seven idolatrous nations whose lands they were about to invade and conquer (Deuteronomy 7:1). The law against intermarriage was instituted to prevent the weakening of the newly developed concept of monotheism introduced by Moses. In talmudic literature (*Sanhedrin* 82a), the prohibition was reinforced by banning social activity between Jews and non-Jews, lest such activity lead to intermarriage. Rabbi Chiya ben Avuya said: "He who is intimate with a heathen woman is as though he had entered into a marriage relationship with an idol."

Despite the fact that in the post-talmudic era (from the early Middle Ages onward) Christians and Muslims were no longer considered idolators (*Mishneh Torah*, Hilkhot Teshuvah 3:5; *Shulchan Arukh*, Yoreh Dei'ah 148:12), laws prohibiting intermarriage between Jew and non-Jew continued in force so as to preserve the integrity and unity of the Jewish community.

Religious Status

In Jewish law (*Sanhedrin* 44a) one who intermarries does not lose his status as a Jew. However, some have maintained that a Jewish man who marries a Gentile woman should not be counted as one of the ten men who constitute a quorum (*minyan*). When a man defies the Torah by intermarrying, it is argued, he should be treated as a Jew who has been excommunicated. In earlier centuries excommunication (*cheirem*) was an effective instrument used by the Jewish community to maintain control over the religious conduct of its members. Often, an excommunicated person was not counted as part of a *minyan* so long as the ban placed upon him remained in effect. Today, the prevailing view is more liberal. Even ultra-Orthodox leaders contend that an intermarried Jew may be counted as part of a *minyan*.

Synagogue Policy

While all Jewish denominations do not allow the non-Jewish spouses of their members to join their congregations, there is generally no particular objection to a non-Jewish spouse attending services or joining in social activities or attending adult classes. Synagogue membership is not granted because, it is argued, if a non-Jew were allowed to become a member, what would prevent the non-Jew from one day holding high office in the synagogue and thus be in a position to set synagogue policy? It is generally felt that a non-Jew who feels close to Jewish life should be willing to convert to Judaism if he or she is eager to participate in setting synagogue policy.

Liberal Reform Attitude

Liberal members of the Reform rabbinate will marry a Jew to a Gentile without demanding that the Gentile first convert to Judaism. The mixed marriage is performed with the hope that the religious ceremony will draw the non-Jew closer to Judaism. Rabbis who follow this practice usually exact a promise from the Gentile partner that the children of the marriage will be raised as Jews. They believe that at some future date—after the non-Jew has become involved in the Jewish community and spent time studying the teachings of Judaism—he or she will request to be admitted as a full-fledged Jew.

The majority of Reform rabbis abide by the 1909 statement (reaffirmed in 1947) of the Central Conference of American Rabbis, which condemns intermarriage as contrary to the traditions and interests of the Jewish religion and hence a practice that should be discouraged by the American rabbinate. The Committee on Jewish Law and Standards of the Rabbinical Assembly (Conservative) does not permit its members to officiate at the marriage of a Jew to a non-Jew, and anyone who does is subject to expulsion.

Burial of Intermarried Couples

Whether the non-Jewish partner of an intermarriage should be permitted to be buried in the same plot as the Jewish spouse has long been debated. Although the Orthodox view, as generally stated, is that a Gentile may not be buried in a Jewish cemetery, exceptions have been made. In an unusual case, the ultra-Orthodox Rabbi Moshe Feinstein ruled (*Igrot Moshe*, Yoreh Dei'ah II:131) that a non-Jewish woman could be buried near her Jewish husband in a Jewish cemetery. The case concerned a woman who had been married to a Jewish man by an Orthodox rabbi. The couple had conducted their lives in keeping with Orthodox teachings. They raised three observant children, two daughters and a son. When the woman died, she was prepared for burial by the Burial Society (*chevrah kaddishah*) in strict Orthodox fashion. But just before the funeral was to take place, a rumor spread that the deceased was not Jewish, that she was the daughter of a non-Jewish woman and that neither mother nor daughter had ever been converted.

The question brought to Rabbi Feinstein was: Should this woman, who had lived as an Orthodox Jew all her life, be allowed burial in a Jewish cemetery? The husband insisted that she be buried in the family plot, next to the grave reserved for him.

Rabbi Feinstein ruled that if two reliable witnesses are able to testify that the mother of the deceased was not Jewish, that neither mother nor daughter ever converted, then the deceased is to be considered non-Jewish. She may, however, be buried in the family plot provided that a space of twelve feet (eight cubits) is left between her grave and the next grave, or if a fence twenty handbreadths high is built around her grave.

The Conservative movement has gone on record as generally opposing the burial of a non-Jew next to his or her Jewish mate. A minority view of its Committee on Jewish Laws and Standards is that if Jews have a family plot and if its members were not forewarned that non-Jewish members of the family may not be buried there, the local rabbi may make an exception. Likewise, he may permit the burial of a non-Jew in the family plot if the non-Jew was close to the Jewish community and sympathetic to its views and practices. However, the majority view is that a symbolic gesture be made to call attention to the situation—namely, to leave one grave unoccupied on either side of the grave of the non-Jew or to surround that grave with shrubbery or a railing.

The Reform attitude is that Gentile relatives may, at the request of the family, be buried in a family plot in a Jewish cemetery.

See Conversion: Rites and Procedures.

Intermediaries

Unlike Christian doctrine, Judaism insists that (with the one exception of Moses who intervened on behalf of the Jewish people when they sinned by worshipping the Golden Calf [Exodus 32:11ff.]), no human can serve as an intermediary between man and God. This cardinal principle of Judaism was first expressed in the Book of Psalms (145:18–19):

> The Lord is nigh unto all them
>   that call upon Him,
> To all who call upon Him in truth
> He will fulfill the desire of them that fear
>   Him
> He will also hear their cry and will save
>   them.

With the emergence of chasidism in the eighteenth century, however, the idea of an individual serving as a conduit between man and God began to be viewed differently. Many chasidic leaders, or *rebbes* ("teachers"), began serving as intermediaries. Disciples of a *rebbe* would make periodic pilgrimages to the leader's home; they would address prayers to him and beg for his intercession.

One of the most respected and adored of the *rebbes* was Dov Ber of Mezirich (1710–1772), also known as the Magid of Mezirich. He was the foremost disciple of the Ba'al Shem Tov, founder of the chasidic movement. So revered was Dov Ber that it was reported that when one of his admirers traveled a long distance to spend time with the Magid and was asked why he could not learn Torah from the *rebbe* of his own village, the admirer replied: "I didn't come here to learn Torah from the *rebbe*. I came to learn how he ties his shoelaces."

To the opponents of the *chasidim*, known as *mitnagdim*, such worship was tantamount to idolatry, and they battled the *chasidim* and their values, which were considered "foreign importations." No individual should be thought of as having semidivine status, they maintained.

Israel: Land and People

Historical Claim

The Jewish claim to the Holy Land dates back to the Bible. In the Book of Genesis (12:1), God commands Abraham: "Go forth from your native land to the land that I will show thee...I will give this land [the land known as Canaan, and later Palestine] to you and your offspring." This covenant between God and the Israelites is repeated several times in the Bible. Even before his death, when Mo-

ses was able to view the Promised Land from afar but not enter it, he reminds the people that the land will belong to them and their children (Deuteronomy 29:9–14).

Jewish ideologists and philosophers have taken God's promise to be immutable: the land is to be Israel's forever. Moses Nachmanides (1194–1270), the foremost scholar of the thirteenth century, expressed this attitude in unmistakable terms. He interpreted the verse in the Book of Numbers (33:53), "And you shall take possession of the land and settle it, for I have assigned the land to you to possess it," to mean that "we may not leave the land in the hands of other nations."

Claim to the Holy Land became ingrained in the Jewish psyche in spite of the fact that for almost two thousand years the land passed through the hands of conqueror after conqueror: Romans, Christian Byzantines, Crusaders, Egyptian Mamelukes, and others. During that period there was a minimal Jewish presence in Palestine, especially in the four holy cities: Jerusalem, Tiberias, Safed, and Hebron. Jews who lived outside the Holy Land nonetheless expressed a yearning to be there in their daily prayers. If this did not materialize in the near future, they affirmed, it most certainly would with the coming of the Messiah.

The Land Is Reclaimed

On May 14, 1948, almost two thousand years after the Second Temple was destroyed and Jewish independence was lost at the hands of the conquering Romans in 70 C.E., a United Nations resolution established Israel as a state. The newly attained independence was not achieved easily. Rather, it was the culmination of intense efforts initiated by Theodor Herzl with the publication of his *The Jewish State* in 1896 and the convening of the First Zionist Conference in Basel, Switzerland, in

1897. After decades of work by Zionists of all religious persuasions, and through the particular dedication of Chaim Weizmann, the Balfour Declaration was issued.

On November 2, 1917, British Foreign Secretary Arthur Balfour (1848–1930), who represented the Zionist Federation, sent a letter to Baron Rothschild, saying that Britain favored "the establishment in Palestine of a national home for the Jewish people" and that Britain would work toward the creation of such a national home. President Woodrow Wilson, of the United States, was a firm supporter of Balfour's position.

In December 1917, a month after the Balfour Declaration had been issued, the British drove the Turks, who then controlled Palestine, out of Jerusalem and took charge of the country. Not until 1920, however, did the League of Nations give Britain the mandate to govern Palestine. Almost thirty years of struggle were to follow before the Zionist dream would be realized.

White Paper

In 1939, Great Britain issued a document declaring that Palestine would become an independent state within ten years. However, this so-called White Paper limited to 75,000 the number of immigrants who would be admitted to Palestine over the next five years. It also restricted Jews from buying land.

Zionists attacked the White Paper, asserting that it betrayed the promise set forth in the Balfour Declaration. In addition, Jews generally condemned the White Paper for not providing refuge for the hundreds of thousands of European Jews whose existence was threatened by the Nazis. The White Paper nonetheless remained British policy, and the matter was referred to the United Nations in 1947.

Partition of Palestine

In 1947, the United Nations drew up borders for a Jewish state and an Arab state in Palestine. The Jews accepted the deal, but the local Palestinian Arabs refused, and on November 29, 1947, with volunteer help from surrounding Arab nations, they began to attack Jewish settlements, blockade roads, and set off explosives in the Jewish sections of major cities.

Jewish defense forces, comprised of fighting members from such groups as the Haganah, Palmach, Irgun, and the Stern Gang (Lechi), fought back. When Israel declared itself a nation on May 14, 1948 (Iyyar 5), the regular armies of five neighboring Arab countries—Egypt, Jordan, Syria, Iraq, and Lebanon—immediately invaded the Jewish state. Although poorly equipped and badly outnumbered, the Jewish forces drove the invaders back on most fronts.

The War of Independence ended in 1949 when Ralph Bunche, the United Nations mediator, arranged an armistice between Israel and the Arabs. Israel lost 6,000 men and women in the war. At the lines where the armies had stopped fighting, the borders were set, leaving the eastern portion of Jerusalem, including the Western Wall of the Temple, in Arab hands. Israel declared the balance of Jerusalem as its capital.

Sinai Campaign

In October 1956, Israel, Britain, and France reached agreement on a coordinated attack against Egypt. It was in this war, known as the Sinai Campaign, that Moshe Dayan made his name. The major Israeli interests were to put a halt to *fedayeen* incursions from Gaza into Israel and to preserve shipping access to Eilat via the Red Sea. The British and French were interested in maintaining freedom of navigation through the Suez Canal in the wake of President Gamal Abdel Nasser's announcement of Egypt's intention to nationalize it. Israel withdrew from both Sinai and Gaza in 1957, with the borders reverting to pre-war status.

The Conflict Continues

Dissatisfied with its subservient status, the Arabs continued to harbor hopes of reclaiming the Land of Israel as theirs exclusively. To achieve this, two major operations were undertaken.

On June 5, 1967, Egypt, Syria, and Jordan took up arms against Israel. However, within a few hours, the Israeli air force had destroyed most Egyptian planes on the ground, before they could take off to engage in battle. Israel's surprise move against Egypt was followed by its ground forces occupying the Sinai and the Gaza Strip. On a second front, Israel flexed its military might by capturing the West Bank and the Old City of Jerusalem, which had been in Jordanian hands since 1948. On a third front, the Israeli army captured the Golan Heights, from which Syrians had often shelled Israeli settlements. The 1967 war lasted from June 5 to June 10 and became universally known as the Six-Day War.

Six years later, the Arab nations tried again to decimate Israel. On Saturday, October 6, 1973, while Israelis were engaged in Yom Kippur prayers, Egypt crossed the Suez Canal and advanced toward Israel while the Syrians attacked from the Golan Heights. Although caught completely off guard, the Israelis, who were outnumbered twelve to one, managed to gain the upper hand in the conflict at a cost of 2,500 dead and many more wounded. The war ended in two weeks with the borders of 1967 still largely intact.

Recolonization of Biblical Lands

In the euphoria following the Six-Day War, Israelis of a nationalist bent clamored for the establishment of a Jewish presence in newly captured lands. Their country's display of military prowess had proven it to be a regional superpower, which translated into political muscle, especially in the United States. The nationalists saw a unique opportunity for Jews to return to the places of the Bible—Hebron, Shilo, Shechem, Beit El—but Israel's leaders were concerned over how the outside world would react. That notwithstanding, the building of Jewish communities in the West Bank—or Judea and Samaria, as Jews refer to it—commenced.

In the late 1960s and early 1970s Jews began to return to Kiryat Arba and Hebron. The settlement movement intensified in 1974, after the Yom Kippur War, with the founding of *Gush Emunim* (Bloc of the Faithful). Gush Emunim drew its spiritual support from Rabbi Zvi Yehuda Kook, head of the Merkaz Harav *yeshivah* in Jerusalem. Rabbi Kook taught that to resettle the ancient Jewish homeland was a religious obligation to be fulfilled at all costs. His followers paid active attention to the verse in Jeremiah (31:16), "Thy sons shall return to their boundaries."

Recolonization of Gush Emunim began on July 25, 1974, at an abandoned railroad station in Sabastia, near the Arab city of Nablus (Shechem). Though expelled by the Israeli army, the settlers returned repeatedly and eventually the Israeli government relented. In time, approximately 150 Jewish communities housing 250,000 Jews sprung up, some housing just a few families, others with tens of thousands of residents. More than any single factor, their presence molds the shape of Middle Eastern politics.

Peace Overtures

After the assassination of Gamal Abdel Nasser (1918–1970), who had led Egypt (known as the United Arab Republic) from 1958 to 1970, Anwar Sadat assumed the presidency. Although as a colonel in the Egyptian army he planned and was responsible for starting the 1973 Yom Kippur War, in 1975 he signed a temporary agreement with Israel in which the two countries pledged to avoid using force to resolve their differences. Then, in November 1977, Sadat surprised the world by announcing that he would go to Jerusalem in search of peace. He was welcomed by Israeli Prime Minister Menachem Begin (1913–1992) and was invited to address the Knesset. In September 1978, U.S. President Jimmy Carter invited Sadat and Begin to meet at Camp David, the presidential retreat in Maryland. This resulted in the signing of a peace treaty between the two adversaries on March 26, 1979. For this achievement, Begin and Sadat were awarded the Nobel Peace Prize.

With the untimely death of Sadat in 1981 at the hands of Egyptian fundamentalist assassins who abhorred his policies, the peace process began to disintegrate. By 1987, impatient Palestinians in Israel began to resort to violence. The actions by Palestinian youths, which involved continual stone-throwing at Israeli soldiers, became known as the *Intifada*, an Arabic term meaning "shaking off." It was a tactic of violent resistance to what Palestinians considered the "violence of occupation." This first *Intifada* spawned the multinational Madrid Conference in 1991. Although it accomplished little, the Madrid Conference marked the first time that a Likud prime minister (Yitzhak Shamir) signaled conciliation to popular Palestinian resistance.

Oslo Peace Accords

In 1993, after several years of Arab violence, a peace agreement was reached between Israel and the Palestine Liberation Organization (PLO). The accord grew out of secret meetings held in Oslo, Norway, between Israel and the PLO. According to its terms, Israel agreed to grant the PLO autonomy over portions of the occupied West Bank (Judea and Samaria) and Gaza—territories captured in the Six-Day War—in exchange for a cessation of the *Intifada* and recognition of Israel's right to exist.

The violence against Israel was called to a halt, and on September 13, 1993, at a White House ceremony presided over by President Bill Clinton of the United States, Israeli Prime Minister Yitzchak Rabin (1922–1995) and PLO Chairman Yasser Arafat (1929–2004) signed a peace accord. Eight months later, on May 4, 1994, in Cairo, Rabin signed an agreement giving the PLO a measure of self-rule in the Gaza Strip and on the West Bank. On October 26, 1994, Israel and Jordan signed a peace treaty at the Aravah Crossing, and shortly thereafter Israel exchanged ambassadors with Jordan.

The Israeli-Palestinian peace process, which was progressing slowly at best, was dealt a serious blow on November 4, 1995. Prime Minister Yitzchak Rabin had just finished delivering a message of peace to an enthusiastic audience at a Tel Aviv rally. As Rabin was leaving the stage, a fanatic Israeli university student, Yigal Amir, shot the prime minister and ended his life. Ironically, the last words uttered by Rabin as he left the stage were, "This is the greatest day of my life."

Prime Minister Rabin was succeeded in office by Labor leader Shimon Peres (1923–), who carried on Rabin's peace initiatives. Peres named Ehud Barak, a former army chief-of-staff, to be his foreign minister. Earlier, Barak had served under Rabin as interior minister.

On June 18, 1996, new elections were held in Israel and, amid rising Palestinian terror attacks, Prime Minister Peres suffered defeat at the hands of Likud leader Benjamin "Bibi" Netanyahu (1949–). Netanyahu had always been suspicious of the motives behind Yasser Arafat's peace overtures. On September 13, 1993, when Rabin joined President Clinton and Arafat on the White House lawn to sign a peace accord, Netanyahu said: "Israel has suffered a national humiliation . . .We are marching toward a PLO state and the destruction of Israel."

Netanyahu's view was shared by Ariel Sharon (1928–), a former army general who was later foreign minister in Netanyahu's government. Sharon said: "He [Rabin] shook the hand of a man [Arafat] who murdered women and children . . ." Sharon urged Israel to stop catering to the PLO, and "to lower the PLO flag and hoist the flag of immigration, the true flag of Israel." He suggested that 1.5 million Jews be brought to Israel from Russia.

In 1998, spurred on by President Bill Clinton, Netanyahu had signed the Wye River Memorandum with Yasser Arafat. The Wye agreement provided for further Israeli control over the West Bank and for relinquishment of control over much of Hebron. Claiming that the PLO was violating Wye by failing to contain terrorist attacks on Israelis, Netanyahu halted Israel's pullback from occupied territories, and the peace process came to a standstill.

New Israeli elections were held on May 17, 1999, and Ehud Barak scored a resounding victory over Netanyahu. He had vowed to follow the peace path of Yitzchak Rabin and, one day after assuming the post of prime minister, declared: "We need to strengthen our country by moving forward to peace agreements [with the Palestinians and Arabs]." In May 2000, Prime Minister Barak fulfilled his campaign pledge and removed all Israeli troops that had been occupying southern Lebanon since 1982.

Barak's attempt to engage Yasser Arafat did not proceed nearly so smoothly. For two weeks in July 2000, under the prodding of President Bill Clinton, Barak and Arafat tried to forge a breakthrough. But even the Israeli offer to yield 94 percent of the West Bank to the Palestinians was deemed unacceptable by Arafat.

In September 2000, Ariel Sharon, a member of the opposition, visited the Temple Mount. This controversial act instigated a second Palestinian resistance period that came to be known as the *Al-Aksa Intifida*. In response to violent Palestinian outbreaks, the Israeli army reoccupied large portions of the West Bank.

New elections were looming, and Barak had lost the confidence of most of the Israeli public in the wake of mounting Palestinian attacks. Nonetheless, injecting new ideas supplied by President Clinton, Barak continued his unsuccessful peace initiatives until his final days in office. In the February 2001 elections, Barak was roundly defeated by Ariel Sharon.

In August 2005, reversing his longstanding position on championing settlement of the Land of Israel, Sharon evacuated all of the Jewish settlements in Gaza (some 9,000 people living in twenty-one communities) and four small settlements in the northern part of Samaria (West Bank). His public motivations were Israel's need to map its own future in the absence of a credible Palestinian peace partner. Critics maintained that the Gaza withdrawal was a smokescreen to divert attention from charges of illegal campaign funding by Sharon's family.

Vital Statistics

The Jewish population of the State of Israel prior to its having gained Independence in 1948 was just below 700,000. Within two years, that population nearly doubled. This was the result of the absorption of hundreds of thousands of immigrants, most of whom had been survivors of the Holocaust.

According to statistics reported in *Jewish Communities of the World*, a 1996 publication of the World Jewish Congress, by 1994 the population of Israel numbered 4.6 million, with most people residing in its three principal cities: Jerusalem, with 577,000 citizens, of whom 412,000 were Jews; Tel Aviv-Jaffa, with a population of 355,000, of whom 340,000 were Jews; and Haifa, with 247,000, of whom 221,000 were Jews.

By the end of 2004, according to Israel government statistics, the country's population numbered approximately 6,869,500, including 5,237,600 Jews. The three largest cities were Jerusalem (706,400), Tel Aviv–Jaffa (371,400), and Haifa (268,300).

Much of the population growth in Israel during the latter part of the twentieth century was the result of an influx of more than one million people from the Soviet Union.

See Zionism.

Isru Chag

First used in the Book of Psalms (118:27), this term literally means "bind the festal procession . . ." and is applied to the day immediately following the major festivals of Passover, Shavuot, and Sukkot. It was then that the pilgrims who had come to Jerusalem to celebrate the holidays began the return trip home.

Jehovah

The Anglicized form of Yehovah, a name for God that is too sacred to be pronounced.

See God, Names of.

Jerusalem

Located 2,700 feet above sea level, the holy city of Jerusalem (in Hebrew, *Yerushala'yim*) has been the political and spiritual capital of the Jewish people for three thousand years. The city became Israel's political capital around the year 1000 B.C.E., when King David, who had ruled over the city of Hebron for seven and one-half years, conquered the area from the Jebusites, as described in II Samuel (5:6–8). He ruled from Jerusalem for thirty-three years, and the city later became known as the City of David.

Solomon succeeded his father, David, as king, and it was in Jerusalem where he built a magnificent Temple on Mount Moriah (II Chronicles 3:1) and placed in it the Holy Ark of the Covenant, which housed the Ten Commandments.

After the death of Solomon, his kingdom split in two, with Jerusalem continuing to be the capital of the two southern tribes, Judah and Benjamin. Samaria (*Shomron*) was selected as the capital of the ten northern tribes.

Between 721 and 715 B.C.E. the ten tribes were taken into captivity by the Assyrians, and in 588 B.C.E. a large portion of the population in southern Palestine, where the remaining two tribes resided, were exiled to Babylonia by King Nebukhadnezzar.

In the ensuing centuries, Palestine passed through the hands of several conquerors, including Persians, Greeks, and Romans. Although for periods of time only a handful of Jews lived in the land, Jews the world over yearned for the eventual return to the land of their ancestors. This hope continued to be ex-pressed in the daily liturgy. Each year, at the end of the Passover *Seder* service, the words "Next year in Jerusalem," were spoken with hope. The feelings of the Jewish people were summed up by these oft-repeated words: "If I forget thee, O Jerusalem, let my right hand wither; let my tongue cleave to my palate if I cease to think of you" (Psalms 137:5).

Hope Realized

In 1891, while serving as the Paris correspondent for the Vienna *Neue Freie Presse*, Hungarian-born Theodor Herzl (1860–1904), an assimilated Jew, became increasingly interested in the plight of his fellow Jews. After the infamous Dreyfus trial of 1894, in which Alfred Dreyfus (1859–1935), a captain on the French general staff was falsely accused and condemned to life in prison for selling secret documents to Germany, Herzl's fight for the founding of a Jewish state by international agreement began. In August 1897 he convened the First Zionist Congress in Basel, Switzerland, and the Zionist movement took root.

After many years of sustained effort by such Jewish leaders as British scientist Chaim Weizmann (1874–1952), on November 2, 1917, Lord Arthur James Balfour, the British foreign secretary, was prevailed upon to issue the famous Balfour Declaration, in which the British government "favours establishment in Palestine a national home for the Jewish people, and will use their best endeavors to the achievement of this object. . . ." President Woodrow Wilson supported Balfour's initiative from the outset, and during Balfour's visit to the United States in the spring of 1917 encouraged him to pursue the course he had set forth.

Finally, on November 29, 1947, the United Nations General Assembly passed a resolution calling for the partition of Palestine into two entities, one to be ruled by Arabs, and the other on which a Jewish state would be established. After two thousand years, Jerusalem would once again be the capital of Israel.

Initially, the Arab nations promised to abide by the partition proposal, but one year later reneged and started a war to regain the portion that had been allotted to Israel. As a result war erupted, and in 1948, in a fierce battle, Jordan occupied the Old City of Jerusalem, which included the Western Wall of the ancient Temple compound. Israel took control of the new city. For nineteen years after the 1948 War of Independence, Jerusalem remained a divided city. In 1967, during the Six-Day War, Israel captured the Old City and Jerusalem was reunited, offering access to everyone to all holy places. To commemorate this auspicious occasion, Jerusalem Day (*Yom Yerushala'yim* in Hebrew), is celebrated each year on the twenty-eighth day of Iyyar.

See Jerusalem Day.

Jerusalem Day

Known in Hebrew as *Yom Yerushala'yim*, this secular holiday is celebrated principally in Jerusalem to commemorate the Israeli victory over the Arab armies in the June 1967 Six-Day War, which resulted in the reunification of East and West Jerusalem. The victory occurred on the twenty-eighth day of Iyyar, and for the first time since the year 70 C.E. the Temple Mount and the Western (Wailing) Wall were under Jewish control.

Jerusalem Day begins with a thanksgiving service at the Western Wall. Torches are lighted in memory of Israeli soldiers who died in the battle for Jerusalem. Since this minor holiday falls during the *sefirah* period (the forty-nine days between the second day of Passover and Shavuot), in some traditional circles the ban on weddings is waived, as on other semiholidays such as Lag Ba-Omer and Rosh Chodesh.

See Sefirah.

Jew

The terms Jew, Israelite, and Hebrew are used interchangeably in Jewish Scripture and in later Jewish literature. "Hebrew" was the first of the three in use.

The Name "Hebrew"

In Genesis 14:13 we are told, "A fugitive brought the news to Abram the *Hebrew* ...," the news being that in the battle of the four kings against the five kings (Genesis 14:1ff.), Lot, the son of Abram's brother, was taken captive. The name Hebrew (*Ivri*), some Rabbis of the Midrash (*Genesis Rabbah* 42:8) speculate, was assigned to Abram (later called Abraham) because he came from the "other side" of the Euphrates River, where Abraham was born. The Hebrew term for "other side" is *eiver*.

The name Ivri is mentioned a number of times in the Book of Genesis in connection with the story of Joseph (Genesis 39:14, 41:12) and in the Book of Exodus in connection with the life of Moses (Exodus 2:11) and in reference to a Hebrew slave (Exodus 21:2). In the Book of Jonah (1:9), the prophet declares, "I am a Hebrew."

The Names "Israel" and "Israelite"

Israelite is a form of Israel, another name of Jacob, son of Isaac, who was so called after his confrontation with an angel, whom he wrestled and overcame. Jacob would not release the angel until the angel blessed him. The blessing of the angel was (Genesis 32:29), "Your name shall no longer be Jacob, but Israel [Yisra'el], because you have contended [*sarita* in Hebrew, from which Yisra'el is derived] with a divine being [the angel] and with men and you have prevailed."

From that time on, Hebrews also became known as Israelites, as noted in the *Shema* prayer (Deuteronomy 6:4): "*Shema Yisra'el...*" Much later, when the third commonwealth was established on May 14, 1948 (5 Iyyar 5708), the name Israel was appropriated.

The Name "Jew"

Jacob had twelve sons. Although Reuben was the eldest, it was Judah, Jacob's fourth son, who emerged as the most prominent. After Joshua conquered the Land of Canaan (later called Palestine) from the indigenous tribes and nations, the land was divided among the twelve tribes that had been the sons of Jacob. Ten tribes settled in the northern part of the country. Joseph's territory was divided between his two sons Ephraim and Menasseh. The tribe of Levi was assigned no specific territory, since it was to be concerned with the needs of the desert Sanctuary and, later, the Jerusalem Temple built by Solomon around 1000 B.C.E. The two tribes to settle in the south were Judah and Benjamin.

King Solomon ruled over the country for forty years. When he died, many disgruntled groups living in the North expressed dissatisfaction with the excessive taxation and with the affluence and favoritism enjoyed by the inhabitants of Jerusalem and the area to the south. Taking advantage of this resentment, under the leadership of Jeroboam, who sought the kingship, the northern tribes rebelled, and the country became divided. Since Judah was the larger and more affluent tribe in the South, that entire territory became known as Judah and its people as Judeans.

At a later date (*c.* 720 B.C.E.), after the ten northern tribes were taken into captivity by the Assyrians and subsequently disappeared, and the southern tribes returned from their exile in Babylonia (*c.* 720 B.C.E.), the name Jew (*Yehudi*) was applied to the whole nation.

In the Book of Esther (2:5), which according to many scholars was composed after the return of the exiles from Babylonia, Mordekhai the Benjaminite is referred to as a *Yehudi*. In an earlier book of the Bible (II Kings 18:28), *Yehudi* appears in the form *Yehudit*, but there it refers to "the language of the kingdom of Judah."

Derogatory Attributions

In the course of time, detractors of the Jews have called them by derogatory names. *Sheeny*, the origin of which is unknown, was common among English-speaking people; *Zhid* or *Zit* among Russians; *Youtre* among the French. Russian Jews referred to a Jew of German origin as *Yehudi* or *Yekke*, and to one of Russian or Lithuanian ancestry as *Yid*. In America, *Kike* has been one of the words of defamation, presumably a form of the word *Keikel*, Yiddish for "circle," because Jewish immigrants who couldn't sign their name in English would make a circle. *Hymie*, a short form of Hyman, a name common among Jews, has also been used.

See Jewish Identity.

Jewish Identity

Jewish law considers a child to be Jewish if the mother is Jewish, regardless of the father's faith. This ruling, first set forth clearly in the Talmud (*Yevamot* 45b), was reinforced by the comment of Rashi, the prominent eleventh-century French authority, who stated: "Since the mother of the child is Jewish, he [the child] is to be counted as one of our brothers."

Rationale for Matrilineal Descent

To support the position that it is the mother's, not the father's lineage that counts in determining whether a child is Jewish, the Rabbis of the Talmud cited the verse in Deuteronomy (7:4): "He [the non-Jewish idolater who is the father of the child] will wean *your* son away from Me [God]." In this verse, say the Rabbis (*Kiddushin* 68b), the words "your son" clearly refer to the child of a Jewish mother, and we must therefore conclude that at all times and in all cases *your son* is Jewish if he is the offspring of a Jewish woman.

A further argument for the mother's lineage serving as the determinant of a child's Jewishness is that at the time of birth one is always certain of the identity of the mother of the child, but one cannot be positive of the identity of the father. Jewish law, therefore, established that if a child's mother is Jewish, the child is Jewish, and that Jewishness is thus passed on to all future generations. The Talmud (*Yevamot* 23a) states very emphatically that a child's status is linked to the mother.

A Jew Forever

Jewish law (*Shulchan Arukh*, Even Ha-Ezer 4:5, 19) adopted the view of the third-century Palestinian rabbi Abba ben Zavda, who said (*Sanhedrin* 44a), "A Jew, even though he sins is still a Jew." He followed that statement with this picturesque comparison: "A myrtle though it stands among reeds is still a myrtle and continues to be so called." In the fifteenth century, Rabbi Solomon ben Simon Duran of Algiers declared categorically that the offspring of a Jewish mother and a Gentile father is Jewish "for all time."

The concept of "once a Jew, always a Jew" is based upon an incident in the Book of Joshua. Under the leadership of Joshua, the Children of Israel began to conquer Canaan, and the first city to be occupied was Jericho. The Israelites had been warned that after the city was captured, no one was to take any war booty for himself; it was all holy and belonged to the Lord. Nonetheless, some disobeyed the order.

One of the violators of the ban was Achan ben Carmi, and he was to suffer death for his sin. Joshua pleaded with Achan to confess his sin (Joshua 7:19). Achan complied and divulged where he had hidden the loot. Although the Bible does not so indicate, the Talmud implies that Joshua convinced Achan that by confessing his sin he would not avoid execution, but he would be assured entry into the next world with a clean slate.

Based on the story of Achan and its talmudic interpretation, a principle of Jewish law was established: one may never think of an errant Jew as being lost to Judaism. There is hope, even until death, that a Jew who has done wrong will confess his sins and repent. For this reason, the door is never closed to his return, and Jewish law insists that a Jew may never be denied his basic rights as a Jew, even if he goes so far as to convert to another religion.

Who Is a Jew?

Soon after the Jewish State was established in 1948, a heated debate ensued in Israel on the question of, "Who is a Jew?" Yitzchak Halevi Herzog (1888–1959), the Chief Ashkenazic Rabbi of Israel at the time, spoke for the traditional view, asserting that according to Jewish law only the offspring of a Jewish mother can be considered a Jew. If the mother is not Jewish, and the father is Jewish, a child born to them is not Jewish; the only way the child can become Jewish is through conversion. For a female, immersion in a ritual bath (*mikveh*) is necessary; for a male, immersion and ritual circumcision are required. The natural-born Jew and the converted Jew, the Chief Rabbi declared, are Jews for all time.

Prime Minister David Ben-Gurion argued that anyone who declares himself Jewish, lives a Jewish life, and is interested in the welfare of the Jews is to be considered a Jew, regardless of the faith of the mother. His reasoning was as follows: We have been Jews without definition for the last 3,000 years, and we shall remain so...By one definition the Jews are a religious community...There is a definition that Jews are a nation...There are Jews without any definition. They are just Jews. I am one of them. I don't need any definition. I am what I am...

To Ben-Gurion, legal status was not the sole criterion for determining who is a Jew. One's emotional connection with Judaism as well as how one is perceived by fellow Jews and by non-Jews must also be considered. This view, shared by many Jews, is summarized in Raphael Patai's *The Jewish Mind*. He states that being Jewish involves "a state of mind." To be a Jew, he says, one has to think or know or feel that he is a Jew and he must be considered by others to be a Jew. Being born of a Jewish mother is not the only determining factor. In recent years, the Reform and Reconstructionist movements have advocated the legitimacy of following patrilineal descent in determining who is a Jew. (*See* Patrilineal Descent.) The Orthodox and Conservative denominations reject this approach.

The Israeli High Court was confronted with the issue of patrilineal descent in 1962 when Brother Daniel (original name, Oswald Rufeisen), a member of the Carmelite Order, requested citizenship under the Law of Return. Daniel was born to Jewish parents in Poland in 1922 and had been an active Zionist during World War II. In 1942, he became a Christian, but continued to consider himself a Jew as well. He then became a monk, and because he loved Israel and had yearned for it since his youth, joined an order that had a chapter in Israel.

When Brother Daniel's application for citizenship under the Law of Return was rejected, he appealed the decision, claiming his rights as the child of a Jewish mother. The High Court, headed by Judge Moshe Silberg, rejected the appeal and emphasized that although according to *halakhah* (Jewish religious law) Daniel is technically a Jew, in the eyes of Jews he is not a Jew. The majority of the justices of the High Court argued: When so many Jews throughout history have sacrificed their lives for their faith, how could one who turned his back on his faith be considered a Jew? The decision of the court was not in strict keeping with Jewish law, but it did express the will of the people.

See Law of Return.

Jubilee Year

The Book of Leviticus (25) mandates that every fifty years, after seven sabbatical (*shemittah*) years have passed, a jubilee year is to be celebrated. As in all sabbatical years, during the course of that year all debts are to be forgiven, all Hebrew slaves are to be granted freedom, and all land is to lie fallow. In addition, in the jubilee year all property is to be returned to the original owner so that no family will be permanently impoverished. The tenth verse of Leviticus 25 was inscribed on the Liberty Bell in Philadelphia, refers to this concept: "And ye shall hallow the fiftieth year, and proclaim liberty throughout the land unto all the inhabitants thereof...."

The jubilee year, which as its name suggests was to be a time of great rejoicing, is known in Hebrew as *yovel* (literally, "ram's horn") because it was ushered in on the tenth day of the seventh month of the fiftieth year. That day is

Yom Kippur, when the ram's horn is sounded to conclude the day of fasting.

The jubilee year was observed during the period of the First Temple, but there is no record of its having been observed in Second Temple times. The Rabbis of the Talmud (*Arachim* 32b) explained that the biblical law requiring celebration of the jubilee year was no longer enforced after the destruction of the First Temple because Leviticus 25:10 makes specific reference to "*all* the inhabitants" of the Land of Israel. Since some of the Tribes of Israel had been exiled when the First Temple was destroyed, and since not all the Jews lived in Palestine, *yovel* could no longer be carried out as prescribed by Scripture.

See Shemittah.

Judaism and Jewishness

Derived from the word *Jew*, the term Judaism is most often defined as "the religion of the Jews." However, beyond being a religious faith. Judaism is a way of life that involves observance of Jewish values, traditions, customs, and the like.

Throughout the ages Jews have expressed their affinity to Judaism through literature—fiction and nonfiction—art, music, and a variety of other cultural means. The writings of the Jews have appeared in the languages of the various countries where Jews have lived. Jews have throughout history felt a strong connectedness to the Land of Israel, which was vouchsafed to Abraham in Scripture and was reclaimed in 1948.

The Jewish religion is inseparable from peoplehood. Jews, whether they be Orthodox, Conservative, Reform, Reconstructionist, or secular, are all part of the community of Israel. And once a person is born to a Jewish mother or is converted to Judaism and has accepted the Jewish way of life, he or she cannot be read out of the Jewish fold, regardless of the offense. The Talmud says (*Sanhedrin* 44a): "A Jew, even if he had sinned, is still a Jew." All Jews are Jews forever, with equal status.

Professor Abraham Joshua Heschel explained this diversity to a group of startled Roman Catholic priests. "Pluralism is the will of God," he said—that is, there are no dogmas to which Jews must subscribe, and there is room for many interpretations.

See Covenant People; Jewish Identity; Reconstructionism.

Justice

The Jewish concept of justice is rooted in the biblical commandment (Deuteronomy 16:20): "Justice, justice shall you pursue." The pursuit of justice was addressed by all the prophets of Israel, yet there is no precise Hebrew word that defines this concept. The closest Hebrew equivalent is *tzedek* and its derivative, *tzedakah*, which is generally translated as "charity." Hence, "to do justice" means to act charitably; to be fair and openhanded; to be fair when judging others; to act honestly in business dealings; to do what is right in the sight of God. The individual who exemplifies all these attributes is characterized as a *tzadik*, a pious, righteous, just person.

See Charity.

Kabbalah

This Hebrew word literally meaning "that which is received" originally referred to the Jewish tradition transmitted from one generation to the succeeding one. The word *kabbalah* applies to the entire body of Jewish learning dating back to Moses, who received the Torah on Mount Sinai and conveyed it to Joshua. Joshua in turn transmitted the Torah to the elders; the elders to the prophets; and the prophets to the Men of the Great Assembly, as indicated at the beginning of chapter 1 of the Ethics of the Fathers.

In the eleventh and twelfth centuries, the term *kabbalah* was applied by mystics to their system of defining the relationship between God, man, and the universe. They believed that the Torah contains the answers to all the mysteries of the universe and that by delving deeply into the holy texts one can find answers to basic truths.

Mission of the Mystics

Kabbalists have been struggling for centuries with questions about the essence of God, the makeup of the universe, the secrets of Creation, and man's place and function in the scheme of things. Kabbalists of diverse backgrounds—Bachya ibn Pakuda (*c.* 1050–*c.* 1120), Moses Nachmanides (1194–*c.* 1270), Abraham Abulafia (1241–*c.* 1291), Joseph Gikatilla (1248–*c.* 1325), Moses Cordovera (1522–1570), Isaac Luria (1534–1572), Chayim Vital (1542–1620), Judah Loew of Prague (*c.* 1525–1609), Moses Chayim Luzzatto (1707–1747), Israel Ba'al Shem Tov (1700–1760), and others—have devoted themselves in various degrees to validating the mystical approach to Judaism by interpreting the words, phrases, and configurations of letters in the Torah, hidden meanings that reveal secrets pertaining to God and His universe.

Mysticism in the Bible

Mystical thinking was noticeable in the apparitions described in the prophecies of Isaiah and Ezekiel. In the Book of Isaiah (chapter 6), the eighth-century B.C.E. Jerusalem prophet, who came from an affluent family but sympathized with the dismal plight of the poor and the underprivileged, answers God's call to confront the leaders of Israel, who had become lax in their morality. Isaiah's mission begins with a vision wherein he sees God "seated on a high and lofty throne, the skirts of His robe filling the Temple. Angels [seraphs, attendants, members of the Heavenly Court that guarded the Heavenly Throne] stood by Him in attendance. Each of them had six wings. With two he [each seraph] covered his face, with two he covered his legs, and with two he would fly. And one would call to the other: 'Holy, holy, holy! The Lord of Hosts! His presence fills the earth....'"

Ezekiel's ministry, which is also aimed at correcting Israel's moral laxity, is also introduced with a remarkable vision of God. The prophet Ezekiel, a member of a priestly family who served in the First Temple in Jerusalem before its destruction, was among the Jews exiled to Babylonia in 597 B.C.E.

Ezekiel's mystical description of the divine throne, similar to Isaiah's but much more detailed, became a basic text for kabbalists of later centuries. In Ezekiel's vision, known as the Divine Chariot (*Merkavah*), the prophet sees four creatures drawing a chariot: "Each figure had four faces and four wings... All had human hands below their wings.... Each had a human face [at the front] and each had the face of a lion on the right side, the face of an ox on the left, and the face of an eagle at the back...." In Ezekiel's vision (chapter 1) the creatures are mobile, each having wheels.

The enigmatic visions of Isaiah and Ezekiel,

the two important First Temple prophets, became the cornerstone of the mystical tradition, which sought to establish a union between man and God. The vision of Ezekiel in particular was seen as the answer to the mystery of Creation and the bond that connects man with God. Some talmudic scholars became very involved in this kind of thinking, but they warned that immersing oneself too deeply in mystical speculation could lead to a misunderstanding of the essence of Judaism (*Chagigah* 11b).

Methods of Interpretation

To avoid assigning too literal an interpretation to the Torah, which would make Judaism appear to be nothing more than a legalistic system devoid of humanity and compassion, kabbalists as far back as talmudic times have subscribed to a method of interpretation known as *hermeneutics*. One of the initiators of this system of extrapolating one conclusion or fact from another was second-century C.E. Rabbi Ishmael ben Elishah.

In the Midrash on Leviticus (the *Sifra*) Ishmael advanced the theory that there are thirteen methods of deriving new applications from the teachings of the Torah. These methods appear in traditional prayerbooks and are recited as part of the early morning service.

The thirteen interpretive methods follow a logic far different from the Aristotelian syllogistic method whereby if A is greater than B, and B is greater than C, then it follows that A is greater than C. Rabbinic hermeneutic logic argues that even if it is true that A is greater than C, that in itself does not mean that the two cannot share commonalities and that what they have in common might not be of extreme significance. By applying such logic to words and phrases that repeat themselves in the Torah, kabbalists have uncovered answers to perplexing questions regarding the nature of God and man and their relationship to one another.

The Bible of Kabbalism

The text that is most closely associated with Kabbalism is the *Zohar* ("Enlightenment"). For many centuries it was believed that the second-century charismatic scholar Rabbi Shimon (Simeon) bar Yocha'i was the "father" of *kabbalah* and author of this work, which is often referred to as the "bible of Kabbalism." It is said that when the Romans put a price on Rabbi Shimon's head for continuing to teach Torah to his students in defiance of the Roman ban on such activity, he and his son hid in a cave for thirteen years. A miracle occurred: a carob tree and a well suddenly appeared, which sustained them. After the death of the Roman ruler, Shimon left the cave with the book he had written: the *Zohar*. Like all other *midrashim* (interpretive books), the *Zohar* is essentially a commentary on the Torah, except that it is infused with mystical interpretation and innuendo.

The claim that Shimon bar Yocha'i authored the *Zohar* was later disputed by reputable scholars who pointed out that many selections incorporated in the text were in fact written by rabbis who lived much later than the second century. The prevailing consensus is that the *Zohar* was composed in the thirteenth century by the Spanish mystic Moses (ben Shem Tov) de Leon (*c.* 1250–1305). According to a statement of his wife, De Leon himself ascribed the book to the highly respected and admired Shimon bar Yocha'i because more people would buy the book if such a prominent name appeared as its author.

The Basic Doctrine

According to kabbalistic belief, God makes Himself known on two levels. On the highest level He is the *Ein Sof*, the Limitless, Infinite Being who, it can be said, has no beginning and no end. As such, God cannot be reached or understood by man directly. It is only through the ten potencies or powers known as "that the *Ein Sof* becomes manifest to mankind. The *sefirot* are the vehicles through which all creation comes about, as they are the source of all cosmic energy and vitality.

The Ten Sefirot

The ten divine potencies that emanate from God, as expounded in the *Zohar*, are:

1. *Keter*—"Crown"
2. *Chokhmah*—"Wisdom"
3. *Binah*—"Understanding"
4. *Chesed*—"Lovingkindness"
5. *Gevurah*—"Power"
6. *Tiferet*—"Beauty"
7. *Netzach*—"Victory"
8. *Hod*—"Splendor"
9. *Yesod*—"Foundation"
10. *Malkhut*—"Sovereignty"

The first three *sefirot* belong to the realm of the *Ein Sof* alone and are too difficult for the human mind even to contemplate. *Keter* is the immediate link between the *Ein Sof* and the other *sefirot* and is said to be the seed from which the process of Creation stems. The second and third *sefirot* are the potencies through which the will of God to create the world is executed—that is, it is through Divine Wisdom and Understanding that He created the world.

The seven lower *sefirot* are said to represent the divine emotions, which are the foundation upon which a just society can be founded. The last of the *sefirot*, *malkhut*, is identi-fied with the *Shekhinah*, the feminine aspect of the godhead.

Representation and Symbolism of the Sefirot

The human body is sometimes said to be a representation on earth of the *sefirot*. This explains the verse in Genesis (1:27) which states that man was created in the image of God. In this view, *keter* is the crown on man's head, *chokhmah* emerges from the brain and *binah* from the heart; man's right arm is *chesed*; and so on.

The *Zohar* links the various *sefirot* to specific colors. Accordingly, white represents *chesed*, red represents *gevurah*, and yellow is the color of *tiferet*.

The *sefirot* have been depicted by some kabbalists as a Tree of Life consisting of three columns. The branches that form the right column contain *chokhmah*, *chesed*, and *netzach*, all of which are characterized as positive, male emanations. The *sefirot* on the left column—namely, *binah*, *gevurah*, and *hod*—are characterized as negative, female emanations. The central column—containing *tiferet*, *yesod*, and *malkhut*—is the balancing, harmonizing force.

The Kabbalistic Renaissance

In the sixteenth century, the town of Safed, in Palestine, was the hub of kabbalistic activity and a renewal of interest in a mystical approach to Judaism. Ashkenazic Rabbi Isaac Luria (1534–1572), also known as the Ari, was the most distinguished of the Safed kabbalists. He did not commit his teachings to writing, but his disciple Chaim Vital (died 1620) recorded them in a volume entitled *Eitz Chayim* ("*Tree of Life*").

According to Lurianic kabbalistic thinking, when the divine light, or creative energy of the *Ein Sof*—the Infinite Being—was channeled into the ten vessels (*keilim*) that were to contain it, only the three upper *sefirot* were strong enough to contain their intensity. When the light reached the seven lower *sefirot*, which did not require as much energy to keep the lower worlds in existence, there was a "breaking of the vessels [*shevirat ha-keilim*]."

When the vessels shattered, it is said, most but not all of the lights returned to the source from which they came. The seven lower vessels were strengthened so that they could now contain the divine energy, but some of the sparks remained free. Many of these holy sparks, as they were called, became trapped by the *kelippot* ("shells, husks"), evil forces that inhabited the demonic side of existence—namely, the *sitra achra* ("Other Side"). The objective of the *kelippot* is to surround and consume what is holy; and it is the role of man, the Lurianic kabbalists maintained, to release the holy sparks from imprisonment. Man is at the center of this war between the holy and the unholy.

In order to release the holy sparks and restore cosmic harmony, man must dedicate himself to carrying out the commandments (*mitzvot*) of the Torah. This will lead to the ultimate redemption of man and *tikkun olam*, the restoration of the world to its proper course.

Tzimtzum

The question of how there is space for the creation of a physical world if God's presence and glory fills the entire world was of great concern to mystics. The doctrine of *tzimtzum* ("contraction") as set forth by the Lurianic kabbalists provides an answer: God purposely contracted Himself, reduced Himself in size, thus creating a vacuum and allowing space for the divine light encased in the *sefirot* to unfold and contribute to the act of creation.

See Sefirot; Tikkun Olam; Tzimtzum; Zohar.

Kabbalat Kinyan

A Hebrew phrase literally meaning "acquiring proprietary rights." The traditional way of sealing a business deal is for each party to a transaction to take hold of the corner of a garment or a handkerchief. It is the equivalent of the modern handshake.

See Handkerchief Ceremony; Kinyan Sudar.

Kabbalat Shabbat

A Hebrew term literally meaning "Welcoming the Sabbath." *Kabbalat Shabbat* is the name of the Friday evening prayers that precede the recitation of the *Ma'ariv* (evening) service that begins with the *Barkhu*.

See Sabbath.

Kaddish

Kaddish is an Aramaic form of the Hebrew word *kadosh*, meaning "holy." Considered to be one of the most important prayers of the liturgy, the *Kaddish* is a paean to God unsurpassed in Jewish literature. Even Jews who are indifferent to many aspects of religious observance deem it a sacred duty to recite the *Kaddish* in memory of a departed mother, father, or other family member.

The Rabbis' Kaddish

The *Kaddish*, which in essence is a sanctification of God's name, was not originally intended as a prayer for mourners. Although the origin of the prayer is obscure, most scholars believe that it was introduced in Temple times to be recited primarily after a Torah study session or a scholarly discourse.

The original form of *Kaddish*—or Great Doxology, as it may be called—has come to be known as *Kaddish of the Rabbis*, *Rabbis' Kaddish*, or *Scholars' Kaddish* (in Hebrew, *Kaddish De-Rabbanan*). The main thrust of the prayer is clearly indicated in its opening words, *Yit-gadal ve-yit-kadash shmei rabbah*, "Glorified and sanctified be God's great name." These words were adopted from the Book of Ezekiel (38:23), in which God says, *Ve-hit-gadalti ve-hit-kadashti*, meaning "I will manifest My greatness and My holiness [and make Myself known to many nations]."

In response to the first words of the *Kaddish*, the congregation says, *Y'hei shmei rabbah mevorakh*, "May His great name be blessed." These words, taken almost verbatim from the Book of Daniel (2:20), came to be regarded by mystics as the essential element of the Great Doxology.

The Talmud (*Berakhot* 3a) comments that when a congregation pronounces the words "May His great name be blessed," God is greatly pleased and says, "Happy is the King who is thus praised in this house." This response was used in the Temple ritual, especially on Yom Kippur, in a slightly variant Hebrew version. When the High Priest uttered the name of God (the Tetragrammaton), the people would cry out: "Blessed be His name whose glorious kingdom is forever and ever." A similar response is found in the *Hallel* (Psalms 113:2).

Today the *Rabbis' Kaddish* is generally recited after the preliminary morning (*Shacharit*) service prior to the *Barukh She-amar* prayer. It is also recited following the Sabbath and holiday *Musaf* service prior to the *Aleinu* prayer.

The Full Kaddish

The *Rabbis' Kaddish* initially was recited by all present after a study session or sermon. When selections from the Talmud became part of the Preliminary Prayers (*Pesukei De-Zimra*) of the morning service, it was considered appropriate to conclude this section with a recitation of the *Kaddish of the Rabbis*. But rather than have the entire congregation recite this *Kaddish*, the privilege was reserved

for mourners, thus giving them an additional exclusive opportunity to recite the *Kaddish*.

On Sabbaths and holidays, after the *Ein Keloheinu* is sung, several selections from the Talmud are read, and once again the *Rabbis' Kaddish* is recited by mourners. At an even later point, the sentiments expressed by the *Kaddish* so appealed to the public that the Rabbis of the post-talmudic period decided to introduce it in yet another form to be recited by the leader (*chazzan* or *ba'al tefillah*) at the conclusion of various sections of the synagogue service.

The *Full Kaddish* (*Kaddish Shalem* in Hebrew) consists of six short paragraphs. It is marked by substituting a paragraph beginning with the word *titkabel* for the fourth paragraph of the *Kaddish* of the Rabbis (which begins with the words *Al Yisra'el*). For this reason, the *Full Kaddish* is sometimes called *Kaddish Titkabel*.

The *titkabel* paragraph beseeches God to accept the prayers and supplications of the whole House of Israel (*titkabel* means "[May the prayers] be acceptable"), a distinctly appropriate conclusion for major sections of the synagogue service. Thus, the *Full Kaddish* is recited at the end of the morning (*Shacharit*) service on the Sabbath and holidays and at the conclusion of all other services after the recitation of the Silent Devotion (*Amidah* or *Shemoneh Esrei* in Hebrew).

Among Syrian Jews it is customary at a *brit* (circumcision) for everyone present who has ever lost a parent to join in reciting the *Full Kaddish*. This is explained as a way of demonstrating that on this day a new Jew has entered the Jewish fold to replace the loss of those being recalled through the recitations of the *Kaddish*.

Aside from the final verse of the *Full Kaddish*, which is translated as "May He who makes peace in His high places make peace for us and for all Israel, and say ye, Amen," the language of the *Kaddish* is Aramaic. For nearly a thousand years, from the time of Ezra in the fifth century B.C.E. until well after the end of the talmudic period, Aramaic was the vernacular of the Jewish masses in Babylonia and Palestine. So that its words should be readily understood, the *Kaddish* was composed in the everyday, spoken language.

The Half Kaddish

After the *Full Kaddish* was introduced to mark the end of major portions of the prayer service, it was considered appropriate to do the same for the smaller prayer units. To distinguish between the two, the *Half Kaddish*, (*Chatzi Kaddish* in Hebrew), consisting of only the first three paragraphs of the *Full Kaddish*, was introduced.

The primary points at which the leader of the service recites the *Half Kaddish* are:

- before the recitation of *Barkhu* at morning services;
- before the *Amidah* is recited at afternoon and evening services;
- before the congregant is called up for the *maftir aliyah*;
- on those occasions when the *maftir* is read from a second scroll, the *Half Kaddish* is recited after the second scroll has been placed on the reading table, and before it is opened for reading. When selections are read from three Torah scrolls on a particular Sabbath, the *Half Kaddish* is recited after the reading has been completed from the second scroll.

In some Sephardic congregations, when readings are conducted from two scrolls, it is customary for the honoree (*oleh*) to recite the *Half Kaddish* after the second Torah has been read.

Sephardim call *Chatzi Kaddish* by the name *Kaddish L'eila* because the last sentence of this short form of the *Kaddish* begins with the Aramaic word *l'eila*.

The Burial Kaddish

Known by its Aramaic name *Kaddish De-Itchadeta* ("*Kaddish of the Resurrection*,") the *Burial Kaddish* is recited by mourners immediately after the coffin is lowered into the grave and is covered with earth. This form of *Kaddish* was introduced by the Rabbis to console mourners by assuring them that death is only a passing stage; that life has meaning and purpose; that we may look forward to the days of the Messiah, when the dead will be revived.

The *Burial Kaddish* differs from the regular *Mourners' Kaddish* in that it makes direct reference to the world to come and to the resurrection of the dead, themes not mentioned in any of the other *Kaddish* forms.

It should be noted that many non-Orthodox rabbis, who do not subscribe to the concept of resurrection in a literal sense, choose to recite the *Mourners' Kaddish* at the cemetery funeral service.

The Mourners' Kaddish

In the early Middle Ages, around the year 1000, the *Al Yisra'el* paragraph was dropped from the *Rabbis' Kaddish* to create another *Kaddish* that would be recited by orphans at designated points in weekday, Sabbath, and holiday services. This version of the *Kaddish* was originally (and often still is) called *Kaddish Yatom*, the "*Orphans' Kaddish*." Today, however, this *Kaddish* is recited not only by orphans but by all mourners.

The earliest reference to the *Kaddish* as a mourner's prayer is found in *Or Zaru'a*, a book by Rabbi Isaac ben Moses of Vienna (1180–1260). The next reference to it appears in the *Machzor Vitry*, dated 1208, where it is noted: "The boy rises and recites the *Kaddish*." Undoubtedly the Rabbis regarded the *Kaddish* as the perfect prayer for mourners, whose faith is being tested by the grievous loss suffered. They compared the mourner's anguish to that of Job, who despite the death of all his children was able to say: "Though He [God] slay me, yet will I trust in Him" (Job 13:15). For this reason the *Kaddish* is often described as "an echo of the Book of Job."

The idea of reciting *Kaddish* for the dead was encouraged by the thirteenth-century kabbalists, who contended that this prayer has the power to redeem the souls of the deceased. This belief may have stemmed from a widespread legend that Rabbi Akiba had helped redeem the soul of a deceased man from the tortures of hell (*Gehinnom*) by teaching a man's son to recite the *Kaddish* at a synagogue service.

In most congregations, the *Mourners' Kaddish* is recited after Psalm 30 of the morning (*Shacharit*) service and after the *Aleinu* at all prayer services.

The *Mourners' Kaddish* has in many ways become the thread that links Jews to their faith and binds the generations. The *Kaddish* declares man's submission to the will of God. It makes no direct reference to death, but infers, as the Talmud (*Berakhot* 60b) points out, that when man's heart is filled with grief and sorrow, he lays his burden in the lap of God by uttering the *Kaddish*, which begins with the words, "Magnified and glorified is His great name." This implies that whatever God decides is good.

Mourners' Kaddish: Rules and Customs

Originally, *Kaddish* was recited only for parents. In time, this practice was extended to include a brother, sister, son, daughter, and spouse. For parents, *Kaddish* is recited for eleven months. For others, it is recited for thirty days.

According to Jewish law the obligation to say *Kaddish* for a parent falls upon the sons of the deceased. Even in the absence of sons, daughters are not required to say *Kaddish*. Orthodox practice suggests that a daughter who wishes to honor her departed father or mother should satisfy her need by listening attentively as others recite the *Kaddish* and by responding "Amen" at the proper time. Such attentiveness is to be regarded as though the daughter had personally recited the *Kaddish*.

Several authorities, however, see no objection to the recitation of *Kaddish* by daughters. The famous chasidic woman *rebbe*, the Maid of Ladamir (1815–1892), an only child, recited *Kaddish* for her father Monesh Werbermacher. When the father of Henrietta Szold, founder of Hadassah, died in 1902, Henrietta and her sisters insisted on saying *Kaddish* for him, contrary to religious practice. Nonetheless, this remains uncommon practice among Orthodox Jews. Women in Conservative, Reform, and Reconstructionist congregations do stand with all mourners to say *Kaddish*.

Talmudic law (*Berakhot* 58b) stipulates that *Kaddish* for a parent be recited for twelve months, noting that "the memory of the dead grows dim after twelve months." However, the belief was prevalent in talmudic times that the wicked are consigned to hell (*Gehinnom*) and are subject to punishment for a maximum of twelve months. To avoid the possibility of people thinking that the parent for whom *Kaddish* was being recited (for a twelve-month period) was wicked, scholars of the caliber of Rabbi Moses ben Israel Isserles (c. 1525–1572) of Cracow reduced the requirement for the recitation of the *Kaddish* for parents to eleven months. By ruling that *Kaddish* for a parent should not be recited for more than eleven months, Rabbi Isserles was removing all possibility of ascribing wickedness to the parent. Even when the Jewish year has thirteen months, as in leap years, *Kaddish*, according to Isserles, should only be recited for eleven months. Most Jews follow the ruling of Isserles.

In most congregations it is customary for all mourners to recite the *Kaddish* in unison. This custom was initiated in Sephardic congregations where most prayers were recited aloud, together with the cantor. After Rabbi Jacob Israel Emden (1697–1776), the foremost authority of his age approved of the practice, it was accepted and followed by most communities. It is also customary among some mourners to take three steps backwards as they recite the concluding verse of the *Kaddish*.

See Ark.

Kallah

A word of uncertain origin, some authorities assume that *kallah* derives from the Aramaic *klalah*, meaning "totality." The Hebrew term *klal Yisra'el* refers to the entire community of Israel. A *kallah* was the name of a large assembly of learned people that gathered for study in Babylonian academies before the Passover and Rosh Hashanah holidays, during the months of Adar and Elul. They attended lectures given by the leading teachers of the Sura and Pumbedita academies (*yeshivot*) on the subject of the approaching holiday, its laws and customs (*Berakhot* 57a).

Abbayei, principal of the academy in Pumbedita from 333 to 338 once said, "The most important part of a *kallah* is a crowd," and the larger the assembly of students, the greater the prestige of the particular academy.

There were no such assemblies in Palestine. The Babylonian community, which was scattered over a more extensive area, seemed to feel the special need for assembling twice a year for group study.

Kallah is also the Hebrew word for "bride."

Kapparot

A Hebrew word literally meaning "atonements, wiping away of sins." The *kapparot* concept evolved from an early belief that it is possible to transfer one's illness, pain, guilt, or sin to another object, living or dead. It is associated primarily with the Yom Kippur holiday when forgiveness from sin is sought.

During the *kapparot* ceremony, still observed by some Jews today, a fowl is waved over the head three times. A man uses a rooster, while a woman uses a hen. In either case the fowl is generally white to symbolize purity.

As the bird is waved overhead, the following words are pronounced: "This is my substitute, my vicarious offering, my atonement. This cock/hen shall meet death, but I shall enjoy a long, pleasant life of peace." This is followed by the reading of selections from the Book of Psalms and the Book of Job. The fowl is then slaughtered and eaten by the owner or is given to the poor.

The primary reason for using a cock or hen in the ceremony was that after the destruction of the Temple no animal used in the sacrificial Temple rites could serve as a symbol of atonement in Jewish life. If a cock or a hen was not obtainable, other animals including geese or fish were used.

The custom of *kapparot*, which is not mentioned in the Talmud, seems to have begun among the Jews of Babylonia. It is alluded to in the writings of the *ge'onim* of the ninth century and became widespread by the tenth century. Although most leading scholars condemned the practice as barbaric, calling it a stupid custom, Rabbi Moses Isserles approved of it, and *kapparot* continued to be observed by German and Polish Jews. But when opposition to its practice mounted, many people began to use coins instead of fowl, and the money was then given to charity.

Karaites

While a number of scholars have advanced the notion that the Karaite sect in Judaism dates back to the end of Second Temple days (first century C.E.) and was associated with groups of the Qumran community whose existence came to light with the discovery of the Dead Sea Scrolls, most scholars have found no credible evidence to sustain this view.

The conventional belief is that in eighth-century Babylonia, under the leadership of Anan ben David, a group of Jews unhappy with the leadership of the *ge'onim* (the religious leaders of Babylonia who often wielded considerable temporal power) broke away from the mainstream rabbinic leadership and organized their own community. They called themselves *Kara'im*, meaning "adherents to *Mikra* [the Hebrew word for Bible]." The Karaites were displeased with the manner in which the Rabbis of the Talmud and those of the post-talmudic era interpreted and, in effect, changed many of the laws prescribed in the Bible.

Beliefs and Attitudes

The Karaites defied rabbinic law and denied the authority of the Talmud. They demanded of their followers, who were located not only in Babylonia but also in Persia, Egypt, and Palestine, strict adherence to the letter of biblical law, which alone is to be considered the word of God. All other laws and regulations were considered rabbinical impositions and hence not valid.

Consequently, Karaites

- did not burn a fire on the Sabbath for light or heat;
- ate cold food on the Sabbath;
- did not permit a non-Jew to work for them on the Sabbath;
- did not permit circumcisions on the Sabbath (circumcisions were performed at the close of the Sabbath so healing would not begin on the Sabbath);
- did not seek medical help because they took literally Exodus 15:26, "I am the Lord who heals you";
- did not observe the postbiblical holiday of Chanukkah;
- did not observe the rituals and ceremonies relating to *tefillin, mezuzah, tzitzit,* marriage, and divorce. All are rabbinic innovations rather than biblical mandates the Karaites argued;
- considered it meritorious to fast on festivals, a belief based on the words of the prophet Amos, "I shall turn your feasts into mourning."

The actual philosophy of Karaism does not differ substantially from normative rabbinic thinking. In the fourteenth century, Karaite philosopher and exegete Aaron ben Elijah (1300–1369), who lived in Nicomedia (Asia Minor), wrote a book entitled *Eitz Ha-Cha'yim* ("Tree of Life"), modeled after Moses Maimonides' *Guide of the Perplexed.* In it he presents the Karaite creed in ten principles:

1. God is the creator and was not Himself created.

2. God created the physical world out of nothing (*ex nihilo*).

3. God is formless and incorporeal, unique and unitary, comparable to nothing in existence.

4. God sent us our teacher Moses.

5. God gave us the Torah through Moses and nothing may be added to it, or subtracted from it, or changed in any way.

6. Every Jew must study the Torah in its original Hebrew language.

7. God also revealed Himself through the prophets.

8. God will resurrect the dead on the Day of Judgment.

9. The individual has freedom of will and is rewarded according to the life he lived.

10. God does not despise those living in exile and they may hope for His help and for redemption through the Messiah of the seed of David.

Scope of the Movement

By the end of the ninth century Anan ben David had assembled a large coterie of followers, but the threat he posed to rabbinic Judaism and its teachers, referred to as Rabbinites, was blunted by the opposition of the greatest scholar of the age, Sa'adya Gaon of Babylonia (882–942). Nevertheless, the fundamentalist approach of Anan did make inroads, albeit modest, into far-flung Jewish communities throughout the world.

At the outset, Palestine itself was the stronghold of the movement, but in the wake of the First Crusade in 1099 and the demolition of Jewish communities in Europe as well as Pal-estine, the center of Karaism moved to the Byzantine Empire, with its capital in Constantinople, where the Orthodox Eastern Church gave Karaites safe haven. Karaism flourished there until the sixteenth century, when it was compelled to seek safer ground and eventually made its way to the Crimean Peninsula, north of the Black Sea and then further north to Lithuania and parts of Poland.

Karaites settled in czarist Russia toward the end of the eighteenth century and became so assimilated that when the Holocaust struck during World War II, Karaites escaped persecution.

By the end of World War II, 7,000 of the 12,000 Karaites in the world lived in Egypt and during the Israeli War of Independence (1948), these Egyptian Karaites imperiled their lives by performing many heroic deeds in behalf of the emerging state of Israel. By 1950, about 3,500 Egyptian Karaites emigrated to Israel, and the State allocated funds for the establishment and administration of Karaite courts that would rule on issues brought by members of the Karaite community

Despite the tacit recognition given the Karaite community in Israel, its members are not considered full Jews. The basic argument is that over the centuries many Karaites have remarried after having been divorced, but the divorce document (*get*) issued by Karaite courts has never met the requirements of rabbinic law. Hence, when a Karaite woman remarried on the basis of a Karaite *get*, the new marriage was really invalid (because the woman who was remarrying was still a married woman in the eyes of Jewish law), and the offspring of the invalid marriage were *mamzerim* (bastards). In Jewish law, only a proselyte or another *mamzer* may marry a *mamzer*.

The view casting the taint of bastardy on all Karaites has not been shared by all scholars.

As far back as the sixteenth century, one of the leading rabbis of Safed, Rabbi David ben Solomon ibn Abi Zimra (also known as the Radbaz), opposed the decision to disallow marriage with Karaites. He offered legal arguments refuting the view of Moses Isserles, and maintained that it is wrong to exclude a sizable group of Jews who sincerely want to be part of the larger Jewish community.

Today there are more than 20,000 Karaites in Israel. Although the issue has not been fully resolved, they are not recognized as a separate community, but they do have a separate *Beit Din* (court) to administer marriages and divorces.

Outside of Israel, small Karaite communities exist in Turkey, France, and the Untied States. In America, the largest Karaite community—about one hundred families—is located in San Francisco.

Kashrut

A term derived from the Hebrew word *kasher* ("ritually fit"), referring specifically to the Jewish dietary laws.

See Dietary Laws.

Kavanah

A Hebrew term with the dual meaning of "intention" and "concentration."

While in its general application *kavanah* is associated primarily with an act of prayer, Professor Ephraim Urbach of Israel, in his volume *The Halakhah: Its Sources and Development*, points out that in talmudic law the concept has important legal ramifications, particularly as it pertains to the Sabbath.

The word *kavanah* appears only once in the Mishnah (*Eruvin* 4:4), where the question is raised as to whether an act in itself or the intention behind an act should determine the culpability of an individual. The answer was

provided by the third/fourth-century Babylonian *amora* Rabbah and his colleagues, who ruled that only one who intentionally commits a transgression is culpable (*Bava Kamma* 26b).

The main thrust of the *kavanah* concept, however, relates to prayer and the degree of concentration that must be expended to have a truly spiritual experience. In his *Duties of the Heart*, the medieval Jewish philosopher Bachya ibn Pakuda wrote: "If one prays with his tongue, and his heart is otherwise engaged, his prayer is like a body without a spirit, like a shell without a kernel."

Preparing for Prayer

In early talmudic times, pious Jews were known to prepare for prayer. The Mishnah says (*Berakhot* 5:1), "Pious men of old used to meditate for one hour before engaging in prayer so that their final thoughts would be properly focused on their Father in heaven." Rabbi Chaninah, a first-century Deputy High Priest (whose function it was to stand next to the High Priest on the Day of Atonement, ready to take over should the need arise), said (*Eruvin* 65a) that he would never pray when in a state of agitation. In the third century, the Babylonian teacher Rav (Abba Arikha) issued this ruling (ibid.): "A person should not pray when his mind is not at ease."

By the time the first authoritative prayerbook was issued by Rabbi Sa'adya Gaon in the tenth century, a whole series of prayers were already being recited by pious Jews who wanted to prepare themselves for the actual prescribed prayers. These preparatory prayers came to be known as *Pesukei De-Zimra*, "Verses of Praise." Sa'adya included them as an appendix to his *siddur* (prayerbook), but later prayerbooks grouped them at the beginning of the liturgy, and they became the opening prayers of the morning service. The *Pesukei De-Zimra* consist of seven Psalms (100, 145–50) plus other prayer compositions, one of which is the *Barukh She-amar* prayer, "Blessed be He who spoke and the world was created."

In later centuries brief introductions to individual prayers were composed. Most noteworthy were those of the sixteenth-century mystics (kabbalists) living in Safed, Palestine. To reach toward God, to adore Him, to revere Him, to strive to become one with (be part of) Him was the essence of the mystic's existence. Accordingly, the kabbalists, more than other pious Jews, insisted that no prayer should be recited and no ritual performed without proper preparation. Some of the familiar short introductions to prayers composed by them are those beginning with *Hineni mukhan u'mezuman* (Behold, I am prepared"), *Yehi ratzon* ("May it be Thy will"), and *Le-sheim yichud* ("For the sake of unification").

The esteemed thirteenth-century scholar Solomon ibn Adret of Barcelona recognized early on that not all Jews would achieve a degree of spirituality that would prepare them for prayer and that not all would be able to appreciate the words being repeated over and over again. He therefore announced that all Jews will be rewarded for prayer if at the least they will bear in mind that there is a God and that all blessings flow from Him. It matters not, he affirmed, if one is ignorant and cannot even pronounce the words of the prayers accurately, or if one word is substituted for another. As long as prayer is being recited with *kavanah*, the person will be rewarded for his or her general intention.

Kedushah

A Hebrew word literally meaning "holiness." The prayer known as *Kedushah* was added to the *Eighteen Benedictions* (called the *Tefillah* in early times and *Amidah* in later times) around the turn of the first century C.E., after the format and content of the liturgy had already been established by the Rabbis of the academy in Yavneh.

The *Kedushah* is mystical in nature, as is evident from its reference to angelic beings who sanctify God's name with the words *Kadosh, kadosh, kadosh*... "Holy, holy, holy, is the Lord God of hosts, the whole earth is full of His glory." These words, which first appeared in the Book of Isaiah (6:3), are recited at every morning and afternoon prayer service.

Kehillah

A variant form of the Hebrew word *kahal*, meaning "congregation" or "community." The Book of Deuteronomy (33:4) uses the expression, "Moses charged us with the Torah, [which is] the heritage of the congregation of Jacob [*kehillat Yaakov*]."

In its widest sense, the term *kehillah* encompasses the entire body of world Jewry; in its most narrow sense, it may refer to a local community, regardless of size. Local communities are often referred to as *kahal kadosh* or *kehillah kedoshah*, "holy community." The term is also sometimes applied to a particular major synagogue within the community.

In the Middle Ages, in the larger communities of Europe, the *kehillah* was autonomous and self-sustaining. Through taxes imposed on members of the community, it established and supported its synagogues and their functionaries, as well as schools and cemeteries. It cared for the sick, the poor, the widow, and the orphan. But the hub of all activity was the synagogue.

At the beginning of the nineteenth century, during the Napoleonic era, the Jewish community and its autonomy changed, as Jews were considered citizens like all other members of the state. Freedom of religious practice was generally guaranteed and compulsory membership in the Jewish community was no longer demanded. Since Jews were free to be part of the community at large, the role of the local Jewish community diminished.

Today, the concept of the "oneness of the Jewish community" carries on, although on a purely voluntary basis. In times of crisis, Jews the world over coalesce to form a united front.

Keiruv

A Hebrew term literally meaning "drawing close," used to describe the concept of outreach, a program employed by the various denominations to encourage nonobservant Jews to embrace religious observance.

Kelippah

Plural, *kelippot*. A Hebrew word literally meaning "shell, husk." According to kabbalistic teaching, demonic forces known as *kelippot* seek to surround the holy sparks and consume them. It is up to man to free the holy sparks from imprisonment. In some literature, the term *kelippot* refers to everything that is evil.

See Kabbalah; Shevirat Keilim.

Keri'ah

A Hebrew term literally meaning "tearing, rending," referring specifically to the Jewish law requiring that, following a death, a garment be torn by close family members as a sign of mourning.

Origins

The custom of *keri'ah* is of biblical origin. When Jacob saw Joseph's blood-stained coat of many colors, he was told by his sons that Joseph was killed by a wild beast. Jacob reacted by tearing his garment (Genesis 37:34).

The Bible also describes how David tore his clothes when he heard of the death of King Saul (II Samuel 1:11). In the Book of Job (1:20), we are told that upon learning of the death of his children, Job "stood up and rent his clothes."

The Talmud (*Moed Katan* 15a) associates the *keri'ah* law with the incident described in Leviticus 10, where Nadav and Avihu, two of the four sons of Aaron, met an untimely death because they had brought an unauthorized sacrifice on the altar. Moses said to his brother, Aaron, and to Elazar and Ittamar (the other two sons of Aaron), "Do not bare your heads and do not rend your clothes [that is, do not carry out the mourning rites] (10:6)." From this verse the Rabbis deduced that since Aaron, Elazar, and Ittamar were specifically ordered *not* to mourn the unworthy Nadav and Avihu, it is implicit that relatives in general *are* obligated to mourn the loss of relatives by rending a garment.

Some scholars consider the rite of rending a garment to have been introduced as a substitute for the pagan practice of bruising one's flesh and shaving off the hair of one's head, referred to in the Book of Deuteronomy (14:1) and in First Kings (18:28). Israelites were warned not to violate their bodies as an expression of grief.

In ancient times, when it was customary for a Jewish mourner to wear black as an expression of bereavement over the loss of a loved one, the Rabbis felt it unnecessary for the mourner to repeat that expression by tearing a garment. Later authorities, however, disagreed and insisted that the mourner rend the garment regardless of its color.

Regulations Pertaining to Keri'ah

The Talmud (*Moed Katan* 25a) prescribes that everyone who witnesses a death must rend a garment immediately. The Rabbis considered a human life to be equal in value to the most holy object: the Torah scroll. And, they reasoned, just as everyone who witnesses the burning of a Torah scroll is required by law to tear a garment to symbolize that they have suffered a serious personal loss, so is everyone who witnesses the expiration of life required to tear a garment. The gender of the deceased and the relationship of the deceased to those present are both irrelevant.

In time, this requirement was modified to include only immediate relatives present in the death-room at the time of death. The change was effected because authorities feared that if the original regulation were allowed to stand, visitors would be discouraged from visiting the terminally ill out of concern that if a death were to occur in their presence, they could be obligated to tear their garments. Sick people would thus be denied the comfort visitors can offer.

Jewish law requires that *keri'ah* be performed for the seven closest relatives: father, mother, son, daughter, brother, sister, spouse. It is for these relatives that one is obligated to formally mourn (Yoreh Dei'ah 340:1).

Generally, the officiating rabbi tears the mourner's garment. In Orthodox circles, however, where it is considered an act of immodesty for a man to touch a woman, one of the women present who can lead the mourner in the *keri'ah* prayer performs the act on the womenfolk.

For parents, the left side of a garment is torn because in ancient times it was believed that the left side is closest to the heart, and parents are closest to the heart of a child. For a son, daughter, brother, sister, and spouse *keri'ah* is performed on the right side of the garment. Strict observance demands that the tear performed for parents be done by hand, although the starting cut may be done with a knife.

Although Jewish law demands that the tear be made in the garment itself (a woman's dress and a man's vest or jacket), since the tear would render an otherwise good garment unusable, it became customary to attach a ribbon to the garment and to cut the ribbon instead of the garment. Justification for this now commonplace practice is based on the *bal tashchit* principle, which considers it wasteful to destroy a useful garment. Those who favor the use of ribbons for *keri'ah* explain that the rite is basically an expression of grief, and the same emotions are felt whether the tear is made on a ribbon or garment.

Many Orthodox Jews find the use of ribbons an absolute violation of Jewish law. Orthodox authority Rabbi Yekutiel Greenwald (see his *Kol Bo Al Aveilut, p. 28*) recommends that if a ribbon has been used for *keri'ah*, a second *keri'ah* be performed on a regular garment before the *shivah* period is over. In such a case, the *keri'ah* blessing need not be repeated. Rabbis of the Spanish-Portuguese community do not perform *keri'ah* on a ribbon. The Committee on Jewish Law and Standards of the Rabbinical Assembly (Conservative) expressly permits the use of ribbons.

After *keri'ah* has been performed, the following blessing is recited by the mourner: *Barukh atah Adonai, Eloheinu melekh ha-olam, Da'yan Ha-Emet*, "Praised be Thou, O Lord our God, King of the universe, who is a true Judge."

See Bal Tashchit; Shivah.

Ketubbah

A Hebrew word literally meaning "writing," referring specifically to the document that a groom gives his bride at the time of marriage. Formalized by Shimon ben Shetach, the first-century B.C.E. leader of Pharisaic Judaism, the *ketubbah* is written in Aramaic, the language of the masses in which of all legal documents of the talmudic period were written.

The *ketubbah* guarantees to the bride that her husband will provide for all of her needs and, should the marriage be dissolved by death or divorce, the man or his estate will provide the woman with a specified amount of money. The obligations of the wife to her husband are not spelled out in the *ketubbah*.

Witnessing the Ketubbah

The *ketubbah* must be signed by two male witnesses not related to the bride or groom. This rule is an extension of Deuteronomy 24:16, which states that a father cannot be put to death based on the testimony of his son.

Although the actual *ketubbah* signing is done privately, before the wedding ceremony begins, the witnesses must be present when it is read aloud under the wedding canopy or under the *chuppah*.

After the reading the *ketubbah*, the document is handed to the groom, who in turn hands it to his bride with the understanding that she keep it in her possession from that day on.

Sometimes a memorial prayer (*El Malei Rachamim*) for deceased parents of the bride and groom is recited at the signing.

Recent Innovations

In modern times, an attempt has been made to address the problem of husbands who refuse to grant their wives a Jewish divorce document (*get*) after the state has granted the couple a civil divorce. The Law Committee of the Rabbinical Assembly (Conservative) has appended a section to the traditional *ketubbah* which states that in the event of the dissolution of a marriage, the couple agrees to appear before a rabbinic court (*Beit Din*) to adjudicate the matter.

In Reform Judaism, the issuance of a *ketubbah*, which had fallen into disuse, has been reintroduced for couples desiring one. In this modified version of the traditional *ketubbah*, mutual obligations of the couple rather than those of the male partner alone have been introduced.

The Ketubbah as Art

As far back as the Middle Ages, illuminated *ketubbot* featuring scenes from the Bible, family coats of arms, mythological characters, and other motifs were created. One of the earliest decorated *ketubbot* was executed in 1392 for an Ashkenazic couple from Kresmir, Austria. However, the best known illuminated marriage contracts began to appear in Italy and neighboring countries in the sixteenth and later centuries.

Designs of *ketubbot* varied from locale to locale and were executed either on paper or parchment. Typical of most were colorful floral designs that served as borders surrounding a handsome hand-lettered text.

Although the use of costly *ketubbot* was out of fashion for many years, in recent times artists have reintroduced the concept, and many young couples have commissioned personalized marriage contracts that reflect their feelings and aspirations.

See Handkerchief Ceremony.

Kevod Ha-Beriot

A Hebrew term literally meaning "honor of fellow humans." This concept, based on the principle that all people are created in the image of God and are to be accorded respect and dignity, is akin to the concept of *kevod tzibur*.

The *kevod ha-beriot* principle was best exemplified by Rabbi Yochanan ben Zakkai, the eminent first-century talmudic scholar of whom it was said (*Berakhot* 17a): "No one ever greeted him first, even a heathen in the street." He made a special effort to greet a passerby first so as to acknowledge the individual's worth and importance.

The minor talmudic tractate *Derekh Eretz Rabbah* (56b) expresses this concept in a pithy, practical way when it cautions: "Let all persons always be in your eyes as robbers [that is, be suspicious of them], but honor each with the same respect accorded [the revered, pious, first-century patriarch] Rabbi Gamaliel." This same ethical principle is expressed succinctly by the motto *Kabdeihu vechashdeihu*, "Respect him and suspect him" (*Kallah Rabbati* 9).

See Kevod Tzibur.

Kevod Ha-Met

A Hebrew term literally meaning "reverence for the dead," referring to one of the two basic principles—the other is *kevod he-chai* ("reverence for the living")—that govern Jewish death and mourning rites.

The *kevod ha-met* principle stems from the concept that man is created in the image of God and any affront to man, even when deceased, is an affront to God. Any action that bestows honor on the dead fulfills the *kevod ha-met* mandate.

When Jewish law requires that a funeral take place within twenty-four hours after a death, it is concerned with *kevod ha-met*, for to leave a body unburied for an extended period of time is considered disrespectful. Viewing the remains before burial was rarely done in Europe except for the lying-in-state of royalty and other notables. Jewish tradition regards such viewing of the deceased in an open casket as incompatible with the concept of *kevod ha-met*.

When Jewish law requires that a person be buried in the earth rather than be cremated, its intention is also to show respect for the dead, who in Jewish tradition must be returned to the earth from which man was created.

Bequeathing an organ of the dead to help the living is, in most cases, considered to be an act that exemplifies *kevod ha-met*, since it enhances the prospects of the return of an ill person to a healthy condition.

The delivery of a eulogy at a funeral is another example, say the Rabbis of the Talmud, of an act performed to honor the dead. Thus, if the deceased willed that a eulogy *not* be delivered at the funeral, the request is generally honored.

See Kevod He-Chai; Nivul Ha-Met.

Kevod He-Chai

A Hebrew term literally meaning "reverence for the living," referring to the concept that is associated with the laws of death and mourning. The essence of the principle is that just as respect must be accorded the deceased (see *kevod ha-met*), due consideration must be given to the grief-stricken survivors. Thus, for example, neighbors are required to prepare a meal of condolence for the bereaved, who otherwise might not bother to prepare food for themselves. In the same spirit, visitors are urged to refrain from paying a condolence call until the third day after burial, so as to give mourners the chance to express their grief privately and to collect their thoughts. The entire seven-day mourning period known as *shivah* similarly focuses on the living rather than the deceased.

See Shivah.

Kevod Tzibur

A Hebrew term literally meaning "honor of the public." One of the guiding principles of Judaism, *kevod tzibur* expresses the concern of the Rabbis of the Talmud and later scholars that

Jews not engage in any behavior that might be considered offensive or undignified, that is, an insult to the congregation. With this as a motivating factor, religious authorities banned certain practices.

Consideration for the feelings of the community is the reason behind using more than one Torah scroll for holiday readings and for readings on special Sabbaths. The Talmud (*Yoma* 70a) explains that on Yom Kippur in Temple times, the High Priest first read two selections from the Book of Leviticus; then he rolled up the scroll, tucked it under his arm, and recited the *maftir* portion (from the Book of Numbers) from memory.

The Rabbis asked why the High Priest did not roll the Torah scroll from Leviticus to Numbers and then read the *maftir* portion from the scroll instead of reciting it from memory. The answer given is *mipnei kevod tzibur*, out of consideration for the feelings of the public. The congregation might have become impatient if it had to sit and wait while the scroll was being rolled. This explains why, on any given Sabbath, as many as three Torot may be read from, all of which must be rolled to the right place in advance of the service.

The sensitivity of the public is also the rationale for opposition to women's participation in religious services. Women were prohibited from leading a service (or from sitting next to men in a congregation) because, as the Talmud (*Berakhot* 24a) explains it, a woman can arouse men sexually when in close proximity and thus interfere with their concentration on prayer. This same concern with public sensitivity is why an improperly clad person, the Talmud (*Megillah* 24b) says, should not be permitted to read the Torah before the congregation.

An illustration of how seriously the concept of *kevod tzibur* was taken in ancient times is found in the conduct of the illustrious Rabbi Akiba. Rabbi Judah reported, "This was the practice of Rabbi Akiba: When he prayed with the congregation, he used to cut it short [referring to the lengthy *Eighteen Benedictions* (*Shemoneh Esrei* prayer), in order not to impose a burden [the term *mipnei torach tzibur* is used] on the congregation. But when he prayed privately, one might leave Akiba's room when he was standing in one corner and praying, and later, upon returning, find him in another," so energetic were the many genuflections and prostrations that Akiba indulged in (*Berakhot* 31a).

The principle of *kevod ha-beriot* differs from *kevod tzibur* in that the former expresses concern for the individual whereas the latter expresses concern for the community at large.

See Tircha De-Tzibura.

Kibbutz

(Plural, *kibbutzim* or *kevutzot*.) A Hebrew word literally meaning "gathering-in," a name attached to the cooperative farming settlements first established in Palestine in 1909, when twelve young pioneers founded Degania near the Sea of Galilee (Lake Kinneret). Members of the cooperative were to share work and earnings equally.

Being the first *kibbutz*, Degania became known as "mother of *kevutzot*." It was the home of Russian-born philosopher A. D. (Aharon David) Gordon (1856–1922), whose teaching greatly influenced the Palestinian Jewish labor movement. Gordon regarded physical labor as the basis of human existence and a return to nature as a psychological and spiritual necessity for the development of human personality.

Soon after the establishment of Degania, other *kibbutzim* began to spring up, until, over time, more than two hundred fifty dotted the country. *Kibbutz* members—popularly called *kibbutzniks*—were taken care of by the cooperative. Housing, education, health care, and child care were provided. Meals were prepared in the *kibbutz* kitchen and served in a community mess hall. Decisions on work assignments were made by a central committee chosen democratically.

Kibbutz members were reputed to be strong and courageous, and did in fact become the backbone of the Israeli armed forces. The IDF (Israel Defense Forces) boasted military leaders of the caliber of Moshe Dayan and Yitzhak Rabin, who were products of *kibbutzim*.

The *kibbutz* movement in Israel continues today, but its popularity has waned. Young people have opted for full independence and opportunities to acquire wealth in private industry.

See Moshav.

Kibbutz Galu'yot

A Hebrew term literally meaning "ingathering of exiles," referring to a concept based upon a prophecy of Ezekiel. In the Book of Ezekiel (chapter 34), speaking in the name of God, the prophet promises to reverse the fortune of the Jews who had been exiled to Babylonia by returning them to their homeland.

In modern times, the concept of return from exile was promoted by leading Orthodox Zionist pioneers such as Rabbi Tzevi Hirsch Kalischer (1795–1874), who considered the return of the exiled Jewish people to the Land of Israel the first step in the redemption of the land. He saw this as a necessary goal if the Jews were to be able to carry out all the commandments (*mitzvot*) that hinge on residency in the land, including restoration of the sacrificial system. Like the secular-minded A. D. Gordon, Kalischer advocated the formation of an agricultural society in Palestine, a pro-

posal advanced in his book *Derishat Tziyon.* (1862).

The Law of Return, which gives every Jew the right to settle in the Land of Israel, is a fundamental law of the State of Israel today.

Kiddush

A Hebrew term literally meaning "sanctification." In order to spiritualize the mundane activity of drinking wine at mealtime, and in order to infuse Sabbath and holiday meals with a sense of holiness, a prayer called the *Kiddush* was introduced between the sixth and fourth centuries B.C.E. by the Men of the Great Assembly. The two major themes expressed in the prayer are Creation and the Exodus, both of which speak to the power of God.

Early Practices

In talmudic times, it was customary to drink wine daily, and the *Borei peri ha-gafen* blessing was always recited first. Before wine was consumed on a Sabbath or holiday, this blessing was expanded to recall the miracles of the Creation and the Exodus.

Up until the destruction of the Second Temple in 70 C.E., the *Kiddush* had been recited only in the home. Soon thereafter, the size of the Jewish community in Babylonia grew as a result of the emigration from Palestine of large numbers of Jews anxious to avoid Roman persecution. Many of these refugees became itinerant peddlers who often found themselves far from home on the Sabbath. To care for these Jews, synagogues opened their doors and provided meals and lodging.

To insure that itinerant Jews who ate their Sabbath and holiday meals in the synagogue would hear the recitation of the *Kiddush*, the prayer was now also recited by the cantor at the conclusion of the synagogue service. (Permanent residents of the town would recite the *Kiddush* privately for their own families at home.) Thus, in Babylonia and other communities outside of Palestine, it became customary for the *Kiddush* to be recited both in the synagogue and the home. In Palestine itself, where wayfaring strangers were not in abundance and where there was little need for Sabbath synagogue hospitality, *Kiddush* was not recited in the synagogue. To this day, synagogues in Israel do not recite the *Kiddush* at the Friday evening service.

Kiddush Protocol and Customs

The Rabbis of the Talmud mandated that the *Kiddush* be recited and wine drunk before the *Hamotzi* blessing is recited. If the *Kiddush*, the blessing over the wine, were to be pronounced after the *Hamotzi* prayer, the *Kiddush* would be superfluous. This is so because the *Hamotzi* blessing, which is recited over bread at the beginning of the meal, covers all the food to be eaten in the course of the meal, including wine (*Pesachim* 105a).

Since talmudic times there has been much debate over whether only red wine can be used for *Kiddush* or whether white wine is an acceptable alternative. Both the Palestinian and the Jerusalem Talmuds discuss the question, concluding that since only strong—that is, red—wine was used on the altar in Temple times, so must red wine be used for *Kiddush*. On the other hand, Joseph Caro, in his *Code of Jewish Law* (*Shulchan Arukh*, Orach Cha'yim 272:4), permits the use of white wine for *Kiddush* but suggests that red wine should be used if possible. In either case, there is no prohibition against using dry wine as opposed to the sweet wines most Jews associate with Jewish ritual.

It is traditional to fill to overflowing the cup of wine over which *Kiddush* is recited. This is often explained as an expression of

hope that life's goodness and bounty will be as abundant as the wine that is being blessed, but a more basic reason is related to the sacrificial system that was operative in Temple times. When burnt- and peace- offerings were made, an entire container of wine was poured onto the altar. After the Temple was destroyed and wine was used in connection with home rituals, a custom developed of filling the cup of wine to its very brim.

When reciting the *Kiddush*, many traditional Jews pick up the wine goblet, which has been filled to capacity, and cup it in both hands. They then remove their left hand and hold the goblet only with their right hand approximately three inches (one *tefach*) above the table. Some people nestle the bottom of the cup in the palm of their right hand and grasp it with five fingers to be in compliance with the verse in the Book of Psalms (145:16), "Thou openest Thine hands and satisfiest every living thing with favor" (*Kitzur Shulchan Arukh* 45:4). Others ascribe the practice to the symbolic five-petaled rose of Sharon in Song of Songs (2:1).

Although it is more common for families to stand rather than sit while the *Kiddush* is recited, this is not, and has not been, a universal practice. The Sephardic and chasidic communities generally follow the practice established by Rabbi Isaac Luria (known as the Ari), who lived in Safed, Palestine, from 1570 until his death in 1572. He believed that one should stand during *Kiddush* because it is an essential part of Sabbath observance. Isaac Luria, comparing the Sabbath to a bride, said that just as when blessings are recited at a marriage ceremony the groom stands next to his bride, so should Jews stand when ushering in the "Sabbath bride."

When returning home from synagogue on the Sabbath or holidays, *chasidim*, as well as those who follow chasidic practice, continue to wear their street hats (usually black felt hats) at least until after reciting the *Kiddush*. Sabbath and holiday meals are formal occasions, and one must dress for them accordingly. Some wear a street hat throughout the meal, while others change to a black skullcap (*yarmulke*) after the *Kiddush* has been recited.

See Berakhah Le-Vatalah; Wine.

Kiddush Ha-Shem

A Hebrew term literally meaning "sanctification of the Name [of God]," which encompasses loyalty to God and observance of his Laws given in the Torah. In its most extreme sense, the concept relates to martyrdom by saintly persons who choose death rather than violate God's law. The biblical basis of this concept of *kiddush Ha-Shem* can be found in Leviticus (22:32): "You shall not profane My holy name; I shall be hallowed among the Children of Israel. I am the God who hallows you."

Kiddush Ha-Shem was exemplified by the ten martyrs whose story is told in the liturgy of the Yom Kippur afternoon (*Musaf*) service. These ten distinguished and courageous rabbis of the first century C.E. defied the Roman laws forbidding the teaching of the Torah. They were apprehended and, as a consequence, were subject to a horrible death.

Kiddushin

A Hebrew term literally meaning "sanctification," referring specifically to the marriage ceremony, which is also known as *nisuin*.

See Nisuin.

Kiddush Levanah

A Hebrew term literally meaning "sanctification of the moon." Since the destruction of the Temple, the arrival of the New Moon has been commemorated through special prayers. On a clear moonlit weekday evening, immediately after the *Ma'ariv* service, congregants assemble outside the synagogue some time between the third day after the crescent of the new moon appears in the sky and the fifteenth day of the new month, when the moon begins to wane. They recite one major prayer, recorded in the talmudic tractate *Sanhedrin* (42a), plus several shorter prayers. The ceremony is also known as *Birkat Levanah*. In some communities, the ceremony is postponed until after Yom Kippur and after the fast days of the month of Tevet and Av are commemorated.

Kiddush Levanah is a ceremony distinct from the *Birkhat Ha-Chodesh* (Blessing of the New Month) ceremony held in the synagogue on the Sabbath prior to the first day of the forthcoming new month. The *Birkhat Ha-Chodesh* is not recited to welcome Tishrei, a month so filled with holidays that it does not require additional blessing.

Kinyan Sudar

A Hebrew term literally meaning "acquisition by handkerchief," a symbolic act whereby one acquires property.

See Handkerchief Ceremony.

Kissing

In the Bible, the kiss is an expression of affection, devotion, and reverence. Esau and Jacob kiss after not seeing each other for a long time; Jacob kisses Rachel when seeing her for the first time; Laban kisses his sons and daughters; Aaron kisses his brother, Moses; Samuel kisses King Saul; Orpah kisses Naomi, her mother-in-law.

The Rabbis of the Talmud (*Genesis Rabbah* 70:12) disapprove of kissing, even labeling it obscene. Rabbi Akiba (*Berakhot* 8b) praises the ancient Medes because when they kissed, they kissed only on the hand, not on the lips. The Talmud (*Shabbat* 13a) notes that when the fourth-century scholar Ulla would return home from his academy, he would kiss his sisters on the hand. And Rashi, in his commentary on *Avodah Zarah* 17a, observes that it is proper conduct, when leaving a synagogue service, for one to kiss his father and mother as well as his teacher.

Moses Maimonides (*Mishneh Torah*, Issurei Biah 21:1, 6) found a biblical basis for condemning physical contact with the opposite sex by interpreting the verse in Leviticus (18:6), "No one shall approach close relatives to uncover their nakedness," to mean that not only are sexual relations between relatives forbidden, but kissing is forbidden as well, even where it does not cause sexual arousal. However, along with most other authorities of his day, Maimonides excluded from this ban the kissing of one's closest relatives—particularly one's mother, wife, daughter, sister, and aunt.

Later codifiers of Jewish law were even more strict and extended the meaning of kissing to include any type of physical contact with the opposite sex because it might lead to sexual arousal. The *Code of Jewish Law* (*Shulchan Arukh*, Even Ha-Ezer 21:1, 2) forbids a man to even smell the scent of a strange woman, to look at her hair, or so much as gaze upon her little finger. Many Orthodox Jews today, particularly the ultra-Orthodox, are meticulous about complying with this law and, accordingly, refuse even to shake hands with members of the opposite sex.

Kissing Religious Objects

From time immemorial Jews have displayed affection for religious articles by kissing them. The Torah is kissed by worshippers when it is carried in procession around the synagogue before the Torah reading. Before reciting the first and last blessings over the Torah, people once kissed the Torah with their lips or touched it with the tips of their fingers and then kissed their fingers. Since the Talmud considered it improper to touch a holy object in this manner, it became customary to touch the corner of the Torah with its mantle or with one's *tallit* (prayershawl), or sometimes to touch the object with a prayerbook and then to kiss the prayerbook. Upon leaving a house, the *mezuzah* is touched by the fingers, which are then kissed. The fringes of the *tallit* are kissed whenever donned. When a holy book (prayerbook or Bible) is picked up after being dropped, it is kissed.

One of the more interesting local customs is followed by Russian Jews, who use their index finger to kiss the *mezuzah* and the little finger to kiss the Torah scroll.

See Prayer.

Kittl

The Yiddish name for the white linen garment originally worn in ancient Palestine on festive days. Also the name of one of the garments in which the deceased is dressed for burial. The whiteness of the garment represents purity.

Today a *kittl* is often worn by the leader of the Passover *Seder* and by clergy and lay Jews during High Holiday services. Rabbis and cantors also don a *kittl* when special prayers for dew (*tal*) and rain (*geshem*) are recited during the *Musaf* service of Shemini Atzeret and Passover. *Tal* is recited on the first day of Passover, *Geshem* is recited on Shemini Atzeret.

The burial *kittl* is called a *sargenes*, or *sarginos*, a word probably related to the German *Sarg*, meaning "coffin." Some linguists see a relationship between *sargenes* and the English word "serge," a strong twilled fabric with a diagonal rib. According to Rashi, the word derives from the Latin *serica* or *sericum*, akin to the old French *sarge* and the Middle English *serge*, and refers to a garment of wool or linen.

A *kittl* is often worn by an Orthodox groom while standing under the wedding canopy (*chuppah*).

Klal Yisrael

See Kallah.

Klei Kodesh

A Hebrew term literally meaning "holy vessels," originally applied to the *menorah* (candelabrum), altars, table upon which the shewbreads (two *challot*) were placed, and all the other appurtenances of the desert sanctuary and the later Temples in Jerusalem. In post-Temple times, the term came to be applied to all Torah ornaments: crowns, pointers, breastplates, and *rimmonim* (which are placed over the two finials). The same name was later applied to the various functionaries (professional and voluntary) who serve the synagogue, much like the various adornments serve the Torah itself.

Knas Mahl

A Hebrew/German term literally meaning "penalty meal." *Knas* is a Hebrew word, commonly used in the Talmud, meaning "penalty, fine." *Mahl* is a German word meaning "meal." In the Middle Ages, the Jews of Germany introduced a celebration at which arrangements were made between the parents of the bride and groom for a forthcoming marriage.

In the course of the meal, discussions were held and marriage arrangements were made by the parents of the couple. Among the decisions reached was the penalty that would be levied against a party who broke the engagement.

The agreed-upon stipulations, the *knas mahl*, also called *tena'im*, were formulated as a written contract, specifying the amount of dowry to be paid, the date and place of the marriage ceremony and other pertinent details.

The signing was concluded by throwing crockery to the ground and shattering it, symbolizing the destruction of the Temple in Jerusalem and serving as a reminder that such will be the fate of the couple if all terms of the agreement are not carried out.

In more recent times the handkerchief ceremony, called *kinyan sudar*, has replaced *knas mahl*.

See Handkerchief Ceremony.

Knesset

This Hebrew word meaning "assembly" is the name by which the legislative body, or parliament, of the State of Israel is called. The word was first used as part of the title of the governing body of Jewish life in the centuries after Ezra the Scribe reinvigorated Jewish life: the *Anshei Knesset Ha-Gedolah*, the members of the Great Assembly.

Established in 1949, the Israeli Knesset has a single house of 120 members elected by citizens over the age of eighteen under a system of proportional representation. The voters choose from candidate lists of the different political parties, and the members of the Knesset are elected according to the number of votes each list receives. Knesset members serve a four-year term, but a majority of the body's members may call a new election before the end of the four years.

The Knesset building in Jerusalem was built in 1966 with money donated by James R. Rothschild. A stunning example of modern architecture, it contains mosaics and tapestries designed by artist Marc Chagall.

See Knesset Ha-Gedolah.

Knesset Ha-Gedolah

A Hebrew term literally meaning "great assembly." During the Second Temple period, from the fifth-century B.C.E. to 70 C.E., the *Knesset Ha-Gedolah* was the supreme authority in matters of religion and law. Established by Ezra the Scribe, this body consisting of one hundred twenty Jewish scholars, known as the *Anshei Knesset Ha-Gedolah* ("Men of the Great Assembly"), was the spiritual center of the Jewish people.

Among its many worthy accomplishments was the establishment of a fixed liturgy for the synagogue (*Berakhot* 33a). During the years of its existence, five distinguished "pairs" (*zugot* in Hebrew) served as its president and vice-president: Yossi ben Yo'ezer and Yossi ben Yochanan; Joshua ben Perachya and Nittai of Arbel; Judah ben Tabbai and Shimon ben Shetach; Shema'ya and Avtalyon; and finally, Hillel and Shammai. These rabbis were the forerunners of the *tanna'im* whose analysis of the Bible established the legal structure of Judaism for the generations that followed.

See Ma'asei Bereishit and Ma'asei Merkavah; Men of the Great Assembly.

Knots

The Book of Daniel (5:12, 16) states that the ability to loosen knots is considered to be among the great feats performed by magicians. This led to the popular superstition that anything that ties or binds can cause an ill effect. For this reason, the ties of a shroud are not knotted, nor is the thread used to sew shrouds.

Kolel

Plural, *kolelim*. A Hebrew word literally meaning "group, assembly, congregation, community." Members of the early *kibbutzim* in Israel were referred to as being part of a *kolel*. A Jewish European community in the eighteenth and later centuries was often referred to as a *kolel*—for example: Kolel Warsaw, Kolel Hungary, Kolel Ashkenazim.

In modern times, the term was applied to another type of community—namely, a community of students in an academy of higher learning who devoted their full day to study. These students, generally married men with families, were supported by wealthy individuals within the community or by family members. The word *kolel* in this sense was coined in 1878 by Rabbi Israel Lipkin (Salanter), of Kovno, Lithuania.

In November 1995, a group of Reform Jews under the leadership of Rabbi Joshua Salzman officially opened a *kolel* in New York City in which sixty men and women dedicated themselves to engage in intensive study of talmudic and auxiliary texts, along the lines established by the Orthodox community.

See Yeshiva.

Kol Ishah

This Hebrew term literally meaning "the voice of a woman" is the name given a talmudic concept (*Berakhot* 24a) which declares that a woman's voice, as well as her legs and hair, are sexually provocative and are not to be exposed to men, lest they be tempted to harbor impure thoughts.

This concept led to the establishment of a divider (*mechitzah*) or balcony in Orthodox synagogues, which would serve to keep women separate from men. Among ultra-Orthodox Jews, the sexes are also separated at the wedding ceremony and wedding dinner. Some Jews have even extended the prohibition of females joining in singing songs (*zemirot*) at family Sabbath meals.

After the assassination of Israeli Prime Minister Yitzhak Rabin in 1996, a program to honor his memory was held in Madison Square

Garden, in New York City. Hearing that Barbra Streisand was scheduled to sing, the ultra-Orthodox said that they would enter the hall only after she had concluded her performance. In the end, Streisand refused to attend.

Kol Nidrei

A Hebrew term literally meaning "all vows." Chanted at the evening service of Yom Kippur, this prayer was composed in post-talmudic times. Written in Aramaic, the vernacular of the Jews of Babylonia, the *Kol Nidrei* asks for the nullification of all vows made to God, innocently or under duress, that one is unable to fulfill. These do not include promises or commitments made to one's fellow man. To be forgiven such trespasses, one must appeal to the person who has been offended or harmed. Since Judaism regards the spoken word as sacred, it introduced the *Kol Nidrei* formula as a means of expressing regret for violating this primary Jewish value and for seeking absolution.

The *Kol Nidrei* is chanted three times by the cantor to a haunting sixteenth-century melody of unknown authorship. Flanking the cantor are two respected members of the congregation, each of whom holds a Torah scroll. The threesome symbolizes a *Beit Din*, a court of law, before whom individuals on trial stand in judgment.

Yom Kippur evening, as well as the entire synagogue service, has come to known as *Kol Nidrei*. To emphasize the holiness of the service men don a prayershawl (*tallit*), which is not normally worn at nighttime services. So that one can recite the blessing over the prayershawl while it is still light, the *Kol Nidrei* service begins before sunset. Furthermore, because *Kol Nidrei* is a legal formula whereby one is released from a vow, and because courts did not function on Sabbaths and holidays, it

was arranged for the *Kol Nidrei* to be recited before sundown.

Attempts to eliminate the *Kol Nidrei* from the service have been made over the years but have failed because of the profound emotional pull of the chant. Although the words themselves are legalistic and hardly apply to modern life, the warm and tender melody has kept the prayer alive.

Korban

Plural, *korbanot*. A Hebrew word literally meaning "that which is brought forth or offered," referring in particular to sacrificial gifts brought to the Temples in Jerusalem. These consisted of animals, fowl, and cereal offerings presented to the Priests (*Kohanim*), who offered them as sacrifices on the Temple altar. The Book of Leviticus discusses the details of this sacrificial system.

See Sacrificial System.

Kosher Dietary Laws

See Dietary Laws.

Kupat Cholim

A Hebrew term literally meaning "fund for the sick," referring to the medical insurance organization established to provide for Jews in ill health. When the State of Israel was established, *Kupat Cholim* became part of the Histadrut, the federation of labor. It functions much like American health maintenance organizations (HMOs).

Kvater, Kvaterin

In the Middle Ages, in addition to the father, the *mohel* (the person who performs the procedure), and the *sandek* (the person who holds the child), two other personalities were invited to participate in the circumcision ceremony. These were the *kvater* and the *kvaterin*, usually a husband and wife or a brother and sister. As assistants to the *sandek*, the *kvater* and the *kvaterin* are thought of as godfather and godmother to the child.

The word *kvater* has been explained as being composed of the Hebrew letter *kaf*, meaning "like" when used as a prefix, and the German word *Vater*, meaning "father." More likely, it is derived from the German *Gevatter*, meaning "godfather." *Kvater* and *kvaterin* are Polish-Yiddish corruptions.

During the circumcision ceremony, the *kvaterin* takes the child from the mother and hands it to the *kvater*. The *kvater* hands the child to the father, and the father then hands the child to the *sandek*, who is seated in a special chair prepared for him. These intermediary steps are required because the husband is not permitted to take the child from the mother, since she is still in a state of impurity from childbirth (as explained in Leviticus 12:1–5).

See Brit.

Kvitl

Plural, *kvitlach*. A Yiddish word meaning "piece of paper or parchment [on which a petition to God is written]." The most commonly known *kvitlach* are those traditionally written by individuals and inserted into cracks of the Western (Wailing) Wall by those seeking to communicate with God.

Among kabbalists, petitions to God are written not by laymen but by a holy person. These *kvitlach* might express a prayer for the speedy recovery of an ill person, the successful delivery of a baby, or the success of a business venture.

In 2000, when Pope John Paul II visited the Wailing Wall, he inserted a *kvitl* in a crack of the wall and uttered a private prayer.

See Amulet.

La'az

Plural, *la'azim*. An acronym for the Hebrew phrase *leshon am zar*, meaning "language of a foreign nation." In his commentaries, Rashi uses many French words spelled out in Hebrew characters. He introduces them with the word *b'la'az*, "in a foreign language," by which he means French. In Rashi's commentary on Jeremiah 2:22, for example, he notes that the Hebrew word *borit*, meaning "soap", is *sabon* in *la'az*.

Labor

According to the Book of Genesis (2:15), man (who is created in God's image) was placed in the Garden of Eden "to till it and to tend it," not to sit idly by and luxuriate. Just as God worked for six days each week and observed the seventh as a day of rest, so must man.

The psalmist speaks of a happy and peaceful person as the one who enjoys the fruits of his labor (Psalms 128), and the Talmud (*Berakhot* 8a) remarks that saintly people divide their waking day into three parts: (1) devoted to prayer, (2) devoted to work, and (3) devoted to the study of Torah.

Since biblical times, the laborer has been invested with honor and dignity. The laborer is expected to earn a day's pay by supplying an honest day of work; to extend less than a maximum effort is considered deceitful. Talmudists believed that labor lends dignity to man (*Nedarim* 45b). No type of work is demeaning; only idleness is degrading (*Bava Batra* 110a). The illustrious Babylonian scholar Rav put it succinctly: "One should even skin carcasses in the marketplace to earn a living and never say, 'I am a great man, such work is beneath my dignity.'" Consequently, it is not unusual to find among the great scholars of the Talmud craftsmen and laborers of all types: Yochanan bar Nappacha was a blacksmith; Yosei ben Chalafta was a leather-worker; Joseph bar Chiya was the owner of palm trees and vineyards; Simon ben Abba was a gravedigger; and Simon ben Lakish, who was known for his brute strength, earned a living in a circus combating wild beasts.

Lag Ba-Omer

Literally, "the thirty-third day of the *omer*," the *omer* being the forty-nine day period between the second day of Passover and Shavuot. *Lag* is an acronym consisting of the Hebrew letters: *lamed*, which has a numerical value of thirty, and *gimmel*, which has a numerical value of three.

The seven weeks between Passover and Shavuot are counted off day by day, and a blessing is recited each night at the conclusion of the evening service. The "counting" ceremony is known as *sefirat ha-omer*. The thirty-third day after the second day of Passover (when the counting begins) is known as Lag Ba-Omer.

Lag Ba-Omer is significant because, according to a tradition recorded in the Talmud (*Yevamot* 62b), during the seven week period between Passover and Shavuot (in the second-century C.E.) thousands of Rabbi Akiba's pupils were overcome by a deadly plague, which abated on the thirty-third day of the period. Consequently, the Rabbis ruled that except for Lag Ba-Omer and Rosh Chodesh (which is a semiholiday) the entire period shall be a period of mourning, and weddings and other joyous celebrations shall not be held.

The father of *kabbalah* (Jewish mysticism) Rabbi Shimon (Simeon) bar Yocha'i (a disciple of Rabbi Akiba), was a brilliant talmudic scholar whose most productive years were from 130 to 160 C.E. According to one tradition, he died in Meron, near Safed, on the eighteenth day of Iyyar, corresponding to the thirty-third day of the *omer* count.

There is a legend that Rabbi Shimon bar Yocha'i hid from the Romans, who were persecuting the Jews, for thirteen years in a cave in the Galilee. There he lived with his son, subsisting on the fruit of the carob tree. Each year, on Lag Ba-Omer, his students would visit him disguised as hunters carrying bows and arrows. In the evening they carried on in festive fashion, lighting a huge bonfire at midnight, then singing and dancing until dawn. On Lag Ba-Omer, the anniversary of the day of Rabbi Shimon's death, this custom is still carried out at his Meron gravesite.

Throughout Israel on Lag Ba-Omer children are free from school. They spend the day enjoying field trips and playing outdoor games. In many villages bonfires are lit, people sit around campfires, dance, sing, and tell stories.

Lamed Vovnik

Also spelled *lamed vavnik*. The Hebrew letter *lamed* has a numerical value of thirty, and the letter *vav* equals six, for a total of thirty-six. In Jewish folklore (*Sanhedrin* 97b; *Sukkah* 45b), thirty-six represents the number of righteous people alive in the world at any one given time, and it is through the merit of these thirty-six saintly people—referred to in the vernacular as *lamed vovniks*—that the world continues to exist. Neither they themselves nor anyone else knows who the thirty-six are; when one *lamed vovnik* dies, another saintly person takes his place.

The concept of the "thirty-sixers" grew out of an interpretation of the verse in Isaiah (30:18), "Happy are all those who wait for Him [God]." The Hebrew word for "Him" is *lo*, composed of the letters *lamed* and *vav*. The *lamed vovnik* is also referred to as a *nistar*, from the Hebrew meaning "hidden [one]."

Although the concept of sainthood does not exist in Judaism in the way that it does in certain Christian denominations, some chasidic sects have assigned what amounts to saintly status to their leaders. The most famous of these was Israel ben Eliezer (1700–1760), also known as the Ba'al Shem Tov, who had lived a life of solitude until his thirty-sixth year, at which time he returned to civilized society and dedicated himself to motivating others to live a life of piety. The fact that this change took place in year thirty-six of the Ba'al Shem Tov's life led many to conclude that he was one of the *lamed vovniks*.

Law and Custom

Law (*halakhah*) and custom (*minhag*) are two inextricably bound forces that fuel the motor of Jewish life. While not always synchronized to operate in perfect harmony, they are the sources of energy that link individual Jews and communities of Jews to one another. A Jew in Bombay will feel comfortable in a Sephardic synagogue in Brooklyn and an Ashkenazic Jew born and bred in Berlin, Germany will feel at home in Berlin, New Hampshire. While there are variations in prayer and differences in chants and cantillation, the basic structure of the synagogue service is alike in all synagogues worldwide.

Relationship of Custom to Law

While Jewish law derives from the Bible and the subsequent interpretations of the law by scholars of the talmudic and later periods, custom derives from the manner in which people carry out the requirements of biblical and rabbinic law.

Unlike law, which is imposed from without, custom takes root and grows from within. That Jews are required to bless the *lulav* along with the other three species on Sukkot is a biblical ordinance, but how the *lulav* is to be waved when the blessing is recited is a matter of *minhag*, of custom, as it evolved within the community. In time, custom takes on an importance of its own, and as far back as talmudic times the warning was issued that custom not be treated lightly. "Do not change [abandon] the custom of your ancestors," says the Talmud (Yerushalmi *Pesachim* 4:1). This attitude is repeated in several tractates and is codified as law in the *Shulchan Arukh* (Yoreh Dei'ah 376:4), where custom is equated with law: "The custom of your ancestors is Torah [Law]."

The Talmud reiterates in a number of places that custom is equal in importance to law. One of the strongest statements in this vein is in the tractate *Bava Metzia* (86b), where Rabbi Tanchum comments, "One should never deviate from established custom. For, behold, when Moses went up to heaven he ate no bread [and acted like a heavenly being (Exodus 34:28)]; and when the Ministering Angels descended to earth [to visit Abraham (Genesis 18:9)], they did eat bread." The point is that one must follow local custom.

The importance of deferring to the practices of a particular locality is indicated several times in the Talmud where questions of law are involved. In the tractate *Eruvin* (14b), when asked which of two blessings should be recited when one drinks water, Rabba ben Chanan replies, "Go out [into the streets] and see what the people are doing [and then you will know which blessing one should recite]." Rabbi Shimon bar Yocha'i associates loyalty to established custom with the biblical verse (Deuteronomy 19:14), "Remove not the ancient landmark which your ancestors have set." To him, adherence to custom is to be viewed as a biblical rather than a rabbinic regulation.

An important example of how reluctant the Rabbis were to change established laws and customs is mentioned in the Talmud (*Beitzah* 4b) in connection with the observance of the major festivals. The question is asked, "Why do Diaspora Jews observe two days of some festivals while in Palestine only one day is observed?" By that time (the fourth century C.E.), after all, the calendar had already been firmly established and there was no longer the need to rely on messengers to report when a New Moon appeared or when holidays should be celebrated.

Variations in Practice

Since not all communities had the same needs, some of the basic customs followed in one community differed markedly from those observed in another. For example, one community may have found it easy to assemble a quorum of ten to constitute a *minyan*, whereas another may have found it difficult. For this reason, the custom of counting the ark as a person evolved. (*See* Minyan.)

Another example of practice being modified to meet a local need can be seen in the action taken by Moses Maimonides (twelfth century) when he was Chief Rabbi of Old Cairo, then called Fostat. Maimonides didn't appreciate the fact that members of the congregation, after finishing the recitation of the *Silent Devotion* (*Amidah*), immediately began talking to one another, creating bedlam in the synagogue. Maimonides learned that Muslims ridiculed Jews for such behavior, and he therefore decided, contrary to talmudic law, to discontinue the long-established practice of having the congregation recite the *Amidah* before the cantor recited it aloud. This innovation of Maimonides, which was introduced to solve a local problem, was followed in all Egyptian synagogues and in some Palestinian synagogues for three hundred years.

Among the customs that have been accepted by some communities but rejected by others are *kapparot* and *tashlikh*. *Kapparot*, which seems to have originated in Babylonia some time after 500 C.E., spread to communities in the East and West. The ceremony involved reciting prescribed prayers on the day before Yom Kippur while waving a chicken over one's head. While many communities accepted the practice, most rabbinic authorities characterized it as barbaric. Yet, Moses Isserles, the renowned Polish commentator on the *Shulchan Arukh*, approved of it. And because of his great influence among German and Polish Jews *kapparot* continued to be practiced on the day before Yom Kippur for many centuries. Some Jews practice it in the same manner to this day, but most have substituted coins for the fowl and give the money to charity.

Tashlikh, a ceremony through which one rids himself of sins by casting crumbs into a stream or river on the afternoon of the first day of Rosh Hashanah, was initially widely practiced by Jews and later denounced by rabbinic authorities, who considered it to be of pagan origin. In recent years many congregations have reintroduced the practice.

See Halakhah; Kapparot; Tashlikh; Talmud.

Law, Jewish

Jewish law, known in Hebrew as *halakhah*, meaning "the way, the path [to proper living]," has its roots in the Bible—specifically in the Torah, the Five Books of Moses, which is also known as the Written Law. Rabbi Simla'i, a third-century Palestinian scholar, and Rabbi Hamnuna, a third-century Babylonian talmudic scholar, stated that there are a total of 613 commandments in the Torah: 365 negative ones, corresponding to the days in one year, and 248 positive ones, corresponding

to the parts of a person's body (*Makkot* 23b). Tradition maintains that all of these laws were dictated by God to Moses when he was atop Mount Sinai.

The Oral Transmission

The first *mishnah* of the talmudic tractate *Avot*, later popularly known as the Ethics of the Fathers, spells out this tradition:

> Moses received the Torah [the Written Law] on Sinai and transmitted it to Joshua, Joshua to the Elders, and the Elders to the Prophets, and the Prophets to the Men of the Great Assembly.

The Men of the Great Assembly (*Anshei Knesset Ha-Gedolah*) consisted of 120 individuals who served as leaders of the Jewish community that returned from the Babylonian Exile around 520 B.C.E., some 800 years after Moses received the Torah on Mount Sinai. Since many additions, omissions, and a variety of interpretations of the text surely occurred during this lengthy period of oral transmission, the Rabbis of the Talmud who devoted a good part of their lives to an explication of the Torah laws, felt free to add their insights and explanations.

From the third century B.C.E. through the sixth century C.E. talmudic scholars studied, debated, and issued rulings that amplified upon the 613 commandments. These laws were instituted as a safeguard or, as it is often described, as a "fence" around the Torah. Prohibitions were added so as to make it difficult for the commandments to be violated.

Codifiers of the Law

One of the principle codifiers of Jewish law, which is dispersed throughout the many pages of the Talmud, was the twelfth-century Spanish-born Moses Maimonides (1135–1204). Maimonides completed his fourteen-volume code of Jewish law, known as the *Mishneh Torah*, meaning "review of the Torah" after ten years of studying and writing. This work—also known as the *Yad Ha-Chazakah*, meaning "strong hand" (the letters *yud* and *dalet*, which spell the Hebrew word *yad*, collectively have a numerical value of fourteen)—was organized by subject and written in Hebrew simple enough to be understood by educated laymen.

Four centuries later, Rabbi Joseph Caro (1488–1575), another Spanish-born scholar, composed his code of Jewish law, which he called the *Shulchan Arukh*, meaning "prepared table." Caro's *Code of Jewish Law*, which presents the laws in an even more concise and popular form than does the work of Maimonides, is divided into four parts: Orach Cha'yim, dealing with everyday life; Yoreh Dei'ah, dealing with the dietary laws and other matters; Even Ha-Ezer, dealing with personal and family matters; and Choshen Mishpat, dealing with civil law. These classifications were first formulated several centuries earlier by Jacob ben Asher (1270–1343), who wrote a code of Jewish law known as *Arba'ah Turim*, meaning "four rows," an expression used in Exodus 28:17. Jacob ben Asher became known as the "Ba'al Ha-Turim."

Caro's code is printed together with notes (glosses) composed by Polish-born Moses Isserles (1525–1572), an Ashkenazic scholar, to balance the views of Caro which were said by some to be partial to the Sephardic tradition by not taking into consideration the practices of the Ashkenazic community.

How Jewish Law Developed

The method by which Jewish law has been interpreted and reinterpreted, expanded and enlarged, over the centuries can be seen from a study of the dietary laws, which are presented in their basic form in Leviticus 11, and also are stated elsewhere in the Torah.

Based on the commandment in the Bible (Exodus 23:19 and Deuteronomy 14:21), "Thou shalt not seethe [cook] a kid in its mother's milk," the Rabbis of the Talmud legislated not only that meat and milk products not be *cooked* together, but that they not be *eaten* together at one meal. They went further and ruled that the same cooking and eating *utensils* must not be used for preparing or serving meat and dairy meals. Undoubtedly, it was the absorbent nature of pottery, from which most dishes were made in early times, that led the Rabbis to prohibit mixing meat and dairy dishes.

Rabbinic laws of this type, which are far more demanding than biblical law, were instituted to serve as a "fence around the Law [*se'yag la-Torah*]" and thus protect biblical ordinances from being violated. The biblical law of not cooking "a kid in its mother's milk" was extended even further by instituting a requirement that one wait a period of time after eating a meat product before eating a dairy product. Depending on the rabbinic authority, the waiting period extends from one hour to six hours.

The Latitude of Halakhah

To some Rabbis of the Talmud and later scholars who followed in their footsteps, *halakhah* was not intended to be stagnant, immutable. Occasionally departing from a strict constructionist approach, they maintained, could lead to a higher good. These authorities drew a distinction between a theoretical law and a ruling that is characterized as *halakhah le-ma'aseh*, "a practical ruling."

The Talmud (*Beitzah* 28b) illustrates this

distinction by relating an incident involving the third/fourth-century Babylonian rabbis Nehemiah ben Yosef and Rava. On a particular holiday Nehemiah saw Rava stropping his *clean* knife against the edge of a reed basket, a method often used to sharpen a knife or to clean a greasy one. The law forbids one from sharpening a knife on a holiday, but one may clean the filth from it.

Rabbi Nehemiah inquired of Rava, "What are you doing?" Are you sharpening your knife or are you removing grease?"

"I am removing grease," replied Rava, offering an answer that was clearly untrue.

When asked to explain why he was telling an untruth, since it was quite evident that his stroking was to sharpen the knife, Rava explained that he was violating the law so as to teach the public a lesson. By performing an obviously unlawful act for which he was rightfully being criticized, he hoped that people would learn the importance of respecting holiday laws rather than taking them lightly.

The Power of Halakhah

Orthodox and Conservative Jews regard the *halakhah* as binding, although the Conservative approach allows its rabbis more latitude in interpreting the law to suit local conditions. Classic Reform Judaism did not consider the *halakhah* as binding at all. But in a 1979 responsum, modern Reform rabbis reconsidered this old view and addressed the question, "What shall be the attitude of Reform Judaism toward practices once discarded?" The Committee on Responsa of the Central Conference of American Rabbis expressed the opinion (*American Reform Responsa*, pp. 3–4) that since the *Code of Jewish Law (Shulchan Arukh)* and its commentaries have "adopted, omitted, and sometimes readopted" many laws, customs, and ceremonies, there is

nothing to prevent Reform Jews from doing likewise. If a new generation finds old, discarded practices meaningful and useful once again, there is no reason why they should not be reintroduced. This applies both to private and synagogue practices. Consequently, today many Reform (and Reconstructionist) Jews will, for example, observe *kashrut* to varying degrees as well as wear a *tallit* and keep their heads covered in the synagogue.

Law of Return

Enacted in 1950 by the Israeli Knesset, the Law of Return guarantees that (1) every Jew has the right to come to Israel as an *oleh* ("immigrant") and (2) an entrance visa shall be granted to every Jew who expresses the desire to settle in Israel, unless the minister of immigration finds the applicant to be engaged in activity directed against the Jewish people or likely to endanger the public health or the security of the State. The *oleh* receives automatic citizenship the moment he or she sets foot in the country.

In March 1970 the Law of Return was amended to define the term "Jew" as a person born of a Jewish mother or who had converted to Judaism and does not profess a different religious faith. The majority view of the Israeli Supreme Court, expressed by the then-president Meir Shamgar, was that "a certificate of conversion issued by any Jewish congregation outside the State of Israel—whether Orthodox, Conservative, or Reform—suffices to require that an applicant be registered as a Jew under the Population Registry Law, 1965. Accordingly, the Registrar may not inquire into the validity of the conversion."

The 1970 amendment to the 1950 Law of Return also stipulated that anyone with one Jewish grandparent has the right to immigrate to Israel and become a citizen. Such an individual has all the rights and privileges of a new immigrant, including free education, health coverage, and financial assistance as do his or her spouse and children, including those who may themselves not be Jewish according to religious law.

In a 1989 ruling, the Israeli Supreme Court held that one who is born Jewish but is a member of a messianic movement such as Jews for Jesus, even though the person may not have formally renounced Judaism, is not eligible for the benefits of the Law of Return.

See Jewish Identity.

Law-of-the-Land Principle

Known by the Aramaic expression *dina de-malkhuta dina*, meaning "the law of the land is the law," this principle was first enunciated in the Talmud (*Nedarim* 28a and *Bava Kama* 27a). The Rabbis recognized that for order to exist within society, people must obey the law of the land. Rabbi Chaninah, the first-century C.E. deputy High Priest, dramatically emphasized the importance of man's respecting the law (Ethics of the Fathers 3:2): "Pray for the welfare of the government. Were it not that people are in awe of it, men would swallow each other alive."

Jewish law, however, forbids any Jew from obeying the law of the land if it contravenes basic moral principles. The Rabbis of the Talmud (*Sanhedrin* 74a) listed three actions that must not be performed even if the government orders one to do so: idolatry, incest (which included adultery), and murder. Anyone who is ordered by the government to violate these prohibitions, the Rabbis advise, *yei-hareig ve-al ya'avor*, "he should allow himself to be killed rather than transgress."

The Law-of-the-Land Principle has been cited by religious authorities making a decision on the permissibility of specific behavior.

For example, through the centuries Jewish law has held that autopsy is forbidden under normal conditions. However, if civil law demands that an autopsy be performed in order to determine the cause of death, the Rabbis have ruled that it may be performed.

An interesting application of this principle occurred in 1806 when Napoleon, emperor of France, had issued a call to notables of the Jewish community to be present at a convocation in Paris to discuss Jewish relations with the French Empire. As a test of the Jews' loyalty, the first session was called for a Saturday, when travel and writing were forbidden. In keeping with the concept of *dina de-malkhuta dina*, rabbis and other observant members of the Jewish communities attended the first session despite the fact that it was on the Sabbath, but they avoided travel and taking notes so at least the letter of Sabbath law could be kept even if its spirit was being violated.

Leap Years

The Jewish calendar is lunar, with 354 days in a year, while the civil calendar is solar, with 365 days. In order to harmonize the two, it became necessary to add one extra month (called Adar II) to the Jewish calendar seven times in nineteen years. A year in which an extra month is added to the calendar is known as a leap year.

See Calendar.

Legal Fiction

Some biblical laws are so difficult to carry out that the Rabbis decided to create a device that would in effect nullify or lessen the demands of these laws so that people would not be tempted to violate them. This device is commonly referred to as "legal fiction." For example, the Bible forbids the taking of interest when making a loan, and this prohibition posed a terrible hardship on those in need of a loan, since few lenders would be willing to make funds available without interest. The Rabbis therefore employed a legal fiction whereby the loan was considered to be an investment on the part of the lender, in return for which the lender was guaranteed a fixed income, which falls into a different category from that of taking interest.

A famous example of the application of legal fiction in Jewish law is the *prosbul*, a novel concept that was introduced by the first-century B.C.E. scholar Hillel the Elder (*Gittin* 34b). A *prosbul* is a legal document which declares that debts, which are required to be cancelled by biblical law in the seventh year (*shemittah*), need not be cancelled. The reasoning is similar to that applied to the above-mentioned ban on taking interest.

Another legal fiction involves the biblical law (Exodus 13:7) requiring that all *chametz* (leavened food) be removed from one's home and ownership for the duration of the Passover holiday. This calls for the sale of all *chametz* that one owns, whether in the home or in warehouses that one leases. Since it is virtually impossible for a person to physically divest of all such property, especially one who owns a granary or liquor establishment, a legal procedure was introduced whereby a Jew would "sell" his *chametz* to a rabbi, who in turn would "sell" it to a non-Jew with the understanding that the sale is only symbolic. The non-Jew is considered the owner of all this *chametz* throughout Passover. Once the holiday is over, however, it is understood that for some monetary consideration the transaction is to be nullified and the *chametz* once again becomes the property of the Jew.

A lesser known legal fiction revolves about the food one may or may not eat if it has been cooked by a non-Jew. Jewish law prohibits the eating of food cooked by a non-Jew without any involvement by a Jew. An exception is made, as noted in the *Mishneh Torah* of Moses Maimonides (Ma'akhalot Asurot 17:13), if a Jew lights the fire. Then, the cooking may be done by a non-Jew. The reason is not given, but it probably stems from the fact that affluent Jewish families were dependent upon non-Jewish maids and servants to prepare meals for the family. This practice is observed to this day by Jewish restaurant owners who follow the strict demands of Jewish law. Their *mashgiach* (*kashrut* supervisor) or some other Jew lights the fire each morning so non-Jews may do the cooking. By lighting the fire, it is *as if* the Jew is a participant in the cooking.

In 1909, Rabbi Abraham Isaac Kook (1865–1935), first Chief Rabbi of Palestine, was faced with the problem of the sabbatical year, in which, according to biblical law, land is to be left fallow. This was devastating to farmers. Kook therefore issued a ruling, not accepted by all rabbis, that the land could be "sold" nominally to a non-Jew, thereby permitting the Jew to cultivate the land. When the year was over, the land would be "repurchased" by the Jewish owner.

Lekhah Dodi

This popular hymn, which literally means "Come, My Beloved," is part of the Friday evening liturgy. Composed by Solomon (Shlomo) Alkabetz (c. 1505–1584), a Salonica-born kabbalist living in Safed, it was made popular by the mystics of that town who went out into the fields to greet, in a symbolic ceremony, the Sabbath bride.

When the hymn is sung during the Friday evening service, it serves as an opportunity to welcome mourners who have been sitting *shivah* and are waiting at the back of the synagogue to be received by the congregation. As the last stanza is chanted, the congregation turns to face the rear and the mourners walk down the aisle to become part of society for the duration of the Sabbath.

When the first letter of each of the eight verses of the poem are placed side by side, they spell out the author's first name and lineage: Shlomo Halevi.

Lesbianism

The Bible does not mention female homosexuality, from which one may infer that lesbianism was practiced little, if at all. Except for references to lesbianism in two talmudic tractates, *Yevamot* (76a) and *Shabbat* (65a), there is no further mention of the subject. In these tractates, the opinion of the third-century Babylonian scholar Huna is repeated. "A woman deeply 'intertwined' with another woman," Huna said, "may not marry a High Priest." This ruling was based on the interpretation of Leviticus 21:14, which requires that a High Priest marry only a virgin, the implication being that the two "intertwined" women had engaged in vaginal intercourse and that the virginity of one or the other had been violated. Moses Maimonides, in his *Mishneh Torah* (Issurei Bi'ah 21:8), offers a more lenient interpretation of the law, claiming that lesbianism does not involve genital intercourse.

See Homosexuality.

Leshon Ha-Kodesh

A Hebrew term literally meaning "holy tongue," a reference to the Hebrew language, the language of the Bible (*Sanhedrin* 21b). It was once customary among some Jews to use no language other than Hebrew when conversing on the Sabbath, the holy day.

Leshon Ha-Ra

Also pronounced *lashon ha-ra*. A Hebrew term literally meaning "evil tongue." Speaking ill of another person, whether true or not, is condemned in the Bible. The Book of Exodus (23:1) states: "You must not spread false rumors." The Book of Leviticus (19:16) says: "You must not go about as a talebearer among your people." Biblical commentators tried to explain why some individuals become lepers by interpreting the Hebrew term for leper, *metzora*, as having been derived from the words *motzi shem ra*, "he who spreads a bad name."

The Rabbis of the Talmud spoke often of the damage caused by those who gossip. The second-century talmudic scholar Rabbi Eleazar ben Perata, who was taken captive by the Romans, asked (*Arachin* 15a): "From whence do we know the great power of the evil tongue?" He answered his own question by saying that we know it from the story of the ten spies who brought back a negative report about Canaan, declaring how impossible it would be to conquer that land. The spies described the ruggedness of the land and its harsh terrain. They were punished for this evil, negative report.

Rabbi Yochanan, quoting Rabbi Joseph ben Zimra said (*Arachin* 15b): "One who bears evil tales is comparable to one who denies the existence of God." And he adds: "Such a person will be stricken with leprosy."

Rabbi Israel Meir Ha-Kohen, a nineteenth-century Lithuanian scholar, wrote an important treatise on the subject of gossip and slander which he entitled *Chafetz Chayim*. The book became so popular that the author himself became known by the title of his work, words taken from the Book of Psalms (34:13): "Who is the man who is desirous of life [*chafetz chayim*] . . . Guard your tongue from evil."

See Musar Movement.

Leviathan

According to talmudic legend (*Bava Batra* 74b), when God formed the world, He created a sea animal called Leviathan. The male and female of the species grew to be so large that God feared that when they mated and bore offspring, they might destroy the whole world. He therefore emasculated the male and killed the female, preserving her flesh in brine, to be served at a sumptuous banquet in Paradise.

Levirate Marriage

The term derives from *levir*, Latin for "brother-in-law"—more specifically, a woman's husband's brother. The Hebrew equivalent is *yavam*.

The institution known as levirate marriage, known as *yibum* in Hebrew, requires that a man marry the childless widow of his brother in order to produce a child who will carry the deceased brother's name. So important is the perpetuation of a name that that which is called incest (in this instance marriage to a sister-in-law) and is forbidden in the Book of Leviticus (18:16) may be engaged in to comply with the law of levirate marriage, which is set forth in the Book of Deuteronomy (25:5–10).

Early Levirate Marriage

Levirate marriage, which was well established in biblical times, was practiced by many Near Eastern peoples, having been introduced by Indo-Europeans between the years 2000 and 1000 B.C.E. This form of matrimony was viewed not as a new union, but rather as a continuation of the woman's first marriage, with the second husband merely serving in place of his brother.

The first biblical mention of levirate marriage is found in Genesis 38, where the story is told of Judah, the son of Jacob. Judah had three sons, Er, Onan, and Shelah. Er was wicked and God slew him (the nature of his wickedness is not specified). Judah told Onan, the elder of the two remaining brothers, that he must fulfill the obligation of levirate marriage by marrying his brother's wife because Er had died childless.

The concept of levirate marriage is detailed in the Book of Deuteronomy in these words:

> If brothers dwell together, and one of them shall die and have no child, the widow shall not be married to another man who is not his [her husband's] kin. Her husband's brother shall come on her [have intercourse with her], and take her to him as a wife, and perform the duty of a husband's brother unto her. And it shall be that the firstborn that she bears shall carry the name of the brother that died so that his name not be blotted out of Israel.

Ceremony of the Removed Sandal

If the brother of the deceased refuses to marry the widow of the deceased, the wife must then go to the gate of the city where the Elders sit and inform them: "My husband's brother refuses to establish a name in Israel for his brother, he will not perform the duty of a *levir* [brother-in-law]."

The Elders then must summon the brother to them, and if he repeats his refusal saying, "I will *not* marry her," the widow must then go up to her brother-in-law in the presence of the Elders, pull the sandal off his foot, spit in his face, and make the following declaration: "So shall be done to a man who refuses to build up his brother's house." Only after this Ceremony of the Removed Sandal, known in Hebrew as *chalitzah*, has been performed is the widow free to marry another man.

Controversy Over Levirate Marriage

Levirate marriage was performed well into the second century C.E. About that time, rabbinic authorities began to question the wisdom of continuing the practice, especially in view of Leviticus 18:16, which declares that marriage between a man and his brother's wife is incest. The Rabbis began to doubt whether a man could really marry his childless sister-in-law purely out of the high motive set forth in Deuteronomy 25:6: to perpetuate his deceased brother's name—without the element of sexual gratification entering into the decision. They ruled that the commandment (*mitzvah*) of *chalitzah* supersedes the commandment of *yibum* (*Yevamot* 39b).

As long as polygamy continued to exist, however, the question of whether someone could fulfill the levirate marriage obligation out of pure motive persisted. Not until Rabbenu Gershom ben Judah of Mainz, Germany, (965–1028) and his synod placed a ban on polygamy, around the year 1000, was levirate marriage abandoned in favor of *chalitzah*. This was a necessary change because up until that time a brother-in-law could have other wives and still marry his widowed sister-in-law. Once polygamy was banned, however, a married brother-in-law could not fulfill the levirate marriage law, for he would then be guilty of bigamy, which is a violation of Jewish law. Consequently, *chalitzah* became the normative practice, and the requirement that a childless widow marry her brother-in-law was abandoned in cases where the brother of the deceased was already married.

This was a welcome change in the law because often the brother-in-law was suspected of marrying the widow for financial gain. Even in the Talmudic period there was concern among the Rabbis that a brother-in-law's intention in marrying his brother's widow might be to acquire the brother's property through marriage rather than to perpetuate the name of the deceased by siring a child who would carry his name.

During the geonic period (approximately 700–1200 C.E.), levirate marriage was practiced in Sura, Babylonia, but *chalitzah* was practiced in Pumbedita, Babylonia. Maimonides, in the twelfth century, favored levirate marriage, and the Sephardic communities in North Africa, Yemen, Persia, and Babylonia followed his lead. However, the grandson of Rashi, Jacob ben Meir (Rabbenu Tam), a contemporary of Maimonides, favored *chalitzah*, and this became the accepted practice in Ashkenazic communities.

Contemporary Practice

Chalitzah is the established practice among Orthodox Jews today. Until the ceremony is performed, the widow is not free to remarry. In Israel in 1953, the Rabbinical Courts Jurisdiction Law was issued: "Where a rabbinical court, by final judgment, has ordered that a man be compelled to submit to *chalitzah* by his brother's widow…the attorney general can compel compliance with the order by [ordering] imprisonment."

The Committee on Jewish Law and Standards of the Rabbinical Assembly (Conservative) suggests that should a couple wish to prevent any future possibility of the wife being subjected to the *chalitzah* requirement, a condition be included in the marriage contract specifying that if the husband dies without children, but with a surviving brother, the marriage be considered null and void.

See Bal Tashchit; Chalitzah.

Levite

The Book of Genesis states that Levi, the son of Jacob and Leah, was the third of Jacob's twelve sons. He was the progenitor of the tribe designated "to carry the Ark of the Lord's covenant, to stand in attendance upon the Lord, and to bless His name" (Deuteronomy 10:8). For this reason, members of the tribe of Levi, the Levites as they were called, were not counted in the census taken to determine who was to serve in the military (Numbers 26:51). They were exempt because their lives were to be dedicated to the service of God.

Members of the tribe of Levi were not awarded any land when the Children of Israel, under Joshua, conquered the Promised Land (Deuteronomy 18:1–2). The land was divided among the other eleven tribes, and each of them allocated parcels of land within their domains on which the Levites could establish homes. The Levites were supported through a tithe, known as *ma'aser* that was levied on the produce of the farmers of Israel.

In time, Levite became a generic term describing two branches of the tribe of Levi: the first, and more prestigious group, consisted of Aaron, the brother of Moses, and his descendants; the second consisted of the other families of the tribe. The former are generally referred to in the Book of Deuteronomy (31:9) as Levitical Priests, or *Kohanim*. They were the group who transported the Holy Ark which housed the Ten Commandments (Deuteronomy 10:8). They also offered sacrifices on the altar, and bestowed a blessing upon the people daily. Gradually, the term Levite came to mean only non-Priests of the tribe of Levi, whose duty it was to sing in the Temple choir and perform the more menial Temple tasks.

See Priesthood; Priestly Benediction; Tithes.

Lex Talionis

A Latin legal term meaning "law of retaliation," referring to a concept that derives from the biblical (Exodus 21:24; Leviticus 24:20) law known as *a'yin tachat a'yin*, "an eye for an eye."

The Rabbis of the Talmud (*Bava Kama* 83b) realized that seeking this kind of justice may have been acceptable in biblical times, but was no longer considered acceptable in the comparatively more enlightened talmudic times. Thus they believed that the intent of the Bible was not to exact justice by committing an identical injustice. Rather, they said, justice should be satisfied through financial recompense: "*a'yin tachat a'yin mamon*."

Lifnim Mi-Shurat Ha-Din

A Hebrew term literally meaning "inside the line of justice." When the Children of Israel were being prepared to enter the Promised Land, they were urged to observe all the laws and commandments imposed upon them by God through Moses. They were specifically enjoined to do "what is good and right in the sight of the Lord" (Deuteronomy 6:18, 12:28). The Rabbis of the Talmud (*Berakhot* 7a, 45b; *Bava Kama* 99b) interpreted this commandment to mean that in order "to satisfy Heaven (God)," *latzeit y'dei Sham'ayim*, one must do not only what is legally right, but also go beyond that to do what is fair and compassionate. This concept became known in Jewish jurisprudence as acting *lifnim mi-shurat ha-din*, that is, beyond the demands of the law (*Bava Metzia* 30b).

As an example: A factory burns down and workers find themselves without income. The employer, who is not legally obliged to pay them, will be acting *lifnim mi-shurat ha-din* if he chooses to do so anyway.

Lilith

According to one legend, Lilith was Adam's first wife, and Eve was created only after Lilith left him and refused to return. Another view of this character is that Lilith is the female demon of the night characterized in the Babylonian Talmud (*Niddah* 24b) as having a human face and wings. In mystical literature she is considered to be queen of the demons and the symbol of sexual temptation. Still another legend contends that Lilith is bent on killing all newborn babies. Some Jews, to protect the child, hang amulets in the room of a woman who has just given birth.

In 1976 a small group of writers and editors launched a Jewish feminist quarterly magazine called *Lilith*, named after positive qualities of the mythological figure. By the early 1970s a number of legends had been created which retold the initial story of Lilith, from the medieval *Alphabet of Ben Sira*. This version holds that Lilith was the first woman, created simultaneously with Adam, and that God intended them to be absolute equals. Adam, however, soon tried to declare himself boss, saying, "I shall lie above you; you shall lie beneath me." Lilith fled the Garden of Eden, and even

though Adam asked God to send ministering angels to bring her back, she refused to return as nothing less than Adam's full partner. Adam says no, begs God for another wife, and Eve arrives, springing from Adam's own body (rib), thus fulfilling male fantasies of parturition. She is the perfect trophy wife: younger than Adam, and less knowledgeable about the world they inhabit.

The kernel of this Lilith story—of a strong woman willing to take risks for the principles of independence and parity—continues to motivate many contemporary Jewish feminists, who, like *Lilith* magazine's editors, point out that the character of Lilith got a bad reputation starting about two hundred years after the *Alphabet* appeared. It is in these later additions to the tale that Lilith is described as a she-demon, because, speculate various scholars, the image of a powerful woman willing to take risks for equality was threatening to men then, as it sometimes is today.

Ma'ariv

Derived from the Hebrew word *erev*, meaning "evening," this is the name given to the daily prayer service that is recited after nightfall. The *Ma'ariv* service is also sometimes called *Arvit*.

Until the beginning of the second century C.E., only two prayer services were held daily: the morning *Shacharit* service and the afternoon *Minchah* service. Noting that the Bible says that the psalmist prayed "evening, morning, and at noonday" (Psalms 55:18) and Daniel prayed "three times a day" (Daniel 6:11), Rabbi Gamaliel II mandated that a *Ma'ariv* evening service be recited daily. His contemporary Rabbi Joshua disagreed, arguing that since a *Ma'ariv* service was not held when the Temple was in existence, it should not be introduced. According to one tradition, it was the patriarch Jacob who, introduced the evening service (*Berakhot* 26b).

The *Ma'ariv* weekday service is shorter than the morning *Shacharit* service, but longer than the afternoon *Minchah* service. The Friday evening *Ma'ariv* service is more extended, containing a prologue beginning with the words *Lekhu neranenah*, "Come, let us sing [praises]."

On weekdays, *Ma'ariv* begins with the *Barkhu* call to prayer. All evening services end with the *Aleinu*, followed by the recitation of the *Kaddish* by mourners.

Ma'asei Bereishit and Ma'asei Merkavah

From the early days of Jewish history, beginning with the prophet Samuel, who anointed Saul king of Israel, through the appearance of Malakhi in the fifth century B.C.E., it was the prophets who kept alive the teachings Moses had received from God on Mount Sinai. It was they who inveighed against the wrongdoing of the people and taught them the meaning and demands of Jewish law, both ritual and ethical. It was they who tried to impress upon people God's creative power and His role in the world as it relates to man.

But when the prophetic era ended at the time of the rebuilding of the Second Temple, there was no respected authority to carry on the teachings of the prophets. Consequently, many false voices were heard. The first-century rabbinic leader Yochanan ben Zakkai later summed up the situation (*Bava Batra* 12a–b): "Ever since the Temple was destroyed, prophecy was taken from the prophets and given to fools and children."

In the fifth century B.C.E. Ezra the Scribe attempted to reform Jewish life. He left his comfortable home in Babylonia, where the Jews had been exiled, and returned to Palestine with a band of followers intent upon reestablishing Mosaic law. One of Ezra's initial efforts was to create an assembly of seventy elders and scholars that became known as the *Knesset Ha-Gedolah* "the Great Assembly."

One of the main tasks of the *Anshei Knesset Ha-Gedolah* ("Men of the Great Assembly"), as the members of the institution were called, was to fill the gap that existed in Jewish spiritual life since the efforts of the last prophets. They tried to instill in the masses love and devotion toward God and the commandments of the Torah. Above all, they had to face the more difficult task of explaining questions that arose with regard to the creation of the world, God's role before and after Creation, the way in which the world is governed, and other esoteric matters. The Rabbis of the Talmud tried to address these issues in the centuries following Ezra and his *Knesset* through the sixty-three volumes of the Babylonian Talmud, the smaller Palestinian (Jerusalem) Talmud, and the later commentaries on the

Talmud. The Rabbis realized that delving into cosmology, the sea of the unknown, was fraught with danger, for it could be harmful to the spiritual well-being of the individual Jew. Thus, even learned scholars were warned not to speculate on these matters.

The content of all such studies, which went under the rubric of *Ma'asei Bereishit* ("Act [work] of Creation") and *Ma'asei Merkavah* ("Act [work] of the Divine Chariot"), involved a world of mysticism and mystery and was therefore kept secret from the general public. It was transmitted only to a chosen few, and these people were permitted to pass this information on to students who were deemed wise and sensitive enough to be taught such speculative matters. Even there, the teacher would discuss the subject matter only in bare outline, avoiding specific details. Actually, little is known about the methodology of such instruction, but in several places the Talmud does allude to the fact that the presentation is always in allegorical form.

One popular story tells of four scholars who entered the "garden [of mystical speculation]." Some exited unscathed, but one—Rabbi Elishah ben Avuyah—questioned too much and too deeply, and as a result became an apostate whose real name was thereafter never mentioned. In referring to him, colleagues used the cognomen *Acher*, meaning "the other one."

The terms *Ma'asei Bereishit* and *Ma'asei Merkavah* were introduced by the Rabbis of the Talmud in the Mishnah of tractate *Chagigah* (2:1), where the parameters of learning in these areas are outlined. The text says: "Whoever probes into four areas, it would have been better had he never been born. These are: what is above, what is beneath, what was before time, and what will be in the hereafter." The Rabbis feared that unnecessary speculation might lead the individual to wrong conclusions with regard to God, the Creator.

Ma'asei Bereishit concerns cosmology as reflected in the first chapter of Genesis. *Ma'asei Merkavah* concerns itself with angelology and attitudes toward the godhead as understood by the devotees of mysticism. It is based upon the mysterious vision of the sixth-century B.C.E. prophet Ezekiel as detailed in the first and tenth chapters of his prophetic book.

In calling attention to Ezekiel's vision of a Divine Chariot, the Rabbis were hoping to explain via a dramatic allegory the nature of God's grandeur, omnipotence, and omniscience. (In chapter 6 of the Book of Isaiah a similar lofty vision of God is unfolded.) In his vision, Ezekiel sees four living creatures, each of which appears to be human in form but has four faces: that of a man, lion, ox, and eagle. Each of the figures has four wings, and under the wings are the hands of humans. The figures are propelled by wheels that are motivated by a spirit residing within. Above these ungainly creatures is a platform, and on the platform rests a great throne-chariot, the *merkavah*. Ensconced on the throne is what appears to be the likeness of the glory of God.

Ezekiel is filled with fear and awe at the sight before him, and then, as he hears a voice speaking to him, he falls to the ground and prostrates himself. The voice then communicates to the prophet a message that is to be delivered to the rebellious people of Israel.

The significance of the throne-chariot vision of Ezekiel is shrouded in mystery, and the Rabbis feared that too much speculation about its mystical meaning might lead to religious skepticism, even apostasy.

Scholars have presented a variety of views in an attempt to explain the intent and purpose of the twin esoteric concepts of *Ma'asei Bereishit* and *Ma'asei Merkavah*. In his *Guide of the*

Perplexed (III:1–7), the outstanding twelfth-century rabbi/philosopher Moses Maimonides considers *Ma'asei Bereishit* an attempt to understand and explain the physical world and the natural order of things, while *Ma'asei Merkavah* offers insights helpful in explaining what transpires in the realm of metaphysics, with its goal of trying to understand the origin and structure of the world-at-large.

See Knesset Ha-Gedolah; Men of the Great Assembly.

Maccabee

The Hebrew word *maccabee* is an acrostic created by joining the first letter of the Hebrew words *Mi kamokha ba-eilim Adonai?*, meaning "Who among the mighty is like Thee, O God?"

According to one theory, "Maccabee" was the battle cry of the Jewish patriots who battled the Syrian-Greeks in 165 B.C.E. According to a second theory, *maccabee* is the Hebrew word for hammer, derived from the root *makav*. Judah, the leader of the revolt against the Syrian-Greeks and the hero of Chanukkah, was given the name Maccabee because of his great strength. He was the son of the High Priest, Mattathias the Hasmonean.

See Chanukkah.

Machzor

Commonly pronounced *machzor*, this Hebrew word literally meaning "cycle" refers to the prayerbooks used in the course of a year on the major Jewish holidays—specifically Rosh Hashanah, Yom Kippur, Pesach, Shavuot, and Sukkot. The most commonly used *machzor* contains the prayers of Rosh Hashanah and Yom Kippur.

See Siddur.

Maftir

The Hebrew word *maftir* and its variant form *haftarah* mean "conclusion," both deriving from the root *patar*, meaning "to be rid of, to be free of, to end, to complete." A person whose life has ended is called a *niftar*, "deceased." To be declared free of guilt or responsibility is to be *patur*.

The person awarded the last Torah honor (*aliyah*) on Sabbaths and holidays is called the *maftir* ("concluder"), and the Torah portion that is read is also called the *maftir*. After the *maftir* portion has been read, the Torah scroll is removed from the reading table and the *maftir* honoree recites the *haftarah*, a selection from the Prophets.

On Sabbaths *maftir* is an additional *aliyah* that follows the seven prescribed ones; on Yom Kippur it is a seventh *aliyah* that follows the prescribed six; and on major holidays it is the sixth *aliyah* that follows the prescribed five. On minor holidays falling on weekdays (Purim, Chanukkah, and the Intermediate Days [Chol Ha-Moed] of Passover and Sukkot) a *maftir aliyah* is not added to the prescribed number (four on Rosh Chodesh and three on Purim and Chanukkah).

On the fast days of Shivah Asar B'Tammuz, Tzom Gedaliah, and Asarah B'Tevet the Torah is read at the morning and afternoon service and three *aliyot* are awarded. A *maftir* is not called up at either service, but at the afternoon service a *haftarah* is read from the Book of Isaiah. On Tishah B'Av, the most important of all the minor fast days, a *haftarah* is read at both the morning and afternoon service. The person honored with the third (final) *aliyah* recites the *haftarah*. At the Yom Kippur afternoon Torah reading, when only three *aliyot* are awarded, the person receiving the third *aliyah* recites the *haftarah*.

See Haftarah; Torah Reading.

Maimouna

Among Moroccan Jews it is customary, on the last night of Passover, to give the holiday a festive send-off. Tables in every home are laden with savory and sweet foods, and scented plants and herbs are distributed throughout the house. Family members as well as friends make the rounds from house to house wishing each other well.

On the day that follows, Maimouna Day, barbecues are held on the beach and a spirit of celebration fills the air, offering thankfulness for having been blessed with an enjoyable Passover.

Mamzer

Plural, *mamzeirim*. Generally defined as "bastard," the origin of the word *mamzer* is uncertain. Some conjecture that it is connected to the Arabic word meaning "rotten, rotten seed."

English dictionaries define a *bastard* as an illegitimate child, that is, one born of a man and woman who are not married to each other. In Jewish law, however, there are several types of *mamzer*. Primarily, a child is a *mamzer* if he or she was born of an adulterous union—specifically, one born to a married woman who has had sexual intercourse with a man who is not her husband. A *mamzer* is also a child born of a woman who has remarried without having obtained a valid Jewish divorce document (*get*) from her first husband. And, finally, *mamzer* refers to a child born of a sexual relationship between a couple forbidden to marry because their marriage would constitute incest.

The Bible (Deuteronomy 23:3) specifies that "a *mamzer* shall not enter into the congregation of the Lord; even until the tenth generation he shall not enter..." This means that only after an extremely long time ("tenth

generation" means an indefinite number of years) will the stigma of bastardy (*mamzeirut*) be erased. The Rabbis considered this rather harsh treatment for innocent individuals who were paying for the sins of their parents and ancestors. And so, while the Rabbis had no power to set aside the severity of the biblical law, they did find a means of softening it and allowing a *mamzer* to marry within the Jewish fold.

Initially, the *mamzer* could marry only another *mamzer*, but by homiletical interpretation of the biblical texts (Numbers 15:15 and Deuteronomy 23:3, 9), the Rabbis concluded that a *mamzer* may also marry a proselyte—a convert to Judaism (*Kiddushin 73a*). The Rabbis made this allowance because they observed that the stigma of proselytism wears off within a generation or two, and by permitting a *mamzer* to marry a proselyte, the stigma of bastardy will disappear more quickly. He or she would be referred to as a descendant of a proselyte rather than as a descendant of a *mamzer*. By the sixteenth century the stigma attached to the *mamzer* was fully dissipated, and it was ruled that "a *mamzer* may be called to the Torah" (*Shulchan Arukh*, Orach Cha'yim 282:3, and the Notes of Isserles).

A child born out of wedlock (to a couple not married to each other but eligible to be married) is not a *mamzer* in the eyes of Jewish law. The offspring is free to marry any Jew.

Artificial Insemination and Bastardy

In the opinion of some Christian theologians and some Western legislators, artificial insemination by a donor other than the husband is to be condemned as immoral. They consider this tantamount to adultery, and a child conceived by AID (Artificial Insemination Donor) is therefore branded a bastard.

Jewish law differs. Bastardy, it maintains, is a label that can be applied only when there has been direct physical contact between a man and a woman. In the case of AID, there is no sexual intercourse, hence Jewish law does not label the resulting offspring a *mamzer*.

See Artificial Insemination; Incest.

Manners

See Derekh Eretz.

Ma'ot Chittim

A Hebrew term literally meaning "funds for wheat," referring to money collected before Passover so that the poor will be able to purchase wheat with which to make *matzah* for the holiday. The ancient custom of donating money to a *ma'ot chittim* fund continues today, governed by the talmudic rule that "those who have enough give, and those who don't have enough take."

Mappah

A Hebrew word literally meaning "covering." Since it is considered disrespectful to leave a Torah scroll uncovered when it is not being read, some congregations place a special cover (*mappah*) over the scroll after each Torah portion has been read. Others use the Torah mantle itself as a cover. The *mappah* is made out of the same material as a Torah mantle or ark curtain and may be decorated in a similar manner.

Marit A'yin

A Hebrew phrase literally meaning "how things appear to the eye" or "what the eye perceives." One of the most important principles in Jewish law, *marit a'yin* is used to describe situations where an observer of an action might misconstrue what he sees. For example, margarine, a purely vegetable prod-

uct, may be served with meat meals, but since its appearance is so much like butter, which may not be eaten with meat products, those who are extremely meticulous about Jewish observance will avoid serving margarine at a meal where meat is also served. The same would apply to serving a nondairy creamer with coffee at a meat meal.

Joseph Caro, compiler of the *Shulchan Arukh* (sixteenth century), did not know about margarine or nondairy creamers, but he was familiar with the use of almond milk (a liquid made from almonds), and he declared (Yoreh Dei'ah 87:3) that it should not be served with a meat meal on account of *marit a'yin*, "for appearance's sake."

The eminent German scholar Rabbi Jacob Emden (1697–1776), in one of his responsa, objects to a woman wearing a wig because, he said, it might appear to people that they are gazing upon her actual hair, which should not be exposed. He was suggesting that the hair be covered with some sort of headgear.

The importance of the *marit a'yin* principle is evident in the following example: Jewish law states that work may be done for a Jew by a Gentile on the Sabbath if it is not done at the express order of the Jew. Thus, a Jew may make a contract with a Gentile to build the Jew a house. They enter into a type of contract called *kablanut*, which establishes no time limit for completion of the work. The Gentile labors at his own pace and on whatever days he chooses.

Such an arrangement is acceptable in Jewish law for the building of a home but not for the building of a synagogue. People seeing work done on the synagogue on the Sabbath might conclude that the leaders of the congregation ordered that the work be performed on the Sabbath, which would be in violation of Jewish law. But when one observes a house under construction, it is generally unknown whether the house is being built for a Jew or a non-Jew.

The Richard Tucker Dilemma

Professor Louis Ginzberg (1873–1953), talmudic scholar at the Jewish Theological Seminary, was asked in a letter addressed to him by Rabbi Israel H. Levinthal, of the Brooklyn Jewish Center whether it was proper for his cantor, Richard Tucker, to be appearing in roles at the Metropolitan Opera House while being employed as cantor in his synagogue.

On October 16, 1944, basing his view on the concept of *marit a'yin*, Ginzberg responded that "while there is no specific prohibition in Jewish law which would prevent a cantor from serving in the synagogue while at the same time appearing in the opera, I do not think the combination is a very healthy one.... People would find it quite strange to see their cantor one day chant the *Ne'ilah* prayer and the following day singing a love duet with some lady." Tucker subsequently relinquished his position at the Brooklyn Jewish Center.

Feinstein Ruling

In a 1984 ruling by the prominent legal authority Rabbi Moshe Feinstein, the *marit a'yin* concept was employed when he was asked by Harvard students whether they could attend their graduation, which was being held on the second day of Shavuot (June 7, 1984). Rabbi Feinstein ruled that although a graduate may walk to the ceremony and be fastidious about not violating Jewish law, those who notice his presence there might be left with the impression that he did, indeed, violate Jewish law by driving to get there. Attendance at the graduation was therefore forbidden.

Marranos

In the late fourteenth and early fifteenth centuries, the Jews of Spain were subject to intense persecution, taunting, and general humiliation. Ultimately, many of these Jews acceded to Christian demands and submitted to baptism in order to save their lives and their fortunes. Some of these *conversos*, or New Christians—in Hebrew, they were called *anusim*, "forced ones"—embraced their new religion, while others professed Christianity publicly but secretly continued to carry out many Jewish practices. These despised people soon came to be known as Marranos, "swine" in Spanish.

Many of the *conversos* were successful in reestablishing themselves as important, influential members of mainstream Spanish society. However, in 1449, anti-Marrano sentiments grew and laws were issued banning New Christians from advancing in society based on their origins. This culminated in the expulsion of the Jews from Spain in 1492 and of the forcible conversion of Portuguese Jews some five years later. Those "criminals" who were suspected of practicing Judaism secretly were tried by the Inquisition and summarily punished.

Many Marranos escaped to England, France, South America, even as far away as India, where many sought to start new lives as Jews, while others found that prospect too painful.

Marranos Today

Today, many centuries after the first Marranos appeared on the scene, their descendants continue to surface. In 1994, a 200-member community of Marranos made themselves known in the remote town of Belmonte, Portugal. They have shed the pretense of being Christian and, under the guidance of a rabbi from Israel, are relearning how to live openly as Jews. Similarly, according to the January 1995 issue of *Dateline World Jewry*, a publication of the World Jewish Congress, in Natal, in northeastern Brazil, twelve Marrano families are shedding their Christian identity.

Since descendants of Marranos who have decided to reclaim their Jewish heritage and wish to identify as Jews are unable to establish with certainty their maternal Jewish ancestry, they are required to undergo the full conversion ceremony, including immersion in a *mikveh* and circumcision for men.

Marriage

In Judaism, marriage has always been considered a sacred institution. From the days of the prophets, it has been viewed as a holy covenant between man and woman, with God as the intermediary. In his code of Jewish law, the *Mishneh Torah* (Hilkhot Sefer Torah 8:2), Maimonides (1135–1204) notes that while one is not permitted to sell his personal Torah scroll even if he needs the money to buy food for his family, he may sell it to acquire the money for the purpose of marrying and having a family.

Holiness, or *kedushah*, is the term with which marriage has always been associated. In fact, today the entire marriage ceremony is referred to as *kiddushin*, "holy matrimony." In Maimonides' classification of the laws, marriage is grouped under "Holiness," while to Nachmanides (1194–c. 1270) a treatise on love and marriage merited the title "Sacred Letter."

Judaism views marriage as the ideal state, a prescription for healthy living and an antidote to loneliness. After Adam was created, God said, "It is not good for man to be alone: I will make for him a companion" (Genesis 2:18). The Talmud adds: "One who does not

have a wife lives without joy, without bliss, without happiness" (*Yevamot* 62b). But even more important than these reasons, in Jewish tradition matrimony is an expression of the fulfillment of the divine plan to propagate the human race: "Be fruitful and multiply and fill the earth" (Genesis 1:28). So important was the fulfillment of this commandment that the Rabbis ruled (*Ketubbot* 17b) that even the study of Torah may be suspended in order to rejoice with, and bring joy to, a bride and groom.

Marriage Age

In talmudic times, eighteen was considered the proper age for marriage (Ethics of the Fathers 5:25). When the economic situation of Jews was good (as in Babylonia of the early centuries C.E.), youthful marriages were common. When conditions were poor (as in Palestine of that same period), young people waited until they could afford to marry.

In the Middle Ages, girls were betrothed as young as age twelve. In Russia of the late nineteenth and early twentieth centuries child marriages were commonly arranged so that boys would not have to serve in the military.

Stages of Marriage

Jewish marriages were originally conducted in two stages. *Eirusin*, the first stage, was the betrothal or engagement. *Nisuin* or *kiddushin*, the second stage, was the wedding itself. Around the twelfth century, the two stages were merged into one ceremony as it exists today.

See Eirusin; Nisuin; Weddings.

Marriages, Prohibited

The Bible contains a long list of prohibited marriages between blood relatives. (The list was later expanded upon by the Rabbis of the Talmud.) These prohibitions are classified as incest because they were practiced by idolatrous nations and were therefore forbidden to the Children of Israel. Leviticus 18:3 warns: "You shall not follow the practices of the land of Egypt where you lived, nor of the land of Canaan, to which I am taking you....I the Lord am your God."

More marriage restrictions apply to a *Kohen*, a member of the priestly family, than to any other Jew. The Rabbis reasoned that just as sacrifices brought by the Priest in the Temple had to be pure (without blemish), so the priestly stock had to remain pure.

The Bible (Leviticus 21:7) prescribes that a *Kohen* may not marry a divorcee. However, the Rabbis of the Talmud concluded that if the marriage has already been contracted, it is valid, but the *Kohen* must forego his priestly privileges.

Special rules apply to the marriage of a *Kohen* and a proselyte. The Book of Leviticus (21:7) stipulates that a Priest shall not marry a woman who is "defiled by harlotry." To the Rabbis of the Talmud, the word "harlot" meant not only "prostitute" but also a woman tainted for any reason. Since proselytes in ancient times came from heathen stock, they were considered tainted. In later rabbinic rulings, the marriage of a *Kohen* to a proselyte was prohibited in the first place, but once consummated was considered valid, with the *Kohen* having to forego his priestly privileges. The offspring of the marriage of a Priest to a divorcee or proselyte were called *chalalim*, meaning "impure ones," those unfit to carry out priestly functions. Non-Orthodox denominations permit the marriage of a *Kohen* to a proselyte.

Although a *Kohen* may not marry a divorcee or a proselyte, he may marry a widow. In biblical times, only High Priests were forbidden to marry widows. (Leviticus 21:14).

Marrying a woman with the same first name as one's mother was avoided by men in talmudic times. Likewise, marrying a man with the same first name as one's father was avoided by women. The Talmud puts it this way: "When he [the husband] calls to his wife [by name], his mother might answer, and this would prove embarrassing." In Jewish tradition, it is disrespectful to call a parent by his or her first name. Rabbi Yehudah He-Chasid (1150–1217), author of *Sefer Chasidim*, emphasized the importance of abiding by this custom so as to avoid violating the commandment of honoring and respecting parents.

Other Rabbinic Prohibitions

A widower is expected to wait for the passing of three major festivals (Passover, Sukkot, and Shavuot) before he remarries. This tradition took root because it was felt that if the widower waited for a cycle of three separate holidays to pass, he would not hastily enter into a second marriage, which he might later regret. However, if a widower has small children and no one to care for them, he may marry immediately after the thirty-day period of mourning (called *sheloshim* in Hebrew) has passed.

A widow was permitted to remarry much sooner than a widower because, in the opinion of the Rabbis, the unmarried lifestyle is much more difficult for a woman than for a man.

A second marriage is permitted only after a Jewish divorce document (*get*) and a civil decree have been obtained. In Reform practice only a civil decree is required.

A man may not remarry a woman whom he had once divorced if she had in the interim been married to another man.

See Incest.

Martyrdom

Derived from the Greek word for "witness," a martyr chooses to suffer or die rather than give up his faith or principles. By so doing, he bears witness to the veracity of his beliefs.

In Jewish tradition, a person who dies a martyr is called a *kadosh*, "a holy person," and that person is said to have died *al kiddush Ha-Shem*, "for the sanctification of God's name" (*Pesachim* 53b). The concept of *chillul Ha-Shem* refers to desecration of the name of God (*Berakhot* 19b).

According to a *midrash*, the first martyrs in Jewish history were the seven sons of Hannah, who along with other Jews had been commanded by Antiochus III (Antiochus Epiphanes), the Syrian-Greek ruler, to eat pork in public. They refused to violate this basic Torah commandment and in 169 B.C.E. were ordered put to death.

About two centuries earlier, Daniel and his three friends—Chananyah, Mishael, and Azaryah—were willing to martyr themselves rather than obey the command of rulers who ordered that they worship idols. But although Daniel was cast into a den of hungry lions and his three friends were thrown into a fiery furnace, miraculously they all emerged unscathed.

Undoubtedly, the most celebrated of all Jewish martyrs were the men who in the second century C.E. defied the Roman edict that anyone who teaches Torah will be put to death. Ten famous rabbis chose to ignore the edict and met martyrdom in the most unspeakable forms. The High Priest Ishmael whose face had been flayed with rakes was the first to die. Rabbi Shimon ben Gamaliel, head of the *Sanhedrin*, was next: his head was severed. Rabbi Akiba met martyrdom after he openly continued to teach Torah to his students. As hot iron combs scraped his flesh, he died with the words of the *Shema* on his lips.

Lesser known martyrs have graced Jewish history. In the Middle Ages, after the massacre of Jews after the First Crusade in 1096, German communities kept a record of these noble souls in books known as *Memorbüchen*.

Although Jewish law considers it sinful to commit suicide, Jewish history has not looked harshly upon those who felt compelled to do so as martyrs. That would include the 960 individuals who held out against the Romans at Masada, and finally took their own lives in 135 C.E. Also in this category is Samuel Zygelbojm, who in 1943 took his own life so that the world would begin to realize what the Nazis were doing to the Jewish people.

See Chillul Ha-Shem; Suicide.

Masada

This Anglicized form of the Hebrew word *metzada* refers to the 1,300-foot-high, mountain fortress situated one mile west of the Dead Sea. Built by Jonathan the Maccabee in the second century B.C.E., Masada was attacked often despite its inaccessibility. After Herod became king of Israel in the year 37 B.C.E., he repaired the fortress, fortifying it with a wall containing thirty-seven high turrets around the flat summit of the mountain. Behind the wall, he built an elaborate palace which he stocked with arms to ensure his safety should he have to take refuge there.

After the fall of Jerusalem and the destruction of the Temple in the year 70 C.E., 960 insurgents under the leadership of Eleazar ben Jair ensconced themselves in Masada and for three years repelled the onslaughts of the powerful Roman army. Finally, when all hope was lost, the resistors committed suicide. When the Romans entered the compound, they found only two women still alive. With the fall of Masada in the year 73, the war against the Romans came to an end. In the years that followed, a Byzantine chapel was built on the site, and centuries later it became a Crusader outpost. Thereafter, it was completely abandoned.

In excavations of the site conducted from 1963 to 1965, archaeologist Yigael Yadin discovered the remains of the elaborate palace built there by King Herod. Archaeologists also discovered the remains of the palace built in the time of the Maccabees. Thus, an aura of sacredness began to envelop the site.

In 1967, after the Israeli-Arab Six-Day War, the memory of Masada was fully resurrected. Because of its association with the heroism of the 960 zealots, it was adopted as the site where inductees into the Israel Defense Forces were sworn in. It also became the site where some Israelis and Jews from all parts of the world brought their sons to celebrate their bar or bat mitzvahs.

Masorah and Masoretic Text

The standard version of the Hebrew Bible used today is known as the Masoretic Text. Scholars refer to it as *textus receptus*, meaning "received text," the text received by one generation from an earlier one. Today's text is the result of an editing process that began some 2,400 years ago with Ezra, the first scribe.

The work of the early scribes (called *soferim*; singular, *sofer*) included counting letters and words of the finished scrolls to ascertain whether anything had been omitted from or added to the text. The actual meaning of the word *sofer* is "counter, one who counts."

Over the centuries, thousands of Torah manuscripts were written by countless scribes, and many variations appeared in the texts. In the post-talmudic period (after 500 C.E.), the importance of establishing a single, normative text of the Torah and of the Bible as a whole became obvious. The scribes who set out to accomplish this were called Masoretes, a form of the word *mesorah*, meaning "tradition" or "that which has been transmitted." Their purpose was to determine and preserve the authentic text of the Bible.

Ascertaining which of the numerous biblical texts in existence was the true original turned out to be a monumental task. Over a period of several centuries, particularly from the eighth through the tenth centuries, Masoretes were actively engaged in sorting through manuscripts and in establishing authenticity. In the great Babylonian cities of Sura and Pumbedita, Masoretic schools were established within the academies of higher learning. There, scholars devoted themselves almost exclusively to purging the biblical text of errors that had crept in as a result of the work of inefficient copyists.

At the same time, in Tiberias, Palestine, two great Masoretic schools appeared on the scene. One was made up primarily of the Ben Asher family and the other of the Ben Naftali family. By the ninth century, the Ben Asher school emerged as the dominant force, and its text became the accepted one.

Besides establishing the content and form of the handwritten scrolls to be used for public readings in the synagogue, the Babylonian and Palestinian Masoretes devoted their attention to the preparation of Bible manuscripts to be used by students. These editions, usually handwritten on both sides of single sheets of parchment, were known as codices (singular, codex). The margins of the codices often contained notations on the spelling, writing, pronunciation, and cantillation of given words. These Masoretic notes are found in most printed Hebrew Bibles in use today.

The oldest text containing the Masoretic alterations is the St. Petersburg Codex of 916

C.E. What is sometimes considered the official Masoretic Text was firmly established by the middle of the sixteenth century when a Hebrew Bible that had been edited by Jacob ben Chayim was published in Venice by Daniel Bomberg, a Christian printer. This Bible, which appeared in 1525, became the model for all future editions.

Some contemporary Bible scholars are of the opinion that there is no one version of the Bible that can accurately be labeled *the* Masoretic Text.

Masquerading

In Jewish tradition, masquerading was banned because it often involved men and women interchanging garments. The prohibition is based on biblical law, "Neither shall a man wear the garments of a woman" (Deuteronomy 22:5). However, toward the end of the fifteenth century, rabbinic authorities made an allowance and permitted masquerading on the joyous holiday of Purim. Under the influence of the Roman carnival, Italian Jews were the first to add masquerading to the celebration of Purim. From Italy the custom spread to many other Jewish communities. Today, masquerading is a prominent feature of the Adloyada Purim Carnival held annually in Tel Aviv. Purim masquerade parties are popular in all parts of the world.

See Adloyada.

Masturbation

In Jewish law, the wasting of human seed through masturbation is considered a violation of the biblical principle of *bal tashchit* ("do not waste").

The Story of Er and Onan

The Book of Genesis (38) relates the story of Judah, the fourth son of Jacob. Judah had three sons, Er, Onan, and Shelah. Er was wicked and God slew him. (The Rabbis in the minor tractate *Kalla Rabbati*, chapter 2, say that Er, spelled *a'yin reish*, when spelled backward is *ra*, meaning "evil.") His wickedness is not specified.

Judah told Onan, the elder of the two remaining brothers, that he must fulfill the obligation of levirate marriage by marrying his brother's wife because Er had died childless. (levirate marriage, or *yibum* as it is called in Hebrew, was a practice followed by many people in the Near East in biblical times, having been introduced into the area by Indo-Europeans between 2000 and 1000 B.C.E.)

The story in Genesis continues: "And Onan knew that the child would not be his. And it came to pass when he went into [had intercourse with] his brother's wife that he spilled it [his seed] on the ground, lest he should give seed to his brother. And the thing which he did was evil in the sight of the Lord, and God slew him" (Genesis 38:1–10). The Rabbis condemn anyone who "brings forth seed for no purpose" because they considered semen to be a valuable resource reserved for a holy task: to populate the world and thus bring glory to God by his creatures (*see Niddah* 43a; *Rosh Hashanah* 12a; and *Shulchan Arukh*, Even Ha-Ezer 23:1–3).

To minimize the incidence of violation, the Rabbis of the Talmud (*Niddah* 13a; *Shabbat* 108b) cautioned that a male who touches his genitals excessively is a sinner. The same applied to wearing tight trousers (*Niddah* 13b) or riding a camel bareback (*Niddah* 14a). These activities generate heat and stimulation and may lead to the spilling of seed.

Stressing the seriousness of the sin of wasting seed, Rabbi Eleazar (*Niddah* 13b) linked the verse in Isaiah (1:15), "When you pray to Me, I [God] will not hear you, for your hands are full of blood [source of human life]," to those who "perform masturbation with their hands." Rabbi Eleazar (ibid. 13a) goes even further and says that "whoever holds his penis while passing water is as though he had brought a flood on the world [and caused its elimination]." He feared that the handling of the penis might cause an erection and lead to the spilling of semen. This is supported by the view of Rav (ibid. 13b), who states: "A man who willfully causes an erection should be placed under the ban." Rabbi Ammi adds: "Such a person is called a renegade, because such is the art of the evil inclination. Today it incites man to do one wrong thing, and tomorrow it incites him to worship idols."

In the minor tractate *Kallah Rabbati* (2), the Rabbis were particularly strong in their condemnation of masturbators. Rabbi Eliezer ben Jacob said: "Whoever masturbates is like one who has committed murder."

The sole talmudic reference to female masturbation appears in the tractate *Megillah* (12a) where Rava mentions the popular saying: "He [masturbates] with a large pumpkin and his wife with small pumpkins," actions that Rava, for some unknown reason, associates with the sinful conduct of King Ahasueros and his wife Vashti.

Despite the traditional proscriptions, modern rabbis tend to favor a more liberal approach toward masturbation. They do not categorize it as "wasting"—or, as some authorities call it, "destroying"—semen if the semen is used for medical testing or for artificially inseminating a man's wife who would otherwise remain infertile. Others, particularly among the non-Orthodox, agree with physicians and psychologists who do not condemn masturbation as an evil act, but consider it a normal, healthy human release.

It is reasonable to assume that the point of

the Onan story in Genesis 38 has been misinterpreted. Traditionally, the story has been taken to be a condemnation of masturbation, but it may very well be no more than a condemnation of the attitude of a selfish brother who refused to carry out the ancient rite of *yibum*, of marrying the childless widow of a brother in order to produce a child with her so as to carry on the deceased brother's name.

See Bal Tashchit; Onanism.

Matriarchs

In Judaism, the wives of the three Patriarchs are known as the Matriarchs. These four women are Sarah, (wife of Abraham) Rebecca, (wife of Isaac) and Rachel and Leah (wives of Jacob).

See Patriarchs.

Matrilineal Descent

Under Jewish law, a child is Jewish if his or her mother is Jewish; if the mother is not Jewish, the child is not Jewish. The religion of the child's father is irrelevant.

So strong is the maternal bond that Jewish law considers a child Jewish even if he or she is brought up by a non-Jew and is unaware of the fact that the maternal lineage is Jewish.

The Talmud (*Yevamot* 45b) is quite explicit in stating that a child born of a Gentile father and a Jewish mother is Jewish. Rashi reinforces this view: "Since the mother of the child is Jewish, he [the child] is to be counted as one of our brothers."

The primary reason advanced in support of using the mother's lineage in determining a child's Jewishness is that one is always certain of the identity of the mother of the child, but one cannot be positive of the identity of the child's father.

In the fifteenth century, talmudist Rabbi Solomon ben Simon Duran of Algiers declared categorically that the offspring of a Jewish mother and a Gentile father is Jewish "for all time." A century later, this opinion was codified as law (*Shulchan Arukh*, Even Ha-Ezer 4:5, 19). In recent years, the Reform movement in the United States officially recognized as Jewish a child whose mother is non-Jewish but whose father is Jewish.

See Patrilineal Descent.

Matzah

Plural, *matzot*. The Bible (Exodus 12:18ff.) mandates that *matzah*—unleavened bread—be eaten on Passover in commemoration of the hasty departure of the Children of Israel from Egypt (Exodus 12:34). *Matzah* has been described as "desert bread"—bread that is made hastily and does not have the time to rise—and to this day it is a staple food of Bedouins living in the Negev, south of Beersheba.

The significance of eating *matzah* on Passover is amplified in Deuteronomy (16:3ff.): "For seven days [after the sacrifice of the paschal lamb] you shall eat unleavened bread...for you departed from the land of Egypt hurriedly—so that you may remember the day of your departure from the land of Egypt as long as you live." The Rabbis (*Pesachim* 120a) interpret this verse to mean that it is mandatory to eat *matzah* on the first night of Passover and optional to eat it for the balance of the week, so long as any leavened (fermented, soured) product *chametz* is not eaten.

After the destruction of the Second Temple in the year 70 C.E., the sacrificial system was abandoned and *matzah* symbolically replaced the paschal lamb that had been consumed by each family on the first night of Passover, at the *Seder* meal.

Method of Preparation

Matzah is a flat, waferlike bread made of any of the following five grains only: wheat, barley, spelt (a primitive species of wheat), rye, and oats. Although these grains are actually *chametz*, which is normally forbidden to be used on Passover, an exception was made so that *matzah* could be baked.

Matzah is made by mixing the flour of one of the five grains with water, then kneading and baking it hastily—within eighteen minutes—so that the dough will not sour and become *chametz*.

Before placing the *matzah* in the oven, perforations are made in the flat dough to allow air to escape and retard fermentation. The perforations also prevent the dough from rising and swelling while baking. Today, handmade *matzot* are perforated quickly with a wheel (called a *reidl* in Yiddish).

Originally all *matzot* were round-shaped. In 1875, a *matzah*-baking machine that made square *matzot* was invented in England. The machine, equipped with an automatic perforator that makes lines about one-quarter to one-half inch apart, was subsequently introduced into the United States. There was initial opposition to the use of this new machine because rumor had it that to satisfy people accustomed to eating round *matzot* the corners of the square matzot were trimmed off. This rounding process was said to prolong preparation time and possibly cause fermentation to set in. Many also argued that milling by heavy machinery causes wheat to give off moisture. They also argued that pieces of dough adhere to the baking surface and thus cause fermentation before the baking process ends.

The type of water used in the baking of *matzah* was once an issue. According to ancient belief expressed in the Talmud (*Pesachim* 94b), at night the sun underneath the earth heats up the wells and streams, and their waters become tepid. Rabbi Judah ordered that such water not be used in the preparation of *matzah* because the tepid water accelerates the process of fermentation. He required that *matzah* be made with *ma'yim she-lanu*, water that has "lodged" or been kept overnight in the home at cool temperatures. Some Jews continue to use only such water in the baking of their *matzah*.

Types of Matzah

Two types of *matzah* are made for Passover use. One type is called *lechem oni*, meaning "poor man's bread" or "bread of affliction," may be used at the *Seder*. *Lechem oni*, which is made from flour and water alone, is the term used for *matzah* in the Bible (Deuteronomy 16:3) and in the Haggadah.

The second type of *matzah* is called *matzah ashirah*, "rich *matzah*," sometimes called "the bread of opulence"—so named because it is made of flour mixed with wine, oil, honey, or eggs instead of water. Only *lechem oni* may be eaten at the *Seder* (*Pesachim* 36a).

Shemurah Matzah

Shemurah matzah—also called *matzah shemurah* or *matzah shel mitzvah*—means "guarded *matzah*." Unlike ordinary *matzah*, *shemurah matzah* is guarded so that it does not make contact with water from the moment the grain is cut until the moment the *matzah* is baked in the oven. To reduce the chances of the *matzah* fermenting, it is prepared in moisture-free (or as dry as possible) premises. During the baking process, all activity is carefully supervised so as not to prolong the procedure needlessly, further reducing the possibility of fermentation setting in. *Shemurah matzah* is generally made completely by hand in special bakeries not otherwise in operation throughout the

year. The cost per pound is, of course, much higher than machine-made *matzah*.

The *matzah* selected for consumption at the *Seder* table is particularly special, and *shemurah matzah* is the only type very observant Jews use. *Chasidim* eat only *shemurah matzah* for the duration of the holiday.

Seder Matzot

The importance of *matzah* is reflected in the fact that three whole *matzot* are displayed on the *Seder* table. One explanation for the use of three is that at regular holiday and Sabbath meals two loaves of bread (*challot*)—symbolic of the showbreads (shewbreads) displayed in two rows by the Priests in Temple days—are placed on the table. On Passover, since bread is not to be eaten, two *matzot* are baked instead. A third *matzah* is added as a reminder of the joyous nature of this holiday of freedom.

The popular explanation is that the three *matzot* represent the three groups in Jewish religious life—Priests, Levites, and Israelites. According to some authorities, including Maimonides and the Gaon of Vilna, only two *matzot* are to be placed on the *Seder* table, with the lower one broken to be used as the *afikomon*.

The First Taste of Matzah

In the Jerusalem Talmud (*Pesachim* 10:1), Rabbi Levi was the first to propose the rule that *matzah* should not be eaten on the day prior to the first *Seder* because doing so removes the novelty of eating *matzah* for the first time at the *Seder* itself. He put it as follows: "One who eats *matzah* on the eve of Passover is like one who has intimate relations with his bride-to-be in his [future] father-in-law's home." Some Jews do not eat *matzah* for an entire month prior to the holiday to further heighten the experience of eating *matzah* for the first time at the *Seder.*

See Chametz; Passover.

Ma'yim Achronim

A Hebrew term literally meaning "last waters," referring specifically to the water one pours on the hands after completing a meal. Just as it is customary to wash the hands *before* sitting down to a meal, so is it customary to pour water over one's fingers *after* the meal is finished and before *Grace After Meals* is recited. This water is known as *ma'yim achronim.* Small pitchers designed as *ma'yim achronim* dispensers are often used at the table to wet the fingers so that one doesn't have to leave the table to wash.

Maimonides, in his *Mishneh Torah,* explains that unlike the washing of hands at the beginning of a meal, which is a religious obligation, the washing of hands at the end of the meal is done for health reasons alone, hence no prayer is recited.

In early times, it was customary to use salt freely. Salt was taken in hand and sprinkled over the food. A residue of salt always remained on the diner's fingers when the meal was over, and if the diner rubbed his eyes, it could result in serious damage. It therefore became customary among Jews to wash the fingers at the end of the meal.

Ma'yim She-lanu

Literally, "water that has rested," with special reference to water that has been drawn from a well before sunset and that has "rested" all night long so that it is at the proper temperature for use in baking matzah. Rashi reminds us (Pesachim 42a) that during the month of Nissan the sun is strong and the well water is warm during the day. Of course, warm water hastens fermentation. By being drawn the night before it is used, the water has a chance to cool off.

In the tractate *Pesachim* (42a), Rav Yehudah says: "A woman must knead unleavened bread only with water that has been kept [rested] overnight [and has had a chance to cool off]."

Mazal

Plural, *mazalot.* This Hebrew word literally means "star" or "constellation" but has taken on the connotation of luck. The Bible makes only one reference to *mazalot* (II Kings 23:5), but the Talmud and later rabbinic literature refer to them often, making the point that man's fate is tied to the position of the stars.

The Midrash (*Genesis Rabbah* 10:6) says: "There is not one blade of grass that is not governed by a *mazal* in heaven that smites it and says to it, 'Grow!'" In the *Zohar* the kabbalists were wont to say, "Everything depends on *mazal*, even a *Sefer Torah* in the ark." This quotation is usually explained as referring to the Torah lucky enough to be selected for the reading of the day, since of the many Torah scrolls in the ark only one is generally removed for the reading.

Another interpretation of this kabbalistic aphorism is that mice often gnawed away at the parchment of Torah scrolls, rendering them unusable at a public reading. If a Torah scroll was spared an attack by mice, it was indeed fortunate, for that scroll might be selected for the Torah reading.

A more mainstream view of *mazal* in Jewish tradition is expressed in the Talmud (*Nedarim* 32a and *Shabbat* 156a), where God says to Abraham, "*ein mazal le-Yisra'el* [The fate of Israel is not dependent on the stars]." The implication is that man's fate is determined by divine providence, not by the position of the stars.

See Zodiac.

Meal of Condolence

It is considered a meritorious deed (*mitzvah*) for neighbors to prepare the first full meal eaten by mourners after returning from a funeral. The Rabbis of the talmudic period reprimanded neighbors who were so callous that they did not prepare food for a neighbor who was grieving after burying his dead. Jewish tradition considers it of great help to a mourner to know that friends are sympathizing with him in his painful loss.

When David mourned the death of his close friend Abner, commander of Saul's army, "all the troops came to urge David to eat something" (II Samuel 3:35). The Hebrew word used here for "to urge to eat" is *le-havrot*, from which is derived the Hebrew name for the meal of condolence, *havra'ah* or *se'udat havra'ah*.

Se'udat havra'ah is also referred to in English as the meal of healing, for it is thought to be of great help in assuaging the grief of mourners. Knowing that one's neighbors and friends are supportive contributes to the process of healing.

The menu of the meal of condolence is designed to include foods that symbolize eternal life: round rolls and bagels, oval eggs, and lentils, all of which reflect the cyclical, eternal, continuous nature of life. After serving these ceremonial foods, a regular meal is eaten (Yoreh Dei'ah 378:9).

A second explanation offered for eating round foods—particularly eggs—is that these items have no mouth, that is, they have no opening. They represent the mourner, still in shock, who has no words for anyone (*Bava Batra* 16b).

The Talmud (ibid.) offers a third explanation for the serving of round and oval foods to mourners who have just returned home from burying their dead. The Rabbis say that the soup of lentils that Jacob made for his father, Isaac, was cooked on the same day on which his grandfather, Abraham, died, and that it was specifically prepared as a meal of condolence for Isaac.

Among Judeo-Spanish Jews—those living in the general area of Turkey and Greece—families sit on the floor when eating the meal of condolence, which consists of olives, eggs, and bread.

The practice among Ethiopian Jews has been for the attendants at the burial, who lay the corpse in the grave and fill it with earth, to return to the house of mourning, where they eat peas and drink coffee.

Among Sephardim in the Syrian and Moroccan communities, it is the Burial Society (*chevrah kaddishah*) that prepares the meal of condolence. Among Syrians, the meal is served after the *keri'ah* ritual has been performed. The rending of the garment takes place in the *shivah* home, not earlier as in most other communities.

See Chevrah Kaddishah.

Mechitzah

This Hebrew word literally meaning "divider, partition" is the name given to the railing, curtain, or other type of divider that separates the women's section from the men's section in Orthodox synagogues. In older synagogues, women were seated in a gallery that extended around the two sides and back of the sanctuary. The most authoritative explanation connects the origin of the custom with the *ezrat nashim*, the women's quarter in the ancient Jerusalem Temples.

Women were separated from men in the synagogue in order to eliminate the possibility of distraction during prayer. In time, the practice of separating the sexes was extended to other social gatherings, even those not associated with a religious service or not held in the synagogue. At some Orthodox weddings, women sit apart from men not only during the ceremony but also during the dinner. The *mechitzah* also separates the men and women during the dancing.

Some authorities, attempting to show how ancient is the practice of separating the sexes, associate it with Noah (Genesis 7). They point to the verse, "Noah and his sons, his wife and his son's wives went into the Ark..." (7:7), to prove that the males and the females entered separately (*Tanchuma Ha-Yashan*, Noach 17). Other authorities are of the opinion that the practice of separating the sexes in the synagogue is related to an episode recorded in the Book of Exodus. Before Moses received the Ten Commandments at Mount Sinai, the Israelites were ordered to remain in a state of purity by staying away from their womenfolk for three days.

The term *mechitzah* is also used to designate the point of separation between the public and private domain.

Mixed pews are commonplace in non-Orthodox synagogues.

See Eruv; Women's Gallery.

Megillah

Plural, *megillot*. Although five books of the Bible—Esther, Lamentations, Song of Songs, Ruth, and Ecclesiastes—are designated *Megillot*, meaning "scrolls," the word *Megillah*, when used without specification, refers to the Scroll of Esther. In early talmudic times, until the year 250 C.E., the Book of Esther, handwritten on parchment, was the only scroll read at a synagogue service.

The Megillah (*Megillat Ester* in Hebrew), as the Scroll of Esther is commonly called, tells the story of Purim, which revolves about the heroic Mordekhai and Esther and the villainous Haman, who sought to destroy the Jews of Persia.

The Megillah is read in the synagogue each year on the fourteenth of the month Adar, after the evening and morning Purim services. The scroll is never read on the Sabbath because the calendar is so arranged that the fourteenth of Adar cannot fall on a Sabbath. In walled cities, such as Shushan in the days of Mordekhai and Esther and Jerusalem even today, the Megillah is read on the fifteenth of Adar only, the day on which the enemy that was intent on destroying the Jews of Persia was defeated. Since the fifteenth of Adar can fall on a Sabbath, the Rabbis ruled (*Megillah* 4a and 4b) that the Megillah not be read on that day, lest the reader carry the scroll to his instructor for last-minute instruction, thus violating the Sabbath law that prohibits the carrying of an object more than six feet in the public domain. To solve the problem the Rabbis ruled that when Purim begins on a Friday night, the reading of the Megillah should be held before nightfall rather than after the evening service. (See also *Mishneh Torah*, Hilkhot Megillah 1:13.)

As the Megillah reading progresses, the parchment on which the text is written is folded over to simulate a letter. The custom derives from the fact that the story of Esther was originally sent out as a letter to all the Jewish communities of the kingdom of Ahasueros (Esther 9:30). The name of God was omitted from the letters, lest the scroll be mishandled, thus desecrating God's name. This is the only book in the Bible in which God's name is not mentioned.

Erasing Haman

Haman epitomizes all enemies of the Jewish people throughout the ages. Thus, whenever Haman's name is uttered during the reading of the Megillah, listeners stomp their feet, sound noisemakers, and the like, in the hope of "erasing" the villain's name. Exodus 17:14 is often quoted in connection with this tradition: "For I will utterly erase the remembrance of Amalek from under the heavens." Haman's ancestors were considered to be Amalekites.

Several commentaries explain why God singles out Amalek from all hostile nations and targets them for destruction: the nation of Amalek is said to be a nation descended from Esau, and the leading force of evil, brazenly defying God and His nation, even after Egypt and all the other nations witnessed God's great powers in freeing the Israelites. Their unprovoked sneak attack on the Israelites is an example of this evil and of the lasting hatred of Esau for Jacob.

Of the various noisemaking methods used in past centuries to erase Haman's name, one of the more interesting is that of writing the name of Haman on two smooth stones or slates and then rubbing and knocking the stones together.

The Tractate Megillah

An entire tractate of the Talmud bearing the name Megillah concerns itself primarily with the Book of Esther, its history, its place in the liturgy, its observance as a festive day, and rules regarding its public reading.

The word *megillah*, as used in the English vernacular term "the whole megillah," refers to a long, drawn-out story of any kind.

See Purim.

Mehadrin min Ha-Mehadrin

A Hebrew term literally meaning "choicest of the choice," used (*Shabbat* 21b) to describe pious and observant persons who carry out Jewish law to the fullest extent. It is also used to indicate that a food product has been pre-

pared in an especially careful manner consistent with Jewish law.

Mekhirat Chametz

A Hebrew phrase literally meaning "selling of *chametz*," referring to a ritual performed prior to the Passover holiday.

See Bedikat Chametz; Chametz; Legal Fiction.

Melaveh Malkah

A Hebrew term meaning "accompanying the queen." In Jewish tradition, the Sabbath is referred to as a bride and as a queen. At the conclusion of the Sabbath, after *havdalah*, a light repast is served, at which time the Sabbath Queen (*Shabbat Ha-Malkah*) is bid farewell in song.

According to legend, the *melaveh malkah* custom originated with King David. David asked God to tell him when he would die, and God answered that it would happen on a Saturday. From that time on, at the conclusion of each Sabbath, David made a party to celebrate his survival.

See Havdalah.

Men of the Great Assembly

Frequently referred to in the Talmud (Ethics of the Fathers 1:1) as *Anshei Knesset Ha-Gedolah*, these men formed a bridge between the prophets and the scribes. During the Second Temple period—approximately 520 B.C.E. to 70 C.E.—the Men of the Great Assembly regulated Jewish life and law. Created by Ezra the Scribe, the size of the assembly varied, but generally consisted of 120 of the most learned members of the community. According to tradition, they decided which books were included in the biblical canon and formulated prayers for the liturgy. They added Purim to the cycle of Jewish holidays and were widely accepted as the spiritual leaders of the Jewish people.

See Knesset Ha-Gedolah; Ma'asei Bereishit and Ma'asei Merkavah.

Menorah

Plural, *menorot*. A Hebrew term literally meaning "candelabrum," referring either to one with seven branches, as was used in the Temples in Jerusalem or to one with nine branches, as is used on the holiday of Chanukkah. The first mention of a *menorah* is found in the Book of Exodus (25:31ff.), where God commands Moses to fashion a seven-branched "lampstand of pure gold" to be used in the Tabernacle. In the Book of Numbers (8:1ff.), there is a description of the duties incumbent upon Aaron and his sons with regard to the kindling of the seven lights of the candelabrum in the Tabernacle. Inasmuch as the seven-branched *menorah* was the centerpiece of the sanctuary in the wilderness as well as of the First and Second Temples in Jerusalem, after the Temples were destroyed it became unacceptable to replicate (*Menachot* 28b) the *menorah* or any of the other Temple appurtenances. As a result, the six-branched *menorah* with a Star of David affixed to the center post became commonplace as a synagogue fixture.

Congregations that do display seven-branched *menorot* today reason that since modern candelabra are electrified, they are quite unlike the original that was cleaned each day, the wicks of which were changed, and to which fresh oil was added.

The nine-branched Chanukkah *menorah*, designed to hold eight lights plus a *shamash*, was a special creation. In modern Hebrew it is known as a *chanukkiyah*.

See Chanukkah.

Menschlichkeit

A Yiddish term from the German *mensch*, meaning "person," and connoting a sensible, mature, responsible person. The concept of *menschlichkeit*—that is, being a good, caring person—is stressed in the rearing of Jewish children.

Mercy and Justice

These twin concepts represent the method by which, in Jewish tradition, God governs the world. The Midrash (*Genesis Rabbah* 12:15) says, "The Holy One said: 'If I had created the world with the attribute of mercy alone, its sins would be great; and if with justice alone, how could the world endure? So I will create it with both justice and mercy.'" There is an ongoing tension between the two attributes.

In the Bible, the full measure of justice is referred to as *midat ha-din*. The full measure of mercy is *midat ha-rachamim*.

See Justice.

Meshumad

A Hebrew word literally meaning "one who destroys," referring specifically to an apostate who weakens Jewish unity through defection. The term is used in the Tosefta (*Chullin* 1:1), a text parallel to the Mishnah that was composed in Palestine. The Babylonian Talmud uses the word *mumar* for apostate.

See Apostate and Apostasy.

Messiah and Messianic Age

The Hebrew word for Messiah is *mashiach*, meaning "the anointed one." The word, however, is sometimes used to refer to an age rather than a person. While belief in the coming of the Messiah is a basic principle of the Jewish faith, the exact nature of the Messiah and the expected time of his arrival as expressed in the Bible, the Talmud, and in later rabbinic writings is often vague and contradictory.

Talmudic Views

The talmudic tractate *Sanhedrin* (98a) presents a variety of views as to when the Messiah will come. The second-century Palestinian scholar Rabbi Chaninah conjectured that the Messiah will not come until conditions are so bad that a fish needed for an invalid's sustenance will be uncatchable because "the seas will be covered with oil."

Chaninah's son, Chama, said the Messiah will not come until things are so bad that Israel has become a powerless people. Rabbi Zeira, quoting Rabbi Chama, said: "The son of David will not come until there are no conceited men in Israel." Rabbi Yochanan of the first century said the Messiah will come "when you see a generation overwhelmed by troubles." On another occasion, he said: "The son of David will come only when there is a generation consisting wholly of righteous people or evil people."

Maimonides' View

In the twelfth century, Maimonides expressed agreement with the talmudic scholar Samuel that "there is no difference between this world and the days of the Messiah except [that in the latter instance] Israel will not be subject to foreign powers [gilui malkhu'yot]" (Berakhot 34b).

While Maimonides speaks of the Messiah as a period of time that will be no different from our age, except that Israel will be in control of its own destiny (Mishneh Torah, Hilkhot Teshuvah 9:2) and Jews will be able to study Torah without molestation, he also conceived of the Messiah as a person, "as a king," who will appear on the scene. This king, a descendant of David, will be wiser than Solomon and possess prophetic powers almost on a par with Moses. He will teach the people and lead them in the way of the Lord. (See Shabbat 63a.)

Maimonides wrote:

Do not think that in the Messianic Age anything will be changed in the world's order, or that some innovation will be in-

troduced. Not at all! The world will continue in its normal course. The words of Isaiah (11:6), "And the wolf shall dwell with the lamb, and the leopard shall lie down with the kid," is to be understood as an allegory, meaning that Israel will live in peace with the wicked among the pagans. All of them will adopt the true faith and will never again steal or destroy. They will obey the commandments and will live peacefully with Israel.

Elijah as Forerunner

According to ancient Jewish tradition, the prophet Elijah never died but merely vanished in heaven, having ascended there in a fiery chariot drawn by fiery horses. The belief grew that someday Elijah would return to earth, and as the forerunner of the Messiah he would prepare the way for a new, great age of peace by resolving all disputes and by preparing mankind for its redemption.

The designation of Elijah as forerunner of the Messiah dates back to his career as the charismatic prophet of the ninth century B.C.E. who dared castigate King Ahab and Queen Jezebel for their evil ways. Elijah was a fierce advocate of God, ever battling the foes of Israel intent upon discrediting God (I Kings 18:17ff.). For this reason, Elijah became the "guardian angel" of the Jewish people and was believed to be the one who will herald the coming of the Messiah. He insisted that Israel must not forsake God, so that the Covenant made between God and Abraham might endure.

Identity of the Messiah

In the talmudic period (beginning with the first century B.C.E.) there was a shift away from the concept of Messiah as a point in time to that of a Messiah being an actual person who would proclaim himself to be the Messiah or would be proclaimed by others to be the precursor of a golden age.

In the tractate *Sukkah* (52a), the theory is advanced that there will be two Messiahs, Mashiach ben Yosef (Messiah son [descendant] of Joseph) and Mashiach ben David (Messiah son [descendant] of David.) Mashiach ben Yosef will appear first, and in his attempt to establish himself as the redeemer he will be killed, making way for the true savior, Mashiach ben David.

Based upon various verses in the Bible, rabbinic authorities concluded that the name of the Messiah will be David. One such verse is in Psalms (18:51): "He [God] gives deliverance to His king and shows kindness to His anointed [*Mashiach*], to David, and to his seed forever." Since the Anointed One will be a descendant of King David, he is also called Tzemach, meaning "offshoot of David" (Jeremiah 23:5).

During the decades preceding and following the destruction of the Second Temple in 70 C.E., oppression of Jews by the Romans was intense, and every sign pointing toward redemption was cherished. In his *Antiquities*, which records the events of that period, the historian Flavius Josephus (c. 37–95 C.E.) tells of the many people who came forward claiming to be the Messiah or suggesting the identity of the Messiah.

One of the most charismatic of these figures in the ensuing centuries was Bar Kokhba, who in the year 132 C.E., during the Jewish revolt against the Roman occupation of Palestine, was proclaimed the Messiah by no less a figure than Rabbi Akiba. Citing the verse in the Book of Numbers (24:17), "There shall come forth a star [*kokhav*] out of [the house of] Jacob," Rabbi Akiba said this refers to Bar Kochba who is to be the Messiah." Most of Akiba's colleagues ridiculed the idea. One of them, Rabbi Yochanan ben Torta, exclaimed, "Akiba, grass will grow from your cheeks [you will be long dead] and still the Messiah will not have come" (Yerushalmi *Ta'anit* 4:3).

Nevertheless, Akiba clung to his belief and left Palestine, traveling to distant Jewish communities in Babylonia, Egypt, North Africa, and Gaul in order to raise funds and rally support for the man he believed to be the Messiah. Akiba even permitted his thousands of students to join the fighting forces of Bar Kochba, most of whom were massacred by the Romans. In 135, at Betar, the rebellion was crushed and Akiba abandoned his belief.

In later centuries, particularly in the Middle Ages when Jewish communities regularly faced persecution and desperately clung to every promise of a better future, they fell prey to the claims of charismatic individuals who promised them salvation. From the time of the first Crusade (1096) onward, many pseudo-Messiahs appeared on the scene. Among the more prominent false Messiahs were David Alroy, who appeared in Mesopotamia in 1147, and Abraham Abulafia, who was active in Sicily in the thirteenth century. In 1391, because of persecution in Spain, Moses Botarel became a popular messianic figure. And following the expulsion of the Jews from Spain in 1492 numerous pseudo-Messiahs surfaced, Shlomo Molcho (1500–1532) being the most famous. Later, one of the most charismatic of all the false Messiahs was Shabbetai Tzevi of Smyrna, Turkey (1626–1676), who in the end converted to Islam. The most recent pseudo-Messiah was Leibele Prossnitz, who appeared in Yemen in 1889.

Met Mitzvah

A Hebrew term literally meaning "*mitzvah* corpse," referring to the obligation to care for an unattended, unidentifiable corpse found lying on a public thoroughfare. The community closest to the site must perform the *mitzvah* (commandment) of burying the dead, said the Rabbis of the Talmud (*Sotah* 14a). Caring for a deceased stranger falls under the Hebrew ethical rubric of *chesed shel emet*, "a true act of kindness," for it is done with no ulterior motive, since there is no way in which the recipient of the kindness—that is, the deceased—can reward the community for its compassionate action.

Tending to an unattended corpse was considered of such high priority that even a High Priest, who was not permitted to come into contact with a corpse unless it was a member of his immediate family, was commanded to become personally involved in the ritual of burying the unidentified person (Leviticus 21:1–4). (See *Berakhot* 19b and *Nazir* 47b.)

See Chesed Shel Emet.

Meturgeman

An Aramaic term literally meaning "translator." So that members of a congregation, who were generally not well versed in Hebrew, would understand the meaning of the Hebrew Torah text as it was read aloud, the *meturgeman* was introduced into Jewish life in the time of Ezra and Nehemiah (fifth century B.C.E.). The Torah reader would recite a Hebrew verse and then pause while the verse was translated by the *meturgeman* into the vernacular (Nehemiah 8:1–8), which was Aramaic in Palestine and Babylonia in biblical and talmudic times. (See Mishnah *Megillah* 4:4. See also *Mishneh Torah*, Hilkhot Tefillah 12:10–14, and *Shulchan Arukh*, Orach Cha'yim 145:1–3.)

The translator of the Hebrew Torah text was not permitted to write out and read his translation to the public because it was feared that people might be misled into thinking that the words being spoken by the translator were actually written in the Torah scroll. The

rule was therefore established that a *meturgeman* must speak extemporaneously (*Mishneh Torah*, Hilkhot Tefillah 12:11).

In talmudic times, the *meturgeman* was often an *amora* and therefore a scholar in his own right. Some in fact were outstanding scholars: Rabbi Chuzpit was the *meturgeman* at the academy of Rabban Gamaliel II; Avdon was appointed by Judah the Prince to be his interpreter; Rabbi Pedat was the interpreter of Rabbi Yossi; Bar Keshita was the *meturgeman* of Rabbi Abbahu; and Judah bar Nachmani was the interpreter of Rabbi Shimon ben Lakish.

Scholars were not appointed to the office of *meturgeman* if they were under age fifty, because younger men were often more interested in proving their mastery at oratory than being accurate in their translation and interpretation.

The use of a public translator of the Torah was discontinued in time for a very practical reason: it lengthened the service unduly. This problem was not terribly acute for the Jews of Palestine, who read the Torah over a period of three years (triennial cycle). But for the Jews of Babylonia and the Jews of the Diaspora, who employed the annual Torah reading cycle, Sabbath readings were often very long. It was therefore decided to dispense with the services of the *meturgeman* and require congregants to review the Hebrew text and its translation in advance of the Sabbath reading. The use of a *meturgeman* still persists to this day in the Yemenite community. In Yemenite synagogues in Israel a *meturgeman* stands beside the *ba'al korei* and translates each verse into Arabic.

The Targum

The accepted Aramaic translation of the Pentateuch ("five books [of the Torah]") was prepared in the first century by a Palestinian proselyte named Onkelos. It was this translation that became the standard text used in the synagogues of Palestine and Babylonia. *Targum Onkelos* was later incorporated into printed copies of the Torah text and is popularly referred to simply as the *Targum*.

A second form of *Targum* was composed in Palestine toward the end of the talmudic period (around 500 C.E.). Known as the *Jerusalem Targum*, its translators not only translated the text into the vernacular, but added explanations and legendary folksy material to make the text more appealing and understandable.

Mezuman

A Hebrew word literally meaning "appointed, invited [to share a meal]." A quorum of three persons is required to have shared in a meal for the preamble to the *Grace After Meals* to be recited. When ten or more have shared in a meal, the word *Eloheinu* is added to the preamble.

See Grace After Meals; Minyan.

Mezuzah

Plural *mezuzot*. A Hebrew word literally meaning "doorpost," referring specifically to the piece of parchment on which two passages from the Bible are inscribed. The parchment is rolled up, inserted in a case so as to protect it from the elements, and attached to a doorjamb.

The Jewish historian Flavius Josephus, who lived in Palestine in the first century C.E., wrote in his *Antiquities*, "The greatest benefits of God are to be written on the doors...in order that His benevolent providence may be made known everywhere." And Moses ben Maimon (Maimonides), the outstanding twelfth-century scholar, wrote in his famous *Mishneh Torah*, "By [complying with] the commandment of the *mezuzah*, man is re-

minded of the unity of God, and is aroused to the love of Him..."

Mezuzah Wordings

In total, the *mezuzah* contains twenty-two handwritten lines. The two passages from the Book of Deuteronomy (6:4–9 and 11:13–21) that are handwritten upon parchment by a scribe (*sofer*) explain the rationale for the *mezuzah*. The first selection begins with the familiar words *Shema Yisra'el, Adonai Eloheinu, Adonai Echad*, "Hear O Israel, the Lord our God, the Lord is One," and ends with the verse, "And you shall write them upon the doorposts of your house and upon your gates." (Sephardim therefore sometimes refer to a *mezuzah* as the *Shema*.) The second begins with the words, *ve-hayah im shamo'a*, "And if you will obey the commandments," and goes on to express the same sentiment as the first section, stating specifically that a *mezuzah* must be affixed to the doorpost of every home.

The word *Shaddai*, meaning God, must be inscribed on the obverse side of every *mezuzah* parchment. The *Zohar*, the bible of kabbalists, which was composed near the end of the thirteenth century by Moses de Leon of Spain, explains the significance of *Shaddai*, by interpreting its spelling—*shin, dalet, yud*—as an acronym of the Hebrew words *shomer daltot Yisra'el*, "protector of the doors of Israel."

The word *Shaddai* is positioned on the obverse side of the point where the second selection (Deuteronomy 11:13) begins (the seventh line from the top).

Placement of the Mezuzah

Only a permanent dwelling requires a *mezuzah*; residences in which one resides for thirty days or less do not (*Yoma* 10a). Within the permanent residence, only rooms in which one eats or sleeps require a *mezuzah*.

Thus, bathrooms, storerooms, closets, garages, and all other areas where people do not actually "live" are excluded. If a room has more than one door leading into it, the *mezuzah* is to be affixed to the door most often used (*Menachot* 33a).

Rabbi Ephraim Oshry, a Lithuanian authority who survived the Holocaust, was asked whether a "home" in a ghetto needs a *mezuzah*. He responded: "Rooms in the ghetto were unbearably crowded; beds were almost literally one on top of another. Such rooms in no way were to be considered normal, permanent dwelling places, because if a person had the option he would leave them as soon as possible. A *mezuzah* is required only on a permanent residence. Thus, a temporary dwelling such as a *sukkah* requires no *mezuzah*. (See his *Responsa From the Holocaust* [1983].)

In past centuries, when synagogues were used only for prayer and study, they did not require a *mezuzah* because their sanctity was self-evident and required no other symbol to mark their holiness (*Berakhot* 47a). However, as synagogues became centers of social activity where food is served, it became necessary to affix a *mezuzah* to their entrances.

In recent years it has become customary to affix a *mezuzah* to the entrances of all public buildings in Israel, since parties and celebrations are often held in these buildings, and they thus fall in the domicile category.

Protecting and Positioning the Mezuzah

In order to protect the writing on the parchment from becoming wet and faded, it became customary to roll up the parchment and insert it in a metal or wooden container with a small opening near the top. The word *Shaddai* was so positioned that it would be visible through the aperture. Today, many modern *mezuzah* cases are elaborately designed, and some do not have apertures to reveal the word *Shaddai*.

To make the *mezuzah* readily noticed, it is always affixed to the right doorpost, as one enters a house or a room, approximately one-third from the top crosspiece (lintel), at eye-level of an average adult. The right jamb was designated for this purpose because most people are right-handed. (See *Menachot* 33a–b for additional details.)

Some scholars believe that the position of the *mezuzah* was arrived at during the early Middle Ages, when there was a debate as to whether the *mezuzah* should be affixed to the doorpost vertically or horizontally. Rashi and his grandson participated in this debate, with Rashi taking the position that the *mezuzah* should be affixed vertically and his grandson, Rabbenu Tam, maintaining that it should be placed horizontally. (See the commentary of Rabbi Meir Ha-Kohen, *Hagahot Maimuniyyot*, on the *Mishneh Torah*, Hilkhot Sefer Torah 10:8.)

The Maharil (Rabbenu Jacob Halevi Mollin), the fourteenth-century German authority, called attention to this dispute between Rashi and his grandson in his famous book on Jewish customs and liturgy entitled *Minhagei Maharil*. He suggested a compromise so as not to belittle either of these two authorities. He proposed that the *mezuzah* be placed on a slant (about a 30-degree angle) with the top facing inward (to the left) on the doorpost. This has been the custom since the seventeenth century, when the Maharil's book was first published and widely distributed.

When Moving

If one sells or rents a house to another Jew, he must not remove the *mezuzot* because the new owner may not be able to secure his own quickly enough. Thus, he will not be living in the house without *mezuzot* on its doorposts. The new owners must acquire their own *mezuzot* within thirty days. To distinguish Israel from the Diaspora, Jews living in Israel are required to affix their own *mezuzot* immediately upon moving into a new home. The Rabbis (Yoreh Dei'ah 286:22) expected anyone living in Israel to be dwelling there on a permanent basis.

If one sells a house to a non-Jew, he must remove all *mezuzot*, lest they be profaned. However, if it is reasonable to believe that the new owner may be offended by such action, the *mezuzot* are not to be removed.

In *Yoma* (11a), Abbayei says that a *mezuzah* on a private home should be checked twice every seven years, and on public buildings twice every fifty years.

As a gesture of reverence, it has become customary to kiss the *mezuzah* upon entering and leaving a home. Many Jews follow the talmudic custom of touching the *mezuzah* with the fingertips, kissing them, and reciting, *Adonai yishmor tzeitchah u-vo'achah mei-ata ve-ad olam*, "May God protect my going out and coming in, now and forever" (Psalm 121:8).

Mystical Beliefs

In talmudic times it was believed that the *mezuzah* possessed protective powers, capable of warding off evil spirits. Later, in the early Middle Ages, under the influence of kabbalists, not only were biblical references cited to prove the mystical powers of the *mezuzah*, but various names of angels were added to the wording on a *mezuzah*.

In medieval times mystics added three cryptogrammic words to the bottom of the obverse side of the *mezuzah*, below the word *Shaddai*. These nonwords—*kozu be-muchsaz kozu*—represent three real Hebrew words, *Yehovah Eloheinu Yehovah*, meaning Jehovah our God is our Lord." (*Yehovah*, the holiest of

God's names, is always pronounced *Adonai*.) This formulation was arrived at by substituting for each Hebrew letter, the letter that follows it. Thus, *Yehovah*, spelled *yud*, *hei*, *vav*, *hei*, became *kaf*, *vav*, *za'yin*, *vav* or *kozu*. Similarly, *Eloheinu* became *b'muchsaz*.

Apparently, the belief that the *mezuzah* possessed magical powers was widespread and was shared and even encouraged by prominent scholars. It is reported that when the thirteenth-century revered Jewish scholar Rabbi Meir of Rothenburg exhorted people to fasten *mezuzot* to their doors, he said: "I am convinced that no demon can harm a house properly provided with a *mezuzah*."

In recent centuries, the Jews from Yemen have followed the practice of removing the *mezuzah* and sacred books from the room of a dying man who is in great pain. The Yemenites believe that the presence of holy objects lessens the power of the Angel of Death. Thus, by removing the *mezuzah*, the Angel of Death is able to take the life of the patient sooner, sparing him suffering.

Midrash

Derived from the Hebrew word *darash*, meaning "to explore, investigate, interpret," *Midrash* is a generic term for a body of post-talmudic literature whose aim is to delve deeply into the Bible, particularly the Torah (Five Books of Moses), and to elucidate its textual and conceptual content.

There are two types of midrashic literature. The *Midrash Halakhah* (*halakhah* means "law") is devoted to explaining the legal aspects of Scripture. This category includes collections such as the *Mekhilta*, a commentary on the Book of Exodus; the *Sifra* (also called *Torat Kohanim*), a commentary on Leviticus; and *Sifrei*, a commentary on Numbers and Deuteronomy.

In the second category of midrashic literature, *Midrash Aggadah* (or *Haggadah*), the major work is *Midrash Rabbah* (also known as *Midrash Ha-Gadol*). It consists of legends, anecdotes, homiletic interpretations, aphorisms, parables, and similar material, and its main purpose is to draw ethical and moral lessons from the biblical text.

The methodology employed by the Rabbis whose views are expressed in midrashic (as well as talmudic) literature was best summarized by Rabbi Chisda, the third-century Babylonian scholar who was a disciple of Mar Ukba: "It is possible to pile mounds upon mounds of expositions and interpretations on each and every stroke [of the letters of the Torah]" (*Eruvin* 21b).

An example of how *Midrash Halakhah* and *Midrash Aggadah* differ in interpreting a biblical verse may be seen in the manner in which they deal with the subject of leprosy. In interpreting the verse, "This shall be the law of the *metzora* on the day of his purification...." the legalistic *Sifra* says that what is important in the verse is the use of the word "day." This means, the Rabbis conclude, that the cleansing may take place only during the day, not at night.

Midrash Aggadah, on the other hand, focuses in on the word *metzora*. Rabbi Yannai says that the word *metzora* is an abbreviated form of three Hebrew words: *motzi shem ra*, meaning "one who spreads a bad name," one who gossips or slanders. This interpretation led the Rabbis to conclude that a person becomes a leper because he cannot control his tongue and is a moral failure who is being punished.

Mikveh

Also spelled and pronounced *mikvah*. A Hebrew word literally meaning "a gathering place of water, a pool," referring specifically to a body of natural water such as a river, lake, or ocean, in which a person ritually purifies him- or herself by immersion (*tevilah*). A pond or a pool that is fed directly by natural springs or indirectly from well water, or one that holds stored water from rains, melted snow, or melted ice, may also be used as a *mikveh*. Water that had been stored in a metal container (*ma'yim she'uvin*) may not feed a *mikveh*, since metallic objects are susceptible to uncleanness. However, metal pipes laying in the earth as a conduit from the water source may be employed, since earth nullifies all susceptibility to ritual impurity.

A tractate of the Talmud known as *Mikva'ot* concerns itself with the rules and regulations pertaining to the *mikveh*. *Mikva'ot* consists of ten chapters and deals with the wells, cisterns, pools, reservoirs, ponds, ditches, or any other gatherings of water to be used for ritual purification.

The *mikveh* structure must be a minimum of two feet square by six feet high and must be filled with at least 191 gallons of natural water, an amount sufficient for average-sized people to immerse themselves fully. If additional water is needed to fill the *mikveh*, it may be drawn from any source.

Function

In biblical times, the *mikveh* was used by men and women for a variety of impurities, many of which are described in the Books of Leviticus (13, 15) and Numbers (19, 31). Today, the *mikveh* is used mainly by women for purification purposes on the seventh day after the menstrual period has ended, and by converts to Judaism as an essential part of the conversion process.

A bride is expected to immerse herself in a *mikveh* prior to the wedding ceremony. The Rabbis explain: just as Israel (the bride) had to be in a state of purity before receiving the Torah, so must a bride be ritually pure before entering into a covenant with her mate.

Although a ritual bath is visited by some observant Jews to purify themselves before major holidays and particularly before the Day of Atonement, members of some chasidic sects immerse themselves every Friday afternoon to prepare for the Sabbath.

Since writing a Torah scroll is a highly sacred activity, it was considered important for a scribe to immerse himself in a *mikveh* before beginning the writing process. Some scribes immerse themselves each day before they begin work, while others do so only on the very first day, at the beginning of the entire undertaking.

Orthodox Jews use a *mikveh* to purify dishes and other serving and cooking utensils that are being used for the first time. Just as everything brought upon the altars of the Temples in ancient times had to be ritually pure, said the Rabbis, so must all kitchen utensils brought to the table—the altar of the home—today. Many hardware stores in the Jewish sections of Brooklyn, New York, have installed *mikva'ot* to satisfy this demand.

Throughout the ages the *mikveh* has traditionally been housed in the synagogue structure, but in recent years many have been erected as independent buildings. These modern *mikva'ot*, sometimes referred to as ritualariums, are often equipped with amenities such as hair dryers, and those in affluent neighborhoods even have cosmeticians, hairdressers, and manicurists on call to service their clients.

In the Orthodox community a group of local women known as "*mikveh* ladies" oversee the monthly visitors to their *mikveh*, checking to see that the immersion is properly executed. In recent years, a number of "watchers" have been trained to keep an eye open for signs of wife-battering, something that has heretofore not been spoken of publicly. This project was initiated by two organizations: the Shalom Task Force and the Jewish Board of Family and Children's Services.

See Niddah; Purity and Impurity; Tohorat Ha-Mishpachah.

Minchah

A Hebrew word literally meaning "gift." In Temple days, the afternoon sacrificial offering (Exodus 29:41; Leviticus 2:4) was called *minchah*, and the same appellation was later given to the afternoon synagogue prayer service that replaced it.

The main feature of the daily *Minchah* service is the silent recitation of the *Amidah* by congregants and its repetition aloud by the cantor. Psalm 145 (*Ashrei*), a song of praise to God, was later added as an introductory prayer. The afternoon service concludes with the recitation of the *Aleinu*, another song of praise to God, and the recitation of the *Kaddish* by mourners.

The Sabbath afternoon *Minchah* service consists basically of a recitation of Psalm 145 (*Ashrei*), the *Amidah*, the *Aleinu*, and the *Kaddish* for mourners. In addition, the *U-va Le-Tziyon* "(May [a redeemer] Come to Zion")* prayer follows the *Ashrei*. The words of *U-va Le-Tziyon*, taken from the Book of Isaiah (59:20), were comforting to Jews whose lives were so often filled with uncertainty and who would once again have to face a hostile outside world once the Sabbath was over.

On Sabbath afternoon, the Torah is read immediately preceding the *Amidah*. Only three Torah honors (*aliyot*) are awarded so as not to extend the service. (In years past, this allowed sufficient time for preachers and teachers to deliver their discourses). During the Torah reading, bar mitzvah and bat mitzvah celebrations are sometimes held.

The (fourth) prayer of the Sabbath afternoon *Amidah* is preceded by a series of special prayers beginning with the words *Atah Echad* ("Thou Art One [and Thy Name is One]").

Minhag

A Hebrew term literally meaning "custom." In Jewish tradition, custom is an outgrowth of the way in which people carry out the requirements of law.

See Law and Custom.

Minyan

Plural, *minyanim*. This Hebrew term, literally meaning "number, count, quorum," was first used in the Talmud (*Berakhot* 6b) where Rabbi Yochanan explains the importance of assembling a ritual quorum for a public prayer service: "Whenever the Holy One, Blessed be He, comes into a synagogue and does not find ten persons there [which is required if the proper congregational responses are to be made when prayers such as *Barkhu* and *Kaddish* are recited], God becomes angry immediately." As corroboration of God's attitude, Rabbi Yochanan cites Isaiah 50:2: "Why, when I came, was no one there; why, when I called, was there no response?"

Rationale

Many theories have been advanced for requiring ten persons to complete a *minyan*. Philo believed that ten was selected because it is the most perfect number, but the Rabbis of the Talmud and other interpreters of the Bible found several biblical bases for the choice of the number ten. The most popular explanation is found in the tractate *Megillah* (23b), where this conclusion is said to be derived from the story of the twelve spies who were

sent out by Moses to scout the land of Canaan to determine if it was safe to invade and conquer. Two of the twelve scouts returned with a favorable report, while ten opposed it, warning that the undertaking would be too hazardous. The ten who opposed the adventure are referred to in the Bible (Numbers 14:27) as *eidah* ("congregation"), hence in Jewish traditional writings a congregation, an *eidah,* must consist of not less than ten people. (See *Sanhedrin* 2b for the significance of the number ten as it applies to a court of law.)

Another interpretation of why ten was selected as the number that constitutes a congregation is based on the first verse of Psalm 82: "God is present in the divine congregation." Here, again, *eidah* is used for "congregation," and the Talmud (*Berakhot* 6a) concludes that "if ten men pray together, God's presence is with them."

The number ten also appears in the story of Boaz and Ruth in the Book of Ruth (4:2), where it is indicated how many people must be present to constitute a legal quorum. Ruth was the daughter-in-law of Naomi, and Boaz, her kinsman, wanted to marry her. There was, however, a closer kinsman who had a prior claim on the widow Ruth. In order to have this kinsman announce publicly his marital intentions vis-à-vis Ruth, Boaz assembled ten men of the elders of the city to sit at the city gates (where courts normally held their sessions and people met for the interchange of news and the adjudication of disputes) to hear from other relatives who may have had a prior claim. The one kinsman who was qualified decided not to take Ruth as his wife, leaving Boaz free to marry her. This biblical account is offered as an explanation of why ten persons are required to constitute a *minyan*, particularly for the recitation of the marriage benedictions.

Other explanations have been offered to explain why the number ten was selected to constitute a quorum. One is that ten of Joseph's brothers were sent by their father, Jacob, to Egypt to buy grain during the years of famine in Canaan. Another is that ten is the minimum number Abraham bargained for with God to save Sodom. God was determined to destroy that wicked city, but yielding to Abraham's appeal (Genesis 18:23–32), God agreed that if even as few as ten righteous people were to be found in Sodom, He would not destroy the city.

Minyan Deficit

Where conditions are such that it is impossible to gather a quorum, services may be conducted with a lesser number. In the Talmud (*Berakhot* 47b), Rabbi Huna says: "Nine people plus the [Torah in the] ark" suffices for a quorum. Rabbi Joshua ben Levi went even further: "Even an infant in a cradle can be counted to a *minyan*. In the post-talmudic period it was considered acceptable to count a boy holding a *Chumash* (Pentateuch) as a member of a *minyan*.

Many authorities, principally Rabbenu Tam (1100–1171), the grandson of Rashi, considered these proposals preposterous and a contravention of the law. (See the Tosafot on *Berakhot* 48a.)

Rabbi Meir of Rothenburg (1215–1293), the great legal authority of thirteenth-century Germany, sharing the view of Rabbenu Tam, ruled that a child should not be counted to a *minyan* even when a quorum is required to say *Kaddish*. He advised: "The best you can do is to leave the synagogue [when some of the assembled wish to count a young boy so as to make a tenth] so you will not be guilty of transgressing the law."

Yet, despite the fact that Joseph Caro's *Code of Jewish Law* (*Shulchan Arukh*, Orach Cha'yim 55:1) ruled that the basic prayers—namely *Kaddish*, *Barkhu*, and *Kedushah*—may not be recited unless ten adults are present, it does include (55:4) the more lenient view that a boy under thirteen—even a boy as young as six, if he is intelligent—may be counted as part of the required quorum. This view did not sit well with Moses Isserles (the Rama), who in his Notes to Caro's *Code* adds: "Even if the boy holds a *Chumash* in his hand, he should not be counted." Then he relents: "However, in case of an emergency there are authorities who are more permissive."

Rabbi Moshe Feinstein (1895–1986) is one of the contemporary authorities who is more permissive in this regard. In his book of responsa entitled *Igrot Moshe* ("Letters of Moses"), he suggests that rather than refrain from conducting a public service for lack of ten men, a boy who is at least twelve years old may be counted. And a Torah scroll, even if it is *pasul* (unfit to read), should lie on the table with a child grasping its handles.

Orthodox congregations do not count women as part of a *minyan*, but Reform congregations do. According to a 1973 decision of the Rabbinical Assembly's (Conservative) Committee on Jewish Law and Standards, individual rabbis have the option, with the consent of their congregation, of counting women as part of a *minyan*.

Entering the Minyan

The phrase "entering the *minyan*" is the way Sephardim refer to a bar mitzvah boy. Once he begins donning his *tefillin*, he is counted as one of the ten persons who make up a prayer quorum.

After the large exodus of Jews from Cuba in the 1960s, a dwindling group of aging men was left in most communities and they were only able to assemble eight men at most for a *minyan*. A quorum of eight was soon given the name "Cuban *minyan*."

See Weddings; Women.

Mipnei Darkei Shalom

A Hebrew term meaning "for the sake of the paths of peace," referring to the concept that espouses maintaining goodwill between the Jewish and non-Jewish communities, within the Jewish community itself, or within a family unit. The term was first used in the Mishnah *Shevi'it* (4:3) in connection with the offering of assistance to Gentiles laboring in the fields in the seventh (*shemittah*) year when fellow Jews could not be helped.

See Goodwill Principle.

Mipnei Kevod Tzibur

A Hebrew phrase meaning "because of the honor of the public," referring to the Jewish concept that the dignity and welfare of the community must always be considered.

See Kevod Tzibur.

Miracles

The question as to whether miracles are possible has long been a subject of debate. A miracle, by definition, is a deviation from the established laws of nature. The Midrash, which contains the thinking of the early rabbis (first to fifth centuries) expresses the view, which is generally accepted in Judaism, that the miracles described in the Bible were not "miraculous" events, but were preordained. Hence, rather than constituting a break with natural law, they were actually a fulfillment of natural law.

The Midrash puts it this way: Rabbi Yochanan said, "God made an agreement with the sea [during the period of Creation] that it would split in half when approached by the Israelites [fleeing from Egypt]."

Rabbi Jeremiah said: "Not only did God make an agreement with the sea, but He made an agreement with all the other things that were created during the six days of Creation. God made an agreement with the sun and the moon that they should stand still in the time of Joshua. God made an agreement with the ravens that they should feed Elijah. God made an agreement with fire that it should not harm Chananiah, Mishael, and Azariah—the three friends of Daniel—when they would be thrown into the fiery furnace at the command of Nebukhadnezzar of Babylonia. God made an agreement with the fish that it should spit out Jonah alive, after it had swallowed him" (*Genesis Rabbah* 5:5; *Exodus Rabbah* 21:6).

While traditional Jews, for the most part, believe in miracles as events that actually happened, some talmudic and post-talmudic authorities were of the opinion that miracles are to be taken as allegorical and poetic expressions of God's greatness. This is evident, for example, from the manner in which the Rabbis interpret the story of Israel's battle with its archenemy, the Amalekites.

The Bible says, "And it came to pass, when Moses held up his hand, Israel prevailed; and when he put down his hand, Amalek prevailed" (Exodus 17:11). The Rabbis of the Talmud wondered about this miraculous event, and concluded that as long as the Children of Israel look up and keep their hearts attuned to their Father in heaven, they will prevail. If they do not look up toward God, they will be defeated (*Rosh Hashanah* 21a).

This allegorical, symbolic interpretation of the Bible was widely accepted by the greatest of scholars, among them Sa'adya Gaon and Moses Maimonides. Maimonides states openly in his *Guide of the Perplexed* (III:46) that the miracles described in the Bible in connection with the careers of the prophets must be understood as prophetic visions, not as literal happenings.

Mi Shebeirakh

These Hebrew words, literally meaning "He [God] who blessed," are the first words of the prayer sometimes recited by the Torah reader or sexton (*gabbai*) after a person has been honored with an *aliyah* (Torah honor). The prayer reads: "May He who blessed our fathers, Abraham, Isaac, Jacob send His blessings upon.... [at this point the honoree's name and the honoree's father's name are inserted]. May the Holy One bless him, and protect him, and deliver him from all trouble and illness. May He send a blessing and success to all his efforts and to those of the whole household of Israel. And let us say, Amen."

The *Mi Shebeirakh* prayer may also be pronounced for someone other than the honoree. If the prayer is being recited for the recovery of an individual, the names of the matriarchs—Sarah, Rebecca, Rachel, and Leah—are substituted for those of the patriarchs. In explaining why the mother's name is used, Yehuda Leib Zirelson (1860–1941), Chief Rabbi of Bessarabia, quotes the Talmud (*Shabbat* 66b) where the scholar Abbayei was told by his mother that when using magical incantations, the mother's name is to be used. Zirelson explains that since a prayer is involved, and prayers must always be spoken in truth, the mother's name is used because one can always be sure who the individual's mother is, while one cannot be absolutely certain who the father is.

Persons for whom the *Mi Shebeirakh* prayer is generally recited include a bar or bat mitzvah celebrant; a groom on the Sabbath before his wedding (who in non-Orthodox congregations is often joined by the bride); the parent of a newborn girl who is being named at the service; and those who are ill or have just recovered from an illness.

In some Sephardic congregations, a *Mi Shebeirakh* is recited after the ark is opened and before the Torah scroll is removed for the Torah reading service.

In recent years, traditional non-Orthodox synagogues that are gender-conscious add the names of the matriarchs to all *Mi Shebeirakh* blessings.

Mishnah

A Hebrew term literally meaning "that which is studied," referring specifically to the body of Jewish literature that forms the first part of the Talmud. The Mishnah explains, interprets, and analyzes the laws set forth in the Torah. It also treats its subjects that relate to Jewish ethics, history, folklore, and ceremonial practice.

The rulings expressed in the Mishnah are those of the *tanna'im* (singular, *tanna*), teachers of the various academies of learning in Palestine during the several centuries before and after the Common Era (C.E.). Judah the Prince (also referred to as Yehudah Ha-Nasi or Judah I), who was born about 135 C.E. and died in the year 220, was the prime figure responsible for the final assembly and editing of the Mishnah text.

Written in a precise, terse Hebrew style, in its edited form the Mishnah is a distillation of the views of the many *tanna'im* (one hundred and forty-eight are mentioned by name) who participated in legal discussions over several centuries. Dissenting views are presented together with the names of their advocates; the majority view, which became law, is presented last.

Judah's accomplishment, which extended for half a century, was built on the scholarship of Rabbi Akiba ben Joseph and Rabbi Meir, who were prime movers of Jewish learning in the Palestinian academy in Yavneh. Akiba, who according to legend did not start studying before the age of forty, was the first to arrange the accumulated lore according to subject matter. Until then, it had been transmitted randomly by word-of-mouth.

Rabbi Meir winnowed the vast number of accumulated laws, traditions, and fables, separating the important from the unimportant. Judah the Prince and his associates added to the efforts of Akiba, Meir, and their associates by further refining and organizing the mass of material into a manageable entity.

The Six Orders

Judah the Prince divided the Mishnah into six *sedarim* (singular, *seder*), or orders:

1. *Zera'im* ("Seeds"), consisting of eleven tractates (*massekhtot* in Aramaic; singular *massekhtah*) devoted to laws pertaining to agriculture, except for the first tractate, *Berakhot*, which deals with food blessings and daily prayers.

2. *Mo'ed* ("Festivals"), consisting of twelve tractates dealing with the holiday seasons of the year.

3. *Nashim* ("Women"), consisting of seven tractates dealing with the laws of marriage, divorce, and vows.

4. *Nezikin* ("Damages"), consisting of ten tractates dealing with civil and criminal law.

5. *Kodoshim* ("Sacred Things"), consisting of eleven tractates devoted to laws concerning ritual slaughtering, sacrifices, sacred Temple objects, and Temple worship.

6. *Tohorot* ("Purifications"), consisting of twelve tractates devoted to laws of ritual purity.

The Six Orders of the Mishnah, called *Shishah Sedarim* in Hebrew, are usually referred to by the Hebrew acronym *Shas*. In all, there are sixty-three tractates in the Mishnah. The contents of the Mishnah are elucidated in the *Gemara*. *See* Gemara.

Tosefta

As the official Mishnah was being compiled, independent Mishnah compilations were also being formed. These were not incorporated into the body of Judah the Prince's work—either because they were unknown to him or because he chose not to include them—and hence they were called Tosefta, meaning "additions, supplementary material." The individual sections of the Tosefta are known by the Aramaic term *baraitot* (singular, *baraita*), meaning "extraneous Mishnah." *See* Tosefta.

See Talmud.

Mishneh Torah

The name of a Hebrew compendium of Jewish law composed in the twelfth century by the most erudite of all talmudic authorities, Moses ben Maimon, better known by the acronym Rambam and by his Greek appellation, Maimonides. Maimonides was born in Cordova, Spain, in 1135, and died in Old Cairo (Fostat), Egypt, in 1204.

The *Mishneh Torah*, meaning "review of the Torah," is also known as *Yad Ha-Chazakah*, meaning "mighty hand," or *Yad* for short. The Hebrew word *yad* has a numerical value of fourteen (*yud* [10] plus *dalet* [4]), the number of volumes in Maimonides' work.

Maimonides' great accomplishment in the *Mishneh Torah* was to organize the immense amount of material in the Talmud by subject matter, thus creating order out of what was previously a loose admixture of law, history, folklore, philosophy, legends, and miscellany spread out over the sixty-three talmudic tractates that comprise the Babylonian Talmud. Maimonides also included the laws that applied to the Temple sacrificial system because he expected that one day the Temple would be rebuilt and the duties of the Priests reinstituted.

In the *Mishneh Torah*, Maimonides, unlike other codifiers of the law, does not present the varying viewpoints of talmudic scholars on any one issue. Rather, he records only that which he believes to be established law. Additionally, he does not list the talmudic sources on which he bases his conclusions, and for this he was criticized severely. His opponents referred to his code as *Yad Ha-Chazakah*, because they felt he was overbearing and strong-handed for not revealing his sources.

Mitnagdim

Singular, *mitnageid*. This Hebrew term literally meaning "opponents [of the chasidic movement]" was coined by the Ba'al Shem Tov (*c.* 1700–1760) and his followers, who were being condemned by Lithuanian Jews under the leadership of Elishah ben Solomon (Zalman) [1720–1797], better known as the Vilna Gaon ("the Sage of Vilna"). The Vilna Gaon considered the views and habits of the *chasidim* to be contrary to Jewish conventional practice, and he went so far as to deny them the right to be called Jews.

Among the main criticisms that the Vilna Gaon and his fellow *mitnagdim* harbored against the Ba'al Shem Tov and his fellow *chasidim* were their denial of the primacy of the talmudic study, the use of the Sephardic liturgy, the strong belief in the supernatural powers of their *rebbes*, and the establishment of separate synagogues. So intense was the opposition toward the *mitnagdim* that the Vilna Gaon issued a ban against the practice of chasidism in Lithuania, and he ordered that its adherents be excommunicated ("placed in *cheirem*") and their literature destroyed.

Despite this overt challenge of the *mitnagdim*, chasidism began to spread, especially after 1772 when the first partition of Poland took place and that country was divided among Russia, Austria, and Prussia. Chasidism that had taken root in Poland began to spill over into these new areas, which had been under the influence of rabbinical Judaism and its prime exponent and leader, the Vilna Gaon.

The opposition of the *mitnagdim* toward *chasidim* lasted until 1797, one year after the last partition of Poland, by which time chasidic sects had met success after success and became dominant in many important communities. The movement became entrenched in White Russia, which in the course of time had become politically cut off from Poland and was under the control of Russia. There, in Lyady, Rabbi Shneur Zalman became the spiritual head of the chasidic movement. Under his influence, chasidism spread into Lithuania, the stronghold of the Vilna Gaon and his followers. And despite all efforts to discredit the *chasidim*—even to the extent of accusing Shneur Zalman of disloyalty to the Russian government and having him arrested and imprisoned in St. Petersburg in 1798—after reviewing his case, Czar Paul I released him.

In 1800, a second effort was made by some *mitnagdim* to defame Shneur Zalman. They claimed, falsely, that he was instructing his followers to fear only God, not the government. As a consequence he was arrested once again and imprisoned until March 29, 1801. At that time Alexander I ascended the throne of Russia; the charges against Zalman were dropped, and he was released from the St. Petersburg "fortress."

In the years following, the influence of chasidism grew and became even more widespread, as the influence of the *mitnagdim* over the masses began to dwindle. In time, the feud between the two groups subsided and both were able to pursue their own goals in peace.

See Cheirem; Excommunication.

Mitzvah

Plural, *mitzvot*. A Hebrew word literally meaning "divine commandment." Originally, the term *mitzvot* applied only to commandments prescribed in the Torah, of which the Talmud (*Makkot* 23b) says, there are 613, often referred to as *taryag mitzvot*. The numerical value of the letters in the term *taryag* is 613.

Of the 613 commandments in the Torah, 248 are positive—such as "Honor thy father and mother" (Exodus 20:12)—and 365 are negative—such as "Thou shall not murder" (Exodus 20:13). Positive commandments are called *mitzvot asei*; negative ones are called *mitzvot lo ta'aseh*. Rabbi Simlai associated the 365 negative commandments with the number of days in the solar calendar and the 248 positive ones with the number of parts in the human body.

In time, the term *mitzvah* was extended to mean "good deed" in a social sense, which is what the Ethics of the Fathers (4:2) means to convey when it quotes the second-century talmudic scholar Ben Azzai as saying, "One *mitzvah* leads to another." Ben Azzai continues: "The reward for performing a *mitzvah* is a *mitzvah*, and the penalty for performing an *aveirah* ["sin"] is an *aveirah*."

One category of commandments are those classified in the Talmud as being required to be performed at a specific time (*mitzvot asei she-ha-zeman gerama*). These are *mitzvot* that must be performed only at a specific time of day, or during the day rather than at night, or on certain days of the year. Women are gen-

erally exempt from carrying out these commandments—such as reciting the morning prayers—because they would interfere with their duties as homemaker and mother. Nevertheless, there are some time-related commandments that a woman is obligated to perform, including lighting Sabbath candles and eating *matzah* on Passover night. It should be noted that the fact that women are *not obligated* to perform certain *mitzvot* does not mean they may not do so voluntarily.

Fearing that Jews might lose sight of the intrinsic value of the commandments, the famous chasidic Kotzker Rebbe said: "The prohibition against idolatry [the second of the Ten Commandments] includes the prohibition against making idols out of *mitzvot*. We should never imagine that the chief purpose of a *mitzvah* is its outer form [its performance] rather than its inner meaning."

See Noahide Laws; Taryag Mitzvot; Women.

Mixed Breeds

Known in Hebrew as *kila'yim*, this concept stems from the biblical law spelled out in Leviticus 19:19 and Deuteronomy 22:11. In these verses, the Israelites are instructed not to mate their animals with others of a different breed, not to sow their fields with two different kinds of seed, and not to make garments in which animal and vegetable threads (wool and linen) are intermingled. The latter is know as *shaatnez*.

All of the above practices were common among heathens and, according to Maimonides, (*Guide of the Perplexed*) are to be avoided because "they are associated with idolatry."

Mizrach

A Hebrew word literally meaning "east," referring specifically to an ornamental plaque on which that word is engraved or handlettered.

Such plaques are placed on a wall in the synagogue or in the home facing in the direction of Jerusalem, which is generally to the east of most Jewish populated countries. According to Jewish tradition, one must face that holy city when engaged in prayer.

According to some scholars, *mizrach* is an acronym derived from the Hebrew expression *mit-tzad zeh ru'ach cha'yim*, meaning "From this side [the east] comes the breath of life."

Mnemonic Devices

The use of certain techniques or formulas to help recall facts and improve memory, known as mnemonics, was widespread in Jewish scholarly circles.

Among the most popular aids to memory is the acronym, in which the first letter of the words to be recalled are formed as a word. For example, in order to remember the three parts of the Bible, which consists of the *Torah*, *Nevi'im* (Prophets), and *Ketuvim* (Holy Writings), the acronym *Tanakh* (*tav, nun, khaf*) was created.

Another frequently used mnemonic device is the acrostic, in which the first letter of each line in a prayer or poem when taken in order spell out a word, a slogan, or the alphabet in sequence. An example of an alphabetic acrostic is the *Ashrei* prayer. Another type of acrostic is found in the Friday night *Lekhah Dodi* prayer, in which the first letter of each stanza, when taken in order, spells out the name of the author of the poem.

See Acrostic.

Modesty

The Jewish concept of modesty is best conveyed by the Hebrew word *tzeniut*, a term used by the prophet Micah (6:8) in the phrase "ve-hatznei'a [a form of *tzni'ut*] lekhet im Elohekha," meaning to "walk humbly before your God."

Humility and modesty are two sides of the same coin, but whereas humility addresses the spiritual nature of man, modesty concerns the material aspects of man's nature. It concerns his physical appetites and predilections, and is measured by how well a person succeeds in distancing himself from ugly and unseemly conduct.

In one reference, the Talmud (*Kiddushin* 40b) says, "He who eats in the street is to be compared to a dog." In the minor talmudic tractate *Derekh Eretz Zuta* (2), one is reminded to "be modest toward everyone, and gentle in speech."

The learned man (*talmid chakham*) is especially warned to be extremely circumspect in his personal habits. The talmudic tractate *Shabbat* (118b) highlights a comment of the saintly editor of the Mishnah, Rabbi Judah the Prince: "The beams of my house have never seen the seams of my shirt." So careful was Rabbi Judah not to expose his bare body that even when he removed his shirt in undressing he pulled it over his head while sitting in bed so that his body remained covered as much as possible.

The talmudic tractate *Berakhot* (62a–b and elsewhere) is replete with instructions for learned Rabbis as to how they should conduct themselves when taking care of their bodily functions. But the main area of concern for modest behavior in the Jewish law and tradition relates to the conduct of women, particularly married women. A married woman is warned not to appear in public in dress that is seductive to men. To expose her bare skin in any way is sexually provocative, says Rabbi Isaac (*Berakhot* 24a). And Rabbi Chisda said, "A woman's leg is sexually exciting." To which Rabbi Samuel added, "A woman's voice is sexually exciting." And Rabbi Sheshet noted that "a woman's hair is sexually exciting."

The comment of Rabbi Sheshet is probably the basis for ultra-Orthodox married women covering their natural hair with a wig (*sheitl* in Yiddish) or a kerchief (*tikhl* in Yiddish). Some of these women shave their heads first.

The overall Jewish attitude toward living a modest life was summed up by the Rabbis in *Pesikta Rabbati* (185b), where the following observation is made: "No one is more beloved of God than a modest person."

Mohel

Plural, *mohalim*. A Hebrew word literally meaning "circumciser," referring to the one who cuts away the foreskin of the penis during the *brit milah* ceremony.

Actually, the first circumciser was Abraham, whom God commanded (Genesis 17:11ff.), "And you shall circumcise the flesh of your foreskin; and that will serve as a sign of the Covenant between Me and you. And throughout the generations, every male among you shall be circumcised at the age of eight days." Abraham then circumcised himself, his son Ishmael, and all his slaves.

The second person to perform a circumcision was Tzipporah, the wife of Moses, who circumcised her son with a stone (Exodus 4:25). The Talmud (*Avodah Zara* 27a) says that Moses completed the circumcision, which is the rabbinic way of declaring that the obligation to circumcise a son belongs to the father and should not be performed by a woman, although it may be delegated to a *mohel*. Later rabbinic authorities declared that a woman is permitted to perform a circumcision if a male *mohel* is not available.

Moses Maimonides, in his twelfth-century code of Jewish law known as the *Mishneh Torah*, ruled that an idol worshipper (*akum* in Hebrew) may not perform a circumcision. Only a member of the Jewish faith may do so.

However, one century earlier, in his commentary on the talmudic tractate *Avodah Zarah* (27a), Rashi went so far as to say that where a Jewish *mohel* or physician is unavailable, a heathen doctor may be trusted to circumcise a Jewish infant because he would not want to hurt his reputation by mutilating his patient's sexual organ. Thus, in actual practice, where a *mohel* or Jewish doctor is unavailable, a Gentile doctor may perform a circumcision in the presence of a rabbi or knowledgeable Jew who is able to recite the Hebrew prayers and name the baby.

(Great Britain's royal family has been calling upon a *mohel* since the time of Queen Victoria (1837–1901) to circumcise its male offspring. Charles, the Prince of Wales, was circumcised by a *mohel* who was also a medical doctor. Critics of circumcision have convinced Prince Charles to abandon the practice, and the younger members of British royalty today are uncircumcised.)

Since 1984 the Reform movement has been licensing medical doctors—including obstetricians, pediatricians, and urologists—to be *mohalim* after concluding a course of study. These doctors must be members of a Reform congregation and must be sponsored by a rabbi. In 1989, the Conservative movement decided to embark upon a similar program. The Orthodox do not have a licensing program for doctors who wish to serve as *mohalim*.

Medieval Superstition

In the early Middle Ages, when a circumcision had to be performed on a Sabbath, it was customary for the *mohel* to place the scalpel under the baby's pillow on Friday before dark so that he would not have to violate the law that prohibits carrying an object in public on the Sabbath.

In the sixteenth century, the practice of

leaving the scalpel under the pillow was extended to all circumcisions, even those performed on a weekday. The custom, not common today, was instituted by kabbalists (mystics), who believed that demons attack newborn infants but are scared off by knives and similar objects.

See Circumcision.

Moneylending

In three instances (Exodus 22:24, Leviticus 25:36–37, and Deuteronomy 23:20–21) the Bible states that an Israelite is forbidden to charge interest when lending money to a fellow Israelite. Deuteronomy specifies that interest may be charged when lending money to a non-Israelite.

The Bible uses two different words, *neshekh* and *ribit*, for interest. *Neshekh*, the more commonly used term, derives from the Hebrew verb meaning "to take a bite" and refers to interest—that is, taken "off the top" of the total sum being loaned. *Ribit*, on the other hand, which derives from the word meaning "increase," refers to accrued interest, a sum added to the principal amount loaned and payable when the loan is due. Both types of interest are forbidden in the Torah.

Moneylending by Jews to non-Jews at reasonable interest rates was never strictly forbidden by Jewish authorities. But when it became urgent for Jews to borrow money from fellow Jews for commercial enterprises, the biblical ban against charging interest was eased by means of a legal fiction known as a *heter iska*, "an allowance to conduct business." The idea was introduced in the community of Nehardea, Babylonia (present-day Iraq), where the loan was characterized as a combination of "trust" and "loan," an instrument that satisfied the needs of both the lender and the borrower without violating Jewish law. By means

of the *heter iska* the lender (creditor) became a limited partner of the borrower (debtor) in the enterprise for which the money was to be used. The lender would then receive a portion of the profits thrown off by the business venture, the proceeds being called dividends rather than interest. (*Bava Metzia* 68b and 104b–105a discusses the subject fully, offering a variety of scenarios in which losses are involved.)

Moneylending in Medieval Society

The medieval Church, which took Holy Scripture literally, forbade its members from making loans that required the payment of interest, a practice called usury. But when economic and political conditions were such that businessmen and rulers of countries were in dire need of money to finance businesses and wars, the Church allowed its followers to turn to Jews for loans. Fortunately for medieval Christian society, Jews of affluence were present in many countries.

After the destruction of the Second Temple in 70 C.E., Jews had settled in a variety of locations and earned a living as farmers, vintners, and craftsmen. But as a result of the Crusades, which began in 1096 and ravaged many Jewish communities throughout Europe, Jewish farms were confiscated and Jews were denied membership in the various crafts and guilds. As a consequence, the major industry open to them was moneylending, an occupation forbidden to Christians.

The positive result of this initially negative situation was that Jews were able to enter the portals of power. Because of the financial needs of the Christian community, many Jews became *Schutzjuden*, German for "protected Jews." Powerful rulers took them under their wing and allowed them access to the inner circles of government, where they became known as *Hofjuden,* or "court Jews." Many of these Jews were instrumental in having oppressive rulings against individual Jews and Jewish communities nullified.

Free-Loan Societies

Many Jews, even today, have heeded the biblical injunction against charging interest on loans to the needy. In the Middle Ages, this concept was institutionalized in most communities through the formation of *gemilut chasadim* societies. These Free-Loan societies lent money interest-free to needy individuals and families, especially to immigrants in need of help to establish themselves in a new environment.

Monotheism

Monotheism, the belief that there is but one God who created and sustains the world, and that He alone is to be adored, worshipped, and emulated is a major Jewish contribution to civilization. It is the signature of Judaism that has left an indelible impression upon civilization. As the German philosopher Arthur Schopenhauer (1788–1860), a vocal critic of most aspects of Judaism, acknowledged, "Judaism cannot be denied the glory of being the only genuinely monotheistic religion on earth."

Monotheism stands in stark contrast to the primitive polytheistic view which maintains that many gods rule the universe, each promoting its own ethical values. And so obsessed had Jews become with this idea of one God as Master of the universe and that no other god may even be compared to Him that the Rabbis of the talmudic period felt it imperative to establish Abraham, the Founding Father of Judaism, as a pure monotheist. And so the Midrash (*Genesis Rabbah* 38:13) depicts him as an iconoclast. He is portrayed

as having grown up in the home of his father, Terah, who was engaged in manufacturing, selling, and worshipping idols. Abraham took strong exception to the activity of his father and smashed the idols that had been prepared for sale. The Rabbis did not want the taint of idolatry to be associated with Abraham, the first Hebrew.

In similar fashion, the authors of the Book of Chronicles, the very last book of the Bible, were anxious to have Moses, the hero of the Exodus, seen in a pure, untainted light. And so, First Chronicles (4:18) introduces the idea that Pharaoh's daughter, who found Moses in the bulrushes along the River Nile when she went out to bathe one morning, was actually a Jewess. It suggests that her name is Bityah, meaning "daughter of God." Under this scenario Moses was brought up by a God-fearing Jewess, not by Egyptian idolators.

The question then arose: How is it possible to claim that Pharaoh's daughter was a Jewess? The Talmud (*Megillah* 13a) offers this explanation: She went down to the river to cleanse herself of her father's idols. To which Rabbi Yochanan adds: "Anyone who repudiates idolatry is a Jew."

The concept of one God to the exclusion of all other gods became engraved upon the consciousness of the Jewish people after it was inscribed on the tablets of the law as the second of the Ten Commandments received by Moses on Mount Sinai. It boldly declared: "Thou shalt have no other gods beside Me. Thou shalt not make unto thee a graven image, nor any manner of likeness, of anything that is in heaven above... Thou shalt not bow to them or worship them..." (Exodus 20:3–6), and once again this concept is reiterated in the famous *Shema* prayer (Deuteronomy 6:4): "Hear, O Israel, the Lord is our God, the Lord is One."

The emphasis placed by Judaism on the idea of the unity—the oneness, the uniqueness—of God, establishing Him as the sole Creator and the Father of all mankind carries with it the implication that all God's children are brothers; that all are created in the image of God. Thus, no one may say, "I am better than you" or "My stock is more distinguished than yours."

This concept runs counter to those advanced by other cultures and religions of the biblical period. The Zoroastrian doctrine of dualism, which states that there are two basic antagonistic forces—good and evil—governing the universe, was propounded in Persia from the seventh to the fifth centuries B.C.E. At that same time, Greeks advanced a pantheistic view, which proposed that God is the total of all the laws, forces, and manifestations of the existing universe. These pagan views were threats to Judaism and the probable reason why the Bible (Deuteronomy 7:3) warns Jews (then called Hebrews or Israelites) not to intermarry with members of pagan nations. The purpose was to prevent the monotheistic character of the then-emerging Jewish nation from being diminished.

Christianity and Monotheism

The Christian belief in the Trinity—the Father, the Son, and the Holy Spirit—has been viewed by Jewish scholars in two ways. To people such as Moses Maimonides (1135–1204), worship of a Trinity is polytheism; he called Christians "heathens," "idolators," violators of the commandment "Thou shalt have no other gods before me" (Exodus 20:3). Maimonides, who was born in Spain but spent most of his life in countries where the dominant religion was Islam, considered only Jews and Muslims to be true monotheists.

Scholars such as the French-born Rabbenu Tam (1100–1171), the grandson of Rashi who spent his life in Christian Europe, accepted the view of Christian theologians, who explained that the Trinity is consistent with the concept of *one* God. To these theologians the three personages are part of the one God; they are not individual gods. Just as spokes of a wheel are not in themselves wheels but components that are integral to the actual wheel, so the three personages are not gods but together they comprise the one God.

The British theologian Rabbi Louis Jacobs summed up the Jewish view of the importance of the monotheistic concept when he wrote in his *A Jewish Theology* (1975), "Judaism stands and falls on the rejection of polytheism as it is incompatible with dualism and trinitarianism."

Moshav

Plural, *moshavim*. A Hebrew word meaning "settlement." Also called *moshav ovdim*, "workers' settlement."

The *moshav* is an agricultural village that combines aspects of both cooperative and private farming. Early experimentation with this form began in Palestine in 1907, but it was during the post-World War I period that the institution really took hold.

Cooperative activities were carried out much as they were on the *kibbutz*, but the *moshav* differed in that it allowed for individual initiative and paid special attention to the integrity of the family unit. Each family lived in its own dwelling.

At the founding of the State of Israel in 1948, there were fifty-eight *moshavim*, but soon the *moshav ovdim* took on additional significance as a way of assimilating huge numbers of immigrants into the population. Members of older settlements helped the newcomers to establish settlements of their own, and by 1956 hundreds more *moshavim* had been established.

As the Jewish state matured, fewer people opted for the lifestyle of the *moshav*, choosing instead lives of complete independence.

Moshav Shitufi

In the late 1930s, those Jews who wanted to live a cooperative life but were unhappy with the extreme collectivism of the *kibbutz* and the emphasis on individual farming of the *moshav* created a type of settlement that blended the positive features of both. This new form of cooperative was called the *moshav shitufi*, or "partnership settlement." The first two *moshavim shitufim* (plural) were Kfar Chittim and Moledet.

Moshav Zekeinim

A Hebrew term meaning "hostel [settlement] for the aged." Concern for the welfare of the elderly who could no longer care for themselves led to the establishment of hostels in which the aged were cared for by the community. These homes for the aged were fixtures in pre-World War II Europe. They are not in evidence in modern society. The word *hekdesh*, meaning "holy place," was often used as a euphemism for the *moshav zekeinim*.

Mourners and Mourning

The human expression of grief over the loss of a close relative or friend dates back to Abraham, of whom the Bible (Genesis 23:2) says, "And Abraham came [to Hebron] to mourn for Sarah [his wife] and to weep for her." Later, we are told, Jacob mourned for "many days" when he was led to believe that his beloved son Joseph was dead. And when Jacob died, there was great wailing and "he [Joseph] mourned for his father for seven days" (Genesis 50:10).

The manner and extent of mourning differs in Jewish law in keeping with the degree and severity of the loss, but the sensitivity of the Rabbis to the trauma experienced by the individual mourner was always in evidence. For this reason words and expressions associated with death and dying were created to soften the shock and lessen the pain. Pleasant-sounding words were substituted for harsher ones, kindlier expressions for abrasive ones.

The softening of the word "death" is noticeable in many Hebrew and Yiddish expressions. The Hebrew word *niftar*, meaning "departed," was commonly used for one who has died, as was the Yiddish expression *Er iz avek tzum oilum ho-emes*, "He is off to the world of truth." The cemetery thus became known as *olam ha-emet*, "world of truth."

The use of euphemistic language by Jewish scholars in matters relating to death is most evident in the very name of the talmudic tractate devoted exclusively to the laws of mourning. Its original title was *Eivel Rabbati*, "Major Tractate on Mourning," a name used until about the tenth century. In the eleventh century, Rashi introduced new terminology by referring to this tractate euphemistically as *Semachot*, meaning "Rejoicings." That name has been used ever since.

Recognizing the severity of the shock experienced by an individual upon learning of the death of a close relative, the Rabbis freed the mourner from prayer and other religious obligations until after the funeral. And they made a distinction between the bereaved's status before and after the funeral. Until the time of burial, the bereaved is called an *onein* (feminine, *onenet*), meaning "distressed one." After burial, the bereaved is referred to as an *aveil* (feminine *aveilah*), "grieving one."

Just as the Rabbis were sensitive to the feelings of the mourner before burial, they were also sensitive to the feelings of the mourner directly after burial. Realizing that the bereaved might require a few days to be alone after the funeral, the Rabbis suggested that, if at all possible, friends not pay condolence calls for the first three days of the initial seven-day mourning period (*shivah*).

See Condolences; Kaddish; Meal of Condolence; Sheloshim; Shivah; Yud Bet Chodesh.

Muktzah

Of talmudic origin, this Hebrew term meaning "edge, outer limit" or "that which is set apart" refers specifically to mundane articles—such as money, tools, or writing materials—that are considered off-limits and thus not to be handled or even touched on the Sabbath and holidays.

The law of *muktzah* also applies to an object that is indirectly associated with work or business, so that a purse or wallet may not be touched on the Sabbath or holidays even if it contains no money. The introduction of these rabbinic enactments (called *gezeirot* in Hebrew) was precautionary. The Rabbis felt that if a person were to be permitted to touch *muktzah* items on the Sabbath, he might inadvertently forget and actually use them.

Later authorities were more flexible in interpreting the rabbinic law of *muktzah*. Moses Isserles (1525–1572), the Ashkenazic authority whose Notes are part of the *Code of Jewish Law*, remarks that a person may carry money on the Sabbath if he finds himself in a situation where he must spend the Sabbath at an inn and is afraid that the money might be stolen if he leaves it unattended in his room (*Shulchan Arukh*, Orach Cha'yim 301:33).

Contemporary authorities in their responsa have eased the law of *muktzah* under special circumstances. When muggings were rampant in New York City in the 1980s, the elderly, being prime targets, were permitted by rabbinic authorities to carry money on the Sabbath because muggers often became violent when they discovered that their victims had no money to give them. Justification for this view was based on the principle that one may violate the Sabbath to save a life.

See Pikuach Nefesh.

Mumar

This Hebrew term meaning "one who changes, deviates" is synonymous with *meshumad*.

See Apostate and Apostasy; Meshumad.

Musaf

A Hebrew word literally meaning "additional," referring specifically to one of the public sacrifices offered in Temple times on Sabbaths, New Moons, and festivals. The *Musaf* sacrifice, which was brought after the morning sacrifice, is recalled by the *Musaf* service, which today is recited in the synagogue following the morning *Shacharit* service.

Musar Movement

Recognizing that *yeshiva* students traditionally spent practically all their time studying talmudic texts, Rabbi Israel Lipkin, who was born in 1810 in Zhagory, Lithuania, believed it necessary to imbue students with moral and ethical values as well. To correct the situation, he introduced a movement that became known as the *Musar* ("ethics, morals") movement.

In 1842, Lipkin—who became known as Salant or Salanter because he grew up and studied in Salant—was appointed head of Yeshiva Tomchei Torah, in Vilna. It was there that he began insisting that time be devoted each day to the study of the moral teachings of Judaism. He also emphasized the importance of Jews being engaged in manual labor and in showing loyalty to their national government.

Lipkin traveled extensively throughout Europe, spreading his message of moral rectitude and establishing societies for the study of ethical literature. These organizations, housed in what were called "Musar houses," also published a journal called *Tenuva* to disseminate Lipkin's ideas.

Lipkin's philosophy was initially rejected by other *yeshiva* leaders, but by the time of his death in 1883, *musar* had taken hold in Lithuanian schools. To this day *yeshivot* of higher learning devote time each day to the study of ethical texts such as *Mesilat Yesharim* by Moses Chayim Luzzatto, and *Or Yisra'el*, the ethical teachings of Lipkin himself.

Music

In biblical times Jews used a variety of musical instruments. The Book of Genesis (4:21) mentions Jubal as "the father of all such as handle the harp and the pipe." In Exodus (15:20), after the successful escape of the Israelites from the pursuing Egyptians at the Red Sea, "Miriam took a timbrel in her hand, and all the women went out after her with timbrels and with dances." The Talmud (*Sotah* 11b) praises the activity of these people, refering to them as "righteous women."

After the rescue, Moses led the Children of Israel in a lengthy song of Thanksgiving (Exodus 15:1ff.) that has become part of the weekday and Sabbath morning service (*Shacharit*). Likewise did the judge Deborah give vent to her joy in song after she and her general, Barak ben Avinoam, were victorious over Sisera, the general of the army of Jabin, king of Canaan, who had attacked Israel.

The Bible refers to a wide variety of musical instruments. Among them are the *kinor* (a stringed instrument) and the *ugav* (possibly a shepherd's flute), both mentioned in Genesis 4:21; the zither, lyre, and bagpipe in Daniel 3:5; and the *tof* (a drum) and *chalil* (flute) in Isaiah 5:12.

Music in the Temples

Many of the one hundred fifty chapters of the Book of Psalms are introduced with the mention of various types of musical instruments. Chapter 4 mentions the *sheminit*; chapters 8, 81, and 84 mention the *gittit*; chapter 22 mentions the *a'yelet ha-shachar*; chapters 45 and 69 mention the *shoshanim*; and several chapters, including 4 and 55, speak simply of "string music."

These instruments and many more were played in the Jerusalem Temple by Levites who also formed a Temple choir. Second Chronicles (5:12–13) records that at the dedication of King Solomon's Temple one hundred twenty Priests blew trumpets and joined singers in extolling God. And throughout the existence of both the First and Second Temples, choral singing and a Temple orchestra playing harps, lyres, trumpets, flutes, and other instruments as the sacrificial rites took place.

After the year 70 C.E., when the Second Temple was destroyed by the Romans and the prayer service of the synagogue totally replaced the sacrificial system of the Temples, all music was banned as a sign of mourning for the loss of Judaism's central sanctuary, its most cherished institution.

The third-century C.E. Babylonian scholar Mar Ukba was asked where in the Torah singing is forbidden (*Gittin* 7a). He responded by quoting a verse from Hosea (9:1): "Rejoice not, O Israel, like other peoples, for you have gone astray from your God." Later commentators expressed the opinion that Mar Ukba was referring only to the singing of secular songs at wild parties, not to singing and playing instruments at weddings and other joyous religious events.

For many centuries the question of reintroducing instrumental music into the synagogue rarely arose. (Cantorial and other forms of vocal music were found objectionable). But in 1818 a Reform layman, Israel Jacobsen, installed an organ in a synagogue that he founded in Seesen, Germany, and the subject became a source of contention between the Orthodox and liberal communities.

The Concepts of Shevut and Chukat Ha-Goy

A primary reason advanced for prohibiting the playing of a musical instrument on the Sabbath and holidays is that it interferes with the Sabbath spirit of "rest," or *shevut*, as demanded by Jewish law. A second reason is that Jews are still in mourning for the destruction of the Temple, and except for joyful occasions such as weddings the use of musical instruments is forbidden. A third reason advanced is that the to use instrumental music in the synagogue would be emulating Christian practice, a concept known as *chukat ha-goy*.

The answer of the non-Orthodox, particularly Reform Jews, to the arguments of the Orthodox establishment is that many Orthodox Jews no longer pay attention to the principle of *chukat ha-goy*. Rabbi Joel Sirkes (1561–1640), a leading rabbi of communities in Poland and Lithuania, wrote in one of his responsa (#127) that only music that is an integral part of the Christian liturgy is forbidden to Jews. In fact, the synagogue in Prague employed instrumental music, even an organ, which was played during the first half of the Friday evening service. Additionally, it was argued, the law that called for mourning over the loss of Jerusalem and the Temples was no longer universally observed.

The ban that the Rabbis of the Talmud had placed upon instrumental and vocal music began to weaken as cantorial music began to develop. Jews found great joy in the cantorial renditions which enhanced the services of the synagogue.

Synagogue Choirs

Early in the seventeenth century, Leon de Modena (1571–1648), an Italian rabbi who also directed a theater and a musical academy in Venice, issued a responsum permitting choral singing in the synagogue if it was not accompanied by instrumental music. This provided a license for itinerant cantors (*chazzanim*) to give concerts in synagogues accompanied by a male choir, usually featuring a boy soprano. This practice continued even into the twentieth century.

Presently, instrumental music has become a permanent part of Reform Jewish worship, and a small number of Conservative congregations have opted for the use of musical instruments to enhance the richness of their service.

See Cantillation; Cantor.

Mysticism

Jewish mysticism has its roots in the Bible, particularly in Ezekiel's vision of a Divine Chariot. The Jewish mystical tradition was spurred on by a desire to discover the origin and structure of the world and to understand the nature of God as He operates the world. The Rabbis of the Talmud warned against such dangerous speculations. Only the elect, the specially trained, were permitted to engage in it at all.

Mysticism was thus taboo for centuries, coming to life only after the appearance of the *Zohar*, a commentary on sections of the Torah (Pentateuch) and parts of the Song of Songs, Ruth, and Lamentations. Its authorship is ascribed to the second-century popular Rabbi

Shimon bar Yocha'i, but the work was actually composed in the thirteenth century by the Spanish kabbalist Moses de Leon, who used Shimon's name as the author in order to stimulate sales.

In the centuries that followed, noteworthy rabbis became attracted to the mystical approach and sought to understand God, to adore Him, and reach toward Him through prayer and service. To strive to become one with God, and thus to be part of Him, was the goal of every mystic. Accordingly, they insisted that no prayer be recited and no ritual performed without adequate preparation. Thus, many of the prayers they recited began with the phrase *Hineni mukhan u'mezuman*, "Behold, I am prepared and ready."

Mystics attempted to uncover the mysteries of the universe by delving into the nature of being and reality and by discovering the relationship of God—the Infinite Being (the *Ein Sof*)—to finite man living in a physical world. They arrived at the conclusion that to reach God and be one with Him man must rid himself of all barriers that separate him from God. These barriers are called *kelippot*, shells or husks that distract man from his effort to connect with God.

The mystics' search for God reached its zenith in the sixteenth century, in Safed, Palestine, when many of the greatest rabbis of the age became devotees of mysticism. These included such luminaries as

- Joseph Caro (1488–1575), codifier of the *Shulchan Arukh*, who claimed that religious secrets were revealed to him by a supernatural messenger.
- Moses ben Yaakov Cordovero (1522–1570), a pupil of Joseph Caro, who maintained that all creation was a unity, with man's soul being the entity that pos-

sesses an image of all the upper worlds. The aim of moral living, therefore, is to unify all the powers of the soul and place them under the control of God and His wisdom.

- Solomon Alkabetz (*c.* 1505–1584), a Hebrew poet, best known for his composition *Lekhah Dodi* ("Come, My Beloved"), a hymn welcoming the beloved Sabbath which is recited in all synagogues at the Friday night service.
- Isaac Luria (1554–1572), born in Jerusalem of a German (Ashkenazic) family, is popularly known as the "Ashkenazi" or the "Ari," the latter being an acronym of Ashkenazi Rabbi Isaac. The Ari was admired for his saintly character and ascetic lifestyle. He was also prone to ecstatic visions in which he fashioned himself a precursor of the Messiah.

 Among the unique mystical concepts he proposed was that of *tzimtzum*, in which God, whose glory and presence fills the whole world, contracts Himself so as to allow space for the formation of a physical world in which man can function. The unity of God and all creation is a fundamental premise of Lurianic mysticism.

- Chayim Vital (1543–1620), in his formative years, was a pupil of Moses Cordovero, and in his mature years became the devoted disciple of the Ari. He recorded all the views of his master and published them in a volume entitled *Eitz Chayim* ("Tree of Life"). Thus were the views of Isaac Luria disseminated far and wide and became known as Lurianic *kabbalah*.

Among the prominent mystics of the post-sixteenth-century era are Judah Loew ben

Bezalel of Prague (c. 1525–1609), famous for his construction by magical means of a *golem*, an automaton in human form; Moses Chaim Luzzatto (1707–1747), a celebrated poet and ethicist best known for his *Mesilat Yesharim* ("The Way of the Righteous"); and Israel ben Eliezer (c. 1700–1760), founder of chasidism, and better known as the Ba'al Shem Tov ("Master of the Good Name") because of his miraculous cures.

See Kabbalah; Sefirot.

Naming: History and Practices

The earliest personal names on record are found in the Bible, and many are still in use in their original form. For the most part, biblical names (which were often based on life experiences of the individual) are easy to understand because their roots are easily traced, usually to the Hebrew. In fact, many are explained in the Bible itself.

The Hebrew root of the name Cain, for example, is *kanah*, meaning "to acquire, to buy." Genesis 4:1 explains that after Eve conceived and bore Cain, she said, "I have acquired [*kaniti*] a male child."

Abraham and Sarah named their son Isaac. Abraham was one hundred years old at the time, and when Sarah was told she was to bear a child, she said, "Everyone who hears about it will *laugh*." The Hebrew root of the name Isaac, *tzachok*, means "laughter."

Scores of such examples can be found in the pages of the Bible. Names sometimes describe a physical attribute (Korach, meaning "bald," or Charim, meaning "flat-nosed"); an inspiring or unusual experience (Moshe was so named because he was "drawn out of the water"); resemblance to or reminders of animal features or characteristics (Yonah, meaning "dove," or Devorah, meaning "bee"); affection or affinity to plants or flowers (Tamar, meaning "palm tree," or Tzemach, meaning "plant"). The Bible also contains many God-centered names (such as Yonatan, meaning "gift of God," or Yoel, meaning "God is willing") and names that express hope for a bright future (Yosef, meaning "may God increase").

Many first names, like surnames, have been borrowed from the names of places. The Bible, of course, has many such examples. Efrat is the place where Rachel died and was buried; Efratah is the name of Caleb's wife in the Book of Chronicles. Ofrah, the name of a city in the Book of Joshua, is also a masculine first name. Ur, a place-name in the Book of Genesis, is a masculine first name that appears in the Book of Chronicles.

The Naming Ceremony

Traditionally, a girl is named in the synagogue on the first Sabbath following her birth. The father is called to the Torah, and after he recites the second Torah blessing, a *Mi Shebeirakh* prayer is recited by the Torah reader or rabbi, in the course of which a Hebrew name is bestowed upon the girl. In many non-Orthodox synagogues, the mother brings the child to the synagogue and joins her husband in receiving the *aliyah* and reciting the Torah blessings.

The naming may also take place at other times when the Torah is being read, such as at the Monday or Thursday morning service or on Rosh Chodesh (New Moon). In recent years, the naming is often done as part of the *shalom bat* ceremony. (*See* Shalom Bat.)

Reform Judaism urges parents to arrange a "Covenant of Life" service either in the home or the synagogue. At the service, which it is recommended be held on the eighth day after birth or, if not feasible, at a later date, the girl is officially named.

The naming of a boy takes place on the eighth day of life at the circumcision (*brit*) ceremony. If the circumcision is delayed for health reasons, the naming is postponed.

Ashkenazic Practice

Ashkenazic Jews refrain from naming a child after a living relative, believing that doing so would rob the living person of a full life. This idea was introduced in the twelfth century by the prominent German mystic Rabbi Yehudah He-Chasid (1638–1700), who associated a person's name with his very soul.

Rabbi Yehudah also originated the idea that a man should not marry a woman with the same first name as his mother. He felt that it might lead to the embarrassing situation of the mother answering her son when the son was actually addressing his wife. Another potential problem could arise were his mother to die. The man would then not be able to name his future child after his mother because his still-living wife carried the same name.

Sephardic Practice

Sephardic Jews (from Spain, North Africa, and the Middle East) do not share the Ashkenazic belief and do name offspring after living relatives.

In the naming of babies, many Sephardim follow this formula:

- The first male child is named for the paternal grandfather.
- The second male child is named for the maternal grandfather.
- The first female child is named for the paternal grandmother.
- The second female child is named for the maternal grandmother.
- In naming an adopted child, the name of the adoptive father or the natural father may be used.

Jews from Morocco and countries such as Turkey, which were once part of the Ottoman Empire, named girls in a home ceremony called *zeved ha-bat* or *zebed ha-bat* ("gift of a daughter"). The ceremony is held as soon as the mother has regained her strength. If the girl is the mother's firstborn, she is generally named Bekhorah or Bukhuretta, or by the diminutive form Buzika. (Firstborn boys are named Bekhor or its pet form, Buki.)

Jews from Spanish-speaking countries often give their daughters a Spanish name such as Fortuna or some form of the name Rose. They do not give girls a Hebrew name. The same is true of Syrian Jews who until recently only bestowed an Arabic first name upon a girl.

The Arabic word for the Hebrew *ben*, meaning "son," is *ibn*. It was customary for Jews living in lands ruled by Arabs in the Middle Ages, particularly Spain, to use the word *ibn* to form a family name, as for example Rabbi Abraham ibn Ezra, Abraham ibn David, and Solomon ibn Gabirol.

Calendar Names

Among both Ashkenazic and Sephardic Jews, it was not uncommon to use names derived from the calendar and holidays. In fact, the Hebrew term for holiday, *yom tov*, is sometimes used as a personal name. In the Middle Ages, it was common to call boys who were circumcised on Purim by the name Mordekhai, in honor of the hero of the holiday. Those born on Tishah B'Av were often named Menachem, meaning "comforter," because the ninth (*tishah*) day of the month Av is a fast day commemorating the destruction of the Temple in Jerusalem, and in the Prophetic portion (Isaiah 40) read in the synagogue on the Sabbath following that fast day the prophet *comforts* Israel. Among the Jews of Eastern Europe, a son born on Chanukkah was often called by the name of the holiday.

Particularly among Sephardic Jews, children born on Yom Kippur were often called Rachamim ("mercy") and those born on Passover were sometimes named Pesach. Shabbat and Shabetai were popular Sephardic names for boys born on the Sabbath. One rabbi, the father of twelve sons, is reported to have named each son after a different Hebrew month.

Celebrity Names

Many names in use today have been adopted because they are the names of celebrities. In this category we include not only contemporary celebrities in the fields of entertainment, sports, music, and politics, but also the great figures of history, political as well as religious, whose charisma was so great that parents named children after them.

Alexander the Great entered Palestine in 333 B.C.E., and according to legend all Jewish boys born in that year were named Alexander in his honor. Although we do not have records indicating how popular that name became among the masses in the years immediately following Alexander's visit, we do know that one Jewish king (Alexander Janneus) and one queen (Salome Alexandra) did use the name. A bit later, in talmudic times, we find the name being used by the scholar Rabbi Alexandri (*Yoma* 53b).

Over the years many Jewish boys have been named Theodor and Herzl, after the founder of modern Zionism, and more recently the names of Israel's popular prime ministers (Ben-Gurion and Golda) have been used.

The custom of naming children after celebrities, however, has never been particularly popular among Jews. In fact, in scanning the Bible one finds that the names of heroes mentioned early in the Bible are not used again by anyone later in the biblical narrative. No one but the original Abraham, Sarah, Isaac, Rebecca, Jacob, Rachel, Leah, Joseph, Moses, Aaron, Miriam, Isaiah, and Jeremiah are so named. The reason for this strange circumstance has not been explained. Nor has it been explained why not even one scholar in the Talmud is named Abraham, Israel, or Solomon, while the names of some of Jacob's sons are used. Of Jacob's sons, the names Dan, Gad, and Asher are not used. Of the prophets,

the names Isaiah, Hosea, Joel, Amos, Ovadiah, Mikhah, Habakkuk, Zephaniah, and Malakhi are not used at all by Rabbis in the Talmud.

It is indeed difficult to explain why Rabbis of the Talmud are named Ishmael, but not one is named Moses. Attempts have been made to explain the use of the name Ishmael, but they are not satisfying. Rabbi Jose (*Genesis Rabbah* 71:3) finds some justification in the explanation that Ishmael is an example of a person whose "name was beautiful but whose actions are ugly." The commentary (Tosafot) on *Berakhot* 7b justifies the use of the name by observing that Ishmael, Abraham's son by his concubine Hagar, was a sinner who repented, and it was, therefore, quite proper to use his name.

Name Changes

Early Jews who became the founders of Christianity changed their Jewish names to identify with their newly formed religion and thereby sever their connection with their Jewish past. Thus, the man once known as Simon bar Jonah came to be known as Peter, and Saul of Tarsus took on the name of Paul.

In earlier biblical times, it was not unusual for an individual to undergo a name change, but then it was for the purpose of elevating the person's status. Among the more prominent examples: Abraham (from Abram), Sarah (from Sarai), Jacob (to Israel), Joshua (from Hosea), Gideon (to Jerubaal), Zedekiah (from Mattaniah), and Jehoiakim (from Eliakim).

Though name-changing is no longer common, there is an old Jewish custom of changing a person's name in time of serious illness. It was hoped that the change of name will cause the Angel of Death to doubt whether the person he is about to visit (who has a different name than expected) is the correct target. Sometimes, if the patient is young, the name Alter ("old one" in Yiddish) or Alterke (for a female) is added to or used as a substitute for the original name. It was believed that the Angel of Death would be confused if, when he is assigned to take action against Alter, and when he finally finds him, the person turns out to be young rather than old as his new name implies. This custom is not widely practiced today.

See Surnames.

Nasi

A Hebrew word literally meaning "prince." The president of the *Sanhedrin* was called *nasi*. Second in command was the *Av Beit Din*, literally meaning "father of the Court." The most prominent of all the *nesi'im* (plural of *nasi*) was Yehudah Ha-Nasi (Judah the Prince), the scholar who edited the Mishnah.

In talmudic times, the term *nasi* was used as designation for the spiritual and political head of Palestinian Jewry. Beginning with the second century C.E., the *nasi* had to be a descendant of Hillel, who was presumed to be of the House of David. He was recognized by the Roman rulers of Palestine as the titular head—the Patriarch—of the Jewish people. In subsequent centuries, in countries such as Spain, the *nasi* was not always a rabbi, but a lay leader.

Presently, the title *nasi* is reserved for the president of the State of Israel.

Nazirites

Pious persons who followed an ascetic lifestyle in order to show devotion to God. A description of the lifestyle of Nazirites is found in the Book of Numbers, chapter 6.

See Asceticism.

Nedavah

A Hebrew term literally meaning "free-will offering," first encountered in the Book of Exodus (35:29) where the Children of Israel brought voluntary gifts of gold, silver, and a wide variety of materials to be used in the building of the Tabernacle that would accompany the Israelites during their forty-year trek through the wilderness on the way to the Promised Land.

In common parlance, a *nedavah* is a donation one makes to a needy individual or to a charitable or religious institution.

Netaneh Tokef

Literally meaning "And let us declare the mighty [holiness of this day]," these are the first Hebrew words of a moving prayer recited on Rosh Hashanah. Its authorship is attributed to Rabbi Amnon of Mainz, Germany, of the tenth/eleventh century, who had been ordered by the local bishop to submit to conversion. Instead of refusing outright and offending the bishop, he asked for three days of grace to consider the matter.

After the three days, Amnon failed to appear. When finally brought before the bishop, he requested that, as punishment, his tongue be cut out so that he would be unable to respond to any questions put to him. Instead, the bishop ordered that the rabbi's limbs be severed, and in that mutilated condition he was carried into the synagogue on the following Rosh Hashanah.

It was then that Amnon recited the soul-stirring *Netaneh Tokef* prayer, in which he proclaimed his total faith in God and His judgments, fully confident that all who believe in Him will find their virtuous lives rewarded by being inscribed in the Book of Life kept by God. The prayer ends on the high note: "Repentance, prayer, and acts of charity can ameliorate the severity of life's decrees."

Neturei Karta

An Aramaic term meaning "Guardians of the City," derived from an incident described in the Jerusalem Talmud (*Chagigah* 1:7). Rabbi Judah the Prince had sent three emissaries—Rabbis Chiya, Ammi, and Ashi—on a tour of inspection to various towns. In one town, when they asked to see the guardians of the city (*neturei karta*), they were pointed to civilian police. "They are not guardians of the city," said the Rabbis. "The real guardians are the scribes, and the scholars are the true *neturei karta*."

The name was adopted in 1935 by Rabbi Amram Blau after he left the Agudat Israel Movement and founded the extreme anti-Zionist Chevrat Ha-Cha'yim ("Society of the Living") association, which later became known as Neturei Karta. This ultra-Orthodox anti-Zionist sect is based in the Mei'ah She'arim quarter of Jerusalem.

The sect refuses to accept the authority and legitimacy of the Jewish State, contending that it is a secular establishment that forcibly took the land from the Palestinians to accomplish their goal. This, they argue, was in violation of Jewish law, which maintains that a Jewish state can come into being only after the arrival of the Messiah. They therefore display no allegiance to the state and consider the PLO (Palestinian Liberation Organization) the rightful owners of the land.

The sect's most recent leader and chief spokesman is Rabbi Moshe Hirsch.

In a 1989 interview, he stated: "The Palestinian people chose the PLO as their representatives, and we are loyal to the PLO and their future state."

Nichum Aveilim

A Hebrew term literally meaning "comforting mourners," referring to the primary Jewish obligation of visiting a mourner during the first seven days of mourning (*shivah*). When a person fulfills this obligation, he is said to be *menachem aveil*, "comforting a mourner."

See Condolences.

Niddah

A Hebrew term literally meaning "menstruating woman." By Torah law, a woman is ritually impure during the period of her menstruation and for seven days thereafter. She may not have sexual relations with her husband during the time of her impurity. While a woman in this state renders ritually impure both people and objects that come in contact with her, she is not prohibited from holding, touching, or kissing a Torah or a *mezuzah*, which contains writings from the Torah. Jewish law states that the words of the Torah are not subject to defilement. So high is the Torah on the ladder of spirituality that nothing can affect its holiness (*Berakhot* 22a).

The prohibition barring a man and woman from having sex during the woman's monthly period is described in the Bible. Leviticus 15:19–24 explains that the woman is in a state of impurity during this period of time, and Leviticus 20:18 says, "If a woman lies with a man in the time of her menstrual flow...both shall be cut off [excommunicated] from their people." Some commentators say that "to be cut off" means "to be ostracized," while others interpret it to mean "to be put to death."

Leviticus 15:19 states that "when a woman has a discharge of blood from her body, she shall remain impure for seven days." The Bible requires that abstention from sex last only seven days, to be reckoned from the day menstruation begins. The Rabbis of the Talmud, however, instituted a stricter code of conduct, ruling that the seven-day period of abstention mentioned in the Bible is to begin *after* the actual flow of blood has ceased. Since the actual flow of blood lasts from four to five days, the seven "clean" (also called "white") days begin at that point, which in most cases means that the total period of abstinence from sex for the average couple is eleven or twelve days. Each woman notes when the flow of blood has ceased and then counts seven more days of abstinence. Orthodox and many Conservative women follow this practice today.

At the end of the period of abstinence, the woman must immerse herself in a ritual bath (*mikveh*) before she may resume having sex with her husband. The talmudic laws referred to here are summarized by Maimonides in his *Mishneh Torah* (Issurei Bi'ah 11:2–4).

In biblical times, when the period of abstinence came to an end, the menstruant offered a sacrifice to the Lord of two turtledoves or two young pigeons. No mention is made in the Bible of the requirement that a woman immerse herself in a *mikveh* to achieve purification, but the Rabbis of the Talmud (in the tractates *Niddah* and *Mikva'ot*) infer this from Leviticus 18, which calls for bathing in water to achieve purification. The talmudic laws pertaining to the menstruant are codified in the *Shulchan Arukh* (Yoreh Dei'ah 183–200).

A variety of reasons have been offered by talmudic and later scholars to explain the significance of maintaining sexual abstinence during the menstrual period. One scholar says that it teaches a lesson in patience. Men who are unable to wait for their wives to be "clean" again, and who indulge in sex while they are still menstruating, should learn the lesson of patience from young trees whose fruit may not be eaten for the first three years (Leviticus 19:23). In his book *A Hedge of Roses,* Rabbi Norman Lamm, president of Yeshiva University, describes the value of the marital bond from succumbing to sexual overindulgence, which can lead to ennui.

The Talmud notes that the enchantment of marriage is heightened if abstinence is observed during the menstrual period (*Niddah* 31b).

See Mikveh; Tohorat Ha-Mishpachah.

Nisuin

Derived from the Hebrew root meaning "to raise up," the term is used primarily to describe the marriage ceremony, in which a man elevates the status of a woman by taking her as his wife. Once married, the responsibility for her maintenance becomes that of her husband rather than her father (Mishnah *Ketubbot* 4:5). The marriage ceremony is also known as *kiddushin* ("holy matrimony").

Nivul Ha-Met

A Hebrew term literally meaning "desecration of the dead" or "violation of the dignity of the dead." A prime example of *nivul ha-met* is exhuming a body for a frivolous reason. The Talmud (*Bava Batra* 154a) relates an incident in which a person died after selling his father's estate. Members of the family protested, claiming that the seller was a minor and had no authority to make the sale. To prove their point, they requested permission from Rabbi Akiba to exhume the body. Akiba declined, responding, "You are not permitted to dishonor him [*le-navlo*]."

Based on Deuteronomy 21:22–23, which states that if a criminal is put to death by hanging, "his body shall not remain all night hanging on the tree, but thou shalt surely bury him that same day," the Rabbis conclude that to mistreat or mutilate the body of a deceased in any way is a violation of scriptural law.

In Jewish law, performing an unnecessary autopsy on the dead is also considered *nivul ha-met*.

See Funeral Practices.

Noahide Laws

Judaism never expected anyone but Jews to abide by all the laws of the Torah, but it did expect that all human beings be governed by elementary moral precepts. Accordingly, based upon the covenant God made with Noah (Genesis 9), in which He promised never again to bring a flood upon mankind, the Rabbis concluded that Gentiles are expected to abide by seven basic laws, termed in Hebrew *sheva mitzvot b'nei Noach*. The first-century talmudist Rabbi Chaninah referred to these laws as Noahide (also spelled Noachide) Laws (*Genesis Rabbah* 34:14).

The Seven Noahide Laws as listed in the talmudic tractate *Sanhedrin* (56a) demand that one:

- behave equitably in all relationships and establish courts of justice.
- refrain from blaspheming God's name.
- refrain from practicing idolatry.
- avoid immoral sexual practices, specifically incest.
- avoid shedding the blood of one's fellow man.
- refrain from robbing one's fellow man.
- avoid eating a limb torn from a live animal.

Maimonides considers a Gentile who observes the Seven Noahide Laws to be a righteous person (*chasid*), and as such he is assured a place in the world to come, like any observant Jew who abides by all 613 precepts of the Torah (*Mishneh Torah*, Hilkhot Melakhim 8:10). Such individuals are characterized as *chasidei umot ha-olam*, "righteous people of the universe."

Over the centuries, the Noahide Laws were generally of intellectual interest to Jews, but in 1980 the Lubavitcher movement made an effort to influence the non-Jewish community to take these laws seriously.

Numbers

Numbers are of great significance in the Jewish tradition. Each of the twenty-two letters in the Hebrew alphabet is assigned a numerical value and plays a role in interpreting the law and understanding the lore of Judaism.

- *alef* equals 1. When it appears at the beginning of a series of numbers, particularly dates, with a small stroke over it, it equals 1,000.
- *bet* equals 2. When it appears without a dot (*dagesh*) in it, it is pronounced *vet*. When it appears before a series of numbers, particularly dates, with a small stroke over it, it equals 2,000.
- *gimmel* equals 3. When it appears before a series of numbers, particularly dates, with a small stroke over it, it equals 3,000.
- *dalet* equals 4. When it appears before a series of numbers, particularly dates, with a small stroke over it, it equals 4,000. It is also used as an abbreviation for *Adonai* (God).
- *hei* equals 5. When it appears before a series of numbers, particularly dates, with a small stroke over it, it equals 5,000. It is also used as an abbreviation for *Adonai* (God).
- *vav* equals 6. When it appears before a series of numbers with a small stroke over it, it equals 6,000.
- *za'yin* equals 7. When it appears before a series of numbers with a small stroke over it, it equals 7,000.

- *chet* equals 8. When it appears before a series of numbers with a small stroke over it, it equals 8,000.
- *tet* equals 9. When it appears before a series of numbers with a small stroke over it, it equals 9,000.
- *yud* equals 10. Also pronounced *yod*. When it appears before a series of numbers with a small stroke over it, it equals 10,000. It is also used as an abbreviation for *Adonai* (God).
- *kaf* equals 20. When it appears without a dot (*dagesh*) in it, it is pronounced *khaf*. When it appears as a final letter (*kaf sofit*) before a series of numbers, its value is 500.
- *lamed* equals 30.
- *mem* equals 40. When it appears as a final letter (*mem sofit*) before a series of numbers, it has a value of 600.
- *nun* equals 50. When it appears as a final letter (*nun sofit*) before a series of numbers, it has a value of 700.
- *samekh* equals 60.
- *a'yin* equals 70.
- *pei* equals 80. When it appears without a dot (*dagesh*), it is pronounced *fei*. When it appears as a final letter (*pei sofit*), before a series of numbers, its value is 800.
- *tzadi* equals 90. Also known as *tzadik*. When it appears as a final letter (*tzadi sofit*) before a series of numbers, it equals 900.
- *kuf* equals 100. Also pronounced *kof*.
- *reish* equals 200.
- *shin* equals 300. It consists of three vertical arms. When a dot appears over the right arm, it is pronounced *shin*. When the dot appears over the left arm, it is pronounced *sin*.
- *tav* equals 400.

Sacredness of Numbers

Numbers have always carried an aura of sacredness in the Jewish tradition and their use was therefore restricted, particularly for counting people. This taboo dates back to the census taken in biblical times. In the Book of Numbers (1:26), the counting of the Children of Israel was undertaken at the command of God. But in II Samuel 24, David ordered an unauthorized census, and as a result, by way of punishment, a severe plague befell the Israelites and seventy thousand people perished. No explanation is offered in the Bible for this severe punishment, but it became the reason for the taboo placed upon using numbers to count people. It was believed that the privilege of numbering people belongs to God alone, and to do so without divine sanction can result only in catastrophe.

Thus, even today, in some communities when it is necessary to determine if ten adult males are present to constitute a *minyan* (quorum) in order to hold a prayer service, the counting is done indirectly, in a negative fashion. As the counter points to each eligible individual, he pronounces in Yiddish: *nisht eintz*, "not one"; *nisht tzvei*, "not two"; *nisht drai*, "not three"; until ten is reached.

Often, in place of negative counting, a ten-word Hebrew verse from the Book of Psalms (28:9) is recited. As the counter points to the first person, he says the word *hoshiya*; he then points to the second person and says *et*; and so on, until *olam*, the tenth and last word in the verse, is reached. In English the verse has eleven words and reads, "Save and bless Thy people, tend them and sustain them forever."

Special Significance of the Number Three

The number three dominates many aspects of Jewish law and lore, beginning with the three patriarchs of the Jewish people:

Abraham, Isaac, and Jacob. It is they who, according to tradition, instituted the three daily prayer services: *Shacharit*, *Minchah*, and *Ma'ariv*. The Bible (Daniel 6:11) tells us that when Daniel prayed to God three times each day, he kneeled and faced Jerusalem.

The number three also represents the totality of the Jewish community, which is comprised of three classes of Jews: Priests (*Kohanim*), Levites (*Levi'im*), and Israelites (*Yisra'elim*). The First Temple in Jerusalem, which was the center of Jewish life for more than one thousand years, was divided into three sections: the open court, where the public assembled; the holy place where the altar stood and sacrifices were offered; and the Holy of Holies, where the Ten Commandment tablets were kept (Exodus 26:33; 27:9).

In the Middle Ages, repeating words or actions three times became an antidote to evil forces that were thought to attack innocent people. Spitting three times was once a widespread practice engaged in by Jews of Eastern Europe. This was a way of negating the effect of an evil sight or pronouncement. Reciting prayers such as the *Kol Nidrei* three times was a popular method of disarming Satan or other forces intent upon doing harm. Marching a bride around a groom three (and in some communities seven) times under the wedding canopy has its origin in the belief that encirclement can protect the groom against demons. For the same reason, during the *kapparot* ceremony conducted by some Jews before Yom Kippur, a hen or a rooster is waved overhead three times as a protective measure.

Kabbalists were particularly enamored of the number three, which they believed was a primary number. They pointed out that the twenty-seven letters in the Hebrew alphabet (twenty-two regular, plus five final letters), are divisible by three, and that the cube of three is twenty-seven (three times three times three).

Mystics found sacred qualities in the number three, for it alone conveys the idea of wholeness and unity; it alone has a distinct beginning, middle, and end. They support this view by observing that the Bible describes the world created by God as consisting of three parts: heaven, earth, and the netherworld. They also call attention to the fact that the number three symbolizes the basic unity that exists between God, the Jewish people, and Torah through the phrase *Ha-Kadosh Barukh Hu, Yisra'el, ve-oraita chad hu*, meaning "God, Israel, and the Torah are one." The three are an inseparable triad.

Rabbis of the Talmud, many of whom were mystics and strong believers in astrology, saw special meaning in the fact that Exodus 19 reports that the Revelation took place on the third day of the third month (Sivan) following the escape from Egyptian bondage. When the Children of Israel reached Mount Sinai, Moses is instructed by God to have the Israelites cleanse and purify themselves in preparation for the momentous event that would take place on the third day after their arrival (Exodus 19:11).

Jewish mystics believe that Sivan, the third day of the third month of the Hebrew calendar—which falls in May-June—was chosen for the physical appearance of God (theophany) and the sixth day of the month (two times three) was chosen for the Revelation of the Torah because they coincide with the appearance of Gemini in the zodiac. A constellation containing the stars Castor and Pollux, Gemini is represented as twins sitting together. That the theophany and the Revelation took place under the twins' sign indicates that the Torah does not belong to the descendants of Jacob (Israel) alone, but also to those of his twin brother, Esau, and hence to all mankind.

Special Significance of the Number Seven

The number seven is mentioned over five hundred times in the Bible. Its preeminence was highlighted early in the Bible, when the seventh day was consecrated as holy, climaxing the six days of Creation.

In Leviticus 23, both Passover and Sukkot were declared to be seven-day festivals. The seven weeks after the first day of Passover were to be counted day by day, culminating in Shavuot, the holiday celebrating the Revelation on Mount Sinai. The Book of Deuteronomy (31:10–13) declares that at the end of every seven-year period the Torah is to be read to all the Children of Israel. In the Book of Nehemiah, we are told that Ezra read the Torah to all the people on the first day of the seventh month and then again on each of the seven days of Sukkot (Nehemiah 8:2 and 8:18).

Because of the many ways in which the number seven is associated with the Torah, it is understandable why seven was selected as the number of Torah honors (*aliyot*) to be awarded on the Sabbath, the most sacred day in the Jewish calendar. Mystics such as Bachya ibn Pakuda (*c*. 1050–*c*. 1120) attributed selection of the number seven to the sun, the moon, and the five planets observed by ancient man, and others saw its importance in the fact that the month falls into four quarters of seven days each.

The number seven is central to two basic institutions described in the Book of Leviticus (25): the sabbatical year and the jubilee year. The sabbatical year (*shemittah*) is observed every seventh year and the jubilee year (*yovel*) on the fiftieth year after seven sabbatical years have passed.

It has also been noted that the seventh month of the year, Tishrei, is the month in which most holidays fall. This led the noted eleventh-century scholar Rashi to assume that there is a connection between the words *sheva* (seven) and the word *sova* (sated), since Tishrei—the seventh month—is sated with holidays.

The magic of number seven is most dramatically demonstrated in Joshua's capture of the city of Jericho. Joshua (6) describes the event: For six days seven Priests carrying seven ram's horns marched before the Ark of the Covenant. On the seventh day they marched around the city seven times, whereupon the city wall collapsed.

The Rabbis of the Talmud summed up the place of the number seven in Jewish life and lore by saying, *kol shevi'in chavivin*, "All sevens are beloved." Thus, the Rabbis of the Talmud (*Shabbat* 67a), who were not averse to superstitious practice, found its employment effective in a prescription to remedy someone suffering from a persistent fever: "Procure seven prickly thorns from seven palm trees, seven wood slivers from seven beams, seven pegs from seven bridges, seven [heaps of] ashes from seven ovens, seven [mounds of] earth from under seven door-sockets, seven specimens of pitch from seven ships, seven handfuls of cumin, and seven hairs from the beard of an old dog, and tie them to the nape of the neck with a white twisted thread."

Seven was set as the number of laws non-Jews were expected to adhere to if they were to earn the appellation "moral people." These laws are called the Seven Noahide Laws. (*See* Noahide Laws.)

At a funeral service, seven was chosen as the number of stops to be made by the procession as the casket is carried to the grave, while Psalm 91 was being recited.

On Sukkot, when it is customary to invite guests to one's *sukkah*, a total of seven "imaginary" guests are invited to dinner, one on each of the seven nights of the holidays. These guests are called *ushpizin*. (*See* Ushpizin.)

Multiples of seven figure prominently in Jewish tradition. In addition to the seven times seven, or forty-nine, days between Passover and Shavuot, there were a total of seven times seven, or forty-nine, years between the beginning of the sabbatical and the jubilee years.

Also, seven times ten, or seventy, was the number of sacrificial bullocks (Numbers 29:12–38) the Israelites were expected to offer as an expression of gratitude. Additionally, seven times ten was the number of elders Moses appointed to assist him in governing the Israelites (Numbers 11:16).

Earlier, the Bible (Genesis 50:3) notes that Egyptians "bewailed" for seventy days when Jacob died, and Joseph mourned him for seven days (Genesis 50:10).

The *Zohar* says there are seventy facets to the Torah, and the Midrash (*Numbers Rabbah* 14:12) speaks often of the seventy nations and seventy languages that were known in ancient times. When the Septuagint, the Greek translation of the Bible, was initiated at the command of King Ptolemy II (285–246 B.C.E.) of Egypt, seventy Jewish scholars were assembled to work on the translation independently of each other.

Eleven times seven, or seventy-seven, is another important number in Jewish tradition. The word *mazal* in Hebrew, meaning "good luck," has a numerical value of seventy-seven.

Special Significance of the Number Ten

The number ten is also of importance in Jewish life and law. The Bible (Ruth 4:2) tells us that when Boaz was ready to marry Ruth, he called together ten elders of the city. Using this as a basis, the Talmud (*Ketubbot* 7b) ruled that a quorum of ten men (*minyan*) should be present when a wedding ceremony is performed.

Ten is also significant as the number of commandments Moses received on Mount Sinai and as the number of martyrs who suffered death at the hands of the Romans in the second century C.E. Ten is also the number of days of repentance between Rosh Hashanah and Yom Kippur, known as the Days of Awe.

Other Numbers of Significance

The number eighteen, composed of the letters *chet* and *yud*, spells out the word *chai*, meaning "life." When contributions are made to a charity, eighteen dollars is a popular amount donated, because it connotes long life. Of its multiple, two times eighteen, or thirty-six, the Rabbis of the Talmud say, "The world exists because of the merit of thirty-six righteous people [*lamed vovniks*] who inhabit the earth in each generation" (*Sukkot* 45b).

Sephardim consider the numbers twenty-six and one hundred and one exceptionally lucky, and often make contributions in these amounts. Twenty-six is the numerical value of Yehovah (*yud* [10], *hei* [5], *vav* [6], *hei* [5]), and one hundred and one is the numerical value of the name of the angel Michael (*mem* [40], *yud* [10], *khaf* [20], *alef* [1], *lamed* [30]).

See Jubilee Year; Shemittah.

Nusach

Plural, *nusachim*. When used in connection with the liturgy of the synagogue, this Hebrew term meaning "arrangement" refers to the melodies to which the prayers and the Torah are chanted. There are two primary *nusachim*: *nusach Ashkenaz* and *nusach Sepharad* (*S'phard*).

Although the name Ashkenaz appears simply

as a personal name of one of Noah's grandsons in Genesis 10:3, since the early Middle Ages, the word has been associated with the Jews of Germany. Their style of prayer, known as the *nusach Ashkenaz*, was later adopted by France as well.

The *nusach* employed in Spain and several nearby countries became known as *nusach Sepharad*. *Sepharad* is mentioned in the Bible (Ovadiah 1:20) as the name of a country, but not as the country we know of as Spain.

See Cantillation.

Ohel

A Hebrew word literally meaning "tent, enclosure," referring specifically to the canopy-like structure erected over the grave of a distinguished scholar or notable. An elaborate *ohel* covers the grave of Moses Maimonides, in Tiberias, Israel, and that of the famous second-century C.E. mystic Rabbi Shimon bar Yocha'i, who is buried on Mount Meron, near Safed. Admirers of these celebrated scholars visit their respective graves each year.

Aside from the association of the word *ohel* with a physical structure, in Jewish law the term relates significantly to the concept of ritual impurity (Numbers 19:13-20), and the belief that a person or thing that is in an enclosure with a corpse becomes impure. The entire tractate of the Talmud, called *Oholot* (plural of *ohel*), devotes its eighteen chapters to the subject of ritual impurity—known as *tumah* in Hebrew—primarily as it relates to foodstuffs and liquids and persons engaged in their preparation.

Most of the laws of *tumah* fell into disuse, especially as they relate to the functioning of the Priests (*Kohanim*) after the destruction of the Second Temple in 70 C.E. The sole exception is the regulation that prohibits Priests from being in close proximity to the dead.

See Priesthood.

Omer

A Hebrew word literally meaning "a measure [of grain]," referring specifically to an amount of the barley crop harvested before Passover and brought as a sacrificial offering to the Temple in Jerusalem on the second day of the holiday. Fifty days later, on Shavuot, the wheat crop was harvested and brought to the Temple as a sacrificial offering.

The forty-nine days between Passover and Shavuot are marked off (counted), day by day, and a special blessing is recited at the *Ma'ariv* (evening) service. This counting is known as *sefirat ha-omer*, "the counting of the *omer*," or simply as *sefirah*.

The Bible (Leviticus 23:15-16) describes the counting in this manner:

> And from the day on which you bring the sheaf offering—the day after the Sabbath ["the Sabbath" meaning the holiday of Passover and "the day after" meaning the second day of the holiday]—you shall count off seven weeks until the day after the seventh week [Shavuot].

According to the twelfth-century philosopher Moses Maimonides, the importance of counting the days between the Exodus from Egypt and the anniversary of the receiving of the Law at Mount Sinai is to indicate that release from bondage is not an end in itself, that liberty without law is a doubtful blessing.

See Lag Ba-Omer; Sefirah.

Onanism

Derived from the name of Onan, a son of Judah, one of Jacob's twelve sons, the term is defined as withdrawal from sexual intercourse before ejaculation, thus resulting in the wasting of seed. In Hebrew, the action is referred to as *hashchatat zera*. The story of Onan is told in the Book of Genesis (38:4-10).

See Bal Tashchit; Masturbation.

Oneg Shabbat

A Hebrew term literally meaning "Sabbath delight." The name of a social gathering held on Sabbath afternoon, at which time lectures are given, games played by children, and songs are sung. The idea was first suggested and instituted by Russian-born Chaim Nachman Bialik (1873-1934), who settled in Israel and became the poet laureate of the Jewish people. He held the first *Oneg Shabbat* in his home in Tel Aviv in 1924.

The name for the celebration was suggested to him by the verse in Isaiah (58:13), *Ve-karata la-Shabbat oneg*, "And you shall call the Sabbath a delight [*oneg*]." The term *Oneg Shabbat* was later applied to the collation following the late Friday evening service or lecture, conducted in many American synagogues.

Onein

A Hebrew word literally meaning "distressed person." During the period of time that begins with the passing of a close relative (father, mother, son, daughter, brother, sister, or spouse) and concludes with the burial of the deceased, the mourner is called an *onein* (feminine: *onenet*; plural *onenim* and *onenot*).

The Rabbis compare the *onein* to an inebriated person, one not in full control, one guided by impulse rather than reason. Because the mind of the *onein* is preoccupied with funeral arrangements and not concerned with the carrying out of religious commandments (*mitzvot*), the Rabbis ruled that the *onein* is not to pray or participate in religious activities of any kind (*Semachot* 10:1 and Yoreh Dei'ah 341:1). He may not be counted as one of the ten adults who constitute a *minyan*.

Some Conservative rabbis argue that banning the *onein* from participating in religious practice is outmoded because local communities and funeral parlors take care of burial needs, and demands made upon mourners is minimal. An *onein* should, therefore, be encouraged to pray and derive from it the solace and comfort it provides.

Because the Sabbath is to be a day of peace and joy, all forms of public mourning are forbidden on this day. Therefore, on the Sabbath,

the *onein* is thus required to carry out the religious duties incumbent upon all Jews (Yoreh Dei'ah 341:1).

Oral Law

The Oral Law (or Oral Torah, as it is sometimes called) consists of the Talmud and Midrash, in which the teachings and laws of the Written Law—the Torah itself—are explained and interpreted. These teachings were transmitted by word-of-mouth from teacher to student for many generations and therefore became known in Hebrew as Torah *she-be'al peh* (literally, "Torah by mouth"). So venerated were the teachings of the Oral Law that the Rabbis began to claim that the Oral Torah, along with the Written Torah, was part of the Revelation at Mount Sinai—if not in every last detail, at least in principle. Not all Rabbis of the Talmud agreed with this theory (*Gittin* 60b), insisting that only the written Torah was the Revelation and hence only it should be transmitted in written form.

By the middle of the first century C.E., as the political situation in Palestine deteriorated and the Roman conquerors prohibited Jewish schools from functioning, it became evident that unless the Oral Law was committed to writing, in time its teachings would be lost forever. When Rabbi Yochanan ben Zakkai, the foremost scholar of this period, realized that the destruction of the Jewish commonwealth was imminent, he managed to obtain permission from the Roman ruler to move his school from Jerusalem to Yavneh, a town located between Joppa (present-day Jaffa) and Ashdod. There, a process of collecting the teachings and traditions of the past began.

Around the year 200 C.E., Rabbi Yehudah Ha-Nasi (Judah the Prince), the political and religious leader of Palestinian Jewry, took over the project and pursued it vigorously. The result was the Mishnah: an orderly compilation of Jewish laws and traditions that had been handed down from generation to generation. In the two and one-half centuries that followed, the Mishnah was studied, analyzed, and interpreted, and these interpretations were edited around the year 500 and set down in final form as the *Gemara*. The Mishnah and *Gemara* together are known as the Talmud, which is the Oral Law committed to writing.

See Mishnah; Talmud; Written Law.

Ordination

The Hebrew word for ordination is *semikhah*, meaning "laying on of hands."

In its original use, the term was associated with an individual who brought an animal to the Temple to be offered as a personal sacrifice of repentance. The Bible (Leviticus 1:4) says, "He shall lay [*ve-samakh* in Hebrew, hence the word *semikhah*] his hand upon the head of the offering." The Rabbis of the Talmud amplify upon the requirement by saying that the person bringing the sacrifice is to press down with both hands, using full strength, between the horns of the animal.

A form of the term *semikhah* is used later in the Bible (Numbers 27:22–23; Deuteronomy 34:9) in a description of the first instance of an individual being ordained. Moses bestowed ordination upon Joshua by laying his hands upon him, thus transferring a portion of his power and spirit to his disciple.

The privilege of being ordained a rabbi applied only to the scholars of Palestine. Scholars of equal knowledge who lived in Babylonia or any other country outside of Palestine could not be ordained and were to bear the simple title *rav*, meaning "master teacher," as opposed to rabbi [*rabi*], meaning "my master or teacher." The rabbis of Babylonia were not authorized to rule on money disputes or levy fines.

The Talmud (*Sanhedrin* 13b–14a) describes how the ordination of a rabbi is to be performed. Three "elders [actually, scholars]" are designated to confer the honor, one of whom officially represents the Patriarch (*nasi*) of Palestine and does the laying on of hands. Once the ceremony is concluded, the candidate is to be called "rabbi" and is granted the privilege of sitting on the *Sanhedrin*, the supreme religious authority in ancient Palestine. He is also authorized, by virtue of his *semikhah*, to rule on all ritual and legal matters and to impose monetary fines when necessary.

Among the better known rabbis of Palestine are Akiva, Meir, Tarfon, Gamliel, and Judah the Prince. Among the distinguished rabbis of Babylonia are Ashi, Samuel bar Abba, Zeira, Papa, and Nachman bar Isaac. Many of the prominent rabbis of Babylonia bore no title at all and were called simply by their first name or by their first name preceded by the word *mar* ("mister").

An ordained rabbi in Palestine was authorized to confer *semikhah* upon his own worthy students. In this manner, Rabbi Yochanan ben Zakkai ordained Eliezer and Joshua and Rabbi Joshua ordained Akiba, and Akiba ordained Meir and Shimon bar Yocha'i.

In the year 425, when the Roman rulers of Palestine abolished the office of Patriarch, the ordination of rabbis was discontinued and the *Sanhedrin* itself ceased operation. It was not until Moses Maimonides appeared on the scene in the twelfth century that any authority even considered the possibility of ordaining a rabbi. Maimonides boldly declared in his code, the *Mishneh Torah*, that ordination could be restored only by unanimous agreement of all the rabbis of Palestine.

In 1538, Jacob Beirav (Berab)—a wealthy scholar who had moved from Spain to Turkey to Egypt to Jerusalem, finally settling in

Safed—was deeply impressed by the growth of the Jewish community of Palestine both in numbers and in the quality of scholarship. This encouraged him to promote a call for the reestablishment of the institution of *semikhah*. Beirav called together twenty-five learned rabbis of Safed, a city in northern Palestine where one thousand Jewish families were living at the time, and they ordained him at his request. Beirav, in turn ordained four other scholars, one of whom was Joseph Caro, the noted author of the *Code of Jewish Law* (*Shulchan Arukh*).

Through his efforts to revive ordination, Beirav had hoped that the ancient *Sanhedrin* would be reconstituted and reassume its function of legislating for world Jewry as in the days of the patriarchate. To accomplish this he sought the acquiescence of the religious leaders of Jerusalem. Beirav was unsuccessful in this effort and the entire scheme fell apart.

Nevertheless, the practice of an individual rabbi conferring *semikhah* on an individual student continued throughout the centuries. In more recent times, seminaries established in Europe and in America adopted the practice of conferring ordination on their students. In the United States, the first major institution that undertook to ordain rabbis was the Orthodox Rabbi Isaac Elchanan Theological Seminary, founded in 1896, which later became a part of Yeshiva University. Others that followed were the Jewish Theological Seminary of America (Conservative); the Hebrew Union College/Jewish Institute of Religion (Reform); and the Reconstructionist College. Smaller academies representing various denominations also confer the title of rabbi.

European countries have their own seminaries where rabbis are ordained, most prominent of which is Jews' College in London, founded in 1856 by Rabbi Nathan Marcus Adler.

Ordination of Women

In 1846, at their conference in Breslau, Germany, Reform rabbis favored the granting of religious equality to women, yet it was not until 1972 that a Reform seminary, Hebrew Union College–Jewish Institute of Religion, ordained Sally Priesand, as the first woman rabbi. The Conservative movement, through its mother-institution, the Jewish Theological Seminary, followed suit, and in 1985 ordained its first female rabbi. (It was later revealed that Henrietta Szold, who later founded Hadassah, the women's Zionist organization, had been permitted, in 1903, to attend classes at the Jewish Theological Seminary, but only on condition that she would not be ordained and that she would not use her knowledge to function as a rabbi.) The Reconstructionist Rabbinical College, which was founded in Philadelphia in 1968 by disciples of Rabbi Mordecai Kaplan, ordained its first woman rabbi in 1974.

Modern Orthodox women have begun making demands that they be allowed to be more participatory in religious life and synagogue affairs, but they have not yet openly demanded the right to be ordained as rabbis. A few congregations, however, have engaged learned women to act as interns, which involves assuming some of the functions of the congregational rabbi, particularly in the field of education.

Opposition Claims

The arguments advanced in the opposition to the ordination of women are primarily twofold.

First, according to Jewish law women may serve as witnesses, and therefore a woman rabbi would not be able to sign as a witness on a *ketubbah* (Jewish marriage contract), on a divorce document (*get*), or on a conversion document.

Second, according to Jewish law women are not obligated to participate in public prayer because their primary obligation is to home and family, and domestic duties would sometimes conflict with the specific times at which prayer must be recited. Since in Jewish law one can carry out a function for others only when he himself is *obligated* to perform that function, a woman is unable to lead a group in prayer, as many rabbis are called upon to do today. With this in mind, in January 1984 the Jewish Theological Seminary made it mandatory for all women who apply for admission to its rabbinical school to take upon themselves the obligation to observe *mitzvot* such as *tallit* and *tefillin*.

See Rabbi.

Organ Transplants

The lifesaving principle (*pikuach nefesh*) has a direct bearing on the subject of organ transplants. Most Jewish authorities agree that when a transplant is likely to save a life, it is permissible. Saving a life or improving the quality of one are of the highest priority in Jewish law, superseding even the laws of Sabbath (*Yoma* 85a).

Proprietary rights an individual has over his own body, and the extent to which he may permit his body to be tampered with in order to save the life of another has been the subject of debate. While the Talmud (Mishnah *Bava Kama* 8:1; 91b) warns that a person may not inflict a wound upon himself or upon others, most authorities would consider it permissible to allow a "wound" (operation) to be inflicted on one's body in order to donate an organ for transplant.

The former Sephardic Chief Rabbi of Israel, Ovadiah Yosef (who served until 1983), was asked whether one can donate a kidney to a person in critical need of a transplant. His response was that one is obligated to donate a kidney if doctors can assure the donor that the operation is likely to succeed and that the donor's health will not be jeopardized. By extension, the Chief Rabbi ruled, all organ transplants that do not put the donor's life or health at risk are permitted under Jewish law (*Yechaveh Daat* III:84). This represents the general view of most rabbinic authorities.

Some authorities have raised objection to transplantation of an organ from the body of a deceased, because the body must be buried in its entirety in order to be in compliance with the commandment, "Thou art dust and unto dust shalt thou return" (Genesis 3:19). To do otherwise would constitute a desecration of the dead (*nivul ha-met*). This objection is countered by the argument that a transplanted organ will eventually be buried with the demise of the recipient.

The permissibility of a Jew's accepting a transplant organ from the body of a non-Jew has not been specifically addressed by religious authorities. However, supporters of the practice point to the fact that since it is permissible for a Jew to accept a heart-valve replacement from the body of a pig (*Shulchan Arukh*, Yoreh Deah 155:3), an animal reviled by Jews, accepting an organ from a non-Jew is certainly acceptable.

Original Sin

The biblically-based concept of Original Sin, which is more relevant to Christian theology than to Jewish thought, stems from the Book of Genesis (2, 3), wherein Adam is warned by God not to eat from the Tree of Knowledge in the Garden of Eden, or he will surely die. The serpent convinces Adam through his wife, Eve, to disobey God's command, and assures him that not only will he not die, but that he will become wiser as a result. Adam and Eve believe the snake, and thereby commit the first sin against God—the "original sin," as Christians call it.

According to Christian teaching (I Corinthians 15:22), the burden of the original sin was lifted from man when Jesus died for him upon the Cross. Jesus was the sacrificial lamb through whom man, born into a state of sin, was saved and restored to an untainted state. This concept of vicarious atonement, which Christians believe was foretold in the prophecy of Isaiah (particularly chapter 53), is at variance with Jewish belief, which holds not only that man was *not* born into sin but that every individual is responsible for his own actions.

Many Christians today, particularly members of the Anglican, Roman Catholic, Lutheran, Methodist, and Presbyterian Churches, maintain that the sin of Adam was transferred to all future generations, tainting even the unborn. Substantiation for this view is found in the New Testament (Romans 5:12) where Paul says, "Wherefore as by one man sin entered into the world, and death by sin; and so death passed upon all men, for that all have sinned." And Paul adds, "By one man's disobedience many were made sinners."

According to Jewish tradition, the people of Israel were later purified from the taint of the sin committed by Adam and Eve when they stood at the foot of Mount Sinai awaiting the descent of Moses with the Ten Commandments, which they eagerly accepted. The Revelation at Sinai enabled the Israelites to conquer the "evil impulse" (*yeitzer ha-ra*), an inborn trait of every human being, and replace it with the "good impulse" (*yeitzer ha-tov*), which is also an innate aspect of the human personality.

The doctrine of original sin is totally unacceptable to Jews (as it is to Fundamentalist Christian sects such as the Baptists and Assemblies of God). Jews believe that man enters the world free of sin, with a soul that is pure and innocent and untainted. While some Jewish teachers in talmudic times believed that death was a punishment brought upon mankind on account of Adam's sin, the dominant view by far is that man sins because he is not a perfect being, and not, as Christianity teaches, because he is *inherently* sinful.

Orlah

The Bible warns the Israelites (Leviticus 19:23), "When you enter the land and plant any tree for food, you shall consider its fruit as forbidden [*orlah* in Hebrew]. Three years shall it be forbidden for you, not to be eaten...."

The term *orlah* is the Hebrew word for foreskin, the part of the male anatomy that is removed during circumcision. Some commentators believe that the fruit of the first three years is forbidden until the tree is "circumcised," meaning much of its growth is cut away and discarded, just as the foreskin of the penis is cut away and discarded. The idea may have been that by thinning its branches, the tree will be healthier and the fruit more abundant after three years. The fruit of the fourth year was to be set aside as an offering to God in keeping with a widespread belief that all new life, whether human, animal, or vegetable, belongs to Him.

See Omer; Pidyon Ha-Ben.

Orthodox Judaism

In a religious context, the term "orthodoxy," which derives from the Greek word meaning "straight [upright] opinion," applies to longstanding and immutable beliefs that must be embraced without question.

In Judaism, Orthodoxy demands unquestioned

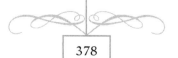

belief that the Torah transmitted to Moses on Mount Sinai was dictated word for word by God, that it contains 613 commandments (*mitzvot*), and that anyone who violates these laws is a heretic.

Rabbi Ishmael ben Elishah, a second-century Palestinian scholar, once said to his disciple Rabbi Meir, who was not only a great scholar but a scribe by occupation (*Eruvin* 13a), "My son, be scrupulous in your work [of writing Torah scrolls], for your work is divine. If you delete even one letter or add even one letter [to the Torah text], you may destroy the entire world."

Rabbi Ishmael was reminding Rabbi Meir of the warning in the Book of Deuteronomy (13:1), "You shall not add anything to what I command you [*lo toseif*] or take anything away [*lo tigra*] from it, but keep the commandments of the Lord your God that I enjoin upon you."

Fulfilling Jewish Law

Recognizing how difficult it would be for people to accept each and every Torah commandment literally, and that they required interpretation, the Rabbis declared that not only was the Torah—the Five Books of Moses—transmitted by God to Moses on Sinai, but all the teachings of future students of the Law are to be considered as if they, too, were imparted by God to Moses on Mount Sinai. Hence, despite the admonition that one may not "add to" or "subtract" from laws of the Bible, the Rabbis did just that via their interpretive teachings and rulings, which are recorded in the Talmud. These rulings, became known as the Oral Law and together with the Torah teachings, which is the Written Law, became part of established Jewish Law (*halakhah*), which is the basis of Orthodox belief.

In the sixteenth century, a code of Jewish law was created by Spanish-born Joseph Caro (1488–1575) and Polish-born Moses Isserles (1525–1572). Based upon work done earlier by Asher ben Yechiel (1250–1327), known as the Rosh, and his son, Jacob (1270–1350), who published a code named *Arba'a Ha-Turim*, the work composed by Caro and Isserles was named the *Shulchan Arukh*, meaning "Prepared Table." In simple, direct fashion it sets forth all the laws that an observant Jew is expected to obey.

Scholars of subsequent centuries—including the likes of Ezekiel Landau (1719–1793), Moses Sofer (1762–1839), Samson Raphael Hirsch (1808–1888), Abraham Kook (1865–1935), and Moshe Feinstein (1895–1986)—have added new rulings and offered new insights and interpretations on the rulings outlined in the earlier codes.

American Orthodoxy

At the very end of the nineteenth century, the Rabbi Isaac Elchanan Theological Seminary (RIETS) was founded in New York City with the mission of educating and ordaining Orthodox rabbis. Named after Isaac Elchanan Spektor (1817–1896), the illustrious Lithuanian-born rabbi who had established a noted *yeshivah* in Kovno, this institution opened its doors in 1895.

Bernard Revel (1885–1940) was appointed head of RIETS in 1915. In 1928, with the establishment of Yeshiva College, the first Jewish college in America, a secular curriculum was offered as well. In time, the curriculum was further expanded and Yeshiva College became Yeshiva University, which ultimately added a medical school, a law school, a business school, and other departments of higher learning.

Polish-born Samuel Belkin (1911–1976), who migrated to the United States in 1929,

joined the faculty of Yeshiva College in 1935 and became a professor in 1940. A scholar who authored several works on the Hellenistic period, Belkin became dean of the school in 1941, and in 1943 he succeeded Bernard Revel as president.

Rabbi Norman Lamm (1927–) assumed leadership of Yeshiva University in 1976, after having served as a professor of Jewish philosophy at the institution. Under his leadership the university continued to grow.

Not of the same stature, but equally acclaimed for its academic programs, is the Hebrew Theological College of Chicago, in Skokie, Illinois. Aside from its rabbinical school, it offers a bachelor's degree, a Master of Hebrew Literature degree, as well as a doctoral program.

The rabbis ordained at these seminaries are considered "modern Orthodox" and are not well received by ultra-Orthodox Jews, who oppose the teaching of secular studies. The ultra-Orthodox, or *chareidi* (literally, "God-fearing"), Jews are very strict in all matters of Jewish observance. The largest enclave of ultra-Orthodox live in the Mei'ah She'arim section of Jerusalem, and in Bnei Brak, near Tel Aviv. Basically anti-Zionist, they do not consider themselves citizens of Israel.

Prominent Orthodox Organizations

The oldest Orthodox synagogue body is the Union of Orthodox Jewish Congregations of America. Founded in 1898, by the 1990s it consisted of 1,500 affiliated synagogues and more than 250 *yeshivot* and day schools. It is the largest Orthodox group that supervises *kashrut* (the dietary laws). Most large national food manufacturers use the **K** symbol on their product labels, thus identifying the products as kosher and under the Union's supervision. A Woman's Branch of the Union was estab-

lished in 1924 and a National Conference of Synagogue Youth in 1954.

Orthodox rabbis belong to one of three major professional organizations: (1) The Union of Orthodox Rabbis in the United States and Canada, popularly known as Agudath Harabonim, the primary activity of which is to promote Judaism by providing assistance to the *yeshivot* in North America. (2) The Rabbinical Council of America (RCA), founded in 1923, whose more than one thousand members occupy pulpits throughout the United States and Canada. (3) The Rabbinical Alliance of America, known as Iggud Ha-Rabbanim, established in 1944, whose membership consists primarily of rabbis who were ordained at the Mesivta Torah Vadaath, in Brooklyn, New York.

Orthodox Defectors: Yotze'im

In recent years an organization known as Hillel (not to be confused with the Hillel that serves Jewish youth on American campuses) was organized to assist ultra-Orthodox youngsters who have abandoned Orthodoxy and opted for the secular world. Having been raised in an environment where the primary emphasis was on Torah study, most of these *yotze'im* ("leavetakers") have found the transition extremely difficult. To help them adapt to a new lifestyle, a group of psychologists, doctors, professors, marriage counselors, and former *yeshivah* students was organized under the name *Ha-Agudah L'Yotze'im Le-She'eilah*, meaning "those who have left because of doubts." (Hillel is an acronym formed from those three Hebrew words.) Members of the group provide monetary and psychological support to these lost souls, guide them in securing a secular education, and assist them in learning a trade and finding employment.

See Halakhah; Law and Custom; Law, Jewish.

Paradise

To encourage Jews to observe the commandments (*mitzvot*) and thus live a godly life, the Rabbis of the Talmud said that those who were loyal to their faith would be rewarded in Paradise. The term derives from the word used in the Greek translation of the Bible (Septuagint) for the Hebrew *Gan Eden* (Garden of Eden). However, some scholars maintain that Paradise derives from the Persian for park or garden.

In Jewish tradition, it was believed that those who did not live righteously would be consigned to *Gehinnom*, or hell, while those who lived righteously would be rewarded after death with a new, happy life in Paradise. In *Ta'anit* 31a, Ulla Bira'a, a disciple of Eleazar, visualized *Gan Eden* as a place in which God sits surrounded by a chorus of righteous people who dance all around Him, and with fingers pointed toward God sing His praises, such as those written in the Book of Isaiah (25:9):

In that day they shall say:
This is our God;
We trusted in Him, and he delivered us.
This is the Lord in whom we trusted,
Let us rejoice and revel in His deliverance.

See Afterlife.

Pardeis

The Hebrew word *pardeis*, literally meaning "tree, garden, orchard," occurs only three times in the Bible. The Greek form is *paradeisos*, akin to Paradise.

Biblical scholars have employed the term *pardeis*—spelled in Hebrew *pei, reish, dalet, samekh*—as an acronym for four methods of interpreting Scripture:

- *pei* stands for *peshat*, meaning "literal translation";
- *reish* stands for *remez*, meaning "allusion, allegory, symbolism";
- *dalet* stands for *derash*, a form of the word *midrash*, meaning "[homiletical] interpretation"; and
- *samekh* stands for *sod*, meaning "secret, mystery."

From talmudic times onward, scholars have employed these four methods to explain obscure and even contradictory biblical words or passages. However, it was not until the end of the thirteenth century that the Spanish Bible scholar and kabbalist Bachya ben Asher ibn Halawa (died 1340) called this fourfold method of analysis to our attention in his commentary on the Pentateuch.

Peshat

Of the four methods of biblical interpretation, *peshat*—the direct, simple, purely literal translation of a text—is most commonly used and preferred. However, because the demands of the Torah were sometimes inequitable, the Rabbis found that following the *peshat* did not always lead to a reasonable interpretation of Scripture. Such was the problem that they came upon in Exodus 21:24, which demands "an eye for an eye." The Rabbis did not consider this an appropriate way to mete out justice, and they found that following one of the other methods of interpretation would lead to a more humane punishment. *A'yin tachat a'yin* ("an eye for an eye"), they said, means that one should pay for the damage done by payment of money (*mamon*).

Derash

Rashi, the twelfth-century French commentator, once stated, "No verse may be deprived of its plain, literal, self-evident meaning." Nonetheless, he did not hesitate to sprinkle his commentary with other types of interpretation when he felt that the literal translation did not sufficiently express the intent of the text. Thus, in order to understand the true meaning of the first verse of the Bible ("In the beginning God created the heaven and the earth..."), the *derash* method must be employed. Based on an analysis of the construction of the word *bara* ("created"), Rashi was convinced that the proper translation of the opening verse is, "In the beginning, when God *began* to create heaven and earth..."

The *derash* method proved to be of immense value when it came to justifying the appointment of David as king of Israel. David was a direct descendant of Ruth, a Moabitess, and the Bible is quite emphatic in warning (Deuteronomy 23:4) that a Moabite shall not be admitted to the congregation of God—to the Jewish fold. How, then, could David become king?

By employing the *derash* method, the Rabbis of the Talmud (*Ketubbot* 7b; *Yevamot* 76b) were able to justify the action. They said: The Bible purposefully uses only the masculine form, Moabite, and therefore the prohibition does not include women. Hence, Ruth's marriage to Boaz, the relative of Naomi, was legitimate, and David's ancestry is untainted.

Remez

The employment of *remez* as a method of understanding a text can be seen in how Rebecca's pregnancy and giving birth to twins (Genesis 23:21–24) are explained. The Rabbis in the Midrash (*Genesis Rabbah* 63:6–7) wondered why Rebecca was so disturbed over

the fact that the twins she was carrying were in constant motion, seemingly struggling (*va-yit-rotzetzu* in Hebrew) to exit the womb. Such movement is not extraordinary, especially with twins. Why, then, was Rebecca so despondent that she had to consult God for an explanation?

To Rashi and the Rabbis before him, Rebecca's discomfort was a sign (*remez*) that Jacob would be superior to Esau, because in the struggle of the two fetuses, says the Midrash, whenever Rebecca passed a place where Torah was being studied, the fetus of Jacob moved energetically, attempting to be first to exit the womb. And whenever she passed a pagan temple, Esau would become restive and anxious to leave the womb.

An earlier example of how *remez* was used to explain a difficult Torah question concerns the behavior of God as He confronted a rebellious Adam. Adam was commanded not to taste the fruit of the Tree of Knowledge, yet he did so at the instigation of his wife, who was misled by the cunning snake. When God calls out to Adam, *"A'yekah?* [Where are you?]," the Rabbis are puzzled. Why would an omniscient God have to ask Adam where he was hiding?

In this confrontation between God and the first man on earth, the Rabbis of the Midrash (*Tanchuma*, Tazria 9) found a lesson for future generations—namely, that through atonement God offers man an opportunity to make amends for the errors of his ways. Through God's innocuous question, He was providing Adam with an opportunity to give vent to his feelings and express regret for the sin of eating the forbidden fruit. God is reminding him that the Gate of Repentance is always open.

Simon ben Lakish, better known as Resh Lakish, was an outstanding third-century Palestinian scholar famous for his brute strength as well as his scholarship, integrity, and compassion. He wanted to establish the practice of visiting the sick (*bikur cholim*) as an important value in Judaism by finding a basis for it in the Torah. The tractate *Nedarim* (39b) details how Resh Lakish found an allusion (*remez*) to this practice in the conduct of Dathan and Abiram, members of the tribe of Reuben. They joined Korach in a conspiracy to denigrate the leadership of Moses and Aaron, claiming that they were power-hungry people who did not deserve to lead Israel. In the course of responding to their charges, Moses says (Numbers 16:29), "If these men die as all men do, or if they continue to be visited [when they are ill] as all men are normally visited, then [be sure that] the Lord has *not* sent me [to be your leader, and Korach is right...]." Rava, a younger contemporary of Resh Lakish, declared that, in accordance with this interpretation, visiting the sick is an important Torah-based commandment.

In searching for an answer to the question of why it was mandated that four cups of wine be consumed by each participant at the Passover *Seder*, Rabbi Yochanan, quoting his teacher Benaiah (Jerusalem Talmud, *Pesachim* 10:1 [68b]), found a *remez* to it in the fact that the Torah uses four different words to describe how Israel will be saved from Egyptian tyranny. God orders Moses (Exodus 6:6,7) to tell the Children of Israel: "I am the Lord. I will remove [*ve-hotzeiti*] you from the oppression of the Egyptians and deliver [*ve-hitzalti*] you from their bondage. I will redeem [*ve-ga'alti*] you with an outstretched arm...And I will take [*ve-lakachti*] you to be My people and I will be your God." Each cup of wine thus serves as a reminder of one of these four references to redemption.

In his commentary on the Torah, Moses ben Nachman, also known as Nachmanides or Ramban, finds in the first word of Exodus 25:10 a *remez* to a deep-rooted Jewish concept. Here, the Torah describes the construction of the Ark and the various vessels that are to be made for the Tabernacle that was to be built. The first word of the verse is *ve'asu*, "and they shall make." But in the construction of the Tabernacle itself, *ve'asu [li]*, "and they shall make [for Me]" (25:8) is used.

Nachmanides sees a *remez* in the use of *ve'asu* and not *ve'asu li* in verse 10. He concludes that the plural form is used here to draw attention to the fact that the holy Ten Commandments were to be housed in the Ark, and in its construction every single Israelite must be involved, either by providing funds or materials or by helping Bezalel, the architect, do the actual labor.

Sod

The form of interpretation known as *sod*— mystical speculation into the meaning of a text—is closely allied to *remez*, and sometimes even to *derash*. This method was employed by mystics, particularly in their efforts to establish that the resurrection of the dead can be deduced from the Torah. Rabbi Simla'i, a first/second-century talmudic scholar, found the message concealed in the verse (Exodus 6:4), "And I [God] have also established My covenant with them [the Patriarchs] to give *them* the land of Canaan." The fact that the verse does not say "to give *you*" but "to give *them*," coupled with the fact that the Patriarchs were already dead, is proof that the Patriarchs will be resurrected in the future. Hence, concludes Rabbi Simla'i (*Sanhedrin* 90b), *techiyat ha-metim* ("resurrection of the dead") is implicitly stated in the Torah.

Sod was also used to answer the question: How do we know that Jacob, even while spending more than two decades under the roof of his idolatrous father-in-law, Laban, was careful about observing all the *mitzvot* (commandments)? Rashi found the answer secreted in the verse (Genesis 32:5) *Im Lavan garti*, "I lived with Laban." The Hebrew word for "I lived" is *garti*, consisting of the letters *gimmel*, *reish*, *tav*, *yud*, which have a numerical value of 613 and are the same letters in the acronym *taryag*, which refers to the *taryag mitzvot*, the 613 biblically-mandated commandments. Hence, Rashi concludes, we have proof that Jacob observed all of the 613 Torah commandments.

This methodology of searching for the hidden meaning of a biblical text by comparing the numerical value of words and phrases was characteristic of the kabbalistic approach employed by mystics and popularized in the *Zohar*. For example, in the *Zohar* the opening words of Genesis 12 are *Lekh lekha*, "Go you forth." Why was it necessary for God to say, "Go *you* forth from the land...," when it would have been perfectly clear and adequate to say *lekh*, "Go forth," without the "you." In this verse the kabbalists found an answer to a gnawing question—namely, at what point was Abraham advised that he would sire a son at age 100? The answer: It was right here, at the time God told Abraham *lekh lekha*—go forth to the land of Canaan.

The kabbalists arrived at this conclusion based on a hidden meaning they detected in the superfluous word *lekha*. The numerical value of all the letters in the phrase *lekh lekha* equals 100, they noted, and from this they concluded that Abraham would father a child at age 100.

In Genesis 12:6 the Spanish commentator Abraham ibn Ezra (1089–1164) found that the word *az* in the phrase *Ve-ha-Kena'ani az ba-aretz* poses a problem, and it would have been better had the word been omitted. *Az*

means "then," and the phrase is to be translated "and the Canaanites were *then* [in the time of Abraham] in the land." That is true, but it is also true that the Canaanites occupied the Land of Israel even in the time of Moses, and they remained there until they were expelled by Joshua.

If the word "then" is kept in the text, it could possibly imply that Moses did not write the Torah, or at least this part of the Torah. He would not have written "the Canaanites were *then* in the land," since they were still there. He would have written simply, "the Canaanites were in the land."

To Ibn Ezra use of the word *az*, "then," is one that harbors a secret meaning.

Karaite Objection

Sects such as the Karaites, who originated in and around Persia in the eighth century C.E., did not use these methods of interpretation and therefore refused to accept the rulings of the mainstream establishment centered in Babylonia. To the Karaites, one is required to accept the Bible in its literal sense. Thus, they said, if the Bible states (Exodus 35:3), "You shall not kindle a fire throughout your settlement on the Sabbath Day," this means that one's house must remain dark for the entire Sabbath day.

It is evident that there are numerous approaches to achieving an understanding and appreciation of the Torah. The Midrash (*Zohar*, Bereishit 36) put it well when it said, "There are seventy faces [facets] to the Torah." To which other Rabbis have added: Whatever any diligent student offers as an interpretation of the Torah may be considered as if it, too, came from Sinai. Professor Abraham J. Heschel summed it up when he wrote: "Judaism is a minimum of revelation and a maximum of interpretation."

Parents, Honoring

The concept of respecting and revering parents, twice mentioned in the Pentateuch, is the fifth of the Ten Commandments. Exodus 20:12 states: "Honor thy father and mother." Deuteronomy 5:16 repeats the commandment. In both cases the reward for honoring parents is long life.

In Leviticus 19:3 a similar admonition is issued, with no reward promised, but here "mother" is mentioned before "father": "Each person shall revere his mother and father... [because] I the Lord am your God."

The Talmud sings the praises of two individuals who displayed extraordinary respect toward their parents. One was a Gentile, a Roman military leader named Dama ben Netina; the other, the second-century talmudic scholar Rabbi Tarfon, an associate of Rabbi Akiba.

When Rabbi Eliezer was asked to what lengths one should go in fulfilling the commandment of honoring father and mother, he responded: "Don't ask me. Ask Dama ben Netina." He went on to explain that once, while seated among the notables of Rome, for no apparent reason Dama's mother tore off a silk garment that her son was wearing and slapped him in the face. Yet, in no way did he put her to shame (*Kiddushin* 31a).

In another instance, when a valuable jasper stone, representing the tribe of Benjamin, fell out of the High Priest's breastplate and was lost, a search was made to find a replacement. When it was learned that Dama ben Netina's family had one, Dama was offered one hundred dinar for it. Dama agreed to sell the stone, but when he went upstairs to get it, he found his father asleep. The keys to the chest in which the stone was kept were under his father's pillow, and he would not disturb him.

Dama told the buyers that he could *not* sell them the stone. They thought he wanted more money and offered him one thousand dinar, but he still refused. Later, when Dama's parents were awake, he called the men back and told them that they could purchase the stone for the original agreed-upon price (Jerusalem Talmud, *Avodah Zarah* 24a and *Pei'ah* 3a). He refused to profit from merely abiding by the commandment to respect one's parents.

Rabbi Tarfon's treatment of his mother is another case in point. The Talmud (*Kiddushin* 31b) reports that whenever she wished to get into bed, he would bend down and let her step on his back to ease her ascent, and he did likewise when she wished to get out of bed.

The Talmud and later codes of Jewish law assert that one demonstrates proper respect toward a father by not sitting in his seat, speaking when he is speaking, or contradicting him. On the affirmative side, the Talmud advises that one should feed, dress, and escort a parent in and out of the house when necessary.

Jewish theologians such as Moses Chaim Luzzatto (1707–1747) were so impressed by the value expressed in the Fifth Commandment that they considered it to be a model for proselytes and for non-Jews. In the twelfth-century, Moses Maimonides wrote that a convert to Judaism must *not* cease respecting his Gentile father. Parents continue to be parents even though one has converted.

The Rabbis of the Talmud (*Kiddushin* 30b) summed up the place of parents in a person's life as follows: "There are three partners in man: the Holy One, blessed be He, his father, and his mother. When a man honors his father and mother, the Holy One, blessed be He, says, 'I ascribe merit to them as though I had dwelt among them and they had honored Me.'" Honoring parents is tantamount to honoring God.

In a responsum (*Igrot Moshe*, Yoreh Dei'ah II:130), Rabbi Moshe Feinstein answered a sick non-Jewish mother of a proselyte who requested that her (now Jewish) daughter visit her with her children. There had been no contact between mother and daughter for twenty years despite the fact that they lived in the same city. Rabbi Feinstein responded that the proselyte should comply with her mother's request and thus fulfill the commandment of honoring parents.

While rabbinic authorities do not all agree that a Jew—whether by birth or by conversion—should observe all the mourning rites for non-Jewish parents, there is general agreement that *Kaddish* should be recited for them as a sign of respect.

Pareve

Foods that are neither meat (*fleishik* in Yiddish) nor dairy (*milchik* in Yiddish), nor derivatives of such products, are called *pareve*, a Yiddish word of uncertain etymology meaning "neutral." They may be used when preparing or serving either meat or dairy meals. *Pareve* products include all kosher fish, all fruits and vegetables and other nonanimal products, and all food products made from them. Also included are all nonanimal, artificial food products such as nondairy creamers and saccharin.

Passover

Passover (*Pesach* in Hebrew) is one of the three Pilgrim Festivals ordained in the Bible. (*See* Pilgrim Festivals.)

Originally, Passover was two separate holidays: an agricultural holiday known as Chag Ha-Matzot ("Festival of Unleavened Bread") and a pastoral holiday called Chag Ha-Pesach ("Festival of the Paschal Lamb"). Both holidays developed independently in the springtime of the year, in the Hebrew month of Nissan (March–April).

Chag Ha-Pesach is the older of the two festivals. In ancient times, when most Jews were still nomadic desert shepherds, Jewish families celebrated the advent of spring by offering an animal sacrifice. At one point in the Bible, before the Exodus, Moses begged Pharaoh to allow the Children of Israel to go out into the wilderness to observe their feast in honor of God.

The agricultural festival, Chag Ha-Matzot, was a spring holiday during which the Jewish farmers of Palestine celebrated the beginning of the grain harvest. Before cutting the grain, they would discard all sour dough (fermented dough was used as yeast to leaven bread).

In the course of time, these two springtime festivals came to be associated with another event that occurred in the springtime of the year: the Exodus from Egypt, known in Hebrew as *Zeman Cheiruteinu*, "the season of our redemption." Chag Ha-Pesach (Exodus 34:25) became identified with the happening in Egypt when God "passed over" the houses of the Children of Israel, who were instructed to dab some of the blood of the paschal lamb on their doorposts, thus identifying them (ibid. 12:21ff.). The homes of the Egyptians were not spared, and the eldest son in each family met his death.

The name Pesach comes from the Hebrew root *pasach*, meaning "paschal lamb" and "pass over." Chag Ha-Matzot (ibid. 23:15) was tied to the hasty departure of the Children of Israel from Egypt, when they "took their dough before it was leavened" (Exodus 12:34).

In the last years of the Second Temple, before 70 C.E., Passover was very popular. The Jewish historian Flavius Josephus and the Roman historian Tacitus estimated that the number of participants who came to Jerusalem to celebrate Passover in the year 65 C.E.

was "not less than three million," a figure that corresponds with the statement in the Talmud (*Pesachim* 64b) describing the census taken by King Agrippa. Agrippa ordered the Temple Priests to set aside one kidney from each offering of the paschal lamb. Since not less than ten people shared in eating each lamb, from the number of kidneys set aside it was estimated that three million Jews were in Jerusalem to celebrate Passover that year (five years before the destruction of the Temple).

Passover Observance

The Bible commands that Passover be observed for seven days. After the exile from Palestine in 70 C.E., when Jews were dispersed throughout the world, an extra day was added. This additional day was necessary because in ancient times the beginning of a new month was determined by the appearance of witnesses who would come to the *Sanhedrin* (Supreme Court) and testify that they witnessed the appearance of the new moon. If the testimony was accepted as reliable, the news was transmitted from Jerusalem by lighting torches atop mountain peaks and hills from one city to another. Since there was much margin for error, an extra day of observance was added to Passover, Sukkot, and Shavuot in order to avoid possible desecration of the holiday should the information not reach all Jews on time.

Most Jews in the Diaspora today observe Passover for eight days, but Reform Jews and some Conservative Jews follow the Israeli practice of observing the holiday for seven days. The additional day observed in the Diaspora is known as Yom Tov Sheini Shel Galuyot.

So as to conclude the holiday on a happy note, many communities have instituted farewell ceremonies. Moroccan Jews end the holiday with a celebration called *maimouna*,

in honor of Maimon, the father of Moses Maimonides. During the evening of the last day, families visit each other and serve freshly prepared *chametz* foods, such as thin pancakes (*mufleita*), stuffed dates, and other sweet delicacies.

Chabad *chasidim* celebrate with a "Messiah's Feast" (*se'udat Mashiach*), expressing faith in the imminent arrival of the promoter of the final redemption. Polish and Galician *chasidim* called their farewell celebration *Beglaiten dem Yom Tov*, "escorting the festival."

Lithuanian Jews, followers of the Gaon of Vilna, celebrate with a meal called "the meal of the Gra," *Gra* being an acronym formed from the Hebrew words "Gaon Rabbi Eliahu."

Passover Dietary Laws

The dietary regulations that apply to Passover differ in many respects from those that are followed throughout the year. The Passover regulations are centered about the concept of *chametz*, meaning "sour." Basically, any food product that is subject to fermentation may not be consumed during Passover and, likewise, all cooking and eating utensils (pots, pans, dishes, forks, spoons, etc.) that have been in contact with *chametz* products during the year may not be used in preparing or consuming Passover meals.

Although many families set aside a complete set of eating and cooking utensils for use only on Passover, the Rabbis felt that such an expense could not be borne by all families, and they therefore introduced a system known as kashering, whereby dishes and utensils can be made ritually kosher.

Methods of Kashering

Four methods of kashering eating and cooking utensils were developed: immersing the item in a large pot containing boiling water; subjecting the article to fire or intense heat until it glows; soaking the article in room-temperature water for three days, changing the water daily; and autoclaving, that is, subjecting the article to superheated steam under pressure so as to reach all cracks and crevices that can not be reached by simple boiling.

In determining which method of kashering is to be used for a particular item, four factors are to be considered:

1. The material from which the article is made. If the material is porous (and therefore absorbent) and cannot withstand the intense heat to which it must be subjected to be made kosher, the item will not be usable for Passover. Included in this category are pottery and earthenware. Nonporous articles, such as metal flatware and glassware of all kinds, can be successfully purged and thereby made kosher for Passover.

2. How the article is constructed. Items that have seams or are assembled from more than one piece—such as flatware with wooden or plastic handles, or pots with curled lips—may not be koshered for Passover because food can lodge in the seams. Conversely, one-piece items may be koshered.

3. The current condition of the item. Regardless of material or construction, any item that is chipped, cracked, or has been mended is not eligible for kashering because food particles that would be difficult to purge may have penetrated it.

4. The temperature of the food that had come in contact with the article. Ordinary glass dishes onto which hot foods were placed during the course of the year cannot be kashered successfully for Passover because if the glass is exposed to intense heat, it would crack. However, glassware used only as receptacles for cold foods can be made kosher for Passover by immersion in water for three days.

Passover Foods

According to the Bible (Exodus 13:6–7), *matzah* is to be eaten throughout the seven-day Passover holiday, and "no leavened bread shall be eaten." The difference between leavened bread which has a tendency to become soured or fermented under certain conditions and unleavened bread is that unleavened bread is made only out of flour and water. It is prepared hastily, not to exceed eighteen minutes before it is placed in the oven to be baked. If it takes more than eighteen minutes to be prepared it has a tendency to ferment and is referred to in Hebrew as *chametz*. Ordinary bread is made with flour and water plus yeast which causes it to rise and prevent fermentation. *Matzah* must have the *potential* of fermenting, but must not be allowed to ferment.

The Five Grains

The Bible itself does not specify which grains may be milled in order to make flour for the making of *matzah*, but the Talmud (*Pesachim* 35a) lists five grains that may be used for this purpose. These are: wheat, barley, spelt (a species of wheat), rye and oats. Apparently, those were the primary grains from which flour was made in talmudic times, even as it is today, two thousand years later. To make flour for the baking of *matzah* from any other products is strictly prohibited.

And the interesting anomaly is that while one of these five grains must be used to make *matzah*, none of them may be used on Passover to make any other product. If one wishes to bake a cake, it must be made from finely ground *matzah* (*matzah* meal).

Sephardic and Ashkenazic Practices

Joseph Caro, the Sephardic author of the *Shulchan Arukh*, states that rice and other legumes (called *kitnit* [plural, *kitni'ot*] in Hebrew) may be consumed on Passover for purposes other than baking *matzah* (Orach Cha'yim 453:1). Sephardic Jews follow this ruling, but the Ashkenazic community, following the lead of Moses Isserles, prohibits the use of rice and legumes *not* because Jewish law bans them directly, but because their use might lead to possible confusion in the kitchen. Specifically, it is feared that flour made from rice or legumes might be stored near flour made from the five permissible grains, and through an error a homemaker wanting to bake *matzah* might use the forbidden rice or legume flour. As a precautionary measure, Ashkenazic authorities have banned the use of rice and legumes in all forms during Passover, while Sephardic authorities have not. Sephardim will therefore eat rice and corn as well as lentils, split peas, soybeans, chickpeas, string beans, and green peas.

In Israeli supermarkets, some kosher-for-Passover products are labeled "for *kitni'ot* eaters only," to warn Ashkenazim that the item may contain a legume.

See Calendar; Chametz; Seder.

Patience

The modern Hebrew term for patience, *savlanut*, meaning "carrying a burden," implies that one must not speak out in anger when troubled by others. In the Bible (Exodus 34:6), one of the characteristics of God, whom man is expected to emulate, is his attribute of being *erekh a'pa'yim*, that is, "long-suffering, patient, slow to anger, and quick to forgive." The sage Hillel, of the first century B.C.E., summed up the significance of this attribute when he remarked that "an impatient man cannot be a teacher" (Ethics of the Fathers 2:6).

Hillel's saintly character, which was modeled after that of the biblical Job, who patiently accepted all adversity, was exemplified in a legend in which two men wagered four hundred coins called *zuzim*. The winner was to be the one who succeeded in trying Hillel's patience to the point that he would react in anger. One of the wagerers posed a series of infantile questions to the great talmudic scholar in an attempt to provoke him, but Hillel answered each question in a kindly manner. Finally, the man said, "Your patient answers have cost me four hundred *zuzim*!" Hillel answered: "It is better that you should lose four hundred *zuzim* than succeed in provoking Hillel to anger" (*Shabbat* 30b–31a).

Patriarchs

The founding fathers of the Jewish people, called *Avot* in Hebrew, are identified in the Book of Genesis. They are Abraham, whose wife was Sarah; Isaac, whose wife was Rebecca; and Jacob whose wives were Rachel and Leah. Some scholars refer to Jacob's twelve sons as Patriarchs as well.

Patrilineal Descent

Owing in part to the Holocaust, in part to the fact that Jewish families are not reproducing at the same rate as in the past, and in part to assimilation, the number of Jews in the world is dwindling. To remedy the situation, many leaders within the Reform movement are of the opinion that Jewish law (*halakhah*) should be modified so as to make it easier to increase the number of Jews in the world. This, they argue, can be accomplished by considering as Jewish the children of a Jewish man and a non-Jewish woman, which is contrary to established Jewish law that considers a person Jewish only if his or her mother is Jewish, or the individual has converted to Judaism.

The argument advanced in favor of patrilineal descent is that there is much within Jewish law and tradition that identifies a child with its father. The Book of Numbers (1:2) states that in taking the census the Children of Israel were to be counted "by their *fathers'* houses." Later, the Book of Numbers (18:1) indicates that priestly status passes from father to son, and also that only sons inherit the estate of the father (Numbers 36).

Additional support for the view that the status of the father is primary is adduced from legislation in the Talmud (Mishnah *Kiddushin* 3:12 [66b, 67a]):

- If a *Kohen* (Priest) marries an ordinary Jewish woman (Israelite), a child born from the marriage is a *Kohen*, like the father. The same applies to a *Levi*.
- If an Israelite marries a woman who is a member of the priestly family, a child born from that union is an Israelite, like the father, not a *Kohen* like the mother.

Advocates of the paternity position also cite the statement of Maimonides who, in discussing the biblical laws [Deuteronomy (25:5ff.)] relating to levirate marriage, says that what makes a surviving brother responsible to marry or release from marriage his deceased brother's widow is the fact that the two brothers have a father in common. The law of levirate marriage does not apply to brothers who have only a mother in common (*Mishneh Torah*, Hilkhot Yibum 3:1).

In his 1999 publication, *The Beginnings of*

Jewishness, Conservative Rabbi Shaye D. Cohen, who for many years taught at the Jewish Theological Seminary of America and later at Brown University, makes a number of observations that would lend support to the position of advocates of patrilineal descent. He notes that

- heroes of the Bible, including Joseph, Moses, David, and Solomon, were all married to non-Jews, but their offspring were considered Jewish.
- up until about 200 C.E., when the Mishnah was formulated by Judah the Prince, Jewish law considered children to be Jewish even if only the father was Jewish.

In March 1983, at the convention of the Central Conference of American Rabbis (Reform), the patrilineal descent concept was introduced by Rabbi Alexander M. Schindler, president of the Union of American Hebrew Congregations. A three-to-one majority voted to recognize as Jewish a child whose mother *or* father is Jewish with the proviso that the child be reared as a Jew and be identified formally and publicly with the Jewish faith. Orthodox and Conservative rabbinic groups have repudiated this Reform position, but it has been advocated by many Reconstructionists. The Reform movement in Israel, which is more traditional than its members in the Diaspora, does not accept patrilineal descent.

See Jewish Identity; Matrilineal Descent.

Peace

The Hebrew word for peace, *shalom*, is also used as a greeting meaning "hello" or "goodbye." So important is the concept of peace in the Jewish tradition that the ancient Rabbis taught (Midrash *Numbers Rabbah* 11:7):

"Great is peace, for God is called Peace." This attribution stems from a statement by the judge and military leader Gideon who, upon achieving a victory over Israel's enemy, built an altar to God and called it *Adonai Shalom*, "God is Peace" (Judges 6:23–24). Rabbi Shimon Ben Gamaliel immortalized the concept when he taught (Ethics of the Fathers 1:18): "The world rests on three foundations: truth, justice, and peace," as it is written (Zekhariah 8:16), "You shall administer truth, justice, and peace within your gates."

In Jewish history one leader stands out more prominently than any other as a man of peace, and that man is Aaron, brother of Moses. The Fathers According to Rabbi Nathan devotes the greater part of chapter 12 lauding the virtues of Aaron as a peacemaker. When Aaron died, the Bible notes (Numbers 20:29), the *entire* house of Israel *wept* for him. When Moses died, the mourning was apparently less intense, for the Book of Deuteronomy (34:8) simply states that the Children of Israel "bewailed" him. The Rabbis inferred from the contrast in wording that Aaron was mourned more intensely because he was more concerned with the welfare of all the people and was devoted to bringing peace into their lives on a very personal level.

The conclusion that Aaron loved peace and pursued it more vigorously than anyone else was also arrived at by the Rabbis assuming that the statement in the Book of Malakhi (2:6) refers to Aaron, although his name is not specifically mentioned there. The verse reads: "The law of truth was in his mouth; unrighteousness was not found on his lips. He walked with Me in peace and uprightness and turned many away from iniquity."

This led Hillel the Great, of the first century B.C.E., to advise (Ethics of the Fathers 1:12): "Be of the descendants of Aaron: love peace and pursue it." A century later, Rabbi Shimon ben Gamaliel (Ethics of the Fathers 1:18) promoted the virtue of peace by emphasizing the teaching of the prophet Zekhariah: "The world endures on three things—justice, truth, and peace, as it is said: 'Truth and the verdict of peace are you to adjudicate in your gates.'"

Of all the prophets who looked forward to and expressed themselves most eloquently on the prospects of a world at peace, Isaiah stands out above all the rest. His memorable prophesy (Isaiah 2:4) is the most oft-quoted. It ends with the famous passage that looks forward to a time when nations "shall beat their swords into plowshares and their spears into pruning hooks; nation shall not lift up sword against nation, neither shall they learn war anymore."

The yearning for peace was given vivid expression by Rabbi Judah the Prince (Yehudah Ha-Nasi), principal editor of the Mishnah in the early part of the third century C.E. He decided that Israel's craving for peace could best be acknowledged by ending the Six Orders of the Mishnah with a quote by Rabbi Shimon ben Chalafta. Rabbi Shimon said: "The Holy One, blessed be He, could find no more appropriate vessel that could hold a blessing for Israel other than peace, as is written (Psalms 29:11): 'The Lord will give strength to His people, the Lord will bless His people with peace.'"

With these words, the last Mishnah of the last tractate of the Talmud, *Uktzin* (3:12), comes to a close.

See Goodwill Principle.

Pentateuch

A Greek word meaning "five books," referring to the first five books of the Bible: Genesis, Exodus, Leviticus, Numbers, and Deuteronomy.

See Bible; Torah.

Pesach Sheini

A Hebrew term literally meaning "Second Passover." In Temple times, for the festival of Passover, Jews traveled to Jerusalem to offer the paschal lamb as demanded in the Torah (Numbers 9:9–14). For those unable to make the trip and offer the sacrifice on the fourteenth of Nissan, the specified time, provision was made for them to do so one month later, on the fourteenth of Iyyar.

Some could not observe the holiday in the month of Nissan because they were in a state of ritual impurity (having been in contact with the dead), and others because they were too far from the sanctuary to arrive in time for the holiday.

Although most of the restrictions of the first Passover apply to Pesach Sheini, according to the Mishnah (*Pesachim* 9:3) a person observing Pesach Sheini is required to eat *matzah* but is not obligated to rid his house of all *chametz*.

Some Jews today still commemorate Pesach Sheini by eating *matzah* on the fourteenth of Iyyar as a reminder of the Exodus. The only change in the liturgy is the omission of the penitential *Tachanun* prayer.

Because more than one Passover was regularly observed in ancient times, the tractate of the Talmud that deals with Passover laws is called *Pesachim* (plural), not *Pesach* (singular).

Pesach Sheini is sometimes referred to as "Minor Passover."

Pharisees

Pharisee is a Greek form of the Hebrew term *parush*, meaning "separated." The group of Jews known as Pharisees (in Hebrew, *Perushim*) were members of a religious/political party organized in Second Temple Days to distinguish themselves from the Sadducees. Whereas the Sadducees believed that only that which is explicitly commanded in the Torah should be accepted as the law governing Jewish life, the Pharisees believed that when God gave the Written Torah on Mount Sinai, He also gave them the Oral Torah, which we call the Talmud. In the Talmud, Torah law is expanded upon and interpreted by Babylonian and Palestinian scholars to make it harmonize with ever-changing societal conditions.

Thus, for example, the Pharisaic rabbis ruled that the biblical statement (Exodus 21:24), *a'yin tachat a'yin*, "an eye for an eye" (*lex talionis*), is not to be taken literally. Rather, the man who inflicts the damage on his fellow man is to compensate the victim for the damage he caused. The Saducees disagreed, insisting that the law as prescribed in the Torah is to be followed to the letter.

Despite the fact that concepts such as "day of judgment" and "resurrection of the dead" are not mentioned in the Torah, the Pharisees promoted them. Such expressions of hope for a better future appealed to the oppressed masses, and they rallied around the Pharisaic leaders, accepting their innovations and interpretations of the Torah text.

Pidyon Ha-Ben

A Hebrew term literally meaning "redemption of the [firstborn] son." The Book of Exodus (13:1–2) explicitly states that "the first issue of every womb [*peter kol rechem*] . . . of beast and man is Mine," and this requirement was clearly understood to apply specifically to the firstborn of a mother, not a father.

The Rabbis interpreted the words *peter rechem* to mean the first male offspring to exit a woman's womb by natural means. This excludes a child born to a woman who has had a miscarriage, as well as to a firstborn that emerged from the womb by means of a Caesarian section.

The law of redemption applies only to firstborn male children, since the Bible specifies "consecrate unto Me every *bekhor*," *bekhor* being the masculine word for "firstborn." Through the redemption ceremony (*pidyon ha-ben*), the firstborn child, who ordinarily was to be dedicated to the service of God—first in the Tabernacle in the desert and later in the Jerusalem Temples—would be freed of that obligation. Only the firstborn of priestly families (*Kohanim*) and Levitical families (*Levi'im*) were subject to this law, thus removing a hardship from the vast majority of people who needed their firstborn to help sustain the family.

The *pidyon ha-ben* ceremony for a firstborn male Israelite, which was formalized during the geonic period (seventh and eighth centuries), is held on the thirty-first day after a child's birth (the day of birth is counted as the first day). At the ceremony, the father of the child pays a Priest (*Kohen*) five pieces of silver (*shekalim*) as outlined in the Book of Numbers (18:15–16). If the thirty-first day is a Sabbath or holiday, the ceremony is postponed until the following day. The thirty-first day was selected because it was considered likely that once the child survived the first month of life, his chances for good health were assured. Therefore, even if a child's circumcision (*brit*) was postponed because of ill health, the *pidyon ha-ben* is nevertheless held on the thirty-first day of his life.

In modern times, five silver dollars are generally given to the *Kohen*, who later returns them to the father or gives them to charity. He does not keep the money because one can never be sure of the true genealogy of a *Kohen*, and it is assumed that Priests are only Priests by presumption.

In cases where the father of the baby to be redeemed is not Jewish and is therefore not qualified to carry out the commandment of *pidyon ha-ben* by reciting the prayer prescribed for this occasion, which include the words *asher kideshanu be-mitzvotav ve-tzivanu* ("[God] Who has sanctified *us* by His commandments and commanded *us* to…)," the Jewish court (*Beit Din*) appoints a surrogate father, who assumes the father's role for the occasion.

The Ceremony

To prepare for the *pidyon ha-ben* ceremony, arrangements must be made for a *Kohen* to be present in the home on the day the firstborn son will be thirty-one days old. Whenever possible, a *minyan* is assembled and seated around a table graced by a covered *challah* and a goblet filled with wine.

The mother then brings in the baby on a pillow and hands him to her husband, who either holds the child in one arm or places him on the table.

The father addresses the *Kohen* in Aramaic, as follows:

> This, my firstborn son, is the firstborn of his mother. The Holy One, blessed be He, has commanded that he be redeemed, as it is written [in the Torah]: "The redemption price for each firstborn son of the age of one month shall be fixed at five sacred silver *shekels*, the equal of twenty *gerahs*." And it is written: "Consecrate every firstborn until Me, whatever is firstborn in Israel, of man or beast, since it belongs to Me."

The *Kohen* then asks the father:

> What would you prefer? To give this child to me and to have me dedicate him to the service of God, or would you prefer to redeem him as demanded by the Torah?

The father then holds up five silver coins and responds:

I wish to redeem my son, and here is the fee the Torah calls upon me to pay. Praised be Thou, O Lord our God, King of the universe, who has commanded us regarding the redemption of the firstborn son.

The father continues with the recitation of the *She-heche'yanu* prayer. Holding the redemption money over the child's head, the *Kohen* says:

I accept this money as a substitute for this child. May he grow up to live a life of love for Torah and God. Just as the act of redemption has been enacted in his behalf, so may his future lead him into a happy marriage and a life of good deeds.

The *Kohen* then places his hands over the child's head and pronounces the ancient *Priestly Benediction*.

The *Kohen* then raises a cup of wine and recites the appropriate blessing. A festive meal (*se'udat mitzvah*) follows.

At a *pidyon ha-ben* ceremony of Sephardim from Syria, Morocco, and the Balkan area, mothers dress in their finest clothing, often in their wedding gowns. Many hang amulets on the walls and doors of the room in which the baby is kept, as well as around the neck of the child. The amulets usually contain the names of angels, such as Gabriel and Mikhael, who are believed to be guarantors of protection from evil spirits.

Reform Judaism does not accept the validity of a hereditary priesthood, and their rabbis, by and large, do not approve of the *pidyon ha-ben* ceremony.

Pidyon Shevu'yim

A Hebrew term literally meaning "redemption of captives." Particularly in the Middle Ages it was common for pirates, slave traders, and religious bigots to kidnap Jews in the hope of exacting a handsome ransom from the Jewish community. It would appear that those engaged in such activity were well aware of the high priority Jewish law and tradition placed upon the value of every Jew.

The Rabbis of the Talmud (*Bava Batra* 8b), based upon a verse in the Book of Jeremiah (15:2), concluded that the redemption of Jewish prisoners (and their slaves) is a positive religious commandment of the greatest importance. Maimonides, in his *Mishneh Torah* (Matnat Aniyim 8:10), considers the ransom of captives a commandment that supercedes even the duty of giving charity (*tzedakah*).

In order to spare a woman captive from immoral indignities, the Rabbis of the Talmud (Mishnah *Hora'yot* 3:7 [13a]) gave priority to ransoming her over that of ransoming a man. In addition, since scholars were not easily replaceable, their ransom was given priority over even that of a king.

One of the most famous cases of a Jew being taken captive occurred in 1286 when the illustrious German talmudist and legal authority Rabbi Meir ben Baruch Rothenberg was arrested by Emperor Rudolf and imprisoned for objecting vigorously to new taxes that were to be imposed. He could have been released upon the payment of a ransom by the Jewish community, but Rabbi Meir refused to allow the payment to be made, not wanting to encourage the enemies of Jews to continue the practice of taking captives. Ultimately, in 1293, Rabbi Meir died in prison, but his body was not released until 1307, when a wealthy resident of Frankfort paid the ransom so that the rabbi might be given a proper burial.

Piety

This concept, encountered in talmudic and post-talmudic literature and known in Hebrew as *chasidut*, predates by many centuries the chasidism of modern times. A *chasid* of this early period, who in Bible times was also known as a *tzadik*, was a person who observed ritual and ethical precepts far beyond what the law demanded.

The Rabbis of the Talmud speak often of "pious men of former generations" (*Bava Kama* 30a) and "pious men of old" (Mishnah *Berakhot* 5:1 [30b]). Scholars refer to these persons by the term *vatikin*, persons of profound spirituality who often lived in groups. The Essenes, of Hasmonean and later times (second century B.C.E.), were one such community. In the time of the Alexandrian philosopher Philo (20 B.C.E. to *c.* 40 C.E.) they numbered about four thousand.

Rabbi Yochanan, in the tractate *Berakhot* (9b), describes *vatikin* as being very careful about the time at which they would recite the *Shema* in the morning. They made sure to finish its recitation just as the sun rose so that the important prayers that followed would be recited, as mandated, in the morning.

According to Hillel, a pious person has to be a learned person (Ethics of the Fathers 2:6). An ignorant person (*am ha-aretz*), it was noted, may have high moral standards, but because of his lack of learning could never associate with learned people and acquire more and more knowledge, an essential ingredient in the makeup of a truly pious person.

The talmudic tractate *Menachot* (41a) describes how "pious men of old" would impose upon themselves a religious regimen not demanded by the law: they would sew the *tzitzit* onto a garment being prepared for them even before the garment was completed.

In the tractate *Nedarim* (10a) Rabbi Judah describes the extent to which the "early" *chasidim* went in order to offer a sacrifice they were not actually required to bring. They wished to bring a sin-offering, but since they had not actually sinned, they would take an oath to become Nazirites, which would include a pledge to abstain from drinking wine. They would then break their promise by drinking some wine, which would make them sinners and thus eligible to bring the sacrifice.

Achieving Piety

In modern times, the true meaning of piety was demonstrated in the life of the founder of chasidism, Israel ben Eliezer, better known as the Ba'al Shem Tov (1700–1760), whose name means "Master of the Good Name." Born in Ukraine, he inclined to a life of solitude and communing with nature, during which time he devoted himself to the study of *kabbalah*. The Ba'al Shem Tov became known for his miraculous cures, which brought him followers that were said to be in the many thousands. His message to them, which he never committed to writing, was that the essence of piety is to lead a godly life, that is, to be just, honest, and kind.

See Chasidism; Chasid Shoteh; Holiness; Lamed Vovnik.

Pikuach Nefesh

A Hebrew term meaning "saving, or prolonging, a life." This basic principle allows one to violate most Jewish laws, including all Sabbath and Yom Kippur prohibitions, in order to save a life. The only exceptions are the three cardinal sins of idolatry, sexual immorality, and murder (*Ketubbot* 19a).

The *pikuach nefesh* allowance is based on two biblical commandments. Leviticus 18:5 says, "Observe My commandments, so that they may be your guide in life." Deuteronomy 30:19 states, "I have set before you life and death, blessing and curse. Choose life so that you and your offspring may live." From these verses the Rabbis of the Talmud (*Yoma* 82a) concluded that there is no higher priority than saving a life—one's own as well as that of a fellow man. And they demonstrate the importance of *pikuach nefesh* through the following legend: When David returned victorious after his battle with Goliath, the women of Israel showered him with their gold and silver jewelry. He set the jewelry aside for future use in the building of the Temple and even during a three-year period of famine did not use it to purchase food for the needy. Because David bypassed the immediate needs of the hungry, who would surely die, for the future needs of the Temple, Solomon, not David, was granted the privilege of building the Temple (Midrash *Pesikta Rabbati* 6:26a).

In the 1980s, the Sephardic Chief Rabbi of Israel, Ovadiah Yosef, was asked whether one can donate a kidney to a person in critical need of a transplant. His response (Yechaveh Da'at III:84) was that one is obligated to donate a kidney if doctors can assure the person that the operation is likely to succeed and that the donor's health will not be jeopardized. By extension, he ruled, all organ transplants that do not put the donor's life at risk or health in danger are permitted under the law of *pikuach nefesh*.

The *pikuach nefesh* concept was put to a practical test when Orthodox members of the Israeli inner cabinet were granted permission by the Chief Rabbis to travel to a meeting on the Sabbath. On January 19, 1991, an Iraqi Scud missile attack was in progress and Prime Minister Yitzhak Shamir found it imperative to confer with his Cabinet about how best to secure the safety of Israeli citizens whose lives were in peril. The safety of the population overrode the prohibition of traveling on the Sabbath.

So basic has the law of *pikuach nefesh* become in Jewish life that one need not consult with any authority before taking action (*Yoma* 83a–84b). Every Jew *must* violate the Sabbath and holidays to save a life, and it is a duty that cannot be delegated to another person.

See Chasid Shoteh.

Pilgrim Festivals

Pesach (Passover), Shavuot (Pentecost), and Sukkot (Tabernacles) are referred to as Pilgrim Festivals because on these holidays all males were required to make a pilgrimage, known as *aliyah l'regel*, to "the place that God will choose" (Deuteronomy 16:16–17). On these three occasions during the year, each man was required to bring to the sanctuary a gift in accordance with his means. Since society in biblical times was primarily agricultural, the gifts brought were from the produce of the land.

The primary sanctuary before Solomon's Temple was built in Jerusalem was located in Shilo, twenty-five miles north of Jerusalem. The biblical term (Exodus 23:14) for the Pilgrim Festivals is *Shalosh Regalim*. The word *regalim*—the plural of *regel*, meaning "foot"—is a reference to the manner in which people journeyed to Jerusalem. *Regel* later took on the meaning of "holiday."

Pilpul

A method of talmudic study employed in academies of higher learning, characterized by subtle dialectics and finespun argumentation.

Pogrom

This Russian word meaning "destruction, desolation, rioting" is widely used to refer to attacks against Jews and their property. Pogroms began in Russia and Poland in the second half of the nineteenth century, encouraged and often instigated by the civil authorities. Prior to that time, anti-Jewish riots were carried out, often on a massive scale, but they were not known as pogroms.

The first major pogrom took place on March 13, 1881, in response to a rumor that Jews were responsible for the assassination of Czar Alexander II. His son and successor, Alexander III, was convinced that "liberal" Jews with revolutionary ideas were responsible for Russia's problems, and he allowed anti-Semitic agitation—already rampant in Germany—to find expression in his own country. Beginning with Easter and continuing into the summer of 1881, the Jewish quarter was invaded and dwellings were looted and demolished. With the support of artisans, laborers, and peasants, riots erupted in hundreds of small Russian localities and large cities, Kiev and Odessa among them.

A second series of pogroms took place between 1903 and 1906, notably in Kishinev; and a third series took place between 1917 and 1921. In all, it is estimated that in over 1,200 incidents in more than five hundred communities some sixty thousand Jews were killed and several hundred thousand wounded. Tens of thousands were able to escape to the West, primarily to the United States.

See Anti-Semitism; Blood Libels.

Polygamy

In the patriarchal society of biblical times, men were permitted to have more than one wife, but a woman could have only one husband.

The Rabbis of the Talmud were convinced that the Torah commandment "to be fruitful and multiply" (Genesis 1:28), although actually addressed to Adam and Eve, applied solely to men. Women bear the children, the Rabbis reasoned, yet it is man's seed that propagates the race. Man was therefore permitted as many wives as would bear him children. But a woman, declared the Rabbis, "cannot be a wife to two men." The Talmud (*Kiddushin* 7a) affirms that a married woman is sanctified (set aside) to one man; she is not to bear the children of any other man. However, based upon a careful analysis of the Mishnah and Tosefta, feminist Judaic scholars have become convinced that this view was not shared by all talmudic authorities.

While the Bible does not encourage polygamy, neither does it forbid it. The Book of Deuteronomy (17:17) warns the future kings of Israel against taking "many" wives, but it never limits the number of wives a man can have concurrently. The patriarch Abraham had two wives; Jacob had two wives, plus two concubines who bore him children; David had at least eighteen wives; and Solomon is reputed to have had one thousand wives (*Sanhedrin* 21a).

Over the course of time, the practice of polygamy began to wane, but it did not disappear. Scholars, such as the fourth-century Rabba of Babylonia, frowned upon the practice and sought to limit it. Rabba ruled (*Yevamot* 65a; *Ketubbot* 62b): "A man may marry other wives, in addition to his first one, provided he has the means to support them."

The warnings of Rabba and others did not succeed in eliminating polygamy. Jews of later centuries, especially those living among Muslims (who accept polygamy), continued to take two or more wives. The majority of Jews living in Christian countries were monogamous, however. The Church steadfastly demanded monogamy of its adherents, based on statements in the New Testament (Titus 1:6 and I Timothy 3:2,12) that advise all who aspire to be bishops and elders of the Church to lead exemplary lives, which includes not taking more than one wife.

The illustrious Rabbenu Gershom ben Yehudah (960–1028) of Mainz, Germany, who because of his brilliance was known as the Me'or Ha-Golah ("Light [Luminary] of the Exile [Diaspora]," sought to establish monogamy as a rule of Jewish law. His goal was to avoid conflict with the Church and to heal family problems created by polygamous marriages. About one thousand years ago, he convened an assembly of rabbis from various European countries, and they issued a ban on polygamy. Anyone who violated the ban, which became known as the *cheirem d'Rabbenu Gershom,* was excommunicated.

In time, the enactment of Rabbenu Gershom's assembly became widely accepted by all Ashkenazic communities. Sephardic Jews, who had close contact with Muslims, did not accept the ruling of Rabbenu Gershom. In his code of Jewish law, the *Mishneh Torah,* Moses Maimonides, a *Sephardi,* does not allude to this ban against polygamy.

In 1950, a rabbinic conference convened in Israel by its Chief Rabbis renewed the ban instituted by Rabbenu Gershom and proclaimed that monogamy is binding upon all Jews. Exceptions were allowed, by special application to the Chief Rabbinate, for immigrants who had come to Israel with several wives from Muslim countries. Marriages that had been contracted before these immigrants entered Israel were not nullified, but all future polygamous marriages were banned.

See Cheirem.

Prayer

In biblical times, offering of sacrifices, characterized as the "service of the altar," was the common means of reaching toward God. Later, expressions of faith and devotion to God took the form of prayer, which came to be called the "service of the heart [*avodah b'leiv*]," as detailed in the tractate *Ta'anit* (2a).

When the First Temple in Jerusalem was destroyed by the Babylonians in the year 586 B.C.E., Jews no longer had a central shrine where sacrifices could be offered. For about seventy years, until the Second Temple was built, the only form of worship was the service of the heart, the verbal service. It was at this point in Jewish history that synagogues were established in various locations.

Originally, the service of the heart consisted largely of extracts from the Bible, particularly the Book of Psalms. In later centuries, many prayers were composed by rabbis and poets, and these have become part of the liturgy as it is known today.

During the post-talmudic period, from about the sixth to the tenth century, religious leaders such as Hai Gaon and Sherira Gaon wrote and collected *piyyutim* (religious poetry), which they incorporated into the prayerbooks that they themselves composed. Many poets (*paitanim* in Hebrew) in the centuries that followed continued to write religious poetry, and these too found a place in the liturgies of particular community synagogues in various parts of the world.

Language of Prayer

The Hungarian authority Rabbi Moses Sofer (1763–1839), author of the *Chatam Sofer,* believed that it is forbidden to pray in any language other than Hebrew and that it is better to recite prayers in Hebrew rather than one's vernacular even if the meaning of the prayers is not understood. Rabbi Sofer's uncompromising attitude, which is certainly not typical of rabbinic scholars, was undoubtedly dictated by his strong opposition to Reform Judaism, which had begun to take root in Europe and introduced prayers in the vernacular.

The classic rabbinic view, to which almost all authorities subscribe, was best expressed by the renowned Spanish authority Solomon ibn Adret (1235–1310), who wrote that it does not matter if one is ignorant and cannot even pronounce the Hebrew words correctly; prayers are heard as long as one recites them with sincerity. Much earlier, the Talmud (*Berakhot* 13a) expressed the same view:

> The *Shema* must be recited as it is written [in the original Hebrew]. This is the opinion of Rabbi [Judah the Prince]. The Sages, however, say that it may be recited in any language...What is the reason of the Sages? It is because the Bible uses the word *hear* in Deuteronomy 6:4 [Hear, O Israel...], implying that you can recite it in any language that you can hear and understand.

While Hebrew was the preferred language of prayer, the Rabbis of the Talmud realized that Hebrew was not familiar to all Jews. They were aware of the very large Jewish community in Alexandria, Egypt, that knew the Greek language, but little if any Hebrew. The Rabbis were also aware of the fact that the community of Jews in Babylonia, where the vernacular was Aramaic, had little knowledge of Hebrew. Even in Palestine itself Aramaic, not Hebrew, was the language of the masses. Nevertheless, poets continued to compose prayers in Hebrew, considered by all to be the holy tongue.

Public vs. Private Prayer

"The king's glory is enhanced by a multitude of people," says the Book of Proverbs (14:28). This statement has been interpreted by scholars from talmudic times onward to mean that God (the divine King) looks with favor upon congregational prayer, and that it is incumbent upon Jews to join in public worship. Rabbi Abba Benjamin, a second-century rabbi, once commented (*Berakhot* 6a): "A man's prayer is heard [by God] only in the synagogue." A century later, Rabbi Yochanan remarked: "Whenever the Holy One, Blessed be He, comes into the synagogue and does not find ten persons [a *minyan*] there, He becomes very angry."

Scholars of later centuries concurred with the view that public prayer is preferred over private prayer. In the eleventh century, Rashi said that a person is *obligated* to pray with a *minyan*. A century later, Moses Maimonides expressed a similar view when he wrote in the *Mishneh Torah*: "God always answers the prayers of a community...Therefore, one should always associate himself with the community and, wherever possible, not pray privately."

Maimonides summarized this generally accepted attitude by adding: "Even if there were sinners among them [the ten members of the *minyan*], God would not despise the prayer of the group." The thirteenth-century scholar Moses ben Nachman (Nachmanides) said that a man should seek out a *minyan* and join it in prayer whenever possible, but that he is not *obligated* to do so.

Prayerful Expressions

Symbols, gestures, and postures of all kinds have figured prominently in religious expression. Often they are as eloquent and meaningful as spoken words. Jewish literature includes many stories that make this point, one of the most poignant, attributed to the Ba'al Shem

Tov, tells of a young boy, the son of a *chasid*, who was unable to speak, and whose education had suffered as a result. When taken by his father to the synagogue on Rosh Hashanah, the boy was unable to respond "Amen" to the prayers like everyone else, so instead he blew a whistle that he carried with him. The boy's father reprimanded him, but the *rebbe* was more understanding. "Your boy's whistling is as acceptable to God as our Amens," he said to the father.

Jews were never encouraged to engage in protracted prayers. Moses received high praise for creating the shortest and most effective prayer when he used five simple words to appeal to God for the recovery of his sister, Miriam, who was suffering from leprosy (Numbers 12:13): "Please God, bring her healing." Many years later, Rabbi Meir remarked (*Berakhot* 61a): "When you pray to God let your words be few."

Genuflecting and Bowing

In Jewish worship, bending the knee and bowing as one pronounces certain benedictions and prayers has long been a sign of reverence for God. The practice was particularly popular when the Priests of Temple times officiated and performed the prescribed rites and rituals, some of which continued in post-Temple times and down to this day.

The Book of Nehemiah (8:5–6) notes that when Ezra read the Torah to the great assemblage in Jerusalem, "He opened the book in the sight of all the people. . . . And Ezra blessed the Lord, the great God. And the people answered: 'Amen, Amen.' They lifted up their hands; and they bowed their heads, and fell down before the Lord with their faces to the ground." The talmudic tractate *Berakhot* (34 a–b) discusses bowing, kneeling, and prostration.

The Mishnah (*Tamid* 7:3) recalls that during the songs sung by the Levites after the morning service in the Temple, the people in attendance prostrated themselves. This practice continued even after the Temple was demolished in 70 C.E.

Even after genuflecting by Jews was discouraged, many individuals felt it satisfying to bow and kneel during prayer. They therefore continued to do so, particularly in the privacy of their homes. The Talmud (*Berakhot* 36a) says of Rabbi Akiba that when he prayed privately, he would begin in one corner of the room, and after a series of kneelings and prostrations would end up in the opposite corner of the room. Many scholars were critical of this degree of genuflecting. Rabbi Chaninah (*Berakhot* 28a), a contemporary of Akiba, believed that if a worshipper simply bows his head, he is showing sufficient reverence.

The Rabbis (*Berakhot* 34a) generally discouraged bowing at the beginning and end of each prayer. They felt that too much bowing is an excessive display of piety.

When the Church adopted kneeling and prostration as a common mode of prayer, Jews tried to avoid such practices so as not to be accused of copying their practices (*see* Chukat Ha-Goy). The only exception was on Yom Kippur, when during the *Musaf* service an account of the ancient Temple service is read. Then the cantor and some members of the congregation kneel and prostrate themselves, as did the High Priest when he officiated.

Contemporary Prayer Postures

Today, most genuflecting and bowing centers about the *Amidah* prayer (the *Shemoneh Esrei*, or *Eighteen Benedictions*). When the first word of the opening phrase (*Barukh atah Adonai*, "Praised [blessed] be Thou, O Lord,") is recited, the knee is bent; the upper torso is bent forward when God's name is uttered.

Jews in the Sephardic community do not follow this practice; in fact, there is practically no genuflecting or bowing that takes place during their prayer service.

When preparing to recite the *Amidah*, it is customary for the worshipper to stand with feet together, as suggested by the talmudic scholar Eliezer ben Jacob, who finds precedence for this practice (*Berakhot* 10b) in the verse in Ezekiel (1:7), "And their feet were straight together."

Yechiel Michael Epstein (1829–1908), author of *Arukh Ha-Shulchan*, offers this explanation for the practice of standing with feet together when engaged in prayer:

> Gentiles join their hands in prayer, signifying that their hands are bound. We express the same idea by putting our feet together when we rise for the [*Eighteen*] *Benedictions*. This symbolizes greater humility, for with the hands bound one can still run for pleasure, but not with feet bound.

When the three words *kadosh, kadosh, kadosh* ("holy, holy, holy") are pronounced during the *Kedushah* portion of the *Amidah*, many worshippers raise themselves on their tiptoes three times, reaching ever upward, a custom based on the repetition of the word *kadosh* three times in Isaiah (6:3)· "Holy, holy, holy is the Lord of hosts; the whole earth is full of His glory." Kabbalists suggested that when reciting the triple sanctification of God's name, one should copy the movement of angels, as described in the Book of Isaiah (6:2): "And with two wings they fluttered about." The raising of one's body when saying the word "holy" symbolizes reaching toward God with one's entire being. The custom of raising oneself on one's toes when saying *kadosh* is not universal, as evidenced by the

Yiddish folksaying *Vi di shul, azoi shpringt men kadosh*, "One raises himself [or does not raise himself] at *kadosh*, in accordance with the tradition of the synagogue."

It is customary to step forward three paces when starting to recite the *Amidah* and move backward three paces when concluding it. This derives from the popular metaphor that likens God to a king. God is the King of Kings. A subject approaches a king with reverence and departs reverently; one never turns one's back on royalty.

The forward movement of the worshipper at the opening of this important prayer (after having taken a few backward steps) has been explained as being derived from the life of Abraham who, when he prayed to God to save the inhabitants of Sodom and Gomorrah (Genesis 18:23), "came forward" to pray.

Swaying While Praying

The custom of swaying (in Yiddish, *schuckln* or, in the Anglicized form, *schuckling*) while praying is explained in the *Zohar*, the "bible" of Kabbalists, written in the thirteenth century. Its author, Moses de Leon, explains the custom through a comment of Rabbi Yosei, who is reported to have asked Rabbi Abba, "Why is it that of all peoples Jews alone are in the habit of swaying the body when they study the Law?" Rabbi Abba answered: "It is proof of the excellence of their souls. The spirit of the man is the candle of the Lord [referred to in Proverbs 20:27]. The light of that candle flickers and wavers [sways] in harmony with the light of the Torah."

In his famous book *The Kuzari*, the twelfth-century Spanish poet and philosopher Yehudah Halevi offers this explanation for swaying: "It often happens that a number of people have to read from one book at the same time [since printed books were not yet available], and each of them is compelled to bend down in order to read a passage, and then must straighten himself again. This resulted in continual bending forward and moving backward [that is, swaying], the book being on the ground." The habit of swaying continued even when books became plentiful.

A third explanation for the origin of swaying is given by the fourteenth-century German-born scholar who later moved to Spain, Rabbi Jacob ben Asher (also known as Ba'al Ha-Turim). In his commentary on the passage, "When the people saw it [Moses receiving the Ten Commandments], they were moved" (Exodus 20:15). "This," he continues, "accounts for the swaying of the body during the study of the Torah, which was received with awe, trembling, and shaking." The verse in Psalms (35:10) is interpreted similarly. The verse reads: "All my bones shall say, 'Who is like unto thee, O Lord?'"

Some authorities valued the practice of swaying, contending that it is no more than the body keeping time to the rhythm of the prayer. Some, however, have objected to it and recommended that all bodily movements should be avoided during prayer, except for a gentle swaying during the recitation of God's praises. Sephardim, by and large, do not sway when they pray. The Italian talmudic scholar Azariah do Fano (1548–1620) was quite emphatic when he ruled categorically, "There should be no swaying when praying." He believed that any movement of the body during prayer interferes with one's concentration on the words being recited.

In his *Arukh Ha-Shulchan*, Rabbi Yechiel Michal Epstein quotes the coauthor of the *Shulchan Arukh*, Moses Isserles (Orach Cha'yim 48:3), as saying that if swaying during prayer helps increase a person's concentration (*kavanah*), he should do so. And if he concentrates better by remaining motionless, he should follow that procedure.

Waving and Hand Gestures

Waving hands or objects during Jewish worship is first mentioned in connection with the sacrificial system. In Leviticus 7:34 and 14:12 there is reference to the sacrifice being "waved" before the Lord. The act of waving has been interpreted as an aid in bringing the offerer of the sacrifice closer to God. Some authorities believed that waving keeps away evil spirits, as in the waving of the *lulav* on Sukkot. Others believe the waving of the palm branch in six directions during prayer (called *na'anuim*) symbolizes the acknowledgement that God is everywhere.

The use of hands is another practice associated with prayer. The Talmud (*Shabbat* 10a) mentions the fact that the scholar Rava "clasped his hands" when he prayed. The *Kohanim* (Priests) also employed their hands when they conferred the *Priestly Benediction* on the congregation. (*See* Priestly Benediction.) In a later period, outstretched hands became symbolic of the priesthood. It is common to find this representation engraved on tombstones of members of the priestly family.

Hands were used especially on Yom Kippur during the recitation of the penitential prayers, *Al Cheit* and *Ashamnu*. These *mea culpa* prayers were accompanied by striking lightly the left breast (supposedly over the heart) with the clenched right hand. Breast-beating was considered a means of reminding one of sins committed, knowingly or unknowingly, and the need for sincere penitence.

When pronouncing a blessing over the lighted candles on Friday evening, thus introducing the Sabbath as a day of peace and rest, hands are cupped and waved in circular fashion three times over the dancing flames.

The intent is to symbolically bring the holy fire into the home or, as some believe, to cast a spell on demons and keep them at bay. Demons cannot penetrate magical circles.

The Standing Position

The formal posture for the recitation of all important prayers and the observance of religious rites is the standing position. This is said to be based on the action of Job who, when notified that all his children had died, stood up to rend his garments (keri'ah) [Job 1:20]. To this day mourners stand when ker'ah is performed and the keri'ah blessing is recited.

As the synagogue service grew longer, it became difficult for congregants to stand for prolonged periods, so only the more important prayers were recited while standing. The longest prayer in the liturgy, the *Eighteen Benedictions*, is recited while standing and is therefore also called the *Amidah*, which means "standing."

There are no hard-and-fast rules as to which prayers must be said while standing. However, it is generally accepted that the *Barkhu*, *Hallel*, *Kedushah*, and in many communities all forms of *Kaddish* are sufficiently important to be recited in a formal standing posture.

Some authorities maintain that prayers in the prayerbook that are derived from the Bible and that are part of the texts students study do not have to be recited while standing because sitting is the normal position for study. This may explain why one does not have to stand while the Torah is read or the *Shema* is recited, but it does not explain why similar portions of the daily morning prayerbook, such as those from Nehemiah 9 and from Exodus 14 and 15, recited prior to the *Barkhu*, are often pronounced in a standing position.

A common practice in most Reform and Conservative congregations is for everyone to rise when reciting the first verse of the *Shema* (Deuteronomy 6:4) to attest to the importance of this selection (from the Torah), which is an expression of Israel's profession of faith. Congregants then resume their sitting posture as the balance of the prayer (Deuteronomy 6:5–9, 11:13–21; Numbers 15:37–41) is recited.

Kiddush Posture

Whether one should stand or sit when reciting the *Kiddush* on Friday nights (and holidays) has been a subject of debate. Sephardic and chasidic communities generally follow the practice established by Rabbi Isaac Luria (known as the Ari), who lived in Safed, Palestine, from 1570 until his death in 1572. He believed that one should stand during the recitation of the *Kiddush* because it is the ceremony that welcomes the Sabbath.

The Ashkenazic community follows the view of sixteenth-century Joseph Caro, author of the *Shulchan Arukh*. Although a Sephardic Jew, he ruled that when one recites the first part of the Friday night *Kiddush* (Genesis 2:1–3), he should stand, and thereafter he should sit. Moses Isserles, the Polish-born commentator, says in his Notes to the *Shulchan Arukh* that it is acceptable to stand but better to sit (Orach Cha'yim 271:10).

Silent Prayers

Congregational prayers, for the most part, are recited silently, perhaps because the Rabbis of the Talmud (*Ta'anit* 2a) considered prayer to be a "service of the heart," and God can know what goes on in a man's heart without his shouting it aloud. This view is based on the verse in the Book of Deuteronomy (11:13) that speaks of *serving* God "with all your heart and all your mind and all your soul." Serving is identified with prayer. The Rabbis support this conclusion by calling attention to the conduct of Hannah, mother of Samuel, who when praying for the birth of a child, "spoke in her heart.... Only her lips moved, but her voice could not be heard" (I Samuel 1:13).

In the Talmud (Mishnah *Berakhot* 3:3 and 4:3), the *Tefillah*, literally meaning "prayer" (also known as the *Amidah*), was recited silently, as were all prayers. The Talmud (*Berakhot* 24b) notes: "He who recites the *Tefillah* so it can be heard [by others] is a person of small faith." The implication is that such a person believes that God will be unable to hear his prayer unless it is recited aloud. Rabbi Huna qualifies this statement by saying that the talmudic statement applies particularly to public, not private prayer, explaining that when one prays aloud in the midst of a congregation he may disturb the concentration of other congregants.

Another reason why prayers are recited silently may be traced to the sin-offering that was brought in Second Temple times. The individual bringing the sacrifice would deliver it to the Priest, and it would be offered on the same side of the altar as all other sacrifices, the side not fully visible to the public. None of the onlookers was able to detect whether the Priest was offering up a sin-offering or one that was brought by an individual who had come to the Temple with an offering of thanksgiving.

This probably led Rabbi Yochanan to ask rhetorically (*Sotah* 32b): "Why was the rule instituted that the *Tefillah* should be recited silently?" His answer: "So as to avoid putting anyone to shame." It was customary for sinners to confess their sins in the course of prayer, and if prayers as a rule were recited aloud, all would hear their confessions. To avoid embarrassment, all prayers were recited silently. The practice today, particularly in congregations that follow the Sephardic rite, is to recite most prayers aloud, along with the cantor.

The Direction of Prayer

The direction one is to face when praying was of concern to the Rabbis of the Talmud. They based their decision on the action of Daniel, of whom it was said (Daniel 6:11) that when he prayed he stood before windows facing Jerusalem. Thus, the Rabbis established the following formula (*Berakhot* 30a): "If one is in the east [of Palestine], he should turn his face to the west; if in the west [of Palestine], he should turn his face to the east; if in the south, he should turn his face to the north; if in the north, he should turn his face to the south. In this way all Israel will be turning their hearts toward one place."

The Temples of Jerusalem were central in Jewish life for about one thousand years, and their practices continued to influence Jewish life for two thousand years following their destruction. As a token of respect, to this day Jews turn in prayer toward Jerusalem. In the Western world, the ark is erected on the eastern wall of synagogues so the congregation will be facing east as it prays. In Eastern countries the architecture is reversed. In Israel proper today, congregants in the Galilee face south, while those in southern Israel face north. In Jerusalem itself, worshippers face the Temple Mount, the site of the ancient Temples.

Priesthood

The Book of Genesis (35:23) records that Jacob had twelve sons, Levi, the son of Jacob and Leah, being the third son born to them.

Levi had three sons: Gershon, Kohath, and

Merari (Exodus 6:16). Kohath had four sons: Amram, Yitzhar, Chevron, and Uziel.

Amram married Yokheved, his father's sister, and she bore him Aaron, Moses, and Miriam.

Aaron and his sons were designated by God (Exodus 29:44) "to serve Me as Priests." They were ordained as Priests (*Kohanim*) in a ceremony that lasted seven days, during which they offered sacrifices to purify themselves from sin and consecrate the altar to the service of God.

Before long, two of Aaron's sons, Nadav and Avihu, violated their vows and offered "strange" offerings on the altar, for which they met an untimely death (Leviticus 16:1ff.). This left Kohath and Merari, Aaron's remaining two sons, and their descendants as Priests eligible to perform the rituals in the Tabernacle in the desert and later in the Jerusalem Temples. Since in time Kohath and his descendants distinguished themselves by performing efficiently and loyally, it was from this family, particularly from the clan of Zadok, that all the High Priests were chosen (Ezekiel 44:15ff.).

All the other members of the tribe of Levi—Levites, as they are formally called (*Levi'im* in Hebrew)—assisted the Priests and performed many sacred tasks including offering sacrifices on the altar, transporting the Holy Ark that housed the Ten Commandments (Numbers 1:49), and purifying the Priests by pouring water on their hands each day before the Priests blessed the people. (*See* Priestly Benediction.)

The High Priest

The most senior of all Priests at any given time was designated as High Priest (*Kohen Gadol*). Scripture (Leviticus 21:10) refers to him as *Ha-Kohen ha-mashu'ach*, "the anointed Priest," because oil had been poured on his head to consecrate him to the service of God. It was mandated (Leviticus 8:6–9) that he wear four special garments in addition to the four ordinary ones Priests were required to wear. The High Priest was required to keep his head covered, not to tear his garments when in mourning, not to allow himself to become profaned (*tamei*) by being in the proximity of a dead person (even his mother or father), and to marry a woman who is a virgin, which excludes divorcées.

The High Priest alone could perform the special *Avodah* service on Yom Kippur, and during the rest of the year he could perform any service he chose, without waiting for his turn, as was required of ordinary Priests. He was required to bring a special meal-offering, called *chavitin*, twice each day, and unlike other Priests he was permitted to serve on the day of death of a close relative.

One *Kohen* was designated as the High Priest's deputy (*segan*), and he took on the duties of High Priest should the High Priest be unable to carry out his duties for any reason.

Purity of Ordinary Priests

The Book of Leviticus (21:6–7) emphasizes that Priests are expected to be in a constant state of holiness since they tend the sanctuary and offer sacrifices to God. Special laws were enacted to ensure that the Priests would always be in a state of ritual purity and thus ready to perform their priestly duties. The principle proscription in this regard was that a *Kohen* not come into contact or be in the proximity of a corpse.

The Bible emphasizes (Numbers 19:11) that all Israelites become ritually impure (*tamei* in Hebrew) if they touch a corpse, whether the deceased is a Jew or a non-Jew. A *Kohen*, however, had special responsibilities and must therefore conform to a higher standard. The Priest becomes ritually impure not only upon touching a corpse but even when entering an enclosure (*ohel* in Hebrew) containing a Jewish corpse. When out of doors the *Kohen* is required to stay a minimum of six feet from a Jewish corpse.

A *Kohen* may attend the funeral of a non-Jew and may visit a non-Jewish cemetery. He may not, however, attend the funeral of a Jew when it is held in an enclosed area, such as a chapel, unless the deceased is a member of his immediate family: mother, father, son, daughter, brother, unmarried sister, and wife. The first six are mandated in Leviticus 21:2, the seventh by a ruling of the Rabbis of the Talmud (*Yevamot* 22b).

A traditional rabbi who is a *Kohen* may not officiate at a funeral held in any enclosed area. If he wishes to be present at the funeral, he must wait outside the building. The rabbi-*Kohen* may visit a cemetery because it is not in an enclosure, but he must distance himself at least six feet from all graves.

Non-Orthodox rabbis who are *Kohanim* do not by and large follow these proscriptions because they believe that the laws of ritual purity and impurity were applicable to Priests only so long as there was hope that the Temple and the sacrificial system might be restored.

In order to satisfy the most strict view relating to the maintenance of the purity of Priests, Hadassah Hospital in Jerusalem has installed double doors to different sections of the building, one of which is always closed when the other is opened. Thus, a *Kohen* is able to visit the sick because the area he is visiting is cut off from the rest of the structure.

El Al, the Israeli airline, has made special efforts to satisfy the sensitivity of the most right-wing members of the Orthodox rabbinate. Coffins containing corpses destined for burial in Israel are transported in special cardboard containers. About three and one-half inches of airspace are left on all sides of the coffin, thus establishing it as a distinctly separate "room" in the cargo hold and thereby allowing members of a priestly family to fly on the same plane.

Priestly Marriages

So as to maintain the purity of priestly families, precise laws pertaining to marriage were instituted. The Bible considers it improper for a Priest to marry a divorced woman or a woman who has converted to Judaism: "They [Priests] shall not marry a woman defiled by harlotry; nor shall they take a divorced woman, for they are holy unto their God" (Leviticus 21:7–8).

To the Rabbis of the Talmud the word "harlot" meant not only "prostitute" but any woman who was tainted for any reason. And since the proselytes in early times came from heathen stock, whose morality was not on a par with the Jewish standard, they were considered tainted. The same reasoning forbids a Priest from marrying a divorcee. The Rabbis felt that a divorced woman is blemished and therefore unsuited to be the wife of a Priest.

Today, only the Orthodox community continues to follow the above rulings. The position of the Rabbinical Assembly (Conservative) is that Priests are generally of uncertain genealogy (*see* Priests by Presumption), and the traditional rulings have lost their validity. They also argue that it is unfair and even embarrassing to admit a proselyte to the Jewish fold and then deny her the right to marry a *Kohen* because of a regulation that may have had validity when the Temple existed but no longer applies. The reestablishment of the Temple, they say, is not anticipated. The Reform and Reconstructionist rabbinate share the Conservative view.

Priestly Privileges and Responsibilities

A *Kohen* is awarded the first Torah honor (*aliyah*) whenever the Torah is read in public (*Moed Katan* 28b). This tradition developed because according to the Bible (Deuteronomy 3:19) the Priests were the first to receive the Torah: "And Moses wrote down the Law and handed it to the Priests. . . ." Reform Judaism does not assign to *Kohanim* higher status than other Jews, and the first *aliyah* is assigned to any member of the congregation.

A Priest is to be given the honor of leading *Grace After Meals* whenever three or more persons have eaten together. He also officiates at the *pidyon ha-ben*, the redemption ceremony of the firstborn male child of a mother. Some authorities are of the opinion that since a *Kohen's* ancestry is probably uncertain, the five silver dollars (*shekalim*) the father gives the Priest should not be kept but returned to the father (Yoreh Dei'ah 305:8 and 306).

The *Kohen* is also privileged to confer a blessing upon the congregation at Sabbath, holiday, and daily services.

Priestly Benediction

In Temple times, Priests (*Kohanim*) would mount a platform (*dukhan* in Hebrew) several times each day and, using the words commanded in the Bible (Numbers 6:24–26), bless the people:

> May the Lord bless thee and keep thee.
> May the Lord cause His countenance
> to shine upon thee and be gracious unto
>   thee.
> May the Lord lift His countenance toward
>   thee and grant thee peace.

This threefold blessing, which is popularly known by its Hebrew name *Birkat Kohanim* (literally, "Blessing of the Priests"), was pronounced daily in the Jerusalem Temples and, later, after the Temples were destroyed, continued to be recited by Priests as part of the synagogue morning prayer service.

The Ceremony

The ceremony during which the *Priestly Benediction* is pronounced is popularly known by the Anglicized term *dukhening*, which is derived from the Hebrew *dukhan*. Most Orthodox congregations *dukhen* (verb form) only on the more important holidays in the Jewish calendar—Rosh Hashanah, Yom Kippur, Passover, Sukkot, Shavuot—when the congregation is generally larger and more spiritually attuned. Non-Orthodox congregations in the Diaspora have discontinued the practice completely, arguing that the genealogy of Priests is no longer certain.

In Israel, communities follow various procedures. In Jerusalem, Bnei Brak, Tel Aviv, and in the southern section of Haifa, the *Birkat Kohanim* is pronounced at the morning service each day. In the rest of Haifa, Safed, and the Galilee, it is generally recited only on Sabbaths and holidays. Most Sephardic congregations in the Diaspora follow this latter procedure.

In the Bible, the removing of shoes is associated with holiness. When approaching the burning bush, Moses is commanded (Exodus 3:5): "Remove your shoes, for the place on which you stand is holy ground." From this evolved a law requiring Priests to perform their Temple duties barefooted. Today, when Priests ascend the pulpit to confer the *Priestly Benediction* upon the congregation, they do so without footwear.

While pronouncing the *Priestly Benediction*, the Priest assumes a posture known as *nesi'at kapa'yim* ("raising of the hands"). He stretches both arms and hands forward, extending the fingers straight ahead and separating the little finger and ring finger of each hand from the other fingers, forming a V shape.

The thumb of each hand is separated from the index finger so that the formation of each hand looks like the Hebrew letter *shin*, the first letter of *Shaddai*, the name of God. Although the custom of spreading the fingers is not mentioned in the Talmud, it is referred to in Midrash *Rabbah*, which comments on verse 2:9 of the Song of Songs: "My beloved [Israel] is like a gazelle or a young deer who stands behind our wall and looks in through the windows; he peers through the latticework." The Rabbis of the Talmud believed this to be an allusion to the Priest as he blessed the people: the "windows" represent the Priest's shoulders and arms, the "latticework" his fingers.

In a later period, outstretched hands became symbolic of the priesthood. It is common to find this representation engraved on tombstones of members of the priestly family.

Talmudic law forbids members of a congregation to look at the Priests when they are pronouncing the *Priestly Benediction*. The tractate *Chagigah* (16b) cautions: "One's eyes will grow weak if he gazes upon the hands of a *Kohen* when he is performing."

The actual origin of the ban against gazing upon Priests as they *duchen* may be found in the Bible, where the Levites are cautioned to avoid witnessing the dismantling of the Tabernacle in the wilderness in preparation for its being carried to the next station. Aaron the High Priest and his sons were assigned the major task of covering the holy vessels. The Levites did the transporting, and they were forbidden to gaze upon any of the holy objects as they were being covered, "lest they die" (Numbers 4:17–20).

The *Kohanim*, too, are cautioned not to tempt the congregation to look at them while they are pronouncing the benediction. The Mishnah (*Megillah* 4:7) explains that Priests with soiled hands (many of them were dyers of fabric) will arouse the curiosity of congregants, who will look at them and thus violate the law. The Talmud (*Megillah* 24b) notes that Joshua ben Levi stated that if the hands of a Priest are spotted or deformed by being curved inward or bent sideways, that individual should not bless the people. Traditionally, the hands of the Priests are washed by Levites before they mount the pulpit to *dukhen*.

The *Shulchan Arukh* (Orach Cha'yim 128:30–31) states that when performing the *Priestly Benediction*, the *Kohen* covers his face and hands with his *tallit* so that no physical blemish can be seen. In Sephardic congregations, it is not uncommon for a father who is not a *Kohen* to drape his *tallit* over the head of a son (or sons) regardless of age while the *Birkat Kohanim* ceremony is being performed. The reason may be to remove the temptation to gaze.

Today, rabbis who are not *Kohanim* often pronounce the *Priestly Benediction* upon a bar or bat mitzvah, upon a couple under the marriage canopy, and also as the concluding benediction at a religious service.

Priests by Presumption

The concept known in Hebrew as *safek Kohen* ("Priest by presumption") dates back to early talmudic times. Maimonides notes that Priests (*Kohanim*) who claimed the right of officiating in the Temple were subjected to vigorous scrutiny. He points out in his *Mishneh Torah* (*Beit Ha-Mikdash* 6:11) that it was the duty of the High Court (*Beit Din Ha-Gadol*) to investigate the genealogy of all claiming to be Priests and to deny priestly privileges to those whose genealogy was not adequately proven or who were afflicted with some sort of physical blemish or disability that would render them unfit. Those who were excluded from priestly service because their genealogy could not be substantiated had to leave the Temple precincts dressed in black, while those whose ancestry could be authenticated robed themselves in white.

Since it became more and more difficult with the passage of time for a Priest to prove that he is a descendant of the family of Aaron of the tribe of Levi, many celebrated scholars considered all Priests to be Priests by Presumption.

Rabbi Jacob Emden, an outstanding eighteenth-century scholar (known as Yavetz), pointed out that the reason why a *Kohen* who officiates at a *pidyon ha-ben* usually returns the five silver dollars (*shekalim*) that he receives from the father of the child being redeemed is because he is only a Priest by Presumption.

The nineteenth-century Hungarian rabbi Yehudah Aszod stated categorically in his volume *Yehudah Ya'aleh* that "*Kohanim* nowadays should be considered as being of doubtful lineage," and he therefore allowed a marriage between a *Kohen* and a *chalutzah*, which was prohibited by rabbinic law.

For the same reason, some authorities within the Orthodox community do not consider it a violation of biblical or talmudic law if a *Kohen* wishes to study medicine, even though doing so would demand his being in proximity of a corpse. They feel that inasmuch as a Priest today is only one by presumption and inasmuch as doctors save lives—the greatest of all *mitzvot*—a *Kohen* should be permitted to study medicine.

There are, however, Orthodox authorities who have vehemently rejected this position. Rabbi Yekutiel Greenwald and Rabbi Moshe Feinstein forbid a *Kohen* from entering the medical profession. They consider the laws of Levitical purity to be as fully in effect today as they were in Temple times. Rabbi Greenwald berated Rabbi Bernard Revel, first president of Yeshiva University, for holding a liberal view in this matter.

According to a *Hadassah Magazine* article (January 2001) by Nadine Epstein, recent research by Karl Skorechi of Haifa, Michael Hammer of Tucson, Arizona, and several London scientists points to a priestly line of Jewish males. The researchers studied the Y chromosome pattern, which passes unchanged from father to son, and distinctive genetic markers on the chromosomes. They determined that half of the Ashkenazic and Sephardic men claiming to be *Kohanim* have the same markers. Their conclusion was that there is a likely possibility that all these men were descendants of a single male *Kohen* or of a group of *Kohanim*.

Persons with surnames such as Cohen, Kane, Kohn, Kahn, Kahan, and Kagan are generally presumed to be of priestly lineage. Persons named Katz or its derivatives, an acronym for *Kohen Tzedek* ("Righteous Priest"), are likewise presumed to be of priestly descent.

See Pidyon Ha-Ben.

Privacy

The right to absolute privacy is rooted in Scripture. The Book of Proverbs (11:13) considers anyone who divulges another person's secrets to be a scoundrel. The Talmud (*Yoma* 4b) emphasizes that "when one reveals something to a second person, the second person has no right to divulge it to a third party without the first party's consent. Rabbenu Gershom, at the end of the tenth century, declared a ban (*cheirem*) on anyone guilty of reading another person's correspondence in order to steal trade secrets. In his *Halakhot Ketanot* (vol. 1, no. 276), the seventeenth-century Palestinian scholar Jacob Hagiz (1620–1674) reminded his flock that "it is forbidden to search out the secrets of one's fellow."

Jewish law considers a man's home his castle and cautions against invading his privacy. This is based on the biblical injunction (Deuteronomy 24:10–11), "When you make a loan of any kind to your countryman, you may not enter his house to seize his pledge [collateral]. You must remain outside, while the man to whom you made the loan brings the pledge out to you."

So careful were the early talmudic scholars about the individual's right to complete privacy, that they ruled (Mishnah *Bava Batra* 3:7) that "no one may build an entrance to his house that faces the entrance of another house...nor may a window be installed facing the window of a neighboring house." One's right to full privacy was codified as law in Maimonides' *Mishneh Torah* (Hilkhot Shekhaynim [5:6]).

The Rabbis of the Talmud (*Sukkah* 49b) distinguished between actions that take place *be-farhesya* (from a Greek word meaning "in public") and those that take place in the privacy of one's home. Joseph Caro, in his *Code of Jewish Law* (*Shulchan Arukh*, Orach Cha'yim 385:3), equates a person who desecrates the Sabbath *be-farhesya* as an atheist and an idolator, but not so one who violates the Sabbath in private. What happens in the privacy of one's home, he believed, was not of public concern. In the talmudic tractate *Sanhedrin* (74b), Rabbi Jacob, quoting Rabbi Yochanan, defined "public" as "a place where a minimum of ten people [a *minyan*] may freely assemble."

Profanation of God's Name

Better known by the Hebrew expression *chillul Ha-Shem*, this concept refers to any action that puts God in a bad light, thus desecrating His name. It is the opposite of *kiddush Ha-Shem*.

God is said to be put in a bad light when a Jew acts dishonorably, for these actions reflect negatively on the entire Jewish people. Since Jews are spoken of as God's Chosen People, poor conduct ultimately reflects poorly on God, who chose Israel and expects from his people the highest standard of moral conduct.

Among the offenses considered demeaning to God is acting dishonestly in one's dealings with non-Jews. The Rabbis (Tosefta on *Bava Kama* 10:15) stated very explicitly: "Stealing from a non-Jew is worse than stealing from a Jew, because it represents the desecration of God's name."

The Rabbis of the Talmud (*Gittin* 88b; *Shulchan Arukh*, Choshen Mishpat 26:1) considered Jews who bring their disputes into non-Jewish secular courts rather than a Jewish court (*Beit Din*) as "wicked people."

The practice of polygamy among Jews was permitted up until the eleventh century, when Rabbi Gershom Ha-Golah of Germany declared the practice to be a *chillul Ha-Shem* and thus forbidden. Continuing polygamy, he said, would make Jews appear immoral in the eyes of their Christian neighbors who had already banned the practice.

See Kiddush Ha-Shem.

Promises

The Torah regards promises made to be of supreme sanctity. When one makes a vow to God, says the Book of Deuteronomy (23:22), it is not to be taken lightly: *motza sefatekha tishmor*, "Guard the utterance of your lips." Here, the Bible speaks of a *neder*, a "vow," which may be either a promise to bring a sacrifice to the Temple or a promise to abstain from an activity, such as eating certain foods for a period of time.

The Book of Numbers (30:3) says: "If a man makes a vow [*neder*] to the Lord to take an oath [the term *shevuah* is used] imposing an obligation on himself, he shall not break his promise. He must carry out all that has crossed his lips."

A Promise Fulfilled

The Bible abounds in examples of oaths and vows and the consequences thereof. One of the most famous examples involves the warrior-judge Jephthah.

In the Book of Judges (11:30ff.), Jephthah, as he undertakes to lead an Israelite army in battle in their effort to conquer the Promised Land, swears that should his mission to defeat the Ammonites turn out to be successful, when he returns from the war he will consecrate to God the first thing that comes forth out of his house. Jephthah returns home victoriously and finds that it is his daughter whom he must sacrifice. He fulfills his promise, exclaiming, "I have opened my mouth unto the Lord, and I cannot go back [on my promise]."

False Promises

The Bible (Deuteronomy 6:13) instructs man to "revere only the Lord, your God, and worship him alone, and swear only by his Name." However, this biblical license to swear was later discouraged by the Rabbis of the Talmud, concerned that untrustworthy individuals would invoke the name of God in vain.

In the talmudic tractate *Bava Metzia* (49a), Rabbi Yosei ben Yehudah stresses: "Let your 'yes' be an honest 'yes' and let your 'no' be an honest 'no.'" To which Abbayei added, "This means one should not say one thing with his mouth and mean otherwise in his heart."

Methods of Absolution

Acknowledging that people frequently did invoke the name of God in vain, the Rabbis introduced a procedure for nullification of vows. The procedure, *hatarat nedarim*, "absolution of vows," is undertaken before a *Beit Din*, a court of law consisting of three men learned in Jewish law. After listening to a person's expression of regret, the court is empowered to confer absolution.

The best known exercise of the absolution rite is what transpires at the *Kol Nidrei* service in Yom Kippur. To constitute a court, two learned elders of the congregation are flanked by the cantor as he intones the *Kol Nidrei* prayer three times, declaring, "All vows and oaths we take, all promises and obligations we make to God between this Yom Kippur and the next we hereby publicly retract and declare our expectation to be absolved of them." It is generally understood that this ceremony nullifies only promises made to God. Anyone who has made unfulfilled promises to his fellow man must be excused by addressing the person directly involved.

Biblical Symbolism

The sacredness of the promise was marked early on in biblical history by a symbolic act that accompanied the affirmation of the vow. In the Book of Genesis (24:2ff.), when Abraham sends his servant on the important mission of finding a wife for his son Isaac, he says to him: "Put your hand *under my thigh* and I will make you swear by the Lord, the God of heaven and the God of earth, that you will not take a wife for my son from the daughters of the Canaanites..."

Rashi, the eleventh-century French Bible commentator, notes (*Shevuot* 38b) that in talmudic times it was customary for one making a sacred promise to take hold of a holy object, such as a Torah scroll or *tefillin*, on which are inscribed passages from the Torah. In earlier times, a man's genitals, which are located under his thigh, were considered his most precious possession. It is through the penis that must be circumcised that he is able to fulfill the commandment *pru u-revu*, "be fruitful and multiply" (Genesis 1:22). Abraham therefore selected his male organ as the object upon which his servant was to take the oath. Interestingly, the Middle English word *testimonium* (testimony) is derived from the Latin literally meaning "testes."

Kabbalists have suggested that when taking an oath, a Jew should hold a copy of the *Zohar*, a book considered so holy that anyone who touches it and swears falsely will die within a few days. This view was not accepted by mainstream Judaism.

A Folk Expression

So deeply ingrained in the consciousness of the Jew was the prohibition against employing God's name indiscriminately that it was common practice for a religious person to preface even the most innocent promises with the words *b'li neder* (or *b'lo neder*), meaning "without promising." Thus, the individual was nullifying his promise in advance, just in case he should be unable to fulfill it for whatever reason.

Prophets and Prophecy

The prophet, in the Jewish tradition, was an unusually gifted and sensitive person selected by God to instruct the Jews on how to follow the right path. Despite the casual reference to Abraham as a prophet (*navi*) in Genesis (20:7), and assertions in the Koran and elsewhere that Abraham was the first prophet, this is contrary to mainstream Jewish thought.

One of the basic principles of Judaism as enunciated by Moses Maimonides in his *Mishneh Torah* (Yesodei Ha-Torah 7:6) is that it was Moses who was the father of all Jewish prophets. Maimonides' view is based on one of the closing verses of the Pentateuch (Deuteronomy 34:10): "Never has there arisen in Israel a prophet like Moses..." And in his monumental work *Religion of Israel*, the prominent Israeli Bible scholar Yechezkel Kaufmann states categorically: "No patriarch is charged with a prophetic mission; the first apostolic prophet is Moses."

The Talmud and Midrash affirm this high regard in which Moses is held, sparing no effort to dramatize his life. In the Talmud (*Sotah* 12a), Rabbi Nehemiah said that when Moses was born and his mother saw "that he was good [*ki tov*]" (Exodus 2:2), she foresaw that he would be worthy of the prophetic gift. Others claim that when he was born, the house was filled with light, a sign that he was close to God, as the Bible (Genesis 1:4) says, "And God saw the light that it was good [*ki tov*]." The Midrash (*Leviticus Rabbah* 6:6) reinforces this view, adding: "Compared to Moses, all the prophets were like the moon compared to the sun."

As added proof of the attributes of goodness and perfection that were associated with baby Moses, some Sages maintained that Moses was born circumcised (*mahul*).

Other Sages of the Talmud were more circumspect in asserting the qualities and characteristics expected to be associated with a prophet. They say (*Shabbat* 92a and *Nedarim* 38a): "The prophetic spirit does not rest upon a person unless he is wise, strong, rich, and tall."

The medieval Spanish philosopher Joseph Albo (*c.*1380–*c.* 1435), in his work *Sefer Ha-Ikarim* (*Book of Root-Principles*), explains that the attribute of a tall stature was expected to be found in a prophet because it is a quality people admire and respect. He adds: "If a person does not have all these qualities, there is no point imbuing him with the prophetic spirit."

The Rabbis of the Talmud taught (*Megillah* 14a) that there were forty-eight male prophets in Jewish history. Most of these—Samuel, Isaiah, Jeremiah, Ezekiel, Hosea, Joel, Amos, Ovadiah, Jonah, Mikhah, Nahum, Habakkuk, Zephaniah, Haggai, Zekhariah, and Malakhi—are well known because they left books bearing their names. Nonetheless, prophets such as Elijah, Nathan, and Elishah—for whom no book carries their name—also figure prominently in Jewish history. Additionally, the Sages added seven women—Sarah, Miriam, Deborah, Hannah, Abigail, Huldah, and Esther—to the list of prophets.

The Rabbis of the Talmud considered an individual a true prophet only if he or she "neither detracted nor added to any law written in the Torah," nor set him- or herself above the law.

With the destruction of the Second Temple in 70 C.E., Rabbi Yochanan asserted (*Bava Batra* 12b): "Prophecy was taken from the [true] prophet and was placed in the possession of fools and children." His view was borne out by the many false prophets who have appeared on the scene over the last two millennia and heaped catastrophe on the Jews in many communities. These were the pseudo-Messiahs such as the seventeenth-century Shabbetai Tzevi, of Smyrna, Turkey, who claimed to carry a special mission from God. All of his prognostications turned out to be false, and according to Deuteronomy (18:21–22) a "prophet" whose words fail to materialize is a false prophet.

Prosbul

Although Jewish tradition asserts that the laws of the Torah are eternal and immutable, economic and social conditions forced the Sages to make changes, sometimes radical ones, in the law.

One such radical change was made in connection with the law of the sabbatical year (*shemittah* in Hebrew). The Bible (Deuteronomy 15:1–3) demands that every seventh year all debts be cancelled. This law was especially hard on poor people who would not be able to obtain loans when the *shemittah* year was approaching. Lenders would certainly not want to lend money if they were not to be repaid.

This law of the sabbatical year was so oppressive that Hillel, the leading scholar of the first century B.C.E., issued a ruling (*takanah*) that became known by its Greek name, *prosbul*. A *prosbul* was a declaration made in court at the time of the execution of a loan. Its terms made it clear that the law of *shemittah*, which ordinarily cancelled loans, would not apply to the specific loan being transacted (Mishnah *Shevi'it* 10:3ff. and *Gittin* 37a).

The court, in effect, guaranteed that it would collect the debt for the lender. This circumvention of biblical law was justified on the basis that it was done *mipnei tikkun ha-olam*, that is, to improve the human condition. The *prosbul* protected the rich against monetary loss and helped the poor by enabling them to secure loans.

The prominent second/third-century scholar Rav (also known as Abba Arikha) took exception to the concept of *prosbul*, declaring that if he had the power, he would have done away with this innovation of Hillel (*Gittin* 36b). Other talmudic authorities, such as the fourth-century scholar Abbayei, were of the opinion that during the period of the Second Temple the law of the sabbatical year was generally no longer in effect.

The *prosbul* enactment is still in effect today. In 1994, a *Beit Din* consisting of three scholars from Yeshiva University granted a *prosbul* to United Mizrahi Bank and Trust Company (UMB), permitting them to collect unpaid bills in a *shemittah* year.

See Shemittah; Tikkun Olam.

Pseudepigrapha

At about the same time that the books of the Apocrypha were being composed (between 200 and 100 B.C.E.), a variety of texts on diverse subjects was being written, but these were not incorporated into the Apocryphal canon. The authorship of some of these works—all of which were classified as Pseudepigrapha ("false writing")—was ascribed to biblical heroes such as Adam, Enokh, Abraham, Moses, Solomon, Isaiah, Daniel, and Ezra. The authorship of others was illusory. The Pseudepigrapha generally deals with the suffering of the Jewish people and their quest for salvation through supernatural means.

How many works can be characterized as pseudepigraphous is open to conjecture, ranging from seventeen to thirty-three or more. Among the best known of these works, which were written in Hebrew or Aramaic and were later translated into Greek, are *The Testaments of the Twelve Patriarchs*, in which the twelve sons of Jacob, mentioned in Genesis 49 and Deuteronomy 33, expand upon their life experiences, and *The Book of Jubilees*, which is an enlarged *midrash* ("commentary") on Genesis 1:1 to Exodus 12:47.

See Apocrypha.

Purim

The fifth-century B.C.E. events that led to the minor Jewish holiday of Purim are recounted in the biblical Book of Esther, also known as the Scroll of Esther or, in Hebrew, as *Megillat Esther*. The scroll is sometimes referred to simply as the Megillah. The name Purim, the Book of Esther explains, derives from the word *pur* (plural, *purim*), meaning "lots"—a reference to the lots drawn by Haman, prime minister of King Ahasueros of Persia, to determine the date on which he would exterminate the Jews of that country. The thirteenth of the Hebrew month Adar was chosen as the day on which the massacre would take place.

Haman's plans were foiled by beautiful Queen Esther and her cousin, Mordekhai. Risking her own life, Esther pleaded before the king for her people, and Haman's order was rescinded. Instead of the Jews of Persia being slaughtered, Haman and his ten sons were hung on the gallows that had been prepared for Mordekhai. Thus, those days of doom were turned "from sorrow to gladness," days to be commemorated by "sending gifts [*mishlo'ach manot*] one to another and presents to the poor (*matanot le-evyonim*)" (Esther 9:22). According to one tradition, two gifts should be sent to a friend, and charity should be given to two poor people.

Shushan Purim

The Book of Esther proclaims the fourteenth day of Adar (usually during the month of March) as a day of celebration. However, in Shushan, the capital of Persia, the Jews did not finish ridding themselves of their enemy until the following day, and so they celebrated Purim on the fifteenth of Adar instead.

Because Shushan was a walled city, it became a rule (Mishnah *Megillah* 1:1) that communities in all walled cities, from the time of Joshua onward, should celebrate the holiday on the fifteenth, which came to be known as Shushan Purim. To this day, Jerusalem, a walled city since early times, observes Purim on the fifteenth, while in other parts of Israel the holiday is celebrated on the fourteenth.

Shabbat Zakhor

The Sabbath immediately before Purim, which is the second of four special Sabbaths that precede the Passover holiday, is called Shabbat Zakhor, "Sabbath of Remembrance." The *maftir*, which is read from a second scroll on that day, begins with the Hebrew word *zakhor* ("Remember what Amalek did to you when you came out of Egypt"). It describes how the Amalekites savagely attacked the weary Children of Israel as they began their trek through the desert toward the Promised Land after leaving Egypt. Because of this, Israel was commanded to always remember (*zakhor*) that occurrence and "to blot out the memory of Amalek from under heaven," a nation representing all the enemies of the Jewish people, who brazenly attacked the Israelites, even after viewing God's miraculous destruction of Egypt.

Ta'anit Esther

The day before Purim, the thirteenth day of Adar, is called Ta'anit Esther, the Fast of Esther, for it was on that day that the Jews of Persia fasted to lend support to Queen Esther, who displayed great courage by approaching King Ahasueros without prior permission, an act punishable by death.

Mordekhai's Day

Purim was once called Mordekhai's Day, and some scholars believe it was merged at some point with another holiday called Nicanor's Day, which in the ancient Jewish calendar preceded Purim by one day. It celebrated the Hasmonean victory over an invader who was intent on desecrating the Jerusalem Temple. Later, Nicanor's Day was associated with

Chanukkah and the Syrian-Greek attempt to subjugate the Jewish nation. Nicanor (died 161 B.C.E.), a general who commanded the Syrian forces of Antiochus IV, was sent to subdue the insurrection of the Hasmoneans. He was killed by Judah the Maccabee on Adar 13, and that date was commemorated as Nicanor's Day.

Celebrating Purim

The major religious rite observed on Purim is the reading of the Megillah in the synagogue on Purim night and again the following morning. The Megillah, which tells the story of the holiday in great detail, is unrolled as it is read and then folded in sections to simulate a "letter," since the Book of Esther was originally sent out as a letter in scroll form to Jews throughout the Persian Empire (Esther 9:26). Each time the name of Haman is mentioned during the Megillah reading in the synagogue, members of the congregation customarily stamp their feet, clap their hands, twirl noisemakers (*groggers*), or slap or beat whatever object is handy. By such action, congregants express a desire to "erase" the wicked Haman's name. Exodus 17:14 says, "For I will utterly erase the remembrance of Amalek from under the heavens." Haman was believed to be a descendant of Amalek.

The Grogger

It is believed that using the *grogger*, a word of Yiddish derivation, as a noisemaker originated in the thirteenth century, and Ashkenazim have continued the practice throughout the centuries. However, when Sephardic Jews from Spain and Portugal settled in Holland at the end of the fifteenth century, they ceased using *groggers* so as not to attract the attention of the Christian population. Today, at New York City's Spanish and Portuguese Synagogue, it is customary to follow the subdued practice of stomping the feet rather than using a noise-maker when Haman's name is pronounced during the reading of the *Megillah*.

Purim Delicacies

An interesting variety of delicacies is prepared for Purim. One authority, Kalonymos ben Kalonymos, in his book *Massekhet Purim*, lists twenty-seven different meat dishes. Most popular of all delicacies eaten on the holiday are the triangular-shaped pastries known as *hamantaschen*, a German word meaning "Haman's pockets." *Hamantaschen* are traditionally filled with fruit, cheese, or a poppy seed mixture.

One explanation for the name of these most popular of all Purim delicacies is that Haman stuffed his pockets with bribe money. Originally, *hamantaschen* were called *mohn taschen*, "poppy seed pockets," a reference to the poppy seed filling commonly used. Poppy seeds became the filling of choice, for *mohn* (manna) sounds like the Hebrew pronunciation of the second syllable of the name Haman.

The three-cornered *hamantasch* pastries are also said to be eaten on Purim as a reminder of the type of hat worn by Haman when he was second-in-command to the king of Persia. A more traditional explanation is that the courage of Queen Esther was derived from her antecedents, and the three-cornered *hamantasch* represents the three patriarchs—Abraham, Isaac and Jacob—the founders of the Jewish people.

Hamantaschen are also called *oznei Haman* ("Haman's ears"), because the hanging of Haman reminded some people of an old practice of cutting off the ears of criminals before hanging. In Holland, *hamantaschen* are called *hamansoren*, and in Italy *orrechi d'Aman*.

Purim Se'udah

Although Purim is classified as a minor holiday, it has been treasured highly in Jewish tradition, and a holiday meal was therefore instituted. The meal, or *se'udah*, is eaten on the afternoon of the holiday, rather than the night before, when a holiday meal is traditionally eaten. A large braided *challah*, called *keylitsh* in Russian, is baked for the occasion. It is said to represent the long ropes used to hang Haman on the gallows.

Another Purim *se'udah* specialty is *kreplach*, triangle-shaped pieces of dough filled with a chopped meat preparation. This dish became appropriate for Purim because the "chopping" of the meat is associated with the noisy greeting accorded Haman whenever his name is mentioned during the reading of the Megillah.

Beans and peas are also associated with Purim. According to one tradition, Esther did not want to eat nonkosher food and therefore only ate beans and peas, as did Daniel and his friends in the court of Nebukhadnezzar (Daniel 1:12). Another explanation is that the eating of legumes was once considered a charm that protected one against harmful spirits.

Among kabbalists and *chasidim*, sweet-and-sour dishes are prepared on Purim to express the unusual dual nature of the holiday, which shifts from a day of mourning and fasting (on the thirteenth of Adar) to a day of joy and celebration (on the fourteenth of Adar). Many Sephardim prepare a Purim pastry called *folares* in Ladino: a jail cell made out of baked dough encases a hard-boiled egg. The "incarcerated" egg represents the imprisoned Haman awaiting execution.

Being a joyous holiday, the drinking of wine on Purim is taken for granted. The victory achieved by Esther began at a "banquet of wine" (Esther 5:6). Because of the great and unexpected victory over Haman, letting one-self go and getting drunk is looked upon kindly and even encouraged. Rava, the renowned Babylonian talmudic scholar, said (*Megillah* 7b) that a man is obligated to drink much wine on Purim, until he reaches the point of no longer being capable of distinguishing (*ad de-lo yada*) between the words "blessed is Mordekhai" and "cursed is Haman."

Purim Joviality

The spirit of joviality led to the institution of a Purim "rabbi" who created and expounded outlandish lessons by manipulating the meaning of otherwise sacred texts. Purim plays called *Purim shpiels* are also presented as public entertainment.

In Jewish tradition, masquerading was banned because it often involved men and women interchanging garments. The prohibition is based on biblical law (Deuteronomy 22:5): "Neither shall a man wear the garments of a woman." However, because Purim was such a great and joyous festival, the Rabbis permitted this breach of biblical law.

Under the influence of the Roman carnival, Italian Jews at the close of the fifteenth century were the first to add masquerading to the celebration of Purim, and from Italy the custom spread to many other Jewish communities. Today, masquerading is a prominent feature of the Adloyada Purim Carnival held annually in Tel Aviv. Purim masquerade parties are popular in all parts of the world.

Among the special prayers recited on Purim, the *Al Ha-Nisim* ("For the Miracles") is most notable. It is recited as part of the *Grace After Meals* and also as part of the *Amidah* prayers that are recited on weekdays. It is not included in the Sabbath or holiday prayerbooks because Purim can never fall on the Sabbath in the Diaspora. The calendar is so

arranged that the fourteenth of Adar is always on a weekday.

Hallel is not recited on Purim as on other holidays, because the reading of the Megillah itself is considered to be a sufficient expression of gratitude for having been saved from annihilation.

Because Purim is a joyous holiday, *shivah* is not observed by mourners on that day. In fact, mourners are expected to visit the synagogue to hear the reading of the Megillah.

Messianic Times

The Midrash *Mishlei* (chapter 19) predicts that in messianic times life will be so blissful that there will be no need to celebrate holidays any longer. All holidays will be erased from the Jewish calendar except Purim. Purim will have to remain to remind people who are unable to conquer their hatred toward all who are unlike themselves that they may expect to experience the fate of Haman, who failed in his effort to destroy the Jewish people.

See Megillah.

Purim Katan

In a leap year, when the extra month Adar II is added to the Jewish calendar, Purim is celebrated in that month, not in Adar I. The fourteenth day of Adar I is then called Purim Katan ("Little Purim"). Some observances practiced on Purim Katan are similar to those observed on Purim proper, such as sending gifts to the poor and fasting on the thirteenth day of the month.

The term "Purim Katan" is also used to characterize a special fast day set aside by a particular community to commemorate a special event that brought them relief from persecution, just as the action of Esther and Mordekhai saved the Jews of Persia.

Karaites always celebrate Purim in Adar I.

See Fasting and Fast Days.

Purity and Impurity

The concepts of purity and impurity were especially important to Jews from early biblical times until the destruction of the Second Temple by the Romans in 70 C.E. That which is ritually clean and pure is called *tahor* in Hebrew; that which is impure is called *tamei.*

The regulations relating to these concepts are found in Leviticus, chapters 11 to 17, and in Numbers, chapter 19. These sections state that leprosy, secretions that issue from sex organs, and corpses (both human and animal) are sources of impurity. Purification is achieved through immersion in a body of natural water, such as an ocean, river, pond, or a pool (*mikveh*) that is fed from a natural water source such as a well.

The persons most affected by the laws of *tumah* (the nominative form of the word *tamei*) are the Priests who, in order to perform their priestly functions, were expected to be in a constant state of *tohorah* (the nominative form of the word *tahor*), meaning "ritually clean."

One of the six divisions of the Talmud, known as Tohorot, is devoted to the subject of ritual purity. One of its twelve tractates is *Niddah*, which details the laws that apply to the menstruant (*niddah* in Hebrew). For approximately two weeks each month, a woman is considered ritually impure and as such may not be in physical contact with her husband until she has visited a *mikveh* and purified herself. (*See* Mikveh *and* Niddah.)

The *Kohen* (Priest) and *niddah* are most affected by the laws of *tumah* and *tohorah*, but the average Jew is at times required to submit to ritual purification through water. This is one of the reasons why one washes the hands before sitting down to a meal or after having visited a cemetery and been in close proximity to a grave.

With the destruction of the Second Temple in the year 70 C.E. and the accompanying dissolution of the sacrificial system, the laws of purity and impurity became a lesser factor in Jewish life, but they continued to affect the evolution of Jewish law.

Handling a Torah Scroll

According to biblical law, a ritually unclean person who touches a Torah scroll would render it unclean and unfit for public reading. However, the prominent first-century talmudic scholar Judah ben Bathyra announced (*Berakhot* 22a): "Words of the Torah are not susceptible to uncleanness." He drew his conclusion from the words of the prophet Jeremiah, who declared (23:29), "Is not my word as fire?" Rabbi Judah interpreted this to mean that just as fire is not susceptible to uncleanness [for the very nature of fire is to purify objects], so a Torah scroll, which contains the word of God, is not susceptible to uncleanness no matter who touches it. Thus, contrary to popular misconception, a woman during her period of impurity may hold or kiss a Torah, just as she is permitted to touch and kiss a *mezuzah*, which contains a parchment with writings from the Torah.

Moses Maimonides amplified upon this ruling of Rabbi Judah when he wrote in his *Mishneh Torah* (Hilkhot Sefer Torah 10:8) that anyone may handle a Torah scroll and read from it, even a non-Jew.

Purification of the Dead

To this day, the belief that the dead are the chief transmitters of ritual impurity is operative in Jewish thinking. For this reason, when preparing the dead for burial, the *chevrah kaddishah* (Burial Society) washes the corpse thoroughly from head to toe. This procedure is called *tohorah.*

Jewish tradition insists that just as the body is washed when it emerges from the mother's womb, so at death must the body be thoroughly cleansed in order that it may be returned to God in a state of purity. Following the purification procedure, the body of the deceased is clothed in white garments in preparation for burial. This is comparable to the procedure followed by the Temple Priests, who had to thoroughly cleanse themselves before donning white garments to perform their sacrificial duties before God.

Using twenty-four quarts of water, the Burial Society must make sure not to neglect any of the orifices or the spaces between fin-gers and toes. The nails must be pared and the hair groomed, but cosmetics may not be used. During the washing procedure, the body of the deceased is not to be placed face down, for this is considered disrespectful. After washing, the corpse is dressed in shrouds and placed in a coffin.

While tradition demands that Jews, particularly observant ones, perform the cleansing of the body of the deceased before burial, in cases where Jews are not available to do this, Gentiles may perform the function, with a Jew supervising the activity.

See Burial Society.

Rabbi

The English equivalent of the Hebrew word *rabi*, meaning "my master, my teacher." The term was used for the first time in Palestine in the first century C.E. to address those rabbis who had been ordained and were eligible to serve as judges on the *Sanhedrin*, the highest court in the land. In talmudic times, scholars of great erudition who were not residents of Palestine were referred to as *rav*, meaning "master, teacher."

In post-talmudic times, men of great learning were ordained and given the title "rabbi," whether they were residents of Palestine or the Diaspora. Centuries later, with the advent of the ordination of women as rabbis in Israel, the question arose as to how they are to be addressed. The accepted term for a male rabbi was *rabi* and the unordained wife of a rabbi was called *rabbanit*. In 1993, the Israeli writer Ruth Almag suggested the title *raba,* and this terminology was eventually accepted by the Hebrew Language Academy.

See Ordination; Rabbinate.

Rabbinate

The Hebrew word for ordination is *semikhah*, meaning "laying on of hands."

The first of two types of *semikhah* refers to an individual who brought an animal to the Temple to be offered as a personal sacrifice of repentance. The Bible (Leviticus 1:4) says, "He shall lay [*samakh* in Hebrew, hence the word *semikhah*] his hand upon the head of the offering." The Rabbis of the Talmud amplify upon the requirement by saying that the person bringing the sacrifice is to press down with both hands using full strength, between the horns of the animal. This ceremony was required of men, but some authorities considered it optional for women.

A second type of *semikhah* is also known as *semikhat zekeinim*, "ordination of the Sages." This concept is first encountered in the Bible (Numbers 11:16 and 24–25) when Moses ordained seventy elders to assist him in governing the Children of Israel. But the first instance of the ordination of an individual occurred when Moses ordained Joshua by laying his hands upon him, thus transferring a portion of his power and spirit upon his disciple (Numbers 27:22 and Deuteronomy 34:9).

The Talmud (*Sanhedrin* 13b–14a) describes how the ordination of a rabbi is to be performed. Three "elders" (actually scholars) are designated to confer the honor, one of whom officially represents the Patriarch (*nasi*) of Palestine and does the laying on of hands. Once the ceremony is concluded, the candidate is to be called "rabbi" and is granted the privilege of sitting on the *Sanhedrin*, the supreme religious authority in ancient Palestine. He is also authorized, by virtue of his *semikhah*, to rule on all ritual and legal matters and to impose monetary fines when necessary.

The privilege of being ordained as a rabbi applied only to the scholars of Palestine. Scholars of equal knowledge who lived in Babylonia or any other country outside of Palestine could not be awarded *semikhah* and were to be designated simply as *rav*, meaning "teacher," as opposed to rabbi [*rabi*], meaning "my teacher." The rabbis of Babylonia were not authorized to rule on money disputes or levy fines.

Among the better known rabbis of Palestine are Rabbi Akiva, Rabbi Meir, Rabbi Tarfon, Rabbi Gamaliel, and Rabbi Judah the Prince. Among the distinguished rabbis of Babylonia are Rav Ashi, Rav Samuel bar Abba, Rav Zeira, Rav Papa, and Rav Nachman bar Isaac. Many of the prominent rabbis of Babylonia bore no title at all and were called simply by their first name or as *mar* ("mister").

An ordained rabbi was authorized to confer *semikhah* upon his own worthy students. In this manner, Rabbi Yochanan ben Zakkai ordained Rabbis Eliezer and Joshua, and Rabbi Joshua ordained Rabbi Akiba, and Rabbi Akiba ordained Rabbis Meir and Shimon bar Yocha'i.

In the year 425, the Roman rulers of Palestine abolished the office of Patriarch, the ordination of rabbis was discontinued, and the *Sanhedrin* itself ceased to be operative. It was not until Moses Maimonides appeared on the scene in the twelfth century that any authority even considered the possibility of ordaining a rabbi. Maimonides boldly declared in his code, the *Mishneh Torah*, that ordination could be restored by unanimous agreement of all the rabbis of Palestine.

In 1538, Jacob Beirav (Beirab)—a wealthy scholar who had moved from Spain to Turkey to Egypt to Jerusalem, finally settling in Safed—was deeply impressed by the growth of the Jewish community of Palestine both in numbers and in the quality of scholarship. This encouraged him to promote a call for the reestablishment of the institution of *semikhah*. Beirav called together twenty-five learned rabbis of Safed, where at the time one thousand Jewish families were living, and they ordained him. Beirav then in turn ordained four other scholars, one of whom was Joseph Caro, the noted scholar who later composed the *Code of Jewish Law* (*Shulchan Arukh*).

Through his efforts to revive ordination, Beirav had hoped that the ancient *Sanhedrin* would be reconstituted and reassume its function of legislating for world Jewry, thereby unifying it as in the days of the Patriarchate. To accomplish this he sought the acquiescence of the religious leaders of Jerusalem. Beirav was unsuccessful in his effort, and the entire scheme fell apart.

Nevertheless, the practice of an individual rabbi conferring *semikhah* on an individual student continued throughout the centuries. In more recent times, seminaries established in Europe and in America adopted the practice of conferring ordination on their students. In the United States, the first major *yeshivah* that undertook to ordain rabbis was the Rabbi Isaac Elchanan Theological Seminary, a part of Yeshiva University (Orthodox); the Jewish Theological Seminary of America (Conservative); the Hebrew Union College–Jewish Institute of Religion (Reform); and the Reconstructionist College. Smaller academies representing various denominations also confer the title of rabbi.

European countries have their own seminaries where rabbis are ordained, most prominent of which is Jews' College in London.

In the early 1970s, the Reform seminary opened its doors to women, and since 1972 over fifty rabbis have been ordained, Sally Priesand being the first. Reconstructionists followed suit in 1974, and the Conservative movement undertook the ordination of women in 1983.

See Ordination; Rabbi.

Rachmanut

A Hebrew term literally meaning "compassion." In Jewish tradition, showing compassion is considered a way of imitating God.

See Compassion.

Reason

The concept of Judaism as a "religion of reason" was popularized by Hermann Cohen (1842–1918), one of the most celebrated German philosophers of the nineteenth/twentieth century. Cohen studied at the Jewish Theological Seminary in Breslau, but left to study philosophy at the University of Berlin.

Cohen was influenced in his thinking by the famous eighteenth-century German philosopher Immanuel Kant, who believed that the role of the philosopher is to uncover the logical base upon which all scientific knowledge is founded.

The idea that physical reality is preceded by thought was expressed in poetic fashion by the sixteenth-century kabbalist Solomon Alkabetz, who composed the *Lekhah Dodi* prayer, sung at every Friday evening service in synagogues the world over. The key phrase is *sof ma'aseh b'machshavah techillah*, "All reality, all activity, starts with thought." What we *see* in the physical world was first *visualized* by the brain.

In his senior years Cohen shifted his thinking from saying all reality is rooted in human reason to say that reality is rooted in God, since man's power to reason originated with God. He no longer viewed God as an idea or a process, but as a Creator who is a pure Being, and that "man is a co-worker with God" in the work of creation. God issued commandments (*mitzvot*) and man is responsible to live by them. He developed the idea that "God" and "man" are correlative terms, meaning that neither one can be fruitfully discussed without discussing the other.

Reconstructionism

Lithuanian-born Mordecai Kaplan (1881–1983), a professor at the Jewish Theological Seminary of America for more than fifty years, was frustrated by his attempts to have Conservative Judaism delineate its difference from Orthodox and Reform Judaism. The Conservative movement, he thought, was without a fresh philosophy or purpose; it could be viewed as an uneasy partnership between right-wing Reform Judaism and left-wing Orthodoxy.

The Reform movement, Rabbi Kaplan believed, had reduced Judaism to a church sect that denied the national element of Jewish life. On the other hand, Orthodoxy was laden with fundamentalist thinking, incapable of meeting the needs of contemporary Jews.

Kaplan thought of Judaism not only as a religion, but also as a civilization. Jews, he contended, are a *people* who share a common heritage—one that includes religion, history, language, dance, art, customs, great literature, and a promising future. Kaplan taught that the laws, customs, and traditions of Judaism were not handed down by God to Moses on Mount Sinai in a supernatural fashion, but that they developed over many centuries and ultimately became hallowed as "God's commandments." To be a good Jew, he taught, one need not subscribe to all facets of Judaism.

Reconstructionist Society Is Formed

In 1922, Kaplan founded and became leader of the Reconstructionist Society for the Advancement of Judaism. In that year he introduced one of his most important innovations: the bat mitzvah ceremony for a girl entering maturity. His daughter, Judith, was the first girl to be so honored.

In the decades that followed, congregations led by rabbis who subscribed to Kaplan's approach to Judaism organized into a federation of congregations and fellowships, and in 1967 the Jewish Reconstructionist Society established a rabbinical college in Philadelphia, where men and women are prepared for the rabbinate and ordained.

Kaplan was roundly criticized by Jews of various stripes—including some of his fellow professors at the Jewish Theological Seminary—for his unorthodox views about God. He conceived of God as a representation of the highest *ideal* of mankind, as a process rather than as a self-existent Being. To him, God was a power, "the power that makes for salvation." Kaplan's description of the customs and ceremonies of Judaism as mere "folkways" irked many traditional Jews.

The Chosen People

Kaplan rejected the doctrine that Jews are God's Chosen People. He urged Jews to no longer regard themselves as chosen, because that implies a sense of superiority. Accordingly, the movement dropped from the traditional Torah blessing the words "Who has chosen us above all peoples..." and substituted "Who has *brought us closer to his service.*" In the Reconstructionist view, this modification expresses the idea of responsibility rather than superiority.

Opponents of the Chosen People concept often point out that the idea has not been considered basic to Judaism by all authorities. Moses Maimonides' Thirteen Articles of Faith, for example, does not allude to the chosenness concept.

Ironically, in the 1990s many Reconstructionist rabbis reconsidered the importance of the Chosen People concept and had the original form of the Torah blessing reinstated.

Among the many books authored by Mordecai Kaplan are *Judaism as a Civilization* (1934), *The Future of the American Jew* (1948), and *The Meaning of God in Modern Jewish Religion* (1962).

Professor Kaplan settled in Jerusalem in 1971. He died in New York in 1983, at the age of 102.

See Excommunication.

Red Heifer

The red heifer, or red cow, known in Hebrew as *parah adumah*, figures prominently in one of the most inexplicable biblical rituals. The Midrash comments (*Numbers Rabbah* 19:3) that

the wise King Solomon admitted that when he came to study the section in the Book of Numbers (19:2ff.) concerning the red heifer, he realized that it was far beyond his comprehension. This section prescribes a specific ritual of purification that one is to undergo after becoming defiled from having come in contact with a corpse. A red cow is slaughtered and burned, and the ashes, mixed with water, are sprinkled on a person on the third and seventh day following his defilement and he is purified. The mysterious aspect of the entire procedure is that the person who handles the ashes and prepares the mixture becomes unclean and remains so until nightfall.

When the first-century talmudic sage Rabbi Yochanan ben Zakkai was asked by a Gentile to explain why the same ashes that purify one person make another (the preparer) impure, he was unable to answer. Later, he said to his students, who had posed the same question: "This is what God decreed, and you must obey His law" (*Numbers Rabbah* 19:8).

The fact that the appearance of a red heifer within a herd was so rare is illustrated in the Talmud (*Kiddushin* 31a), which relates that a pious non-Jew named Dama ben Netina refused to disturb his father's sleep in order to retrieve the key to his vault that was kept under his father's pillow. Dama could have made a large amount of money if he had access to the vault, but he refused to dishonor his father by awakening him. The Talmud then adds that because of the respect shown his father, as a reward a red heifer was born in Dama's herd the following year.

The Mishnah (*Parah* 3:5) says that the ritual of the red heifer was enacted once by Moses, once by Ezra, and thereafter only a few more times.

As a reminder that a ritually unclean person must cleanse himself and be in a state of purity before partaking of the Passover sacrifice, Shabbat Parah is celebrated on one of the Sabbaths before Passover, and the biblical portion relating to the red heifer is read in addition to the regular Torah reading.

Reform Judaism

Israel Jacobson, a wealthy German layman who lived in Seesen, Germany, is acknowledged as the father of Reform (or, as it is sometimes called, Liberal) Judaism. Although Jacobson himself was an observant Jew, he was profoundly influenced by the equally Orthodox but highly cultured Moses Mendelssohn (1729–1786), a person well educated in philosophy, mathematics, Latin, French, and English. Mendelssohn believed that Jews, who for so long had exhibited a ghetto mentality, needed to expand their horizons and begin to appreciate world culture, especially German. His Lithuanian-born contemporary Elijah ben Solomon (Zalman), better known as the Vilna Gaon, was greatly displeased with Mendelssohn's approach, favoring a student's concentrated application to talmudic studies.

The innovative Jacobson organized a small congregation in his home in 1815. The liturgy of the congregation's prayer service was abbreviated, organ music was introduced, prayers and hymns were chanted in the vernacular, and a sermon was delivered in German. Jacobson gradually attracted quite a few adherents to this new form of religious service, and the appeal of a modified type of Jewish service spread to other parts of Germany. Consequently, Reform temples were established in Hamburg and Berlin. However, it was not until Abraham Geiger (1810–1874) appeared on the scene and became the rabbi of a congregation in Wiesbaden, Germany, that rabbis began to play an active role in the dissemination of Reform views and practices.

Geiger instituted liturgical reforms in his own congregation, and in 1837 convened the first conference of Reform rabbis. Three more such conferences were held between 1837 and 1846, the result of which was a greater emphasis being placed on the prophetic nature of Judaism. The conference participants regarded Judaism as a religion with a mission to reform the world, which meant that Jewish nationalism was to be discouraged. Accordingly, all references to a return to Zion were eliminated from the prayerbook.

The Reform conferences also led to other departures from traditional practice. Riding to the synagogue on the Sabbath was considered permissible, and observance of a second day of holidays, introduced in postbiblical times, was replaced by the biblically mandated one day of observance.

Reform Judaism Reaches America

By the middle of the nineteenth century Reform Judaism was widespread in Germany and was beginning to develop a following in the United States. In 1824, some members of the Orthodox Beth Elohim Congregation in Charleston, South Carolina, which adhered to Sephardic ritual, became dissatisfied with their type of service and advocated adoption of some of the practices of Germany's Reform Jewry. They decided to shorten the service, translated Hebrew prayers into English, and instituted a weekly Sabbath sermon.

The majority of Beth Elohim members were opposed to the proposed changes, so the Reform element withdrew from the congregation, organized the Reformed Society of Israelites, and conducted the first Reform synagogue service in America. Although this effort failed, by 1841 the Beth Elohim membership began to see things the Reformer's way and modified their service to conform to the Reformers' requirements. Thus, Beth Elohim became the first Reform congregation in America.

Other congregations in large American cities quickly followed the lead of the Charleston congregation: in 1842 Har Sinai in Baltimore was established as a Reform congregation, and in 1843 Temple Emanu-El in New York was organized.

Rabbi Isaac Mayer Wise (1819–1900) was a prime mover of the Reform movement in the United States. Wise came to America from Bohemia in 1846, and soon thereafter was called to occupy the pulpit of an Orthodox congregation in Albany, New York. After several years there, Wise began to preach sermons that did not comport with traditional Orthodox beliefs of members of the congregation. His sermons were more in line with the Reform views of Geiger. Wise was forced to resign, and along with his supporters organized a Reform congregation in Albany.

In 1854, Isaac Mayer Wise was called to occupy the pulpit of Congregation Bene Yeshurun, in Cincinnati, Ohio. Of the 75,000 Jews in all of America at that time a considerable number lived in Cincinnati, and most of those were of German extraction.

Before long, Wise began to realize that unless the Reform congregations in America were to form an association where they could support each other and exchange ideas, the movement would not flourish, and so in 1873 all like-minded congregations were invited to meet in Cincinnati. Thirty congregations responded, and the Union of American Hebrew Congregations (UAHC) was formed. In 1997, the UAHC boasted a membership of over 850 congregations.

Isaac Mayer Wise, who became known as the father of Reform Judaism in the United States, was convinced that unless a school was established to train Reform rabbis, Reform Judaism would not take root in America. He encouraged the UAHC to found a seminary, and in 1875 Hebrew Union College (HUC) was established in Cincinnati, with Wise as its first president. In 1950, a seminary established in New York in 1922 by Rabbi Stephen S. Wise (no relation), called the Jewish Institute of Religion (JIR), merged with HUC. Both institutions continued to conduct classes and ordain rabbis as before.

Today, the UAHC supports or sponsors many subsidiary groups, including the National Federation of Temple Youth (NFTY), which runs summer camps and other activities for Jewish youth, and the World Union for Progressive Judaism (WUP), which seeks to strengthen Reform Judaism, particularly in Europe and Israel.

Additionally, among the various auxiliary groups affiliated with the UAHC are the National Federation of Temple Sisterhoods (1913), the National Federation of Temple Brotherhoods (1923), the National Association of Temple Secretaries (1943), and the National Association of Temple Educators (1955).

Establishment of the CCAR

In addition to what he had already accomplished, Rabbi Isaac M. Wise had one other goal: to unite all Reform rabbis into a professional group. This he accomplished in 1889, when in Detroit, Michigan, at a meeting of Reform rabbis, the Central Conference of American Rabbis (CCAR) was established. Rabbi Wise was promptly elected as the organization's first president, a capacity in which he served until his death in March 1900, at age 81.

Classical Reform Judaism

The earliest Reform rabbis sought to free their followers from what they considered antiquated Jewish beliefs and practices. They insisted on promoting primarily the universal ethical teachings advanced by the prophets, and offered members of the movement the option of accepting or rejecting traditional religious practices, as each saw fit.

In 1885, when Kaufmann Kohler (1843–1926), rabbi of Temple Beth El in New York City, recognized a breach developing between the more liberal and more conservative Reform rabbis, he convened a meeting of about two dozen rabbis in Pittsburgh, Pennsylvania, the purpose of which was to establish a creed to which Reform Jews should subscribe. Known as the Pittsburgh Platform, the conclusions of this meeting became the beliefs held by Reform Jews for more than half a century.

The Pittsburgh Platform

The Pittsburgh Platform affirmed that

- the God concept was the highest ever achieved by man;
- the Bible, important as it is, with its powerful moral and ethical teachings, reflects many ideas that are primitive and should be discarded;
- the laws of *kashrut* (dietary laws) and the idea of priestly purity are of no value, and only practices and ceremonials that enhance our lives should be retained;
- the dawn of a Messianic Age should be measured by advances in human freedom and the growth of culture;
- Jews are not a nation, but a religious community, and all Zionist aspirations for a Jewish homeland in Palestine should be abandoned and discouraged;

- all beliefs in a heaven and hell, and all anticipation of the resurrection of the physical body after death should be rejected.

The Columbus Platform

A strong shift in the views of Reform rabbis began to take place in 1937, and a definite movement to the right was in evidence. At the 1937 convention of the Central Conference of American Rabbis, held in Columbus, Ohio, the membership voted to replace the long-held Pittsburgh Platform with one that acknowledged the centrality of tradition and ceremonialism in Judaism as well as aspirations for a Jewish state in Palestine.

Innovative Decisions

A 1979 responsum addressed the question, What shall be the attitude of Reform Judaism toward practices once discarded? The CCAR's Committee on Responsa expressed the opinion that since the *Code of Jewish Law* (*Shulchan Arukh*) and its commentaries have "adopted, omitted, and sometimes readopted" many laws, customs, and ceremonies, there is nothing to prevent Reform Jews from doing likewise. If a new generation finds old, discarded practices once again meaningful and useful, there is no reason why they should not be reintroduced. This applies both to private practices and to synagogue practices. Thus, today, many Reform Jews don a *tallit*, put on *tefillin*, wear a headcovering (*kippah*) in the synagogue, and observe the dietary laws (*kashrut*) to varying degrees.

Ordination of Women

One of the major innovations of Reform Judaism was the ordination of women as rabbis and cantors. In 1972, the Hebrew Union College in Cincinnati ordained the first woman rabbi, and soon thereafter, in 1974, the Reconstructionist rabbinical college in Philadelphia followed suit. By 1984, the HUC had ordained seventy-two women. Ten years later, in 1984, after much heated debate, the Conservative Jewish Theological Seminary of America ordained its first woman rabbi.

The 1997 Miami Beach Platform

The most dramatic turnabout in the Reform attitude toward Israel and Jewish ritual practice took place in 1997. At its convention held in Miami Beach, Florida, on June 24, the CCAR adopted a new Zionist platform, which stated:

> We encourage *aliyah* [immigration] to Israel in pursuance of *Yishuv Eretz Yisra'el* [the program providing for settling the Land of Israel]. Only in *Medinat Yisra'el* [the State of Israel] do Jews bear the primary responsibility for the governance of society, and may realize the full potential of their individual and communal religious strivings.

See Confirmation; Conversion; Conservative Judaism; Orthodox Judaism; Patrilineal Descent.

Reincarnation

The concept of reincarnation, which holds that the soul inhabits another body after death, was shared by many ancient peoples, particularly those of Hindu belief. Most Jewish authorities condemned the doctrine as having no basis in either the Bible or Talmud. Sa'adya Gaon (882–942), in his *Emunot Ve-Dei'ot*, characterized it as un-Jewish, while other rabbis labeled it heathen superstition. Nevertheless, mystics of the school of Rabbi Isaac Luria of Safed (died 1572) accepted reincarnation as basic kabbalistic doctrine.

The concept of reincarnation asserts that certain souls require cleansing from sin, and to accomplish this they must pass into another body or substance after death. Sometimes a soul must pass through several bodies before its sins are completely atoned for.

Many kabbalists believe that adults and even little children suffer because they have sinned as adults in a prior life. This notion was expressed as recently as August 7, 2000 by Rabbi Ovadiah Yosef, spiritual leader of Israel's council of Torah sages. In a sermon preached on that date, he made the controversial statement that the six million Jews who perished in the Holocaust died because they were reincarnations of sinners.

See Gilgul.

Rending Garments

See Keri'ah.

Repentance

The Jewish concept of repentance (*teshuvah* in Hebrew, literally meaning "return") acknowledges that a sinner has the power—through prayer, fasting, and rededication—to change the direction of his or her life.

In the Book of Deuteronomy (4:29), the Israelites are assured that if they search for God with heart and soul, they will surely find Him, even if they had abandoned Him by worshipping other gods. The prophet Jeremiah (3:22) so reassures the Children of Israel: "Return, O rebellious children. I will hear of your backslidings." (*See* Jeremiah 29:13 and Isaiah 55:6.) The Rabbis of the Talmud likewise promoted the concept of *teshuvah*. The third-century talmudic scholar Chama bar Chaninah proclaimed (*Yoma* 86a): "Great is repentance, for it brings healing to the world."

The belief that a sinner is never to be considered incorrigible has its roots in a dramatic incident related in the Book of Joshua (chapter 7). (*See* Jewish Identity.)

The Talmud (*Sanhedrin* 44a) says: "A Jew is a Jew despite the fact that he may have sinned." Elsewhere (*Berakhot* 34b and *Sanhedrin* 99a), the Talmud is praiseworthy of one "who returns to the straight path" (known in Hebrew as *ba'al teshuvah* or *chozer bi-teshuvah*) by declaring that a *ba'al teshuvah* rates even higher than a righteous person who has never sinned. It takes great strength and fortitude for one to admit mistakes and follow a new path.

Maimonides, in his *Mishneh Torah* (Hilkhot Teshuvah 2:2 and 5:1), asserts that it is within the power of every person to rise to noble heights or sink into a life of sin. To sin is to abandon the goals implied by the term "godly living;" and to be a repentant, to be a *ba'al teshuvah*, is to return and embrace noble goals once again.

The Midrash (*Song of Songs Rabbah* 5:2) characterizes the traditional Jewish attitude toward *teshuvah* by imagining God saying to Israel, "My sons, open for me a gate of repentance no bigger than the eye of a needle, and I will enlarge it into an opening [of forgiveness] through which wagons and carriages can pass." This, add the Rabbis, comports with the popular belief that "if a man pursues the path to purify himself, he is assisted from heaven."

See Confession of Sins; Shabbat Shuvah; Ten Days of Repentance.

Respect

See Derekh Eretz; Kevod Ha-Beriot; Kevod Ha-Met; Kevod He-Chai; Kevod Tzibur; Tircha De-Tzibura.

Responsa Literature

In 499 C.E., after its final editing by Ravina II, the Babylonian Talmud was closed to further additions. The task of compiling and editing this massive work had begun two generations earlier under the leadership of Rav Ashi, headmaster of a prestigious academy in Sura, Babylonia.

Following the redaction of the Talmud, difficult questions on matters of Jewish law continued to be asked of local rabbis, who in many cases felt it best to seek the advice of a more knowledgeable rabbinic authority. When the authority lived far away, the query was transmitted via carrier, usually a merchant or businessman, who would deliver the question (*she'eilah* in Hebrew; plural, *she'eilot*) upon his arrival at the destination. After having obtained a written response (*teshuvah*; plural, *teshuvot*), the carrier would commence his return journey, periodically stopping and sharing the contents of the communication with interested students.

Over the centuries, many responsa were lost, some as a result of natural disaster or the hostile acts of anti-Semites. But many thousands of communications did survive, and together they comprise the body of work commonly referred to in Hebrew as *she'eilot u-teshuvot*, or Responsa Literature.

The Geonic Period

Talmudic references (*Yevamot* 105a, *Chullin* 95b, *Sanhedrin* 29a) reveal that Babylonian and Palestinian scholars sought each other's advice on matters of law and ritual via personal visitations or written communications. Nonetheless, the actual responsum period is said to have begun in earnest after the redaction of the Talmud in the sixth century and to have flourished through the entire geonic period, which ended in the eleventh century. During this time, the *ge'onim* (singular, *ga'on*, meaning "his eminence") headed academies of learning in Babylonia, principally in the cities of Sura and Pumbedita, situated along the Euphrates and Tigris rivers. They personally addressed obvious questions, but those of a more difficult nature were often brought to the attention of the large gathering of students and scholars that assembled twice a year, once during the month of Adar (usually March) and once during the month of Elul (usually August).

The months of Adar and Elul are known as *yarchei kallah* ("*kallah* months"), the word *yarchei* meaning "months" and the word *kallah* being associated with both the Hebrew root *kalol*, meaning "all-inclusive," and the word *kahal*, meaning "congregation." During the *yarchei kallah* months, the work of farmers and agricultural merchants was relatively light, and they were therefore able to devote themselves to study. During the same time, scholars and students would review a selected tractate of the Talmud and listen to lectures. Principals of the academies would read aloud the more difficult questions that had been received via courier, and they would solicit observations from the large number of highly educated individuals in the assembly.

The comments would be noted by a scribe, and the headmaster would then forward the response to the questioner, once again via courier. As the messengers made their way through various territories en route to their ultimate destinations, the contents of the communications would be shared with local rabbis.

Among the earliest responsa on record were those written by Natronai Gaon and his successor, Amram Gaon. Natronai, who served as the principal of the academy in Sura from 853 to 856, dealt mainly with the one hundred blessings an observant Jew is obligated to recite daily and also with the order of the synagogue service. He maintained contact with community leaders in Spain and North Africa, and his writings were largely in reply to their questions. Approximately five hundred responsa have been attributed to Natronai.

Amram Gaon, principal of the academy in Sura from 856 to 874, devoted himself to synagogue liturgy and prepared the first authoritative prayerbook, the *Siddur of Rav Amram Gaon*. In addition to setting forth the sequence of prayers to be recited, it included extensive notes and comments.

When Egyptian-born Sa'adya Gaon (882–942) was appointed head of the academy in Sura in 928, he carried on the work of Amram Gaon by perfecting a *siddur* for the lay worshipper. In addition, Sa'adya was a brilliant theologian and philosopher of whom Louis Ginzberg, professor of Talmud at the Jewish Theological Seminary of America in the mid-twentieth century, said, "Anything he touched in the wide range of his studies bears the stamp of his personality and originality."

Many of the queries addressed to Sa'adya related to the Jewish calendar and especially to the status of the growing Karaite community, which bound itself by biblical law but was unwilling to accept rulings and interpretations advanced by talmudic and later rabbinic authorities.

The geonic period was brought to a close by two celebrated scholars of the tenth and eleventh centuries: Sherira Gaon (906–1006) and his son and successor, Hai Gaon (939–1038). Both maintained contact with Jewish communities in North Africa and Spain, even as they served as principals of the elite academy of learning in Pumbedita.

Sherira is especially noted for responses to queries from scholars in the North African city of Kairouan, near Tunis, who were anxious to learn more about the history of the Talmud and the early geonic period. Hai, on the other hand, was often questioned by students and rabbis about claims that rearranging the letters of the divine name can make one invisible, a theory he dismissed as preposterous. It is estimated that Hai responded to more than one thousand *she'eilot*, some in consultation with his father.

With the influence of the *ge'onim* at a virtual end, centers of Jewish life began to emerge in North Africa and Spain, in Germany and France, even in Italy. The religious authorities in these locales gradually replaced Babylonian scholars as the individuals to whom questions on matters of Jewish law and practice were addressed.

The Rishonim

The first group of authorities to whom questions were addressed during the post-*geonic* era were called the *rishonim*, meaning "first ones." Primary among them was Rashi (1040–1105), an acronym of Rabbi Shlomo Yitzchaki (Isaac). Born in Troyes, France, Rashi lived during the time of the First Crusade, which was wending its way through Europe en route to the Holy Land in the hope of rescuing the Holy Sepulchre from the Muslim "infidels." As the mobs increased, they began to attack Jews in the communities through which they marched.

Many Jews attempted to resist the menacing hordes and were put to death, while others survived by converting to Christianity. When asked whether such converts were still to be considered Jews, Rashi answered unequivocally by citing the talmudic (*Sanhedrin* 44a) statement, "A Jew, even if he sins, is still a Jew."

In addition to being known for important responsa, which were published in a volume entitled *Teshuvot Rashi* ("Responses of Rashi"),

this great scholar's fame is owed more to his commentaries on the Bible and most of the tractates of the Babylonian Talmud. Rashi's facility at explaining a difficult word or passage of text earned him the title *parshandata*, Aramaic for "expositor par excellence."

Another of the outstanding *rishonim* was the learned Jacob ben Meir (1100–1171), son of Rashi's eldest daughter. He was given the appellation Rabbenu Tam, meaning "perfect master," as testimony to the high esteem with which he was regarded by French Jewry. (The word *tam* was first used in Genesis 25:27, where Jacob is described as an "*ish tam*," a wholesome, upright, perfect man.) Rabbbenu Tam's father was the esteemed Rashbam (Rabbi Samuel ben Meir), a renowned scholar in his own right.

When Rabbenu Tam's family home in Ramerput, France, was destroyed by the Crusaders in 1147, he finally settled in Troyes, where he excelled in his studies and was regarded by some as superior in learning even to his grandfather, Rashi. His many *tosafot* (additional talmudic comments), which corrected inaccuracies in the text of the Talmud, were collected into his *Sefer Ha-Yashar* along with many of his responsa.

A third luminary of the distinguished *rishonim* period was Rabbi Isaac ben Jacob of Fez (1013–1103), better known by the acronym Alfasi ("of Fez"). Under the leadership of the Alfasi, the North African town of Fez became a center of talmudic studies that produced many scholars. That closely knit community later received many Jews who fled persecution in Spain in 1391 and 1492.

Born in Algeria in 1013, the Alfasi studied in the academy in Kairouan and later settled in Fez, where he became the town's leading rabbi. In 1088, advanced in years, he settled in Lucena, Spain. Respected there as a man of great learning, he served as the community's chief rabbi until his death in 1103.

The Alfasi received many questions from near and far, and they were later published in a collection simply called *Responsa*. The three hundred twenty *she'eilot u-teshuvot* contained in that work deal with civil law as well as with religious rites and ceremonies. Maimonides, in particular, relied upon the rulings of the Alfasi in preparing his famous *Mishneh Torah*. He found the Alfasi's judgment to be almost faultless. Maimonides refers to Joseph ibn Migash, one of the Alfasi's students, as one of his most influential teachers.

Maimonides (1135–1204), popularly referred to as the Rambam, an acronym of Rabbi Moshe ben Maimon, was undoubtedly the most eminent of the *rishonim*. Born in Cordova, Spain, in 1335, he is remembered primarily for his monumental *Guide for the Perplexed*, written in Arabic, and his *Mishneh Torah*, a code of Jewish law, written in Hebrew. Maimonides authored commentaries on both the Bible and the Talmud while at the same time serving as rabbi in Fostat (Old Cairo), Egypt, and also as physician to the royal family.

Remarkably, he still found time to teach and answer the many *she'eilot* received from neighboring countries. The most famous of these was a letter from Obadiah, a former Catholic priest who had converted to Judaism. When Obadiah's own teacher refused to accept him as a full Jew owing to the fact that he was not born Jewish, Obadiah sought outside help. In response, Maimonides reprimanded Obadiah's teacher sternly and advised the convert, "Go tell your teacher that he owes you an apology. And tell him that he should fast and pray and ask God to forgive him for what he said to you...."

Although the responsa of Maimonides deal generally with basic human values and with philosophical and theological questions, they also discuss many purely ceremonial aspects of Judaism. Among the issues expounded upon are whether one should pray in a room without windows and whether congregants must stand when the Ten Commandments are read aloud from the Torah at a synagogue service.

In addition to the Rambam, Rashi, Rabbenu Tam, and the Alfasi, another great scholar of the period was the Spanish-born Rabbi Moses ben Nachman (1194–1270), popularly known by the acronym Ramban. He is noted for his commentaries on the Bible and Talmud, but he is also known for a responsum concerning the status of an apostate, a question the Rambam also addressed. The Ramban ruled that an apostate is officially considered a Jew, since "a Jew who has sinned [including an apostate] is still a Jew," according to the Talmud.

A collection of responsa erroneously attributed to the Ramban was actually the work of his disciple Solomon ben Abraham Adret, popularly called by the acronym Rashba. Born in 1235 to a wealthy family in Barcelona, Spain, Adret is characterized as the most famous respondent in Jewish history. He was widely acclaimed not only as the Rabbi of Barcelona, but also as the Rabbi of Spain itself.

None of the great *rishonim* is said to have entertained as many questions as did Adret. His *she-eilot u-teshuvot*, which number in the thousands, consist of queries from many communities in Europe, Africa, and Asia Minor. While Adret appreciated the teachings of Maimonides, he disagreed with him on several basic issues. In one responsum, for example, contrary to the position of the Rambam, he issued a ban on students under age thirty studying Greek philosophy, characterizing those who pursue such studies as "uprooting the law of God." He also disagreed with Maimonides' acceptance of the Aristotelian position that because of the complete regularity in the forces of nature the world would never come to an end. To the contrary, Adret believed, as did Rabbis of the Talmud and Midrash, that the world would indeed have an end.

The Later Rishonim

The responsum literature continued to grow in the fourteenth and fifteenth centuries, in large part due to the contributions of such scholars as the Maharil, Rabbi Meir of Rothenburg, Elijah Mizrachi, and David ibn Abi Zimar.

Jacob ben Moses Ha-Levi Möllin (1365–1427), better known as the Maharil, an acronym of Moreinu Ha-Rav Rav Yaakov Ha-Levi, lived in Mainz, Germany, where he succeeded his father as chief rabbi. During those years, Central Europe was reeling from the effects of the Black Plague. Ironically, although the Jewish communities themselves were suffering great losses, it was the Jews who were accused of starting the deadly disease in order to exterminate the Christian population of Germany.

Some of the Maharil's *teshuvot*, which were collected by his disciple Zalman of St. Goar into a volume entitled *Sefer Maharil*, discuss ways of reconstructing the devastated communities. Others focus on the importance of maintaining the traditional customs of a community and on the possibility of introducing new prayers and melodies to the synagogue liturgy.

Rabbi Meir of Rothenburg (1215–1293), another of the latter *rishonim*, is regarded by many as the most illustrious talmudic authority of the second half of the thirteenth century. He was also one of the most prolific writers of responsa, having answered approximately one thousand queries, which run the gamut from civil and religious law to personal questions about ritual practice. The subjects covered include inheritance, buying and selling, hiring employees, and marriage and divorce.

Born into a large family of scholars in Worms, Germany, in his youth Meir was sent to a famous academy in Mainz to pursue his studies. Later, he went to France to study under Yechiel of Paris, a leading scholar. It was there, in 1242, that Meir witnessed the heartbreaking scene of confiscated copies of the Talmud being publicly burned. Meir then returned to Germany where he settled in Rothenburg, becoming its chief rabbi for forty years.

Elijah Mizrachi (*c.* 1455–*c.* 1525), chief rabbi of the entire Turkish empire and one of the last of the prominent *rishonim*, was author of two volumes of responsa. His rulings included such controversial topics as whether it was appropriate to place a ban on a person who instructed Karaites in secular studies and whether a synagogue was rendered contaminated as a result of a homosexual act between a sexton and a boy having taken place there. In both instances, Mizrachi ruled in the negative.

The last of the major *rishonim* was David ibn Abi Zimar (1479–1573), known by the acronym Radbaz. Born in Spain, in his early youth he spent time in Jerusalem and ultimately settled in Egypt, where he served as rabbi for forty years. The Radbaz was not only a great master of the Talmud, but also a renowned kabbalist. He believed that behind the words of the Torah often lies profound mystical meaning, and this view is reflected in many of his responsa, of which he authored a staggering number.

The Acharonim

The activities of the *rishonim* ended in the middle of the sixteenth century with the publication

of Joseph Caro's *Shulchan Arukh*. Born in Spain, Caro (1488–1572) later settled in Palestine, where in 1525 he organized a *yeshivah* and became a devotee of kabbalism. He once claimed that religious secrets were revealed to him by an angel.

Caro's rulings tended to accentuate the views of the Sephardic community, and in order to make them more acceptable to all Jews, the final editions of Caro's code also incorporated the rulings of Ashkenazic authorities. The author of this supplementary information was Moses Isserles (1525–1572), a native of Cracow, Poland. His work was entitled *Mappah* ("tablecloth"), for it sought to cover the *Shulchan Arukh* ("prepared table") with additional information.

These two sixteenth-century scholars dedicated themselves more to compiling codes of religious law than to conducting correspondence with individuals. That was the domain of a group of scholars referred to as the *acharonim*, "the later ones," among whom were Jacob Emden, Ezekiel Landau, Moses Sofer, Solomon Kluger, and Isaac Elchanan Spektor. The *acharonim* dominated the scene from the seventeenth to the twentieth centuries.

Also known by the acronym Yavetz, Jacob Emden (1697–1776) was the chief rabbi of Emden, Germany, hence the surname. Difficulties with some prominent local personalities forced him to leave the pulpit after four years of service, and in 1732 he returned to his birthplace in Altona and started a printing business. Emden had earned a reputation as a great scholar, so queries on many subjects continued to be sent to him. His basic interest remained *halakhah*, about which he wrote forty books.

Polish-born Ezekiel ben Yehudah Landau (1713–1793), who served as rabbi of the community in Prague from age thirty-one until his death, is another of the most prolific writers of responsa of all times. His answers to queries covering many aspects of personal and communal life were published in a volume entitled *Noda Bi-Yehudah* (using his father's first name), but he probably is most remembered for instituting the Sumptuary Laws, which established guidelines for how much money should be spent on social religious affairs. He also issued instructions as to how military conscripts should conduct themselves in the observance of Jewish law.

Another of the great *acharonim*, Rabbi Moses Sofer (1763–1839), was born in Frankfort-on-the-Main but gained great fame while serving for thirty-six years as rabbi of the community in Pressburg, Hungary. Opposed to change, Chatam Sofer, as he signed his responsa, vigorously condemned the fledgling Reform movement that was emerging in Germany and gaining strength in Hungary. He even opposed moving the *bimah* from the center of the room to an area close to the ark, a practice some Orthodox synagogues had initiated.

One of the interesting queries addressed to the Chatam Sofer regarded the images or letters that sometimes appear on the gilt-edged pages of a bound book. When the book is closed, one can see the images or letters, but when the book is opened they disappear. The specific question was whether such a book may be read on the Sabbath or whether the opening and closing of the book constitutes an erasure, which would be a violation of Sabbath law.

Another of the great *acharonim* was Solomon Kluger (1783–1819). Born in Komarow, Poland, Kluger died in Brody, Galicia, where he served as chief rabbi, judge, and preacher for almost fifty years. Many of the questions he addressed involved interpersonal relationships.

One responsum for which Kluger is particularly noted concerns the requirement that a man, when divorcing his wife, place the Jewish divorce document (*get*) directly into the woman's hands. If a pressing reason makes this impractical, such as the fact that the two live a considerable distance apart, Kluger finds it acceptable that the *get* be sent via an agent.

Russian-born Isaac Elchanan Spektor (1817–1896) served congregations not only in White Russia but also in Lithuania. He was appointed chief rabbi of Kovno, Lithuania, where he founded and led a *yeshivah* that became increasingly famous as his status as a legal authority grew. So highly regarded was Spektor that an Orthodox rabbinical school established in New York City in 1895 was named the Rabbi Yitzchak Elchanan Theological Seminary (RIETS), later to become part of Yeshiva University. Spektor tended to be lenient in his interpretation of Jewish law, and many of his responsa were aimed at finding a solution to the gnawing *agunah* problem. The *agunah*, literally "a chained" woman, may not remarry unless her husband presents her with a *get*, directly or through an agent. If, out of stubbornness or maliciousness, a husband refuses to grant a *get*, the woman is left in limbo. Neither Spektor nor scholars who followed him were able to advance a solution acceptable to all legal authorities, and today the *agunah* continues to be left in the unfortunate situation of being unable to remarry.

The Cairo Genizah

In 1896, Dr. Solomon Schechter, a lecturer in Talmud at Cambridge University, traveled to Egypt to examine a cache of books, manuscripts, and leaflets stored in the *genizah* ("hiding place") located on the second floor of the Ezra Synagogue in Old Cairo (Fostat), where Moses Maimonides had served as rabbi in the twelfth century. As Jewish law dictates, sacred writings and artifacts were to be kept until they could be accorded proper cemetery burial. Among the items found in the Cairo Genizah were incomplete manuscripts and loose pages containing responsa from leading scholars in various countries.

Dr. Schechter returned to England with thousands of documents and fragments, and these were distributed to Judaic scholars for further examination and analysis.

Contemporary Respondents

Among the most influential contributors to contemporary responsum literature was Rabbi Moshe Feinstein (1859–1986), founder and head of the Tiferet Yerushala'yim Rabbinical Academy in New York City. This leading Orthodox thinker of the twentieth century authored six volumes of responsa, entitled *Igrot* [letters] *of Moshe*. Typical of the questions addressed by him are: May one dishwasher be used for meat and dairy dishes? Is it proper to celebrate a Bat Mitzvah as one does a Bar Mitvah? Is a marriage performed by a Reform rabbi valid, since the witnesses to the *ketubbah* are probably Sabbath violators? Does one display a lack of faith in God by taking out an insurance policy?

The leading Reform writer of responsa in the twentieth century was Solomon B. Freehof, formerly of Rodef Shalom Temple, in Pittsburgh, Pennsylvania. Representative of the questions addressed in his eight volumes of responsa are: May a non-Jewish doctor perform a circumcision? May a man who has remarried say *Kaddish* for his first wife? May a woman submit to cosmetic surgery, since it may lead to unnecessary bodily injury? Is occasional participation in gambling and state lotteries permitted? Should homosexuals be encouraged to establish their own congregations?

The responsa committee of the Conservative movement's Rabbinical Assembly of America also addresses questions on matters of Jewish law and practice, but their rulings have not been made available to the general public in published form.

The Responsa Project

In 1963, Professor Aviezri Fraenkel, following a conversation with Irving Kuttof of Minneapolis, Minnesota, founded the Responsa Project at the Weizmann Institute of Science, in Rehovot, Israel. Realization of the project, which later was transferred to Bar Ilan University, was the joint research effort of Professors Fraenkel, Yaacov Choueka, and Nachum Dershowitz.

In its early stages, the focus of the effort was solely on creating a computer database into which the questions and answers that comprise the Responsa Literature would be entered. A special committee was established to sort through the large quantity of material and decide which texts to include in light of their relevance, scope, and accessibility. The Responsa Project, also known as the Global Jewish Database, grew to become the largest collection of data of its kind. It now includes the full text of the Bible and its principal commentaries, the Babylonian Talmud with Rashi's commentary and Tosafot, the Jerusalem Talmud, Maimonides' *Mishneh Torah*, the *Shulchan Arukh* with commentaries, *midrashim*, 369 books of responsa, and the Talmudic Encyclopedia. All of this material is available on compact disk.

See Yarchei Kallah.

Resurrection

Although belief in the resurrection of the dead first entered Jewish thought in the sixth century B.C.E. under the influence of the Persians who ruled Palestine, it took several centuries for the concept to take root among Jews. The concept is represented in Hebrew by the term *techiyat ha-metim*, meaning "revival of the dead," although Jewish scholars and theologians have never been in agreement as to the precise meaning of the term. Would the dead be revived and restored to full physical life, or would only "souls" be revived while bodies remain as dust?

Biblical References

The Bible itself carries few references to resurrection of the dead, the most famous being the vision of the prophet Ezekiel (37), which describes a valley of dry bones that will come to life again. The concept is also referred to in the Book of Daniel (12:2–3): "And many of those who sleep in the dusty earth shall awake, some to everlasting life, others to everlasting reproach and contempt." Isaiah expressed the same sentiment (26:19): "Oh, let Your dead revive! Let corpses arise! Awake and shout for joy..."

Isaiah's hopeful scenario is not shared by the author of the Book of Job, who says (5:7): "Man, born of woman, is short-lived and burdened with trouble. He blossoms like a flower and withers; he vanishes like a flower and does not endure." Job, who was once wealthy and successful, has lost most of his family and all his riches and is now steeped in grief, beyond consolation. The author sees him as a man representative of all people, as one who does not stand a chance of redemption, considering all the forces of nature aligned against him. To Job, to believe in or hope for a new life after death is futile.

Not until the fourth century B.C.E., when the Greeks conquered Palestine and the influence of Plato and others began to be felt, did the doctrine of resurrection start to become

accepted by Jews. It was embraced particularly by those who battled for their lives and honor when they opposed the domination of the Syrian-Greeks in the second century B.C.E. Loss of life was so great during these battles that the survivors found it necessary to cling to a belief in a world to come where the righteous would return to life.

At this point in history, the two major Jewish sects debated whether the doctrine of resurrection should be accepted as a basic article of faith. The Sadducees believed that only that which is explicitly commanded in the Bible should be accepted. Since belief in the resurrection of the dead is not specifically advocated in the Pentateuch, they denied the doctrine. The Pharisees, however, believed that the words of the Torah are subject to interpretation, and they affirmed the belief in resurrection.

The strongly stated view of the Pharisees was adopted by the later Rabbis of the Talmud (*Sanhedrin* 90a): "Anyone who denies that the doctrine of resurrection of the dead is a Torah-based commandment excludes himself from the Jewish fold and will have no share in the world to come." This teaching, introduced as one of the *Eighteen Benedictions* (*Shemoneh Esrei*), became a cardinal belief of Judaism. In the twelfth century, Maimonides included it in his Thirteen Principles of Faith.

From the Maccabean period (second century B.C.E.) onward, the concept of heaven and hell was coupled with an ever-growing belief that not only does the soul survive death, but that one day the body will come to life again and be reunited with the soul. One of the first to advance this idea was Gabicha ben Pasisa, the fourth-century B.C.E. spokesman of Palestinian Jewry during the reign of Alexander the Great, who said: "If what never existed before now can exist, why cannot that which did once exist come to life again?" Ben Pasisa's view of resurrection as a physical happening was the traditional Jewish view for many centuries.

Moses Maimonides, the prominent twelfth-century philosopher and rabbinical scholar, was one of the first to cast doubts on the accepted view of resurrection. His revolutionary idea as to the nature of resurrection was first presented in his commentary on the first *mishnah* of the tenth chapter of the tractate *Sanhedrin*, where he emphasizes that the concept of resurrection must be thought of in an allegorical sense and that the statements of the Rabbis regarding physical life in the hereafter are not to be taken literally.

Therefore, says Maimonides, when one comes across a statement of the Rabbis that seems to conflict with reason, one ought to stop and think about it "because you must surely understand that it is but a riddle or a parable." To illustrate, Maimonides reminds us of the oft-quoted comment of the talmudic scholar Rav on the afterlife (*Berakhot* 17a): "The future world is not like this world. In the future world there is no eating or drinking, or propagation or business transactions, or jealousy, or hatred, or competition, but the righteous sit with their crowns on their heads feasting on the brightness of the divine presence."

To Maimonides, saying that the righteous will "sit with their crowns on their heads" is but an allegorical way of affirming that the righteous will be rewarded by experiencing the heightened spiritual and intellectual pleasure of knowing and understanding God. Only the soul of man is capable of such experience; it is beyond the physical realm (*Mishneh Torah*: Hilkhot Teshuvah 8:2).

This is how Maimonides interprets the statement of Rabbi Eleazar (*Ketubbot* 111b): "The ignorant will not be resurrected." He explains that for man to merit life in the hereafter he must nourish his soul in the here-and-now by serious and intensive study, for study leads to righteous living, and righteous living leads to a healthy soul that will enjoy immortality.

The equation of study and learning with life in the hereafter was first suggested by Hillel the Great, who said (Ethics of the Fathers 2:6): "An ignorant man cannot be truly pious." The idea was further embellished upon by later Rabbis of the Talmud, who added (*Berakhot* 18a–b): "The righteous, even after death, are referred to as living."

Today, the more liberal wings of Judaism (Reform, Reconstructionist, and part of the Conservative movement) do not believe in physical resurrection of the dead. They have affirmed in its place the concept of the immortality of the soul. Orthodox and Conservative prayerbooks have retained references to the resurrection of the dead and leave it to the worshipper to apply his own interpretation to the concept.

See Afterlife; Gilgul.

Revelation

The term "revelation," which has no precise Hebrew equivalent, refers to the way in which God communicates with man as well as the substance of that contact. In the Jewish tradition, revelation is generally linked principally to the events that occurred on Mount Sinai. The primary source of information about the revelation on Mount Sinai is the Torah itself. Exodus (19) describes how, after being enslaved in Egypt for centuries, the Children of Israel escape from the "house of bondage" and are miraculously guided in safety through the Sea of Reeds (often confused with the Red Sea). They approach Mount Sinai in the third month after leaving Egypt.

Moses ascends the mountain while the Children of Israel are encamped below. God reveals Himself to Moses and tells him that the Israelites will be His Chosen People, a holy nation, if they will conduct their lives in purity and be steadfast in their loyalty to Him. This loyalty is to be manifested by the observance of the Torah's commandments (*mitzvot*).

When Moses comes down from the mountain and delivers God's message to the Israelites assembled below, they respond in unison: "All that God has spoken, we will do." Moses returns to the mountaintop and conveys this response to God. Whereupon God instructs Moses to return to his people and lead them through three days of ritual preparation, at which point God will "come down and appear before them."

Early on the third day there is thunder and lightning, and a thick cloud appears on the mountain. A thunderous blast of the *shofar* (ram's horn) is heard, and everyone in the camp trembles. God descends from the heavens and appears on the summit of Mount Sinai. He calls to Moses, and Moses goes up to meet Him. Moses receives the Ten Commandments and takes them down from the mountaintop to transmit them to the Children of Israel.

Matan Torah

The essence of the Revelation on Mount Sinai as described in the Bible and accepted by traditional Jews is that God reveals Himself to Moses and then reveals the Torah to the Children of Israel through Moses. This reception is known in Hebrew as *Matan Torah*.

Although it is universally accepted that something awesome happened on Mount Sinai, not all Jews interpret the events in the same way. While all believe that in the wilderness of

Sinai the Jewish people came into possession of the Torah, the precise nature of its original form, how it was received by Moses from God, and how it was transmitted by Moses to the people of Israel are open to speculation.

The Rabbis (Midrash *Tanchuma* on Bereishit 1:1) offer a wide range of views about the origin of the Torah. There are those who believe that the Torah is older than the world itself, that it existed for 947 generations before the world was created. In fact, they maintain that since the Torah is the epitome of wisdom, God consulted and was guided by it when He decided to create the world.

At the other end of the spectrum are traditionalists who believe that the Torah is a God-inspired document, that its truths are divinely revealed and that it consists of a record of how the earliest Jews conceived of the creation of the world and how they view the relationship between man and his Creator. To them, its essential purpose is to explain how God manifested His presence in history.

Traditionalists can be divided into three groups:

1. *Strict constructionists*. This group is represented by Rabbi Samson Raphael Hirsch (1808–1888), a German scholar and the founder of neo-Orthodoxy. While Hirsch agrees with Maimonides that what took place at Sinai is incomprehensible, he maintains that every word of the Written Law (Torah) and the Oral Law (Talmud) must be taken literally because both were supernaturally revealed. To strict constructionists, when the Bible says, "And the Lord spoke to Moses," it is to be taken to mean that the Lord actually spoke.

2. *Loose constructionists*. Theirs is the approach to Scripture of the twelfth-century Moses Maimonides. While Maimonides affirmed that what took place on Sinai is beyond human comprehension, he insisted that all biblical descriptions of God as hearing, seeing, speaking, and making appearances must not be taken literally. "To anthropomorphize God is an act of sacrilege," said Maimonides, adding that "whoever conceives of God as a corporeal being is an apostate."

3. *Modernists*. Included in this group are contemporary theologians who believe that the Torah is divinely inspired and was written by God-inspired men of exceptional spirituality, men of the caliber of Moses. While modernists believe that the Torah is divine and in that sense comes "from heaven" (*min hashama'yim*), they do not necessarily believe that every word or phrase or sentence in the Torah need be taken literally. They remind us of the statement of Rabbi Yosei, a disciple of Rabbi Akiba, that the verse in Exodus (19:3) which describes Moses as "going up" and God as "coming down" from the mountaintop is to be taken figuratively, not literally. In the view of Rabbi Yosei, Moses did not go up and God did not come down (*Sukkah* 5a).

Traditionalists have never spoken with one voice. All authorities do agree, however, that an extraordinary event took place at Mount Sinai, one that transformed the Jewish people from an idolatrous nation into a God-loving one.

The Louis Jacobs Debacle

Although Maimonides believed sincerely that only a simpleton would maintain that every statement in the Bible is to be taken literally, in the 1960s Orthodox scholar Louis Jacobs was rejected as a suitable principal for Jews' College, Anglo-Jewry's rabbinic training seminary, for holding this very belief. In his *We Have Reason to Believe* (1957), he wrote that in light of modern theories about the evolution of Hebrew Scripture it is folly to believe that "the Torah simply dropped down from heaven after having been dictated by God to Moses on Mount Sinai." The argument of Rabbi Jacobs that the words of the Torah have always been subject to interpretation did not prevail.

Reaffirmation of the Covenant

The Revelation was a reaffirmation of God's covenant entered into with Abraham (Abram). The Book of Genesis (12:1–3) describes the Covenant: Abraham is instructed to go forth and spread God's name throughout the world, and as a reward he and his descendants will be blessed forever. Centuries later, during the course of the Revelation at Sinai, the covenant was reaffirmed and its terms restated (Exodus 19:5–6): If Israel will be faithful to God and obey the commandments, God will treasure them and reward them. As God's Chosen People, they will become a kingdom of Priests and a holy nation.

The Revelation on Mount Sinai is celebrated on the festival of Shavuot. The connection between the giving of the Torah on Sinai with Shavuot was made by the Rabbis of the Talmud after they observed that the agricultural festival of Shavuot and the events at Mount Sinai occurred in the same season of the year. Once this association had been firmly established, the one-time agricultural holiday became the annual occasion to celebrate the giving of the Torah. Torah study sessions are held all through the night of the holiday, and the holiday is highlighted as a time for Jewish affirmation.

See Covenant People; Shavuot.

Revenge

At the beginning of the Christian era, when esteemed talmudic scholar Hillel was asked by a heathen to sum up in one sentence the entire teachings of the Torah, he quoted the majestic statement from the Book of Leviticus (19:18) that is popularly known as the Golden Rule. It reads, "You shall love your neighbor as yourself." What generally goes unnoticed is that the first half of that verse contains a highly important negative comment "You shall not take vengeance or bear a grudge [*lo tikom ve-lo titor*] against your kinfolk."

The lesson drawn from this verse was emphasized by the prophets Isaiah (34:8, 35:4), Jeremiah (46:10, 51:6), and Ezekiel (25:14,17), among others who preached that when one engages in seeking retribution against one who has defamed him, he is treading on the prerogatives of the Divine. Only God can seek retribution; only God can accuse, punish, or forgive. This position is detailed often in the Torah, and never more directly than in the Book of Deuteronomy (32:41), where we read, "I will wreak vengeance upon those who are My enemies."

While biblical commentators generally acknowledge that it is in God's hands to exact revenge, and that it is wrong for man to "play God" in situations that call for vengeance against those who have committed wrongs, there are cases when man is allowed to intervene to defend God's name. In the talmudic tractate *Yoma* (23a), the famous Rabbi Yochanan bar Nappacha taught, "Any scholar who does not avenge himself and retains anger like a serpent [when God's name is being defamed] is no true scholar." He is obligated to intervene, and God will be pleased by his support.

One such instance is recorded in the Book of Numbers (25:ff.), where the Israelites had backslided and allowed themselves to be enticed by the idolatrous women of Moab and Midian to engage in immoral activity. Based upon the commentary in the tractate *Sanhedrin* (106a), Rashi states that after these women invited the Israelites to eat and drink with them to excess, the men tried to cohabit with them, but the women opened their gowns and drew forth their local idols, known as Ba'al Pe'or, demanding that the Israelites first bow down to them.

Verse 25:3 records how the Israelites became attached to these idols and God ordered Moses to kill all the sinners. And Pinchas, Aaron's grandson, does likewise to an Israelite who flouts the moral code (25:14). God is pleased with the actions of Moses and Pinchas, although it was uncommon for humans to perform acts reserved for the divine.

A second instance may be found in the Book of Esther, where after Haman's plot to annihilate all the Jews in the kingdom of Ahasueros is foiled by Esther and her cousin Mordekhai, on God's orders the Jews are granted the right to kill all their enemies throughout ancient Persia. God is pleased to allow the Jews the privilege of performing the task He generally reserves for Himself.

Revenge vs. Bearing a Grudge

In the tractate *Yoma* (23a), the Rabbis attempt to explain the distinction between taking revenge (*nekamah*) and bearing a grudge (*netirah*). The following example is given:

If a man asks his fellow to lend him a sickle and he refuses, and then on the next day the second person asks the first to lend him his axe, and he replies, "I will not lend it to you, just as you did not lend me your sickle," that is revenge. But if a man asks his fellow to lend him his sickle and he refuses, and the following day the second man asks the first to lend him a garment, and he replies, "Here it is. I am not like you," that is not bearing a grudge.

Maimonides, in his *Mishneh Torah* (Hilkhot Dei'ot 7:7–8), explains that a wise person will refuse to take revenge because it is worthless to make an issue over worldly things. One is simply magnifying the importance of a "sickle" by doing so. He also understands, as Rabbi Louis Jacobs explains in his *What Does Judaism Say About...* (1973), that the prohibition against bearing a grudge is a means of avoiding the more serious offense of taking revenge. This, Maimonides posits, is the proper approach if society is to be well established.

The Italian kabbalist Moshe Chaim Luzzatto (1707–1747), in his *Path of the Upright* (*Mesilat Yesharim*), distinguishes between revenge and bearing a grudge. He says that to take revenge is to return evil for evil, while bearing a grudge is to remind a person of the evil he has done to another, although the victim is willing to repay him with kindness.

The Book of Romans in the New Testament, written by the learned Jew Saul of Tarsus (later known as Saint Paul), who became devoted to the teachings of Jesus and labored to spread them to Gentiles and Jews living in Rome, understood and preached the very same message of Judaism on the subject of revenge. His famous teaching (Romans 12:19), "Vengeance is mine, I will repay, saith the Lord," is identical to the Hebrew words in the Book of Deuteronomy (32:35), *li nakam ve-shilem*. Vengeance is not an activity mortal man should be devoted to. Rectifying wrongs is within God's domain.

Historian Emanuel Ringelbaum (died 1944), who lived in the Warsaw ghetto during the Nazi occupation, was able to write in his diary, even after being incarcerated in a concentration camp, that vengeance is the Lord's prerogative. If this were not the case, he explains, "the vanquished would in turn plan their own vengeance, and so it would go on forever." This has been the prevailing Jewish view since biblical times.

Reward and Punishment

The concept of divine justice, of reward for good deeds and punishment for evil actions, is referred to in Deuteronomy 11:13–21, which is the second paragraph of the *Shema* prayer:

> If you will obey My commandments that I command you this day, to love the Lord your God and to serve Him with all your heart and soul, then I will provide rain for your land in its proper time…and you will eat and be satisfied. Beware, lest your heart be led astray and you will serve other gods and bow down to them. The Lord's anger will burst forth against you and He will seal the heavens so there will be no rain and the earth will not yield her produce. And you will soon perish from the good land the Lord is giving you.

Divine retribution, or *theodicy*—a word coined by the German philosopher Gottfried Leibnitz (1710)—is the hallmark of all Torah legislation. With the exception of the Book of Job, whose hero is punished not because of a fault of his own but because of a wager between God and Satan, the books of the Bible all attest to this belief in divine justice. Reward or punishment for actions does not always follow immediately, nor is it clearly discernible; but it is sure to come, if not in this world, then in the next. In the tractate *Kiddushin* (39b), Rabbi Jacob notes that there is not a single precept in the Torah where the reward for its fulfillment is immediate. Its reward will come when resurrection takes place.

Two classic views on the concept of reward and punishment were expressed by the twelfth-century Moses Maimonides and the fifteenth-century Joseph Albo, both Spanish philosophers. Maimonides presents the following as his eleventh Principle of Faith: "I believe with complete faith that the Exalted One rewards those who observe the commandments of the Torah and punishes those who transgress them. The greatest reward is to enter the world to come, and the greatest punishment is extinction."

Joseph Albo, in his *Sefer Ha-Ikarim* (*Book of Root-Principles*), considered reward and punishment to be one of the primary principles of Jewish faith.

See Afterlife; Resurrection; Sin.

Righteous Judge

The concept of God as a Righteous Judge (*Da'yan Ha-Emet* in Hebrew) is prominent in Jewish theology and is expressed pointedly in the prayer recited on Rosh Hashanah immediately following the sounding of the *shofar*. The prayer begins with the words "Today the world was created [*ha-yom harat olam*]" and continues, "On this day all creatures of the universe stand in judgment before Thee." The Righteous Judge concept emphasizes the equality of all people, rich and poor, free and enslaved. All stand before God to be judged for their conduct. As a person reaches out to God in sincerity, expressing remorse for past misdeeds, he or she can expect compassion from the Righteous Judge, who treats people mercifully and compassionately.

Following the loss of a loved one, at the time of rending a garment, the *Barukh Da'yan Ha-Emet* blessing—"Praised be Thou, O Lord our God, King of the universe, who is a Righteous Judge"—is pronounced. These words, uttered at a time of intense grief, bear testimony to the fact that the mourner harbors no blame against God for his misfortune and that God's judgment is being accepted.

Right vs. Left

In Jewish tradition, the right side, which represents strength, power, and victory, is favored over the left. The Bible expresses this sentiment in the Book of Exodus (15:6): "Your right hand, O Lord, is majestic in power; Your right hand, O Lord, shatters the enemy." It is reinforced in the Book of Psalms (118:16): "The right hand of the Lord is exalted; the right hand of the Lord is triumphant."

Any number of additional examples are to be found in Scripture to support the view that the right hand and right side are preferred to the left. In Genesis 48, Joseph brings his sons Manasseh and Ephraim to his father, Jacob, for a blessing. Joseph stations Manasseh, the older son, opposite Jacob's right side so that Jacob will be forced to bless him with his right hand. But Jacob preferred Ephraim to Manasseh, and so he crosses his hands, resting his right hand on Ephraim, the younger son.

Leviticus 8:22–26 describes one of the ceremonies connected with the sacrificial system. Moses dabbed the blood of the sacrificial ram on the lobe of Aaron's right ear, on the thumb of his right hand, and on the great toe of his right foot. Moses then followed the same procedure with the sons of Aaron. (Other sig-

nificant references in the Bible portraying the power of the right hand are to be found in Exodus 15:12 and Psalms 18:36; 139:10.)

Over the centuries the right side came to assume such significance in Jewish ritual that the Talmud (*Shabbat* 61a) prescribes that one must put on his right shoe first. When washing one's hands before pronouncing a blessing, water is to be poured on the right hand first. *Tefillin* is placed on the left arm (by right-handed persons), leaving the right hand free to wrap the *tefillin* straps around it. A *mezuzah* is affixed to the right, not the left, doorpost as one enters a room.

A Torah scroll is always carried in the right arm. This view was first expressed by fourth-century Babylonian scholar Rava (*Berakhot* 62a), who based his ruling on Deuteronomy 33:2: "The Lord came from Sinai...lightning flashing from His right." The Rabbis believed that this refers to the side from which God handed the Torah to Moses on Mount Sinai. This view is also expressed in the *Zohar*, where Rabbi Judah declared that the Torah was given from the side of power, the right side (*Parashat Yitro* 81a). In the minor tractate *Soferim* (3:10), the Rabbis ruled that when a Torah is passed from one person to another, it must be received on the right side.

The Talmud (*Berakhot* 62a) also notes that when one cleans himself after evacuating, he should use his left hand, not his right hand. Rabba bar Chama says that this method should be followed "because [food] is brought to one's mouth by the right hand [and the right hand should be kept in a state of purity]."

In answer to the question, How does one honor his teacher? The Rabbis responded (*Derekh Eretz Rabbah* 4:2), "When both are walking along the way, the student must place himself to the left of his teacher and not to the right [so that his teacher's right hand will be free to greet passersby]."

The early Romans had a similar conception of the importance of the right side. They believed that the left side represented evil. In fact, linguists maintain that the English word *sinister*, meaning "wicked" or "evil," is derived from the Latin word meaning "left side."

Rishon Le-Tziyon

Literally, "the first in Zion." An honorable title bestowed upon the Sephardic Chief Rabbi of Israel.

Rodef

This Hebrew word meaning "pursuer" is closely associated with the term *din rodef*, or "law of the pursuer." The term *din rodef* was first used in the talmudic tractate *Sanhedrin* (72b–73b), where it describes a situation in which a man is being robbed and fears for his life. To save himself, the victim attacks the criminal and kills him. The Rabbis consider the action justified, explaining that nothing is more important than saving a life, especially one's own.

In contemporary times, the law of the pursuer was invoked by Yigal Amir, who assassinated Prime Minister Yitzhak Rabin at a rally in Tel Aviv's Square of the Kings on Saturday night, November 4, 1995. Amir, a law student at Bar-Ilan University, defended his action as being in accordance with the law of the pursuer. Rabin had subscribed to the Oslo Peace Accords, which, Amir argued, put the lives of the people of Israel in jeopardy. Although Amir's reasoning was rejected by Jews as a whole, some activist rabbis did support it.

Rosh Chodesh

A Hebrew term literally meaning "head of the month" or "new moon," referring to the beginning of the Jewish month, which in ancient times (Isaiah 66:23 and II Kings 4:23) was widely celebrated.

In the Jewish calendar there are twenty-nine days in some months and thirty days in others. Since the moon makes one revolution around the earth every twenty-nine and one-half days, the New Moon actually appears every thirtieth day. When a month has twenty-nine days, the first day of the next month is considered Rosh Chodesh. However, when a month has thirty days, the New Moon actually appears on the thirtieth day of that month, not on the first day of the next month. Therefore, the arrival of the New Moon at the end of a thirty-day month is celebrated for two days: on the first day of the new month and also on the thirtieth day of the preceding month. In such cases, the new month starts with the second day of the New Moon celebration.

In ancient times the arrival of Rosh Chodesh was marked by the offering of special sacrifices in the Jerusalem Temple. When the Temples were destroyed and the sacrificial system was discontinued, the Temple ritual of the New Moon could no longer be carried out, and observance of the occasion continued only in a minor way. Most of its observances became associated chiefly with the liturgy: additional prayers (*Musaf*) were added to the morning service; the *Hallel* prayer was recited; the *Ya'aleh Ve-Yavo* prayer was added to the *Amidah*; and a special Torah reading was conducted.

On the Sabbath before the appearance of the New Moon, a special prayer called *Birkhat Ha-Chodesh* is recited in the synagogue.

Women, in particular, think of Rosh Chodesh as their holiday. In the Middle Ages pious women used to refrain from working on Rosh Chodesh (see *Shulchan Arukh*, Orach Cha'yim [417:1]), a custom based on the belief that when the Golden Calf was built, women refused to heed their husbands' requests to contribute their gold jewelry. Among the responsa of Rabbi Meir of Rothenburg (1215–1293) is one in which a questioner asks, "Is there a custom of abstaining from work on Saturday night and Rosh Chodesh?" Rabbi Meir responds, "There is a custom of women refraining from working on the day of the New Moon."

In recent years, women have begun to reclaim Rosh Chodesh as their holiday and have established new rituals to mark the occasion.

See Calendar.

Rosh Hashanah

A Hebrew term literally meaning "head of the year," referring specifically to the Jewish New Year. Jewish tradition postulates that Rosh Hashanah is the birthday of the world and a day of judgment when man must account for his actions during the past year and contemplate how well he has lived up to the values of Judaism. If he has fallen short, he must mend his ways in the year ahead so that the Book of Life, where God is said to record the deeds of each individual, will reflect a positive balance. Rosh Hashanah is therefore referred to as Yom Ha-Zikaron, "Day of Remembrance."

Although the Bible refers to Tishrei, the month in which Rosh Hashanah is celebrated, as the seventh month, it is in fact the first month of the *religious* new year. Nissan, the month in which Passover falls and in which the first crops of the post-winter season are harvested, is considered the first month of the agricultural new year.

The Bible (Leviticus 23:24) describes Rosh Hashanah as a one-day holiday to be observed on the first day of the seventh month, on the day of the arrival of the New Moon. In early centuries, testimony of witnesses was re-

quired to determine the official date of arrival of the New Moon, and then messengers were sent forth to notify outlying communities. If the witnesses were to arrive too late for the distant communities to be notified on time, those living far from Jerusalem would miss the correct day of observance of the holiday. In order to protect against this, Rosh Hashanah was made a two-day holiday, and the two days were considered one long day (*yoma arichta* in Aramaic) to confirm to the biblical call for a one-day holiday.

Once the calendar was firmly established by Hillel II in 359 C.E., the Jews of Palestine reverted to the practice of observing Rosh Hashanah for only one day. However, the observance of the holiday for two days had become so firmly established that Jews in the Diaspora retained the two-day holiday. When, in the Middle Ages, many European Jews began settling in Palestine, they brought with them their practice of observing Rosh Hashanah for two days, and soon all residents of Palestine began to observe Rosh Hashanah for two days, a practice that continues to this day. Most Reform Jewish congregations have adopted the biblical practice of celebrating Rosh Hashanah for only one day.

Penitential Period

The first day of Rosh Hashanah is the first day of the Ten Days of Repentance, which concludes with Yom Kippur. (The penitential period in the Jewish calendar actually starts at the beginning of Elul, one month before Rosh Hashanah.) These ten days have special significance because, as the liturgy of the High Holidays reminds the worshipper, it is during this period that God passes judgment on every individual; final judgment is reserved for Yom Kippur.

The Ten Days of Repentance are regarded

as man's last opportunity, through his actions, to influence God to reconsider an unfavorable decision (*Rosh Hashanah* 16b). For this reason, as Yom Kippur nears, the Rosh Hashanah greeting *Leshanah tovah tikateivu*, "May you be *inscribed* in the Book of Life for a good life," is changed to *Gemar chatimah tovah*, "May you be *sealed* in the Book of Life for a good life."

Synagogue Observance

Rosh Hashanah morning services—which can last from two to six hours depending on the congregation—stress the concept of "return to God," who in His mercy is willing to receive the penitent, forgive his sins, and offer him an opportunity to begin the New Year with a clean slate. According to the Talmud (*Rosh Hashanah* 16a), God's decision is not made in haste. The gates of repentance remain open until the Day of Atonement, at which time the final decree is established: "Who will live and who will die; who will be serene and who will be disturbed; who will be poor and who will be rich; who will be humbled and who will be exalted."

The wearing of a white robe during High Holiday services is a longstanding tradition. White is symbolic of humility and purity of thought. When the High Priest entered the Holy of Holies on the Day of Atonement, rather than dressing in his usual golden vestments, he wore simple white linen garments.

The white robe, called a *kittl* in Yiddish, is worn on Rosh Hashanah and Yom Kippur not only by rabbis and cantors but by some members of the congregation. The tradition was inspired by the statement in the Book of Isaiah, which is read on Rosh Hashanah: "Though your sin be as scarlet [hence real and uncontestable], they shall be as white as snow [after repentance]" (Isaiah 1:18). It has also become traditional to replace the colored ark curtain (*parokhet*), the Torah mantles, and pulpit covers, with white ones.

The most impressive and important Rosh Hashanah synagogue ritual is the blowing of the ram's horn (*shofar*). One other dramatic moment occurs during the *Musaf* service when the cantor chants, "We bend the knee and prostrate ourselves before the King of Kings." As he utters these words as part of the *Aleinu* prayer, he kneels and touches his forehead to the ground. In some congregations many worshippers do the same.

The Rosh Hashanah service contains many poems, called *piyyutim* in Hebrew (singular, *piyyut*), that were written over the centuries. (*Piyyut* is the Hebraic form of the Greek word that gave us the English word "poet.")

Rosh Hashanah Foods

The eighth chapter of the Book of Nehemiah speaks of Rosh Hashanah as a holy day on which sweets should be eaten. In that chapter, Ezra and Nehemiah address the congregation of Israel on the first day of Tishrei, which is Rosh Hashanah, saying to them:

> This day is holy unto the Lord your God; mourn not, weep not . . . Go your way and eat the fat, and drink the sweet, and send portions unto him for whom nothing is prepared, for this day is holy unto our Lord.

The fifteenth-century scholar Rabbi Jacob Levi Mollin of Germany, also known as the Maharil, interpreted the words "drink the sweet" to mean that Jews should use honey at their Rosh Hashanah meals on the first day of Tishrei. The serving of sweet side dishes and desserts on the holiday is said to stem from the Maharil's interpretation.

At mealtime, family members and guests dip a piece of apple or *challah* in honey and recite the phrase, "May the New Year be as good and sweet as honey." The normal year-round procedure of dipping *challah* in salt before tasting it is not followed on Rosh Hashanah.

Honey cake, called *lekach* ("portion") in Hebrew, is a traditional East European holiday food. Honey cake is served with the hope and prayer that those who observe Jewish traditions will be blessed with "a goodly portion."

Carrot *tzimmes*, a honey-sweetened carrot preparation, is served on Rosh Hashanah to express the hope for a sweet year. The Yiddish word for carrot is *meiren*, which also means "to multiply," thus expressing the hope for a productive year in which man's blessings may be multiplied. Another explanation is that when the carrots are sliced, they become coin-shaped; and since carrots are also golden-colored, they are a symbol of prosperity.

The *t'einah*, mentioned in Genesis, is a variety of fig that is particularly known for its sweetness and ripens in Israel in August, shortly before the Rosh Hashanah holiday. (Another variety, *pagim*, ripens later in the year and is not as sweet.) Since Rosh Hashanah is associated with the creation of the world and the first humans, it is logical that the species of fruit (according to one tradition) that Adam and Eve tasted in the Garden of Eden would be linked to the New Year holiday.

Observant Jews often deny themselves certain fruits—such as grapes, pomegranates, and apples—all summer long so that they may eat them for the first time on the second night of Rosh Hashanah. (The pomegranate is particularly popular because it has many seeds, thus symbolizing the hope that the year ahead will be one in which man will be privileged to perform many worthy deeds.) At that time, the *She-heche'yanu* prayer, which expresses thanks for having reached this important moment in life in good health and peace, is recited.

Chasidim serve beets on Rosh Hashanah. The basis for this practice is to be found in the Talmud (*Hora'yot* 12a) where the scholar Abbayei says that at the beginning of the year a person should eat pumpkins, leeks, beets, dates, etc., for these grow in abundance and are good omens. Another reason why *chasidim* serve beet roots or beet leaves on Rosh Hashanah is that the Hebrew word for beet, *selek*, is similar in origin to the Hebrew word *she-yistalku* in the phrase *She-yistalku oivaynu* ("May we rid ourselves of our enemies"), an expression used on Rosh Hashanah.

Some Jews refrain from eating nuts on Rosh Hashanah because *egoz*, the Hebrew word for nut, has the same numerical value as *cheit*, the Hebrew word for sin. *Egoz* has a value of seventeen, and *cheit*, if spelled without the *alef*, also has a value of seventeen.

In Jewish tradition, it became customary to serve fish, which is associated with productivity, as part of the holiday meal. The head of a fish is served, symbolizing the hope that greatness and leadership may be man's lot in the coming year. The tradition is associated with the promise of God in the Book of Deuteronomy (29:13) that those who observe the commandments of the Torah will be blessed: "The Lord will make you the head and not the tail; you will always be on top and not on bottom."

See She-heche'yanu; Shofar; Tashlikh.

Sabbath

The institution of the Sabbath, a day set aside for rest and worship, dates back to early biblical times. The importance of the Sabbath is emphasized in both the Book of Exodus and the Book of Deuteronomy, where its observance is listed as the fourth of the Ten Commandments.

In Exodus (20:8–11) the Sabbath is underscored as a day of rest, because it was on that day that all the acts of Creation were completed and God "rested." Deuteronomy (5:12–15) describes the Sabbath as a day of rest during which one should remember the time when the Israelites were slaves under Pharaoh in Egypt, after which God freed them from oppression by means of his "mighty hand."

To the Rabbis of the Talmud and later generations, the Sabbath became the focus of the Jewish religion, and they introduced regulations and ordinances designed to keep it a day free from the intrusion of mundane matters. An entire 312-page tractate of the Babylonian Talmud is devoted to the many regulations by which the day is to be governed.

The Sabbath has thus become the most holy day in the Jewish calendar, even more so than Yom Kippur, the Day of Atonement. The penalty for violating the fast day of Yom Kippur is excommunication (Leviticus 23:29–30), whereas the penalty for desecrating the Sabbath is death (Exodus 31:15), a clear indication that the Sabbath is considered more holy than Yom Kippur.

In the Torah, there are more reminders about the Sabbath observance than about any other matter, with the possible exception of idolatry. The Sabbath may be violated only for the sake of saving of a life (*pikuach nefesh*).

The Sabbath in Legend

So central had the fourth of the Ten Commandments become in Jewish life that many legends grew up around it to emphasize its importance. In one legend, God speaks to the Children of Israel, saying, "My children, if you are willing to accept the Torah and observe its precepts [*mitzvot*], I will grant you a most precious gift."

"And what is this precious gift to be?" ask the Children of Israel.

"The world to come," is the reply.

"Tell us what the world to come is like," retort the Children of Israel.

God responds, "I have already given you the Sabbath. The Sabbath is a taste of the world to come."

In other legends, non-Jews are heard expressing interest in the manner in which Jews find peace and tranquility on this special day of the week. The Talmud (*Shabbat* 119a) describes how Roman Emperor Hadrian (117 to 138) once asked his friend Rabbi Joshua ben Chananiah, "Why does the food you eat on the Sabbath have such a fragrant odor?"

The rabbi responded, "It is because we have a certain spice, called Sabbath. We put that into our food and it gives it a delightful flavor and odor."

"Give us some of that spice," said the emperor.

"I can't," replied the rabbi. "It works only for those who observe the Sabbath, but for anyone else it is of no use."

So important did the observance of the Sabbath become to the ancient Rabbis that the famous Shimon bar Yocha'i was prompted to say that by honoring the Sabbath, Jews can find the path to personal salvation. "If Israel were to observe but two consecutive Sabbaths," he said (*Shabbat* 118a), "the world would be redeemed." Rabbi Yochanan went even further, saying, "He who observes the Sabbath as prescribed by law is forgiven, even if he practices idolatry."

A Day of Celebration

The Sabbath has been compared to a bride. Rabbi Isaac Luria, the sixteenth-century mystic of Safed, took this personification of the Sabbath bride literally. Late on Friday afternoons, he and his disciples would march in a procession to the outskirts of the town to greet the queen, the Sabbath bride, with song.

The uniqueness and holiness of the day is celebrated in traditional homes by sharing in a festive meal on an elaborately set table covered with a white tablecloth. Two *challot* are placed on the table. (*See* Challah.) The Talmud (*Pesachim* 100b in the *Tosafot*) describes the custom of covering the Sabbath table with a white cloth as a reminder of the manna that covered the earth during the sojourn of the Israelites in the desert after the exodus from Egypt. Another explanation is that the two rows of showbreads (*challot*) that were continuously on display in the Tabernacle were laid out on a "pure table," as the Bible puts it. White is a symbol of purity.

Before sunset the homemaker conducts a candlelighting ceremony, invoking the biblical commandment to keep the Sabbath holy. Before the meal is begun, the *Kiddush* is recited. A prayer of sanctification, the *Kiddush* stresses two themes: creation and freedom— God as the creative power that sets man free. God and freedom are interrelated. During the meal, in many homes, Sabbath songs (*zemirot*) are sung.

Orthodox and some Conservative synagogues hold an early (just before sundown) Friday evening service called *Kabbalat Shabbat* ("receiving the Sabbath"). Non-Orthodox institutions usually hold a late Friday evening service, which is followed by an *oneg Shabbat* at which refreshments are served.

At the Sabbath morning synagogue services (*Shacharit and Musaf*), the weekly portion of the Torah is read. Seven Torah honors (*aliyot*) are awarded in traditional synagogues. Toward the end of the day, an afternoon prayer service (*Minchah*) is held at which three people are called to the Torah. A minimum of nine verses is then read from the *sidrah,* at least three for each *aliyah.*

Following the afternoon service, a third repast (*se'udah shelishit*) is often served, at which time songs are sung and a short lecture on the Torah reading of the week or some other topic is presented. Finally, the evening (*Ma'ariv*) service is held, which concludes with the *havdalah* ceremony. At this point, the Sabbath is officially over.

Upon returning home from the synagogue, some families enjoy a post-Sabbath meal called *melaveh malkah*, meaning "accompanying the Sabbath Queen [on her departure for the week]."

Special Sabbaths

A number of Sabbaths are celebrated during the year to call attention to special times in the Jewish calendar. These include Shabbat Chazon, Shabbat ha-Chodesh, Shabbat Ha-Gadol, Shabbat Kallah, Shabbat Mevarkhim, Shabbat Nachamu, Shabbat Parah, Shabbat Rosh Chodesh, Shabbat Shekalim, Shabbat Shirah, Shabbat Shuvah, and Shabbat Zakhor. (*See individual entries.*)

Sabbath Restrictions

The Bible forbids only three types of Sabbath activity (known in Hebrew as *melakhah*): plowing a field and harvesting its produce (Exodus 34:21); making a fire (Exodus 35:3); and gathering wood (Numbers 15:32–36).

The caution against making a fire on the Sabbath is preceded by the statement, "Whoever does any work on the Sabbath shall be put to death." No biblical explanation is offered for the imposition of the death penalty upon those who performed work on the Sabbath, nor is the term "work" defined in the Bible.

The Rabbis (Mishnah *Shabbat* 7:2) explain the meaning of "work" by declaring that thirty-nine categories of work are to be avoided on the Sabbath. These include growing and preparing food; making clothing by shearing, weaving, washing, bleaching, spinning, dyeing, tanning, and curing; building structures or demolishing them; and transporting goods in the public domain. Secondary prohibitions were also applied to such activities as the *handling* of tools or instruments involved in the above-mentioned work. Thus, writing and erasing were prohibited among a host of other minor activities.

Law of Muktzah

One category of activity introduced by the Rabbis of the Talmud is labeled *muktzah*, meaning "setting apart." This refers to the prohibition against handling, or even touching, articles that are part of the regular workaday routine.

The law of *muktzah* applies also to any object that is even indirectly associated with work or business. Thus, a purse or wallet may not be touched even if it contains no money; a pencil may not be touched even if one has no intention of writing with it. The introduction of these rabbinic enactments (*gezeirot* in Hebrew) was precautionary. The Rabbis felt that if a person is permitted to touch *muktzah* items on the Sabbath, he might inadvertently forget and actually use them.

Later authorities proved themselves flexible in interpreting the law of *muktzah*. Moses Isserles (1525–1572), the Ashkenazic authority whose notes are part of the *Code of Jewish Law*, remarks that a person may carry money on the Sabbath if he finds himself in a situation where he must spend the Sabbath at an inn and is afraid that the money might be stolen if he leaves it unattended in his room (*Shulchan Arukh*, Orach Cha'yim 301:33).

Contemporary authorities in their responsa have applied this ruling to the problem of muggings. The elderly, being prime targets, have been permitted by rabbinic authorities to carry money on the Sabbath since it is established that muggers often become violent when they discover that their victims are without money.

Concepts of Shevut and Eruv

In order that the Sabbath be a day of complete rest, the Rabbis (Mishnah *Beitzah* 5:2) enacted a law known as *shevut* (derived from the word *shabbat*, meaning "rest"). The Mishnah says: "The following acts are culpable as a *shevut*: one may not climb a tree, nor ride a beast, nor swim, nor clap one's hands, nor slap [the thighs], nor dance." In each case the act is banned not because it is a violation of the law in itself, but because it might *lead* to a violation of the law.

The Talmud goes on to explain that if one climbs a tree, he might pluck a fruit, and that would be a violation of Sabbath law. If one rides on an animal, he might cut off a branch (to use as a whip), and this would be a violation of law. In the same vein, the Rabbis forbade the blowing of the *shofar* on the Sabbath, lest the *shofar* blower carry the instrument in public to his teacher for last-minute instruction, thus violating the law against carrying on the Sabbath. Through such secondary prohibitions the Rabbis sought to create "fences" or "curbs" that would protect Sabbath law from being violated.

Thus, strict constructionists of Jewish law forbid swimming on the Sabbath on the grounds that one might splash water from the river, lake, or pool, which in turn might create a furrow or depression in the adjacent ground, and this would be a violation of Sabbath law against digging in the earth. If this can be avoided, swimming is permitted (Orach Cha'yim 339:2), although some authorities would still ban swimming lest the swimmer sit on the wet bathing suit and *squeeze* water from it.

The ban on playing baseball, basketball, and similar sports on the Sabbath falls into the same category. It is argued that one might be tempted to carry the ball out of one's private property into the public domain, and such carrying from one domain into the other is a Sabbath violation. Even when played in the private domain (which is permissible), the ball might hit soft earth and create a depression or hole, which would constitute a violation. For these reasons, Joseph Caro (1488–1575), author of the *Shulchan Arukh* (Orach Cha'yim 308:45), declares it forbidden to play ball on the Sabbath and holidays.

A controversy with regard to handclapping on the Sabbath arose when Rabbi Judah the Prince's son Shimon was being honored on the Sabbath prior to his marriage. Rabbi Meir saw members of the congregation clapping the back of their hands (not in the normal fashion), and he said to Rabbi Judah, "My master, has the Sabbath been suspended?"

Ovadiah of Bertinoro, the fifteenth-century Italian commentator on the Mishnah, theorized that the clapping of hands and dancing are prohibited only because these activities involve music. Musical instruments were used to accompany dancing, and people clapped hands and kept beat by slapping their sides. Since a musical instrument might break while the activity was in progress, and one might be tempted to fix it on the spot (and by so doing violate Sabbath law), dancing and clapping hands were prohibited as a precautionary mea-

sure. Thus it became customary to refrain from applauding in the synagogue at the conclusion of sermons and speeches on the Sabbath.

The hardships imposed by many of the Sabbath prohibitions led to the development of the *eruv* ("amalgam, mixture") concept. One of its purposes is to transform the public domain into a private domain. On the Sabbath, the carrying of objects is prohibited in the public domain but permitted in the private domain. An *eruv* was established by drawing a wire or a nylon cord around the entire perimeter of a specific area, thus establishing a private zone in which objects may be carried on the Sabbath, baby carriages pushed, etc. (See *Eruv* for more about this concept.)

Fire vs. Electricity

The Bible (Exodus 35:3) specifically prohibits the making of a fire—and, by extension, cooking—on the Sabbath. However, since tradition demands that Sabbath be "a day of delight," some hot or warm food is usually served. Observant families will keep one or more of the stove burners at a moderate temperature and place a metal sheet (called a *blech* in Yiddish) over the burners so that cooked food can be kept warm.

Orthodox and Conservative Jews consider inviolable the biblical ban on lighting a fire on the Sabbath. There is a difference of opinion, however, among Conservative Jews as to whether *electricity* is to be characterized as fire. The traditional position is that electricity is fire because, like fire, electricity is used to heat, illuminate, and cook. Accordingly, its use on the Sabbath is forbidden.

While a minority of the Committee on Law and Standards of the Rabbinical Assembly (Conservative) agrees with the traditional position, the majority is of the opinion that electricity is not fire and that its use is therefore not a violation of Sabbath law. (The Reconstructionist movement shares this view.) It permits the turning on and putting off of electric lights, radios, television sets, and the like because use of these modern inventions enhances the joy of the Sabbath and reduces personal discomfort. Permission to turn on electric stoves or appliances to warm food is not included in this decision, because the use of such heating devices can result in cooking.

Almost all observant Jews agree that it is permissible to program a timer to turn lights on and off during the Sabbath. Some also program their radios and television sets. However, Rabbi Moshe Feinstein, in his book of responsa (*Igrot Moshe*, Orach Cha'yim 23), permits the use of a timer to switch electric lights on and off on the Sabbath only because it is now a widely accepted practice among Orthodox Jews. But he opposes its use for preprogramming an electric stove or food warmer to heat precooked food on the Sabbath—this despite the fact that the warming of precooked food is permissible on the Sabbath. Feinstein is apprehensive that use of the timer in connection with the warming of food might ultimately lead to use of the timer for other unnecessary activities, such as putting a television on and off.

Recognizing the need to perform certain essentials on the Sabbath, such as milking cows, turning on sprinklers in the fields, and so on, Orthodox *kibbutzim* in Israel long ago adopted a preprogrammed system of timing devices that turn machines on and off automatically, thus avoiding any unnecessary violation of the Sabbath.

Ovadiah Yosef, Israel's former Sephardic Chief Rabbi, ruled that trained monkeys may turn off lights or do other domestic chores forbidden to Jews on the Sabbath. However, he emphasized that only a borrowed monkey, dog, or other animal capable of performing such tasks may be used. One's *own* beast must be allowed to rest, as per the biblical commandment. The accepted practice, however, is that a non-Jew may be engaged prior to the Sabbath to perform any of these duties (*see* Shabbes Goy).

Traveling on the Sabbath

From very early talmudic times, the Rabbis recognized that if Jews were to be able to maintain contact with the outside world, it would be necessary for them to travel on the Sabbath. Because of the distances between cities and the length of time required to cross large bodies of water, it would have been impossible for Jews to carry on normal business dealings or to engage in social or charitable activities if they had not been able to travel on the Sabbath.

The Talmud (*Shabbat* 19a) stipulates that one may not set out on a journey by ship unless he boards the ship at least three days before the Sabbath begins. This applies only to trips made for business or social purposes. If the purpose of the trip is charitable—to raise funds for a Torah institution, to collect funds for orphans and widows, to ransom a captive, or to carry out similar *mitzvot* (religious precepts)—the Rabbis permit one to board the ship immediately before the onset of Sabbath (*Erev Shabbat*). The above laws were codified in the sixteenth century in Joseph Caro's *Code of Jewish Law* (*Shulchan Arukh*, Orach Cha'yim 248:1–2).

Today, the Orthodox community is vigorously opposed to any form of travel on the Sabbath while the non-Orthodox are divided on the issue. By a majority vote of its Committee on Law and Standards, the Conservative rabbinate granted its constituents permission to travel to the synagogue on the Sabbath and holidays in order to attend services, but not for any other purpose. By "travel" the Committee means riding in a vehicle, not driving one. The ruling, reported in full in the 1950 *Proceedings of the Rabbinical Assembly*, is based on the fact that travel on the Sabbath does not violate any direct biblical or rabbinic law and that it is better to join fellow Jews in worship than to engage in prayer alone.

Those who oppose the ruling argue that traveling on the Sabbath and holidays violates the spirit of holiness associated with these days, and that granting permission to travel in a car may lead to violations of Jewish law. If one is permitted to travel to the synagogue on these days, they fear, he may grow accustomed to the idea of traveling and eventually will do so for other purposes, including shopping and doing business. Some also argue that riding in a car may lead to *driving* a car, and when one drives he must turn the ignition key to start the motor, which involves starting a fire (combustion), which is a violation of biblical law.

Treatment of Sabbath Violators

Many differences of opinion have been expressed over the centuries as to how a violator of Sabbath law should be treated and, in fact, who is to be considered a true violator of the law. While the death penalty for Sabbath violators no longer applies, the most extreme Orthodox view, expressed by Moses Maimonides, equates a Jew who desecrates the Sabbath with an idolator and an atheist. This equation is also made in the *Shulchan Arukh* (Orach Cha'yim 385:3).

The Rabbis (*Eruvin* 69a; *Shulchan Arukh*, Orach Cha'yim 385:3) considered a person who violates Sabbath law *publicly* to be in the category of the worst of all apostates who have flouted Jewish law. They considered such a person a much greater threat to the future of

Judaism than he who violates the Sabbath in the privacy of his own home, because by his actions he may encourage others to sin.

Condemnation aside, virtually no Orthodox authority has banned a Sabbath violator from participation in Jewish religious and social life. While Orthodox authorities (*Igrot Moshe*, Orach Cha'yim 23) will not allow a non-Orthodox Jew (especially one reputed to be a Sabbath violator) to sign as a witness on a *ketubbah*, they will count a non-Orthodox Jew as part of a *minyan*.

Mourning on the Sabbath

According to Jewish tradition, any activity that would impinge upon the joy and peace of the Sabbath has been taboo. Thus, while instrumental music was an integral part of the prayer service in Temple times, once the Temple was destroyed it was not carried over into the synagogue service. In modern times, many liberal congregations have come to believe that the richness and joy music brings to the service adds to the Sabbath spirit, and that mourning on the Sabbath is contrary to Jewish tradition.

Because the Sabbath was intended to engender joy, mourning for a relative is not permitted on the Sabbath (and holidays), for Isaiah (58:13) says that the Sabbath must be kept as "day of delight." No intrusion, not even death, may interfere with this goal. Hence, when the Sabbath day comes during the week of *shivah*, all mourning is suspended for the duration of the Sabbath, although it is counted as one of the seven days of mourning. On these days a mourner dresses up appropriately, attends synagogue, and carries on somewhat normally until nightfall, at which time mourning resumes.

The Christian Sabbath

In explaining why Christians changed the Sabbath day from Saturday to Sunday, the Talmud describes how prayers and fasting by Jewish laymen accompanied the offering of various sacrifices in the Temple on every day of the week except Sunday. Rabbi Yochanan, the leader of Jewry during the trying years of 66–70 C.E., immediately prior to the destruction of the Second Temple, explained (*Ta'anit* 27b) why sacrifices were not offered on Sunday: "So as not to offend the Nazarenes." Rashi comments: "They [the Nazarenes or Christians] made Sunday their holy day."

Although it would appear from the comment of Rabbi Yochanan that Sunday became the day of rest for Christians soon after the death of Jesus, it was actually not until the year 321 that it became official. In that year Constantine, the emperor of Rome—the first Roman emperor to embrace Christianity—declared Sunday a legal holiday, the official day of worship for all Christians, thus replacing the Sabbath as proclaimed in the Ten Commandments (Exodus 20:8). Henceforth, the Sabbath was to be celebrated on the first day of the week (Sunday), the day on which, in Christian tradition, Jesus rose from the dead. The change of the Sabbath day from Saturday to Sunday marked a complete break between Christianity and Judaism, its mother religion.

Although today most Christian sects observe Sunday as the Sabbath, the Seventh-Day Adventists continue to observe the Sabbath on Saturday because they believe that God's commandment, "Remember the Sabbath Day," refers to the seventh day of the week.

Sabbatical Year

Known in Hebrew as *shemittah*, this concept is based upon the biblical ordinance (Exodus 23:10–11) requiring that the land be allowed to rest (lie fallow) every seventh year.

See Shemittah.

Sacrificial System

Along with all ancient people who offered animal sacrifices to curry favor with and express gratitude to a deity, Jews brought offerings to God from earliest times until the Second Temple was destroyed by the Romans in 70 C.E. These sacrifices, which are detailed in the Book of Leviticus, consisted primarily of burnt offerings, which represented man's total subservience to God; peace offerings, which expressed man's gratitude for God's beneficence; sin offerings, which expressed man's regret over being neglectful of God's commandments; and community offerings, which were sacrificed on behalf of the well-being of the entire congregation of Israel. Not all offerings were animal; some were offerings of grain and cereals.

Jews from all over Palestine and even surrounding areas would make a strong effort to journey to Jerusalem on one of the three major festivals (Passover, Sukkot, and Shavuot), at which time they would bring their offerings so as to fulfill the commandment in the Book of Exodus (23:17), "Three times a year all your men shall appear before God, the Lord."

After the destruction of the Second Temple, the synagogue became the center of religious life, and an expanded worship service emphasizing offerings of the heart became the substitute for the Temple sacrificial system. Nevertheless, Jews continued to include in their prayers a yearning for the rebuilding of the Temple and the reintroduction of the old sacrificial system.

Even as late as the twelfth century, Moses Maimonides continued to hope that the

Temple would be rebuilt and sacrifices reintroduced. He believed so strongly in this that his code of Jewish law, the *Mishneh Torah*, details procedures to be followed, so that when the Messiah arrives and the Temple service is restored, the Priests will know how to carry out their duties. In his *Guide of the Perplexed* (III:32), Maimonides explains that the original purpose of the sacrificial system—namely, "to wean away the primitive Israelites from idolatrous worship, to give its followers purity and holiness by teaching them to suppress sensuality, to guard against it and to reduce it to a minimum"—was still valid.

On the other hand, another codifier of the law, the sixteenth-century Joseph Caro, devotes no space to this subject in his *Code of Jewish Law (Shulchan Arukh)* and clearly did not anticipate the restoration of the sacrificial system.

While theoretically Orthodox Jews look forward to the restoration of the sacrificial system, and their prayerbooks continue to express this, few have taken the idea literally. In the 1930s, the Chief Rabbi of Palestine, Abraham I. Kook, who believed that the coming of the Messiah was imminent, proposed that a school be established to train Priests in the practical conduct of Temple ritual. However, he found no support for the idea and abandoned it. However, in Israel today, there is an organization that is recreating the Temple artifacts in preparation for the Messiah.

Reform and Reconstructionist prayerbooks have eliminated all prayers referring to the sacrificial system. Conservative prayerbooks retain these prayers but cast them in the past tense, which is a way of taking note of the sacrificial system only as a historical fact and part of Jewish tradition.

Sadducees

The Sadducees (in Hebrew, *Tzedokim*), a religious/political party organized around 200 B.C.E., consisted mainly of the wealthier and more aristocratic members of the Jewish community. The Priests (*Kohanim*), who were in charge of all Temple activity, including its lucrative sacrificial system, were primary members of this group. The actual name *Tzedokim* was adopted because the High Priest Tzadok was the person called upon by King David to install Solomon as his successor.

The Sadducees were strict constructionists. They believed the words of the Torah to be inviolate; they must be accepted literally and are not subject to modification or interpretation. Thus, the Sadducees contended, the Shavuot holiday must always fall on a Sunday because Leviticus 23:15 says that it is to be observed fifty days after Passover, and the counting is to begin on "the day after the Sabbath." The Pharisees contended that the word "Sabbath" in that verse means the Passover *holiday*, while the Sadducees take Sabbath to mean the first actual Sabbath day after the beginning of the Passover holiday.

The Sadducees rejected immortality of the soul, resurrection, and life after death, concepts not mentioned in the Torah. The approach of the Pharisees, who supported these beliefs, was more acceptable to the masses, and consequently Pharisaic Judaism survived even when the Temple was destroyed in 70 C.E. At this point, when the sacrificial system could no longer be sustained and the power of the priestly clan was totally diminished, the Sadducees ceased being a viable religious/political power.

Traditional Judaism rejected the views of the Sadducees, although Jewish cults such as the Samaritans and Karaites continue to follow their rulings to this day.

Salt

The use of salt in Jewish ritual is first mentioned in the Book of Leviticus (2:13), which declares, *Al kol korbankha takriv melach*, "On all your [meal] offerings shall you sprinkle salt" (Leviticus 2:13). And the Talmud (*Menachot* 20a, b) extended this requirement to include all sacrifices. Since sacrifices were not always eaten immediately by the Priest or the offerer, the preservative qualities of salt were effective in retarding food spoilage.

Salt in general was important throughout biblical and later times. Treaties were sealed with salt; the Bible (Numbers 18:19) speaks of "an everlasting covenant of salt," signifying the establishment of a solemn permanent bond of lifelong loyalty; and from the Book of Ezekiel (16:4) we learn that newborn babes were rubbed with salt, a practice still current in the Orient. The Talmud (*Yerushalmi Hora'yot* 3:5) says, "The world can get along without pepper, but it cannot get along without salt." Homer called it "divine" and Plato described it as a substance of the gods.

So common and inexpensive was salt that the Midrash (*Lamentations Rabbah* 1:7) relates that an Athenian in Jerusalem once gave a child a penny and asked him teasingly to bring something of which he could eat his fill and have plenty left over to take on his journey. The child brought him salt.

When the Temple was destroyed and sacrifices were no longer offered, the table in the home assumed the role of the altar. The Talmud (*Berakhot* 55a) says, "A man's table is like the altar that brings atonement" to which the Babylonian scholar Rav (*Berakhot* 44a) adds, "A meal with no salt is no meal."

The custom of dipping bread in salt evolved as a memorial to the sacrificial system. Medieval commentators expressed the view that salt must be set on the table before every meal because it protects one against Satan. Kabbalists (mystics) believed that dipping bread in salt and reciting the *Hamotzi* blessing render evil spirits powerless to harm man. Some kabbalists were in the habit of dipping bread in salt three times because God's name, Yehovah (spelled *yud, hei, vav, hei),* has the numerical value of twenty-six (*yud* equals 10; *hei* equals 5; *vav* equals 6), and *three* times twenty-six is seventy-eight, which is the numerical value of *melach*, the Hebrew word for salt.

In present-day Israel, the mayor of Jerusalem often greets distinguished visitors at the entrance of the city with an offering of bread and salt. Arabs, to this day, seal agreements with bread and salt.

Salt Water

In Jerusalem of the first and second centuries, it was customary at mealtime to dip a vegetable (hors d'oeuvre) in salt water. This was probably done at least partially for health reasons: salt was known to have antiseptic as well as seasoning value.

At the Passover *Seder*, salt water is used as a solution in which to dip first a vegetable (*karpas*) and later, before the meal, a hard-boiled egg. The salt water is said to serve as a reminder of the many salty tears shed by the Israelites during their years of bondage in Egypt.

See Bread.

Salvation

The *Nishmat Kol Chai* ("The soul of all living beings") prayer, which is recited as part of the morning service on Sabbaths and holidays and is also prominent in the Passover *Seder* ritual, expresses the essence of the Jewish concept of salvation:

The soul of all living beings shall bless Your Name, O Lord our God. . . . You are

God and aside from You we have no king, redeemer, or savior; no liberator, rescuer, or sustainer.... You have redeemed us from Egypt and liberated us from the house of bondage... You saved us from the sword and from the plague, and spared us from severe disease.

Salvation by definition is the deliverance of man from dire situations, particularly those involving intense suffering, or the spiritual rescue from the consequences of sin. Many early religions, Judaism included, envisioned the nascent world as a place of purity and perfection, a Garden of Eden in which everything required for a free and happy life was present, a place where peace and harmony would reign. But then, Adam and Eve, tempted by the serpent, succumbed and sinned, displaying disobedience toward their Maker. The ideal state was shattered. Man now had to toil for his daily bread, and childbirth, which was to have been an easy experience, became painful.

According to Jewish tradition, man would be able to redeem himself only by obtaining God's forgiveness; and this could be accomplished only by subjugating himself to God's will through the observance of His commandments (*mitzvot*). While professing a belief in God is an essential part of Judaism, more important than belief is observance. Being actively observant and committed to carrying out the rites and rituals of Judaism are prerequisites to achieving salvation.

Judaism differs from Christianity in that the latter requires a mere belief in Jesus as God incarnate—as a being who was crucified, suffered death, and was resurrected from the dead. His death atoned for all the sins of mankind. Little or no action is called for on the part of the believer. In Judaism, salvation comes only in response to personal effort and the performance of good deeds.

In the Jewish tradition, salvation has, in addition to its personal element, a national aspect that is emphasized in the various books of the prophets. Jeremiah and Zekhariah, for example, address themselves to the worst catastrophe suffered by Jews in the course of their history, namely, the exile from the land of their fathers, known in Hebrew as the *galut*. "Because of our sins we were exiled from our land" are the stark words employed by the prayerbook in describing the event. But the promise of return was never abandoned, and the words of Jeremiah (31:9ff.) have ever been on the lips of loyal Jews:

He who scattered Israel will gather them,
And will guard them as a shepherd his
    flock.
For the Lord will ransom Jacob,
Redeem him from one too strong for
    him....

They shall return from the enemy's land.
And there is hope for the future.
Your children shall return to their old
    boundaries.

See Messiah and Messianic Age.

Samaritans

In 586 B.C.E. the Babylonians destroyed the First Temple, which had been built by King Solomon in 960 B.C.E., and forced most Jews to leave Palestine. Those who remained behind included a group who lived in Samaria (hence the name Samaritans) in an area today called Nablus (Shekhem in Hebrew).

In 530 B.C.E., the Persians conquered the Chaldeans, who then ruled over Babylonia. The benevolent Persian king, Cyrus, allowed the Jews who had been exiled to Babylonia in 586 to return to Palestine. When they did, they wanted to rebuild the Temple. The Samaritans offered to help, but their offer was refused on the grounds that during the fifty-six years when Jews were in Babylonian exile, the Jews who remained behind in Palestine became idol worshippers, followers of the customs and rituals of the Chaldeans. As a result, animosity developed between the Samaritans and the rest of the Jewish population, one that was to last for centuries. Maimonides categorized the idol-worshipping Samaritans as Gentiles, and to the present time are still not recognized as Jews.

Samaritans consider Mount Gerizim, overlooking Nablus, to be the holy mountain on which the intended sacrifice of Isaac (known as the *Akeidah*) was to have taken place. In 332 B.C.E., having been granted permission by Alexander the Great, the Samaritans built a temple on Mount Gerizim. The temple was later destroyed by John Hyrcanus, but to this day Samaritans assemble on this mountaintop to celebrate the Passover holiday in the manner prescribed in the Bible, that is, by offering the paschal lamb as a sacrifice. Like the Karaites, the Samaritans do not accept the validity of postbiblical, rabbinic law.

The minor talmudic tractate *Kutim* (2:7) concludes by asking when the Jewish community at large will be able to accept the Samaritans as full-fledged Jews. The answer given is, "When they abandon their belief in Mount Gerizim [as a holy mountain], acknowledge Jerusalem as the holy city, and believe in the resurrection of the dead." (*See Sanhedrin* 90b for more on the rabbinic attitude toward Samaritans.)

In the fourth and fifth centuries, the Samaritan community in Palestine numbered over one million. By 1917 the number had dwindled to less than one hundred fifty, most of whom survived by selling ancient parchments. By 1995 the Samaritan population was 574, half of whom lived on Mount Gerizim on the West Bank, and the other half as Israeli citizens in Holon, near Tel Aviv.

Sanctification

See Kiddush Ha-Shem.

Sandek

A title derived from the Greek word *syndikas,* meaning "someone who represents another." At the circumcision ceremony (*brit*), the circumcisor (*mohel*) represents the father, whose duty it is to circumcise his own son. The *sandek* is the person designated to take the place of the father and hold the child in his lap during the circumcision.

The *sandek* is often referred to as a godparent. He is also called the *ba'al brit*, "master of the circumcision ceremony," because of his central role.

Sanhedrin

This Hebrew term derived from the Greek *synedrion*, meaning "assembly, council," refers to the higher courts of law that administered justice in the latter part of the Second Temple period in Palestine. They handled most capital cases and other serious violations of the law. The talmudic tractate describes two kinds of major court. The highest court, the Great Sanhedrin, consisted of seventy-one ordained scholars and met in the *Lishkat Ha-Gazit* ("Chamber of Hewn Stones") in the Jerusalem Temple. The Lower (Lesser) Sanhedrins, of which there were several, consisted of twenty-three members and met in Jerusalem and other parts of the country.

Before the Temple was destroyed in the year 70 C.E., the High Priest presided over the

Great Sanhedrin, but afterward it was headed by the Patriarch, an acclaimed scholar and community leader who was given the title *nasi*, meaning "prince."

The most distinguished leader ever to hold the post of *nasi* was the second/third-century Rabbi Judah the Prince, known also as Yehudah Ha-Nasi. Judah was the scholar who, in the early part of the second century C.E., edited and finalized the Mishnah, the code of Jewish law upon which the entire Talmud is based. So highly regarded was he that during his lifetime he was addressed as Rabbenu Ha-Kadosh, "Our Holy Teacher." In rabbinic literature he is simply called "Rabbi. "

Second in stature to the *nasi* was the deputy *nasi*, known in Hebrew as *Av Beit Din*, literally "Father of the Court." His function was to preside over the court in the absence of the *nasi*.

The Great Sanhedrin not only handled capital cases, as did the Lower Sanhedrins on occasion, but it was also empowered to grant permission for the country to go to war and also to judge cases involving a king, a High Priest, and false prophets. Rulings of the Lower Sanhedrins were appealed to the Great Sanhedrin, and the decision on this "Court of Seventy-one" was deemed binding.

Below the courts of twenty-three, there also existed courts consisting of three rabbinically ordained experts (*mumchim*) in Jewish law who were authorized to adjudicate civil cases, those involving business disputes in which fines could be imposed. In addition, courts of three lay judges (*hedyotim* in Hebrew) were authorized to hear civil cases in which fines were not involved.

The entire *Sanhedrin* court system ceased when the Patriarchate (office of the *nasi*) was abolished by the Romans in the year 425, which meant that rabbis could no longer be ordained. One attempt to revive the act of or-

dination, long defunct, was attempted in the 1530s by Jacob Beirav, a man of great wealth and great learning, but his attempt met with failure.

In 1807, at the request of Napoleon Bonaparte, a Jewish assembly of seventy-one members was convened in Paris for the purpose of having the assembly declare that no Jewish law compromising the loyalty of Jews to the French state would be enacted.

See Nasi; Ordination.

Satan

In the biblical Book of Job, Satan prompts God to test Job in order to determine if he is sincerely loyal to God or is simply loyal because he had been successful. In the Talmud and Midrash, Satan is portrayed as the force behind God's desire to test Abraham by asking him to offer his son Isaac as a sacrifice.

In the postbiblical era, Satan begins to emerge as an even more violent and destructive personality. The First Book of Enokh—one of the books in the Pseudepigrapha, composed between 200 and 100 B.C.E.—depicts Satan as one of the fallen angels who came down to earth from heaven, seduced the beautiful women of mankind, and begat children with them.

The third-century scholar Shimon ben Lakish depicted Satan as the Evil Inclination and as the Angel of Death. And in the tractate *Berakhot* (60a), Abbayei warns: "Open not your mouth to Satan," lest harm befall you.

Throughout Jewish history, many proposals were made suggesting how Satan may be rendered ineffective. The Talmud (*Rosh Hashanah* 16b) relates that on Rosh Hashanah the ram's horn (*shofar*) is blown in order to confuse Satan and minimize the opportunity for him to bring charges before God on the Day of Judgment. When Satan hears the loud blast of the *shofar*, he will become so confused that he will believe that the Messiah has come and that his influence and power over God will have come to an end.

Some scholars have explained that the new month of Tishrei is not announced publicly (*mevorkhim ha-chodesh*) as are all other months so as to confuse Satan. Satan will be unaware that during the coming month Jews will be petitioning God for forgiveness at Rosh Hashanah and Yom Kippur services. Hence, Satan will not appear to testify against them as he is wont to do whenever Jews petition God.

In Jewish folklore, much of Satan's activity centers about the birth of a child. Many amulets have been created to curb his influence. The approaching *brit* (circumcision) is a particularly hazardous time, and ceremonies have been put in place to counteract the potential damage that Satan may cause.

Among Sephardic Jews, the *shalom zakhar* ceremony is held on the night before the circumcision. Sephardim believe that the presence of a group of people will deter Satan, who is eager to prevent Jews from observing the rite of circumcision. The Ashkenazic community, which does not share this belief, observes the *shalom zakhar* celebration on the Friday night following the child's birth.

Savora'im

Also spelled *sabora'im*. An Aramaic term literally meaning "interpreters." An honorable title given to Babylonian scholars in the post-talmudic era, from approximately 500 to 600. The main activity of the *savora'im* was to explain to students in their academies the intricacies of discussions encountered in the Talmud text and to clarify the various opinions expressed. Since not all legal rulings of the Talmud were firmly established by the

tanna'im and *amora'im*, these unresolved problems were left to the *savora'im* (and later the *ge'onim*) to deal with.

Rabbi Yossei of Pumbedita was the last of the Babylonian *amora'im* and the first of the *savora'im*.

Scribe

See Sofer.

Sects

See Chasidism; Essenes; Karaites; Neturei Karta; Sadducees; Samaritans.

Seder

A Hebrew word literally meaning "order," most commonly used in reference to the festive home service held on the first evening of Passover (Pesach). Jews who observe the second day of the festival as a full holiday conduct a *Seder* on the second evening as well. This is common practice in the Diaspora, but in Israel all Jews celebrate a *Seder* only on the first night of the holiday, since only the first and last days of the seven-day holiday are full holidays. The five intermediate days are semiholidays, commonly referred to as Chol Ha-Moed. In the Diaspora, most Reform Jews as well as some Conservative Jews follow the Israeli practice.

Holiday Origins

The original Passover celebration was not a *Seder* but a festival observed by nomadic people to celebrate the advent of spring. At this festival, held on the fourteenth day of the month Nissan (usually in April), each family took a lamb and slaughtered it. After roasting the animal, it was shared that night (when the first *Seder* is now held) by all members of the family (Exodus 12:8).

For many centuries after the exodus from

Egypt, the family paschal lamb celebration was abandoned; but when Josiah became king of Israel in 640 B.C.E., the celebration was reintroduced (II Kings 23). The High Priest at the time, Chilkia, showed Shafan, the royal scribe, a Book of the Law (Torah scroll) that he had discovered in the Temple during its renovation. From the scroll, the king learned for the first time of the ancient paschal lamb ritual held each spring; and when the Temple renovation was completed, he ordered a great celebration in Jerusalem at which thousands of lambs and other animals were slaughtered. The Bible notes: "For no such Passover had been kept since the days of the Judges."

In ensuing centuries, when the Jerusalem Temples were fully active, Jews from all over the area would flock to Jerusalem and offer paschal lamb sacrifices. Jews outside of Jerusalem celebrated the holiday simply by eating a festive meal. In time, ceremonies, symbolic foods, psalms, and songs were added to the celebration, somewhat resembling the modern *Seder*.

Postbiblical Celebrations

Once the Second Temple in Jerusalem was destroyed by the Romans in the year 70 C.E., the sacrificial system came to an end and prayer services (which had been conducted even while the Temple still existed) replaced it. In order to restore the Passover festival to its former meaningful position in Jewish family life, later in the first century C.E. Rabbi Gamaliel II, president of the *Sanhedrin*, proclaimed: "Anyone who has not said these three words on Passover has not done his duty: *pesach* [paschal lamb], *matzah* [unleavened bread], *maror* [bitter herbs]." Scholars interpret his statement as meaning that Jews are obligated to eat these three items and to recite the Haggadah, the *Seder* prayerbook, in

which the symbolism of each is explained.

The tractate *Pesachim* (99b) added two other core elements that have become part of Jewish tradition: not less than four cups of wine shall be served and *Seder* participants are to recline when eating the Passover meal.

The Haggadah and the Seder Meal

The prescribed order (*seder*) of the Passover eve celebration is detailed in the Haggadah, which means "narrative," the narrative that basically recounts the story of the exodus from Egypt.

Over the centuries many practices, prayers, and songs were incorporated into the Haggadah in order to enhance the spirit of the festivities. Ceremonies that would involve children and keep them interested were introduced.

Seder Garb and Posture

Participants at a *Seder* generally wear formal garb. The leader sometimes wears a white robe called a *kittl*, which symbolizes luxury and freedom, the end result of the Israelites' liberation from bondage and exodus from Egypt. Sephardim do not follow this practice.

During the *Seder* the leader, and sometimes other participants, recline against a pillow placed on the left side. The custom of eating while reclining on the left side is of Persian origin and symbolizes freedom and independence. Greek and Roman patricians also followed this practice, and Jews who lived in their midst adopted it as a meaningful expression of their desire to lead a free, unharried existence. The custom is referred to in the talmudic tractate *Berakhot* (42a) and commented upon by Rashi and Tosafot.

While the Mishnah (*Pesachim* 10:1) requires that even the poorest person in Israel not eat on the first night of Passover unless he reclines, later authorities consider it a practice unworthy of emulation. Rabbi Yechiel Michal Epstein (1835–1905), author of the *Arukh Ha-Shulchan*, commented (Orach Cha'yim 472:3) that many of his illustrious predecessors have pointed out that the custom of leaning on a pillow at the *Seder* is meaningless. More recently, Rabbi Menachem Kasher (1895–1983) noted in his Haggadah that to the modern mind eating in this manner is "the way of the sick [who are bedridden]" and thus "not a practice to emulate."

Seder Tray

The centerpiece of the *Seder* table is a tray with six circular indentations, on which are displayed symbolic foods that are referred to as the Haggadah is read during the *Seder* service. The tray is generally placed atop a three-pocketed container that houses three whole *matzot*. The three *matzot* represent the three classes of Jews: Priest (*Kohen*), Levite (*Levi*), and Israelite (*Yisra'el*). Each *matzah* is used at a different point of the *Seder*, as indicated in the Haggadah.

The foods displayed on the *Seder* tray are:

- *Maror* (bitter herbs). Either the head of a horseradish or some grated horseradish is displayed to symbolize the bitter conditions under which the enslaved Israelites lived in Egypt.
- *Karpas*. A Hebrew word derived from either the Greek or Persian and referring to a vegetable. It may be cucumber, lettuce, radish, parsley, potato, or any other vegetable in season.

  At a specific point during the *Seder* meal, the vegetable designated as *karpas*—a reminder of the association of Passover with springtime and the rebirth of nature—is dipped in salt water and eaten by each *Seder* participant. This cus-

tom dates back to Jerusalem of the first and second centuries, when it was common to begin a formal meal by passing around vegetables as hors d'oeuvres.

Since *karpas* is eaten toward the beginning of the *Seder* service and there is a long wait until the main meal, in some Sephardic families it is customary to serve substantial amounts of broccoli, asparagus, or other green vegetables to satisfy the hunger of the participants.

- *Charoset*. The Talmud (*Pesachim* 116a) describes *charoset*, a word of uncertain origin and meaning, as a food mixture that recalls the mortar that the Children of Israel made from straw during their enslavement in Egypt. Some scholars say the word is a form of the Hebrew word *cheres*, meaning "clay," an allusion to its claylike color.

  In the Mishnah, commentators describe *charoset* as consisting of nuts and fruits, pounded together and mixed with vinegar (*Pesachim* 10:3). A small amount is served together with the bitter herbs (*maror*) to reduce the pungency of the *maror*.

  In his Notes to Joseph Caro's sixteenth-century *Code of Jewish Law*, Polish-born Moses Isserles mentions apples as the main ingredient in *charoset* (*Shulchan Arukh* Orach Cha'yim 473:5). Rabbi Ovadiah of Bertinoro (1440–1516), the leading rabbi in Italy and later in Jerusalem, speaks of figs as the main ingredient. Heinrich Heine, in his early nineteenth-century novelette *The Rabbi of Bachrach*, describes the *charoset* prepared in a German household as consisting of raisins, cinnamon, and nuts.

  Nowadays, the Ashkenazic version of *charoset* generally consists of chopped apples, walnuts, and cinnamon, to which wine is added. The Sephardic version is made from chopped nuts, dates or figs or other dried fruit, wine, and a variety of spices, including ground ginger and cloves. However, the ingredients vary widely from community to community throughout the world: some Yemenites add sesame or pomegranate seeds; Italians and Egyptians frequently add bananas; Greeks, Spaniards, and Poles use almonds.

- *Zero'a* (shankbone). A roasted bone, symbolic of the mighty arm of God that punished the Egyptians and persuaded Pharaoh to free the Israelites.

- *Beitzah* (egg). The roasted hardboiled egg that is placed on the *Seder* tray is symbolic of the regular festival sacrifice brought in the days when the Temple stood in Jerusalem. On Passover, in addition to this regular sacrifice (*korban chagigah* in Hebrew), the paschal lamb was offered as a second sacrifice.

  Some authorities have interpreted the use of the roasted egg as a sign of mourning for the loss of the two Temples that once stood in Jerusalem—the first destroyed by the Babylonians in 586 B.C.E., the second by the Romans in 70 C.E. With the Temples destroyed, sacrifices could no longer be offered. The egg symbolizes this loss.

- *Chazeret* (vegetable). Carrying the same symbolism as the *maror*, this is usually a radish or some other vegetable that has a slightly bitter taste.

  The reason for placing a bitter herb in addition to *maror* on the *Seder* tray has been related to the biblical verse, "They shall eat it [the paschal lamb] with un-

leavened bread and bitter herbs" (Numbers 9:11). It has been explained that since the Book of Numbers speaks of herbs in the plural form (*merorim*), this *chazeret* was included on the *Seder* tray in addition to the *maror* vegetable.

Not all authorities considered it mandatory to use *chazeret* as a *Seder* symbol. Rabbi Isaac Luria, the sixteenth-century mystic also known as the Ari, used *chazeret*, while the equally famous eighteenth-century scholar Rabbi Elijah of Vilna, better known as the Vilna Gaon, did not. Practically all *Seder* trays manufactured today have six compartments (indentations), one reserved for *chazeret*.

In 1981, under the leadership of Susannah Heschel, Jewish feminists wishing to have their movement represented at the *Seder* began the practice of placing an orange on the table along with the other symbolic foods. Professor Heschel invited her guests to "take a segment of orange, make the blessing over fruit, and eat it as a gesture of solidarity with Jewish lesbians, gay men, and others who are marginalized within the Jewish community."

In recent years, feminists have also adopted the custom of placing a wine goblet on the table next to the Elijah Cup. The cup has been named Miriam's Cup, giving credit to the sister of Moses, who was hidden in the bulrushes by his mother, Yocheved (Exodus 2:1–4).

Salt Water

Twice during the Passover *Seder* service, food is dipped in salt water and then eaten by the participants. On the first occasion it is the *karpas*—which, as stated above, may be cucumber, radish, or another vegetable in season—that is so treated. Later, immediately preceding the *Seder* meal, a whole, halved or quartered hard-boiled egg is dipped in the salt water and then eaten as an hors d'oeuvre. Vinegar is sometimes used as a substitute for the water.

Handwashing

According to ancient practice recorded in the Talmud, hands are washed before food is dipped into a liquid or sauce. Since during the *Seder* each participant dips the *karpas* into salt water, it was customary for each person to first wash his hands. This practice remains part of the *Seder* ritual. A pitcher of water is carried around the table by the mistress of the house, and water is poured onto the hands of each participant. In some households the participants leave the table to wash their hands.

The Centrality of Wine

According to an ancient custom, at Sabbath and festival meals two cups are filled with wine: one for the recitation of the *Kiddush* and the other to be held aloft by the master of the house while he leads in the *Birkat Ha-Mazon* (*Grace After Meals*). Since Passover, the Festival of Freedom, is such a significant holiday in the Jewish calendar, two additional cups of wine were added to the *Seder* celebration, and these are also served to each participant.

Additional explanations have been offered for the custom of drinking four cups of wine at the *Seder*, the most popular being that the four cups are drunk because the Bible uses four different verbs in describing the drama of redemption from slavery in Egypt. The four references to the redemption can be found in the Book of Exodus (6:6–7):

1. I will *bring* you out of Egypt.
2. I will *deliver* you from their bondage.

3. I will *redeem* you with an outstretched arm.
4. I will *take* you to Me for a people.

At an Ashkenazic *Seder*, a blessing is recited before drinking each of the four cups. Among Sephardim, however, a blessing is not recited over the second and fourth cups. The blessing over the first cup (*Kiddush*) and the third cup (following *Grace After Meals*) was considered sufficient to cover the second and fourth cups as well.

Because eminent scholars such as Rabbi Akiba consider all the people of Israel to be royalty (*Shabbat* 128a), it became customary in some households for each person to pour the wine for the person seated next to him, and to be served, just as royalty is served by others (*Arukh Ha-Shulchan* 272:1).

The Four Questions

One of the highlights of the Passover *Seder* is the asking by a child of the Four Questions. Known in Hebrew as the *Arba Kushiyot* and in Yiddish as the *Fier Kashes*, they begin with the words *Ma nishtanah?* ("Why is this night different?"). The practice, mentioned in the Talmud (Mishnah *Pesachim* 10:4), was introduced to involve children in the proceedings of the evening. If no children are present, an adult may recite the questions.

The involvement of children in the Passover *Seder* was actually mandated in Exodus 12:26–27:

And when your children ask you, "What do you mean by this rite?" you shall say, "It is the Passover sacrifice to the Lord, because He passed over the houses of the Israelites in Egypt when He smote the Egyptians, but saved our houses."

Thus, the education of children became a primary objective of the *Seder* service.

The Four Questions, as they are recited today, are:

- Why is it that on all other nights during the year we eat either bread or *matzah*, but on this night we eat only *matzah*?
- Why is it that on all other nights we eat all kinds of vegetables, but on this night we eat bitter herbs?
- Why is it that on all other nights we do not dip even once, but on this night we dip twice?
- Why is it that on all other nights we eat either sitting or reclining, but on this night we eat in a reclining position?

The questions asked in Temple times were quite different. Originally, there were only three questions, the first relating to the eating of *matzah*, the second to the eating of roast meat from the paschal lamb, and the third to the practice of double dipping. Scholars believe that a fourth question, the one related to eating bitter herbs, was later added so as to harmonize the number of questions with the *four* cups of wine and the *four* sons mentioned in the narrative.

After the Temple in Jerusalem was destroyed in the year 70 C.E. and the sacrificial system was ended, the question relating to roast meat was eliminated and in its stead the question about reclining was interposed. So as to express the feeling of freedom experienced by the Israelites after the exodus, the Jews copied the conduct of Romans, who leaned on pillows when enjoying a festive meal.

To answer the Four Questions, the leader of the service, accompanied by all the participants, recite the story of the enslaved Israelites and the exodus from Egypt.

The Ten Plagues

Many early societies believed that evil spirits could be bribed with wine. Accordingly, some wine was always spilled from the cup before any of its contents was drunk. This practice was carried over to the Passover *Seder*, where a small amount of wine is traditionally spilled from each participant's cup when the name of each of the ten plagues is pronounced. This has been explained as an expression of sorrow for the pain caused the Egyptians by each plague.

In most households, instead of spilling the wine directly from the goblet into a saucer, a drop at a time is removed with the small finger and tapped into the saucer. The use of the finger is said to be a reminder of the verse in Exodus (8:15) in which Pharaoh's magicians, unable to duplicate the miracles performed by Moses, had to admit that it was the "finger of God" that executed the miracles that eventually made the Exodus possible. In more recent times it has become customary among some to dip the stem end of a spoon into the wine and deposit droplets onto a plate.

Edda Servi Machlin, in *The Classic Cuisine of the Italian Jews*, reports that in her native village of Pitigliano, in the Tuscany region of Italy, it was customary up until World War II to keep all the windows open during the recitation of the ten plagues. The drops that were removed from each wine goblet were thrown out of the window to ward off evil spirits that may want to enter the home and harm the inhabitants.

Hillel's Sandwich

Immediately preceding the Passover *Seder* meal, it is customary to eat *charoset* and *maror* sandwiched together between two pieces of *matzah*. Introduced by Hillel the First, who was born in Babylonia in 75 B.C.E. and who later studied in Jerusalem, the sandwich originally also included *pesach*, meat of the paschal lamb that was offered on the Temple altar during Passover.

Afikomon

During the early part of the Passover *Seder* service, the leader breaks off a piece of the middle *matzah* that is under the *Seder* tray. This *matzah*, called the *afikomon* (derived from the Greek *epikomion*, meaning "dessert"), is placed in a napkin or bag, to be shared by everyone as dessert after the meal has been served.

Traditionally, the *afikomon* represents the paschal lamb, which in ancient times was to be the last taste to linger in one's mouth after the *Seder*. After the destruction of the Second Temple in 70 c.e., when the sacrificial system was no longer in force, the *matzah* symbolically replaced the paschal lamb in the *Seder* ritual and was to be the last taste of the evening.

The present-day custom of setting aside a piece of *matzah* for the *afikomon* is only 700 years old. When the Mishnah (*Pesachim* 10:8), which was composed about 1,800 years ago, says that "one must not conclude the paschal meal by saying, 'Now to the *afikomon*,'" it is referring not to the dessert but to "the entertainment." In those times the Greek aristocracy, after serving a lavish meal, would engage in serious discussion about issues of the day and would follow it by calling for the entertainment, which was known as the *epikomion*. This involved wild dancing and revelry, of which the Rabbis did not approve. They therefore interpreted the word *epikomion* to mean "dessert" rather than "entertainment."

In order to make the *Seder* more exciting for children, the custom evolved of allowing youngsters to "steal" and hide the *afikomon*. Since the *Seder* could not continue until a piece of the *afikomon* was eaten by everyone,

the leader had to search for it. If he could not find it, he would offer a gift to the children, and they would fetch the *afikomon* from its hiding place. In some families the leader hides the *afikomon*, and the children receive a gift if they find it.

When the *afikomon* is finally returned, the leader of the *Seder* breaks it into small pieces, which he distributes to everyone at the table. After the *matzah* is consumed, the *Seder* continues with the recitation of the *Grace After Meals*.

Exotic Customs

In the Middle Ages, many superstitious people believed that the *afikomon* had the power to drive off evil spirits. They would therefore hang a piece of leftover *afikomon* on the walls of their homes and synagogues. They would also place a piece in a pouch and carry it on their person as a good luck charm.

Jews in Kurdistan used to mix pieces of the leftover *afikomon* in their rice, flour, and salt canisters. The pieces of *matzah*, they believed, would insure that their food containers would never be empty.

Many Jews from North Africa, particularly Morocco, believe that the *afikomon* has the power to calm the stormy sea, and they carry a piece with them whenever they travel by boat. When the sea becomes rough, they throw the piece of *afikomon* into the water. Some also hang pieces of *afikomon* on the walls of their homes as protection against fire.

Awaited Guest

After the *Grace After Meals* (Birkat Ha-Mazon) has been recited and the *afikomon* (dessert) has been distributed, a special decorative goblet known as *koso shel Eliyahu* ("the cup of Elijah") is filled with wine. At that point, the front door to the house also is opened.

Elijah was the great prophet of Israel who dominated the Palestinian scene about twenty-eight centuries ago. He was the conscience of Israel during the reign of King Ahab and Queen Jezebel, a couple who promoted idol worship. Because Elijah battled the pagan influences that threatened to discredit God, he was looked upon as the forerunner of the Messiah.

Miriam's Cup

In the 1980s, taking their cue from the practice of Jews of the geonic period (sixth to tenth centuries), one supported by Moses Maimonides in his *Code of Jewish Law* (*Mishneh Torah*, Hilkhot Chametz u-Matzah 8:10), which permitted adding a fifth cup of wine to the *Seder* celebration, women activists introduced the idea of placing a wine goblet next to the one reserved for Elijah. It was called Miriam's Cup, after the sister of Moses who, like her brother, was esteemed in Jewish tradition as a prophet (Exodus 15:20). Since it was Miriam who stood guard over the crib of Moses when he was hidden among the reeds in the waters of the Sea of Reeds, and because according to tradition it was "Miriam's Well" that miraculously accompanied the Hebrews during their long trek through the desert and from which waters were drawn to quench the thirst of the weary travelers (the well is alluded to in Numbers 21:16–18), it was deemed fitting that deference be paid her on this Festival of Freedom.

Since Miriam is identified more with water than with wine, after the second cup of wine has been drunk, the females at the *Seder* table fill Miriam's cup with water poured from their own glasses. In some homes, the cup is then passed around to all participants as the leader describes the role of Miriam in the story of Exodus.

Wine and Blood Libels

Over the course of history, the use of red wine at the *Seder* led to the leveling of blood-libel accusations against Jews. Charges were made that Jews drink the blood of Christian children at the *Seder* or use it in the baking of *matzah*. Such accusations were always proven unfounded, yet as late as the first part of the twentieth century in Messina, New York, such an accusation was leveled. The rabbi of the town was questioned when a Christian girl happened to disappear at Passover time. The girl was found unharmed the next day, and the town mayor apologized publicly.

Instances such as this encouraged the use of white wine at the *Seder*, which is permitted according to the *Code of Jewish Law* (*Shulchan Arukh*, Orach Cha'yim 272:4 and 472:1); several rabbinic authorities even forbade the use of red wine. However, the Rabbis of the Talmud recommended that red wine, which was considered superior, be used for holiday celebrations. (*See* Blood Libels).

Concluding Seder Songs

The *Seder* service as it is presented today in all Haggadot ends with a series of songs, including *Ki Lo Na'eh, Adir Hu, Echad Mi Yodei'a*, and *Chad Gadya*. Consisting of lively lyrics and melodies, these songs were added to the Haggadah in the Middle Ages, primarily to keep the children interested. Apparently all of these songs were not yet part of the *Seder* liturgy in the twelfth century because Maimonides does not mention them when he lists in his *Mishneh Torah* (following chapter 8 of the section entitled Hilkhot Chametz u-Matzah) the prayers and poems to be recited.

The authors of most of these compositions are unknown. It is known, however, that *Adir Hu* was sung in France and Germany in the fifteenth century, and *Echad Mi Yodei'a* probably was composed in the fifteenth or sixteenth centuries. The *Chad Gadya* jingle is an adaptation of a sixteenth century German poem.

While the songs are widely sung in Hebrew, Jews of North Africa sing *Chad Gadya* in Judeo-Arabic. East European Jews, in some locales, have been known to sing *Echad Mi Yodei'a* in Yiddish. Some families in America have been singing the *Chad Gadya* with Chinese modality, leading in to the final rousing hopeful prognostication: *Le-shanah ha-ba'ah bi-Yerushala'yim*, "Next Year [may we meet] in Jerusalem!"

See Bedikat Chametz; Elijah's Cup; Matzah; Passover; Salt.

Sefirah

A Hebrew word literally meaning "counting," referring to the counting of the *omer*, the forty-nine days between the second day of Passover and Shavuot.

See Omer.

Sefirot

Literally "numbers, countings." A concept developed by kabbalists to elucidate the ten qualities that constitute the essence of God and through which He governs the world. These instruments, entirely spiritual in nature, form a basic unity, although they are not all operative at the same time. Man's purpose in life is to reach for God by incorporating these attributes into his own life.

See Bedikat Chametz; Kabbalah; Shekhinah; Shevirat Keilim.

Selichot

A Hebrew term literally meaning "pardons," referring to the penitential prayers recited on fast days and especially during the period that commences on the first day of Elul (the month before Rosh Hashanah) and extends until after Yom Kippur, approximately six weeks later.

A special midnight *Selichot* service is generally held on the Saturday night preceding Rosh Hashanah, unless Rosh Hashanah falls on a Monday or Tuesday. In that case, the midnight *Selichot* service is held one week earlier on Saturday night. The *Selichot* custom arose because the psalmist declared: "At midnight I will rise to give thanks unto Thee [God]" (Psalms 119:62).

Semikhah

A Hebrew word meaning "laying on of hands." The term originally related specifically to the sacrificial system (Leviticus 3:2) but later became associated mainly with ordination.

See Ordination.

Sephardim

Also spelled *Sepharadim* and *Sefardim*. Singular, *Sephardi*, *Sepharadi*, or *Sefardi*. *Sepharad*, a form of the word *Sephardim*, is first used in the Book of Ovadiah (1:20), where it appears as a place-name. It was believed to be a locale in northern Palestine to which exiles from Jerusalem were deported after the destruction of the First Temple in 586 B.C.E.

In the Middle Ages, the term Sephardim took on new meaning and became associated with the Jews of Spain, around the same time that the word *Ashkenazim* (singular, *Ashkenazi*) became identified with Jews who lived in Germany and environs. The actual word *Ashkenaz* appears for the first time in the Book of Genesis (10:3), where it is the name of a son of Gomer, who was a son of Noah.

In its strict sense, the term *Sepharadi* (and its variants) refers only to those Jews who trace their ancestry to Spain. However, considerable confusion has been generated by the recent tendency to characterize all non-Ashkenazi

Jews, and primarily Oriental Jews (known in Hebrew as *Eidot Ha-Mizrach*, "Communities of the East") from Arabic-speaking countries (for example, Syria, Lebanon, Egypt, Iraq, Yemen), as Sepharadim. Such practice was reinforced with the establishment of a dual Ashkenazi and Sepharadi chief rabbinate in Palestine during the British Mandate period. Non-Ashkenazi, "Oriental" Jews affiliated with the Sephardic Chief Rabbi, thereby permanently blurring the distinction between Sepharadim and Oriental Jews.

Most rigorous contemporary historians define the Sephardic community as descendants of those Jews who for centuries lived peacefully and productively in Spain under Muslim rule. In the fifteenth century, however, as political power in the land shifted from Muslim hegemony to Christian control, conditions began to change. The monarchs Ferdinand and Isabella were guided by their Christian counselor and religious fundamentalist mentor, Torquemada, who ordered Jews to convert to Christianity or be burned at the stake. Many Jews, preferring life to death, professed Christianity outwardly but secretly practiced Judaism. These Jews were called *conversos* or *marranos* (meaning "swine" in Spanish) because they were always under suspicion of being insincere in their conversion.

In 1492, most Spanish Jews were expelled from the country and settled mainly, but not exclusively, in neighboring Portugal, both areas being part of the Iberian Peninsula. But within five years the claws of the Christian inquisitors reached out into Portugal as well, where the same fate befell its Jewish population. In 1497, a mass migration of Jews began in Portugal.

The exodus of Jews from Spain and Portugal followed two courses. Those Jews who were expelled from Spain in 1492, except for those who settled in Portugal, found domicile in Morocco, France, Italy, and various parts of the Ottoman Empire, primarily Turkey. These Jews were called Eastern Sephardim. Those who settled in northern Morocco spoke a combination of Spanish, Hebrew, and Arabic, called Haketia, a language all but forgotten today. Those who settled in the Ottoman Empire continued speaking Spanish, but absorbed within their vocabulary hundreds of words from Turkish, French, Italian, Greek, and Arabic. Their language became known as Ladino, Judeo-Spanish, Judezmo, or Espanyol, meaning "Spanish of the Jews." (See below.)

Spanish Jews who had settled in Portugal and were later also expelled from that country eventually made their homes primarily in Holland and England. These Western Sephardim, as they were called, were among the first Jews to settle in America, as early as the seventeenth century. The first synagogue built in America was New York City's Mill Street Synagogue, constructed in 1730. Officially it was known as Congregation Shearith Israel (which traces its roots to 1654), but it was more popularly called The Spanish and Portuguese Synagogue.

Sephardim have developed a synagogue vocabulary different from that of Ashkenazim. They use the word *Arbit (Arvit)* for the Ashkenazic *Ma'ariv* (the evening service); *heikhal* for *aron* (ark); *(e)snoga* for *shul* (synagogue); *haggadah* for *Seder*; *hashkabah* for *hazkarah* (prayer for the dead); *Kippur* for *Yom Kippur*; *Sefer* for *Sefer Torah*; *teivah* for *bimah* (reading table); *tefillot* for *siddur* (prayerbook).

In Israel today, the Sephardic pronunciation of Hebrew is the official style of speech, even by those who have emigrated from countries where the Ashkenazic style had been current.

Ladino

Written primarily in Hebrew characters, Ladino is based on Castilian-Spanish. But it also contains a variety of words and expressions culled from other languages, including Greek, Turkish, Portuguese and, to a lesser extent, Hebrew and Aramaic.

The first book printed in Ladino was issued in Constantinople in 1510. This was followed by a variety of religious works, novels, magazines, and newspapers. The language is still used today by pockets of Sephardim in parts of the Balkans and in Israel, although the number is steadily dwindling. Today, the only Ladino language publication is issued in Israel by Moshe Shaul. Called *Aki Yerushalayim*, ("Here Jerusalem"), it has been in existence since 1978. With a worldwide circulation of over one thousand, the magazine is issued two or three times a year. Half of the printed copies are sent free to libraries in several countries.

Yitzchak Navon, Israel's fifth president, is one of the few notable Ladino-speaking Sephardim in the world. He is the president of the National Authority for the Preservation of Ladino Culture.

Conservative estimates place the number of Ladino speakers in the world at sixty thousand, although some scholars place the number as high as four hundred thousand. In Israel, the largest number reside in Jerusalem, Lod, and Bat Yam. In America, pockets of Ladino-speaking Jews live in New York City, Los Angeles, Seattle, and southern Florida.

Septuagint

This Greek word meaning "seventy" is the name given to the third-century B.C.E. Greek translation of the Pentateuch, the Torah. In Hebrew it is called *Targum Ha-Shivim* ("Translation of the Seventy"). In later centuries, when the balance of the Bible was translated into Greek, the term Septuagint was applied to the entire Bible, although originally it referred to the Torah alone.

The earliest Jewish record of how the Hebrew Bible came to be translated into Greek is found in *Antiquities of the Jews*, by Flavius Josephus, a Jewish historian who lived in Jerusalem and Rome during the first century C.E. In this first history ever written about the Jews, Josephus tells of the beneficent King Ptolemy Philadelphus, who ruled over Palestine and Egypt in the third century B.C.E.

Demetrius, the king's librarian, wanted to assemble a great library and was eager to include a copy of all books that existed anywhere in the world. The king supported Demetrius in this goal.

Demetrius learned that there were many books of law belonging to the Jews that should be in the king's library but were written in a language not understood by the Greeks. Aristeas (Aristeus), an intimate friend of the king, had long been disturbed over the plight of the many thousands of Jewish captives who lived in lands ruled by King Ptolemy. He suggested to the king that a letter be sent to Elazar, the High Priest in Jerusalem, requesting that scholars be selected to prepare a Greek translation of the Pentateuch. As an inducement, Aristeas suggested that Ptolemy free the Jewish slaves.

To make sure that the final translation would be free of errors or outside influence, Demetrius proposed to the king that the High Priest select seventy-two scholarly elders, six from each of the twelve tribes of Israel, and that they be housed in Alexandria in seventy-two individual rooms, where each would write his own independent translation.

A letter ("The Letter of Aristeas") making this request was dispatched by the king to the High Priest. Elazar accepted Ptolemy's proposal. The plan was executed and, miraculously, all seventy-two translations turned out to be identical.

The story of how the Septuagint came to be written as detailed above is not accepted as fact by most scholars. Some believe that "The Letter of Aristeas" was actually written during the Hasmonean period, around 165 B.C.E. Others believe the date of writing to be around 80 B.C.E. Later, the Rabbis of the Talmud do refer to such a letter. They indicate their belief in its authenticity and in the fact that the Greek translation of the Torah was composed under divine guidance.

Most contemporary scholars believe that the Greek translation came about in the same natural way as did the Aramaic translation (the *Targum of Onkelos*) in the first century C.E. The Aramaic translation was composed because the masses of Jews living in Palestine, whose spoken language was Aramaic, were no longer able to understand the Torah reading, which was conducted in Hebrew. Similarly, when the Jews of Alexandria, Egypt (whose vernacular was Greek), were no longer proficient in Hebrew, the Torah reading had to be translated for them into Greek.

Why the names Septuagint and *Targum Ha-Shivim* should have been selected to designate the Greek translation of the Torah is quite inexplicable in view of the fact that according to the accepted tradition seventy-two persons were said to be involved in the translation. Some scholars theorize that the use of seventy rather than seventy-two was a matter of convenience; that seventy is a round number, much easier to remember. Others hold to the view that the number seventy replaced seventy-two because it is a cardinal number and much easier to record. Still others believe it was chosen because seventy is a multiple of two important numbers in the Bible: seven and ten.

What seems to have been overlooked by biblical scholars is that the minor tractate *Sefer Torah* (1:8), whose compiler lived in the early part of the third century, before the final editing of the Mishnah, records a view noted nowhere else: that *seventy* elders translated the Torah into Greek. This would explain why the Septuagint is called *Targum Ha-Shivim*.

It should be noted that the number seventy is highly significant in Jewish history and tradition. Seventy persons were in Jacob's entourage when he went to Egypt (Exodus 1:5). When Jacob died, he was mourned for seventy days (Genesis 50:3). Seventy elders assisted Moses (Numbers 11:16). Gideon had seventy sons (Judges 8:30). The *Zohar* says there are seventy facets to the Torah.

The Rabbis of the Babylonian Talmud were concerned about the propriety of having a Greek translation of the Torah. Some expressed the view that while *tefillin* and *mezuzot* may be written in any language, the Torah may be written only in Hebrew. However, Rabbi Shimon ben Gamaliel, first-century C.E. president of the *Sanhedrin*, said that the Torah may be written in Greek as well as in Hebrew. He reasoned that this should be done out of respect for King Ptolemy, the Greek ruler of Palestine who in the middle of the third century B.C.E. had been very kind to the Jews. The view of Rabbi Shimon prevailed. (Mishnah *Megillah* 1:8 and *Bava Kama* 83a.)

The Palestinian Talmud (*Megillah* 1:9) explains why the Rabbis agreed to make an exception in the case of the Greek language. They felt that Greek is a rich language, sufficiently elastic to capture the flavor and nuances of the Hebrew text. A Greek translation of Scripture, it was believed, would reflect honor on the Torah and help propagate its message.

Some dissidents (*Soferim* 1:7–8) rejected this notion and characterized the day on which the Torah was rendered into Greek as "a sad day for the Jewish people, a day comparable to the day on which Israel decided to worship the Golden Calf."

In the twelfth century, Moses Maimonides emphasized that permission was given to write Torah scrolls in Greek but not in any other language (*Mishneh Torah*, Hilkhot Tefillin, u-Mezuzot, ve-Sefer Torah 1:19).

The Vulgate

The Latin translation of the Hebrew Bible, known as the Vulgate, was made by Saint Jerome around the year 400 C.E. In preparing the translation, Jerome asked his Hebrew teachers to share with him the interpretations of Scripture that were current in the synagogue.

The name Vulgate, derived from the Latin *vulgatus*, meaning "common, usual," was adopted because the translation was written in the everyday language of the common man. The Vulgate translation was widely accepted, and in 1546 the Council of Trent proclaimed it as the "authentic" Bible of the Latin Church that "none should dare or presume to reject under any pretext whatsoever."

Se'udah Ha-Mafseket

A Hebrew term literally meaning "the meal that interrupts or separates," specifically the last meal eaten before the Yom Kippur fast begins. The term is first used in the tractate *Ta'anit* (30a) and harks back to the statement in Leviticus (23:32): "And you shall afflict your souls [fast] on the ninth day [of Tishrei]," where the word "ninth" is not taken literally, for the Yom Kippur fast day was on the tenth of the month, not the ninth.

The Talmud explains that we begin fasting on the ninth day, while it is yet daytime, by having a small meal. After a short interruption, more food is consumed. This is the

seu'dah ha-mafseket. Rabbi Chiya from Difti explains (*Rosh Hashanah* 9a): "If a man eats and drinks on the ninth day [of Tishrei], Scripture credits him as if he had fasted on both the ninth and tenth [Yom Kippur]." The eating and drinking on the ninth day is called "fasting" in Leviticus.

Se'udah Shelishit

A Hebrew term literally meaning "third meal," referring specifically to the third and final meal of the Sabbath, called by many *shalashudis*, *shalosh se'udos*, or *shalosh se'udot*.

Traditionally, three meals are eaten on the Sabbath. This custom is based on the fact that the verse in Exodus (16:25), describing the miracle of the manna in the desert uses the word *ha-yom* ("today") three times: "And Moses said: Eat it [the manna] today, for today is a Sabbath unto the Lord, today you will not find it [manna] in the field." The first Sabbath meal is eaten on Friday night; the second on Saturday around noontime, after the morning service; and the third late in the afternoon, usually after the *Minchah* service.

The *se'udah shelishit* is generally very simple. *Challah*, herring or herring salad, simple cakes, and beverages are served. It is common for a member of the congregation to sponsor the meal to commemorate a marriage, a *yahrzeit* (anniversary of death), or other milestone. Songs (*zemirot*) are sung and sometimes a lecture on some aspect of the Torah portion of the week is offered.

Se'udat Mitzvah

A Hebrew term first used in the tractate *Pesachim* (49a) by Rabbi Shimon, literally meaning "commandment meal" and referring to the meal served in conjunction with the performance of a *mitzvah* such as a *brit*, a *pidyon ha-ben*, a betrothal, and in more recent times, a bar or bat mitzvah. A *se'udat mitzvah*—or *mitzvah meal*, as it is sometimes called—is often held upon the completion of a unit of the Torah or a talmudic tractate.

The meal served after the wedding ceremony as well as during the week after the wedding is also called *se'udat mitzvah*. Usually served in the home in the presence of the bride and groom, the repast is accompanied by blessings and prayers appropriate to the occasion.

Many Orthodox authorities do not characterize the meal celebrating a bat mitzvah as a *se'udat mitzvah* because the bat mitzvah is not a religious requirement. They argue that when a girl reaches her majority (twelve years and one day), she is not obligated to put on *tefillin* (phylacteries), nor is she counted to a *minyan* (religious quorum) or given an *aliyah* (Torah honor) as are boys who have reached the age of bar mitzvah.

See Mitzvah; Sheva Berakhot; Siyyum; Siyyum Bekhorim.

Sex and Sexuality

The obligation to perpetuate life is explicitly set forth in the early pages of the Bible. Genesis 1:27–28 states that after creating man and woman, "God blessed them and said to them, 'Be fertile and increase. Fill the earth and master it.'" This is the first commandment in the Torah. Much later Isaiah says, "God formed the earth so that it shall be inhabited" (45:18).

The Rabbis of the Talmud went even further. They declared that, beyond the propagation of the race, sex is to be enjoyed (*Ketubbot* 14a). A man is obligated to satisfy his wife's sexual needs (referred to as *onah* in the Bible [Exodus 21:10]), and this must be done with respect and consideration (ibid. 62b and *Pesachim* 49b). To deny one's wife sexual pleasure is grounds for compelling a man to issue a divorce. Maimonides elaborates, emphasiz-

ing that just as a man may not deny his wife sexual satisfaction, so may a woman not withhold sex from her husband (*Mishneh Torah*, Hilkhot Ishut 15:1).

The term *onah* (literally "time") traditionally has been taken to refer to the appropriate time for sex, that is, when copulation will most likely result in impregnation. That "time" is immediately after the *niddah* (menstruation) period is over, which begins seven days after the menstrual period has ended.

The concept of *onah* is emphasized in the Book of Deuteronomy (24:5), in which a man who takes a new wife is instructed not go into military service but to stay at home for one year "to make his wife happy." The Talmud (*Chagigah* 5b) even approves of a certain degree of frivolity during sex between a husband and wife.

The responsibility of a husband to satisfy his wife sexually and the frequency of such activity was a matter of concern to the Rabbis of the Talmud and later rabbinic authorities. The tractates *Yevamot* (62b) and *Ketubbot* (61b and 62b) spell out a variety of views:

1. Rabbi Joshua ben Levi said: "Whoever knows his wife to be a God-fearing woman and does not "visit" her is called a sinner, for it is written (Job 5:24), "And thou shalt know that thy tent [home] is in peace." Rabbi Joshua elaborated, saying that it is a man's duty to satisfy his wife sexually before going on a journey.

2. If a man took a vow not to have intercourse with his wife, the School of Shammai ruled that she must consent to the deprivation for a period of two weeks; the School of Hillel says, one week. After this period, if the husband refuses to have sex, the wife can demand that her husband divorce her.

3. Students may go away to study Torah without their wives' permission for a period of thirty days; laborers for only one week.

4. The conjugal duty of a man toward his wife is as follows: "Every day for unemployed or retired persons; twice a week for laborers; once a week for ass-drivers; once in thirty days for camel-drivers; and for sailors once in six months. These are the rulings of Rabbi Eliezer (Ketubbot 62b).

Defining Sex

In Numbers 5:13, sexual activity between a man and a married woman is described as "a man lay with her carnally [producing emission of seed]." The Hebrew term shikhvat zera is used in this connection, and Abbayei and Rava analyze its meaning in discussing the question of natural and unnatural intercourse (Sotah 26b). One view maintains that the term sexual intercourse is to be applied only when the penis is inserted into the vagina. The other view is that even external contact is to be considered coitus. Oral sex would not be considered sexual intercourse according to the first view. This apparently is the definition offered by modern dictionaries.

The view that Jewish law approves of sexual intercourse between married people only when there is a possibility of the woman conceiving is clearly incorrect. Joseph Caro's Code of Jewish Law (Shulchan Arukh, Even Ha-Ezer 23:5) states that the biblical ban on "wasting seed" (hashchatat zera) does not apply to intercourse with a sterile woman so long as the intercourse is normal and artificial barriers (contraceptive devices) are not placed in the womb to bar the seed from entering.

Rabbi Moses Isserles (1525–1572), in his notes to Caro's code, is quite explicit when he comments that although the purpose of marriage is to have children, a man may marry a woman who cannot bear children (Even Ha-Ezer 1:3). Several centuries earlier, Rashi (1040–1105) had commented that "a wife has the right not to be ignored [sexually]" even if she is unable to bear children (Ketubbot 60b).

Many of Rashi's predecessors, including Sa'adya Gaon in the tenth century, and many of his successors, such as Moses ben Nachman (Nachmanides) in the thirteenth century, agreed that sex is to be an honest expression of love that deepens the marital bond between husband and wife and provides personal satisfaction for both mates. There can be nothing reprehensible about the sex act, said these rabbis, since God's holy men in the Bible engaged in it with His approval.

Nachmanides, in fact, wrote a letter about marriage to a friend, which appeared in book form under the name Iggeret Ha-Kodesh ("Epistle of Holiness"), in which he said, "Hurry not to arouse passion until her mood is ready. Begin in love and let her semination [orgasm] take place first."

The Rabbis believed that just as a man emits semen, so does a woman—obviously confusing the vaginal secretions produced by a woman when her clitoris is stimulated or she has otherwise been brought to the apex of passion. Rabbi Ammi said (Niddah 31a): "If the woman emits her semen first, she bears a male child; if the man emits his semen first, she bears a female child." Rabbi Kattina went further: "I could make all my children to be males." His colleague, Raba, explaining how this is done, said (31b): "One who desires all his children to be males should cohabit twice in succession," meaning that at that point she will be fully aroused and will eject her "semen" first.

As late as the sixteenth century, five centuries after Rashi, Ovadiah ben Jacob Sforno, an outstanding Italian Bible commentator and physician, continued to express the belief that if a woman produces seed first, her child will be a boy. In his commentary on Leviticus 21:2, he explains that her seeds are produced in the genital fluids she emits during intercourse.

Appropriate Times for Sex

There are specific times when sexual activity is recommended and others when it is strictly forbidden. Fast days (Yom Kippur, Tishah B'Av, etc.) and the *shivah* period following the loss of an immediate family member are mournful times, and sex is therefore totally banned. However, abstinence is particularly important during the eleven- or twelve-day interval following the start of a woman's menstrual period. (*See* Niddah.)

Because the Sabbath is the holiest and most peaceful day of the week, Jewish tradition considers it an appropriate time for sexual intercourse between husband and wife. This was based on the answer Rabbi Judah (quoting Rabbi Samuel) gave as an answer to the question, How often should scholars perform their marital duties? (*Ketubbot* 62b.) Rashi suggests that Friday night is ideal because "it is a night of delight, relaxation, and joy." Nachmanides, in *Iggeret Ha-Kodesh*, repeats this idea, explaining that Friday night is a time of heightened spirituality, and sexual union between husband and wife is most suited for this time of the week.

Sexual Temptations

Starting with a premise stated in the talmudic tractate *Niddah* (31b) that it is natural for a man to pursue a woman but not for a woman to pursue a man, the Rabbis have laid down many guidelines for women instructing them to avoid being seductive to men and to remain chaste. While men are cautioned not to gaze even at the little finger of a woman because that is tantamount to peering at her "secret place" (*Berakhot* 24a), and that one should not walk behind a woman even if she be his own wife—because her movements can be sexually arousing—the main caution is directed at the woman.

The Rabbis (*Berakhot* 24a and *Kiddushin* 70a) warned women to be careful in their dress, that no part of their flesh, including their hair, be exposed to public view: Rabbi Chisda said a woman's leg induces sexual excitement; Rabbi Samuel said that listening to a woman's voice is sexually exciting; Rabbi Sheshet said a woman's hair is sexually exciting.

All this applies to women whether married or single, but especially to married women. It also applies to women whether pretty or ugly (*Avodah Zarah* 20a).

The fear of avoiding a situation where sexual arousal is possible extended to the teaching profession. Maimonides summed up the rule in his *Mishneh Torah* (Hilkhot Talmud Torah 2:4) when he said that a bachelor should not teach children because their mothers come to pick them up and a woman should not teach young children because their fathers come to pick them up.

Sex Outside of Marriage

Talmudic and later authorities were deeply concerned about the issue of living together out of wedlock. The Rabbis of the Talmud (*Sanhedrin* 21a) established the requirement that before a couple could live together it was necessary that the woman receive from her man a *ketubbah* (marriage contract). In the fourteenth century, Rabbi Jacob ben Asher, author of the *Tur*, the code of Jewish law upon which the *Shulchan Arukh* is based, wrote (Even Ha-Ezer 26) that if a man lives with a woman merely for sex, this is simple lewdness.

Some contemporary authorities, in expressing their disapproval of unmarried couples living together, cite the talmudic admonition against a man being alone in an enclosure with a woman other than his wife (*Avodah Zarah* 36b). This is interpreted to mean that a man is forbidden to have sexual relations with anyone except a spouse.

However, recognizing how strong is man's desire for sexual gratification and how powerless he sometimes is to control it, talmudic authorities were not quick to condemn sexually active single persons. Although the Rabbis of the Talmud considered premarital sexual activity sinful, they did display an understanding of man's sexual needs. One tractate, for example, records the rather unorthodox observation of Rabbi Assi: "In the beginning, the evil [sexual] inclination [*yeitzer ha-ra*] is [thin and fragile] like a spider's thread, but in the end [as it continues to spin its thread] it becomes as strong as a rope that pulls a wagon." (*Sukkah* 52a.) To Rabbi Assi, sexual need is a force to be reckoned with.

Also in the Talmud, we find the view of Rabbi Ela'i the Elder. He believed that a person is not evil if he cannot control his sexual passions, but he also believed that the person should act discreetly. "If a man sees that he is being overwhelmed by sexual desire," said Rabbi Ela'i (*Chagigah* 16a), "he should go somewhere where he will not be recognized, and there should dress himself in black garments [so he will not be recognized], and do what his heart desires, but let him not defame God by conducting himself in that manner publicly."

Despite these sympathetic sentiments, Jewish tradition is firmly opposed to premarital

and extramarital sex. Possibly the most emphatic expression of this mainstream view is found in the tractate *Sanhedrin* (75a) where a physician suggested that a man who became infatuated with a certain woman be allowed to have intercourse with her. The Rabbis emphatically said no. In his *Mishneh Torah* (Hilkhot Ishut 1:4), Moses Maimonides reminds us that fornication (sex outside of marriage) is punishable by flogging. One must bear in mind, however, that this twelfth-century scholar was one of the few Jewish authorities to deprecate the sex act. He adopted the view of the Greek philosopher Aristotle, contending that sexual intercourse should be regarded with contempt and be engaged in only at rare intervals (*Guide to the Perplexed* III:49). At the same time, he affirmed that just as a man may not deny his wife sexual satisfaction, so may a woman not withhold sex from her husband (*Mishneh Torah,* Ishut 15:1).

Prohibited Practices

The Bible itself is very outspoken in its condemnation of certain types of sexual activity—specifically, adultery, incest, rape, intercourse with animals, and homosexual practices. It makes no mention of lesbianism per se. It is also quite direct in its prohibition of intercourse between a man and his wife during her menstrual period and for the seven days of ritual uncleanliness that follows. These laws are spelled out in detail primarily in chapter 18 of the Book of Leviticus.

See Birth Control; Homosexuality; Incest; Kissing; Niddah; Onanism.

Se'yag La-Torah

A Hebrew term literally meaning "boundary to the Torah."

In order to stem the tide of Jews forsaking the law, and in order to prevent assimilation, beginning in the second century B.C.E. the Rabbis of the Talmud (Yerushalmi *Kiddushin* 4:12) introduced precautionary legislation. This legislation involved establishing a boundary, or fence, around Jewish law in order protect it.

One such precautionary measure aimed at limiting social contact between Jews and non-Jews involved the drinking of wine that had been handled by Gentiles. Since the wine prepared by non-Jews was once used in connection with idolatrous practices, Jews had long been forbidden to drink their wine. The Rabbis reasoned that even though idolatry was no longer the issue, the ban against drinking wine prepared by Gentiles should continue in order to minimize social contact with outsiders that might lead to intermarriage.

Another Torah safeguard relates to the dietary laws. Based on the commandment in the Bible (Exodus 23:19 and Deuteronomy 14:21), "Thou shalt not seethe [cook] a kid in its mother's milk," the Rabbis of the Talmud legislated not only that meat and milk products not be cooked together, but also that they not be served together at one meal.

In establishing boundaries, the Rabbis paid most attention to laws relating to Sabbath observance, particularly to the question of "work." Regulations were established prohibiting otherwise permissible activities so as to minimize the possibility of the Sabbath being violated. Among the activities banned for this reason are the playing of musical instruments, dancing, swimming, and the carrying of objects from the private to the public domain.

See Wine.

Shaatnez

Although the word *shaatnez* is of uncertain origin (some scholars believe it derives from the Greek), in the Hebrew Bible the term refers to a mixture of diverse species. The first reference to *shaatnez* can be found in the Book of Leviticus (19:19): "You shall not permit your cattle to mate with a different species of animal; you shall not sow your field with two varieties of seeds; and you shall not wear garments made of a mixture of two kinds of materials [fibers]."

The Book of Deuteronomy (22:11) specifies which mixture of fibers is prohibited: "You shall not wear a garment containing wool and linen." Because of this specification, the Rabbis of the Talmud ruled that the law of *shaatnez* refers only to garments made of a mixture of animal and vegetable fibers. However, wool or linen may be mixed with cotton, silk, and other fibers in the manufacture of products other than clothing. Shrouds may be made of *shaatnez* because the dead are free of all commandments (Yoreh Dei'ah 301:1; 351:1).

Rationale

Certain biblical laws cannot be explained logically, and the law of *shaatnez* was believed to be one of them. In analyzing Leviticus 19:19, biblical commentator Rashi said that the law pertaining to the mixing of breeds defies logic. It is to be considered a *chok,* a mandatory divine decree for which no reason is given or required, one that must be obeyed without question, just as one obeys a king's command. On the other hand, Maimonides (twelfth century), Nachmanides (thirteenth century), and other scholars did offer explanations.

Maimonides said that the wearing of garments containing mixed fibers is forbidden because heathen priests wore garments made of vegetable and animal materials. For Priests to do so would be a violation of the general law against imitating heathen customs.

Nachmanides, in his commentary on Leviticus 19:19, suggests that all species were made by God at the time of Creation and that any attempt to create a new species by mixing breeds is a defiance of God's will and therefore forbidden.

Practice

Chasidim, particularly in the eighteenth century, were meticulous about adhering to the laws of *shaatnez*, and some would not wear wool garments at any time, lest some linen material was mixed in with it. They wore only silk garments. On the other hand, *chasidim* who lived in Minsk (White Russia) prior to World War II wore only pure linen garments made from cloth imported from China and thus were sometimes called Chinese *chasidim*.

Today, a few small clothing manufacturers who cater to an ultra-Orthodox clientele are careful to produce garments that do not contain the forbidden mixture of fibers. There is also a segment of the Orthodox community that buys off-the-rack garments in general clothing stores and then removes and replaces all threads that are not of the same species as the basic material itself.

Additional Stringency

Columbia University Professor Eli Ginzberg, son of the esteemed scholar Louis Ginzberg of the Jewish Theological Seminary, describes in his *Keeper of the Law* the fastidiousness with which his grandfather, Rabbi Isaac Ginzberg, would observe the laws of *shaatnez*. Once, at the age of seventy, he was traveling with his wife on a train from Bad Homberg, near Frankfort, to Amsterdam. Suspecting that the upholstered seats on the train may have been made of *shaatnez* material, he stood for eight hours, the full duration of the trip. The learned rabbi was adhering to a stringency applied by some ultra-Orthodox Jews to not make use of any fabric comprised of *shaatnez*

in addition to the actual prohibition of not wearing *shaatnez* close to one's body.

Shabbat Chazon

Literally, "Sabbath of prophesies." The Sabbath on which the Torah portion Devarim (Deuteronomy 1:1–3:22) is read in the synagogue is so called because the first Hebrew words of the prophetic reading (*haftarah*) of that day is "the prophesies [vision] of Isaiah."

Devarim is always read on the Sabbath before Tishah B'Av, and the *haftarah* reading Isaiah 1:1–27 was selected to accompany it, because that Torah portion speaks of the catastrophe that befell Jerusalem as a result of Israel's sinfulness. The prophet foresees the possibility of redemption if Israel turns back to God in sincere repentance. This is the third of the Three *Haftarot* of Rebuke, and it is chanted in the mournful style associated with the Book of Lamentations (*Eikhah*).

Verse 1:21 is chanted to the *Eikhah* tune.

Shabbat Ha-Chodesh

Literally, "Sabbath of the New Moon." Also called Parshat Ha-Chodesh, meaning "portion of the New Month." This special Sabbath is so called because it occurs closest to the beginning of the month of Nissan, the month in which the important holiday of Passover is celebrated.

Shabbat Ha-Gadol

Literally, "the Great Sabbath," so called because it immediately precedes the great festival of Passover (*Shulchan Arukh*, Orach Cha'yim 430:1). A second explanation for the choice of the name is that the prophetic portion (*haftarah*) recited on this Sabbath is from Malakhi 3:4–24, which speaks of the "great day" that is to come, a day in which the ninth-century B.C.E. prophet Elijah, renowned as the great healer and peacemaker, will reappear. According to Jewish tradition, Elijah will herald the coming of the Messiah and usher in an age in which the world will enjoy the blessings of freedom, peace, and love.

Shabbat Kallah

Literally, "Sabbath of the bride." In some Sephardic communities, the Sabbath before Shavuot, the holiday on which the Torah was given to Israel, is so named because in Jewish tradition the Torah is compared to a bride and the people of Israel to a bridegroom. On Shavuot, the two were wed.

Sephardim designate the Sabbath that precedes a wedding as Shabbat Kallah. Some Ashkenazi Jews also recognize the Shabbat before a wedding as Shabbat Kallah. Girlfriends of the bride have a small party with the bride and keep her company during her last weekend as a single woman.

Shabbat Mevarkhim

Literally, "Sabbath of the blessing [of the new month]." On the Sabbath prior to the arrival of a new Hebrew month, a member of the congregation carries a Torah to the reader's desk and holds it upright while the cantor intones the blessing for the new month that is to be ushered in.

Shabbat Nachamu

Literally, "Sabbath of consolation." The seven weeks between Tishah B'Av and Rosh Hashanah are known as Shivah D'Nechemta, the "Seven [Sabbaths] of Consolation." This seven-week period that follows the Three Weeks of Rebuke was instituted to offer consolation to a despondent and despairing people who had just seen their holy Temple destroyed.

During this period, the prophetic reading on each Sabbath is a selection from the Book of Isaiah. On the first of these Sabbaths the reading is from Isaiah 40:1–26, the first words of which are *Nachamu, nachamu, ami,* "Comfort ye, comfort ye, My people." Hence, that Sabbath became known as Shabbat Nachamu.

See Shivah D'Nechemta.

Shabbat Parah

Literally, "Sabbath of the cow." The third of the four special Sabbaths that precede Passover is so called because the *maftir* selection from the Book of Numbers (19:1–22) that is read on that day deals with the ritual of the *parah adumah,* the young red cow (heifer) that in Temple times was first sacrificed and then burned on a pyre. Its ashes were dissolved in fresh water and sprinkled upon anyone who had come into contact with a corpse, thus purifying that individual and making it possible for him to partake of the Passover sacrifice (the paschal lamb).

See Maftir; Red Heifer.

Shabbat Rosh Chodesh

Literally, "Sabbath of the New Month." When the New Moon falls on a Sabbath, the occasion is celebrated by reading a selection from the Book of Numbers (28:9–15) from a second Torah scroll. The selection details the sacrifices offered on Sabbath and Rosh Chodesh. Depending on the calendar, Shabbat Rosh Chodesh may be celebrated several times in one year. The *haftarah* read on Shabbat Rosh Chodesh is from chapter 66 of the Book of Isaiah, where reference is made to the significance of celebrating the New Moon.

Shabbat Shekalim

Literally, "Sabbath of the coins," usually celebrated on the Sabbath before the month of Adar. This special Sabbath was introduced in

Temple times in order to remind Jews of their obligation to support the Temple by contributing a half-shekel for its maintenance and for the purchase of sacrificial animals.

Shabbat Shirah

Literally, "Sabbath of song." This is the Sabbath on which the Torah portion Be-shalach (Exodus 13:17 to 17:16), which describes the successful crossing of the Children of Israel through the Sea of Reeds (Red Sea) and their escape from the pursuing Egyptian army, is read. Appreciating their new-found freedom, Moses and the Children of Israel gave expression to their emotions in what has come to be known as *Shirat Ha-Yam*, "Song of the Sea."

Shabbat Shuvah

This Hebrew term literally meaning "Sabbath of return (repentance)" refers to the Sabbath between Rosh Hashanah and Yom Kippur, at which time the prophetic reading is from the Book of Hosea (14:2), which begins with the words *shuvah Yisra'el*, "Return, O Israel [unto the Lord your God"]. This Sabbath is sometimes referred to as Shabbat Teshuvah.

Shabbat Zakhor

Literally, "Sabbath of remembrance." Falling immediately before Purim, this is the second of four special Sabbaths that precede Passover. The maftir Torah reading on this Sabbath, taken from the Book of Deuteronomy (25:17–19), describes how the Amalekites attacked the Children of Israel as they began their trek through the desert toward the Promised Land after leaving Egypt. Because of the savagery of the attack upon the weary Israelites, Israel was commanded to always remember (*zakhor*) that occurrence and "to blot out the memory of Amalek from under heaven."

During the *Shacharit* (morning) service on this Sabbath, Sephardim recite the poem *Mi Kamokhah* ("Who Is like Thee [O God])," composed by the twelfth-century Spanish poet Yehudah Halevi. The poem retells the Purim story of Mordekhai, Esther, and Haman. Sephardim therefore refer to Shabbat Zakhor as Shabbat D'Mi Kamokhah. Every stanza in the long poem ends with a biblical reference and concludes with the word *lo*.

Shabbes Goy

A Yiddish term derived from the Hebrew, literally meaning "Sabbath Gentile," referring to a non-Jew who is employed to perform certain activities forbidden to Jews on the Sabbath, such as turning lights on and off. The practice stems from the prohibition recorded in the Mishnah *Shabbat* (16:18) which states that a Jew may not ask a non-Jew to perform an activity on the Sabbath that he (the Jew) may not perform. When a non-Jew is to be so engaged, he must be instructed of his tasks before the Sabbath.

Owing to the advent of the timer and other electronic gadgetry, few Jews today require the services of a *Shabbes goy*. In earlier times, on the afternoon before Yom Kippur, in the vestibule of most Orthodox synagogues, collection plates for a variety of organizations and study groups within the community were placed on long tables covered with white tablecloths. One of the plates was designated for donations to help defray the fees paid to the *Shabbes goy*, an indication of the importance of his service.

Mario Cuomo, former governor of New York, among other prominent people, recalls with delight how he served as a *Shabbes goy* for a Jewish family. General Colin Powell, who grew up in the 1950s in Hunts Point, a Jewish section of the South Bronx of New York City, writes in *My American Journey* (1995), "On

Friday nights I earned a quarter by turning the lights on and off at the Orthodox synagogue, so that worshippers could observe the Sabbath ban on activity." In 1952, in Memphis, seventeen-year-old Elvis Presley became the personal *Shabbes goy* of Rabbi Alfred Fruchter and his family. Elvis refused to accept money for his services, saying that it was his pleasure to help the rabbi keep his Sabbath (*New York* magazine, August 25, 1997).

Shacharit

A Hebrew word literally meaning "morning [hours]." Originally, *Shacharit* was the name of the early morning sacrifice brought daily in the Temple in Jerusalem. After the destruction of the Temple in 70 C.E., it was adopted as the name of the early morning prayer service.

The weekday morning *Shacharit* service begins with the donning of the *tallit* (prayer-shawl) and *tefillin* (phylacteries) by adult members of the congregation and the recitation of appropriate prayers to accompany the performance of these rites. In traditional congregations a series of prayers called the *Pesukei De-Zimra*, "Verses of Praise," most of which are selections from the Book of Psalms, are then recited. This is followed by the *Barukh She'amar* ("Blessed Is He Who Said") prayer, which introduces the main body of prayers of the morning service.

The core of the *Shacharit* service consists of the *Barkhu*, the *Shema,* and the *Amidah*, the Silent Devotion. The *Amidah* ends with *Sim Shalom*, a prayer for peace, preceded by the *Priestly Benediction* (*Birkat Kohanim*), which is recited daily in Jerusalem synagogues and on the Sabbath and/or holidays in the Diaspora.

Shadkhan

Also spelled *shadchan*. Plural, *shadkhanim* or *shadchanim*. A Hebrew term referring to a matchmaker. Long considered an honorable profession among Jews, the *shadkhan* is looked upon as one engaged in doing God's work. This is evident from a talmudic legend (*Genesis Rabbah* 68:4) describing a conversation between a Roman matron and Rabbi Yosei ben Chalafta, a second-century scholar who was a disciple of Rabbi Akiba.

"What has your God been doing since He finished making the world?" asked the matron.

"He has been matching couples," the rabbi answered.

"That isn't so difficult," said the woman. "I can do as well."

"You may think it is simple," said Rabbi Yosei, "but it is as difficult as the splitting of the Red Sea."

Unmoved by the rabbi's argument, the Roman matron set out to prove her point. She took one thousand male slaves and one thousand female slaves, lined them up in rows, separated them into couples, and joined the couples' hands in matrimony. The next morning they descended upon her in droves, one with a smashed head, another with gouged-out eyes, a third with a broken leg. The couples demanded that the marriages be annulled.

The matron conceded the point to the rabbi.

Although in more recent times the *shadkhan* has come to be thought of disparagingly, marriage brokers were traditionally an asset to the Jewish people because Jews as a whole were so often denied mobility. The matchmaker was permitted to move about freely and thus was able to bring together people from various communities who might otherwise never have met. Some of the most illustrious rabbis and scholars (for example, the fifteenth-century

Jacob ben Moses Halevi Mollin, the Maharil) made their living as *shadkhanim*.

When a matchmaker is successful in arranging a marriage, it is said that he has performed a *shidukh*.

Shai Olamot

A Hebrew term literally meaning "three hundred and ten worlds." *Shai*, spelled *shin yud*, has a numerical value of 310.

In the last Mishnah of the Talmud (*Uktzin* 3:12), Rabbi Joshua ben Levi says, "In the world to come, the Holy One, blessed be He, will cause each righteous person to inherit 310 worlds." This will be their reward for having made the study of Torah their chief delight in life.

Shalashudis

See Se'udah Shelishit.

Shalom

A Hebrew word literally meaning "peace." *See* Greetings and Salutations.

Shalom Bat

A Hebrew term literally meaning "welcome [to a] daughter." In an effort to match the attention that traditionally has been lavished upon the newborn male child, Jewish feminists have created ceremonies to welcome the female child. Most have used the term *brit*, "covenant," as part of the ceremony names (*brit bat*, "covenant of the daughter"; *brit shalom*, "covenant of peace"; *brit kedushah*, "covenant of holiness"; etc.), and some have incorporated the word *simchah*, meaning "joy," or *shalom*, meaning "welcome," into the names (such as *shalom bat* and *simchat ha-bat*). The terms *shalom bat*, "welcome to the daughter," and *shalom nekeivah*, "welcome to the female" (to match *shalom zakhar*), are preferred by many who feel that the word *brit* should be reserved exclusively for the male *brit milah*, "covenant of circumcision."

The ceremony of welcome is generally held on a Friday night after the child is one month old, the age at which Jewish law considers the newborn to be viable. A definitive ceremony has not been established, so each family fashions its own.

Shalom Zakhar

A Hebrew term literally meaning "welcome to the male child," referring to a celebration held upon the birth of a boy. According to the Talmud, as soon as a male child comes into the world, peace comes into the world. Of kabbalistic origin, the *shalom zakhar* celebration was introduced by the Jews of Eastern Europe, particularly Germany, in the fifteenth century. It became customary for relatives, friends, and members of the local congregation to visit the home of new parents on the Friday night after the birth of a boy. The guests were served wine, cider, beer, cake, fruit, cooked beans, and peas. The cantor of the congregation led the guests in song, and the rabbi often delivered a brief discourse.

The *shalom zakhar* is held on the Friday night following the birth of a boy or, among Sephardic Jews, on the night before the circumcision. Sephardim believe that the presence of a group of people will deter Satan, who is eager to prevent Jews from observing the rite of circumcision. Cooked legumes, such as beans and peas, are served because it is believed that these foods are effective charms against evil spirits intent upon harming children.

A similar ceremony, not much practiced these days, is called *ben zakhar*. The name derives from the statement in the Book of Jeremiah (20:15), "A boy [*ben zakhar*] is born unto you."

Shalosh Regalim

The Hebrew term referring to the three Pilgrim Festivals when Jews came by foot (and by other means) to a sanctuary to offer thanks to God. The three festivals are Pesach (Passover), Sukkot (Tabernacles), and Shavuot (Pentecost), as noted in Exodus 23:14.

See Pilgrim Festivals.

Shamash

A Hebrew word literally meaning "server," the term for the extra arm on a candelabrum (*menorah*) whose flame is used to "serve" the others by kindling them from its fire. The first *shamash* was the seventh branch of the seven-branched candelabrum of the Tabernacle in the desert and later in the Temple in Jerusalem.

A ninth candle was added to the eight-branched Chanukkah *menorah* because the eight primary candles of the *menorah* may not be used for practical purposes. By having a ninth candle to light the others, one will not be tempted to use any of the eight primary candles for such a purpose.

The word *shamash* is also used to describe the sexton of a synagogue whose function it is to serve the needs of worshippers. On occasion, he also leads the service and reads the Torah.

Sharing

See Zeh Ne'heneh Ve-Zeh Lo Chaser.

Shas

A Hebrew acronym formed from the letters *shin* and *samekh*, which are the first letters of the term *Shishah Sedarim*, meaning "six orders [of the Mishnah]." The Mishnah (first part of the Talmud) is divided into six sections or orders:

1. *Zera'im*, dealing with the subject of tithes, Temple offerings, and agricultural matters.
2. *Moed*, dealing with holidays of all types.
3. *Nashim*, dealing with marriage and divorce.
4. *Nezikin*, dealing with legal matters.
5. *Kodoshim*, dealing with the Temple sacrificial system.
6. *Tohorot*, dealing with questions of ritual purity.

The term *Shas* is also used to refer to the entire Talmud, Mishnah plus *Gemara*.

See Talmud.

Shatz

An acronym formed from the initial letters of the Hebrew term *shli'ach tzibbur*, meaning "public messenger," referring to the person who leads a prayer service.

See Shli'ach Tzibur.

Shavuot

A Hebrew term literally meaning "weeks." It is the name of the spring holiday that is celebrated seven weeks after the beginning of Passover. Shavuot falls on the sixth day of Sivan, usually in late May or early June. It is celebrated for one day in Israel and for two days in the Diaspora.

One of the three Pilgrim Festivals mentioned in the Bible, Shavuot is known by many names. In the Book of Exodus (23:16), it is called Chag Ha-Katzir, meaning "harvest festival," because it was a holiday observed when the first cuttings of the wheat harvest were brought as a sacrifice. A special sacrifice of two loaves of bread baked from the new crop was offered in the Temple. In the Book of Numbers (28:26), Shavuot is known as Chag Ha-Bikkurim, meaning "festival of first fruits."

In the Talmud (*Megillah* 32a), the only name by which Shavuot is known is Atzeret, meaning "assembly." According to the description of the holiday in the Mishnah (*Bikkurim* 3), the village people of Palestine would first assemble in the largest town of the district and bring their first ripe fruits to the Temple, where they would be welcomed by the Levites with song.

Although seven weeks separate the two holidays, the tractate *Pesachim* (42b) refers to Shavuot as *Atzeret Shel Pesach*, "the concluding season of the Passover festival." To the Rabbis of the Talmud, the relationship of Shavuot to Passover was the same as that of Shemini Atzeret to Sukkot. Even though a separate holiday, Shemini Atzeret was considered the last day of Sukkot; Shavuot was considered the end of Passover, concluding the forty-nine-day *sefirah* period, which begins on the second night of Passover.

The third-century C.E. scholar Rabbi Eleazar said (*Pesachim* 68b) that all authorities agree on the necessity of rejoicing with good food and wine on Atzeret because on that day the Torah was given to Israel. Thus, Shavuot became known as *Zeman Matan Torateinu*, the "time of the giving of the Torah."

Shavuot became increasingly associated with the Revelation on Mount Sinai because it had lost its significance as a purely agricultural holiday. The Jews of Palestine had become an urban people, and to keep the holiday alive it became necessary to associate the Shavuot holiday with a historical event.

Shavuot is also known as Pentecost, from the Greek meaning "holiday of fifty days." This word is used by Christians in commemoration of the gathering of Jesus' disciples and a large band of followers to hear St. Peter tell the story of his resurrection and ascension to heaven. Christians observe this fiftieth day on the seventh Sunday after Easter.

Length of Observance

The Bible (Leviticus 23:15–16) describes Shavuot as a one-day holiday. As with other holidays, because of the uncertainty of the calendar, communities outside of Israel traditionally observe the holiday for one extra day. However, Reform congregations and some Conservative ones follow the Israeli practice.

There is an opinion that Shavuot was always observed as a two-day holiday. This is based on the difference of opinion expressed in the Talmud (*Shabbat* 86b). The Rabbis taught: "The Torah was given to Israel on the sixth day of Sivan, but Rabbi Yosei maintained that it was on the seventh."

Synagogue Observance

A number of novel features were introduced into synagogue decor and liturgy to celebrate Shavuot. First, many synagogues are decorated with greenery in keeping with the belief that Mount Sinai was a green mountain covered with trees and shrubs when the Torah was given to Moses. Some early authorities disapproved of this custom, claiming to do this was an imitation of certain Christian customs, such as displaying greenery on Christmas. This is rebutted by the talmudic argument (*Rosh Hashanah* 2a) that Shavuot is a judgment day for trees, and displaying green plants is not an imitation of non-Jewish practices.

Following the evening service, or a few hours thereafter, it has become customary in many synagogues for congregants to devote all or a good part of the night to Torah study. This practice, which was introduced by medieval kabbalists is known as *tikkun leil Shavuot*.

At the Shavuot morning service, a special long poem (*piyyut*), written in Aramaic and known as *Akdamut*, is chanted to a special tune before the Torah reading. The opening words, *akdamut milin*, meaning "first words," plead for God's approval to speak, among other things, of His love for Israel and Israel's faithfulness to the Torah. The poem was composed in the eleventh century by Meir ben Isaac Nehora'i, of Orléans, France.

The Torah reading for (the first day of) Shavuot includes the section from the Book of Exodus (20:2–14) that enumerates the Ten Commandments. While these commandments were recited daily in Temple times, when the Temple was destroyed its recitation was not included in the prayerbook out of fear that some Jews might claim that only these commandments, not the entire Torah, were given to Moses on Mount Sinai (*Berakhot* 12a).

Although the custom today is to rise when the Ten Commandments are read from the Torah, during the Middle Ages there were protests against this practice by those concerned that undue importance would be attached to them.

On the first day of Shavuot, the Book of Ruth (*Rut*), one of the five *megillot*, is read aloud. Several reasons have been offered to explain why this book of the Bible was selected: (1) The story of Ruth and Boaz takes place in the spring, at harvest time, which is when Shavuot falls; (2) Ruth was the ancestor of King David, and according to a tradition mentioned in the Talmud, David was born and died on Shavuot; and (3) Since Ruth expressed her loyalty to her mother-in-law, Naomi, and accepted her religion, it was appropriate to read the story of her life on Shavuot, the holiday of the Torah.

Because the Torah and Jewish loyalty are so intimately linked with Shavuot, in many Eastern European communities it was once customary to introduce children three to five years of age to Hebrew school studies on Shavuot. The children were then treated to cakes, honey, and sweets "so the Torah might be sweet on their lips."

The Reform movement introduced the idea of confirming children thirteen to sixteen years of age on Shavuot. Many more conservative congregations have adopted the confirmation ceremony, at which boys and girls confirm their loyalty to Judaism.

Shavuot Foods

On Shavuot, some families serve a round *challah* at the holiday meal while others use the traditional braided Sabbath *challah*. A ladder design is sometimes placed on top of the loaf to commemorate the giving of the Torah on Mount Sinai. The ladder design was chosen because the numerical value of the Hebrew word for Sinai is the same (130) as that of the Hebrew word for ladder (*sulam*). The ladder symbolizes the ascent of Moses to heaven to receive the Ten Commandments.

The eating of cheese products on Shavuot has been a longstanding Jewish tradition. One explanation is that dairy foods (and honey) should be eaten on the day the Torah was received on Mount Sinai because the words "honey and milk under thy lips" in the Song of Songs (4:11) imply that, like milk products and honey, the words of the Torah lift man's spirits.

Another explanation for the use of dairy products on Shavuot is based on Exodus 23:19: "The choicest first-fruits shalt thou bring to the House of the Lord. Thou shalt not seethe [cook] a kid in its mother's milk." The fact that the verse mentions meat (a kid) and milk is taken to mean that the two main dishes served at the holiday meal are to be a dairy dish, followed by a meat dish.

A third explanation for the dairy tradition on Shavuot is based on a legend which maintains that when the Israelites reached their homes after receiving the Torah on Mount Sinai, they had little time to prepare a meat meal (since a good deal of time is needed for the kosher slaughtering of an animal). Instead, they hastily put together a dairy meal, which could be more quickly prepared.

Serving two cheese *blintzes*, representing the two tablets of the Ten Commandments, is a popular Shavuot dish.

Triangular-shaped *kreplach* ("dumplings") are also a popular Shavuot dish. Three is a prominent number in Jewish tradition: there are three patriarchs (Abraham, Isaac, Jacob); three parts to the Bible (Torah, Prophets, Holy Writings); and three types of Jews (Priests, Levites, Israelites). Also, the Torah was given to the Israelites in the third month (Sivan) through Moses, the third child of his parents.

Shloshet Yemei Hagbalah

The three days before Shavuot are known as *Shloshet Yemei Hagbalah*, meaning "three days of bounds." That characterization stems from the text of Exodus 19:10–13, where God says to Moses, "Go to the people, prepare them to be holy today and tomorrow...that they may be ready for the third day, for on the third day [the sixth of Sivan] God will come down [to Mount Sinai] before the eyes of all the people. Fix boundaries for all the people and say to them, 'Be careful not to go up the mountain or even touch its border, for you shall be put to death.'"

The three days of separation were the third, fourth, and fifth of Sivan; the sixth day of the month is Shavuot The third, fourth, and fifth of Sivan, along with the first day of the month, Rosh Chodesh, were all declared semiholidays. This left the second day of the month unaccounted for and undistinguished.

In order not to neglect the second day of Sivan entirely, the Rabbis gave it the special designation *Yom Ha-Meyuchas*, meaning "the choice day." Because it was discovered that Yom Kippur always fell on the same day of the week as the second day of the month of Sivan, it too was considered a semiholiday. (See *Shabbat* 87a.)

Although weddings are prohibited on most of the fifty days between Passover and Shavuot, they are permitted on *Shloshet Yemei Hagbalah*.

See Tikkun Leil Shavuot.

Shaygetz and Shiksa

Shaygetz is a Yiddishized form of the Hebrew word *sheketz*, meaning "an abomination," a term originally applied to insects and other unpleasant forms of life that crawl on the earth (Leviticus 11:20, 23) and are forbidden as food. Anything taboo or abominable became known as *sheketz*. Since intermarriage with non-Jews is taboo, the term was applied to them. *Shaygetz* is a masculine form and *shiksa* (actually *shiktza*) is the feminine form.

Shechitah

A Hebrew word literally meaning "slaughtering," referring specifically to the ritual slaughtering of animals in accordance with the Jewish dietary laws. The *shochet*, or slaughterer, must be an observant Jew who is well-versed in the law and has been technically trained to perform his duties.

The knife a *shochet* uses is called a *chalif*. For the slaughtering of mammals, a twenty-inch blade is used; for fowl, a six-inch blade.

The knife must be razor-sharp, free of all nicks. When the slaughterer performs his act, he draws the knife across the throat of the animal, severing the jugular vein in one swift stroke. The animal dies instantly and painlessly as a maximum amount of blood leaves its body in one gush. The carcass must be drained of as much blood as possible because of the biblical injunction against consuming blood, which symbolizes the very soul of man (Leviticus 3:17).

The work of the *shochet* is checked by an examiner (*mashgiach*) to see if Jewish law has been adhered to.

There are many Jewish rituals that women do not practice even though they are legally permitted to do so, one of which is serving as a *shochet*.

In Britain, the Royal Society for the Prevention of Cruelty to Animals has campaigned for years to ban *shechitah*, but the effort has failed. Similar unsuccessful attempts were made in South Africa and France, where actress Brigitte Bardot led the charge.

Swiss Chief Rabbi Yisrael Levinger, a veterinary physiologist, the leading world authority on *shechitah*, is the author of the definitive work on the subject. Published in 1995, it is entitled *Shechitah in the Light of the Year 2000*.

In 1997 Denmark's right-wing Progressive Party instigated an inquiry to determine whether *shechitah* should be banned as cruel and inhumane treatment of animals, but the effort was in vain.

Presently, only three countries formally outlaw *shechitah*: Switzerland, where it has been banned since 1893; Norway, since 1929; and Sweden, since 1937.

She-heche'yanu

A Hebrew term literally meaning "[God] Who has enabled us to survive," this is the name given to a blessing of appreciation recited on various occasions.

The *She-heche'yanu* blessing—*Barukh atah Adonai, Eloheinu melekh ha-olam, She-heche'yanu, ve-ki'yemanu, ve-hi'giyanu la-zeman ha-zeh*, "Praised be Thou, O Lord our God, King of the universe, who has kept us alive, and sustained us, and enabled us to reach this season" was introduced to encourage Jews to offer thanks for first-time happenings. It is a prayer of gratitude recited upon the annual advent of a holiday, or when a rite or ritual is observed for the first time in the year, or upon eating a fruit for the first time in a season.

The *She-heche'yanu* benediction is also recited when one puts on a new garment, whether it is a dress, suit, coat, or pair of shoes. The Rabbis, however, have insisted that when an article is made from the skin of an animal, a benediction is not to be recited, because wearing such a product flies in the face of the biblical commandment to treat animals kindly (Exodus 20:10 and Deuteronomy 22:4).

The *She-heche'yanu* blessing is recited on the first day of all holidays in Israel and in the Diaspora.

In recent years, the family of a bar and bat mitzvah join in reciting this blessing when this rite of passage is celebrated.

Sheitl

Also pronounced *shaitl*. In biblical times women covered their heads with scarves or veils as a sign of chastity and modesty. To expose a woman's hair was a way of expressing humiliation (Numbers 5:18; Isaiah 3:17 and *Berakhot* 24a). In early talmudic times it became common practice for married women to keep their heads covered (*Sanhedrin* 58b). Rabbi Sheshet said (*Berakhot* 42a): "A woman's hair is sexually exciting." To be out of doors with head uncovered was a serious breach of law and custom, and it constituted sufficient grounds for a man to divorce his wife without his being required to pay her any of the monies normally due her upon divorce, as stipulated in the marriage contract (*Ketubbot* 72a).

Some talmudic scholars regarded the wearing of a headcovering as an expression of guilt for the sin of Eve (Genesis 3:7–8).

To emphasize the importance of a woman keeping her hair covered, the Talmud relates the story of a pious woman named Kimchit, who was the mother of seven sons, each of whom became a High Priest. When asked why she thought she was blessed with so many distinguished sons, she replied, "Because the beams [posts] of my house never saw my hair" (*Yoma* 57a).

The *Code of Jewish Law* (*Shulchan Arukh*, Orach Cha'yim 75:2) states: "Married women always keep their heads covered; unmarried women do not have to keep their heads covered." The purpose of the legislation is to make perfectly clear to men the marital status of a female.

Today, only ultra-Orthodox women keep their heads covered at all times. Some wear a scarf, called a *tikhl* in Yiddish; others wear a *sheitl*. Some chasidic women wear hats and sheitls together.

In some chasidic communities, it is customary for a bride to cut off all her hair before her wedding and to keep her head shaved indefinitely, covered only by a *tikhl*. In Israel today, a trend has begun among Orthodox young women to throw a "*tikhl* party" for a friend who has become engaged. The bride-to-be's friends bring various hats and headcoverings, and in a spirit of fun they try on each other's gifts.

See Headcovering.

Shekhinah

Literally meaning "indwelling," this term is derived from the Hebrew root "to dwell." It is a synonym for God created by the Rabbis of the Talmud to describe God's closeness to the people of Israel (Exodus 25:8). The Talmud (*Megillah* 29a) describes His immanence and omnipresence by saying, "Come and see how beloved is Israel before the Omnipresent [God], for wherever they went into exile the Shekhinah went with them; in Babylon, the Shekhinah was with them..."

While philosophers such as Sa'adya Gaon, Moses Maimonides, and Judah Halevi interpreted the *Shekhinah* in an impersonal way (as a Divine Light or Divine Influence), kabbalists personified the *Shekhinah*, even interpreting it as the feminine aspect of the godhead. They considered the last of the ten *sefirot*, called *Malkhut* ("Sovereignty"), to be identical with the *Shekhinah*.

Feminists point to the characterization of the *Shekhinah* as the feminine aspect of God as proof that God should not be thought of in strictly male terms.

Shelom Ba'yit

This Hebrew term literally meaning "household peace" is sometimes rendered as *shlom ba'yit* or, incorrectly, as *shalom ba'yit*. First used in the Talmud (*Shabbat* 23b), it reflects the ideal that peace and harmony should prevail in family relationships and within the Jewish community at large.

The concept of *shelom ba'yit* was addressed in a 1926 responsum of Rabbi Solomon Friedmann of Lemburg. The question posed was whether it is proper to count to a ritual quorum (*minyan*) a person who had profaned the Sabbath or had shaved with a razor and should therefore be denied a Torah honor (*aliyah*). Rabbi Freidmann argues that to deny any Jew an *aliyah*, and thus treat him as a Gentile, will cause strife in the community and violate the principle of *shelom ba'yit*.

Shelosha De-Puranuta

Literally meaning "three of rebuke," this Hebrew/Aramaic term refers to the themes expressed in the prophetic portions (*haftarot*) read from the Book of Jeremiah on the three Sabbaths prior to Tishah B'Av. These readings relate to the sinfulness of Israel that led to the destruction of the Temple, for which the prophet is rebuking them. The original Aramaic term is *Telat De-Puranuta*.

Sheloshim

A Hebrew word literally meaning "thirty." The Rabbis of the Talmud prescribed that after the first week of intense mourning (*shivah*), the remainder of the first month also be set aside to grieve the loss of a member of the immediate family. The one-week period of *shivah* plus the additional mourning period that follows it are known as *sheloshim*.

The *sheloshim* period commences on the day the deceased is buried and concludes after morning prayers have been recited on the thirtieth day after burial. For those mourning close family relatives other than parents, the mourning period ends officially at this point. However, those mourning the death of a parent are obliged to observe mourning rites for a full year, although the recitation of the *Kaddish* prayer itself ends after eleven months.

During the first thirty days after the death of a close relative, mourners are not permitted to marry. An exception is made in cases where final marriage arrangements had been completed before the death occurred.

See Shivah; Yud Bet Chodesh.

Shema

A Hebrew word literally meaning "hear." The prayer known as the *Shema* is a basic Jewish prayer because it expresses the Jewish affirmation of faith in One God. The *Shema* consists of three biblical selections that are recited at every morning and evening prayer service. The first selection, taken from the Book of Deuteronomy (6:4–9), begins with the familiar words *Shema Yisra'el, Adonai Eloheinu, Adonai Echad*, "Hear O Israel, the Lord is our God the Lord is One," thus proclaiming the unity of God as a basic principle of Judaism. It then goes on to encourage Jews to commit themselves totally to love God, to follow His precepts, and to transmit that message to their children. This first verse of the *Shema*, say the Rabbis of the Talmud (*Berakhot* 15b), must be recited aloud and distinctly if one is to fulfill his religious obligation.

The second paragraph of the *Shema* (Deuteronomy 11:13–21) instructs Jews to affirm their belief in one God by placing a *mezuzah* on their doorposts and by wearing *tefillin* (phylacteries) on their arms and foreheads during prayer at specified times.

The third paragraph (Numbers 15:37–41) tells the Children of Israel that their life purpose is to be a holy people. To remind them that God's commandments must always be observed, they must wear fringes (*tzitzit*) on their garments.

The sentence that follows the first verse of the *Shema* is *Barukh Sheim kevod malkhuto le'olam va'ed*, "Blessed be His glorious Name forever and ever." This nonbiblical statement appears for the first time in the Talmud in connection with the Yom Kippur afternoon service (known as the *Avodah*) conducted by the High Priest. In the presence of a large congregation, the High Priest, standing in the Temple Court, confessed his sins. As he did so, he pronounced the sacred and ineffable name of God (*Yehovah*) that no one but the High Priest was permitted to utter. Upon hearing this, the congregation responded aloud, enthusiastically, "Blessed be His glorious Name forever and ever." This response was repeated three times (*Yoma* 35b).

At prayer services conducted in Babylonian synagogues in Temple times, it was customary to intone the second sentence of the *Shema* silently so as not to detract from the importance of the biblical verses that preceded and followed it. This was also the practice of the Jews of Palestine. However, when the Christians who lived among them (there were no Christians in Babylonia) accused the Palestinian Jews of enunciating secret, heretical doctrines, Jews began to recite the second sentence of the *Shema* aloud.

Today, all Orthodox and some Conservative congregations follow the practice of Babylonian Jewry and recite the *Barukh Sheim Kevod* silently throughout the year. But on Yom Kippur, as a reminder of the enthusiastic response of the ancient congregation of Israel to the confession of sins by the High Priest, all congregants in all congregations recite the *Barukh Sheim Kevod* aloud.

A fanciful explanation for reciting the second sentence of the *Shema* aloud only on Yom Kippur has been offered by mystics. They say that when Moses went to heaven to receive the Ten Commandments, he heard the angels respond aloud to the first sentence of the *Shema* with the words *Barukh Sheim Kevod*. When the angels discovered that men on earth had been doing likewise, they objected, arguing that earthlings are sinners and hence not entitled to the privilege of responding to the *Shema* as are sinless angels. However, say the mystics, since Yom Kippur is a day on which sins are forgiven and men become like angels, all may respond aloud to the *Shema*.

In many editions of the prayerbook, and in the Torah itself, the last letter of the first word of the *Shema* (*a'yin*) and the last letter of the last word of the *Shema* (*dalet*) are written in bold, large script. Taken together, the *a'yin* of *Shema* and the *dalet* of *Echad* form the word *eid*, meaning "witness," are a reminder that Jews are duty bound to serve as witnesses to God's sovereignty by leading exemplary lives.

Many pious Jews prolong the sounding of the last word of the first verse of the *Shema*—the *echad*, meaning "one [God]." In the tractate *Berakhot* (13b), Rabbi Symmachus explains: "Whoever prolongs the word *echad* will have his life prolonged."

To intensify concentration when reciting the *Shema*, many Jews, especially Sephardim, cover their eyes with a corner of their prayershawl. The Talmud (*Berakhot* 13b) notes that when Rabbi Judah the Prince recited the *Shema*, he would "pass his hand over his eyes as a sign that he accepts the yoke of the kingdom of heaven."

The traditional practice is to remain seated when reciting the *Shema*, because these verses are taken directly from the Bible, a book that is studied in schools, and students sit when studying. (This also explains why the congregation does not stand while the Torah is being read.) Reform congregations and most Conservative congregations, however, consider the *Shema* so important that when the first verse is recited, the congregation does stand.

Because of the importance ascribed to the *Shema*, it became a popular bedtime prayer that is taught to children at a very young age. This practice may have its origin in a comment by the talmudic authority Joshua ben Levi, who said (*Berakhot* 4b), "Though a person has recited the *Shema* in the synagogue, it is a religious obligation to recite it again before going to bed."

In many European communities, Jews believed that the *Shema* possessed magical powers that afford protection to those who are vulnerable. They would therefore conduct a vigil in the home of a newborn whose circumcision was scheduled for the next day. The gathering was called *Wachnacht*, a German word meaning "night of watching." Schoolchildren would be invited to encircle the crib and recite the *Shema* prayer along with adults, who then spent the night in study. This circle of protection, of kabbalistic origin, is similar in purpose to many other Jewish customs where encirclement is practiced as a means of warding off evil spirits.

The *Shema* consists of 248 words (when the three introductory words, *El Melekh Ne'eman*, are added to the 245 words in the body of the text). This has been associated with the belief that the human body has 248 parts. Based on this, it was said that if we recite the *Shema* with sincerity, God will watch over our bodies and bless us with good health. This led to the old Yiddish adage that a person who is absolutely sincere is acting *mit alleh ramach eivorim*, "with all 248 limbs." (The word *remach* is an acronym consisting of the letters *reish* [200], *mem* [40], and *chet* [8], for a total of 248.)

See Mezuzah; Monotheism.

Shemini Atzeret

From the Hebrew literally meaning "Assembly of the Eighth Day," referring specifically to the holiday celebrated on the eighth day after the seven days of Sukkot. Contrary to common misconceptions, Shemini Atzeret is a separate one-day holiday, not the eighth or last day of Sukkot. None of the Sukkot ceremonials apply to it.

Shemini Atzeret is prescribed in the Book of Leviticus (23:36) with these few words: "On the eighth day you shall hold a holy convocation; you shall do no work on it." At a later date, the communities in the Diaspora added a second day to Shemini Atzeret, which became known as Simchat Torah, "the Festival of Rejoicing in the Torah." In Israel, Simchat Torah is celebrated on Shemini Atzeret.

Observance

In ancient times, to celebrate the Sukkot holiday, Jews traveled by foot or by horse-drawn carriage to the Temple in Jerusalem. There, they offered thanks to God. After Sukkot, before returning to their homes, the pilgrims remained in Jerusalem for one more day. On that day, Shemini Atzeret, special prayers were recited and sacrifices were brought in the Temple.

In later years, aside from the assigned synagogue Torah reading for Shemini Atzeret, it became customary to read one of the five scrolls, Ecclesiastes. According to tradition, Ecclesiastes (*Kohelet* in Hebrew), was composed by King Solomon in his old age, at a point when he was frustrated and despondent. Its content, often pessimistic, was found to be an accurate expression of the mood of the masses who had just experienced the long holiday period beginning with Rosh Hashanah and concluding with Sukkot, during which much soul-searching was demanded.

If one of the intermediate days of Sukkot falls on a Sabbath, Ecclesiastes is read on that day rather than on Shemini Atzeret.

See Simchat Torah.

Shemittah

A Hebrew term meaning "release, abandonment." According to the Bible (Exodus 23:10–11 and Leviticus 25:1–7), the land in Israel must be allowed to lie fallow every seventh year. The seventh year is known as *shemittah*, a sabbatical year, a year of rest for both the land and the people who work it. Whatever grows in unattended fields of the land during the *shemittah* year is to be left for the poor.

The Bible (Deuteronomy 15:1–3) also requires that in every seventh year all debts be cancelled. This law was especially hard on poor people who would not be able to obtain loans when the *shemittah* year was approaching. Lenders would certainly not want to lend money if they might not be repaid. In fact this law of the sabbatical year turned out to be so oppressive that Hillel, the leading scholar of the first century B.C.E., issued a ruling that became known by its Greek name, *prosbul*. A *prosbul* was a declaration made in a court at the time of the execution of a loan. Its terms made it clear that the law of *shemittah*, which ordinarily cancels loans, would not apply to the specific loan being transacted.

The law of the sabbatical year also requires that every Hebrew slave—man or woman—be released. So that the slaves would not be released empty-handed, they were to be supplied liberally "of thy flock and from thy threshing-floor and winepress" (Deuteronomy 15:12–14).

In modern times, the need for Jews to grow food in Israel became acute, and observance of the sabbatical year problematic. To cope with the situation, rabbinic authorities have permitted Jewish farmers, via a legal fiction, to sell their land to non-Jews for the *shemittah* period. This allowed them to cultivate the land as nonowners. The chief proponents of this innovation were Rabbi Isaac Elchanan Spektor of Kovno (1817–1896), the foremost authority of his age, and Rabbi Abraham I. Kook (1865–1935), Chief Rabbi of Palestine. Today, most, but not all, rabbinic authorities subscribe to this ruling.

In recent years, other methods were intro-duced to ease the heavy economic and social load imposed by the *shemittah* requirements. One method was the early sowing of crops (before Rosh Hashanah) and another was the growing of crops by hydroponics or other soil-less methods. Throughout the *shemittah* year, the Orthodox Israeli press lists shops selling permitted fruits and vegetables that were either grown on non-Jewish soil or imported.

The fiftieth year, after seven sabbatical years, is called the *yovel* (literally, "ram's horn") or jubilee, year (Leviticus 25:8ff.).

As an outgrowth of the *shemittah* concept, it has become customary for professionals such as rabbis and professors to be allowed the freedom every seventh year to enjoy a "sabbatical" (either the whole or part of the year) to refresh themselves by pursuing their studies without other responsibility, or by traveling to enhance their knowledge.

See Jubilee Year; Prosbul.

Shemoneh Esrei

A Hebrew term literally meaning "eighteen," a name given to one of the most important prayers in the liturgy.

See Amidah; Eighteen Benedictions.

Shemurah Matzah

Also referred to as *matzah shemurah* or *matzah shel mitzvah*, this Hebrew term literally meaning "guarded *matzah*" refers to special *matzah* that is watched from the moment the grain is cut to the moment the *matzah* is baked in the oven. To reduce the likelihood of the *matzah* fermenting (fermented food is prohibited on Passover) the *matzah* is prepared in moisture-free (or moisture-reduced) premises. During the baking process, all activity is carefully supervised so as not to prolong the procedure, thus reducing the possibility of fermentation to set in.

According to the Rabbis of the Talmud (*Pesachim* 120a), the positive obligation to eat *matzah* applies only to the first night of Passover, although it is quite clear that bread and leavened products may not be eaten at any time during the holiday. For this reason, the *matzah* selected for consumption at the *Seder* table is particularly special, and *shemurah matzah* is the only type very observant Jews use.

Shemurah matzah is generally made completely by hand in special bakeries not otherwise in operation throughout the year. The cost per pound is considerably higher than machine-made *matzah*.

Sheva Berakhot

A Hebrew term literally meaning "seven blessings," the name given to the benedictions that are recited by the rabbi or cantor at the conclusion of a traditional wedding ceremony and then again during the *Grace After Meals* that is recited as part of the wedding dinner. Usually, seven guests are invited to participate, each of whom recites one of the seven blessings. The *Sheva Berakhot*, which is also called *Birkat Chatanim* ("Blessing of the Bridegrooms"), expresses thanks for the gift of life and for the union of a son and daughter in Israel; it also expresses the hope that joy and contentment will reign in the home of the newlyweds.

A tradition developed to repeat these blessings each day for seven days after the day of the wedding. A ritual quorum (*minyan*) assembles each day with the bride and groom present, and after a meal is served the seven blessings are recited as part of the *Grace After Meals*. (The Talmud [*Ketubbot* 8b] makes reference to the requirement that a *minyan* be present all seven days.)

This custom of celebrating a marriage for seven days is associated with Jacob, who was misled into believing that his seven years of service to Laban would win him the hand of Rachel in marriage. Instead, he discovered belatedly that it was Leah, Rachel's sister, whom Laban was planning to have him marry. But when Jacob insisted that he wanted Rachel to be his wife, Laban said (Genesis 29:27), "Wait until the bridal week of this one [Leah] is over and we will give you that one [Rachel] also, provided you serve me for seven more years." The Rabbis interpreted this to mean that the wedding celebration should last for a whole week. Judges 14:12 speaks of wedding celebrations as lasting a whole week.

If one marries a widow or a divorcee, the celebration is held for only three days, and the Seven Benedictions are recited only on the first day.

The newlyweds leave for their honeymoon after the *Sheva Berakhot* days have ended. In some circles, upon the couple's return from their honeymoon, it is customary for family and friends to greet them at the door of their new house and to give them a loaf of bread, expressing the hope that food will never be lacking in their home.

Shevirat Keilim

A Hebrew term literally meaning "breaking of the vessels." A mystical concept formulated by the famous sixteenth-century kabbalist Rabbi Isaac Luria, better known as the Ari of Safed. He proposed the idea that the whole universe is in need of repair and redemption because the lower vessels (*sefirot*) of Creation were unable to contain the intense energy of the divine light. Hence, they shattered, resulting in a dispersion of some of the holy sparks. Since then the world has been imperfect.

To the modern scholar of mysticism Gershom Scholem (1897–1982), author of *Major Trends in Jewish Mysticism*, the shattering of the vessels "...is the cause of that inner deficiency which is inherent in everything that exists and which persists as long as the damage is not mended. For when the bowls [vessels] were broken...the fiendish nether-worlds of evil, the influence of which crept into all stages of the cosmological process, emerged from the [shattered] fragments [*kelippot*] which still retained a few sparks of the holy light....In this way the good elements of the divine order came to be mixed with the vicious ones."

See Kabbalah; Kelippah.

Shevut

This Hebrew term literally meaning "rest, abstinence from work [on the Sabbath]" is an important rabbinic concept relating to the type of work that may and may not be performed on the Sabbath. In the Talmud, the term is applied to activities that are not specifically banned in the Torah but that may interfere with carrying out the Sabbath as a complete day of rest.

The word *shevut* is also an acrostic for the talmudic expression *sheiv ve'al ta'aseh*, "Sit and do not do [any work]."

See Sabbath; Seyag la-Torah.

Shira'yim

A Yiddish word meaning "leftovers," derived from the Hebrew word *she'ar*, meaning "the rest of" or "the leftover."

From each course of a Sabbath and holiday meal, a chasidic *rebbe* would leave over some food, which his disciples and others who had joined him at the table would anxiously seize. The *rebbe's* followers considered it a *segulah*—a sign of good fortune and a redemptive act—to eat *shira'yim* from the *rebbe's* table.

Shivah

A Hebrew term literally meaning "seven," referring to the seven-day mourning period for close relatives—mother, father, son, daughter, sister, brother, spouse—that begins when mourners return from the cemetery after burial. Like the chapel and cemetery funeral services, the *shivah* period is marked by simplicity. During this time of intense grieving, which is commonly referred to a "sitting *shivah*," pleasurable activities are avoided.

The establishment of seven days as the first stage of mourning is based on an interpretation of a verse in Amos (8:10):

> And I will turn your feasts into mourning, and all your songs into lamentations; and I will bring sackcloth upon all loins, and baldness upon every head; and I will make it as the mourning for an only son; and the end thereof is a bitter day.

The Rabbis interpret the words of Amos to mean that just as feasts (Passover and Sukkot) were celebrated for seven days, so must the initial period of mourning last seven days. A seven-day mourning period is also associated with Joseph, who mourned for his father, Jacob, for that length of time (Genesis 50:10).

Kabbalists believe that the soul remains bound to the physical body for seven days after death and refuses to release it. The soul, it is believed, flits repeatedly from the home of the deceased to the cemetery, not allowing the departed to be at ease. After the *shivah* period has ended, the soul accepts reality and disattaches from the corpse.

Shivah Customs

Shivah is not observed on the Sabbath or holidays, for these are days of joy. Mourners may leave their homes to attend synagogue services, but they are not offered a Torah honor (*aliyah*) because the blessing a person recites when being so honored expresses a feeling of good fortune. For the mourner, this is not in keeping with the reality of the moment.

A memorial candle or lamp is kept burning for the duration of *shivah*. Some Sephardim keep a memorial light burning throughout the entire first year of mourning. Burning a candle in the house of mourning is a custom that dates back to the thirteenth century. In Jewish tradition, a flame symbolizes the soul of man reaching ever upward. This is suggested by the verse in Proverbs (20:27), "The soul of man is the lamp of the Lord." By lighting a candle and keeping it burning throughout the *shivah* period, it is believed that the soul of the departed is aided in its journey heavenward.

When the patriarch Rabbi Judah the Prince (135–220 C.E.), editor of the Mishnah, was on his deathbed, he called for his sons and instructed them that "the light [which he used during his lifetime] shall continue to burn in its usual place" (*Ketubbot* 103a). This, say some commentaries, is the basis for the custom that a light be kindled in the house of mourning. However, scholars find no reference to such a practice being employed by Jews before the thirteenth century.

Sometime after the thirteenth century, it also became customary to place a towel and a glass of water near the memorial candle. According to popular belief, this would appease the Angel of Death, who might want to wash his sword in the water and dry it with the towel. There also existed the belief that man's soul returned to cleanse itself in the water. Nineteenth-century scholars condemned this practice and forbade it.

During the week of *shivah*, mourners are expected to refrain from all sexual activity. They also are expected to refrain from unnecessary grooming, including shaving or having their hair trimmed. Bathing for cleanliness is permitted, but bathing for mere pleasure is forbidden. Mourners are not to wear leather shoes, which were once considered symbols of luxury, nor are they to change their clothes unnecessarily. They are not to engage in business activity unless their livelihoods are at stake. In fact, mourners are not to leave their houses during *shivah*, except for emergencies or if there is not enough sleeping space to accommodate all the mourners.

In some communities mourners still follow a rarely observed practice of placing a bit of sand or earth in their shoes when leaving the house of mourning. The discomfiture is a reminder that they must return as soon as possible once their urgent business is concluded.

In the Babylonian Talmud (*Moed Katan* 15 a, b), the third-century Palestinian scholar Bar Kapparah states that a mourner is required to turn over his bed (*kefiyat ha-mitah* in Hebrew) so that it is not in a normal position, thus discouraging sexual activity. In time this practice was abandoned because it was feared that non-Jews would consider it some form of sorcery.

Covering Mirrors

The custom of turning mirrors toward the wall during *shivah* or covering them with a cloth may have replaced *kefiyat ha-mitah*. Among the other reasons advanced for turning or covering the mirrors, the most popular is that mirrors are associated with personal vanity. During mourning, it is not appropriate to be concerned with personal appearance.

The covering of mirrors has also been explained as an expression of the mourner's belief that despite the great loss just suffered, he refuses to blame God. To see oneself in a sorry state, as a grieving mourner, is not a compliment to God, since man was created in the image of God. One more reason given for the covering of mirrors is that prayer services are held in the house of mourning, and it is forbidden to pray in front of a mirror. (Synagogues are not decorated with mirrors.)

Mourners' Stools

During *shivah* mourners customarily sit on low benches. According to some scholars, this ancient custom, widespread in talmudic times (*Bava Metzia* 59b), is based on the Bible's description of Job, who, having suffered misfortune, was comforted by friends who sat with him on "the earth." Today, mourners do not sit directly on the earth; rather, they sit as close to the earth as possible, usually on wooden stools. Jewish law merely demands that mourners not sit on chairs of normal height, a way of demonstrating that the mourners have reached a low point in life because of the loss of a loved one. Some explain the custom as a way of expressing the desire to stay close to the earth in which a loved one is now buried.

Sephardic Jews do not use stools to the same extent as do Ashkenazim. Jews who follow the Moroccan and Judeo-Spanish (Turkey, Greece, etc.) tradition sit directly on the floor, while Syrians sit on the floor but use thin pillows to reduce the hardship.

Mourners appreciate receiving well-wishers during the *shivah* week, but tradition dictates that visitors wait until the third day before making a *shivah* call so as to allow mourners a period of time to be alone with their thoughts.

Duration of Shivah

Mourning is not observed on the Sabbath, which in Jewish life is a day of delight (*oneg*). Tradition demands that Jews express joy and fulfillment on the Sabbath (and holidays), and mourning is therefore suspended an hour or so before sunset on Fridays for the duration of the Sabbath (although it is counted as one of the seven days of mourning). On this day mourners dress up, attend synagogue, and carry on somewhat normally until nightfall on Saturday, at which time mourning is resumed.

Since under Jewish law part of a day is considered equal to a whole day, if a mourner sits *shivah* for as little as one hour on the day of the funeral, that is considered as one full day of *shivah*. The same is true on the seventh day: if a mourner sits *shivah* for only an hour it is considered a full day. Generally, on the seventh day, mourners sit on their stools for a short while after the conclusion of the morning service. They then receive words of consolation from visitors. With this, the *shivah* period is considered ended. In some communities, it is customary for mourners to walk together around the block (or for a short distance) at the end of the *shivah* period. The walk symbolizes their return to society and the real world from which they have withdrawn for a week.

Many Jews follow an unfounded practice of sitting *shivah* for a child who has intermarried or converted to another religion. This is neither demanded nor encouraged by Jewish law, because the principle of "once a Jew always a Jew" (*Sanhedrin* 44a) holds true even in these cases.

See Apostate and Apostasy; Condolences; Keri'ah; Sheloshim; Yud Bet Chodesh.

Shivah Asar B'Tammuz

A Hebrew term literally meaning "seventeenth [day] of Tammuz." It is the name of one of the minor fast days in the Jewish calendar.

See Fast of the Seventeenth of Tammuz.

Shivah D'Nechemta

The seven weeks between Tishah B'Av and Rosh Hashanah are known as Shivah D'Nechemta, the "Seven [Sabbaths] of Consolation." This seven-week period following the Three Weeks of Rebuke was instituted to offer consolation to a despondent and despairing people. The Rabbis considered the prophecies of the Second (Deutero–) Isaiah to be most suited for this purpose. From his home in Babylonia, this sixth-century B.C.E. prophet promised Israel that although God punishes His people for disloyalty, He rewards them and shows them compassion when they return to Him with renewed faith.

This message runs through each of the prophetic portions (*haftarot*) of consolation recited during the seven Sabbaths after Tishah B'Av. These *haftarot*, beginning with Shabbat Nachamu on the Sabbath after Tishah B'Av, are: Isaiah 40:1–26 for the Torah portion Ve-Etchanan; Isaiah 49:14–51:3 for Eikev; Isaiah 54:11–55:5 for Re'ei; Isaiah 51:12–52:12 for Shoftim; Isaiah 54:1–10 for Ki Teitzei; Isaiah 60:1–22 for Ki Tavo; and Isaiah 61:10–63:9 for Nitzavim (or Nitzavim/Va-Yeilech). Nitzavim is always read on the Sabbath before Rosh Hashanah.

Shli'ach Tzibur

A Hebrew term literally meaning "messenger of the congregation," referring to the individual—professional or layman—who leads a congregation in prayer. The term *shatz* is an acronym formed from of the first letter of each of the words *shli'ach tzibur*. *Ba'al tefillah*, meaning "master of prayers," is a synonym for *shli'ach tzibur*.

Shloshet Yemei Hagbalah

See Shavuot.

Shnudder

A Yiddish word that is a corruption of the Hebrew word *she-nadar*, as used in the phrase *ba-avur she-nadar*, "because he has pledged." These words are part of the *Mi Shebeirakh* prayer, often recited in traditional synagogues after a person has received a Torah honor (*aliyah*) and pledged a donation to the synagogue or some other charity. A person who makes such a pledge is said "to *shnudder*."

Shofar

Plural, *shofrot*. A Hebrew word literally meaning "horn," referring to the natural wind instrument that is blown in the synagogue on Rosh Hashanah. The horn of a ram, sometimes called *yovel* in the Bible, is most commonly used because it is associated with the ram that Abraham used as a substitute sacrifice for his son Isaac (Genesis 22:13). Horns of cows are not used because cows are associated with the worship of the Golden Calf. In Temple times the horn of an antelope was sometimes used (*Rosh Hashanah* 26b).

In earliest times the *shofar* was used by Jews to command the attention of the masses. The Bible says that at Mount Sinai (Exodus 19:13) the *shofar* was blown to assemble the people. The Bible also describes the *shofar* as being sounded to intimidate an enemy and declare war. However, in biblical times, the *shofar* was most frequently used to herald the beginning of each new month. The Book of Psalms (81:4) reminds us of this custom when it says, "Blow the horn [*shofar*] on the New Moon, on the full moon for our festival day."

On the occasion of the New Moon, staccato blasts were sounded. However, on the New Moon of the seventh month—the month Tishrei, when Rosh Hashanah is celebrated—long blasts were sounded. The Bible (Leviticus 23:14) explains the long blasts as marking the beginning of a special period—a period of holy convocation—when major Jewish holidays (Rosh Hashanah, Yom Kippur, Sukkot) were to be celebrated. Today it is sounded throughout Elul, the month preceding the High Holidays, to make people aware of the approaching Days of Awe.

In talmudic times it was customary to blow a *shofar* both to announce the approach of the Sabbath (*Shabbat* 35b) and to announce a death so people might assemble for the funeral (*Moed Katan* 27a).

To Philo, the prominent first-century Jewish philosopher, the *shofar* was a reminder of the giving of the Torah as well as the instrument used in wartime to signal an army to advance or retreat. But the Talmud, advancing a more mystical interpretation, states that the *shofar* is blown in order to confuse Satan and thus prevent him from bringing any charges against Jews before God on the Day of Judgment.

Shofar-blowing on the High Holidays

According to tradition, one hundred blasts of the *shofar* are sounded on Rosh Hashanah, a custom associated with Rabbi Meir's comment that a Jew must recite one hundred blessings every day (*Menachot* 43b). Since hearing the *shofar* is considered a blessing ("Blessed is the people who know [appreciates] the sound of the *shofar*" [Psalms 89:16]), the one hundred blasts were introduced.

Three types of blast are sounded from the *shofar*: *teki'ah*, a single long blast; *teruah*, nine staccato blasts; and *shevarim*, three wavering or undulating sounds (*Rosh Hashanah* 33b).

Over the centuries, scholars have disagreed over the number of *shofar* blasts to be sounded and the proper pattern to be followed. One established sequence is: *teki'ah, shevarim-teruah, teki'ah/teki'ah, shevarim, teki'ah/teki'ah, teruah,*

teki'ah. On Rosh Hashanah, this sequence of ten blasts is sounded three times after the Torah reading, immediately before the *Musaf* service. The same sequence, with variations depending on local custom, is again sounded at three points during the *Musaf* service: after *Malkhuyot*, in which God's kingship is affirmed; after *Zikhronot*, in which God's Covenant with Israel is affirmed; after *Shofrot*, in which the belief in the coming of the Messiah is affirmed.

Finally, a series of forty blasts is sounded at the end of the Rosh Hashanah service in those congregations that follow the tradition that demands that one hundred blasts be heard on Rosh Hashanah. However, it is common practice to sound only the first two series of thirty blasts.

At the end of the *Ne'ilah* service (final service of Yom Kippur) one long blast of the *shofar* concludes the day of fasting. The extended blast expresses the feeling of the worshippers that they have extended themselves spiritually during the long day of prayer and are now resolved to implement the new insights gained.

Shomer

A Hebrew word literally meaning "watchman, guard." As a sign of respect, the body of the deceased is never left unattended from the time of death until burial.

The term *shomer* (and its feminine form, *shomeret*) has other applications as well. It is used by the Orthodox community to describe the person who stays close to a bride and groom for the seven days prior to their wedding to make sure they conduct themselves properly, and it is used in the expression *shomer Shabbos* or *shomer Shabbat* to describe a person who observes the Sabbath.

See Burial Society.

Shomer Negi'a

Literally meaning "guarding against touch," this concept is based on the prohibition in Leviticus 18:19, "Do not come near a woman during her period of impurity to uncover her nakedness."

The idea took on new meaning in the late 1960s and 1970s, when the sexual revolution was in full swing, and many Orthodox young men and women no longer married in their late teens and early twenties. To counter the trend toward premarital sex, Orthodox rabbis began to emphasize the concept that all physical contact between the sexes, even touching, is to be avoided.

Shrouds

Known in Hebrew as *takhrikhim*, shrouds are the garments in which a deceased is dressed for burial. Sephardim refer to *takhrikhim* as *cortar mortaza*, "cloth cut for the dead."

There is no evidence in the Bible that in early times the dead were buried in shrouds. The witch of Endor (I Samuel 28:14) saw the prophet Samuel arise from the grave clad in a robe, which the Midrash (*Leviticus Rabbah* 26:7) assumes was his normal, everyday clothing, noting that Samuel's mother had made a robe for him when he was a boy (I Samuel 2:19).

In talmudic (*Sanhedrin* 90b) and post-talmudic times, the concept of resurrection and the afterlife became increasingly popular among Jews, and it was believed that by wearing loose, unknotted garments—rather than normal street clothing—one would be better prepared for the resurrection.

It is not until the seventeenth century that we find the first allusion to the practice of dressing the dead in unknotted clothes—that is, shrouds. This reference appears in the classic work *Ma-avar Yabok*, by the Italian mys-

tic Aaron Berechya of Modena (died 1639), which contains laws and prayers pertaining to the sick and terminally ill, plus laws of mourning. In time, the use of shrouds became a strongly entrenched practice in Jewish life. Today, even secular Jews are often appalled at the idea of burying relatives in anything but shrouds.

Traditionally, shrouds are sewn only by women and are made of inexpensive muslin, flax (linen), or cotton. The color white was selected because it is the symbol of purity and forgiveness. This symbolism dates back to the prophet Isaiah, who said (1:18):

> Be your sins like crimson,
> They can turn snow-white.
> Be they red as dyed wool,
> They can become [white] like fleece.

Not all talmudic and post-talmudic scholars have felt bound by the custom of using only white for shrouds, and over the years black, red, and other colors also have been used. Rabbi Yochanan, the third-century talmudist, was one of those who did not feel tied to the "white" tradition. He left these instructions before his death: "Do not bury me in white or black shrouds, but in colored ones" (*Genesis Rabbah* 100:2).

Yochanan assumed that white was chosen for those destined for heaven and black for those destined for hell. Not being sure of his final destination, Yochanan did not want to offend the righteous in heaven or the wicked in hell, so he requested burial in colored shrouds. From the sixteenth century on, white has been the accepted color for shrouds. (Yoreh Dei'ah 352:2).

While the word *takhrikhim* is often thought of as referring to the white gown in which the deceased is dressed, it actually refers to all seven garments in which the deceased is dressed by the *chevrah kaddishah*:

1. Trousers (*mikhnas'ayim*), which extend from the abdomen to the soles of the feet and are generally sewn across the bottom of each leg. The trousers are put on the corpse by two members of the *chevrah kaddishah* and are loosely tied around the waist and ankles. The ties around the waist are twisted (without forming knots) to form the Hebrew letter *shin*, the first letter of *Shaddai* (God).

2. A slipover blouse with sleeves (*ketonet*). The garment is tied at the neck so that the ties form the letter *shin*.

3. A coat (*kittl*), which may be either an open-front or a slipover garment. If the deceased had worn a *kittl* during his lifetime (such as at High Holiday services or at the Passover *Seder*), that particular garment is used, but all fastening devices are first removed. Like the *ketonet*, the *kittl* is tied at the neck to form the letter *shin*.

4. A sash (*avnet*), which is wrapped around the *kittl* three times and is tied in the same manner as the *ketonet*.

5. A prayershawl (*tallit*), usually the one worn in the deceased's lifetime. If the deceased did not own a prayershawl, the Burial Society provides one. Usually, one of the fringes of the *tallit* is cut off, thereby rendering it invalid, and the ornamental neckband (*atarah*) is removed. The *tallit* is draped over the *kittl*.

6. A headcovering (*mitznefet*), resembling a full-length hood, which is drawn over the entire head and neck until it reaches the *ketonet*.

7. A large sheet (*soveiv*), in which the entire dressed corpse is wrapped.

Some communities follow a slightly different procedure, but the preceding is commonly accepted practice.

Although the Bible (Leviticus 19:19 and Deuteronomy 22:11) prohibits the wearing of garments made from a mixture of wool (animal) and linen or cotton (vegetable) fibers (such a mixture is called *shaatnez* in Hebrew), shrouds for the dead may be made of *shaatnez* because the dead are obviously exempt from observing all commandments (Yoreh Dei'ah 301:1 and 351:1).

Jewish tradition demands that shrouds be made without pockets. Although it is not specifically prescribed by Jewish law, since the sixteenth century it has been customary to make shrouds pocketless as an expression of opposition to the ancient practice of heathen peoples who took with them into their tombs precious stones and utensils in preparation for a new physical life after death. The Ethics of the Fathers (Pirkei Avot 6:9) states: "In the hour of man's departure from this world, neither silver nor gold nor precious stones nor pearls accompany him, but only Torah and good works."

Shtadlan

Plural, *shtadlanim*. A Hebrew word literally meaning "an intercessor, go-between." An individual, usually a person of wealth and influence who, particularly in the Middle Ages, interceded with royalty and governmental powers to lighten the burden imposed upon Jews who were overtaxed, whose residency was limited to certain districts, or whose means of livelihood were restricted.

Jews in governmental service, court Jews, and well-to-do merchants often acted as *shtadlanim.* Among the noted *intercessors* in Jewish history were Gracia Nasi and members of the Nasi family who in the sixteenth century influenced the Sultan of Turkey to support the cause of the Marranos. In the eighteenth century Moses Mendelssohn of Germany interceded with the Duke of Schwerin to alleviate the condition of his Jewish subjects. In the nineteenth century Moses Montefiore was the *shtadlan* for the oppressed Russian masses.

Shulchan Arukh

Literally meaning "prepared (set) table," the *Shulchan Arukh* is the authoritative code of Jewish law composed by the Spanish scholar Joseph Caro (1488–1575). In this work, all laws governing the life of a Jew—from birth to death—are laid out in a well-organized fashion.

Prior to the death of Moses Maimonides (1205), the most outstanding codifier of Jewish law was Isaac ben Jacob Alfasi (1013–1103), of Fez, North Africa. He was popularly known as the Alfasi, "the man of Fez." After the death of Maimonides, the two most outstanding codifiers of the law were Asher ben Yechiel (1230–1327), popularly known as the Rosh, and his son Jacob (1270–1350), also known as Ba'al Ha-Turim, after his code, which was named *Arba'ah Turim* ("four rows").

Jacob ben Asher's compendium was divided into four parts:

- Orach Cha'yim, which deals with the laws of prayer and man's daily conduct.
- Yoreh Dei'ah, which deals with the dietary laws, laws of ritual purity, and laws of mourning.
- Even Ha-Ezer, which deals with personal and family matters, including the laws of marriage and divorce.

- Choshen Mishpat, which deals with civil and criminal law and the administration of justice.

Joseph Caro undertook to abbreviate and simplify the *Arba'ah Turim* and also to take into account the views of previous codifiers of the law, primarily those of the Alfasi, Maimonides, and Asher ben Yechiel. Where there was lack of unanimity, Caro sided with the two who agreed.

Since Joseph Caro as well as Asher ben Yechiel, his son Jacob, Maimonides, and the Alfasi were all Sephardic scholars, Caro was accused of ignoring the views of French and German legal authorities. As a result, Moses Isserles (1520–1572) of Poland, known by the acronym Rema or Rama, wrote supplementary notes to the *Shulchan Arukh* which he called the *mappah*, meaning "tablecloth [for the 'prepared table']." The Notes of Isserles, often referred to as "glosses," set forth the views of Ashkenazic scholars and present the customs of their communities. On occasion, Caro and Isserles do not agree, in which case Sephardim follow Caro and Ashkenazim follow Isserles.

The combined Caro-Isserles *Shulchan Arukh* is the standard code of Jewish law. Unchallenged for the past four hundred years, adherence to its laws has become the test of Jewish fidelity.

Shushan Purim

A Hebrew term literally meaning "Purim [of the city] of Shushan."

In the Book of Esther, a distinction is made between Jews who live in walled cities and those who live in unwalled cities. The rule in the Mishnah (*Megillah* 1:1) is that since Shushan, the capital of Persia, was a walled city, all cities known to be walled since the days of Joshua were to celebrate Purim on the fifteenth day of the month of Adar, the same date on which it was observed in Shushan in the days of Mordekhai and Esther (Esther 9:18). All other cities were to celebrate the holiday on the fourteenth of Adar. Jerusalem is a walled city; therefore, in that city Purim is celebrated on the fifteenth, not the fourteenth of Adar. For this reason, the day after Purim became known as Shushan Purim.

In leap years, when there is an extra month of Adar (Adar I and Adar II), Purim is always celebrated during the second Adar.

Siddur

A Hebrew word literally meaning "order [of prayers]," the term used for the prayerbook that contains the entire weekday liturgy. The special prayerbook used on the High Holidays, and to some extent on all major festivals, is called a *machzor*, meaning "cycle [of prayers]." The rabbinic scholars of the seventh and later centuries, known as the *ge'onim*, used the name *Seder Tefillah* ("order of prayers") for their prayerbook, which included the complete liturgy for the entire year.

It took centuries for the *siddur* to evolve into its present form. Initially, in Temple times, in addition to sacrifices that were offered as a way of showing devotion to God, two prayers were mandated to be recited each morning and evening: (1) The *Shema*, consisting of three paragraphs from the Book of Deuteronomy (6:4–15) beginning with the words "Hear O Israel," which became the cornerstone of Jewish worship, and (2) the *Eighteen Benedictions*, known in Hebrew as *Shemoneh Esrei* or the *Amidah*.

The origin of the *Shemoneh Esrei* is shrouded in mystery. Many scholars trace its beginnings to the period between 533 B.C.E., when the Babylonian exiles returned to Palestine,

and 332 B.C.E., the period of Persian dominance, when Alexander the Great arrived at the gates of Jerusalem. The Talmud itself (*Megillah* 17b) quotes Rabbi Yochanan as stating that "one hundred and twenty elders [the Men of the Great Assembly], among whom were many prophets, drew up the eighteen benedictions in a fixed order." So central to Jewish worship was the recitation of these extended blessings that the name *Tefillah* ("prayer") became the name by which these prayers were called in early Jewish literature.

An additional blessing was added to the eighteen when in the first century C.E. Rabbi Gamliel I, president of the *Sanhedrin*, realized that Judeo-Christians, known as *minim*, were having an undue influence on the loyalty of Jews. He asked for a volunteer to compose a prayer condemning the *minim*. Rabbi Samuel the Lesser volunteered and composed the nineteenth prayer that begins with the words "And to the slanderers [of the Jews] let there be no hope" (*Berakhot* 28b).

Beginning with the geonic period (seventh century), new prayers and poems were composed by writers known as *paitanim* ("poets"). They wrote about God's justice and mercy, about man's sinfulness and opportunities for repentance, and about hope in a future Messianic Age.

While Orthodoxy today does not add to or modify any of the traditional prayers, prayerbooks have been published by the non-Orthodox community with many additions, deletions, and modifications.

Sidrah

Plural, *sidrot*. A Hebrew term literally meaning "order," referring specifically to the weekly Torah portion read in the synagogue on the Sabbath. The Torah is divided into fifty-four *sidrot*, one of which is read each week, although on occasion two *sidrot* are combined and read on a single Sabbath. The name of each *sidrah* consists of one or more words taken from the first verse of the Hebrew text. The term *parashah* ("chapter") is synonymous with *sidrah*, although the latter is used primarily by Ashkenazim and the former by Sephardim.

See Torah Reading.

Simchat Beit Ha-Sho'eivah

A Hebrew term literally meaning "celebration of water-drawing [from the spring]," referring specifically to the celebration that was held in Temple times at night at the end of the first day of Sukkot and on the remaining days of the holiday, except for the Sabbath. At the beginning of the holiday, Priests would fill a golden flask with water from the Siloam pool, located near Jerusalem. Each morning, after the sacrifice was offered (*Yoma* 26b), some of the water was poured into a bowl next to the altar. This act of water libation, called *nisukh ha-ma'yim* in Hebrew, was intended to induce the heavenly forces to bless Israel with a rainy season that would nourish the crops of the fields.

The main celebration of the event after the first day of Sukkot was such a high-spirited one that it prompted the Rabbis to say (*Sukkah* 51a), "He who has not seen the rejoicing at the place of the water-drawing has never seen rejoicing in his life." Featured in the celebration were lighted torches that illuminated the huge plaza known as *ezrat nashim*, which measured some 200 square feet (135 x 135 cubits). The Priests and Levites would descend from their court to the Court of Women, where the masses were assembled. An untold number of Levites with harps, cymbals, lyres, and trumpets would play their instruments, sing songs, and dance all night long.

The water-drawing ceremony was rejected by the Sadducees, who argued that there is no basis for it in the Torah. But the Pharisees maintained that it was *Torah min ha-shama'yim*, a divine law given to Moses by God on Mount Sinai.

See Women's Gallery.

Simchat Torah

A Hebrew term literally meaning "rejoicing over the Torah," referring specifically to a holiday first celebrated in talmudic times when the Babylonian custom of completing the reading of the Torah in one year was common practice. Although the Talmud (*Megillah* 31a) refers to Simchat Torah as "the second day of Shemini Atzeret," in reality it is an independent holiday created in postbiblical times to celebrate the completion of the annual reading of the Torah.

Simchat Torah is celebrated as a full holiday only in the Diaspora. In Israel and in most Reform congregations in the Diaspora, it is observed as part of Shemini Atzeret.

In the synagogue, Simchat Torah is celebrated with much merriment. All persons are called to the Torah for an *aliyah* (Torah honor). The last part of the Book of Deuteronomy, followed immediately by the first part of the Book of Genesis, is read from two different Torah scrolls to express the never-ending cycle of Torah reading. Before the Torah is read, all the scrolls are taken from the ark and carried in joyful procession (called *hakafot* in Hebrew) seven times around the synagogue. Worshippers take turns carrying the scrolls; children carrying flags generally follow the adults in procession; youngsters are given candy to symbolize the sweetness of the Torah's teachings.

In the synagogue on Simchat Torah morning, everyone present, including children, is called upon to recite the Torah blessings, either individually or in groups. In larger congregations, small groups hold separate Torah readings in separate rooms so as to allow everyone to receive an individual *aliyah*.

As on Purim, on Simchat Torah it is acceptable for one to lose oneself in revelry in the synagogue. Congregants often consume liberal amounts of wine or liquor and then let themselves go, singing and dancing and merrymaking.

Two distinctive Torah honors are awarded on Simchat Torah. The recipient of the first honor is called the *chatan Torah*, the "bridegroom of the Torah," and for him the final portion of the Book of Deuteronomy is read. The person awarded the second honor is called the *chatan Bereishit*, the "bridegroom of Genesis," and for him the first portion of the Book of Genesis is read from a different Torah scroll.

Among the *aliyot* given that morning is one known as *im kol ha-ne'arim*, "with all the children." It is so named because all the children in the synagogue accompany the honoree to the pulpit and join him as he recites the Torah blessing. A large *tallit* is held over all their heads while this Torah portion is chanted.

Sin

The Bible uses three terms for sin. *Cheit* is the most common, appearing in various forms more than 300 times. *Avon* and *pesha* are synonymous biblical terms, *avon* appearing 229 times and *pesha* 93 times. *Aveirah* is a synonym that occurs for the first time in the Talmud (*Sotah* 3a) where Resh Lakish says: "A person does not commit a sin [*aveirah*] unless some silly notion [*shetut*] enters his mind."

Cheit, the most commonly used term, literally means "missing the mark," that is, living an unfocused religious life. Theoretically, anyone who fails to live up to any one of the 613

Torah commandments (*taryag mitzvot*) is a sinner and may expect punishment commensurate with the violation, even to the extent of being excommunicated. In biblical times, for the most grievous of sins the punishment was death.

Moses Maimonides is more lenient in his approach to the sinner when he states in his commentary on the Mishnah that if a person observes *one* of the 613 commandments properly, with love, he merits life in the world to come.

Judaism categorically rejects the Christian notion of original sin. St. Augustine (354–430) was the first theologian to teach that man is born into this world in a state of sin. The basis of this belief is found in the Bible (Genesis 3:17–19), where Adam is described as having disobeyed God by eating the forbidden fruit of the Tree of Knowledge in the Garden of Eden. This was the original sin.

Historian Abraham Geiger, in his *History of Judaism* (1865), disagreed, proudly proclaiming: "Judaism has not allowed the doctrine of original sin to be grafted onto it."

Judaism, from the time of Moses, has taught that a third party cannot bring absolution or salvation to an individual. Moses asked God that he alone be allowed to accept the punishment for Israel's sin of worshipping the Golden Calf (Exodus 32:33). God responded that whosoever has sinned shall suffer. This view was reiterated in Deuteronomy (24:16): "The fathers shall not be put to death for the children, neither shall the children be put to death for the fathers; every man shall be put to death for his own sin." The prophets Jeremiah (31:29–30) and Ezekiel (18:2) repeat this view.

While Judaism definitely opposes the idea that one human being can vicariously atone for another, it does not completely rule out vicarious atonement through animals or other objects. The Bible speaks of the *sa'ir la-azazel*, the scapegoat that bore the sins of the Children of Israel and was sent out into the desert on Yom Kippur (Leviticus 16:10). To this day, the practice of *kapparot*—in which a hen, rooster, or money is used as a medium through which one rids himself of sins—is still in vogue in some Jewish communities.

Confession of sins is necessary for atonement, and many penitential prayers have become part of the daily liturgy as well as that of the High Holidays when the words *ashamnu* ("we have sinned") or *al cheit* ("for the sin of...") are recited. They are accompanied by beating the left breast (over the heart) with the right hand. This breastbeating is not intended to inflict pain but to remind one of the words being uttered and to encourage sincere penitence.

Early on, however, the Mishnah (*Yoma* 8:9) reminds us that while the confession of sins on Yom Kippur may absolve one from guilt, such confession applies only to sins committed against God. To be forgiven for sins committed against a fellow man, one must ask for forgiveness directly from the individual who was offended.

See Confession of Sins; Kapparot; Original Sin.

Sinai

The name of the desert through which the Children of Israel wandered for forty years after the exodus from Egypt before they reached the Promised Land. Also, the name of the mountain upon which Moses received the Ten Commandments (Har Sinai). The exact location of the mountain is uncertain, but there is a strong belief that it is Gebel Musa located near St. Catherine's Monastery, in the southern Sinai desert.

In Jewish literature, Mount Sinai is located

in a desert known by six different names. Using homiletic license, the Talmud (*Shabbat* 39a–b) explains the basis for each name:

- *Tzin*, because God announced His commandments there. The name is associated with the word *tzivah*, meaning "He commanded."

- *Kadesh*, because Israel was sanctified there. The name is connected with the word *kadosh*, meaning "holy, sanctified."

- *Kadmut*, because the Torah, which had existed from the time of Creation, was finally revealed there. *Kadmut* is associated with the word *kedem*, meaning "early, ancient."

- *Paran*, because it was there that the numbers of Israelites greatly increased. The name is related to the word *paru*, meaning "and they multiplied."

- *Sinai*, because it was there that God's hatred of heathens began. The name is connected with the word *sin'ah*, meaning "hatred [toward idolators]."

- *Choreiv (Horeb),* because the annihilation of heathens was decreed there by God. The name is connected with the word *churban*, meaning "desolation, destruction."

According to the Bible, it was at Mount Sinai that God entered into a covenant (*brit* in Hebrew) with Israel. The terms of the covenant are simple and direct: if Israel accepts the Torah and abides by all of its commandments (*mitzvot*), God promises that Israel will be his treasured people (*Am Segulah*) and that He will serve as their protector and savior (Exodus 19:5ff.).

The Sinai Selection

The Rabbis of the Talmud wondered why a small, insignificant mountain such as Sinai should have been chosen as the site where an event as momentous as the Revelation should take place. After much long discussion, they agreed that the choice was meant to convey an important message to mankind (*Numbers Rabbah* 1:7). They envisioned a scenario in which the various mountains carried on a dispute that went as follows:

Mount Tabor said to Mount Hermon, "I am most deserving to have God's Presence [*Shekhinah* in Hebrew] rest upon me, because in the days of Noah, when the earth was inundated by flood, only my peak remained above water while all other mountain tops were submerged."

Mount Hermon replied to Mount Tabor, "I am the one upon whom God's Presence should rest, for when the Children of Israel passed through the Red Sea (Sea of Reeds), it was I who enabled them to accomplish this remarkable feat. I placed myself in the middle of the sea, making it possible for the Israelites to pass through on dry land. Even their clothes did not get wet."

Mount Carmel was silent. It settled down partly on the shore and partly on the sea, thinking to itself, "If the *Shekhinah* appears on the sea, it will rest upon me; and if it will come to the mainland, it will rest upon me."

A voice then rang out from heaven: "The *Shekhinah* will not rest upon high mountains that are so proud. It will rest upon a low modest mountain that does not look upon others with disdain. It will rest upon Sinai because it is the smallest and most self-effacing of all."

When this decision was announced, the other mountains protested, "Are we to receive no reward for our good intentions?" "You too will be rewarded," God replied. "Upon you,

Mount Tabor, I will aid Israel in the days of Deborah, and upon you, Mount Carmel, I will support Elijah in his battle with Ba'al."

The Rabbis add that Mount Sinai was shown preference over the other mountains not because of its humility alone, but also because it had never been used for idol worship. Idol worshippers established altars only on tall mountains, hoping thereby to be closer to their gods.

Siyyum

A Hebrew word literally meaning "completion." *Siyyum* refers to the celebration held to commemorate the end of a period of learning or the completion of study of a tractate of the Talmud or a book of the Bible.

Among the various "celebrations of completion," most notable are *siyyum bekhorim*, "celebration of the firstborn; the *siyyum* to celebrate the ending of a year of study in school; and *siyyum Ha-Shas*, held upon completion of studying the entire Talmud. Of these, only the *siyyum bekhorim* is biblically mandated.

See Se'udat Mitzvah; Siyyum Bekhorim.

Siyyum Bekhorim

A Hebrew term referring to a celebration in honor of the firstborn. To commemorate and express gratitude for the sparing of the firstborn of Israel prior to the exodus from Egypt, the day preceding Passover became a fast day to be observed by the firstborn male in each family. In time, the requirement changed: the fast was excused if the firstborn undertook to study a talmudic tractate and to complete his studies on the day before Passover. In practice (and with exceptions), the studying was and is assumed by the local rabbi, who on the morning of the first *Seder* night of Passover assembles all the firstborn of the community. After morning prayers, the group joins the rabbi in reviewing the last section of the tractate that he had been studying in anticipation of the occasion. The rabbi or anyone who has studied the tractate delivers a short discourse about the significance of Passover during the morning service, and this is followed by a festive repast. This meal, called *se'udat mitzvah*, relieves all firstborn who have participated in the service from fasting for the balance of the day.

See Se'udat Mitzvah.

Slavery

Under biblical law, slaves who were purchased or obtained as a result of warfare belonged to their master as would any other piece of property. The owner was allowed to chastise his slave or beat him, but not so severely as to cause death (Exodus 21:20).

According to the Bible, poverty-stricken Hebrews who had sold themselves into slavery had to be treated more humanely; after six years of enslavement they were offered freedom. However, those who preferred to remain with their master were released when the jubilee year arrived (Leviticus 25:39ff.).

The institution of slavery continued into the talmudic period (200 B.C.E. to 500 C.E.), and the tractate *Gittin* (8b; 43b; 77b; etc.) has much to say about the treatment of slaves. After the talmudic period, when Jews no longer had a land of their own, the issue of Jews holding other Jews in bondage ceased to be an issue. However, when the question of slavery arose during the presidency of Abraham Lincoln (1861–1865), some Jews supported the practice while others condemned it.

Rabbi Morris J. Raphall, a proponent of slavery, never failed to chastise Lincoln from the pulpit for his advocacy of abolition. From 1861 onward, in sermon after sermon, Raphall attempted to convince his flock and the population at large that slavery was sanctioned by

the Bible. In an 1861 sermon entitled "The View of Slavery," he said: "When you remember that Abraham, Isaac, Jacob, and Job—the men with whom God conversed—were slaveholders, does it not strike you that you are guilty of something very little short of blasphemy [by opposing slavery]?"

Likewise, Rabbi Isaac Mayer Wise (1819–1900, the leading American Reform Rabbi of that time, a staunch Democrat with pro-Southern leanings, did not hesitate to express pro-slavery sentiments to his predominantly Republican membership in Cincinnati. He urged Jews to vote the Democratic ticket and support the Dred Scott decision, which held that Congress "had no right to prohibit slavery in the territories," thus angering many of his members.

Other rabbis, such as Reform rabbi David Einhorn (1809–1879) and his more traditional colleague in Baltimore, Maryland, Benjamin Szold (1892–1902) [father of Henrietta Szold, founder of Hadassah], attacked Raphall for his anti-abolitionist sermons, reminding him that to enslave human beings created in the image of God constituted a rebellion against God.

In one of Einhorn's sermons, he called slavery "the cancer of the Union" and went on to say, "Does the Negro not have less ability to think, to feel, to will? Does he have less of a desire to happiness?...Slavery is immoral and must be abolished."

In his *Seminary Addresses and Other Papers*, Romanian-born Solomon Schechter (1847–1915), who became president of the Jewish Theological Seminary of America in 1901, had this to say about the Great Emancipation, "We are grateful to God for having given us such a great soul as Lincoln, who under God gave his nation a new birth of freedom...."

Sneezing

In biblical times, and for centuries thereafter, it was generally believed that a person was made of flesh (*basar*) and spirit or soul (*ru'ach*). When God created man, the Bible (Genesis 2:7) says, "He [God] blew into his [man's] nostrils the breath of life, and he [man] became a living being."

Thus, it was believed, the soul of man is in his breath and the nostrils are the apertures through which life enters and leaves the body. According to Jewish legend, until the time of the patriarch Jacob people did not become ill before dying. They simply sneezed and life departed. Sneezing was believed to signal the approach of death.

It was also believed by early Jews as well as other peoples that sneezing was the work of evil spirits determined to take a man's life and that the spirits could be frustrated by uttering biblical quotations or other expressions. Jews have been known to respond to a sneeze with the verse uttered by Jacob on his deathbed, "For thy salvation have I hoped, O Lord" (Genesis 49:18) or by exclamations such as "God bless you" or *Gezundheit*, meaning "to your health."

Sofer

A Hebrew word literally meaning "scribe" (plural, *soferim*), referring to the skilled calligrapher who executes the most sacred ritual documents connected with Jewish ritual and law. A *sofer* hand-letters sheets of parchment that are sewn together to form Torah scrolls; writes parchments that are placed inside phylacteries (*tefillin*) and *mezuzot*; and writes divorce documents. Jewish law requires that a scribe be both learned and pious.

Since the primary function of a *sofer* has always been to write Torah scrolls, the word *sofer* has also taken on the meaning of "one who counts." The Talmud informs us that the earliest scribes, beginning with Ezra (Ezra 7:6), were cautioned to review the text they were transcribing carefully. They were to count the letters, words, and verses they had written to make sure that nothing has been added or omitted. If the count was correct, the scribe could be sure that their work was errorless. (*Eruvin* 13a and *Kiddushin* 30a) The *Code of Jewish Law* (*Shulchan Arukh*, Orach Cha'yim 31:20) applies this same rule to scribes who write other religious documents.

In biblical times the right hand and the right side were considered superior, and the Rabbis therefore encouraged right-handed persons to become scribes. They based this on Scripture, pointing to Deuteronomy 6:8–9, which says, "And you shall bind them for a sign upon your hand....," referring to the *tefillin* that right-handed people were to wrap around their left hand, using the right hand to do the binding. Although in the Pentateuch the commandment relates to *tefillin*, the Rabbis of later centuries associated it with the writing of a Torah scroll.

Today, the generally accepted view is that a left-handed *sofer* is permitted to write a Torah scroll because the left hand of a left-handed person is equal in strength to the right hand of a right-handed person (*Shabbat* 103a, *Berakhot* 152a).

Traditionally, a woman is not permitted to be a Torah scribe because a scroll may be read in public only if written by one who is eligible to read it publicly (*Shulchan Arukh*, Yoreh Dei'ah 281:3). Since women in post-talmudic times were not permitted to read the Torah before a congregation, they were not permitted to write a Torah. Today, however, in non-Orthodox synagogues women often read the Torah at services and some women affiliated with these denominations have undertaken the task of becoming scribes.

Writing a Torah Scroll

Since writing a Torah scroll is a holy activity, it is considered proper for a *sofer* to prepare for the task by immersing himself in a ritual bath (*mikveh*). Some scribes immerse themselves each day before they begin work, while others do so only on the first day of a new undertaking.

The conscientious scribe, as he writes a scroll, is ever mindful of the verse in Exodus (15:2), "This is my God and I will glorify Him." The scribe proves that he is glorifying God, says the Talmud (*Soferim* 3:13), by writing a beautiful scroll with choice ink and a fine reed pen or quill, on a selected, well-prepared piece of parchment.

Before setting quill to parchment, the scribe declares that he is writing the Torah to sanctify the name of God. And each time, before he writes the name of God, he says aloud, "I am writing this holy scroll to sanctify God's holy name" (*Shulchan Arukh*, Yoreh Dei'ah 274:1).

The Rabbis ruled (*Megillah* 18b) that a scribe, when writing a Torah scroll, must have an accurate copy of the Torah text set before him and must pronounce each word aloud as he writes it. In early times the scribe referred to a handwritten scroll or codex; today he uses a printed copy of the Pentateuch.

The scribe may not write from memory, nor may anyone dictate the words of the Torah to him. This ensures that the scribe will concentrate intently on the sacred words of the Torah as he writes them. By constantly referring to a correct text, his mind is prevented from wandering, which could result in words being written mechanically and possibly incorrectly. If any one of the 304,805 letters in the Torah is written incorrectly, the scroll may not be used for a public reading, until corrected.

If the Torah were to be dictated to the scribe, frequent errors might occur owing to mishearing or lack of familiarity with the text. For example, if the single word *eilav* ("to him") were dictated in the Sephardic pronunciation, the word would be sounded as *elav*. This pronunciation could lead the scribe to believe that two separate words, *el av* ("to the father") had been dictated.

In Temple times, a Torah scroll that was reputed to be one hundred percent accurate was available for consultation. According to one tradition it was from this "Temple Scroll" that the High Priest would read on Yom Kippur, and it was this same Torah that was used by scribes as a guide when writing a new scroll (Rashi on Mishnah *Moed Katan* 3:4.) Over the centuries, scribes have always consulted a master text. Maimonides, the twelfth-century authority, revealed (*Mishneh Torah*, Hilkhot Sefer Torah 8:4) that when he wrote his own personal Torah, he used as a guide a copy of the Torah text that had been worked on and approved by the Ben Asher family of Tiberias.

When printing was introduced, a book called *Tikkun* was published. This carefully edited printed text of the Pentateuch became the standard reference book for scribes. To avoid mistakes when writing a scroll, the scribe would read aloud a sentence from the *Tikkun* and then proceed to write it.

Scribal Errors

No matter what precautions are taken, in the writing of a scroll the enormity of the scribe's task makes mistakes inevitable. The common errors of scribes are classified as either *dittographic*, made by writing the same letter or word twice; *haplographic*, made by omitting one or two identical letters or words that rightfully follow each other; or *homoioteleutonic*, made by omitting a few words or lines that appear again farther on in the passage. The scribe's eye picks up on the repeated words and as a result fails to include the words in between.

Minor errors are easily corrected by the scribe by scratching out the incorrect writing with a sharp blade. When a major error is made, the entire piece of parchment must be discarded and rewritten. Such an error involves the omission or misspelling of God's name. In Jewish law, erasing God's name is an affront to God. When such an error is made, the entire sheet of parchment is invalid and may not be used.

The third-century C.E. Palestinian talmudic scholar Rabbi Ammi (*Ketubbot* 19b) warned that the owner of a Torah is behaving disrespectfully if he permits errors in a scroll to remain uncorrected for thirty days. Moses Maimonides, in his *Mishneh Torah* (Hilkhot Sefer Torah 7:12), repeats this caveat and rules that if errors are not corrected within that timeframe, the Torah should be stored in a *genizah* (storage room) until such time that it can be buried.

Several views are held by the Rabbis of the Talmud (*Menachot* 29b) about how many errors a Torah scroll may contain before it is considered invalid and must be buried in a cemetery. One view is that if any column within the scroll contains three or more errors, the entire Torah must be buried. Another view is that this applies only if there are four errors in a column. For obvious practical reasons, it is current practice not to bury an entire Torah regardless of the nature or quantity of errors in a column. Rather, the defective leaf (*yeriah*) of the scroll is removed and replaced with a newly written unit.

Sofer Stam

A Hebrew term for a scribe who writes Torah scrolls, *tefillin*, and *mezuzah* parchments. *Stam* is an acronym formed from the first letter of the Hebrew words *sifrei Torah* (plural of *sefer Torah*), *tefillin*, and *mezuzot* (plural of *mezuzah*). The expression *otiyot stam* refers to the type of script used in the writing of Torah scrolls, *tefillin*, and *mezuzot*.

Sotah

A Hebrew word literally meaning "suspected woman" or "errant wife." The term is derived from the verb *satah*, meaning "to turn aside," which appears in the Book of Numbers (5:12): "If a man's wife go astray [*sisteh*]..." A woman who is suspected by her husband of marital infidelity must submit to the ordeal of drinking bitter water, and her reaction to it is said to establish her guilt or innocence. The tractate of the Talmud named *Sotah* offers detailed information relating to the ordeal of bitter water as practiced by the early Hebrews. The Bible itself gives no instance of the test ever being carried out.

See Adultery.

Soul

The Hebrew words *neshamah* and *nefesh*, both of which mean "breath" or "breath of life," are most frequently used for soul, although the term *nefesh* is also used for the entire physical body (Exodus 1:5).

Neshamah is used early in the Book of Genesis (2:7). When Adam was created, the Bible says: "He [God] blew into his nostrils the breath of life, and he became a living being." This verse led to the belief that essence of man's soul is his breath.

According to some Rabbis of the talmudic era, the *neshamah* ascends to heaven upon the demise of the body and resides with God. Other spirits continue to wander the earth after burial, sometimes returning to the interred body, with which it longs to be reunited. (See *Pesikta Rabbati*, Piska 12:1.)

In the twelfth century, Moses Maimonides evoked a fierce controversy by stating that the soul *alone*, not the body, is immortal, thus deeply offending traditionalists who were convinced that at some point after death the body is resurrected. (See Maimonides' *Mishneh Torah*, Teshuvah 8.)

The son of Maimonides expanded upon his father's view by saying that when philosophers speak of matter never being completely destroyed, they mean that it assumes new form. In like manner, he says, man's nature, spirit, or soul is not propelled into oblivion after death. It merely assumes the new form, that of pure intelligence. Since earthly man has no experience in such matters, it is difficult for him to grasp the concept of a pure spirit totally independent of bodily form.

Neshamah Yeteirah

In the talmudic tractate *Beitzah* (16a), third-century Palestinian scholar Rabbi Shimon ben Lakish made a connection between the soul and the Sabbath, suggesting that on that day of peace and rest God gives man an extra soul (*neshamah yeteirah*) so as to enable him to experience an extra dose of pleasure. Once the Sabbath ends and the extra soul departs, the *havdalah* service, marking the separation of the holy from the mundane, is held. The odor of the spices that are smelled during the *havdalah* service are said to mitigate the sadness resulting from the departure of the extra soul.

See Afterlife; Havdalah; Resurrection.

Soul-searching

See Cheshbon Ha-Nefesh.

Spices

Spices (*besamim* in Hebrew) played an important role in the carrying out of Jewish customs and ceremonies since biblical times. The Bible (Exodus 30:23–25, 34) describes the special altar constructed in the Tabernacle for the burning of incense as well as the choice of spices (myrrh, cinnamon, aromatic cane, cassia wood) that were blended together with olive oil to create the sacred anointing oil used by the Priests to consecrate the sanctuary in the wilderness and all its utensils. Other aromatic spices mentioned are stacte, onycha, galbanum, and frankincense.

Later books of the Bible make reference to spices and lotions used by women to make themselves more attractive and beautiful. The Song of Songs (3:6) speaks of women "perfumed with myrrh and frankincense," and the Book of Esther (2:12) describes women anointed with "oil of myrrh."

The use of spices is an integral part of the *havdalah* ceremony.

See Havdalah.

Spitting

Spitting is a universally recognized expression of contempt that was also employed by Jews in talmudic times to condemn evil practices and evil-doers. Although Rabbis railed against such practices, spitting persisted, most notably, when reciting the section of the *Aleinu* prayer that refers to idol worshippers.

See Aleinu.

Star of David

The Hebrew term for the six-pointed Star of David is *Magen David*, literally meaning "Shield of David." The origin of this symbol is uncertain and probably has no connection whatsoever with King David, although according to one tradition King David used a six-pointed shield.

In early times, the hexagram—two equilateral triangles superimposed one on the other—

as used on Roman mosaic pavements as a decorative design, but this carried no special significance. Its earliest use in a synagogue dates back 1,800 years, when it appeared next to a five-pointed star (pentagram) and a swastika on a frieze in the Synagogue of Capernaum. In sixth-century Italy, the Star of David emblem appeared for the first time on a tombstone. For the most part, however, the six-pointed star has been used by members of other faiths, particularly Hindus, to whom the triangle pointing upward symbolizes man, and the triangle pointing downward symbolizes woman.

In the Middle Ages (1300–1700), Jewish mystics (kabbalists), who used the terms "Shield of David" and "Shield of Solomon" interchangeably, associated the symbol with feats of magic in general. Not until the seventeenth century, in Prague, was the Star of David used as a specifically Jewish emblem. At that time, it appeared as the official seal of the Jewish community on printed prayerbooks and on official documents of various kinds. Only in the nineteenth century did the *Magen David* become widely used on religious articles of all types.

In 1897, the First Zionist Congress adopted the Star of David as its symbol, and in 1948 it became the central emblem on the flag of the new State of Israel.

Aside from the variety of religious articles on which the Star of David is used as ornamentation (Torah mantles, ark curtains, etc.), it is also popular as an article of jewelry, usually suspended from a necklace. Despite its widespread use, the "Jewish star" holds no religious sanctity. To most wearers it is a symbol of their identification with the Jewish people.

Jewish comedian David Brenner, who wears a small Magen David on a gold chain explains, "I wear it in memory of the more than 1,000,000 Jewish children murdered by the Nazis in World War II." When asked if he personally knew any of the children, he replied, "I knew every one of them."

Even some non-Jews have been known to wear a Star of David charm on a neckchain, among them the Mormon senator of Utah, Orrin Hatch, and the legendary jazz musician Louis Armstrong. Hatch explains that he wears the *Magen David* because it serves to remind him of "the awful tragedy of the Holocaust perpetuated on the Jews." When Armstrong was a teenager in New Orleans, the Karnofsky family, local coal merchants, hired him to be a delivery boy. They took a strong liking to him and took him under their wing, even lending him five dollars to buy his first coronet. So appreciative was Louis of the kindness shown by this Jewish family that he wore a Star of David necklace for his entire life.

Stones

Stones are associated with many significant episodes in Jewish history. When Jacob was in flight from his brother, Esau, on his way to Haran (Genesis 28:10), he stopped to spend the night in the field. "He took one of the stones of the place and put it under his head" as a pillow. In the verse, the Hebrew word used for "stone" is *even*. Shortly thereafter (Genesis 28:12), the Bible describes Jacob's famous dream in which he sees a ladder reaching from heaven to earth and "angels of God were ascending and descending upon it." The Sages comment that the stones began arguing, each saying, "Upon *me* shall this righteous man rest his head."

When, after working for him for twenty years, Jacob finally leaves the home of his uncle and father-in-law, Laban, Jacob makes a peace pact with Laban by first setting up a pillar of stone and then telling his kinsmen to gather stones and make a mound, which would become a symbol of the pact (Genesis 31:44–48). In this verse the Hebrew word used for stone is *sela*.

Stones also played an important part in the life of Moses, who along with his brother, Aaron, was denied entry into the Promised Land because Moses struck a rock rather than speak to it, as instructed by God (the Hebrew word used in the verse is *even*) (Numbers 20:11–12).

The heaping of stones over a grave dates back to the story of Achan (Joshua 7:26), who was put to death for his evil actions. Here the purpose of using stones was not to perpetuate his memory, but rather to keep his evil soul incarcerated. In rabbinic times, it was still customary to cast stones upon the coffin of one who had died in a state of excommunication.

The Falasha Jews of Ethiopia once carried out a practice of heaping stones over a grave and sometimes planting a young tree nearby as a symbol of the renewal of life. This was done in keeping with an ancient belief that death is the beginning of a person's new life.

Stones as a Way of Remembering

In order to bridge the chasm that separates the deceased from its soul, and to satisfy the need of the impatient soul for recognition, since the sixteenth century it has become common practice after visiting a gravesite to place one or more small stones on the monument of a loved one as a way of saying that the dead have not been forgotten. In some locales it became customary to leave grass instead of stones on the grave marker.

Today, when one visits the grave of the famous sixteenth-century Rabbi Judah Loew ben Bezalel of Prague (creator of the Golem), one finds that it is covered with mounds of small stones placed there by visitors who have beseeched the saintly rabbi to intercede with God in their behalf.

Some cemeteries today follow the practice of placing an urn filled with small white stones at the cemetery entrance so visitors may use them after having visited a gravesite.

The movie *Schindler's List* (1993), directed by Steven Spielberg concludes with a dramatic scene in which some of the 1,100 Jews whom Oskar Schindler saved during the Holocaust, as well as some of their relatives, parade past their hero's gravesite. Each person places a stone on Schindler's tombstone, signifying that his life is remembered and treasured.

After the assassination of Prime Minister Yitzhak Rabin in 1995, and his burial on Mount Herzl, where great Israeli leaders such as Theodor Herzl, Golda Meir, and Chaim Herzog are buried, it became customary that all new army recruits be brought to Rabin's grave. There, they are informed about his outstanding political and military career, and as they prepare to leave the site, they line up and place stones on the Israeli hero's monument.

See Tombstones.

Strangers, Treatment of

The talmudic tractate *Bava Metzia* (59b) warns no less than thirty-six times against taunting or mistreating a stranger by word or deed, because "you know the feelings of a stranger, for you yourselves were strangers in the land of Egypt" (Exodus 23:9). The Book of Deuteronomy (10:19) goes still further, stating, "You must *love* the stranger, for you were strangers in the land of Egypt." Only a people that had been enslaved for hundreds of years can truly appreciate how lonely a newcomer to a community can be.

Moses Maimonides, the twelfth-century authority, was appalled at the treatment of Obadiah, a convert to Judaism, at the hands of his teacher, and Maimonides castigated the teacher severely. In his *Mishneh Torah* (Hilkhot Dei'ot 6:4), Maimonides affirms how much God Himself loves the stranger and quotes the Book of Deuteronomy (10:17–18), "For the Lord your God...loves the stranger, providing him with food and clothing." In the section of his code covering the laws of mourning (Hilkhot Aveilut 14:2), Maimonides says, "The reward for welcoming strangers is greater than the reward for all the other commandments. It is a practice that Abraham, our father, exercised when he gave wayfarers food to eat and water to drink and escorted them. Offering hospitality to wayfarers is greater than receiving the Divine Presence."

See Conversion: Historical Background.

Stumbling-Block Principle

This important concept in Jewish law is based on two verses in the Bible. Leviticus 19:14 states, *Lifnei iver lo titen mikhshol*, "Thou shalt not place a stumbling block before the blind." Deuteronomy 27:18 adds, "Cursed be he who misleads the blind." The stumbling-block principle does not simply emphasize the obvious, namely, that one should not place a physical obstruction in the path of a blind person. Its overriding purpose is to instruct Jews to refrain from deceiving or misleading the weak, the ignorant, and the unsuspecting. It is also intended to refrain from leading the unwary along a path that may cause them to violate Jewish law.

The Talmud asks, "How do we know that it is wrong for a man to offer a cup of wine to a Nazirite [who has vowed never to taste wine and liquor]?" And it answers, "Because it is stated, 'Thou shalt not place a stumbling block before the blind'" (*Avodah Zara* 6b; *Pesachim* 22b). Tempting one to sin is a violation of the stumbling-block principle.

One example of how this principle works concerns the treatment of children. The Rabbis (*Moed Katan* 17a) warned that a man should not punish his son by striking him, lest the boy be provoked to strike back. By striking the boy, the parent would be placing a stumbling block before the child, because it might result in the boy speaking or acting disrespectfully, thus violating the positive commandment to honor parents.

In a second example, the Talmud (*Bava Metzia* 75b) states that if one lends money to another and there are no witnesses to the transaction, the lender is guilty of violating the law against placing a stumbling block before the blind. The reasoning is that if the creditor does not insist that witnesses be present when he makes the loan, he is tempting the borrower to lie at some future date about having borrowed the money. Jewish law therefore insists that witnesses be present when a loan is made, so as to remove a potential stumbling block from the path of the borrower.

A contemporary example was offered by the renowned authority Rabbi Moshe Feinstein (1895–1986) when the question arose about the permissibility of Jewish students to attend their graduation exercises that were to be held on June 7, 1984, the second day of Shavuot.

Rabbi Feinstein did not allow the graduates to attend. One of the reasons he gave was that it would be a violation of the law against placing a stumbling block in the path of the blind. He pointed out that members of the graduates' families, who may be less meticulous about the observance of Jewish law, and others who are ignorant of its provisions, might get into their cars and drive to the ceremony. By inviting them, the graduate would, in effect, be setting up a stumbling block before the blind. He would be causing them to violate the law which prohibits travel on Sabbath and holidays.

Following similar reasoning, in 1996 the Religious Affairs Ministry in Israel rejected a request to keep open Rachel's Tomb on the Sabbath so that people might pray there. After consulting with the Chief Rabbi, the ministry decided not to grant the request because it would result in a desecration of the Sabbath. If the site, near Bethlehem, were opened, the ministry argued, visitors would travel there and Jewish security guards would have to work.

Suicide

Jewish law considers the taking of one's life a grave offense. The Talmud (*Semachot* 2) says:

> For him who takes his own life, fully conscious of his action [the Hebrew word is *b'daat*], no funeral rituals are to be observed... There is to be no rending of clothes and no eulogy. But people should line up for him [at the end of the burial ceremony] and the mourner's blessing should be recited [as the mourners pass through] out of respect for the living. The general rule is: Whatever rites are [normally] performed for the benefit of the survivors should be observed; whatever is [normally] done purely out of respect for the dead should not be observed.

Jewish law does not place all suicides in the same category. One grouping includes those who take their lives while in full possession of their physical and mental faculties. A second category includes those who act on impulse or under severe mental or physical strain. Jewish law describes an individual in this second category as an *anuss*, "one under compulsion" and hence not responsible for

his actions. All burial and mourning rites are observed for him only.

The first *anuss* in Jewish history was King Saul, who, after being defeated by the Philistines on Mount Gilboa, realized what would happen to him if he were taken alive. He therefore impaled himself on his sword (I Samuel 31:4). This action gave rise to the expression *anuss k'Shaul*, meaning "as distressed as Saul."

Joseph Caro, in his *Code of Jewish Law* (*Shulchan Arukh*, Yoreh Dei'ah 345:3), and most authorities of subsequent generations have ruled that the majority of suicides are to be considered as distressed as Saul and thus as having acted under compulsion. As such, they are not responsible for their actions and are to be buried and mourned like the average Jew who has met a natural death. However, there is no question that a mentally competent person who commits suicide is not to be excused for his actions. Tradition requires that his grave be located at least six feet distant from other graves or in a special section close to the perimeter of the cemetery. This tradition was not followed by all communities. The Falashas of Ethiopia, for example, were more demanding and forbade burial of all suicides in a Jewish cemetery. They usually buried their suicides at a site very close to the place where the body was found.

Among scholars who were more lenient in the handling of suicides, the ruling of Rabbi Moses Schreiber (1762–1839) stands out. The celebrated Ukrainian, in his book *Chatam Sofer* (Yoreh Dei'ah 326), ruled that if a suicide occurred in a respectable family that would suffer shame and humiliation if the incident became widely known because they would not be observing mourning rites, it is permissible to sit *shivah* and carry out the various laws and customs.

The more liberal branches of Judaism to-day—Conservative, Reform, and Reconstructionist—regard suicide as the act of a mentally unstable person who should not be held responsible for his or her actions. Consequently, they accord full funeral and mourning rites to such individuals.

Sukkah

Plural, *sukkot*. A Hebrew word literally meaning "hut, booth," referring specifically to the temporary structure erected by the Israelites during their sojourn in the desert.

See Sukkot.

Sukkot

Singular, *sukkah*. A Hebrew word literally meaning "booths, huts." The name of the festival known in English as Tabernacles, which derives from the Latin word *tabernaculum*, meaning "temporary shelter." Sukkot is variously transliterated as Succos, Succoth, and Sukkoth. In Hebrew, the holiday is also sometimes referred to as *Zeman Simchateinu* ("season of our joy").

One of the three Pilgrim Festivals (Exodus 23:17) that attracted Jews to Jerusalem from all parts of the country, Sukkot is observed on the fifteenth day of Tishrei, two weeks after Rosh Hashanah, usually during the month of September. When the Temple was in existence, Jews brought with them the first crops of the season, a portion of which was offered as a sacrifice and the balance used by the priestly families. Only after this obligation was fulfilled were the new season's crops to be used as food.

Although Sukkot, like Passover and Shavuot, was originally an agricultural holiday, the Bible also ascribes to it definite historical roots: "You shall live in booths seven days in order that future generations may know that I made the Israelite people live in booths when I brought them out of the land of Egypt" (Leviticus 23:42–43). The holiday thus commemorates the forty-year trek of the Israelites through the desert to the Promised Land. In Israel, Sukkot is celebrated for seven days as prescribed in the Bible. In the Diaspora it is observed for eight days. Reform Jews follow the biblical tradition and observe Sukkot for seven days.

The Sukkah Structure

The huts (*sukkot*) built by the Israelites in the wilderness were hastily constructed, temporary abodes. To serve as a reminder of those structures, the *sukkah* today consists of loosely assembled walls made from wood panels or canvas, which are supported by wood or metal posts. The interior is decorated with fruits, vegetables, and artistic hangings of various kinds. The roof of the *sukkah* usually consists of branches, shrubs, cornstalks, straw, or slats of wood. To be a valid *sukkah*, the covering must be sufficiently dense that there will be more shade than sunlight inside the structure during the day, and yet not so dense that the bright stars will not be visible at night. The Hebrew name for the *sukkah* covering is *s'khakh,* which literally means "covering."

By "dwelling" in a *sukkah* for the duration of the holiday Jews recapture the feeling of insecurity experienced by the Israelites in the desert. Some Jews not only take their meals in the *sukkah* throughout the week, but also sleep there. It is traditional to start building one's *sukkah* immediately after the concluding service on Yom Kippur. A blessing is recited when the structure is completed and ready for use. Since a *sukkah* is a temporary structure, one is not required to affix a *mezuzah* to it (*Sukkah* 8b).

In explaining the value of building a *sukkah*,

Maimonides comments on the biblical injunction stated in Leviticus (23:42). He writes: "Man should remember his days of adversity when enjoying days of prosperity. He will thereby be inclined to thank God repeatedly and to lead a modest and humble life. Therefore, on the holiday of Tabernacles we leave our comfortable homes to dwell in booths and remember that this had once been our lifestyle."

Aside from erecting a *sukkah* structure itself, the holiday is marked by reciting a prayer over four species of plants, as prescribed in Leviticus 23:40: "And you shall take on the first day [of the holiday] the fruit of goodly trees, branches of palm trees, and boughs of thick trees [myrtle branches], and willows of the brook, and you shall rejoice before your God seven days."

During the Sukkot morning synagogue service, congregants march around the synagogue as they hold the four species. This is a carryover of a tradition that began in Temple times when upon completion of the sacrificial offerings, the *etrog* and *lulav* were carried joyously around the altar, while the people sang with loud, firm voices (Psalms 118:25):

We beseech Thee, O Lord, save us now!
We beseech Thee, O Lord, make us now
    to prosper!

Today, a similar procession is held after the *Musaf* service in Ashkenazic synagogues and after *Hallel* in Sephardic synagogues.

See Four Species; Hoshanah Rabbah; Shemini Atzeret; Simchat Torah; Ushpizin.

Sumptuary Laws

From talmudic times through the Middle Ages, individual Jews were often criticized by the Jewish community at large for throwing lavish parties, furnishing their homes ostentatiously, and wearing gaudy jewelry.

The Talmud (*Berakhot* 30b, 31a) describes the wedding feast made in the fifth century C.E by Rabina for his son. The rabbis present were growing unduly merry, so Rabina brought out a very expensive crystal cup and threw it to the ground, smashing it before their very eyes. The sudden noise shocked the merrymakers and reminded them of the importance of conducting themselves in a sober and socially acceptable manner.

Rabbi Solomon Luria, the sixteenth-century Polish rabbinic authority known as the Maharshal, condemned unbridled religious celebrations, which he claimed were often held just for the purpose of enabling guests to stuff themselves with food and to carry on in an uninhibited, wild fashion.

The extravagance of individual Jews not only offended the Jewish community at large, but earned the scorn of many Christians who considered such conduct immoral. Consequently, Jewish communities, especially those in Italy, at various times in history established what came to be known as Sumptuary Laws. These laws restricted the number of people who could be invited to private parties, the types of food that might be served, the amount of jewelry one could wear, and the type and number of wedding gifts one could give.

In recent times it has become customary among some Jews to curtail the lavishness of their celebrations and instead to donate to charity ten to twenty percent of the amount that would normally have been spent on food and entertainment. Leading ultra-Orthodox rabbis have suggested that only 400 invited guests be seated at a *chassunah se'udah* (wedding) and that the menu consist of not more than three courses followed by a regular dessert; a Viennese table and a bar are to be avoided. The Rabbinical Council of America, noting that recent sociological studies have revealed that ten to fifteen percent of Jews are alcoholics, recommends that hard liquor not be served in synagogues regardless of the occasion.

Superstition and Magic

Although many Jewish authorities are uncomfortable with having Jewish customs, laws, and practices explained as being connected with superstitious actions and beliefs, these elements are clearly an integral part of the Jewish past. The Talmud does not hesitate to describe some actions and attitudes of the Rabbis as being associated with the world of demons and spirits.

The tractate *Shabbat* (156a–b) devotes considerable attention to the question of planetary influence. Rabbi Chaninah believed that "planetary influence affects one's wisdom and wealth." Rabbi Yochanan disagreed, maintaining that: "Israel is immune from planetary influence." This attitude, expressed in Hebrew as *ein mazal le-Yisra'el*, is considered to be the more acceptable view. Joseph Caro's *Code of Jewish Law* (*Shulchan Arukh*, Yoreh Dei'ah 179:1) states that "one should not consult astrologers," because many Jews continued to believe that their fate is determined by the stars.

Superstitious belief among Jews was pervasive in talmudic and later times. The tractate *Berakhot* (55a), for example, states that "three persons need protection ['against evil spirits' is added by Rashi]: a sick person, a bridegroom, and a bride." The tractate *Hora'yot* (13b) cautions that a man who walks between two women will forget all he has learned, and the tractate *Pesachim* (111a) warns that if a menstruant woman walks between two men

early during her period, she will cause the death of one of them. Rabbi Yossi (*Berakhot* 19a) advises: "One should never speak in a way as to give an opening to the Satan [*Al tiftach peh la-Satan*]."

Sages (*ge'onim*) of the post-talmudic era were strong believers in the possibility of achieving magical results through the manipulation of the various names of God. Even Maimonides (1135–1204), who rejected a belief in demons, accepted predictions based on biblical verses. But he opposed the addition of cryptograms to the *mezuzah* parchment, condemning the practice as sheer superstition.

Nevertheless, the masses associated magical qualities with the *mezuzah,* which led to a popular Yiddish folksaying, "*Vi a shed far a mezuzah,*" meaning "like a demon [*shed*] in front of a *mezuzah*." In other words, the demon is totally ineffective when facing a *mezuzah* on a doorpost; the inhabitants need have no fear. The biblical passages inscribed on the *mezuzah* parchment will protect them.

Rabbi Meir of Rothenburg, the most outstanding scholar of the second half of the thirteenth century, was among those who believed in the magical qualities of the *mezuzah,* and he exhorted people to fasten *mezuzot* to their doors. He wrote: "I am convinced that no demon can harm a house properly provided with a *mezuzah*. . . In our house we have close to twenty-four *mezuzot*."

Nachmanides (1194–1270), whose commentary on the Bible reveals him as being very rationalistic, does not hesitate to say that if a menstruating woman stares in a mirror of polished iron, drops of blood will appear on it (Leviticus 18:19).

Superstition has found its way into practices accepted as routine today. Breaking a glass at a wedding ceremony, the bride walking around the groom seven times, and various customs associated with the Passover *afikomon* are based on ancient superstitious belief.

See A'yin Ha-Ra; Demonology; Mezuzah; Satan.

Surnames

Until the beginning of the nineteenth century, particularly during the Napoleonic era, Jews in Eastern Europe and Russia were not legally required to carry a surname. Jews were known by their first name and their father's first name—such as Abraham ibn ("son of" in Arabic) Gabirol or Moshe ben ("son of" in Hebrew) Maimon.

Hapsburg ruler Joseph the Tolerant, anxious to integrate the residents of Jewish ghettos into mainstream Christian society, decreed in 1787 that Jews follow the Christian style and adopt surnames. Similar laws were enacted throughout Europe in the ensuing decades.

Most commonly, Jews chose surnames that were the actual name, or some form of the name, of the town or city in which they lived. Thus, Jews who lived in Posen took the surname Posner or Posnansky, while a Jew from Berlin might call himself Berlin or Berliner, and a Jew from Poland might assume Polish, Pollack, or Polansky as a surname.

Jews sometimes adopted the name of their trade or occupation. Thus, Cooper or Cooperman was assumed by persons who worked with copper (derived from the German *Kupfer*), and a cantor might become known as Cantor, Chazan, Chasan, or Shatz, an acronym formed from the Hebrew words *shli'ach tzibur*, meaning "deputy [messenger] of the people."

Quite often, the surname chosen was simply a patronymic form of one's first name. This was accomplished by adding a suffix meaning "son of" to an already established first name. Thus, from Jacob might come Jacobs or Jacobson; from David, Davidson or Davidowitz; from Isaac and its Yiddish form Itzig, Isaacs, Isaacson, and Itzkowitz.

See Naming: History and Practices.

Surrogate Motherhood

The concept of surrogate motherhood, wherein a woman agrees to have the fertilized egg of another woman implanted in her womb, to be carried to term, was totally unknown before the middle of the twentieth century. The question of whether a woman is permitted to "rent" her body for such purposes has not yet been sufficiently discussed.

The unofficial Orthodox view, expressed by Rabbi Moshe Tendler, professor of medical ethics at Yeshiva University in New York, is to condemn the practice, describing it as a form of enslavement and thus a violation of biblical law.

The Committee on Jewish Law and Standards of the Conservative Movement, considers the practice permissible but advises that before the procedure is undertaken, social and psychological factors be considered. It also makes the point that if the surrogate mother is not Jewish, the child would have to submit to conversion.

A law enacted by the Israeli Knesset in March 1996 stipulates that in surrogate motherhood the sperm must come from the father who will raise the child, and that the surrogate mother, who must be unmarried, may accept money only to cover basic expenses. This ruling was overturned in September of that year when an expanded Supreme Court ruled by a vote of seven to four that a woman named Ruti Nahmani could use her eggs, fertilized *in vitro* by the sperm of her estranged husband, so that she could have a child through surrogate motherhood, even though her ex-husband objected.

Symbols

As is true for other religions and ethnicities, a broad array of symbols has become associated with Jews and the Jewish way of life. Some symbols foster group identity; others have religious significance; and still others simply add color and festivity to holidays and ceremonies. Among the most common symbols are the *shofar*, the Star of David, the Torah and its adornments, the *mezuzah*, ornaments associated with the Sabbath (*challah*, candlesticks and *havdalah* accessories), the *Seder* tray and its components, and the four species used during Sukkot.

Because of the biblical prohibition against anthropomorphism, the image of God is not found in any Jewish symbol. Although not specifically banned, representations of biblical heroes such as Moses or David are also not traditionally depicted.

See the index for symbols relating to specific customs and celebrations. See also Flags and Emblems.

Synagogue

Derived from the Late Latin and Greek, meaning "assembly, a bringing together," the term *synagogue* refers to the place where Jews gather for worship or religious study. Corresponding Hebrew terms are *beit knesset*, meaning "house of assembly," *beit tefillah*, "house of prayer," and *beit midrash*, "house of study." These terms emerged over the centuries as the function of the synagogue changed and became the center of communal life. The Yiddish name for synagogue is *shul*, derived from the German *Schule*, meaning "school." The term *Beit Mikdash Me'at*, meaning "Holy Temple in Miniature," was first used as a synonym for synagogue by the prophet Ezekiel (11:16).

Origin and Development

Scholars believe that the synagogue was originated in Babylonia by the Jews who were exiled there after the destruction of the First Temple in 586 B.C.E. When the exile ended some seventy years later and the Second Temple was built, the returnees brought with them modes of worship that they had developed during the exile, and these became part of the Temple regimen. Prayer services coexisted alongside the restored sacrificial system.

The prayer service in the Second Temple was held in an area known as *Lishkat Ha-Gazit*, "Chamber of Hewn Stones." It was the same area in which the Great Sanhedrin, the supreme legislative and judicial body of the Jewish people, carried out its deliberations. The Talmud (*Berakhot* 11b and *Tamid* 32b) reveals that each morning, at dawn, after the *Kohanim* (Priests) offered the morning sacrifice, a service consisting of a recitation of the Ten Commandments followed by the three paragraphs of the *Shema* and several other prayers was conducted in the Chamber of Hewn Stones.

Originally this service was only part of the daily activity within the Temple, but later it took on a life of its own as worship services began to be conducted in various towns and villages outside the Temple precincts in structures built for that specific purpose. Many of the physical features of the Temple were transferred to the synagogue. In the Temple of Jerusalem, the Priest offered his daily *Priestly Benediction* from a platform, called a *bimah* or *dukhan*, located in the center of the room. This setup was copied by the synagogue, and to this day Orthodox synagogues are so arranged. Within the Temple compound there was a section known as *ezrat nashim* ("Court [Quarters] of Women"), where large celebrations were held. At one point, a gallery for women was built around it, a feature copied by all Orthodox synagogues.

Some of the names of synagogue prayer services were borrowed from the Temple sacrificial system. *Minchah*, the name of the afternoon sacrifice, became the name of the afternoon synagogue service, and *Musaf*, the additional sacrifice brought on Sabbaths, New Moons, and holidays, became the name of the service conducted on these occasions following the Torah reading.

Physical Structure

Over the centuries, many questions arose as to the overall physical structure of the synagogue. Because the Book of Daniel (6:11) says that when Daniel prayed he looked out of his window, the Rabbis suggested that all synagogues are to have windows. The *Shulchan Arukh* (Orach Cha'yim 90:4) states that it should have twelve windows, corresponding to the Twelve Tribes of Israel. It also advises that it be the tallest structure in town (ibid. 150), a requirement that often could not be fulfilled because of the opposition of the Church. Another requirement was that the ark be on the east or west wall (depending on geographical location) so that all prayers be directed toward the holy city of Jerusalem.

Rabbi Ezekiel Landau (1713–1793) of Prague, author of *Noda Bi-Yehuda* (Orach Cha'yim 18), said that a synagogue may be built in any shape, even octagonally. Generally, a synagogue's architecture reflects the style of the particular locale in which it is situated.

As far back as talmudic times, the synagogue reflected the demography of the Jewish community at large. The tractate *Sukkah* (51b) indicates that in the large Alexandrian synagogue in Egypt there was separate seating for the various trades. In the Middle Ages separate synagogues were established by tailors, bakers, and other tradespeople. There also existed synagogues in which almost all congregants were *Kohanim*. Such divisions are no longer in vogue.

Greenery in the Synagogue

The ark area of modern synagogues, especially on the holiday of Shavuot, is often decorated with green plants and flowers. Some authorities associate this custom with the belief that Mount Sinai, on which the Torah was given, was once a green mountain covered with trees and shrubs.

Some authorities, including the Gaon of Vilna, were well aware of this association but forbade the introduction of greenery into the synagogue because they considered it an imitation of certain Church and home rites (such as the use of Christmas trees and wreaths). This view, however, did not prevail, and for most authorities greenery carried a positive symbolism. They associated the greenery with the baskets of first fruits brought to the Temple on Shavuot.

See Art and Sculpture; Simchat Beit Ha-Sho'eivah; Women's Gallery.

Tachanun

A Hebrew term literally meaning "supplication." The penitential prayers known as *Tachanun* are recited on Monday and Thursday mornings, when the Torah is read. They are not recited on the New Moon (Rosh Chodesh) and festivals.

Tachanun consists of a number of prayers introduced in the Middle Ages that plead for God's mercy and grace and ask for salvation from the hands of one's enemies. Similar prayers were recited in the earlier talmudic period (first to sixth centuries), at which time worshippers would fall to the ground and prostrate themselves (as is done even today during the Yom Kippur *Musaf* service). However, because synagogues were often too small and space was inadequate for such posturing, it became customary to lean one's head on the left arm when reciting these prayers. The left arm was designated because it was a reminder of the daily sacrifice offered in Temple times when the sacrificial animal was laid on its left side to be slaughtered.

The *Tachanun* is not recited on joyous or sorrowful days, including Friday afternoons, the afternoon of the day preceding a holiday (except for Chanukkah), Rosh Chodesh (the beginning of a new month), the entire month of Nissan (when Passover is celebrated), Lag Ba-Omer, from the beginning of Sivan through the Shavuot holiday, Tishah B'Av, the Fifteenth of Av, on the morning before Rosh Hashanah, from the morning before Yom Kippur through the Sukkot festival, the fourteenth and fifteenth of Adar (Purim) in normal and leap years, and on the Fifteenth of Shevat (Chamishah Asar Bi-Shevat).

Tagin

This Aramaic word meaning "daggers" is used to describe the daggerlike crowns used by scribes as embellishments to decorate seven of the twenty-two letters of the Hebrew alphabet when writing a Torah scroll. The seven letters are *shin, a'yin, tet, nun, za'yin, gimmel,* and *tzadi.* Most have three *tagin* and some have one. There is also a tradition that the letters *bet, dalet, kuf, chet, yud,* and *hei* should be adorned with one *tag.* Because of their daggerlike appearance, *tagin* are also known as *ziyunim,* meaning "weapons."

The Rabbis of the Talmud were of the view that the idea of decorating letters of the Torah with *tagin* was inspired by God Himself. The Talmud (*Menachot* 29b) records a legend in which Moses ascends to heaven and finds God engaged in affixing *tagin* to the letters of a Torah scroll. Moses asks, "Why are You doing this? Is this necessary? What additional meaning do they convey that is not already implicit in the Torah itself?" And God answers, "After many generations a man named Akiba will appear and he will heap upon each *tag,* piles of new interpretations to the Torah itself."

Maimonides (*Mishneh Torah,* Hilkhot Sefer Torah 7:9) was of the opinion that *tagin* are used to beautify the writing of a Torah scroll and have no other significance. The Ashkenazic authors of the Magen Avraham and the Be'er Heiteiv commentaries on the *Shulchan Arukh* (Orach Cha'yim 36:3) state that a scroll is not valid if it does not have *tagin* on the appropriate letters. They considered the use of *tagin* to be a requirement that cannot be ignored because they were part of the original transmission from God to Moses.

Modern scholars tend to agree with Maimonides that *tagin* are nothing more than calligraphic flourishes introduced by early scribes in order to enhance the beauty of the Torah lettering. While this may be the case, the fact that *tagin* are dagger-shaped—like the letter za'yin—might carry significance. The dagger is a device one uses to protect himself and his property, and the early Rabbis saw it as an instrument that could protect the Torah from those who would violate it in any way.

In the New Testament, tagin are referred to as tittles (Matthew 5:18).

Tal

Literally meaning "dew," this is the Hebrew name of a special prayer composed in the eighth century by the poet Eleazar Kallir, who resided in Tiberias. It is recited during the Musaf service on the first day of Passover, when the rainy season has ended and dew is needed to nourish the crops during the forthcoming dry summer months. Before the Musaf service begins, the rabbi and cantor don a white robe and cap.

Each stanza of the Tal prayer begins and concludes with the word tal, and the verses are arranged as a reverse alphabetic acrostic, beginning with tav and ending with alef.

See Geshem.

Tallit

Also pronounced tallis. Plural forms are tallitot and talleisim. In the Book of Numbers (15:37–41) God says to Moses, "Speak to the Children of Israel and bid them to affix fringes (tzitzit) to the corners of their garments...that ye may look upon it [them] and remember all the commandments of the Lord..." The outergarment, which Jews wore as a matter of course, became the instrument on which these fringes are to be attached to serve as a visible reminder that God's commandments must be observed.

The Book of Deuteronomy (22:12) expands in this law and specifies that these fringes are to be placed on the four corners of a garment. This proved to be a problem in

Palestine in talmudic times when the Roman government occupied and ruled the country. Many Jews adopted the Roman style and wore togas, blanket-like coverings that did not have easily accessible four corners on which to attach tzitzit. (It was likewise a problem many years later, in the Middle Ages, when in many European localities four-cornered garments were a rarity, and the tzitzit observance began to wane.)

In Palestine the problem was solved by the introduction of the tallit, with its distinct four corners on which the tzitzit could be hung. It became the reminder to observe the mitzvot ("commandments") called for in Numbers and Deuteronomy. Kabbalists spoke of the tallit as a special garment that inspires awe and reverence during prayer. Its distinctive and impressive appearance led Rabbi Jeremiah to say (Shabbat 10a), "a lawsuit does not officially begin until the judges wrap themselves in their prayershawls." The litigants were impressed by the solemnity of the occasion, and the goal of achieving just results was enhanced.

However, since it was cumbersome for the average Jew to walk about all day long with this type of large overgarment, the tallit was worn only when prayers were recited, and in its stead a small undergarment, called a tallit katan ("small tallit"), was created. Fringes were attached to the four corners of the tallit and the garment was worn all day long. Actually, during prayertime observant Jews would be wearing two tallitot at the same time.

When the Tallit Is Worn

The tallit is worn only during the day, when there is sufficient light for the fringes to be easily noticed. The biblical commandment requires that the fringes be seen. Only on Yom Kippur eve, because of the holiness of the day, is the *tallit* worn at night, and even then it is donned before nightfall (before the *Kol Nidrei* is recited) so the prayer over the *tallit* can be recited during daylight.

The leader of the service, the cantor (*chazzan*) or *ba'al tefillah*, wears a *tallit* whenever he leads the congregation in morning and afternoon prayers. At the weekday *Ma'ariv* (evening) service, the leader does not wear a *tallit*. However, for Sabbath and holiday evening prayers he does wear a *tallit*, so as to honor the special day.

Fabric and Color

Deuteronomy 22:10 states: "Thou shalt not wear a garment in which wool [an animal product] and linen [a vegetable product] have been mixed together." The mixture of an animal product and a vegetable product, called *shaatnez* in Hebrew, is forbidden. Therefore, a silk or woolen *tallit*—which is made of material derived from an animal—must have silk or woolen fringes (*tzitziot*); they may not be fringes made from cotton, a vegetable product. A rayon *tallit* may have any type of *tzitziot*, since rayon is synthetic and hence a neutral product. Since a *tallit* is usually made of wool, silk, or the neutral rayon, woolen *tzitziot* may be used on all prayershawls.

Blue is the most popular color used for the stripes that are dyed into the fabric of a *tallit*. Blue is a reminder of the blue thread that was once added to the fringes (*tzitziot*). Numbers (15:38) is explicit: "...attach to the fringe of each corner of the garment a thread of blue." The Talmud (*Menachot* 43b) suggests that blue was a favorite color of Jews because they lived near the Mediterranean Sea, a large body of water known for its blue hue. Blue is also a reflection of God's throne, which is believed to be decorated with sapphires.

In *Sotah* (17a) Rabbi Meir explains why, of all colors, blue was specified to be one of the threads of the *tzitzit*. He says: "Blue resembles the color of the sea, and the sea resembles the color of heaven, and heaven resembles the color of the Throne of Glory." He then quotes verses from Exodus 24:10 and Ezekiel 1:26 to substantiate his view.

Today, a blue thread is no longer added to each fringe because the source of that dye (*tekheilet*) has long been considered questionable. Instead blue has become the color of the *tallit* stripes, although most Orthodox Jews wear only black-striped *tallitot*. Recently, the murex snail, found in the Mediterranean Sea, has been identified as the source of the *tekheilet* dye, and therefore one sometimes sees a thread of blue in the fringes.

The Atarah

Literally meaning "round headpiece" or "crown," the *atarah* is the neckband sewn to the top of the *tallit*. Some *atarot* (plural) are made of small silver squares or fancy metallic embroidery, but most are fashioned out of simple fabric. The following *tallit* blessing is embroidered on the neckband: *Barukh ata Adonai, Eloheinu melekh ha-olam, asher kideshanu be-mitzvotav, ve-tzivanu le-hitatef ba-tzitzit* ("Praised be Thou, O Lord Our God, King of the universe, who has sanctified us by His commandments and commanded us to drape ourselves with a fringed garment").

Donning the Tallit

Before draping themselves with their prayershawls, some worshippers lay the folded prayershawl over their left shoulder, take hold of all the fringes, and recite the *tallit* blessing. They then open the *tallit* fully and, with both arms extended, cover their forehead, chin, and mouth, leaving only their eyes exposed. After a pause, the *tallit* is draped in a normal manner over both shoulders. This procedure, known as *atifat Yishm'eilim*, "the draping of Ishmaelites," was introduced by Babylonian Jews, who borrowed it from Arabs living in Babylonia during pre- and post-talmudic times (*Moed Katan* 24a).

The word for shoulder in Hebrew is *shekhem*, from which root the word for early rising (*hashkem*) is derived. Thus, the idea of associating the "shoulder" with performing one's religious duties at the earliest moment after arising in the morning became linked, symbolically representing one's strength with religious commitment. The prophet Zephaniah (3:9), in anticipating a time when all people will acknowledge the sovereignty of God, says:

> For I will then make the peoples pure of speech, so that they all invoke the Lord by name and serve him with one shoulder [*shekhem echad*].

The significance of the shoulder in prayer ritual was observed by Rabbi Israel Mowshowitz in his book *A Rabbi's Rovings* (1986). During a trip to Thailand he noted that when walking into temple grounds, Buddhist monks uncover their right shoulder, and when they leave they cover it. They consider the shoulder to be a symbol of strength, and by their action they indicate that they are prepared to place all their strength and power in the service of Buddha.

Some Jews pray with the *tallit* draped over their heads, a practice based on the statement in the Tosefta (*Tohorot* 4:1), "It is customary for scholars and their students not to pray without first wrapping themselves in their prayershawls." This is in keeping with the *tallit* benediction, which concludes with the words *le-hitateif be-tzitzit*, "to drape oneself with *tzitzit*."

Most Orthodox and many Conservative Jews believe that a *tallit* must cover most of a person's body if it is to qualify as a "garment" on which fringes may be hung. Most non-Orthodox Jews, however, wear the scarflike *tallit*. They consider this adequate because the commandment calls for the wearing of *tzitziot*, not for the wearing of the *tallit*. Joseph Caro's *Code of Jewish Law* (*Shulchan Arukh*) states that the minimum size of a *tallit* should be that which is large enough "to cover a small child able to walk."

Among Orthodox and some Conservative Jews, the bride presents her groom with a gift *tallit* before the wedding. This custom is based on an interpretation of two biblical verses. Deuteronomy (22:12) states, "You shall make fringes on the corners of your garments," which is the reason for the creation of the *tallit*. This verse is immediately followed by the words, "If a man takes a wife..." The inference drawn is that a *tallit* with fringes must be presented by a bride to her husband-to-be.

A large *tallit* is often used as the canopy (*chuppah*) under which a couple is married. It is also used on Simchat Torah to cover all the children (*kol ha-ne'arim*) when they are called to the Torah for an *aliyah*.

In some congregations, a *tallit* is also spread above the *chatan Torah* ("Bridegroom of the Torah") and the *chatan Bereishit* ("Bridegroom of Genesis") when they receive their *aliyot* on Simchat Torah to conclude and initiate a new Torah reading cycle.

In talmudic times, the *tallit* signified a person's station in life. Judges wrapped themselves in a *tallit* so that they would be constantly reminded of the gravity of their assignment (*Shabbat* 10a). It was also an indication of a person's marital status. Unmarried men did not wear a *tallit*. Today, the practice relating to unmarried men wearing *tallitot* varies with each community. In many Orthodox synagogues, an unmarried man does not wear a *tallit*. In Oriental communities, an unmarried man does wear a *tallit*. When leading the congregation in prayer and when being honored with an *aliyah*, all men wear a *tallit* (Orach Cha'yim 17:3).

Women and the Tallit

One would expect women, like men, to be obligated to carry out the biblical commandment of wearing fringes on one's garment, since it would not interfere with their daily routine. In fact, some Rabbis of the Talmud (*Menachot* 43a) believed that women are indeed so obligated. Rabbi Judah the Prince attached *tzitziot* to the aprons of all women in his household. However, since women in ancient times generally did not wear the type of four-cornered garment worn by men—the type on which fringes could be sewn—the wearing of *tzitziot* by women never took root. In addition, most authorities consider the law of *tzitziot* to belong to the category of commandments that must be performed at a specific time of day (during daylight hours) and from which women are therefore exempt.

Now and again, throughout the ages, women have voluntarily taken upon themselves the obligation of wearing *tzitziot*. One such classic case was the Maid of Ladamir, a chasidic woman *rebbe* born in Russia in the early part of the nineteenth century. She wore a *tallit* and *tefillin* every morning, defying rabbinic authorities who tried to stop her.

Today, in some Conservative and Reconstructionist synagogues women do occasionally wear prayershawls (*tallitot*) with fringes during services, although this is not a common practice. In some Reform congregations, *b'not mitzvah* wear a *tallit*, as do women who are called to the Torah.

Burial Rites

When a man dies, he is buried in the *tallit* he wore during his lifetime, particularly if he wore it on a regular basis (Yoreh Dei'ah 351:2). According to some authorities (Yoreh Dei'ah 51:12), one of the *tzitziot* is cut off so as to render the *tallit* invalid (*pasul*). The point being made is that the obligations of Jewish law are no longer required of the deceased, and to enclose a perfectly valid *tallit* in his coffin would be "mocking the dead."

Some noted authorities, including the eighteenth-century scholar Rabbi Joel Sirkes (the Bach), contend that one need not cut off a fringe to render the *tallit* defective. It is sufficient to tuck one of the fringes into a corner pocket, thus hiding it from view, or to tie all four fringes of the *tallit* together, thereby rendering it unfit for normal use (*Chokhmat Adam* 157:1).

In addition to the *tzitziot*, the neckband (*atarah*) is sometimes removed from the *tallit* of the deceased before burial.

Talmid Chakham

Plural, *talmidei chakhamim*. A Hebrew term literally meaning "wise student." The Talmud (*Berakhot* 64a) says, "Students [disciples] of the wise [*talmidei chakhamim*] increase peace in the world," as it says (Isaiah 54:13), "All thy children shall be taught of the Lord, and great shall be the peace [happiness] of thy children."

The Hebrew term *lamdan*, "learned person," is applied particularly to one who is very knowledgeable in biblical and talmudic studies. The *lamdan* is held in high esteem in Jewish society.

See Am Ha-Aretz.

Talmud

A Hebrew term literally meaning "learning," used to designate the Oral Law, which is a commentary on the Written Law, better known as the Torah.

Interpreting the Torah

For Israel to fulfill itself as God's Chosen People, it had to remain loyal to the teachings of the Torah. Since the biblical prescriptions and proscriptions are not always sufficiently clear or specific or enforceable, the Rabbis interpreted the Bible so that what they considered to be the true intent of the text would be revealed. Of all the works that have been produced to explain the Bible, the Talmud is undoubtedly the most important.

The first part of the Talmud, known as the Mishnah, consists of the teachings of the *tanna'im* ("teachers"). The *tanna'im* were scholars and sages who lived prior to 220 C.E. In compiling the Mishnah, Judah the Prince (135–220), his co-editor Nathan, and their associates sifted through, evaluated, and edited a vast number of legal opinions that had been expressed over the centuries in the academies of learning, primarily in Palestine.

The second part of the Talmud, known as the *Gemara*, is a commentary on the Mishnah. The scholars whose views are presented in the discussions in the *Gemara* are known as *amora'im*, meaning "interpreters" or "speakers." For the most part they lived in Babylonia, where the great academies were situated following the destruction of the Temple in 70 C.E. and continued to operate during the Roman occupation of Palestine. The *Gemara* of the Babylonian scholars was edited and finalized by Rav Ashi, principal of the academy in Sura (375–427), and by his successor, Ravina II (474–499), around the year 500 C.E. Together with the Mishnah it comprises the Babylonian Talmud.

A second Talmud, the Palestinian (or Jerusalem) Talmud, was also created. The Mishnah of Rabbi Judah the Prince is the central text of this work as well. However, the *Gemara* of the Palestinian Talmud consists of the discussions that took place among the *amora'im* in the academies of learning in Palestine. The redaction of the Jerusalem Talmud was begun by Rabbi Yochanan of Tiberias in the middle of the third century, and it continued after his death (*c.* 279) by such Sages as Jeremiah, Jonah, and Yossi bar Zavda. The work continued until 359, at which point it began to assume its final form.

The academies that continued to flourish in Palestine, primarily in Tiberias, during the Roman occupation in the early centuries C.E., were not equal in stature to those of Babylonia, and the Palestinian Talmud therefore enjoys lesser status than the Babylonian Talmud.

The Palestinian Talmud, which is often called by its Hebrew name, Yerushalmi, meaning "of Jerusalem," is only about one-quarter the size of the Babylonian Talmud, which is often referred to as the Bavli, meaning "of Babylonia." It should be noted that only in recent centuries have scholars begun to study the Yerushalmi. *Yeshiva* students to this day are engaged primarily in studying the Bavli.

Contents of the Talmud

The Talmud is encyclopedic, containing the views and opinions of thousands of scholars. Within its pages is information covering almost every conceivable area of human interest—information presented specifically in order to help Jews understand their legal and moral responsibilities as proclaimed in the Bible. The overriding purpose of the interpreters of the Bible was to preserve the uniqueness of the Jewish people, to make sure that they remained loyal to the Covenant by observing all the commandments (*mitzvot*) of the Torah. To the Rabbis of the Talmud this meant that a system of law had to be established that would train Israel to carry out the mission of being a holy, godlike people. Jews would have to be protected from alien influences that might lead them away from God.

The Oral Tradition

The discussions and rulings of the Rabbis did not always exist in the written form. Since it was forbidden (*Gittin* 60b) to commit to writing anything but the Torah itself, the arguments and opinions of the Sages had to be passed on by word-of-mouth from father to son, from scholar to disciple, from teacher to pupil. These spoken teachings came to be known as the Oral Law, in contradistinction to the Bible, which was called the Written Law.

By the second half of the fourth century C.E., because it was feared that the massive body of knowledge that comprised the Oral Law might be forgotten, the ban was lifted and the Oral Law was finally put into written form.

Understanding the Talmud

The Talmud, which is in reality the first code of Jewish law, presents problems to the student because the issues under discussion are often extremely complex, and the final decision pertaining to a particular law is often difficult to pinpoint. It was these factors that prompted the writing of many commentaries on the Talmud.

For the first five hundred years following the final editing of the Talmud—from the years 500 to 1000—great scholars, particularly in Babylonia, continued the process of interpreting the Bible. As they explained and commented on the text of Talmud, they gained new insights from its teachings. This period is known as the geonic period, and its scholars are called *ge'onim* (singular, *ga'on*, meaning "his eminence"). Among the better-known *ge'onim* are Hai, Sherira, and Amram, each of whom headed an academy of learning in a Babylonian city.

These scholars, as well as those who followed them for approximately the next five centuries—until about the middle of the sixteenth century—were known as the *rishonim*, meaning "first ones." In addition to studying and analyzing the Talmud, they wrote commentaries on it and answered questions addressed to them by rabbis and teachers from all over the world.

Among the more celebrated scholars of the post-geonic period (after the year 1000) was the North African Isaac ben Jacob of Fez (1013–1103), better known as the Alfasi and the acronym Rif; the French-born Solomon ben Yitzchak (1040–1105), better known by the acronym Rashi; his grandson Rabbenu Tam (100–1170); Moses ben Maimon (1135–1204) of Spain and Egypt; Moses ben Nachman (1194–1270) of Spain, also known as Nachmanides and by the acronym Ramban; and Meir ben Baruch of Rothenberg, Germany (1220–1293). The numerous scholars who wrote commentaries of the Talmud after the sixteenth century were known as the *acharonim*, meaning "the later ones."

Printed Editions

Until 1517, when Christian merchant Daniel Bomberg, a native of Antwerp, Belgium, set up a Hebrew press in Venice, Italy, and printed an edition of the Bible in Hebrew with the commentaries of Rashi, Ibn Ezra, David Kimchi, and Gersonides, Hebrew classics existed only in manuscript form. Due to the bigotry of medieval popes, carloads of Talmud manuscripts were often consigned to flames, and the only complete manuscript that remained dated back to 1334. Known as the Munich manuscript, it was kept in the possession of the Vatican.

In 1520 Bomberg received permission from Pope Leo X to issue a printing of the complete Babylonian Talmud based on this Munich manuscript. The Church, however, scrutinized Bomberg's effort to make sure that the modifications it had made in the text during the years it was engaged in censoring the talmudic text remained unchanged. Thus, a word such as *goy*, which has the simple meaning of "nation" was construed to be a defamatory synonym for Christian, was replaced with *akum*, an acronym for the Hebrew words *oveid kokhavim u-mazalot*, "worshippers of stars and constellations." By using *akum*, the Vatican made it clear that the reference was not to Christians but to idolators.

The format of Bomberg's edition of the Bavli became the model for future printings. The numbering of pages in the Babylonian Talmud began with page two, the first page being the title page. Rashi's commentary was placed next to the spine with the other major commentary, the *tosafot*, being placed in the outer margins. Rashi was so placed to ensure that if the book became damaged Rashi's words would be the last to be affected. Another reason for the placement of the Rashi text in the gutter of each page is suggested by Jonathan Rosen in his 2000 publication, *The Talmud and the Internet*. He writes: "Rashi's commentary is so prized that it appears on the inside margin of every page of Talmud so that, as I was taught in Hebrew school, if you should, God forbid, drop your Talmud in a puddle, Rashi would at least be farthest from the mud."

The first edition of the Yerushalmi was printed by Bomberg in 1524, and its first page, unlike the Bavli, begins with number one (*alef*).

The best printed editions of the Bavli and Yerushalmi in later years were issued by the Romm Publishing House, which was founded by Baruch ben Joseph Romm of Grodno, Lithuania. In 1789 he established the first Hebrew printing press, which he later moved to Vilna. In 1835 his son Menachem was instrumental in producing the first acclaimed Vilna Talmud, also known as the Vilna Shas, which became a model for future editions.

Recent Talmud Editions

After a hiatus of several centuries, renewed attention was accorded the study of the Talmud, and numerous commentaries and translations began to appear. In the twentieth century alone, translations have appeared in English, French, Portuguese, and German. A French translation of the Yerushalmi was prepared by M. Schwab in eleven volumes at the end of the nineteenth century.

For several decades, the 1935 thirty-five-volume English translation, published by the Soncino Press in London, dominated the scene. In 1946, at the end of World War II, not a single copy of the Talmud was to be found anywhere in Western Europe. In 1948, Rabbi Philip Bernstein, special advisor on Jewish affairs to General Joseph McNarney, U.S. military commander in Germany, requested that the army print fifty sets of the Talmud. The request was approved.

Toward the end of the century, the masterful English translation and commentary (which was first issued in Hebrew) began to appear under the editorship of Rabbi Adin Steinsaltz. As of the year 2000, seventeen volumes had appeared covering all or part of the tractates *Ta'anit*, *Bava Metzia*, *Sanhedrin*, and *Ketubbot*. In 1990 Mesorah Publications,

Ltd., began publication of the Bavli, with its own translation of the text accompanied by "Notes" and "Insights."

Talmudic Tractates

The six orders (*sedarim* in Hebrew; singular, *seder*) of the Mishnah (called *Shishah Sedarim* in Hebrew or *Shas* for short) are divided into sixty-three tracts or tractates, called *massekhtot* (singular, *massekhtah*) in Aramaic. The orders of the Mishnah are *Zera'im*, *Mo'ed*, *Nashim*, *Nezikin*, *Kodoshim*, and *Tohorot*.

In both the Babylonian (*Bavli*) and Jerusalem (*Yerushalmi*) Talmud, each *mishnah* is usually followed by a *gemara* commentary, but in many instances the *mishnah* stands alone. Such is the case with the popular tractate Ethics of the Fathers, known in Hebrew as *Avot* or *Pirkei Avot*.

These are the six orders of the Talmud and their tractates:

THE FIRST ORDER: ZERA'IM ("SEEDS")

Laws relating to agriculture as well as blessings and daily prayers.

1. *Berakhot* ("Benedictions"), the first of the twelve tractates in the order Zera'im, consists of nine chapters and deals with laws and regulations pertaining to the most important prayers in the liturgy, such as the *Shema*, and also to blessings to be recited for various foods, fragrances, and sights.

2. *Pei'ah* ("Corner"), consisting of eight chapters, deals with the laws relating to the harvesting of the corners of the field as well as sheaves that were forgotten during harvest and were to be left for the poor, as prescribed in Leviticus 19:9–11 and Deuteronomy 24:19–22. Includes some treatment of the laws of charity.

3. *Demai* ("Doubtfully Tithed Produce"), consisting of seven chapters, analyzes the problems of doubtful produce— that is, fruit, grain, and other products of the earth about which there is uncertainty as to whether or not the tithe had been paid.

4. *Kil'ayim* ("Mixtures"), consisting of nine chapters, deals with prohibited mixtures of seeds, animals, plants, and cloth for garments. It also discusses the laws prohibiting the grafting of different species of plants and the cross-breeding and yoking of animals, as prescribed in Leviticus 19:19 and Deuteronomy 22:9–12.

5. *Shevi'it* ("The Sabbatical Year"), consisting of ten chapters, deals with the land-laws that apply to the seventh year, the sabbatical year. The seventh year is a year of "rest" for the land, as prescribed in Exodus 23:10–12; 25:2– 8 and Deuteronomy 15:1–4.

6. *Terumot* ("Heave Offerings"), consisting of eleven chapters, deals with the offerings brought by the Children of Israel to God. It sets down the rules indicating from which of these offerings the Priest was entitled to take a share, as prescribed in Numbers 18:8, 12, 24, 26 and Deuteronomy 18:4.

7. *Ma'aseirot* ("Tithes"), consisting of five chapters, deals with the tithes to be given to the Levites and also with products not subject to tithes, as prescribed in Numbers 18:21–26.

8. *Ma'aser Sheini* ("Second Tithe"), consisting of five chapters, deals with

problems arising out of the second tithe, which was to be consumed in Jerusalem. It discusses how this tithe is to be brought and how it is to be redeemed, as prescribed in Leviticus 27:30 and Deuteronomy 14:22–29 and 26:12.

9. *Challah* ("Dough"), consisting of four chapters, deals with those cereals of which a portion (*challah*) belongs to the Priest. It discusses how much dough must be removed by the baker and given to the Priest, as prescribed in Numbers 15:18–21.

10. *Orlah* ("Uncircumcised Fruit"), consisting of three chapters, deals with the "uncircumcised" or forbidden fruit of trees, which was not to be eaten during the first three years of growth, as prescribed in Leviticus 19:23–26.

11. *Bikkurim* ("First Fruits"), consisting of three chapters, deals with fruits that may be brought to the Temple as first-fruit offerings and the ceremonies involved. These fruits include wheat, barley, grapes, figs, pomegranates, olives, and dates, as prescribed in Exodus 23:19 and Deuteronomy 26:1–12.

THE SECOND ORDER: MO'ED ("FESTIVAL")

Laws applying to the Sabbath, festivals, and fast days.

1. *Shabbat* ("Sabbath"), consisting of twenty-four chapters, deals with Sabbath laws, particularly prohibitions against all forms of work, as prescribed in Exodus 16:22–30, 20:10, and 23:12ff.

2. *Eruvin* ("Mergings"), consisting of ten chapters, deals with laws relating to carrying objects from the private to the public domain on the Sabbath, as well as to which sections of a town can be artificially combined so as to increase the distance that a person may walk without violating the Sabbath.

3. *Pesachim* ("Passover"), consisting of ten chapters, deals with the laws pertaining to Passover, as prescribed in Exodus 12:1; Leviticus 23:4; and Numbers 9:1.

4. *Shekalim* ("Coins"), consisting of eight chapters, deals with monies collected as a Temple tax and the usage to which they were put, as prescribed in Exodus 30:12–16. In the Babylonian Talmud, this fourth tractate in the order *Mo'ed* contains no *gemara*.

5. *Yoma* ("Day of Atonement"), consisting of eight chapters, deals with the laws pertaining to the Temple service on Yom Kippur and the laws of fasting, as prescribed in Leviticus 16:3–34 and Numbers 29:7–11.

6. *Sukkah* ("Booth"), consisting of five chapters, deals with laws pertaining to valid and invalid *sukkot* and the proper handling of the *etrog* and *lulav*, as prescribed in Leviticus 23:34 and Numbers 29:12.

7. *Beitzah* ("Egg"), consisting of five chapters, deals with the different types of work permitted and prohibited on holidays, as prescribed in Exodus 12:16 and Leviticus 23:3–36. It derives its name from the first word in the tractate. This tractate is sometimes referred to as *Yom Tov* (holiday).

8. *Rosh Hashanah* ("New Year"), consisting of four chapters, deals with questions

relating to the calendar in general and specifically to the Jewish New Year, as prescribed in Leviticus 23:24 and Numbers 29:1.

9. *Ta'anit* ("Fast Days"), consisting of four chapters, deals with the laws of public fasts and the liturgy of such days.

10. *Megillah* ("Scroll"), consisting of four chapters, deals with the reading of the Scroll of Esther and the observance of Purim.

11. *Mo'ed Katan* ("Minor Festivals"), consisting of three chapters, deals with the intermediate days of the Passover and Sukkot holidays. It also deals in great detail with laws pertaining to mourning.

12. *Chagigah* ("Festival Offering"), consisting of three chapters, deals with the obligation to make pilgrimages to Jerusalem and the type of sacrifices to be brought by pilgrims, as prescribed in Exodus 23:14 and Deuteronomy 16:16–18.

THE THIRD ORDER: NASHIM ("WOMEN")

Deals basically with the laws pertaining to marriage, although two of the tractates (*Nedarim* and *Nazir*) deal with other subjects.

1. *Yevamot* ("Levirate Marriages"), consisting of sixteen chapters, deals with the laws of levirate marriages. It is also the main source for laws pertaining to forbidden marriages, as prescribed in Deuteronomy 25:5 and Leviticus 18.

2. *Ketubbot* ("Marriage Contracts"), consisting of thirteen chapters, deals with the laws of marriage and with the financial and personal obligations and rights of a married woman and her husband, as prescribed in Exodus 21:10.

3. *Nedarim* ("Vows"), consisting of eleven chapters, deals with vows and methods of annulling them, as prescribed in Numbers 30:3–16.

4. *Nazir* ("Nazirite"), consisting of nine chapters, deals with the laws pertaining to the Nazirite and the offerings he brings, as prescribed in Numbers 6:2–21.

5. *Sotah* ("Suspected Woman"), consisting of nine chapters, deals with the (laws pertaining to a) wife suspected of adultery, as prescribed in Numbers 5:11–31.

6. *Gittin* ("Bill of Divorce"), consisting of nine chapters, deals with all the laws pertaining to the granting and execution of divorces, as prescribed in Deuteronomy 24:1–5.

7. *Kiddushin* ("Betrothals"), consisting of four chapters, deals with the modes of betrothal and conditions to be fulfilled for a marriage to be valid. It also contains laws relating to the acquisition of slaves and property, and injunctions pertaining to the relationship between parents and children.

THE FOURTH ORDER: NEZIKIN ("DAMAGES")

Deals with civil and criminal law, including the composition of courts and judicial procedure. Ethical matters are also treated.

1. *Bava Kama* ("First Gate"), consisting of ten chapters, is the first of three tractates dealing with injuries and damages caused by a man or his beast, for which the man is responsible, as

prescribed in Exodus 21–22 and other biblical passages.

2. *Bava Metzia* ("Middle Gate"), consisting of ten chapters, deals with the laws concerning lost property, trusts, the prohibition of usury, buying, selling, lending, hiring, and renting, as prescribed in Exodus 22 and 23:3; Leviticus 19:13; 25:14, 36; Deuteronomy 22:1–4; and elsewhere.

3. *Bava Batra* ("Last Gate"), consisting of ten chapters, deals with the various ways of taking possession of property, the right of preemption, laws of partnership, inheritance, and the laws regarding legal documents.

   The above three tractates were known as *Nezikin* before they were subdivided.

4. *Sanhedrin* ("Courts"), consisting of eleven chapters, deals with the composition of the courts, procedures, examination of witnesses, administration of criminal law, and capital punishment. Some sections deal with man's place in the world to come.

5. *Makkot* ("Lashes"), consisting of three chapters, is a continuation of the tractate *Sanhedrin*. It deals with offenses punishable by administering thirty-nine lashes. It also discusses the punishment of false witnesses (Deuteronomy 25:2) and the laws relating to the cities of refuge (Numbers 35:10 and Deuteronomy 19:9).

6. *Shevuot* ("Oaths"), consisting of eight chapters, deals with oaths taken in private or administered by the court, as prescribed in Exodus 22:6–10.

7. *Eiduyot* ("Testimonies"), consisting of eight chapters, consists of a compilation of laws and decisions on various subjects. This tractate, sometimes called *Bechirta* ("Chosen"), does not contain a *gemara*.

8. *Avodah Zarah* ("Idolatry"), consisting of five chapters, contains the regulations that govern the avoidance of contact with idols and idol worshippers, as prescribed in Deuteronomy 4:25.

9. *Ho'rayot* ("Decisions"), consisting of three chapters, deals with problems arising out of wrong decisions rendered by authorities and acted upon by individuals in connection with the type of sacrifices that were brought for the expiation of sins, as prescribed in Leviticus 4 and 5. It also deals with the conduct of rabbinical courts.

10. *Avot* ("Ethics of the Fathers"), consisting of six chapters of ethical maxims of the *tanna'im*, is the only tractate that deals with moral rather than legal conduct. It is often referred to as *Pirkei Avot* ("Chapters of the Fathers") and does not contain a *gemara* commentary on the Mishnah.

THE FIFTH ORDER: KODOSHIM ("HOLY THINGS")

Laws pertaining to the sacrifices brought in the Temple.

1. *Zevachim* ("Sacrifices"), consisting of fourteen chapters, deals generally with the laws governing the sacrifices brought in the Temple. It discusses types of offerings, sprinkling of the blood, and burning of the fat, as prescribed in Leviticus 1–4.

2. *Menachot* ("Meal Offerings"), consisting of thirteen chapters, deals with the

meal offerings and other types of sacrifices brought in the Temple, as prescribed in Leviticus 2. It also discusses the laws pertaining to *tzitzit* and *tefillin*.

3. *Chullin* ("Secular Things"), consisting of twelve chapters, deals with the method of slaughtering animals for general domestic use. It also discusses animal diseases and the rules pertaining to the mixing of meat and dairy dishes.

4. *Bekhorot* ("Firstborn"), consisting of nine chapters, discusses laws regarding the firstborn of animals and humans. It specifies which blemishes of firstborn animals make them unfit as sacrifices and also details the laws of inheritance with regard to a firstborn son, as prescribed in Exodus 13:2, 12 and Numbers 18:15–19.

5. *Arakhin* ("Evaluations"), consisting of nine chapters, deals with the evaluation of persons and things dedicated to the Temple. It details the amount that must be paid to redeem an article that had been pledged to God, as prescribed in Leviticus 27:2–27.

6. *Temurah* ("Exchange"), consisting of seven chapters, discusses the laws bearing on the substitution of an ordinary animal for one already dedicated to the altar, as prescribed in Leviticus 27:10–27.

7. *Keritot* ("Excisions"), consisting of six chapters, deals with sins committed intentionally that are subject to the punishment of excommunication (*karet*) and which sacrifices are to be brought for sins committed inadvertently, as prescribed in Genesis 17:14 and Exodus 12:15.

8. *Me'ilah* ("Trespass"), consisting of six chapters, deals with the sin of the mundane use of objects or property that belongs to the Temple, as prescribed in Leviticus 5:15–17.

9. *Tamid* ("Daily [Sacrifice]"), consisting of seven chapters, deals with the ritual of the daily burnt offering sacrificed in the Temple, as prescribed in Exodus 29:38–42 and Numbers 28:2–8.

10. *Middot* ("Measurements"), consisting of five chapters, deals with the size and shape of the Temple, describing its courts, halls, chambers, gates, and the uses of its various courtyards and chambers.

11. *Kinnim* ("Bird's Nests"), consisting of three chapters, deals with the doves brought as sin-offering or burnt-offering sacrifices, as prescribed in Leviticus 1:14; 12:8; 14:22–31; 15:14–30; and Numbers 6:9.

THE SIXTH ORDER: TOHOROT ("RITUAL PURITIES")

Deals with laws of ritual purity and impurity. No *gemara* exists for this order, with the exception of the tractate *Niddah*.

1. *Keilim* ("Vessels"), consisting of thirty chapters, deals with ritual uncleanness as it pertains to furniture, garments, and vessels of all types, as prescribed in Leviticus 11:33–36.

2. *Oholot* ("Tents"), consisting of eighteen chapters, deals with the laws of ritual impurity that apply to tents or other dwelling places that may have housed a dead body, human or animal, as prescribed in Numbers 19:14–22.

3. *Nega'im* ("Leprosies"), consisting of fourteen chapters, deals with the laws of leprosy, the contamination it causes, and the method of purification, as prescribed in Leviticus 13 and 14.

4. *Parah* ("Heifer"), consisting of twelve chapters, deals with laws pertaining to the red heifer, as described in Numbers 19. It deals with the cow's age requirement, traits, and preparation for slaughter.

5. *Tohorot* ("Purifications"), consisting of ten chapters, deals with (laws pertaining to) uncleanness of various kinds, particularly with the lesser degrees that last only until sunset, as prescribed in Leviticus 11:24–28.

6. *Mikva'ot* ("Ritual Baths"), consisting of ten chapters, deals with the ritual baths, their construction, the sources of their water, and the laws of ritual immersion, as prescribed in Leviticus 15.

7. *Niddah* ("Menstruant"), consisting of ten chapters, deals with ritual impurity among women because of menstruation or childbirth, as prescribed in Leviticus 12:2–8 and 15:19–31.

8. *Makhshirin* ("Preparations"), consisting of six chapters, deals with conditions under which liquids such as dew, water, wine, oil, blood, milk, and honey cause defilement, as prescribed in Leviticus 11:34–39.

9. *Zavim* ("Discharges"), consisting of five chapters, deals with bodily secretions, the defilement they cause, as well as the method of purification by which a defiled person can be purified, as prescribed in Leviticus 15:2–18.

10. *Tevul Yom* ("Daytime Immersion"), consisting of four chapters, deals with specific problems of the person who has taken the prescribed ritual bath but must wait until sunset before he can be regarded as completely cleansed.

11. *Yada'yim* ("Hands"), consisting of four chapters, deals with the laws of the ritual washing of hands.

12. *Ukatzim* ("Stalks, Stems"), consisting of three chapters, deals with the problems relating to the ritual impurity of stems and the fruit attached to them.

MINOR TRACTATES

In addition to the sixty-three tractates listed above, there are fifteen tractates that have not been accepted as full-fledged books of the Talmud. These are known as *massekhtot ketanot* ("minor tractates") and also as *massekhtot chitzoniot* ("extracanonical tractates"). In many editions of the Babylonian Talmud these are appended toward the end of the order *Nezikin*, following the Ethics of the Fathers (*Avot*). These were not finalized until geonic times (eighth and ninth centuries), some three to four centuries after the main body of the Talmud was redacted.

1. *Avot d'Rabbi Natan* ("The Fathers According to Rabbi Nathan"), a supplement and commentary on *Avot*, it consists of forty-one chapters.

2. *Soferim* ("Scribes"), a collection of laws detailing rules for the writing of a Torah scroll and how it is to be read; also contains laws pertaining to the liturgy of the Sabbath, holidays, and fast days.

3. *Eivel Rabbati*, meaning "Great Mourning," is better known by its euphemistic name *Semachot*, meaning "Happy

Times." In fourteen chapters, it details laws concerning burial and mourning.

4. *Kallah* ("Bride"), consisting of one chapter, deals with betrothal, marriage, and moral purity and chastity.

5. *Kallah Rabbati* ("Great Tractate on Brides"), consisting of ten chapters, the first two of which are commentaries on *massekhet Kallah*, while some of the others are devoted to questions of good manners and sundry subjects.

6. *Derekh Eretz Rabbah* ("Great Tractate on Good Manners") is the title of two independent tractates consisting of eleven chapters and dealing with the subject of moral and ethical conduct.

7. *Derekh Eretz Zuta* ("Lesser Tractate on Good Manners"), consisting of ten chapters, is directed primarily at the good behavior expected of scholars.

8. *Perek Ha-Shalom* ("Chapter on Peace"). This material appears in editions of the Talmud as the last of the eleven chapters of *Derekh Eretz Zuta*, but is actually a separate tractate on the theme of peace. It discusses the degeneracy that will prevail preceding the coming of the Messiah.

9. *Geirim* ("Strangers"), a law manual relating to converts (proselytes) referred to as *geirim* (singular, *ger*), consists of four chapters that detail how converts are to be admitted into the Jewish community and how they are to be treated.

10. *Kutim* ("Samaritans") contains two brief chapters that address the question of how the Samaritans are to be treated. The Samaritans were an alien population sent into Samaria by the Assyrian ruler Sargon in 720 B.C.E. in order to neutralize the area and prevent an uprising. They intermingled with the Jewish population and accepted Jewish practices.

11. *Avadim* ("Slaves") is composed of three chapters, in which the treatment of Hebrew slaves and the method of their release from bondage are discussed.

12. *Sefer Torah* ("Torah Scroll"), consisting of five chapters, deals with the preparation and the correct way to handle sacred scrolls, particularly the Torah.

13. *Tefillin* ("Phylacteries"), consisting of one chapter, presents the rules dealing with the materials and languages that may be used in writing *tefillin* scrolls.

14. *Tzitzit* ("Fringes"), consisting of one chapter, details the laws pertaining to a *tallit* (prayershawl) and the fringes to be attached to its four corners.

15. *Mezuzah* ("Doorpost Scroll"), consisting of two chapters, discusses the laws pertaining to the writing of the parchment scroll and the manner in which it is to be attached to the doorpost.

Talmud Torah

A Hebrew term literally meaning "the study of Torah," which is central to the Jewish tradition. The Talmud (Mishnah *Pei'ah* 1:1) equates the study of Torah with all the great goals to which one can aspire, such as the practice of charity and the making of peace. The Ethics of the Fathers (6:2) states, "One cannot call himself free unless he engages in the study of Torah."

Moses Maimonides, in his *Mishneh Torah* (Hilkhot Talmud Torah 1:8, 10) writes: "Every man is obligated to study Torah whether he is poor or rich, of sound health or ailing, full of the vigor of youth or very old and feeble…until the day of death."

"Talmud Torah" is the name commonly used to describe a religious school where Hebrew studies are conducted.

Tanakh

A Hebrew acronym formed from the first letter of each of the Hebrew words *Torah*, *Nevi'im*, and *Ketuvim*, the three divisions of the Bible. The Torah consists of the Five Books of Moses (Pentateuch), which are the first five books of the Bible. *Nevi'im* consists of the twenty-one books of the Prophets. *Ketuvim* consists of the thirteen books of the Hagiographa, or Holy Writings. There are a total of thirty-nine books in the *Tanakh*.

See Bible.

Tanna

Plural, *tanna'im*. This Aramaic term literally meaning "teacher" applies explicitly to those Sages whose discussions and rulings are recorded in the first part of the Talmud, known as the Mishnah. The last of the *tanna'im* was Judah the Prince (Yehudah Ha-Nasi), who in the first part of the third century assembled, edited, and committed to writing the teachings of his colleagues.

The first Rabbis who carried the title *tanna* were disciples of the eminent first-century C.E. scholars Hillel and Shammai. Among the earliest *tanna'im*, those whose presence was widely known between the years 10 and 80 C.E., were Akavya ben Mehalalel, Rabban Gamaliel the Elder, Chaninah the Chief Priest, Shimon ben Gamaliel, and Yochanan ben Zakkai.

The next prominent group of teachers whose views and rulings are included in the Mishnah are Rabban Gamaliel II (of Yavneh), Zadok, Dosa ben Harkinas, Eliezer ben Jacob, Eliezer ben Hyrcanus, Joshua ben Chananiah, Eleazar ben Azariah, and Judah ben Bathyra. Their years of activity extended from 80 to 120 C.E.

A third group, who were active between 120 and 140 C.E., consisted of Rabbis Tarfon, Yishmael, Akiba, Yochanan ben Nuri, Yossi the Galilean, Shimon ben Nanos, Judah ben Bava, and Yochanan ben Baroka.

The fourth generation of *tanna'im* extended from the death of Akiba, in 140 C.E., to that of Shimon ben Gamaliel, around 165 C.E. These teachers included Rabbis Meir, Judah ben Ila'i, Yosei ben Chalafta, Shimon ben Yocha'i, Eleazar ben Shammua, Yochanan Ha-Sandlar, Eleazar ben Jacob, Nehemiah, and Joshua ben Karcha.

The *tanna'im* active from 165 to 200 include Nathan the Babylonian, Symmachus, Judah the Prince (also called Judah I), Yossi ben Judah, Eleazar ben Shimon, and Shimon ben Eleazar.

The sixth and last generation of *tanna'im* were active from 200 to 220 C.E. Because these scholars, contemporaries and disciples of Judah the Prince, are not mentioned by name in the Mishnah, they are often called semi-*tanna'im*. They are, however, identified in the Tosefta, a body of scholarship that parallels the Mishnah.

Targum

A Hebrew term literally meaning "translation." As used in rabbinic literature, *targum* refers to a translation of the Bible in Aramaic, the vernacular of the populace. When the term is used alone, it refers to *Targum Onkelos*, a popular translation of the Torah. The Talmud (*Megillah* 3a) ascribes its authorship to Onkelos the proselyte, a contemporary of Rabbi Akiba of the first/second century C.E. Another Aramaic translation, one that gained wide popularity in the first century B.C.E., was that of Yonatan ben Uziel, a notable disciple of Hillel the Elder. This translation covers the Prophets and Holy Writings (Nevi'im and Ketuvim).

Kurdistani Jews, who speak Aramaic, refer to their language as Targum.

Taryag Mitzvot

Taryag—spelled tav, reish, yud, gimmel—is a coined word having a numerical value of 613 (tav equals 400, reish equals 200, yud equals 10, gimmel equals 3). The number of mitzvot ("commandments") in the Torah is said to be 613. This view was expressed by the third-century Palestinian amora Simlai (Makkot 23b), who delivered a sermon in which he said, "Six hundred and thirteen mitzvot were communicated to Moses, three hundred sixty-five positive ones, corresponding to the days of the year, and two hundred forty-eight negative ones, corresponding to the parts [joints, bones, organs, etc.] of the body."

Rabbi Hamnuna (ibid. 24a) asked, "What is the biblical basis for Simlai's statement?" He concluded that it is based on Deuteronomy 33:4, which says "Moses commanded us a Torah...," Torah having a letter value of 611. To this number are to be added the first two of the Ten Commandments [but not reckoned in Simlai's figure] because we heard them directly from the mouth of the Almighty."

The first list of the Taryag Mitzvot appears in a volume entitled Halakhot Gedolot, by Rabbi Shimon Kayyara, a ninth-century Babylonian scholar (ga'on). Later versions of the Taryag Mitzvot were composed by Sa'adya Gaon, Maimonides, Nachmanides, among others. The compilation of Maimonides, written in Arabic and entitled Sefer Ha-Mitzvot, is the most famous.

The lists of mitzvot compiled by the various scholars differ in content. Maimonides, for example, omits aliyah (settling in Israel) as a positive commandment, while Nachmanides includes it. Maimonides probably omitted aliyah because he himself did not abide by it. In 1165, after settling in Acre, Palestine, for a few years, he moved to Egypt, never to return. When he died, his disciples brought him back to the Holy Land for burial in Tiberias.

Sefer Ha-Bahir, the thirteenth-century book on kabbalah, says that if one counts the letters in the (Hebrew) Ten Commandments, one finds that they add up to 613. It also notes that all the letters of the Hebrew alphabet—except for the ninth letter, tet—are represented in the Ten Commandments. The reason for the omission, say the mystics, is that the tet is shaped like a snake, and a snake, as in the Garden of Eden story, is an instrument of evil.

See Mitzvah.

Tashlikh

A Hebrew term literally meaning "casting off." On the afternoon of the first day of Rosh Hashanah (or the second day if the first day falls on a Sabbath), Jews gather at a body of water to empty their pockets, in which crumbs had been placed, and recite penitential prayers, including the verse from the Book of Micah (7:19), "And Thou wilt cast [ve-tashlikh] all their sins into the depths of the sea." The first direct reference to this custom was made by Rabbi Jacob ben Moses Ha-Levi Mollin (also known as the Maharil, c. 1360–1427), which led some scholars to assume that it did not originate before the fourteenth century.

Other scholars claim that the custom of tashlikh originated much earlier. This is based on the fact that most of the prominent scholars of the Middle Ages expressed disapproval of the practice because it was associated with the pagan custom of emptying crumbs from one's pockets in order to give the devil "its due" and being spared the harm that it might inflict. Primitive man believed that evil spirits lived in streams and wells and could be placated with gifts of food.

The prevailing feeling of those who observe *tashlikh* today was once expressed by Rabbi Isaiah Hurwitz, a renowned kabbalist who lived at the end of the eighteenth century. In his *Two Tablets of the Covenant* he wrote that it is foolish for Jews to assume that they can shake off their sins by emptying their pockets into a stream. Nevertheless, Hurwitz did accept the concept of ridding oneself of sins. He felt that visiting a fish-carrying stream can serve as a reminder that in many ways man is like a fish, that he must be wary lest he be trapped as easily as a fish can be ensnared.

Orthodox Jews today observe *tashlikh*, as do an increasing number of Conservative congregational members. Reform Jews, who discarded the practice early in the twentieth century, have returned to it in varying degrees.

Tashlikh ceremonies differ around the world. The Jews of Kurdistan, for example, follow a practice of reciting penitential prayers near a river and then jumping into the water and swimming around, instead of merely shaking crumbs out of their pockets.

Tattoos

The Book of Leviticus (19:28) explicitly prohibits tattooing: "You shall not cut into your flesh [in mourning] for a dead person, nor etch any marks into your skin; I am the Lord."

Ancient peoples of the Near East often cut into their skin and mutilated their bodies to demonstrate grief. They also cut into their skin and filled the incisions with indelible dyes, creating tattoos of the deities they worshipped. These practices were forbidden to Jews not only because they represented pagan worship, but also because they ran counter to the biblical prohibitions against spilling blood and mistreating man's God-given body. (See Maimonides' *Mishneh Torah*, Hilkhot Avodat Kokhavim 12:11; *Makkot* 21a.)

Since tattooing in modern times involves pricking the skin rather than cutting into it, and since idolatry is no longer practiced among civilized people, some authorities question whether the biblical ban against tattooing still applies.

Unfounded statements have been made that Jews with tattoos are not to be buried in a Jewish cemetery.

Techiyat Ha-Metim

A Hebrew term literally meaning "revival of the dead."

See Resurrection.

Tefillah

This Hebrew word literally meaning "prayer" is also one of the names for the most important prayer recited in talmudic times, popularly known as the *Shemoneh Esrei*, or *Eighteen Benedictions*.

The Mishnah *Sotah* (7:1) rules that most prayers must be recited in Hebrew, but the *Tefillah*, the *Shema*, and *Birkat Ha-Mazon* (*Grace After Meals*) are so important that they may be recited in any language.

See Eighteen Benedictions; Tefillin.

Tefillin

The word *tefillin* is a plural form of *tefillah*, meaning "prayer." It also has a secondary meaning of "to judge" or "intercede." Since *tefillin*, small leather boxes containing selections from Scripture, are worn only as a pair, they are referred to primarily in the plural form.

In the New Testament (Matthew 23:5), *tefillin* are called "phylacteries," derived from the Greek *phylakterion*, meaning "safeguard." The implication is that *tefillin* are amulets. While in early societies jewelry and other objects were worn on the head, hands, and arms to protect against evil spirits, there is no evidence that this ever applied to the wearing of *tefillin*.

The Purpose of Tefillin

The Torah (Exodus 13:16) uses the word *totafot*, meaning "symbols," for *tefillin*. The choice of the word *totafot* explains the basic purpose of *tefillin*: to serve as symbols of faith and devotion. The head cube and its contents symbolize intellectual loyalty, while the arm cube is a reminder that the worshipper must serve God with all his might and strength.

Tefillin are worn on the upper arm and forehead when reciting weekday morning prayers. Since the Sabbath and holidays in themselves are observed to affirm one's devotion to God, *tefillin* are not worn on those days. Furthermore, if it were required that *tefillin* be worn on the Sabbath, a person might be tempted to carry them to the synagogue, and carrying on the Sabbath is forbidden (*Shabbat* 61a).

Some Jews, particularly *chasidim* and Sephardim, believe that the intermediate days of holidays (Chol Ha-Moed) are holy and hence must be observed fully, as are the first and last days of Passover and Sukkot. Accordingly, they do not put on *tefillin* at any time during these holidays. However, those who work on Chol Ha-Moed do put on *tefillin*, but remove them before reciting the selection of Psalms known as *Hallel*. Recitation of *Hallel* is in itself a reminder that the day is holy.

In Israel today, the Sephardic practice of not wearing *tefillin* on the intermediate days of holidays has gained acceptance, and the Israeli Ashkenazic community does not don *tefillin* on these days as well.

In talmudic times, and presumably for some years afterward, men—especially scholars—wore *tefillin* all day long (*Moed Katan* 26a). The prominent first-century scholar Yochanan ben Zakkai once remarked (*Yoma* 86a) that he never walked more than four cubits (six feet) without wearing *tefillin*. He considered it a profanation of God's name to do so. Rabbi Zeira, a fourth-century scholar, made a similar statement (*Megillah* 28a). Abbayei, the third/fourth-century scholar, noted (*Berakhot* 30b) that scholars always study Torah while wearing *tefillin*. Since scholars were constantly engaged in studying or thinking Torah thoughts, it became customary for learned people to wear *tefillin* all day long (*Menachot* 36b and *Shabbat* 49a, 127b). It was said that Abba Arikha (Rav), the illustrious disciple of Rabbi Judah the Prince, was never seen walking four cubits without carrying a scroll of the Torah, without a garment to which *tzitzit* are attached, and without wearing *tefillin*. (*Mishneh Torah*, Hilkhot Tefillin 4:25)

An incident described in the Talmud illustrates how Rabbi Judah, who while on a mission to Rome in behalf of the Jews of Palestine showed respect for his *tefillin*. He was invited to the home of a Roman matron, and before entering, removed his *tefillin*. Commentators explained (*Shabbat* 127b) that there were idols in the house and Joshua did not want to bring sacred articles into such an environment.

The Content of Tefillin

Each *tefillin* cube contains four passages from the Bible, handwritten on parchment by a scribe (*sofer*). The selections are from Exodus 13:1–10, Exodus 13:11–16, Deuteronomy 6:4–9, and Deuteronomy 11:13–21.

The boxes must be square, black, and made

of the skin of a kosher animal. Traditionally they are no smaller than the width of two fingers, but no particular size is mandated (*Arukh Ha-Shulchan* 32:74). The text must be written with specially prepared black ink. The cube for the arm contains the four passages on one piece of parchment, while the head cube has four separate parchments.

In France, a difference of opinion developed between the disciples of Rashi (1040–1105) and the disciples of his grandson, Jacob ben Meir (1100–1171), popularly known as Rabbenu Tam, over the arrangement of the four parchments that were placed in the cube worn on the head. The question was, Should the parchment on which Deuteronomy 11:13–21 is written be placed before or after the parchment on which Deuteronomy 6:4–9 is written?

The majority sided with Rashi's followers, who believed that the order of the Torah should be followed. Thus, from left to right, the order should be Exodus 13:1–10; Exodus 13:11–16; Deuteronomy 6:4–9; and Deuteronomy 11:13–21. Rabbenu Tam's followers contended that the last two sections should be reversed so that Exodus 13:11–16 and Deuteronomy 11:13–21 would be next to each other. Both, they argued, begin with the Hebrew word *ve-hayah*, "and it shall come to pass," and therefore belong side by side.

To satisfy both views, many ultra-Orthodox Jews wear both types of *tefillin* in the course of the morning service. Until the end of the *Amidah* prayer they wear the Rashi-style *tefillin*. For the remainder of the service they wear the Rabbenu Tam version.

Attached to the head and arm cubes are leather straps two to three feet in length. These leather straps are called *retzu'ot* (plural) in Hebrew. The strap (singular, *retzu'ah*) of the head cube hangs loosely, while the strap of the arm cube is wound around the arm seven times. The reason why it is wound seven times is because there are seven Hebrew words in the verse "Thou openest thy hand and satisfiest every living creature" (Psalms 145:16).

After being wound around the arm, the end of the strap is wound three times around the hand and three times around the ring finger and middle finger, forming the Hebrew word *Shaddai*, meaning "God." The winding of the strap three times is also traced to the fact that Hosea (2:21–22) uses the word "betroth" three times to spell out God's triple commitment to Israel:

> And I will betroth thee unto Me forever;
> Yea, I will betroth thee unto Me in
>   righteousness, and in justice,
> And in lovingkindness and in
>   compassion.
> And I will betroth thee unto Me in
>   faithfulness;
> And thou shalt know the Lord.

Right-handed vs. Left-handed People

Right-handed people wear the hand *tefillah* on the left hand, while left-handed people wear it on the right hand. According to one interpretation, this practice is based on a reading of the Hebrew word *yadkha*, meaning "your hand," which appears in the verse "And you shall bind them for a sign upon *your hand*" (Deuteronomy 6:8). If the Hebrew letter *hei* is added to the end of the word *yadkha*, the word can then be divided into two words, pronounced *yad kei-hah*, meaning "the weaker hand." According to this interpretation, the hand *tefillah* is to be wrapped around the weaker hand—the left hand of a right-handed person and the right hand of a left-handed person.

Another reason for wearing the *tefillah* on the weaker hand is that in the Book of Deuteronomy, the verse "And thou shalt bind them for a sign upon thy hand" (6:8) is followed by "And thou shalt write them upon the doorposts of thy house" (6:9). From the order of these verses, the Rabbis concluded that "the hand that binds must be the same hand that writes." Hence, if one writes with his right hand, he must wind the straps of his *tefillah* with his right hand (*Menachot* 37a).

Jews who follow Sephardic practice wind the *tefillin* around the arm in an overhand (clockwise) fashion, while the Ashkenazic practice uses a counterclockwise motion.

Cube Designs

The head cube, which is called *tefillah shel rosh* in Hebrew, has the Hebrew letter *shin* embossed on two of its sides. Various explanations have been offered for this practice, but most probably the *shin* simply stands for *Shaddai*. Interestingly, the *shin* embossed on the left side of the head cube has one extra vertical stroke, four rather than the three embossed on the right side. The extra stroke was probably added to the *shin* on the left side of the cube to indicate to the maker of the *tefillin* the order in which the four parchments are to be inserted. It has also been noted that the seven vertical strokes that make up the two *shins* are equal in number to the number of times the *retzu'ah* is wound around the arm.

The hand cube has no embossing.

Posture and Blessings

The correct posture of the individual when donning *tefillin* has been the subject of debate. Kabbalists were of the opinion that one should be seated as the *tefillin* are put on. However, the sixteenth-century Polish authority Rabbi Solomon Luria protested this practice, asserting that all the great Rabbis of the Talmud put on their *tefillin* while standing, and one should not deviate from this custom. The common practice today is to don the *tefillin* while standing.

The Talmud (*Berakhot* 60b) prescribes that a special blessing be pronounced when mounting each of the *tefillin*. When putting on the hand *tefillah*, one should say, "Blessed is He who has sanctified us with His commandments and commanded us to put on *tefillin*." And when putting on the head *tefillah*, he should say, "Blessed is He who has sanctified us with His commandments and commanded us concerning the commandment of *tefillin*."

Even though in Jewish law *tefillin* are considered more holy and more important than a *tallit*, the *tallit* is always put on first. The reason for this sequence is that Jewish law follows the rule that whichever rite is practiced more often is performed first. The *tallit* is used every day of the week; *tefillin* are not worn on the Sabbath or on holidays.

In talmudic and geonic (post-talmudic) times, *tefillin* were worn by rabbis and scholars all day long. Therefore, they put on the *tefillin* before the *tallit* in accordance with its primary status. Later, when *tefillin* were worn only at morning prayers, the *tallit* was put on first and was removed after the *tefillin* had been removed.

Women and Tefillin

According to talmudic law, women are exempt from performing rituals that must be carried out at a specific time of the day. Since *tefillin* are worn during the morning service, women are free from this obligation, although they may assume the obligation voluntarily if they so wish.

The more probable reason for the exemption of women is that it is considered improper to wear a holy object like *tefillin* when one is in a state of impurity. Due to the menstrual cycle, women are periodically ritually impure.

In *Berakhot* 2:2 [146] of the Palestinian Talmud, Rabbi Yochanan bar Nappacha offers a different explanation. He notes that since the verses in Deuteronomy (11:18–19) relating to *tefillin* emphasize that they are to serve as symbols to "teach your sons [*b'neikhem*]," and the text does not say "your daughters [*b'noteikhem*]," this is proof that only those to whom Torah must be taught (male children) are responsible to don *tefillin*. Women, who are not obligated to study Torah, are not required to wear *tefillin*.

In ancient times, some women were known to wear *tefillin*. The Talmud (*Eruvin* 96) notes that Michal, daughter of King Saul, donned *tefillin*. But in the sixteenth century Rabbi Moses Isserles, in his commentary on the *Code of Jewish Law*, ruled that this practice is to be banned. His ruling has been generally observed, although there have been women in history who have worn a *tallit* and *tefillin* despite the disapproval of the rabbinate.

One such case was the Maid of Ladamir, a chasidic woman *rebbe* born in Russia in the early part of the nineteenth century. She wore a *tallit* and *tefillin* every morning. Rabbinic authorities tried to stop her from carrying on "in the manner of a man," but she defied them.

The Maid of Ladamir moved to Palestine, where she continued to attract a small coterie. Until the very end of her life, she could be seen scurrying early in the morning from her home in Mea Shearim to the Wailing Wall, dressed in *tallit* and *tefillin*, to recite her morning prayers.

In recent decades, despite the objections of some authorities, women of all denominations have taken upon themselves the obligation to pray with *tefillin* every day.

Tefillin and Mourning

When *tefillin* are dropped, one experiences a sense of mourning. Jewish law (*Shulchan Arukh*, Orach Cha'yim 44:1) demands that the person who drops them should fast on that day. In some communities, it is customary for all present when the incident happens to fast as well.

Tefillin are not worn by mourners from the time one learns of a death in the immediate family until the first or second day of the seven day *shivah* period, depending upon which authority one accepts. The wearing of *tefillin* is considered a symbol of joy, not at all compatible with mourning.

Teiku

An acronym formed from the Hebrew/Aramaic words *Tishbi yetareitz kushiyot ve-aba'yot*, meaning, "The Tishbite will explain all difficulties and questions."

The ninth-century B.C.E. prophet Elijah, of the kingdom of Israel, was known as the Tishbite, after his birthplace, Tishbi, in the Transjordan area. According to the prophet Malakhi (3:23–24), Elijah will bring reconciliation between the fathers and sons "before the coming of the great dreadful day of the Lord." As a result of his prophecy, Jewish tradition marked Elijah as the harbinger of the Messiah, who will be the ultimate deliverer and savior of Israel and will usher in a period of universal peace.

The term *teiku* is used in the Talmud when a debate between scholars on a question of law cannot be resolved. It was argued that it be left standing, unanswered, until Elijah the all-knowing prophet reappears and solves the problem.

Some scholars are of the opinion that *teiku* is an Aramaic word, akin to the Hebrew word *takum*, meaning "let it stand."

Teivah

A Hebrew term literally meaning "box." The first use of the term is in the Book of Genesis (6:14), where God commands Noah to "make a *teivah* [box or ark] of gopher wood." The *teivah*, a rudderless structure not intended to be navigated by man, was intended to house Noah's family and a selection of animals during the flood. God alone was to be its navigator and hence a sense of holiness was attached to it.

It is therefore entirely understandable that the box or ark that was later to house the Ten Commandments, and still later the Torah scrolls, was called an *Aron Ha-Kodesh*, "a holy ark." Sephardic Jews call the ark *Teivah*.

As far back as early talmudic times, the lectern from which the *shli'ach tzibur*, the leader of the service or cantor, was to officiate was placed on a level lower than the ark housing the Torah. Hence, the Mishnah *Berakhot* 5:3 (34a) refers to one as "going down before the *teivah*." In non-Orthodox synagogues today, the lectern from which the service is led is generally on the same level as the ark itself.

Temples, First and Second

The first of two Jewish Temples that sat atop Mount Moriah in Jerusalem, built by King Solomon at great expense, was dedicated about 964 B.C.E. The Second Book of Chronicles (36:17) refers to the structure as *Beit Ha-Mikdash*, "the House of the Sanctuary," while the First Book of Kings (6:1 and elsewhere) simply refers to it as the *Ba'yit*, "the House [for God]." The holy Ark of the Covenant, which held the Ten Commandments and had been carried throughout the forty-year sojourn of the Israelites through the desert, was now housed in the Holy of Holies of this elaborate structure.

In his dedication prayer, Solomon acknowledged that the Ark now residing in the Holy of Holies symbolized God's presence. He said (I Kings 8:13), "I have now built for Thee [God] a stately house, a place where Thou may dwell forever."

Chapters 6 and 7 of First Kings describes the exterior and interior of the elaborate Temple structure in full detail, noting that it required seven years to construct a regal edifice where sacrifices could be brought.

The country prospered under Solomon, but upon his death the monarchy split. Ten of the twelve tribes occupied the northern territories, with Samaria as its capital; two of the twelve tribes, Judah and Benjamin, occupied the south, with Jerusalem as its capital. The northern territory became known as Israel, and the southern ones as Judea.

In 721 B.C.E., the Assyrians attacked the kingdom of Israel and exiled most of its inhabitants. Their whereabouts remain a mystery to this day.

In 597 B.C.E., Nebukhadnezzar, the mighty king of the East, conquered Palestine and forced the Judeans to surrender. He drove many of the noble families into exile in Babylonia and appointed Zedekiah king, hoping that he would be loyal. But Zedekiah threw his lot with Egypt and rebelled against Nebukhadnezzar and the Babylonians. The Babylonians reacted with force, and in 586 B.C.E. murdered multitudes, besieged Jerusalem, and destroyed Solomon's Temple. Thousands of Jews were exiled to Babylonia, where they joined the thousands exiled there earlier in 597.

Nebukhadnezzar had no intention of eradicating the Jewish people; he was simply anxious to command their loyalty. Consequently, all of the Jewish refugees in Babylonia were able to establish a viable, if disjointed community. With the support of prophets like Isaiah and Ezekiel, the exiled Jews kept alive the hope that the God of Israel would one day restore them to their land.

The day was not long in coming when the power of the Babylonians diminished and Persia, under King Cyrus, became the dominant power in the region. In the second year of his reign (537 B.C.E.), Cyrus issued an edict allowing the exiled Judeans to return to Judah and rebuild their Temple in Jerusalem, a policy continued by his successor, King Darius.

After eighteen years of slow, hard work punctuated by many disappointments, the task of rebuilding the Temple was complete. Quite clearly, this Second Temple, built by a poor community, was in no way comparable to the grand and glorious Temple of Solomon.

In the year 516, exactly seventy years since the First Temple was destroyed and about twenty-one years after the first group of Babylonian exiles was allowed to return to Judea, the modest new Temple began to function. Priests, with the assistance of Levites, began offering sacrifices on the altar, and Jews from towns and villages began to stream into Jerusalem, where they ascended the Temple Mount to watch the sacrificial rituals and hear the Levites sing songs of praise to God.

The Second Temple functioned until its destruction by the Romans in the year 70 C.E.

Tena'im

A Hebrew term literally meaning "stipulations." As far back as talmudic times, after a marriage was arranged, the family of the bride and groom met and an agreement was drawn up, which was at first called *shidukhin* and later *tena'im* (*Kiddushin* 12b). Terms of the marriage stipulated the amount of the dowry to be paid and the date and place of the wedding.

To seal the deal, the parties involved in the marriage-to-be take hold of a kerchief (called a *kinyan* in Hebrew), thereby signifying symbolically that they will fulfill all conditions specified in the *tena'im*. After the eleventh century, the agreement, oral at first, was committed to writing. In some communities today, the mothers of the bride and groom take hold of a plate and break it over a chair. The noise, it is believed, will scare off the evil spirits that may be anxious to disrupt the happy occasion.

See Handkerchief Ceremony; Knas Mahl.

Ten Commandments

The Bible recounts that after Moses had spent forty days and nights communing with God atop Mount Sinai, he descended with two stone tablets upon which were engraved the words of the Ten Commandments, also known by the Greek name *Decalogue* ("Ten Words").

The Torah itself (Deuteronomy 4:13 and 10:4) refers to the Ten Commandments as *Aseret Ha-Devarim* ("The Ten Words"), while the Talmud (*Berakhot* 11b) uses the term *Aseret Ha-Dibrot* ("The Ten Statements"), possibly because the very first verse of the Ten Commandments is an actual statement affirming the existence of God.

The Golden Calf

When Moses descended from the mountain, he found that the Israelites, believing that Moses would not return after such a long absence, had convinced Aaron, Moses' brother, to erect a Golden Calf for them to worship.

Upon observing the Israelites dancing joyfully around the Golden Calf, Moses hurls the

Ten Commandments to the ground, shattering them at the foot of the mountain. He takes the idol and sets it afire until it turns into a molten mass, which he later grinds into a powder. He then mixes the powder with water and makes the people drink from it as atonement for their evil deed (Exodus 32:20).

The Second Decalogue

After pleading with God to forgive His errant people, Moses is ordered once again to go to the top of Mount Sinai, where, after forty more days and nights, he receives a second set of the Ten Commandments (Exodus 34:28). These tablets were then (as prescribed in Deuteronomy 10:2) placed in the ark that was carried by the members of the tribe of Levi. This tribe was so honored because its members did not participate in either the building or the worshipping of the Golden Calf. Rather, they helped Moses punish the sinners (Deuteronomy 10:8).

According to tradition (*Bava Batra* 14b; *Berakhot* 5b), not only was the second set of Ten Commandments stored in the ark, but the broken pieces of the shattered first tablets were kept there as well. When the First Temple was erected by King Solomon, the Ten Commandments were housed in the Holy of Holies, a room in the Temple the High Priest alone was permitted to enter but once a year, on Yom Kippur.

The Lost Tablets

At some point, the Ten Commandments disappeared. One theory is that King Josiah, the sixteenth king of Judah who reigned between 637 and 608 B.C.E., during a period of religious reform, had hidden them to prevent possible capture by an enemy. Another theory is that the prophet Jeremiah hid them on Mount Nebo, from which Moses was able to view the Promised Land before his death (Deuteronomy 34:1–3).

Although the Talmud (*Menachot* 28b) specifically prohibits duplicating the rooms and verandas of the Jerusalem Temples, as well as their tables and seven-branched candelabra (*menorot*), it says nothing about replicating the two Tablets of the Law. Why the replication of the Decalogue is permitted is not definitely known, but it may relate to the fact that the people never actually saw the tablets. The Ten Commandments were stored in the Holy of Holies, an area off-limits to everyone excluding the High Priest.

Decalogue Text

The text of the Ten Commandments as it appears in Exodus (20:1–14) is as follows:

I

I the Lord am your God who brought you out of the land of Egypt, the house of bondage.

II

You shall have no other gods beside Me. You shall not make for yourself a sculptured image, or any likeness of what is in the heavens above, or on the earth below, or in the waters under the earth. You shall not bow down to them or serve them. For I, the Lord your God, am an impassioned God, visiting the guilt of the parents upon the children, upon the third and upon the fourth generations of those who reject Me, but showing kindness to the thousandth generation of those who love Me and keep My commandments.

III

You shall not swear falsely by the name of the Lord your God; for the Lord will not excuse one who swears falsely by His name.

IV

Remember the Sabbath day and keep it holy. Six days you shall labor and do all your work, but the seventh day is a Sabbath of the Lord your God: you shall not do any work—you, your son or daughter, your male or female slave, or your cattle, or the stranger who is within your gates. For in six days the Lord made heaven and earth and sea, and all that is in them, and He rested on the seventh day; therefore the Lord blessed the Sabbath day and hallowed it.

V

Honor your father and your mother that your days may be prolonged on the land that the Lord your God is giving to you.

VI

You shall not murder.

VII

You shall not commit adultery.

VIII

You shall not steal.

IX

You shall not bear false witness against your neighbor.

X

You shall not covet your neighbor's house: you shall not covet your neighbor's wife, or his male or female slave, or his ox or his ass, or anything that is your neighbor's.

The Text in Deuteronomy

The Ten Commandments as they appear in the Book of Deuteronomy (5:6–18) are different from those in Exodus in several respects. In Deuteronomy, the commandment relating to the Sabbath begins with the words "Observe the Sabbath day" instead of "Remember the Sabbath day." And after the words "your male and female slaves," Deuteronomy employs the words "your ox or your ass, or any of your cattle, or the stranger in your settlements, so that your male and female slaves may rest as you do. Remember that you were a slave in the land of Egypt and the Lord your God freed you from there with a mighty hand and an outstretched arm; therefore, the Lord your God has commanded you to observe the Sabbath day."

These words do not appear in the Ten Commandments of Exodus.

Finally, the last commandment (verse 18) has a slight variation. Deuteronomy reads, "You shall not covet your neighbor's wife. You shall not crave your neighbor's house, or his field, or his male or female slaves, or his ox, or his ass, or anything that is your neighbor's."

In Exodus (20:14), "Your neighbor's house" appears before "your neighbor's wife."

Christian Versions

The Ten Commandments, which do not appear in the New Testament, are accepted by all Christians as the word of God, although some denominations number them differently. *The Interpreter's Bible*, which presents the Holy Scriptures in accordance with the King James Version acceptable to most Christian denominations, considers the first commandment to be, "You shall have no other gods before Me," and the second commandment to read, "You shall not make a graven image...you shall not bow down to them..."

Roman Catholics and Lutherans combine the first and second commandments and make up for it by separating the tenth commandment into two parts. They consider "You shall not covet your neighbor's house" to be the ninth commandment and "You shall not covet your neighbor's wife" to be the tenth commandment.

Synagogues Readings

The Ten Commandments form part of the synagogue Torah reading several times in the course of one year. They are read on the Sabbaths when the Torah portion Yitro is read (Exodus 18:1–20:23) and when Va-etchanan is read (Deuteronomy 3:23–7:11). They are also read on the first day of Shavuot, the holiday that celebrates the giving of the Torah on Mount Sinai.

Posture During Ten Commandments Reading

While most authorities favor standing when the Ten Commandments are read, others share the view of Maimonides that standing might lead people to think that all parts of the Torah are not of equal importance, that only the Decalogue was revealed to Moses on Mount Sinai and is deserving of special respect. In his responsa (no. 46), Maimonides ruled that although the Jews of Babylonia (present-day Iraq) followed the practice of standing when the Ten Commandments are being read, it is prohibited to stand if all through the rest of the year one sits when the Torah is being read.

In Temple Times

In Second Temple times, after the Priests offered the daily morning sacrifice (Sabbath included), a prayer service was held. During this service, the Ten Commandments were recited as a reminder of the Revelation on Sinai (Mishnah *Tamid* 5:1).

After the destruction of the Second Temple in the year 70 C.E., the reading of the Decalogue was transferred to the liturgy of the synagogue. The Samaritans and the emerging Christian community began to spread the idea that the sole reason for including the Ten Commandments in the Temple prayer service or the later synagogue liturgy was that it alone was the part of the Torah that had been revealed on Mount Sinai and that it alone was sacred.

To make the point that all parts of the Torah were revealed on Mount Sinai and were of equal importance, the Rabbis of Palestine eliminated the Ten Commandments from the liturgy. Around 400 C.E., Rav Ashi enacted a similar ruling for Babylonian Jewry. Other communities throughout the world followed suit, the Jews of Egypt being the last to remove the Ten Commandments from the prayerbook. Nevertheless, isolated congregations continued to recite it as part of the prayer service.

When the prominent thirteenth-century Spanish Rabbi Solomon ben Adret (the Rashba) of Barcelona, Spain, tried to reintroduce the Decalogue into his daily service, his attempt was vehemently opposed. To this day, all traditional prayerbooks exclude the Ten Commandments from the liturgy.

See Taryag Mitzvot.

Ten Days of Repentance

The ten days beginning with Rosh Hashanah and concluding with Yom Kippur are known in Hebrew as *Aseret Yemei Teshuvah,* the "Ten Days of Repentance." These days have special significance because during this time, Jewish tradition contends, God passes judgment over every individual, reserving final judgment for Yom Kippur.

The Ten Days of Repentance are regarded as a Jew's last chance to influence God to reconsider an unfavorable decision (*Rosh Hashanah* 16b). For this reason, the pre-Yom Kippur holiday greeting, *Leshanah tovah tikateivu,*

"May you be *inscribed* in the Book of Life for good," is changed to *G'mar chatimah tovah*, "May you be *sealed* in the Book of Life for good."

See Numbers; Repentance.

Ten Lost Tribes

After the conquest of the Promised Land by Joshua, Moses' successor, the land was divided among the Twelve Tribes of Israel. The ten tribes that occupied the northern part of the country were conquered by the Assyrians between 732 and 721 B.C.E. and were sent into exile. Many of the deportees settled in Assyria, but most were dispersed to a variety of unknown places. From time to time, world travelers have claimed to have located members of these ten lost tribes, but without presenting credible evidence. According to one tradition, the Ten Lost Tribes of Israel were exiled to places beyond the legendary Sambatyon River, which all week long is turbulent but on the Sabbath rests (*Genesis Rabbah* 11:5; *Sanhedrin* 65b).

Eldad Ha-Dani, a ninth-century traveler, reported having found these exiles in a mountainous area of Africa. David Reuveni, the sixteenth-century adventurer, appeared in Venice in 1524 appealing for help from the Christian powers against the Moslems, claiming that he was sent by his brother who was king of the tribe of Reuben. Other travelers have reported locating the Ten Tribes in South America and Japan. In 1994, new arrivals in Israel claimed to be descendants of the Tribe of Manasseh. None of these claims has been substantiated.

In an essay in *The Jerusalem Post* (October 22, 2001), Shalva Weil wrote that a Bukharian Jewish barber traveling to Kabul, Afghanistan, in 1935, came across nomadic Pathan tribesmen who claimed to be descendants of the Children of Israel. They wore jackets embroidered on the back with a Chanukkah lamp, wore beards, and claimed to be "sons" of the tribe of Ephraim. The barber was also told that they placed *mezuzot* on their doorposts and lit candles on Friday night. Scholars who subsequently have investigated the matter were convinced that the tribesmen could be long-lost "cousins" of the Jews.

See Tribes of Israel.

Ten Martyrs

Referred to in Hebrew as *asarah harugei malkhut*, the ten martyrs of the second century C.E. were leading rabbis who defied the orders of the Romans to cease teaching Torah to students in their academies and discontinue all Jewish observances.

The precise identity of the ten martyrs is uncertain, but the names as listed in the High Holiday prayerbook generally include Akiba ben Joseph, Ishmael ben Elishah, Eleazar ben Dama, Chaninah ben Teradyon, Judah ben Bava, Chutzpit the Interpreter, Yesheivav ben Chakinai, Shimon ben Gamaliel, and Yishmael the High Priest (*Berakhot* 61b).

The Talmud (*Berakhot* 61b) describes the cruel death administered to many of these rabbis. Akiba's death was typical. He was taken out of his cell when the hour had come for the recital of the *Shema*. As his flesh was being mutilated with iron combs, Akiba's soul left his body as he uttered the word *echad* ("one"), the final word of the *Shema*.

Tereifah

A Hebrew word literally meaning "torn," referring specifically to an animal that has been attacked and mutilated by another animal and for that reason is not fit for food. This is in accordance with the statement in Exodus 22:30, "You shall not eat any flesh that is torn of beasts [killed by other beasts in the open field]." In time, the concept was extended to include all unfit—that is, nonkosher—foods and utensils. *Treif* is the colloquial way of pronouncing *tereifah*.

Eating a limb torn from a living animal is one of the seven prohibitions in the Noahide Code, incumbent upon all non-Jews.

See Dietary Laws.

Terumah

A Hebrew term literally meaning "raised up, separated," referring specifically to a gift or offering of money or property that was dedicated to a specific religious purpose. The half-shekel that was collected from the Israelites when taking the census was called *terumah l'Adonai*, "an offering to the Lord" (Exodus 30:13).

In ancient times, when the sacrificial system was in vogue, the gifts of animal and farm produce that were set aside for the Priests (*Kohanim*) were called *terumah*. The Book of Numbers (18:8ff.) ordains that a portion of the yearly harvest be separated and brought to the Priest for his support. The quantity brought depended on the generosity of the farmer.

See Tithes.

Teshuvah

See Repentance.

Tetragrammaton

From the Greek meaning "four letters," this is a reference to the four Hebrew letters that spell out God's name, Yehovah, which in Jewish law is too sacred to be spoken aloud.

See God, Names of.

Tevilah

A Hebrew term literally meaning "immersion." It is through this religious rite of ablution, repeatedly mentioned in the Torah, that one who has become ritually unclean purifies

him- or herself. The *tevilah* ritual involves immersion in a body of living water , as opposed to drawn water. (Living water is derived from a natural source, such as a river or lake, whereas drawn water has been previously collected and stored.) The use of a *mikveh* in which the ablution is to take place was ordained by Ezra (*Berakhot* 22b). Dishes and pots are also purified by immersion in a *mikveh*.

See Mikveh.

Thirteen Attributes of Mercy

The Book of Exodus (32:19) describes how, after waiting forty days for Moses to return from Mount Sinai, the Children of Israel turned to Aaron and implored him to build a Golden Calf that they might worship. Aaron was pressured by the people to comply. When Moses finally descended the mountain with the Ten Commandments, he was so angered that he threw the tablets to the ground and shattered them.

After a brief interval, Moses ascended the mountain to receive a second set of tablets. Before Moses began his descent, God taught him the *Shelosh Esrei Midot Ha-Rachamim*, "Thirteen Attributes of Mercy," which was to be intoned in order to win God's forgiveness and thereby avoid a second Golden Calf calamity. This penitential prayer (*selichah*; plural, *selichot*), which begins with the words *Adonai, Adonai, El rachum ve-chanun*, "God, O God, merciful and compassionate One," is explained in the Talmud (*Rosh Hashanah* 17b) as deriving from Exodus 34:6–7. There, an allusion is made to the grievous sin of the Israelites who forced Aaron to build a Golden Calf.

The "Thirteen Attributes of Mercy," which today is recited on Yom Kippur as well as when a calamity is thought to be imminent, actually ascribes *ten* attributes to God. The explanation of why the ten are traditionally referred to as thirteen is that the three names of God at the beginning of the prayer (*Adonai, Adonai, El*) are counted as individual attributes, increasing the number to thirteen.

The attributes are as follows:

- He is compassionate.
- He is gracious.
- He is slow to anger.
- He is abundant in kindness.
- He is abundant in truth.
- He is a preserver of kindness for thousands of generations.
- He forgives iniquity.
- He forgives willful sin.
- He forgives error.
- He cleanses sinners.

Thirteen Principles of Faith

Over the centuries, prophets and rabbis have set forth principles (or articles) of faith that they believe constitute the core of Judaism and which may therefore not be compromised by any Jew. The most famous is that of Spanish rabbi, scholar, and philosopher Moses Maimonides (1135–1204). Later theologians, such as Joseph Albo (*c.* 1380–*c.* 1435), using the creed of Maimonides as his basis, have set forth their own basic principles of faith.

In his commentary on the Mishnah portion known as *Cheilek*, which in the Jerusalem Talmud begins the tenth chapter of the tractate Sanhedrin and in the Babylonian Talmud begins the eleventh chapter of the tractate, Maimonides presents Thirteen Articles of Faith that every Jew must believe in order to be assured of a portion (*cheilek*) of the world to come. These principles later became the basis of the *Yigdal* hymn, composed in the year 1300 by Daniel ben Judah, which was incorporated into the *siddur* (prayerbook) and is part of the daily morning (*Shacharit*) liturgy.

The earliest printed edition of the declaration of Maimonides was issued in Naples, in 1492, by the Italian publisher Joshua Solomon Soncino.

The following are Maimonides' Thirteen Principles of Faith:

Principle No. 1

I believe with complete faith in the existence of the Creator, blessed be He, who is perfect in all aspects of existence; that He is the cause of all things in existence, and nothing can exist without Him.

Principle No. 2

I believe with complete faith that the Creator, blessed be He, is One and totally unique, unlike any other species or entity. He alone is our God who was, is, and ever will be.

Principle No. 3

I believe with complete faith that the Creator, blessed be He, is not a physical being and that physical attributes such as movement and rest do not apply to Him.

Principle No. 4

I believe with complete faith that the Creator, blessed be He, is the absolute first, and that everything else that exists is not first in relation to Him.

Principle No. 5

I believe with complete faith that the Creator, blessed be He—and may He be exalted—is the only One worthy of worship, and that his greatness should be made known to all.

Principle No. 6

I believe with complete faith that within the human race there are prophets, individuals of outstanding merit and great intellect, from whom prophecy emanates.

Principle No. 7

I believe with complete faith that the prophecy of Moses our teacher, peace be upon him, was true and that he was the father of all the prophets, both those who preceded him and those who followed him. All are subordinate to him in rank, for he was chosen by God.

Principle No. 8

I believe with complete faith that the entire Torah, which is found in our hand today, is from Heaven and is the same one that was given through Moses.

Principle No. 9

I believe with complete faith that this Torah will not be abrogated and that no other Torah will come from God. One may not add to it or delete any part of it. This applies to the Written Torah and the Oral Law.

Principle No. 10

I believe with complete faith that the Exalted One knows the actions of all men and does not neglect them.

Principle No. 11

I believe with complete faith that the Exalted One rewards those who observe the commandments of the Torah and punishes those who transgress them. The greatest reward is to enter the world to come, and the greatest punishment is extinction.

Principle No. 12

I believe with complete faith in the coming of the Messiah, and even though he may tarry, I look forward every day to his coming.

Principle No. 13

I believe with complete faith that there will be a resurrection of the dead.

See Faith.

Three Weeks

For three weeks during the summer months, traditional Jews observe a period of semi-mourning to commemorate the razing of Jerusalem and the destruction of the First and Second Temples. Strict observance demands that music not be played, weddings not be held, personal grooming be curbed (no haircuts), and new clothing not be worn.

The period extends from the seventeenth day of Tammuz (Shivah Asar B'Tammuz) through the ninth day of Av (Tishah B'Av). During the final nine days of this three-week period, mourning is most intense; and during the days prior to Tishah B'Av, many abstain from consuming meat and wine, both symbols of luxury and joy.

See Fast of the Seventeenth of Tammuz; Fast of the Ninth of Av.

Tikkun Chatzot

A Hebrew term literally meaning "midnight prayers of repair," consisting principally of selections from the Book of Psalms that recall the destruction of the Jerusalem Temples. The prayers—particularly Psalms 79 and 137—are an appeal to God to "repair" the schisms that plague the Jewish community. The Rabbis of the Talmud attributed the disastrous fate of the Temples to senseless hatred and antagonism among Jews. Some pious Jews interrupt their sleep at midnight to recite these prayers, which they hope will restore God's presence in their midst.

Tikkun Leil Shavuot

The *Zohar*, ascribed to the second-century mystic Rabbi Shimon bar Yocha'i, says that it behooves a man to study Torah on the night that Israel received the Torah, and in the sixteenth century Solomon Alkabetz of Safed introduced the custom of preparing to celebrate Shavuot by staying up all night to study the Torah.

The tradition of studying in order to perfect one's spiritual self for the holiday is still observed in synagogues in a variety of forms, but few people stay up for the entire night. One of the books used on this night, known as *Tikkun Leil Shavuot*, is an anthology of readings assembled from biblical, talmudic, and kabbalistic sources. The term is also used to identify the night of study itself.

Tikkun Olam

Also rendered as *tikkun ha-olam*. A Hebrew term literally meaning "repairing [perfecting] the world" a concept rooted in the biblical commandment "Justice, justice, shalt thou pursue" (Deuteronomy 16:20). The idea was expanded upon in the Talmud, particularly by Hillel the Elder of the first-century B.C.E. (Mishnah *Gittin* 4:2) .

Rabbi Gamaliel applied the concept of *tikkun olam* when ruling on a case in which a man who had issued a divorce decree (*get*) to his wife, then changed his mind before the messenger delivering the *get* reached her. The husband appeared before a court of three judges and asked that they declare his divorce null and void, which they did. The wife, who was never properly notified of the annulment, had remarried in the meantime. Rabbi Shimon declared the man's action inappropriate and condemned it *mipnei tikkun ha-olam*, because it was an obstacle to the concept of perfecting the world, which demands that justice be done (*Gittin* 32a).

The *tikkun olam* concept is expressed in the *Aleinu* prayer, which is recited at the conclusion of every religious service through the words *Le-takkein olam be-malkhut Shaddai*, "to perfect the world through the sovereignty of the Almighty." This concept, which has been attributed to the talmudic scholar Rav, became an important aspect of kabbalistic thinking of the sixteenth-century Ashkenazic mystic of Safed, Isaac ben Solomon Luria (1534–1572), also known as the "Ari." He taught that the act of "perfecting" or "repairing" the world and restoring it to its pristine state can come about by the individual perfecting his inner self as well as the world he inhabits.

See Kabbalah.

Tircha De-Tzibura

This Aramaic term meaning "public inconvenience" refers to a principle of Jewish law that is applied to many areas of ritual practice. This is the reason why on those Sabbaths and holidays when Torah portions are read from two different parts of the Pentateuch, two scrolls are removed from the ark. If only one were removed, the congregation would be inconvenienced by having to wait while the scroll is being rolled from one place to another, thus trying the patience of congregants.

Another example of *tircha de-tzibura* is described in *Sanhedrin* 7b, where Mar Zutra the Pious, elderly and unable to walk quickly, was carried shoulder-high through the throngs of people assembled for prayer so that the congregation would not have to wait for him to reach the podium on his own. The Talmud (*Berakhot* 31a) also describes a custom followed by Rabbi Akiba. When he prayed with the congregation, he used to cut his prayers short so as not to keep the congregation waiting for the service to continue.

Tishah B'Av

A Hebrew term literally meaning "the ninth of Av," the most important fast day in the Jewish calendar next to Yom Kippur.

See Fast of the Ninth of Av.

Tithes

The Bible demands that a portion of the wealth acquired by man be returned to God. In earliest biblical times, the amount to be returned to God from one's annual income— that is, from an increase in the value of one's agricultural products or livestock—was one-tenth. This was called a "tithe," from the Old English word meaning "one-tenth." The literal Hebrew equivalent, as used in the Bible, is *ma'aseir* (plural, *ma'aseirot*).

The earliest biblical reference to tithing is found in the Book of Genesis (14:18–20), where four kings, led by Chedorlaomer of Elam, made war against five kings, one of whom was Bera of Sodom, ruler of the region in which Abraham's nephew, Lot, lived. Chedorlaomer and his three fellow-kings defeated the armies of the five kings, and Lot was taken prisoner. When Abraham learned of this, he assembled a small army, pursued the victors, and subdued them decisively, taking much booty and gaining the release of Lot.

Not wanting to retain all of the booty for himself, Abraham turned over one-tenth of all that he had profited from his victory to Melchizedek, king of Salem, who was not involved in the conflict but who was a respected "priest of God Most High."

Three Types of Tithes

The Book of Deuteronomy spells out in detail three types of tithes that were to be proffered on a triennial basis. The "first tithe," known in Hebrew as *ma'aseir rishon*, was given to the Levites, who had not been allo-cated land to be cultivated or farmed when Canaan was divided among the various tribes. Their lives were to be dedicated to the service of God. Of this group of Levites, the *Kohanim* (Priests), direct descendants of Aaron the High Priest, were first allowed one-tenth of the *ma'aseir rishon* agricultural produce, which is called *terumah* or *terumat ma'aseir*, known in English as the "heave offering." The remaining portion was divided among the rest of the Levites.

The owner of the produce was permitted to give the tithe to any Levite he wished, but the Levite had to set aside one-tenth of his *ma'aseir rishon* for a Priest.

After *terumah* had been given to the Priests and the Levites had received their portion of the *ma'aseir rishon* tithe, a "second tithe," known in Hebrew as *ma'aseir sheini*, was set aside to be brought to Jerusalem by the farmer. There, he and his family consumed it or else redeemed it for money, which was then consecrated to the Temple (Deuteronomy 14:22ff.). The second tithe was given during the first, second, fourth, and fifth years of the seven-year *shemittah*, or sabbatical, cycle.

In the third and sixth year of the seven-year cycle, a "poor-man's tithe," called *ma'aseir ani* in Hebrew, was set aside from the remaining agricultural produce of the previous tithing year and was distributed to the needy.

Tohar Ha-Neshek

A Hebrew term literally meaning "purity of [military] arms," a concept postulated after the 1967 Six-Day War when Israel routed the Egyptian, Syrian, and Jordanian armies. As a result of this war, in which the Israel Defense Forces (IDF) demonstrated military superiority, it became evident to those concerned with maintaining a high level of Jewish morality that a new code of modern warfare needed implementation, lest the aggressive appetite of Jewish soldiers go unfettered.

The new type of warfare Israeli soldiers were called upon to conduct raised the moral consciousness of the military leadership and impelled them to establish new rules of military conduct. The Israeli soldier was taught that regardless of how the enemy conducts itself, the soldier must abide by the concept of *tohar ha-neshek*. Accordingly, a soldier is not to attack the enemy without sufficient provocation; a soldier is not to maim the enemy without good reason; a soldier is not to kill the enemy except in self-defense.

Tohorat Ha-Mishpachah

A Hebrew term literally meaning "family purity," a concept that expresses the importance of adherence to the laws of sexual abstinence during a woman's menstrual period.

The period of abstinence commences with the onset of the woman's menstrual period and extends for its duration plus an additional seven days, often referred to as "clean days" or "white days." At the end of this average ten- to twelve-day period, the woman immerses herself in a ritual bath (*mikveh*), after which sexual relations may be resumed.

Most Orthodox women today follow the laws of *tohorat ha-mishpachah*, as do a lesser number of Conservative women. Reconstructionists as well as Reform Jews find the laws incompatible with modern living.

See Mikveh; Niddah.

Tokheichah

In two portions of the Torah, the Children of Israel are warned that if they do not obey the commandments of God, they will be reprimanded and severely punished. These two portions of maledictions known collectively as the *Tokheichah*, meaning "rebuke," are found in the books of Leviticus (26:14–39) and Deuteronomy (28:15–68).

The *Tokheichah* spells out the punishments in stark detail, and when these passages were recited aloud as part of the Torah reading, the congregation became filled with fear. It therefore became customary to recite them quickly and in a subdued tone.

Congregants were reluctant to be called to the Torah for an *aliyah* when the *Tokheichah* passages were to be read, so it became customary to give these honors to the poor, who were not often called to the Torah because they could not afford to pledge the money usually expected of one given an *aliyah*. Since this was demeaning to the poor, at a later date it became the practice for the reader, the sexton, or the rabbi to take this *aliyah*. When the *Tokheichah* was read, a person called to the Torah was not called by name, as was the normal practice.

In one synagogue during the Middle Ages, it was reported that a Torah was allowed to lie open on the reading table for several hours before a congregant would step forward, accept the *aliyah,* and pronounce the Torah blessings.

In some synagogues, when the episode of the Golden Calf (Exodus 32) is read, it is the practice to do so in low tones. In Sephardic synagogues, when the two verses from the second paragraph of the *Shema* (Deuteronomy 11:13–21) describing the curses that will result from disobedience to God's commandments are read, the Torah reader likewise recites them in barely audible tones.

In recent times, the fear associated with being called to the Torah when unpleasant portions are read has diminished, and most people will not refuse such an *aliyah*.

Tombstones

The common Hebrew word for tombstone, *matzeivah*, is first used in the Book of Genesis (35:20). In later biblical times, the word *tziyun*, meaning sign, was used to designate a grave marker. In II Kings 23:17, King Josiah is said to have seen a *tziyun* over the grave of a prophet. This term is rarely used today.

In rabbinic literature, in addition to the more common appellation *matzeivah*, the tombstone placed on a grave is often called *nefesh* (literally, "soul"). According to a widespread ancient Jewish belief, the soul hovers over the spot where a person is buried. This belief, promoted by the foremost kabbalist of the sixteenth century, the Ari of Safed, suggests that the soul continually floats over the grave. To honor the soul and give it a specific area within which to dwell, the grave is marked by erecting a tombstone over it.

In the Jewish tradition, the custom of erecting a tombstone over a grave dates back to biblical times. It is first mentioned when Rachel, Jacob's wife, died on the road to Bethlehem and Jacob "set up a pillar upon her grave."

The Talmud (*Sanhedrin* 48a and Mishnah *Shekalim* 2:5) refers to the custom when it records the second-century scholar Nathan as saying that when money has been collected for the burial of a particular individual and there is money left over, that money should be used to erect a monument over the person's grave. In *Moed Katan* (5a), Shimon ben Pazzi proves that a gravesite should have a marker on it by citing a quotation from the Book of Ezekiel (39:15): ["And when they pass through . . . the land] and one sees a man's bone, then shall he set up a sign by it."

In Jewish tradition, the tombstone was erected for two reasons. First, it served as a sign of respect and remembrance for a departed relative; second, it served as a warning to Priests (*Kohanim*) that this was an area they must avoid. Priests, according to biblical law, were rendered impure if they had come in contact with or had come close to a corpse, unless the deceased was an immediate relative. In Temple times, this meant that the defiled Priest was unfit to carry out his priestly duties until he purified himself.

Inscriptions on Tombstones

At the outset, tombstones were engraved principally with the name of the deceased, the date of birth and death, and perhaps a brief phrase of adulation. As time went on, adornments were added; symbols representing the vocation of the deceased were common. The tombstone of a Priest (*Kohen*) might often have an engraving of outstretched hands, representing the *Priestly Benediction*. Tombstones of Levites might be engraved with a laver or cup, symbolizing a function of the Levites: to pour water on the hands of the *Kohen* before he offers the *Priestly Benediction*. Likewise, the tombstone of a *sofer* (scribe) might be adorned with an engraving of a quill.

Legal Restrictions

The placement on tombstones of photographs or engraved photographic likenesses is forbidden by almost all authorities. However, the Law Committee of the Conservative Rabbinical Assembly ruled that a "face relief is permissible as long as it is not disproportionate to the size of the total gravestone."

Expensive monuments are considered ostentatious, and rabbis urge that only very simple headstones be erected. To reinforce their view, they quote a verse from the Book of Proverbs (22:2): "The rich and the poor meet together in death. The Lord is Maker of them all." There is also a view that an ostentatious tombstone undermines belief in the coming of the Messiah and the resurrection of the dead.

Although erecting a tombstone is not mandatory under Jewish law, it has become common practice to do so as a way of honoring the dead. The time that should elapse between burial and the setting of the monument varies widely, extending from a point immediately after the seven-day *shivah* period to the end of the first year of mourning. Among Israelis today, monuments are usually erected after the thirty-day mourning period (*sheloshim*).

The most popular practice is to wait a full year before erecting a tombstone. First, this allows sufficient time for the earth on the grave to settle so that the heavy stone will not sink into the ground. Second, it allows for mourners to complete the full year of mourning for parents.

Superstitions

A theory favored by scholars is that the erection of tombstones grew in popularity in the Middle Ages because people believed that ghosts attached themselves to the deceased in the coffin and denied the corpse a peaceful rest. It became customary to fill the grave with earth and set a marker on it, before the ghost could enter the coffin and attach itself to the deceased.

Another superstition involved the reading of inscriptions on monuments. The tractate *Hora'yot* (13b) states that one who reads an inscription on a tombstone will have his ability to study affected.

Joshua Trachtenberg, in his *Jewish Magic and Superstition*, quotes a commentator as saying: "I have seen scrupulously pious men place a stone on a tombstone, and they explained that by doing so the ill-effect of reading the inscription on the stone is nullified."

See Stones.

Torah

A Hebrew word meaning "instruction," "teaching," or "law." Genesis 26:5 uses Torah to mean "instruction," as does Leviticus 6:2 and Deuteronomy 4:44. Isaiah 2:3 uses the word to mean "law," referring to the laws (commandments) of the first five books of the Bible. At times the word Torah is descriptive of the entire gamut of Jewish religious literature from earliest times to the present. A learned person is called a *ben Torah*, literally "a son of the Torah" (*Yevamot* 46a).

Torah, in its most colloquial usage, is the name assigned to the first five books of the Bible, consisting of Genesis, Exodus, Leviticus, Numbers, and Deuteronomy. The Greek word for Torah is *Pentateuch*, meaning "five books [of the Torah]," and a popular Hebrew designation is *Chumash*, derived from the word meaning "five."

The Talmud (*Shabbat* 31a) calls the Torah that was transmitted to Moses by God on Mount Sinai *Torah she-bikhtav*, "Written Law," in contrast to the Talmud, which is characterized as *Torah she-be'al peh*, "Oral Law." The latter designation was used to describe the Talmud because until the third century the Sages would not allow any part of the Jewish heritage to be committed to writing for fear that it would interfere with the superiority and sanctity of the Torah itself. When it was realized that the precious content of the Oral law would be forgotten and lost forever, the ban was lifted.

Torah Origin

Most traditional Jews accept literally the statements in the Book of Exodus (19) that the Torah was revealed to Moses on Mount Sinai. They also accept the belief of the Rabbis, stated in the Ethics of the Fathers (1:1), that "he [Moses] conveyed it [the Torah] to

Joshua; Joshua to the Elders; the Elders to the Prophets; and the Prophets to the Men of the Great Assembly."

Many scholars question whether the Torah that we have today is identical with the one transmitted to Moses by God. In fact, it is evident from the Midrash that there was more than one version of the Torah in existence as far back as the second century C.E.

Genesis Rabbah (9:5) records that "in the Torah of Rabbi Meir," a disciple of Rabbi Akiba, the phrase *ve-hinei tov me'od*, "and behold it was very good" (Genesis 1:31), referring to God's evaluation of His acts of Creation at the end of the sixth day, was to be read *ve-hinei tov mavet*, "and death was very good," because the spelling in Rabbi Meir's version was *mem, vav, tav* ("death"), not *mem, alef, dalet*, as the Bible spells it today.

Authenticity of the Text

Speculation has been rife over the ages as to the authoritativeness of the Torah text. Not until the ninth century, when Moses ben Asher and his son, living in Tiberias, Palestine, edited and produced a version of the text, did an official text of the Bible come into being. This became known as the Masoretic (from the word *mesorah*, meaning "tradition") Text. In the twelfth century, the illustrious Moses Maimonides used the Ben Asher text, from which he made his own handwritten copy, and thenceforth it became universally accepted.

School of Higher Criticism

Scholars such as the Dutch-born Baruch Spinoza (1632–1677) questioned the theology and factual accuracy of many of the stories and statements of the Torah. These scholars, who became known collectively as the School of Higher Criticism, pointed out many internal contradictions and inconsistencies in the text, such as those found in the story of Noah and the ark. In Genesis 6:19 Noah is told to bring two of each animal—one male and one female—into the ark, but in Genesis 7:2 he is told to bring seven pairs of each animal into the ark. As to the number of days the rain fell to create the flood, Genesis 7:17 says forty whereas Genesis 7:24 says one hundred fifty.

A frequently cited example of confused chronology relates to the Tower of Babel story. In Genesis 10:5 the text refers to different nations speaking separate languages, while in the next chapter (11:1), the Bible says, "Everyone on earth spoke the same language and the same words."

Another example of muddled chronology is found in connection with God's order to Moses to build a Tabernacle (*mishkan* in Hebrew). This is related in Exodus, chapter 25. The story relating to the erection of a Golden Calf appears later, in chapter 32. Logically, the instructions concerning the building of the Tabernacle should have appeared after, not before, the Golden Calf incident because the Tabernacle was built in order to atone for the idolatry of the Golden Calf. It was to be a physical structure that the people of Israel could identify with God, where they might experience his presence, thus eliminating the tendency to worship idols.

Higher Critics explain the reason for much of the redundancy and inconsistency of the Torah text by proposing that it consists of four separate documents (hence known as the Documentary Theory) written at different times and then laced together by an editor, thus creating the present Torah.

Nevertheless, despite all the critical theories about the origin of the Torah, its authenticity, and its many baffling inconsistencies relating to chronology, a 1993 report of the Guttman Institute for Applied Social Research in Israel found that fifty-four percent of Jewish adults in Israel believe in the literal Torah text and also believe in *Torah min ha-shama'yim*, "the Torah from Heaven;"—that is, the Torah as it was revealed by God to Moses on Mount Sinai.

The popular traditional view of today is consistent with the view expressed by the third-century Babylonian scholar Menashe bar Tachlifa, who, quoting his famous teacher, Rav, said (*Pesachim* 6b): "There is no such thing as [an incident having occurred] earlier or later in the Torah." To them, the fact that the chronology of the Torah is not precise was of little consequence.

The Torah Scroll

The Torah is the holiest artifact in Jewish life, so holy in fact that it is beyond contamination. No unclean person or object that comes into physical contact with it can render it unclean. Nevertheless, it is treated with the greatest reverence and respect.

Torah scrolls are housed in a closet called an *Aron* ("ark, chest") or *Aron Ha-Kodesh*, "holy ark," when not being used at a religious service. The ark is located on a raised platform (*bimah*) situated in front of every sanctuary.

The Torah scroll is handwritten by a scribe (*sofer*) on parchment: the skin of a kosher animal, usually a sheep, calf, or goat. Each Torah is made up of many sheets of parchment (or leather) generally ranging in height from 18 to 22 inches. The parchments are sewn together and then rolled up to form a scroll. The thread used, called *gidin*, is made from the dried veins of a kosher animal, stretched until they are of proper thickness.

To make the parchment suitable for the writing of a scroll, the hide of a kosher animal is cured and made smooth so it will accept the specially prepared ink. If the ink peels off the parchment, the scroll is invalid and must be repaired before it can be used at a public reading.

Traditionally, Torah scrolls and other religious articles are written with black ink. Black is a symbol of modesty; other colors, particularly gold, smack of ostentation. Gold ink used in a scroll would recall the gold that was used in fashioning the Golden Calf (Exodus 32), an act deplored in Jewish tradition.

Torah Ornaments

In Jewish tradition, the statement in Exodus 15:2, "This is my God and I will glorify Him," was taken to mean that special honor and respect is to be shown God by serving Him through the use of religious articles that are beautifully made. This applies especially to Torah ornaments—including breastplates, crowns, mantles, pointers, and the like—all of which are considered sacred because they come into direct contact with the holy scroll.

The Rabbis (*Shulchan Arukh*, Yoreh Dei'ah 282:11, 12; *Mishneh Torah*, Hilkhot Sefer Torah 10:4) ruled that a Torah ornament may not be sold unless the funds realized from their sale are to be used for the purchase of a new Torah scroll or for other books of the Bible. The legal principle at work here is *ma'alin ba-kodesh ve-lo moridin*, that is, it is permissible to elevate the status of a sacred object but not reduce it.

The Breastplate

This shieldlike Torah ornament represents the gold breastplate (*choshen* or *tass*) worn by the High Priest in biblical and Temple times (Exodus 28:15). Usually made of silver and measuring approximately eight by ten inches, a breastplate may be decorated in a variety of ways. Some have four rows of precious or semiprecious stones, as did the High Priest's breastplate, on which was engraved the name of each of the twelve sons of Jacob. Others carry simple engravings or applied ornaments. A chain is attached to the breastplate so that it can be draped over the two finials extending from the top of the scroll.

A more elaborate breastplate sometimes has soldered to it a small silver box containing silver plates on which the names of holidays and special Sabbaths are engraved. The plate bearing the name of the holiday or Sabbath being celebrated is placed in front of the others to indicate to the cantor or Torah reader that this particular Torah scroll has been prepared for the day's reading and is therefore to be removed from the ark first.

Crowns

Decorative crowns that fit over each of the two finials (wooden poles) of the Torah rollers to which the parchment scroll is attached are known in Hebrew as *rimmonim* (singular, *rimmon*), literally meaning "pomegranates," an illusion to the ornament's customary shape. The finials are also referred to as *rimmonim*. Synonyms for *rimmonim* are *atzei cha'yim* (singular, *eitz cha'yim*) and *kitrei Torah* (singular, *keter Torah*). A single large crown that fits over both finials is also referred to as a *keter Torah*.

Since the Torah is the holiest object in Jewish life, it is natural to "crown" it with the symbol of kingship. Hai, a tenth-century scholar and community leader was the first to make reference to the use of a crown as a Torah ornament.

Torah crowns are usually decorated with small bells. These are reminiscent of the robe (*ephod*) worn by the High Priest, which was adorned with golden bells (Exodus 28:31–33). Some modern authorities are of the opinion that the bells were introduced by Jewish communities in the East, where it was believed evil spirits are warded off by the noise of bells. Other scholars are of the opinion that bells were attached to Torah ornaments so that when one hears them, the person will know that the Torah is being carried in a procession and that it is appropriate to assume a standing position.

The prominent thirteenth-century Spanish authority Rabbi Solomon ibn Adret of Barcelona writes in one of his responsa that on Simchat Torah in some Spanish communities it was customary to place the Torah crowns on the heads of children and on the heads of those called up to the Torah to recite Torah blessings.

The Mantle

The Talmud (*Shabbat* 133b) states that it is obligatory to write a beautiful scroll and to wrap the finished scroll in beautiful silk. Great care was taken to conform to the statement in Scripture "This is my God and I will glorify Him" (Exodus 15:2), which was explained by the Rabbis to mean that God is glorified and honored by being served with handsome religious articles made with love and care. The tractate *Sanhedrin* (100a) relates that Levi ben Samuel and Rabbi Huna ben Chiya were repairing the mantles of scrolls belonging to Rabbi Judah's academy.

The function of the Torah mantle, which may be made out of a variety of colorful materials, is both to protect the scroll and to beautify it. White is used for holidays, particularly the High Holidays, and blue and maroon are the more common colors used year-round.

Mantles are embroidered by hand or by machine with a variety of symbols and biblical phrases. Among the popular decorative symbols used are the Ten Commandments, lions, crowns, Stars of David, menorahs, flowers, and wreaths. The name of the individual who donated the Torah and/or the mantle to the synagogue is frequently embroidered on the bottom of the mantle or on its lining.

Since it is not considered proper to touch the Torah parchment with bare hands (*Megillah* 32a), some persons receiving an *aliyah* (Torah honor) will touch it with the edge of the Torah mantle and then kiss the mantle before reciting the first and last Torah blessings.

Eastern Sephardim—those from Iraq, Iran, Syria, Egypt, Yemen, and other countries in the area—do not use a Torah mantle. Instead, they lay a long piece of silk fabric along the entire underside of the Torah parchment. This prevents the scratching or erasure of the Torah's letters, which would render the Torah invalid (*pasul*). The entire scroll is then set into a *tek* (or *tik*), a cylindrical metal or wooden box lined with velvet, and the Torah is read in an upright position. The word *tik*, derived from the Greek for "casing," is used in the *Code of Jewish Law* (*Shulchan Arukh*, Orach Cha'yim 154:3). Its diminutive form, *tekel*, is used by Ethiopian Jews.

Non-Eastern Sephardic congregations—including those of Spain, Portugal, and the North African countries—line the underside of their Torah scrolls with silk but do not house them in cylindrical containers. Rather, they cover the scrolls with cloth mantles, as do Ashkenazim.

The Pointer

In the Jewish tradition, the *yad*, meaning "hand," represents God's power and protective spirit, as expressed by the prophet Ezekiel (37:1) In a call to prophesy, Ezekiel says, "The hand of the Lord came upon me."

The Torah pointer, which is also called a *yad*, is shaped like a hand with the index finger extended. Probably first introduced in Germany in the sixteenth century, it is generally made of wood, solid silver, or silver tubing and extends approximately six to eight inches. At the end of the unit is a sculpted right hand with an outstretched index finger.

Although in Jewish law a Torah scroll is not subject to impurity and does not lose its sacredness even if an impure person touches it, it became customary not to touch a scroll with bare hands so as to accord it the utmost respect. As the Torah reader reads from the scroll, he uses the *yad* to point to each word so that the recipient of the *aliyah* can follow the reading closely. The Torah reader always holds the Torah pointer in his right hand and stands to the left of the person being honored with the *aliyah*, making it easier for the honoree to follow the words of the Torah as they are pointed to. In Jewish tradition, the right hand and right side are favored over the left.

The above notwithstanding, left-handed Torah pointers are sometimes used. In the Jewish Cultural Museum in the Caribbean island of Curaçao's Mikvé Israel-Emanuel Synagogue, a left-handed pointer can be seen on display.

Among Arabic-speaking Jews, especially those of North Africa, the *yad*, with five fingers extended, became a popular amulet, often worn on a necklace. In Judeo-Arabic, *yad* is called *chamsa*, meaning "five."

The Gartl

Fashioned from a length of material two to three inches wide, the *gartl* ("girdle" in Yiddish) is used to secure a rolled-up Torah scroll. Sometimes it is made from the swaddling clothes worn by a baby at his circumcision (*brit*). The clothes are cut into strips, sewn together, and then embroidered or painted with the child's name, date of birth, and expressions of good luck. The binder made from them is saved and used on the Torah that is read on the day of the boy's bar mitzvah.

The practice of wrapping (swaddling) newborn babies with narrow bands of cloth was popular in the Middle Ages. Among the Jews of Germany, the mother of a newborn boy would come to the synagogue on the fourth Sabbath after the birth of her son and present a *gartl* (*wimpel* in German) fashioned from the swaddling clothes in which her son was wrapped at his *brit*. On this same fourth Sabbath, the father received an *aliyah* and bestowed a secular name upon his son, the Hebrew name having already been announced at the *brit*.

Gartls for which there was no immediate need were stored in the synagogue ark. They were tied around Torah scrolls that were awaiting correction by a scribe and were therefore not to be used.

In some Sephardic congregations, the *gartl* that has been removed from the Torah that was to be read on Sabbath is rolled up and passed among the women of the congregation. As each woman receives it, she kisses it, presses it to her eyes, and meditates for a few moments. It is hoped that the *gartl* and the holiness with which it is imbued by virtue of its having touched the Torah will assist in bringing a satisfying response to the personal prayers being uttered.

In some communities the Torah *gartl* is called *mappah*.

See Aliyah to the Torah.

Torah Reading

The first recorded law pertaining to the time and manner in which the Torah is to be read publicly is found in Deuteronomy 31:10–12. After Moses wrote down the words of the Torah, he instructed the Priests as follows:

[At the end of] every seventh year [the *shemittah* year] at the Feast of Booths [Sukkot]...you shall read this Torah aloud in the presence of all Israel...that they may hear and so learn to respect the Lord your God and to observe faithfully every word of this Torah. [The Torah was actually read in the beginning of the eighth year, after seven years had passed. See Rashi on Deuteronomy 31:10.]

Neither the Torah itself nor the later Rabbis explain why the Torah was to be read publicly only once every seven years, but its concurrence with the sabbatical year offers an explanation. In the sabbatical year, the land was to be left fallow, and farmers therefore had little work to do. Thus, greater numbers of Jews were able to make the annual pilgrimage to the central sanctuary in Jerusalem without the pressure of having to return home to tend to their farms. This allowed ample time to listen to the reading of the Torah.

Ezra's Innovations

When, in the fifth century B.C.E., Ezra introduced the concept of public Torah readings, each person who was called to the Torah read his own portion aloud, but only the first and last reader recited a blessing. The Mishnah (*Megillah* 21a), which was codified in the third century C.E., notes that the first Torah blessing was recited by the recipient of the first Torah honor (*aliyah*) and the concluding blessing was recited by the recipient of the last *aliyah*.

By the end of the third century C.E., this practice had changed somewhat. The Talmud says, "Nowadays all [who are called to read from the Torah] recite a blessing before and after they read their portions (ibid. 21b)." This was ordained by the Rabbis of the Talmud so that the public should not be misled. The Rabbis were concerned that those who come to the synagogue after the Torah reading had already begun might notice that some persons (those receiving the second, third, and later *aliyot*) were reading from the Torah without first having pronounced a blessing. The latecomers might be left with the impression that it is not necessary to recite a blessing before one reads from the Torah. Likewise, congregants who leave the synagogue before the Torah reading had ended, without having heard anyone recite the second (concluding) blessing, might be misled into thinking that it is not necessary to recite a blessing after the Torah reading has been completed.

It would appear that the custom of having all persons who are called to the Torah recite blessings before and after the reading developed after the ninth century. The reason is not clear, but it may have been introduced to afford members of the congregation an additional opportunity to respond "Amen" to important blessings.

Before reciting the first and last blessings over the Torah, honorees once kissed the scroll with their lips, or they touched it with the tips of their fingers and then kissed their fingers. Since the Talmud considered it disrespectful to touch a holy object in this manner, it became customary to touch the Torah parchment with the corner of one's *tallit* (prayer-shawl), or sometimes with a prayerbook, and then to kiss these religious objects.

Ezra chose the Sabbath and holidays—periods of rest—as days on which the Torah should be read to the public. The people had much free time and could listen with clear minds. Monday and Thursdays were chosen because those were the days when Jews came to Jerusalem from outlying farm areas to market their produce. Ezra took advantage of these opportunities to transmit the Torah messages to a larger group of people.

A second theory for Ezra's decision that a public reading of the Torah take place on Monday and Thursday as well as on Sabbaths is that according to Exodus 15:22 the Israelites in the desert were unable to find water for three days. They complained to Moses, and Moses appealed to God. God promised them relief if they would observe His commandments. Thus, as a reminder, no more than three days should elapse without the Torah being read.

A third theory, put forth by Rabbi Israel Meir Ha-Kohen (1838–1933), author of the *Mishnah Berurah*, suggests Mondays and Thursdays are especially propitious days for supplication (*y'mei ratzon*). According to one tradition (*Mishnah Berurah*, Orach Cha'yim 134:1), it was on Thursday that Moses went up to Mount Sinai to receive the Ten Commandments, and on Monday that he returned with them. Although neither the Talmud nor the codes discuss this question directly, it is likely that the Torah was not read at night owing to poor lighting conditions. Jewish law mandates that he who reads the Torah must *see* each word as he reads it, otherwise the reading is invalid. When candles were the only source of light, the Torah was not read at night on the Sabbath or holidays because it would have been necessary to move the candles around, which would be a violation of Jewish law.

The Reading Cycles

Although in Jewish tradition the entire Bible is considered the word of God, the first five books, the Pentateuch, is considered more sacred than the Prophets and the Holy Writings (*Megillah* 21b and Rashi on *Megillah* 23a). For this reason, the Pentateuch is read publicly in its entirety in the course of one synagogue year, while only selected portions of the Prophets and Holy Writings (Hagiographa) are read.

The earliest reference to a Torah reading cycle is found in the Talmud (*Megillah* 29b). In Palestine of the early centuries of the Common Era, it was customary to follow a triennial cycle. The entire Torah was divided into 154 or 155 weekly portions, depending on the calendar year, and was read in sequence over a three-year period, one-third each year. This is known as a triennial cycle.

At about the same time, among the Jews of Babylonia, a different tradition emerged. The Pentateuch was divided into fifty-four portions, all of which were read in the course of one year. This annual reading cycle, not the triennial reading cycle, became the standard for world Jewry. After the ninth century, the annual cycle was adopted for the most part in Palestine as well.

Today, some Conservative and Reform congregations follow the triennial cycle. However, all Orthodox and most Conservative congregations employ the annual cycle.

The weekly portion that is read from the Torah on Sabbath is known by two names: *sidrah* and *parashah*. The words *sidrah* (plural, *sidrot*) and *parashah* (plural, *parashot* or *parashiyot*) are used interchangeably.

The Torah Reader

Originally, in Temple times and in early talmudic times, each person called to the Torah read his own portion. Later, when the majority of people were not proficient in reading the unvocalized Torah text, one capable person read the Torah portions for all, so as not to embarrass the less learned Jews. This was a procedure later followed even for those who were knowledgeable enough to read their own portion.

The Torah reader is called a *ba'al korei* or *ba'al keriah* in Hebrew, both terms meaning "master of the reading." Since the text of the Torah scroll is not vocalized, the reader must be adept at reading the words correctly. When reading the Torah before the congregation, the person must use the correct melody (*trop*), which requires a great deal of preparation.

In the *Shulchan Arukh* (Orach Cha'yim 142:1), both Joseph Caro and Moses Isserles express the opinion that if an experienced *ba'al korei* is not present to read the Torah, an inexperienced member of the congregation may be called upon to perform the task, despite the fact that many errors will be made. The synagogue officials (*gabba'im*) who stand at his side are expected to guide the reading and correct any errors that are made.

Women as Readers

While the law (*Shulchan Arukh*, Yoreh Dei'ah 281:3) explicitly states that a woman may not *write* a Torah scroll for public use, it is quite clear that she may *read* the Torah at a public service. Nevertheless, many authorities, particularly Maimonides (*Mishneh Torah*, Hilkhot Tefillah 12:17), found such permissiveness objectionable and ruled that a woman should not read the Torah publicly *mipnei kevod tzibur*, that is, because it would be offensive to the congregation, which is not accustomed to having women officiate.

Another argument advanced for denying women the privilege of reading the Torah publicly is that menstruants are sometimes in a state of ritual impurity. However, the Talmud is quite explicit in stating that "the words of the Torah are not subject to ritual impurity." No one can render a Torah impure by touching it.

Positioning the Torah

In Sephardic congregations it is traditional to read from the Torah while the scroll stands vertically on the reading table. This practice may have evolved out of a practical need, since it is Sephardic custom to encase each Torah scroll in a hinged wooden or metal container known as a *tik*. Handling the Torah in its heavy casing is much easier when the scroll stands upright. When opened, the Torah portion to be read is exposed. The Torah parchment may be rolled from section to section by manipulating two finials (*atzei cha'yim*) that protrude from the top of the case. (Finials on Sephardic scrolls in a *tik* do not protrude on the bottom.)

The practice of standing scrolls upright may also have come about because in earlier centuries congregants did not have individual copies of the Pentateuch, and the only way to follow the Torah reading was to stand close to the reader and follow the reading from the upright scroll.

By far the more common procedure today, which is followed by all Ashkenazic congregations, is to lay the Torah flat on the reading table.

The Gabba'im

The Talmud (*Soferim* 14:14) notes that it would be demeaning for the Torah to rest on the reading table without being flanked by an honor guard. It was therefore ruled that two *gabba'im* (singular, *gabbai*) should stand on either side of the reading table while the Torah is being read. The Torah reader and these officials are said to represent the three patriarchs—Abraham, Isaac, and Jacob—whose names are often invoked during prayer.

The Jerusalem Talmud (*Megillah* 4:11) explains that just as God, Moses, and the congregation of Israel were present at Sinai when the Torah was transmitted to Moses, so at every reading must a trio be present when the Torah is read to the public. Hence, the Torah reader, who represents Moses (the transmitter), is flanked by two *gabba'im*, who represent God and Israel.

Since it is essential that a Torah reader chant the text of a Torah scroll in accordance with the established cantillation, in some Sephardic congregations, particularly among the Yemenites, a *gabbai* who stands next to the *ba'al korei* indicates through hand movements when the reader's voice should rise or be lowered, when a note should be extended, and when it should be curtailed. Rashi (eleventh century) mentions this practice in his commentary on the Talmud. He recalls seeing Jews from Palestine who had settled in France motion with the right hand to indicate the pattern of the melody when the Torah was being read (*Berakhot* 62a).

The Aliyot

Before a selection from the Torah is read aloud by the *ba'al korei*, a congregant is called up to the reading table to pronounce the Torah blessings before and after the portion is read. The "calling up" is known as *aliyah* in Hebrew (plural, *aliyot*).

While it is well-established in Jewish law that a Torah scroll is so sacred that it is not subject to impurity no matter who touches it (*Berakhot* 22a), to ensure that an attitude of respect toward sacred ritual objects would always prevail and that their sanctity would not be compromised, it became widespread custom to refrain from touching the Torah script with the bare hand. It became traditional that when one is called to the Torah to recite the blessings, the Torah reader points with a Torah pointer, called a *yad* ("hand"), to the portion being read. Before pronouncing the blessing, the person who has received the *aliyah* touches the Torah script with the fringes of the *tallit* or with a prayerbook or with the Torah binder (*gartl*) and then kisses the object that touched the script.

Although the precise origin of the fringe-touching custom is unknown, it is generally assumed to be derived from the fact that the numerical value of the word *tzitzit*, 600, when added to the number of knots and strings in each fringe (13), adds up to 613, the number of commandments in the Torah.

Torah Etiquette

Jewish law and custom demand that the Torah scroll be approached and handled with the utmost respect and reverence. When a scroll is removed from the ark for a public reading and is transferred to the prayer leader, and then by the leader to the individual who is to lead the procession, it is handed from one to another so as to be received in the right arm. The practice is based on the comment of the *Zohar* on Deuteronomy 33:2, "... from His [God's] right hand issued a fiery law for them," which signified that the Torah (the Law) was given by God to Moses in his right hand, thus establishing the right side and right hand as symbolic of God's majesty and glory. For this reason, whenever the Torah is carried in procession around the synagogue before the Torah reading begins, it is carried in the right arm. The procession begins by walking down the right aisle and then circling the synagogue once. The Torah is then taken to the reading table. When the scroll is returned to the ark after the Torah has been read, the reverse order is followed.

It is customary in many congregations for a Torah scroll to be closed while the Torah blessings are recited. The Talmud (*Megillah* 32a and *Soferim* 13:8) as well as the *Mishneh*

Torah of Maimonides (Hilkhot Tefillah 12:5) describe two procedures in this regard.

According to the second-century Palestinian scholar Rabbi Meir, a person called up to the Torah should open the scroll, look at the words where the reading is to begin, close the scroll, recite the first Torah blessing, and then unroll the scroll for the reading to begin. After the portion is read, the scroll is once again rolled closed, and the honoree recites the final blessing. Rabbi Meir believed that the scroll should *not* be left open while the Torah blessings are recited because if the eyes of the honoree should be cast downward, toward the open scroll, people might assume that the blessings he is reciting are being read from the Torah itself, when in fact the blessings are not written in the Torah.

Rabbi Judah did *not* believe that the Torah scroll has to be rolled closed when the blessings are recited. He was convinced that no one would ever think that the Torah blessings are written in the Torah scroll.

Although Rabbi Judah's procedure was the more accepted one, both practices have been followed by different communities over the centuries. Ashkenazic Jews generally follow the protocol outlined by Rabbi Meir, although some cover the Torah scroll either with its mantle or a special Torah cover called a *mappah* when the Torah blessings are recited. The *mappah* is made out of the same material as a Torah mantle or ark curtain and may be decorated in a similar manner. Sephardic Jews generally do not roll the Torah scroll closed when the blessings are recited, nor do they cover it.

When reciting Torah blessings, some individuals turn their heads to one side or close their eyes. Some do this in order to intensify concentration, while others do so to indicate to those watching that they are not reading the Torah blessings from the Torah itself. Nonetheless, this practice is not approved of by many authorities because it gives the impression that one is flaunting his piety. It falls into the same category as excessive bowing and genuflection during prayer, a practice condemned in the *Code of Jewish Law* (*Shulchan Arukh*, Orach Cha'yim 113:1, 3).

When a special *Mi Shebeirakh* prayer is recited for a person after receiving an *aliyah*, the scroll is covered with the Torah mantle or smaller covering, the *mappah*. The Chafetz Chaim (Israel Meir Kagan 1835–1933) explained that one is showing proper respect for the Torah by not allowing the scroll to remain uncovered and unattended while not in actual use. (See *Shulchan Arukh*, Orach Cha'yim 139:5, and *Mishnah Berurah*, note 20 on this section, for the comment of the Chafetz Chaim.)

See Aliyah to the Torah.

Tosafot

A Hebrew word literally meaning "additions." While the commentary of Rashi, the eleventh-century French scholar, appears on the gutter (spine) side of each page of the Babylonian Talmud, a commentary called Tosafot appears on the other side. It contains explanatory notes relating to textual interpretations that sometimes conflict with those of Rashi.

The scholars whose views are expressed in this commentary—referred to as *Ba'alei* ("Masters") *Ha-Tosafot*—are French and German rabbis who lived from the twelfth to the fourteenth centuries. Among the earliest and most prominent of these Tosafists, as they are called in English, are Rashi's sons-in-law and grandsons. One daughter, Miriam, was the wife of Tosafist Rabbi Judah ben Nathan. Another daughter, Yocheved, married Rabbi Meir ben Samuel of Ramerupt, who was one

of the earliest Tosafists in the north of France and the father of four sons who became great scholars. Of these four, two were also prominent Tosafists: Rabbi Samuel ben Meir, better known as the Rashbam, and Rabbi Jacob ben Meir Tam, widely known as Rabbenu Tam, who was acclaimed as the greatest scholar of his day.

The most prominent Tosafist after Rabbenu Tam was his pupil and relative Isaac ben Samuel Ha-Zakein of Dampierre. Isaac was succeeded by a pupil of his by the name of Samson ben Abraham of Sens (died about 1235). He, along with other thirteenth-century French Tosafists, is credited with having collected and edited the commentaries of all of the other Tosafists, many of whom were situated in far-flung communities. The writings of the Tosafists appear in only thirty-eight of the sixty-three tractates of the Babylonian Talmud.

Of the great number of Tosafists, only forty-four are known by name.

Tosefta

An Aramaic term literally meaning "additions, supplements, extensions," referring to a collection of rabbinic teachings similar to those in the Mishnah but which were not included in the final edition of the Mishnah, which was edited by Judah the Prince. The teachings in the Tosefta are called *baraitot* (singular, *baraita*), an Aramaic word meaning "outside."

Most authorities consider the actual compiler or editor of the Tosefta to be Chiya bar Abba, the third-century Babylonian-born scholar who moved to Palestine and studied under Judah the Prince in his academy at Sepphoris. Among the prominent scholars of the Tosefta are Polemo, Issi ben Judah, Eleazar ben Yossi, Yishmael ben Yossi, Judah ben Lakish, Chiya, Acha, and Abba (Arikha).

Like the Mishnah, the Tosefta is divided into six orders (*sedarim*) and the same names are used: *Zera'im*, *Mo'ed*, *Nashim*, *Nezikin*, *Kodoshim*, and *Tohorot*. However, whereas the six orders of the Mishnah are subdivided into sixty-three tractates, the Tosefta, does not include *Avot* (Ethics of the Fathers), *Kinnim*, *Middot*, and *Tamid*, all of which are part of the order *Nezikin*.

The best known edition of the Tosefta was published by M. S. Zuckermandl in 1880 based on the Erfurt manuscript. A new critical edition with commentary was prepared in 1955 by Professor Saul Lieberman of the Jewish Theological Seminary of America.

Transmigration of Souls

See Gilgul.

Tribes of Israel

Jacob, son of Isaac and grandson of Abraham, was the progenitor of the tribes of Israel. It was from his twelve sons—Reuben, Shimon, Levi, Judah, Issachar, Zebulun, Dan, Naphtali, Gad, Asher, Joseph, and Benjamin—that the twelve tribes of Israel emerged. Each of these, except for Levi and Joseph, had a tribe named for them and were awarded specific portions of the Promised Land. The tribe of Levi was excluded because it was to become a special group dedicated to the service of God without ownership of any land. Joseph's portion was divided between his two sons, Ephraim and Manasseh, which became independent tribes.

Under the leadership of Joshua, who divided the territory of Canaan among the tribes, two and one-half tribes—Reuben, Gad, and half of Manasseh—were granted territory in Transjordan. All the others settled in what later became known as Palestine.

After the death of King Solomon, the country was divided, with Judah, Shimon (and most of Benjamin) constituting the southern kingdom and the other tribes constituting the northern kingdom. In 732 and 721 B.C.E., when Assyria invaded the country, the ten northern tribes were driven into exile. The whereabouts of the ten lost tribes has never been fully ascertained.

See Ten Lost Tribes.

Truth

The Hebrew word for truth, *emet*, is spelled *alef, mem, tav*—the first, middle, and last letters of the Hebrew alphabet. To the Rabbis of the Talmud, who interpreted the words of the Bible, this was significant, for they saw in this combination of letters the alpha and omega of Judaism. Judaism stands or falls on *emet*—truth.

Jeremiah was one of the early prophets to recognize the validity of this concept and very clearly and pointedly associates the very essence of God with truth. "The Lord God is Truth" (10:10) is the way the prophet expressed it. Rabbi Chaninah, a third-century scholar, echoed Jeremiah's words when he said, "The seal of God is Truth" (*Shabbat* 55a and *Yoma* 69b). The same thought was emphasized a century earlier by the respected Shimon ben Gamaliel, who said, "The world continues to exist because of three things: justice, truth, and peace" *Avot* (1:18). The Palestinian Talmud (*Ta'anit* 4:2, 68a) expands upon the concept and emphasizes that the three are linked: "When justice is done, truth is achieved and peace prevails."

The twelfth-century Spanish scholar Maimonides, in his *Mishneh Torah* (Hilkhot Sanhedrin 23:9), was even more direct in linking truth with justice and peace. "A judge who renders true judgments may be said to have set the world in order."

The expressions of the above noted rabbis reminds one of the third of the Ten Commandments, "You shall not bear false witness against your neighbor," found in Exodus 20:13. Several chapters later (Exodus 23:7–8), the Bible makes it clear that to bear false witness means accepting a bribe by a judge, oppressing a stranger, and the like. The opposite of truth is *sheker*, falsehood, lying.

A prayer taken verbatim from the *Zohar* and attributed to the kabbalist Shimon bar Yocha'i makes the following statement about the place of truth in Jewish life: "I do not put my trust upon any angel but upon the God of heaven, who is the God of truth, whose Torah is truth, whose prophets are prophets of truth, and who abounds in deeds of goodness and truth . . ." Recited on Sabbaths and holidays before the Torah is removed from the ark for public reading, this prayer begins with the Aramaic words *Brikh Sh'meih* ("Blessed is the Name"), from which its title derives.

White Lies

It is quite apparent that the Rabbis of old considered any deviation from the truth and any embroidery of the truth to be a serious breach of proper conduct. They spoke of such behavior as an "opening wedge to sin" (*Sanhedrin* 29a), and it is for this reason that they tried to cover up the activity of the third patriarch, Jacob. The story, related in chapter 27 of the Book of Genesis, describes Jacob's father, Isaac, as being old, with faulty vision. He calls his firstborn son, Esau, who was a hunter, to go out and fetch some game so that he might prepare a sumptuous meal for his father. As a reward, Esau would receive a blessing.

Rebecca, the mother of Jacob and Esau, favored Jacob, her younger son. When she overhears the promise her husband, Isaac, makes to Esau, she plots for the blessing to be given to Jacob, not to Esau. She herself prepares a delectable dish for Isaac and then, dressing Jacob in a hairy coat to simulate Esau's hairy body, she has Jacob take the dish to Isaac.

Being nearly blind, Isaac is unable to recognize that Jacob is standing before him. He touches his son and feels a hairy body, but is doubtful about the voice.

Isaac then asks, "Which of my sons are you?" And Jacob answers, "I am Esau, your firstborn son, I have done as you requested."

This was a blatant lie, but not wanting history to see one of its patriarchs portrayed as having lied, the Rabbis put a new spin on the response of Jacob, thus attempting to make the full lie appear to be a half-lie.

Thus we find commentators such at the eleventh-century French rabbi Rashi explaining that what Jacob had in mind when he answered his father was, "It is I who am bringing you the food you requested, although Esau is your firstborn son." The twelfth-century Spanish Bible commentator Abraham ibn Ezra explains away Jacob's lie by suggesting that while saying aloud, "I am Esau, your firstborn son," the thought in Jacob's mind was, "I am [me]. Esau [is] your firstborn son."

Room for Flexibility

Although the concept of truth is central to Jewish thinking and was always at the core of Jewish values, the Rabbis felt it absolutely essential that some room be left for flexibility. The second-century Palestinian talmudic scholar Ishmael ben Elishah, in teaching his students the importance of creating and maintaining family harmony (*shelom ba'yit*), commented: "How great is the establishment of peace, for even God almighty deviated from the truth in order to preserve it" (*Yevamot* 65b).

Rabbi Ishmael had in mind an incident in

the life of the first patriarch and his wife Sarah (Genesis 18:1–15). Abraham was one hundred years old and Sarah was ninety, much too old to conceive and give birth to a child. Abraham offers hospitality to three angels in the guise of men, who assure Abraham that at this time, next year, his wife will give birth to a son.

Overhearing the conversation, Sarah laughs to herself, saying, "After I have been worn out, is there to be [sexual] pleasure for me? And *my husband* is old!" God then appears and says to Abraham, "Why did Sarah laugh and say, 'Shall I really give birth now that *I* am old?'"

Sarah's actual words were, "My *husband* is old," but here God quotes her as having said, "...now that I [Sarah] am old." Quite clearly, God was making an untrue statement. But for the sake of peace between husband and wife, Scripture [that is, God] changed Sarah's original characterization of her husband as old so that it would appear as if she was speaking about herself. This led the disciples of Rabbi Ishmael to teach that peace is so precious a commodity that for its sake even God deviated from the truth (*Bava Metzia* 87a).

Truth and Compassion

In Jewish tradition, truth must be accompanied by compassion. Thus, for example, while the Talmud (*Semachot* 3:5 and *Shabbat* 153a) and the *Code of Jewish Law* (*Shulchan Arukh*, Yoreh Dei'ah 344:1) condemn eulogies that are blatantly untrue or significantly distort the truth, it does not condemn eulogies that embellish slightly on the truth.

The disciples of Shammai and Hillel differed over how a bride is to be greeted and serenaded at her wedding. The students of Shammai said: "You describe her as she is." She is not to be called beautiful if she is ugly. The School of Hillel maintained: "You praise her and speak of her as graceful and beautiful," even if that is false (*Kallah Rabbati* 10:1).

In the same spirit, if a critically sick person inquires as to the health of a family member who had died, one is justified in withholding the truth, even outright lying, so as not to aggravate the physical health of the patient.

Tu B'Av

A Hebrew term literally meaning, "the fifteenth of [the Hebrew month] Av," the name of a very minor Jewish holiday that is no longer observed but was celebrated as a joyous day in talmudic times. The Talmud (Mishnah *Ta'anit* 4:8) describes the holiday in this way: Rabban Shimon ben Gamaliel said, "There were no happier days for Israel than the fifteenth of Av and the Day of Atonement, for on those days the young women in Jerusalem would come out dressed in borrowed white garments so that no one [who could not afford fancy clothes] would be embarrassed by not having such clothing...And the daughters of Jerusalem went forth to dance in the vineyards. And what did they say? 'Young man, lift up your eyes and see what you should choose for yourself. Set your sights not on beauty, but on family...'"

Some scholars believe that Tu B'Av represented an effort to cancel the biblical prohibition of a man from one tribe marrying a woman from a different tribe, lest any property she might receive as inheritance from her father's estate pass over to her husband's tribe. Tu B'Av has also been associated with the defeat of Bar Kochba by the Romans when he led an aborted revolt in 135 C.E. As punishment, the Romans prohibited Jews from burying their dead. After three years, the ban was lifted on the fifteenth of Av, when a new Roman emperor assumed power. Thus, the day was marked as a happy occasion.

Tu Bi-Shevat

A Hebrew term literally meaning "the fourteenth of [the Hebrew month] Shevat," the name of a minor Jewish holiday that ushers in the spring season.

See Chamishah Asar Bi-Shevat.

Tza'ar Ba'alei Cha'yim

A Hebrew term literally meaning "the pain caused to living creatures," used in connection with the basic biblical concept of prevention of cruelty to animals, which is embodied in several specific laws. These include giving animals a day of rest along with humans (Exodus 20:10); helping an animal with a heavy burden (Exodus 23:5); not muzzling an ox while it works in the field, thus denying him food (Deuteronomy 25:4); not harnessing the donkey to the stronger ox in order to plow a field (Deuteronomy 22:10); not removing eggs or fledglings from a nest in the presence of the mother (Deuteronomy 22:6–7).

Jewish law concedes that while it may be necessary to use an animal for food, it is not permissible to take an animal's life merely to provide man with luxuries. To kill an animal for the purpose of using its fur for a coat or its skin to make leather shoes is considered inconsistent with the spirit of Jewish law. However, since the wearing of such garments is considered a necessity, the rule is that one is not to recite the blessing of thanksgiving (She-heche'yanu) when wearing such apparel for the first time, as is normally required.

The second-century talmudic scholar Rabbi Shimon ben Eleazar was disturbed that some people doubted the superiority of man over beast. He remarked (*Kiddushin* 82b): "Throughout my entire life I never witnessed a deer gathering fruit, a lion carrying a burden, or a fox acting as a shopkeeper. Yet, they all manage to live without trouble. Now, if these animals who were created to serve man can be sustained without any effort on their part, how much more so am I entitled to live and be sustained without working and without anxiety."

The prevailing mood among the Rabbis of the Talmud, however, is more generous toward animals. Based on the biblical statement, "And I will provide grass in the fields for your cattle and you shall eat and be satisfied" (Deuteronomy 11:15), they concluded that a person may not eat his own meal before he has fed his animals. (See *Gittin* 62a; *Berakhot* 40a.)

The Midrash *Tanchuma* (Noach 7) calls attention to the statement in the Book of Genesis (8:1), "God remembered Noah and all the beasts and cattle that were with him in the ark..." and reminds us of the verse in the Book of Proverbs (12:10), "A righteous man knows the needs of his beast."

In the Torah, God shows mercy toward animals, just as He shows mercy toward man. When He was prepared to destroy the world because the generation of the flood proved itself to be wicked, God equated man and animal, as the Bible states (Genesis 6:7), "The Lord said: 'I will blot out from the earth the men whom I created—men together with beasts...for I regret that I had made them." But when it came time to act, God showed mercy toward man [by saving Noah and his family] and toward animals [by taking them into the ark as well]—as it is written: "And God remembered Noah and all the beasts..."

Rabbi Akiba, one of the noble martyrs of Jewish history, ruled that it is even forbidden to take the life of a wild animal without giving it a fair trial before a court of twenty-three judges, the same as for a human being. Undoubtedly, this was pure hyperbole, not to be taken literally, but it did call attention to the need to respect all living creatures. The Talmud (*Chullin* 60b) discourages hunting, especially for sport.

In his classic work *Guide of the Perplexed* (III:48), the twelfth-century scholar Moses Maimonides points out that "since it is necessary that animals be killed in order to have food, they should be killed in the quickest manner; that it is forbidden to torment them...for animals feel very great pain, there being no difference in the pain felt by animals and man."

Moses Nachmanides, the noted thirteenth-century rabbi, observes: "The reason for the prohibitions [pertaining to cruelty to animals] is to teach us the trait of compassion, that we are not to soil our human souls by being cruel."

Force-feeding

In the early part of the twentieth century a dispute developed between rabbinic authorities in Eastern Europe over the question of whether Jewish farmers are permitted to force-feed geese in order to fatten them and thus enlarge their livers. The sale of goose livers was an important source of income for East European Jews. Nonetheless, the prevailing rabbinic view was that the force-feeding of geese violates the biblical principles of *tza'ar ba'alei cha'yim* and must therefore be avoided.

After 1948, raising fowl, including geese, became a major industry in Israel. The Israelis discovered that they could benefit substantially by fattening geese through force-feeding and selling the enlarged livers to European markets. The legality of this practice was brought before the Chief Rabbinate, and the ban on force-feeding was lifted for purely financial gain. This decision was deemed in keeping with the talmudic principle, *Ha-To-rah chasah al mamonam shel Yisra'el*, "The Torah protects [is concerned with] the money [economic interests] of Jews" (*Chullin* 49b).

Animal Experimentation

Rabbinic authorities generally permit experimentation on animals if the purpose is to find a cure for man's ills or to serve man's interests in some positive way. They do, however, insist that every precaution be taken to prevent inflicting unnecessary pain on the animals. In this vein, in his notes to Joseph Caro's *Code of Jewish Law* (*Shulchan Arukh*, Even Ha'ezer 5:14), Moses Isserles rules that it is permissible to pluck feathers from living geese (to be used by a scribe to write a Torah scroll, for example). However, he urges that the practice be avoided because it would appear to be an act of cruelty.

Rabbi Ezekiel Landau of Prague (1713–1793) was asked by a Jew who had inherited a vast estate in which there were large wooded areas housing many wild animals whether he was permitted to hunt these animals. Landau's answer given in his volume of responsa titled *Noda Bi-Yehuda* (Yoreh Dei'ah II: 10) was that the wanton killing of animals for sheer pleasure is forbidden. However, if the purpose is to make use of the animal in a way that enhances a person's life—such as providing him with a living by selling or using parts of the animal or providing him with the opportunity to conduct scientific experiments—the killing of an animal is permitted.

A contemporary view on the use of animals for man's benefit was expressed by Rabbi Moshe Tendler, professor of talmudic law and chairman of the biology department at Yeshiva University (*The Jewish World*, October 7–13, 1994): "It is absolutely a misreading of Torah literature to speak of animal rights. Animals were given in this world to serve man, and that hierarchy is a fundamental belief in Torah Judaism. There are no animal rights, but human obligations, which are to use animals for the benefit of man according to prohibitions against causing animals pain and against wastefulness. . . . The greatest *mitzvah* a person can do is to use an animal to save a human life."

See Hunting.

Tzadik

Plural, *tzadikim*. A Hebrew term, first used in the Bible (Genesis 18:23), literally meaning "righteous one." Any righteous person may be called a *tzadik*, but among *chasidim* "The Tzadik" is the leader of a sect who is thought of as the intermediary between man and God. He is believed to be a holy man whose every movement and action is divinely inspired. *Chasidim* often travel great distances to spend a Sabbath listening to The Tzadik teach, to seek his advice, or simply to be in his presence at mealtime. The Tzadik, who is more commonly called Rebbe, leaves over some food from each course, which is divided among his followers. This pittance of food, called *shira'yim* ("leftovers") is believed to be a good-luck charm with redemptive powers.

See Piety.

Tzedakah

A Hebrew term literally meaning "justice or righteous," which encompasses the concepts of charity and compassion.

See Charity; Compassion.

Tze'enah U-Re'enah

Meaning "Come out, you women, and see..." the words *tze'enah u-re'enah* were adopted from a phrase in the Song of Songs (3:11) and became the name of a category of literature composed for women not as well educated as men. Written in Yiddish, *Tze'enah U-re'enah* is a free translation of the Torah, interspersed with legends and ethical teachings.

The most popular book of this type is the *Teitsch Chumash*, written by Jacob Ashkenazi (1550–1626), of Janow, Poland.

Tziduk Ha-Din

A Hebrew term literally meaning "justification of the ruling [of God]."

During the funeral, as the coffin is carried from the hearse to the grave, the *Tziduk Ha-Din* prayer is recited following the recitation of Psalm 90, which begins with the words *Tefillah le-Moshe* ("A Prayer for Moses"), and Psalm 91, which begins with the words *Yoshev be-Seiter Elyon* ("He who dwells in the Shelter of the Most High").

Of talmudic origin, the *Tziduk Ha-Din* prayer dates back to the period of time when the Romans persecuted the Jews in the second century C.E. Bar Kochba led a failed attempt to retake Palestine from Roman control. Three martyrs of that period—Rabbi Chaninah ben Teradyon, his wife, and his daughter—died as they uttered words from the biblical books of Deuteronomy and Jeremiah. Through these words they were expressing their undying faith in God and His administration of justice (*Avodah Zara* 18a).

Rabbi Chaninah spoke first, reciting the verse from the Book of Deuteronomy (32:4): "The Rock [God]. His deeds are perfect, all His ways are just." Chaninah's wife continued: "A God of faithfulness, lacking in wrongdoing, just and right is He." And their daughter concluded with words from Jeremiah (32:19): "Great in counsel and mighty in deed [is God] whose eyes see all the ways of men, to repay every one in accordance with his conduct, and according to the fruit of his deeds."

These verses were embellished in the

course of time and became the foundation of the *Tziduk Ha-Din* prayer as we know it today. The prayer opens with Deuteronomy 32:4 and includes selections from the Talmud and later rabbinic writings expressing the same theme: justification of God's judgment.

Moses Maimonides ascribed great importance to the *Tziduk Ha-Din* prayer when he noted that its essence—our acceptance of God's decree—is a fundamental principle of the Jewish faith. Christianity made the concept central to their faith and expressed it in a prayer ascribed to Jesus, "Thy will [not ours] be done."

Moses Isserles, in the *Code of Jewish Law* (Yoreh Dei'ah 34:4), indicates that in most communities it is customary to recite the *Tziduk Ha-Din* and *Kaddish* only for a child who has attained the age of one year. The commentator Be'er Heiteiv disagrees, noting that in most congregations these prayers are said for a child who has lived for more than a full month.

In addition to being recited at the burial service, the *Tziduk Ha-Din* is also recited by individuals paying a graveside visit on various occasions. Traditionally, the prayer is not recited at funerals on days when the *Tachanun* penitential prayer is omitted from the synagogue service. On these days, Psalm 16, which opens with the words *Mikhtam ["Epigram"] le-David*, is often substituted for the *Tziduk Ha-Din* by traditional Jews.

See Tachanun.

Tzimtzum

This kabbalistic term meaning "contraction, shrinkage" was introduced by Rabbi Isaac Luria (1534–1572), known as the Ari of Safed, and was recorded by his devoted disciple Chaim Vital. This central doctrine of *kabbalah* attempts to explain how there is room for a physical world to exist if, as Isaiah (6:3) quoting the angels puts it, "God's presence fills the whole world."

The answer of Lurianic kabbalists is that God purposely contracted himself to allow space for man and his world to exist. God, they contended, purposely did this, so as to make man responsible for the world and its condition. And if the world is imperfect and there is evil in the world, it is man's doing and man must correct it by a process known as *tikkun olam*, "the fixing [repair] of the world."

The concept of *tzimtzum* actually antedates the Ari by many centuries. Commenting on Exodus 25:8, in which God says to Moses, "And they shall make for Me a sanctuary that I may dwell among them," the Rabbis in the Midrash wondered how God could fit into the tabernacle (sanctuary), since it is written (I Kings 8:27), "The heavens and the heaven of heavens are not spacious enough to contain My presence." God's response was, "I will go down to earth and contract Myself so that I will fit into the sanctuary."

Gershom Scholem, in his *Major Trends in Jewish Mysticism* (1941), sums up the significance of the *tzimtzum* concept:

> *Tzimtzum* is one of the most amazing and far-reaching conceptions ever put forward in the whole history of kabbalism. *Tzimtzum* originally means "concentration" or "contraction," but if used in kabbalistic parlance, it is best translated by "withdrawal" or "retreat." To the kabbalists of Luria's (the Ari's) school, *tzimtzum* does not mean the concentration of God at a point, but his retreat away from a point.... It means briefly that the existence of the universe is made possible by a process of shrinkage in God.

> *See* Kabbalah.

Tzitzit

A Hebrew term literally meaning, "fringe, tassel." Although *tzitzit* is the singular form and *tzitziot* the plural, *tzitzit* is commonly used in the plural sense. *Tzitzit* are attached to the four corners of the *tallit* (prayershawl) worn by males at most religious services and to the *tallit katan* ("small *tallit*"), also known as *arba kanfot* ("four corners"), which is worn as an undergarment.

The requirement that *tzitzit* be applied to the four corners of a garment is biblical in origin. In the Book of Numbers (15:37–41) God says to Moses, "Speak to the Children of Israel, and tell them to attach fringes [*tzitzit*] to the corners of their garments" so that they will be reminded of God's commandments and thus avoid evil conduct. Israel was created to be a holy nation, and the *tzitzit* are worn as a reminder of its mission to serve as a model of righteous living to humanity. The commandment regarding *tzitzit* is repeated in the Book of Deuteronomy (22:12), where the Hebrew word for fringes is *gedilim*, and the commandment specifies that they be placed on the *four* corners of a garment.

The seriousness with which the commandment to wear *tzitzit* has been accepted by Jews since early times was enunciated by the fourth-century Rabbi Joseph bar Rabba. He was once asked, "Which commandment of the Torah is your father most careful to observe?" He replied, "The commandment of *tzitzit*—fringes." Rabbi Joseph related that one day, while his father was standing on a ladder, one of the threads of his *tzitzit* was torn, and he would not descend from the ladder until it was replaced with a whole fringe (*Shabbat* 118b).

Many pious Jews have taken literally the injunction in Numbers (15:39) to look at them [the fringes] and recall all the commandments of the Lord..." They interpret this statement as meaning that the fringes of the *tallit katan* must be exposed so that they are visible at all times.

This view had not been universally held by all Orthodox Jews. The former Sephardic Chief Rabbi of Israel, Ovadiah Yosef, wrote in a responsum (*Yechaveh Daat* 1) that the tradition among Sephardim is that the *tzitzit* should not be exposed at any time. To Ovadiah Yosef the commandment in the Book of Numbers that fringes be "seen" means that they be seen when one puts them on each morning, at which time he recites the appropriate blessing.

Much earlier, the eighth-century Karaite cult, which took the words of the Bible literally, did not hang *tzitzit* on the four corners of their garments, but attached them to a wall in their houses, where they were always visible, thus complying with the requirement to "look at them."

The Blue Cord

When making a fringe, four threads are used, three of equal length and one much longer. These are pulled through a hole made in each corner of the garment, folded over and tied with a series of double knots so that in the final product each fringe consists of eight loosely hanging strings of equal lengths with five knots. The details are provided in the *Shulchan Arukh*, Orach Cha'yim 11:14.

As described in Numbers (15:38), each fringe should have "a cord of blue [*petil tekheilet*]" attached. The dye used originally to make the blue (*tekheilet*) color was obtained from a mollusk whose identity is no longer known. The hard-shelled snail, called *chilazon* in Hebrew, issued a secretion from which the dye was made. Since the dye was no longer obtainable in talmudic times, the Rabbis suspended the requirement that a blue thread be part of the fringes, agreeing that white wool threads alone would suffice.

In the tractate *Sotah* (17a) Rabbi Meir comments on why a thread of *blue* was part of the fringes on a prayershawl. He says: "Blue resembles the color of the sea, and the sea resembles the color of heaven, and heaven resembles the color of the throne of God."

For centuries, scientists have tried to identify more accurately the snail from which the blue dye was made. In recent years the murex snail, found in the Mediterranean Sea, has been identified as the source of the *tekheilet* dye. Murex is the genus name of a flesh-eating snail found in warm sea waters. Some species yield a purple substance formerly valued as a dye.

Tzitzit and Mitzvot

Because the reason for wearing *tzitzit* is to "remember all the commandments," Rashi associated the word with the 613 commandments (*taryag mitzvot*) of the Torah. He noted that the numerical value of the Hebrew word *tzitzit* is 600, and when one adds to that the eight threads and five knots that make up each fringe, the total is 613.

Eleazar ben Judah of Worms (Germany), a noted twelfth/thirteenth-century poet, scholar, and kabbalist (also known as Eleazar Rokeach because he was a spice-dealer), belonged to a circle of mystics known as *Chasidei Ashkenaz*. They offered guidance on how the love of God can be attained through an understanding of what the eight strings of each of the *tzitzit* represent:

1. The first thread, representing the eyes, teaches one not to sin by desiring everything one's eyes see.

2. The second thread, representing the ears, teaches one not to listen to gossip or false reports or profanity.

3. The third thread, representing the throat, teaches one not to eat abominable food.

4. The fourth thread, representing the mouth and tongue, the organs of speech, reminds one not to utter vain words and only to speak the truth.

5. The fifth thread, representing the hands, teaches one not to rob or steal and to open one's hands to the needy.

6. The sixth thread, representing the feet, cautions one not to be a talebearer or follow false gods.

7. The seventh thread, representing the sexual organs, reminds one to be fruitful and multiply, and to avoid adultery.

8. The eighth thread, representing the nose, reminds one to refrain from smelling the scent of idols, but to smell the sweet odor of the myrtle branches as part of Sabbath observance. It also reminds one to avoid anger, which traditionally is associated with the nose.

See Tallit.

Tzom Gedaliah

A Hebrew term literally meaning "Fast of Gedaliah," a minor fast day that falls on the third day of the Hebrew month of Tishrei.
See Fast of Gedaliah.

Ululating

From the Latin *ululatus*, a ululating sound, that of wailing or wavering, commonly made by Jewish women of Sephardic heritage (primarily from countries such as Syria, Iran, and Iraq) when a bar mitzvah or bridegroom is called to the Torah, or when a baby girl is being named at a synagogue service. The sound is believed effective in scaring off evil spirits that are prone to make appearances at happy occasions with the express purpose of disturbing or harming the celebrants.

Unveiling

A graveside service during which a monument to the deceased is formally dedicated. Before the service begins, a piece of cloth (a veil) is draped over the stone so as to conceal the inscription. At one point in the service, a family member is called upon to remove the cloth and unveil the stone. At this point, the inscription, seen by the public for the first time, is read aloud. A *minyan* need not be present at an unveiling. However, if the *Kaddish* prayer is to be recited by family members, a quorum must be present.

Although monuments have been erected over graves for many centuries, the custom of conducting a special unveiling ceremony was instituted toward the end of the nineteenth century in England and later in the United States to formalize and dignify the erection of the monument. The British use the term "tombstone consecration," whereas Americans have adopted the term "unveiling."

There is no religious obligation that an unveiling be held, and it is not necessary that a rabbi officiate. Anyone able to recite the selected psalms and deliver a eulogy, if one is desired, may conduct the ceremony.

Although an unveiling may be held at any time after the monument has been erected,

most families wait about one year so as to give the earth a chance to settle.

Jewish law discourages the serving of food in a cemetery because such activity is considered disrespectful to the deceased. Nevertheless, in some communities, refreshments—generally limited to wine, liquor, cookies, and cake—are offered. Those present raise a glass of spirits and wish others *Le-cha'yim*, "to life."

See Tombstones.

Upsherenish

A Yiddish term meaning "cutting off." Many Orthodox Jews, especially *chasidim*, allow a boy's hair to grow until his third birthday, at which time the father gives the child his first haircut, making sure to leave the *pei'ot*—side-locks—intact. This is the point at which the boy officially begins Torah studies. On occasion, relatives and friends of the child are invited to participate in the *upsherenish* ceremony by snipping an additional lock of hair. A barber is often present to straighten the cutting so that the child will look presentable.

Students of Jewish folklore explain that the *upsherenish* tradition arose among Jews who believed that evil spirits are poised to attack boys, but not girls. In order to confuse the spirits as to the child's gender, a boy's hair is allowed to grow long.

In recent years, some Reconstructionist families have adopted the *upsherenish* custom and celebrate it as a joyous moment in a family's life.

Ushpizin

Ushpiz is an Aramaic term used in the Talmud (*Moed Katan* 9b) to designate an inn. In the tractate *Yoma* (12a), the word *ushpizin* is used to describe an innkeeper, but the term gradually took on the meaning of "guests" of the innkeeper. Since guests at an inn are temporary visitors, the term became associated with guests invited to one's *sukkah*, which is a temporary dwelling. Aside from family and friends, kabbalists introduced the concept of inviting seven celebrated heroes of the Jewish past as guests to dinner, one on each of the seven nights of the holiday.

On the first night of Sukkot, Abraham is invited, for it is he who welcomed strangers into his home, just as is done on Sukkot. On the second night of Sukkot, the special guest is Isaac, the son of Abraham and Sarah. On the third night of the holiday, the imaginary guest is Jacob, the father of twelve sons who in turn became the heads of the twelve tribes of Israel. The fourth guest is Joseph, for whom Jacob made a coat of many colors. On the fifth night of Sukkot, Moses, the great emancipator who led the Children of Israel out of Egypt so that they could become a free people, is invited into the *sukkah*. On the sixth night of the holiday, Aaron, the loyal brother of Moses, is welcomed, and on the seventh and last night of Sukkot, David, the king of Israel who built the city of Jerusalem, where the Temple was later erected, is invited into the *sukkah*.

In recent years feminists have commemorated the contributions of Jewish women to Jewish survival by adding to the male *ushpizin* seven women who, in Jewish tradition, are lauded as prophetesses or individuals of noble character. These *ushpizot*, as they are called, include Sarah, Miriam, Deborah, Hannah, Abigail, Hulda, and Esther.

Veiling the Bride

Better known by the Yiddish-Hebrew term *badekn di kallah*, this is a custom whose origin has been traced to biblical times. The ceremony takes place in the bride's dressing room immediately prior to the wedding itself. After the groom raises the veil of the bride and identifies her as the woman of his choice, he lowers the veil over her face. The officiating rabbi then blesses the bride and recites one or more appropriate verses from the Bible. One popular verse is, "O sister! May you be the mother of thousands of myriads" (Genesis 24:60), a blessing bestowed upon Rebecca when it was agreed that she was to be Isaac's wife. The popularity of this particular verse relates to the traditional explanation of the origin of the veiling custom itself.

According to tradition, the veiling custom is associated with the incident in the Book of Genesis where Abraham's servant, Eliezer, is sent to find a wife for Isaac. He chooses Rebecca, and when Isaac comes to meet her for the first time, Rebecca says, "Who is this man who walks in the field to meet us?" The servant replies, "It is my master, Isaac" (24:65), whereupon Rebecca takes her veil and covers her face.

A second traditional explanation is that since Jacob was misled into thinking that he was marrying Rachel, when in fact it was a veiled Leah whom he was marrying, the bridegroom must always see the bride unveiled before the wedding ceremony.

Students of Jewish folklore believe that the use of a veil by a Jewish bride may be an adaptation of a Roman custom. Among Romans, the bride wore a full-length veil, which was later used as her burial shroud.

Vengeance

In Jewish thought, seeking to take revenge upon someone who has harmed an individual or a group is sometimes condoned and sometimes condemned.

In the Book of Deuteronomy (25:17–19), Israel is cautioned to remember that, after they fled Egypt, Amalek denied them passage through their land. And then, unafraid of God's retribution, how the Amalekites first attacked the straggling Israelite women and children who were making their way through the desert. Israel was then exhorted, "You shall blot out the memory of Amalek from under the heavens. Do not forget!" Similar words of condemnation of the arch enemy of Israel are found in the Book of Exodus (17:14–16).

Vengeance upon the Amalekites was exacted many years later. In the Book of Esther (8:13), after the downfall of Haman (a descendent of Amalek according to Jewish tradition), who had planned to exterminate all the Jews in the Persian kingdom of Ahasueros, the Jews again are urged to "avenge themselves of their enemies." They did so by attacking all of their foes within the kingdom (Esther 9).

The view of retaliating forcefully against a wrongdoer was supported by some of the later sages of the Talmud but was disapproved of by others. In the tractate *Yoma* (23a), Rabbi Yochanan, quoting his teacher Rabbi Shimon ben Yehotzadak, said, "Any scholar who does not avenge himself and become angry like a serpent [and strike out against an intruder] is no real scholar." Rabbi Yochanan felt that misconduct should not be allowed to go unavenged.

His colleague Rava, however, was much more conciliatory. He maintained that "one who is willing to overlook offenses against others will have his offenses overlooked as well." Clearly, this view is more in keeping with the admonition in the Book of Leviticus (19:18), "Do not take vengeance or bear a grudge." Vengeance is the prerogative of God, as implied in Deuteronomy 5:9.

Viddui

A Hebrew term literally meaning "declaration" or "confession [of sins]," referring to the tradition of expiating one's sins before an anticipated death.

See Confession of Sins.

Wachnacht

A German word meaning "night watch." In Europe, particularly in Germany, it was customary to conduct a night-long vigil before the circumcision of a baby. Schoolchildren would be invited to surround the crib and recite the *Shema* ("Hear, O Israel") prayer along with adults, who then spent the night in study. This circle of protection is of kabbalistic origin and, as is true of many other Jewish customs where encirclement is practiced, its original purpose was to ward off evil spirits.

See Shema.

War, Symbols of

In Jewish ritual, the use of an iron implement or any other object symbolic of war is forbidden. The ban dates back to biblical times, when stones could not be used in constructing the altar if they had been shaped with iron tools. The Book of Exodus (20:22) states, "And if you make Me an altar of stone, do not build it of hewn stones, for if you apply your sword [iron tool] to it, you have profaned it."

In the writing of ritual objects such as a Torah scroll or *mezuzah* or *tefillin* parchments, the use of steel writing implements is avoided. Scribes originally used reeds, but later they favored feathers from a kosher animal, primarily the goose. The scribe prepares the quill by shaving the thick end of the feather shaft to a fine point and then slitting the tip lengthwise. This allows the scribe to fashion an instrument that will make fine letters or broad ones, as needed.

Wasted Blessings

See Berakhah Le-Vatalah.

Weddings

The origins of the marriage ceremony as we know it today are obscure. An oblique reference to a marriage feast is made in Genesis (29:21), when Jacob asks Laban to give him Rachel as a wife, for whom he had paid with seven years of service. Later in the Bible, there are references to brides, bridegrooms, wedding feasts, and wedding processions.

The Bible does not specify a formal manner in which a marriage is to take place. However, we learn from the Rabbis of the Talmud (Mishnah *Kiddushin* 1:1) that a marriage could be entered into unceremoniously by mutual agreement. The man gives the woman money (or something of value) or a signed contract stipulating his agreement to marry her. Or he could enter into marriage though the act of sexual intercourse.

The second/third-century Babylonian scholar Rav, also known as Abba Arikha, objected to the third method and ordered any rabbi who validated a marriage through intercourse to be flogged. As a result, the two remaining methods became standard. During the wedding ceremony, as practiced to this day, the man gives his bride a written document—a *ketubbah*—spelling out his obligation to support her financially along with something of discernible value—such as a ring. Originally, a coin was used.

A Public Event

Because marriage is a sacred event in communal as well as in family life, after the eighth century it became customary to require that a *minyan*—a ritual quorum of ten men—be present when a wedding ceremony is held. In support of this new requirement, it was pointed out that when Boaz was ready to marry Ruth (Ruth 4:2), he called together ten of the elders of the city.

Although it is generally agreed among authorities that it is preferable to have a *minyan* present at a wedding, if less than ten men are present the ceremony is still legally binding. This view was expressed by Rabbi Ezekiel Landau, the prominent eighteenth-century rabbi of Prague, in his *Noda Bi-Yehudah* (Even Ha-Ezer 1:56).

The Modern Ceremony

In a contemporary traditional ceremony, after the clergy have taken their position under the canopy (*chuppah*), the groom arrives and is positioned facing the right side of the rabbi (and cantor, if one is present). When the bride arrives later, she is positioned to the right of the bridegroom. This arrangement is sometimes said to derive from an interpretation of the verse in Psalms (45:10), "The queen stands on your right hand in fine gold of Ophir." In Jewish tradition, the bride is a queen and the groom a king.

The reason why the groom precedes the bride to the *chuppah* relates to the giving of the Ten Commandments at Mount Sinai. Just as God (the bridegroom) came forth to receive Israel (the bride), so the groom takes his place under the canopy first, ready to receive the bride.

Among members of the Orthodox community, the groom will on occasion wear a white robe, or *kittl*, during the wedding ceremony. The stark whiteness symbolizes purity, a reminder to the groom that the new life upon which he is about to embark must be pure and clean.

After the wedding principals (parents, groomsmen, bridesmaids, etc.) have taken their places, the rabbi (or cantor) recites the initial prayers over a cup of wine, from which the groom and then the bride sip.

In Orthodox ceremonies, the bride, sometimes escorted by her mother, will encircle the groom three times. This practice is based on the verses in the Book of Hosea (2:21–22)

in which God speaks to Israel and says, "And I will *betroth* thee unto Me forever; and I will *betroth* thee unto me in righteousness, and in justice, and in lovingkindness, and in mercy; and I will *betroth* thee unto me in faithfulness, and you shall know the Lord." The use of the word "betroth" three times is the basis for the encirclement three times.

In some Orthodox ceremonies, it is customary for the bride to encircle the groom *seven* times. The number seven is considered holy and significant, as it represents the seven days of the week; the seven *aliyot* that are distributed each Sabbath during the Torah reading; the Seven Benedictions recited to conclude the wedding ceremony, the seven weeks between Passover and Shavuot, and so on.

The Ring

The bridegroom then places the marriage band on the forefinger of the bride's right hand. The ring will reach only to the finger's second joint, and the bride keeps it in that position until the ceremony is over. The practice of placing the ring on the forefinger of the bride's right hand is thought to have been introduced by the eminent fifteenth-century German Rabbi Moshe Mintz. The index finger was designated because it is the most prominent; the ring that is placed upon it is easily visible to the witnesses who have signed the *ketubbah*.

The ring the groom gives the bride must be of determinable value. A ring containing diamonds, rubies, or ornamentation cannot be easily estimated by an inexperienced person. If given a jewelled or otherwise ornamented ring by her groom, a naïve bride might erroneously think she is receiving something of great value. Judaism protects the bride by suggesting that a simple, unadorned ring be used.

At this point the marriage declaration—*Ha-rei at me-kudeshet li be-taba'at zo ke-dat Moshe ve-Yisra'el*, "Behold, thou art consecrated unto me with this ring, in accordance with the laws of Moses and Israel"—is pronounced by the groom.

In recent years, it has become customary for the bride also to place a ring on the finger of the groom during the marriage ceremony. Although some object to this practice on grounds that it is not traditional or that it might appear as if the bride were returning the ring given to her by the groom, there is no legal basis for the prohibition.

When a double-ring ceremony is conducted, the bride places the ring on one of the groom's fingers but does not (except in the Reform tradition) utter the same words used by the groom, since he alone is *obligated* to give his mate a ring and to make a legal declaration to that effect. In many cases the bride will simply say, "Behold, you are consecrated unto me with this ring," to which she may also add some personal words.

The Ketubbah

The Jewish marriage contract, the *ketubbah*, is then read aloud by the officiant. After the reading, he hands the document to the groom, who in turn hands it to his bride with the understanding that she keep it in her possession from that day on. At Reform weddings, a simple Certificate of Marriage is generally used in place of the *ketubbah*.

After the *ketubbah* is read, the concluding blessings, known in Hebrew as the *Sheva Berakhot*, are recited over a second cup of wine.

The officiating clergyman then places a glass wrapped in paper or cloth on the floor. The groom crushes the glass with the heel of his foot, and all present shout "*mazal tov!*" After the crushing of the glass, the formal wedding ceremony is over. During the recessional, the bride and groom are sometimes showered with rice and nuts, which in some cultures are considered symbols of fertility.

Among more traditional Jews, following the ceremony it is customary for the newlyweds to seclude themselves in a private room. The custom is called *yichud* in Hebrew, meaning "union, joining, togetherness."

Wedding Fasting

The idea of fasting on one's wedding day became traditional because of the statement in the Jerusalem Talmud, where the opinion is ventured that the sins of a king, a prince, and a groom are forgiven on the day they enter their new lives. Fasting is a way of asking for forgiveness for past sins.

While in some communities both bride and groom fast on their wedding day, in others only the bridegroom fasts. It was believed that if the groom were not required to fast, he might join his friends in the prenuptial celebration and become inebriated, placing him in poor condition to carry out the legal formalities involved in the wedding ceremony. Since it is considered less likely that the bride's friends will imbibe, or that they will induce the bride to imbibe, she is not required to fast.

If the ceremony is held at night, the fast is broken when the first stars appear. Fasting is not observed on Rosh Chodesh, Purim, Chanukkah, and other minor holidays.

Marriage Days

Over the centuries there has been much debate as to which day of the week is the most propitious for holding the wedding ceremony. According to an ancient tradition, Tuesday—the third day of Creation—is the best day because on that day God reviewed what he had created up until that time and said, *Ki tov*, "It is good."

Among other days that have been designated for marriages are Wednesday (for virgins); Thursday (for widows); and Friday, which leads into the Sabbath, the day of rest.

Weddings among the Sephardim of Morocco usually take place on Wednesday night, which is actually Thursday (*yom chamishi*), the fifth day of the week. Moroccans consider *chamishi* (the fifth *aliyah*) to be the most prestigious of all Torah honors, and a bar mitzvah is awarded this *aliyah*.

Some Sephardim, primarily Syrians, arrange for marriages to be held during Elul, the month before the High Holy Days. Elul is considered a month for love because the word *Elul* is an acronym formed from the first letters of the Hebrew words in the Song of Songs, *Ani le-dodi, ve-dodi li*, "I am my beloved's, and my beloved is mine."

Prohibited Marriage Days

In Jewish law and tradition there are also specific days and periods when marriages are forbidden. Although there is no explicit prohibition against holding a wedding between Rosh Hashanah and Yom Kippur, weddings traditionally are not performed during this time. The ten-day period between these fall holidays is one for serious introspection, and the spirit of levity generally manifested at wedding celebrations is considered to be inconsistent with the somber mood that should prevail during this period.

With several days excepted, the seven-week period between Passover and Shavuot is considered a time of semi-mourning, and weddings are prohibited. One theory, advanced by students of folklore, traces the ban to a Roman superstition against celebrating marriages in May. Romans believed that during this month the souls of the departed return to earth and disturb the living. But Jewish sources attribute the ban to the plague that befell thousands of Bar Kochba's soldiers, who were Rabbi Akiba's students. Bar Kochba led a rebellion against the Roman occupation of Palestine, which met with disaster in 135 C.E. (*Yevamot* 2b).

Marriages are also traditionally prohibited during a three-week period in summertime—from the seventeenth of Tammuz (Shivah Asar B'Tammuz) to the ninth of Av (Tishah B'Av). During this time in the year 586 B.C.E., the Babylonians breached the walls of Jerusalem and destroyed the First Temple. Ever since, on these days, except for the New Moon (Rosh Chodesh), weddings are not held.

Marriages may not be performed on Sabbaths and major festivals but are permitted on minor holidays, including Chanukkah and Purim. They may also not be performed on the Intermediate Days of Passover and Sukkot (Chol Ha-Moed).

There are varying opinions as to which days in the seven-week period between Passover and Shavuot are to be excluded from the marriage ban. All agree that marriages may be performed on festive days such as Lag Ba-Omer (the thirty-third day of the *sefirah* period), the New Moon of Iyyar, and from the New Moon of Sivan until Shavuot. But not all agree on which of the other days between Passover and Shavuot weddings may be held. In some communities, with the exceptions mentioned here, weddings are totally banned.

Most Sephardim ban weddings from Passover to Lag Ba-Omer but permit them thereafter. Some however, particularly those of Spanish-Portuguese extraction, permit weddings during the entire month of Nissan as well as on Rosh Chodesh Iyyar and Sivan, on Lag Ba-Omer, and on the three days prior to Shavuot.

In other communities, weddings may be held during the first two weeks of *sefirah* (from Passover until the New Moon of Iyyar), but are prohibited from that time until the New Moon of Sivan. And in still other communities, weddings may not be held for the first two weeks after Passover, but they may be held after Rosh Chodesh Iyyar.

In 1949, the Committee on Law and Standards of the Rabbinical Assembly (Conservative) favored the eighth- and ninth-century tradition of forbidding weddings from the second day of Passover (16 Nissan) until Lag Ba-Omer (18 Iyyar). Subsequently, the committee shortened to less than two weeks—from the beginning of Passover until 27 Nissan (Yom Ha-Sho'ah)—the period during which weddings and other festive celebrations are prohibited. It ruled that the remainder of the *sefirah* period is "to be considered as any other time of the year."

Reform Judaism does not ban weddings on *sefirah* days or on fast days. However, with regard to Tishah B'Av, the *Reform Manual* says, "On the grounds of historical consciousness, marriages should be avoided by Reform rabbis on the ninth of Av, even though the Reform Synagogue does not officially recognize the day as a fast day."

See Circles and Circling; Eirusin; Glassbreaking; Ketubbah; Marriage; Nisuin; Sheva Berakhot; Yichud.

Western Wall

Known in Hebrew as Kotel Ha-Ma'aravi, the Western Wall is all that remains of the wall associated with the Second Temple, which was destroyed by the Romans in 70 C.E. The Second Temple, which had been built by the poor Jews who had returned from the Babylonian Exile toward the end of the sixth century B.C., paled in comparison to the beauty, grandeur, and opulence of the First Temple, which was dedicated by King Solomon around 964 B.C.E.

In the second half of the first century B.C.E., Rome had appointed Herod, a non-Jew, to be king of the Jews. Herod was addicted to building magnificent structures throughout Palestine, including heathen temples. When he saw the poor state of the Second Temple, he undertook to renovate it so as to make it worthy of its name—a Temple to God. Herod completed renovation of the basic structure in a year and one half, but it took many years for the interior to be fully refurbished. The actual completion was accomplished during the rule of Roman procurator Albinius (62–64 C.E.).

When Herod's Temple was finally completed, people said, "Anyone who has not seen the Temple of Herod has never seen a beautiful building in his life" (*Bava Batra* 4a). The Rabbis of the Talmud describe its interior as having been constructed of blue, yellow, and white marble.

But Herod felt that his beautification of the Temple would be incomplete unless a promenade area was also constructed. And so he built a huge retaining wall along the western side of the Temple and filled it with earth so a larger assembly area would exist where the large number of Jews who come together on the important holidays might congregate. This promenade became known as the Temple Mount.

What remains today of the Western Wall are twenty-six rows of huge stones of various sizes above ground level, plus another nineteen rows below ground level. The large plaza where today Jews and others gather to pray and insert petitionary notes (*kvitlach*) into the cracks of the wall was completed after the 1967 Six-Day War when the area was retaken from the Jordanians, who had ruled it for nineteen years, since the 1948 War of Independence.

With the exception of the comment of the fourth-century *amora* Tanchuma bar Abba, who is presumed to be the editor of the Midrash *Tanchuma*, nary a reference is made to the Western Wall in rabbinic literature. It was not until the sixteenth century, when Jews began to visit Jerusalem in significant numbers, that it became customary for them to stop at the Wall to pray, petition God, shed tears, and mourn the destruction of the demolished Temple. Hence, the name the Wailing Wall was conferred upon the site, which had attained an aura of holiness.

The sentiment expressed by Tanchuma bar Abba in the fourth century was now recalled. He had said (Midrash *Tanchuma*, Exodus 10): "God's presence was never absent from the western wall of the holy Temple." Jews were now being reminded that the Holy of Holies, in which the tablets of the Ten Commandments were kept, was situated in the western part of the Temple, not too distant from Herod's retaining wall. Thus, sanctity was conferred upon the western wall erected by Herod, as if it were the western wall of the Temple itself.

Palestinians in Denial

The following is an Islamic religious ruling (*fatwa*) issued by the Mufti of Jerusalem, Akramah Sabri. Broadcast on February 20, 2001, on the Palestinian Authority's Voice of Palestine radio, the ruling denies that Jews had any connection with the Wall, which they claim belongs to Islam:

> According to international law, this is an Islamic holy place, because El-Buraq Wall is part of the wall of the Al-Aqsa mosque. In addition, Mohammed established its holiness on the night of the Isra and the Me-araj when he tied El-Buraq [a horse with a human face] who carried him from Mecca to Jerusalem, to that wall. There-

fore, we establish that the Wall belongs to Islam and has no connection to the Jews.

There are many explanations for why the Jews cry at the Wall. According to one tradition, they cry because they have not kept the Ten Commandments of our lord Moses, peace be upon him. According to another version, they cry because the prophet Mohammed was an Arab and not a Jew. It is for this reason that they call it the "Wailing Wall."

One issue that will have to be agreed upon before a final settlement between Israelis and Palestinians can be reached is the exact dimensions of the Western Wall. Writing in the Hebrew daily *Ha'aretz*, military analyst Ze'ev Schiff framed the dispute in these words:

> What is the length of the Western Wall? Is it confined to the wall facing the space traditionally used by Jews for prayer, which is only 58 meters, or does it include the entire western retaining wall of the Temple Mount? The Palestinians demand that any diplomatic settlement adhere to the shorter length, known as "the Wailing Wall." Israel insists on "the Western Wall" . . . whose length is 485 meters.

Wine

From earliest times, wine was served as a palliative to lessen stress. In the Book of Proverbs (31:6), it is advised to "give strong drink to him that is ready to perish and wine unto the bitter of soul." In Jewish tradition it thus became popular, during the meal of condolence after a funeral, to offer the bereaved a "cup of consolation" (Jeremiah 16:7).

Although the excessive use of wine is deplored early in the Bible, when consumed in moderation wine is considered a blessing to man. "Wine cheers the hearts of men," says the psalmist (Psalms 104:15). The talmudic scholar Eleazar Ha-Kappar (*Ta'anit* 11a) elaborates upon this, saying that a Nazirite who has foresworn the use of wine is called a sinner because he denies himself that which was created by God as a source of enjoyment to man. Elsewhere, the Talmud adds, "When man avails himself of God's gifts, he brings cheer to God" (*Berakhot* 35a).

Jews are expected to add joy to every Sabbath and holiday meal by beginning it with the recitation of a prayer of sanctification—the *Kiddush*—over a cup of wine. At the same time, the Rabbis have consistently cautioned that overindulgence may lead to drunkenness, and drunkenness can lead to speaking out of turn and revealing confidential information.

They accentuated this caution by equating the Hebrew words *ya'yin* meaning "wine," and *sod*, meaning "secret." The numerical value of each word is seventy. This led Rabbi Chiya to comment, "When wine goes in [to one's body], secrets come out" (*Sanhedrin* 38a). The Priests, who had to be completely focused in the Sanctuary, were not permitted to drink wine before officiating (Leviticus 10:8–11).

The only time intoxication is permitted in Jewish life is on Purim.

Kosher Wine

According to Jewish law, wine touched by non-Jews is deemed nonkosher. This ruling dates back to talmudic times, when Gentiles were considered to be idolaters and wine libations were integral to the worship of heathen gods. The prohibition was aimed at reducing social contact between Jews and non-Jews, and as a result reduce the incidence of intermarriage.

Although Christians and Muslims are no longer considered idol worshippers, the ban against using wine prepared by them continues to be in force. The Talmud (*Avodah Zarah* 55b–60a) refers to such wine as *ya'yin nesekh*, "wine used for libations [on heathen altars]." The Rabbis found a basis for the banning of wine prepared by non-Jews in verses in Deuteronomy (32:38) and Daniel (1:8).

The only time wine prepared by idolators was permissible to Jews was when it had been previously boiled (*Avodah Zarah* 29b). The rationale is that idolators never used boiled wine in their sacrificial system.

Ya'yin mevushal, the Hebrew term for boiled wine, appears on most labels of wines produced by companies such as Kedem and Manischewitz. Wine manufacturers such as Carmel do not print these words on their labels, because idol worship is no longer prevalent, and the concept of *ya'yin nesekh* no longer applies.

The Committee on Jewish Law and Standards of the Rabbinical Assembly (Conservative) considers all wine produced today by Gentiles as *stam yeinam* ("ordinary wine"), not *ya'yin nesekh,* since wine processing is automated and no human being touches the wine during production. Conservative authorities do not require rabbinic certification for wine to establish its kosher status.

The concept of *ya'yin nesekh* does not apply to beer and grain spirits, products never used in heathen worship.

See Adloyada; Kiddush; Seder; Weddings.

Witnesses

In Jewish law, no less than two witnesses (*eidim* in Hebrew; singular, *eid*), must offer testimony (*eidut*) before a conviction can be pronounced. This is based on the biblical passage (Deuteronomy 19:15), "A single witness may not validate guilt against a person....A case can be valid only upon the testimony of two or more witnesses." This law applies to all criminal cases and most civil cases. (See Numbers 35:30 and Deuteronomy 17:6).

The Talmud (*Sanhedrin* 27a) states that anyone who fits the category of *rasha*, such as robbers and professional gamblers, are disqualified to serve as witnesses. Maimonides points out in his *Mishneh Torah* (Hilkhot Eidut 9:1) that among those also disqualified to serve as witnesses are women, slaves, relatives, minors, the insane, the deaf, and the blind.

The talmudic version of the right established by the U.S. Constitution protecting every individual against self-incrimination was advanced by the third/fourth-century scholar Rabba ben Joseph, who said, "Every man is considered a relative to himself and no one can declare himself to be wicked [*rasha*]" (*Sanhedrin* 9b).

Sabbath Violators

According to talmudic law, a Jew who violates the Sabbath publicly is labeled an apostate, one no longer to be trusted. Rabbis who are strict adherents of Jewish law will not permit such a violator to sign as a witness on a Jewish marriage contract (*ketubbah*). Ultra-Orthodox rabbis such as Moshe Feinstein (1895–1986) have ruled as invalid marriages performed by Reform rabbis, because the Reform *ketubbot* are presumed to have been witnessed by Sabbath violators (*Igrot Moshe*, Even Ha-Ezer 76).

Most of the rules pertaining to witnesses and their testimony is presented in the talmudic tractate *Eiduyot*.

Women

In biblical times society was patriarchal. The Jewish woman occupied a position subordinate to that of the Jewish male, her function being to serve man. When a woman married, she became the property of her husband. In fact, the original word for marriage was *kinyan*, meaning "acquisition," although the word used for marriage today is *kiddushin*, meaning "sanctification." Jacob may have loved Rachel when he married her, but he had to "buy" her from his father-in-law, Laban, by working for him for many years (Genesis 29:18). A family in biblical times was called *beit avot*, a term literally meaning "house of the fathers" (Exodus 12:3), which implied that a man's estate had to be transferred to his sons and could not be inherited by his daughters.

The law prohibiting women from inheriting a father's property was introduced so that at some future date, when the tribes of Israel occupied the land of Canaan, the portion of land awarded to each tribe was to be secure. One way that a tribe might suffer the loss of land is through marriage. If a man and woman of different tribes married, all property in the wife's name would automatically become the husband's property. Thus, to minimize the loss of land by tribes, women were not permitted to inherit property.

The Five Protesters

In early biblical times this inequity was protested by the five daughters of Zelophechad of the tribe of Manasseh (Numbers 27:1ff.), who were not permitted to inherit their father's estate even though he had no male offspring. The daughters brought their complaint to Moses, who appealed to God for a ruling. According to a legend in the tractate *Bava Batra* (116a–119b) the five siblings were learned individuals and were able to offer some convincing emotional arguments. Moses presented their protest to God, repeating the appeal of the sisters, in which they argued: "Surely God's love is not like that of mortal man. A mortal man prefers sons to daughters, but He who created the world extends His love to women as well as to men."

The daughter's appeal succeeded and God justified their claim (27:7). Thenceforth, it was decreed that in a situation where there are no male heirs a daughter may inherit a father's estate.

But this victory in the battle for equality did not extend to all areas of life in which women were involved. Although a third-century Babylonian scholar such as Rabbi Chisda proudly proclaimed, "Daughters are dearer to me than sons" (*Bava Batra* 141a), the fact is that when a male child was born, everyone rejoiced and recited prayers of thanksgiving, but when a girl was born, parents and relatives were less celebratory (*Berakhot* 59b; *Niddah* 31b).

In fact, some scholars mistakenly believed the women have "weak minds" (*da'atan kallah*), characterizing them as lightheaded (*Shabbat* 33b) and incapable of learning (*Yerushalmi Pesachim* 1:4).

These extreme claims were contradicted by the fact that Beruriah, daughter of the illustrious second-century scholar Chaninah ben Teradyon and wife of Rabbi Meir, is cited in the Talmud as having mastered three hundred laws in one day (*Pesachim* 62b).

In *Eruvin* 63a Rabbi Eliezer consults with his wife, Imma Shalom, who was a sister of Rabban Gamliel. In *Bava Metzia* 59b she instructs him on how to control his movements when pouring out his feelings of grief during the recitation of certain prayers.

On Teaching Torah to Women

Drawing upon explicit biblical texts, the Rabbis of the Talmud and later times pointed to several passages to make the argument that a man's primary responsibility is to teach Torah to his sons, not his daughters. Among the verses cited are:

- "And thou shalt tell thy son on that day [Passover], saying: 'It is because of that which the Lord did for me when I came forth out of Egypt'" (*Exodus* 13:8).

- "...Do not forget the things you saw with your own eyes...and make them known to your children and your children's children" (*Deuteronomy* 4:9). The Hebrew word for children in this verse is the masculine *banekha*, not the feminine *b'notekha*.

- "A wise person is instructed by his father" (*Proverbs* 13:1).

- "Train up a child in the way he should go..." Here the masculine *na'ar* is used for child, not the feminine *na'arah*" (*Proverbs* 22:6).

While such verses from the Bible have been cited by the earliest talmudic scholars to prove that a man's only obligation is to teach his son Torah, it is evident from the *mishnah* in *Nedarim* (4:3) that it was important for a man to also teach Torah (*Mikra*) to his daughters.

Ben Azzai, the second-century Babylonian scholar, was clearly a strong proponent of this view. In the tractate *Sotah* (20a) he declared: "A man is obligated to teach his daughter Torah so that if she is ever in a situation where she is forced to drink the bitter waters, she will know that her having studied Torah will accrue to her merit."

How Women Earn Merit

Ben Azzai was referring to the case of a man, described in Numbers 5:11ff., who had suspected his wife of infidelity but had no proof of her guilt. Nevertheless, the accusation by the husband was sufficient to make his suspected wife (called a *sotah*) endure the ordeal of "bitter waters." She was forced to drink a concoction in which earth from the floor of the Tabernacle was mixed with water. If the woman was guilty of infidelity, the water would have a vile, bitter taste, and the woman's body would undergo dreadful physical changes. If she was innocent, the drink would not taste bitter and would have no physical effect on her.

The *mishnah* in *Sotah* continues to explain that even if the wife were guilty, the bitter waters would have no effect upon her if she had earned some merit in the past. The punishment would be postponed for as long as three years. And what type of merit could she have earned? The merit of having studied Torah. To Ben Azzai, this merit was sufficient justification for a father to teach his daughter Torah.

Ben Azzai's contemporary, Rabbi Eliezer, took an opposite view, insisting that "whoever teaches his daughter Torah teaches her immorality (*tiflut*)," suggesting that she might not be discouraged from leading a profligate life once she has learned that punishment for such behavior would be delayed as much as three years because she had studied Torah.

The question of how women earn merit was also addressed by the Babylonian scholar Rav, who said, "Women earn special merit by making their children go to synagogue to learn Bible and their husbands go to the *beit midrash* to study Mishnah, and by waiting for their husbands until they return" (*Berakhot* 17a).

Because of a woman's primary role as homemaker and nurturer of children and supporter of her husband, Jewish law freed her from the responsibility of abiding by all 248 of the positive commandments. (She is, however, expected to abide by all 365 negative commandments.) This, in essence, is the reason why a man recites the oft-objected-to morning blessing ending in the words *shelo asani ishah*, "Thank God for not making me a woman." The Rabbis, who were all male, were expressing thanks for the privilege of carrying out all the *mitzvot* demanded in the Torah.

Nevertheless, women who fulfilled the special role that was assigned to them were highly praised. For the guidance they gave the family and support they lent their husbands they were called "righteous women" and accorded honor and respect. The Rabbis of the Talmud state: "Women are endowed with more intelligence than men," and "A man should love his wife as himself and respect her more than himself" (*Niddah* 45b and *Yevamot* 62b respectively). Rabbi Judah the Prince was known to be especially careful in giving women proper respect. The Talmud (*Ketubbot* 103a) recalls that when this celebrated leader of Jewry was approaching death, he assembled his sons and said to them, "Be careful to show respect to your mother."

Observances Incumbent Upon Women

Because of a woman's special duties in the home, especially her involvement with the daily task of raising children, a delineation was made between the positive Torah commandments that had to be carried out at a specific time of day or month or year and those not timebound. The timebound positive (commandments), from which women are exempt, are called *mitzvot asei she-ha-zeman gerama* (Mishnah *Kiddushin* 1:7).

The tractate *Rosh Hashanah* (33b–34a) posits as a primary positive timebound commandment the donning of *tefillin*, a ritual carried out in the morning, when women are occupied at home. And by extension, reasoned third-century Babylonian *amora* Acha bar Yaakov, women are exempt from studying Torah. He bases this conclusion on the verse in Exodus (13:9) "And it [the *tefillin*] shall be for a sign upon thine hand and for a memorial between thine eyes, that the Torah may ever be in thy mouth." From this, one may infer that the whole Torah is compared to *tefillin*, and just as putting on *tefillin* is an affirmative commandment limited to a specific time-frame, so is the study of Torah.

Despite the fact that women are generally exempt from observing positive timebound commandments, the Talmud (*Berakhot* 20b) requires them to recite the prayer over wine (*Kiddush*) on the Sabbath, basing this exception on two different words used in reference to the Sabbath in the two versions of the Ten Commandments. Exodus 20:8 commands the Children of Israel to "*remember* the Sabbath Day," while Deuteronomy 5:12 commands them to "*observe* the Sabbath Day." Citing this, the Rabbis established the principle that whoever has to *observe* also has to *remember*, and since women have to observe the Sabbath by abstaining from work, so must they remember the Sabbath by reciting the prayer of sanctification over wine.

Nevertheless, in many homes only the male head of the household recites the *Kiddush*, while all present, women included, fulfill their obligation by responding "Amen" to the prayer and then tasting wine from the leader's cup. This is consistent with the talmudic law (*Rosh Hashanah* 29a) that permits an individual to perform a religious act in behalf of another as long as both are obligated to perform that act. In some households today each person recites the *Kiddush* individually, while in others only males do so. In still others, all present recite the *Kiddush* in unison. A woman dining alone is obligated to recite the *Kiddush*.

In various other talmudic tractates scholars added to the list of time-bound command-ments which a woman is expected to observe. They include fasting on Yom Kippur (*Sukkah* 28a), eating *matzah* on Passover and celebrating the festivals (*Kiddushin* 34a), reading the Scroll of Esther on Purim (*Megillah* 4a), and drinking four cups of wine at the Passover *Seder* (*Pesachim* 108a).

Inappropriate Permissible Activities

There are many Jewish rituals that women do not practice even though they are legally permitted to do so. For example, although in theory Jewish law allows a woman to act as a ritual slaughterer (*shochet*), this is traditionally a male occupation and women are discouraged from entering it (*Shulchan Arukh*, Yoreh Dei'ah 1).

Jewish law also permits a woman to act as a *mohel* (ibid. 264:1), but tradition does not consider performing circumcisions an appropriate female occupation. This attitude prevails, notwithstanding the fact that early in the Bible (Exodus 4:25) Tzipporah, the wife of Moses, circumcised her son.

Lighting Sabbath and Chanukkah Candles

The main, but not exclusive, obligation for lighting Sabbath candles belongs to women. The traditional explanation is found in the Talmud (*Shabbat* 31b), where Rashi comments that because a woman was responsible for man's downfall (by Eve, who at first was tempted by the snake), causing "the light of the world to be dimmed," it is woman's obligation to light the candles and bring back that primordial light. But, if for some medical or other legitimate reason the woman of the house cannot carry out the candlelighting duty, the obligation rests upon the man. Single men, as well as women, who run independent households are obligated to light Sabbath candles.

The primary obligation to light Chanukkah candles rests with the master of the house (*Shulchan Arukh*, Orach Cha'yim 671). However, despite the fact that the lighting ceremony must be performed at a given time, and despite the fact that women are exempt from performing timebound positive commandments (*Shabbat* 23a), women are obligated to light Chanukkah candles, since they, too, witnessed the miracle of Chanukkah (Orach Cha'yim 675:4).

The Polish authority Abraham Gombiner (1635–1683), in his authoritative *Magen Avraham* commentary on the *Shulchan Arukh*, comments that this means that a woman may light Chanukkah candles not only in her own behalf but also in behalf of her entire family.

Wearing a Tallit

One would expect women, like men, to be obligated to carry out the biblical commandment of wearing fringes on one's garment, since it would not interfere with their daily routine. However, since women in ancient times generally did not wear the type of four-cornered garment (*tallit*) worn by men—the type on which fringes (*tzitziot*) could be attached—the wearing of *tzitziot* by women never took root. In addition, most authorities considered the law of *tzitziot* to belong to the category of commandments that must be performed at a specific time of day (during daylight hours) and women are therefore exempt.

Through the ages women now and again have voluntarily taken upon themselves the obligation of wearing *tzitziot*. Today, in some Conservative and Reconstructionist synagogues women do occasionally wear prayer-shawls (*tallitot*) with fringes during services, although this is not a common practice.

Nevertheless, since the wearing of a *tallit* with fringes was seen as not necessarily interfering with a woman's performance of her daily household duties, some Rabbis, as far back as the talmudic period, believed that women should wear fringes on their garments (*Menachot* 43a). In fact, the illustrious Rabbi Judah the Prince is said to have personally attached fringes (*tzitziot*) to his wife's apron and to the aprons of all women in his household. But as far as is known, this practice was not copied by other authorities.

In recent years the egalitarian movement has influenced the non-Orthodox Jewish community significantly, and women have taken it upon themselves the obligation to carry out many of the rituals once reserved only for men. Prominent among these are the donning of a *tallit* and *tefillin*.

Wearing Tefillin

The wearing of *tefillin* is based upon commandments in Exodus 13:9 and 13:16, and Deuteronomy 6:8 and 11:18. In these verses, Jews are mandated to place a symbol "on their hand and between their eyes" as a reminder of God's commandments. Nowhere is it indicated that this law applies only to men. However, as in the case of the *tallit*, the Rabbis of the Talmud ruled that since *tefillin* are worn at a specific time, during the morning service, women are free from this obligation. Nonetheless, in recent years the wearing of *tefillin* has become popular among some non-Orthodox women.

Regarding the position of feminists who today are taking upon themselves the obligation of carrying out *mitzvot* from which Jewish law has exempted them, Nehama Leibowitz, the learned teacher of biblical studies, responded vehemently when once asked if she wanted to put on *tefillin*: "Have I already fulfilled all the *mitzvot* that I am obligated to fulfill with respect to the treatment of my fellow persons? Have I fulfilled my allotment of *chesed*? Am I lacking in *mitzvot* that I am obligated to fulfill, that I should need to lay *tefillin*?"

It has become increasingly commonplace for women studying for the rabbinate or cantorate in non-Orthodox seminaries to pray each morning while wearing *tefillin* and a *tallit*.

Wearing a Headcovering

It is customary for married Orthodox women to wear a headcovering at all times, out of concern that her exposed hair be sexually arousing to men. The question was posed (*Berakhot* 24a) as to whether a wig suffices as a headcovering, or whether a veil, hat, or kerchief must be worn.

Some Orthodox scholars permit the wearing of a wig on the grounds that the Talmud only disapproves of a woman displaying her *own* hair. Others, citing the appearance principle (in Hebrew, *marit a'yin*), are of the opinion that a woman may not wear a wig without covering it. The rationale: a man might be misled into thinking that he is looking at the woman's own hair and is thereby violating the talmudic prohibition against gazing at the hair of a woman (*Shulchan Arukh*, Orach Cha'yim 75:1–2).

Women as Witnesses

The Talmud (Mishnah *Shevuot* 4:1 [30a]) rules that only men may testify in court. When the question is posed, "How do we know [that women are ineligible as witnesses]?" the answer given is that since Deuteronomy 19:17 states, "And the two *men* shall stand," we know that witnesses must be men (*Shevuot* 30a). This view was supported by Moses Maimonides who, in his *Mishneh Torah*, comments

that when the Bible refers to witnesses, it uses the masculine plural form (*eidim*), implying that it is only men who can serve as witnesses (Hilkhot Eidut 9:2).

Some scholars offer a more practical reason for prohibiting women from serving as witnesses. They argue that since in most cases women were supported totally by their husbands and were not property owners, that if a woman had been allowed to testify and her testimony proved inaccurate, damages levied against her could not be collectible as they would in a case involving a man who gave false testimony.

It should be noted that in post-talmudic times women could appear as witnesses in cases where they were particularly knowledgeable, such as those involving an *agunah* (*Sotah* 47b).

In Reform and Reconstructionist Judaism women have been granted full parity with men. They are counted as part of a *minyan*, act as rabbis and cantors, and may sign as witnesses on all religious documents. Conservative Judaism has granted women many of these rights, but not the right to sign as a witness.

Counting Women in a Minyan

The Talmud does not discuss whether a woman may be counted as part of a *minyan*. It is only in the codes that appeared many centuries later that she is denied this right. The reason given is that women have important responsibilities to home and family that exempt her from attending public prayer services. Since she is exempt from this responsibility, eligibility to be counted in the quorum (*minyan*) is denied.

In 1973, the Rabbinical Assembly's Committee on Law and Standards (Conservative) ruled that the decision as to whether women should be counted as part of a *minyan* be left to the individual congregation and its rabbi. Many Conservative rabbis prefer to follow the law as enunciated in the minor tractate *Soferim* (10:17), namely that a *minyan* for a prayer service must consist of ten adult males. Conservative rabbis who favor counting women as part of a *minyan* base their opinion on a passage in tractate *Megillah* (23a): "All are to be counted in the seven [who may be called up to read the Torah on Sabbath], even a woman and a minor..."

Although liberal rabbis acknowledge that this last statement refers only to the *minyan* required for the Sabbath Torah reading, they emphasize that the reading is an essential part of the synagogue service; and since women once enjoyed the honor of receiving *aliyot* and reading from the Torah, this privilege of being counted as equal with men should be restored and even extended to include women when counting individuals to a *minyan* for a prayer service. Orthodox congregations do not count women, while Reform and Reconstructionist congregations do.

Receiving Aliyot

In talmudic times women who were sufficiently educated received *aliyot* and read from the Torah just as men did (*Megillah* 23a). In that period (first centuries C.E.), those who were called to the Torah not only recited the Torah blessings but also read their own individual portions. However, the Rabbis were concerned that if a woman was given an *aliyah* while some men present in the congregation had not received one, the impression might be left that the men were insufficiently learned to read the unvoweled text of the Torah, and this would cause both them and the congregation embarrassment. Therefore, invoking the "honor of the public" (*kevod tzi-*

bur) principle, the Rabbis denied women the privilege of being awarded *aliyot*.

Other reasons were advanced for not permitting women to appear before men on the *bimah*. Rabbi Samuel said (*Berakhot* 24a) that to listen to a woman's voice (*kol ishah*) is sexually provocative and would interfere with a man's concentration on his prayers.

However, as late as the thirteenth century we find a responsum of Rabbi Meir of Rothenburg (1215–1293) in which he answers a question addressed to him by Rabbi Asher ben Moses which would indicate that in some instances women were awarded *aliyot*. Meir says that if there are no *Yisra'elim* at a Sabbath service, women and children *may* be called up to the Torah. And, if there are only *Kohanim* present and no women are present, the Torah cannot be read. It is apparent from this responsum that at least at one time, in some German communities, women were invited to recite the Torah blessings. Today, many Conservative and all Reform and Reconstructionist congregations award *aliyot* to women because they no longer regard as valid the prohibition based on *kevod tzibur*. Since the individual who is called to the Torah no longer reads the Torah portion, the original reason of potentially causing embarrassment is no longer applicable.

The Evolving Status of Women

The role of women began to change somewhat after the destruction of the Second Temple, especially in Jewish communities outside Palestine. While many scholars in the academies of learning in Palestine and Babylonia continued to disparage women, leaders of Jewry in other countries, especially in Egypt and its metropolis, Alexandria, treated women with great respect and allowed them to play a prominent role in Jewish life.

Inscriptions on a large fourth-century synagogue in Alexandria indicate just how active women were. In seven out of fourteen inscriptions, only women are mentioned, and in the remaining seven both women and men are mentioned. The men list the contributions of their wives, their children, and their mothers-in-law.

Basically, from talmudic times onward, the status of women in Jewish life continued virtually unchanged until, in the year 1000, Rabbenu Gershom of Mainz, Germany, a leading rabbi of the day, convened a synod of prominent rabbis that enacted legislation prohibiting a man from having more than one wife simultaneously, which is not prohibited in the Bible. He also enacted legislation that would prevent a man from divorcing a wife without her consent. (If he tried, she could refuse to accept the *get*, the divorce document.) But despite this monumental change in the law, it would be a long time before the status of women would be significantly improved.

The Beth Jacob Schools

One of the early pioneers in the drive for providing a Jewish education for girls in modern times was Sarah Schenirer (1883–1935). Her father was a follower of the chasidic Rabbi of Belz, but unlike most *chasidim* he believed his daughter should receive religious instruction, and he therefore hired a teacher to tutor her once or twice a week. Sarah became quite learned and was able to study not only the Bible but rabbinic texts.

Sarah considered it unfair that only boys should receive a formal Jewish education while girls were being neglected. She believed that it was necessary for Jewish girls to receive a good education if they were to be able to transmit their Jewish heritage to the children they would be rearing.

At the start of World War I, Sarah and her family fled to Vienna, Austria, where she attended lectures by one Rabbi Dr. Flesch, a modern progressive rabbi whose talks inspired her to open a religious school for women. This she did in 1917 when, following the war, she returned to her hometown of Cracow. She received encouragement from such notables as the Rebbe of Belz, the Rebbe of Ger, and the Chafetz Chaim. She began teaching a few very young children in her home, and by 1918, as her reputation as a fine teacher spread, twenty-five older girls began coming to her for religious instruction. Thus was founded her first school, which was named Beth Jacob (House of Jacob).

By 1929, with the aid of Agudat Israel, 147 schools for girls were established in Poland, and twenty schools in Lithuania, Latvia, and Austria. By 1937, in Poland alone, 248 schools were opened with an enrollment of 35,000 girls. By the end of World War II Beth Jacob schools were opened in Israel, England, Switzerland, Belgium, France, Uruguay, Argentina, and the United States.

Little is known of Sarah's personal life. It has been reported that she was once married, but divorced her husband because he was not sufficiently observant. After a brief illness, Sarah Schenirer died in 1935 in a Vienna hospital, at the age of fifty-two.

Bat Mitzvah

In a desire to give formal recognition to girls who had reached maturity by age twelve, in 1922 Rabbi Mordecai Kaplan, the founding father of the Reconstructionist movement, introduced a bat mitzvah ceremony in his New York City synagogue, the Society for the Advancement of Judaism (SAJ). The girl celebrating her bat mitzvah was Dr. Kaplan's daughter, Judith.

The practice quickly spread to other non-Orthodox congregations, first to those affiliated with the Conservative movement and later to Reform congregations. Modern Orthodox congregations did not follow suit, but did acknowledge that at age twelve in a girl's life she is considered an adult and is bound by all *mitzvot* to which an adult woman is obligated.

Orthodox Opposition to Bat Mitzvah

Among ultra-Orthodox rabbis there is a wide range of attitude on the subject of recognizing the bat mitzvah celebration in a formal religious manner. At one extreme, Rabbi Moshe Feinstein was opposed to anyone holding, or even attending, a bat mitzvah celebrated in the synagogue or even at a party on private premises. He considered the celebration nonsensical. *Hevel* is the descriptive Hebrew word he used (*Igrot Moshe* on Orach Cha'yim 1:104).

The Chief Rabbi of France, a Sephardic Jew, opposed the ritual, but with far less vituperation. On the other hand, the Sephardic Chief Rabbi of Israel, Ovadiah Yosef, held a view that was quite liberal. While he did not believe that the ceremony should be held during the formal synagogue service, he did believe that the day should be marked by a festive meal that could legitimately be called a *se'udat mitzvah,* a religious meal of celebration (*Yechaveh Da'at* II:29 and *Yabi'a Omer* 6, on Orach Cha'yim 29).

Modern Orthodox Jews, following the lead of Rabbi Yosef, do celebrate a young girl's coming of age at a *kiddush* after the Sabbath service. At that time, the girl delivers a short speech, called a *d'var Torah,* often related to the *sidrah* that was read in the synagogue that morning. Sometimes the *d'var Torah* is given at a party held at another location.

Ordination of Women

In 1846, at their conference in Breslau, Germany, Reform rabbis favored the granting of religious equality to women, yet it was not until 1972 that a Reform seminary, Hebrew Union College—Jewish Institute of Religion, ordained Sally J. Priesand as the first woman rabbi. By 1984 it had ordained a total of seventy-two women rabbis.

The Conservative movement, which also aspired toward greater equality, did not grant women the right to be candidates for ordination at the Jewish Theological Seminary until 1984. In 1985, it ordained Amy Eilberg as the first woman rabbi. In 1903 Henrietta Szold, who later founded Hadassah, the women's Zionist organization, had been permitted to attend classes at the Jewish Theological Seminary, but on condition that she would not be ordained and would not use her knowledge to function as a rabbi.

The Reconstructionist Rabbinical College, which was founded in Philadelphia in 1968 by disciples of Rabbi Mordecai Kaplan, stands for granting women full equality with men "in all matters of ritual." In 1974, it ordained Sandy Eisenberg Sasso as its first woman rabbi.

In the Orthodox community, ordination for women has not yet been accepted. Nonetheless, some of the greatest Orthodox scholars are women. Outstanding among them is Nehama Leibowitz (1905–   ), sister of the late Hebrew University Professor Yeshayahu Leibowitz (1903–1994), who commented on the esteem in which his sister is held: "The greatest revolution of the twentieth century is the entrance of women into the world of learning."

In recent years it has become increasingly commonplace for women to study Talmud and the *Code of Jewish Law (Shulchan Arukh).* In an article in *Moment* magazine (December 1993), Blu Greenberg, a highly educated Orthodox feminist and author of *How to Run a Traditional Jewish Household*, made the following striking statement:

> Orthodox women should be ordained because it would constitute a recognition of their new intellectual accomplishments and spiritual attainments; because it would encourage greater Torah study; because it offers wider female models of religious life.

Greenberg's wish has not come to fruition, but a number of Orthodox congregations have added to their rabbinic staff female scholars known as *yo'eitzot* ("advisors"). They supplement the work of the rabbi by being available for guidance, particularly to female members of the congregation.

See Education; Mechitzah; Ordination; Purity and Impurity; Shekhinah; Tallit; Tefillin; Women's Gallery.

Women's Gallery

The special section set aside for women in Orthodox synagogues has its origin in the First and Second Temples, dating back some 3,000 years. The largest Temple assembly area, measuring approximately 200 x 200 feet (135 square cubits), was called *ezrat nashim*—the "Court [Quarters] of Women."

The area was probably so named because more women than men would congregate there at one time, since men were permitted to occupy other Temple areas whereas women were not. When men wished to bring a sacrifice, they could enter the adjoining Priestly Court, which abutted the altar area where sacrifices were brought. Women had to remain with their sacrifices at the gate of the Priestly Court, where a Priest (*Kohen*) would be waiting to receive them.

On Sukkot in particular, throngs would come to the Temple to celebrate the special water libation ceremony, at the conclusion of the first day of the holiday. Because of the crowds, which brought men and women in close proximity, the Sages decided that it would be wise to build a gallery around the perimeter of the Women's Court and have the women confined to that area. Apparently, the Rabbis feared that such close contact between men and the women would lead to sexual misconduct (*Sukkah* 51b).

The gallery was removed after the Sukkot holiday, but the practice of separating men from women continued. Historical records indicate that by the thirteenth century the establishment of a separate women's section in the synagogue was widespread.

Today, only Orthodox synagogues separate men from women during prayer.

See Mechitzah; Simchat Beit Ha-Sho'eivah.

Written Law

According to tradition, the Jewish religion began with the Revelation on Mount Sinai (Exodus 19:5–6). God appeared to Moses on the mountaintop, and there He revealed the laws and doctrines the Jews were to follow if they were to become a "holy nation." Until talmudic times, these were the only laws permitted to be recorded in writing, hence the name Written Law, known in Hebrew as *Torah she-bikhtav*.

See Oral Law; Torah.

Yahrzeit

Derived from the German *Jahrzeit*, meaning "anniversary," the Yiddish word *yahrzeit* was first used by the early Christian Church to denote an occasion honoring the memory of the dead. It was not employed by Jews until the Middle Ages, although the custom of remembering parents and teachers on the anniversary of death dates back to talmudic times (*Nedarim* 12a).

The first Jew to employ the term *yahrzeit* to denote the anniversary of a death was the fourteenth-century German scholar Rabbi Jacob Mollin (the Maharil), who used it in his writings. Sephardim use the word *nachalah* for *yahrzeit*. In modern Hebrew, Yom Ha-Shanah is the term used.

The primary ceremonies connected with *yahrzeit* observance are the lighting of a twenty-four hour memorial lamp, the leading of a religious service by the mourner if capable, receiving an *aliyah* when the Torah is read that day or week, and, most important, the recitation of *Kaddish* at all services held on that day. While it was once considered an act of piety for one to fast on the day *yahrzeit* is observed for a parent, this custom is no longer widely practiced. Many people choose to visit the graves of loved ones.

While the occasion of *yahrzeit* is often thought of as sad, the charismatic second-century talmudic authority Shimon Bar Yocha'i, who is considered to be the author of the *Zohar*, thought of it as a time for celebration. He left instructions that his death be memorialized joyfully, and his *yahrzeit* date became known as *Yom Hilula de-Rabbi Shimon bar Yocha'i*, "a day of celebrating the life of Rabbi Shimon bar Yocha'i." To this day, many of his followers make a pilgrimage on Lag Ba-Omer, the day of Rabbi Shimon's death, to his grave on the top of Mount Meron in the Galilee, where they study and celebrate his life.

This positive attitude toward death has roots in early Jewish literature. The Midrash (*Ecclesiastes* 7:4) makes the following comment: "When a person is born, all rejoice; when he dies, all weep. It should not be so. When a person enters this world, there should be no rejoicing, because it is not known how he will develop; it is not known whether he will be righteous or wicked, good or bad. However, when he dies with a good name and leaves the world in peace, there is cause for rejoicing." That is what King Solomon meant when he said, "Better is the day of death than the day of birth."

It was in this spirit that the minor tractate *Eivel Rabbati*, meaning "Great Mourning," was renamed *Semachot*, meaning "rejoicing."

Viewing death as a time to rejoice and remember fondly was reflected in Sholom Aleichem's request in his will that on his *yahrzeit* family members should assemble at his gravesite and read some of his more humorous stories.

See Birthdays.

Yamim Nora'im

A Hebrew term literally meaning "days of awe," introduced by the German scholar Rabbi Jacob ben Moses of Mollin (*c.* 1360–1427), also known as the Maharil. It refers specifically to the ten-day period between Rosh Hashanah and Yom Kippur when, according to the Talmud (*Rosh Hashanah* 16a), all man's actions of the past year are reviewed by God, who judges whether the individual's deeds have been meritorious and what fate is in store for each person in the coming year. These awesome days are also known as *Aseret Yemei Teshuvah*, "Ten Days of Repentance," for during this period man can still influence God's judgment.

In the Talmud (*Rosh Hashanah* 16b), Rabbi Yochanan summarized what transpires during these fateful days: "Three books are opened on Rosh Hashanah for the evaluation of man: The Book of Life of the completely wicked, The Book of Life of the completely righteous, The Book of Life of those in between. The perfectly righteous are immediately promised a good life in the future. The perfectly wicked are immediately condemned to death. Judgment of those in between is deferred until Yom Kippur, when a final decision is made as to which category they are to be assigned.

Yarchei Kallah

This Hebrew term meaning "*kallah* months" is the name assigned to Elul and Adar, the months preceding Rosh Hashanah and Passover, when the work of farmers was relatively light. During this period thousands made their way to the Babylonian academies, where they engaged in Torah study and attended lectures, especially about the forthcoming holidays (*Berakhot* 6a). The practice was ongoing in Babylonia between the first and tenth centuries C.E.

The word *kallah* may stem from the Hebrew word *kalol*, meaning "all inclusive" and referring to the conglomerate of individuals who assembled in the academies for an extended period of study.

See Kolel.

Yashan and Chadash

The Hebrew words *yashan* and *chadash*, meaning "old" and "new" respectively, represent a rabbinic concept based upon statements in Leviticus, chapters 23:9–14 and 26:10.

In Leviticus 23, the Israelites are promised that if they obey all the commandments of God, when they enter the Promised Land the grain harvest will be so plentiful that the granaries will always be full. Thus, Rashi comments, the overabundance of the old crop, which will improve with age, will make it impossible to accommodate the new.

The Bible here specifies that the Israelites were to bring to the Priest (*Kohen*) a portion of the new crop in the amount of one *omer* before the rest of the harvest could be used. The Priest would offer the grain as a meal-sacrifice to God. Once this offering was brought, all new grain (*chadash*) cut from the fields could be consumed by the farmer, but up until that time only *yashan*, grain harvested before that point, could be used.

In the Talmud (*Pesachim* 10b–11a), compiled when the Temple no longer existed, the Rabbis associate the concept of *yashan* and *chadash* with the removal of leaven from the home on the fourteenth of Nissan. All grain harvested from the fields after that point in time was considered *chadash* and therefore could not be consumed until the following season.

The Rabbis of later generations ruled that the laws of *yashan* and *chadash* did not apply to Jews living in the Diaspora. Yet many Orthodox Jews continued to abide by the talmudic ruling. Professor Louis Ginzberg of the Jewish Theological Seminary recalls that his father, Rabbi Isaac Ginzberg, honored this principle.

Professor Ginzberg relates the story of how in 1884, when he was thirteen years old, his father took him on a six-day trip from Neustadt to enroll as a student at the Telzer *yeshivah*. On one of the nights, they stopped at an inn in the town of Plunge. Although they had not eaten for many hours, Rabbi Isaac would not consume the bread they offered because he could not be sure that it had not been made from *chadash*—from new grain. Apparently, he did not agree with many authorities who ruled that the laws of *yashan* and *chadash* do not apply to Jews living in the Diaspora, as do most ultra-Orthodox Jews to this day.

Yavneh and Yaknehaz

Two acronyms used to remember the sequence of events and blessings that are part of the *havdalah* service following the Sabbath and festivals. *Yavneh* represents the four Hebrew letters *yud, vet, nun,* and *hei. Yud* stands for *ya'yin,* meaning "wine"; *vet* (or *bet*) stands for *besamim,* meaning "spices"; *nun* stands for *ner,* meaning "candle" or "light", and *hei* for *havdalah,* meaning "separation [of the holy from the mundane]." These are the four parts of the *havdalah* service.

Yaknehaz, spelled *yud kuf nun hei za'yin,* serves as a reminder of the five *Havdalah* blessings recited when the Sabbath coincides with a holiday. *Yud* for *ya'yin* (wine); *kuf* for *Kiddush,* the blessing recited over the wine; *nun* stands for *ner* (candle); *hei* for *havdalah.* The *za'yin* stands for *zeman,* meaning "[holiday] time," a reference to the special *She-heche'yanu* prayer that is recited on the first day of a holiday.

Since the word *yaknehaz* sounds so much like the German expression *jag den Hase,* meaning "hunt the hare," artists in medieval times who illustrated books, particularly Haggadot, drew hunting scenes. Sholom Aleichem took advantage of the odd-sounding word and made it the name of a town in some of his stories.

See She-heche'yanu.

Yeitzer Ha-Ra

A Hebrew term literally meaning "the evil inclination," specifically that inborn tendency in man that leads him to perform destructive and evil acts. A common prayer is, "May the evil impulse not dominate my life" (*Berakhot* 60b). The opposite concept is *yeitzer ha-tov.*

Yeitzer Ha-Tov

A Hebrew term literally meaning "the good inclination," specifically the drive in man to aspire to perform good deeds. The term is often expressed in a prayer, such as, "Cause me to cleave to the good inclination and to a good friend" (*Berakhot* 60b). The opposite concept is *yeitzer ha-ra.*

Yekum Purkan

By the eleventh century, when Jewish life in Babylonia had reached its peak, the influence of the *ge'onim* began to wane, and legal authorities in Europe and North Africa rose to prominence. At that time an unidentified author composed a prayer in Aramaic that became known by its first words, *yekum purkan,* meaning "may salvation arise [from Heaven]."

The prayer asks that God's blessings be conferred on "the principals of academies of learning," and on "the exilarchs [*roshei galuta*]," those appointed to manage the secular affairs of the community in captivity in Babylonia. It was therefore quite fitting that the prayer be recited as long as the leaders of the failing Babylonian communities had power and influence. But, oddly, today the *Yekum Purkan* is still recited in Ashkenazic synagogues before the *Musaf* service on the Sabbath and holidays. Sephardic congregations generally do not include the prayer in their liturgy.

See Gaon.

Yeshivah

Plural, *yeshivot.* Derived from the Hebrew word meaning "to sit," the *yeshivah* is a school in which students of all ages and all levels of erudition spend many hours each day engaged in Jewish studies. Traditionally, in the more advanced schools the focus is on the

Talmud and codes of Jewish law, although in modern academies Bible and history are also part of the curriculum.

The most elementary type of *yeshivah*, the *yeshivah ketanah* ("small" *yeshivah*), was designed to serve children of elementary school age. *Yeshivot* of this type became common in America at the beginning of the twentieth century, although they existed for many centuries in a number of European and North African countries.

In the United States today, these junior schools are open every day of the week except the Sabbath, from 8:00 AM or 9:00 AM, until approximately 7:00 PM. On Friday, classes are let out at noon so that students can prepare for the Sabbath. Judaic studies are generally taught until 3:00 PM, and after a short rest period the English curriculum is begun. One of the oldest and most prominent of these schools is the Rabbi Jacob Joseph School (RJJ), which originated on New York City's Lower East Side.

Discipline in *yeshivot* is strict, and until recently the rule of "spare the rod and spoil the child" was taken literally by many of the instructors. Yiddish novelist Chaim Grade (1910–1982), in his novel *Yeshiva* (1967, translated into English in 1976 by Curt Leviant), describes the *yeshivah* as that "institution of Jewish learning which inspired, shaped, and sometimes stained the lives of countless Jewish youths."

Adult Study Academies

For the most part, *yeshivot* were established for adult study. The earliest of these were founded in the major Babylonian cities of Sura and Pumbedita during the Second Temple period. The *yeshivot* did not gain prominence until after the destruction of the Second Temple in 70 C.E., reaching their peak during the talmudic and geonic periods, from about 200 to 1000 C.E. The heads of these academies were called *ge'onim* (singular, *ga'on*), meaning "illustrious ones." The distinguished scholar Sa'adya Gaon headed the academy at Sura, while Sherira Gaon and his son Hai Gaon were the respected heads of the academy in Pumbedita.

In subsequent centuries, similar centers of study were established throughout Europe and North Africa. Usually, the Chief Rabbi of the city was the dean of the school, this being part of his rabbinic responsibilities. The community itself maintained these institutions of higher learning, but wealthy families contributed to their support and invited students, many of whom had come from distant cities and countries, to spend Sabbaths and holidays with them.

One of the characteristics of the adult *yeshivah*, then and now, is that each of its students studies with a partner in a buddy system known as *chavrutah*. In keeping with a warning issued by the talmudic scholar Rabbi Eliezer, students are required to study out loud. Eliezer had one student who studied silently and after three years forgot all that he had learned (*Eruvin* 54a. *See Ta'anit* 7a).

As the Jewish population made its home in Europe in the early and later Middle Ages, *yeshivot* were established in every major city. The *yeshivah* of Moses ben Nachman (Nachmanides) was established in Gerona, Spain, and that of Solomon ibn Adret in Barcelona. The *yeshivah* of Rabbenu Tam, grandson of Rashi, was founded in France. In Mainz, Rabbenu Gershom Me'or Ha-Golah established one of the more prestigious German academies. From the sixteenth century onward, *yeshivot* were established by prominent rabbis in Poland, Hungary, and other countries.

The academies of Lithuania were the most

outstanding because of the style and intensity of instruction. The most renowned of these was led by the great talmudist Elijah ben Solomon [Zalman] (1720–1979), better known as the Vilna Gaon. Because he refused to accept a rabbinic position and the remuneration that came with it, the Vilna Gaon's reputation for saintliness and talmudic scholarship was widespread. Many *yeshivot* in Europe and later in America were modeled after his.

Yeshivot in America

One of the earliest of the adult *yeshivot* to be established in America was Yeshivat Etz-Chaim, which opened its doors in New York City in 1896. It was later renamed Yeshivat Rabbenu Yitzchak Elchanan, after the celebrated Russian talmudic scholar Isaac Elchanan Spector (1817–1896), who had led congregations in various White Russian towns and later established a noted *yeshivah* in Kovno (Lithuania). The institution grew into what later became Yeshiva University.

One of the junior *yeshivot* in America was named after an illustrious Kovno rabbi, Israel (Salanter) Lipkin (1810–1883), founder of the Slobodka *yeshivah* in Lithuania and initiator of the *Musar* movement. Its purpose was to emphasize the study of ethics and morality and the strengthening of inner piety, to which *yeshivot* had heretofore paid little attention. The Salanter Yeshiva, later established in the Bronx, New York, was named after him.

By the end of the twentieth century there were hundreds of junior and senior *yeshivot* throughout North America. With the exception of those under ultra-Orthodox auspices, secular studies are part of each day's curriculum.

Most *yeshivot* today are under Orthodox sponsorship, but in recent decades the Conservative movement's Solomon Schechter schools have established a greater presence. In recent years, even the Reform movement has begun to establish day schools with heavy concentration on Judaic studies.

Hesder Yeshivot

In Israel, where many of the students in Orthodox *yeshivot* are exempt from serving in the military, more than a dozen Orthodox academies of learning, known as *hesder* ("orderly") *yeshivot*, were established. In these academies, an orderly arrangement was made so that students could voluntarily fulfill their years of military service while continuing their studies.

See Kolel; Musar Movement; Orthodox Judaism.

Yibum

According to Torah legislation a man is required to marry his deceased brother's widow if she is childless. This institution, rarely observed in modern times, is referred to in Hebrew as *yibum*.

See Levirate Marriage.

Yichud

A Hebrew term literally meaning "union, joining, togetherness." In the Orthodox tradition, after the glass is broken at the end of the wedding ceremony, the couple leaves the gathering and spends five or ten minutes alone together in a private room. Since the bride and groom have fasted all day, they now partake of a small snack. In early days, *yichud* involved actual consummation of the marriage. This practice has long been abandoned.

See Weddings.

Yichus

This Yiddish term of Hebrew origin applies to one who has a good pedigree, who stems from a scholarly or prestigious family. The concept frequently comes into play when considering a prospective marriage partner.

Yigdal

A Hebrew term literally meaning "May He be exalted," the name given to a popular liturgical hymn in praise of God. Authored around the year 1300 by Daniel ben Judah of Rome, the *Yigdal* originally was recited at the beginning of the daily morning service, but later it was adopted as the concluding hymn for the Sabbath and holiday morning services as well.

Yigdal is based on the Thirteen Principles of Faith expressed by Moses Maimonides in his introduction to the Mishnah *Sanhedrin*, chapter 10.

See Ani Ma'amin.

Yizkor

A Hebrew term literally meaning "May He [God] remember." Also referred to as *Hazkarat Neshamot* ("remembering the souls"), this is the name of the Hebrew memorial prayer in which departed family members are lovingly recalled. The third-fourth century Palestinian scholar Ammi Said (*Shabbat* 55a), "There is no death without sin [*ein mitah b'lo cheit*], the implication being that our deceased relatives are in need of our prayers in order to prevail upon God to allow them to enter Paradise. Each of the *Yizkor* prayers recited on the three Pilgrim Festivals articulate this theme.

Although the earliest reference to the *Yizkor* service is found in the eleventh-century *Machzor Vitry*, composed by Rabbi Simcha ben Samuel of Vitry, a pupil of Rashi, some scholars believe that the service dates back to the Maccabean period (165 B.C.E.), when Judah the Maccabee and his soldiers prayed for their fallen comrades and brought sacrifices to the Temple in Jerusalem to atone for their sins (II Maccabees 22:39–45).

Most scholars, however, are of the opinion that *Yizkor* was introduced as a formal part of the prayer service in the aftermath of the First Crusade (1096), when many thousands of Jews were murdered indiscriminately by Christians who were making their way to the Holy Land to wrest it from the Moslems. The *Yizkor* prayer expresses the hope that these innocent martyrs would appeal to God in behalf of the suffering masses everywhere.

The German community was particularly hard-hit by the mad antics of the frenzied Crusaders whose battle cry was, "Kill a Jew and save your soul." Wanting to memorialize their dead, the Germans recorded all names of Jews who were martyred by the Crusaders into a *Memorbuch*, "Book of memories." On Yom Kippur and other major festivals, it was customary to read the names of the deceased publicly during services.

Opposition to Yizkor

Hai Gaon (939–1038), the most eminent Babylonian scholar of the eleventh century, together with his prominent pupil Nissim ben Jacob, opposed the custom of praying for the dead on festivals and on Yom Kippur. They also opposed donating charity in memory of the dead, as is pledged during the *Yizkor* service. These scholars believed that the only things important to God are the good deeds that each individual actually performs in his lifetime. One cannot be saved through the good deeds or prayers of ancestors or others.

The Sephardic community did not suffer the ravages of the Crusaders and, in keeping with the ruling of Hai Gaon, did not feel the need to introduce a *Yizkor* prayer. In recent times, to accommodate members of their communities with Ashkenazic antecedents, some Sephardic synagogues do conduct a special memorial service but only after the formal holiday service is concluded.

Although originally a memorial prayer was recited in the synagogue only on Yom Kippur, it later became customary to recite *Yizkor* on the three major holidays: Pesach, Shavuot, and Sukkot (Shemini Atzeret in the *Diaspora*), when the concept of salvation through prayer and charity became popular. In many Reform congregations, *Yizkor* is recited only on Yom Kippur and the last day of Passover.

Although it is considered preferable for the individual to recite the *Yizkor* prayer at a public service in the synagogue, where a quorum of ten adults (*minyan*) is present, it is also permissible to recite the prayer in the privacy of one's home. *Kaddish*, however, may not be recited unless a *minyan* is present.

Many Jews are under the impression that *Yizkor* may not be recited during the first year after a death in the family, but no such prohibition exists. *Yizkor* may be recited beginning with the very first holiday following the death of a loved one, even if only one month has elapsed. Since *Yizkor* is a positive statement of faith in God and an expression of love for a departed relative, there is no valid reason to postpone its recitation for an entire year.

In most congregations, worshippers who have not lost a close relative leave the synagogue during the recitation of *Yizkor*, although there is no requirement to do so.

Yoma Arichta

An Aramaic term literally meaning "one extended day." Of all holidays in the Jewish calendar, only Rosh Hashanah is celebrated on the first day of a month. Since in early times the first day of the month (Rosh Chodesh in Hebrew) could only be ascertained through the testimony of witnesses who declared that they had sighted the new moon, and who then relayed the sighting via messengers sent out to communities far from Jerusalem, Jews living in distant places would often receive the news belatedly and fail to observe the holiday on time. Rosh Hashanah, a one-day biblical holiday falling on the first day of the month, was therefore extended to a two-day holiday, and the two days were considered to be *yoma arichta*, one long day. The second day of the holiday is not widely observed by Reform Jews.

See Berakhah Le-Vatalah.

Yom Ha-Atzma'ut

Literally meaning "day of independence," this holiday was recently added to the Jewish calendar in order to commemorate the establishment of the State of Israel. It is celebrated on the fifth day of the Hebrew month Iyyar, because it was on this day, corresponding to May 14, 1948, that Israel achieved statehood. Not since the year 70 C.E., when the Second Temple was destroyed by the Romans, had Israel been an independent nation.

Yom Ha-Atzma'ut is celebrated throughout Israel by holding spectacular parades and lavish festivities. Increasingly, it has become an important Diaspora holiday as well, although many congregations, particularly the ultra-Orthodox, have been unwilling to assign to it a religious dimension. Unlike modern Orthodox, Conservative, and Reform Jews, they have been unwilling to introduce special prayers of thanksgiving into the prayer service of the day.

Yom Ha-Sho'ah

Literally "a day of tragedy and destruction," which was established by the Israeli Knesset on April 12, 1951 (the 27th day of the Hebrew month of Nissan) as a memorial day for the victims and heroes of the Holocaust.

See Holocaust Remembrance Day.

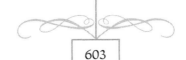

Yom Kippur

Literally meaning "Day of Atonement," Yom Kippur is a solemn day of prayer and fasting observed annually on the tenth day of the Hebrew month Tishrei, as mandated in the Book of Leviticus (23:27) and repeated in the Book of Numbers (29:7). No manner of work may be done, and one is instructed to "afflict his soul" on that day by fasting and seeking atonement for sinfulness.

While it is popularly believed that Yom Kippur is the holiest day in the Jewish calendar, the Sabbath is in fact on a higher plane of sanctity. The Bible makes it clear that the penalty for violating Yom Kippur is excommunication (Leviticus 23:29), whereas the penalty for violating the Sabbath is death (Exodus 31:14).

All mature, healthy adult Jews are obligated to fast on Yom Kippur. Girls under age twelve and boys under age thirteen are not so obligated, but they are usually trained to fast for part of the day after age ten or eleven.

Yom Kippur Calendar Days

While all other fast days that fall on the Sabbath are postponed to Sunday, Yom Kippur must be observed on its appointed day. The calendar was designed so that the tenth of Tishrei should not fall on a Friday, Sunday, or Tuesday.

If Yom Kippur were to fall on a Friday, it would be impossible to prepare food for the Sabbath. If it were to fall on a Sunday, it would be impossible to do on the Sabbath all that is necessary to prepare for the fast. If it were to fall on a Tuesday, Hoshanah Rabbah would fall on the Sabbath, and the requirement that willows (aravot) be beaten could not be observed, for this would be a violation of the Sabbath.

Pre- and Post-Holiday Foods

At the pre-holiday meal, the challah served is sometimes decorated with birds, expressing the hope that as winged creatures fly heavenward with ease and grace, so will man's prayers reach God and be answered favorably. Similar challot are made for Rosh Hashanah. Triangular-shaped dumplings known as kreplach, usually filled with chopped meat, chopped onion, and seasonings, are also served at the pre-fast meal.

Since water is not drunk during the twenty-five hour Yom Kippur fast, at the post-Yom Kippur break-the-fast meal salty herring is often served to induce thirst and thus encourage the individual to restore the fluids needed by the body. Rav Yehudah, in the tractate Avodah Zarah (27a), was probably the first to suggest this when he said, "Small fish in brine is good after fasting."

Preparing for Sukkot

In Jewish folklore, the belief is prevalent that following Yom Kippur Satan will make one final effort to entrap Jews and cause them to sin. To convince Satan that they are resolved to fulfill all religious obligations, immediately after the break of the Yom Kippur fast many Jews begin to construct a sukkah for the approaching Sukkot holiday.

Yom Kippur Dress

Among the activities considered pleasurable and therefore banned on the solemn day of Yom Kippur are the wearing of leather shoes, bathing, eating, and sexual intercourse. The wearing of leather apparel was a luxury in ancient times, and it therefore became customary to wear uncomfortable rubber or canvas shoes on Yom Kippur to mark it as a "day of affliction" (Leviticus 23:27). Many people, unaware that it is the leather that is banned, mistakenly wear sneakers with leather sides.

Others consciously continue to wear leather shoes, maintaining that leather is no longer considered a luxury.

At Yom Kippur services, a prayershawl (*tallit*) is worn throughout the day by those who customarily wear one. While on all other holy days and Sabbaths a *tallit* is not worn during an evening service (except for the officiating clergy), on Yom Kippur a *tallit* is donned to accentuate the holiness of the day. The prayershawl is actually donned before nightfall, so that the blessing over it can be recited while it is still light. The opening *Kol Nidrei* prayer itself is also recited before sunset.

Many men, in addition to the rabbi and cantor, wear a white robe called a *kittl* throughout the day. White is a symbol of purity, a state all worshippers hope to achieve as a result of the long day of prayer, meditation, and confession of sins.

Religious Services

Five synagogue services are held in the course of the twenty-five-hour Yom Kippur holiday. *Kol Nidrei*, meaning "all vows," which begins before sundown, opens the holiday. The last service, called *Ne'ilah*, meaning "closing of the gates," concludes it.

In addition to the *Kol Nidrei* and *Ne'ilah* services, a morning service called *Shacharit* is held. This is followed by a *Musaf* ("additional") service, at which the martyrdom of ten rabbis who were put to death by the Romans for teaching Torah is recounted and during which the Temple service once conducted by the High Priest is recalled. A *Minchah* (afternoon) service follows.

Between the *Shacharit* and *Musaf* services, a Torah reading is conducted from two scrolls. Six Torah honors (*aliyot*) are awarded, plus an additional one—the *maftir*. A Torah reading is conducted a second time during the *Minchah*

service, at which three persons are awarded *aliyot*. The person receiving the third *aliyah* chants a prophetic portion (*haftarah*) from the Book of Jonah.

The story of Jonah was selected for the *haftarah* reading because God is represented there as the God of all nations. The concept of the universality of God is emphasized throughout the High Holiday liturgy. The Book of Jonah also addresses itself to another High Holiday theme: that man can abandon his evil ways, accept responsibility for his actions, and return to God.

After the *Ne'ilah* service is concluded, the day of prayer and fasting ends with the sounding of the *shofar*.

See Kapparot; Kol Nidrei; Se'udah Ha-Mafseket.

Yom Kippur Katan

For a short while in the sixteenth century, a minor fast day known as Yom Kippur Katan, meaning "the small Yom Kippur," was observed by a group of students and followers of the kabbalist Rabbi Moses of Cordovero (1522–1570). Cordovero was a colleague of the famous mystic Rabbi Isaac Luria, better known as the Ari. Both had settled in Safed after having spent time in Jerusalem. But while the more inhibited Luria left it to his disciples to spread his kabbalistic teachings, Cordovero took his teachings to Italy, and from Italy to Germany.

Cordovero believed that man must rid himself of guilt by confessing his sins more than once a year on Yom Kippur. Maintaining that a confession should be made monthly, he introduced a fast day to be observed each month on the day before Rosh Chodesh. Special prayers pleading for forgiveness (*selichot*) were uttered so as to purify man's soul and allow him to face a new month in purity. The concept never caught on with the public-at-large, although in a few kabbalistic circles the custom is still followed.

Details of the Yom Kippur Katan observance were brought to light by the Eastern European scholar and kabbalist Isaiah Horowitz (c. 1565–1630) who wrote about it in his classic *Shnei Luchot Ha-Berit* ("Two Tablets of the Covenant"), a deeply ethical work concerning Jewish customs, ceremonies, and beliefs presented from a kabbalistic viewpoint.

See Rosh Chodesh.

Yom Tov

This Hebrew word literally meaning "good day" is the generic term for all Jewish holidays, with specific reference to the three Pilgrim Festivals—Passover, Shavuot, and Sukkot.

Yom Tov Sheini

This Hebrew term literally meaning "second day of a holiday" is a shortened form of the phrase Yom Tov Sheini Shel Galuyot, "the second festival day of the Diaspora." In lands outside of Israel, one extra day was added to the three Pilgrim Festivals (Pesach, Shavuot, and Sukkot) because of the uncertainty of the calendar. But even after the calendar was fixed in the fourth century C.E. and it was certain when each holiday would begin, it was customary for Jews in the Diaspora to retain this added day. The reasoning was that one should not deviate from customs established by one's ancestors.

Moses Maimonides, in his *Mishneh Torah* (Kiddush Ha-Chodesh 5:5), reiterates this talmudic principle when he says, "Be careful: do not treat the customs of your fathers lightly." This attitude was further reinforced by Moses Isserles who, in his Notes to the *Shulchan Arukh* (Yoreh Dei'ah 376:4), says that established custom is equal in importance to established law.

Reform Jews living in the Diaspora do not observe Yom Tov Sheini, whereas Conservative and Orthodox Jews do.

See Calendar, Diaspora.

Yordim

A Hebrew term meaning "those who have gone down," referring specifically to Israeli citizens who have left Israel and settled in the Diaspora. Most of the *yordim* retain their Israeli citizenship and sometimes return to their homeland to vote in national elections.

Yud Bet Chodesh

A Hebrew term literally meaning "twelve months," referring specifically to the year-long mourning period for those who have lost a parent. While those mourning the loss of a relative other than a parent observe only the thirty day mourning period known as *sheloshim*, the Rabbis of the Talmud felt that a full year is required to adequately grieve for a parent.

Unlike the *shivah* and *sheloshim* periods, which commence on the day of burial, the twelve-month mourning period is counted from the date of death according to the Jewish calendar and extends through the first anniversary of that date. Thus, for one who dies on the first day of Nissan, the twelve-month period concludes at the end of the first day of Nissan one year later. *Kaddish*, however, is recited for only eleven months.

When a death occurs in a Hebrew leap year, a year with thirteen months (containing an Adar II in addition to Adar I), the twelve-month mourning period is considered complete at the end of Adar I, after twelve months have elapsed from the date of death.

See Kaddish; Mourners and Mourning, Sheloshim; Shivah.

Zaka

A Hebrew acronym for *Zihui Korbanot Ason* ("Identification of the Victims of Disaster"). Overseen by a band of seven ultra-Orthodox rabbis, this organization consists of over nine hundred members, each volunteering to attend a three-month course of study in which they are taught how to handle bodies and body parts that have been blown up by suicide bombers and how to identify them for burial in accordance with the strict demands of Jewish law (*halakhah*).

The Jerusalem Post of September 22, 2003, has an extensive report by Mitchell Ginsburg detailing the operation of this unique organization of dedicated volunteers that are the first to appear at the scene of a terrorist attack.

Zeh Ne'heneh Ve-Zeh Lo Chaser

A Hebrew phrase literally meaning "this one [person] gains satisfaction and the other [person] suffers no loss." This guiding principle of ethical behavior, of talmudic origin (*Bava Kama* 27a; *Sanhedrin* 8:2), in effect suggests that one go out of his way to help a fellow human being, especially when the person will lose nothing by so doing.

Among the cases cited in the Talmud is one in which a person occupies an unoccupied house without the owner's permission. The Talmud says that the squatter does not have to pay the owner rent because the premises were not occupied and the owner loses nothing while the squatter gains. Another case concerns the owner of a piece of property that abuts a neighbor's plot that is up for sale. The ruling is that if the neighbor is willing to pay the seller as much as any other potential buyer, he must receive preference, since the buyer gains much by having two contiguous pieces of land, while the seller loses nothing.

In modern times, the *zeh ne'heneh ve-zeh lo chaser* principle has been invoked by those who suggest that one may donate an organ to an ill person if the donor will not suffer ill-health thereby. The principle is also sometimes applied to inanimate objects, as when a burning candle is used to light the wick of an unlit candle. The intensity of the burning candle is not diminished, while the unlit one benefits from its flame. In fact, it is sometimes said, the former finds itself empowered by the light emanating from the latter.

Zeikher Le-Churban

This Hebrew expression meaning "in remembrance of the devastation" was introduced after the destruction of Jerusalem and the Second Temple in 70 C.E. at the hands of the Roman emperor Titus. The expression derives from the verse in the Book of Psalms (137:5): "If I forget thee, O Jerusalem, let my right hand wither; let my tongue cleave to my palate if I cease to think of thee, if I do not keep Jerusalem in my memory even at my happiest hour."

Many practices were instituted to perpetuate the memory of the Temple and serve as a reminder of its catastrophic end. The talmudic tractate *Bava Batra* (60b) cautions that when painting or plastering their houses, Jews should leave unfinished a small area above the entrance measuring one square cubit (approximately eighteen inches). In the same reference—as a sign of mourning for the lost sanctuary—women are advised not to wear all of their fine jewelry at one time, and a bridegroom is instructed to place ashes on his forehead, on the spot where the *tefillin* is worn.

Additionally, as a remembrance of the devastation that befell the Temple, the rabbis of the Talmud ruled that the custom of having a bride and groom wear crowns be discontinued.

At a later date, the Jews of Spain permitted the use of a crown made of olives because olives, their national fruit, have a bitter taste that will serve as a reminder of the loss of Jerusalem and the Temple.

One major ruling of the fourth-century amora Abbayei cautioned (*Avodah Zarah* 43a) that "a person should not construct a house after the design of the Temple...or a candelabrum after the design of the Temple candelabrum [which had seven branches]...." One was to be continually cognizant of the terrible loss Jews suffered with the destruction of the Temple.

Zekhut Avot

A Hebrew term literally meaning "the merit of the fathers," referring to the patriarchs Abraham, Isaac, and Jacob. The concept implies that we are not always worthy of the good life we enjoy, and only by virtue of the meritorious lives of our earliest ancestors has our fate been blessed (Ethics of the Fathers 2:2). Later, the concept of *zekhut avot* was extended to encompass all meritorious forebears. Ralph Waldo Emerson captured the spirit of this ancient Jewish concept when he wrote, "Every man is an omnibus on which all his ancestors are seated."

Zemirot

A Hebrew term literally meaning "songs," specifically those of a religious nature that are sung at the dinner table, particularly on the Sabbath. The practice of singing *zemirot* was introduced by the kabbalists of the sixteenth century, primarily by Isaac Luria (the Ari) of Safed. The kabbalists wanted to infuse the Sabbath with a joyful spirit and spiritual significance.

Zionism

In 1891, Nathan Birnbaum (1864–1937), a Viennese-born journalist, coined the word "Zionism" as a name by which to identify a new movement whose goal it was to reestablish a national Jewish homeland in Palestine. The term derives from the Hebrew word *Tziyon*, which is used often in the Bible to refer to the Land of Israel.

As early as 1882, several years before Theodore Herzl (1860–1904) appeared on the international scene, Nathan Birnbaum advocated Jewish nationalism in his writings, and these served as a basis for expressing the Zionist ideology. Subsequently, he worked alongside Herzl for several years, and in 1899 became the first general secretary of the newly formed World Zionist Organization. However, soon thereafter he broke ranks with Herzl, disagreeing about the goal of "*political* Zionism." Birnbaum, along with such prominent figures as Achad (Ahad) Ha-Am (1856–1927), the Ukrainian-born essayist and philosopher, and other members of the Chovevei Zion ("Lovers of Zion") movement, favored a Jewish state that would emerge naturally through the growth of a Jewish spiritual and cultural presence in the Holy Land. A Jewish state, they believed, would emerge only after enough Jews settled in Palestine to form a majority. By the time the Third Zionist Congress of 1899 ended, it was evident that Herzl's views, which foresaw a political solution to the problem of Jewish homelessness and persecution, would prevail.

Herzl on the Scene

It was not until 1894, when Alfred Dreyfus (1859–1935), an army officer on the French general staff, was falsely accused of selling military secrets to the Germans, that young Viennese journalist Theodor Herzl became interested in Jewish affairs. He had been sent by his newspaper *Neue Freie Presse* to cover the Dreyfus trial being held in Paris. Emotionally stirred by the anti-Semitic Parisian mobs that heaped scorn on Dreyfus the Jew, despite the clearly trumped up charges under which Dreyfus was tried and convicted, Herzl was determined to be more involved in the fate of his fellow Jews, with whom he had had little association in the past. He was particularly affected by Emile Zola's classic *J'Accuse*, in which the writer exposed the evident failure of the French judicial system to render a just verdict.

Herzl was likewise moved to action by statements made by Georges Clemenceau (1841–1929), who was premier of France from 1906 to 1909 and again from 1917 to 1920. Clemenceau condemned the 1894 military tribunal that found Dreyfus guilty and sentenced him to life in prison and banishment to Devil's Island, off the coast of French Guiana. After years of effort to see that justice be done, in 1906 Dreyfus was finally declared innocent.

The Jewish State

Clearly in reaction to the injustice of the Dreyfus decision, in 1896 Herzl dashed off a pamphlet entitled *The Jewish State*, in which he argued that anti-Semitism would be overcome only when Jews are recognized as a nation and have their own independent state.

In 1897, at a time when the total Jewish population of Palestine was 50,000, Herzl convened the First Zionist Congress, in Basle, Switzerland. By 1914, that number had grown to 100,000, the Arab population being 500,000. The administration of Palestine was then in the hands of a hostile Ottoman Empire.

At the end of World War I, following the conquest of Palestine by the British in 1917, Foreign Secretary Arthur James Balfour issued the Balfour Declaration, which recognized the Jewish aspiration for a homeland in Palestine and called for the "facilitation" of establishing there a "Jewish national home."

Despite the pronouncement of Lord Balfour, officials in charge of the administration of Palestine instituted restrictions on *aliyah* (immigration) to Palestine. These continued throughout World War II, during which time the Nazis decimated one-third of the Jewish people.

In November 1947, the General Assembly of the United Nations voted to partition Palestine. The Jewish community accepted the plan, but the Arabs opposed it. The British Mandate ended with the establishment of the State of Israel on May 14, 1948.

Immediately, a War of Independence had to be waged against the regular armies of Egypt, Jordan, Syria, Lebanon, and Iran, who had taken up arms against an ill-equipped Israeli army. After fifteen months of bloody battles and the loss of over 6,000 Israeli lives, the Israel Defense Forces prevailed.

With the establishment of the state, the focus of Zionism shifted to providing support for the flow of immigrants from countries where Jews were being, or had been, oppressed. Great effort was also made to encourage all other Jews to make *aliyah* and settle in Israel, where they were assured a more meaningful life.

Zionist Leaders

Many outstanding leaders have shaped the Zionist movement. The following, reflecting a variety of perspectives, were highly instrumental in bringing the state of Israel to full bloom:

Louis Dembitz Brandeis (1856–1941), American-born U. S. Supreme Court Justice, appointed in 1916 by President Woodrow

Wilson, was honorary president of the Zionist Organization of America from 1918 to 1921 and of the World Zionist Organization from 1920 to 1921. Brandeis helped establish the Palestine Economic Corporation and the Palestine Endowment Fund, both devoted to building Palestine's economy.

Ze'ev (Wolf) Gold (1899–1956), Polish-born rabbi and noted preacher who served as president of Mizrachi (the religious Zionist organization) in America before settling in Palestine in 1935. He was a member of the executive committee of the Jewish Agency and president of the Mizrachi World Organization, which came into being in 1902, specifically to counter the position of secular Zionists. Quite appropriately, its slogan was: "The Land of Israel for the people of Israel according to the Torah of Israel."

Nahum Goldmann (1894–1982), Russian-born leader who represented the Jewish Agency at the League of Nations from 1935 to 1939. He served as president of the World Jewish Congress from 1953 to 1977 and as president of the World Zionist Organization from 1955 to 1968. In a 1915 address he proclaimed, "The Jewish Renaissance has come—the nation is reborn, and the Jewish state in its beginning is already here."

Israel Goldstein (1896–1986), American-born pulpit rabbi in New York City who did most of his Zionist work in the United States before settling in Israel in 1960. He served as president of the Zionist Organization of America, the World Confederation of General Zionists, and the U. S. branch of the Jewish National Fund. From 1948 to 1949 he was a member of the Jewish Agency Executive and its treasurer.

Aharon David Gordon (1856–1922), Russian-born philosopher who became the spiritual icon of the Zionist movement in Palestine. At age fifty-eight he moved to Palestine, where he worked as a farmhand on *kibbutzim* Petach Tikvah, Rishon Le-Tziyon, and Degania. He preached what has been called a religion of labor: "Too long have the hands been the hands of Esau and the voice the voice of Jacob. It is time for Jacob to use his hands." Gordon's ideas attracted many settlers to Palestine in the early 1900s, during a period that has been named the Second Aliyah (wave of immigration).

David Ben-Gurion (1886–1973), Russian-born founding father of the Jewish state. At age twenty he went to work the land of Palestine as a pioneer and soon thereafter founded, along with others, Achdut Ha-Avodah, a socialist political party. Ben-Gurion served as its delegate to the 1920 Zionist Conference. Later he was a founder of the Mapai Party and was chairman of the Jewish Agency of the World Zionist Organization. In 1948, David Ben-Gurion became the first prime minister of the newly formed Jewish state.

Tzevi Hirsch Kalischer (1795–1874), a rabbi who for fifty years served the community of Thorn, in Prussia. He was a nationalist who believed that the redemption of the Jews from oppression would be the result of natural activity, not the advent of a Messiah. In his 1962 book, *Derishat Shalom* ("Search for Peace"), Kalischer advocated the establishment of a Jewish agricultural society in Palestine, a goal he believed had to be achieved before the coming of the Messiah. His views influenced the thinking of many Zionist leaders and Hebrew writers, including Moses Hess (1812–1875) and Peretz Smolenskin (1842–1885).

Emma Lazarus (1849–1887), born in New York City, grew up in the comfortable home of her parents, who were descendants of Sephardic Jews who had arrived in America even before the American Revolution. Emma was a rather frail child who spent most of her days indoors, where she received private tutoring and developed a love of classic literature. As she matured, she began to write poetry that was good enough to attract the attention of Ralph Waldo Emerson, to whom she dedicated her second volume, *Admetus and Other Poems* (1871).

The condition of the Jews of Russia, who had suffered through the pogroms of 1881 and 1882, awakened in her a concern for her fellow Jews. George Eliot's novel *Daniel Deronda,* with its portrayal of a Jewish family's quest to return to Zionism, spurred Lazarus on to pay regular visits to Ward's Island, where Jewish immigrants were housed. She felt their plight deeply and was inspired to write her famous poem *The New Colossus*, with its stirring words: "Give me your tired, your poor/your huddled masses yearning to breathe free…"

Lazarus's passion for her own people continued to grow and Zionist poems began to pour from her pen, the *Banner of the Jew* being the most famous. Among its most memorable lines are: "Wake, Israel, wake! Recall today the glorious Maccabean rage…Let but a new Ezra rise anew, to lift the banner of the Jew."

Emma Lazarus never married. After a lengthy illness, she died in 1887 at the young age of thirty-eight. Memorial services were held for her in all of New York's synagogues.

Golda Meir (1898–1978), born on May 3, 1898, in Kiev, Ukraine, one of eight children born to Moshe and Bluma Mabovitz. In 1903, her father, a skilled cabinetmaker, left for the United States to seek his fortune in Milwaukee. Three years later, he was joined by the rest of his family. By age eighteen, Golda had completed high school and a teacher training course.

While still in her teens, Golda was attracted to both Zionism and socialism. And in 1917, at age nineteen, she met and married a sign painter named Morris Myerson. Convinced that her future lay in Palestine, in 1921 Morris reluctantly agreed to settle on a *kibbutz*, but he never adjusted, and in 1945 the two separated.

Over the years Golda became deeply involved in the burgeoning labor movement of the *yishuv* (Jewish community), and by 1940 she had become head of the political department of Histadrut, the major Jewish labor federation. When, in June 1946, the British, then in control of Palestine, arrested most of the Jewish political leaders, Golda became acting head of the Jewish Agency's Political Department. On May 14, 1948, she became one of the signatories to Israel's Proclamation of Independence. She was the only woman to serve as a member of the Provisional Council of the State of Israel and of Israel's first legislature.

In September 1948, Golda was appointed ambassador to the Soviet Union, and upon her arrival ignited a spontaneous pro-Israel demonstration of love in which 40,000 Russian Jews participated.

In January 1949, Golda Mabovitz Myerson was elected to the first Knesset as a member of Ben Gurion's Mapai party. Four months later she was appointed Minister of Labor, a position she held until 1956. In that year she changed her name to the more Israeli-sounding Golda Meir.

In 1969, Golda Meir became prime minister of Israel. The country grew economically under her leadership, even as she established new programs to reduce the gap between rich and poor. She was reelected in 1973, but retired in 1974 after a commission questioned her judgment relating to the conduct of the 1973 Yom Kippur War.

Golda died in 1978, at age eighty, after a long bout with cancer. Upon her death, television journalist Walter Cronkite said: "She is the strongest woman to head a government in our time and for a very long time past."

Manya Wilbushewitz Shochat (1880–1961), founder of the first *kibbutz* in Palestine, was born near Grodno, Byelorussia, to a wealthy, deeply religious father who had a profound interest in technology. He and his more free-thinking wife raised eight children, Manya being the youngest. She, like most of her siblings, identified with the social revolutionaries of the time, and because of her activity was arrested in the summer of 1899. Upon her release, Manya formed the Jewish Independent Labor Party, which was dissolved two years later, in 1903. But her goal of organizing Jewish workers in such a manner that they would work the land and be self-sustaining remained with her.

In 1904, at the urging of her brother Nachum, who had settled in Palestine, Manya visited the country, fell in love with it, and in 1907, together with her future husband, Yisrael Shochat, established a farm in Sejera, in the Lower Galilee, where she was also able to implement the socioeconomic plan on which she had been working for years. This was actually the first *kibbutz* established in Palestine. In 1948, after the state was established, she joined the left-wing Mapam Party and settled in Tel Aviv, where she was engaged in social work until her death in 1961.

Abba Hillel Silver (1893–1963), Lithuanian-born American rabbi who, at various times between 1938 and 1948, served as president of the Zionist Organization of America, the United Jewish Appeal, and the United Palestine Appeal. He was one of the major spokesmen before the United Nations during the Palestine Hearings of 1947, representing the Central Conference of American Rabbis, which he then headed.

Henrietta Szold (1860–1945), the eldest of eight daughters of Rabbi Benjamin Szold, a prominent leader of the Baltimore Jewish community. Henrietta was born shortly after her family arrived in the United States from Hungary. She began teaching by age seventeen and at age nineteen was writing articles for Jewish magazines, having been taught by her father Hebrew, Bible, Talmud, and Jewish history.

In 1893, Szold became secretary of the editorial board of the Jewish Publication Society (JPS), and in time she assumed the post of editor of its publications, working in that capacity until 1916. For many years, she worked closely with Professor Louis Ginzberg of the Jewish Theological Seminary of America, who wrote many of the articles for the *Jewish Encyclopedia*, and she translated his monumental multivolume *Legends of the Jews* from German into English. Henrietta hoped he would ask her to marry him, but that never materialized.

In 1909, Henrietta and her widowed mother visited Palestine for the first time. About her visit, she wrote: "If I were ten years younger, I would feel that my field is here. I think Zionism is a more difficult aim to realize than I ever did before...[but] if not Zionism, then nothing...then extinction of the Jews."

Henrietta Szold returned to the United States and continued to serve as editor of JPS. Having become an ardent Zionist, she was determined to alleviate the miserable health conditions she observed during her visit to Palestine. In 1912, she organized Hadassah, initially known as the Women's Zionist Organization, which supported hospitals, schools, and clinics throughout the country.

In 1920, Szold returned to Palestine to supervise Hadassah's activities, expecting to remain for only two years. Instead, she spent the rest of her life there, providing health services to both Arabs and Jews. In 1934, she delivered an address at the cornerstone laying of the Hadassah Hospital on Mount Scopus in Jerusalem.

When the Nazis rose to power in Germany, Szold became a leader of Youth Aliyah, a movement started by Recha Freier to bring children and young people out of Germany (and later all of Europe) and settle them in Palestine. Between 1933 and 1945 300,000 children were thus saved.

Henrietta Szold, who never married, died on February 13, 1945.

Chaim Weizmann (1874–1952), Russian-born chemist who moved to England in 1904 to teach chemistry at Manchester University. As a young man, he attended the First Zionist Conference, which met in Basle, Switzerland, in 1897. There he met Theodor Herzl, who favored establishing a Jewish state through negotiations with important governments. Weizmann believed that the state had to first find the support of Jews the world over. In 1920 he was elected president of the World Zionist Organization and in 1948 became the first president of the State of Israel.

Stephen S. Wise (1874–1949), a U. S. rabbi who in 1922 founded New York's Jewish Institute of Religion, which in 1950 merged with the Hebrew Union College, in Cincinnati, Ohio. He was a founder of the Federation of American Zionists, which later became the Zionist Organization of America. Wise also founded the American Jewish Congress and served as its president from 1925 to 1929 and again from 1935 to 1949.

Zodiac

From the Greek meaning "circle," the zodiac is defined as an imaginary belt in the heavens that extends about eight degrees on either side of the apparent path of the sun and which includes the path of the moon and eight principal planets. It is divided into twelve equal parts, or signs, each named for a particular constellation and represented in most cases by animals.

In Jewish literature, reference to the signs of the zodiac is first found in the *Sefer Yetzira* ("Book of Creation"). There the constellations, known in Hebrew as *mazalot*, are named as follows: *Taleh* for Aries ("ram"), *Shor* for Taurus ("ox"), *Te'omim* for Gemini ("twins"), *Sartan* for Cancer ("crab"), *Aryeh* for Leo ("lion"), *Betulah* for Virgo ("virgin"), *Mozna'yim* for Libra ("scales"), *Akrab* for Scorpio ("scorpion"), *Keshet* for Sagittarius ("bow"), *Gedi* for Capricorn ("goat"), *Deli* for Aquarius ("water bucket"), and *Dagim* for Pisces ("fish").

Each of the zodiacal signs corresponds to a month in the Jewish calendar, and in talmudic times the rabbis attempted to explain the origin of the signs' names and associated many of them with important events in Jewish history. For example, the *Taleh* ("lamb"), the sign of Aries, is associated with the paschal lamb that was offered in the month of Nissan. The sign for Tishrei, the month in which Rosh Hashanah and Yom Kippur fall, the period when man's conduct is judged, is Libra, meaning "scales" in Latin.

See Calendar.

Zohar

Literally meaning "brilliance, enlightenment," the *Zohar*, sometimes known as "Book of Splendor," is the bible of kabbalists. Its authorship has been attributed to the second-century scholar Rabbi Shimon bar Yocha'i, although most authorities believe that it was composed in the thirteenth century by the Spanish-born kabbalist Moses (ben Shem Tov) de Leon (*c.* 1250–1305).

Written in a language that is partly Aramaic and partly Hebrew, the *Zohar* is a compilation of fragments from a variety of manuscripts arranged as a commentary on most of the weekly portions read from the Torah each Sabbath. The commentary reflects the view that, man's suffering notwithstanding, the supreme worth of Judaism is unquestionable. The interpretations of the Torah offered by the *Zohar* are rife with the promise of a speedy redemption. The assurance that past oppression can be overcome by drawing close to God made the *Zohar* the premier textbook of medieval Jewish mysticism.

Zugot

Singular, *zug*. This Hebrew term literally meaning "pairs" is the name given to pairs of legal scholars who lived between the Maccabean and Herodian periods (150–30 B.C.E.) and who preceded the *tanna'im*. The period of the *zugot* begins with Yosei ben Yoezer and ends with Hillel.

Five such "pairs" of scholars served as president and vice-president of the *Sanhedrin*. They were Yosei ben Yoezer and Yosei ben Yohanan, who lived during the time of the Maccabean wars of independence; Joshua ben Perachya and Nittai of Arbela, contemporaries of John Hyrcanus; Judah ben Tabbai and Simon ben Shetach, contemporaries of Alexander Yannai and Queen Salome; Shemaiah and Avtalyon, contemporaries of Hyrcanus II; and Hillel and Shammai, contemporaries of King Herod.

According to tradition, the first name in each "pair" was the president (*nasi*) of the *Sanhedrin* and the other was the deputy judge of the court (*Av Beit Din*).

The Hebrew word *zivug*, meaning "pairing," is traditionally used when a boy and girl are matched to become husband and wife.

Index

A

Aaron ben Asher, 89
Aaron ben Elijah, 286–287
Aaron the High Priest, 56–57, 246, 314. *See also* Levites
  on compromise, 123
  death of, 391
  denied entry into Israel, 512
  garments of, 157
  God, communications with, 164
  Golden Calf and, 43, 544, 549
  Korach vs., 383
  lineage of, 290, 405
  menorah kindled by, 334
  Moses and, 297
  as peacemaker, 391
  sacrificial blood dabbed on, 442
  ushpizin and, 577
Abandonment of Torah. *See* Yotze'im
Abba, 67, 401
Abba Arikha, 23, 539
Abba bar Mammel, 212–213
Abba Benjamin, 399
Abba ben Zavda, 275
Abbahu, 78, 176, 230
Abba Joseph, 257
Abbayei, 68, 158, 209–210, 608
  on assemblies, 285
  on education, 161
  on mezuzot, 340
  on promises, 411
  on prosbul of Hillel, 413
  on Rosh Hashanah foods, 446
  on Satan, 458
  sexual relations, definition of, 473
  on tefillin, 539
  on using mothers' names in prayers, 346
Abbreviations. *See* Acronyms
Abed-Nego, 14
Abelson, Rabbi Kassel, 175
Abigail, 577
Abiram, 383
Abnormalities, physical, 2, 263
Abolition, 506
Abortion, 1–2
Abraham (Patriarch), 85, 86. *See also* Patriarchs
  as Abram, 273
  Akeidah, the, 10–11, 85, 457, 458, 496
  as an angel, 205

  angels and, 25, 231, 305, 569
  astrology, as believer in, 52
  Christians as descendants of, 32
  circumcision of, 26, 116, 118, 351
  converts, as common name of, 133
  covenant with God, 266, 439
  death of, 80, 92, 93, 123
  as father of all Jews, 130
  God, covenant with, 12, 136, 266, 439
  Hagar and, 25
  hospitality of, 259, 513
  Isaac and, 184, 361
  lekh lekha commandment, 384
  man's fate and, 330
  as Muslim patriarch, 118
  as prophet, 412
  pseudepigrapha and, 414
  Sarah and, 41, 245
  as slaveholder, 506
  Sodom and, 344
  symbolic promises and, 411
  ushpizin and, 577
  war of four kings and, 553
  white lie of God and, 257
  wives of, 397
Abraham ben David of Posquières, 28, 63, 75
Abrahams, Israel, 121, 240
Abram, 273. *See also* Abraham (Patriarch)
Absalom, 238
Abstinence. *See also* Nazirites
  from food, 410–411
  from sexual relations. *See also* Niddah laws
  from wine, 586
Abulafia, Abraham, 336
Abun, Rabbi, 124
Abundance, 446
Abuse, physical, 342
Abyssinia. *See* Ethiopia
Academies of learning, 22–23, 526. *See also* Chavrutah;
    Kolelim; Schools; Yeshivot
  Babylonian. *See* Pumbedita, Babylonia; Sura,
    Babylonia
  kolelim, 300, 429, 598
  Palestinian. *See* Palestinian scholars
Acco, 187
Acha bar Yaakov, 196
Achan ben Carmi, 275, 512
Acharon acharon chaviv, 2

Acharonim, 432–434, 527. *See also* Caro, Joseph;
    Responsa Literature; Rishonim era
Achdut Ha-Avodah, 610
Acher, 36, 177, 317
Acronyms, 2–3. *See also* Mnemonic devices
Acrostics, 3, 350
Actions, 182, 288–289, 422. *See also* Commandments
Adam (first man), 80, 86, 137. *See also* Garden of Eden
    burial of, 92
    chronology of the world and, 86
    confrontation with God, 382
    creation of, 212, 507, 509
    from the earth, 138
    Eve, influenced by, 240
    figs eaten by, 446
    fruitful and multiply commandment, 397
    Gabriel and Mikhael as best men of, 26
    Lilith and, 314–315
    loneliness of, 322
    Original Sin of, 377–378, 456, 503
    pseudepigrapha and, 414
    Sefer Razi'el and, 24
Adar, 83–85, 309, 414, 429, 501, 598. *See also* Leap
    years; Purim
Ad de-lo yada, 417
Addictions, 202
Adding to laws, 379
Addis Ababa. *See* Ethiopia
Address, Rabbi Richard, 175
Adir Hu (song), 466
Adler, Cyrus, 128
Adler, Morris, 138
Adler, Rabbi Hermann, 138–139
Adler, Rabbi Nathan Marcus, 376
Adloyada Purim Carnival, 3, 326, 417
Admetus and Other Poems (Lazarus), 611
Adonai, 3, 212–213, 367, 550. *See also* God
Adon Olam, 4
Adoption, 4, 60, 133–134, 362
Adornment. *See* Beauty and beautification; Flowers
Adoshem, 214
Adret, Rabbi Solomon ben Abraham, 399, 431–432
Adultery, 4–5, 262, 475, 546. *See also* Mamzeirim; Sotah
    abortion permitted in case of, 1
    AID (Artificial Insemination Donor) equated with, 49,
        319–320
    penalty for, 91, 139
    pikuach nefesh and, 395
    sotah, 4–5, 509, 531, 588–589
    tzitzit as reminder against, 575
    yeihareig ve-al ya'avor, 309
Adulthood, status of. *See* Bar mitzvah; Bat mitzvah
Advancement of Learning (Bacon), 260
Affliction, Day of, 604. *See also* Yom Kippur
Afikomon, 23, 329, 465, 518. *See also* Passover

Afolim, 173
A fortiori, 244–245
Afterlife, 5–7, 441, 498, 499. *See also* Gilgulim; Heaven;
    Reincarnation; Resurrection; World to come
Afternoon. *See* Erev Shabbat; Minchah (prayers); Musaf
    (services)
Age of Messiah. *See* Messiah and Messianic Age
Aggadah, 7–8, 227, 244, 341. *See also* Haggadah
Aging, 8, 44, 199–200. *See also* Hekdeish; Life; Moshav
    Zekeinim
Agreements. *See* Compromise; Covenants
Agriculture
    laws pertaining to. *See* Zera'im (Mishnah tractates)
    Nissan as first month of the agricultural new year, 444
    pilgrim festivals and, 386, 396, 439, 482–483, 515
    tithing, 553
    Zera'im (tractate) on, 482
Agrippa, King, 387
Agudath Harabonim, 380
Agudat Yisrael, 594
Agunot, 9–10, 37, 153, 245–246, 434, 592
Ahab, King, 335, 466
Ahasueros, King, 28, 188, 327, 332, 414.
    See also Purim
Ahavat Yisra'el, 10, 106
AID (Artificial Insemination Donor), 49–50, 319–320
AIDS virus, 117
AIH (Artificial Insemination Husband), 49–50, 259,
    319–320
Airplane travel by Kohanim, 406
Akavya ben Mahalalel, 109, 177
Akdamut (poem), 10, 484
Akeidah, the, 10–11, 85, 457, 458, 496. *See also* Moriah,
    Mount
Akh le-Tzara. See Greenwald, Rabbi Yekutiel
Akiba (Rabbi), 8
    on the Apocrypha, 34
    Avinu Malkeinu (prayer), 55
    on Bar Kokhbah, 336
    capital punishment, opposition to, 91
    clothing of, 157
    on divorce, 153
    on free will, 197
    as gabba'ei tzedakah, 205
    Kaddish and, 284
    Lag B'Omer and, 303
    martyrdom of, 324. *See also* Ten martyrs
    on Medes, 297–298
    on nivul ha-met, 366
    ordination by, 421
    plague on students of, 583
    prayers of, 294, 400
    on royalty, 463
    tagin story and, 521
    Tale of Four Scholars and, 36

tircha de-tzibura of, 552
on treatment of animals, 570–571
Akiba ben Joseph, 346–347, 548
Aki Yerushalayim (Shaul), 469
Akrab, 613
Akum, 11, 528. *See also* Idolatry and idol worshippers
Al-Aksa Intifida, 270
Al-Aqsa mosque, 585
Albinius, 584
Albo, Joseph, 155, 412–413, 441, 550
Al Cheit (prayer), 11, 79, 125, 402, 504. *See also*
    Ashamnu (prayer)
Alcohol. *See* Drinking; Wine
Aleichem, Sholom, 597, 599
Aleinu (prayer), 11–12, 316, 445, 510, 552
Aleph, 17, 21, 161, 367. *See also* Hebrew language
Alexander I, Czar, 348
Alexander II, Czar, 397
Alexander III, Czar, 397
Alexander Janneus, 363
Alexander the Great, 363, 457, 501
Alexander Yannai, 614
Alexandri, 363
Alexandria, Egypt, 68, 146–147, 399, 520, 593–594
Alfasi of Fez, 430–431, 500, 527
Algiers, Purim of, 187
Al-Ha-Nisim (prayers), 12, 417
Aliyah (Torah honor)
    bar/bat mitzvah and, 62
    blessings of, 564–565
    chamishi, 583
    chatan Bereishit and Torah, 108
    of exilarchs, 181
    fathers of newborns, 361
    gabba'im, distributed by, 202
    golel, 227
    of mamzeirim, 319
    mourners and, 493–494
    to poor and poverty, 554
    Priests (Kohanim), 135, 407
    on Sabbath, 370, 448
    to Sabbath violators, 487–488
    to shnudder, 496
    on Simchat Torah, 502–503
    tallit worn during, 525
    Tokheichah and, 554
    women, given to, 15–16
Aliyah (to Israel) , 12–13, 267, 270, 398, 427, 609. *See
    also* Jewish identity and status; Kibbutzim; Zionists
    and Zionism
Aliyah l'regel, 396. *See also* Pilgrim Festivals
Aliyot (Torah honors). *See* Aliya
Alkabetz, Rabbi Solomon, 310, 359, 422, 552. *See also*
    Lekhah Dodi (prayer)
Al Kiddush Ha-Shem. *See* Kiddush Ha-Shem; Martyrdom

Allegories, 317, 381–383, 436–437. *See also* Aggadah
All Saints' Day, 113
Allusions. *See* Remez
Almag, Ruth, 420
Almond milk, 320
Alonso, King. *See* Inquisition, Spanish
Alpha, 17
Alphabet, Hebrew, 3, 17–21. *See also* Hebrew language;
    specific letters by name
Alphabet of Ben Sira, 315
Al Pi Shechata, Yisra'el Hu, 39
Alroy, David, 336
Altars, 67–68, 95–96, 153, 455, 580. *See also* Sacrifices
Altruism. *See* Chesed
Aluf, 17
Amalek and Amalekites, 333, 345, 415, 479, 578
Amalgam. *See* Eruvin
Amen (response), 15, 21–22, 400
Amen ba, 3, 164
American Jewish Congress, 613
American Jewish life. *See also* Diaspora; United States
    Ashkenazim and, 52
    black Jews, 183
    demographics, 131
    education, 163–164, 601
    Karaite community, 288
    Ladino population, 469
    Orthodoxy in, 379–380
    Reform Judaism and, 423–427
    slavery question and, 506
    Western Sephardim, 468
    Zionist movements of, 609–613
Am ha-aretz, 22
Amharic, 182. *See also* Falashas
Amidah. *See* Eighteen Benedictions
Amir, Yigal, 187–188, 269, 443
Ammi, 365, 473, 509, 602
Ammonites, 411
Amniocentesis, 2
Amnon, Rabbi of Mainz, 364
Amora'im, 22–23, 59, 204, 337, 526. *See also specific
    amora'im by name*
Amorites, 229
Amos (prophet), 111, 286, 493
Amram, son of Kohath, 405
Amram Gaon, 429, 527
Am Segulah. *See* Chosen People
Amulets, 23–24, 143, 302, 315, 394, 459, 465, 539. *See
    also* Segulot
Anaf eitz avot, 196
Analogies, verbal. *See* Gezeirah shavah principle
Anan ben David, 286–287
Anav. *See* Humility
Ancestry. *See* Customs and law; Lineage
Angels, 24–27. *See also specific angels by name*

Abraham and, 305, 569
Abraham as, 205
amulets, names in, 24
Azazel, 57
of conception, 197–198
of death, 143, 174, 340, 363–364, 458, 494
  names, changing of to confuse, 143, 363–364
  Satan as, 458
  shivah period and, 494
  Yemenite customs and, 174
Elijah the Prophet as guardian angel of Israel, 335
evil, 23–24, 26–27. See also Demons and demonology
ladder of Jacob and, 156, 511
Ma'asei Merkavah on, 317
man in world to come compared to, 6
man's emulation of, 401
seraphim, 25
Shema (prayer) and, 489
visions of, 278
Anger, 53, 389, 575. See also Vengeance
Aniel, 26
Ani Ma'amin, 27
Animals, 558. See also Anthropomorphism of God;
    Sacrifices; specific animals by name
  Chullin (tractate) on, 533
  constellations and, 613
  fibers from, 476–477, 523
  firstborn, 533
  hide of, 486, 558. See also Leather
  images of prohibited, 47–48
  intercourse with, 475
  kosher, 149, 172. See also Kashrut; Pork
  Sabbath and, 451
  sacrifices of, 420, 453, 521. See also Sacrifices
  slaughtering of. See Slaughtering
  Temurah (tractate), 533
  tereifah, 61, 548–549
  treatment of, 27, 260, 570–572
Anim Zemirot, 27
Aninut, 27, 355, 374, 542. See also Burial; Mourners and
    mourning
Annihilation. See Holocaust; Purim
Anniversary of death. See Yahrzeits
Annulment of marriage, 10. See also Get (divorce
    document)
Annulment of vows, 410–411, 412, 531
Anointed one. See Messiah and Messianic Age
Anointing oil, 510
Anointment of High Priest, 405
Anokhi, 21
Anshei Knesset Ha-Gedolah. See Great Assembly
Anski, Solomon, 159
Antelopes, 496
Anthropomorphism of God, 27–28, 179, 211, 438, 519
Anti-Defamation League, 33

Antidemonic charms, 23–24
Antidemonic Psalm, 23, 56, 145, 181, 238
Antiochus Epiphanes, 99, 105, 149, 318, 324. See also
    Chanukkah
Antiquities of the Jews, 336. See also Josephus, Flavius
Anti-Semitism, 28–33. See also Diaspora; Holocaust
  anti-Marrano, 321
  arba kanfot and, 41
  Black Plague and, 432
  burning of books and, 528
  converts, initiated by, 128
  Crusades, the, 336, 430
  derogatory attributions to Jews, 274
  Dreyfus trial, 31–32, 272, 608–609
  expulsion from Spain (1492), 321
  Messiah, hopes for, 336
  pogroms, 397, 611
  Zionism and, 32
Anti-Zionism, 13, 107, 380
Anusim, 321. See also Marranos
Anuss, 514–515
Apikores, 33–34, 35
Apion, 76
Apocrypha, 34–35. See also Pseudepigrapha
Apostates and apostasy, 11–12, 28, 35–39, 334, 431,
    452, 495, 587
Apotropos, 4
App, Austin J., 253
Apparitions. See Ghosts
Appearance of God, 369
Appearances, 39–41. See also Clothing; Hair and
    haircutting
Applauding, 450
Apples, 446. See also Fruits and fruit trees
Aquarius (zodiacal sign), 85, 613
Arabic-speaking countries, Jews from, 468
Arabs, 238, 239–240, 609. See also Muslims
Arafat, Yasser, 269–270
Arakhin (tractate), 533
Aramaic, 283, 291–292, 301, 399, 470, 536
Aravot. See Four species; Willows
Ara'yot, 262
Arba'ah Turim (Ba'al Ha-Turim), 307, 379, 500
Arba Imma'hot, 41. See also specific Matriarchs by name
Arba kanfot, 41, 574
Arba kosot, 383, 460, 463, 466. See also Passover
Arba kushiyot, 463–464
Arba minim, 41, 516
Arbit, 468. See also Ma'ariv (prayers)
Arbitration, 41–42, 123. See also Courts, Jewish
Arbor Day, 42, 98. See also Chamishah Asar Bi-Shevat
Archangels. See Angels; Demons and demonology
Ari, the, 106, 280–281, 605
  on bal tashchit, 58
  exorcism of dybbuks, 159

on gilgulim, 210
on Kiddush (prayer), 296, 403
as mystic, 359
on reincarnation, 427
Sabbath observance of, 448
Seder of, 462
shevirat keilim concept, 492
on souls and graves, 555
on tefillin, 541
on tikkun olam, 552
tzimtzum concept and, 573
zemirot of, 608
Aries (zodiacal sign), 85, 613
Aristeas, 469–470
Aristobulus II, King of Judea, 166
Aristotle, 1, 432, 475
Ark of the Covenant, 42–46, 543, 558. See also
    Tabernacle
    High Holidays curtains, 445
    Holy of Holies and, 543
    minyan, counted in, 45–46, 305, 344
    placement of, 520
    respect for, 44–45
    Sephardic term for, 468
    teivah, referred to as, 543
    Ten Commandments, fragments placed in, 8, 545
Ark of Noah, 543
Armageddon, 46–47, 215. See also Gog and Magog
Arme, 241
Arms, 521
Armstrong, Louis, 511
Armucella, 241
Aroma. See Scents
Aron Ha-Kodesh. See Ark of the Covenant
Arrangement. See Nusachim
Art and sculpture, 47–48, 545. See also Beauty and
    beautification
Artificial insemination, 48–50, 259, 319–320, 327
Arukh Ha-Shulchan (Epstein), 461
Arur, 21
Arvit, 468. See also Ma'ariv (prayers)
Aryans. See Nazis
Aryeh, 613
Asarah B'Tevet, 50–51, 185–186, 254, 318. See also
    Fasting and fast days
Asarah harugei malkhut. See Ten martyrs
Asceticism, 51, 364. See also Essenes; Nazirites
Aseret Ha-Dibrot, 544. See also Ten Commandments
Aseret Yemei Teshuvah, 51, 547, 597–598. See also Elul;
    Repentance
Ashamnu (prayer), 51–52, 79, 125, 402, 504. See also Al
    Cheit (prayer); Yom Kippur
Asher ben Moses, 340
Asher ben Yechiel, 48, 63, 379, 500
Ashes, 189, 478. See also Cremation

Ashi (Rav), 181, 203, 204, 365, 428, 526, 547
Ashkenazi, Jacob, 572
Ashkenazim, 52, 409, 467, 500
Ashkenazi Rabbi Isaac. See Ari, the
Ashrei (prayer), 3, 52, 350
Assembly, 53, 285, 300, 410, 429, 598. See also Atzeret;
    Community; Congregations; Knesset Ha-Gedolah;
    Knesset, Israeli; Sanhedrin; Shemini Atzeret;
    Synagogues
Assi, 239, 475
Assimilation, 184, 235–236, 389, 475–476, 518. See also
    Intermarriage
Assisted suicide, 173–175, 340. See also Suicides
Association. See Chavrutah; Chevrah
Assyrian Empire, 21, 34, 129, 146, 180, 272, 543, 548
Astrology, 52–53, 84–86, 369, 517, 613. See also
    Constellations; Hebrew calendar; Kabbalah and
    kabbalists; Moon; Mystics and mysticism; Stars;
    Sun; Zodiac
Aszod, Rabbi Yehudah, 409
Atarot, 523, 525. See also Tallitot
Atheism, 35, 410, 452
Atifat Yishm'eilim, 524
Atonement. See also Repentance; Sins and sinners; Yom
    Kippur
    of Adam (first man), 382
    Christian beliefs of, 456
    deathbed, 125–126
    for Golden Calf, 545
    handwashing as, 235
    intermediaries for, 503–504
    Original Sin and, 378
    reincarnation and, 427
    through sacrifice and prayer, 125
Attendants, mikveh, 342
Attributes of God, 64, 280, 467, 487, 492, 549–550
Atzei cha'yim, 564
Atzeret, 53, 483. See also Shavuot; Shemini Atzeret
Auctioning of aliyot, 16–17
Aufruf, 15, 53–54
Augustine, Saint, 503
Auschwitz, 251, 252, 254. See also Concentration camps
Austrian expulsion of Jews, 147
Authenticity of the Torah, 35, 557–558
Authority. See Beit Din; Courts, Jewish; Rabbis
Autoclaving, 388
Auto de fe, 30
Autopsies, 54–55, 309, 366
Av (month), 84, 85–86
Avadim (tractate), 536
Av Beit Din, 65, 364, 458, 614. See also Beit Din
Avdon, 337
Aveilut, 55, 123–125, 355. See also Menachem aveil;
    Mourners and mourning
Aveirah, 503. See also Sins and sinners

Avihu (son of Aaron), 290, 405
Avinadav, 43
Avinu Malkeinu (prayer), 55
Avnet, 499
Avodah b'leiv, 398. *See also* Prayers and blessings
Avodah of the Temples, 55–56. *See also* High Priest
Avodah zarah, 532. *See also* Idolatry and idol worshippers
Avon, 503. *See also* Sins and sinners
Avot. *See* Patriarchs
Avot (Ethics of the Fathers), 529, 532, 535
Avot d'Rabbi Natan (tractate), 535
Avraham. *See* Abraham (Patriarch)
Avtalyon, 244, 614
A'yelet ha-shachar, 357
A'yin, 19, 368, 521
A'yin ha-ra, 56
A'yin tachat a'yin, 314, 381, 392
Azariah do Fano, 402
Azaryah, 26, 324
Azazel, 56–57
Azharot (poem), 10
Azlu, 57

B

Ba'al (vs. Elijah), 505
Ba'al brit, 457. *See also* Sandek
Ba'alei Ha-Tosafot, 566. *See also* Tosafot
Ba'al Ha-Rachamim, 122
Ba'al Ha-Turim, 307, 500
Ba'al korei, 16, 45, 58, 90, 232, 563, 564. *See also* Cantors
Ba'al Peor, 440
Ba'al Shem Tov, the, 2, 105–116, 159, 278, 304, 348, 360, 395, 400
Ba'al tefillah. *See also* Ba'al korei; Cantillations; Shli'ach tzibur
    bareheaded, 240
    defined, 58, 68
    Eighteen Benedictions, repetition of, 164
    as holy vessels, 249
    Kaddish of, 282
    objections to, 358
    Sephardic customs for, 226
    surnames and, 518
    tallitot worn by, 523, 525
    Yom Kippur services of, 400
Ba'al teki'ah, 58. *See also* Shofar
Ba'al teshuvah, 58, 112, 428. *See also* Repentance
Babies. *See also* Children; Circumcision; Pregnancy
    aliyot (Torah honors) given to fathers of sons, 14
    ben zakhar, 481
    conversion to Judaism of, 133–134
    converts compared to, 133
    death of, 573

demons, protection against, 143, 481, 490, 580
    fetuses, 1–2, 473
    Lilith, danger to, 315
    naming of, 15, 117, 250, 361
    protection of, 23, 56, 121, 166, 315, 394
    quorum, counting in, 344
    salt rubbed on, 455
    shalom bat ceremony, 361, 481
    shalom zakhar, 143, 459, 481
    Wachnacht, 115, 490, 580
Babylonia. *See also* Destruction of the Temples; Nebukhadnezzar, King
    Babylonian Talmud, 146, 526, 527. *See also* Talmud
        on apostates and apostasy, 35
        baraitot and, 59
        daf yomi, 141
        Ezra the Scribe and, 316–317
        final editing of, 204, 428
        first printing of, 528
        Rashi's commentary and, 566
        on the Sabbath, 447
    exile, 5, 146, 189, 215, 272, 457, 519, 543–544. *See also* Men of the Great Assembly
    ge'onim of, 286
    levirate marriage practices, 313
    Persians and, 456–457
    responsa literature of, 428–430
    savora'im, 459
    scholars of, 146, 375–376, 536
        Amora'im, 8, 22–23. *See also* Rava (Rabba)
    Shema (prayer) recitation, 489
    Torah reading customs, 563
Bach, the. *See* Sirkes, Rabbi Joel
Bachya ibn Pakuda, 6, 109, 278, 288, 370, 381
Bacon, Francis, 260
Bad. *See* Demons and demonology; Omens
Bad dreams, 187
Badekn di kallah, 58, 97, 578
Baghdad, Purim of, 187
Bagpipe, 357
Balconies, 300
Balfour Declaration, 267, 272, 609
Ball games, 450
Bal tashchit, 58, 160, 291, 373. *See also* Birth control
Bal tosif, 58–59. *See also* Chasid shoteh
Banner of the Jew (Lazarus), 611
Bans. *See* Cheirem; Excommunication
Baptism, 32, 321. *See also* Converts and conversion
Baraitot, 59, 347, 567. *See also* Mishnah; Tosefta, the
Barak, Ehud, 269–270
Barak ben Avinoam, 357
Bardot, Brigitte, 486
Barefoot, 407
Bareheaded. *See* Hair, covering of; Headcoverings
Bareikh, 173. *See also* Prayers and blessings

Bari, archbishop of, 130
Bar Ilan University, 435
Bar Kapparah, 21, 239, 494
Bar Ka'yamah, 1
Bar Keshita, 337
Barkhu (prayer), 316, 343, 344, 480
Barkiel, 26
Bar Kokhba revolt, 128, 189, 336, 569, 572–573, 583
Barley, 98, 189, 328, 373, 388. *See also* Grains; Seven species of Israel
Bar mitzvah, 59–60
    confirmation vs., 60, 126
    conversion of adopted children and, 134
    haftarah readings and, 15
    honors given to parents at, 4
    maftir given to, 15
    Masada, celebrations at, 325
    Mi Shebeirakh (prayer) for, 346
    Priestly Benediction for, 408
    as quorum member, 344–345
    se'udat mitzvah and, 472
    She-heche'yanu (blessing) for, 486
    tefillin and, 229
    Torah scroll gartls made for, 561
Barriers to immersion, 132
Barukh (blessed), 21
Barukh, Book of, 34
Barukh ben Neriah, 34
Barukh She'amar (prayer), 289, 480
Barukh She-petarani, 60
Basar (flesh), 507. *See also* Body; Meat
Basar lavan, 149. *See also* Pork
Basel, Switzerland, 266, 272
Bastards and bastardy, 1, 5, 61, 287–288
Batei Mikdash, 249. *See also* Temples
Batel b'shishim, 61
Bath, Ritual. *See* Mikveh
Bathing, 494, 604. *See also* Shaving; Tohorot
Bat kol, 244
Bat mitzvah, 4, 61–62
    confirmation vs., 126
    conversion of adopted children and, 134
    haftarah readings and, 15
    introduction of, 422, 594–595
    maftir given to, 15
    Masada, celebrations at, 325
    Mi Shebeirakh (prayer) for, 346
    Priestly Benediction for, 408
    Sephardic customs for, 15
    se'udat mitzvah and, 472
    She-heche'yanu (blessing) for, 486
    tallitot worn by, 525
Battered Women, 62–63
Battle. *See* War
Bava Batra (tractate), 532

Bava Kama (tractate), 531–532
Bava Metzia (tractate), 532
Bavli, 526. *See also* Babylonian Talmud; Talmud
Bea, Augustin Cardinal, 32
Beans, 98, 416
Beards, 107, 112, 238, 487–488, 548. *See also* Hair and haircutting; Pei'ot
Beasts. *See* Animals
Beauty and beautification, 64. *See also* Art and sculpture
    atarot, 523, 525
    erasure of images on Sabbath and, 433
    with flowers, 191–192
    of Haggadot, 227, 599
    hiddur mitzvah, 64, 246
    in kabbalah, 280
    of ketubbot, 292
    Knesset building, Jerusalem, 299
    of mezuzot cases, 339
    Star of David, 510–511
    of Sukkot, 515
    of synagogues, 520
    tagin, 521–522
    women's spices and lotions, 510
Bechirta (tractate), 532
Be-di-avad, 135
Bedikat chametz, 64, 73. *See also* Chametz
Bedouins, 328
Beds, 494
Bedtime, 489–490
Beer, 586. *See also* Drinking
Be'er Heiteiv, 521, 573
Beets, 446
Be-fanav, 95
Be-farhesya, 37, 191, 410. *See also* Public vs. private
Be fruitful and multiply. *See* Fruitful and multiply commandment
Begin, Menachem, 86, 253, 269
Beginning, 10
Beginnings of Jewishness, The (Cohen), 390
Beglaiten dem Yom Tov, 387
Behavior. *See* Conduct
Bei'ah, 173
Beilis Trial, 76
Beirav, Jacob, 375–376, 421, 458
Beit avot, 93, 587. *See also* Cemeteries
Beit cha'yim, 93. *See also* Cemeteries
Beit Din, 64–65. *See also* Jewish law
    Beit Din Shel Esrim ve-Shalosh, 65
    Birkat Ha-Levanah and, 70
    conversions and, 131
    get documents and, 9–10, 207–208
    under Hadrian's rule, 208
    Ho'rayot (tractate) on, 532
    of Karaites, 288
    ketubbot, 10

prosbul and, 414
punishment by. *See* Capital punishment;
        Excommunication
of Yom Kippur, 301
Beit Ha-Mikdash, 543. *See also* Temples
Beit kevarot, 92. *See also* Cemeteries
Beit knesset, 65, 519. *See also* Synagogues
Beit midrash, 65
Beit mikdash me'at, 519. *See also* Synagogues
Beit olam, 93. *See also* Cemeteries
Beit sefer, 65
Beit Shemesh, 68
Beit Yosef. *See* Caro, Joseph
Beitzah, 173, 462, 530
Bekhorim
        birthright of, 72–73, 568. *See also* Inheritance
        first fruits, 189
        names of, 362
        pidyon ha-ben, 135, 392–394, 407, 409
        ta'anit bekhorim, 185–186, 188, 505
        tractate of, 533
Bel and the Dragon, 34
Belief. *See* Dogma and Judaism; Prayers and blessings
Beliefs and Opinions (Sa'adya Gaon), 203
Belkin, Samuel, 379–380
Bells, 559
Belts. *See* Gartls
Belzer, Isaac, 163
Belzer chasidim, 107, 242
Ben, 362
Ben Ami, 133
Ben Asher family, 325, 508
Ben Azzai, Rabbi Shimon, 349, 588
Ben brit, 136. *See also* Covenant People
Benches for mourners, 495
Benedictions. *See* Prayers and blessings
Benedictions (tractate), 529
Ben Eleazer, 228
Benevolence. *See* Kindness; Zeh ne'heneh ve-zeh lo chaser
Ben Ezra Synagogue, 206
Ben-Gurion, David, 276, 363, 610, 611
Benjamin (tribe of), 255, 272, 274, 567
Ben Ka'yamah, 1
Ben Naftali text, 325
Benshn Goimel. *See* Birkat Ha-Gomel (prayer)
Bent nun (letter), 19. *See also* Nun (Hebrew letter)
Ben Torah, 556
Bent pei (letter), 19. *See also* Pei/fei
Bent tzadi (letter), 19. *See also* Tzadi
Ben zakhar, 481
Berakhah Le-Vatalah, 16, 66
Berakhot. *See* Prayers and blessings
Berakhot (Mishnah tractate), 347, 529. *See also* Mishnah
Bera of Sodom, 553
Bereavement. *See* Mourners and mourning

Berechya, Aaron of Modena, 498
Be-reishit bara, 136. *See also* Creation
Bernstein, Rabbi Philip, 528
Beroka (Rabbi), 121
Beruriah, 162, 588
Besamim, 510. *See also* Spices
Besht, the. *See* Ba'al Shem Tov, the
Bestiality, 91
Bet, 161
Beta, 17
Beta Israel. *See* Falashas
Betar, 189, 336
Beth Elohim Congregation, Charleston, 424–425
Beth Hillel. *See* Hillel
Beth Jacob Schools, 162, 594
Beth Shammai. *See* Shammai
Betrothal, 173, 531, 536. *See also* Eirusin; Weddings
Betulah (zodiacal sign), 613
Bet/vet (letters), 17, 20–21, 367, 521
Bezalel, 42, 383
Bialik, Chaim Nachman, 7–8, 373–374
Biber hats, 242
Bible. *See* New Testament; Septuagint; Tanakh; Torah
Biblical law, 309–310. *See also* Jewish law
Biblical names, 361, 363. *See also* Names and naming
Biers, 119. *See also* Coffins
Bigamy. *See* Polygamy
Bikkurim. *See* First fruits
Bikkurim (tractate), 530
Bikur cholim, 67, 122, 383, 406. *See also* Illness
Bimah, 13, 16, 44–45, 67–68, 294, 433, 468, 519, 558
Binah, 107, 280
Binding. *See* Knots
Binding, the. *See* Akeidah, the
Birds, 36, 47–48, 149, 533, 604. *See also* Chickens
Birkat Chatanim (prayers), 492. *See also* Sheva Berakhot
        (blessings)
Birkat Ha-Chamah (prayer), 68–69
Birkat Ha-Chodesh (prayer), 69, 297, 443
Birkat Ha-Gomel (prayer), 15, 69–70
Birkat Ha-Levanah (prayer), 70
Birkat Ha-Mazon (prayer). *See* Grace After Meals
Birkat Ha-Minim (prayer), 164
Birkat Kohanim (prayer). *See* Priestly Benediction
Birnbaum, Nathan, 608
Birth, 23, 53, 56, 72, 275, 315, 327, 419. *See also*
        Babies; Firstborn son; Jewish identity and status;
        Pregnancy
    impurity following, 302
    Niddah (tractate) on, 534
    Original Sin and, 456
Birth control, 70–72, 473
Birthdays, 72, 84
Birthright, 72–73, 568. *See also* Firstborn son;
        Inheritance

Bitter and bitterness, 84, 464, 509, 588–589
Bi'ur (Mendelssohn), 236
Bi'ur chametz, 73
B'la'az, 303
Black, 121–122, 157, 242, 290, 409, 558. *See also*
	Headcoverings
Black Jews, 183. *See also* Falashas
Black Plague, 432
Blades, 509. *See also* Knives
Blair, Tony, 254
Blame. *See* Vengeance
Blasphemy, 91, 108
Blau, Rabbi Amram, 365
Blech, 73, 450
Bleich, Rabbi J. David, 2, 49, 117, 175, 263
Blemishes, 533. *See also* Purity and impurity
Blessings. *See* Prayers and blessings
B'li a'yin ha-ra, 56
Blindness, 263, 513, 568
B'li neder, 412
Blintzes, 485
Bloc of the Faithful, 268
Bloise, France blood libel, 76
Blood, 75–76
	body, removal from. *See* Embalming
	circumcision and, 116–117, 132
	defilement by, 534
	hemophilia, 118
	kashering process and, 151
	menstrual. *See* Menstruation
	of sacrifices, 121
	shedding. *See* Murder and murderers
	slaughtering and, 150, 486
	tattoos and, 538
Blood-avenging relatives, 119
Blood libels, 28–29, 76–77, 139–140, 466
Blood relatives, 50. *See also* Family and family life;
	Forbidden relationships
Blouses, 499
Blue, 120–121, 523, 574–575
B'nai Zakin Sar Shalom, 183
B'nei Berak, 380
B'nei Noach. *See* Noahide Laws
Boaz, 103, 232, 343, 382, 484, 580
Body. *See also* Afterlife; Autopsies; Birth; Corpses; Death;
	Health; Medical intervention; *specific body parts by*
	name
	basar, defined, 507
	cleanliness of. *See* Hygiene
	correspondence to commandments, 306, 349, 537
	correspondence to Shema (prayer), 490
	covering of. *See* Clothing; Modesty
	gartls to separate regions of, 107
	images of, 47–48
	paganism and, 290

physical expressions of during prayers, 399–404
	reincarnation and, 427
	right vs. left side of, 442–443
	sefirot represented by, 280
	souls and, 7, 493, 509–510
	tefillin in direct contact with, 250
	during Torah study, 402
	tzitzit as representative of, 575
Boethusians, 164
Bogeret, 61
Bokser (carob), 98
Bokser, Rabbi Ben Zion, 243–244
Bologna, Italy, 202
Bomberg, Daniel, 208, 326, 527–528
Bondage. *See* Slavery (Egyptian); Slavery (Hebrew)
Bonfires, 304. *See also* Torches
"Book of Creation", 613
Book of Life, 444, 445, 548, 598. *See also* Rosh
	Hashanah; Yom Kippur
Book of Remedies (Maimonides), 193. *See also* Maimonides,
	Rabbi Moses
Book of Root-Principles (Albo), 155, 412–413
"Book of Splendor", 614. *See also* Zohar, The
Book of Transmigration of Souls (Vital), 210
Books, 178, 245
Boone, Pat, 94
Booths. *See* Sukkot; Tabernacle
Booty of war, 553
Borerut, 42
Borrowing. *See* Loans
Botarel, Moses, 336
Boundaries, 475–476, 485. *See also* Eruvin
Bowing, 73, 400–401, 445, 566. *See also* Idolatry and
	idol worshippers
Bows, 613
Box. *See* Aron Ha-Kodesh
Boys. *See also* Children; Sons
	bar mitzvah, 59–60
		confirmation vs., 60, 126
		conversion of adopted children and, 134
		haftarah readings and, 15
		honors given to parents at, 4
		maftir given to, 15
		Masada, celebrations at, 325
		Mi Shebeirakh (prayer) for, 346
		Priestly Benediction for, 408
		as quorum member, 344–345
		se'udat mitzvah and, 472
		She-heche'yanu (blessing) for, 486
		tefillin and, 229
		Torah scroll gartls made for, 561
	shalom zakhar, 143, 459, 481
Braids of challot, 96
Brain, 142, 422
Brandeis, Louis Dembitz, 609–610

Brandenburg concentration camp, 251
Bratzlav chasidim, 106, 107
Brazen serpents, 77
Bread, 77–79, 78. *See also* Grace After Meals; Passover
    of affliction, 329. *See also* Matzot
    breaking bread, 78
    challah. *See also* Bread
        embarrassment of, 88
        Kiddush over, 97
        overview of, 95–97
        for pidyon ha-ben ceremony, 393
        for Sabbath and holidays, 258, 416, 446, 448,
            484, 604
        showbreads symbolized by, 329
        slicing, 79
        as symbol of Jewish unity, 519
        tractate of, 530
    derekh eretz of eating, 146
    Four Questions and, 464
    given to newlyweds, 492
    Hamotzi (blessing), 66, 74, 78, 97, 231, 296, 455
    handwashing prior to eating, 78, 233–234, 418, 534
    health benefits of, 193
    pat lechem, 231
    sacrifice of. *See* Grains
    salt and, 455
    shewbreads, 95–96, 250
    tashlikh ceremony and, 306, 537–538
    unleavened. *See* Matzot
    wine and, 78
Breaking of fasts, 604
Breastbeating, 11, 79, 402, 504
Breastfeeding, 71
Breastplate of the High Priest, 190–191, 385
Breastplate of Torah, 558
Breathing, 142, 509. *See also* Sneezing
Brenner, David, 511
Breslau conference (Reform movement), 376, 595
Bribery, 568
Bridegrooms. *See also* Chatan Bereishit; Chatan Torah;
    Marriage; Weddings
    aliyot (Torah honors) given to, 2, 14, 15, 54
    circled by bride, 56, 581
    clothing, 299
    demons, protection against, 143–144, 369, 517
    gifts from brides, 524
    as kings, 581
    Mi Shebeirakh (prayer) for, 346
    myrtle worn by, 191–192
    shomer of, 497
    zeikher le-churban and, 607–608
Brides. *See also* Marriage; Weddings
    aufruf, participation in, 54
    beauty of, 569
    circling of the bridegroom, 56, 144, 581

demons, protection from, 143–144, 517
    facial hair and, 228
    gifts to bridegrooms, 524
    kallah, defined, 285
    mikveh immersion by, 341–342
    myrtle for, 196
    as queens, 581
    Sabbath compared to, 296, 310, 333, 448
    shomeret of, 497
    Torah compared to, 478
    veiling of, 58, 97, 578
    zeikher le-churban and, 607–608
Brit. *See* Circumcision; Covenant People
Britain. *See* Great Britain
Brit bat, 481
British Mandate period, 468, 609
Brit milah. *See* Circumcision
Broiling, 150
Brother Daniel, 276
Brothers-in-law. *See* Levirate marriage practices
Brothers of Joseph. *See* Twelve Tribes of Jacob
Buber, Martin, 110
Buddhist monks, 524
Bukhara, Uzbekistan, 228
Bul, 84
Bullocks, 371. *See also* Sacrifices
Bunam, Rabbi Simchah, 137
Bunche, Ralph, 267
Burial, 5, 79–81, 200–201. *See also* Cemeteries;
    Cremation; Death; Kevod ha-met
    aninut and, 27
    autopsies and, 54
    Bar Kokhbah rebellion and, 569
    blood of deceased and, 76
    Burial Society, 81–82, 418–419, 497
    coffins, valuables in, 58
    demons and, 144–145
    Eivel Rabbati (tractate) on, 535–536
    ghosts, prevention of, 209
    of holy objects, 46, 81, 206, 254, 434, 509
    of intermarried couples, 265
    Jewish law of, 166–167
    Kaddish De-Itchadeta, 283. *See also* Kaddish (prayer)
    in kittls, 298
    met mitzvah, 336–337. *See also* Chesed shel emet
    mourner prior to. *See* Aninut
    of non-Jews, 265
    organ transplants and, 377
    shrouds, 120, 121, 300, 419, 476, 498–499
    of suicides, 514–515
    tallit and, 525
    tattoo myth and, 538
    of victims of suicide attacks, 607
Burning, execution by, 29, 91, 140. *See also* Capital
    punishment

Burning bush, 211, 407
Burning of books and Torah scrolls, 291, 528
Burning of the chametz, 64
Burnt offerings, 78, 95, 453, 533. *See also* Sacrifices
Burundi, 191
Business affairs. *See also* Kinyan sudar; Labor (work)
   chazakah claim, 109
   good faith and, 182
   mourner, forbidden to conduct, 27, 494
   Nezikin (tractate) on, 532
   objects of, 356, 449
   Sabbath travel and, 451
Butter, 40
Buying and selling. *See also* Business affairs
   of aliyot, 16–17
   of chametz, 98, 333
   of a home, 339–340
   Nezikin (tractate) on, 532
   for sabbatical years, 310
   of Torah ornaments, 558
Buzika, 362
Byzantine Empire, 92, 287, 325

C

Cabinet. *See* Ark of the Covenant
Cadavers. *See* Corpses
Caduceus, 77
Caesarea, 22
Caesarian sections, 392
Cain, 361
Cairo Genizah, 206, 434
Cake, 95, 389
Calendar. *See* Hebrew calendar
Callah. *See* Brides
Calligraphers. *See* Scribes
Camel, 326
Camp David Accords, 269
Canaan, 263, 274, 357, 384. *See also* Palestine (history of)
Cancer (zodiacal sign), 85, 613
Candles and candlelighting, 75, 87–89. *See also*
       Chanukkah; Torches
   eternal light, 169, 231
   for havdalah service, 237–238, 599
   light of Torah represented by, 44
   memorial candles, 494, 597
   menorahs, 99–100
   by Pathan tribesmen, 548
   as protection from demons, 143–144
   Sabbath, 402–403, 448, 562
   souls compared to, 401
   as symbol of Jewish unity, 519
   torches, 143–144
   women's obligation in, 349, 590
   zeh ne'heneh ve-zeh lo chaser principle and, 607

Candy, 54, 59. *See also* Sweets and sweetness
Canon. *See* Tanakh
Canopies. *See* Chuppah; Oholot
Cantillations, 89–90, 232, 564. *See also* Cantors;
       Nusachim; Torah readings
Cantors. *See also* Ba'al korei; Cantillations; Shli'ach tzibur
   bareheaded, 240
   defined, 58, 68
   Eighteen Benedictions, repetition of, 164
   as holy vessels, 249
   Kaddish of, 282
   objections to, 358
   Sephardic customs for, 226
   surnames and, 518
   tallitot worn by, 523, 525
   Yom Kippur services, 400
Capek, Karel, 76–77
Capitalis, 241
Capital punishment, 90–92, 177, 448–449, 452, 503
   for adultery, 5
   burial of one guilty of, 93
   by crucifixion, 139–140. *See also* Crucifixions
   Jewish methods of, 29, 140
   Sabbath violation and, 604
   Sanhedrin and, 65, 139–140, 457–458
   shivah not observed for executed criminals, 39
Capricorn (zodiacal sign), 84, 613
Captives, 394, 451. *See also* Slavery (Egyptian); Slavery
     (Hebrew)
Carbon monoxide, 251
Card games, 102, 202–203
Cardinal sins of Judaism, 395. *See also* Adultery;
     Idolatry and idol worshippers; Murder and
     murderers
Carmel, Mount, 505
Carmelite Order, 276
Carmel wines, 586
Carnivals, 3, 326, 417
Caro, Joseph, 359, 376, 421, 433. See also *Code of Jewish
     Law* (Caro)
Carob, 98
Carrots, 446
Carrying on the Sabbath, 167–169, 356, 449–450, 476, 530
Cars. *See* Travel
Carter, Ben Ammi, 183
Carter, Jimmy, 269
Cassiel, 26
Castilian-Spanish. *See* Ladino
Castor, 369. *See also* Astrology
Castration, 70–71
Catholic Church and Catholicism, 34–35, 154, 181, 208,
     546–547. *See also* Christians and Christianity
Cave of Makhpelah, 92, 93
CCAR (Central Conference of American Rabbis), 132,
     264, 390, 425–427, 612

Celebrations. *See also* Bar mitzvah; Bat mitzvah;
        Circumcision; Confirmation ceremony; Holidays;
        Pidyon ha-ben; Weddings
    secular, 357
    Sumptuary Laws and, 433, 516–517
    on yahrzeits, 597
Celebrity names, 363
Celestial beings. *See* Angels
Celibacy, 92. *See also* Tohorat ha-mishpachah
Cemeteries, 92–94. *See also* Burial; Death
    ashes, burial of, 138–139
    etiquette of, 93–94
    food in, 93, 576
    funerals in, 198
    handwashing and, 56, 94, 145, 201, 234–235, 261,
        418
    military, 199
    Priests prohibited from, 94, 115, 406, 555
    tattoo myth and, 538
Censoring of literature, 11
Census, 314, 368, 387, 390
Central Conference of American Rabbis (CCAR), 132,
        264, 390, 425–427, 612
Cereal, 95. *See also* Grains
Ceremony of the Removed Sandal, 95, 312–313. *See also*
        Levirate marriage practices
Certificate of marriage, 582. *See also* Ketubbot
Certification, kosher, 151, 586
Chabad, 106–107, 348, 387. *See also* Chasidim and
        chasidut
Chadash and yashan, 598–599
Chad Gadya (song), 24, 94, 466–467. *See also* Passover
Chafetz Chayim, 562, 566
Chagall, Marc, 299
Chaggai (prophet), 258
Chag Ha-Bikkurim, 189, 483. *See also* Shavuot
Chag Ha-Katzir, 482. *See also* Shavuot
Chag Ha-Matzot, 386. *See also* Passover
Chag Ha-Pesach, 386. *See also* Passover
Chag Ha-Urim, 99. *See also* Chanukkah
Chagigah (tractate), 531
Chai, 94–95, 104
Chained woman. *See* Agunot
Chairs, 117, 166, 495
Chalakah, 229
Chalalim, 323
Chaldeans, 456–457
Chalif, 485–486. *See also* Slaughtering
Chalil, 357
Chalitzah, 38, 95, 312–313. *See also* Levirate marriage
        practices
Challah. *See also* Bread
    embarrassment of, 88
    Hamotzi (blessing), 66, 74, 78, 97, 231, 296, 455
    handwashing prior to eating, 78, 233–234, 418, 534

Kiddush over, 97
overview of, 95–97
for pidyon ha-ben ceremony, 393
for Sabbath and holidays, 258, 416, 446, 448, 484,
        604
showbreads symbolized by, 329
slicing, 79
as symbol of Jewish unity, 519
tractate of, 530
Challenger space shuttle, 89
Chalutzah, 409. *See also* Levirate marriage practices
Chama (fourth century), 170
Chama (third century), 249
Chama bar Chaninah, 427
Chama ben Chaninah, 212, 335
Chamah (sun), 68
Chamber of Hewn Stone, 65, 457, 519. *See also* Great
        Sanhedrin
Chametz
    batel b'shishim and, 61
    bedikat chametz, 64
    bi'ur chametz, 73
    chadash and yashan and, 598
    Chag Ha-Matzot and, 386–389
    contemporary observance of, 148
    fermentation, 329, 330, 386–388
    kitni'ot and, 389
    matzot and, 328
    mekhirat chametz, 98, 310, 333
    overview of, 97–98
    Pesach Sheini and, 392
    yeitzer ha-ra and, 97–98
Chamin, 194
Chamishah Asar Bi-Shevat, 42, 85, 98
Chamsa, 560. *See also* Amulets
Chananyah, 26, 324
Change
    abandonment of the Torah. *See* Apostates and
        apostasy
    man's capacity for, 46. *See also* Repentance
Chaninah (Rabbi), 21–22
    on angels, 25
    on free will, 197
    kavanah of, 288
    on law-of-the-land, 309
    on Messianic Age, 334–335
    on Noahide Laws, 367
    on planetary influence, 517
    on prayers, 400
    on truthfulness, 567
Chaninah ben Papa, 197
Chaninah ben Teradyon, 162, 572, 588
Chanukkah, 99–102
    aliyot (Torah honors) given on, 14
    babies born on, 362

Book of Judith, 34, 101
candlelighting blessings, 75
date of, 84
dreidel game, 102, 202
eulogies during, 171
Karaites and, 286
maftir of, 318
menorahs, 99–100
Nicanor's Day, 415
overview of, 248
prayers and blessings of, 12, 230
on Sabbath, 100
Sukkot and, 99
Syrian customs, 231
Chanukkat Ha-Ba'yit, 102
Chanukkiyah, 99, 334, 548. *See also* Menorahs
Chapels, non-Jewish, 199
Chareidim, 380. *See also* Orthodoxy
Charim, 361
Charity, 66, 102–104, 572. *See also* Chesed;
          Donations
    blessings not required for, 74
    boxes, 104–105
    collection of, 202
    death, saves from, 105
    in honor of the dead, 602
    justice and, 277
    kapparot and, 285–286, 306
    in lieu of lavish celebrations, 516
    ma'ot chittim, 320
    matanot le-evyonim, 414
    Mazon, 60
    in multiples of eighteen, 371
    in multiples of twenty-six, 371
    nedavah, 364
    Netaneh Tokef (prayer) and, 364
    organizations for, 60
    overview of, 102–105
    Pei'ah (tractate) on, 529
    pidyon shevu'yim, superseded by, 394
    pledges of, 496
    from the poor, 122
    "poor-man's tithe", 553
    Sabbath travel and, 451
    Thursdays as day of generosity, 53
    tzitzit as reminder of, 575
Charles, Prince of Wales, 351
Charms, 23–24, 94, 112, 511
Charoset, 461–462, 464–465
Chasdiel, 26
Chasidei Ashkenaz, 575
Chasidei umot ha-olam, 105–108, 367
Chasidim and chasidut, 395. *See also* Righteousness
    birthday celebrations of, 72
    clothing and headcoverings of, 242, 297, 477

facial hair and, 228–229
growth of, 348
leaders of, 266, 493, 572
mitnagdim vs., 266, 348–349
Passover customs, 329, 387
Satmar chasidic sect, 13, 107, 113, 242
Chasid shoteh, 108
Chastity, 536
Chatam Sofer (Schreiber). *See* Sofer, Rabbi Moses
Chatan. *See* Bridegrooms
Chatan Bereishit, 108, 192, 503, 524
Chatan Torah, 108, 192, 503, 524
Chatzi Kaddish, 283. *See also* Kaddish (prayer)
Chatzitzah, 132
Chavitin, 405. *See also* Sacrifices
Chavrutah, 108, 600. *See also* Yeshivot
Chavurah, 108. *See also* Chevrah
Chazakah, 109
Chazeret, 462
Chazir. *See* Pork
Chazzan. *See also* Ba'al korei; Cantillations; Shli'ach
          tzibur
    bareheaded, 240
    defined, 58, 68
    Eighteen Benedictions, repetition of, 164
    as holy vessels, 249
    Kaddish of, 282
    objections to, 358
    Sephardic customs for, 226
    surnames and, 518
    tallit worn by, 523, 525
    Yom Kippur services, 400
Chederim, 65, 109, 163. *See also* Education
Chedorlaomer of Elam, 553
Cheese, 101, 152, 484–485. *See also* Dairy foods
Cheilek (tractate), 550
Cheirem, 109, 153, 177, 398, 409, 594. *See also*
          Excommunication
Cheit, 503. *See also* Sins and sinners
Chelbo (Rabbi), 129
Chelmo extermination camp, 252
Chemical depilatories, 228
Cherubim. *See* Keruvim
Chesed, 26, 109, 231, 280, 337. *See also* Charity
Cheshbon ha-nefesh, 109
Cheshvan, 83–84
Chet, 18, 368, 521
Chevrah, 108, 110
Chevrah kaddishah, 110, 418–419, 499, 607. *See also*
          Burial; Purity and impurity
Chevrah rodfei tzedek, 81
Chevrat chesed ve-emet, 81
Chevrat gomlei chasadim, 81
Chevrat Ha-Cha'yim, 365
Chevrat Rabbi Shimon bar Yocha'i, 81

Chevron (son of Kohath), 405
Chewing cud, 149
Chickens, 40, 101, 285–286, 306, 369, 504
Chickpeas, 389
Chief Rabbinate, Israeli, 51, 246, 468
Chilazon, 120, 523, 574–575
Childbirth. *See* Birth; Pregnancy
Children. *See also* Babies; Daughters; Education;
    Family and family life; Heirs; Pregnancy; Sons;
    Youth
   aliyot (Torah honors) given to, 16–17, 503
   birth control used by, 71
   childless marriages. *See* Levirate marriage practices
   commandment to beget. *See* Fruitful and multiply
     commandment
   conversion to Judaism of, 133–134
   discipline of, 162–163, 600
   of Essenes, 51
   fasting and fast days, 186, 604
   Four Questions asked by, 463–464
   Kaddish, recital of, 4
   Kiddushin (tractate) on, 531
   marriages of, 322
   naming of, 312–313, 363–364
   out of wedlock, 319
   Passover and, 465
   prayers for, 404
   of Priests and divorcees, 323
   protection of, 23
   quorum, counting in, 344
   Shema (prayer) and, 489–490
   Youth Aliya, 613
Chilkia the High Priest, 460
Chillul Ha-Shem, 110, 142, 177, 324, 410
Chinese chasidim, 477
Chisda (Rabbi), 157, 341, 350, 474, 588
Chiya (bar Rav) of Difti, 471
Chiya (Rabbah), 586
Chiya bar Abba, 204–205, 239, 365, 566
Chiya ben Avuya, 264
Choice. *See* Free will
Choirs, 357–358
Chok (chukim), 476
Chokhmah, 107, 280. *See also* Wisdom
Chol, 250
Cholent, 194
Chol Ha-Moed, 14, 110, 248–249, 318, 459, 531, 539,
   583
Choreiv, 504
Chosen People, 32–33, 110–111, 180, 410, 422, 439,
   504. *See also* Covenant People
Choshen Mishpat, 307, 500, 558–559. *See also Code of
   Jewish Law (Caro)*
Choueka, Yaacov, 435
Chovevei Zion, 608

Chovot Ha-Levavot. See Bachya ibn Pakuda
Chozer Bi-Teshuvah, 112. *See also* Teshuvah (return)
Christians and Christianity. *See also* Jesus Christ; Non-Jews
   Abraham (Patriarch), as descendants of, 32
   on the Apocrypha, 34–35
   Byzantine Empire, 92, 287, 325
   Chosen People, Jewish nation recognized as, 32–33
   Christmas, 202–203, 483, 520
   circumcision of, 118
   confirmation and, 126
   dogma of, 155
   Dominicans, 179
   Gentiles, referred to as, 206–207
   giftgiving of, 101–102
   Halloween celebrations, 113
   headcoverings and, 241
   influence on Jewish prayers, 12
   interest payments, prohibition of, 352–353
   intermarriage with, 264–265
   Jesus as God incarnate, 456
   Jewish communities under control of, 468
   on Jews as the Chosen People, 111
   Judeo-Christians, 501
   on justice of God, 573
   Latin translation of the Hebrew Bible, 471
   monogamy of, 397–398
   monotheism of, 11
   New Testament, 67
   New Year's Day (secular), 112–113
   Noahide Laws, 105, 255, 366, 367, 370, 549
   Original Sin and, 377–378
   Pentecost, 483
   prayers of, 400, 401
   Sabbath of, 453
   Seventh-Day Adventists, 453
   sexual relations, views on, 92
   Shema (prayer) and, 489
   on sins and sinners, 503
   Ten Commandments and, 546–547
   Ve-la-malshinim (prayer) vs., 164
Chromosomes, 263, 409
Chronology of the World, The (Yosei ben Chalafta), 86. *See
   also* Hebrew calendar
Chug Ivri, 112
Chukat ha-goy, 112–113, 191–192, 357–358. *See also*
   Christians and Christianity
Chukim, 113–114. *See also* Red heifer
Chul. *See* Chutz la-aretz
Chullin (tractate), 533
Chumash, 344, 556. *See also* Five Books of Moses
Chuppah, 114–115, 192, 292, 369, 492, 517, 524, 581.
   See also Weddings
Churban, 504. *See also* Holocaust
Church bells, 210
Churches, 48. *See also* Christians and Christianity

Church of St. Mary of Zion at Axam, 43
Chutz la-aretz, 115. *See also* Diaspora
Chutzpit the Meturgeman, 36
Chuzpit, Rabbi, 337
Cincinnati, Ohio, 425
Circles and circling. *See also* Hakafot; Kapparot; Weddings
    under the chuppah, 369, 517, 581
    demons and, 143, 403
    Kike as name for Jewish immigrants, 274
    machzorim and, 318
    renewal of life and, 96
    Wachnacht, 115, 490, 580
    zodiac and, 613
Circumcision, 79, 115–119
    of Abraham (Patriarch), 26
    banning of, 116
    of British Royalty, 351
    clothing of baby for, 46
    of converts, 131–132, 275, 322
    of Falashas, 182
    gartls made from ceremonial clothing of, 560–561
    hatafat dam brit, 117, 132
    of Jesus Christ, 112
    Kaddish recited at, 282
    Karaite observance of, 286–288
    mohel, 116–117, 132, 301, 457, 590
    of Moses, 412
    naming of baby and, 361
    orlah, 378
    pidyon ha-ben and, 393
    on Sabbath, 143, 351–352
    Satan and, 143, 459, 481
    shalom zakhar, 143, 459, 481
    Syrian prohibition of, 99
    Wachnacht, 115, 490, 580
Circumstantial evidence, 91
Cities of refuge, 119, 532
Citizenship, Israeli. *See* Law of Return
Citron, 41, 64, 182, 194–196, 516, 530. *See also* Arba
    minim
City of David, 272. *See also* Jerusalem
City of refuge, 119, 532
Civil calendar, 83–84, 87, 112–113
Civility. *See* Derekh eretz
Civilization, Judaism as, 422–423
Civil law
    adultery, definition of, 4
    agunot and, 9
    Choshen Mishpat, 307, 500
    contrary to moral principles, 309
    divorce and, 154, 207
    for Jews, 410
    mumchim and, 458
    Nezikin (Mishnah tractates), 347, 531–532
    remarriage following, 323

    testifying against Jews, 177
    witnesses for, 587
Civil rights of Jews, 251
Claims. *See* Jewish law; Property
Class. *See* Jewish identity and status
Classic Cuisine of the Italian Jews, The (Machlin), 464
Clean days, 554. *See also* Tohorat ha-mishpachah
Cleaning the home for Passover, 64. *See also* Passover
Cleanliness and cleansing, 116, 173, 191, 260–261, 442.
    See also Bathing; Purity and impurity
Clemenceau, George, 609
Clemens, Flavius, 133
Clement XIV, Pope, 76
Clinton, Bill, 269–270
Clothing. *See also* Hair, covering of; Headcoverings;
    Jewelry and charms; Modesty; Shaatnez; Shoes
    cleanliness of, 261
    colors of, 157
    derekh eretz and, 145
    dignity and, 158
    men prohibited from wearing women's, 326
    mourning, 121
    non-Jewish customs of, 112
    Purim, 417
    red, 121
    She-heche'yanu (blessing) for, 486
    during shivah period, 494
    of the soul, 143
    tzitzit, 157
    women's, 157–158, 417
    for Yom Kippur, 604–605
Coats. *See* Kittls
Code of Jewish Law (Caro). *See also* Caro, Joseph; Jewish
    Law; *Mappah* (Isserles)
    on aging, 8
    on apostates and apostasy, 35, 38
    on birth control, 71–72
    on breaking bread, 78
    on candles, 44
    on cemeteries, 93
    on customs and law, 305
    on Eighteen Benedictions, 165
    on euthanasia, 174
    on funeral practices, 198
    on genuflection, 566
    on hagbahah, 17
    on hair coverings, 487
    on handwashing, 234, 261
    on hashchatat zera, 473
    on headcoverings, 239, 241
    on heathens, 113
    on Kiddush (prayer), 296, 403
    on kitni'ot, 389
    on kosher animals, 150
    on mirrors, 158

on names of God, 214
on niddah, laws of, 366
on non-Jewish parents, 134
numbering of pages and chapters, 172–173
overview of, 307, 379, 433, 500
on Passover observance, 466
on physical contact with opposite sex, 298
on planetary influence, 517
on prohibitions against graven images, 47–48
on quorums, 344
Reform Judaism and, 308, 426
on Sabbath laws, 450, 451
sacrificial system, not addressed in, 454
on scribes, 507
on shaving the face, 228
on standing before the Torah, 45
study of, 163
on suicides, 514
on synagogue structure, 520
on tallitot, 524
on Torah readings, 563
on willows, 197
on women and tefillin, 542
Codices of the Bible, 325–326, 508
Codifiers of Jewish law, 306–307
Coffins, 58, 80, 112, 115, 119–120, 198, 199, 293, 406.
    See also Burial
Cohabitation, 154, 474–475. See also Sexual relations
Cohen, Gerson D., 126, 128
Cohen, Hermann, 421–422
Cohen, Rabbi Shaye D., 390
Coins, 286, 306, 449, 478–479, 530, 580. See also
    Money
Collection of funds. See Charity
Colors, 120–122, 157, 190, 280, 498. See also Beauty and
    beautification
Columbus Platform, 426
Comfort. See Compassion; Menachem aveil; Mourners
    and mourning
Commandments. See also Bar mitzvah; Bat mitzvah;
    Jewish law; religious articles; specific
    commandments by name; Taryag mitzvot; Ten
    Commandments; Torah
  adding to, 59, 413
  aliyot (Torah honors) as, 13
  bikur cholim, 67, 122, 383, 406
  blessings and prayers over, 66, 74
  correspondence to the body, 306, 349, 537
  defined, 122
  education of, 160
  forgiveness from God and, 456
  as "good deeds", 349
  hiddur mitzvah, 64
  kavanah and, 288–289
  lo toseif, lo tigra, 379

loyalty to God and, 437
man's partnership with God and, 422
as means of tikkun olam, 281
mitzvot lo ta'aseh, 10
mourner, exemption from, 27
name of Mt. Sinai and, 504
non-Jews and, 16. See also Noahide Laws
oneinim not obligated in, 355, 374
preparation for. See Handwashing
protection from harm by performance of, 36
Sabbath travel and fulfillment of, 451
sins, as results of, 74
study of Torah as, 13
time-related, 137, 231, 349, 376, 525, 541
tzitzit correspondence to, 575
women not obligated in, 162
Commitment ceremonies for homosexuals, 257
Commitments. See Vows
Committee on Jewish Law and Standards, 128, 451–452,
    518, 584, 586
Communal regulations. See Hasagat gevul
Communal sins, 51–52, 55
Communications of Torah learning. See Responsa
    Literature
Communication with God, 156. See also Prayers and
    blessings; Prophets and prophecy (Nevi'im);
    Revelation at Sinai
Community, 289–290. See also Assembly; Kehillah; Public
    vs. private; Quorum
Community offerings, 453. See also Sacrifices
Community of Israel, 369. See also Israelites;
    Kohanim; Levites
  kolelim, 300, 429, 598
  mipnei kevod tzibur, 293–294, 345, 563, 593
  Pittsburgh Platform on, 426
  shelom ba'yit and, 487–488
  taxes for, 289
Companionship. See Chavrutah; Chevrah
Compassion, 27, 102, 122, 260, 421, 441–442, 550,
    569, 570–572. See also Charity; Condolences;
    Derekh eretz; Mercy
Compendium on Medical Ethics (Jakobovits), 142. See also
    Jakobovits, Rabbi Immanuel
Compensation. See Money, fines of
Compromise, 123, 339. See also Arbitration
Concentration and intentions. See Kavanah
Concentration camps, 27, 32, 251–253, 441. See also
    Holocaust
Conception, 1–2, 197–198, 473. See also Birth control;
    Pregnancy
Conclusion (complete). See also Totality
  acharon acharon chaviv, 2
  haftarah and, 318
  maftir and, 318
  mashlim aliyah and, 2

of meals. *See* Grace After Meals; Ma'yim achronim
of the Sabbath. *See* Havdalah service
of Talmud tractate. *See* Siyyum
Torah as complete, 59
of Torah readings. *See* Hagbahah and gelilah
Conclusion (judgment). *See* Appearances
Concubines of Jacob, 397
Condolences, 123–125, 201, 356, 365, 495. *See also*
    Mourners and mourning; Shivah
Condoms, 70
Conduct. *See* Derekh eretz; Kevod tzibur; Modesty;
    Reward and punishment
Confession of sins. *See* Atonement; Repentance; Sins and
    sinners; Yom Kippur
Confirmation ceremonies, 60, 126, 484
Conflict. *See* Arbitration; War
Congregation Bene Yeshurun, Cincinnati, 425
Congregations, 289–290. *See also* Quorums; Rabbis;
    Synagogues
    as an eidah, 343. *See also* Quorums
    establishment of, 398
    family life and, 184
    functionaries of, 202, 205–206, 299, 346, 563, 564
    for homosexuals, 256
    hospitality of, 295–296
    mipnei kevod tzibur, 293–294, 345, 563, 593
    non-Jews and, 264
    prayers of, 399
    tircha de-tzibura and, 552
Congregation Shearith Israel, 468
Conjugal duties. *See* Sexual relations
Consecration
    Chanukkah and, 99
    firstborn. *See* Pidyon ha-ben
    first fruits, 189
    of sanctuary in the wilderness, 510
Conservative Judaism, 126–128, 387, 422, 601
Consolation, 478, 585. *See also* Menachem aveil;
    Mourners and mourning
Consonants. *See* Alphabet, Hebrew
Constantine, Emperor, 29, 453. *See also* Roman
    government and Romans
Constantinople, 287
Constellations, 11, 317, 330, 370, 517, 613. *See also*
    Hebrew calendar; Kabbalah and kabbalists; Moon;
    Mystics and mysticism; Stars; Sun
Construction, 40, 320–321
Consummation of marriage, 114, 580, 601
Contamination. *See* Purity and impurity
Contra Apionem, 76
Contraceptive devices. *See* Birth control
Contracts. *See* Jewish law
Conversation, 124–125. *See also* Speech
Conversos. *See* Marranos
Converts and conversion. *See also* Baptism

Abraham (Patriarch) as father of, 130
Amnon, Rabbi of Mainz, martyrdom of, 364
children of surrogate mothers, 259
to Christianity, 30, 35, 147, 178, 208, 245, 275, 321,
    468. *See also* Inquisition, Spanish
circumcision of, 117, 275
Constantine, illegal under, 29
of Falashas, 183
forced, 129, 430
geirei ara'yot, 129
Geirim (tractate) on, 536
historical background, 128–131
honoring parents and, 385–386
intermarriage and, 264
kindness to, 122, 245, 406
Law of Return and, 308
of Marranos back to Judaism, 322
marriage to mamzeirim, 5, 319
marriage to Priests and, 135, 323, 406–407
mikveh immersion by, 131–132, 275, 322, 341
name changes by, 363
Obadiah the convert, 130, 431, 512–513
rites and procedures, 131–135
shivah for, 495
stigma of, 319
witnesses of, 376
Convictions. *See* Courts, Jewish; Jewish law; Punishment
Cooking. *See also* Kashrut
    eruv tavshilin, 168
    grounds for divorce and, 153
    kashrut and, 152, 307, 476
    non-Jews, food cooked by, 310
    Passover, 387–389
    Sabbath, 73, 286–288, 450–451
    utensils for, 342
Cooperatives. *See* Kibbutzim
Copenhagen Haggadah, 227
Copper laver for Priests, 233
Copper serpents, 77
Cordovera, Moses, 278, 359
Corner (tractate), 529
Corpses, 366, 373, 405–406, 409, 418, 422, 478, 497,
    555. *See also* Death
Corruption. *See* Sins and sinners
Cortar mortaza, 498. *See also* Shrouds
Costumes and masquerading, 326, 417
Cotton, 157, 349, 523
Council. *See* Sanhedrin
Council of Trent (1546), 471
Counting, 325, 368, 507. *See also* Numbers and values;
    Quorums
Counting of the omer. *See* Sefirat ha-omer
Courtesy. *See* Derekh eretz; Tircha de-tzibura
Court Jews, 135, 353, 499–500
Court of Seventy-one. *See* Great Sanhedrin

Court of Twenty-three, 65

Court of Women. *See* Ezrat nashim

Courts, Jewish, 22, 180, 301, 522, 531–532. *See also*
  Civil court; Jewish law; Justice

Courtyards, 167–169. *See also* Public vs. private

Covenant People, 136, 152, 439, 504. *See also* Chosen
  People; Jewish people

Covenants. *See also* Circumcision; Marriage
  Covenant of Life service, 361
  covenant of the daughter, 481
  salt and, 455

Cows, 114, 422–424, 451, 476, 478, 534. *See also*
  Golden Calf

Crabs, 613

Creation, 136–138. *See also* Adam (first man); Days of the
  week; Eve (first woman)
  of angels, 25
  anthropomorphism of God and, 28
  Chronology of the World, The, 86
  Darwinian theory, 137–138
  days of, 68–69
  of evil spirits, 143
  evolution vs., 176–177
  fish and, 193
  Hebrew alphabet and, 20
  interpretations of, 382
  Kiddush (prayer) and, 295
  Ma'asei Bereishit, 317–318
  of man, 507
  preordained miracles and, 345
  Rosh Hashanah and, 446
  Sabbath and, 447
  seven, significance of, 370
  shaatnez and, 477
  of the sun and moon, 68
  three, importance of number, 369
  Torah preceding, 438
  translations of, 557

Crediting. *See* Interest payments

Cremation, 80, 138–139, 293

Cremona, Italy, 202

Crescas, Rabbi Chasdai, 198

Criminal law, 347, 531–532, 587

Criminals, 79, 366. *See also* Punishment; Stealing

Crimson. *See* Red

Crockery, breaking, 299

Cronkite, Walter, 612

Crops. *See* Harvest

Crosses. *See* Crucifixions

Crown (in kabbalah), 280

Crowns (of Torahs), 558, 559

Crucifixions, 11, 28, 29, 30, 139–140, 378. *See also* Jesus
  Christ

Cruelty to animals. *See* Tza'ar ba'alei cha'yim

Crumbs. *See* Bread; Chametz; Tashlikh ceremony

Crusades, the, 30, 324, 325, 352, 430, 602

Crusts of bread, 78

Crying, 171, 455, 584–585

Cryptograms, 517

Cuban minyan, 344–345

Cubes of tefillin, 539–541. *See also* Tefillin

Cud, 149

Culture, 277, 424. *See also* Haskalah movement

Cuomo, Mario, 479

Cup of Elijah, 166. *See also* Passover

Cups, Kiddush, 296. *See also* Kiddush (prayer)

Cups, washing. *See* Handwashing

Curaçao, 144

Curbs around the Torah, 358, 493

Cures. *See* Amulets; Medical intervention; Miracles

Curses on Jewish people, 3, 21, 173, 554. *See also*
  Demons and demonology

Cursing of parents, 91

Curtains of the ark, 46

Customs and law, 74, 304–306, 422, 426, 606. *See also*
  Chukat ha-goy

Cyrus the Great of Persia, 146, 456–457, 544

D

Dachau, 32. *See also* Holocaust

Dafina, 194

Daf Yomi, 141

Dagesh, 17, 18, 19

Daggers, 521–522

Dagim, 613. *See also* Fish

Dairy foods, 61, 101, 152, 307, 320, 476, 484–485, 534.
  See also Kashrut

Dalet, 17, 161, 367, 521

Dama ben Netina, 385, 422

Damages, 347, 381, 392, 531–532

Damascus Affair, 76

Dan (tribe of), 182

Dancing, 450, 476, 503, 569

Danger, 69–70. *See also* Birkat Ha-Gomel (prayer);
  Demons and demonology; Pikuach nefesh

Daniel
  on angels, 25–26
  Bel and the Dragon, 34
  den of lions and, 324
  dreams, interpretations of, 156
  prayers of, 316, 369, 404, 520
  pseudepigrapha and, 414
  Song of the Three Holy Children, 34
  Susanna and the Elders, 34
  telata gavrei and, 14

Daniel, Brother, 276

Daniel ben Judah, 155, 550, 602

Daniel Deronda (Eliot), 611

Dargesh, 119

Darius, King, 28, 544
Dark Forces, Prince of, 24
Darkness, 87, 143–144. *See also* Night
Darwinian theory, 137–138
Dateline World Jewry, 322
Date palm. *See* Palm branches
Dates (fruit), 189. *See also* Seven species of Israel
Dathan, 383
Daughters, 2, 184–185, 284, 361, 481, 587–588. *See also* Bat Mitzvah; Children; Girls; Women
Davav, 141
Davenen, 141. *See also* Prayers and blessings
David, King, 128
    on aging, 8
    appointment as king, 382
    Ark (of the Covenant) and, 43
    birth and death of, 484
    census ordered by, 368
    eulogies delivered by, 170
    on euthanasia, 173
    Goliath and, 396
    headcovering of, 238
    High Priest as descendant of, 247
    image of, 519
    Jerusalem, rule over, 272
    keri'ah by, 290
    lamentations of, 254
    marriage of, 390
    melaveh malkah, origin of and, 333
    Messianic Age and, 335–336
    nesi'im as descendants of, 364
    Shield of David, 510–511
    ushpizin and, 577
    wives of, 397
David ben Zimri, 182
David ibn Abi Zimra, 95. *See also* Radbaz
Davis, wife of Maurice, 138–139
Dayan, Moshe, 267, 295
Da'yan Ha-Emet, 441–442
Da'yanim. *See* Beit Din
Da'yeinu (song), 141. *See also* Passover
Day of Atonement, 445, 530. *See also* Yom Kippur
Day of Judgment, 258, 392, 444, 458–459, 497. *See also* Hoshanah Rabbah; Rosh Hashanah
Day of Remembrance, 444. *See also* Rosh Hashanah
Days, 84. *See also* Hebrew calendar
Day schools, 601
Days of Awe, 51, 109, 371, 444–445, 496–497, 547–548, 583, 597–598. *See also* Elul; Repentance; Rosh Hashanah; Yom Kippur
Days of Messiah. *See* Messiah and Messianic Age
Days of the week, 53, 68–69. *See also specific days by name*
Dead Sea Scrolls, 169, 286. *See also* Essenes
Dearborn *Independent*, 31–32

Death, 65, 142. *See also* Afterlife; Burial; Capital punishment; Cemeteries; Heaven; Hell; Inheritance; Kaddish (prayer); Mourners and mourning; Murder and murderers; Orphans; Resurrection; Widowers; Widows; World to come; Yahrzeits
    Angel of Death, 143, 174, 340, 363–364, 458, 494
    announcement of, 497
    of an apostate, 39
    atonement before, 125–126
    autopsies, 54–55, 309, 366
    birth compared to, 419
    birth of another, preceding, 72
    black and, 121
    candles and, 87–88
    charity saves from, 105
    chesed shel emet and, 109, 231, 336–337
    communication with the dead, 209
    corpses, 366, 373, 405–406, 409, 418, 422, 478, 497, 555
    cremation, 80, 138, 293
    deathbed, protection from evil eye, 56
    declaration of, 142
    demons and, 143–145
    by drownings, 9, 108
    of the Egyptian firstborn, 186, 188
    embalming, 76, 80, 165–166
    euthanasia, 173–175, 340
    of fetus, 1
    of the goat on Yom Kippur, 57
    handwashing and, 94, 145, 201, 234–235, 261, 418
    Hazkarah (prayer) for, 166, 238, 468
    impurity and, 114, 533
    interim period following. *See* Aninut
    ketubbot stipulations, 292
    kevod ha-met, 54, 79, 82, 93, 198, 293, 366, 377, 419
    of Levites, 408
    met mitzvah. *See* Chesed shel emet
    mezuzot in room of, 340
    neshama and, 509–510
    of newborns, 117–118
    niftar, defined, 318
    nivul ha-met, 54, 79, 198, 366, 377
    of non-Jewish parents, 134–135
    Original Sin and, 377–378
    poor equated with, 94
    Priests and proximity to, 373
    as punishment. *See* Capital punishment
    as renewal, 512
    Sabbath violation and, 447
    for sexual relations with a niddah, 365
    sneezing and, 507
    spices and, 192
    suicides, 39, 171, 173–175, 252, 324, 340, 514–515

ten martyrs, 36, 123, 297, 324, 371, 548, 572, 605
  Viddui (prayers) prior to, 579
  "zikhrono li-verakhah" expression, 3
Deborah (judge), 357, 361, 505, 577
Debts, 276, 310, 413–414, 491. *See also* Interest
      payments; Loans
Decalogue, 142, 544. *See also* Ten Commandments
Decapitation, execution by, 91. *See also* Capital
      punishment
Decay. *See* Embalming
Deceit, 142, 513. *See also* Chillul Ha-Shem; Lying; Truth
      and truthfulness
Decorations. *See* Art and sculpture; Beauty and
      beautification
Decorum in synagogue, 202
Decrees. *See* Excommunication; Judgment
Dedication. *See* Consecration
Deeds. *See* Actions; Commandments
Deer, 209
Defection. *See* Apostates and apostasy; Converts and
      conversion
Defilement. *See* Purity and impurity
Deformities, 2, 263
Degania, 294
Degel, 190. *See also* Flags and emblems
Dei'ah, 107
De Leon, Moses, 279, 338, 359, 401, 614
Deli (zodiacal sign), 613
Delight. *See* Oneg Shabbat
Deliverance. *See* Exodus (from Egypt); Redemption
Delury, George, 175
Demai (tractate), 529
Demetrius, 469
Demographics of Jewish population, 131, 271
Demons and demonology, 142–145. *See also* Magic;
      Satan; Superstition
  afikomon to ward off, 465
  angels, 26–27
  cemeteries and, 94, 234
  circles and circling as protection against, 115, 403
  Code of Jewish Law, chapters of, 172–173
  darkness and, 87
  death and, 143–145
  defined, 443
  Er, son of Judah and, 326
  evil eye, 15, 121
  four species, warding off with, 196
  funeral practices to divert, 200
  hand gestures and, 402
  invocation of God's names, 214–215
  kelippot, 290
  knives, scared by, 352
  left, represented by, 443
  Lilith, 315
  Messianic Age and, 335

  mezuzot vs., 517
  nighttime funerals and, 80
  noise and, 144, 544, 559, 576
  number three as antidote to, 369
  origin of, 143
  protection against, 23–24, 56, 115, 215, 231, 340,
        481, 490, 576, 580
  protection of newborn from, 394
  sitra achara (Angel of Death), 281
  snakes as instrument of, 537
  sneezing and, 507
  in water, 538
  weddings and, 143–144, 210–211
  wine and, 237, 464
Denial of pleasure. *See* Asceticism
Deniers of the Holocaust, 253
Denmark, 486
Denunciation of Judaism. *See* Apostates and apostasy;
      Converts and conversion, to Christianity
Deputy High Priest, 288
Deputy judge of Av Beit Din, 614
Derash, 381–382. *See also* Midrash
Derekh eretz, 145–146, 293, 350, 404, 536. *See also*
      Conduct; Kevod tzibur; Menschlichkeit; Modesty
Derishat Shalom (Kalischer), 610
Derishat Tziyon (Kalischer), 295
Dershowitz, Nachum, 435
Descent, Jewish. *See* Jewish identity and status; Law of
      Return; Matrilineal descent; Patrilineal descent
Desecration of the body, 290, 538. *See also* Nivul ha-met
Desecration of the name of God, 177, 545. *See also*
      Chillul Ha-Shem
Desecration of the Sabbath. *See* Sabbath, violation of
Desert, 96, 328, 466, 515, 562. *See also* Matzot; Sinai,
      Mount
Design. *See* Beauty and beautification
Destroying seed, 49–50, 70–72, 473
Destruction, 334, 504. *See also* Death
Destruction of the Temples. *See also* Temples
  Ark, location of following, 43
  end of prophetic era and, 316
  fast days to commemorate. *See* Asarah B'Tevet;
        Tishah B'Av
  First Temple, 456
  jubilee year and, 277
  mourning for, 125, 357–358
  Second Temple, 5, 46, 544
  Tikkun Chatzot (prayers), 551
  weddings and, 210–211, 299
  zeikher le-churban, 607–608
Detzakh, adash, b'achav, 2. *See also* Ten Plagues
Devarim (Torah portion), 477
Devash. *See* Honey
Deveikut, 146. *See also* Chasidim and chasidut; Kelippot
Devir, 254. *See also* Holy of Holies

Devorah (judge), 357, 361, 505, 577
Devotion to God. *See* Faith
Dew, 298, 522, 534
Diaspora, 114, 146–147. *See also* American Jewish life; Anti-Semitism; Exile
    chadash and yashan and, 598–599
    compared to one without a God, 12
    mezuzot and, 340
    ordination of rabbis within, 420
    Passover observance in, 387, 459
    Priestly Benediction recitation, 407, 480
    as result of sins, 456
    return from. *See* Aliyah (to Israel)
    Rosh Hashanah in, 444
    Shekhinah within, 487
    Simchat Torah and, 502
    two-day festival observance, 305, 387, 606
    yoma arichta and, 603
    Yom Ha-Atzma'ut in, 603
    yordim, 606
Dice (gambling), 202
Dietary laws. *See* Kashrut
Dignity. *See* Derekh eretz; Honor and dignity; Kevod ha-beriot; Kevod ha-met; Kevod he-chai; Kevod tzibur
Dimi ben Chama, 110–111, 192
Dimona, Israel, 183
Din. *See* Justice
Dina de-malchuta dina. *See* Law-of-the-land principle
Dining. *See* Meals
Dinosaurs. *See* Fossils
Din rodef, 443
Dipping in salt water, 464
Direction of prayer, 404, 520
Disappearance of a husband. *See* Agunot
Disbeliever. *See* Apikores; Atheism
Discarding of religious articles, 46, 81, 206, 254, 434, 509
Discharges of fluids, 473–474, 534. *See also* Semen
Disciples. *See* Students
Discipline of children, 162–163, 600
Discrimination. *See* Anti-Semitism
Disease. *See* Illness
Disfigurement. *See* Abnormalities, physical; Autopsies; Desecration of the body
Dishes, 299, 307, 342, 549
Dishonesty. *See* Chillul Ha-Shem; Lying; Stealing
Disputes. *See* Compromise; Courts, Jewish
Dissection. *See* Autopsies
Distance. *See* Eruvin
Dittographic, 508
Dividers. *See* Mechitzah
Divination. *See* Astrology
Divine Chariot of God, 278–279, 317–318

Divine energy, 281
Divine Light, 492. *See also* Shekhinah
Divine name of God, 430
Divine providence, 330
Divine retribution, 441
Divine revelation. *See* Revelation at Sinai
Divine sparks, 281, 290
Divine Understanding, 280
Divine Wisdom, 280
Divorce, 152–154
    of Falashas, 182
    Gittin (tractate) on, 531
    Karaites and, 182, 286, 287–288
    ketubbot stipulations, 292
    lack of sexual fulfillment and, 472
    marriage to Priests and, 135, 323, 405, 406–407
    Nashim (Mishnah tractates), 482
    remarriage, 323, 492
    spousal abuse and, 63
    Takanot d'Rabbenu Gershom, 178, 245–246
Doctrine. *See* Dogma and Judaism
Doctors, 117, 351, 409. *See also* Medical intervention
Documentary Theory, 557
Documents, 214, 310, 532. *See also* Get (divorce document); Ketubbot; Scribes
Dogma and Judaism, 154–156. *See also* Belief
Dogs, 145, 350, 451
Domain, 45. *See also* Eruvin; Property; Public vs. private
Dominicans, 179
Donations
    for artificial insemination, 49–50, 319–320
    monetary. *See* Charity
    of organs, 293, 607
Doorposts. *See* Mezuzot
Doors, 18
Dorff, Rabbi Elliot N., 63
Dough. *See* Bread; Challah
Doughnuts, 101
Dov Ber of Mezerich, 106
Doves, 533
Dovevot, 141
Dowries, 232, 299, 544. *See also* Handkerchief ceremony
Drawing close. *See* Keiruv
Drawings. *See* Art and sculpture
Drawn waters, 24
Dreams, 156–157
Dred Scott decision, 506
Dreidel game, 102, 202
Dress code, 107, 113, 157–158, 474
Dressing, personal, 350
Dressing of the Torah. *See* Gelilah
Dreyfus trial, 31–32, 272, 608–609
Drinking, 3, 146, 374, 417, 585, 586. *See also* Fasting and fast days; Wine
Driving on the Sabbath, 424, 451–452. *See also* Travel

Drownings, 9, 108
Druids, 113
Drums, 357
Duach, 3
Dukhening, 158, 407, 519. *See also* Priestly Benediction
Dura Europos, 48
Duran, Rabbi Simon, 16–17, 327–328
Duran, Rabbi Solomon ben Simon, 275
Dust to dust, 80, 138
Duties of the Heart (Bachya ibn Pakuda), 288
D'var Torah, 158–159. *See also* Sermons
Dybbuks, 159. *See also* Demons and demonology

E

Eagles, 317
Ears, 416, 575
Earth
    burial in, 80, 119, 138, 166, 200, 293
    Garden of Eden in, 243
    nullification of impurity and, 341
    as origin of life, 138
    in shoes of mourners, 494
Earthenware. *See* Pottery
East, 26, 404, 520
Easter, 76
Eastern Sephardim, 468
Eating, 350. *See also* Food; Meals
Ecclesiastes, Book of, 125, 227, 490
Ecclesiasticus, 34
Echad Mi Yodei'a (song), 466–467
Echad of Shema (prayer), 489. *See also* Shema (prayer);
        Unity of God
Eclipse, 53
Ecology, 160
Eden, Garden of, 22, 203. *See also* Adam (first man); Eve
        (first woman)
    earthly, 243
    fruit of, 195, 446
    man's role in, 303
    Original Sin and, 377–378, 456, 503, 590
    snakes in, 537
    vision of by Ulla Bira'a, 381
    wooden coffins, origin of, 119
Editions, Bible. *See* Masorah and Masoretic text
Education, 160–164. *See also* Beit Midrash; Schools;
        Teachers and teaching; Torah; Torah study
    age to begin, 576
    in America, 163–164
    beit sefer, 65
    cheder, 109
    family bonding and, 184
    Haskalah movement and, 236
    historical transmission of Torah, 278
    menschlichkeit, 334

obligation of, 161, 542, 588
    Passover Seder as, 227, 463–464
    Shavuot as starting point of, 484
    of trade, 161
    of women, 161–162, 163–164
Effort, 456
Efrat, Israel, 361
Eger, Rabbi Akiba, 39
Eggs (of chickens), 173, 192, 416, 455, 462, 463, 530
Eggs (Ovum). *See* Artificial insemination; Host-mothers
Egoz, 54, 446
Egypt. *See also* Exodus (from Egypt); Wilderness
    Babylonian conquest of, 180
    Cairo Genizah and, 206, 434
    circumcision practices, 116
    compassion toward, 122
    embalming, 166
    enslavement of Jewish people, 28
    idolatry and, 263
    Israel vs., 268
    Jacob's death and, 371
    Karaites and, 287
    modern peace with Israel, 269
    Moses and the burning bush, 211
    pre-Exodus celebration of Passover, 386
    references to in Aleinu (prayer), 12
    salvation from, 383
    Sinai Campaign, 267–268
    Six-Day War (1967), 92, 268–269, 273, 553–554, 584
Egyptian Hallel (psalms), 230. *See also* Hallel (prayers)
E-he-yeh Asher E-he-yeh, 212. *See also* God
Eichmann, Adolph, 92
Eidah, 343
Eidim, 586. *See also* Witnesses and testimony
Eidot Ha-Mizrach, 468
Eiduyot (tractate), 532, 587
Eighteen, significance of, 94, 104, 371
Eighteen Benedictions, 22, 73, 164–165
    Al Ha-Nisim, 12
    Ashamnu, 52
    genuflecting and bowing during, 400–401
    Kedushah (prayer), 289, 401
    morning prayers and, 480
    overview of, 404, 491, 501, 538
    of Purim, 417
    resurrection doctrine and, 436
    of Rosh Chodesh, 443
    of Sabbath Minchah services, 342–343
    standing during, 403
Eikhah, 189
Eilberg, Amy, 595
Einhorn, Rabbi David, 506
Ein Keloheinu (prayer), 3, 165
Ein Sof, 280–281, 359–360. *See also* Ten sefirot
Eirusin, 165, 322. *See also* Marriage

Eiruv. *See* Eruvin
Eisenstadt, Meir, 45
Eish, 89. *See also* Candles and candlelighting
Eitz Chayim (Vital), 280–281, 359
Eitz Ha-Cha'yim (Aaron ben Elijah), 286–287
Eivel Rabbati (tractate), 535–536, 597
Eiz azal, 57
El, 212–213. *See also* God
El (name of God), 550
Ela'i the Elder, 475
El Al (Israeli airline), 406
Elazar (Rabbi), 108, 129, 483
Elazar, son of Aaron, 290
Elazar the High Priest, 469–470
El-Buraq Wall, 585
Eldad Ha-Dani, 548
Elderly, 8, 449
Eleazar (Rabbi), 21, 36, 61, 97, 233, 326–327, 436–437
Eleazar ben Jair, 324
Eleazar ben Judah of Worms, 575
Eleazar ben Zadok, 196
Eleazar Ha-Kappar, 586
Eleazer ben Yosi, 204
Eleazer Rokeach, 575
Elections, Knesset, 299
Electric candles, 89
Electricity, 450–451
Electric menorahs, 100, 334
Eliezer (Rabbi), 55, 161–162, 385, 421, 473, 588, 600
Eliezer (servant of Abraham), 25, 578
Eliezer ben Azariah, 91
Eliezer ben Hyrcanus, 85, 91, 157
Eliezer ben Jacob, 68, 327, 401
Eliezer son of Yosei, 244
Elijah ben Solomon. *See* Vilna Gaon, the
Elijah the Prophet, 5, 165
    Ba'al, battle with, 505
    chair of, 117. *See also* Circumcision
    cup of, 462, 465–466
    as forerunner of the Messiah, 335, 466, 478, 542
    role of, 184
    teiku, 542–543
Elimelekh, 232
Eliot, George, 611
Eliphaz the Temanite, 124
Elishah ben Avuyah, 36, 161, 177, 317
Elishah ben Solomon. *See* Vilna Gaon, the
El Malei Rachamim (prayer), 165, 200, 238, 292
Eloha, 212–213. *See also* God
Elohim, 212–213. *See also* God
Elokeinu, 214
Elokim, 214
El Rachum Ve-Chanun, 122
Elul, 84, 86, 246–247, 429, 444, 496–497, 583, 598.
    See also High Holidays

Embalming, 76, 80, 165–166
Embarrassment, 88, 323, 362, 404, 514. *See also*
    Ceremony of the Removed Sandal; Kevod tzibur;
    Kindness
Emblems and flags, 190–191, 510–511
Embryos, 1–2. *See also* Artificial insemination
Emden, Rabbi Jacob, 1, 24, 40, 285, 320, 409, 433
Emergencies. *See* Pikuach nefesh
Emerson, Ralph Waldo, 608, 611
Emet. *See* Truth and truthfulness
Employment. *See* Labor (work)
Emptiness, 12
Emulation of God, 212
Emunah. *See* Faith
Emunot Ve-Dei'ot (Sa'adya Gaon), 203, 427
Enclosed mem. *See* Final letters
Encroachment. *See* Hasagat gevul
End of days. *See* Messiah and Messianic Age
Endor, witch of, 498
Enemies, 122, 288, 442, 446. *See also* Vengeance; War
Energy, divine, 281
Engagement, 299, 480–481, 487, 544, 601–602, 614.
    See also Eirusin
England. *See* Great Britain
English language. *See* Vernacular
Enjoyment. *See also* Asceticism
Enlightenment. See *Zohar, The*
Ennui, 366
Enokh, 5, 414, 458
Enough. *See* Da'yeinu (song)
Enslavement. *See* Slavery (Egyptian); Slavery (Hebrew)
Entertainment, 465. *See also* Celebrations
Entrance to homes, 410
Environmentalism, 58, 98
Ephod, 559
Ephraim (son of Joseph) , 232, 442, 567
Ephraim (tribe of) , 274, 548
Ephraim ben Isaac, 150, 157
Ephron the Hittite, 92, 93, 245
Epicurus, 33
Epikomion, 465
Epilepsy, 263
"Epistle of Holiness" (Nachmanides), 473
Epitropos, 4
Epstein, Nadine, 409
Epstein, Rabbi Yechiel Mikhael, 45, 195, 401, 402, 461
Equality, 105, 119–120, 162, 315. *See also* Bat mitzvah;
    Women
Equinox, vernal, 68
Er (son of Judah), 58, 312, 326–327
Erasure, 433, 509
Erekh a'pa'yim, 389
Erev. *See* Ma'ariv (prayers)
Erev rav, 167–169
Erev Shabbat, 451. *See also* Sabbath

Erfurt manuscript, 567
Errors in Torah scrolls, 508–509
Eruvin, 167–169, 449–450, 530
Ervah, 262
Esau, 2, 72, 297, 333, 369, 382, 511, 568
Esnoga, 468. *See also* Synagogues
Espanyol, 468–469
Esrim Ve-Arba'ah, 67
Essenes, 51, 164, 169, 395
Estates. *See* Inheritance
Esther and Book of Esther, 3, 28, 34, 87, 214, 227,
    414–417, 440, 531, 577, 578. *See also* Purim
Eternal light, 169, 231
Eternity. *See* Afterlife; Heaven
Ethics, 169–170, 531–532, 536, 607. *See also* Derekh
    eretz; Moral standards; Truth and truthfulness
Ethics of the Fathers, 22, 169, 529, 532, 535
Ethiopia, 13, 43
Etrogim, 41, 64, 182, 194–196, 516, 530. *See also* Arba
    minim
Eugenius IV, Pope, 30
Eulogies, 80, 170–172, 198, 293, 569
Euphemisms, 172–173
Euthanasia, 173–175, 340
Evaluations (tractate), 533
Eve (first woman), 92, 137, 195. *See also* Garden
        of Eden
    Adam, influence over, 240
    Cain and, 361
    figs eaten by, 446
    fruitful and multiply commandment, 397
    hair coverings as result of sin of, 487
    Lilith and, 314–315
    Original Sin and, 377–378, 456, 590
Even Ha-Ezer, 275, 307, 500. See also *Code of Jewish Law*
        (Caro)
Evening. *See* Ma'ariv (prayers); Night
Even Tekumah, 23, 511–512. *See also* Stones
Evil inclination. *See* Yeitzer ha-ra
Evil spirits (demonology). *See* Demons and demonology
Evil tongue. *See* Leshon ha-ra
Evolution, 137–138, 176. *See also* Creation
Exchange (tractate), 533
Excommunication, 30, 177–180. *See also* Apostates and
        apostasy
    of chasidim by the Vilna Gaon, 348
    Cheirem de-Rabbenu Gershom, 153, 245, 398
    intermarriage and, 264
    Keritot (tractate) on, 533
    for sexual relations with a niddah, 365
    stones upon coffins and, 512
    Yom Kippur violation and, 447, 604
Execution. *See* Capital punishment
Exhumation, 366
Exilarchs, 180–181, 599

Exile, 42, 86, 146–147, 180–181, 456, 487, 599. *See also*
        Destruction of the Temples; Diaspora
Ex nihilo. *See* Creation
Exodus (Book of). *See* Five Books of Moses
Exodus (from Egypt) , 85, 460. *See also* Five Books of
        Moses; Haggadah; Passover; Slavery (Egyptian);
        Wilderness
    Amalek and, 333, 415
    arba kosot representative of, 383, 463
    erev rav, 167–169
    Kiddush (prayer) and, 295
    matzah as commemoration of, 328
    in merit of righteous women, 162
    music in celebration of, 357
    remembrance of, 447
    Ten Commandments and, 545, 546
    Torah description of, 437
Exorcism, 159, 180. *See also* Demons and demonology
Explication de texte, 158–159
Expressions. *See* Euphemisms; Greetings and salutations
Extracanonical tractates, 534–535
Extramarital sex, 475
Eye (needle), 20
Eye, evil. *See* A'yin ha-ra
Eye-for-an-eye principle, 314, 381, 392. *See also*
        Vengeance
Eyes, 19, 238, 330, 408, 575. *See also* Marit a'yin; Sight
Eyewitnesses. *See* Witnesses and testimony
Ezekiel (prophet), 46–47, 215, 278–279, 295, 317, 435,
        503
Ezra the Scribe, 13, 34, 233, 507
    on immersion, 549
    Knesset Ha-Gedolah, 299, 300, 316, 333
    Masoretic text and, 325
    prayers of, 400
    pseudepigrapha and, 414
    public Torah reading introduced by, 561–562
    red heifer ritual enacted by, 422
    on Rosh Hashanah, 445
    Torah readings by, 370
Ezrat nashim, 181, 502, 519–520, 596. *See also*
        Mechitzah

F

Fabric, forbidden mixtures of, 35
Faces, 261, 408
Facial hair, 228, 487–488. *See also* Hair and haircutting
Fairness. *See also* Ethics; Justice
Faith. *See* Dogma and Judaism; Prayers and blessings;
        Righteousness
Faitlovitch, Jacques, 183
Falashas, 182–183, 512, 514
Fallopian tubes. *See* Artificial insemination
Fallow land. *See* Sabbatical years

Falsehood, 411, 575. *See also* Leshon ha-ra

False messiahs, 336, 413. *See also* Bar Kokhba revolt

Family and family life, 184–185. *See also* Brothers-in-law;
    Children; Fathers and fatherhood; Grandparents;
    Jewish identity and status; Mothers and
    motherhood; Parents; Tohorat ha-mishpachah

    aliyot (Torah honors) given to blood relatives, 15

    beit avot, 587

    death of. *See* Mourners and mourning

    Even Ha-Ezer, 307, 500

    forbidden marriages and, 262–263, 322–323. *See also*
        Incest; Levirate marriage practices

    shelom ba'yit, 487–488, 568–569

    surnames, 409, 518

    testimony, prohibition of by blood relatives, 15

Family Purity. *See* Niddah laws; Tohorat ha-mishpachah

Farmers and farming, 22, 84, 429, 476, 491, 570–572,
    598. *See also* Agriculture

Fasputshes, 101

Fasting and fast days, 185–189. *See also* Asceticism;
    Minor fast days; Tishah B'Av; Yom Kippur

    Asarah B'Tevet, 50–51, 185–186, 254, 318

    Chanukkah, during, 171

    communal, 186–187

    Cordovera, Moses on, 605–606

    dreams fasts, 157

    of Esther, 186, 187, 188, 415, 416. *See also* Purim

    of the Fifth Month. *See* Tishah B'Av

    of the Firstborn, 185–186, 188, 505

    of the Fourth Month. *See* Shivah Asar B'Tammuz

    of Gedaliah, 185–186, 188, 318, 575

    Karaites and, 286

    maftir of, 318

    meals before and after, 604

    of the Ninth of Av. *See* Tishah B'Av

    personal fasts, 187

    Purim Katan, 417

    as repentance, 427–428

    by Sanhedrin members, 91

    of the Seventeenth of Tammuz. *See* Shivah Asar
        B'Tammuz

    of the Seventh Month, 185–186. *See also* Yom Kippur

    sexual relations prohibited on, 474

    Shivah Asar B'Tammuz, 185–186, 189, 318, 495, 551

    of Speech, 187

    Ta'anit (tractate), 531

    ta'anit chalom, 157

    Ta'anit Ha-Dibur, 187

    of the Tenth Month. *See* Asarah B'Tevet

    Tishah B'Av, 185–186, 189

    on wedding day, 582, 601

    on yahrzeits, 597

    Yoma (tractate), 530

    Yom Kippur, 185–186, 471, 604

Fate, 7, 197, 330, 517. *See also* Judgment

Father of the Court, 65. *See also* Beit Din

Fathers According to Rabbi Nathan, The, 391

Fathers and fatherhood. *See also* Children; Family and
    family life; Parents

    AID (Artificial Insemination Donor) and, 50

    bar mitzvah blessings, 61

    circumcision by, 351, 457

    commandment to beget children, 50. *See also* Fruitful
        and multiply commandment

    education of children, responsibility of, 161, 588

    honoring. *See* Parents, honoring

    kissing, 298

    names of in Mi Shebeirakh (prayer) and, 346

    naming of newborn, 15, 361

    of newborn sons, 14

    patrilineal descent, 134

    sandek as representative of, 457

    teachers compared to, 162

Fats, 151

Fear, 161, 239. *See also* A'yin ha-ra; Demons and
    demonology

Feast of Weeks. *See* Shavuot

Feathers, 571, 580

Fedayeen incursions, 267

Federation of American Zionists, 613. *See also* Zionist
    Organization of America

Fedoras, 242

Feet, 261, 396, 401, 415–416, 575. *See also* Shoes

Feinstein, Rabbi Moshe

    on AID (Artificial Insemination Donor), 50

    on bat mitzvah celebrations, 62, 595

    on blood transfusions, 76

    contribution to Orthodox beliefs, 379

    on honoring parents, 385–386

    on ketubbot, 37

    on Kohanim as doctors, 409

    on marit a'yin, 321

    on intermarried couples, 265

    overview of, 434

    on quorums, 344

    on Sabbath laws, 451, 513–514

    on witnesses to marriages, 587

Fei/pei, 19, 368

Female homosexuality, 255, 311

Feminine attributes of God, 487

Feminists, 315, 462, 466, 481, 577, 591–592

Fences around the Torah, 306, 307, 475–476

Fennel, 23

Ferdinand, King, 468. *See also* Inquisition, Spanish

Fermentation, 329, 330, 386–388. *See also* Leavened
    foods

Fertility issues, 48–50, 70–72, 259, 319–320, 327, 473,
    518. *See also* Fruitful and multiply commandment;
    Pregnancy

Festival of first fruits, 483. *See also* Shavuot

Festival of Freedom. *See* Passover
Festival of Lights, 99. *See also* Chanukkah
Festivals. *See* Holidays
Festivals (tractate), 530
Festive meals. *See* Se'udat mitzvah
Fetuses, 1–2, 473
Fever, 370. *See also* Illness
Fez, North Africa, 430–431
Fibers. *See* Shaatnez
Fields. *See* Farmers and farming
Fier Kashas, 463–464
Fifteenth day of Av, 85–86, 569
Fifth Commandment. *See* Honoring parents
Figs, 446, 461
Final letters, 18, 19, 20, 368. *See also* Alphabet, Hebrew
Final Solution. *See* Holocaust
Final war. *See* Armageddon
Financial justice, 314
Fingernails, 237
Fingers, 18, 296, 298, 408, 464, 560, 581. *See also* Hands; Handwashing
Finials of Torah scrolls, 559, 564
Finkelstein, Louis, 126, 128
Fins, 149–150
Fire. *See also* Candles and candlelighting; Capital punishment; Cooking; *entries at* Burning
    for cooking by non-Jews, 310
    havdalah service and, 599
    impurity and, 418
    for kashering process, 388
    Sabbath, forbidden on, 384
    Sabbath, violation of, 75, 448–449, 450–451, 452
    torches, 143–144
Firstborn son
    apostates, rights of, 38
    Bekhorot (tractate) on, 533
    birthright of, 72–73, 568
    death of, 386
    fast of, 185–186, 188, 505
    named after deceased father, 312–313
    pidyon ha-ben, 135, 392–394, 407, 409
First fruits, 189–190, 233, 520, 530
First Temple. *See* Destruction of the Temples; Temples
First Zionist Congress (1897), 266–267, 272, 510–511, 609, 613
Fish, 604
    danger and, 538
    fishes and fox parable, 8
    kosher, 149–150
    Leviathan, 312
    representations of, 19
    Rosh Hashanah, eaten on, 446
    on the Sabbath, 193–194
    zodiacal sign of, 85, 613
Five, 231

Five Books of Moses, 2, 66–67, 340–341, 379, 536, 556. *See also* Torah
Flagellation, 51
Flags and emblems, 190–191, 510–511
Flames. *See* Candles and candlelighting; Torches
Flatware, kashering, 388
Fleckeles, Rabbi Eleazar, 164–165
Fleishik. *See* Meat
Flesch, Rabbi Dr., 594
Flesh, 143, 290
Flogging, 191, 475
Flood in time of Noah, 367, 505, 543
Flour, 98. *See* Grains
Flowers, 114, 120, 191–192, 296, 483, 520. *See also* Gardens
Flutes, 357
Folares, 416
Food, 192–194. *See also* Bread; Cooking; Grace After Meals; Kashrut; Meals; Wine
    abstention from, 328–329. *See also* Fasting and fast days
    blessings for, 75, 231
    in cemeteries, 93, 576
    chasidim, prepared by, 108
    derekh eretz of, 145–146
    expenses of, 158
    for guests, 513. *See also* Hospitality
    for the poor, 205
    reclining and, 460–461
    right hand used to eat, 442
    for Sabbath and holidays, 247–248, 258, 416, 445–446, 447, 448, 450, 484–485
    salt and, 455
    Sumptuary Laws and, 516–517
Forbidden foods. *See* Nonkosher food
Forbidden fruit. *See* Orlah
Forbidden mixtures of food, 61
Forbidden pleasures. *See* Asceticism
Forbidden relationships, 262–263, 531. *See also* Adultery; Incest; Levirate marriage practices
Forced conversions, 129, 430. *See also* Marranos
Ford, Henry, 31–32
Foreigners. *See* Gentiles; Immigration
Foreskin, removal of. *See* Circumcision; Orlah
Forest celebrations, 112–113
Forgiveness, 157, 456, 467, 504, 549, 550, 582, 605. *See also* Atonement; Repentance
Forli, Italy, 202
Form, 7. *See also* Anthropomorphism of God; Art and sculpture
Fornication, 474–475
Fortune. *See* Mazal
Fossano, Italy, 187
Fossils, 176
Fostat, Egypt, 206, 305
Foundation (in kabbalah), 280

Fountain, 56
Four-cornered garments. *See* Tallitot; Tzitzit
Four Questions of Passover, 463–464. *See also* Seder
Four Sons of Passover, 464
Four species, 59, 194–197, 516, 519
Fowl, 101, 149, 151, 571. *See also* Meat; Slaughtering
Fox and fishes parable, 8
Fraenkel, Aviezri, 435
Fragrance. *See* Scents
France, 31–32, 147, 267–268, 272, 595, 608–609
Frankel, Rabbi Zacharias, 126–127
Frankincense, 510
Freedom. *See also* Free will; Slavery (Egyptian); Slavery
        (Hebrew)
    abolition and, 506
    kittls symbolizing, 460
    Maimonides on, 373
    Passover as celebration of, 329
    Sabbath observance and, 448
    Yom Ha-Atzma'ut, 230, 603
Freedom, Festival of. *See* Passover
Freehof, Rabbi Solomon B., 50, 256, 434
Free-loan societies, 353
Free will, 197–198, 364, 378
Freier, Recha, 613
Freud, Sigmund, 256
Fridays, 171, 481, 583, 604. *See also* Kabbalat Shabbat;
        Sabbath
Friedlander, David, 236
Friedmann, Rabbi Solomon, 487–488
Friendship. *See* Chavrutah; Chevrah
Fringes. *See* Tallitot
Fruchter, Rabbi Alfred, 480
Fruitful and multiply commandment, 66, 70–72, 92,
        184–185, 312–313, 322, 397, 473, 575. *See also*
        Children; Pregnancy
Fruits and fruit trees. *See also* Bikkurim; Four species;
        Harvest; *specific fruits by name*; Trees
    bal tashchit and, 58
    Chamishah Asar Bi-Shevat, 98
    charoset and, 461–462
    eaten by Adam and Eve, 446
    fallen, 103
    festival of first fruits, 483. *See also* Shavuot
    health benefits of, 193
    orlah, 378
    preservation of, 160
    She-heche'yanu (blessing) for, 486
    Ukatzim (tractate) on, 534
Full Hallel (psalms), 230. *See also* Hallel (prayers)
Full Kaddish, 282–283. *See also* Kaddish (prayer)
Funerals, 145. *See also* Mourners and mourning
    common practices, 198–201, 293
    flowers at, 192
    Hazkarah (prayer), 166, 238, 468
    humility and simplicity of, 120
    preparation for, 374
    Priests, attendance by, 406
    processions, 231, 370
    Tziduk Ha-Din (prayer), 572–573
    wine as consolation, 585
Fur, 570. *See also* Hunting

G

Gabba'im, 202, 205–206, 346, 563, 564
Gabbai of Alexandria, Egypt, 68
Gabicha ben Pasisa, 436
Gabriel, 25–26, 394
Gad (tribe of), 567
Galatians, 92. *See also* New Testament
Galut. *See* Diaspora; Exile
Gamal, 17
Gamaliel (Rabbi), 36, 222, 293, 420, 536, 552
Gamaliel II (Rabbi), 164, 316, 337, 460, 536
Gamblers and gambling, 102, 202–203, 587
Gamliel (Rabbi), 164, 375, 501, 588
Gamma, 17
Gan Eden. *See* Garden of Eden
Ganganelli, Cardinal Lorenzo, 76
Ganze, 102
Gaon. *See* Geonic period
Gaon of Vilna. *See* Vilna Gaon, the
Gaon Sar Shalom, 144–145, 200
Garden of Eden, 22, 203. *See also* Adam (first man); Eve
        (first woman)
    earthly, 243
    fruit of, 195, 446
    man's role in, 303
    Original Sin and, 377–378, 456, 503, 590
    snakes in, 537
    vision of by Ulla Bira'a, 381
    wooden coffins, origin of, 119
Gardens, 381–384. *See also* Flowers; Fruits and fruit
        trees; Trees
Garlic, 193
Garments. *See* Clothing
Gartls, 107, 226, 560–561, 565
Gas chambers, 251–252. *See also* Concentration camps
Gates of Repentance, 382, 445. *See also* Atonement
Gay. *See* Homosexuality
Gaza, 267–268, 269–270. *See also* Palestine (history of)
Gebel Musa, 504
Gebruchts, 203
Gedaliah, Fast of, 185–186, 188, 318, 575
Gedi, 613
Gedilim, 41, 574. *See also* Tzitzit
Geese, 101, 571, 580
Gefilte fish, 193. *See also* Fish
Gehakte herring, 194. *See also* Fish

Gehinnom, 57, 203–204, 284–285, 381, 426. *See also*
    Afterlife
Geiger, Rabbi Abraham, 126–127, 424–425, 503
Geirei ara'yot, 129. *See also* Converts and conversion
Geirim (tractate), 536. *See also* Converts and conversion
Gelilah, 17
Gelt, 101–102
Gemachs, 206. *See also* Tzedakah
Gemara, 22–23, 204, 374–375, 526. *See also* Mishnah;
    Talmud; Torah study
Gematriah, 17–21, 204–205, 367–371. *See Hebrew*
    alphabet for numerical value of each letter
Gemilut chasadim, 104, 205–206. *See also* Charity
Gemini (zodiacal sign), 85, 369, 613
Gender of fetus, 1–2, 473
Genealogy. *See* Lineage
Geneivat da'at. *See* Deceit
Generosity, 53. *See also* Donations
Genesis. *See* Five Books of Moses
Genetics, 263, 409
Genitalia, 173, 326–327, 412. *See also* Seed
Genizah, 46, 81, 206, 254, 434, 509
Gentile court. *See* Civil law
Gentiles, 206–207, 385–386, 457, 476. *See also*
    Christians and Christianity; Non-Jews
Genuflection, 400–401, 566
Geonic period, 59, 203, 286, 428–435, 459, 501, 517,
    527, 599. *See also* Pumbedita, Babylonia; Scholars;
    Sura, Babylonia
Gerer chasidim, 107, 242
Gerizim, Mount, 457
Germans and Germany, 31, 33, 324, 424, 467, 602. *See*
    also Ashkenazim; Holocaust
Gershom ben Yehuda. *See* Rabbenu Gershom
Gershon (son of Levi), 404–405
Geshem, 55, 207, 258, 298, 502, 522. *See also* Rain
Gesher Ha-Cha'yim (Tucatzinsky), 142
Gestures, 232, 399–404, 566. *See also* Greetings and
    salutations
Get (divorce document), 9–10, 153–154, 207–208,
    245–246, 292, 323, 376, 434, 487. *See also* Divorce
Gevatter, 302
Gevurah (in kabbalah), 280
Gezeirah shavah principle, 244–245
Gezeirot of muktzah, 356, 449
Gezel. *See* Theft
Gezundheit, 507
Ghettos, 31, 208–209, 339, 424. *See also* Holocaust;
    Pogroms
Ghosts, 79, 209, 556. *See also* Demons
    and demonology
Gibeah, 255
Gibson, Mel, 33
Gideon, 214, 391
Gidin, 209, 558

Gifts, 101–102, 103, 113, 342, 396, 414. *See also*
    Charity; Minchah (prayers)
Gikatilla, Joseph, 278
Gilboa, Mount, 209
Gilgulim, 209–210. *See also* Afterlife; Ibbur;
    Reincarnation
Gilui ara'yot, 262. *See also* Incest
Gilui malkhu'yot, 335. *See also* Messiah and Messianic
    Age
Gimmel, 17, 102, 161, 367, 521
Ginsburg, Mitchell, 607
Ginzberg, Eli, 477
Ginzberg, Louis, 180, 321, 429, 598, 612
Ginzberg, Rabbi Isaac, 477
Girdles. *See* Gartls
Girls. *See also* Children; Women
    bat mitzvah, 4, 61–62
        confirmation vs., 126
        conversion of adopted children and, 134
        haftarah readings and, 15
        introduction of, 422, 594–595
        maftir given to, 15
        Masada, celebrations at, 325
        Mi Shebeirakh (prayer) for, 346
        Priestly Benediction for, 408
        Sephardic customs for, 15
        se'udat mitzvah and, 472
        She-heche'yanu (blessing) for, 486
        tallitot worn by, 525
    education of, 161–162, 163–164
    fruitful and multiply commandment, 184–185
    inheritance denied to, 587–588
    Kaddish recited by, 284
    mashlim aliyah for, 2
    naming of, 346, 361
    shalom bat ceremony, 361, 481
    of Zelophechad, 587–588
    zeved ha-bat, 362
Gittin (tractate), 506, 531
Gittit, 357
Giving of the Torah. *See* Revelation at Sinai
Glassware
    breaking of, 56, 144, 210–211, 516, 517, 582
    kashrut and, 152, 388
Glatt kosher, 211. *See also* Kashrut
Gleaning, 103
Global Jewish Database, 435
Glorification of God, 170, 508, 565. *See also* Kaddish
    (prayer); Prayers and blessings
Goats, 56–57, 613
God, 211–215. *See also* Creation; Torah
    Abraham, covenant with, 12, 266
    angels of. *See* Angels
    anger of, 343
    appearance of, 369

attaching oneself to, 146
attributes of, 27–28, 64, 280, 467, 487, 492. See also
    Ein Sof; Thirteen Attributes of Mercy
communication with man. See Dreams
compassion and mercy of, 122
defense of name of, 439–440
defined, 211–212
denial of, 34
devotion to. See Faith
Divine Understanding, 280
Divine Wisdom, 280
fear of, 8
glorification of, 47–48
gratitude to. See Thanksgiving prayers
holiness of, 43
humility of, 260
image of, 317
imitation of, 249
Job and, 458
justice of, 572–573
Kingship of, 22, 445
Land of Israel, God as instrument of return to, 13
love of, 10, 146, 575
man and, 212, 385, 422, 495
ministers of. See Angels
moral law, as source of, 33
names of, 18, 23–24, 177, 212–215, 332, 545. See
    also Berakhah Le-Vatalah; Chillul Ha-Shem;
    Kiddush Ha-Shem
nature and, 179
Oneness of, 155. See also Ein Keloheinu (prayer);
    Monotheism; Shema (prayer)
praise for. See Prayers and blessings
Presence of (Shekhinah). See Shekhinah
as Righteous Judge, 441–442
right hand of, 442
sacrifices to. See Sacrifices
sanctification of name of. See Kiddush Ha-Shem
tagin story and, 521
tests by. See Akeidah; Job
Throne of Glory, 120, 523
Torah readings and, 564
visions of, 278
Godparents. See Kvater and kvaterin; Sandek
Gods. See Idolatry and idol worshippers
"God's Acre", 93
Go'el ha-dam, 119
Gog and Magog, 46–47, 215. See also Armageddon
"Going Up". See Aliyah (to Israel); Aliyah (Torah honor)
Goitein, S. D., 206
Golah. See Diaspora
Golan Heights, 268
Gold, Ze'ev (Wolf), 610
Golden Calf, 43, 265, 544–545. See also Ten
    Commandments, breaking of the tablets

building of the Tabernacle and, 557
ink for Torah scrolls and, 558
Levites abstention from building, 42
Moses and, 503
reading of portion about, 554
sadness represented by, 471
Shofrot and, 496
Thirteen Attributes of Mercy and, 549
women and, 444
Golden Rule, 215–216, 439
Goldmann, Nahum, 610
Goldstein, Israel, 610
Golel, 216, 226–227. See also Hagbahah and gelilah
Golem, 216–217, 360
Goliath, 396
Gombiner, Abraham, 591
Gomer, 467
Gomorrah, 401
Good and goodness. See also Righteousness
    goodwill principle, 217–218, 293–294, 345, 563, 593
    inclination toward, 378, 599
    luck, 85. See also Amulets; Segulot
    nuts, symbolized by, 54
    olam she-kulo tov, 5
Good deeds, 349. See also Commandments
Goodwill principle, 217–218, 293–294, 345, 563, 593
Gordon, Aharon David, 294, 295, 610
Goren, Rabbi Shlomo, 49, 89, 183
Gospels. See New Testament
Gossip, 341, 575. See also Leshon ha-ra
Government, 309, 356, 599
Goyim, 218, 528. See also Non-Jews
Grace After Meals, 12, 75, 79, 97, 218–219, 407, 417,
    492
Gracia Nasi, 500
Grade, Chaim, 600
Graham, Billy, 253
Grains, 98, 328, 373, 386, 453, 586, 598–599. See also
    Bread; Drinking; Sacrifices
Grandparents, 13, 251, 362
Grapes, 189. See also Seven species of Israel; Wine
Grass-tossing, 81, 219–220. See also Burial
Gratitude. See Sacrifices; Thanksgiving prayers
Gratz, Rebecca, 163
Graven images, 47–48
Gravesites, 86, 115, 220, 373, 406, 512, 555. See also
    Cemeteries
Great Assembly, 160, 164, 227, 299
Great Britain, 32, 65, 147, 267–268, 351, 486
Great Doxology, 281–282. See also Kaddish (prayer)
Great Hallel (psalms), 230. See also Hallel (prayers)
Great Sabbath, 477
Great Sanhedrin, 64–65, 457–458. See also Sanhedrin
Greeks
    eating while reclining, 460

epikomion, 465
homosexuality and, 255
language, 399
philosophy of, 431–432, 435–436
Septuagint translation of the Bible, 371, 469–471
Greenberg, Blu, 595–596
Greenery, 483, 520. *See also* Flowers; Trees
Green peas, 389
Greenwald, Rabbi Yekutiel, 80, 291, 409
Greetings and salutations, 220–224, 293
gezundheit, 507
in a house of mourning, 124–125
le-cha'yim, 576
of Rosh Hashanah, 445
"shalom", 390
of Yom Kippur, 445, 547–548
Gregorian calendar, 83–84, 87
Gregory VII, Pope, 29–30
Gregory X, Pope, 76
Gribenes, 101
Grief. *See* Mourners and mourning
Grivn, 101
Groggers, 333
Grooming. *See* Bathing; Shaving
Grooms. *See* Bridegrooms
Grudges, 439–441. *See also* Vengeance
Grynszpan, Herschel, 251
Guarded matzah, 329. *See also* Matzot
Guardian angels, 335. *See also* Angels
Guardians of the City, 365
Guarding, 497
Guests, 15, 576–577. *See also* Hospitality
Guide for the Perplexed of the Time (Krochmal), 236
Guide of the Perplexed (Maimonides), 27, 109, 454. *See also* Maimonides, Rabbi Moses
Guilt, 318. *See also* Atonement; Confession of Sins; Kapparot; Original Sin; Sins and sinners; Tokheichah
Gush Emunim, 268
Guttman Institute for Applied Social Research, 148, 557–558
Gypsies, 252

H

Ha-Agudah L'Yotze'im Le-She'eilah, 380
Ha-Am, Ahad, 77, 608
Habakkuk, 182
Hadasim. *See* Myrtle
Hadassah College of Technology, 101
Hadassah Hospital, Jerusalem, 406, 613
Hadassah Magazine, 409
Hadassah organization, 376, 595, 612–613
Hadrian, Emperor of Rome, 36, 86, 208, 447
Hafsakah, 75

Haftarah readings, 225–226
bar mitzvah readings, 59–60
bat mitzvah readings, 62
children, given to, 17
of consolation, 496
maftir given to, 14, 318
of Shabbat Chazon, 477
Three Haftarot of Rebuke, 477, 488
of Yom Kippur, 605
Haganah, 238
Hagar, 25
Hagbahah and gelilah, 17, 226–227
Haggadah, 2, 180, 227, 341, 460, 468, 599. *See also* Passover
Hagiographa, 227, 536. *See also* Holy Writings (Ketuvim)
Hagiz, Rabbi Jacob, 410
Haifa, Israel, 271
Hai Gaon, 203, 234, 398, 429–430, 527, 559, 600, 602
Hair and haircutting
beards, 107, 112, 238, 487–488, 548
covering of, 40, 158, 298, 300, 320, 350–351, 474, 486–487, 592. *See also* Headcoverings
cutting, prohibitions of, 27, 51, 113, 494. *See also* Nazirites
overview of, 227–229
pei'ot, 58, 107, 228, 229, 576
removal of, 158
upsherenish, 229, 576
Hakafot, 115, 229, 502, 516
Ha-Kalir, Eleazar, 207
Hakamah, 226–227
Haketia, 468
Hakhnasat orchim. *See* Hospitality
Ha-Kohen, Rabbi Israel ben Meir, 195, 311
Ha-Kohen, Rabbi Meir, 78
Ha-Kohen ha-mashu'ach, 405. *See also* High Priest
Halakhah, 7–8, 229–230. *See also* Customs and law; Jewish law
Halakhah: Its Sources and Development (Urbach), 288
Halakhot Gedolot (Kayyara), 537
Halb, 102
Halevi, Rabbi David, 76
Halevi, Rabbi Shlomo, 3. *See also* Lekhah Dodi (prayer)
Halevi, Rabbi Yehuda, 197, 401–402, 479, 487
Half Hallel (psalms), 230. *See also* Hallel (prayers)
Half Kaddish, 283
Half-shekel contribution to Temple, 479, 549
Half-siblings. *See* Incest
Hallel (prayers), 95, 108, 196, 230, 443, 516, 539
Halloween, 113
Halva'yat ha-met, 199, 230–231. *See also* Funerals
Haman, 3, 97, 188, 332–333, 414–417, 578. *See also* Amalek and Amalekites; Purim
Hamantaschen, 416
Ha-Me'agel, Choni, 115

Ha-mitzri, Solomon, 31
Hammer, 318
Hammer, Michael, 409
Hamnuna (Rabbi), 239, 306, 537
Hamotzi (blessing), 66, 74, 78, 97, 231, 296, 455
Hamsa, 231
Ha-Nappach, 23
Ha-Nasi, Yehuda. *See* Judah the Prince
Hancock, Graham, 43
Handkerchief ceremony, 232–233, 281, 544. *See also*
    Kinyan sudar; Knas mahl
Hand matzot, 492. *See also* Matzot
Hands
    challot in shape of, 97, 258–259
    clapping on Shabbos, 450
    gestures, 232, 402–403
    hand gestures, 90, 232, 564
    handshaking, 298
    khaf/kaf, represented by, 18
    Kiddush and, 296
    kissing, 298
    of Kohanim, 215
    nesi'at kapa'yim, 407–408
    during prayer services, 401
    of Priests, 402, 408
    right hand favored, 233–234
    ritual washing of. *See* Handwashing
    semikhah and, 375, 420
    Shema (prayer) and, 489
    tzitzit as representative of, 575
    yad (Torah pointer), 560
Handwashing
    cemeteries and, 56, 94, 145, 201, 234–235, 261, 418
    cleanliness and, 261
    ma'yim achronim, 234, 330
    before meals, 78, 233–235, 418, 534
    of Priests, 405
    right before left, 442
    at the Seder, 463
Hanging of Haman, 414, 416
Hannah (mother of Samuel), 404, 577
Hannah, sons of, 324
Haplographic, 508
Happiness, 414–417. *See also* Joy
Haran, 25, 511
Harlem, New York, 183
Harlotry, 323, 406
Harm. *See* Danger; Demons and demonology; Vengeance
Har Megiddo, 46–47
Harmony. *See* Peace
Har Sinai Congregation, Baltimore, 425
Harvest. *See also* Farmers and farming; Fruits and fruit
    trees; Sacrifices
    chadash and yashan, 598
    first fruits, 189

    season of, 84
    Shavuot and, 482
    Sukkot and, 515
    terumah, 549
Hasagat gevul, 235
Hashchatat zera, 49–50, 235, 373, 473. *See also* Bal
    tashchit; Birth control
Ha-Shem, 213, 214, 235. *See also* God
Hashkabah (prayer), 166, 468. *See also* Hazkarah
    (prayer); Yizkor services
Hashkem, 524
Hasidism. *See* Chasidim and chasidut
Haskalah movement, 235–237
Hasmoneans, 99, 415. *See also* Maccabees
Hatafat dam brit, 117, 132
Hatarat nedarim, 411
Hatch, Orrin, 511
Hatred. *See* Anti-Semitism; Vengeance
Hats, 40, 107, 241, 297
Havdalah service, 89, 237–238, 333, 448, 510, 519, 599
Haven. *See* City of refuge
Havlagah, 238
Hazkarah (prayer), 166, 238, 468. *See also* Yizkor
    services
Hazkarat Neshamot, 602. *See also* Yizkor services
Hazlitt, William, 156
Hazzan. *See* Chazzan
Head, 20, 400–401, 541. *See also* Hair and haircutting;
    Hair, covering of; Tefillin
Headcoverings, 40, 53, 93, 107, 112, 238–243, 297,
    405, 499, 524. *See also* Hair, covering of
Head of the Exiles. *See* Exilarchs
Heads (of words). *See* Roshei teivot
Heads (of fish), 446
Health, 149, 234, 330, 393. *See also* Illness; Medical
    intervention
Hearing, 399. *See also* Shema (prayer)
Hearses, 199. *See also* Funerals
Heart (human), 142, 377. *See also* Breastbeating;
    Kavanah
Heart (of palm trees), 196. *See also* Lulav
Heat, 388, 450–451. *See also* Fire
Heathens. *See also* Chukat ha-goy; Idolatry and idol
    worshippers
    akum, description, 11
    Chanukkah and, 99
    deference to old, 8
    Gentiles, referred to as, 206–207
    Halloween, 113
    homosexuality and, 255
    mixed breeds practice, 349
    pederasty of, 129
    pork and, 148
    Romans, 112–113
    shaatnez worn by, 476

Sinai, Mount and, 504
Sylvester new year celebrations, 112–113
Heaven, 243–244. *See also* Afterlife; Zodiac
  ascent to, 87, 182
  Azazel, 57
  blue representing, 523
  color of, 575
  Divine Throne, 278
  Heavenly Court. *See* Angels
  Heavenly voice, 244
  ladder of Jacob and, 25
  manna from, 96
  min ha-shama'yim, 438
  Pittsburgh Platform on, 426
  reward for one who does not practice astrology, 52–53
  Torah min ha-shama'yim, 558. *See also* Revelation at
    Sinai
  tzimtzum concept and, 573
  Yizkor services and, 602–603
Heave Offerings (tractate), 529, 553
Hebrah chased va-emet, 81
Hebrew, as name of Jews, 273. *See also* Jewish identity
    and status
Hebrew Bible. *See* Tanakh
Hebrew calendar, 83–87, 305, 362, 531, 606. *See also*
    specific days by name
Hebrew language
  alphabet, 161, 367–368, 369, 521–522. *See also*
    Scribes
  chug ivri, 112
  leshon ha-kodesh, 311
  prayers in, 398–399, 538
  Sephardic pronounciation of, 468
  Yiddish vs., 235–236
Hebrew Language Academy, 420
Hebrew Loan Societies, 206. *See also* Charity
Hebrew names, 15, 117, 361–362
Hebrew-Phoenician Torah Script, 21
Hebrew schools, 163–164. *See also* Education
Hebrew slaves, 536
Hebrew Theological College of Chicago, 380
Hebrew Union College (HUC), 126, 127, 376, 421, 425,
    426–427, 595, 613
Hebron, 80, 92, 93, 270
He-chasid, Rabbi Yehuda, 27, 323, 361–362
Hedge of Roses, A (Lamm), 366
Hedonism, 33
Hedyotim, 458
Hei, 18, 23, 102, 367, 521
Height of man, 412–413
Heikhal, 42, 468. *See also* Ark of the Covenant
Heine, Heinrich, 260, 461
Heirs. *See* Inheritance
Hekdeish, 244. *See also* Aging
Hell, 57, 203–204, 284–285, 381, 426. *See also* Afterlife

Hellenism, 99. *See also* Chanukkah
Hemophilia, 118
Hemorrhoids, 173
Hens, 285, 369, 504. *See also* Chickens
Herbs, 23. *See also* Maror
Hereditary characteristics, 263
Heresy, 20–21, 178–180. *See also* Boethusians; Darwinian
    theory; Essenes; Excommunication; Sadducees
Hermeneutics, 244–245, 279
Hermon, Mount, 505
Herod, King, 324–325, 584, 585, 614
Heroes, 363
Herring, 194. *See also* Fish
Hertz, Rabbi Joseph H., 137, 176, 213
Herzl, Theodor, 32, 104–105, 190–191, 266–267, 272,
    363, 608–609, 613
Herzog, Rabbi Yitzchak Halevi, 154, 183, 275
Heschel, Abraham Joshua, 8–9, 277, 384
Heschel, Susannah, 462
Hesder yeshivot, 601
Hespeid, 245. *See also* Eulogies
Heter iska, 352. *See also* Interest payments
Heter mei'ah rabbanim, 153, 245–246. *See also* Divorce
Hevel, 62, 145, 199–200
Hevel va-rik, 11–12
Hezekiah, King of Judah, 77
Hidden. *See* Apocrypha; Kabbalah and kabbalists; Lamed
    vovniks
Hiddur mitzvah, 47–48, 64, 158, 246. *See also* Beauty
    and beautification
Higher Criticism, School of, 557
High Holidays, 246. *See also* Elul; Rosh Hashanah;
    Sukkot; Yom Kippur
  ark coverings for, 46
  cantillations of, 90
  kittls, 121, 207, 298, 445
  overview, 247–248
  season of, 84
  Shofrot and, 497
  Ten Days of Repentance, 51, 109, 371, 444–445,
    496–497, 547–548, 583, 597–598
  Tishrei and, 69
High Priest, 246–247. *See also* Aaron the High Priest;
    Priests (Kohanim)
  cities of refuge and, 119, 532
  defined, 246
  Deputy High Priest, 288
  education of, 160
  garments of, 405, 558–559
  Great Sanhedrin and, 457–458
  hair of, 227–228
  Holy of Holies and, 43
  Kimchit, sons of, 487
  lineage of, 405
  marriage of, 50, 311, 405

met mitzvah and, 337
overview of, 405
parents of, 405
Torah reading by, 294
Yom Kippur services of, 56, 246–247, 255, 400, 405, 445, 488–489
Hillel
on agunot, 9
on Chanukkah, 100
on fruitful and multiply commandment, 184–185
on Golden Rule, 439
nesi'im as descendants of, 364
on New Year for Trees, 98
on piety, 395
on praising a bride, 258
prosbul of, 413–414, 491
titles of, 536
Hillel (for yotze'im), 380
Hillel, School of
on divorce, 153
on obligation to have children, 71
on praising a bride, 569
on sexual relations, 472
Hillel II, 83, 444
Hillel the Elder, 614
on education, importance of, 160
patience of, 389
prosbul, 310
on tikkun olam, 552
Hillel the First, 464–465
Hillel the Great
exegetical interpretations of, 244
on peace, 391
on piety, 437
Hindenburg, Paul von, 251
Hindquarters, 151, 209
Hinduism, 427, 511
Hineni mukhan u'mezuman (prayer), 359
Hiring, 532. See also Work
Hirsch, Rabbi Moshe, 365
Hirsch, Rabbi Samson Raphael, 83, 247, 379, 438
History of Judaism (Geiger), 503. See also Geiger, Rabbi Abraham
Histadrut, 301, 611
Hitler, Adolf, 32, 187, 251–252. See also Holocaust; Nazis
Hittites, 92, 93
Hod (in kabbalah), 280
Hoffman, Rabbi David, 24
Hofjuden, 135, 353
Holidays, 247–249. See specific holidays by name
Beitzah (tractate) on, 530
burial before, 171
candles and candlelighting, 87–89
clothing for, 158, 297

conclusion of. See Havdalah service
in the Diaspora, 444
eruv tavshilin, 168
Falasha observance of, 182
family bonding and, 184
as family celebration, 184
fixed dates of, 83, 444
knives and, 308
Moed (tractate) on, 347, 482
mourning prohibited on, 495
naming and, 362
second day of, 177, 424, 444
She-heche'yanu (blessing) for, 486
shivah and, 493
space travel and, 89
tallitot worn on, 523
tefillin and, 539
Torah readings on, 562
wine for, 586. See also Kiddush (prayer)
yoma arichta and, 603
Holiness. See Holy and holiness
Holiness Code, the, 8, 250
Hollekreisch, 250
Holocaust, 251–254, 609
concentration camps, 27, 32, 251–253, 441
denial of, 253
Diaspora following, 147
Hitler, Adolf, 32, 187, 251–252
Holocaust Remembrance Day. See Yom Ha-Sho'ah
Kaddish for victims of, 51, 254
Karaites and, 287
Nazis, 32, 92, 187, 208–209, 251–252, 324
patrilineal descent as result of, 389
reincarnation of sinners and, 427
remembrance of, 254, 511
White Paper and, 267
Yad Vashem, 105, 208–209, 252, 254
Yom Ha-Sho'ah, 248, 252, 254, 603
Youth Aliya movement during, 613
Holocaust Memorial Museum, Washington, D.C., 252
Holofernes, 101
Holy and holiness, 249–250. See also Piety; Purity and impurity; Temples
hierarchy of sanctity, 249–250
Holiness Code, the, 250
Kedushah (prayer), 289
kedushah, defined, 249
Kodoshim (Mishnah tractates), 347
marriage and, 322
name of Mt. Sinai and, 504
objects of, 254, 411–412. See also Genizah
shoes, removal of, 407
tzitzit as reminder of, 574
war vs. unholy, 281
Holy Box. See Aron Ha-Kodesh

Holy Land. *See* Land of Israel
Holy of Holies, 43, 46, 247, 254–255, 543, 545. *See also*
    Temples
Holy Sepulchre, 30, 430. *See also* Crusades, the
Holy Writings (Ketuvim), 14, 255, 536. *See also* Tanakh
Homeland, Jewish. *See* Israel (biblical); Israel (modern
    state); Zionists and Zionism
Homer, 455
Homes. *See* Houses
Homicide. *See* Murder and murderers
Homoioteleutonic, 508
Homosexuality, 91, 255–257, 432, 462, 475
    lesbianism, 255, 257, 311, 462, 475
Honesty, 257–258, 395. *See also* Ethics
Honey, 205, 445–446, 484, 534
Honeymoons, 492
Honor and dignity. *See also* Aliyah (Torah honor)
    labor and, 303
    of the living, 82
    mipnei kevod tzibur, 293–294, 345, 563, 593
    white lies and, 257–258
Honoring parents, 323, 385–386, 513
    apostates and, 39
    Dama ben Netina, 422
    non-Jewish, 134–135
    Ten Commandments and, 546
Honoring the dead, 54, 79, 82, 93, 198, 293, 366, 377,
    419
    eulogies, 171
    Rashi on, 112, 120, 192
Honors of the Torah. *See* Aliyah (Torah honor); Gelilah;
    Hagbahah and gelilah
Hoods, 499
Hoover, J. Edgar, 253
Hooves, 149
Hope. *See* Ani ma'amin; Faith; Prayers and blessings
Ho'rayot (tractate), 532
Horeb, 504
Horns. *See* Shofar
Horoscopes, 52. *See also* Astrology
Horowitz, Isaiah, 200, 606
Horseradish, 461
Hosafot, 14, 258
Hosea (prophet), 152, 182, 540, 581
Hoshanah Rabbah, 44, 97, 191, 197, 229, 258–259, 604
Hospice care. *See* Hekdeish; Illness
Hospitality, 259, 295–296, 513
Host-mothers, 259, 518. *See also* Artificial Insemination
Hotels, 113
House Assigned for the Living, 93. *See also* Cemeteries
House of Israel. *See* Falashas
House of prayer, 519. *See also* Synagogues
Houses
    bet, represented by, 17
    building of, 40, 320–321

    dedication of, 102
    of mourning. *See* Shivah
    non-Jewish customs of, 112
    Passover preparations, 64
    privacy of, 410
    Temple represented by, 95–96
    zeikher le-churban and, 607–608
How to Run a Traditional Jewish Household (Greenberg),
    596
HUC (Hebrew Union College), 126, 127, 376, 421, 425,
    426–427, 595, 613
Hugh of Lincoln, 76
Hulda, 577
Humans. *See* Man (humans)
    form of. *See* Anthropomorphism of God; Golem;
        Graven images
Humiliation. *See* Embarrassment
Humility, 260, 350, 401, 445, 505. *See also* Modesty;
    Purity and impurity
Huna, (Rav), 45–46, 157, 181, 239, 311, 344, 404
Huna bar Nathan, 181
Huna ben Chiya, 559
Huna ben Joshua, 241
Hunting, 19, 260, 571–572, 599
Hurwitz, Rabbi Isaiah, 538
Husbands. *See also* Marriage
    abuse of wives, 62–63
    AIH (Artificial Insemination Husband), 49–50
    get (divorce document), refusal to give, 9–10
    multiple wives of. *See* Polygamy
    obligations of, 292
Husks (kelippot), 359
Huts. *See* Sukkot
Hydroponics, 491
Hygiene, 260–261. *See also* Cleanliness; Ritual
    cleanliness
Hymie, 274
Hymns. *See* Prayers and blessings; Songs and singing
Hyrcanus, John, 457, 614
Hyrcanus II, 614

I

Ibbur, 262
"Ibn" as family name, 362
Ibn Ezra, Abraham, 24, 53, 136, 143, 384, 568
Ibn Gabirol, Solomon, 4
Ibn Plat, Joseph, 74
Identity, Jewish. *See* Jewish identity and status
IDF (Israel Defense Forces), 3, 295, 325, 601, 609
Idleness, 303
Idolatry and idol worshippers, 262, 290, 382, 538. *See
    also* Chukat ha-goy; Heathens
    akum, description, 528
    apostates and, 35–39

Avodah Zarah (tractate), 532
Ba'al Pe'or, 440
Bel and the Dragon, 34
of brazen serpents, 77
as cardinal sin, 262
circumcision by, 351
Diaspora compared to, 12
Elijah the Prophet vs., 466
eradication of, 11
facial hair and, 228
flowers and, 191–192
forgiveness for, 447
geirei ara'yot and, 129
graven images and, 47–48
incest and, 263, 323
intermarriage and, 263–264
masturbation compared to, 327
mitzvot made into, 349
mountains used for, 505
Noahide Laws and, 367
pikuach nefesh and, 395
repentance from, 427
Sabbath violation and, 410, 452
Samaritans and, 457
spitting as condemnation of, 510
sun-worshipping, 68
Ten Commandments and, 545
tzitzit as reminder against, 575
wine libations and, 476, 586
yeihareig ve-al ya'avor, 309
Iggeret Ha-Kodesh (Nachmanides), 473, 474
Iggud Ha-Rabbanim, 380
Ignorance, 16, 22, 395, 399, 437, 513
Igrot Moshe (Feinstein), 434. See also Feinstein, Rabbi
Moshe
Ikutz, 195. See also Citron
Illegitimacy. See Mamzeirim
Illiteracy, 16. See also Ignorance
Illness. See also Birkat Ha-Gomel (prayer); Euthanasia;
Health; Medical intervention; Pikuach nefesh
Angel of Death and, 24
bikur cholim, 67, 122, 383, 406
blessings over recovery from, 69
deathbed atonement, 125–126
demons, protection from, 143
Jacob (Patriarch) and, 507
Mi Shebeirakh (prayer) and, 346
names, changing of, 143, 363–364
prayers and blessings for, 174–175
protection from evil, 517
sneezing and, 507
standing before the Torah, 45
truth withheld from patients, 569
Viddui (prayers) and, 579
Illuminated documents. See Beauty and beautification

Illustrious one. See Geonic period
Images on tombstones, 555
Imaginary guests. See Ushpizin
Imitation of God, 170, 249. See also Holy and holiness
Im kol ha-ne'arim (aliyah), 503
Imma'hot. See Arba imma'hot
Imma Shalom, 588
Immersion. See also Purity and impurity
apostates, immersion of, 38
converts, immersion by, 131–132, 275, 322, 341
for kashering process, 387–388
Mikva'ot (tractate), 341–342, 534
preceding Revelation, 132, 342, 369
scribes and, 508
tevilah, defined, 549
virgin impregnated within, 50
of women, 341–342, 366, 418, 554. See also Tohorat
ha-mishpachah
Immigration. See Aliyah (to Israel)
Immorality. See Idolatry and idol worshippers
Immortality. See Afterlife; Resurrection
Impatience. See Patience
Implantation. See Artificial insemination
Impoverished. See Poor and poverty
Impregnation. See Ibbur; Pregnancy
Impulses. See Yeitzer ha-ra; Yeitzer ha-tov
Impurity. See Purity and impurity
Inanimate objects. See Anthropomorphism of God
Incense, 510
Incest, 50, 91, 262–263, 309, 312, 313, 323, 367, 475.
See also Mamzeirim
Inclinations
evil, 97–98, 378, 458, 599. See also Satan
free will and, 197
good, 378, 599
Income, 153, 235, 257, 553, 571. See also Labor (work);
Sales and selling
Inconvenience. See Tircha de-tzibura
Independence. See Freedom
Independence Day. See Yom Ha-Atzma'ut
Individuals, rights of. See Hasagat gevul
Inebriation. See Wine, excessive
Infants. See Babies
Infertility, 473. See also Fertility issues
Infidelity. See Adultery; Sotah
"Infidels". See Crusades, the
Infinite Being. See Ein Sof
Influence, Divine. See Shekhinah
Ingathering of exiles. See Aliyah (to Israel)
Inheritance, 2, 4, 38, 72–73, 134, 313, 390, 532, 533,
587–588. See also Birthright
Injury. See Damages; Illness
Ink for Torah scrolls, 558
Innkeepers, 576–577
Innocence. See Purity and impurity

Innocent III, Pope, 30
"In Our Time" papal document, 32
Inquisition, Spanish, 30–31, 147, 468. *See also* Spain
Insanity, 153
Insignias. *See* Flags and emblems
Instruction. *See* Education; Torah
Instruments, musical, 357–358
Insults, 177
Insurance, medical, 301
Intelligence, 6–7, 53, 510, 588
Intentions. *See* Kavanah
Intercalating, 83–84. *See also* Hebrew calendar
Intercourse. *See* Sexual relations
Interest on loans, 30, 309–310. *See also* Loans
Interest payments, 352–353
Interfaith cooperation, 199. *See also* Non-Jews
Interim period following death, 7
Intermarriage, 262, 263–265
    children of, 134
    Conservative Judaism policy on, 128
    conversion and, 129, 264
    dietary laws as means of prevention, 148
    patrilineal descent and, 390
    pidyon ha-ben and, 393
    precautions against, 476, 586
    shaygetz and shiksa terms for, 485
    shivah, 495
Intermediaries, 265–266, 503–504, 572
Intermediate Days. *See* Chol Ha-Moed
International School for Holocaust Studies, 208–209
Interpretation of Jewish law, 306–308, 340–341. *See also*
        Jewish law
Interpretation of Scripture, 22, 244–245, 279, 381–384,
        438–439, 459, 526. *See also* Babylonia, academies
        of learning; Translations of the Hebrew Bible
Interpreters, 337–338. *See also* Translations of the Bible
Interpreters Bible, The, 546
Interruption, 75
Intifada, 269–270
Intimacy. *See* Sexual relations
Intoxication. *See* Wine, excessive
Introduction, 10
Introspection, 247. *See also* Repentance
Investments, 309–310
Invisibility, 430
In vitro fertilization, 49–50, 518
Iraq War (1990–1991), 396
Iron implements, 580
Irrationality. *See* Chok (chukim)
Irving, David, 253
Irving, Deborah, 253
Isaac (Patriarch), 86. *See also* Patriarchs
    Abraham's death and, 123
    Akeidah, the, 10–11, 85, 457, 458, 496
    angels and, 25

burial of, 92
deception of by Jacob, 568
marriage of, 184, 578
name of, 361
Rebecca and, 41
as slaveholder, 506
ushpizin and, 577
Isaac, Rabbi of Vienna, 38, 92, 240
Isaac, Rabbi Shlomo. *See* Rashi
Isaac ben Jacob, Rabbi. *See* Alfasi of Fez
Isaac ben Moses, Rabbi, 284
Isaac ben Samuel Ha-Zakein, 566
Isaac the Blind, 262
Isabella, Queen, 468. *See also* Inquisition, Spanish
Isaiah (prophet), 11–12
    on color white, 46
    on Creation, 92
    on fruitful and multiply commandment, 472
    mission of. *See* Kabbalah and kabbalists
    on peace, 391
    pseudepigrapha and, 414
    on purity, 498
    on resurrection of the dead, 435
    Shabbat Chazon and, 477
    Shivah D'Nechemta, 496
    on sins, 121
Ishah. *See* Women
Ishmael ben Elishah, 116, 172, 244, 279, 379, 568–569
Ishmael, High Priest, 324
Ishmael (Rabbi), 54
Ishmael (son of Abraham), 118, 363
Isi'im. *See* Essenes
Islam, 130, 585
Israel (biblical), 12, 184, 266, 274, 548, 567, 587–588.
        See also Wilderness
Israel (modern state), 266–271. *See also* Jewish people;
        Palestine (history of); Zionists and Zionism
    aliyah to, 12–13
    Arab claims to, 267–270
    Birkat Kohanim in, 407
    black Jews community, 183. *See also* Falashas
    British Mandate period, 468
    chalitzah enforced by courts, 313
    chareidi population of, 380
    Chief Rabbis, 468
    commandments to live in, 295
    death penalty and, 91–92
    dreidels of, 102
    earth used for burial, 82
    entrance visas to, 308
    establishment of, 12–13, 266–267, 608–609, 611
    Euthanasia Law, The, 175
    flag of, 190–191, 511
    Hebrew language of, 468
    holiday observance of, 128, 387

Jewish connectedness to, 277
Jewish population, 271
Karaites and, 287–288
kashrut observance, 148
Ladino population, 469
mayor of Jerusalem, 455
mezuzot and, 340
Middle East peace efforts, 269–270
military of. *See* IDF (Israel Defense Forces)
name appropriated, 274
Neturei Karta vs., 365
peace with Palestinians, 585
president, 364
Priestly Benediction recited in, 480
reforestation of, 105
requirement to live on the land, 12–13
Rishon Le-Tziyon, 443
Samaritan population, 457
shemittah observance in, 310, 491
Sinai Campaign, 267–268
Six-Day War (1967), 92, 268–269, 273, 553–554,
    584
status of Jews and, 275–276
Supreme Court, 65, 308
UN General Assembly resolution to establish, 267–
    268, 272–273
War of 1973, 268–269
Yad Vashem, 105, 208–209, 252, 254
Yom Ha-Atzma'ut, 230, 603
Yom Ha-Sho'ah, 248, 252, 254, 603
Yom Yerushala'yim, 273
yordim of, 606
Israel ben Eliezer. *See* Ba'al Shem Tov, the
Israel Defense Forces, 3, 295, 325, 601, 609
Israel Independence Day, 230, 603
"Israelite Apostate", 35. *See also* Apostates and apostasy
Israelites, as name of Jews, 13, 160, 273–274, 329, 369,
    390, 461. *See also* Jewish identity and status
Isru Chag, 271
Isserlein, Rabbi Israel, 154, 240
Isserles, Rabbi Moses, 14, 45, 145
    on apostates and apostasy, 39
    on burials, 80
    on *Code of Jewish Law*, 307, 500
    on customs and law, 606
    on funeral practices, 200
    on gifts to non-Jews, 113
    on glassbreaking at weddings, 211
    on Jewish identity, 38
    on Kaddish (prayer), 285, 573
    on kapparot, 286, 306
    on Karaites, 288
    on Kiddush (prayer), 403
    Mappah, 433
    on marriage, 473

on muktzah, 356, 449
on names of God, 214
on non-Jewish customs, 112
overview of, 379
on Passover observance, 389, 461
on physical abuse of women, 63
on quorums, 344
on shaving the face, 228
swaying during prayer, 402
on Torah readings, 563
on treatment of animals, 571
Italy, 464
Ittamar, son of Aaron, 290
Iyyar, 84, 85

J

J'Accuse (Zola), 609
Jacob (Patriarch). *See also* Patriarchs; Tribes of Jacob
    angels and, 25, 273–274
    birthright of, 72
    blessings of, 181, 232, 442
    burial of, 92, 119
    death of, 166, 371, 470, 493
    deception of Isaac by, 568
    dreams of, 156
    Egypt, travel to, 86, 470
    Esau and, 2, 297, 333, 511
    heritage of, 289
    Israel, known as, 273–274
    Joseph and, 290
    Laban and, 383–384
    ladder of, 25
    Ma'ariv (prayers) introduced by, 316
    marriage of, 184, 578
    peace pact with Laban, 511–512
    Revelation of the Torah and, 369
    as slaveholder, 506
    sons, blessing of, 190
    superiority over Esau, 382
    ushpizin and, 577
    weddings of, 492, 580
    wives of, 41, 297, 397, 587
Jacob (Rabbi), 6, 37, 410, 441
Jacob ben Asher, 307, 402, 474–475, 500
Jacob ben Chayim, 326
Jacob ben Meir, 540. *See also* Rabbenu Tam
Jacob ben Moses Ha-Levi Möllin. *See* Maharil, the
Jacob Joseph of Polonnoye, 106
Jacobs, Rabbi Louis, 439, 440
Jacobsen, Israel, 358, 424
Jahrzeit, 597
Jail, 94. *See also* Prisoners
Jakobovits, Rabbi Immanuel, 54, 71, 142, 259
Jasmine, 191

Jebusites, 272
Jehovah. *See* Yehovah
Jehovah's Witnesses, 252–253
Jellinek, Adolf, 249
Jephthah, 411
Jeremiah (amora), 345
Jeremiah (prophet), 13, 182, 456, 503, 545
Jeremiah (Rabbi), 13, 23, 34, 51, 108, 418, 522, 526, 567
Jericho, 177, 275, 370
Jeroboam, 274
Jerome, Saint, 471
Jerusalem, 272–273. *See also* Israel (biblical); Israel (modern state); Temples
    Ark (of the Covenant) brought to, 43
    Babylonian attack on, 189
    Le-shana ha-ba'ah bi-Yerushala'yim, 467
    mayor of, 455
    Megillah readings within, 332
    as modern capital of Israel, 267
    mourning for, 121
    population of, 271
    prayers in direction of, 43–44, 350, 369, 404, 520
    Purim celebrations of, 414–415, 501
    siege of. *See* Asarah B'Tevet
    Temples of, 272
    zeikher le-churban and, 607–608
Jerusalem Day, 273
Jerusalem Talmud, 51, 59, 526. *See also* Talmud
Jerusalem Targum, 338. *See also* Targum
Jesus Christ
    accusations of references to in Aleinu (prayer), 12
    circumcision of, 112, 118
    crucifixion of, 11, 28–29, 30, 33
    as God incarnate, 456
    Jews as Christ-killers, 139–140
    on justice of God, 573
    Original Sin and, 378
    Passover, arrest on, 29
    resurrection of, 483
    statues of, 47
    Sunday as Sabbath and, 453
    Yeshu (Hebrew name), 12
Jewelry and charms, 158, 511, 516, 607. *See also* Amulets
Jewish Agency, 610, 611
Jewish calendar. *See* Hebrew calendar
Jewish communities. *See* American Jewish Life; Ashkenazim; Sephardim
Jewish courts. *See* Courts, Jewish
Jewish Encyclopedia, 612
Jewish Free School, 236
Jewish homeland. *See* Israel (biblical); Israel (modern state); Zionists and Zionism
Jewish identity and status, 273–277. *See also* Apikores;

Apostates and apostasy; Assimilation; Bar mitzvah; Bat mitzvah; Birthright; Chosen People; Circumcision; Converts and conversion; Covenant People; Israel (modern state); Kohanim; Levites; Priests (Kohanim)
    chair charms, 94
    derogatory attributions, 274
    dietary laws and, 148
    emotional connection to Judaism and, 276
    of Falashas, 182–183
    of forced converts, 430
    host-mothers and, 259
    intermarriage and, 264, 495
    Karaites and, 287–288
    Law of Return and, 13, 308–309
    of mamzeirim, 319
    marital, 524–525
    names, changing to elevate, 363
    Nuremberg Laws, 251
    overview of, 274–276
    patrilineal descent, 276
    retained for sinners, 430, 431
    Sabbath observance and, 36–37
    of Samaritans, 457
    sinning and, 428
    symbols of, 511, 519
    Yehudi, Jews known as, 274
    yichus, 601–602
Jewish Institute of Religion (JIR), 376, 425, 613. *See also* Hebrew Union College
Jewish law. *See also* Anshei Knesset Ha-Gedolah; *Code of Jewish Law* (Caro); Commandments; Cooking; Justice; Mishnah; Takanot; Talmud; Torah; Witnesses and testimony
    abandonment of. *See* Apostates and apostasy
    analyzing of. *See* Talmud
    bal tosif, 58–59
    converts to. *See* Converts and conversion
    customs and, 304–306
    food regulations. *See* Kashrut
    halakhah, defined, 229, 307–308
    interpretations of. *See* Responsa Literature
    Midrash Halakhah and, 340–341
    overview of, 306–308
    Positive Historical Judaism and, 127
    violation of. *See* Pikuach nefesh
Jewish Life in the Middle Ages (Abrahams), 121
Jewish Magic and Superstition (Trachtenberg), 200, 556
Jewish Medical Ethics. See Jakobovits, Rabbi Immanuel
Jewish Mind, The (Patai), 276
Jewish National Fund, 104–105, 610
Jewish nationalism. *See* Zionists and Zionism
Jewish people. *See* Jewish identity and status
Jewish Publication Society (JPS), 612
Jewish quarters. *See* Ghettos

Jewish Reconstructionist Foundation, 111, 180. *See also*
    Reconstructionist movement
Jewish State, The (Herzl), 266, 609
Jewish status. *See* Jewish identity and status
Jewish Theological Seminary of America (JTS), 126,
    127–128, 375–376, 421, 595
Jewish War, The. See Josephus, Flavius
Jews and Their Lies (Luther), 111. *See also* Luther, Martin
Jews' College, London, 376, 421, 439
Jews for Jesus, 309
Jezebel, Queen, 335, 466
Job, 124, 173
    faith of, 284
    grief of, 435
    keri'ah by, 290
    mourning of, 403, 495
    punishment of, 441
    Satan and, 26, 458
    as slaveholder, 506
Johanan (Rabbi). *See* Yochanan (Rabbi)
John Paul II, Pope, 33, 302
John XXIII, Pope, 32, 111
Jonah (Rabbi), 23, 526
Jonah, Book of, 605
Jonathan (son of King Saul), 170, 254
Jonathan bar Nappacha, 23
Jonathan the Elder, 23
Jonathan the Maccabee, 324–325
Jordan, 268, 272–273
Jose (Rabbi), 192, 363
Jose ben Chaninah, 68
Joseph (the righteous), 2, 56
    blessing from Jacob, 181
    brothers of, 257
    coffin of, 119
    death of, 166
    division of Israel and, 567
    dreams, interpretations of, 156
    Jacob and, 290, 371, 442, 493
    Jericho, capture of, 370
    marriage of, 390
    Mashiach ben Yosef, 336
    name of, 361
    territory of, 274
    ushpizin and, 577
Joseph bar Chiya, 303
Joseph bar Rabba, 574
Joseph ben Zimra, 2
Joseph ibn Migash, 431
Joseph the Tolerant of Hapsburg, 518
Josephus, Flavius, 29, 336
    Contra Apionem, 76
    on crucifixions, 139
    on embalming, 166
    on Essenes, 51

on false Messiahs, 336
on mezuzot, 338
on Passover celebrations, 386–387
on the Septuagint, 469
Joshua (biblical), 177, 274, 275, 278, 375, 420, 567
Joshua (Rabbi), 240, 316, 421
Joshua ben Chananiah, 447
Joshua ben Gamala, 161, 162
Joshua ben Korcha, 42, 123
Joshua ben Levi, 23, 161, 239, 344, 408, 472, 481, 489
Joshua ben Perachya, 614
Josiah, King, 460, 545, 555
Joy, 85, 87, 121–122, 173, 414–417, 452
JPS (Jewish Publication Society), 612
JTS (Jewish Theological Seminary), 427
Jubal, 357
Jubilee year, 276–277, 370–371, 491, 506
Judah (disciple of Rav), 193
Judah (son of Jacob), 58, 274, 312, 326
Judah (tribe of), 272, 274, 567
Judah, Rabbi of Regensburg, 173
Judah bar Nachmani, 337
Judah ben Bathyra, 418
Judah ben Ila'i, 161, 204
Judah ben Lakish, 43
Judah ben Nathan, 566
Judah ben Simon, 26, 176
Judah ben Tabbai, 614
Judah I. *See* Judah the Prince
Judah Loew ben Bezalel of Prague, 359–360
Judah the Ammonite, 133
Judah the Maccabee, 99, 318, 415, 602. *See also*
    Chanukkah; Maccabees
Judah the Pious, 263
Judah the Prince, 181, 204, 263, 329, 364, 604. *See also*
    Mishnah
    on aliyah to Israel, 13
    on aliyot to the Torah, 565
    baraitot and, 59
    on blessings, 195
    on conduct of scholars, 350
    death of, 174, 494
    on deference to old, 8
    on early chasidim, 395
    on hospitality, 259
    leadership of, 458
    marriage of son, 450
    Mishnah compiled by, 346–347, 374–375, 458, 526.
        See also Mishnah
    neturei karta and, 365
    on nutrition, 192
    overview of, 536
    on peace, 391
    on separation of unmarried men, 256
    on sexual relations, 474

on Shema (prayer), 399, 489
on synagogues, 68
tefillin of, 539
Torah given from right side of God, 442
on water for matzot, 329
on women and tallitot, 525, 591
Judaism. *See* Jewish identity and status; Jewish law;
    Jewish people
Judaism and Healing, Halakhic Perspectives (Bleich), 175.
    See also Bleich, Rabbi J. David
Judaism as civilization, 422–423
Judaism Eternal (Hirsch), 247
Judaism: Profile of a Faith (Bokser), 243–244
Judea, 543
Judenkaiser, the, 135
Judenrein, 251
Judenstadt (Jewish State), 190–191. *See also* Herzl,
    Theodor
Judeo-Christians, 501
Judeo-Italian, 141
Judeo-Spanish, 468–469
Judges and judicial procedure, 202, 522, 524, 531–532,
    568. *See also* Courts, Jewish
Judgment. *See also* Appearances; Beit Din; Justice
    Day of (Messianic), 6. *See also* Resurrection
    Days of Awe, 371, 496–497, 597–598
    God as Righteous Judge, 441–442
    Hallel and, 230
    interim period following death, 7
    justice and, 42, 104
    Netaneh Tokef (prayer) on, 364
    ordination and, 375
    Pharisees on, 392
    sealed on Hoshana Rabbah, 258
    Yom Kippur and, 444–445
Judith, Book of, 34, 101
Justice, 277. *See also* Courts, Jewish; Ethics; Jewish law;
    Judgment; Piety
    faith and, 182
    financial, 314
    as foundation of the world, 567
    midat ha-din, 334
    Noahide Laws and, 367
    piety and, 395
    tzedakah and, 102, 104, 572
    Tziduk Ha-Din (prayer) and, 572–573

K

K (kosher symbol), 151
Kabbalah and kabbalists, 278–281. *See also* Astrology;
    Chasidim and chasidut; Radbaz; Sefirot, ten;
    Zohar, The
    amulets, 23–24
    astrology, rooted in, 53
        Ba'al Shem Tov and, 395
        Caro as, 433
        Chasidei Ashkenaz, 575
        evolution and, 176
        exorcism of dybbuks, 159
        kavanah and, 289
        kvitlach and, 302
        on reincarnation, 427
        on salt, 455
        shevirat keilim concept, 492–493
        Shield of David and, 511
        sod Bible interpretation, 381, 383–384
        ten sefirot, 64, 280, 467, 487, 492
        three, importance of number, 369
        on Tikanta Shabbat, 3
        on tikkun olam, 552
        tzimtzum concept and, 573
        Yom Kippur Katan and, 605–606
Kabbalat kinyan, 281
Kabbalat Shabbat, 281, 448
Kabdeihu vechashdeihu, 293
Kablanut, 40, 320–321
Kaddish (prayer), 4, 22, 200, 281–285
    for an apostate parent, 39
    for babies, 573
    for Holocaust victims, 51
    Jewish Libyan customs, 231
    Ma'ariv (prayers) and, 316
    Mourners', 281–285, 488, 603, 606
    for non-Jewish parents, 386
    quorum for, 343, 344, 603
    response by congregation to, 282
    at unveilings, 576
    women's recitation of, 284
    on yahrzeits, 597
    Yom Ha-Sho'ah, not recited on, 254
Kadesh, 504
Kadmut, 504
Kadosh, 249, 289, 324. *See also* Holy and holiness
Kaf/khaf, 18, 302, 368
Kaftziel, 26
Kagan, Israel Meir. *See* Chafetz Chayim
Kahal, 146. *See also* Diaspora
Kalischer, Rabbi Tzevi Hirsch, 295, 610
Kallah (assembly), 285, 429, 598
Kallah Rabbati (tractate), 536
Kallir, Eleazer, 522
Kalol, 598
Kalonymos ben Kalonymos, 416
Kal va-chomer principle, 244–245
Ka'mei'a, 23
Kanah, 361
Kant, Immanuel, 422
Kaplan, Judith, 62, 422, 594
Kaplan, Rabbi Mordecai, 61–62, 111, 179–180, 198,

376, 422–423, 594. *See also* Reconstructionist
    movement
Kapparot, 285–286, 306, 369, 504. *See also* Circles and
    circling
Kapporet (valance for ark), 46
Karaites, 286–288
    on candlelighting, 88
    divorces of, 182
    marriages of, 182
    Mizrachi, Elijah on, 432
    pardeis interpretations, objections to, 384
    Purim celebrations of, 417
    Sa'adya Gaon vs., 429
    Sadducees and, 454
    on tzitzit, 574
Karnofsky family, 511
Karpas, 455, 461, 463
Kasher, Rabbi Menachem, 461
Kashrut. *See also* Shochet
    animals, kosher, 149, 172
    appearance principle and, 40
    batel b'shishim, 61
    blood, prohibition of, 75–76
    certification, 151, 586
    defined, 288
    Falasha observance of, 182
    family bonding and, 184
    gidin, 209, 558
    glatt kosher, 211
    kashering process, 150–151, 387–388
    kosher style, 151
    marit a'yin and, 40–41
    mashgichim, 310, 486
    meat, 150–151
    meat and milk combinations, 61, 112, 152, 307, 320,
        476, 485, 533
    mehadrin min ha-mehadrin, 333
    Noahide Laws and, 549
    nonkosher food, 35, 41, 61, 75, 121, 416, 548–549
    overview of, 147–152
    pareve, 40, 151, 320, 386
    Passover, 148, 151, 387–389. *See also* Chametz
    Pittsburgh Platform on, 426
    of religious articles, 147
    safeguards of, 476
    slaughtering, 38, 150, 347, 485–486, 533, 590
    source of law, 148
    tereifah, 61, 548–549
    Union of Orthodox Jewish Congregations of America,
        380
    of wine, 586
    Yoreh Dei'ah, 307, 500
Katri, 181
Kattina (Rabbi), 473
Katz as surname, 409

Katznelson, Berl, 247
Kaufmann, Yechezkel, 170, 412
Kavanah, 288–289, 402–404
Kayyara, Rabbi Shimon, 537
KD (kosher symbol), 151
Kedem wines, 586
Kedushah (holiness), 249, 289. *See also* Holy and
    holiness
Kedushah (prayer), 289, 344, 401
Keeper of the Law (Ginzberg), 477
Kefiyat ha-mitah, 494
Kehillah, 289–290. *See also* Community; Congregations
Keikel, 274
Keilim (tractate), 533
Keilim of God. *See* Vessels, holy
Keiruv, 107, 290
Kelippot, 229, 281, 290, 359, 493. *See also* Shevirat ha-
    keilim
Kerchieves, 351. *See also* Hair, covering of
Keren Ka-yemet Le-Yisra'el, 104–105
Keri, 173
Keri'ah (tearing of the garment), 58, 121, 290–291, 403.
    See also Mourners and mourning
Keritot (tractate), 533
Keruvim, 25. *See also* Angels
Ke-she-nishtamed, 38
Keshet, 613
Keter (in kabbalah), 280
Ketiv, 173
Ketonet, 499
Ketubbot, 10, 291–292
    beautification of, 47–48
    chalitzah, avoidance of, 313
    cohabitation and, 474
    homosexuality and, 255
    Ketubbot (tractate), 531
    overview of, 582
    as validation of marriage, 580
    witnesses of, 37, 147, 232–233, 292, 376, 581, 587
Ketuvim (Holy Writings), 3, 227, 536
Kever avot, 86
Kevod ha-beriot, 292–293, 294. *See also* Derekh eretz
Kevod ha-met, 54, 79, 82, 93, 198, 293, 366, 377, 419.
    See also Autopsies
Kevod he-chai, 293
Kevod tzibur, 293–294, 593. *See also* Mipnei kevod
    tzibur; Tircha de-tzibura
Kevorkian, Jack, 175
Kevutzot. *See* Kibbutzim
Keylitsh, 97, 416
Keys, 97
Khaf/kaf, 18, 368
Khazars kingdom, 130
Khitan, 118
Kibbutz galu'yot, 295. *See also* Aliyah (to Israel)

Kibbutzim, 294–295, 300, 451, 610, 612. *See also*
    Moshav
Kichah, 245
Kiddush (prayer), 97, 249, 259, 295–297, 403, 448, 463.
    See also Wine
Kiddush Ha-Shem, 110, 297, 324. *See also* Martyrdom
Kiddushin, 165, 249, 297, 322, 366, 531, 587. *See also*
    Marriage; Nisuin; Weddings
Kiddush Levanah, 297
Kidnapping, 91, 394
Kidney transplants, 377, 396
Kike, 274
Kila'yim, 349
Kil'ayim (tractate), 529
Killing. *See* Hunting; Murder and murderers
Kimchit the pious woman, 487
Kindness, 53, 395, 486, 550. *See also* Ethics
King James Bible, 546
Kingship of God, 22, 401, 445, 559
Kingship of Israel, 227–228, 394. *See also specific kings*
    by name
King's Orchard. *See* Paradise
Kinnim (structure), 533
Kinor, 357
Kinyan sudar, 232–233, 245, 281, 297, 299, 544, 587.
    See also Knas mahl
Kippot, 74, 426
Kippur, 468. *See also* Yom Kippur
Kiryat Arba, 92. *See also* Hebron
Kishinev, 397
Kislev, 83–84
Kissing, 297–298, 340
Kitchens, kosher, 152, 342. *See also* Kashrut
Kitni'ot, 98, 389
Kittls, 121, 248, 298–299, 445, 460, 499, 581, 605
Kitvei Ha-Kodesh. *See* Ketuvim (Holy Writings); Tanakh
Kiv'yakhol, 28
Klalah, 285
Klal Yisrael, 299
Klei kodesh, 249, 299. *See also* Cantors; Rabbis; Sextons
Klein, Rabbi Isaac, 150
Kluger, Rabbi Solomon, 433–434
Knas mahl, 232, 299. *See also* Weddings
Kneeling, 73
Knesset, Israeli, 4, 299, 518
Knesset Ha-Gedolah, 300, 316–317
Knives, 143, 150, 308, 351–352
Knots, 300, 498, 574–575. *See also* Tzitzit
Knowledge, 3, 107, 179, 203, 421–422. *See also*
    Education; Torah study
Kodesh Kodoshim, 249. *See also* Holy of Holies
Kodoshim (tractate), 347, 482, 532–533, 567. *See also*
    Mishnah
Kof, 368
Kohanim. *See* Priests (Kohanim)

Kohath (son of Aaron), 405
Kohath (son of Levi), 404–405
Kohelet. *See* Ecclesiastes, Book of
Kohen Gadol. *See* High Priest
Kohler, Rabbi Kaufmann, 60, 426
Kolelim, 300, 429, 598. *See also* Yeshivot
Kol Ha-Neshamah, 257
Kol ishah, 300–301, 350, 474, 593
Kol Nidrei (prayer), 248, 301, 369, 411, 605
Kol shevi'in chavivin, 370
Kook, Rabbi Abraham Isaac
    on art on religious objects, 48
    on autopsies, 54
    on Creation, 137
    on cremation, 138
    on evolution, 176
    on Falashas, 183
    on Messianic Age, 454
    on sabbatical years, 310, 491
Kook, Rabbi Zvi Yehuda, 268
Koppel, 241. *See also* Headcoverings
Korach, 361, 383
Koran, the, 118, 412
Korban chagigah, 462
Korbanot, 301. *See also* Sacrifices
Kosher dietary laws. *See* Kashrut
Kosher for Passover. *See* Passover
Kotel Ha-Ma'aravi. *See* Western Wall
Kotzker Rebbe, 349. *See also* Gerer chasidim
Kovno yeshiva, 434
Kreischen, 250
Kreplach, 258, 416, 485, 604
Kresmir (Austria) ketubbah, 292
Kristallnacht, 251
Krochmal, Nachman, 236
Kuf, 20, 368, 521
Kugels, 194
Kuppah, 205, 301. *See also* Gemilut chasadim
Kurdistani Jews, 536, 537
Kutim (tractate), 536
Kuttof, Irving, 435
Kuzari. See Halevi, Rabbi Yehuda
Kvater and kvaterin, 116–117, 301–302. *See also*
    Circumcision
Kvitl (card game), 203
Kvitlach (notes), 258–259, 302, 584
K'zayit, 97

L

La'az, 303
Laban, 25, 156, 297, 383–384, 511–512, 580, 587
Labor (birth). *See* Birth
Labor (work), 303. *See also* Business affairs; Income;
    Kibbutzim; Salary; Sales and selling

defined, 167–169, 449
on holidays, 530
infringement upon, 235
objects of, 356
Original Sin and, 456
on Rosh Chodesh, 443–444
by saintly people, 303
Salanter, Rabbi Israel on, 356
surnames and, 518
treatment of animals and, 571
wives, time spent away from, 473
Labor camps, 252–253. *See also* Concentration camps
Ladders, 25, 96–97, 156, 205, 484, 511
Ladimir, Maid of, 525
Ladino, 468–469
Lag Ba-Omer, 81, 85, 303–304, 583, 597
Lake Kinneret, 294
Lamb, paschal, 85
Lamdan, 525. *See also* Scholars
Lamed, 18, 368
Lamed vovniks, 304, 371
Lamentations, Book of, 90, 227
Lamm, Rabbi Norman, 256, 366, 380
Land. *See* Farmers and farming
Landau, Rabbi Ezekiel ben Yehudah, 54, 228, 260, 379,
433, 520, 571, 581
Land of Canaan, 43
Land of Israel. *See* Israel (biblical); Israel (modern state)
Languages. *See also* Euphemisms; Hebrew language;
Translations of the Hebrew Bible
of the ancient world, 371
of angels, 25
Haketia, 468
la'az, 303
Latin, 141, 471
of prayer, 25, 398–399
Tower of Babel and, 557
Yiddish, 141, 235–236, 572
Lanzmann, Claude, 252
Lasers for circumcision, 118
Lashes, 532. *See also* Flogging
Later rishonim, 432. *See also* Rishonim era.
Latin, 141, 471
Latkes, 101
Lau, Rabbi Yisroel Meir, 131
Laughter, 361
Lavishness, 516–517
Law. *See* Civil law; Courts, Jewish; Jewish law
Law of Anatomy and Pathology, The, 55
Law of Return, 13, 38, 276, 295, 308–309, 347. *See also*
Aliyah (to Israel)
Law-of-the-land principle, 309
Lay leaders (parnassim), 14
Lazarus, Emma, 611
Leaders and leadership, 17, 299. *See also* Lamed

vovniks; Lay leaders (parnassim); Nesi'im; Priests
(Kohanim); Rabbis; Scholars
League of Anti-Semites, 31
League of Nations, 267, 610
Leah (Matriarch), 92, 327, 578. *See also* Arba Imma'hot
Leap years, 83–84, 85, 285, 309, 501, 606. *See also* Adar
Learned. *See* Aging; Wisdom
Learning. *See* Education; Teachers and teaching; Torah
study
Leather, 248, 260, 486, 494, 540, 558, 570, 604–605
Leavened foods, 329, 330, 386–388. *See also* Chametz
Leavetakers, 380
Lebanon, 270
Lebov, Myrna, 175
Le-cha'yim (salutation), 576
Lechem ha-panim, 95–96. *See also* Showbreads
Lechem mishneh, 96
Lechem oni, 329. *See also* Matzot
Lectures. *See* Sermons
Leeser, Rabbi Isaac, 127
Left vs. right, 442–443, 507, 540–541, 560
Legal documents. *See* Documents
Legal fiction, 98, 309–310, 352, 491
Legal guardians, 4
Legal matters, 98
Legal processes. *See* Civil law; Courts, Jewish; Jewish law
Legends of the Jews, 612
Legitimacy. *See* Jewish identity and status
Legs, 300, 350, 474
Legumes, 98, 389, 416, 481
Leibnitz, Gottfried, 441
Leibowitz, Nehama, 591–592, 595
Leibowitz, Yeshayahu, 7, 595
Leikh La-azazel, 57. *See also* Hell
Lekach, 446
Leket, 103
Lekhah Dodi (prayer), 3, 310–311, 350, 359, 422
Lekh lekha (commandment to Abraham), 384
Lekhu neranenah (prayer), 316
Lending. *See* Debts; Loans
Lentils, 193, 389
Leo (zodiacal sign), 85, 613
Leo X, Pope, 528
Leprosy, 153, 263, 311, 341, 400, 418, 534
Lesbianism, 255, 257, 311, 462, 475
Leshon am zar, 303
Leshon ha-kodesh, 311. *See also* Hebrew language
Leshon ha-ra, 311
Leshon nekiyah, 172
Lesser Sanhedrin, 65
Lessons. *See* Aggadah; Education; Teachers and teaching;
Torah study
"Letter of Aristeas, The", 469–470
Letters and documents. *See also* Get (divorce document);
Ketubbot; Scribes

banned, 178
God's name in, 214
kvitlach, 258–259, 302, 584
reading others', 178, 245, 409
"writing quickly", 2
Letters of the Hebrew Alphabet. *See* Acrostics; Gematriah;
    Hebrew language; Roshei teivot
Lev, 196
Levantador, 226–227
Levi (Rabbi), 20–21, 119–120, 329
Levi (tribe of), 274
Leviant, Curt, 600
Leviathan, 312
Levi ben Samuel, 559
Levinger, Chief Rabbi Yisrael, 486
Levinthal, Rabbi Israel, 321
Levirate marriage practices, 38, 95, 262, 312–313, 326–
    327, 390, 531
Levites, 246, 313–314. *See also* Priests (Kohanim)
    aliyot (Torah honors) given to, 13, 16
    Ark (of the Covenant), carrying of, 42
    division of Israel and, 567
    duties of, 405, 408
    education of, 160
    Golden Calf and, 545
    lineage of, 404–405
    matzot representing, 329
    music of, 357–358, 502
    natural inheritance of status, 4
    non-Priests, 314
    as one-third of Jewish community, 369
    patrilineal descent and, 390
    pidyon ha-ben exemption, 393
    prayers of, 164
    represented by matzot at Seder, 461
    retirement of, 8
    songs of, 400
    tithing for, 103, 529–530, 553
Leviticus. *See* Five Books of Moses
Levivot, 101
Levi Yitzchak of Berdichev, 102, 106
Lex talionis, 56, 314. *See also* Eye-for-an-eye principle
Liberal Judaism. *See* Reform Judaism
Liberia, 183
Liberty. *See* Freedom
Liberty Bell, 276
Libra (zodiacal sign), 84, 613
Lieberman, Saul, 10, 180, 567
Life. *See also* Afterlife; Aging; Birth; Creation
    aging, 8
    commandment to choose, 173
    compared to Torah scrolls, 291
    desire for, 311
    eighteen, significance of, 104, 371
    free will and, 197

gematriah of, 205
life-for-a-life principle, 119
renewal of, 96, 512
seven worlds passed through, 199–200
Life-support systems, 174–175
Life-threatening experiences. *See* Birkat Ha-Gomel
    (prayer); Danger
Lifnim mi-shurat ha-din, 314
Light, 137, 143–144, 211, 281, 401. *See also* Candles and
    candlelighting; Sun; Torches
Light, Divine. *See* Shekhinah
Lightning, 437
Light of Israel, The (Belzer), 163. *See also* Musar
Likutei Amarim, 106
Lilienblum, Moses Leib, 236
Lilies, 191
Lilith, 314–315
Li nakam ve'shilem, 441
Lincoln, Abraham, 506
Lineage, 184, 251, 274–276, 308–309, 393, 608. *See also*
    Family and family life
Linen, 35, 114, 157, 349, 476–477, 523. *See also*
    Shaatnez
Lintels. *See* Mezuzot
Lions, 129, 190, 317, 324, 613
Lipkin, Rabbi Israel. *See* Salanter, Rabbi Israel
Lips. *See* Kissing
Lipschutz, Rabbi Israel, 176
Liquor, 517. *See also* Drinking
Lishkat Ha-Gazit, 65, 457, 519. *See also* Great Sanhedrin
Literal Bible translations, 381, 384, 392, 438–439, 454.
    See also Pharisees
Literature, 11, 277, 572
Lithuanian chasidim, 107
Lithuanian yeshivot, 600–601
Litigation. *See* Courts, Jewish
Liturgy. *See* Poets and poetry; Prayers and blessings
Livelihood. *See* Income; Labor (work)
Living, the, 361–362
Living waters, 24. *See also* Water
Living wills, 175
Loans, 30, 103–104, 309–310, 410, 513, 532. *See also*
    Debts
Lodging. *See* Hospitality
Lo'eg la-rash, 94
Logic. *See* Chok (chukim)
Loneliness of Adam, 322
Longfellow, Henry Wadsworth, 93
Lord. *See* God
Lost Tribes of Israel, 146, 274, 543, 548, 567
Lot, 25, 26, 255, 273, 553
Lo tehorah, 172. *See also* Treif
Lo tigra, 379
Lo tikum ve-lo titor, 439–441
Lo toseif, 379

Lots (purim), 414–415. *See also* Purim
Love and lovingkindness. *See also* Gemilut chasadim
    Elul as month of, 583
    as foundation of the world, 55
    of God, 10, 146, 575
    in kabbalah, 280
    Nachmanides on, 322
    sexual relations as expression of, 473
    Shema (prayer) and, 155
    of strangers, 512
Lovers of Zion movement, 608
Lower Sanhedrin, 457. *See also* Sanhedrin
Loyalty, 11, 437, 484. *See also* Tests by God
Lubavitcher chasidim, 106–107, 242, 367. *See also*
    Chabad
Lubavitcher Rebbe, The, 72, 107
Luck. *See* Mazal
Luke, Book of, 29, 140. *See also* New Testament
Lulav, 94–95, 182, 194–197, 304–305, 402, 516, 530.
    See also Four species
Luminary of the Diaspora, The, 38
Lunar calendar, 309. *See also* Hebrew calendar
Lungs of kosher animals. *See also* Kashrut
Luria, Rabbi Isaac. *See* Ari, the
Luria, Rabbi Solomon, 40, 71, 240–241, 278
Luther, Martin, 31, 111
Lutherans, 546–547. *See also* Christians and Christianity
Luxury, 248, 460, 494, 516–517, 551, 604–605
Luzzatto, Rabbi Moses Chaim, 278, 357, 360, 385, 440
Lying, 257–258, 308, 410. *See also* Truth and
    truthfulness
Lyre, 357

M

Ma'alin ba-kodesh ve-lo moridin, 250, 558
Ma'ariv (prayers), 73, 164, 297, 369, 468. *See also* Prayers
    and blessings
    of the Sabbath, 62, 281, 316, 448
Maaseh Book, 159
Ma'asei Bereishit and Ma'asei Merkavah, 316–318
Ma'aser, 103, 314, 553. *See also* Tithing
Ma'aser Sheini (tractate), 529–530
Ma-avar Yabok (Berechya), 498
Mabovitz, Golda. *See* Meir, Golda
Maccabees, 34, 190, 318, 324–325, 415, 602, 614. *See*
    also Chanukkah
Machlin, Edda Servi, 464
Machzorim, 48, 318, 501. *See also* Prayerbooks
Machzor Vitry, 284, 602
Madison Square Garden, New York, 141, 300–301
Madrid Conference, 269–270
Maftir, 2, 14–17, 59, 283, 294, 318, 415, 605. *See also*
    Haftarah readings; Torah readings
Magbi'ah, 226–227. *See also* Hagbahah and gelilah

Magen Avraham (Gombiner), 521, 591
Magic, 121, 300, 340, 517–518. *See also* Demons and
    demonology
Magic Square Amulet, 24. *See also* Amulets
Magid of Mezirich, 266
Magog and Gog, 46–47, 215
Maharil, the, 87, 90, 216–217, 234, 243, 339, 432, 537
    as matchmaker, 481
    on mezuzot, 339
    on Rosh Hashanah, 445
    on yahrzeits, 597
    on Yamim Nora'im, 597
Maharshal, 516
Mahul, 412. *See also* Circumcision
Maid of Ladamir, 284, 525, 542
Maids, 310
Maimonides, Rabbi Moses
    613 Commandments, list of, 12, 537
    on afterlife, 6–7, 243
    Alfasi of Fez and, 431
    on aliyah to Israel, 12, 537
    amulets, condemnation of, 24
    on angels, 27
    on anthropomorphism, 28
    on apostates and apostasy, 39
    on astrology, 53
    banned writings of, 178–179
    on blades for shaving, 228
    on blessings, 74, 75
    Cairo Genizah and, 206, 434
    on candlelighting, 89
    changes to Amidah, 305
    on circumcision, 119, 351
    on clothing of men, 158
    on conversion, 130, 131, 134
    on Creation, 137
    on customs and law, 606
    on death of newborns, 118
    on demons, 143
    on dietary laws, 148
    on dreams, 156
    on Eighteen Benedictions, 165
    on eruvin, 167–168
    on fasting, 187
    on food cooked by non-Jews, 310
    on free will, 197
    on gambling, 202
    on Gentile term, 207
    on graven images, 47
    gravesite of, 373
    Guide of the Perplexed, 109
    on health and well-being, 193
    on homosexuality, 256, 311
    on immortality of the soul, 510
    on impurity, 418

on justice of God, 573
on kashrut, 149
on levirate marriages, 313, 390
on Ma'asei Bereishit and Ma'asei Merkavah, 318
maimouna celebration and, 387
marriage classification, 322
Masoretic text used by, 557
on ma'yim achronim, 330
on meat and milk, 112
on Messianic Age, 335
on mezuzot, 338
on miracles, 345
Mishneh Torah, overview of, 347–348
on mixed breeds, 349
name of, 2
on Noahide Laws, 105, 366, 367
Obadiah the convert and, 512–513
on ordination, 375, 421
overview of, 431
on Passover observance, 466
on personal conduct, 146
on physical contact with opposite sex, 298
on pidyon shevu'yim, 394
on pleasures in life, 51
on priesthood, 408–409
on privacy rights, 410
on prophets and prophecy, 345, 412
on quorum for prayer, 399
on repentance, 428
on resurrection of the dead, 436–437
on Revelation, 179, 438–439
on revenge, 440
on reward and punishment, 441
rishonim era and, 527
on Sabbath desecration, 37, 452
on sacrificial system, 453–454
on Samaritans and idolatry, 457
on Sanhedrin, 122
on Seder matzot, 329
on sefirat ha-omer, 373
on sexual relations, 472, 475
on shaatnez, 476
on Shekhinah, 487
on sins and sinners, 503
on Sukkot, 516
on superstition, 517
on tagin, 521
on teachers, 474
on Ten Commandments, 547
Thirteen Principles of Faith, 155, 422
Torah scroll of, 508
on Torah scrolls, 509
on Torah study, 535–536
on translations of the Torah, 471
on treatment of animals, 571

on truthfulness, 142, 567
on tzedakah, 103
on wifebeating, 63
on witnesses, 22, 587, 592
on women as Torah readers, 563
Maimonides Rabbi's Training College, 127
Maimouna, 319, 387
Maimuni, Abraham, 7
Major Trends in Jewish Mysticism (Scholem), 492–493, 573
Makav, 318
Makhshirin (tractate), 534
Makkot, 228, 532
Malakhi (prophet), 152, 184, 258, 477–478, 542
Malakhim. See Angels
Malkhut (in kabbalah), 280, 487
Malkot. See Flogging
Malshinim, 164
Mammals. See Animals
Mamzeirim, 160, 287–288, 319. See also Adultery
Man (humans). See also Adam (first man);
        Anthropomorphism of God; Jewish people
    angels and, 25, 401
    communications from God. See Dreams
    created in image of God, 25, 47–48, 54, 495
    Creation and, 193, 212
    in Ezekiel's vision, 317
    God and, 212
    partnership between man and God, 422
Man (male). See Fathers and fatherhood; Husbands; Men;
        Patrilineal descent
Mana, Rabbi of Sepphoris, 124
Manasseh ben Israel, 53
Manasseh, king of Judah, 34
Manasseh (son of Joseph), 232, 442
Manasseh (tribe of), 274, 548, 567, 587–588
Mandate period in Israel, 267
Manifestations of God. See Attributes of God
Manischewitz wines, 586
Ma nishtanah, 463–464
Manna, 96, 141, 448, 471
Manners. See Conduct; Derekh eretz; Menschlichkeit
Mantle, Torah, 46, 226, 320, 558, 559–560, 561, 565
Ma'ot chittim, 320
Ma'oz Tzur (song), 101
Mapai Party, 610, 611
Mapam Party, 612
Mappah. See Mantle, Torah
Mappah (Isserles), 433, 500. See also Isserles, Rabbi
        Moses
Mar (son of Ravina), 210
Mar (title), 22, 375, 420
Mar bar Ameimar, 196
Mar-Cheshvan, 84
Margarine, 40, 320

Mari bar Rachel, 133
Marit a'yin, 40, 320–321, 592. *See also* Stumbling-block
    principle
Mark, Book of, 29, 139. *See also* New Testament
Marking commissioner of Palestine, 180
Maror, 460, 461, 464–465
Marr, William, 31
Marranos, 30, 321–322, 500. *See also* Spain
Marriage, 322–323. *See also* Adultery; Bridegrooms;
    Brides; Divorce; Husbands; Ketubbot; Sexual
    relations; Wives
  abstention from, 51. *See also* Asceticism
  age of, 322
  of children born out of wedlock, 319
  Christian view of, 92
  consummation of, 114
  conversion and, 5, 129, 319
  to divorcees, 492
  of Falashas, 182
  first year of, 472
  forbidden, 262–263, 531
  for homosexuals, 256, 311
  Kallah (tractate) on, 536
  of Karaites, 182, 286, 288
  knas mahl, 299
  of mamzeirim, 5, 319
  modesty of married women, 474
  to more than one woman, 4
  mourning and, 488
  multiple wives. *See* Polygamy
  name of spouses and, 323, 362
  Nashim (Mishnah tractates). *See* Mishnah
  Nashim (tractate) on, 482
  of Priests, 405, 406–407, 409
  prohibited, 322–323
  sexual relations outside of, 474–475
  shadkhanim, 480–481
  tallit as symbol of, 525
  of teachers, 163
  validation of, 245
  of widows, 38, 492, 583
Mar Samuel, 23
Martyrdom, 297, 324
  of Amnon, Rabbi of Mainz, 364
  Bar Kokhbah rebellion, 324–325
  Isaac as symbol of, 11
  ten martyrs, 36, 123, 297, 324, 371, 548, 572, 605
  Yizkor and, 602
Mar Ukba bar Nechemia, 181, 357
Mar Zutra the Pious, 552
Masada, 324–325
Mashgichim, 310, 486. *See also* Kashrut
Mashiach. *See* Messiah and Messianic Age
Mashiah, Shlomo, 49
Mashlim aliyah, 2

Masorah and Masoretic text, 173, 325–326, 557. *See also*
    Torah
Masquerading, 326, 417
Massekhet Purim (Kalonymos), 416
Massekhtot, 347. *See also* Mishnah; Talmud
Massekhtot ketanot, 534–535
Master teacher title, 375. *See also* Ordination; Rabbis
Masturbation, 58, 129, 326–327, 373. *See also* Artificial
    insemination
Matanot le-evyonim, 414. *See also* Purim
Matan Torah, 437–438. *See also* Revelation at Sinai
Matchmaking, 480–481. *See also* Shidukhin
Mathematics. *See* Hebrew calendar
Mather, Increase, 35
Matnito, 59
Matriarchs (mothers), 92, 327, 346, 363. *See also* Leah;
    Rachel; Rebecca; Sarah
Matrilineal descent, 274, 327–328. *See also* Jewish
    identity and status
Matrimony. *See* Marriage
Mattathias the Hasmonean, 99, 318. *See also* Chanukkah;
    Maccabees
Matter, destruction of, 7
Matthew, Book of, 28–29, 139. *See also* New Testament
Matthew, Wentworth A., 183
Maturity, 134, 228, 334, 422. *See also* Confirmation
    ceremonies
Matzeivah, 555. *See also* Tombstones
Matzot, 328–330, 388. *See also* Passover
  as amulet, 23
  blessing for, 74
  blood libels and, 76, 466
  Four Questions and, 464
  Hillel's sandwich, 464–465
  lechem oni, 329
  matzah ashirah, 329
  matzah meal, 389
  obligation of, 460
  Pesach Sheini and, 392
  for Seder, 461
  as symbol of purity, 98
  women's obligation in, 349
Mausoleums, 80
"May a Redeemer Come to Zion" (prayer), 342
Ma'yim. *See* Water
Ma'yim achronim, 234, 330
Ma'yim cha'yim, 24
Ma'yim she-ein la-hem sof, 9
Ma'yim she-lanu, 329, 330
Ma'yim she'uvim, 24, 341
Ma'yim she-yeish la-hem sof, 9
Mazal, 52, 330, 371, 613. *See also* Zodiac
Mazon, 60
McNarney, General Joseph, 528
Meal-offerings, 405, 455, 532–533. *See also* Sacrifices

Meals. *See also* Food; Kashrut; Se'udat mitzvah
    conclusion of. *See* Grace After Meals; Ma'yim
          achronim
    d'var Torah for, 158
    family life and, 184
    feeding animals prior to, 570
    handwashing prior to, 78, 233–234, 418, 534
    meat and milk combinations, 307, 476
    moderation in eating, 192
    of mourners, 189
    pat lechem, 231
    right hand used to eat, 442
    salt and, 455
    Se'udah Shelishit, 448, 471, 481
    for visitors, 295–296
    waiting period between milk and meat, 152
Me'arat Ha-Makhpelah, 80
Mea She'arim, Jerusalem, 80, 380
Meat. *See also* Shochet; Slaughtering
    abstention from, 51, 551
    accidental combinations with milk, 61
    hindquarter, 151
    hunting for, 260
    kashering process, 150–151
    Noahide Laws and, 367
    nutrition of, 192–193
    for Purim, 416
    raw, 78
    on the Sabbath, 194
Meat and milk combinations, 112, 152, 307, 320, 476,
    485, 533
Mechitzah, 300. *See also* Women's Gallery
Medes, 297–298
Mediators. *See* Tzadikim
Medical insurance, 301
Medical intervention. *See also* Autopsies; Doctors; Health;
    Illness; Science
    abortions and, 1–2
    caduceus as symbol of medicine, 77
    flowers as medicine, 191
    Jewish Medical Ethics. See Jakobovits, Rabbi Immanuel
    Karaites and, 286
    masturbation and, 327
    organ transplants, 293, 607
    surrogate motherhood, 259, 518
Medinat Yisra'el. *See* Israel (biblical); Israel (modern state)
Meditation. *See* Kavanah
Mediterranean Sea, 523
Mediterranean Society, A (Goitein), 206
Megiddo, Mountain of, 46–47
Megillah (Scroll of Esther), 230, 332–333, 415–416, 531.
    See also Esther and Book of Esther; Purim
Mehadrin min ha-mehadrin, 333
Mei'ah berakhot, 73
Mei'ah She'arim, Jerusalem, 80, 380

Me'ilah (tractate), 533
Mein Kampf (Hitler), 251
Meir (Rabbi), 346–347, 557
    on aliyot to the Torah, 565
    Beruriah (wife of), 588
    on blessings, 73, 497
    on blue tzitzit, 523
    on color blue, 120
    ordination of, 421
    on Sabbath laws, 450
    on tzitzit, 575
    wife of, 162
Meir, Golda, 363, 611–612
Meir ben Baruch of Rothenberg, 16, 432
    on aliyot for women, 340
    on beautification of religious objects, 47–48
    on breaking bread, 78
    on headcoverings, 240
    on magic, 517
    on mezuzot, 340
    on quorums, 344
    rishonim era and, 527
    on Rosh Chodesh, 444
    on storing Torah scrolls, 44
    on wifebeating, 63
Meir ben Isaac Nehora'i, 484
Meir ben Isaac of Worms, 10
Meir ben Samuel of Ramerupt, 566
Meiren, 446
Meir the scribe, 379
Mekhilta, 340
Mekhirat chametz, 98, 333
Melach. *See* Salt
Melakhah. *See* Sabbath
Melamed, 109. *See also* Chederim; Education; Teachers
    and teaching
Melaveh malkah, 333, 448
Melchizedek, king of Salem, 553
Melodies of the Torah. *See* Cantillations
Mem, 18–19, 368
Memorbüchen, 324, 602
Memorials, Holocaust, 252, 254
Memory and remembrance
    of Amalek, 333, 479
    angel of, 26
    candles during shivah, 494
    mnemonic devices, 350
    naming of babies and, 362
    of Passover, 328. *See also* Seder
    Rosh Hashanah as day of, 444
    of the Sabbath, 453
    Shabbat Zakhor, 415, 479
    of slavery in Egypt, 447
    stones and, 512
    of Torah, 600

yahrzeits, 15, 84, 171, 186, 597
Yizkor services, 166, 238, 602–603
Yom Ha-Atzma'ut, 230, 603
Yom Ha-Sho'ah, 248, 252, 254, 603
zeikher le-churban, 607–608
"zikhrono li-verakhah" expression, 3
Men. See Bridegrooms; Fathers and fatherhood;
    Husbands; Widowers
Menachem, 86, 362
Menachem aveil, 124–125, 365. See also Mourners and
    mourning
Menachot (tractate), 532–533
Menashe bar Tachlifa, 558
Mendelssohn, Moses, 111, 155–156, 236, 424, 500
Men of the Great Assembly, 227, 237, 278, 306, 333. See
    also Knesset Ha-Gedolah; Ma'asei Bereishit and
    Ma'asei Merkavah
Menorahs (menorot), 88–89, 99–100, 169, 334, 548,
    590–591, 608. See also Chanukkah
Menschlichkeit, 334. See also Derekh eretz
Menstruation. See also Mikveh
    superstition and, 517
    tefillin and, 542
    tohorat ha-mishpachah laws, 302, 341–342,
        365–366, 418, 472, 474, 534, 554
    touching the Torah and, 563
Mental competence, 514–515
Merari (son of Aaron), 405
Merari (son of Levi), 405
Merchants, 499–500. See also Labor (work); Sales and
    selling
Mercy
    angel of, 26
    El Malei Rachamim (prayer), 166
    God as Righteous Judge, 441–442
    justice and, 42, 334
    killing and. See Euthanasia
    midat ha-rachamim, 334
    Thirteen Attributes of Mercy, 549–550
    Yom Kippur and, 362
Mergings (tractate), 530
Meron, Mount, 303–304, 373, 597. See also Shimon bar
    Yocha'i
Mesachek be-kuvya, 202
Meshach, 14
Meshulachim, 104
Meshumad, 35, 334. See also Apostates and apostasy
Mesilat Yesharim (Luzzatto), 357, 360, 440. See also
    Luzzatto, Rabbi Moses Chaim
Mesivta Torah Vadaath, 380
Mesorah. See Masorah and Masoretic text
Mesorah Publications, Ltd., 528–529
Messiah and Messianic Age, 6, 22, 334–336. See also
    Redemption; World to come
    afterlife and, 6

anticipation of, 453–454
Ari, the as a precursor to, 359
Armageddon and, 47
belief in, 556
delay in coming of, 129
as descendant of King David, 128
Elijah as forerunner of, 166, 184, 466, 542
Jeremiah's prophecy of, 456
Kalischer, Rabbi Tzevi Hirsch on, 610
Maimonides' Twelfth Principle of Faith, 27
Mashiach ben David, 336
Mashiach ben Yosef, 336
Messianic movements, 309
Neturei Karta and, 365
Perek Ha-Shalom (tractate) on, 536
Pittsburgh Platform on, 426
Purim and, 417
Reconstructionist views on, 180
Satan and, 459
Schneerson, Rabbi Menachem Mendel promoted as,
    107
se'udat Mashiach, 387
Shofrot (prayers) and, 497
Messina, New York blood libel, 77, 466
Met. See Corpses
Metal coffins, 120
Metal utensils, 388
Met mitzvah, 336–337. See also Chesed shel emet
Meturgeman, 337–338
Metzada. See Masada
Metzitzah b'feh, 117. See also Circumcision
Metzora. See Leprosy
Mevorkhim ha-Chodesh, 459
Mezuman, 338
Mezuzot, 338–340
    blessing for, 74
    chanukkat ha-ba'yit and, 102
    cryptograms and, 517
    God's name in, 215
    holiness of, 250
    Karaites and, 286
    kissing, 298
    language of, 470
    niddah status of women and, 365, 418
    of Pathan tribesmen, 548
    placement of, 101, 442
    Shema (prayer) and, 488
    sofer of, 507
    as symbol of Jewish unity, 519
    as tashmishei kedushah and, 254
    temporary dwellings and, 515
    tractate of, 536
Miami Beach Platform, 427
Micah, 260, 350
Michael (angel), 371

Michal, daughter of Saul, 542
Midat chasidut. See Gemilut chasadim; Piety
Midat ha-din. See Justice
Midat ha-rachamim, 334. See also Mercy
Middle East peace process, 269–270. See also Israel
     (modern state)
Middot (tractate), 533
Midian, 440
Midnight prayers, 551
Midrash, 340–341, 345, 381–382
Mi Kamokhah (prayer), 479
Mikdash, 249. See also Temples
Mikhael, 25–26, 104, 205, 394
Mikhnas'ayim, 499
Mikra. See Bible; Tanakh
Mikveh. See also Purity and impurity
     apostates, immersion of, 38
     converts, immersion by, 131–132, 275, 322, 341
     for kashering process, 387–388
     Mikva'ot (tractate), 341–342, 534
     preceding Revelation, 132, 342, 369
     scribes and, 508
     tevilah, defined, 549
     virgin impregnated within, 50
     of women, 341–342, 366, 418, 554. See also Tohorat
          ha-mishpachah
Mikveh Israel Congregation, Philadelphia, 127
Mikvé Israel-Emanuel Synagogue, Curaçao, 144
Milah. See Circumcision
Milchik. See Dairy foods
Milgrom, Jacob, 148
Military, 199, 314, 322, 433, 512, 553–554. See also IDF
     (Israel Defense Forces); Soldiers; War
Milk. See Dairy foods
Mill Street Synagogue, New York, 468. See also
     Congregation Shearith Israel
Milton, John, 57
Min, 35
Minchah (prayers), 73, 316. See also Prayers and
     blessings
     Eighteen Benedictions, 164
     institution of, 369
     origin of, 520
     overview of, 342–343
     Sabbath, 59, 448
     of Yom Kippur, 605
Mind. See Brain; Souls
Minhagei Maharil. See Maharil, the
Minhagim, 343. See also Nusachim
Minhagim (Tyrnau), 229
Min ha-shama'yim, 438
Minim, 501
Ministering angels. See Angels
Minor fast days. See also Fasting and fast days
     aliyot (Torah honors) given on, 14

Asarah B'Tevet, 50–51, 185–186, 254, 318
     dawn to sundown, 186
     Shivah Asar B'Tammuz, 185–186, 189, 318, 495, 551
     Tzom Gedaliah, 185–186, 188, 318, 575
Minors. See Children
Minor talmudic tractates, 534–535
Minor Purim, 187
Mintz, Moses, 250, 581
Minyan, 59, 343–345
     apostates not counted in, 37–38
     ark counted as member of, 45–46, 305, 344
     counting people for, 368
     intermarriage and, 264
     oneinim not counted in, 374
     for pidyon ha-ben ceremony, 393
     prayers of, 399
     public assembly defined by, 410
     Sabbath observance and, 37, 452, 487–488
     for Sheva Berakhot (blessings), 492
     for wedding ceremonies, 580–581
     women counted in, 344, 592–593
Mipnei darkei shalom, 345. See also Good and goodness;
     Goodwill principle
Mipnei kevod tzibur, 293–294, 345, 563, 593
Miracles, 12, 101, 179, 180, 345, 395, 464
Miriam (daughter of Rashi), 566
Miriam (sister of Moses), 357, 400, 405, 462, 466, 577
Mirrors, 158, 494–495
Miscarriages, 23, 392
Mischlings, 251
Mishael, 26, 324
Mi Shebeirakh (prayer), 346, 361, 496, 566
Mishlo'ach manot, 414. See also Purim
Mishnah, 22–23, 161, 346–347, 374–375, 390, 458,
     482, 526. See also Baraitot; Gemara; Judah the
     Prince; Talmud; Tanna'im; Tosefta, the
Mishnah Berurah. See Ha-Kohen, Rabbi Israel ben Meir
Mishneh Torah (Maimonides), 307, 347–348. See also
     Amora'im; Maimonides, Rabbi Moses
Mishpachah. See Family and family life
Mistreatment of animals, 27, 260, 570–572
Mistreatment of corpses. See Autopsies; Nivul ha-met
Mitnagdim, 108, 266, 348–349
Mit-tzad zeh ru'ach cha'yim, 350
Mitznefet, 499
Mitzvah meals. See Se'udat mitzvah
Mitzvot. See Commandments
Mitzvot lo ta'aseh. See Negative commandments
Mixed breeds, 349
Mixed marriage. See Intermarriage
Mixtures (of prohibited fabrics). See Shaatnez
Mixtures (of prohibited foods). See Milk and meat
     combinations; Shaatnez
Mixtures (tractate). See Eruvin
Mizrach, 349–350

Mizrachi, Elijah, 432
Mizrachi World Organization, 610
Mnemonic devices, 2, 350. *See also* Acrostics
Moab and Moabites, 382, 440. *See also* Ruth, Book of
De Modena, Leon, 7, 205, 358
Modern Orthodox Judaism, 376, 380. *See also*
    Orthodoxy
Modesty, 350–351. *See also* Clothing; Derekh eretz;
    Humility
    aleph, represented by, 21
    black and, 558
    kol ishah, 300–301, 350, 474, 593
    rescue of women and, 108
    sexual temptations and, 474
    shomer negi'a, 498
    of Sinai, Mount, 505
    Torah readings and, 294
    of women, 158
Mo'ed Katan (tractate), 347, 482, 530–531, 567. *See also*
    Mishnah
Mohalim, 351–352. *See also* Circumcision
Mohammed, 585. *See also* Islam
Mohel, 116–117, 132, 301, 457, 590. *See also*
    Circumcision
Mohn taschen, 416
Mokh, 71
Molcho, Shlomo, 336
Mollin, Rabbi Jacob Levi, 87, 90, 216–217, 234, 243,
    339, 432, 537
    as matchmaker, 481
    on Rosh Hashanah, 445
    on yahrzeits, 597
    on Yamim Nora'im, 597
Mollusk. *See* Snails
Molokh. *See* Gehinnom
Moment magazine, 595
Mondays, 14, 53, 186, 521, 562
Money. *See also* Luxury
    fines of, 420
    gelt, 101–102
    for kapparot, 286, 306, 504
    lending, 30
    as muktzah, 356, 449
    as payment for damages, 381, 392
    Sumptuary Laws, 433
    as validation of marriage, 245, 580
Moneylending, 352–353
Monis, Judah, 35
Monkeys, 451
Monogamy, 397–398
Monotheism, 11, 353–354
Montefiore, Moses, 500
Months, 69, 84–86. *See also* Hebrew calendar; Rosh
    Chodesh; *specific months by name*
Monuments. *See* Gravesites

Moon, 443. *See also* Lunar calendar; Rosh Chodesh;
    Zodiac
Moore, George Foot, 5
Morais, Sabato, 127
Moral standards. *See also* Kevod tzibur; Modesty
    Derekh Eretz Rabbah (tractate) on, 536
    God as source of, 33
    Holiness Code, the, 250
    Kallah (tractate) on, 536
    Kiddush Ha-Shem, 110, 297, 324. *See also*
        Martyrdom
    non-Jews and. *See* Noahide Laws
    tohar ha-neshek, 553–554
Mordechai ben Hillel, 63
Mordekhai (author of *Ma'oz Tzur*), 101
Mordekhai the Jew, 3, 214, 274, 332–333, 362, 414,
    417. *See also* Purim
Moreh Nevuchei Ha-Zeman, 236
Moreh Nevukhim (Maimonides). **See also** *Guide of*
    the Perplexed (Maimonides); Maimonides, Rabbi
    Moses
Morgenstern, Dr. Julian, 80
Moriah, Mount, 10, 272, 543
Morning prayers. *See* Shacharit (prayers)
Moroccan customs, 2, 319, 387
Mortar, 461
Mosaic Law. *See* Jewish law
Moses. *See also* Exodus (from Egypt); Revelation at Sinai
    Aaron and, 297
    Amalekites battle and, 345
    birth of, 412
    blessing upon Israelites, 190
    brazen serpents and, 77
    breaking of the tablets, 43, 254
    burning bush and, 211
    children of, 185
    circumcision of son by, 351
    on compromise, 123
    copper laver construction, 233
    daughters of Zelophechad and, 587–588
    death of, 266, 391
    elders of, 371
    ethics discourses, 169–170
    as first prophet, 412
    God, spoken with, 164
    God's covenant reaffirmed by, 136
    Golden Calf and, 265, 503, 544–545, 549
    halakhah le-Moshe mi-Sinai, 229–230
    Hebrew alphabet and, 20
    hidden by Miriam, 462
    historical transmission of Torah and, 278
    humility of, 260
    image of, 519
    instructions for Torah readings, 561
    instructions to fashion a menorah, 334

Korach vs., 383
like an angel, 305
lineage of, 405
marriage of, 390
Miriam and, 466
name of, 361
naming after, 363
ordination by, 420
ordination of Joshua, 375, 420
Pinchas and, 440
prayers of, 400
pre-Exodus celebration of Passover, 386
pseudepigrapha and, 414
red heifer ritual enacted by, 422
represented at Torah readings, 564
rescue of, 26
rock struck by, 512
sacrificial blood dabbed on Aaron by, 442
Shema (prayer) and, 489
Shirat Ha-Yam, 479
sons of Aaron and, 290
tablets, breaking of, 247
tagin story and, 521
Thanksgiving, song of, 357
Torah, Revelation of, 20, 205, 306, 384, 437–439
ushpizin and, 577
Moses ben Asher, 557
Moses ben Jacob of Coucy, 142
Moses ben Maimon. *See* Rambam
Moses ben Nachman. *See* Nachmanides, Rabbi Moses
Moses ben Tzevi, 107. *See also* Satmar chasidic sect
Moses of Cordovero, 605–606
Moshav. *See* Kibbutzim
Moshav Zekeinim, 355. *See also* Aging
Moshe. *See* Moses
Moshe ben Maimon, Rabbi. *See* Maimonides, Rabbi Moses
Moslems. *See* Muslims
Mothers and motherhood. *See also* Children; Family and
        family life; Parents; Pregnancy
    honoring. *See* Parents, honoring
    kissing, 298
    matrilineal descent, 184
    names of in Mi Shebeirakh (prayer) and, 346
    naming of girls, 361
    non-Jews, 134
    protection from evil eye, 56
    surrogate motherhood, 259, 518
Motion during prayer, 399–404, 566
Mot yumat, 91. *See also* Capital punishment
Motzi shem ra, 311. *See also* Leshon ha-ra
Mount Herzl cemetery, 512
Mourners and mourning, 556. *See also* Death; Fasting and
        fast days; Kaddish (prayer); Orphans; Sefirat ha-
        omer; Shivah; Widowers; Widows; Yahrzeits
    aninut, 27, 355, 374, 542

apostates, not observed for, 39
aveilut, 55, 123–125, 355
black and, 121
clothing of, 157, 452
comforting, 86, 122
condolences, 123–125, 201, 356, 365, 495
derekh eretz amongst mourners, 146
Eivel Rabbati (tractate) on, 535–536
executed criminals, not observed for, 39
flowers and, 192
haircutting and, 227
harm to mourners by ghosts, 79
headcoverings and, 238, 240, 242–243
by the High Priest, 405
of Job, 403
keri'ah (tearing of the garment), 58, 121, 290–291,
        403
kevod ha-met, 54, 79, 82, 93, 198, 293, 366, 377,
        419
kevod he-chai, 293
leaving house of mourning, 40–41
meals of, 189, 462
mitzvot, exemption from for onein, 27
Mo'ed Katan (tractate) on, 531
mourning rites, 4
music banned during, 357–358
nichum aveilim, 124–125, 365. *See also* Mourners and
        mourning
of non-Jews, 112, 386
by Priests, 405–406
prohibited periods of, 495
on Purim, 416, 417
on the Sabbath, 374, 452
sheloshim, 55, 171, 323, 488, 556, 606
of suicides, 39, 514–515
talmudic tractate on, 173
tefillin and, 542
Temples, destruction of, 125, 210–211, 299, 357–
        358, 462, 607–608. *See also* Fasting and fast
        days
Three Weeks, 85, 478, 551, 583
weddings prohibited during, 583
when apostasy occurs, 38–39
Yizkor services, 166, 238, 602–603
yud bet chodesh, 44, 606
Mouths, 19, 575. *See also* Speech
Movement during prayer, 399–404, 566
Moving, mezuzot and, 339–340
Mowshowitz, Rabbi Israel, 524
Mozna'yim, 613
Mufti of Jerusalem, 585
Muktzah, 356, 449, 476
Multiple wives. *See* Polygamy
Mumar, 35, 334, 356. *See also* Apostates and apostasy
Mumchim, 458

Munich manuscript, 528

Murder and murderers. *See also* Anti-Semitism
autopsies and, 55
capital punishment for, 90–91
as cardinal sin, 262
of fetus, 1
masturbation compared to, 327
mercy killing. *See* Euthanasia
Noahide Laws and, 367
physical abuse of women and, 63
pikuach nefesh and, 395
Ten Commandments and, 546
unintentional, 119
yeihareig ve-al ya'avor, 309

Murex snail, 523

Murray, Kathleen, 56

Musaf (services), 3, 356
Kaddish of, 282
origin of, 520
of Rosh Chodesh, 443
of Rosh Hashanah, 445, 497
of Sabbath, 448
Yekum Purkan (prayer) and, 599
of Yom Kippur, 57, 255, 400, 605

Musar, 163, 169, 356–357, 601. *See also* Ethics; Leshon
ha-kodesh; Moral standards

Music, 357–358, 450, 452, 476, 502. *See also*
Cantillations; Songs and singing

Muslims. *See also* Arabs; Non-Jews
Cave of Makhpelah, control of, 92
circumcision practices, 118
Crusades and, 30, 430
intermarriage with, 264–265
Jewish communities under control of, 468
monotheism of, 11
polygamy of, 397–398

Mutilation, 54, 538. *See also* Autopsies

Muvchar, 196

My American Journey (Powell), 480

Myerson, Morris, 611

Myrrh, 510

Myrtle, 41, 112, 120, 191–192, 194–197, 516. *See also*
Arba kanfot

Mystics and mysticism, 20, 358–360, 383. *See also*
Angels; Astrology; Kabbalah and kabbalists;
Secrets of the Torah

N

Naamat, 63

Na'anuim, 402. *See also* Lulav

Na'arah, 61. *See also* Bat Mitzvah

Nablus, 456

Nachalah, 597. *See also* Yahrzeit

Nachamu, nachamu ami, 86

Nachman (Rabbi), 230

Nachman bar Isaac, 53, 213, 239

Nachmanides, Rabbi Moses, 7, 278
on aliyah to Israel, 12, 537
on astrology, 53
on birth control, 71
on construction of the Tabernacle, 383
deathbed atonement, 125–126
on headcoverings, 243
on Jewish claims to Israel, 266
on marriage, 322, 473
overview of, 431
on quorum for prayer, 399
rishonim era and, 527
on sexual relations, 474
on shaatnez, 476–477
on superstition, 517
on treatment of animals, 571
on world of souls, 243
yeshiva of, 600

Nachman of Bratzlav, 106

Nadav (son of Aaron), 290, 405

Nahmani, Ruti, 518

Nakedness, 262

Names and naming
acrostics, 3
of boys. *See* Circumcision
of converts, 133
of girls, 346, 362
of Haman, 333
history and practices, 361–364
illness, changing as result of, 143, 363–364
of parents, 323
secular, 250
of spouses, 323, 362
surnames, 409, 518

Names of God, 18, 23–24, 177, 212–215, 332, 509,
517, 545. *See also* Berakhah le-vatalah; Chillul Ha-
Shem; Kiddush Ha-Shem

Naomi, 133, 232, 297, 484. *See also* Ruth, Book of

Napoleonic era, 289–290, 309, 458

Nappacha, Isaac, 14

Narcissus, 191

Narrative. *See* Aggadah

Nashim (tractate), 347, 482, 531, 567. *See also* Mishnah

Nasi family of Turkey, 500

Nasi of Palestine (Prince), 17, 22, 65, 364, 375–376, 420,
458, 614. *See also* Judah the Prince

Nasser, Gamal Abdel, 268, 269

Natal, Brazil, 322

Nathan the Babylonian, 526, 555

National Authority for the Preservation of Ladino
Culture, 469

National Federation of Men's Clubs, 127

National Federation of Temple Youth (NFTY), 425

National Jewish Population Survey of 1990, 131

Natla, 233. *See also* Handwashing

Natronai Gaon, 429

Natural births, 392. *See also* Birth

Natural remedies, 193. *See also* Health

Natural selection. *See* Evolution

Natural waters. *See* Mikveh

Nature, 160, 179, 345, 359, 432. *See also* Beauty and beautification

Navon, Yitzchak, 469

Nazarenes, 453. *See also* Christians and Christianity

Nazirites, 51, 227, 364, 395, 513, 531, 586. *See also* Asceticism

Nazis, 32, 92, 187, 208–209, 251–252, 324, 613. *See also* Holocaust

Nebo, Mount, 545

Nebukhadnezzar, King, 42, 86, 93, 146, 156, 188, 543–544. *See also* Babylonia

Neckchains. *See* Amulets

Neckties, 107, 113

Necromancy, 209

Nedarim, 531. *See also* Annulment of vows; Vows

Nedavah, 364

Needy. *See* Charity

Nefesh, 1, 119, 555. *See also* Souls

Nega'im (tractate), 534

Negative commandments, 10, 306, 349. *See also* Commandments

Negative counting, 368

Nehardea, Babylonia, 22–23, 47, 181, 352

Nehemiah (Book of), 445

Nehemiah (Rabbi), 412

Nehemiah ben Yosef, 308

Neighbors. *See* Property

Ne'ilah, 45, 497, 605. *See also* Yom Kippur

Nekamah, 439–440. *See also* Revenge

Ner, 89. *See also* Candles and candlelighting; Light

Ner ma'aravi, 169

Ner tamid, 169, 231

Neshamas. *See* Souls

Neshekh, 352. *See also* Interest payments

Nesi'at kapa'yim, 407–408

Nesi'im. *See* Nasi (Prince)

Nes la-goyim, 250

Netaneh Tokef (prayer), 96, 364

Netanyahu, Benjamin, 270

Netilat yada'yim (blessing), 233. *See also* Handwashing

Netirah, 439–440. *See also* Grudges

Neturei Karta, 365

Netzach (in kabbalah), 280

Neumann, Abraham, 48

Neumark, Rabbi David, 60

Neutral. *See* Pareve foods

Neutralization of forbidden mixtures. *See* Batel b'shishim

Nevi'im (Prophets), 3, 536. *See also* Tanakh

Newborns. *See* Babies

New Christians. *See* Marranos

New Colossus, The (Lazarus), 611

New Moon. *See* Rosh Chodesh

New Testament, 31, 67, 378. *See also* Christians and Christianity

New Year (Jewish). *See* Rosh Hashanah

New Year (tractate), 530–531

New Year for Trees, 98

New Year's Day (secular), 112–113

New York Times, The, 253

Nezikin (tractate), 347, 482, 531–532, 567. *See also* Mishnah

Nicanor's Day, 415

Nichts, 102

Nichum aveilim, 124–125, 365. *See also* Mourners and mourning

Niddah laws, 302, 341–342, 365–366, 418, 472, 474, 534, 554. *See also* Menstruation; Mikveh

Niddui, 177. *See also* Excommunication

Nieces, 263

Niftar, 172, 318. *See also* Death

Night. *See also* Ma'ariv (prayers)
    angel of conception and, 197–198
    Creation of, 176
    delineation of days and, 84
    funerals and demons, 80
    Lilith as female demon of, 315
    midnight prayers, 551
    sunset, 84, 89
    temperature of, 329, 330
    Torah study during, 483, 552

Night of Broken Glass (Kristallnacht), 251

1948 War of Independence, 273, 584

1967 Six-Day War, 92, 268–269, 273, 553–554, 584

1973 War, 268–269

Nineteenth benediction, 164

Ninety-five Theses. *See* Luther, Martin

Nishmat Kol Chai (prayer), 455–456

Nissan, 84, 85, 330, 444, 598. *See also* Passover

Nissim ben Jacob, 602

Nistar, 304

Nisuin, 165, 322, 366. *See also* Kiddushin; Marriage; Weddings

Nisukh ha-ma'yim, 502

Nitl Nacht, 202–203

Nittai of Arbela, 614

Nitzavim (haftarah portion), 496

Nivul ha-met, 54, 79, 198, 366, 377. *See also* Autopsies

Noah, 86, 467, 505, 543, 557, 570

Noahide Laws, 105, 255, 366, 367, 370, 549

Noda Bi-Yehudah (Landau), 433, 520, 571, 581. *See also* Landau, Rabbi Ezekiel ben Yehudah

Noi mitzvah, 158. *See also* Hiddur mitzvah

Noise, 144, 174, 210, 333, 415–416, 544, 559, 576

Nondairy creamer, 40, 320, 386
Non-Jews. See also Arabs; Christians and Christianity;
        Civil law; Jewish identity and status; Moslems
    acceptance from. See Assimilation; Haskalah
        movement
    akum, description, 11
    aliyot (Torah honors), prohibition of, 16, 66
    burial of, 265
    chametz sold to, 98, 310
    chukat ha-goy, 112–113
    circumcision by, 351
    deceit toward, 142
    emigration·to Israel, 13
    fathers. See Matrilineal descent
    food cooked by, 310
    Gentiles, referred to as, 206–207
    gifts to, 113
    hekdeish care of. See Illness
    as host-mothers, 259
    interest charged to, 352–353
    Kaddish for, 386
    Law of Return and, 309
    mourning, 386
    Noahide Laws, 105, 255, 366, 367, 370, 549
    Nuremberg Laws and, 251
    organ transplants from, 377
    as pallbearers, 199
    patrilineal descent and, 390
    pidyon ha-ben and, 393
    righteousness of, 253
    Sabbath and, 36, 447
    sabbatical years and, 310, 491
    selling homes to, 340
    shaygetz and shiksa terms for, 485
    stealing from, 410
    as surrogate mothers, 518
    synagogue attendance and, 41, 264
    tohorah performed by, 419
    Torah scrolls and, 418
    wine touched by, 586
    work done by on Sabbath, 40, 320–321
Nonkosher food. See also Kashrut
    animals, 61, 548–549
    apostates and, 35
    blessings and, 75
    Daniel, not eaten by, 416
    Esther, not eaten by, 416
    gidin of, 209
    markets, 41
    punishment for selling. See Civil law
    tomatoes as, 121
Nonporous articles, kashering, 388
North, 26, 144, 210–211
Norway, 486
Nose and nostrils, 142, 507, 509, 575. See also Scents

Nostra Aetate, 32
Notarikon, 2
Notes. See Kvitlach (notes)
Nullification of forbidden mixtures.
        See Batel b'shishim
Nullification of marriage. See Get (divorce document)
Nullification of vows. See Kol Nidrei (prayer)
Numbers (Book of). See Five Books of Moses
Numbers and values, 325, 367–371, 507. See also
        Gematriah; specific numbers by name
Nun (Hebrew letter), 3, 19, 102, 368, 521
Nuna, 19
Nuremberg Laws, 251. See also Holocaust
Nuremberg war crimes trial, 253
Nuriel, 26
Nursing mothers, 71
Nurturing. See Children
Nusachim, 89–90, 371–372. See also Cantillations
Nutrition, 192–193. See also Food
Nuts, 54, 59, 446, 461–462

O

Oaths. See Vows
Oats, 98, 328, 388. See also Grains
Obadiah the convert, 130, 431, 512–513
Oberammergau, Germany, 33
Objects, holy. See Holy and holiness, objects of
Objects, inanimate. See Anthropomorphism of God
Obligation. See Commandments
Occupations, 518. See also Labor (work)
Oceans, 9. See also Water
Offense. See Revenge; Sins and sinners
Offerings. See Sacrifices
Offspring. See Children
Ofrah, 361
Oholot, 373, 406, 533. See also Gravesites
Oil, 87–88, 99, 169, 193, 405, 534. See also Candles and
        candlelighting
Olam ha-ba. See World to come
Olam ha-emet, 5
Olam ha-menuchah, 5
Olam ha-nefashot, 5, 243
Olam she-kulo tov, 5
Old age, 8
Old City of Jerusalem, 268, 273. See also Jerusalem;
        Western Wall
Old Testament. See Tanakh
Oleh. See Aliyah (to Israel); Aliyah (Torah honor)
Olives, 100, 189, 193, 608. See also Oil; Seven species of
        Israel
Omens, 53, 156, 446. See also Mystics and mysticism;
        Superstition
Omer
    Lag Ba-Omer, 81, 85, 303–304, 583

offerings, 373, 598
    sefirat ha-omer, 273, 303, 370–371, 373, 467, 483,
        583
Omnipresence of God. See Shekhinah
Onah, 472–473. See also Sexual relations
Onanism, 58, 312, 326–327, 373. See also Hashchatat
        zera; Masturbation
Oneg Shabbat, 373–374, 448, 495
One hundred prayers per day, 164, 497
"One Hundred Rabbis" principle, 153
Onein, 27, 355, 374, 542. See also Aninut
Oneness of God. See Monotheism
Onions, 141, 193
Onkelos, 133, 338, 470, 512, 536–537
On the Jews and Their Lies (Luther), 31. See also Luther,
        Martin
Open mem. See Final letters
Opera, 321
Operation Desert Storm, 56
Operation Moses, 183
Operations (medical), 377, 396. See also Medical
        intervention
Opinions. See Dogma and Judaism
Oppenheimer, Samuel, 135
Oppression. See Anti-Semitism; Redemption; Slavery
        (Egyptian); Slavery (Hebrew)
Orach Cha'yim, 307, 500. See also Code of Jewish Law
        (Caro)
Or Adonai (Crescas), 198. See also Crescas, Rabbi Chasdai
Oral Law, 306, 374–375, 379, 392, 438, 529–535, 556.
        See also Gemara; Jewish law; Mishneh Torah;
        Talmud; Torah
Oranges, 462
Orators, 22
Orchards. See Fruits and fruit trees; Paradise
Orchestras. See Music
Ordination, 22, 65, 375–377, 380. See also Rabbis
    abolished by Roman government, 458
    of exorcists, 181
    overview of, 375–377, 467
    by Reconstructionist movement, 422
    by Reform Judaism, 425
    semikhah, defined, 375–377
    of women, 163–164, 376–377, 421, 422, 426–427,
        595–596
Organ donations, 293, 607
Organ music, 358, 424
Organs (body), 55, 167, 293, 607
Oriental Jews, 468
Original Sin, 377–378, 456, 503, 590
Origins of life. See Creation; Evolution
Orlah, 378, 530
Ornaments, Torah, 226, 299, 558–561
Orot Ha-kodesh, 176. See also Kook, Rabbi Abraham
        Isaac

Orpah, 297
Orphans, 4, 122, 162, 451. See also Kaddish (prayer)
Orrechi d'Aman, 416
Orthodoxy, 126, 151, 378–380, 422, 600–601
Or Yisra'el (Belzer), 163, 357
Or Zaru'a (Isaac of Vienna), 38, 240, 284
Oshry, Rabbi Ephraim, 46, 339
Oslo Accords, 269, 443
"Other One, The". See Acher
Other Side. See Satan
Otiyot stam, 509. See also Scribes
Otot, 190. See also Flags and emblems
Outreach, 107, 290
"Outside Books", 34
Ovadiah of Bertinoro, 450, 461
Oveid kokhavim u-mazalot, 11
Oveir la'asiyatam, 195
Ovum. See Artificial insemination; Host-mothers
Ownership. See Property; Public vs. private
Oxen, 18, 85, 317, 613
Oznei Haman, 416

P

Paganism, 99. See also Idolatry and idol worshippers
Pagim, 446
Pain, 27, 150, 173–175, 260, 340, 427, 456. See also
        Illness
Paintings. See Art and sculpture
Pairs. See Shidukhin; Zugot
Pairs of the Anshei Knesset Ha-Gedolah, 300
Paitanim, 501. See also Poets and poetry
Palestine (history of), 608–610. See also Canaan; Israel
        (modern state)
    Arabs, 267–270, 365, 585
    headcoverings and, 240
    Roman occupation of, 5, 28. See also Roman
        government and Romans
Palestine Economic Corporation, 610
Palestine Endowment Fund, 610
Palestinian scholars, 8, 22–23, 375, 526. See also Talmud
    Ezra the Scribe and, 316–317
    ordination of, 375–376, 420
    overview of, 536
    responsa literature of, 428
    Shema (prayer) recitation, 489
    triennial cycle of Torah readings, 337
    Yavneh academy, 346
Pallbearers, 199. See also Funerals
Palm branches, 41, 94–95, 194–197, 516. See also Four
        species
Pancakes, potato, 101
Panim, 213. See also Face
Pans and pots, 307, 388, 549
Pants, 107

Papacy (Catholic Church), 29–33, 528
Pappus ben Judah, 8
Parables. *See* Aggadah
Paradise, 7, 36, 312, 381. *See also* Garden of Eden; World
    to come
Paradise Lost (Milton), 57
Parah adumah. *See* Red heifer
Paran, 504
Parashot (Torah readings), 501–502, 563
Parchments, 37, 338, 507–509, 539–540, 558. *See also*
    Scribes; Tefillin
Pardeis, 381–384. *See also* Farmers and farming; Fruits
    and fruit trees; Paradise
Pardoning. *See* Forgiveness; Selichot (prayers)
Parents. *See also* Adoption; Babies; Family and family life;
    Fathers and fatherhood; Grandparents; Mothers
    and motherhood
    adoption, 4
    bar mitzvah, role in, 59
    calling by name, 323
    cursing, crime of, 91
    godparents. *See* Kvater and kvaterin; Sandek
    honoring, 4, 134–135, 385–386, 422, 513, 546
    Kaddish for apostates, 39
    Kiddushin (tractate) on, 531
    mourning of, 4, 284–285, 488, 606. *See also* Kaddish
        (prayer); Mourners and mourning
    as partners with God, 385
Pareve foods, 40, 151, 320, 386. *See also* Kashrut
Parnassim, 14
Parokhet, 445
Parshandata, 430. *See also* Rashi
Parshat Ha-Chodesh, 477
Parties, 516–517. *See also* Celebrations
Parush, 392
Pasach. *See* Passover
Paschal lamb, 85, 328, 386, 392, 462. *See also* Matzot;
    Passover
    afikomon representative of, 465
    circumcision preceding, 132
    Four Questions of Passover and, 464
    Hillel's sandwich and, 465
    origin of custom of, 459–460
    sacrifice of, 478
    Samaritan sacrifice of, 457
Passion of the Christ, The, 33
Passion Play, 33
Passive euthanasia, 173–175, 340
Passover. *See also* Omer; Sefirat ha-omer; Slavery
    (Egyptian)
    aliyot (Torah honors) given on, 14
    appointed time of, 83
    babies born on, 362
    bedikat chametz, 64
    bi'ur chametz, 73

burial following, 171
Chad Gadya (song), 24, 94, 466–467
Chol Ha-Moed of, 318
cleaning the home for. *See also* Passover
clothing for, 121, 298, 460
Conservative Judaism policy on, 128
dietary laws of, 387–389
extra day added to, 387, 606
as family celebration, 184
fasting on, 186
food of, 151
history and significance of, 386–389
Israel, observance in, 128
Isru Chag, 271
Jesus Christ's arrest on, 29, 139–140
lulav saved for, 196, 387–389
maftir of, 17
Maimouna, 319
omer offering brought before, 373
overview of, 248
Pesachim (tractate), 530
Pharisees on, 454
post-Temple observance, 460
prayers and blessings of, 230, 455–456
pre-Exodus celebration of, 386
Sabbath of, 227
sacrifices of, 190, 423, 453, 462. *See also* Paschal lamb
Samaritans and, 457
Seder
    Da'yeinu (song), 141
    Elijah's Cup, 166
    Four Sons of Passover, 464
    Haggadah, 2, 180, 227, 341, 460, 468, 599
    handwashing and, 234
    Jerusalem, hopes for, 272
    salt water, 455
    seven, significance of, 370–371
    Shavuot, concluded by, 53
    Tal (prayer), 522
    Torah portions preceding, 477–478, 479
    Yizkor services of, 602–603
    Yom Tov, defined, 606
Pasul, 344, 525
Patai, Raphael, 276
Patar, 318
Pathan tribesmen, 548
Path of the Upright (Luzzatto), 440
Patience, 366, 389, 550
Patients. *See* Illness
Pat lechem, 231. *See also* Bread
Patriarch (office of). *See* Nasi (Prince)
Patriarchs (fathers), 389. *See also* Abraham; Arba
    Imma'hot; Isaac; Jacob
    burial of, 92
    hamantaschen, represented by, 416

names of in Mi Shebeirakh (prayer) and, 346
naming after, 363
number three and, 368–369
represented at Torah readings, 564
resurrection of, 383
telata gavrei represented by, 14
zekhut avot, 608
Patrilineal descent, 134, 276, 328, 389–390. See also
   Jewish identity and status
Patur, 318
Paul, Saint, 11, 51, 92, 118, 363, 378, 440–441. See also
   New Testament
Paul I, Czar, 348
Peace, 390–391. See also Compromise; Good and
   goodness; Goodwill principle
   arbitration and, 42
   as foundation of the world, 567
   Messianic Age and, 335
   mipnei kevod tzibur, 293–294, 345, 563, 593
   pact between Jacob and Laban, 511–512
   with Palestinians, 585
   prayers for, 480
   Sabbath as day of, 452
   sacrifices of, 453. See also Sacrifices
   "shalom" translation, 481
   shelom ba'yit, 487–488, 568–569
   talmidei chakhamim and, 525
   white lies and, 257–258
Peas, 98, 416
Pederasty, 129
Pei'ah, 103, 529
Pei/fei, 19, 368
Pei'ot, 58, 107, 228, 229, 576
Penalties. See Punishment
Pendant-charms. See Amulets
Penis. See Circumcision; Genitalia
Penitence. See Repentance; Yom Kippur
Pens. See Writing instruments
Pentateuch, 381–384, 391, 508, 536, 556. See also Five
   Books of Moses; Septuagint; Torah
Pentateuch and Haftorahs (Hertz), 176. See also Hertz,
   Rabbi Joseph H.
Pentecost, 483. See also Shavuot
Pepper, 455
Perata, Rabbi Eleazar, 311
Perception. See Appearances
Perek Ha-Shalom (tractate), 536
Peres, Shimon, 269–270
Perfection of the world. See Tikkun olam
Peri'ah, 117
Permission. See Heter mei'ah rabbanim
Persecution. See Anti-Semitism; Punishment
Persia and Persians, 29, 460, 500–501. See also Esther
   and Book of Esther; Purim
Personal appearance. See Appearances; Clothing; Hygiene

Personal conduct. See Conduct; Derekh eretz
Perushim. See Pharisees
Pesach. See Paschal lamb; Passover
Pesachim (tractate), 392, 530
Pesach Sheini, 392
Pesat, Rabbi, 337
Pesha, 503. See also Sins and sinners
Pesharah. See Compromise
Peshat, 381
Pesikta Rabbati, 351
Pesukei De-Zimra (prayers), 288–289, 480
Peter, Saint, 118, 363, 483
Peter kol rechem, 392. See also Firstborn son
Petil tekheilet, 120, 523, 574–575
Pharaoh, 28, 72, 156. See also Egypt
Pharisees, 5–6, 392, 436, 502
Philistines, 43
Philo of Alexandria, 137, 154–155, 343, 497
Philosophy, 179, 203, 421–422, 431–432, 435–436. See
   also Aristotle
Photographs, 48, 555
Phylacteries. See Tefillin
Physical abnormalities, 49, 72
Physical abuse of women, 62–63, 153
Physical appearance. See Modesty
Physical contact with opposite sex, 291, 298, 498. See
   also Niddah laws
Physical resurrection of the dead. See Resurrection
Physical world. See World (earthly)
Physicians, 117, 409. See also Medical intervention
Pictures. See Art and sculpture; Photographs
Pidyon ha-ben, 135, 392–394, 407, 409
Pidyon shevu'yim, 394, 451
Piety, 240–241, 395, 400, 437, 566. See also Chasid
   shoteh; Chasidim and chasidut; Holy and holiness;
   Justice; Lamed vovniks
Pigeon sacrifices, 366. See also Sacrifices
Pigs, 148, 149, 321, 324, 377. See also Kashrut
Pikuach nefesh, 55, 356, 377, 395–396, 409, 443, 447,
   571–572
Pilate, Pontius, 28–29, 33, 139
Pilgrim Festivals, 396, 453, 531, 602–603, 606. See also
   Passover; Shavuot; Sukkot
Pill, the, 71–72
Pillows, 460–461, 464, 511
Pilpul, 396
Pinchas, 440
Pincus ben Yair, 260–261
Pious people, 2, 6, 53, 108, 303, 333. See also Chasidim
   and chasidut; Gemilut chasadim; Martyrdom;
   Righteousness
Pirkei Avot, 529, 532, 535
Pisces (zodiacal sign), 85, 613
Pittamim, 195. See also Citron
Pittsburgh Platform, 426

Pius IV, Pope, 30–31
Pius X, Pope, 32
Pius XI, Pope, 32, 76
Piyyutim, 398–399, 445. *See also* Prayers and blessings
Places as names, 361
Plagues (Ten), 2, 185–186, 188, 464
Plagues (upon Jews), 145, 368
Planets. *See* Astrology; Constellations; Earth; Moon; Sun
Plants. *See* Flowers; Gardens; Trees
Plaques, Mizrach, 349–350
Plastic, kashering, 388
Plates, breaking of, 299, 544
Platform. *See* Bimah
Plato, 455
Pledges, 410. *See also* Loans
PLO (Palestine Liberation Organization), 269–270, 365
Plots. *See* Cemeteries
Plow, 18
Pockets, 499
Poets and poetry, 3, 350, 398–399, 445, 466, 501. *See also* Prayers and blessings
Pogroms, 397, 611
Pointers for Torahs, 558, 560
Poison, 24
Poland, 397
Police, 365
Political Zionism. *See* Zionists and Zionism
Pollux, 369. *See also* Astrology
Polygamy, 153, 178, 245–246, 313, 397–398, 410, 594
Polytheism. *See* Idolatry and idol worshippers
Pomegranates, 189, 247, 446. *See also* Seven species of Israel
Pontshkes, 101
Pools. *See* Mikveh
Poor and poverty, 60. *See also* Hebrew slaves
    aliyot (Torah honors) given to, 554
    bikkurim offerings, modern reenactment of, 190
    burial of, 119
    charity from the poor, 122
    equated with death, 94
    food for, 205
    Hebrew slaves and, 506
    matanot le-evyonim, 414
    Pei'ah (tractate) on, 529
    "poor-man's tithe", 103, 553
    sabbatical years and, 276
    Shemittah and, 491
Population and demographics in Israel, 271, 389–390
Population Registry Law, 308
Pork, 148, 149, 321, 324, 377. *See also* Kashrut
Porous articles, kashering, 388
Portugal, 147, 321, 468
Posek, Rabbi Hillel, 211
Positive Commandments, 306, 349. *See also* Commandments

Positive Historical Judaism, 127
Possessed. *See* Dybbuks
Possessions. *See* Property
Post-mortem dissection. *See* Autopsies
Posture during prayer, 403, 407–408, 541
Potato latkes, 101
Pottery, 307, 388, 549
Powell, Colin, 479–480
Power (electricity). *See* Electricity
Power (strength), 280, 442
Practices, non-Jewish. *See* Chukat ha-goy
Praise for God, 25, 56. *See also* Prayers and blessings
Prayerbooks, 318. *See also* Bible; Haggadah
    beautification of, 47–48
    dropped, 298
    for kissing the Torah, 298, 565
    Reconstructionist, 180
    of Sa'adya Gaon, 288
    Sephardic term for, 468
    siddurim, defined, 501
    Siddur of Rav Amram Gaon, 429
    Ten Commandments excluded from, 547
    unusable. *See* Genizah
    of the Vilna Gaon, 226
Prayers and blessings, 22, 73–75, 347, 398–404. *See also* Poets and poetry; Psalms; *specific prayers by name*; Thanksgiving prayers; Torah readings
    acrostics within, 3
    adding to, 59
    of aliyot (Torah honors) given to, 561–562
    Amen response, 21–22
    atonement through, 125. *See also* Yom Kippur
    bar mitzvah, 61
    berakhah, source of term, 73
    "blessed", 21
    carrots representative of, 446
    in cemeteries, 94
    for death, 175
    end of, 3
    for exorcism, 181
    genuflecting of, 400–401
    headcoverings and, 240–241
    introductions to, 288–289
    from Jacob to Joseph, 181
    Jerusalem, in direction of, 43–44, 350, 369, 404, 520
    kavanah during, 288–289, 359, 402
    kvitlach and, 302
    language of, 25, 398–399
    Men of the Great Assembly and, 300, 333
    mirrors and, 495
    mourner, exemption from, 27
    one hundred a day, 164, 497
    oneinim not obligated in, 355, 374
    physical expressions of, 399–404
    recited simultaneously, 15

as repentance, 427–428
for the ruling government, 309
sacrifices, in lieu of, 56, 398, 453
speaking during, 165
as testimony to God, 15
in the vernacular, 126, 398–399, 424, 538
Prayer services. *See* Congregations; Services; Synagogues
Prayershawl. *See* Tallitot
Preaching. *See* Sermons
Precautions. *See* Birth control; Fences around the Torah
Predetermination. *See* Free will
Pregnancy, 1–2, 23, 143, 195, 472. *See also* Babies;
      Birth control; Conception; Fruitful and multiply
      commandment
Preliminary prayers. *See* Pesukei De-Zimra (prayers)
Premarital sex, 474–475, 498
Presents. *See* Gifts
Preservation principle, 160
Preservation stone, 23
Preserving life. *See* Pikuach nefesh
President Masaryk Tells His Story (Capek), 76–77
President of Israel, 364
Presley, Elvis, 480
Pride. *See* Dignity
Priesand, Sally J., 376, 421, 595
Priestly Benediction, 21–22, 59, 70, 181, 228, 232, 261,
      402, 407–408, 480, 519
Priests (Kohanim). *See also* Levites
      airplane travel by, 406
      aliyot (Torah honors) given to, 13, 16
      assistants to. *See* Levites
      cemeteries, prohibited from, 94, 115, 555
      challah given to, 95–96, 530
      clothing of, 122
      dead, proximity to, 373
      face coverings of, 408
      garments of, 157
      hair of, 228
      hands of, 215, 233
      headcoverings of, 238
      lineage of, 393, 405
      marriage of, 135, 323, 405, 406–407, 409
      matzot representing, 329, 461
      menorah kindled by, 334
      natural inheritance of status, 4
      omer offering brought before, 598
      as one-third of Jewish community, 369
      overview of, 404–407
      patrilineal descent and, 390
      pidyon ha-ben ceremonies and, 393
      preparation for reintroduction of sacrifices, 454
      Priests by Presumption, 406, 408–409
      privileges and responsibilities of, 407
      purity of, 405–406
      as rabbis (modern times), 406

Reconstructionist views on, 180
rights of denied to apostates, 37
as Sadducees, 454
Sanhedrin investigations of, 122
terumah gifts to, 549
tithes given to, 553
tumah laws and, 373, 418
white clothing for, 419
wine prohibited to, 586
Primordial light, 590
Prince. *See* Nasi
Principles, Jewish. *See* Chosen People; Commandments;
      Customs and law; Dogma and Judaism; Faith;
      Jewish law; Monotheism; Prayers and blessings;
      Torah; Values, Jewish
Prisoners, 94, 394. *See also* Slavery (Hebrew)
Proceedings of the Rabbinical Assembly (1950), 451–452
Processions. *See* Funerals
Produce. *See* Fruits and fruit trees; Harvest
Productivity, 446
Profanation of God's Name, 367, 410. *See also* Chillul
      Ha-Shem
Prolonging life. *See* Pikuach nefesh
Promised Land. *See* Land of Israel
Promises. *See* Annulment of vows; Vows
Pronouncing the names of God, 213–214
Prop (support), 19
Propagation. *See* Fruitful and multiply commandment
Property. *See also* Inheritance
      acquiring, 245
      burial sites as, 93
      chazakah claim, 109
      Jewish people as God's possession, 110
      Me'ilah (tractate) on, 533
      Nezikin (tractate) on, 531–532
      organ transplants and, 377
      ownership of chametz and, 310
      sabbatical years, returned during, 276
      slaves as, 506
      transfers of, 232
      wives as, 587
Prophets and prophecy (Nevi'im), 14, 20, 156, 316, 345,
      363, 412–413. *See also* Elijah the Prophet; *specific
      prophets by name*; Tanakh
Prosbul, 310, 413–414, 491. *See also* Sabbatical years,
      debts and
Proselytes. *See* Converts and conversion
Prosperity, 238, 446
Prossnitz, Leibele, 336
Prostitutes, 323, 406
Prostration, 400–401, 445, 521. *See also* Idolatry and idol
      worshippers
"Protected Jews", 352–353
Protection from evil powers. *See* Amulets; Demons and
      demonology; Psalms; Segulot

Protestantism, 31, 208. *See also* Christians and Christianity

Protocols of the Elders of Zion, The, 31–32

Prozdor, 6

Pru u-revu. *See* Fruitful and multiply commandment

Psalmist, The (King David). *See* David, King

Psalms. *See also* Hallel (prayers); Poets and poetry;
      Prayers and blessings
  acrostics within, 3
  antidemonic, 23
  Ashrei (prayer) and, 52
  music and, 357
  as protection from evil eye, 56
  Psalm 114, 230
  Psalm 115, 230
  Psalm 116, 230
  Psalm 119, 81–82
  Psalm 136, 230
  Psalm 19, 238
  Psalm 91, 23, 56, 145, 181, 199–200, 370
  used in place of counting with numbers, 368

Pseudepigrapha, 414. *See also* Apocrypha

Ptolemy II, King, 371, 469, 470

Public vs. private. *See also* Community
  carrying, 332
  mezuzot for, 339, 340
  prayers and, 399, 404
  privacy and, 409–410
  private violation of the Sabbath, 36–37
  Sabbath and, 36–37, 167–169, 452

Pulpit, 13, 16, 294. *See also* Bimah

Pumbedita, Babylonia, 22, 203, 285, 313, 429, 600. *See also* Babylonia

Punishment. *See also* Excommunication; Hell; Penalties
  afterlife and, 5–6
  aveirah for an aveirah, 349
  of children, 513
  eye-for-an-eye principle, 381
  of Job, 441
  leprosy as, 341
  plagues, 368
  for sex outside of marriage, 475
  for sodomy, 256
  tokheichah and, 554

Purgatory. *See* Hell

Purification. *See* Immersion; Purity and impurity

Purim. *See also* Amalek and Amalekites
  Adloyada Purim Carnival, 3, 326, 417
  Ahasueros, King, 327
  aliyot (Torah honors) given on, 14
  anti-Semitism, beginning of, 28
  babies born on, 362
  costumes and masquerading of, 326
  date of, 85
  drinking on, 586
  Falashas, not observed by, 182

Fast of Esther, 186, 187, 188, 415
  foods of, 97
  Halevi, Rabbi Yehuda, 479
  light and, 87
  maftir of, 318
  Megillah (tractate), 531
  Minor Purim, 187
  overview of, 248, 414–417
  prayers and blessings of, 12, 230
  Purim Katan, 187, 417
  revenge by Jews, 440
  Sabbath and, 332
  Shabbat Zakhor preceding, 479
  Vashti, 327

Purity and impurity. *See also* Cleanliness; Repentance
  chalalim, 323
  of corpses, 373, 418–419, 478
  definitions of, 418
  of divorced women, 323, 406
  following childbirth, 302
  gravesites, 115
  handwashing
    cemeteries and, 56, 94, 145, 201, 234–235, 261, 418
    cleanliness and, 261, 442
    ma'yim achronim, 234, 330
    before meals, 78, 233–235, 418, 534
    of Priests, 405
    right before left, 442
    at the Seder, 463
  kittls representative of purity, 121, 248, 298–299, 445, 460, 499, 581, 605
  matzah as symbol of, 98
  mikveh
    apostates, immersion of, 38
    converts, immersion by, 131–132, 275, 322, 341
    for kashering process, 387–388
    Mikva'ot (tractate), 534
    preceding Revelation, 132, 342, 369
    scribes and, 508
    tevilah, defined, 549
    virgin impregnated within, 50
    of women, 341–342, 366, 418, 554. *See also* Tohorat ha-mishpachah
  oholot, 373
  overview of, 418–419
  Passover sacrifice and, 423
  Pesach Sheini and, 392
  of Priests, 323, 405–406
  Priests (Kohanim) and, 373
  of the red heifer, 114, 422–424, 478, 534
  as result of homosexual acts, 432
  Revelation, prior to, 437
  tamei, 172, 418
  tohorot, 82, 173, 347, 418–419, 482, 533–534, 567. *See also* Chevrah kaddishah

tomatoes as, 121
of Torah scrolls, 558, 563
white as symbol of, 46, 121, 157, 445, 448, 498
of women. *See* Niddah laws
Purses, 449
Pursuer, law of, 443
Pushkes, 104–105

Q

Quills, 208, 571, 580
Qumran community, 169, 286. *See also* Essenes
Quorums, 59
apostates not counted in, 37–38
ark counted as member of, 45–46, 305
counting people for, 368
intermarriage and, 264
for Kaddish, 603
oneinim not counted in, 374
for pidyon ha-ben ceremony, 393
prayers of, 399
public assembly defined by, 410
Sabbath observance and, 37, 452, 487–488
for Sheva Berakhot (blessings), 492
for wedding ceremonies, 580–581
women and, 344
Yizkor services and, 603

R

Raba (title), 420
Rabba (Rava), 3, 397
Rabba bar Chama, 442
Rabba ben Chanan, 305
Rabba ben Joseph, 587
Rabbah, 288
Rabbana, 180
Rabbanit, 420
Rabbenu Gershom Me'or Ha-Golah, 38, 153, 178, 245,
  398, 409–410, 594, 600
Rabbenu Ha-Kodesh, Judah the Prince as, 458. *See also*
  Judah the Prince
Rabbenu Tam
  on birth control, 71
  on levirate marriages, 313
  on mezuzot, 339
  on quorums, 344
  rishonim era and, 430, 527
  on storing Torah scrolls, 44
  on tefillin, 540
  as Tosafist, 566
  yeshiva of, 600
Rabbi Isaac Elchanan Theological Seminary, 376, 379,
  421, 601. *See also* Yeshiva University
Rabbi Jacob Joseph School (RJJ), 600

Rabbinical Alliance of America, 380
Rabbinical Assembly of America, 92, 128, 256, 344, 435,
  592–593. *See also* Conservative Judaism
Rabbinical Council of America (RCA), 380, 517
Rabbinical courts. *See* Beit Din
Rabbinical laws, 286, 307, 457. *See also* Gezeirot of
  muktzah; Jewish law
Rabbi of Bachrach, The (Heine), 461
Rabbis. *See also* Beit Din; Ordination; Sermons
  Agudath Harabonim, 380
  Chief, 468
  as holy vessels, 249
  homosexuality of, 256
  Iggud Ha-Rabbanim, 380
  as klei kodesh, 299
  Kohanim as, 406
  overview of, 420–421
  Purim "rabbis", 417
  Rishon Le-Tziyon, 443
  talmidei chakhamim, 525
  title of, 22, 420
  women as. *See* Ordination, of women
Rabbis' Kaddish, 281–282. *See also* Kaddish (prayer)
Rabbi's Rovings, A (Mowshowitz), 524
Rabin, Yitzhak, 187–188, 269–270, 295, 300–301, 443,
  512
Rabina, 160, 516
Rabinowicz, Rabbi H., 138
Rachamim. *See* Mercy
Rachel (Matriarch), 2, 297, 327, 361, 555, 578, 580,
  587. *See also* Arba Imma'hot
Rachel's Tomb, 514
Rachmanut, 421. *See also* Compassion; Mercy
Rachmiel, 26
Racial purity. *See* Nazis
Rackman, Emanuel, 10
Rackman, Honey, 10
Radbaz, 288, 432
Rain, 24, 55, 207, 258, 298, 502, 522
Raising of the Torah, 126–127. *See also* Hagbahah and
  gelilah
Raisins, 54
Ram, 11, 85, 613. *See also* Shofar
Rama. *See* Isserles, Rabbi Moses
Ramatchal, 3
Rambam. *See* Maimonides, Rabbi Moses
Ramban. *See* Nachmanides
Ramchal. *See* Luzzatto, Rabbi Moses Chaim
Rams horns, 276–277, 496. *See also* Shofar
Ran, 174
Ransoms, 394, 451
Rape, 475
Raphael, 26
Raphall, Rabbi Morris J., 506
Rapoport, Rabbi Solomon J., 236

Rasha, 587. *See also* Robbers; Sins and sinners
Rashba, the, 66, 90, 547
Rashbam, 430, 566
Rashi
    on bal tosif, 59
    Bavli Talmud printing and, 528
    on Bible interpretations, 382
    on birth control, 71
    b'la'az, 303
    on burials, 145, 298–299
    on candlelighting, 88–89
    on cantillations, 232
    on comforting the mourner, 124–125
    commentaries on the Torah, 566
    on Creation, 137
    on death of newborns, 118
    on demons, 143
    on dreams, 157
    on eating while reclining, 460
    on evil, protection from, 517
    on fetus, status of, 1
    on funeral practices, 198, 200
    on Hallel, 108
    on headcoverings, 240, 242
    on honoring the dead, 112, 120, 192
    on immorality of Moab and Midian women, 440
    on Jacob (Patriarch), 383–384, 568
    on kissing, 298
    on matrilineal descent, 327
    on mezuzot, 339
    name of, 2
    on promises, 411–412
    on quorum for prayer, 399
    on Rebecca's pregnancy, 382
    rishonim era and, 430, 527
    on sexual relations, 473, 474
    on tefillin, 540
    on Tishrei, 370
    on Torah readings, 90, 564
    on tzitzit, 575
    on wisdom, 161
Rav (Abba Arikha), 23, 47
    on afterlife, 6, 436
    Aleinu, composition of, 11
    Birkat Ha-Chodesh, 69
    on Chanukkah, 100
    on chronology of the Torah, 558
    on discipline, 163
    on food, 192
    on hospitality, 259
    kavanah and, 288
    knife, cleaning, 308
    on labor, 303
    as marketing commissioner, 180
    on marriage, 580

    on masturbation, 327
    ordination title, 375
    on Paradise, 243
    on prosbul of Hillel, 413
    on salt, 455
    on tikkun olam, 552
Rava (Rabba), 3, 6
    on bikur cholim, 383
    on chavrutah, 108
    on heaven, 182
    on humility, 260
    on masturbation, 327
    prayers of, 402
    on Purim, 417
    sexual relations, definition of, 473
    on vengeance, 578
Ravad, 28, 63, 75
Ravina, 203, 204
Ravina II, 428, 526
"Rav" title, 22, 420. *See also* Rabbis
Razi'el (angel), 205
Razors, 228, 487–488
Readers. *See* Ba'al Korei
Reading. *See* Hebrew language; Torah readings; Words, Hebrew
Reading table. *See* Bimah
Reason, 179, 203, 421–422. *See also* Science; Understanding
Rebbes. *See* Chasidim and chasidut; Teachers and teaching
Rebecca (Matriarch), 92, 327, 382, 568, 578. *See also* Arba Imma'hot
Rebellion. *See* Heresy
Rebuke. *See* Three Haftarot of Rebuke; Tokheichah
Receiving of the Torah. *See* Revelation at Sinai
Rechabites, 51
Reclining, 460–461, 464
Reconciliation, 42
Reconstructionist movement, 179–180, 257, 376, 421, 422–423, 427, 595. *See also* Kaplan, Rabbi Mordecai
Red, 121, 280, 445, 498
Redemption, 284, 295, 447, 463, 614. *See also* Exodus (from Egypt); Messiah and Messianic Age; Salvation
Redemption of the firstborn son, 407. *See also* Pidyon ha-ben
Red heifer, 114, 422–424, 478, 534. *See also* Chukim
Red Sea, 345, 357, 437, 479, 480, 505
Reform Judaism
    Central Conference of American Rabbis statement on intermarriage, 264
    Columbus Platform, 426
    Committee on Responsa of the Central Conference of American Rabbis (1979), 308

Conservative Judaism and, 126
Haskalah movement and, 236
holiday observance of, 387
Kaplan, Rabbi Mordecai on, 422
ketubbot of, 587
ordination of women, 376
organ music and, 358
overview of, 424–427
patrilineal descent and, 389–390
Pittsburgh Platform, 426
Sofer, Rabbi Moses vs., 433
vernacular, prayers in, 399
Refuge, cities of, 119, 532
Regalim, 396. *See also* Pilgrim Festivals
Regret. *See* Repentance
Reich. *See* Germans and Germany; Nazis
Reidl, 328
Reincarnation, 427. *See also* Afterlife; Gilgulim
Reish, 20, 368
Relatives. *See* Family and family life
Relief funds. *See* Charity
Religion and peoplehood, 277
Religion of Israel (Kaufmann), 412
Religious Affairs Ministry in Israel, 514
Religious articles
    beauty of, 47–48, 64
    buying and selling of, 249–250
    hiddur mitzvah, 47–48
    hierarchy of sanctity, 249–250
    holiness of, 254
    kashrut of, 147
    kissing, 298
Religious obligations. *See* Commandments
Rema. *See* Isserles, Rabbi Moses
Remarriage. *See also* Marriage
    agunot, forbidden to, 9
    divorce and, 154, 207
    following childless marriage. *See* Levirate marriage
        practices
    ketubbah of original marriage and, 37
    to Priests (Kohanim), 135, 405, 406–407
    to spouse after divorce, 323
    without a get. *See* Mamzeirim
Remembrance. *See* Memory and remembrance
Remez, 381–383
Remorse. *See* Repentance
Rending garments, 403, 441–442
Renting, 339–340, 532, 607
Repair of the world. *See* Tikkun olam
Repentance. *See also* Atonement; Rosh Hashanah; Yom
        Kippur
    of apostates, 38
    ba'al teshuvah, 58, 112, 428
    flogging and, 191
    by Ishmael, 363

Netaneh Tokef and, 364
overview of, 427–428
on Rosh Hashanah, 445
Shabbat Shuvah, 479
Ten Days of Repentance, 51, 109, 371, 444–445,
        496–497, 547–548, 583, 597–598
Reports, 3
Reproduction. *See* Fertility issues; Fruitful and multiply
        commandment; Pregnancy
Rescue of women, 63, 108
Resh Lakish, 22, 161, 382–383, 503
Reshut, 45
Resnick, Judith, 89
Resolution. *See* Arbitration
Respect. *See* Honor and dignity
Responsa (Alfasi), 431. *See also* Alfasi of Fez
Responsa Literature, 428–435
Responsibility, 10, 11, 170, 318, 366, 422. *See also*
        Ethics; Free will
Rest, day of. *See* Sabbath
Rest, world of, 5
Restaurants, 310
Resurrection. *See also* Afterlife
    autopsy and, 54
    Burial Kaddish and, 283
    and cremation, opposition to, 138–139
    gilgul mechilot,, 209–210
    gilgul neshamot, 210
    grass-tossing and, 81
    of Jesus Christ, 483
    overview of, 435–437
    Pharisees, promotion of, 392, 454
    Pittsburgh Platform on, 426
    Reconstructionist views on, 180
    reward in, 441
    Sadducees on, 454
    shrouds as preparation for, 498
    of the soul only, 510
    Torah sources for, 383
    views on, 244
Retaliation, 238. *See* Vengeance
Retirement and aging, 8
Return to Judaism, 38, 58, 112, 275, 428, 479. *See also*
        Repentance
Retzu'ot, 540–541
Reuben (son of Jacob), 274
Reuben (tribe of), 548, 567
Revel, Rabbi Bernard, 379, 409
Revelation at Sinai, 306, 556–558. *See also* Shavuot;
        Written Law
    circumcision preceding, 132
    days of the week of, 562
    Gemini and, 369
    immersion preceding, 132, 342, 369
    Jews as the Chosen People, 110–111

Kaplan, Rabbi Mordecai on, 422
location of, 504
Maimonides, Rabbi Moses on, 179
Oral Law and, 374
Original Sin, purification from, 378
Orthodox view of, 379
overview of, 437–439
preparation for, 485
from the right side of God, 442
Shema and, 489
shofar used at, 496
Shofrot and, 497
swaying during, 402
taryag mitzvot and, 537
Ten Commandments and, 544
three, importance of number, 369
weddings compared to, 581
Revenge. *See* Vengeance
Reverence for the Dead. *See* Kevod ha-met
Reward and punishment, 5–6, 349, 441. *See also* Heaven;
    Hell
Ribbons, 291
Ribit, 352. *See also* Interest payments
Rice, 98, 389
Rich. *See* Wealth and wealthy
Rich matzah, 329. *See also* Matzot
Riding on the Sabbath, 424
RIETS (Rabbi Isaac Elchanan Theological Seminary), 434
Rif. *See* Alfasi of Fez
Righteous Judge, 441–442
Righteousness, 22, 197. *See also* Faith; Piety;
    Resurrection; Scholars
  of ba'al teshuvah, 428
  Book of Life and, 598
  burial of person of, 93
  Exodus in merit of women, 162
  lamed vovniks, 304, 371
  Messianic Age and, 335
  Noahide Laws and, 367
  of non-Jews, 105, 207, 253
  reward for, 6, 381, 436–437
  in Sodom, 344
  tzedakah and, 102
  world to come as reward for, 481
Right-handedness, 442–443, 507, 540–541, 560, 565
Rights of individuals. *See* Hasagat gevul
Rights of the apostate, 37–38. *See also* Apostates and
    apostasy
Rimmonim, 559
Ringelbaum, Emanuel, 441
Rings (circles). *See* Circles and circling
Rings (jewelry), 245, 581–582
Rioting. *See* Pogroms
Rishonim era, 430–432, 527. *See also* Acharonim; Later
    rishonim; Responsa Literature

Rishon Le-Tziyon, 443, 468
Rites of Birth, Marriage, and Death Among the Semites
    (Morgenstern), 80
Ritualariums. *See* Mikveh
Ritual cleanliness. *See* Handwashing; Hygiene; Mikveh;
    Purity and impurity; Tohorat ha-mishpachah
Ritual law. *See* Jewish law
Ritual objects. *See* Holy and holiness, objects of
Ritual quorum. *See* Minyan
Rituals. *See* Holidays
Ritual slaughterers. *See* Shochet
Rivers, 306, 329, 537–538. *See also* Mikveh; Water
RJJ (Rabbi Jacob Joseph School), 600
Robbers. *See* Stealing
Rock of Ages (song), 101
Rocks. *See* Stones
Rodeamentos, 115
Rodef, 443
Rolling of the Torah. *See* Gelilah
Rolling through underground passages, 209–210
Roman Catholics. *See* Catholic Church and Catholicism
Roman government and Romans. *See also* Palestine
    (history of); Ten martyrs
  afterlife, views on, 5
  ban on teaching Torah, 279, 374
  clothing, influence on, 522
  crucifixions by, 29, 139. *See also* Jesus Christ,
      crucifixion of
  destruction of Second Temple, 544
  eating while reclining, 460, 464
  exile by, 146
  flags and emblems of, 190
  Halloween, 113
  heathen practices of, 112–113
  Hebrew calendar, effect on, 83
  ordination abolished by, 458
  Patriarchate abolished by, 458
  on right vs. left, 443
  Roman matron and Rabbi Yosei ben Chalafta, 480
  Sanhedrin under, 65
  Temple, destruction of, 46, 86
  ten martyrs, 36, 123, 297, 324, 371, 548, 572, 605
  Torah study forbidden by, 8
  wedding customs of, 578
Romm Publishing House, 528
Roosters, 285, 369, 504. *See also* Chickens
Roots, Aromatic, 23
Rosen, Jonathan, 528
Roses, 191, 296
Rosh (Asher ben Yechiel), 48, 63, 379, 500
Rosh (head), 20
Rosh Chodesh, 297. *See also* Moon
  aliyot (Torah honors) given on, 14
  declaration of, 496, 603
  fixed dates of, 83, 305

maftir of, 318
overview of, 443–444
Passover observance and, 387
prayers and blessings of, 230
sacrifices of, 478
during sefirat ha-omer, 303
selichot and, 605–606
Shabbat Rosh Chodesh, 478
weddings held on, 186
women's observance of, 443–444
Roshei galuta, 180–181, 599
Roshei teivot, 2–3
Rosh ha-mateh ha-kelali, 3
Rosh Hashanah, 497. *See also* Elul; High Holidays;
    Tashlikh ceremony
aliyot (Torah honors) given on, 14
binding of Isaac, reading of, 11
foods of, 96, 247–248, 445–446, 604
God as Righteous Judge, 441–442
Netaneh Tokef, 96
overview of, 247–248, 444–446
prayers and blessings of, 230, 445, 467
Psalm 91 story, 145
Satan as witness on, 459
Shabbat Shuvah following, 479
tashlikh ceremony, 306
Ten Days of Repentance following, 51, 444–445
tractate of, 530–531
yoma arichta and, 603
Rosh Hashanah Le-Ilanot, 98
Rosner, Fred, 175
Rothenberg, Rabbi Meir ben Baruch, 394
Rothschild, Amschel, 135
Rothschild, Baron, 267
Rothschild, James R., 299
Round foods, 189, 328
Royal Society for the Prevention of Cruelty to Animals,
    Britain, 486
Royalty, 120, 351, 463. *See also* Court Jews; Kingship of
    Israel
Ru'ach, 507. *See also* Souls; Spirituality
Rudolf, Emperor, 394
Rufeisen, Oswald, 276
Rulings. *See* Courts, Jewish; Law; Takanot
Rumors. *See* Leshon ha-ra
Russia, 13, 32, 54, 270, 271, 287, 322, 397
Russian Jews, 348
Ruth, 90, 103, 128, 133, 227, 232, 343, 382, 484, 580
Rye, 98, 328, 388. *See also* Grains

S

Sa'adya Gaon, 53, 197, 203, 287, 288, 345, 427, 429,
    473, 487, 600
Sabastia, 268

Sabbath. *See also* Challah; Eruvin; Kiddush (prayer)
aliyot (Torah honors) on, 14, 370
Avinu Malkeinu not recited on, 55
births and deaths on, 53, 362
brides, compared to, 296, 310, 333, 448
burial before, 171
candlelighting, 75, 87–89, 115, 349, 402–403, 448
Chanukkah on, 100
Christian Sabbath, 453
circumcision on, 116, 143, 351–352
clothing for, 121, 158, 297
commandments of, 546
conclusion of. *See* Havdalah service
Conservative Judaism policy on, 128
Creation and, 143, 193
as day of rest, 358
declaration of, 497
demons and, 145
desecration of, 513–514
doves, 533
end of. *See* Havdalah service; Melaveh malkah
erasure on, 433
Falasha observance of, 182
family bonding and, 184
as family celebration, 184
fasting on, 186, 188
food of, 73, 193–194, 447, 448
Friday night services, 62
headcoverings for, 242
immersion preceding, 342
Jesus Christ's arrest on, 29, 139–140
Kaddish of, 282
Karaite observance of, 88, 286–288, 384
kavanah and, 288
Kiddush, 259
leshon ha-kodesh spoken on, 311
Ma'ariv (prayers), 316
maftir of, 318
manna and, 471
marit a'yin and, 40–41, 320–321
meals of, 300, 448, 471, 481
Minchah service, 342
mourning prohibited on, 374, 493, 495
Napoleon's test of Jewish loyalty and, 309
neshama yeteirah of, 510
observance as condition of witness, 37
Pharisees on, 454
pikuach nefesh and, 377, 396
prayers and blessings of, 3, 14, 27, 164, 180,
    407–408, 443, 448, 455–456. *See also* Musaf
    (services)
Priestly Benediction, 480
Purim and, 332
Reform Judaism and, 424
restrictions of, 356, 358, 448–452, 493

Sadducees on, 88, 454
safeguards of, 476
sexual relations on, 474
Shabbat (tractate), 530
Shabbat Chazon, 17, 477
Shabbat D'Mi Kamokhah, 479
Shabbat Ha-Chodesh, 477
Shabbat Ha-Gadol, 477–478
Shabbat Kallah, 478
Shabbat Mevarkhim, 478
Shabbat Nachamu, 478, 496
Shabbat Parah, 17, 422, 478
Shabbat Rosh Chodesh, 478
Shabbat Shekalim, 478–479
Shabbat Shirah, 479
Shabbat Shuvah, 17, 479. See also Repentance
Shabbat Zakhor, 17, 415, 479
Shabbes goy, 479–480
shomer Shabbos status, 497
songs of, 448
space travel and, 89
special Sabbaths, 448
Syrian prohibition of, 99
tallitot worn on, 523
tefillin and, 539, 541
timers used for Sabbath, 479
Torah readings of, 13, 501–502, 562
violations of, 36–37, 91, 410, 447, 452, 476,
    487–488, 513–514, 587, 604
violations of, permitted, 67
weddings prohibited on, 583
wine for, 586. See also Kiddush (prayer)
work done by Gentile on, 40, 320–321
Yom Ha-Atzma'ut on, 230
Sabbath Queen. See Melaveh malkah
Sabbatical years, 160, 310, 370–371, 413–414, 453, 529
Sabri, Akramah, 585
Sachiel, 26
Sacred. See Holy and holiness
Sacrifices. See also Temples
    Akeidah, the, 10–11, 85, 457, 458, 496
    animals, 371, 521
    atonement through, 125
    of barley, 373
    Bekhorot (tractate) on, 533
    blood of, 121
    of bread, 482
    burnt, 78
    burnt offerings, 95
    cereal, 95
    by converts, 131
    crucifixion of Jesus and, 11
    davenen and, 141
    first fruits, tractate on, 530
    hand gestures during, 402

by High Priest, 56–57
    Ho'rayot (tractate) on, 532
    Kodoshim (tractate) on, 347, 482
    Minchah offerings, 342
    Mishneh Torah, laws compiled in, 348
    by Moses, 442
    Musaf, 356
    music during, 357
    of Nadav and Avihu, 405
    of the nazir, 51
    nedavah donations, 364
    by niddah, 366
    omer, 373, 598
    origin of prayers and, 520
    overview of, 453–454
    paschal lamb, 392, 457, 462, 478
    Passover, 423
    personal, 375, 420
    of Pilgrim Festivals, 453
    prayers and blessings in lieu of, 56, 67–68, 126, 398,
        453
    reintroduction of, 453–454
    of Rosh Chodesh, 443, 478
    salt and, 78, 97, 455, 462
    semikhah and, 420
    Shacharit, 480
    sin-offerings of early chasidim, 395
    of Sukkot, 515, 516
    Sundays, not offered on, 453
    Syrian-Greek interference with, 149
    Temple, 55–56
    Terumah (tractate), 529
    thanksgiving, 69
    vows and, 410–411
    wine and, 296
    Zera'im (tractate) on, 482
    Zevachim (tractate), 532
Sadducees, 5, 88, 164, 212, 269, 392, 436, 454, 502
Safed, 280, 359, 376, 421
Safety, 449. See also Pikuach nefesh
Saffron, 191
Sages. See Scholars
Sagi-nehor, 172
Sagittarius (zodiacal sign), 84, 613
Saintly. See Pious people
Saints (Christian), 47, 113
Sa'ir la-azazel, 504
SAJ (Society for the Advancement of Judaism), 594
Sala, Abba the Great, 209–210
Salanter, Rabbi Israel, 163, 300, 601
Salanter Yeshiva, 601
Salary, 153. See also Income
Sales and selling. See Labor (work)
Salome, Queen, 614
Salome Alexandra, 363

Salt, 78, 97, 151, 234, 330, 446, 455
Salt water, 455, 461, 462–463
Salvation, 455–456. *See* Redemption
Salzman, Rabbi Joshua, 300
Samael, Prince of Dark Forces, 24, 26. *See also* Satan
Samaria, 272
Samaritans, 83, 454, 456–457, 536, 547
Sambatyon River, 548
Samekh, 19, 368
Samson, 227
Samson ben Abraham of Sens, 566
Samson ben Zadok, 240
Samuel (prophet), 47, 156, 209, 297, 316, 498
Samuel (Rabbi), 181, 335, 350, 474, 593
Samuel ben Meir, 430, 566
Samuel ben Nachman, 162
Samuel ben Uri Phoebus, 50
Samuel the Lesser, 501
Sanctification of God's name, 508. *See also* Kiddush Ha-Shem
Sanctuary. *See* Ark of the Covenant; Tabernacle; Temples
Sand, 494
Sandals, 232, 312–313. *See also* Levirate marriage
    practices; Shoes
Sandek, 116–117, 301–302, 457. *See also* Circumcision
Sanhedrin. *See also* Nasi (Prince)
    capital punishment and, 91, 139
    judges of, 420
    nasi of, 364
    ordination and, 375–376
    overview of, 457–458
    priestly heritage, investigations of, 122
    reconstitution efforts, 376
    Roman government, under, 29
    Rosh Chodesh, announcement of, 83, 387
    Sanhedrin Ketanah, 65
    tractate of, 532
    zugot of, 614
Sapphires, 523. *See also* Blue
Sarah (Matriarch), 25, 92, 93, 133, 257, 327, 361, 569,
    577. *See also* Arba Imma'hot
Sarajevo Haggadah, 227
Sargenes, 298. *See also* Kittls
Sargon, 536
Sarna, Nahum M., 213
Sartan, 613
Sashes, 499
Sasso, Sandy Eisenberg, 595
Satan, 26. *See also* Demons and demonology; Sitra achara
    (Angel of Death)
    Angel of Death and, 24
    confusion of, 497
    Gog and Magog dominated by, 215
    Job and, 441, 458
    Kol Nidrei vs., 369
    newborns and, 459

    overview of, 458–459
    rebellion against, 57
    salt as protection against, 455
    superstition and, 517
    Tishrei and, 69
Satisfaction of sexual needs. *See* Onah
Satmar chasidic sect, 13, 107, 113, 242
Saturdays, 53, 145. *See also* Sabbath
Saul, King, 138, 170, 173, 209, 254, 297, 316, 514
Saul, Rabbi Abba, 170
Saul of Tarsus, 440–441. *See also* Paul, Saint
Saving of lives, 67. *See also* Pikuach nefesh
Savlanut, 389
Savora'im, 459. *See also* Babylonia
Scales, 149–150, 613
Scalpel, 351–352. *See also* Knives
Scapegoats, 114, 504. *See also* Chukim
Scarlet, 445
Scarves. *See* Hair, coverings of
Scents, 23, 191, 194–195, 237–238, 298
S'chach, 515
Schechitah. *See* Slaughtering
Schechter, Solomon, 127, 156, 206, 434, 506, 601
Schenirer, Sarah, 162, 594. *See also* Beth Jacob Schools
Schiff, Ze'ev, 585
Schindler, Rabbi Alexander M., 390
Schindler's List, 253, 512
Schneerson, Rabbi Menachem Mendel, 62, 107, 176
Schneerson, Rabbi Yosef Yitzchak, 107
Scholars. *See also* Beit Din; Geonic period; Knesset Ha-
    Gedolah; Rabbis; Torah study
    aliyot (Torah honors) given to, 14
    Beruriah as, 162
    clothing of, 158
    derekh eretz of, 146, 536
    eulogies for, 171
    headcoverings of, 239
    insulting, 177
    as laborers, 303
    neturei karta description, 365
    personal habits of, 350
    ransoming of, 394
    semichat zekeinim, 420
    talmidei chakhamim, 525
    tefillin of, 539, 541
    zugot of, 614
Scholars' Kaddish, 281–282. *See also* Kaddish (prayer)
Scholem, Rabbi Gershom, 492–493, 573
School of Higher Criticism, 557
Schools, 163–164. *See also* Beit Midrash; Day Schools;
    Education; Talmud Torah; Teachers and teaching;
    Yeshivot
Schorr, Joshua Heschel, 236
Schorsch, Ismar, 128
Schreiber, Rabbi Moses. *See* Sofer, Rabbi Moses

Schuckling, 401–402
Schutzjuden, 352–353
Schwadron, Rabbi Shalom Mordechai, 49
Science, 179, 203, 421–422. *See also* Medical
 intervention
Scissors, 228
Scorpio (zodiacal sign), 84, 613
Screw, 18
Scribes, 325. *See also* Ezra the Scribe; Hebrew language;
 Writing instruments
 accuracy of, 379
 apostates and, 37
 for get documents, 207–208
 mikveh immersion by, 342
 neturei karta description, 365
 overview of, 507–509
 quills for, 571
 Soferim (tractate) on, 535
 for tefillin, 539
 for Torah scrolls, 558
 women as, 563
 writing implements of, 580
Scroll of Esther, 414. *See also* Esther and Book of Esther
Scrolls. *See* Torah
Sculpture. *See* Art and sculpture; Idolatry and idol
 worshippers
Scutes, 150
Sea, Red. *See* Sea of Reeds
Sea animal. *See* Leviathan
Sea-dragons, 136–137
Sea of Galilee, 294
Sea of Reeds, 345, 357, 437, 479, 480, 505
Seas, 9, 120, 335, 523, 575. *See also* Water
Seasons, 83
Second Aliya, 610. *See also* Aliyah (to Israel)
Second Passover. *See* Pesach Sheini
Second Temple era, 543. *See also* Destruction of the
 Temples; Temples; Western Wall
Secret Jews. *See* Marranos
Secrets of man, 205, 409–410, 586
Secrets of the Torah, 381, 383–384. *See also* Gematriah;
 Kabbalah and kabbalists
Secular court. *See* Civil law
Secular names, 250, 561
Secular studies, 600–601
Sedarim of the Mishnah, 529–535, 567
Seder. *See also* Passover
 arba kosot, 41
 Chad Gadya (song), 24, 94, 466–467
 fifth cup for Seder, 466
 Hillel's sandwich, 464–465
 lechem oni for, 329
 matzot for, 328–330, 492
 origins of, 459–460
 Sephardic term for, 468

 songs of, 466–467
 tray, 461–462, 519
Seder Olam (Yosei ben Chalafta), 86
Seder Tefillah (prayerbook), 501
Seed. *See also* Fruitful and multiply commandment
 hashchatat zera, 49–50, 373
 Jews as seed of Abraham, 136. *See also* Covenant
  People
 preservation principle and, 58
 surrogate motherhood and, 259, 518
Sefarim Chitzonim, 34
Sefer Ha-Bahir, 210, 537
Sefer Ha-Gilgulim (Vital), 210
Sefer Ha-Ikarim (Albo), 155, 412–413, 441
Sefer Ha-Minhagim (Mollin), 243
Sefer Ha-Mitzvot (Maimonides), 537
Sefer Ha-Yashar (Rabbenu Tam), 430. *See also* Rabbenu
 Tam; Talmud
Sefer keritut, 207. *See also* Get (divorce document)
Sefer Maharil, 432. *See also* Maharil, the
Sefer Mitzvot Gadol (Moses ben Jacob), 142
Sefer Razi'el, 24
Sefer Refuot (Maimonides), 193. *See also* Maimonides,
 Rabbi Moses
Sefer Torah. *See* Torah scrolls
Sefer Torah (tractate), 470, 536
Sefer Yetzira, 613
Sefirat ha-omer, 273, 303, 370–371, 373, 467, 483, 583.
 See also Lag Ba-Omer
Sefirot, ten, 64, 280, 467, 487, 492
Segan, 405
Segulot, 493. *See also* Amulets
Sejera, Palestine, 612
Sela, 512
Selek, 446
Self-control, 148
Self-defense, 554
Self-denial. *See* Asceticism
Self-incrimination, 587
Self-reckoning. *See* Cheshbon ha-nefesh
Selichot (prayers), 467, 549, 605
Selling and buying. *See also* Business affairs
 of aliyot, 16–17
 of chametz, 98, 333
 of a home, 339–340
 Nezikin (tractate) on, 532
 for sabbatical years, 310
 of Torah ornaments, 558
Semachot (tractate), 173, 535–536, 597
Semag (Moses ben Jacob), 142
Semen. *See* Artificial insemination; Seed; Sexual relations
Semikhah. *See* Ordination
Seminaries. *See* Schools; Yeshivot
Semitic languages. *See* Amharic; Hebrew language
Sennacherib, King, 34

Sensual pleasure, 33
Separate domain, 45
Separation ceremony, 599. *See also* Havdalah service
Separatism and Jewish identity, 148
Sepharad nusach. *See* Nusachim
Sephardim, 409, 443, 467–469, 500, 576
Sepphoris academy, 22, 86
Septuagint, 35, 469–471. *See also* New Testament; Old
     Testament
Seraphim, 25, 278. *See also* Angels
Sermons, 45, 127, 158–159, 374, 424. *See also* D'var Torah
Serpents, 77, 456
Servants, 310. *See also* Slavery (Egyptian)
Services. *See* Minyan; Prayers and blessings; Priests
     (Kohanim); Synagogues
Service to God. *See* Sacrifices
Settlement (immigration). *See* Aliyah (to Israel)
Settlement (legal). *See* Courts, Jewish
Settlements (Israeli), 268–270
Se'udah Ha-Mafseket, 471, 604
Se'udah shelishit, 448, 471
Se'udat mitzvah. *See also* Food; Siyyum
     for bat mitzvah celebrations, 62, 595
     bread and, 78
     at circumcision ceremonies, 117
     overview of, 471–472
     for pidyon ha-ben ceremony, 394
     of Purim, 416
     siyyum, following, 188, 505
     for weddings, 492
Seven, significance of, 370–371, 373, 492, 493, 517, 581
Seven Benedictions. *See* Sheva Berakhot (blessings)
Seven Noahide Laws, 105, 255, 366, 367, 370, 549
Seven Sabbaths of Consolation, 478
Seven species of Israel, 189
Seven stops during funerals, 199–200
Seventeenth of Tammuz, Fast of, 189
Seventh-Day Adventists, 453. *See also* Christians and
     Christianity
Seventy. *See* Septuagint
Seventy, significance of, 8, 371, 470
Seventy languages of ancient times, 371
Seventy nations, 371
Sevivon (dreidels), 102, 202
Sextons, 249, 482
Sexual organs, 173, 326–327, 412, 575. *See also* Seed
Sexual relations, 66. *See also* Adultery; Birth control;
     Kissing; Physical contact with opposite sex;
     Pregnancy
     abstinence from. *See* Tohorat ha-mishpachah
     AIH (Artificial Insemination Husband) and. *See also*
          Pregnancy
     birth control and, 70–72, 473
     celibacy, 92
     Christian view of, 92

circumcision, effect on, 118–119
conjugal duties of a husband, 472–473
consummation of marriage, 114, 580
defined, 473–474
excretions from, 418
following immersion, 365–366
foods, influence on, 193
gender of fetus and, 473
homosexuality, 91, 255–257, 432, 462, 475
     lesbianism, 255, 257, 311, 462, 475
immorality of Moabite and Midianite women, 440
Incest, 475
Jewish laws of, 162
Jewish view of, 92
Lilith as symbol of temptation, 315
niddah laws, 475
Noahide Laws and, 367
onanism, 373
overview of, 472–475
provocation of, 300, 350, 486–487. *See also* Modesty
in public, 191
rape, 475
refusal of as grounds for divorce, 153
shivah, prohibited during, 494
sins, considered as, 92
as validation of marriage, 580
Yom Kippur, prohibited on, 604
Se'yag la-Torah, 475–476
Sforno, Ovadiah ben Jacob, 474
Shaatnez, 35, 114, 157, 349, 476–477, 499, 523, 529.
     See also Chukim
Shabbat. *See* Sabbath
Shabbat (tractate), 530
Shabbat Chazon, 17, 477
Shabbat D'Mi Kamokhah, 479
Shabbat Ha-Chodesh, 477
Shabbat Ha-Gadol, 477–478
Shabbat Kallah, 478
Shabbat Mevarkhim, 478
Shabbat Nachamu, 478, 496
Shabbat Parah, 17, 422, 478
Shabbat Rosh Chodesh, 478
Shabbat Shekalim, 478–479
Shabbat Shirah, 479
Shabbat Shuvah, 17, 479. *See also* Repentance
Shabbat Zakhor, 17, 415, 479
Shabbes goy, 479–480
Shacharit (prayers), 73, 316. *See also* Musaf (services);
     Prayers and blessings
     Eighteen Benedictions, 164
     institution of, 369
     Kaddish of, 282
     Mourners' Kaddish, 284
     overview of, 480
     position during, 403

Psalm 136, 230
  of Sabbath, 448
  sacrifices, 480
  in Second Temple era, 519
  of Yom Kippur, 605
Shaddai, 212, 214–215, 232, 338–339, 540–541. *See also* God
Shadkhanim, 480–481. *See also* Shidukhin
Shadrach, 14
Shafran, 460
Shai Olamot, 481
Shaitl. *See* Sheitls
Shalashudis. *See* Se'udah Shelishit
Shalom, 214, 481
Shalom bat ceremony, 361, 481
Shalom nekeivah, 481
Shalom zakhar, 143, 459, 481
Shalosh Regalim, 396, 482. *See also* Pilgrim Festivals
Shamash, 100, 169, 334, 482. *See also* Menorahs
Shama'yim, 213. *See also* Heaven
Shame. *See* Embarrassment
Shamgar, Meir, 308
Shamir, Yitzhak, 269–270, 396
Shammai, 9, 100, 184–185, 258, 536, 614
Shammai, School of, 71, 472, 569
Shamor, 26
Shamriel, 26
Shankbone, 462
Shapiro, Rabbi Meir, 141
Sharansky, Natan, 187–188
Sharon, Ariel, 270
Shas, 141, 347, 482, 505, 529–535. *See also* Gemara; Mishnah; Talmud
Shatz, 482, 496, 518. *See also* Shli'ach tzibur
Shaul, Moshe, 469
Shaving, 27, 290, 351, 487–488, 494. *See also* Facial hair; Hair and haircutting
Shavu'a ha-ben, 116. *See also* Circumcision
Shavuot, 248. *See also* Omer; Revelation at Sinai; Ruth; Sefirat ha-omer
  Akdamut (poem), 10, 484
  aliyot (Torah honors) given on, 14
  Atzeret, referred to as, 53
  Azharot (poem), 10
  Book of Ruth and, 227
  burial following, 171
  as Chag Ha-Bikkurim, 189
  confirmation and, 126
  Conservative Judaism policy on, 128
  date of, 85
  extra day added to, 387, 483, 606
  first fruits and, 189
  flowers and, 192
  foods of, 97
  Israel, observance in, 128

Isru Chag, 271
  laws and customs of, 483–485
  maftir of, 17
  names of, 482–483
  overview of, 482–485
  Passover and, 53, 483
  prayers and blessings of, 230
  Revelation of at Sinai celebrated, 439
  sacrifices of, 373, 453
  Sadducees on, 454
  seven, significance of, 370–371
  Shabbat Kallah preceding, 478
  Tikkun Leil Shavuot, 552
  Torah readings on, 547
  Torah study on, 483
  Yizkor services of, 602–603
  Yom Tov, defined, 606
Shaygetz and shiksa, 485
Sheba, Queen of, 182
Shechitah. *See* Slaughtering
Shechitah in the Light of the Year 2000 (Levinger), 486
She'eilot, 428
Sheeny, 274
Sheets, 499
She-heche'yanu (blessing), 61, 100, 260, 394, 446, 486, 570, 599
Sheidim. *See* Demons and demonology
Sheitls, 40, 158, 320, 351, 486–487, 592. *See also* Hair, covering of
Shekalim, 393, 407, 409, 530
Sheker, 568. *See also* Lying
Sheketz, 485
Shekhem, 456, 524
Shekhinah
  headcoverings and, 239
  Holy of Holies and, 255
  malkhut (in kabbalah) and, 280
  menorah lighting and, 100
  Mikhael and, 26
  overview of, 487
  Sinai, Mount and, 505
  Tale of Four Scholars and, 36
  tears of for divorce, 153
  Western Wall and, 585
  in world to come, 6
  Yom Kippur and, 43
Shelah (son of Judah), 312, 326
Shellfish, 148, 150. *See also* Kashrut
Shells. *See* Kelippot
Shelom ba'yit, 487–488, 568–569
Shelosha De-Puranuta, 488
Shelosh Esrei Midot Ha-Rachamim, 549
Sheloshim, 55, 171, 323, 488, 556, 606. *See also* Mourners and mourning; Shivah
Shema (prayer), 22, 155

Akiba (Rabbi) and, 324, 548
headcoverings and, 240
Jews as Israelites, 274
language of, 399
mezuzot and, 338
morning prayers and, 480
origin of, 501
position during, 403
on reward and punishment, 441
vatikin recitation of, 395
virgin of Nazareth, 488–490
Wachnacht, 115, 490, 580
Shemaiah, 244, 614
Shem Ha-Meforash, 213
Shemini Atzeret, 53
aliyot (Torah honors) given on, 14
Ecclesiastes and, 227
Geshem (prayer), 207
overview of, 248, 490
as separate from Sukkot, 248
Simchat Torah and, 490, 502
Sukkot and, 59, 483
Yizkor services of, 602–603
Sheminit, 357
Shemittah, 345, 370–371, 413–414, 490–491, 529, 553,
    561. See also Jubilee year
Shemoneh Esrei. See Eighteen Benedictions
Shemurah matzah, 329, 491–492. See also Matzot
She-nadar, 496
She-nishtamed, 38
Sherira Gaon, 203, 398, 429–430, 527, 600
Sheshet (Rav), 172, 181, 185, 350–351, 474
Sheva. See Seven, significance of
Sheva Berakhot (blessings), 492, 582
Sheva mitzvot b'nei Noach. See Noahide Laws
Shevarim, 497. See also Shofar
Shevat, 84, 85, 449–450
Shevi'it (tractate), 529
Shevirat ha-keilim, 281, 492–493. See also Kelippot
Shevuah, 411. See also Oaths
Shevuot (tractate), 532
Shevut, 358, 493. See also Sabbath
Shewbreads, 95–96, 250. See also Challah
Shidukhin, 480–481, 544, 601–602, 614
Shield of David, 510–511
Shield of Solomon, 511
Shikhvat zera, 473. See also Sexual relations
Shiksa, 485
Shila (Rabbi), 23, 91, 139
Shilo, 396
Shimon (Rabbi), 471–472
Shimon (tribe of), 567
Shimon, son of Judah the Prince, 450
Shimon Bar Yocha'i, 81, 279, 614
    on Eighteen Benedictions, 164

on established customs, 305
gravesite of, 373
Lag B'Omer and, 303–304
ordination of, 421
on Sabbath, 447
on Shavuot, 552
on truthfulness, 568
on yahrzeits, 597
Zohar attributed to, 359
Shimon ben Azzai, 36
Shimon ben Chalafta, 391
Shimon ben Eleazer, 570
Shimon ben Gamaliel, 123, 129, 324, 391, 470, 567, 569
Shimon ben Lakish, 23, 204, 303, 458, 510
Shimon ben Pazzi, 555
Shimon ben Shetach, 161, 162, 291
Shimon ben Yehotzadak, 578
Shimon ben Zomah, 36
Shimon the Just, 55
Shin/sin, 20, 102, 215, 232, 368, 408, 499, 521, 541
Shinui, 200
Ships, 451
Shirat Ha-Yam (song), 479
Shira'yim, 493, 572
Shir Ha-Kavod (hymn), 27
Shishah Sedarim, 529–535. See also Mishnah
Shivah, 356. See also Mourners and mourning; Sheloshim
candles during, 494
counting days of, 606
eulogies on, 171
headcoverings and, 242–243
kefiyat ha-mitah, 494
keri'ah and, 291
kevod he-chai and, 293
mirrors, 494–495
for non-Jewish parents, 135
for one who has converted, 495
for one who has intermarried, 495
overview of, 493–495
prohibitions during, 494
on Purim, 417
Sabbath and, 310–311, 452
sexual relations prohibited on, 474
stools for mourners, 495
when apostasy occurs, 38–39
Shivah Asar B'Tammuz, 185–186, 189, 318, 495, 551.
    See also Fasting and fast days
Shivah D'Nechemta, 478, 496
Shkeil, Samuel ben Abraham, 187
Shli'ach tzibur, 90, 482, 496, 518. See also Ba'al tefillah
Shloshet Yemei Hagbalah, 485. See also Shavuot
Shluchim, 107
Shnei Luchot Ha-Berit (Horowitz), 605–606
Shneur Zalman, Rabbi of Lyady, 106, 348. See also
    Chabad

Shniyot incest offenders, 263

Shnudder, 496

Shoah. *See* Holocaust

Shoah Foundation, 253

Shochat, Manya Wilbushewitz, 612

Shochet. *See* Slaughtering

Shoelaces, 242

Shoes. *See also* Feet
    color of, 121
    leather, 248, 260, 486, 494, 540, 558, 570, 604–605
    non-Jews customs related to, 112
    Priests and, 407
    right before left, 113, 442
    sandals, 232, 312–313. *See also* Levirate marriage
        practices
    of scholars, 158

Shofar
    ba'al teki'ah, 58
    during Elul, 246, 247
    for exorcism, 159
    Falashas, not observed by, 182
    overview of, 496–497
    Revelation at Sinai and, 437
    of Rosh Hashanah, 11, 445
    Sabbath prohibition of, 449
    Satan confused by, 458–459
    as symbol of Jewish unity, 519
    on Yom Kippur, 277, 605

Shomer, 81–82, 497

Shomer negi'a, 498

Shomron. *See* Samaria

Shor, 613

Shoshanim, 357

Shoshanta, 195

Shoulders, 524

Shouting. *See* Hollekreisch

Shovels, 200, 235

Showbreads, 95–96, 448

Shpiels, Purim, 417

Shrinkage of God. *See* Tzimtzum

Shrouds, 120, 121, 300, 419, 476, 498–499. *See also*
    Burial; Tohorot

Shtadlanim, 499–500

Shtreimels, 242

Shul, 519. *See also* Synagogues

Shulchan Arukh (Caro). *See Code of Jewish Law* (Caro);
    Isserles, Rabbi Moses

Shuls, 468. *See also* Synagogues

Shushan, 332

Shushan Purim, 414–415, 500–501. *See also* Purim

Sickness. *See* Illness

Siddurim. *See* Prayerbooks

Siddur of Rav Amram Gaon, 429

Sidelocks. *See* Pei'ot

Sidrot, 501–502, 563. *See also* Torah readings

Sifra, 340

Sifrei, 340

Sifrei Torah. *See* Torah scrolls

Sight, 522–523, 574. *See also* Eyes

Silberg, Moshe, 276

Silence, 187, 244–245, 252, 254. *See also* Speech

Silent prayers, 403–404. *See also* Eighteen Benedictions;
    Prayers and blessings

Silk, 157, 476–477, 523

Silver, 393

Silver, Abba Hillel, 612

Simcha ben Samuel of Vitry, 602

Simchat Beit Ha-Sho'eivah, 502, 596

Simchat ha-bat, 481

Simchat Torah, 490. *See also* Torah
    aliyot (Torah honors) given on, 14
    chatan Bereishit, 108
    chatan Torah, 108
    flowers and, 192
    hakafot of, 229
    overview of, 248, 502–503
    as separate from Sukkot, 248
    Shemini Atzeret and, 490, 502
    tallit as chuppah, 524
    Torot, parade of, 44

Simla'i (Rabbi), 306, 349, 383, 537

Simon ben Abba, 303

Simon ben Lakish. *See* Resh Lakish

Simon ben Shetach, 614

Simon of Trent, 76

Simon the Just, 122, 205

Simple nun (letter), 19. *See also* Nun.

Simple pei (letter), 19. *See also* Pei/fei

Simple tzadi (letter), 19. *See also* Tzadi

Sim Shalom (prayer), 480

Sinai, Mount, 27–28. *See also* Shavuot
    celebration of. *See* Shavuot
    challah as reminder of, 97
    flowers of, 483, 520
    gematriah of, 205
    halakhah le-Moshe mi-Sinai, 229–230
    humility of God and, 260
    location of, 504
    overview of, 504–505
    Revelation of the Torah, 306, 556–558
        circumcision preceding, 132
        days of the week of, 562
        Gemini and, 369
        immersion preceding, 132, 342, 369
        Jews as the Chosen People, 110–111
        Kaplan, Rabbi Mordecai on, 422
        location of, 504
        Maimonides, Rabbi Moses on, 179
        Oral Law and, 374
        Original Sin, purification from, 378

Orthodox view of, 379
overview of, 437–439
preparation for, 485
from the right side of God, 442
Shema and, 489
shofar used at, 496
Shofrot and, 497
swaying during, 402
taryag mitzvot and, 537
Ten Commandments and, 544
three, importance of number, 369
weddings compared to, 581
suspended over Jewish nation, 111
Sinai Campaign, 267–268
Sinews. See Gidin
Singing, 314, 576. See also Cantors; Prayers and blessings
Single men, 239, 256
Sinister, 443. See also Demons and demonology
Sins and sinners. See also Apostates and apostasy;
        Atonement; Fasting and fast days; Penitence;
        Repentance; Sacrifices; Yom Kippur
burial of, 93
change and, 46
confession of, 125–126, 504
        Al Cheit, 11
        Ashamnu, 51–52, 125, 402, 504, 579
        Avinu Malkeinu, 55
        Eighteen Benedictions, 164
        shame and, 404
exile as result of, 456
Jewish status retained, 275, 430
Keritot (tractate) on, 533
man's responsibility for, 378
mitzvot as result of, 74
nuts representing, 446
Original Sin and, 377–378, 456, 503, 590
overview of, 503–504
punishment. See Punishment
quorum, praying within, 399
as red, 121
reincarnation and, 427
remorse for, 55
sacrifices and, 453. See also Sacrifices
sex considered as, 92
sin-offerings, 395, 404
sins as punishment for sinning. See Punishment
of speech, 11
as synagogue members, 256
tashlikh ceremony, 306
tempting others, punishment for. See Civil law
terms for, 503
Yizkor services and, 602
Sin/shin, 102, 368
Sirat, Rabbi René-Samuel, 62
Sirkes, Rabbi Joel, 358, 525

Sisera, 357
Sisters-in-law. See Levirate marriage practices
Sitra achara (Angel of Death), 24, 281. See also Satan
Sitting, 44–45, 403, 541, 599
Sivan, 84, 85, 369, 485
613 Commandments, 167, 384, 503, 537, 575. See also
        Commandments
Six-Day War (1967), 92, 268–269, 273, 553–554, 584
Six orders of the Mishnah, 347. See also Mishnah
Siyyum, 141, 188, 505–506. See also Se'udat mitzvah
Skeptic. See Apikores
Skin (of animals). See Leather
Skin (of man), 143, 350, 538. See also Modesty
Skorechi, Karl, 409
Skullcaps, 107, 297. See also Headcoverings
Sky, 120. See also Heaven; Moon; Stars
Slander, 501. See also Leshon ha-ra
Slaughtering, 38, 150, 347, 485–486, 533, 590
Slavery (Egyptian), 84, 86, 97, 141, 447, 512. See also
        Seder
Slavery (Hebrew), 276, 394, 491, 506, 531, 536
Slavery (of Greece), 469
Slaying, 29, 140. See also Capital punishment; Murder
        and murderers
Sleep, 56. See also Dreams
Slonimsky, Henry, 198
Smell. See Nose and nostrils; Scents
Smith, Reverend Bailey, 111
Smooth. See Glatt kosher
Snails, 523, 574
Snakes, 378, 537
Sneezing, 507
Snoga, 468. See also Synagogues
Socialism. See Zionists and Zionism
Socializing with non-Jews, 148, 264, 476, 586. See also
        Intermarriage
Social ostracism of Jews. See Anti-Semitism
Society for the Advancement of Judaism (SAJ), 594
Society of Lovingkindness and Truth, 81
Society of Pursuers of Justice, 81
Society of the Living, 365
Socks, 107
Sod, 381, 383–384, 586. See also Secrets of the Torah
Sod Ha-Ibur, 83
Sodom and Sodomites, 25, 26, 255, 344, 401, 553
Sodomy, 129, 256
Sofer. See also Mezuzot
Sofer (scribe). See Scribes
Sofer, Rabbi Moses, 514
        on apostates and apostasy, 39
        on autopsies, 54
        on birth control, 71
        contribution to Orthodox beliefs, 379
        on language of prayer, 398–399
        overview of, 433

Reform Judaism vs., 433
  on standing before the Torah, 45
Solar calendar, 309. *See also* Civil calendar
Soldiers, 9, 554. *See also* Military
Solomon, King, 86. *See also* First Temple
  blessings of, 232
  on death, 597
  on discipline, 162–163
  Ecclesiastes, Book of, 490
  Jerusalem, rule over, 272
  marriage of, 390
  pseudepigrapha and, 414
  on red heifer, 422
  rule of, 274
  Sheba, Queen of and, 182
  Shield of Solomon, 511
  Temple, First, 42–43, 543
  Wisdom of Solomon, 34
  wives of, 397
Solomon ben Yitzchak. *See* Rashi
Solomon ibn Adret, 157, 288–289, 559, 600
Soloveitchik, Rabbi Joseph B., 171
Soncino Press, 528, 550
Song of Songs (Torah reading), 90, 191, 227, 296, 572
Songs and singing, 608. *See also* Music; Prayers and
      blessings
  kol ishah, 300–350, 474, 593
  of Levites, 400
  Sabbath, 448, 608
  for the Seder, 466–467
  Shabbat Shirah, 479
  Shir Ha-Kavod, 27
  Song of the Three Holy Children, 34
"Son of the Covenant", 136. *See also* Covenant People
Sons. *See also* Bar Mitzvah; Children
  aliyot (Torah honors) given to fathers of newborns, 14
  firstborn
    apostates, rights of, 38
    Bekhorot (tractate) on, 533
    birthright of, 72–73, 568
    death of, 386
    fast of, 185–186, 188, 505
    named after deceased father, 312–313
    pidyon ha-ben, 135, 392–394, 407, 409
  Four Sons of Passover, 464
  fruitful and multiply commandment, 66, 70–72, 92,
      184–185, 312–313, 322, 397, 473, 575
  hope for, 2
  "Ibn" as part of family name, 362
  obligation to teach Torah to, 542
  of scholars, 14
Sons (of Jacob), 86, 290, 389, 404–405. *See also* Twelve
    Tribes of Jacob
Soroka Hospital, Beersheba, 118
Sorrow. *See* Mourners and mourning

Sotah, 4–5, 509, 531, 588–589. *See also* Adultery
Souls, 509, 510. *See also* Afterlife; Judgment; Sins and
      sinners; Spirituality
  body and, 7, 493, 509–510
  candles, compared to, 401
  creation of, 143
  evil spirits and, 143
  of fetus, 1
  flames as representation of, 494
  immortality of, 437. *See also* Resurrection
  Mourners' Kaddish and, 284
  names and, 361
  nefesh, defined, 509
  neshama, defined, 509
  olam ha-nefashot, 5
  overview of, 509–510
  purity of, 378
  ru'ach, defined, 507
  techiyat ha-metim and, 435
  tombstones referred to as, 555
  transfer of. *See* Ibbur; Reincarnation
Sour. *See* Leavened Foods
South, 26
Southern Baptist Conference, 111
Sova, 370
Soveiv, 499
Sovereignty (in kabbalah), 280, 487
Soviet Union. *See* Russia
Soybeans, 389
Space travel, 89
Spain, 30–31, 147, 189, 321–322, 430, 467, 468, 500.
      See also Marranos; Sephardim
Spanish and Portuguese Synagogue, The, 468. *See also*
      Congregation Shearith Israel
Sparks, divine, 281, 290, 492–493
Speaking. *See* Speech
Species, four. *See* Arba minim
Species of Israel, 189
Speech, 11, 22, 146, 165, 187, 305. *See also* Derekh
      eretz; Eulogies; Euphemisms; Sermons; Silence
Spektor, Rabbi Isaac Elchanan, 9, 80, 138, 379, 434, 491,
      601
Spelt, 98, 328, 388. *See also* Grains
Sperm. *See* Artificial insemination; Seed
S'phard nusach. *See* Nusachim
Spices, 64, 192, 237–238, 510, 599
Spielberg, Steven, 253, 512
Spies on land of Israel, 343
Spilling of wine, 237–238
Spine, 19
Spinoza, Baruch (Benedict), 7, 118, 155, 179, 557
Spirit. *See* Souls
Spirits, evil. *See also* Demons and demonology
Spirituality, 318, 507. *See also* Souls
Spitting, 95, 312–313, 369, 510

Splendor (in kabbalah), 280
Split hooves, 149
Split peas, 389
Splitting of the sea, 345. *See also* Exodus (from Egypt);
    Sea of Reeds
Spodik, 242
Sports, 260, 450, 571–572
Spousal abuse, 342
Spring celebrations, 459, 461
Springs. *See* Mikveh
Squatters, 607
Stam yeinam, 586. *See also* Wine
Standing, 44–45, 403, 541, 547
Star of David, 191, 510–511, 519
Stars, 11, 330, 336, 515
State of Israel. *See* Israel (modern state)
Statues, 47–48. *See also* Civil law; Jewish law
Status, Jewish. *See* Bar mitzvah; Bat mitzvah; Jewish
    identity and status
Status of religious articles, 249–250
St. Catherine's Monastery, 504
Stealing, 142, 202, 257, 367, 410, 546, 575, 587
Steam, 388
Steel, 580
Steinberg, Rabbi Abraham Menachem, of Brody, 112
Steinsaltz Talmud, 528
Stellen, 102
Sterility. *See* Infertility
Stimulation. *See* Sexual relations
Stones, 511–512, 556, 580. *See also* Tombstones
Stoning, 29, 91, 140. *See also* Capital punishment
Stools for mourners, 495
Stories. *See* Aggadah; Haggadah
St. Petersburg Codex, 325–326
Straight Look at the Third Reich, A (App), 253
Strangers, 512–513, 536. *See also* Converts and
    conversion; Met mitzvah
Strangling, 29, 91, 140. *See also* Capital punishment
Streams, 306, 329, 537–538. *See also* Water
Streisand, Barbra, 301
Strength, 442, 524
String beans, 389
String music, 357–358
Students. *See also* Beit Midrash; Education; Teachers and
    teaching; Torah study
    converts as, 131
    kolelim, 300, 429, 598
    ordination of, 375–377, 421
    talmidei chakhamim, 525
    time spent away from wife, 473
    walking with teachers, 443
Studies in Judaism (Schechter), 156. *See also* Schechter,
    Solomon
Stumbling-block principle, 513–514. *See also* Marit a'yin
Sturgeon, 150, 157

Subtracting from laws, 379
Success, 238, 446
Sudara, 239
Suez Canal, 268
Suffering. *See* Anti-Semitism; Pain; Redemption; Slavery
    (Egyptian); Slavery (Hebrew)
Sufganiyot, 101
Suicide bombers, 607
Suicides, 39, 171, 173–175, 252, 324, 340, 514–515
Sukkot
    aliyot (Torah honors) given on, 14
    booths, building of, 515–516
    burial following, 171
    Chanukkah and, 99
    Conservative Judaism policy on, 128
    extra day added to, 387, 606
    fasting on, 186
    Israel, observance in, 128
    Isru Chag, 271
    overview of, 248
    prayers and blessings of, 230
    preparations for, 604
    sacrifices of, 453, 515, 516
    seven, significance of, 370–371
    Shemini Atzeret and, 483
    Simchat Beit Ha-Sho'eivah, 502, 596
    Sukkah (tractate) on, 530
    Temple offerings on, 190
    as temporary dwellings, 339
    ushpizin, 576–577
    Yizkor services of, 602–603
    Yom Tov, defined, 606
Sulam. *See* Ladders
Sumptuary Laws, 433
Sun, 84, 89, 328–329, 330. *See also* Solar calendar;
    Zodiac
Sundays, 53, 453, 604
Sunday schools, 163. *See also* Education
Sunset, 84, 89. *See also* Night
Supernatural. *See* Mystics and mysticism
Superstition, 24, 56, 76–77. *See also* Demons and
    demonology; Heathens
Supervision of kashrut. *See* Mashgichim
Supplications. *See* Prayers and blessings
Supreme Court (of Israel), 65, 131, 308
Supreme Court (Temple Era). *See* Sanhedrin
Sura, Babylonia, 22–23, 144–145, 203, 285, 313, 428,
    429, 526, 600. *See also* Babylonia
Surnames, 409, 518
Surrogate fathers, 393
Surrogate motherhood, 259, 518
Survivors of the Shoah Visual History Foundation, 253
Susanna and the Elders, 34
Suspected women. *See* Sotah
Swaying while praying, 401–402

Swearing. *See* Vows
Sweden, 486
Sweets and sweetness, 54, 59, 445–446, 484, 502
Swimming, 132, 449–450, 476
Swine. *See* Marranos; Pork
Switzerland, 486
Sword, 18, 24, 29, 494
Swordfish, 150
Sylvester new year celebrations, 112–113
Symbols. *See also* Flags and emblems
    holiday foods and, 446, 461–462
    of kosher foods, 151
    tefillin as, 539
    in Torah, 381–383
    of war, 580
Symmachus (Rabbi), 489
Synagogue of Capernaum, 511
Synagogues. *See also* Ark of the Covenant; Community;
    Prayers and blessings
    Beit Knesset, referred to as, 65
    bimah, 13, 16, 44–45, 67–68, 294, 433, 468, 519,
        558
    building of, 40, 320
    churches, differentiated from, 48
    decorations of, 47–48
    driving to on the Sabbath, 424
    funerals in, 198
    Kiddush recited in, 295–296
    liquor served in, 517
    mechitzah, 300. *See also* Women's Gallery
    mezuzot for, 339
    physical structure of, 42–45, 334, 404, 519–520, 543
    Sephardic term for, 468
    services attended by non-Jews, 41
    Temples represented by, 453
    traveling to on the Sabbath, 451–452
    weddings held in, 112
Syrian-Greeks, 99, 149, 436. *See also* Chanukkah
Syrian Jewish community, 131
Szold, Henrietta, 284, 376, 595, 612–613
Szold, Rabbi Benjamin, 506, 612

T

Ta'anit. *See* Fasting and fast days
Tabernacle, 42
    Ark curtains as partition, 46
    building of, 557
    construction of, 383
    dismantling of, 408
    festival of. *See* Sukkot
    God's presence in, 573
    lechem ha-panim, 95–96
    menorah, 334
    nedavah donations, 364

Tabernacles. *See* Sukkot
Tables, 448, 455
Tablets. *See* Ten commandments
Tabor, Mount, 505
Tachanun (prayers), 521, 573
Tacitus, 386–387
Tagin, 521–522
Tahor. *See* Tohorot
Tails of fish, 446
Takanot, 153, 203, 413–414. *See also* Rabbenu Gershom
Takhrikhim (shrouds), 498
Tal (prayer), 298, 522
Taleh, 613
Tall, 412–413
Tallitot, 41, 298, 522–525. *See also* Arba kanfot
    beautification of, 64
    blessings for, 75
    for burial, 499
    as a chuppah, 114
    as inspiration for flag of Israel, 191
    for kissing the Torah, 298, 562, 565
    for Kol Nidrei, 301
    non-Jews, given to, 41
    Reform Judaism on, 426
    for Shacharit (prayers), 480
    tallit katan, 522
    tefillin and, 541
    tzitzit and, 522, 536, 574
    used during Priestly Benediction, 408
    women and, 376, 525, 591
    for Yom Kippur, 605
Talmidei chakhamim, 525. *See also* Scholars
Talmud. *See also* Responsa Literature; Torah study
    age to begin study of, 161
    aggadah, 7–8, 227, 244, 341
    as basis of Orthodox belief, 379
    completion of tractate. *See* Siyyum
    daf yomi, 141
    Ezra the Scribe and, 316–317
    first printing of, 208
    halakhah component, 7–8
    Mishneh Torah and, 347. *See also* *Mishneh Torah*
    names of tractates, 173
    Oral Law, overview of, 374–375
    overview of, 525–529
    Pesachim (tractate), 392
    Revelation of at Sinai, 438
    study of. *See* Torah study
    teiku, 542–543
    tosafot, 430
    tractates, 529–535
Talmud and the Internet, The (Rosen), 528
Talmud Torah, 163, 535–536. *See also* Education; Torah
    study
Talne Rebbetzin, 171

Tam, Rabbenu Jacob, 63

Tamar, 361. *See also* Palm branches

Tamchui, 205. *See also* Gemilut chasadim

Tamei, 172, 418. *See also* Purity and impurity

Tamid (tractate), 533

Tammuz, 84, 85. *See also* Shivah Asar B'Tammuz

Tanakh, 3, 14, 127, 161, 350, 371, 536. *See also*
    Apocrypha; Prophets and prophecy (Nevi'im);
    Torah

Tanchum (Rabbi), 305

Tanchuma bar Abba, 585

Tanna'im, 22–23, 59, 204, 346–347, 526, 536. *See also*
    Mishnah

Tannu rabbanan, 59

Tanya, the, 106

Tapestry. *See* Art and sculpture

Tarfon, Rabbi, 385

Targum Ha-Shivim, 469–470. *See also* Septuagint

Targum of Onkelos, 337–338, 470, 536–537

Tarphon (Rabbi), 91

Taryag mitzvot, 349. *See also* 613 commandments

Tashbetz (Meir ben Baruch of Rothenburg), 240

Tashlikh ceremony, 306, 537–538

Tashmishei mitzvah, 254

Tass, 558–559

Tassels. *See* Tzitzit

Taste, 192, 329–330, 465. *See also* Food

Tattoos, 538

Taurus (zodiacal sign), 85, 613

Tav (letter), 20, 368

Taxes, 202, 289, 530. *See also* Court Jews

Taz, 45

Teachers and teaching. *See also* Education; Gemara; Rabbis
    Amora'im, 22–23
    Bar Yocha'i, Rabbi Shimon, 279
    compared to fathers, 162
    forbidden by Roman government, 8
    kissing, 298
    of Ma'asei Bereishit and Ma'asei Merkavah, 317–318
    marriage of, 163, 474
    ordination by, 375, 421
    training of, 162
    walking with students, 443
    women as, 376, 596

Te'amim, 89. *See also* Cantillations

Tears, 171, 455, 584–585

Techiyat ha-metim, 383, 435–437, 538. *See also*
    Resurrection

Techorim, 173

Tefillah. *See* Prayers and blessings

Tefillah, the, 501. *See also* Eighteen Benedictions; Prayers
    and blessings

Tefillah shel rosh, 541

Tefillin
    bar mitzvah, donned at, 344

in cemeteries, 94

Chol Ha-Moed, not worn on, 110

dropped, 186

God's name in, 215

haircutting and, 229

holiness of, 250

Karaites and, 286

language of, 470

Maid of Ladamir and, 525

Menachot (tractate) on, 533

mourning and, 542

overview of, 538–542

parchments written by apostates, 37

placement of, 442

pre-bar mitzvah training, 59

Rabbenu Tam, 540

Rashi, 540

Reform Judaism on, 426

sabbath and, 541

for Shacharit (prayers), 480

Shema and, 488

sofer of, 507

tallit and, 541

as tashmishei kedushah and, 254

tractate of, 536

women and, 376, 541–542, 591–592

Tefillot. *See* Prayers and blessings

Tehillah, 52. *See also* Ashrei (prayer)

Tehillim. *See* Psalms

Teiku, 542–543

T'einah, 446

Teitelbaum, Rabbi Joel, 107. *See also* Satmar chasidic sect

Teitelbaum, Rabbi Moshe, 113. *See also* Satmar chasidic
    sect

Teitsch Chumash (Ashkenazi), 572

Teivah, 468, 543. *See also* Bimah

Tek (Torah cover), 560, 564

Tekheilet, 120, 523, 574–575

Teki'ah, 497. *See also* Shofar

Telata gavrei, 14

Telat De-Puranuta, 488

Tel Aviv-Jaffa, 271

Television, 451

Temperature, 329, 330, 388

Temple Emanu-El, New York, 425

Temple Mount, 270, 584. *See also* Western Wall

Temples, 543–544. *See also* Destruction of the Temples;
    Sacrifices; Sanctuary; Synagogues
    Amidah recitation and, 501
    annulment of promises, 410–411
    ark curtains, 46
    as Batei Mikdash, 249
    Chanukkah and, 99
    choir of, 357
    destruction of, 146, 189. *See also* Tishah B'Av

duplication of, 46
First, 42–43, 46, 84, 543. See also Solomon, King;
    Tishah B'Av
half-shekel contribution to Temple, 479
journeys to. See Pilgrim Festivals
King David and, 396
klei kodesh, 299
Kodoshim (Mishnah tractates), 347
Levites (non-Priests), 164, 314
location of, 272
menorah, 334
music in, 357
paschal lamb sacrifices, 460
Passover celebrations of, 386–387
physical structure of, 533, 543
pidyon ha-ben ceremony, 393
prayers for rebuilding of, 453–454
prayers in direction of, 43–44, 404
Priestly blessings. See Priestly Benediction
rebuilding of, 457
sacrifices. See Sacrifices
Second, 519, 544, 584
Shema recitation and, 501
shewbreads, 95–96, 250
Simchat Beit Ha-Sho'eivah, 502
Sukkot festival, 490
tables as, 95–96
Ten Commandments, recitation of, 547
three sections of, 369
timeline of, 86
Torah scrolls of, 508
Temptation, 315, 474, 513. See also Sexual relations
Temurah (tractate), 533
Ten, significance of, 371. See also Quorums
Tena'im, 232, 299, 544. See also Handkerchief ceremony;
    Weddings
Ten Commandments. See also Golden Calf; Jewish law;
    Revelation at Sinai; Torah
    aleph, beginning with, 21
    Ark of, 42–43, 383, 545
    breaking of the tablets, 8, 25, 43, 247, 544–545, 549
    decalogue, referred to as, 142
    false witnesses and, 568
    graven images, prohibition of, 47–48
    overview of, 544–547
    recitation of, 484
    Sabbath and, 447
    significance of ten, 371
    synagogue readings of, 547
    text of, 545–547
Ten Days of Repentance, 51, 109, 371, 444–445,
    496–497, 547–548, 583, 597–598. See also Elul;
    Repentance; Rosh Hashanah; Yom Kippur
Tendler, Rabbi Moshe, 117, 518, 571–572
Tendons, 209

Ten Lost Tribes of Israel, 146, 274, 543, 548, 567
Ten martyrs, 36, 123, 297, 324, 371, 548, 572, 605
Ten plagues, 2, 185–186, 188, 464. See also Passover
Ten sefirot, 64, 280, 467, 487, 492. See also Ein Sof
Ten spies, 311
Tent. See Canopies; Oholot
Tenuva (journal), 357
Te'omim, 613
Tereifah, 61, 548–549. See also Kashrut; Nonkosher food
Terminal illnesses. See Illness
Territory. See Property
Terrorist attacks. See PLO; Suicide bombers
Teruah, 497. See also Shofar
Terumah, 103, 529, 549, 553. See also Tithing
Teshuvah (return). See Ba'al Teshuvah; Repentance
Teshuvot (responsa), 428
Teshuvot Rashi, 430. See also Rashi
Testaments of the Twelve Patriarchs, 414
Testes, 173, 412. See also Seed
Testimony. See Witnesses and testimony
Tests by God, 10–11, 85, 457, 458, 496
Test-tube babies. See In vitro fertilization
Tet, 18, 213, 368, 521
Tetragrammaton, 213, 282, 549. See also God; Names of
    God; Yehovah
Tevet, 84. See also Asarah B'Tevet
Tevilah, 549. See also Immersion; Mikveh
Tevul Yom (tractate), 534
Textus receptus, 325
Thanksgiving prayers. See Al-Ha-Nisim (prayer); Birkat
    Ha-Gomel (prayer); She-heche'yanu (blessing)
Theft. See Stealing
Theodicy, 441
Thirteen. See Bar Mitzvah
Thirteen Attributes of Mercy, 549–550. See also Selichot
    (prayers)
Thirteen Principles of Faith, 27, 155, 436, 441, 550–551,
    602. See also Faith; Maimonides, Rabbi Moses
Thread. See Gidin; Knots
Three, significance of, 44, 368–369, 485, 581
"Three gentlemen" (telata gavrei), 14
Three Haftarot of Rebuke, 477, 488
Three Weeks, 85, 478, 551, 583. See also Tishah B'Av
Throat, 575
Throne of God, 26, 120, 523
Thunder, 437
Thursdays, 14, 186, 521, 562, 583
Ti'amat, 136–137
Tiberian system, 89
Tiberias, 22–23, 325, 373, 526
Ties, 107, 113
Tiferet (in kabbalah), 280
Tiferet Yisra'el, 176
Tik (Torah cover), 560, 564
Tikanta Shabbat (prayer), 3

Tikhl, 40, 158, 351, 487. *See also* Hair, covering of
Tikkun (Pentateuch), 508
Tikkun Chatzot (prayers), 551
Tikkun leil Shavuot, 483, 552. *See also* Shavuot
Tikkun olam, 212, 281, 552, 573
Time-related commandments, 137, 231, 349, 376, 525, 541
Timers used for Sabbath, 451, 479
Tiptoes during prayer, 401
Tircha de-tzibura, 552. *See also* Kevod tzibur
Tishah B'Av, 85. *See also* Fasting and fast days; Three Weeks
    aliyot (Torah honors) given on, 14
    babies born on, 362
    defined, 553
    fast of, 185–186, 189
    Lamentations and, 227
    maftir of, 318
    overview of, 248
    parokhet removed on, 46
    sexual relations prohibited on, 474
    Shabbat Chazon preceding, 477
    Shivah D'Nechemta, 478
    Three Haftarot of Rebuke, 477, 488
    Three Weeks and, 551
    weddings prohibited on, 583, 584
    Yom Kippur and, 244–245
Tishbite. *See* Elijah the Prophet
Tishrei, 69, 84, 297, 370, 444, 459, 496–497. *See also* Yom Kippur
Tithing, 103, 314, 482, 529–530, 553. *See also* Terumah
Titkabel, 282. *See also* Kaddish (prayer)
Titles. *See also* Ordination
Titus, 607
Tobit, Book of, 34
Toes, 401. *See also* Feet; Shoes
Tof, 357
Togas, 522
Tohar ha-neshek, 553–554
Tohorat ha-mishpachah laws, 302, 341–342, 365–366, 418, 472, 474, 534, 554. *See also* Menstruation; Mikveh
Tohorot, 82, 173, 347, 418–419, 482, 533–534, 567. *See also* Chevrah kaddishah; Cleanliness; Purity and impurity
Tohu va-vohu, 136. *See also* Creation
Tokheichah, 554
Toldos Aharon chasidim, 107
Toldot Adam Ve-Chavah (Yerucham), 16
Toledot Chag Simchat Torah (Yaari), 229
Tomatoes, 121
Tombstones, 555–556, 576. *See also* Gravesites
Tongue, 575. *See also* Speech
Tops (dreidels), 102, 202
Torah, 66–67. *See also* Aliyah (Torah honor); Ark of the

Covenant; Commandments; Five Books of Moses; Jewish law; Responsa Literature; Revelation at Sinai; Talmud; Tanakh; Ten commandments
    abandonment of. *See* Apostates and apostasy; Atheism
    acceptance of by Jewish people, 110
    adding to, 59, 413
    authenticity of the Torah, 557–558
    bride compared to, 478
    burial of, 81
    Documentary Theory, 557
    dropped, 298
    Festival of Rejoicing in. *See* Simchat Torah
    forgotten, 8
    as foundation of the world, 55
    giving of. *See* Shavuot
    Greek translation of, 371, 469–471
    as halakhah le-Moshe mi-Sinai, 230
    historical transmission of, 278
    holiness of, 249
    kissing, 298
    love of, 10. *See also* God, love of.
    Moses, writing of by, 384
    origin of, 21, 556–557. *See also* Revelation at Sinai
    ornaments, 299
    overview of, 556–558
    as part of Tanakh, 536
    Pittsburgh Platform on, 426
    Priests, received by, 407
    respect for, 44–45
    Revelation of at Sinai, 20, 21
    seventy facets of, 371
    she-ba'al peh. *See* Oral Law
    spacing between words, 20
    standing before the Torah, 44–45
    sweetness of, 502
    as symbol of Jewish unity, 519
    telata gavrei represented by, 14
    Torah she-be'al peh, 556. *See also* Oral Law
    Torah she-bikhtav, 556, 596. *See also* Written Law
    wisdom, as source of, 44
    Written Law, 230, 306, 374, 379, 438, 556, 596
Torah mantles, 46, 445
Torah readings. *See also* Aliyah (Torah honor); Haftarah readings
    cantillations, 89–90, 232, 564
    conclusion of reading of, 2
    covering during breaks in, 320
    cycles of, 562–563
    etiquette of, 565–566
    following seven-year period, 370
    God's name, pronounciation of, 213
    by High Priest, 294
    naming of babies at, 361
    overview of, 561–566
    proper attire for reader, 294

of Rosh Chodesh, 443
Rosh Hashanah, 11
Sabbath, 448
Shavuot, 10
spacing between words, 20
of Ten Commandments, 547
tircha de-tzibura and, 552
Tokheichah, the, 554
triennial cycle of, 337
by women, 563
yad (Torah pointer) for, 560
of Yom Kippur, 605
Torah scrolls, 558
accuracy of, 379
burning of, 291
carrying of, 442
in cemeteries, 94
dropped, 186
gartls for, 107
gidin, 209, 558
hakafot with, 229
held by children, 344
impurity and, 418
kevod tzibur and, 294
life compared to, 291
mantle of, 46, 445
niddah status of women and, 365
selling of, 322
Sephardic, 226
Sephardic term for, 468
sofer of, 507–509
storing of. See Ark of the Covenant
tashmishei kedushah and, 254
"Temple Scrolls", 508
unusable. See Genizah
writing of. See Scribes
Torah study. See also Education; Scholars; Students;
        Talmud; Teachers and teaching; Wisdom
age to begin, 161, 576
Beit Midrash, 65
chavrutah for, 108
daf yomi, 141
by farmers, 429, 598
forbidden by Roman government, 8
Gemara, 204
kallah, 285
kolelim, 300, 429, 598
obligation of, 13, 535–536
piety and, 395
prophets and, 316
as protection of the Jewish People, 8
resurrection as reward for, 437
on Shavuot, 439, 483
swaying during, 401–402
Syrian prohibition of, 99

by women, 588
world to come as reward for, 481
yarchei kallah months, 429
Torah Umesorah, 163. See also Education
Torat Kohanim, 340
Torches, 83, 87, 143–144, 387
Torquemada, 468. See also Inquisition, Spanish
Torture. See Crucifixions
Tosafot, 430, 460, 528, 566. See also Talmud
Tosefta, the, 35, 59, 347, 536, 566–567. See also Mishnah
Totafot, 539. See also Symbols; Tefillin
Totality, 285
Touch. See Physical contact with opposite sex
Tov. See Good and goodness
Towels, 494
Tower of Babel, 557
Trachtenberg, Joshua, 200, 556
Tractates of the Mishnah, 347. See also Mishnah
Tractatus Theologico-Politicus, 155. See also Spinoza,
        Baruch (Benedict)
Trade, 161, 520. See also Business affairs; Labor (work)
Traditional Judaism. See Conservative Judaism
Traits, inborn. See Yeitzer ha-ra; Yeitzer ha-tov
Trani, Rabbi Isaiah da, 71
Transcription. See Scribes
Transfusions, blood, 76
Transgressions. See Sins and sinners
Transjordan, 567
Translation of the Talmud, 528–529
Translations of the Hebrew Bible, 556–558. See also
        Interpretation of Scripture; Vernacular
    Aramaic translation of the Hebrew Bible, 470
    of Five Books of Moses, 337–338
    Latin, 471
    meturgeman, 337–338
    Targum Onkelos, 536
    Translation of the Seventy, 35, 469–471. See also
        Septuagint
    Tze'enah U-re'enah, 572
    Yonatan ben Uziel, 536
Transmigration of souls. See Gilgulim; Reincarnation
Transmission of the Torah, 379, 437–438. See also
        Revelation at Sinai; Torah
Travel, 69, 396, 451–452, 472
Treasured people. See Chosen People
Treaties. See Covenants
Tree of Knowledge, 203, 377–378, 382. See also Garden
        of Eden
Tree of Life, 280
Tree of Life (Aaron ben Elijah), 286–287
Tree of Life (Vital), 280–281, 359
Trees, 85, 98, 105, 160, 483, 520. See also Fruits and
        fruit trees
Treibening, 151
Treif. See Nonkosher food

Treitschke, Heinrich Von, 31
Tribes of Jacob. *See* Twelve Tribes of Jacob
Tribunals, 91. *See* Sanhedrin
Triennial cycle of Torah readings, 337, 563
Trop (Torah readings), 89, 563. *See also* Cantillations
Trousers, 107, 326, 499
Truth and truthfulness, 391, 567–569. *See also* Deceit
    as attribute of God, 550
    compassion and, 569
    eulogies and, 171
    as foundation of the world, 567
    mothers' names in prayers and, 346
    olam ha-emet, 5
    tzitzit as reminder of, 575
    white lies, 568
Tu B'Av, 569
Tu Bi-Shevat, 85, 98, 196, 570
Tucatzinsky, Rabbi Yechiel, 142
Tucker, Richard, 321
Tudela, Benjamin of, 31
Tuesdays, 53, 582–583
Tuition, 163. *See also* Education
Tumah, 373. *See also* Purity and impurity
Tur (Rabbi Jacob ben Asher), 474
Turei Zahav, 45. *See also* Taz
Turks, 267
Turtledove sacrifices, 366. *See also* Sacrifices
Twelve spies, 343
Twelve Tribes of Jacob, 272, 567. *See also specific tribes by name*
    breastplate of High Priest and, 559
    flags and emblems of, 190
    intermarriage between, 569
    Jacob's blessing to, 190
    land of Israel divided between, 274
    split of, 543
    territories of, 184, 314, 587–588
Twenty-six, significance of, 104
Twersky, Rebbetzin, 171
Twins. *See* Esau; Gemini; Jacob (Patriarch)
Two-letter Words, 20
Two Tablets of the Covenant (Hurwitz), 538
Tying. *See* Knots
Tyrnau, Rabbi Isaac, 229
Tza'ar ba'alei cha'yim, 27, 260, 570–572
Tzachok, 361
Tzadi, 19, 368, 521
Tzadikim, 106, 159, 572. *See also* Chasidim and chasidut; Piety; Righteousness
Tzadkiel, 26
Tzadok (High Priest), 454
Tzahal, 3
Tzava Haganah Le-yisra'el, 3
Tzedakah. *See* Charity
Tzedek, 277. *See also* Justice

Tzedokim. *See* Sacrifices
Tze'enah U-re'enah, 572
Tzemach, 336, 361. *See also* Messiah and Messianic Age
Tzeniut. *See* Modesty
Tzeva'ot, 212. *See also* God
Tzevi, Shabbetai, 336, 413
Tzibur. *See* Congregations; Mipnei kevod tzibur
Tziduk Ha-Din (prayer), 572–573
Tzimmes, 446
Tzimtzum, 281, 359, 573. *See also* Kabbalah and kabbalists
Tzin, 504
Tzion, 608. *See also* Zionists and Zionism
Tzipporah (wife of Moses), 351, 590
Tzipori academy, 86
Tzitz Eliezer; A Compendium of Jewish Halakhic Principles (Waldenberg), 174–175. *See also* Waldenberg, Rabbi Eliezer Yehuda
Tzitzit, 41, 157. *See also* Arba kanfot; Tallitot
    adding to, 59
    blue cord of, 574–575
    of early chasidim, 395
    gematriah of, 565, 575
    Karaites and, 286
    kissing, 298
    Menachot (tractate) on, 533
    overview of, 574–575
    Shema and, 488
    tractate of, 536
    women and, 525
Tziyun, 555
Tzom Gedaliah, 185–186, 188, 318, 575
Tzom Shetikah, 187

U

Ubar yerekh imo, 1
Ugav, 357
Ukatzim (tractate), 534
Ukba. *See* Mar Ukba bar Nechemiah
Ukrainian challah, 96–97
Ulla (Rabbi), 14, 255, 298
Ulla Bira'a, 381
Ultra-Orthodox Jews. *See* Orthodoxy
Ululating, 576
UMB (United Mizrahi Bank and Trust Company), 413
Unborn Children. *See* Abortion; Fetuses
Unclean. *See* Purity and impurity
Uncles, 263
Undergarments. *See* Arba kanfot
Understanding, 107, 280. *See also* Reason
Unfaithfulness. *See* Adultery
Unidentified corpses. *See* Met mitzvah
Unintentional murder, 119
Union of American Hebrew Congregations (UAHC), 256, 425. *See also* Reform Judaism

Union of Orthodox Jewish Congregations of America, 151, 380. *See also* Orthodoxy
Union of Orthodox Rabbis, 180. *See also* Orthodoxy
United Arab Republic. *See* Egypt
United Jewish Appeal, 612
United Kingdom. *See* Great Britain
United Mizrahi Bank and Trust Company (UMB), 413
United Nations General Assembly, 267–268, 272–273, 609, 612
United Palestine Appeal, 612
United States
    American Jewish life. *See also* Diaspora
        Ashkenazim and, 52
        black Jews, 183
        demographics, 131
        education, 163–164
        Karaites community, 288
        Ladino population, 469
        Orthodoxy in, 379–380
        Reform Judaism and, 423–427
        slavery question and, 506
        Western Sephardim, 468
    death penalty of, 91–92
    Holocaust Memorial Museum, Washington, D.C., 252
    support for Israel, 267, 272
United Synagogue of America, 127. *See also* Conservative Judaism
Unity of God, 338, 360, 488, 489, 573. *See also* Shema (prayer)
Unity of Jews. *See* Community
Universe. *See* Astrology; Creation; Earth; Moon; Stars
Universities, 191
University of Maryland, 102
Unlearned. *See* Ignorance; Illiteracy
Unleavened dough. *See* Chametz
Unmarried men, 239, 256
Unveilings, 576. *See also* Cemeteries
Un zaiglach, 197
Upsherenish, 229, 576
Ur, 361
Urbach, Professor Ephraim, 288
Uriel, 26
Urim ve-tumim. *See* Breastplate of the High Priest
Ushers. *See* Gabba'im
Ushpizin, 370–371, 576–577. *See also* Sukkot
Usury, 30, 352, 532. *See also* Interest payments
Utensils (for cooking), 307, 387–388
Utensils (for writing). *See* Writing instruments
Uva Le-Tziyon (prayer), 342
Uziel, Rabbi Ben Zion, 1, 138, 211
Uziel, son of Kohath, 405
Uzzah, 43

V

Valance of ark curtain, 46
Valley of Hinnom, 203–204. *See also* Gehinnom
Valuables, 58. *See also* Jewelry and charms
Values, Jewish. *See* Charity; Chesed; Compassion; Derekh eretz; Ethics; Family and family life; Good and goodness; Honor and dignity; Jewish identity and status; Justice; Kindness; Mercy; Moral standards; Peace; Righteousness; Truth and truthfulness
Values of letters. *See* Gematriah
Vanity, 12, 145, 199–200
Vasectomy, 70–71
Vashti, Queen, 327. *See also* Purim
Vater, 302
Vatican. *See* Catholic Church and Catholicism; Papacy (Catholic Church)
Vatikin, 395
Vav, 18, 213, 367
Veal, 40
Vegetables, 192, 349, 455, 461, 462, 464, 476–477, 523
Vegetation. *See* Flowers; Fruits and fruit trees; Gardens; Harvest
Veiling the bride, 58, 97, 578
Veins, 209, 558
Ve-la-malshinim (prayer), 164
Vengeance, 439–441, 578. *See also* City of refuge; Grudges
Venice, Italy, 208
Verbal analogies. *See* Gezeirah shavah principle
Verein für Kultur und Wissenschaft, 236–237
Vernacular. *See also* Aramaic; Translations of the Hebrew Bible; Yiddish
    of Five Books of Moses, 337–338
    names, 362
    prayers in, 126, 398–399, 424, 538
    sermons in, 127
    Talmud translations, 528–529
    Tanakh, translation into, 127, 236, 371, 469–471
Vernal equinox, 68
"Verses of Praise". *See* Pesukei De-Zimra (prayers)
Vessels, holy, 280–281, 408. *See also* Kelippot; Klei kodesh
Vestibule, Earth as, 6
Vet/bet (letter), 17, 367
Victoria, Queen, 351
Victory, 280, 442
Viddui (prayers), 125, 579
Vilna Gaon, the, 105, 107–108, 226, 329, 348, 424, 462, 520, 601
Vilna Shas, 528
Violation of Jewish law. *See* Sabbath
Virgin of Nazareth, 26
Virgins, 50, 86, 311, 613
Virgo (zodiacal), 86, 613
Virtue. *See* Pious people

Visas to Israel, 308
Vishnitzer chasidim, 242
Visiting. *See* Bikur cholim; Guests; Hospitality; Shivah
Vital, Rabbi Chaim, 58, 106, 210, 278, 280–281, 359, 573
Vocal music. *See* Cantors
Voices of women, 300–301, 350, 474, 593. *See also* Songs and singing
Volhynia, Ukraine, 259
Voltaire, François, 31
Vows, 410–412, 531, 532. *See also* Annulment of vows; Kol Nidrei (prayer); Marriage
Vulgate, 471

W

Wachnacht, 115, 490, 580
Wages. *See* Income
Wailing (ululating), 576
Waiting period between milk and meat, 152, 307
Waldenberg, Rabbi Eliezer Yehuda, 49, 174–175
Walkin, Rabbi Aaron, 49
Walking, 167–169, 443
Walled cities, 332, 414–415, 500–501
Wallets, 449
Walls of Jericho, 370
War, 43, 433, 458, 496, 497, 506, 580. *See also* Military; Peace
Ward's Island, 611
Warnings. *See* Azharot (poem)
War of 1967, 92, 268–269, 273, 553–554, 584
War of 1973, 268–269
War of four kings, 553
War of Independence for Israel, 267, 287, 609. *See also* Israel (modern state)
Warsaw Ghetto, 209, 254. *See also* Holocaust
Washing, ritual. *See* Handwashing; Mikveh
Wasted blessings. *See* Berakhah le-vatalah
Wastefulness. *See* Bal tashchit
Wasting seed, 49–50, 373
Wasting time, 231
Watchmen, 81–82, 497
Water. *See also* Handwashing; Mikveh
    defilement by, 534
    in the desert, 562
    drownings, 9, 108
    evil spirits and, 538
    fasting and, 604
    flour and, 98, 328–329. *See also* Fermentation
    immersion in. *See* Mikveh
    for kashering process, 387–388
    ma'yim achronim, 234, 330
    ma'yim cha'yim, 24
    ma'yim she-ein la-hem sof, 9
    ma'yim she-lanu, 329, 330

ma'yim she'uvim, 24, 341
ma'yim she-yeish la-hem sof, 9
mem (letter), represented by, 19
Passover and. *See* Chametz
purity and, 114
rain, 24, 55, 207, 258, 298, 502, 522
salt water, 455
Sea of Galilee, 294
Sea of Reeds, 345, 479, 505
seas, 9, 120, 335, 523, 575
shivah period and, 494
Simchat Beit Ha-Sho'eivah, 502, 596
sotah and, 509, 588–589
streams, 306, 329, 537–538
tashlikh ceremony and, 306, 537–538
water libation ceremony, 502, 596
wells, 329, 330, 466
Waves. *See* Water
Waving hands during prayer, 402–403
Way of the Righteous, The. *See* Mesilat Yesharim (Luzzatto)
Weakness. *See* Illness
Wealth and wealthy, 53, 103, 119, 499–500. *See also* Charity; Court Jews
Weaving. *See* Art and sculpture
Weddings. *See also* Bridegrooms; Brides; Marriage; Sheva Berakhot (blessings)
    blessings at, 97, 296
    bride circling groom under chuppah, 56
    circling of the bridegroom, 115, 369
    clothing, 299
    demons and, 144
    fasting on day of, 186, 582
    on fifteenth day of Av, 85–86
    flowers and, 192
    glass, breaking of, 56, 210–211, 517
    honeymoons, 492
    ketubbah, signing of, 292
    men and women divided at, 300
    music and, 357–358
    overview of, 580–584
    Priestly Benediction for, 408
    prohibited days for, 583–584
    protection from evil eye during, 56
    quorum for, 343, 371
    rings for, 581–582
    sefirat ha-omer, prohibited during, 485
    Shabbat Kallah, 478
    Sumptuary Laws and, 516–517
    synagogues, held in, 112
    Three Weeks, not held during, 85
    torches and, 87
    Tuesdays as preferred day for, 53
    white clothing for, 121
    zeikher le-churban and, 607–608

Wednesdays, 53, 583
Weekdays. *See* Havdalah service; *specific days of the week*
Weekly Torah readings, 501–502, 563. *See also* Torah
        readings
Weeks, 482. *See also* Hebrew calendar
We Have Reason to Believe (Jacobs), 439
Weil, Jacob, 56
Weil, Shalva, 548
Weizmann, Chaim, 267, 272, 613
Weizmann Institute of Science, 435
Welfare of the community, 293–294, 345, 563, 593
Wells, 329, 330, 466. *See also* Living waters; Mikveh; Water
Werbermacher, Monesh, 284
Wertheimer, Samson, 135
Wessely, Naphtali Herz, 236
West, 26, 520
West Bank, 268, 269–270
Western lamp, 169
Western Sephardim, 468
Western Wall, 267, 273, 302, 404, 584–585. *See also*
        Temples
What Does Judaism say About . . . (Jacobs), 440
Wheat, 98, 189, 328, 388. *See also* Chametz; Grains;
        Seven species of Israel
Whipping. *See* Makkot
White, 121–122
        for burial, 419
        chesed represented by, 280
        clothing, 207, 248, 445, 605
        fowl for kapparot, 285
        priestly garments of, 409
        of Priests, 419
        purity and, 581
        shrouds and, 498
        as symbol of purity, 46, 121, 157, 445, 448, 498
White days, 554. *See also* Tohorat ha-mishpachah
White lies, 257–258, 568. *See also* Lying; Truth and
        truthfulness
White Paper, 267
White Russia, 348. *See also* Russian Jews
"Whole megillah, the", 333
Wickedness, 197, 598. *See also* Demons and demonology
Wicks. *See* Candles and candlelighting
Widowers, 323
Widows, 38, 122, 323, 451, 492, 583. *See also* Agunot;
        Levirate marriage practices
Wiesbaden, Germany, 424
Wiesel, Elie, 253
Wife. *See* Agunot; Sotah; Women
Wigs, 40, 158, 320, 351, 486–487, 592. *See also* Hair,
        covering of
Wilbushewitz, Nachum, 612
Wilderness, 42–43, 57, 77, 334, 364, 479, 510. *See also*
        Sukkot
William of Norwich, 76

Will of God, 170
Willows, 41, 191, 194–197, 258, 604. *See also* Four species
Wilson, Woodrow, 267, 272, 609–610
Wimpel, 561
Windows, 410, 520
Wine. *See also* Drinking; Kiddush (prayer)
        abstention from, 51, 227, 364, 395, 513, 551, 586
        alcoholism and, 517
        arba kosot, 383, 460, 463, 466. *See also* Passover
        blessings for, 231
        blood libels and, 76, 466
        bread and, 78
        in charoset, 462
        at circumcision ceremonies, 117
        defilement by, 534
        Elijah's Cup, 166
        fifth cup for Seder, 466
        Gentiles and, 476
        havdalah service and, 237–238, 599
        Holofernes, given to, 101
        lucidity and, 204–205
        overflowing, 296
        overview of, 585–586
        on Passover, 41, 383, 463
        for pidyon ha-ben ceremony, 393–394
        for Purim, 416–417
        red vs. white, 466
        on Simchat Torah, 503
        spilling of wine, 464
        stam yeinam, 586
        touched by non-Jews, 586
        for weddings, 144, 581
        ya'yin mevushal, 586
Wings of angels, 401
Wisdom. *See also* Scholars; Torah study
        arrogance and, 260
        Chabad tenet, as, 107
        Divine Wisdom, 280
        havdalah service and, 238
        in kabbalah, 280
        of nature. *See also* Kabbalah and kabbalists
        old in. *See* Aging
        speaking and, 146
        Torah as source of, 44, 161, 438
        words of. *See* Aggadah
Wisdom of Ben Sira, 34
Wisdom of Jesus, Son of Sirach, 34
Wisdom of Solomon, 34. *See also* Solomon, King
Wise, Rabbi Isaac Mayer, 126, 127, 425, 506
Wise, Rabbi Stephen S., 425, 613
Witches, 250. *See also* Demons and demonology
Witch of Endor, 498
Witnesses and testimony. *See also* Courts, Jewish; Judgment
        am ha-aretz not accepted for, 22
        blood relatives and, 15

in capital punishment cases, 91
to conversions, 131
derekh eretz of, 145
for divorce proceedings, 207
Eiduyot (tractate), 532
false, 532, 546, 568
gambling as disqualifier, 202
to God, blessings on Torah as, 15
of a husband's death, 9
kashrut of, 147
of ketubbot, 37, 147, 232–233, 292, 376, 581, 587
for loans, 513
of marriages, 581
martyrdom and, 324
overview of, 586–587
qualifications of, 587
Rosh Chodesh, announcement of, 83, 387, 444, 603
Sabbath observance of, 37, 452
Satan as, 69, 458–459
Shema and, 489
testimonium, defined, 412
women as, 376, 592
Wives. See also Marriage; Women
modesty of, 350–351
multiple. See Polygamy
as property, 587
of rabbis, 420
sotah, 4–5, 509, 531, 588–589. See also Adultery
support of husbands, 162
Wolfson, A., 154
Womb. See Birth
Women. See also Daughters; Girls; Man (humans);
Marriage; Modesty; Niddah laws; Pregnancy;
Tohorat ha-mishpachah; Widows; Wives
aliyot (Torah honors) given to, 15–16, 593
candlelighting, 88, 590–591
as cantors, 90
circumcision by, 351
clothing of, 157–158. See also Clothing
determination of gender, 1
education of, 161–162, 163–164
as educators, 376
equality and. See Bat Mitzvah
gematriah of ishah, 205
hair of. See Hair, coverings of; Headcoverings
intelligence of, 588
Kaddish recited by, 284
kol ishah, 300–301, 350, 474, 593
literature for, 572
men walking between, 517
mitzvot obligations, 349
Nashim (Mishnah tractates). See also Mishnah
ordination of, 163–164, 376–377, 421, 422,
426–427, 595–596
overview of, 587–596

pulpit, prohibited from, 16, 294
quorums and, 344
as rabbis, 420
ransoming of, 394
Rosh Chodesh as holiday of, 443
scribes, prohibition of, 507, 563
shochet, prohibition of serving as, 486
spices and lotions of, 510
tallitot and, 525, 591
tefillin and, 541–542, 591–592
time-related mitzvot, exemption from, 349
Torah readings by, 563
tzitzit and, 525
ululating, 576
as witnesses, 376, 592
Women's Gallery, 181, 502, 519–520, 596. See also
Mechitzah
Women's League of Conservative Judaism, 127
Women's Zionist Organization. See Hadassah
organization
Wood, 119–120, 388
Wool, 35, 114, 157, 349, 476–477, 523. See also
Shaatnez
Words, Hebrew, 20. See also Acronyms; Acrostics; Hebrew
language
Work. See Kibbutzim; Labor (work); Livelihood
World (earthly), 176, 573
bet (letter), represented by, 21
compared to world to come, 6
creation of. See Creation
four cardinal directions in, 26
origin of, 20–21
perfection of. See Tikkun olam
three foundations of, 55
tzimtzum concept and, 573
World Confederation of General Zionists, 610
World Jewish Congress, 33, 322, 608, 610
World to come. See also Afterlife; Gehinnom; Heaven
Angel of Death, slaying of, 24
Ashrei and, 52
bet, represented by, 21
for Gentiles, 367
for non-Jews, 105
preparation for, 6
resurrection doctrine and, 436
as reward, 503
reward in, 441
Sabbath observance and, 447
Sanhedrin (tractate) on, 532
Shai Olamot, 481
talmudic views on, 6
Tetragrammaton pronounced in, 213
understanding of. See Mystics and mysticism
world of souls, 243
World Union for Progressive Judaism (WUP), 425

World War II. *See* Holocaust
World Zionist Organization, 610, 613
Worship. *See also* Prayers and blessings
    of art, 47–48
    of idols. *See* Idolatry and idol worshippers
Wounds, 377, 396
Wreaths. *See* Flowers
Writing instruments, 208, 356, 449, 541, 571, 580. *See also* Scribes
Writings. *See* Letters and documents
Writing the names of God, 213–214
Written Law, 230, 306, 374, 379, 438, 556, 596. *See also* Commandments; Revelation at Sinai; Torah
Wye River Memorandum, 270

X

Xerxes, 28. *See also* Purim

Y

Ya'aleh Ve-Yavo (prayer), 443. *See also* Eighteen Benedictions (prayer)
Yaari, Rabbi Avraham, 229
Yad. *See* Hands
Yad (Torah pointer), 226, 560, 564
Yada'yim (tractate), 534
Yad Ha-Chazakah, 179, 347. *See also* Mishneh Torah
Yadin, Yigael, 325
Yadkha, 540
Yad Vashem, 105, 208–209, 252, 254
Yagel, Abraham ben Chananiah, 202
Yah, 212–213. *See also* God
Yahrzeits, 15, 84, 171, 186, 597. *See also* Memory and remembrance
Yahweh, 212–213. *See also* God
Yaknehaz, 599
Yamim Nora'im, 597–598. *See also* High Holidays
Yannai (Rabbi), 23, 121, 192, 206, 341
Yannai, King Alexander, 161
Yarchei kallah, 429, 598
Yards. *See* Eruvin
Yarkah be-fanav, 95. *See also* Ceremony of the Removed Sandal
Yarmulkes, 107, 297. *See also* Headcoverings
Yashan and chadash, 598–599
Yavam, 312. *See also* Levirate marriage practices
Yavetz. *See* Emden, Rabbi Jacob
Yavneh academy, 164, 289, 346, 374
Yavneh and Yaknehaz (havdalah ceremony), 599
Ya'yin, 586. *See also* Wine
Y chromosome pattern, 409
Years. *See also* Hebrew calendar
    calculating, 86–87
    New Year, Jewish. *See* Rosh Hashanah

New Year, secular. *See* New Year's Day (secular)
    sabbatical. *See* Shemittah
Yeast, 388
Yechiel of Paris, 432
Yehovah, 87, 104, 205, 212–213, 272, 340, 371, 455, 489. *See also* God; Names of God
Yehudah Ha-Nasi. *See* Judah the Prince
Yehudah Ya'aleh (Aszod), 409
Yehudi, 274. *See also* Jewish identity and status
Yeihareig ve-al ya'avor, 309
Yeitzer ha-ra, 97–98, 378, 458, 599. *See also* Satan
Yeitzer ha-tov, 378, 599
Yekarah de-chayei, 82
Yekarah de-shichvah, 82
Yekke, 274
Yekum Purkan (prayer), 181, 599
Yellow, 280
Yemen, 130
Yemenite customs, 337
Yeriah, 509
Yerucham (Rabbi), 16
Yerushala'yim. *See* Jerusalem
Yerushalmi Talmud, 526, 528. *See also* Talmud
Yeshamiel, 26
Yeshiva (Grade), 600
Yeshivat Etz-Chaim, 601
Yeshivat Rabbenu Yitzchak Elchanan, 376, 379, 421, 601
Yeshiva University, 376, 379–380, 601. *See also* Rabbi Isaac Elchanan Theological Seminary
Yeshivot, 163, 380, 382, 396, 599–601. *See also* Academies of learning; Chavrutah; Education; Kolelim; Musar
Yeshu, 12, 118. *See also* Jesus Christ
Yesod (in kabbalah), 280
Yevamot (tractate), 531
YHWH, 213. *See also* God
Yibum, 38, 114, 312, 313, 326–327, 601. *See also* Chukim; Levirate marriage practices; Sexual relations
Yichud, 114, 582, 601
Yichus, 601–602
Yid, 274
Yiddish, 141, 235–236, 572
Yigdal (prayer), 155, 550, 602
Yishgalenah, 173
Yishkavenah, 173
Yishuv, 611
Yishuv Eretz Yisra'el. *See also* Aliyah (to Israel)
Yisra'el. *See* Israel (biblical); Israel (modern state)
Yisra'elim, 13, 160, 273–274, 329, 369, 390, 461. *See also* Jewish identity and status
Yitzchaki, Rabbi Shlomo. *See* Rashi
Yitzhar (son of Kohath), 405
Yizkor services, 166, 238, 602–603
Yochanan (Rabbi), 2

on angels, 25
on arba kosot of Passover, 383
on breaking bread, 78
on comforting the mourner, 124
on compassion toward Egyptians, 122
on Days of Awe, 598
deference to old, 8
on demons, 80
on Eighteen Benedictions, 164, 501
on Israel as Chosen People, 110
Jerusalem Talmud and, 526
on leshon ha-ra, 311
on Messianic Age, 335
on miracles, 345
on Nazarenes, 453
on planetary influence, 517
on prayer, 399, 404
on prophecy, 413
on public assembly, 410
on a quorum, 37
on quorums, 343
on Sabbath, 447
on shrouds, 498
on vatikin, 395
on vengeance, 578
Yochanan bar Nappacha, 56, 161, 303, 439–440, 542
Yochanan ben Torta, 336
Yochanan ben Zakkai, 42, 243
on end of prophetic era, 316
exegetical interpretations of, 244
on hell, 204
on kevod ha-beriot, 292–293
ordination by, 421
recitation of sacrificial procedures, 56
on the red heifer, 114, 422
tefillin of, 539
Yavneh academy, establishment of, 374
Yochanan Ha-Sandler, 161
Yocheved, daughter of Rashi, 566
Yod. See Yud
Yo'eitzot, 596
Yoel, 361
Yokheved, wife of Amram, 405
Yoma (tractate), 530
Yoma arichta, 444, 603
Yom Ha-Atzma'ut, 230, 603
Yom Ha-Meyuchas, 485
Yom Ha-Shanah, 597. See also Yahrzeits
Yom Ha-Sho'ah, 248, 252, 254, 603. See also Holocaust
Yom Ha-Zikaron, 444. See also Rosh Hashanah
Yom Huledet, 72. See also Birth
Yom Kippur, 604–605. See also Fasting and fast days;
    High Holidays
aliyot (Torah honors) given on, 14
babies born on, 362

calendar and, 485
circumcision on, 116
clothing for, 298, 604–605
fast of, 185–186, 471, 604
flogging before, 191
High Priest, service on, 43, 282, 405
immersion preceding, 342
judgment on, 444–445, 598
maftir of, 318
Memorbüchen and, 602
men compared to angels on, 489
Musaf services, 57, 297
Netaneh Tokef (prayer), 96
overview, 247–248
post-fast meals, 604
prayers and blessings of, 230, 400, 605
pre-fast meal, 604
Priestly attire on, 157
recitation of sacrificial procedures, 56
Satan as witness on, 459
Selichot, 467, 549–550
Sephardic term for, 468
sexual relations prohibited on, 474
Shabbat Shuvah preceding, 479
Shabbes goy, collection of funds for, 479
Shema (prayer) and, 488–489
shofar, 277
Simon the Just, service of, 122
tallitot worn on, 522–523
Ten Days of Repentance, 51
ten martyrs, 123
Tishah B'Av and, 244–245
violation of, 447, 604
Yizkor services of, 602–603
Yoma (tractate), 530
Yom Kippur Katan, 605–606
Yom Kippur War, 268–269, 612
Yom Tov, defined, 606. See also Holidays
Yom Tov Sheini, 387, 606
Yom Yerushala'yim, 273
Yonah, 361
Yonatan ben Uziel, 361, 537
Yordim, 606
Yoreh Dei'ah, 307, 500. See also Code of Jewish Law
    (Caro)
Yoreid lifnei ha-teivah, 68
Yosef. See Joseph (the righteous)
Yosef, Rabbi Ovadiah
on artificial insemination, 49
on art on religious objects, 48
on bat mitzvah celebrations, 62, 595
on Falashas, 183
on names of God, 214
on organ transplants, 377, 396
on reincarnation, 427

on Sabbath laws, 451
on tzitzit, 574
Yosei (Rabbi), 401, 438, 483
Yosei ben Chalafta, 86, 303, 480
Yosei ben Yehudah, 411
Yosei ben Yoezer, 614
Yosei ben Yohanan, 614
Yosei ben Zimra, 311
Yossei of Pumbedita, 459
Yossi bar Zavda, 23, 526
Yotze'im, 380
Young People's League, 127
Youth. *See* Children
Youth Aliya, 613
Youtre, 274
Yovel (horn), 496. *See also* Shofar
Yovel (jubilee year), 491, 506
Yud, 18, 368, 521
Yud Bet Chodesh, 55, 606. *See also* Mourners and
mourning

Z

Zabla, 42
Zadok, 247, 405
Zahlenquadrat, 24
Zaka, 607
Zakhor. *See* Memory and remembrance
Zakhriel, 26
Zal (zikhrono li-verakhah), 3
Zalman of St. Goar, 432
Zavim (tractate), 534
Za'yin, 18, 367, 521–522
Zedekiah, King, 543
Ze'eirah (Rabbi), 78, 246, 335, 539
Ze'era, Rabbi Eleazar, 121
Ze'ev, Rabbi Binyamin of Arta, 234–235
Zeh ne'heneh ve-zeh lo chaser, 607
Zeikher le-churban, 607–608
Zekhariah (prophet), 185, 258, 391, 456
Zekhut avot, 608
Zelophechad, daughters of, 587–588
Zeman Cheiruteinu, 386. *See also* Passover
Zeman Matan Torateinu, 483. *See also* Shavuot

Zeman Simchateinu, 515. *See also* Sukkot
Zemirot. *See* Songs and singing
Zephaniah (prophet), 524
Zera'im (Mishnah tractates), 347. *See also* Mishnah
Zera'im (tractate), 482, 529–530, 567. *See also* Mishnah
Zera kodesh, 136
Zeresh, 3. *See also* Purim
Zerika, Rabbi, 233
Zero'a, 462
Zevachim (tractate), 532
Zeved ha-bat, 362
Zevi, Shabbetai, 336
Zhid, 274
Zihui Korbanot Ason, 607
Zikhrono li-verakhah, 3
Zionist Organization of America, 610, 612, 613
Zionists and Zionism, 608–613. *See also* Israel (modern
state)
    Anti-Zionism, 13, 107, 380
    First Zionist Congress (1897), 266–267, 272, 510–
        511, 609, 613
    Hadassah organization, 376, 595, 612–613
    Herzl, Theodor, 32, 104–105, 190–191, 266–267,
        272, 363, 608–609, 613
    Jewish identity and, 277
    kibbutz galu'yot, 295
    Reform Judaism and, 426–427
Zirelson, Rabbi Yehudah Lev, 154, 346
Zit, 274
Zithers, 357
Zivug, 614
Ziyunim, 521
Zodiac, 84–86, 369, 613. *See also* Astrology; Hebrew
    calendar
Zohar, The, 164–165, 279–280, 330, 338, 358–360, 371,
    384, 401, 412, 442, 568, 614. *See also* Kabbalah
    and kabbalists
Zola, Emile, 609
Zolti, Rabbi Bezalel, 113
Zuckermandl, M. S., 567
Zugot, 300, 614
Zunz, Leopold, 126–127, 236–237
Zygelbojm, Samuel, 324
Zyklon-B, 251

About the Author

Alfred J. Kolatch, a graduate of the Teachers' Institute of Yeshiva University and its College of Liberal Arts, was ordained by the Jewish Theological Seminary of America, which subsequently awarded him the Doctor of Divinity degree, *honoris causa*. From 1941 to 1948 he served as rabbi of congregations in Columbia, South Carolina, and Kew Gardens, New York, and as a chaplain in the United States Army.

Rabbi Kolatch has authored more than fifty books, the most popular of which are *The Jewish Book of Why* and *The Second Jewish Book of Why*, *The Jewish Book of Why: The Torah*, *The Jewish Mourner's Book of Why*, *Handbook for the Jewish Home*, *The New Name Dictionary*, *The Comprehensive Dictionary of English and Hebrew First Names*, *The Family Seder*, and *The Jewish Child's First Book of Why*. Among his recent works are *Great Jewish Quotations: By Jews and About Jews*, *The Presidents of the United States & the Jews*, *What Jews Say About God*, and *Masters of the Talmud: Their Lives and Views*.

In addition to his scholarly work, Rabbi Kolatch has served as president of the Association of Jewish Chaplains of the Armed Forces and as vice-president of the interdenominational Military Chaplains Association of the United States.